Thomas Cook

International Air Travel Handbook

1998

A guide to the world's major airports,
their facilities and transport connections

Thomas Cook

Published by Thomas Cook Publishing
The Thomas Cook Group Ltd
P O Box 227
Thorpe Wood
Peterborough PE3 6PU
United Kingdom

ISBN 0 900341 15 8

Text, maps and diagrams ©1998 The Thomas Cook Group Ltd

All rights reserved. No part of this publication may be reproduced, stored in a retrieval system or transmitted, in any form or by any means, electronic, mechanical, recording or otherwise, without the prior permission of the publishers. All requests for permission should be made to the Head of Publishing at the above address.

Whilst every care has been taken in compiling this publication, using the most up-to-date information available at the time of going to press, all details are liable to change and cannot be guaranteed. The Publishers cannot accept any liability whatsoever arising from the use of the information contained in this publication or from errors or omissions in it, however caused. Views and opinions expressed in this publication are not necessarily those of the Thomas Cook Group Ltd.

Managing Editor: Stephen York
Project Editor: Bernard Horton

Compilers:
A-Z of Air Travel: David Wickers (Chief travel correspondent,
    London *Sunday Times*)
Country by Country travel facts: Ros Renwick, CMC Publishing
Airports:
North America-Kirk D. Schneider, California Transit Publications
Rest of World-Giovanna Battiston

Additional editorial help: Joan Lee, Caroline Horton

Maps drawn by:
Kirk D. Schneider, California Transit Publications
Caroline Horton
ESR Ltd, Byfleet, Surrey, UK
World time zone map supplied by and copyright of
    Oxford Cartographers, Eynsham, Oxford, UK

Text typeset in Avant Garde and Classical Garamond BT using
    Quark Xpress® for Windows®
Maps drawn using GST Designworks® and Macromedia
    Freehand®

Printed in Great Britain by Fisherprint Ltd, Peterborough

Acknowledgements:
The publishers wish to express their gratitude to the many officials and executives of airports around the world, and colleagues within the Thomas Cook Worldwide Network and elsewhere in the travel industry, who have generously given their time and advice in checking the facts contained in this publication.

We welcome all comments, criticisms and suggestions from readers and invite you to use the Reader Survey form at the end of this book to tell us how we can make future editions more helpful to you, the traveller. In particular, if you have information on any airport which you feel will make this work more useful for future readers, please share it with us. All communications will be acknowledged and a free copy of the next edition will be presented to the most informative contributors. Write to:
The Project Editor, International Air Travel Handbook, Thomas Cook Publishing, P O Box 227, Thorpe Wood, Peterborough PE3 6PU, United Kingdom
Fax: 01733 (+44 1733 international) 503596.
E-mail: *publishing@thomascook.com*

Contents

Introduction	5
How to use this book	6
Abbreviations and symbols	9
Airline and currency codes	11
World time zones map	13

SECTION ONE: AIR TRAVEL FACTS

Facts and updates on air travel for 1998

Country by country travel facts	14
The A to Z of air travel	43

SECTION TWO: AIRPORT DIRECTORY

Guide to major airports of the world, arranged alphabetically

Aberdeen	57
Abu Dhabi	58
Adelaide	59
Alicante	60
Amsterdam	61
Terminal Plans, City Map	
Ankara	64
Athens	65
City Map	
Atlanta	67
City Map	
Auckland	69
Bahrain	70
Baltimore-Washington	71
Bangkok	72
Barcelona	75
City Map	
Beijing	77
City Map	
Belfast-International	78
Berlin-Tegel	80
City Map	
Birmingham	82
Bogota	84
Boston	85
Airport Map, City Map	
Bridgetown	88
Bristol	89
Brussels	90
Terminal Plans, City Map	
Bucharest	92
Budapest	93
City Map	
Buenos Aires	95
City Map	
Cairns	96
Cairo	97
Calgary	98
Cape Town	99
City Map	
Caracas	102
Cardiff	103
Casablanca	104
Chicago-Midway	105
Chicago-O'Hare	106
Airport Map, City Map, Terminal Plan, Region Map	
Colombo	110
Copenhagen	111
City Map	
Dallas/Fort Worth	113
Airport Map	
Darwin	115
Delhi	116
Airport Map	
Denver	118
Dubai	119
Dublin	120
Düsseldorf	122
Region map	
East Midlands	124
Edmonton	125
Frankfurt	126
Airport Map, Terminal Plans, Region Map, City Map	
Geneva	130
City Map	
Glasgow	131
Gothenburg	133
Halifax	134
Hamburg	135
Harare	137
Helsinki	137
Hong Kong	139
City Map	
Honolulu	140
Houston	142
Istanbul	143
Jakarta	145
Jeddah	146
Johannesburg	147
Karachi	148
Kiev	149
Kingston	150
Kuala Lumpur	151
Lagos	153
Las Vegas	154
Leeds-Bardford	155
Lisbon	156
Liverpool	157
London-City	158
City Maps	

London-Gatwick	160	New York-La Guardia	214	Stockholm-Arlanda	266
Region Map, Airport Map, Terminal Plans		*Airport Map*		Strasbourg	268
		New York-Newark	216	Stuttgart	269
London-Heathrow	164	Nice	217	Sydney	270
Airport Map, Terminal Plans		*City Map*		*Terminal Plans, City Map*	
London-Stansted	173	Norwich	219	Taipei	272
Los Angeles	174	Orlando	220	Teesside	274
Airport Map, City Map, Terminal Plan, Region Map		*Region Map*		Tel Aviv	275
		Osaka-Kansai	222	Tenerife	276
Lyon	178	Oslo	223	Tokyo-Natita	277
Madrid	180	Palma de Mallorca	225	*Airport Map, Terminal Plans, City Map, Region Map*	
City Map		Paris-Charles de Gaulle	226		
Malta	182	*Airport Map, Terminal Plans, Region Map, City Map*		Toronto	281
Manchester	183			*Airport Map, Terminal Plans, City Map*	
Manila	185	Paris-Orly	234		
Melbourne	186	*Airport Map, Terminal Plans*		Toulouse	285
Mexico City	187	Perth	237	Vancouver	286
City Map		Philadelphia	238	*City Map*	
Miami	189	Prague	239	Vienna	288
Airport Map, City Map Terminal Plan		Reykjavik	241	*City Map*	
		Rio de Janeiro-International	242	Warsaw	290
Milan-Linate	192	*City Map*		*City Map*	
City Map		Riyadh	243	Washington DC-Dulles	291
Milan-Malpensa	194	Rome	244	*Terminal Plans, City Map, Region Map, Airport Map*	
Region Map		*City Map*			
Minneapolis/St Paul	195	St Louis	247	Washington National	294
Montréal-Dorval	197	St Petersburg	248	Zürich	296
City Map		*City Map*		*City Map*	
Montréal-Mirabel	199	San Diego	250		
Moscow-Sheremetyevo	200	*City Map*			
Terminal Plans, City Map		San Francisco	252		
Mumbai (Bombay)	202	*Airport Map, Terminal Plans, City Map*			
Munich	203				
City Map		Santiago	256		
Nairobi	205	São Paulo	257		
Nassau	206	Seattle	258		
Newcastle	207	Seoul	260		
New Orleans	208	Singapore	261		
New York-JFK	209	*Airport Map, Terminal Plans, City Map*			
Airport Map, Terminal Plans, City Map, Region Map					

SECTION THREE: DESTINATION INDEX

International destinations and their connections to gateway airports

Destination index 297

READER SURVEY

Reader survey 319

INTRODUCTION

The *Thomas Cook International Air Travel Handbook* is an air traveller's companion built around a directory of the world's main gateway airports. It is an annually updated (and enlarged) publication which we hope will be a valuable information source for international air travellers and travel industry professionals.

The book is divided into three sections.

Section One, Air Travel Facts, gives information of use to international air travellers. 'Country by country travel facts' is a list of essential travel data for every country which has an airport featured in the main directory of airports in Section Two, arranged in alphabetical order of countries. Facts were correct at time of publication but may be subject to change at any time. In the case of information on passport and visa regulations, the reader is strongly advised to check in detail, well before the intended date of travel, that his or her documentation meets the country's current requirements; the facts given here should not be taken as a complete and definitive statement which applies to every individual's case. 'The A to Z of air travel', written by David Wickers, chief travel correspondent of the London *Sunday Times*, is a review of some of the topics of most interest to air passengers, both frequent flyers and less experienced travellers.

Section Two, the Airport Directory, describes over 100 'gateway' airports across the world, and is arranged alphabetically by the name of the airport city. Facts are presented in a standard order, as explained below. Where a category of information, such as 'Airport Hotels', or specific details, such as opening times or fares, are missing from an airport's entry, this means either that no features of the kind exist at that airport or that no up-to-date information was available to us at the time of compilation. The directory was compiled using a variety of sources, including a questionnaire addressed to the airport administration; every airport in this section was sent a full listing of the data intended for publication, and most reviewed and corrected it where necessary, but not every airport took this opportunity.

One of the ways in which we hope the book will be of most use is in detailing the onward surface transport links from airports, not only to the nearby city centre but also further afield. In addition, we have provided an overview of onward air connections from the major air gateways to 'regional' airports, which may be smaller, more local ones or large international airports which are a short flight time away.

Both the ground transport links and the regional air connections are summarised in **Section Three** of this book, the Destination Index. Here we have listed in one alphabetical sequence all the destinations, large and small, which can be reached by the air and ground transport services described in the main directory, together with basic details of the connections.

We have abbreviated many terms in the directory, such as the names of days of the week, and have used symbols for frequently recurring items such as transport types, or to replace introductory words such as 'Phone number' or 'Journey time'. The diagrams of airports and terminals also make liberal use of symbols. All abbreviations and symbols are listed on p. 9. Although we realise that it can be frustrating to have to refer to such lists in order to decipher the information, we hope that the saving in space and verbal and visual clutter more than compensates, and that remembering the abbreviations and symbols will become easy with continued use of the book. As an aid to familiarity, the main textual symbols are explained at the bottom of each double page spread.

We apologise in advance for instances where we have failed to describe a feature of interest to the reader, or where we have inadvertently published out-of-date facts; we will be grateful for all feedback on such cases, and still more grateful if you can supply us with more up-to-date or complete information for the next edition of this handbook. Please use the Reader Survey form on page 319; all replies will be acknowledged and those judged particularly helpful will earn their contributor a free copy of the next edition.

How to Use This Book

General Notes

These apply to Sections Two and Three alike. **Hours** between which a transport service operates (first and last departures), or during which facilities are open, are introduced by the ☾ symbol and use the 24-hour clock, e.g. 1500 is 3 p.m. Round-the-clock service is denoted by '24 hr'. Daily, monthly or seasonal restrictions on opening or operational hours are shown by additions such as 'Mon–Fri', 'Jan–Mar', 'Summer', after the timings; e.g. '☾0600–1800 Mon–Fri; 0800–1800 Sat' means 'Open 6 a.m. to 6 p.m. Monday to Friday and 8 a.m. to 6 p.m. Saturday'; this also implies no opening on Sundays. Unless a restriction on days of the week is shown, it can be assumed that the service or facility is open every day of the week.

The **frequency** of a ground transport service is prefixed by the symbol » and is usually expressed by the interval between departures – e.g. '»20 min' means that the transport departs every 20 minutes – or by a note such as '3 per day', i.e. there are only 3 departures during the day. Air transport frequencies are stated differently: 'Several per day' indicates that there are at least 2 flights on *every* day of the week, including weekends (there may in fact be many more flights per day than this); 'At least daily' means that there is at least 1 flight on every day of the week (some days may have more); 'Several per week' indicates that there are at least 2 flights each week. Approximate **journey times** for any kind of transport are introduced by the symbol ⊃.

Details of operating hours, frequency and journey times given in this book are deliberately restricted to approximations which will not date significantly over the year of publication, and are intended to give the reader a broad overview of the connections available and their convenience. All timetable details are subject to frequent changes in detail, and of course services may be added or withdrawn by operators during the currency of this issue. It is essential to use a regularly updated timetable, such as the *Thomas Cook European Timetable* for European rail or the *OAG Airline Guide* for air travel, or the services of a travel agency, to plan a journey in detail.

Fares of transport, where known, and **costs** of facilities, are prefixed by the symbol ◇ and expressed in local currency using the IATA abbreviations (see page 12). Again, these cannot be guaranteed during the lifetime of this volume; air and rail fare structures, in particular, are usually too complex to be detailed and should be checked before travelling.

Section Two: Airport Directory

Data is presented in Section Two under the same headings and in the same order for each airport, as follows.

Basic Details

Airport name, standard three-letter **designator code**, and **country** in which the airport is situated (with a cross-reference to the country's general data in Section One).

Telephone national code number to use when calling from outside that country (after dialling your own international access code, e.g. 00 from the United Kingdom).

This is followed by the area code applicable to the airport (note, this is often different from the area code of the nearby city). The form given is the one to use when dialling from inside the country – when dialling to the area from abroad any initial '0' should be dropped – for instance, to call Paris from inside France use area code '01', from outside France use area code '1'. All the other phone numbers quoted in an airport's description can be assumed to be within the same phone area as the airport: i.e. do not add the area code if dialling one of these numbers from the airport itself. Where this is not the case, we show the necessary area code in brackets – dial this as well as the number. This also applies to freephone and local-rate prefixes such as 800 in the USA or 0345 in the UK.

Local time for the airport is given for summer and winter (approximately April to September and October to March in the northern hemisphere, the opposite in the southern hemisphere; exact changeover dates vary by country and region). It is expressed as GMT plus or minus, i.e. the airport time is ahead or behind Greenwich Mean Time by the specified number of hours. For instance, GMT+7 means that the airport is at 7 p.m. when Greenwich is at noon; GMT-9 means that it is at 3 a.m. when Greenwich is at noon. See also the map of world time zones on page 13.

The full postal address of the airport follows, and then the phone and fax numbers of the airport administration. If the airport has an Internet e-mail address and/or a World Wide Web site, their addresses are quoted next.

Finally, the approximate **location** of the airport is given, in terms of distance from its parent city or cities.

Terminals and Transfers

Terminals lists the terminals as named by the airport. Where there is one un-named terminal we call it 'Main Terminal'. What constitutes a terminal is defined by each airport and may be a separate building or just a section of one main building. For each terminal we list the airlines which use it; if a whole class of airlines or flights apply, we simply say e.g. 'All international flights', 'All domestic departures', and so on, without listing all the airlines by name. Next, the **layout** of the main subdivisions of the terminal is briefly described if known, e.g. 'Two levels; Level 1 Arrival, Level 2 Departure'.

Minimum transfer times are the minimum times to allow for transferring between international and domestic flights. Official times are determined and published by IATA. There are numerous exceptions and special cases for certain airlines and destinations due to security or immigration procedures, or airport layout. Times for changing from international flight to a domestic one may be longer than simply changing from one international flight to another, depending on the prevailing customs and immigration practices. The time quoted in this book for 'International' is the official time for changing between two international flights, or from an international flight to a domestic one, or vice versa; where these differ, we have taken the longest of the three. The times given for 'Domestic' are those for changing from one domestic flight to another. If you intend to change between two flights and the interval between their arrival and departure times is close to the minimum transfer time we have given, you should check with your airline or travel agent for possible exceptions which might apply. Transfer between terminals for multi-terminal airports details the mode of transport and its frequency, the terminals and other areas connected by the service, and fare ('Free' if no fare). Often 'terminals' are in the same building and this heading is inapplicable.

INFORMATION

Flight enquiries indicates any phone numbers provided for all flights from the airport; where airlines have specific local numbers for their own flights, these are listed next. If no local number is given, there may be a freephone or other central number for use within the entire country – refer to your airline's literature.

Information and help desks gives the name or type of the desk, its terminal and location within terminal (and how many within that location if more than one), its phone and fax numbers and opening hours, and the type of information it dispenses. Where a desk will make hotel bookings this is also indicated.

EMERGENCIES

Details are given for calling or locating **police** and **medical assistance** at the airport, and reporting/claiming **lost property** (i.e. property lost at the airport – missing flight baggage is best reported direct to the airline's representation at the airport). Location of service (if accessible to the public), phone number and hours of availability are given. Remember that we also give the airport's national emergency numbers in 'Country by country travel facts', Section One.

AIRPORT FACILITIES

Data on all of the facilities follows the pattern: type of facility; terminal and location in terminal; opening hours. The location of public telephones is not recorded, as these tend to be plentiful throughout most airports. For **Money**, we have categorised facilities as: ATM (automatic teller machine, cash dispenser, etc.), i.e. any machine accepting a credit or debit card to dispense cash in local currency; Bureau de change, i.e. a facility mainly concerned with exchanging currency and cashing traveller's cheques, but possibly also offering other services; and Bank, offering money-changing and often a wider range of financial services.

Food and drink defines catering facilities in broad categories, as: Bar, offering mainly alcoholic refreshment (possibly with light snacks); Restaurant, providing formal cooked meals and seating (may be self-service); Café/light meals, covering most other possibilities, ranging from coffee shops to burger bars and stalls in a food court. **Shopping** identifies the types of outlet of most interest to the traveller, including travel agencies, hairdressers and pharmacies, but we have not always detailed gift and general merchandise shops; if many such shops are grouped at the airport they are listed as 'Shopping mall'. 'Supermarket' implies a range of food and groceries. Duty-free shops are always noted separately, and classified as 'Duty-free, departure', i.e. for purchases on leaving the country, which is the norm, and 'Duty-free, arrival', for those countries where it is permitted to buy tax-free items on entering the country. **Luggage** covers trolleys and carts, porter services, left luggage (baggage deposit) offices and self-use luggage lockers. In these instances we have added details of cost, where known.

DISABLED TRAVELLERS

We indicate the existence of a standard range of facilities for passengers with physical impairments, and locations or contact details where known. The airport may also have extra facilities which are less easily categorised.

SMOKING POLICY

Covers restrictions on smoking, or areas where smoking is permitted in a generally non-smoking airport.

SPECIAL PASSENGER LOUNGES

Many airlines, and some airport authorities, provide lounges for the use of their most favoured passengers, or for VIPs or CIPs (commercially important persons). We indicate the name of the providing airline, the name of the lounge, the terminal and location, and in many cases a note of which passengers are permitted to use the lounge. Sometimes an airline permits equivalent passengers of other airlines to use its lounge: this is indicated in our text by the two-letter codes of the qualifying airlines (see p. 10 to decipher unfamiliar codes).

CONFERENCE AND BUSINESS FACILITIES

Most large international airports provide some facilities for business travellers who wish to hold meetings, work or have an office base during their stay at the airport. This section gives the name of the facility, its location, its phone and fax numbers, its opening hours and its range of services according a standard classification (there may be additional services not falling into these categories).

AIRPORT HOTELS

This covers only hotels actually at or very near the airport, suitable for an overnight stay between flights, for instance. Many other hotels in the nearby city and suburbs may be almost as convenient. Details given include name (usually omitting the word Hotel), phone and fax numbers, capacity (rooms or guests), and the existence of a courtesy bus from terminal to hotel (where none is shown, it may simply be that the hotel is too near the terminals for one to be necessary).

CAR RENTAL

Companies operating from the airport are listed with company name, location of the booking desk (not the pick-up point), and local phone number. If no local number is given, there may be a freephone or other central number for use within the entire country – refer to your car rental company's literature.

HOW TO USE THIS BOOK

CAR PARKING

Car parks are categorised as Short-stay (intended for parking for less than a day), Long-stay (for longer-term parking, generally further away from the terminals but cheaper), and Off-airport (companies operating long-term car parks some distance away from the airport, with courtesy shuttle transport). Details include location or associated terminal, number of spaces, and costs per hour, day or week, etc. as appropriate. Names and phone numbers of off-airport operating companies are also given where known.

TAXIS AND CHAUFFEUR-DRIVEN CARS

Information on **Taxis** includes the pick-up point, a local phone number and cab company name where needed, and the approximate journey time and fare to the nearby city centre. The fare should be queried and if possible confirmed before travelling in the taxi. Always use officially licensed taxis. **Chauffeur-driven cars** lists companies which hire out a car and driver by the hour, day, etc.. Since destinations of hired cars are variable by definition, journey times are not indicated, but hire rates are, where known.

PUBLIC TRANSPORT

This sections covers all public ground transport services which have *direct connections with the airport*. Many more train and bus services than we list will usually be available from the centre of the airport's parent city; many of these, and airport-to-city links, are scheduled in detail in the *Thomas Cook European* and *Overseas Timetables*, and other publications.

Services are classified as: **Airport to airport**, i.e. surface transport links to other airports, however far away; **City and suburbs**, covering all routes which give access not only to the nearby city centre but also to outlying suburbs and business areas around the city; **Courtesy and special transport**, defined as any special services laid on to take arriving passengers directly to specific trade fairs, events and tourist destinations (note: courtesy buses to city centre hotels are not included in this edition, though it is hoped they will feature in subsequent editions); and **Other towns and cities**, direct connections from the airport to other town or cities within a few hours' journey time. Within each of these categories services are listed in order of destination.

In addition to destination category and name, the listing includes the type of transport, the operator and service code (e.g. bus number), frequency of service, hours of operation (first and last departure times), journey time, one-way adult fare and any special comments or additional information, e.g. information phone numbers or further connections. See 'General Notes' above regarding rail fares. Types of transport are classified as bus, limousine, train, metro, tram, helicopter or water transport. By 'limousine' we denote vans, minibuses and other light buses which typically operate on demand and along specified routes or to specified destinations but not necessarily to a definite schedule. The distinction between limousines, buses and taxis is not always easy to define, but generally limousine or van services exist to accept several passengers for different destinations along a defined route or within a defined area, buses run to more fixed stops and schedules, and taxis are intended for hire by one party only to an exact destination. Services providing a 'limousine' in the sense of a luxury hired car are covered in Taxis and Chauffeur-driven cars. By 'metro' we mean an urban light rail system, such as the London Underground, Chicago 'El' or the U-Bahn in various German cities. More mainline services, such as German S-Bahn, are classified as 'rail'.

REGIONAL AIR CONNECTIONS

This section lists all cities to which there is a flight or flights of approximately 1 hour or less from the gateway airport. Because of the likelihood of changes to the flight schedules during the currency of this book, details of frequency are deliberately generalised (see 'Frequency' under 'General Notes' above). This section is intended to give an overview of links to onward destinations with airports in the region of the main gateway. It does not imply that no direct service to the regional airport is possible, and airline timetables or a travel agent will indicate whether this is also an option. Many of these regional airports are themselves international airports, and may include some of the other gateways described in this book. For instance, London and Amsterdam are within one another's 'region' in this sense and are shown as such in their respective Regional Air Connections listings. Travellers are thus made aware that it is possible to reach London by onward connection from Amsterdam and vice versa; more favourable fares, choice of airline or flight times may give a good reason for preferring such a routing to a direct flight.

SECTION THREE: DESTINATION INDEX

This section lists all the destinations covered in the Public Transport and Regional Air Connections tables of all of the gateway airports, in one alphabetical sequence. For each destination it provides: the name of the gateway airport from which the destination can be reached (and a cross-reference to the relevant pages in Section Two for further details); the transport type; the frequency; and the journey time. The Destination Index thus makes it possible to find lesser-known places around the world and identify the gateway airport(s) to use in reaching them; bear in mind that there may also be direct flights from your home airport which are not listed. It also shows the choice of transport modes available for the onward journey, and enables you to compare, say, relative timings and frequency of air and rail services between two cities. Again, it is important to remember that this index deals only with connections direct from the gateway airports; by making a short journey into the nearest city centre you will often increase the range of onward destinations available.

TRAVELLER'S NOTES

This section contributes miscellaneous information about the airport or destination which we think will be of use or interest to air travellers. Any advice, tips or items of interest that readers wish to contribute for the next edition from their own experience of the airports or destination cities will be welcomed, and credited by name. Please use the feedback form on page 319 for this.

ABBREVIATIONS AND SYMBOLS

ABBREVIATIONS · ABRÉVIATIONS · ABKÜRZUNGEN · ABBREVIAZIONI · ABREVIATURAS · AFKORTINGEN

approx	approximately · environ · ungefähr · circa · aproximadamente · ongeveer	Nov	November · novembre · November · novembre · noviembre · november
Apr	April · avril · April · aprile · abril · april	NW	North-west · nord-ouest · Nordwesten · nord-ovest · noroeste · noord-west
Arr	Arrivals · arrivée · Ankunft · arrivo · llegada · aankomsten	Oct	October · octobre · Oktober · ottobre · octubre · oktober
Aug	August · août · August · agosto · agosto · augustus	Pub Hol	Public holidays · fêtes légales · Feiertäge · giorni festivi · días festivos · feestdagen
avg	average · moyenne · durchschnittlich · medio · medio · gemiddelde	S	South · sud · Süden · sud · sur · zuid
Dec	December · décembre · Dezember · dicembre · diciembre · december	Sat	Saturday · samedi · Samstag · sabato · sábado · zaterdag
Dep	Departures · départ · Abflug · partenza · salida · vertrek	SE	South-east · sud-est · Südosten · sud-est · sureste · zuid-oost
E	East · est · Osten · est · este · oost	Sep	September · septembre · September · settembre · septiembre · september
Feb	February · février · Februar · febbraio · febrero · februari	stn	station · gare · Bahnhof · stazione · estación · station
Fri	Friday · vendredi · Freitag · venerdì · viernes · vrijdag	Sun	Sunday · dimanche · Sonntag · domenica · domingo · zondag
hr	hour(s) · heure(s) · Stunde(n) · ora, ore · hora(s) · uur, uren	SW	South-west · sud-ouest · Südwesten · sud-ovest · suroeste · zuid-west
Jan	January · janvier · Januar · gennaio · enero · januari	Thu	Thursday · jeudi · Donnerstag · giovedì · jueves · donderdag
Jul	July · juillet · Juli · luglio · julio · juli	Tue	Tuesday · mardi · Dienstag · martes · dinsdag
Jun	June · juin · Juni · giugno · junio · juni	UK	United Kingdom · Royaume-Uni · Vereinigtes Königreich · Regno Unito · Reino Unido · Vereenigde Koninkrijk
km	kilometres · kilomètres · Kilometer · chilometri · kilómetros · kilometer	USA	United States of America · États-Unis · Vereinigte Staaten · Stati Uniti · Estados Unidos · Vereenigde Staten
m	metres · mètres · Meter · metri · metros · meter	W	West · ouest · Westen · ovest · oeste · west
Mar	March · mars · März · marzo · marzo · maart	Wed	Wednesday · mercredi · Mittwoch · mercoledì · miércoles · woensdag
min	minutes · minutes · Minuten · minuti · minutos · minuut		
Mon	Monday · lundi · Montag · lunedì · lunes · maandag		
N	North · nord · Norden · nord · norte · noord		
NE	North-east · nord-est · Nordosten · nord-est · noreste · noord-oost		

SYMBOLS · SYMBOLES · ZEICHEN · SIMBOLI · SÍMBOLOS · TEKENS

General · Général · Allgemeines · Generale · General · Allgemeen

- ✆ phone number · numéro de téléphone · Telefonnummer · numero di telefono · número de teléfono · telefoonnummer
- ℱ fax number · numéro de fax · Faxnummer · numero di fax · número de fax · faxnummer
- ⏱ hours of operation or service · heures d'ouverture ou de service · Öffnungs- oder Betriebszeiten · ore di apertura o di operazione · horas de abertura o de servicio · openings- of bedieningstijden
- » frequency of service · fréquence du service · Häufigkeit des Betriebs · frequenzia di servizio · frecuencia del servicio · dienstfrequentie
- ⊃ journey time · durée du trajet · Reisedauer · durazione del percorso · duración del recorrido · reisduur
- ◇ cost or one-way fare · prix ou tarif (aller) · Preis oder Fahrpreis (einfach) · prezzo o prezzo di biglietto (andata) · kosten of reisprijs (enkele)

Transport · Transport · Verkehr · Trasporti · Transportes · Vervoer

- ✈ air · avion · Flugzeug · aereo · vuelo · lucht
- 🚆 rail · train · Bahn · ferrovia · tren · trein
- 🚌 bus · autobus · Bus · autobus, pullman · autobús · bus
- 🚐 limousine · minibus · Kleinbus · minibus · microbús · auto
- Ⓜ metro, subway · métro · U-bahn · metropolitana · metro · metro
- 🚋 tram · tramway · Straßenbahn · tram · tranvía · tram
- 🚁 helicopter · hélicoptère · Hubschrauber · elicottero · helicóptero · helicopter
- 🚢 water transport · bateau ou hydroglisseur · Fähre · battello · barco · waterbus

Abbreviations and Symbols

Airport Maps · Cartes des aéroports · Flughafenpläne · Piante degli aeroporti · Planos de los Aeropuertos · Plattegronden Luchthavens

P Long stay car park · stationnement à longue terme · Parkplätze (langdauer) · Parcheggio (lungo termine) · aparcamiento (largo plazo) · Parkeergelegenheid lang termijn

P Short stay car park · stationnement à courte terme · Parkplätze (kurzdauer) · Parcheggio (breve termine) · aparcamiento (corto plazo) · Parkeergelegenheid kort termijn

Taxi

Bus stop · Arrêt de bus · Bushaltestelle · Fermata dell' autobus · Parada de autobuses · Bushalte

M Metro station · Station de métro · U-Bahnhaltestelle · Stazione della metropolitana · Estación de Metro · Metro-station

Railway station · Gare ferroviaire · Bahnhof · Stazione ferroviaria · Estación de ferrocarril · Spoorwegstation

Petrol station · Station-service · Tankstelle · Stazione di rifornimento · Estación de servicio · Benzine station

Car rental pick-up · Location de voitures (pick-up) · Mietwagenabholung · Autonoleggio · Alquiler de coches (recogida) · Autoverhuur

Hotel

Boarding gates · Portes d'embarquement · Flugsteigen · Cancelli d'imbarco · Puertas de embarque ·

Customs · Douane · Zoll · Dogana · Aduana · Douane

Passport control · Passeports · Paßkontrolle · Controllo dei passaporti · Control de Pasaportes · Paspoortcontrole

Airline ticket desks · Vente de billets · Flugscheinverkauf · Biglietterie degli aerolinee · venta de billetes · Ticketbalies

Currency exchange · Bureau de change · Geldwechsel · Cambio · Cambio · Wissel

Smoking zone · Zone fumeurs · Raucherzone · Zona per fumatori · Zona fumador · Roken toegestaan

Check-in desks · Enregistrement · Abfertigung · Banchi accettazioni · Facturación · Incheckbalies

Lift · Ascenseur · Fahrstul · Ascensore · Ascensor · Lift

Luggage lockers · Casiers · Schließfächer · Armadietti per bagagli · Consigna automática · Bagagekluizen

Meeting point · Point de rendez-vous · Treffpunkt · Punto di reunione · Punto de reunión · Trefpunt

Airline information · Renseignements aériens · Fluglinienauskunft · Informazioni degli aerolinee · Información de líneas · Vluchtlijninlichtingen

Tourist information · Renseignements de tourisme · Touristeninformation · Informazioni turistiche · Información turística · Toeristische inlichtingen

Lost property · Bureau des objets trouvés · Fundbüro · Ufficio oggetti smarriti · Oficina de objetos perdidos · Bureau van gevonden voorwerpen

Police · Police · Polizei · Polizia · Policía · Politie

First aid · Secours d'urgence · Sanitätswache · Pronto soccorso · Primeros auxilios · Eerste hulp

Post office · Poste · Postamt · Ufficio postale · Oficina de correos · Postkantoor

Telephones · Téléphones · Telefon · Telefoni · Teléfonos · Telefoon

Supermarket · Supermarché · Supermarkt · Supermercato · Supermercado · Supermarkt

Florist · Fleuriste · Blumenladen · Fiorista · Floristería · Bloemenkiosk

Transfer desk · Correspondances · Umsteigeschalter · Mostrador de transbordo · Overstapbalie

Phones for disabled · Téléphones pour handicapés · Telefone für Behinderte · Telefoni per gli handicappati · Teléfonos para los discapacitados · Telefoon voor gehandicapten

Duty-free shops · Boutiques hors-taxe · Zollfreiverkauf · Negozi duty-free · Tiendas libres de impuestos · Belastingvrije winkels

Duty-paid shops · Boutiques à cadeaux · Geschenkeladen · Articoli da regalo · Regalos · Cadeauwinkels

Tobacco shop · Tabac · Tabakwaren · Tabaccaio · Tabaquería · Tabac

Book shop · Librairie · Buchhandel · Libreria · Librería · Boeker

Pharmacy · Pharmacie · Apotheke · Farmacia · Farmacia · Apotheek

Hairdressers · Salon de coiffure · Friseur · Parruchiere · Peluquería · Kapsalon

Restaurant · Restaurant · Restaurant · Ristorante · Restaurante · Restaurant

Bar

Café

Toilets · Toilettes · Toiletten · Tolette · Servicios · Toiletten

Baby care facilities · Chambre d'enfants · Kinderzimmer · Camera dei bambini · Guardería · Moeder en baby ruimte

Chapel · Chapelle · Andachtsraum · Cappella · Capilla · Kapel

Gym · Gymnase · Fitneßraum · Palestra · Gimnasio · Gymzaal

Meeting rooms · Salles de réunion · Besprechungszimmer · Sale per riunioni · Salones de reuniones · Vergaderruimtes

VIP lounge · Salon d'accueil aux VIP · VIP-Halle · Salone VIP · Salón VIP · VIP lounge

Airline lounge · Salon pour passagers · Warteraum · Sala d'aspetto · Sala de espera · Wachtruimte

Left luggage · Consigne des bagages · Gepäckaufbewahrung · Deposito bagagli · Consigna · Bagagedepot

Baggage reclaim · Réception des bagages · Gepäckausgabe · Recupero bagagli · Recogida de equipajes · Teruggeven van bagage

Disabled travellers' facility · Installation pour handicapés · Einrichtung für Behinderte · Attrezzature per viaggiatori andicappati · Instalaciones para viajeros discapacitados · Voorzieningen voor gehandicapten

Moving walkway · Tapis roulant · Rollsteg · Marciapiede mobile · Pasilio móvil

Stairs · Escalier · Treppe · Scala · Escalera · Trappen

Escalator · Escalier roulant · Rolltreppe · Scala mobile · Escalera rodante · Roltrap

Ramp · Rampe · Rampe · Rampa · Rampa · Helling

Business centre · Centre pour voyageurs d'affaires · Geschäftsreisenderzentrum · Centro per viaggiatori d'affari · Centro para viajeros de negocios · Business center

Fax Fax

AIRLINE AND CURRENCY CODES

City maps · Plans des villes · Stadtpläne · Piante delle città · Planos de las ciudades · Stadsplattegronden

	Tourist information · Office de tourisme · Verkehrsverein · Ufficio di Turismo · Oficina de turismo · Toeristische inlichtingen
✉	Post office · Poste · Postamt · Ufficio postale · Oficina de correos · Postkantoor
†	Church · Église · Kirche · Chiesa · Iglesia · Kerk
🚌	Bus station · Gare routière · Busbahnhof · Stazione autobus · Estación de autobuses · Busstation
M	Metro station · Station de métro · U-Bahnhaltestelle · Stazione della metropolitana · Estación de metro · Metro station
✝	Cathedral · Cathédrale · Dom · Duomo · Catedral · Kathedraal

AIRLINE AND CURRENCY CODES

AIRLINE CODES

Code	Airline	Code	Airline	Code	Airline	Code	Airline
2V	Amtrak	B2	Belavia	FR	Ryanair	KP	Kiwi International Airlines
3D	Palair Macedonian Airlines	BA	British Airways	FV	Viva Air	KQ	Kenya Airways
3M	Gulfstream International	BD	British Midland Airways	GA	Garuda Indonesian Airlines	KU	Kuwait Airways
3Q	Yunnan Airlines	BE	Centennial Airlines	GD	Taesa	KW	Carnival Airlines
3S	Shuswap Flight Center	BF	Markair	GF	Gulf Air	KX	Cayman Airways
3V	Waglisla Air	BG	Biman Bangladesh Airlines	GH	Ghana Airways	LG	Luxair
4D	Air Alma	BI	Royal Brunei Airlines	GY	Guyana Airways	LH	Lufthansa
4H	Hanna's Air Saltspring	BO	Bouraq Indonesia Airlines	HA	Hawaiian Airlines	LJ	Sierra National Airlines
5E	BASE Regional Airlines			HE	LGW Walter	LM	ALM Antillean Airlines
5V	Community Express	BQ	Eurobelgian Air	HF	Hapag Lloyd	LO	Lot Polish Airlines
6U	Air Ukraine	BR	Eva Air	HM	Air Seychelles	LR	LACSA
6W	Wilderness Airline	BT	Air Baltic	HP	America West Airlines	LT	LTU International Airways
7F	First Air	BU	Braathens S.A.F.E.	HV	Transavia	LX	Crossair
7L	Air Belfast	BW	BWIA International	HY	Uzbekistan Airways	LY	El Al Israel Airlines
7P	APA International Air	CA	Air China	IB	Iberia	LZ	Balkan Bulgarian Airlines
7S	Region Air	CH	Benidji Airlines	IC	Indian Airlines		
8D	Awood Air	CI	China Airlines	IG	Meridiana	MA	Malev Hungarian
8K	Air Ostrava	CO	Continental Airlines	II	Business Air	MD	Air Madagascar
8M	Mahalo Air	CP	Canadian Airlines Internat'l	IJ	TAT European Airlines	ME	Middle East Airlines
8P	Pacific Coastal Airlines			IL	Istanbul Airlines	MH	Malaysian Airlines
9C	Gillair	CU	Cubana	IR	Iran Air	MI	Silk Air
9K	Cape Air	CX	Cathay Pacific Airways	IW	AOM French Airlines	MK	Air Mauritius
9L	Colgan Air	CY	Cyprus Airlines	IY	Yemen Airways	ML	Aero Costa Rica Acori
9M	Central Mountain Air	CZ	China Southern Airlines	IZ	Arkia Israeli Arlines	MP	Martinair Holland
9P	Pelangi Air			JD	Japan Air System	MS	Egyptair
AA	American Airlines	DE	Condor	JE	Manx Airlines	MU	China Eastern Airlines
AC	Air Canada	DI	Deutsche BA	JI	Midway Airlines	MX	Mexicana
AD	Lone Star Airlines	DL	Delta Airlines	JK	Spanair	MZ	Merpati Nusantara Airlines
AF	Air France	DM	Maersk Air	JL	Japan Airlines		
AH	Air Algérie	DP	Air 2000	JM	Air Jamaica	N5	Nations Air Express
AI	Air India	EH	SAETA	JN	Rich International Airways	NG	Lauda-Air
AM	Aeromexico	EI	Aer Lingus	JP	Adria Airways	NH	All Nippon Airways
AN	Ansett Australia	EK	Emirates	JU	Jat Yugoslav Airlines	NI	Portugalia
AO	Aviaco	EN	Air Dolomiti	JY	Jersey European Airlines	NJ	Vanguard Airlines
AQ	Aloha Airlines	ET	Ethiopian Airlines			NK	Spirit Airlines
AR	Aerolineas Argentinas	EX	Dallas Express	K4	Kazakhstan Airlines	NQ	Orbi Georgian Airways
AS	Alaska Airlines	F9	Frontier Airlines	KB	Druk-Air	NS	Eurowings
AT	Royal Air Maroc	FF	Tower Air	KE	Korean Airlines	NW	Northwest Airlines
AV	Avianca Colombian Airlines	FI	Icelandair	KI	Air Atlantique	NZ	Air New Zealand
		FJ	Air Pacific	KJ	British Mediterranean	OA	Olympic Airways
AY	Finnair	FL	AirTran Airways	KL	KLM	OH	Comair
AZ	Alitalia	FQ	Air Aruba	KM	Air Malta	OK	CSA Czechoslovak

11

Airline and Currency Codes

OS	Austrian Airlines	RG	Varig Brazilian	TK	Turkish Airlines	VM	Regional Airlines
OU	Croatia Airlines	RI	Mandala Airlines	TP	Air Portugal TAP	VN	Vietnam Airlines
OV	Estonian Air	RJ	Royal Jordanian Airlines	TQ	Transwede Airways	VO	Tyrolean Airways
OZ	Asiana Airlines			TT	Air Lithuania	VP	VASP
P9	Topair	RK	Air Afrique	TU	Tunis Air	VR	T.A. de Cabo Verde
PD	Pem-Air	RN	Euralair	TW	TWA (Trans World Airlines)	VS	Virgin Atlantic
PE	Pine State Airlines	RO	Tarom Romanian Air			W3	Swiftair
PK	Pakistan Internat'l Airlines	RP	Macair	TZ	American Trans Air	W5	Tajikistan International
		RQ	Air Engadiana	UA	United Airlines	W7	Western Pacific Airlines
PL	Aeroperu	SA	South African Airways	UB	Myanmar Airways Internat'l	W9	Eastwind
PN	Air Martinique	SD	Sudan Airways			WA	Newair
PR	Philippine Airlines	SG	Sempati Air	UD	Hex'Air	WN	Southwest
PS	Ukraine Internat'l Airlines	SK	Scandinavian Airlines	UG	Tuninter	WO	World Airways
		SN	Sabena World Airlines	UK	Air UK	WP	Aloha Islandair
PX	Air Niugini	SQ	Singapore Airlines	UL	Air Lanka	WT	Nigeria Airways
Q7	Qatar Airlines	SR	Swissair	UM	Air Zimbabwe	WV	Air South
QD	Grand Airways	SU	Aeroflot	UN	Transaero Airlines	WW	Whyalla Airlines
QF	Qantas Airways	SV	Saudia	UP	Bahamasair	XT	Air Exel
QK	Air Nova	SW	Air Namibia	US	USAir	YE	European Air Charter
QQ	Reno Air	SY	Sun Country	UX	Air Europa	YP	Aero Lloyd
QS	Tatra Air	SZ	China Southwest	UY	Cameroon Airlines	YV	Mesa Airlines
QV	Lao Aviation	TA	Taca International Airlines	V4	VLM	YW	Air Nostrum
R9	Air Charter			VA	VIASA Venezuelan	YX	Midwest Express
RA	Royal Nepal Airlines	TE	Lithuanian Airlines	VD	Air Liberté	ZB	Monarch Airlines
RB	Syrian Arab Airlines	TG	Thai Airways	VF	British World Airlines	ZI	Aigle Azur
				VJ	Royal Air Cambodge	ZK	Great Lakes

Currency Codes

The following abbreviations have been used throughout Section Two for the currencies in which payments and fares are expressed. These are the official IATA codes used on airline tickets and other international documents. The actual abbreviation used within a country for its own currency is usually different, e.g. the pound sterling is normally written as '£' within Britain, the Spanish peseta is usually abbreviated to 'Pta' within Spain

Abbreviation	Country	Unit of currency	Abbreviation	Country	Unit of currency
AED	United Arab Emirates	Dirham	ITL	Italy	Italian Lira
ARS	Argentina	Argentinian Peso	JMD	Jamaica	Jamaican Dollar
ATS	Austria	Austrian Schilling	JPY	Japan	Yen
AUD	Australia	Australian Dollar	KES	Kenya	Kenyan Shilling
BEF	Belgium	Belgian Franc	KRW	Korea (South)	Won
BEV	Venezuela	Bolivar	LKR	Sri Lanka	Sri Lanka Rupee
BHD	Bahrain	Bahraini Dinar	MAD	Morocco	Dirham
BRC	Brazil	Cruzeiro	MXN	Mexico	Nuevo Peso
BSD	Bahamas	Bahamian Dollar	MYR	Malaysia	Ringgit
CAD	Canada	Canadian Dollar	NGN	Nigeria	Naira
CHF	Switzerland	Swiss Franc	NLG	Netherlands	Guilder
CLP	Chile	Chilean Peso	NOK	Norway	Norwegian Krone
CNY	China P. R.	Ren Min Bi Yuan	NZD	New Zealand	NZ Dollar
COP	Colombia	Colombian Peso	PHP	Philippines	Philippine Peso
CZK	Czech Rep.	Czech Koruna	PKR	Pakistan	Pakistani Rupee
DEM	Germany	Deutsche Mark	PLZ	Poland	Zloty
DKK	Denmark	Danish Krone	PTE	Portugal	Escudo
EGP	Egypt	Egyptian Pound	RUR	Russia	Russian Rouble
ESP	Spain	Peseta	SAR	Saudi Arabia	Saudi Riyal
FIM	Finland	Markka	SEK	Sweden	Swedish Krona
FRF	France	French Franc	SGD	Singapore	Singapore Dollar
GBP	United Kingdom	Pound Sterling	THB	Thailand	Baht
GRD	Greece	Drachma	TRL	Turkey	Turkish Lira
HKD	Hong Kong	HK Dollar	TWD	Taiwan	New Taiwan Dollar
HUF	Hungary	Forint	USD	United States of America	US Dollar
IDR	Indonesia	Rupiah	VND	Viet Nam	Dong
IEP	Ireland (Rep. of)	Punt	ZAR	South Africa	Rand
ILS	Israel	Shekel	ZWD	Zimbabwe	Zimbabwe Dollar
INR	India	Rupee			

SECTION ONE • AIR TRAVEL FACTS

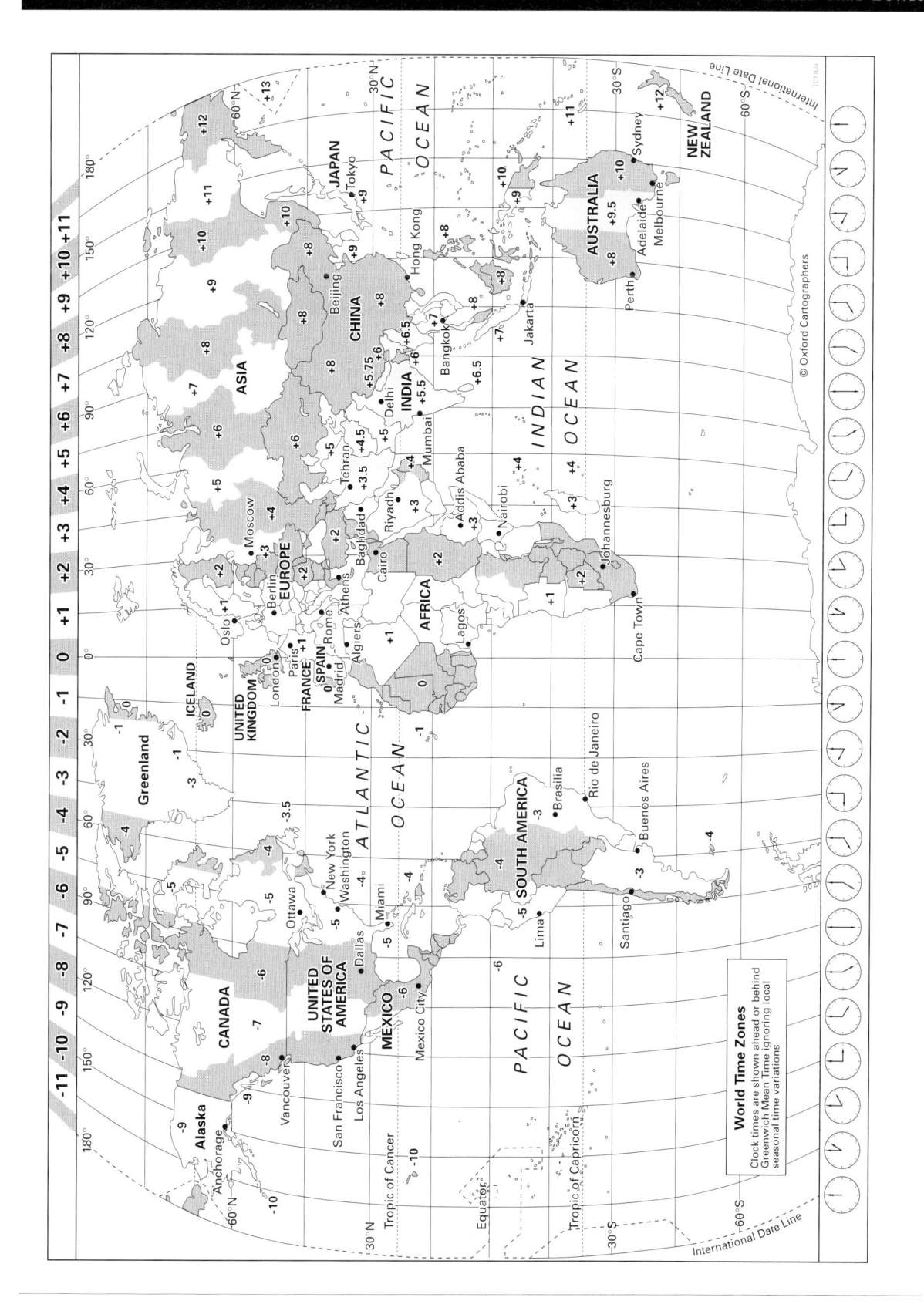

WORLD TIME ZONES

COUNTRY BY COUNTRY TRAVEL FACTS

ARGENTINA

Capital Buenos Aires
Language Spanish is the official language. English, German, French and Italian are sometimes spoken.
Standard time GMT-3
Climate Varies from sub-tropical in the north to sub-Antarctic in the south. The main central area is temperate, but it can be hot and very oppressive with high humidity between mid-December and February.
Health Precautions against Malaria, Hepatitis A, Typhoid and Polio recommended. Tap water generally safe to drink.
Passports and visas Valid passports required by all except nationals of Brazil, Bolivia, Chile, Paraguay and Uruguay holding identity cards. Visas required by all except nationals of Algeria, Austria, Barbados, Belgium, Bolivia, Brazil, Canada, Chile, Colombia, Costa Rica, Denmark, Dominica, Dominican Rep., Ecuador, Eire, El Salvador, Finland, France, Germany, Greece, Guatemala, Guyane, Haiti, Honduras, Hong Kong, Hungary, Italy, Jamaica, Japan, Liechtenstein, Luxembourg, Malta, Mexico, Monaco, Nicaragua, Netherlands, Norway, Paraguay, Peru, Poland, Portugal, Spain, Sweden, Switzerland, Turkey, UK, Uruguay, USA and Yugoslavia. Visas are generally issued for tourist and transit purposes only. Visas are required by all nationals if travelling for business reasons and personal application at the Consulate is necessary. Documentation: Return ticket required by Australia, Japan and others. May be subject to change at short notice. Contact the Consular authority before departure.
Customs regulations (inbound) From Bolivia, Brazil, Chile, Paraguay and Uruguay: Residents returning after a stay of less than 1 year abroad, persons arriving under contract for stays of less than 1 year and tourists: Goods and articles up to the value of 100 US dollars including the following: 200 cigarettes and 20 cigars, 1 ltr of alcoholic beverages and 2 kg of foodstuffs. From countries other than those above: Residents returning after a stay of less than 1 year abroad and tourists, immigrants and persons working under contract from any country for stays of over 1 year: Goods and articles up to the value of 200 US dollars including the following: 400 cigarettes and 50 cigars, 2 ltr of alcoholic beverages and 5 kg of foodstuffs.
Prohibited/ restricted: All animals and birds coming from Africa or Asia (excluding Japan). All birds belonging to the parrot family. Fresh foodstuffs particularly meat, dairy products and fruit, explosives, inflammable items, narcotics, obscene and pornographic material.
Currency Nuevo Peso (ARS) = 100 Centavos
Postage Postcard /airmail letter, approximately 1.00 ARS Post boxes are red or blue.
Telephone codes Inward 54 + Bahía Blanca 91, Buenos Aires 1, Mar del Plata 23. Outward 00. Call boxes are blue/turquoise. Special tokens required. Phonecards also available.
Thomas Cook Travellers' Cheque Collect call Emergency number +44 1733 318950
Mastercard Global Service Toll-free Emergency number 08002 2002
Driving International licence required, plus insurance and proof of ownership for imported vehicles. Drive on the right. Speed limit 80 k/hr (110 k/hr on motorways (highways)).
Business hours Banks: 1000-1600 Mon-Fri. Offices: 0900-1900 Mon-Fri. Shops: 0900-1900 Mon-Fri, 0900-1300 Sat.
Public holidays Jan 1; May 1, 25; June 10, 20; July 9; Aug 17; Oct 12; Dec 8, 25; also Holy Thursday and Good Friday.

AUSTRALIA

Capital Canberra
Language English and many minority languages.
Standard time Lord Howe Island GMT+11 (+10½ from 30 Mar to 26 Oct); Australian Capital Territory, New South Wales GMT+11(+10 from 30 Mar to 26 Oct); Victoria GMT+11(+10 from 30 Mar to 26 Oct); Tasmania GMT+11(+10 from 30 Mar to 26 Oct); Queensland GMT+10; South Australia GMT+10½(+9½ from 30 Mar to 26 Oct); Northern Territory GMT+9½; Western Australia GMT+8.
Climate Varies greatly with latitude, from tropical in Darwin to temperate in Tasmania. Overall, the climate is warmer than that of most of the USA and Europe.
Health Yellow Fever vaccination required if arriving from an endemic or infected area (infants under one year exempt). Tap water safe to drink.
Passports and visas Passports required by all and should be valid at least 6 months beyond the date of stay. Visas required by all except Australian and New Zealand passport holders and passengers passing through Australia in transit to a third country by same or connecting aircraft within 8 hours of arrival and holding tickets with confirmed onward reservations, all documents required for next destination and not leaving the transit lounge and provided (a) they are nationals of Austria, Belgium, Brunei, Canada, Denmark, Eire, Fiji, Finland, France, Germany, Greece, Indonesia, Italy, Japan, Kiribati, Korea Rep. (south), Liechtenstein, Luxembourg, Malaysia, Malta, Nauru, Netherlands, Norway, Papua New Guinea, Philippines, Portugal, Singapore, Solomon Islands, Spain, Sweden, Switzerland, Thailand, Tonga, Tuvalu, UK, USA, Vanuatu, Western Samoa and Zimbabwe. (b) holding passports issued by the Government of the Federal States of Micronesia or the Republic of the Marshall Islands. (c) holding Taiwanese normal passports. Overnight stay is not permitted in Melbourne and Sydney. Limited transit facilities in Darwin. All passengers other than Australian and New Zealanders transiting Australia by sea must be in possession of visas.
Documentation: 1 photograph for visa. Passports must contain 2 unused facing pages for Australian Visas and entry stamps.
Customs regulations (inbound) 250 cigarettes, 1.125 ltr alcoholic beverages, dutiable goods to the value of AUD 400. It is illegal to import ivory and products from endangered species. Most animals and plants, and items of animal or plant origin (including foods) are prohibited imports. Strict regulations also on non-prescribed drugs, weapons and foodstuffs.
Currency Australian Dollar (AUD) = 100 Cents
Postage Postcard AUD 0.70-1.00, Airmail letters AUD1.20 depending on destination. Aerogramme AUD 0.70. Post boxes are red.
Telephone codes Inward 61 + Adelaide 8, Brisbane 7, Cairns 7, Canberra 6, Darwin 8, Hobart 3, Melbourne 3, Perth 9, Sydney 2, Townsville 77. Outward 0011. Call boxes are generally stainless steel and glass with an orange stylized 'T' symbol; international

calls can be made from most payphones. 10 cent, 20 cent, 50 cent, 1 dollar and 2 dollar coins accepted (also phonecards).
Thomas Cook Travellers' Cheque Toll-free Emergency number 1 800 127 495
Mastercard Global Service Toll-free Emergency number 1 800 120 113
Driving Own national licence valid for bona fide tourists; International Permit recommended if national licence is in a language other than English. International Permit compulsory for long-term periods. Licence should be carried at all times when driving. Seat belts must be worn by driver and all passengers. Drive on the left. Speed limit 60 k/hr in urban areas, 100 k/hr elsewhere (110 k/hr in Western Australia, no upper limit in Northern Territory). Traffic regulations vary from state to state.
Business hours Banks: 0930-1600 Mon-Thurs, 0930-1700 Fri. These hours vary throughout the country. Offices: 0900-1730 Mon-Fri. Shops: 0900-1730 Mon-Fri, 0900-1700 Sat, some large stores open Sun.
Public holidays Jan 1, 26; Apr. 25; Dec 25, 26; also Good Friday, Easter Monday, Queen's Birthday (except Western Australia). In addition, there are a number of holidays celebrated in individual states, territories and localities.

AUSTRIA

Capital Vienna (Wien)
Language German. English is widely spoken in tourist areas.
Standard time GMT+2 (GMT+1 Oct-Mar)
Climate Moderate continental climate, warm summers, winters sunny and cold with moderate snowfalls.
Health No compulsory vaccinations. Tap water safe to drink.
Passports and visas Passports required for all except: Nationals of EU countries with a valid ID card. Nationals of Andorra, Liechtenstein, Malta, Monaco, San Marino and Switzerland who may enter with a valid ID card. Holders of passports expired a maximum of 5 years issued to nationals of Liechtenstein, Norway, Switzerland, and the UK. Visas are required by all except: Nationals of Great Britain, Australia, Canada, USA, EU countries, Japan and those referred to under passport exemptions above. Nationals of Argentina, Bahamas, Barbados, Bolivia, Brazil, Chile, Colombia, Costa Rica, Croatia, Cyprus, Czech Republic, Ecuador, El Salvador, Guatemala, Hungary, Iceland, Israel, Jamaica, S Korea, Malaysia, Mexico, New Zealand, Panama, Paraguay, Poland, Seychelles, Singapore, Slovak Republic, Slovenia, Trinidad & Tobago, Tunisia, Uruguay and Venezuela for various lengths of stay (contact Embassy). Others should check.
Customs regulations (inbound) Travellers from within EU countries need not complete Customs formalities. Goods bought outside the EU or in EU duty-free shops; 200 cigarettes or 50 cigars or 100 cigarillos or 250gm tobacco, 1 ltr spirits or 2 ltr sparkling or fortified wine, 2 ltr still table wine, 60ml perfume, 250ml toilet water, other commodities duty free to a value of ATS2400; ATS1000 from the Czech Republic, Slovakia or Slovenia.
Currency Schilling (ATS) = 100 Groschen.
Postage Post offices can be recognised by a golden trumpet symbol and are often located close to the station or main square. They all handle poste restante (Postlagernde Briefe). Nationwide hours are Mon-Fri 0800-1200 and 1400-1800, but offices in major towns tend to stay open during lunch and on Sat. The main post offices in cities frequently open 24 hrs. Stamps (Briefmarke) can also be purchased at Tabak/Trafik shops. Airmail letter (priority to Europe) ATS 7, postcard and non priority ATS 6.50.
Telephone codes Inward 43 + Vienna 1, Salzburg 662, Innsbruck 512. To call international enquiries and operator: tel: 0222 16118. Post office phone counters can give the correct area codes to use locally. National enquiries and operator: tel: 0222 16 11. Emergencies: Police: 133; Fire: 122; Ambulance: 144. Most boxes have instructions in English and most international operators speak it. Telephone cards, slightly cheaper than cash, available from post offices, stations and some shops; metered phones in post offices where payment is made afterwards. Long distance calls are approximately 35% cheaper between 1800 and 0800 and public holidays.
Thomas Cook Travellers' Cheque Local Call Charge Emergency number 0660 6266
Mastercard Global Service Toll-free Emergency number 0600 8235
Driving Drive on right. Priority is given to those coming from the right, except when you are on a major road. Trams always have priority. Speed limit is 30-50 k/hr in villages, 100k/hr on other roads and 130 k/hr on motorways. Third party insurance is obligatory. Seatbelts are compulsory. Children under 12 years are not permitted in front seats.
Business hours Banks: in Vienna - Mon, Tue, Wed, Fri 0800-1230 and 1330-1500/1700, Thurs 0800-1230 and 1330-1730 (some stay open through the lunch hour). Elsewhere, the norm is Mon-Fri 0800-1200 and 1400-1700. Offices: 0800-1700 (Many offices and factories close at 1200/1300 on Fridays). Shops: Mon-Fri 0800-1830, Sat 0800-1300 (in larger towns many stay open until 1700 on the first Sat of the month and may have 1 weekday late night opening. Shops in small villages may close 1 afternoon per week).
Public holidays 1, 6 Jan; Easter Mon; 1 May; Ascension Day; Whit Mon; Corpus Christi; 15 Aug; 26 Oct; 1 Nov; 8, 25, 26 Dec. Many people take unofficial holidays on Good Fri, 2 Nov (schools only), 24 Dec and 31 Dec. Holidays falling on a rest day will not be celebrated on another weekday.

BAHAMAS

Capital Nassau
Language English
Standard time GMT-5
Climate Tropical, tempered by ocean location. Temperatures 20°C - 30°C. Rainfall 600-1000 mm per annum, (most falling May-Nov when occasional tropical storms may occur).
Health Yellow Fever vaccination required by all arriving from endemic areas. Precautions against Hepatitis A, Typhoid and Polio recommended. Tap water generally safe to drink.
Passports and visas Passports required by all except nationals of Canada, Cayman Is., Falkland Is., Gibraltar, Hong Kong, Pitcairn Is., St. Helena, Turks & Caicos Is., UK and Virgin Is. (British), for a temporary visit of no longer than 3 weeks. U.S. citizens may visit for up to 8 months. All passport-free visitors must carry sufficient identification to satisfy the Bahamas Immigration Authorities on entry and valid documentation to enable them to re-enter their country of domicile. Visas required by all except nationals of (a) Anguilla, Antigua, Australia, Bangladesh, Barbados, Belgium, Belize, Bermuda, Botswana, Brunei, Canada, Cayman Is., Cyprus, Dominica, Falkland Is., Gambia, Ghana, Gibraltar, Greece, Grenada, Guyana, Hong Kong, Iceland, India, Italy, Jamaica, Japan, Kenya, Kiribati, Lesotho, Liechtenstein, Luxembourg, Malawi, Malaysia, Maldives, Malta, Mauritius, Montserrat, Nauru, Netherlands, New Zealand. Nigeria, Norway, Papua New Guinea, Pitcairn Is., St. Helena, St. Kitts-Nevis, St. Lucia, St. Vincent, San Marino, Seychelles, Sierra Leone, Singapore, Solomon Is., Sri Lanka, Swaziland, Sweden, Switzerland, Tanzania, Tonga, Trinidad & Tobago, Turkey, Turks & Caicos Is., Tuvalu, Uganda, UK, USA, (for a stay of up to 8 months), Vanuatu, Virgin Is. (British), Western Samoa, Zambia and Zimbabwe (for a stay of up to 8 months). (b) Austria, Denmark, Eire, Finland, Germany, Israel and Mexico (for a stay of up to 3 months). (c) Argentina, Bolivia, Brazil, Chile, Costa Rica, Ecuador, El Salvador, Guatemala, Honduras, Nicaragua, Panama, Paraguay, Peru, Uruguay and Venezuela (for a stay of up to 2 weeks).
Documentation: 2 photographs for visa. All visitors must hold sufficient funds for their stay, and be in possession of onward or

return tickets.
Customs regulations (inbound) Persons aged 18: 200 cigarettes or 50 cigars or 454gm tobacco or 100 cigarillos, alcoholic beverages not exceeding 1 ltr of spirits or not more than 2 ltr spirits if at least 1 ltr is the product of a Caribbean country. Prohibited/restricted: narcotics, firearms, flick knives.
Currency Bahamian Dollar (BSD) = 100 cents
Postage BSD 0.45-0.60 according to destination. Airmail letter BSD 0.40 Post boxes are red. Telephone codes Inward 1242 (Callers from North America and the Caribbean do not need to dial the initial 1) Outward 1 (Caribbean, Canada and USA), 011 (all other destinations). Call boxes are blue and require 25 cent coins, credit cards or phonecards.
Thomas Cook Travellers' Cheque Collect call Emergency number+44 1733 318950
Mastercard Global Service Toll-free Emergency number 1 800 307 7309
Driving Own national licence valid for visitors staying for up to 3 months and who are not employed in the Bahamas. Drive on the left. Speed limit 48-64 k/hr.
Business hours Banks: 0930-1500 Mon-Thur. 0930-1700 Fri. Offices: 0900-1700 Mon-Fri. Shops: 0930-1730 Mon-Fri, 1000-1600 Sun.
Public holidays; Jan 1; July 10; Oct 12; Dec 25, 26; also Good Friday, Easter Monday, Whit Monday, Labour Day, Emancipation Day (1st Mon in Aug).

BAHRAIN

Capital Manama
Language Arabic, English may also be spoken.
Standard time GMT+3
Climate Hot and humid in summer, mild and humid in winter. Rainfall is negligible.
Health Yellow Fever vaccination required if arriving within 6 days after leaving or transiting infected areas (infants under one year exempt). Precautions against Cholera, Hepatitis A, Typhoid and Polio recommended. Tap water safe to drink.
Passports and visas Passports required by all. Israeli passport holders are prohibited at all times. Visas required by all except nationals of Kuwait, Oman, Qatar, Saudi Arabia and United Arab Emirates; also UK British-born nationals for a maximum of 4 weeks (providing their full passport is valid for 6 weeks). Documentation: 2 photographs for visa.
Customs regulations (inbound) 400 cigarettes or 50 cigars or 226gm of tobacco products for personal use, 2 bottles of alcoholic beverages for non-Muslim passengers only. 227 ml perfume. Prohibited/restricted: Firearms, ammunition, drugs, jewellry subject to import permits. Goods of Israeli origin.
Currency Bahrain Dinar (BHD) = 100 Fils
Postage Postcard 150 Fils, airmail letter 200 Fils. Post boxes are red.
Telephone codes Inward 973. No area codes. Outward 00. Call boxes are green. 100-Fil coins required.
Thomas Cook Travellers' Cheque Collect call Emergency number+ 44 1733 318950
Mastercard Global Service Toll-free Emergency number 800 087
Driving International licence required. Drive on the right. Speed limit 70 k/hr.
Business hours Banks: 0730-1200, and usually 1530/1600-1730/1800 Sat-Wed. 0730-1100 Thur. Government Offices: 0700-1415 Sat-Wed, closed Thurs & Fri. Commercial Offices: 0800-1530 (or 0800-1300 and 1500-1700) Sun-Wed. Shops: 0800-1230 Sat-Thur, 1530-1830 Sat-Tue, 1530-2100 Wed & Thur.
Public holidays Jan 1; Dec 16; also Eid al Fiter (3 days), Eid al Adha (3 days), El Hijra, Ashoora (2 days) and Prophet's Birthday.

BARBADOS

Capital Bridgetown
Language English. Local Bajan dialect is also spoken.
Standard time GMT - 4
Climate Tropical, tempered by ocean location. The rainy season lasts from July-Nov. Temperatures 22°C - 30°C throughout the year.
Health Yellow Fever vaccination required if arriving within 6 months from infected areas (infants under one year exempt). Precautions against Hepatitis A, Typhoid and Polio recommended. Tap water safe to drink.
Passports and visas Passports required by all except citizens of Canada and USA who embark in their home country for stays not exceeding 3 months, hold valid return tickets and who have a naturalisation certificate or original birth certificate accompanied by a driving licence with photograph or employment identification with photograph. Passports must be valid at least 6 months beyond the date of entry into Barbados. Visas required by all except nationals of EU countries (except nationals of Spain who can stay for 28 days and nationals of Portugal who do need a visa) for stays of up to 6 months; Nationals of Commonwealth countries for stays of up to 6 months (except nationals of India, Pakistan, and South Africa where special conditions apply). Note: Contact the High Commission for a complete up to date list as many other countries do not require visas for varying durations of stay. Documentation: 2 photographs for visa. All visitors must hold sufficient funds for their stay and be in possession of onward or return tickets.
Customs regulations (inbound) Tobacco and alcoholic beverages for persons of 18 years or older: 100 cigarettes or 50 cigarellos or 100 cigars, 1 litre of alcoholic beverages, 150gm of perfume, gifts to the value of BBD100. Prohibited/restricted: Firearms and ammunition. Permits required for import of plants and animals. Plants subject to inspection on arrival.
Currency Barbadian Dollar (BBD) =100 cents
Postage Postcard BBD1.20. Airmail letter BBD1.25. Post boxes are red.
Telephone codes Inward 1246 (callers from North America and the Caribbean do not need to dial the initial 1) Outward 1 (Caribbean, Canada and USA), 011 (all other destinations). Call boxes are clear glass. 25 cent coins required. N.B. External calls can be made from call boxes but must be collect or made by credit card/phonecard.
Thomas Cook Travellers' Cheque Toll-free Emergency number 1 800 223 7373
Mastercard Global Service Toll-free Emergency number 1 800 307 7309
Driving Barbados permit required (BBD10 - issued on production of valid international or national licence). Drive on the left. Speed limit 35 k/hr (or lower) in urban areas, 80 k/hr on major speedways, 60 k/hr elsewhere.
Business hours Banks: 0800-1500 Mon-Thur, 0800-1300 and 1500-1700 Fri. Shops: 0800-1600 Mon-Fri, 0800-1300 Sat (food shops open longer on Sat and Sun). Offices: 0800-1600 Mon- Fri
Public holidays Jan 1, 21; Nov 30; Dec 25, 26; also Good Friday, Easter Monday, Whit Monday, May Day, Emancipation Day (1 Aug), Kadooment Day (First Mon in August), and UN Day (First Mon in October).

BELGIUM

Capital Brussels (Bruxelles/Brussel).
Language Belgium has three official languages, in different areas: Dutch (north), French (south) and German (east). Most Belgians speak both French and Dutch. Many (especially the young) also speak some English and/or German.
Standard time GMT+2 (GMT+1 Oct-Mar)

SECTION ONE: AIR TRAVEL FACTS

COUNTRY BY COUNTRY TRAVEL FACTS

Climate Temperate, with best weather between Apr and Oct. Winters range from mild to severe.

Health No compulsory vaccinations required. Rabies present in rural areas. Tap water safe to drink.

Passports and visas Passports required for all except: Nationals of EU countries with a valid ID card. Nationals of Andorra, Liechtenstein, Malta, Monaco, San Marino and Switzerland who may enter with a valid ID card. Visas are required by all except: Nationals of Great Britain, Australia, Canada, USA, EU countries, Japan and those referred to under passport exemptions above. Nationals of Argentina, Brazil, Brunei, Chile, Costa Rica, Cyprus, Czech Republic, Ecuador, El Salvador, Guatemala, Honduras, Hungary, Iceland, Israel, Jamaica, S. Korea, Malawi, Malaysia, Mexico, New Zealand, Nicaragua, Norway, Panama, Paraguay, Poland, Singapore, Slovak Republic, Slovenia, Turkey (if resident in an EU country and have a residence permit valid for a further 4 months), Uruguay, Vatican City and Venezuela.

Customs regulations (inbound) Travellers from within EU countries need not complete Customs formalities. Goods bought outside the EU or in EU duty-free shops; 200 cigarettes or 50 cigars or 100 cigarillos or 250gm tobacco, 1 ltr spirits or 2 ltr sparkling or fortified wine , 2 ltr still table wine, 60ml perfume, 250ml toilet water.

Currency Belgian Franc (BEF) = 100 Centimes.

Postage Major post offices (Postes/Posterijen/De Post) open 0900-1700 Mon-Fri (some also open Fri evening and Sat morning). Stamps can be purchased at most places that sell postcards. Postboxes are smallish and bright red.

Telephone codes Inward 32 + Brussels 2, Antwerp 3, Ostende 59, Ghent 9. To call abroad from Belgium; tel: 00. National operator; tel: 1307 (1207 in Flemish areas). International operator; tel: 1304 (1204 in Flemish areas). International operators speak English. Emergencies: Police: 101; Fire/Ambulance: 100. Coin boxes and phonecard/credit card booths all have English instructions. Phonecards are available at rail stations, post offices and some tobacconists. Most international calls are reduced Mon-Sat 2000-0800 and all day Sun. Numbers prefixed 077 are at premium rates.

Thomas Cook Travellers' Cheque Emergency number Free 1 800 1 2121

Mastercard Global Service Toll-free Emergency number 0800 1 5096

Driving National driving licences are acceptable. Green Card insurance is required. Foreign-registered vehicles must display a nationality badge. Drive on the right, trams have priority. Speed limits: 50kph in built-up areas, 90 kph on main roads, 120 kph on motorways. Fire extinguishers and emergency triangle must be carried.

Business hours Banks: Mon-Fri 0900-1200, 1400-1600 (some banks are open 0900-1200 Sat). Offices: Mon-Fri 0830-1730. Shops: Mon-Sat 0900/1000-1800/1900 (often later Fri/Sat). Many establishments close for lunch 1200-1400.

Public holidays Jan 1; Easter Mon; May 1; Ascension Day; Whit Mon; July 21; Aug 15; Nov 1, 11; Dec 25. Also Flemish community holiday, July 11, French community holiday Sep 27 and German community holiday, Nov 15.

BRAZIL

Capital Brasilia

Language Portuguese. French, German, Italian and English are also spoken.

Standard time Fernando de Noronha GMT-2; SE Coast, Goias, Bahia, Brasilia GMT-2(-3 from 16 Feb to 05 Oct); NE Coast States and Eastern Para GMT-3; Mato Grosso, Mato Grosso do Sul GMT-3(-4 from 16 Feb to 05 Oct); NW States, Western Para and Amazonas GMT-4; Acre GMT-5.

Climate Varies from tropical with high humidity in the north to temperate in the south. Rainy seasons occur Jan-Apr in the north; Apr-July in the north east; Nov-Mar in the Rio/São Paulo area.

Health Yellow Fever vaccination required if arriving within 6 days after leaving or transiting infected areas (infants under 9 months exempt). Polio immunisation required for children between three months and 6 years of age. The dosage of vaccine must be clearly indicated on the certificate. Malaria risk exists throughout the year below 900m in Acre and Rondônia states, States of Amapà and Roraima, and in some rural areas of Amazonas, Goiás, Maranhão, Mato Grosso and Pará states. Precautions against Malaria, Hepatitis A, Typhoid and Polio, also Yellow Fever (except for infants under one year), recommended. In the event of an outbreak of Yellow Fever in the northern Amazon region, bus services entering the area are halted for all passengers to be compulsorily vaccinated. Tap water generally safe to drink.

Passports and visas Passports required by all, except nationals of Argentina, Chile, Paraguay and Uruguay who may enter on a National Identity Card if entering from that country. Passports must be valid for at least 6 months. Visas required by all except nationals of Argentina, Austria, Bahamas, Barbados, Belgium, Chile, Colombia, Denmark, Ecuador, Eire, Finland, Germany (Federal Rep.), Greece, Grenada, Iceland, Italy, Liechtenstein, Luxembourg, Monaco, Netherlands, Norway, Paraguay, Peru, Portugal, Spain, Suriname, Sweden, Switzerland, Trinidad & Tobago and Uruguay, UK, providing they hold onward or return tickets. Transit visas required by all whose stay exceeds 24 hours. Documentation (for visa): Tourists require 1 photograph plus a letter from their bank proving means of maintenance or a return or onward air ticket. Visitors on business require 1 photograph plus a letter from their firm giving full details and confirming financial responsibility for, and the good character of, the applicant. Visas will not be granted if the validity of the passport expires within 6 months.All visitors must hold onward or return tickets or evidence of sufficient funds for a ticket to their country of origin.

Customs regulations (inbound) 400 cigarettes and 250gm tobacco and 25 cigars. Bought before arriving in Brazil: 2 ltr alcoholic beverage. Bought for personal use in Duty-Free Shop on arrival: total value not exceeding 500 US dollars, alcoholic beverages restricted to 3 bottles wine, 2 bottles Champagne and 2 bottles spirits.

Currency Brazilian Cruzeiro Real (BRL) = 100 Centavos

Postage Postcard or airmail letter BRL 0.84. Post boxes are yellow.

Telephone codes Inward 55 + Belém 91, Belo Horizonte 31, Brasilia 61, Curitiba 41, Fortaleza 85, Porto Alegre 512, Recife 81, Ribeirão Prêto 16, Rio de Janeiro 21, Salvador 71, São Paulo 11. Outward 00. Colour of call boxes varies with area. Tokens required (available from news stalls).

Thomas Cook Travellers' Cheque Collect call Emergency number +44 1733 318950

Mastercard Global Service Toll-free Emergency number 000811 887 0553

Driving International Permit required. Imported vehicles must be accompanied by certificate of ownership proving that the vehicle has been legally exported from the country of origin, and declaration that the vehicle will be re-exported within 90 days. (Failure to comply with this regulation could result in seizure of vehicle). Drivers of such vehicles must carry their passport/identity card and own national licence. Drive on the right. Speed limit 80 k/hr on secondary roads, 100 k/hr on motorways (highways).

Business hours Banks: 1000-1630 Mon-Fri. Offices: 0800-1800 Mon-Fri, Shops: 0900-1900 Mon-Fri, 0900-1300 Sat, shopping centres 1000-2200 Mon-Sat, 1500-2200 Sun.

Public holidays Jan 1, 20 (Rio), 25 (S. Paulo), 26 (Santos); Feb 2 (P. Alegre); Mar 19 (Fortaleza); Apr. 21; May 1; July 2 (Salvador); July 16 (Recife); Aug 15 (B. Horizonte); Sep 7, 8 (Curitiba, Santos, Vitória); Oct 12; Nov 2, 15; Dec 8 (Belém, B. Horizonte, Brasilia, Campinas, Fortaleza, Manaus, Recife, Salvador); 24, 25; also Carneval (Mon & Tue before Ash Wednesday), Ash Wednesday, Holy Thursday, Good Friday, Holy Saturday, Corpus Christi.

BULGARIA

Capital Sofia
Language Bulgarian. English is spoken in resorts. Turkish, German, French and Russian may also be spoken.
Standard time GMT+3 (GMT +2 26 Oct- 28 Mar)
Climate Summers are the warmest with some rainfall. Winters are cold with snow. Rain falls frequently in the Spring and Autumn.
Health Precautions against Hepatitis A, Typhoid, Tetanus and Polio recommended. Yellow fever vaccination required if arriving from infected areas. An AIDS test may be required if stay is longer than 1 month. Tap water is drinkable, but bottled water is advisable.
Passports and visas Full passports valid for at least 6 months at the time of departure are required by all. Visas are required by all except: Nationals of EU Countries, Iceland, Leichtenstein, Norway and Switzerland for a visit for up to 30 days. Nationals of CIS (former USSR), Nationals of EU Countries, Iceland, Leichtenstein, Norway and Switzerland provided, Cuba, Czech Republic, Estonia, Hungary, Latvia, Lithuania, Mongolia, Poland, Romania, Slovak Republic, Tunisia, former Yugoslavia. Nationals of the USA. Nationals of EU countries, Australia, Canada, Japan and New Zealand, on a pre arranged holiday. Nationals of Bahrain, Cyprus, Hong Kong, Israel, Kuwait, Oman, Qatar, Saudi Arabia, Singapore, S Africa, S Korea, Taiwan, UAE, and Zimbabwe on a pre arranged holiday. Documentation: Those seeking multiple entry visas for business require letter from applicants own company plus letter from Bulgarian partner to be endorsed by the Bulgarian Chamber of Commerce.
Customs regulations (inbound) Persons aged 18 +: 250gm tobacco products, 1 ltr spirits, and 2 ltr wine, 100gm perfume, gifts up to a reasonable amount. Prohibited/Restricted: Arms, ammunition, narcotics, pornography.
Currency Bulgarian Lev (BGL) = 100 Stotinki
Postage Post offices open Mon-Fri 0900-1700, Sat 0900-1200. Stamps can also be purchased from shops, and booths. Post boxes are red and yellow. Airmail letter approx BGL1000.
Telephone codes Inward 359 + Sofia 2, Blagoevrad 73, Bourgas 56, Devnia 519, Gabrovo 66, Lovetch 68, Plovdiv 32, Rousse 82, Smolian 301, Stara Zagora 42, Varna 52, Veliko Tarnovo 62. Outward 00. International Operator 0123. Emergency numbers: Police: 166; Fire: 160; Ambulance: 150. Public telephones are generally attached to walls and most require phonecards (local calls only).
Thomas Cook Travellers' Cheque Collect call Emergency number + 44 1733 318950
Mastercard Global Service Collect call Emergency number 1 314 542 7111 (USA)
Driving International Driving Licence advisable, but most national licences are valid for short journeys. A 'Green' card is compulsory. Drive on right. Speed limits: 100k/hr highways, 80k/hr roads, 40/60 K/hr in urban areas.
Business hours Banks: Mon-Fri 0800-1130, 1400-1800, Sat 0830-1130. Offices: Mon-Fri 0800-1800. Shops: Mon-Fri 1000-2000, Sat 0800-1400.
Public holidays 1 Jan; 3 Mar; Good Friday, Easter Monday; 1, 24 May; 25 Dec.

CANADA

Capital Ottawa
Language English, French.
Standard time Newfoundland (Island) GMT-3½ (-2½ from 6 Apr to 26 Oct); Atlantic Zone GMT-4 (-3 from 6 Apr. to 26 Oct); Eastern Québec GMT-4; Eastern Zone GMT-5 (-4 from 6 Apr. to 26 Oct); Western Ontario GMT-5; Central Zone GMT-6 (-5 from 6 Apr. to 26 Oct); Saskatchewan GMT-6; Mountain Zone GMT-7 (-6 from 6 Apr. to 26 Oct); Part of NE British Columbia GMT-7; Pacific and Yukon Zone GMT-8 (-7 from 6 Apr. to 26 Oct).
Climate Basically temperate, with severe winters (especially inland and in the north) and warm summers. Rainfall can be heavy on the Pacific Coast.
Health No vaccinations required. Tap water safe to drink.
Passports and visas Passports required by all except nationals of France (residing in and entering from St. Pierre & Miquelon) and USA, and residents of Greenland entering from Greenland. Passports issued by the All Palestine Government or by Bophuthatswana, Ciskei, Transkei or Venda are not valid for entry into Canada. Visas required by all except nationals of Andorra, Antigua & Barbuda, Argentina, Australia, Bahamas, Barbados, Belgium, Belize, Bermuda, Botswana, Brunei, Cayman Is., Costa Rica, Cyprus, Denmark, Dominica, Eire, Falkland Is., Finland, France, Germany (Federal Rep.), Gibraltar, Greece, Grenada, Hong Kong, Iceland, Israel, Italy, Japan, Kenya, Kiribati, Lesotho, Liechtenstein, Luxembourg, Malawi, Malaysia, Malta, Mexico, Monaco, Montserrat, Nauru, Netherlands, New Zealand, Nicaragua, Norway, Papua New Guinea, Paraguay, Pitcairn Is., St. Helena, St. Kitts & Nevis, St. Lucia, St. Vincent, Samoa (Western), San Marino, Saudi Arabia, Seychelles, Singapore, Solomon Is., Spain, Suriname, Swaziland, Sweden, Switzerland, Tonga, Trinidad & Tobago, Turks & Caicos Is., UK, USA, Uruguay, Vanuatu, Vatican, Venezuela, Virgin Is. (British), Zambia and Zimbabwe, or persons who are in transit through Canada on a flight which stops in Canada solely for the purpose of refuelling. Documentation: Varies with nationality of applicant. All visitors must hold onward or return tickets.
Customs regulations (inbound) 200 cigarettes and 50 cigars/cigarillos and 400 tobacco sticks and 200 grams tobacco (minimum age to carry tobacco is 18 years), 1.14 ltr spirits or wine or 24 cans or bottles of beer or ale (minimum age to carry alcohol is 18 years in some states and 19 years in others). Gifts valued at more than CAD 60 subject to duty. No restrictions on the import or export of foreign or local currency if declared. Prohibited/restricted: Revolvers, pistols, fully automatic firearms, some foodstuffs, livestock, pets, plants and furs. Quarantine regulations apply.
Currency Canadian Dollar (CAD) = 100 Cents
Postage Postcard or airmail letter to USA (up to 30gm) CAD 0.52; elsewhere (up to 20gm) CAD 0.90. Post boxes are red.
Telephone codes Inward 1 + Calgary 403, Edmonton 403, Halifax 902, Montréal 514, New Brunswick 506, Niagara Falls 416, Ottawa 613, Québec 418, Toronto 416, Vancouver 604, Victoria 604, Winnipeg 204. Outward 011. Call boxes (internal calls and calls to USA only - colour varies with province/territory) accept coins, phonecards and credit cards.
Thomas Cook Travellers' Cheque Emergency number Free 1 800 223 7373
Mastercard Global Service Toll-free Emergency number 1 800 307 7309
Driving International Permit required. Imported vehicles must be accompanied by the registration documents, and in the case of rented vehicles, the rental agreement or letter of authorisation from the owner. Third-party insurance compulsory. Vehicles imported from overseas must have the underside steam-cleaned or high-pressure water washed in the country of origin immediately prior to shipment. The wearing of seat belts by driver and all passengers is compulsory, except in N.W.Territories and Yukon. The use of dipped headlamps during certain hours of daylight is compulsory in some provinces and territories. Drive on the right. Speed limit 50 k/hr in urban areas, 80 k/hr on main roads, 100 k/hr on motorways (highways).
Business hours Banks: 1000-1500 Mon -Fri (some banks in major centres have extended hours - check locally). Offices: 0900-1700 Mon-Fri. Shops: 0930-1730/1800 Mon-Sat, 1200-1700 Sun.
Public holidays Jan 1; July 1; Nov 11; Dec 25, 26; also Good Friday, Easter Monday, Victoria Day (penultimate Mon in May),

SECTION ONE: AIR TRAVEL FACTS **COUNTRY BY COUNTRY TRAVEL FACTS**

Labour Day (first Mon in Sep) and Thanksgiving (second Mon in Oct). Additional regional holidays: Alberta - Heritage Day. British Columbia - British Columbia Day. Manitoba, New Brunswick, North West Territories, Ontario, Saskatchewan - Civic Holiday. Newfoundland - Commonwealth Day, (Mon Mar 9) St. Patrick's Day (Mon prior to Mar 18), St. George's Day (nearest Mon to Apr. 24), Memorial Day (Jul 1) Discovery Day (Mon prior to July 5), Orangeman's Day (Thurs prior to July 16). Québec - June 24. Yukon - Discovery Day (Mon Aug 1).

CHILE

Capital Santiago
Language Spanish. English is also widely spoken.
Standard time Mainland GMT-3 (-4 from second Sun in Mar to second Sun in Oct); Isla de Pascua (Easter Island) GMT-5 (-6 from second Sun in Mar to second Sun in Oct)
Climate Varies from hot and arid in the north to very cold in the far south. The central areas have a Mediterranean type of climate, with a pronounced rainy season from May to Aug. The area southwards from Puerto Montt is one of the wettest and stormiest areas of the world.
Health No compulsory requirements. Precautions against Rabies, Hepatitis A, Typhoid and Polio recommended. Tap water generally safe to drink, but it is advisable for the tourist to use bottled water and avoid eating unwashed vegetables, fruit and seafood.
Passports and visas Passports required by all except nationals of Argentina, Brazil, Colombia, Paraguay and Uruguay who hold an identity card and whose visit is for tourist purposes only and nationals of Taiwan, Mexico and Peru who have an official travel document issued by the organisation of American States. Passports have to remain valid for 6 months after departure. Note: Passports of children must contain a photo and state the nationality. Visa requirements are subject to change at short notice therefore it is advisable to check with the Chilean Consulate for the latest information. Documentation: Tourism Card required by all (valid 90 days - extendable by a further 90 days - obtainable on entry. All nationals under 18 years travelling alone must obtain written permission from their parent or guardian. This must be presented to the Chilean Consul in their country of origin. Nationals of Argentina under 21 years travelling alone must produce similar written permission on entering Chile.
Customs regulations (inbound) All travellers (including infants) 400 cigarettes + 500gm pipe tobacco + 50 large or 50 small cigars, reasonable quantity of perfume for personal use, + for travellers aged 18+, 2.5 ltr alcoholic beverages. Prohibited/restricted: the importation of animal or vegetable products into Chile is prohibited.
Currency Chilean Peso (CLP) = 100 Centavos.
Postage Postcard or airmail letter from CLP 300-450 according to destination and weight. Post boxes are only available at Post offices.
Telephone codes Inward 56 + Santiago 2, Valparaíso 32. Outward 00. Emergency 133. Call boxes vary in colour but are mainly transparent. Special token or 100 Peso coin or card (bought in kiosks usually near phone booths) required. Long distance calls have to be made through a carrier.
Thomas Cook Travellers' Cheque Collect call Emergency number + 44 1733 318950
Mastercard Global Service Toll-free Emergency number 1230 020 2012
Driving International Permit required except for Argentinian and Chilean licence holders. Imported vehicles must be accompanied by registration documents and proof of ownership. In cases where the driver is not the owner of the vehicle, authorisation declared in the presence of an attorney must be presented to the Chilean Consul in the country of origin. Drive on the right. The wearing of seat belts is obligatory. Speed limit 50 k/hr in cities, 100 k/hr elsewhere.
Business hours Banks: 0900-1400 Mon-Fri. Offices: 0900-1900 Mon-Fri. Shops: 1000-1930/2000 (lunchtime closing in provinces 1300-1430) Mon-Fri, 1000-1400 Sat, 1000-2100 Mon-Sun (Malls).
Public holidays Jan 1; May 21; June 29; Aug 15; Sep 11, 18, 19; Oct 12; Nov 1; Dec 8, 25; also Good Friday and Corpus Christi.

CHINA (PEOPLE'S REPUBLIC)

Capital Beijing (Peking)
Language Mandarin Chinese. Cantonese, Fukienese, Xiamenhua and Hakka. English may sometimes be spoken.
Standard time General GMT+8; Tibet GMT+6.
Climate Varies greatly with latitude; in the north it is extreme, ranging from -15°C in Jan to 40°C in July/Aug. The west and parts of the north and central areas are arid and desert-like; in the south the climate is sub-tropical monsoon type, with mild winters and hot, wet summers.
Health Yellow Fever vaccination required by travellers arriving from endemic areas (infants under one year exempt). Precautions against Malaria, Hepatitis A, Typhoid and Polio recommended. Visitors are advised to take throat lozenges with them, especially if travelling to industrial regions. Tap water unsafe to drink.
Passports and visas Passports required by all. Visas required by all except for visitors entering via Gongbei from Macau for the purposes of visiting Zhuhai and/or Zhongshan and whose stay does not exceed 5 days. (Such visitors need only produce passport and complete an entry card at Gongbei). Visitors entering by means other than that above require a tourist (L) or business (F) visa. Tourists entering on a full package tour organised by a tour operator authorised by the China International Travel Service (CITS) will normally have their visas arranged by the operator; individual tourists should apply to their nearest Chinese Embassy with the correct documentation (see below). Business visitors should apply to their local Chinese Embassy at all times with the required documentation. It is a punishable offence to attempt to conduct business without a valid business visa. Transit visas are not required by those who continue their journey to a third country by the same or first connecting aircraft within 24 hours, providing onward confirmed tickets are held. Requirements may change at short notice. Contact the embassy before departure. Documentation: 1 recent photograph. Individual tourists must supply evidence of a valid onward or return ticket, or the receipt from the purchase of travellers cheques from the Bank of China, to a minimum value of GBP 600 in the applicants name. Business visitors must supply an official letter or telex of invitation from an authorised governmental organisation (ministries, provincial governments, or state-run national import/export organisations etc.). In some instances, this letter or telex may be sent direct to the embassy through which the visa application is to be made.
Customs regulations (inbound) 400 cigarettes, 2 ltr alcohol, reasonable quantity perfume for personal use. A notional limit of 1000m video film and 72 rolls of still film. Foreign currency in excess of 5000 US dollars must be declared. Prohibited/restricted: illegal narcotics, pornographic, religious or anti-government literature, radio transmitters/receivers, exposed but undeveloped film. Baggage declaration forms must be completed on arrival noting down all valuables. A copy must be given to customs when leaving the country.
Currency Yuan (Renminbi) (CNY) = 10 Chiao/Jiao or 100 Fen
Postage Postcard CNY 1.60. Airmail letter: charges vary with weight. Post boxes are green.
Telephone codes Inward 86 + Beijing 10, Dalian 411, Guangzhou 20, Shanghai 21. Outward 00. Call boxes are for internal calls only. International calls can be made from post office call boxes.
Thomas Cook Travellers' Cheque Collect call Emergency number + 44 1733 318950

COUNTRY BY COUNTRY TRAVEL FACTS

SECTION ONE • AIR TRAVEL FACTS

Mastercard Global Service Toll-free Emergency number 10 800 110 7309 (only certain provinces)
Driving Neither foreign licences nor an International Permit are recognised in China; intending motorists are required to take a test which comprises written and practical sections and is conducted in Chinese. An interpreter can be arranged if required. Drive on the right. Speed limit: motorways 110 k/hr, urban 30 k/hr.
Business hours Banks: 0930-1200, 1400-1700 Mon-Fri, 0900-1700 Sat. Offices: 0800-1130, 1300-1700 Mon-Fri. Shops: 0900-1900 Mon-Sun (some shops stay open until 2200).
Public holidays: Jan 1; May 1; Oct 1, 2; also Spring Festival (Jan/Feb) - 3 days.

COLOMBIA

Capital Santa Fe de Bogota
Language Spanish. Local Indian dialects and English are also spoken.
Standard time GMT-5
Climate Tropical on the coast and in the north; considerably cooler in the mountains.
Health Cholera, Smallpox and Yellow Fever vaccinations required if visiting the Amazonas, the Llanos Orientales or the Pacific Coast regions. Malaria risk exists all year. Precautions against Malaria, Hepatitis A, Typhoid and Polio, also Yellow Fever (except for infants under one year) recommended. Tap water generally safe to drink, but bottled water recommended.
Passports and visas Passports required by all, and must be valid for 6 months beyond date of departure.
Visas: Required by nationals of Australia, Cyprus, Dominican Republic, Greece, Guyana, Jamaica, Morocco, New Zealand, South Africa & Turkey. All other tourists will be granted a 90-day visa provided they have a valid passport, a return/onward travel ticket and proof of enough financial means for their visit. Full visa (referable to Bogota - approximately 6 weeks delay) required for stays over 90 days and by business visitors unless their visit does not involve the signing of documents, the payment or reception of fees, or the visit to working sites in rural areas, when a tourist visa can be issued. Documentation: Visa applications must be supported by proof of occupation; additionally 1 photograph required for full visa.
Customs regulations (inbound) 200 cigarettes, 50 cigars, 500gm tobacco, 2 bottles wine or spirits, reasonable quantity of perfume and toilet water for personal use.
Currency Colombian Peso (COP). All visitors should carry a minimum of 30.00 US dollars per day of intended stay.
Postage Postcard COP 800. Airmail letter (20 grams) COP 1200. International Post boxes are yellow (all Post boxes are located at Post offices).
Telephone codes Inward 57 + Barranquilla 58, Bogota 1, Cali 2, Cartagena 5. Outward 90. Call boxes are orange. 10 - 20 - 50 -Peso coins required.
Thomas Cook Travellers' Cheque Collect call Emergency number +44 1733 318950
Mastercard Global Service Toll-free Emergency number 980 12 1303
Driving International Permit required. Drivers must be insured against third-party risk. Drive on the right. Speed limit 60 k/hr.
Business hours Banks: 0900-1500 Mon-Fri. Offices: 0830-1730 Mon-Fri. Shops: 0900-2000/2100 (0900-1800/1900 in smaller villages) Mon-Sat, 0900-1700 Sun.
Public holidays Jan 1, 6*; Mar 19*; May 1; June 29*; July 20; Aug 7, 15*; Oct 12*; Nov 1*, 11*; Dec 8, 25; also Holy Thursday, Good Friday, Ascension Day*, Corpus Christi*, Sacred Heart of Jesus*. When holidays marked '*' fall on a day other than Mon, the public holiday occurs the following Mon.

CZECH REPUBLIC

Capital Prague (Praha).
Language Czech (spoken with Bohemia and Moravia). English, German, Slovak and Russian are also spoken.
Standard time GMT+2 (GMT+1 Oct-Mar)
Climate Weather tends to be changeable although winter conditions are likely to be the most settled. Winter temperatures at or below zero and snow is normal. Summers moderately warm.
Health Immunisation against Hepatitis A, Tetanus and Polio recommended. Emergency health treatment is free to foreigners. Food and water are safe.
Passports and visas Full passports valid for at least 8 months at the time of application are required by all except nationals of Germany who can enter with a valid national ID card. Visas are required by all except: Nationals of EU countries (except those with the endorsement British Overseas Citizen who do require a visa) Nationals of Bulgaria, Croatia, Cyprus, Estonia, Hungary, Iceland, Latvia, Lithuania, Former Yugoslav Republic of Macedonia, Malta, Monaco, Norway, Poland, San Marino, Slovak Republic, Slovenia, Switzerland and Vatican City. Nationals of Cuba, S Korea, and Malaysia. Nationals of CIS (except nationals of Armenia, Azerbaijan, Georgia, Tajikistan and Uzbekistan who do need a visa). Nationals of Romania who have been invited by a Czech national and have a stamp from the respective aliens police and immigration service office. Others should check.
Customs regulations (inbound) Persons aged 18+: 200 cigarettes, 100 cigarellos, 50 cigars, 250gm tobacco, 1 ltr spirits, and 2 ltr wine, 500ml perfume or 250ml toilet water, gifts up to value CZK 3,000. Prohibited/Restricted: Arms, narcotics, pornography. All items of value (eg cameras and tents) must be declared on arrival to allow clearance on departure.
Currency Czech Korunas (CZK) = 100 Hellers.
Postage Usual post office opening hours are 0800-1900. Stamps are also available from newsagents and tobacconists. Airletter CZK8, postcard CZK6.
Telephone codes Inward 420 + Prague 2, Brno 5. Information: 121 (national) 0135 (international). Emergencies: Police: 158; Fire: 150; Ambulance: 155 (Prague)
Thomas Cook Travellers' Cheque Collect call Emergency number + 44 1733 318950
Mastercard Global Service Collect call Emergency number 1 314 542 7111 (USA)
Driving International Driving Licence advisable, but most national licences are valid. Carry vehicle's registration document, passport or ID and driving licence at all times. It is obligatory to carry first aid kit, red warning triangle and replacement light bulbs, and to display national identification sticker. 'Green' card recommended. Drive on right. Trams have right of way. Speed limits: 130k/hr motorways, 90k/hr roads, 50k/hr in urban areas. All accidents must be reported to police.
Business hours Banks: Mon-Fri 0800-1800. Offices: Mon-Fri 0800-1600. Shops: Mon-Fri 0800-1800, Sat 0800-1200 (in Prague, shops often stay open longer). Food shops usually open earlier. Food and souvenir shops often open on Sun.
Public holidays 1 Jan; Easter Mon; 1, 8 May; 5-6 July; 28 Oct; 24-26 Dec

DENMARK

Capital Copenhagen (København).
Language Danish. English, German and French may also be spoken.
Standard time GMT+2 (GMT+1 Oct-Mar)
Climate Mild maritime climate, generally free of extremes. Summers warm and sunny, winters rarely severe, with snow late December-February.

Health No compulsory vaccination requirements. Food and water safe.
Passports and visas Passports required by all except; nationals of Austria, Belgium, France, Germany, Greece, Italy, Liechtenstein, Luxembourg, The Netherlands, Portugal, Spain, and Switzerland in possession of a national identity card: nationals of Finland, Iceland, Norway and Sweden in possession of identification papers if travelling entirely within Scandinavia: nationals of Bosnia-Herzegovina in possession of a valid identity card valid for at least 6 months beyond length of stay with a valid visa. Visas required by all except Andorra, Argentina, Australia, Austria, Belgium, Bermuda (BDTC passports only), Brazil, Brunei, Canada, Chile, Costa Rica, Croatia, Cyprus, Czech Republic, Ecuador, El Salvador, Estonia, Finland, France, Germany, Greece, Guatemala, Honduras, Hungary, Iceland, Republic of Ireland, Israel, Italy, Jamaica, Japan, Republic of Korea, Latvia, Liechtenstein, Lithuania, Luxembourg, Malaysia, Malta, Mexico, Monaco, The Netherlands, New Zealand, Nicaragua, Norway, Panama, Paraguay, Poland, Portugal, San Marino, Singapore, Slovakia, Slovenia, Spain, Sweden, Switzerland, UN Laissez Passer, United Kingdom (if right of abode or British Citizen), Uruguay, USA, Vatican City, Venezuela.
Customs regulations (inbound) Visitors from EU member countries need not complete customs formalities. Non-EU visitors should check notices at point of entry for information on tobacco, alcoholic beverages, foodstuffs and other goods on which there are entry restrictions. Meat or meat products and some species of fish can not be imported into Denmark.
Currency Danish Krone (DKK) = 100 re.
Postage Most post offices in big towns open Mon-Fri 0900/1000-1700/1800, Sat 0900-1200. Stamps are also available from newsagents. Postboxes (postkasse) are red, with a yellow horn and crown.
Telephone codes Inward 45, no area codes. Outward 00. National operator: 141. National directory enquiries: 118. International operator/directory: 113. All emergencies: 112. Telephone booths usually take both coins and phonecards (available from DSB kiosks, post offices and news-stands).
Thomas Cook Travellers' Cheque Local Call Charge Emergency number 800 1 01 10
Mastercard Global Service Toll-free Emergency number 8001 6098
Driving Full driving licence required (National driving licence is acceptable). Nationality sticker must be displayed. Visitors taking their own car are advised to obtain a 'Green' card. Drive on the right. At junctions and roundabouts give way to pedestrians; cyclists using far-right lane have right of way. Speed limits: 110k/hr motorways, 80k/hr, 50k/hr in built-up areas. Driving after consuming any alcohol is illegal. Car Hire available only to drivers over the age of 20 (sometimes 25) holding an international credit card.
Business hours Banks: Mon-Fri 0930-1700 (Thur 0930-1800). Shops typically: Mon-Thur 0900-1730, Fri 0900-1900/2000, Sat 0900-1300/1400. Many have longer hours.
Public holidays 1 Jan; Maundy Thur-Easter Mon; Great Prayer Day (fourth Fri after Easter); Ascension Day; Whit Sun-Mon; the afternoon of Constitution Day (5 June); 24, 25, 26 Dec

EGYPT

Capital Cairo
Language Arabic. English and French are widely spoken in cities and tourist areas.
Standard time GMT+2 (+3 from 25 Apr. to 26 Sep.)
Climate Cool and dry in winter (Nov-Mar), with cold nights and daytime temperatures around 18°C; in summer, day temperatures can rise to over 40°C. Rainfall is negligible, except on the coast. Dusty winds from the Sahara prevail during April.

Health Yellow Fever vaccination required if arriving from an infected country. Precautions against Malaria, Bilharzia, Rabies, Cholera, Hepatitis A, Typhoid and Polio recommended. Tap water generally safe to drink.
Passports and visas Passports required by all and must be valid at least 6 months beyond the date of intended stay in Egypt. Visas required by all except: Nationals of Bahrain, Djibouti, Guinea, Libya, Mauritania, Oman, Qatar, Saudi Arabia, Sudan, UAE, and Yemen for a stay not exceeding 90 days. Nationals of Malta and Jordan (if holding a passport valid for at least 5 years) for a stay not exceeding 30 days. Transit passengers continuing their journey to a third country within 24 hours, providing they hold tickets with confirmed seats and do not leave the airport. Visas for most people can be obtained at airport on arrival, please check with relevant embassy. Tourist and business, single and multiple entry types granted. Documentation: 1 photograph for visa. Confirmed onward tickets should be held. Letter required to verify package tour or purpose of business. All visitors must register with the police within one week of arrival. This registration is generally arranged by the hotel.
Customs regulations (inbound) 200 cigarettes or 25 cigars or 200gm tobacco, 2 ltr alcoholic beverage, reasonable quantity of perfume, gifts to value of EGP500. Prohibited/restricted: firearms, narcotics, drugs, cotton. Note: all cash, travellers cheques and gold over EGP500 must be declared on arrival.
Currency 1 Egyptian Pound (EGP) = 100 Piastres
Postage Postcard EGP0.85. Airmail letter EGP0.85. Post boxes are blue for airmail and red for local mail.
Telephone codes Inward 20 + Alexandria 3, Aswan 97, Cairo 2, Port Said 66, Suez 62. Outward 00. Call box colour yellow. 5 or 10 Piastres coins required + phone cards.
Thomas Cook Travellers' Cheque Collect call Emergency number + 44 1733 318950
Mastercard Global Service Toll-free Emergency number 1 314 542 7111 (USA)
Driving International Permit required. Imported vehicles must be insured against third-party risk and be accompanied by a Carnet de Passage (not usually granted to vehicles over 5 years old). Drive on the right. Speed limit 60 k/hr in cities, 90 k/hr on highways.
Business hours Banks: 0830-1500 Sun-Thur. Offices: 0900-1400 Sat-Thur. Shops: 0900-1230, 1600-2000 (1900 in winter) Sat-Thur. Shops in tourist areas open 7 days a week.
Public holidays July 23; also Union Day, Sham el Nasseem, Sinai Liberation Day, Labour Day, Liberation Day, Bainam Feast, Army Day, Suez Day.

FINLAND

Capital Helsinki (Helsingfors).
Language Finnish and Swedish. Some English and German is spoken, especially in Helsinki.
Standard time GMT+3 (GMT+2 Oct-Mar)
Climate Central and south: warm summers and long cold winters. north: snow cover between mid-Oct-mid-May with limited daylight.
Health No compulsory vaccinations required, immunisation against Polio and Tetanus recommended.
Passports and visas Passports required by all except the following nationals providing they hold a valid ID card; Austria, Belgium, Denmark, France, Germany, Italy, Luxembourg, The Netherlands, and Sweden, Iceland, Liechtenstein, Norway and Switzerland. Visas are required by all except nationals of Great Britain (holders of British Hong Kong passports do require a visa), Australia, Canada, USA, EU, Japan. Note: Many other nationals do not require visas - check with the nearest authority for a complete up to date list of visa requirements for Finland.
Customs regulations (inbound) 17+ years: 200 cigarettes or 50 cigars or 250gm tobacco products, 20+ years: 1 ltr strong alco-

holic beverages or 2 ltr mild alcoholic beverages + 2 ltr wines + 15 ltr beer. Food, plants, medicine and works of art will be subject to restrictions.
Currency Finnish Markka (FIM) = 100 Penniä.
Postage Most post offices (posti) open at least Mon-Fri 0900-1700. The logo is a posthorn on a yellow background. Stamps can also be purchased from many shops and hotels. Postboxes are yellow.
Telephone codes Inward 358+ Helsinki 9, Lapland 16, Vaasa 6 (area codes are in the process of being phased out). Outward 990. National directory: 118. International directory: 92 090. All emergencies: 112. International operator: 020 222. Most operators speak English. Phone booths accept phone cards and credit cards; purchase a Tele card which can be used nationwide. Tele booths have a button for English instructions. Phonecards are sold by newsagents and tourist offices as well as Tele offices. Calls are cheapest at weekends and 2200-0800 Mon-Fri.
Thomas Cook Travellers' Cheque Collect call Emergency number + 44 1733 318950
Mastercard Global Service Toll-free Emergency number 08001 156234
Driving National or International Licence required. Drive on right.
Business hours Banks: Mon-Fri 0915-1615, with regional variations. Offices: Mon-Fri 0800-1615. Shops: Mon-Fri 0900-1800, Sat 0900-1400/1500. Stores and food shops: Mon-Sat 0900-1800/2000. Some Sunday opening.
Public holidays 1, 6 Jan; Good Fri; Easter Sun-Mon; May Day Eve and Day; Ascension Day; Whitsun; Midsummer Eve and Day (Juhannus); All Saints' Day; 6 Dec (Independence Day), 24, 25, 26 Dec

FRANCE

Capital Paris
Language French. Many people can speak a little English, particularly in tourist locations.
Standard time GMT+2 (GMT+1 Oct-Mar)
Climate North and central: moderate climate, south and Mediterranean coast: hot summers, mild winters, mountain regions: fine summers, wet, cold winters.
Health No compulsory vaccinations. Tap water safe to drink.
Passports and visas Passports required for all except: EU nationals plus nationals of Andorra, Liechtenstein, Monaco and Switzerland if in possession of a passport expired for a maximum of 5 years or a valid national ID card. Visas required by all except: nationals of Great Britain, Canada, the EU, USA, Japan, Andorra, Argentina, Armenia, Bermuda, Brunei, Chile, Croatia, Cyprus, Czech Republic, Hungary, Iceland, Israel (not including French Overseas Territories), S Korea, Liechtenstein, Malta, Monaco, New Zealand, Norway, Poland, San Marino, Singapore, Slovak Republic, Slovenia, Switzerland, Uruguay, and Vatican City providing their stay does not exceed 3 months in metropolitan France or 30 days in French Overseas Territories. Note: British citizens who have retained their Commonwealth passport may require a visa. Check with the visa section of the Consulate.
Customs regulations (inbound) Travellers from within EU countries need not complete Customs formalities. Goods bought outside the EU or in EU duty-free shops; 200 cigarettes or 50 cigars or 100 cigarillos or 250gm tobacco, 1 ltr spirits or 2 ltr sparkling or fortified wine , 2 ltr still table wine, 60ml perfume, 250ml toilet water, 9-10 lts beer. Gold jewellry, other than personal jewellry below 500gm in weight must be declared. Restrictions on beef, firearms and art / cultural goods.
Currency French Franc (FRF) = 100 Centimes.
Postage Most post offices (PTT: Poste et Telecommunications) open Mon-Fri 0800-1200 and 1430-1900; Sat 0800-1200, but the ones in city centres usually remain open over lunch. Logo: yellow with 'La Poste' in blue. Postboxes are mustard yellow and fixed to walls. Stamps can also be purchased from any café or shop with a red Tabac sign. Letters to 20 gm/postcards FRF3 to EU countries, FRF 4.30 elsewhere.
Telephone codes Inward 33+ Regional code: Paris 1, north-west France 2, north-east France 3, south-east France 4, south-west France 5 +8-figure subscriber number. Old numbers 16 and 161 no longer used. Outward 00. Phone boxes are clear glass. Most phone boxes have instructions in English. Many post offices have metered phones, pay at end of call. Some phone booths take coins, others credit cards and phonecards - available from post offices and some tobacconists. Domestic calls are cheapest Mon-Fri 2230-0800, Sat after 1400 and Sun. Operator - national: 13, international 14. Directory enquiries: 12. Emergencies: Police 17, Fire 18, Ambulance 15.
Thomas Cook Travellers' Cheque Toll-free Emergency number 0800 90 8330
Mastercard Global Service Toll-free Emergency number 0800 90 1387
Driving National licence is sufficient. Nationals from the EU are strongly advised to take a 'Green' card. The car registration documents must also be carried. Front and rear seat belts must be worn. Drive on the right. Priority from right applies in urban areas and at cross-roads; it does not apply to roundabouts. Speed limits: 50 k/hr urban roads, 90 k/hr main roads, 110 k/hr dual carriageways, 130 k/hr motorways.
Business hours Banks: Mon-Fri or Tues-Sat 0900-1200 and 1400-1600/1700. They usually close early on the day preceding a public holiday. Offices: 0900-1200/1300 and 1400-1700/1800. Shops: Tues-Sat 0900-1200 and 1430-1830. A few open Mon and through the midday break, especially food shops, which also frequently open Sun morning and stay open late.
Public holidays Jan 1; Easter Sun and Mon; May 1, 8, Ascension Day; Whit Sun-Mon; July 14; Aug 15; Nov 1, 11; Dec 25. When these fall on Tues or Thur, many places also close Mon or Fri.

GERMANY

Capital Berlin
Language German; English and French are widely spoken in the West, especially by young people, less so in the East.
Standard time GMT+2 (GMT+1 Oct-Mar)
Climate Moderate central European climate, eastern region has colder winters with more snow and frost. Rainfall fairly even throughout the year.
Health No compulsory vaccinations. Tap water safe for drinking.
Passports and visas Valid passports required for all except holders of National Identity Card issued to nationals of Belgium, Denmark, France, Germany, Greece, Italy, Luxembourg, The Netherlands, Portugal, Republic of Ireland and Spain, Austria, Finland, Iceland, Liechtenstein, Malta, Monaco, San Marino and Switzerland. Visas not required by nationals of countries referred to under passport exemptions above, plus nationals of Andorra, Argentina, Bolivia, Brazil, Brunei, Chile, Colombia, Cook Islands, Costa Rica, Croatia, Cyprus, Czech Republic, Ecuador, El Salvador, Guadeloupe, Guam, Guatemala, Honduras, Hungary, Israel, Jamaica, Kenya, S Korea, Macau, Malawi, Malaysia, Martinique, Mexico, New Caledonia, New Zealand, Norway, Panama, Paraguay, Peru, Poland, Puerto Rico, Reunion, St Pierre & Miquelon, Singapore, Slovak Republic, Slovenia, Sweden, Uruguay, Vatican City and Venezuela.
Customs regulations (inbound) Travellers from within EU countries need not complete Customs formalities. Goods bought outside the EU or in EU duty-free shops; 200 cigarettes or 50 cigars or 100 cigarillos or 250 g tobacco, 1 ltr spirits or 2 ltr sparkling or fortified wine , 2 ltr still table wine, 60ml perfume, 250ml toilet water, goods value up to ECU90. Danish visitors must spend at least 36 hrs in Germany before taking their allowances home.
Currency Deutschmark (DEM) = 100 Pfenning.
Postage The usual post office hours are Mon-Fri 0800-1800, Sat

0800-1200 and the main post office in each town has a poste restante facility. Post boxes are yellow.
Telephone codes Inward 49+ Berlin 30, Bonn 228, Munich 89, Hamburg 40, Frankfurt 69. Outward 00. To call the international operator: 0010; national operator: 010; directory enquiries: 001188. Emergencies: Police: 110; Fire: 112; Ambulance: 112. Phone booths are yellow and use coins, cards or both. In theory the Eastern and Western systems have been integrated, but the Eastern phone system still has some catching up to do. If you have important calls to make, make them in the West where the system is very efficient. Black telephone boxes have instructions in English and most operators speak it.
Thomas Cook Travellers' Cheque Toll-free Emergency number 0130 85 9930
Mastercard Global Service Toll-free Emergency number 0130 81 9104
Driving Speed limits: Motorways unlimited (maximum 130k/hr recommended), outside built-up areas 100k/hr, built-up areas 50k/hr. Drive on the right. Priority from the right. National driving licence valid for up to 1 year or IDP. Car registration details should be carried and EU citizens taking their own cars are strongly advised to take their 'Green' card.
Business hours These vary from place to place and are not standard even within one city. Generally, Banks: Mon-Fri 0830-1300 and 1400/1430-1600 (until 1730 Thur). Hours have been shorter in the East, but are changing. Offices: 0830-1700 Mon-Fri. Shops: Mon-Fri 0900-1830 (until 2030 Thur) and Sat 0900-1400.
Public holidays 1, 6 Jan (some regions only); Good Fri; Easter Sun-Mon; 1 May, Ascension Day; Whit Sun-Mon; Corpus Christi*; Ascension of the Virgin Mary (15 Aug*);Day of Unity (3 Oct);Day of Reformation (31 Oct, some regions only) Day of Prayer (third Wed in Nov); 24 Dec (unofficial holiday) 25 Dec; 26 Dec (afternoon). *Catholic feasts, celebrated only in the south.

GREECE

Capital Athens (Athinai)
Language Greek; Most people connected with tourism will speak some English, German, Italian or French. Station and street signs are usually in English as well as Greek characters.
Standard time GMT+3 (GMT+2 Oct-Mar)
Climate Summers warm/hot with a distinct three month dry period. Snow in winter in mountain regions, rare on islands.
Health Yellow Fever vaccination if arriving within 6 days from or via infected areas (except infants under 6 months). Tetanus immunisation recommended. Water varies in quality but is safe to drink.
Passports and visas Passports valid for at least 6 months required by all except EU citizens carrying a valid EU National Identity Card who have sufficient funds for the length of their stay. Visas are required by all except: Nationals of Great Britain, Australia, Canada, USA, EU, Japan for a period of 3 months; Nationals of Andorra, Argentina, Chile, Croatia, Cyprus, Czech Republic, Ecuador, Hong Kong, Hungary, Iceland, Israel, Liechtenstein, Malta, Mexico, New Zealand, Nicaragua, Norway, Poland, San Marino, Slovak Republic, Slovenia, S Korea, Switzerland, St Christophe, Taiwan (China) for a period of up to 3 months; Nationals of Brazil, El Salvador, and Uruguay for a period of up to 2 months; Nationals of Peru for a period of up to 1 month; Nationals of Singapore for a period of up to 2 weeks. Note: Visitors using chartered tickets, leaving Greece on an overnight trip to another country, may risk having their return tickets invalidated by the authorities. Turkish nationals are not permitted to enter Greece at all if their passports indicate that they have visited or intend to visit Turkish occupied Northern Cyprus.
Customs regulations (inbound) Travellers from within EU countries need not complete Customs formalities. Goods bought outside the EU or in EU duty-free shops; 200 cigarettes or 50 cigars or 100 cigarillos or 250 g tobacco, 1 ltr spirits or 2 ltr sparkling or fortified wine , 2 ltr still table wine, 60ml perfume, 250ml toilet water. The export of Antiques is prohibited unless permission is obtained from the Archaelogical Service in Athens. The import of plants is prohibited and only 1 surf-board per person is allowed (if entered in passport).
Currency Greek Drachmar (GRD) = 100 lepta
Postage Post offices, marked by a circular yellow sign, normally open Mon-Fri 0800-1400, and in Athens Sat 0800-1200. They can change money, Eurocheques and travellers cheques. Stamps can be bought in street kiosks and most general stores.
Telephone codes Inward 30+ Athens 1, Rhodes 241, Corfu 661. To call abroad from Greece: tel: 00. Emergencies: General Emergency: 100; Police: 100/109; Fire: 199; Ambulance 150/166; Tourist Police (24 hr, English-speaking); 171; Operator 100; International Operator 162. Some phone booths use phone cards.
Thomas Cook Travellers' Cheque Toll-free Emergency number 00 800 4412 8366
Mastercard Global Service Toll-free Emergency number 00 800 11 887 0303
Driving National driving licence for EU citizens only. Minimum driving age is 18. Speed limits 50km/h built up areas, 110 km/h outside built up ares, 120 km/h motorways.
Business hours Banks: (usually) Mon-Fri 0800-1400, with longer hours in busy tourist areas in peak holiday season. Shops set their own hours; in summer most close from around midday until early evening.
Public holidays 1, 6 Jan; Shrove Mon; 25 Mar; Easter; May Day; Day of the Holy Spirit; 15 Aug; 28 Oct; 25, 26 Dec Everything closes for Easter (Orthodox calendar: the dates may not coincide with the western Easter).

HONG KONG

Language Chinese (Cantonese), English
Standard time GMT+8.
Climate Monsoon, with cold dry winters (Dec-Feb), temperate springs (Mar-May), hot humid summers (May-Sept), when up to 2000mm of rain can be expected, and warm, but not too humid autumns (falls) (Sept-Dec).
Health No compulsory requirements. Precautions against Hepatitis A, Typhoid and Polio recommended. Tap water generally safe to drink. Following the termination of the UK/Hong Kong Reciprocal Health Care Agreement in 1997, UK visitors should purchase health insurance before travelling to Hong Kong.
Passports and visas Passports required by all. Passports issued by the Governments of Bophuthatswana, Ciskei, Emirate of Oman State, Korea P.D.R. (North), Taiwan, Transkei, Turkish Federal State of Cyprus, Venda and Yemen Royalist Authorities not recognised. Those travelling on such passports should obtain a Declaration of Identity (Affidavit in lieu of passport). Visas required by all except nationals of Algeria, Andorra, Angola, Anguilla, Antigua, Australia, Austria, Argentina, Bahamas, Bahrain, Bangladesh, Barbados, Belgium, Belize, Bénin, Bermuda, Bhutan, Bolivia, Bosnia, Botswana, Brazil, Brunei, Burkina Faso, Burundi, Cameroon, Canada, Cape Verde Rep., Cayman Is., Central African Rep., Chad, Chile, Colombia, Comoro Is., Congo People's Rep., Costa Rica, Côte d'Ivoire, Croatia, Cyprus, Denmark, Djibouti, Dominica, Dominican Rep., Ecuador, Egypt, Eire, El Salvador, Equatorial Guinea, Eritrea, Estonia, Ethiopia, Falkland Is., Finland, France, Gabon, Gambia, Germany, Ghana, Gibraltar, Greece, Grenada, Guatemala, Guinea, Guinea Bissau, Guyana, Honduras, Iceland, India, Indonesia, Israel, Italy, Jamaica, Japan, Jordan, Kenya, Kiribati, Korea Rep. (South), Kuwait, Latvia, Lesotho, Liberia, Lithuania, Liechtenstein, Luxembourg, Madagascar, Malawi, Malaysia, Maldive Is., Mali, Malta, Mauritania, Mauritius, Mexico, Micronesia, Moçambique, Monaco, Montserrat, Morocco, Nauru, Nepal, Netherlands, New Zealand, Nicaragua, Niger, Nigeria, Norway, Oman, Pakistan, Panama,

Paraguay, Peru, Philippines, Poland, Portugal, Qatar, Rwanda, St. Kitts-Nevis, St. Helena, St. Lucia, St. Vincent & the Grenadines, Samoa (Western), San Marino, São Tomé & Príncipe, Saudi Arabia, Sénégal, Seychelles, Sierra Leone, Singapore, Slovenia, Solomon Is., South Africa, Spain, Sri Lanka, Suriname, Swaziland, Sweden, Switzerland, Tanzania, Thailand, Togo, Tonga, Trinidad & Tobago, Tunisia, Turkey, Turks & Caicos Is., Tuvalu, Uganda, United Arab Emirates, UK, Uruguay, USA, Vanuatu, Venezuela, Virgin Is. (British), Yemen Republic, Re, Zambia and Zimbabwe. Documentation: None required for a visa. Identification (with a photograph) should be carried at all times, especially when travelling to the New Territories or outlying islands.
Customs regulations (inbound) Overseas visitors: 200 cigarettes or 50 cigars or 250 gm tobacco, 1 ltr wine or spirits, 60 ml perfume, 250 ml toilet water. Residents: 100 cigarettes or 25 cigars or 125 gm tobacco, 1 ltr still wine, 60 ml perfume, 250 ml toilet water. Prohibited/restricted: non-prescribed drugs without a doctor's certificate. Strict regulations control import of animals - check with Dept of Agriculture and Fisheries - and the import/export of ivory. Import licences required for narcotics, certain medicinal drugs, arms and ammunition, fireworks, strategic commodities, textiles, animals, plants, meat and poultry.
Currency Hong Kong Dollar (HKD) = 100 Cents
Postage Postcard or airmail letters HKD 3.10 up to 10 grams. Post boxes are red.
Telephone codes Inward 852. No area codes. Outward 001. Call boxes are orange-yellow. 1 HKD coins required. International calls may be made from booths in most Hong Kong Telephone Co., International Call Office, and Cable and Wireless Sales Office. 1 HKDcoins or phonecard (available in Sales Offices and at CSL shops) required.
Thomas Cook Travellers' Cheque Toll-free Emergency number 800 2505
Mastercard Global Service Toll-free Emergency number 800 966677
Driving International Permit or own national licence valid. Minimum age 18 years. Drive on the left. Drivers must carry their driving licence plus 1 form of identification bearing a photograph. Speed limit 50 k/hr.
Business hours Banks: 0900-1630 Mon-Fri, 0900-1330 Sat. Offices: 0900-1700 Mon-Fri, 0900-1300 Sat. Shops: 0900-2000 Mon-Sun (times vary considerably).
Public holidays Jan 1; Dec 25, 26; also Chinese New Year (Jan/Feb -3 days), Good Friday, Easter Saturday and Monday, Day following Ching Ming (Apr), Tuen Ng Festival (May/June), SAR Establishment Day (July 1), Sino-Japanese War Victory Day (Aug), Day following Mid-Autumn Festival (Sept/Oct), Chung Yeung Festival (Oct), National Day (Oct 1), day following National Day (Oct 2).

HUNGARY

Capital Budapest
Language Hungarian (Magyar). German is widely understood and some English and French are spoken in the tourist areas.
Standard time GMT+2 (GMT+1 Oct-Mar)
Climate Continental climate, warm in summer and very cold in winter.
Health No compulsory vaccinations, Immunisation for Polio and Tetanus recommended. Tap water safe to drink.
Passports and visas All visitors require full passports except nationals of France and Germany holding a national identity card. All passports must be valid for at least 6 months. Visas are required by all except: Nationals of Canada, USA, Japan for a stay of up to 90 days; Nationals of the UK for a stay of up to 6 months; Nationals of Austria, Finland and Spain for a stay of up to 30 days; Nationals of Argentina, Bulgaria, Chile, Costa Rica, Ecuador, Iceland, Israel, S Korea, Liechtenstein, Monaco, Norway, Poland, Seychelles, S Africa, Switzerland, and Uruguay for a stay of up to 90 days; Nationals of CIS (with the exception of citizens of Uzbekistan who do need a visa), Bosnia-Herzegovina, Croatia, Cuba, Cyprus, Czech Republic, Estonia, Latvia, Lithuania, Malaysia, Malta, Nicaragua, Romania, San Marino, Slovak Republic, Slovenia, Yugoslavia, (Serbia and Montenegro) for a stay of up to 30 days; Nationals of Singapore for a stay of up to 14 days.
Customs regulations (inbound) 250 cigarettes or 50 cigars or 250gm tobacco; 2 ltr wine and 1 ltr spirits, minimum age 16 years, as part of 'travel luggage'. In addition, 1 ltr spirits and 1 ltr wine and 5 ltr beer, 500 cigarettes or 100 cigars or 500g tobacco allowed 'customs free'.
Currency 1 Forint (HUF) = 100 fillérs. You can buy Currency at banks and official bureaux (ATM machines are now becoming more widely available), but take care not to buy too much as officially you can only change back 50% of what you changed originally. Keep all receipts. Acceptance of credit cards is becoming more widespread and most large hotels offer the facility. Eurocheques and travellers' cheques are accepted in small denominations.
Postage The postal service is fairly slow but reliable; it is undergoing improvements. Postboxes are red. Post offices open 0800-1800 Mon-Fri.
Telephone Inward 36+ Budapest 1, Szeged 62, Vesprém 88. International calls 00, International operator 09. Emergencies: Police: 107; Fire: 105; Ambulance: 104. Phone boxes use 10 and 20 HUF coins or phonecards.
Thomas Cook Travellers' Cheque Toll-free Emergency number 00 800 11501
Mastercard Global Service Toll-free Emergency number 00 800 12517 Note: the symbol / indicates that you will hear a second dial tone prior to entering the remaining digits.
Driving Pink national UK licence is accepted, but an International driving licence is required if a green licence is held. Drivers must carry car's registration and insurance documents. A first-aid kit, red warning triangle and replacement light bulbs must be carried. Speed limit built up area 50 km/h, other road 80km/h, dual carriageway 100 km/h, motorway 120 km/h
Business hours Banks: 0800- 1500 Mon-Thur, 0800-1300 Fri. Food shops and supermarkets generally open 0600/0700-1800/1900 Mon-Frri. Other shops open around 0900/1000-1800 Mon-Fri, 0900-1300 Sat.
Public Holidays 1 Jan; 15 Mar; Easter Mon; 1 May; Whit Mon; 20 Aug; 23 Oct; 25, 26 Dec.

ICELAND

Capital Reykjavik
Language Icelandic. English and Danish are also widely spoken.
Standard time GMT
Climate Tempered by the Gulf Stream, summers are mild and winters cold. The weather is generally changeable throughout the year.
Health No compulsory vaccinations required. Tap water is safe to drink.
Passports and visas Passports valid for at least 3 months after date of departure required by all except: Nationals of Denmark, Estonia, Finland, Latvia, Lithuania, Norway and Sweden. Nationals of the following countries providing they hold a valid ID card; Austria, Belgium, France, Germany, Italy, Liechtenstein, Luxembourg, The Netherlands, and Switzerland for tourist visits not exceeding 3 months. Visas are required by all except nationals of Great Britain (holders of British Hong Kong passports do require a visa), Andorra, Australia, Austria, Bahamas, Barbados, Belgium, Botswana, Brazil, Brunei, Darussalam, Canada, Chile, Cyprus, Czech Republic, France, Germany, Greece, Grenada, Hungary, Ireland Rep, Israel, Italy, Jamaica, Japan, S Korea, Lesotho, Liechtenstein, Luxembourg, Malawi, Malaysia, Malta, Mexico, Monaco, Netherlands, New Zealand, Poland, Portugal,

San Marino, Seychelles, Slovakia, Slovenia, Solomon Is, Spain, Swaziland, Switzerland, Trinidad & Tobago, United States, Uruguay, Vanuatu and Vatican City.
Customs regulations (inbound) 18+ years: 200 cigarettes or 250gm tobacco products, 20+ years: 1 ltr spirits and 1 ltr wine or 6 ltr beer instead of either the wine or spirits. Restricted/Prohibited: Firearms, drugs, uncooked meats, milk and eggs, live animals (without permit).
Currency Icelandic Krona (ISK) = 100 Aurar.
Postage Post offices open Mon-Fri 0830-1630. Stamps can also be purchased from souvenir shops. Postboxes are red.
Telephone codes Inward 354. No area codes. Outward 00. International Operator 115, International Directory Enquires 114, Local Operator 119, Local Directory Enquires 118. All Emergencies: 112. Phone booths are clear glass and accept coins, phone cards and credit cards.
Thomas Cook Travellers' Cheque Collect call Emergency number + 44 1733 318950
Mastercard Global Service Collect call **Emergency number** 1 314 542 7111 (USA)
Driving International Driving Permit is recommended. Drive on right. Minimum driving age 17 years. Note: Many roads have a gravel surface with poor road markings. Speed limits: 30 k/hr in towns, 50/90 k/hr other roads.
Business hours Banks: Mon-Fri 0915-1600. Offices: Mon-Fri 0900-1700. Shops: Mon-Fri 0930-1800, Sat 1000-1400/1600.
Public holidays 1 Jan; Maundy Thur, Good Fri, Easter Sun-Mon; 23 Apr; 1 May; Ascension Day; Whit Mon; 17 Jun (Independence Day); 3 Aug; 24 (pm only), 25, 26, 31(pm only) Dec.

INDIA

Capital New Delhi
Language Hindi, English. There are also 14 official regional languages and many more unofficial languages.
Standard time GMT+5½.
Climate Tropical, except in the Himalayan regions. The monsoon season occurs June-Sep, except in the south east coastal areas which have only a weak monsoon Jun-Sep and a strong monsoon mid-Oct to mid-Nov.
Health Yellow Fever vaccination certificate required if arriving within 6 days after leaving or transiting endemic areas. Malaria risk exists throughout the year. Precautions against Cholera, Malaria, Hepatitis A, Typhoid, Polio and Tetanus recommended. Bubonic plague, meningitis, tick born relapsing fever, dengue fever, visceral leichmaniasis, filariasis and Hepatitis B are also prevalent. Tap water unsafe to drink.
Passports and visas Passports required by all. Visas required by all except nationals of Bhutan and Nepal, persons of Indian origin holding South African Rep. passports and tourists in direct transit by air who resume their journey by the next regular scheduled flight (max. stay 72 hours), and who hold confirmed onward tickets. This facility does not apply to business travellers who intend to conduct business while in India. Documentation: 3 photographs. Business visitors must supply a letter giving full details of the purpose of the visit. Special permits are required to visit Assam, Darjeerling, Sikkim and certain other frontier regions; also for Lakshadweep and the Andaman and Nicobar Islands.
Customs regulations (inbound) 200 cigarettes or 50 cigars or 250gm tobacco, 1 ltr alcohol, 250ml toilet water. Declare any expensive electrical items such as camcorders and computers. Plants, narcotics, fireworks, gold and silver bullion and coins not in current use are prohibited.
Currency Rupee (INR) = 100 Paise. Foreign currency and travellers cheques may be imported without restriction, but amounts in excess of 2500 US dollars must be declared on entry. Currency and cheques not so declared may not be exported. A tax of INR750 is levied on departures by air to Afghanistan, Bangladesh, Bhutan, Maldives, Myanma, Nepal, Pakistan and Sri Lanka, of INR300 to European destinations and of INR100 to all other destinations.
Postage Postcard INR3.50. Airmail letter INR12.50. Post boxes are red.
Telephone codes Inward 91 + Bombay (Mumbai) 22, Calcutta, 33, Madras 44, Delhi/New Delhi 11. Outward 900. Call boxes (internal calls only) are red. 50-Paise coins required.
Thomas Cook Travellers' Cheque Collect call Emergency number + 44 1733 318950
Mastercard Global Service Toll-free Emergency number 1 314 542 7111 (USA)
Driving International Permit required. Drive on the left. Speed limit 40 k/hr in cities, 80 k/hr on highways.
Business hours Banks: 1000-1400 Mon-Fri, 0930-1300 Sat. Offices: 0900-1700 Mon-Fri, 0930-1300 Sat. Shops: 0930-1900 Mon-Fri, 0900-1400 Sat.
Public holidays Jan 1, 26; Aug 15; Oct 2; Dec 25; also Good Friday and Diwali/Deepavali. In addition, there are many holidays and festivals which are celebrated in certain regions and states only.

INDONESIA

Capital Jakarta
Language Bahasa Indonesian and 250 local dialects. Dutch and English are also spoken.
Standard time Western Zone (Sumatra, Java, West and Central Kalimantan) GMT+7; Central Zone (East and South Kalimantan, Sulawesi, Bali and Nusa Tenggara including Timor) GMT+8; Eastern Zone (Malaku and Irian Jaya) GMT+9.
Climate Warm and humid. May-Sep is dry; Oct-Apr the monsoon season, with most rain falling Jan-Feb. The hills are cooler, but wetter.
Health Yellow Fever vaccination may be required if arriving from an endemic country. Precautions against Cholera, Hepatitis A, Malaria, Typhoid and Polio recommended. Bilharzia and Rabies exist. Tap water unsafe to drink.
Passports and visas Passports required by all, and must be valid at least 6 months beyond the date of stay. Visas required by all except nationals of Australia, Austria, Belgium, Brazil, Brunei, Canada, Denmark, Eire, Finland, France, Germany, Greece, Iceland, Italy, Japan, Korea Rep., Liechtenstein, Luxembourg, Malaysia, Malta, Netherlands, New Zealand, Norway, Philippines, Singapore, Spain, Sweden, Switzerland, Thailand, Turkey, UK, USA, arriving for touristic purposes, and nationals of any country travelling for conference purposes who have documentary proof of approval from the Indonesian government, provided the passport is valid at least 6 months beyond the date of departure from Indonesia, that confirmed or onward tickets are held, and that entry and exit is made through a recognised port or airport. Visas for nationals of China (People's Rep.), Israel, Yemen (P D R) Ukraine and Lithuania will be referred to Jakarta for authorisation, incurring a delay of 4-6 weeks. Portuguese nationals will be refused admission under all circumstances. Maximum permitted stay: tourists - 2 months (non-extendable); Business visitors - 5 weeks; transit - 5 days. Documentation: 2 photographs for a visa. Business visitors (all nationals) require a letter from their firm giving full details of the business to be transacted, date of arrival in Indonesia, and confirming financial responsibility for the applicant. Onward or return tickets must be held. Special permit required to visit Irian Jaya and Timor.
Customs regulations (inbound) 200 cigarettes, 50 cigars or 100gm tobacco, less than 2 ltr alcohol (opened). Prohibited/restricted: narcotics, arms and ammunition, television sets, Chinese publications, medicines and pornography. Cameras and jewellry must be declared on arrival. Advisable to fully label all tablets and first aid items and to carry proof of purchase.
Currency Indonesian Rupiah (IDR) = 100 Sen.
Postage Postcard IDR600 (approx.). Airmail letter IDR900

(approx.). Post boxes are yellow.
Telephone codes Inward 62 + Bandung 22, Denspasar 361, Jakarta 21, Padang 751. Outward 001 or 008. Call boxes are light blue. 50- or 100- Rupiah coins required.
Thomas Cook Travellers' Cheque Collect call Emergency number + 44 1733 318950
Mastercard Global Service Toll-free Emergency number 001803 1 887 0623
Driving International Permit required. Minimum age 18 years. Drive on the left. Speed limit 40 k/hr in cities, 80 k/hr on highways.
Business hours Banks: 0900-1600 Mon-Fri. Offices: 0900-1600/1700 Mon-Fri. Shops: 0830-2000/2100 Mon-Sun.
Public holidays Jan 1; Apr. 18; Aug 17; Dec 25. Also Ascension of Christ, Eid ul Fitr, Eid ul Adha, Hijra, Prophet Mohammad's Birthday and Ascension, Waisak Day and the Balinese Saka New Year (Nyepi).

IRELAND, REPUBLIC OF (EIRE)

Capital Dublin
Language English, Irish (Gaelic)
Standard Time GMT + 1 (GMT Oct - Mar)
Climate Temperate, changeable climate with mild summers and cool winters. Winters reasonably mild with little snow.
Health No compulsory vaccinations. Tap water safe for drinking.
Passports and visas British citizens born in UK, travelling from Britain do not need passport, though carrying official form of identification (driving licence) is recommended. EU visitors and nationals of Leichtenstein, Monaco and Switzerland with national ID card do not need a passport. Visas required by all except: Nationals of Australia, Canada, USA, EU, Japan, Andorra, Argentina, Bahamas, Barbados, Botswana, Brazil, Chile, Costa Rica, Cyprus, Czech Republic, Ecuador, El Salvador, Fiji, Gambia, Grenada, Guatemala, Guyana, Honduras, Hungary, Iceland, Israel, Jamaica, Kenya, S Korea, Lesotho, Liechtenstein, Malawi, Malta, Mauritius, Mexico, Monaco, Nauru, New Zealand, Nicaragua, Norway, Panama, Paraguay, Poland, San Marino, Sierra Leone, Singapore, S Africa, Slovak Republic, Slovenia, Swaziland, Switzerland, Tanzania, Tonga, Trinidad & Tobago, Uruguay, Vatican City, Venezuela, W Samoa, Zambia and Zimbabwe.
Customs regulations (inbound) Travellers from within EU countries need not complete Customs formalities. Goods bought outside the EU or in EU duty-free shops; 200 cigarettes or 50 cigars or 100 cigarillos or 250gm tobacco, 1 ltr spirits or 2 ltr sparkling or fortified wine , 2 ltr still table wine, 60ml perfume, 250ml toilet water.
Currency Irish Punt (IEP) = 100 Pence
Postage Sealed IEP0.32 within Europe, IEP0.52 outside Europe, unsealed/postcard IEP. 0.28. Postboxes are green.
Telephone Inward 353+ Dublin 1, Galway 91, Cork 21, Donegal 73, Tipperary 62. Directory enquiries 1190, international enquiries 1198, emergencies 999.
Thomas Cook Travellers' Cheque Collect call Emergency number + 44 1733 318950
Mastercard Global Service Toll-free Emergency number 1 800 55 7378
Driving Valid national driving licence or IDP required. Owners taking their own cars into Ireland require the vehicles registration book, nationality plates and insurance for the Republic. Drive on left. Road classifications: National Primary (maps and signs show N followed by numbers 1-25), National Secondary (N number over 50) and Regional (R).
Business hours Banks: 1000-1600 Mon-Fri. Offices: 0900-1700 Mon-Fri. Shops: 0900-1730 Mon-Sat (plus late night Thur, Fri, Sat to 2100).
Public holidays 1 Jan, 17 Mar, Good Friday, Easter Monday, first Mon in May, first Mon in Jun, first Mon in Aug, last Mon in Oct, 25 Dec, 26 Dec.

ISRAEL

Capital Jerusalem
Language Hebrew. Arabic, English, French, German and Spanish are also spoken.
Standard time GMT+2(+3 from 30 Mar to 14 Sep).
Climate Mediterranean in character, but can be extremely warm in mid-summer. The hills are generally cooler, the south is warm in winter and hot in summer. Most rainfall occurs in winter (Nov-Mar). There is little rainfall in the south.
Health No compulsory requirements. Precautions against Hepatitis A, Typhoid and Polio recommended. Tap water safe to drink.
Passports and visas Passports required by all, and should be valid for at least 6 months beyond the date of arrival in Israel. Visas required by all except nationals of Argentina, Australia, Austria, Bahamas, Barbados, Belgium, Bolivia, Brazil, Canada, Central African Rep., Chile, Colombia, Costa Rica, Denmark, Dominican Republic, Ecuador, Eire, El Salvador, Fiji, Finland, France, Germany, Gibraltar, Greece, Haiti, Hong Kong, Hungary, Iceland, Italy, Jamaica, Japan, Korea Rep. (South), Lesotho, Liechtenstein, Luxembourg, Maldive Is., Mauritius, Mexico, Netherlands, New Zealand, Norway, Paraguay, Philippines, St. Kitts-Nevis, San Marino, South Africa Rep., Spain, Suriname, Swaziland, Sweden, Switzerland, Trinidad & Tobago, UK and USA . Documentation: Contact nearest Israeli Embassy. Note: Visitors should carry passports at all times and be awarw that passengers boarding flights in Israel can be subject to lengthy personal questioning by security officials.
Customs regulations (inbound) Per adult aged 17 years and above, 250 cigarettes or 250gm tobacco products, 2 ltr wine, 1 ltr spirit, 250ml cologne or perfume, gifts valued at not more than 125 US dollars. Prohibited/restricted: Drugs, counterfeit coins, gambling machines, games of chance, pornography. Certificate required for fresh meat, animals, arms, broadcasting equipment, medicine, raw materials, flowers, plants, seeds.
Currency New Israeli Shekel (ILS) = 100 New Agorot
Postage Airmail letter and postcard ILS1.70 (varies according to weight and destination). Post boxes are red.
Telephone codes Inward 972 + Eilat 7, Haifa 4, Jerusalem 2, Nazerat 6, Tel Aviv 3. Outward 00. Call box colour varies and phonecards/special tokens (obtainable from post offices) are required for long-distance calls.
Thomas Cook Travellers' Cheque Toll-free Emergency number 177 440 8424
Mastercard Global Service Toll-free Emergency number 177 101 8873
Driving International Permit or own national licence valid. Licences printed in a language other than English or French must be accompanied by a Certificate of Confirmation in Hebrew. Drive on the right. Speed limit 40-50 k/hr in urban areas, 90 k/hr elsewhere.
Business hours Banks: 0830-1230 & 1600-1730 Mon-Tue & Thur, 0830-1230 Wed, 0830-1200 Fri. Offices: 0900-1700 Sun-Thur, 0900-1500 Fri. Shops: 0800-1900 Sun-Thur, 0800-1500 Fri. (Muslim stores close Fri, Jewish stores close Sat).
Public holidays All public holidays commence at sunset on the day before the holiday and end at sunset on the day of the holiday. See calendar for exact dates of principal Jewish Festivals). Purim* (Feb/Mar); Pessah (Mar/Apr) - 1st and 7th days; Independence Day (Apr/May); Jerusalem Liberation Day (May/June); Shavu'ot (May/June); Rosh Hashana (Sep/Oct) - 2 days; Yom Kippur (Sep/Oct); Hanukka* (Nov/Dec) - 1st and 7th days; Tu B'Shevat* (Jan/Feb). * Most shops and businesses remain open.

SECTION ONE: AIR TRAVEL FACTS

COUNTRY BY COUNTRY TRAVEL FACTS

ITALY

Capital Rome (Roma)
Language Italian . German, French and English may be spoken in cities and tourist areas.
Standard time GMT+2 (GMT+1 Oct-Mar)
Climate Summers usually hot and dry, mountain areas cold, wet and snowy in winter, costal areas mild.
Health No compulsory vaccinations, Tetanus immunisation recommended.
Passports and visas Passports required for all except nationals of Austria, Belgium, Finland, France, Germany, Greece, Luxembourg, The Netherlands, Portugal, Spain, Sweden, Andorra, Liechtenstein, Monaco, San Marino, and Switzerland carrying a National Identity Card. Visas are required by all except: Nationals of the EU, Australia, Canada, USA, Japan. Nationals of Andorra, Argentina, Bermuda, Bolivia, Bosnia, Herzegovina, Brazil, Chile, Colombia, Costa Rica, Croatia, Cyprus, Czech Republic, Ecuador, El Salvador, Guatemala, Hondura, Hong Kong, Hungary, Iceland, Jamaica, Kenya, S Korea, Liechtenstein, Macedonia, Malaysia, Malta, Mexico, Monaco, New Zealand, Norway, Paraguay, Poland, San Marino, Singapore, Slovak Republic, Switzerland, Uruguay, Vatican City, Serbia and Montenegro for stays not exceeding 3 months. Nationals of Venezuela for visits not exceeding 60 days. Nationals of Israel for stays not exceeding 30 days.
Customs regulations (inbound) Travellers from within EU countries need not complete Customs formalities. Goods bought outside the EU or in EU duty-free shops; 200 cigarettes or 50 cigars or 100 cigarillos or 250gm tobacco, 1 ltr spirits or 2 ltr sparkling or fortified wine , 2 ltr still table wine, 60ml perfume, 250ml toilet water.
Currency Italian Lira (ITL)
Postage Usual post office hours are Mon-Fri 0800-1830, Sat 0800-1145 (no Sat opening in many small places). Stamps are available from post offices, tobacconists and some gift shops in resorts. Poste restante is possible at most post offices, but you have to pay a small amount when you collect.
Telephone codes Inward 39+ Milan 2, Rome 6, Turin 11, Vatican City 66982, Genoa 10. For English information and assistance for intercontinental calls (outside Europe): 170. English information on calling Europe and the Mediterranean area: 176. Local operator assistance (European countries): 15. Local directory enquiries: 12. Emergencies: Fire: 115; Police, Ambulance and other services: 113.
The phone system is in a constant state of overhaul, with frequently changing numbers ranging from two to eight digits. Directories may list two numbers - try both. If they are of different lengths, the longer is likely to be the new one. Most public phones have instructions in English and take coins, phonecards or both. Cards are available from either automatic machines near the phones, tobaconists, or news-stands. Some international calls can be made by phonecard, otherwise go to an office of the state phone company, SIP. Often there are branches at stations or near the main post office. Older phones take only tokens (gettoni); tokens are available from whoever owns the phone, or an automatic dispenser nearby. Gettoni are often accepted as small change, so don't be surprised if you are given some instead of small denomination coins.
Thomas Cook Travellers' Cheque Local Call Charge Emergency number 1678 72050
Mastercard Global Service Toll-free Emergency number 1678 70866
Driving EU Licence required, or national licence with translation. A 'Green' card must be carried (or other insurance). Drive on right. Motorway/Autostrada users are charged a toll. Use of horn prohibited in built-up areas except in emergency - flash car lights instead as a warning.
Business hours Banks: Vary greatly, but in general, Mon-Fri 0830- 1330 and 1530-1930. Shops: (usually) Mon-Sat 0830/0900-1230/1300 and 1530/1600-1900/1930. In July/Aug many close Mon morning or Sat afternoon.
Public holidays All over the country: 1, 6 Jan; Easter Mon; 1 May; 15 Aug (virtually nothing opens); 1 Nov; 8, 25, 26 Dec. Regional saints' days: 25 Apr in Venice; 24 June in Florence, Genoa and Turin; 29 June in Rome; 15 July in Palermo; 19 Sept in Naples; 4 Oct in Bologna; 6 Dec in Bari; 7 Dec in Milan.

JAMAICA

Capital Kingston
Language English. Local patois is also spoken.
Standard time GMT-5.
Climate Tropical, humid. Temperature range 25°C-35°C (coolest and driest period Dec-Mar).
Health Yellow Fever vaccination required if arriving within 6 days after leaving or transiting infected areas (infants under one year exempt). Precautions against Hepatitis A, Typhoid and Polio recommended. Tap water generally safe to drink.
Passports and visas Passports required by all. Visas required by all except nationals of Anguilla*, Antigua*, Argentina@, Australia*, Austria#, Bahamas*, Bangladesh*, Barbados*, Belgium#, Belize*, Bermuda*, Botswana*, Brazil@, Brunei*, Canada, Cayman Is*., Chile@, Costa Rica@, Cyprus*, Denmark#, Dominica*, Ecuador@, Falkland Is.*, Finland#, France#, Gambia*, Germany#, Ghana*, Gibraltar*, Greece@, Grenada*, Guyana*, Hong Kong*, Iceland#, India*, Israel*, Italy@, Japan@, Kenya*, Korea Rep.(south)@, Kiribati*, Lesotho*, Liechtenstein#, Luxembourg#, Malawi*, Malaysia*, Malta*, Mauritius*, Mexico#, Montserrat*, Nauru*, Netherlands#, New Zealand*, Nigeria*, Norway#, Papua New Guinea*, Pitcairn.*, Portugal@, St. Helena*, St. Kitts-Nevis*, St. Lucia*, St. Vincent*, Samoa (Western)*, San Marino#, Seychelles*, Sierra Leone*, Singapore*, Solomon Is*., South Africa, Spain@, Suriname@, Swaziland*, Sweden#, Switzerland#, Tanzania*, Tonga*, Trinidad & Tobago*, Turkey#, Turks & Caicos Is.*, Tuvalu*, Uganda*, UK*, Uruguay@, USA , Vanuatu, Venezuela (14days), Virgin Is. (British)*, Zambia* and Zimbabwe* holding onward or return tickets and evidence of sufficient funds to support themselves.(* 6 months , # 3 months, @ 30 days). Visas will be issued on arrival to nationals of the following (period to be determined by Immigration Control), providing they hold a valid passport, confirmed onward or return tickets and two photographs: Albania, Armenia, Azerbaijan, Belarus, BosniaHerzegovina, Bulgaria, Croatia, Czech Republic, Estonia, Hungary, Kazakhstan, Kyrgystan, Lithuania, Latvia, Moldova, Poland, Russian Federation, Slovakia, Slovenia, Tajikistan, Turkmenistan, Ukraine and Uzbekistan. Documentation: 1 photograph (2 for nationals needing visas at all times) and duplicate copy of visa form 'J'.
Customs regulations (inbound) 200 cigarettes or 50 cigars or 250gm tobacco, 1 ltr alcohol (excluding rum), 360ml toilet water, 180ml perfume, gifts to value USD600 (after each 48 hour visit). Restricted/Prohibited: Firearms, explosives (without permit). Plants & flowers (without permit), fruits, vegetables, coffee, rum, honey, meat, dangerous drugs.
Currency Jamaican Dollar (JMD) = 100 cents.
Postage Postcard JMD8. Airmail letter JMD12.50 (Europe) Airmail letter JMD16.00 (Other countries). Post boxes are red (it is advisable to use post offices & agencies).
Telephone codes Inward 1876 (no area codes within Jamaica, local numbers have 7 digits only). For calls from Canada and USA the initial '1' should be omitted. Outward - direct dial (code113 1) to Canada and USA; direct dial (code113 011) to other destinations: via operator (dial 113 0). From private phones an authorization code is required for all overseas calls. Call boxes (internal calls only) are white or blue. Phone cards required.
Thomas Cook Travellers' Cheque Local Call Charge Emergency

27

number 1 800 223 7373
Mastercard Global Service Toll-free Emergency number 0800 307 7309
Driving Own national licence valid if visit is less than 3 months. Drive on the left. Speed limit 48 k/hr.
Business hours Banks: 0900-1400 Mon-Thu, 0900-1600 Fri. Offices: 0700-1700 Mon-Fri. Shops: 0900-1700 Mon-Sat.
Public holidays Jan 1; Dec 25, 26; also Ash Wednesday, Good Friday, Easter Monday, Labour Day, Emancipation Day, Independence Day and National Hero's Day.

JAPAN

Capital Tokyo
Language: Japanese. Some English.
Standard time GMT+9.
Climate Varies considerably from Hokkaido and N.W. Honshu (cold winters with heavy snow), to the south of Kyushu (sub-tropical).
Health No compulsory requirements. Precautions against Hepatitis A, Typhoid and Polio recommended. Tap water generally safe to drink.
Passports and visas Passports required by all. Japanese authorities do not recognise passports of Chinese residents of Taiwan, Korea P.D.R. (North) or collective passports. Visas required by all except nationals of Andorra, Argentina, Austria, Bahamas, Barbados, Belgium, Canada, Chile, Colombia, Costa Rica, Croatia, Cyprus, Denmark, Dominican Rep., Eire, El Salvador, Finland, France, Germany, Greece, Guatemala, Honduras, Hungary, Iceland, Iran, Israel, Italy, Lesotho, Liechtenstein, Luxembourg, (FYRO) Macedonia, Malta, Mauritius, Mexico, Netherlands, New Zealand, Norway, Portugal (except passports originally issued in present or former Portuguese Colonial Territories), San Marino, Singapore, Slovenia, Spain, Suriname, Sweden, Switzerland, Tunisia, Turkey, UK, USA, Uruguay and for touristic purposes only. All UK passport holders with passport endorsed 'Holder is subject to control under the Commonwealth Immigration Act' or 'This passport is issued on behalf of...' require visas.
Documentation: Visa applicants should contact the Consulate General of Japan directly for details of necessary documents, as document requirements vary depending on nationality and purpose of visit.
Customs regulations (inbound) Persons aged 20+ (Residents) 200 cigarettes or 50 cigars or 250gm tobacco, 3 bottles alcoholic beverage, 57ml perfume, (Non-residents) 400 cigarettes or 100 cigars or 50gm tobacco, 3 bottles alcoholic beverages, 57ml perfume. Prohibited/restricted: Articles which infringe upon rights in patents, utility models, designs, trade marks, copyright or neighbouring right. Counterfeit, altered or imitated articles of coins, paper money, banknotes or securities. Firearms and ammunition, narcotics, stimulants (including Vicks Inhalers and Sudafed), psychotropic substances, obscene articles and publications. Some plants, meats and animals without relevant health certificates; all plants and animals must be presented to the quarantine officer.
Currency Japanese Yen (JPY).
Postage Postcard JPY90-110. Airmail letter JYP130-170. Post boxes are red.
Telephone codes Inward 81 + Hiroshima 82, Kobe 78, Nagasaki 958, Nagoya 52, Osaka 6, Tokyo 3. Outward 001. Call boxes (internal calls only) are blue, red and yellow. 10-Yen coins required (yellow boxes also accept 100-Yen). Newer (green) call boxes are being introduced which accept 10- and 100-Yen coins or a magnetic prepaid card which can be purchased from most shops. International calls can be made from payphones with gold panel.
Thomas Cook Travellers' Cheque Collect call Emergency number + 44 1733 318950
Mastercard Global Service Toll-free Emergency number 0031 11 3886

Driving International Permit required. Drive on the left. Speed limit 40 k/hr in urban areas, 100 k/hr on highways.
Business hours Banks: 0900-1500 Mon-Fri. Offices: 0900-1700 Mon-Fri. Shops: 1000-1900 Mon-Sun.
Public holidays Jan 1, 15; Feb 11; Mar 21; Apr 29; May 3-5; Jul 20; Sep 15, 23; Oct 10; Nov 3, 23; Dec 23. On May 1 (May Day) some manufacturers and companies are closed, but shops are open. During the period Dec 29-Jan 3, government offices and many companies and shops close.

KENYA

Capital Nairobi
Language Swahili, English.
Standard time GMT+3.
Climate Tropical, hot and humid on the coast, more temperate inland. There are two rainy seasons in Nairobi; May-June and Nov-Dec.
Health Yellow Fever vaccination required if arriving within 6 days after leaving or transiting infected areas. Precautions against Meningitis, Hepatitis A, Cholera, Malaria, Typhoid and Polio, also Yellow Fever (except infants under one year), recommended. Tap water generally safe to drink, but bottled water advised on Safari. Swimming in rivers and lakes is not advised.
Passports and visas Passports required by all. Visas required by all except nationals of Anguilla, Antigua, Bahamas, Barbados, Belize, Bermuda, Botswana, Brunei, Canada, Cayman Is., Cyprus, Denmark, Eire, Ethiopia, Falkland Is., Finland, Germany, Ghana, Gibraltar, Grenada, Hong Kong, Italy, Jamaica, Kiribati, Lesotho, Malawi, Malaysia, Malta, Mauritius, Montserrat, Nauru, New Zealand, Norway, Papua New Guinea, Pitcairn Is., St. Helena, St. Kitts-Nevis, Samoa (Western), San Marino, Seychelles, Sierra Leone, Singapore, Solomon Is., Spain, Swaziland, Sweden, Tanzania, Tonga, Trinidad & Tobago, Turkey, Turks & Caicos Is., Tuvalu, Uganda, Uruguay, Vanuatu, Virgin Is. (British) and Zambia. Transit visas not required by passengers continuing their journey to a third country providing they hold confirmed onward tickets and do not leave the airport. Documentation: Visa applications require 2 photographs, plus a letter of recommendation from a reputable tour operator, or letter of invitation from friends, relatives or business associates, or a personal letter explaining reason for visit.
Customs regulations (inbound) Persons aged 16+ 200 cigarettes or 50 cigars or 225gm tobacco, 1 bottle wine or spirits, 568ml perfume. Firearms and ammunition require police permit. Prohibited/restricted: Gold, diamonds. Hunting is banned in Kenya. It is a very serious offence to buy and attempt to export ivory, animal skins and stuffed animals.
Currency Kenyan Shilling (KES) = 100 cents.
Postage Postcard KES33. No post boxes except at post offices.
Telephone codes Inward 254 + Mombasa 11, Nairobi 2, Malindi 123. Outward 000. Call boxes (local calls only) are red.
Thomas Cook Travellers' Cheque Collect call Emergency number + 44 1733 318950
Mastercard Global Service Collect call Emergency number 1 314 542 7111 (USA)
Driving International Permit required (own national licence valid if endorsed at the Road Transport Office). Drive on the left. Speed limit 110 k/hr.
Business hours Banks: 0900-1500 Mon-Fri, 0900-1100 Sat (first & last Sat of month). Offices: 0800-1300, 1400-1700 Mon-Fri. Shops: 0800-1700 Mon-Sat.
Public holidays Jan 1; May 1; June 1; Oct 10, 20; Dec 12, 25, 26; also Good Friday, Easter Monday and Eid el Fitr.

SECTION ONE: AIR TRAVEL FACTS

COUNTRY BY COUNTRY TRAVEL FACTS

MALAYSIA

Capital Kuala Lumpur
Language Bahasa Malaysian, English.
Standard time GMT+8.
Climate Tropical, though cooler in the hills. Average rainfall 2500mm per annum. Weather is generally hot and humid; wettest period Nov-Jan.
Health Yellow Fever and Cholera vaccination required if arriving within 6 days after leaving or transiting endemic areas or a country with infected areas (infants under one year exempt). Precautions against Cholera, Malaria, Hepatitis A, Typhoid and Polio recommended. Tap water generally safe to drink.
Passports and visas Passports required by all and must be valid for at least 6 months beyond the date of stay. Visas required by all except nationals of Afghanistan, Albania, Algeria, Anguilla, Antigua, Argentina, Armenia, Australia, Austria, Azerbaijan, Bahamas, Bahrain, Barbados, Belgium, Belize, Belarus, Benin, Bermuda, Bolivia, Bosnia Herzegovina, Botswana, Brazil, Brunei, Bulgaria, Burundi, Cameroon, Canada, Cayman Is., Chad, Chile, Colombia, Congo, Costa Rica, Croatia, Czech Republic, Denmark, Dominica Rep., Djibouti, Ecuador, Egypt, Eire, El Salvador, Estonia, Falkland Is., Finland, France, Gabon, Gambia, Georgia, Germany, Ghana, Greece, Greenland, Grenada, Guatemala, Guam, Guinea, Guyana, Hong Kong, Hungary, Iceland, Indonesia, Iran, Iraq, Italy, Jamaica, Japan, Jordan, Kazakstan, Kenya, Korea Rep. (South), Kuwait, Kyrgyzstan, Laos, Latvia, Lebanon, Lesotho, Liechtenstein, Lithuania, Luxembourg, Libya, (FYR) Macedonia, Malawi, Mauritius, Maldovia, Montserrat, Morocco, Nauru, Netherlands, New Zealand, Norway, Oman, Palestine passport holders, Peru, Philippines, Pitcairn Is., Poland, Qatar, Romania, Russia, St. Helena, Saudi Arabia, San Marino, Singapore, Slovakia, South Africa, Spain, Sweden, Switzerland, Syria, Tajikistan, Thailand, Tunisia, Turkey, Turks & Caicos Is., Turkmenistan, UAE, UK, Ukraine, USA, Uzbekistan, Virgin Is. (British), Yemen P.D.R. Nationals of Israel are not allowed to obtain visas. Documentation: 3 photographs for visa, 3 forms. Visitors must be in possession of adequate funds and should hold onward or return ticket.
Customs regulations (inbound) 200 cigarettes or 50 cigars or 225gm tobacco, 100 matchsticks, 1 ltr wine or spirits or malt liquor, pefumes to value of MYR200 (opened), gifts and souvenirs not exceeding value MYR200. Visitors must declare valuables and may be required to pay a deposit. Restricted/prohibited: All goods from Israel, indecent or obscene print, cloth bearing the imprint or reproduction of any verses of the Koran. The trafficking of illegal drugs in Malaysia carries the death penalty.
Currency Ringgit (MYR) = 100 Sen
Postage Postcard 20-55 Sen (according to destination). Airmail letter 40-75 Sen (according to weight and destination). Post boxes are red.
Telephone codes Inward 60 + Kuala Lumpur 3, Penang 4, Johor Bahru 7, Kuala Terengganu 9, Kota Kinabalu 88, Kuching 82. Outward 00. Call boxes are orange. Most public telephones require a release button to be pressed when the called number responds. 10-Sen coins required.
Thomas Cook Travellers' Cheque Collect call Emergency number + 44 1733 318950
Mastercard Global Service Toll-free Emergency number 800 804594
Driving International Permit required. Drive on the left. Speed limit 50 k/hr in cities, 110 k/hr on highways.
Business hours Banks: 1000-1500 Mon-Fri, 0930-1130 Sat. Offices: Gov 0830-1430 Mon-Fri, 0800-1300 Sat, Commercial 0900-1700 Mon-Fri, some open Sat. Shops: 0900-1900/2200 Mon-Sun (some 24 hr shops also operate)
Public holidays Johor, Kedah, Kelantan, Perlis and Terengganu 5, elsewhere 7; May 1; Aug 31; Dec 25; also Chinese New Year, Wesak Day, Yang di Pertuan Agong's Birthday, Hari Raya Puasa, Hari Raya Haji, Awal Muharram, Deepavali (except Labuan and Sarawak) and Birthday of the Prophet Muhammed. There are also many State holidays which are celebrated in individual or several States.

MEXICO

Capital Mexico City
Language Spanish. English is widely spoken.
Standard time Central and East GMT-6 (-5 From 6 Apr to 26 Oct); Baja California Sur, Sinaloa and Sonora GMT-7 (-6 From 6 Apr to 26 Oct); Baja California Norte GMT-8 (-7 From 6 Apr to 26 Oct)
Climate Varies from tropical lowlands to hot deserts. There is little rainfall in the north, but rainfall is heavy in the tropical areas.
Health Yellow Fever vaccination is required for travellers over 6 monrths old if arriving from an endemic country. Precautions against Malaria, Hepatitis A, Typhoid and Polio recommended. Cholera is a serious risk - precautions strongly recommended (travellers arriving within 2 weeks of having visited an infected area are required to have a vaccination certificate). Tap water unsafe to drink.
Passports and visas Passports must be valid for six months from the date of entry into Mexico and are required by all except nationals of USA, Canada and Japan who can present a birth certificate or other valid national ID card with photograph. Visas - no brief account of the complex visa requirements will be useful. Readers are advised to check the requirements which relate to them with the appropriate consular authority. Documentation: Tourists must hold a return ticket. Business visitors must submit a letter from their firm stating the specific nature of the business to be transacted in Mexico, the names and addresses of the firms to be visited, and which firm will be financially responsible for the applicants fees and salary while in Mexico. In certain cases, business cards can be issued by the Consulate. These are valid for 90 days between the date of issue and the first entry into Mexico. Holders may enter Mexico as many times as required during this validity. Requirements may change at short notice. Contact the embassy before departure.
Customs regulations (inbound) Persons aged 18+ 400 cigarettes or 2 boxes cigars or reasonable quantity of pipe tobacco, 3 bottles wine or spirits, reasonable quantity of cologne, perfume and lotions for personal use. Photo, cine or video-recording equipment and up to 12 rolls film or cassettes. Prohibited/restricted: Firearms and ammunition require special permit.
Currency Mexican Nuevo Peso (MXN) = 100 Centavos
Postage Postcard/Airmail letter. Cost varies according to size, weight, destination and class of service. Post boxes are green.
Telephone codes Inward 52 + Acapulco 748, Guadalajara 3, Mexico City 5, Monterrey 8, Puerto Vallarta 322. Outward 98. Call boxes are all-glass. 1-Peso coins required.
Thomas Cook Travellers' Cheque Toll-free Emergency number 95 800 223 7373
Mastercard Global Service Toll-free Emergency number 95 800 307 7309
Driving IDP or own national licence valid for own or rented car. Imported cars must be accompanied by proof of ownership. Drive on the right. Speed limit 100 k/hr.
Business hours Banks: 0900-1330 Mon-Fri, some banks are open Sat afternoons. Offices: 0900-1800 Mon-Fri (times can vary). Shops: 0900-1800 Mon-Sat and some Sun opening in commercial centres (Mexico City), 0900-1400 & 1600-2000 Mon-Fri (rest of country).
Public holidays Jan 1; Feb 5; Mar 21; May 1, 5, 10 (half day); Sep 16; Oct 12; Nov 1, 2, 20; Dec 12, 25, 31; also Holy Thursday and Good Friday.

COUNTRY BY COUNTRY TRAVEL FACTS SECTION ONE • AIR TRAVEL FACTS

MOROCCO

Capital Rabat
Language Arabic with some Berber. French is widely spoken with Spanish in the North. English is understood in the North.
Standard time GMT.
Climate Mostly dry with high temperatures. The mountains are cooler. Inland is cooler than the coast.
Health No compulsory requirements. Precautions against Cholera, Malaria, Hepatitis A, Typhoid, Polio and Bilharzia recommended. Tap water generally safe to drink.
Passports and visas Passports required by all, and must be valid for three months beyond the date of entry into Morocco. Visas required by all except nationals of Andorra, Argentina, Australia, Austria, Bahrain, Brazil, Canada, Chile, Congo Peoples Rep., Côte d'Ivoire, Denmark, Egypt, Eire, Finland, France, Germany, Greece, Guinea, Iceland, Indonesia, Italy, Japan, Liberia, Liechtenstein, Mali, Malta, Mexico, Monaco, New Zealand, Niger, Norway, Oman, Peru, Philippines, Puerto Rico, Qatar, Romania, Sénégal, Spain, Sweden, Switzerland, United Arab Emirates, UK, USA, and Venezuela. Transit visas not required by passengers continuing their journey to a third country on the same day by the same or first connecting aircraft, providing they do not leave the airport, except nationals of Algeria, Angola, Bénin, Burundi, Ethiopia, Guinea Bissau, India, Iran, Iraq, Jordan, Korea P D R (North), Kuwait, Lebanon, Libya, Madagascar, Malawi, Mozambique, Pakistan, Rwanda, Sudan, Syria, Togo, Tunisia, Turkey, Yemen Arab Rep., Yemen P D R and Zimbabwe who require a visa at all times and who must obtain special authorisation from Rabat before a visa can be granted. Documentation: 4 photographs and 4 completed forms for visa.
Customs regulations (inbound) Adults only: 200 cigarettes or 50 cigars or 250gm tobacco, 1 ltr spirits, 1 ltr wine, 50gm perfume.
Currency Moroccan Dirham (MAD) = 100 Centimes
Postage Postcard MAD1.80. Airmail letter MAD2.80. Post boxes are yellow.
Telephone codes Inward 212 + Agadir 8, Casablanca 2, Fes 5, Marrakech 4, Rabat 7, Tanger 9. Outward 00. Call boxes are grey. 50-Centime, 1- and 5-Dirham coins accepted.
Thomas Cook Travellers' Cheque Collect call Emergency number + 44 1733 318950
Mastercard Global Service Toll-free Emergency number 1 314 542 7111 (USA)
Driving International Permit or own national licence valid. Minimum age 18. Drive on the right. Speed limit 100 k/hr. Vehicles may be imported for up to 6 months on presentation of registration documents. Green card required, or alternatively insurance may be obtained at port of entry.
Business hours Banks: 0830-1130 & 1430-1700 Mon-Fri (winter) 0800-1530 (summer), (These hours may vary during Ramadam). Offices: 0830-1200 & 1400-1800 (winter) 0800-1600 (summer). Shops: 1000-1300 & 1430-2000 Mon-Sat.
Public holidays Jan 1, 11; Mar 3; May 1, 23; July 9; Aug 14, 20; Nov 6, 18; also the following religious holidays; Aid El Fitre (29 or 30 Jan), Aid El Adha (6 or 7 April), Moharrem (29 April) Prophet's Birthday (6 or 7July).

NETHERLANDS

Capital Amsterdam (administrative) and The Hague (Den Haag) (legislative).
Language Dutch. English, French and German are also spoken.
Standard time GMT+2 (GMT+1 Oct-Mar)
Climate Moderate continental climate, summers warm/hot, winters mild/cold.
Health No compulsory vaccinations. Tap-water safe to drink.
Passports and Visas Passports required for all except EU citizens (except Finland and Sweden) carrying an EU National Identity Card, which must be valid for at least 3 months after the last day of the intended visit. Visas are required by all except: Nationals of Australia, Brunei, Costa Rica, Ecuador, Guatemala, Honduras, Jamaica, Malawi, Malaysia, Nicaragua, Panama, Paraguay, Singapore, and Venezuela for up to 3 months. Nationals who do not require a visa to visit a country which is a signatory to the Schengen Agreement. The following do not require visas for any of the Schengen member states; EU nationals, Andorra, Argentina, Brazil, Canada, Chile, Cyprus, Czech Republic, Hungary, Iceland, Israel, Japan, Liechtenstein, Malta, Mexico, Monaco, New Zealand, Norway, Poland, San Marino, Slovak Republic, Slovenia, S Korea, Switzerland, Uruguay, Vatican City.
Customs regulations (inbound) Travellers from within EU countries need not complete Customs formalities. Goods bought outside the EU or in EU duty-free shops; 200 cigarettes or 50 cigars or 100 cigarillos or 250gm tobacco, 1 ltr spirits or 2 ltr sparkling or fortified wine , 2 ltr still table wine, 60ml perfume, 250ml toilet water.
Currency Guilder (NLG) = 100 cents. Guilders were once known as florins and price tags usually show 'f' or 'fl'.
Postage The post office logo is 'ptt post' (white on red). Most open Mon-Fri 0830-1700 and some Sat 0830-1200. Parcels can be sent only from major post offices.
Telephone codes Inward 31+ Amsterdam 20, Rotterdam 10, Eindhoven 40, The Hague 70. Outward 00. Operator; tel: 06 0410. International directory; tel: 06 0418. National directory; tel: 06 8008. All emergencies (free): 06 11. Booths have a white ptt telecom logo and instructions in English. Most booths are green and take phone cards (available from post offices, VVV and NS). Recorded messages in Dutch are often followed by the English version. International calls are cheapest weekday evenings (after 2000) and all day Sat, Sun. A few numbers prefixed '06' are free, but most are at premium rates, '0900' numbers are also free.
Thomas Cook Travellers' Cheque Toll-free number 0800 022 8630
Mastercard Global Service Toll-free Emergency number 0800 022 5821
Driving EU licence or national driving licence required. 'Green' card is advisable but not compulsory. Drive on the right. Minimum age 18 years. Front seat belts, and rear if fitted must be worn. Driving after drinking any amount of alcohol forbidden.
Business hours Banks: Mon-Fri 0900-1600/1700 (later Thur). Offices: Mon-Fri 0830-1700. Shops: Mon-Sat 0900/0930-1730/1800 (until 2100 Thur or Fri). Many close Mon morning and one afternoon a week.
Public holidays 1 Jan; Good Friday-Easter Mon; 8 May (Liberation Day), 19 May; Ascension Day; Queen's Day; Whit Sun-Mon; 25, 26 Dec.

NEW ZEALAND

Capital Wellington
Language English and Maori.
Standard time North Island, South Island GMT+13 (+12 from 14 Mar to 5 Oct); Chatham Island GMT+13hr 45min (+12hr 45min from 14 Mar to 5 Oct).
Climate Generally temperate, with no extremes of heat or cold, although the northern part of the North Island can be very warm in summer (Dec-Feb).
Health No compulsory requirements. Tap water safe to drink.
Passports and visas Passports required by all. Passports must be valid at least 3 months beyond the intended departure from New Zealand. Passports issued by Democratic Kampuchea, the Democratic People's Republic of Korea, the Turkish Republic of North Cyprus, the Maori Kingdom of Tetiti, the 'Bantustan' republics in South Africa (Bophuthatswana, Ciskei, Transkei, Venda) and official and diplomatic Taiwanese passports are unac-

ceptable for entry to New Zealand. Passports issued by the World Service Authority, Tongan Protected Persons passports, and Rhodesian passports issued before Apr. 18 1980 are also unacceptable for entry to New Zealand. N.B. Passport must be held and a special permit obtained by all nationals wishing to visit Tokelau; a permit to leave and re-enter Samoa (Western) will also be necessary for such visits. Visas required by all except (for up to 3 months unless stated) nationals of Australia, Austria, Belgium, Brunei, Canada, Cook Is., Czech Rep., Denmark, Finland, France (Metropolitan), French Polynesia (1 month), Germany , Greece, Iceland, Indonesia, Italy, Japan, Kiribati, Liechtenstein, Luxembourg, Malaysia, Malta, Monaco, Nauru, Netherlands, New Caledonia (1 month), New Zealand (including Niue and Tokelau), Norway, Portugal (applicable only if holder has right to re-enter Portugal for permanent residence), Singapore, South Africa, Spain, Sweden, Switzerland, Thailand, Tuvalu, UK (6 months) and USA (not applicable to U.S. possessions and protectorates), holding return or onward tickets. Australian citizens travelling on Australian passports do not require visas and are exempt from permit requirements. Australian residents with current Australian resident return visas do not require visas and are granted residence permits on arrival. N.B. Visas for New Zealand issued by Ghanaian Immigrations Authorities in Accra to nationals of Ghana and other nationals are not valid for entry into New Zealand. Documentation: Confirmed onward or return tickets and proof of sufficient funds (NZD1000 per month of stay, or NZD400 if accommodation is prepaid), must be held by all visitors.
Customs regulations (inbound) Persons aged 17+: 200 cigarettes or 50 cigars or 250gm tobacco or combination of these to max. weight of 250gm, 4.5ltr wine or beer, 1.125ml spirit. Prohibited/restricted: Drugs or narcotics, food, plants or parts of plants, biological specimens, flick knives, swordsticks and knuckledusters, and other prohibited articles.
Currency New Zealand Dollar (NZD) = 100 Cents
Postage Postcard NZD1. Aerogramme NZD0.70-0.85. Post boxes are white, red and black.
Telephone codes Inward 64 + Auckland 9, Christchurch 3, Dunedin 3, Invercargill 3, Queenstown 3, Rotorua 7, Wellington 4. Outward 00. Call boxes (international calls can be made from push-button payphones) are glass and metal coloured blue for coinphones, green for cardphones and yellow for credit card phones. 10- 20- and 50 cent coins accepted (minimum charge 20 cents).
Thomas Cook Travellers' Cheque Toll-free Emergency number 0800 44 0112
Mastercard Global Service Toll-free Emergency number 0800 44 9140
Driving International Permit or own national licence valid. Minimum age 15 years (21 for rental cars). Drive on the left. Speed limit 100 k/hr.
Business hours Banks: 0900-1630 Mon-Fri. Offices: 0900-1700 Mon-Fri. Shops: 0900-1730 Mon-Fri, 0900-1230 Sat, some Sun opening.
Public holidays Jan 1,2; Feb 6; Oct 27; Dec 25, 26; also Good Friday, Easter Monday, 2 June, Labour Day.

NIGERIA

Capital Abuja
Language English. There are over 250 local languages.
Standard time GMT+1.
Climate Generally tropical, with high humidity; in the north there is a well-defined dry season with hot winds blowing from the Sahara.
Health Yellow Fever vaccination required by all arriving from an infected country (infants under one year exempt). Precautions against Cholera, Malaria, Meningitis, Hepatitis A, Typhoid, Polio and Yellow Fever recommended.
Passports and visas Passports required by all. Visas required by all except nationals of Bénin, Burkina Faso, Cameroon, Cape Verde, Côte d'Ivoire, Gambia, Ghana, Guinea, Guinea Bissau, Liberia, Mali, Mauritania, Niger, Sénégal, Sierra Leone and Togo. Transit visas not required by passengers continuing their journey to a third country within 48 hours providing they hold confirmed onward tickets. Documentation: 2 photographs for visa. All visitors must hold onward or return tickets.
Customs regulations (inbound) Aged 18+ 200 cigarettes or 50 cigars or 200gm tobacco, 1ltr spirits, small quantity perfume. Prohibited/restricted: Sparkling wines.
Currency Nigerian Naira (NGN) = 100 Kobos
Postage Post offices open 0730-1700 Mon-Fri, 0800-1300 Sat. Post boxes are red. Airmail letter approx NGN20.
Telephone codes Inward 234+ Lagos 1, Kano 64, Abuja 9. Outward 009. Payphones only accept cards and are a variety of colours.
Thomas Cook Travellers' Cheque Collect call Emergency number + 44 1733 318950
Mastercard Global Service Toll-free Emergency number 1 314 542 7111 (USA)
Driving International Permit required plus 2 photographs. Secondary roads are often impassable during the raining season. Car hire is only available from 5 star hotels.
Business hours Banks: 0800-1500 Mon, 0800-1330 Tue-Fri. Offices: 0730-1530 Mon-Fri . Shops: 0800-1700 Mon-Fri. 0800-1630 Sat (some shops and offices in Muslim areas close at 1300 on Fridays).
Public holidays 7; Jan 1, 18; Oct 1; Dec 25, 26; also Good Friday and Easter Monday.

NORWAY

Capital Oslo
Language Norwegian, Lappish (in the north). The majority of people also speak some English.
Standard time GMT+2 (GMT+1 Oct-Mar)
Climate Changeable, fine dry summers with long daylight hours, Arctic winter climate in highlands with severe frost, snow and strong winds.
Health No compulsory vaccinations. Tetanus immunisation recommended. Tap water safe to drink.
Passports and Visas Passports required by all except: Nationals of the EU, Austria, Finland, Iceland, Liechtenstein, Sweden, Switzerland if holding a National Identity Card. Note: Expired passports can not be considered as valid travel documents. Visas required by all except: Nationals of Australia, Canada, USA, the EU and Japan. Nationals of Andorra, Argentina, Austria, Bahamas, Barbados, Belize, Bermuda, Bolivia, Botswana, Brazil, Brunei, Chile, Costa Rica, Croatia, Cyprus, Czech Republic, Dominica, Dominican Republic, Ecuador, Haiti, Honduras, Hungary, Iceland, Israel, Jamaica, Japan, Kenya, Kiribati, S Korea, Liechtenstein, Lesotho, Lithuania (for tourists only), Macau, Malawi, Malaysia, Malta, Mauritius, Mexico, Monaco, Namibia, New Zealand, Nicaragua, Niger, Panama, Paraguay, Peru, Poland, San Marino, Seychelles, Singapore, Slovak Republic, Slovenia, Solomon Island, St Kitts & Nevis, St Lucia, St Vincent & The Grenadines, Surinam, Swaziland, Sweden, Switzerland, Tanzania, Thailand, Trinidad & Tobago, Tuvalu, Uganda, Uruguay, Vatican City, Venezuela, Zambia and Zimbabwe.
Customs regulations (inbound) European residents aged 16+: 200 cigarettes or 250 gm tobacco and 200 cigarette papers . Non-EU residents: twice this allowance. Age 18+: 2 ltr beer and 2 ltr wine not exceeding 22% proof. Anyone aged 20+ may substitute 1 ltr spirits not exceeding 60% proof or 1 ltr wine.
Currency Norwegian Krone (NOK) = 100 Ore. On slot machines, femkrone means a NOK5 coin and tikrone a NOK10 piece.
Postage Post offices generally open Mon-Fri 0800/0830-1600/1700, Sat 0830-1300. Postboxes have a red posthorn and

crown on yellow boxes for local mail and reverse the colours for other destinations.
Telephone codes. Inward 47. No area codes. Directory enquiries 180 for the Nordic countries, 181 for other countries. Local operator 117. Telekorten (phonecards) are available from Narvesen and post offices. A few card phones do now accept credit cards; green or red booths for phone cards. Instructions in English. Free information service; tel: 80 03 10 32. Overseas calls are cheapest 2200-0800 and at weekends.
Thomas Cook Travellers' Cheque Local Call Charge Emergency number 800 11 005
Mastercard Global Service Toll-free Emergency number 800 12697
Driving National licence or International Driving Permit required along with the vehicle's log book. 'Green' card is strongly recommended.
Business hours Banks: Mon-Fri 0900-1600, Sat 0900-1200. Some in Oslo open later, while some rural banks have shorter hours. Offices: 0800-1600 Mon-Fri. Shops: Mon-Fri 0900-1600/1700 (Thur 0900-1800/2000), Sat 0900-1300/1500, but many open later.
Public Holidays 1 Jan; Maundy Thur-Good Fri; Easter Sun-Mon; 1, 17 May (Constitution Day); Ascension Day; Whit Sun-Mon; 25, 26 Dec.

PAKISTAN

Capital Islamabad
Language Urdu, English. Also regional languages plus numerous local dialects.
Standard time GMT+5
Climate Tropical, except in the hills. Generally dry apart from the monsoon season (June-Sep).
Health Yellow Fever vaccination required if arriving from or via any part of a country with infected areas (infants under 6 months exempt providing the mother has proof of her own vaccination before the child was born). Malaria risk exists throughout the year. Precautions against Diptheria and TB, Malaria, Meningitis, Hepatitis A & B, Tetanus, Cholera,Typhoid and Polio recommended. Tap water unsafe to drink.
Passports and visas Passports required by all. Israeli passport holders are prohibited at all times. Passports issued by Taiwan are not recognised. Nationals of Afghanistan who have previously visited or transited through India will be refused entry. Passports must be valid for 6 months. Visas required by all except nationals of Iceland, Maldives Republic, Singapore, S Korea, Trinidad & Tobago, W Samoa and Zambia for a stay of 90 days or less. Nationals of Nepal for a stay of 30 days or less. Documentation: Requirements may be subject to short term change. Contact the relevant authority before departure.
Customs regulations (inbound) 200 cigarettes or 50 cigars or 500gm tobacco, 250ml toilet water and perfume (opened). Prohibited/restricted: Alcoholic beverages, fruit, plants, matches. The export of antiques is prohibited.
Currency Pakistani Rupee (PKR) = 100 Paisa
Postage Postcard PKR15 (to Europe). Airmail letter from PKR17 depending on weight. Post boxes are yellow.
Telephone codes Inward 92 + Faisalabad 41, Gilgit 572, Hyderabad 221, Islamabad 51, Karachi 21, Lahore 42, Multan 61, Rawalpindi 51, Peshawar 521, Skardu 575. Outward via operator or from ISD Public Call Offices (PCO) or 00. Call boxes (internal calls only) are red, and situated in Post Offices and Telegraph Offices only. Card Phone booths (internal calls) on main business streets. Public telephones elsewhere are generally situated in "Customer Service Centres" in general stores and shops, identified by a sign displaying 'PCO' on green boards. Coin phones are not provided. Emergency numbers Police 15, Fire 16, Ambulance 115.
Thomas Cook Travellers' Cheque Collect call Emergency number + 44 1733 318950
Mastercard Global Service Toll-free Emergency number 1 314 542 7111 (USA)
Driving International Permit and own national licence required. Tourists may import a vehicle free of duty for up to 3 months if accompanied by a 'Carnet de Passage en Douane'. All cars must be insured and registered. Minimum age 18 years. Drive on the left. Speed limit 65 k/hr.
Business hours Banks: 0900-1300 and 1500-2000 Sun-Thur, closed Fri 0900-1100 Sat. Offices: Private offices 0900-1700 Mon-Thur and Sat, 0900-1230 and 1430-1700 Fri. Government offices 0900-1700 Mon-Thur and Sat, 0900-1230 Fri. Shops: 0930-1300 & 1500- 1830 Sat-Thur.
Public holidays Jan 29-31; Feb 17, Mar 23; June 8, 9; Jul 1, 16; Aug 14; Sep 6, 11; Nov 9; Dec 25, 26, 31; also Jumat-ul-Wida, Eid-ul-Fitr (2 days), Eid-ul-Adha (2 days), Ashura and Eid-e-Milad-un-Nabi (Birthday of Prophet).

PHILIPPINES

Capital Manila
Language Filipino, English, Spanish.
Standard time GMT+8.
Climate Tropical. The dry season (Mar-June) is hot and dusty, but humid; wet season (July-Oct) has heavy rains and typhoons. Remainder of year is cooler and drier.
Health Cholera vaccination required if arriving from infected areas. Yellow Fever vaccination required if arriving within 6 days after leaving or transiting infected areas (infants under one year exempt). Precautions against Diptheria and TB, Hepatitis A & B, Japanese B encephalitis, Tetanus, Bilharzia, Cholera, Malaria, Typhoid and Polio recommended. Tap water generally safe to drink.
Passports and visas Passports required by all and must have a remaining validity of at least 12 months beyond entry date. Visas required by all except transit passengers. Tourists and business travellers will not require visas providing they have a valid passport for at least 1 year and onward tickets, providing their stay does not exceed 21 days. Note: Certain nationalities will rerquire pre arrival approval by the authorities in Manila before visas can be issued. Check with the Embassy before making travel arrangements. Documentation: Return ticket required. Requirements may change at short notice. Contact the Embassy before departure.
Customs regulations (inbound) 400 cigarettes or 2 tins tobacco, 2 ltr alcoholic beverages, small quantity of perfume. Prohited/restricted: Firearms and ammunition, explosives, drugs, gambling machines, articles of gold, silver and previous metals without an indication of the fineness of quality, ivory, pornography, seditious or subversive material, adulterated or misbranded articles of food or drugs.
Currency Philippine Peso (PHP) = 100 Centavos
Postage Postcard PHP10. Airmail letter PHP20. Post boxes only at post offices.
Telephone codes Inward 63 + Cebu 32, Davao 82, Manila 2, Cagayan de Oro 8822. Outward 00. Public telephones accept 1- or 2-peso coins, but for international calls, PLDT offices provide a cheaper service.
Thomas Cook Travellers' Cheque Collect call Emergency number + 44 1733 318950
Mastercard Global Service Toll-free Emergency number 1 800 1 111 0061
Driving International Permit or own national licence valid up to 90 days. Minimum age 18 years; maximum 85 years. Drive on the right. Speed limit 40 k/hr in urban areas; 70 k/hr on highways.
Business hours Banks: 0900-1600 Mon-Fri. Offices: 0800-1200 & 1300-1700 Mon-Fri. Shops: 0930-2000 Mon-Sat.
Public holidays Jan 1; Feb 25; May 1, 6; June 12; Nov 1, 30, ; Dec 25, 30, 31; also Holy Thursday and Good Friday, Day of Valour,

SECTION ONE: AIR TRAVEL FACTS

COUNTRY BY COUNTRY TRAVEL FACTS

National Heroes Day (last Sun of Aug).

POLAND

Capital Warsaw (Warszawa).
Language Polish; many older Poles speak German or French, while younger Poles (particularly students) are more likely to speak English in tourist areas. Russian is widely understood, but not popular.
Standard time GMT+2 (GMT+1 Oct-Mar)
Climate Moderate continental climate, warm summers, cold winters with snow.
Health No compulsory vaccinations, Tetanus immunisation recommended. Tap water generally safe to drink except in Warsaw.
Passports and Visas All visitors require full passports which must be valid for at least six months after planned departure date from Poland. Visas required by all except: Nationals of the UK for tourist or business visits not exceeding 6 months. Nationals of all other EU countries for periods not exceeding 90 days. Nationals of Andorra, Argentina, Bolivia, Costa Rica, Croatia, Cyprus, Czech Republic, Honduras, Iceland, Liechtenstein, Latvia, Lithuania, S Korea, Malta, Monaco, Nicaragua, Norway, San Marino, Slovak Republic, Slovenia, Switzerland, Uruguay and the USA for visits not exceeding 90 days. Nationals of Bulgaria, Cuba, Estonia, Hungary, Macedonia (FYROM), Mongolia, Romania, for visits not exceeding 30 days. Nationals of CIS countries providing they hold an official invitation or voucher from travel agencies (except nationals of Uzbekistan) who do require a visa. Customs regulations (inbound) Persons aged 18+: 250 cigarettes or 50 cigars or 250 gm tobacco, 2 ltr wine and 1/2 ltr other alcoholic beverage and 5 ltr beer.
Currency Zloty (PLN) = 100 Grozy.
Complete a currency declaration form on arrival if bringing in more than ECU2000. Any Polish money you have left can be re-converted when you leave. The most useful foreign currencies are Sterling, US dollars or Deutschmarks.
You are unlikely to be able to change travellers' cheques or Eurocheques other than at large banks or certain Kantor exchange offices. Kantor sometimes give better rates than banks and their opening hours are longer. Credit cards are now accepted. Thomas Cook will also be able to change your travellers' cheques, free of charge in the case of Thomas Cook travellers' cheques, at: Orbis Travel, ul. Marszalkowska 142, Warsaw.
Postage Post offices (Poczta) open Mon-Sat 0700/0800-1800/2000 (main offices). In each city, the post offices are numbered (the main office is always 1) and the number should be included in the post restante address. Post boxes are green (local mail), blue (air-mail), or red (long-distance mail).
Telephone codes Inward 48+ Gdansk 58, Krakow 12, Warsaw 22. International calls 901, English speaking operator 903. Outward 00. Emergencies: Police 997; Fire 998; Ambulance 999.
Until recently public telephones were operated exclusively by telephone tokens on sale at post offices and Ruch kiosks. Newer telephones operate on telephone cards.
Thomas Cook Travellers' Cheque Collect call Emergency number +44 1733 318950
Mastercard Global Service Toll-free Emergency number 0800 111 1211
Driving International Driving Permit recommended. Car registration card and 'Green' card recommended. Speed limit 70k/hr.
Business hours Banks: Mon-Fri 0800-1500/1800. Offices: Mon-Fri 0800-1600. Shops: Mon-Fri 0800/1100-1900, Sat 0900-1300. Food shops: Mon-Fri 0600-1900, Sat 0600-1300.
Public holidays 1 Jan; Easter Sun-Mon; 1, 3 May; Corpus Christi; 15 Aug; 1, 11 Nov; 25, 26 Dec.

PORTUGAL

Capital Lisbon (Lisboa).
Language Portuguese. English, French and German are spoken mostly in tourist areas.
Standard time GMT+1 (GMT Oct-Mar)
Climate Temperate climate, summers very sunny, especially in south.
Health A yellow fever vaccination certificate is required from travellers over 1 year of age arriving in or destined for the Azores or Madeira if coming from infected areas. Otherwise no compulsory vaccinations. Tapwater unsafe outside main towns.
Passports and Visas Passports required for all except nationals of Austria, Belgium, Denmark, Finland, France, Germany, Greece, Iceland, Ireland, Italy, Leichtenstein, Luxembourg, Malta, The Netherlands, Norway, Spain, Sweden, and Switzerland holding a National Identity Card. Visas are required by all except: Nationals of EU countries for stays of up to 3 months. Nationals of Australia and Japan for stays of up to 2 months. Nationals of Andorra, Argentina, Bermuda, Chile, Costa Rica, Croatia, Cyprus, Czech Republic, Hungary, Iceland, Israel, Liechtenstein, Malta, Mexico, Monaco, New Zealand, Norway, Poland, San Marino, Slovak Republic, Slovenia, Switzerland and Uruguay for stays of up to 3 months. Nationals of Ecuador, S Korea, and Malawi for stays of up to 2 months. Nationals of Brazil for stays of up to 6 months. Nationals of other countries should consult the Portuguese Consulate for further information.
Customs regulations (inbound) Travellers from within EU countries need not complete Customs formalities. Goods bought outside the EU or in EU duty-free shops; 200 cigarettes or 50 cigars or 100 cigarillos or 250gm tobacco, 1 ltr spirits or 2 ltr sparkling or fortified wine, 2 ltr still table wine, 60ml perfume, 250ml toilet water. No restriction on items for personal use, except meat. Domestic animals must have medical documents to prove free from serious diseases (rabies etc).
Currency Escudos (PTE) = 100 Centavos. In written form, the $ sign comes between the Escudos and the Centavos, where there would normally be a decimal point.
Postage 'Correio' indicates both post-boxes and post offices. Most post offices open Mon-Fri 0900-1800, Sat 0900-1300, although the smaller ones close for lunch and are not open Sat. Most large post offices have a poste restante facility. Stamps (selos) can be purchased from anywhere with a sign depicting a red horse or a white circle on a green background.
Telephone codes Inward 351+ Lisbon 1, Oporto 2. Local and overseas operator 118. All Emergencies: tel: 115. Kiosks that take phonecards are as common as coin-operated ones. Surcharge for using phones in hotels etc. If you want to make an international call, the easiest way is to go to a post office: the clerk assigns a booth and times the call. Pay at the end. The phone system is being upgraded and you may find some numbers have changed.
Thomas Cook Travellers' Cheque Toll-free Emergency number 0505 44 9095
Mastercard Global Service Toll-free Emergency number 0501 11 272
Driving International Driving Permit recommended, but foreign licences are accepted. Third party insurance is compulsory and a 'Green' card must be obtained. Seat belts and red warning triangle compulsory. Drive on right. It is customary to sound horn when overtaking. Speed limit; motorways 120k/hr, locally 60k/hr.
Business hours Banks: Mon-Fri 0830-1500. Offices: Mon-Fri 0900-1300, 1500-1900. Shops: Mon-Fri 0900/1000-1300, 1500-1800/1900, Sat 0900-1300. Shopping centres in cities often open daily 1000-2300 or later.
Public holidays 1 Jan; 24 Feb, Shrove Tues; Good Fri; 25 Apr; 1 May; 10 June; Corpus Christi; 15 Aug; 5 Oct; 1 Nov; 1, 8, 25 Dec. In addition, there are a number of local holidays for the days of the

33

patron saints, for example, 13 June in Lisbon and 24 June in Oporto.

ROMANIA

Capital Bucharest
Language Romanian. Hungarian and German in border areas. English and French may be spoken by those involved with tourism and business.
Standard time GMT+3 (GMT +2 26 Oct- 28 Mar)
Climate Summer: inland is hot but the exterior is cooled by a sea breeze. Winters are mildest along the coast. Snow can fall throughout most of the country.
Health Precautions against Cholera, Diptheria, Meningitits, Hepatitis A, Typhoid, Tetanus and Polio recommended. Tap water is drinkable, but bottled water is advisable.
Passports and visas Full passports valid for at least 3 months after return are required by all. Visas are generally required. Contact the Embassy for an up to date list of those nationalities which do not require a visa. Return ticket required.
Customs regulations (inbound) Persons aged 18 +: 2 boxes cigarettes or 200gm tobacco , 2 ltr spirits, 4 ltr wine or beer, gifts up to a value of ROL200000. Prohibited/Restricted: Ammunition, explosives, narcotics, pornography, uncanned meats, animal and dairy products. The import and export of local currency is prohibited.
Currency Romanian Leu (plural Lei) (ROL) = 100 Bani
Visitors are advised to take hard currency, particularly US Dollars which are popular. Sterling can be easily exchanged in most resorts.
Postage Post offices open Mon-Fri 0700-2100. Stamps can also be purchased from shops and newsagents. Post boxes are red or yellow. Postcard approx ROL2000-3000.
Telephone codes Inward 40 + Bucharest 1, Arad 57, Baia Mare 62, Brasov 68, Cluj-Napoca 64, Constanta 41, Craiova 51, Galati 36, Iasi 32. Outward 00, or use International Operator Assistance (dial 971). Internal collect calls, dial 991. Emergency numbers: Police: 955; Fire: 981; Ambulance: 961. Call boxes are orange and accept phonecards issued by Romtelecom or ROL100 coins, but not credit cards.
Thomas Cook Travellers' Cheque Collect call Emergency number + 44 1733 318950
Mastercard Global Service Collect call Emergency number 1 314 542 7111 (USA)
Driving International Driving Licence or national licences required. A 'Green' card is compulsory. Drive on right. Speed limits: 80k/hr highways, 60 k/hr in urban areas. Note: road conditions are poor in some areas.
Business hours Banks: Mon-Fri 0900-1200, and 1300-1500 for currency exchange only. Offices: Mon-Fri 0700-1530. Shops: Mon-Sat 0600/0800-1800/2100, Sun 0900-1300.
Public holidays 1, 2 Jan; Easter Monday (Orthodox Easter); May Day; 1, 25, 26 Dec.

RUSSIA (RUSSIAN FEDERATION)

Capital Moscow (Moskva)
Language Russian. Regional languages also spoken in many areas. English, French or German are spoken by some people.
Standard time Moscow, St Peterburg, Astrakhan GMT+3 (+4 From last weekend in Mar to last weekend in Oct); Samara, Volgograd GMT+4 (+5 From last weekend in Mar to last weekend in Oct); Chelyabinsk, Yekaterinburg GMT+5 (+6 From last weekend in Mar to last weekend in Oct); Omsk, Novosibirsk GMT+6 (+7 From last weekend in Mar to last weekend in Oct); Krasnoyarsk GMT+7 (+8 From last weekend in Mar to last weekend in Oct); Irkutsk, Ulan Ude GMT+8 (+9 From last weekend in Mar to last weekend in Oct); Chita, Yakutsk GMT+9 (+10 From last weekend in Mar to last weekend in Oct); Khabarovsk, Vladivostok GMT+10 (+11 From last weekend in Mar to last weekend in Oct); Magadan, Yuzhno-Sakhalinsk GMT+11 (+12 From last weekend in Mar to last weekend in Oct); Petropavlovsk-Kamchatsky GMT+12 (+13 From last weekend in Mar to last weekend in Oct).
Climate Varies widely, ranging from warm summers in the south and west to bitterly cold winters in the north and east. Day temperatures during January may remain below -25C in Moskow.
Health No compulsory requirements. Precautions against Diptheria. Tap water unsafe to drink in many areas. Health insurance recommended. HIV test required for stays of more than 3 months.
Passports and visas Passports required by all. Return ticket required. Requirements may be subject to short term change. Contact the relevant authority before departure. All travellers are advised to contact the nearest Russian Embassy or Consulate for up to date details. Carry ID at all times.
Customs regulations (inbound) Complete customs declaration form on arrival, keep receipts when changing money. Persons aged 18+ 200 cigarettes or 100 cigars or 500gm tobacco products, 1 ltr alcoholic beverages, reasonable quantity perfume for personal use, goods to value USD5000 for personal use only. Prohibited/Restricted: Photographs and printed matter directed against the CIS, weapons / ammunition, narcotics, pornography, live animals, fruit and vegetables.
Currency Russian Rouble (RUR) = 100 Kopecks
Postage Post boxes are blue (local are red).
Telephone codes Inward 7 + Archangel 818, Chelyabinsk 3512, Ekaterinburg 3432, Irkutsk 3952, Kaliningrad 0112, Khabarovsk 421, Kirov 8332, Moscow 095, Murmansk 8152, Novgorod 8160, Novosibirsk 3832, Perm 3422, St. Petersburg 812, Rostov 8632, Smolensk 8122, Vladivostok 4232, Volgograd 8442. Outward 810 in Moscow, elsewhere via operator. Direct dial available from post offices, some hotels and international telephone boxes only.
Thomas Cook Travellers' Cheque Collect call Emergency number + 44 1733 318950
Mastercard Global Service Toll-free Emergency number 1 314 542 7111 (USA)
Driving National licence with authorised translation or International Permit required. Minimum age 18 years. Drive on the right. Speed limit 60-80 k/hr in urban areas, 90 k/hr on highways, 100 k/hr on motorways.
Business hours Banks: 0930-1730 Mon-Fri. Offices: 0900-1800 Mon-Fri. Shops: 0900-1700 Mon-Sat.
Public holidays Jan 1, 2, 7; Mar 8; May 1, 2, 9; Jun. 12; Nov 7, 8.

SAUDI ARABIA

Capital Riyadh.
Language Arabic. English is spoken in business circles.
Standard time GMT+3.
Climate Desert. In the west it is hot and humid for most of the year; in the east it is hotter, but humid only in summer; the Central Plateau is very hot and dry. Rain, which falls very rarely, occurs as short heavy storms Nov-Apr.
Health Yellow Fever vaccination required if arriving within 6 days after leaving or transiting infected areas. Malaria risk exists all year. Precautions against Hepatitis A, Cholera, Malaria, Meningitis, Bilharzia, Typhoid and Polio recommended. Tap water generally safe to drink.
Passports and visas Passports required by all except Muslim Pilgrims holding 'Pilgrim Passes', tickets and other documents for their onward journey entering the country via Jeddah or Dahran. Passports must be valid for at least 6 months beyond the date of intended stay. Israeli passport holders and holders of passports containing evidence of a visit to Israel are prohibited at all times.

SECTION ONE: AIR TRAVEL FACTS

COUNTRY BY COUNTRY TRAVEL FACTS

Jewish visitors may also be refused entry. Passengers not complying with Saudi conventions of dress and behaviour, including those who appear to be in a state of intoxication. Visas required by all except: Nationals of Bahrain, Kuwait, Oman, Qator and UAE and holders of re-entry permits issued by the Saudi-Arabian government. No tourist visas. Transit visas not required by passengers continuing their journey to a third country by the same or first connecting aircraft providing they hold confirmed onward tickets and do not leave the airport. Documentation: 1 photograph for visa.
Customs regulations (inbound) 600 cigarettes or 100 cigars or 500gm tobacco, reasonable quantity of perfume, food stuffs in easy-to-open containers, no alcohol. Prohibited/restricted: Alcoholic beverages (also applies to transit passengers), pig meat, contraceptives, firearms, cultured or natural pearls, drugs, diet pills, horses, live birds, religious books and material.
Currency 1 Saudi Rial (SAR) = 100 Halalah
Postage Postcard SAR1. Airmail letter SAR1.50-2.00, according to destination. Post boxes are at post offices only.
Telephone codes Inward 966 + Jeddah 2, Makkah 2, Riyadh 1. Outward 00. Police 999. Call boxes are beige, green, red, black & green, black & red. Coins of 50-Hallalah and 1-Rial accepted, some take phonecards and credit cards.
Thomas Cook Travellers' Cheque Collect call Emergency number + 44 1733 318950
Mastercard Global Service Toll-free Emergency number 1 314 542 7111 (USA)
Driving International Permit required or National licence accompanied by officially sanctioned Arabic translation required (for short period only; Saudi licence must be obtained for longer stays). Foreign nationals are not permitted to drive commercial vehicles. Minimum driving age 25 years. Women are not allowed to drive any vehicle. Drive on the right. Speed limit 30-50 k/hr in urban areas; 100-110 k/hr on highways. In the event of an accident, vehicles must not be moved until the police arrive, irrespective of inconvenience to other road users. Drivers must remain with their vehicle.
Business hours Banks: 0830-1200 & 1700-1900 Sat-Wed, 0830-1200 Thur. Offices: 0900-1300 & 1600-2000 Sat-Thur, (during Ramada, 2000-0100) 0730-1430 Sat-Wed (Government offices). Shops: 0900-1300 & 1630-2000 Sat-Thus (during Ramada, 2000-0100).
Public holidays Eid ul Fitr and Eid ul Adha.

SINGAPORE

Capital Singapore
Language English, Malay, Mandarin, Tamil.
Standard time GMT+8.
Climate Tropical; generally hot and humid with little variation throughout the year. Rainfall occurs year-round with Nov-Jan the wettest period.
Health Yellow Fever vaccination required if arriving within 6 days after leaving or transiting infected or endemic areas (infants under one year exempt). Precautions against Cholera, Hepatitis A, Typhoid and Polio recommended. Tap water generally safe to drink. Women more than 6 months pregnant must obtain a social visit pass prior to arrival.
Passports and visas Passports required by all. Visas: Most nationals arriving in Singapore will be granted a 1 month visa-free visit, providing that they are holding a valid national passport valid for 6 months from date of departure, confirmed onward/return tickets and documentation for the next country to be visited, have sufficient funds for their stay and continue their journey within 14 days. This facility is not available to nationals of Afghanistan, Algeria, Armenia, Azerbaijian, Belarus, Cambodia, China (People's Rep.), India, Iraq, Jordan, Kazakhastan, Kyrgyzstan, Laos, Lebanon, Libya, Moldova, Russia, Syria, Tajikistan, Tunisia, Turkmenistan, Ukraine, Uzbekistan, Vietnam, Yemen and Stateless Persons resident in the above-mentioned countries, holders of Hong Kong Documents of Identity, and holders of Refugee Travel Documents, who require visas at all times. N.B. All nationals visiting Singapore for the purposes of conducting seminars/lectures, participating in an exhibition or trade fair in order to demonstrate merchandise, or engage in any business with a view to selling products/goods/properties require a 'Professional Visit Pass'. Application should be made at least 6 weeks prior to intended visit. Documentation: 2 photographs for visa. Onward or return tickets and sufficient funds for their stay. Expectant mothers who are 24 weeks pregnant or more require a Social Visit Pass for Expectant Mothers, these take about 6 weeks to complete. Business visitors require a letter from their firm giving details of the business to be conducted and confirming financial responsibility for the applicant. For a Professional Visit Pass (see above), applicants must submit a letter giving full description of the nature of the work to be performed in Singapore, including dates, venues etc. The name, address and Identity Card number of the sponsor in Singapore should also be provided.
Customs regulations (inbound) No tobacco products duty free. Persons 18+ 1 ltr wine , 1 ltr beer, 1 ltr spirits. No limit on perfume. Import of chewing gum prohibited.
Currency Singapore Dollar (SGD) = 100 Cents
Postage Postcard SGD0.50. Aerogramme SGD0.50. Post boxes are white.
Telephone codes Inward 65. No area codes. Outward 00. Call boxes (internal calls only - colour varies) require 10 cent coins.
Thomas Cook Travellers' Cheque Toll-free Emergency number 800 4481 115
Mastercard Global Service Toll-free Emergency number 800 1100 113
Driving International Permit or own national licence valid, together with passport or identity card. Drive on the left. Speed limit 50 k/hr (80 k/hr on expressways).
Business hours Banks: 1000-1500 Mon-Fri, 1100-1600 Sat. Offices: 0830-1800 Mon-Fri. Shops: 0930-2100 Mon-Sun.
Public holidays Jan 1; May 1; Aug 9; Dec 25; also Chinese New Year, Good Friday, Vesak Day, Hari Raya Puasa, Deepvali, Hari Raya Haji.

SOUTH AFRICA, REPUBLIC OF

Capital Pretoria (administrative), Cape Town (legislative), Bloemfontein.
Language English, Afrikaans. Xhosa, Sotho, Zulu and Tswana also spoken regionally by a high proportion of the population, many of whom do not speak English or Afrikaans.
Standard time GMT+2.
Climate Varies with area: Cape Town - Summer (Dec-Mar) warm (very warm in Feb) and windy, Winter (May-Sep) often cloudy with rain; Mosselbaai/Port Elizabeth - rainfall evenly distributed throughout the year; Johannesburg/Pretoria and High Veldt - Summer hot and sunny with storms (often thundery), Winter - warm, dry and sunny; Natal - Summer very hot with high humidity, Winter temperate.
Health Yellow Fever vaccination required if arriving from infected area. Malaria risk exists all year in certain areas of Mpumalanga (Lowveld), Gauteng (Transvaal) and Kwa-Zulu/Natal and tablets must be taken by all visitors before entering any of these regions. Precautions against Malaria, Meningitis, Cholera, Hepatitis A, Typhoid and Polio recommended. Tap water generally safe to drink.
Passports and visas Passports required by all, and must be valid for 6 months beyond the date of departure from South Africa. Visas required by all except citizens of Argentina, Australia, Austria, Barbados, Belgium, Belize, Bénin, Bolivia, Botswana, Brazil, Canada, Cape Verde, Chile, Comoros Is., Congo, Costa Rica, Cyprus, Denmark, Egypt, Eire, Equador, Finland, France, Gabon,

Germany, Greece, Hungary, Israel, Ivory Coast, Japan, Jordan, Kenya, Korea Rep. (South), Lesotho, Liechtenstein, Luxemburg, Malawi, Malaysia, Malta, Mauritius, Mexico, Namibia, Netherlands, New Zealand, Norway, Paraguay, Perù, Portugal, Senegal, Seychelles, Singapore, Solovakian Rep., Spain, St. Helena, Swaziland, Sweden, Switzerland, Thailand, Turkey, UK, Uruguay, USA, Venezuela and Zambia. Special regulations apply to persons visiting South Africa who intend to be professionally active, journalists, religious workers, lecturers, as well as those contemplating any employment must apply for visas, work or entry permits. Religious workers and those connected with the media require visas or entry permits for holiday visits. Documentation: 2 photographs required in support of each visa application. Business visitors require a letter from their firm. All visitors must hold onward or return tickets and sufficient funds for their stay.
Customs regulations (inbound) 400 cigarettes, 250gm tobacco, 50 cigars, 1 ltr spirit, 2 ltr wine, 50ml perfume, 250ml toilet water, goods to the value of ZAR500. ZAR500 in currency notes can be imported, unlimited foreign currency (declare on arrival). Prohibited/restricted: narcotic and habit-forming drugs, obscene literature, firearms, ammunition, 2nd hand military clothing, foodstuffs, honey.
Currency South African Rand (ZAR) = 100 Cents
Postage 10g Airmail letter ZAR1.70. Post boxes are red.
Telephone codes Inward 27 + Cape Town 21, Durban 31, Johannesburg 11, Pretoria 12. Outward 09. Call boxes (international calls can be made from specified boxes) are orange or blue for coin boxes (20 cent, 50 cent and ZAR1 coins accepted) and green for card phones.
Thomas Cook Travellers' Cheque Toll-free Emergency number 0800 99 8175
Mastercard Global Service Toll-free Emergency number 0800 99 0418
Driving Own national licence valid provided it is printed in English and carries the photograph and signature of the holder as an integral part of the licence. Otherwise International Permit required. Minimum age to drive a hire car 21 (23 stipulated by some companies). Drive on the left. Speed limit 60 k/hr in urban areas, 100 k/hr on main roads and 120 k/hr on motorways (highways).
Business hours Banks: 0830-1530 Mon-Fri, 0800-1130 Sat. Offices: 0730/0830-1630/1700 Mon-Fri. Shops: 0800-1900 Mon-Fri, 0800-1700 Sat, some Sun opening as well.
Public holidays Jan 1; Mar 21; Apr. 27; May 1; June 16; Aug 9; Sep 24; Dec 16, 25, 26; also Good Friday and Family Day (Easter Monday).

SOUTH KOREA (REPUBLIC OF KOREA)

Capital Seoul
Language Korean
Standard time GMT+9.
Climate Temperate, with dry, warm and pleasant weather in spring and autumn. Winter can be bitterly cold, and summer very hot and humid. Heavy rains usually occur during July.
Health No compulsory requirements. Malaria risk exists May-Oct. Precautions against Cholera, Hepatitis A, Typhoid and Polio recommended. Tap water generally safe to drink. Foreigners wishing to stay more than 90 days may need to supply an AIDS-free certificate.
Passports and visas Passports required by all. Visas: Not required for tourism or business purposes for up to 15 days, except for nationals of Albania, Bulgaria, Cambodia, China (P.R.), C.I.S., Cuba, Czechoslovakia, Hungary, Japan, Korea (P D R), Laos, Mongolia, Phillipines, Poland, Romania, Viet Nam and Yugoslavia. Visa required for periods in excess of 15 days except for nationals of:- 1). Up to 1 month: Tunisia. 2). Up to 2 months: Italy, Lesotho, Portugal. 3). Up to 90 days: Austria, Bahamas, Bangladesh, Barbados, Colombia, Costa Rica, Denmark, Dominica, Eire, Finland, France, Germany, Grenada, Haiti, Hungary, Iceland, Liberia, Morocco, Norway, Peru, St Lucia, St Kitts, St Vincents, Singapore, Spain, Sweden, Thailand, Turkey, UK. 4). Up to 3 months: Belgium, Greece, Luxembourg, Malaysia, Mexico, Netherlands, Pakistan, Surinam, Switzerland. Documentation: 1 photograph for visa.
Customs regulations (inbound) 200 cigarettes, 50 cigars, 250gm pipe tobacco (the total quantity not to exceed 500gm), 1 bottle alcoholic beverages (not to exceed 1 ltr), 57ml perfume, gifts to value of KRW300,000, personal effects (clothing, toiletries).
Currency Won (KRW)
Postage Postcard KRW350. Airmail letter KRW440. Post boxes are red.
Telephone codes Inward 82 + Mokp'o 631, Pusan 51, Seoul 2. Outward 001. Call boxes are blue and grey. Phone card or 10-50-100 Won coins required.
Thomas Cook Travellers' Cheque Collect call Emergency number + 44 1733 318950
Mastercard Global Service Toll-free Emergency number 0078 1 1 887 0823
Driving International Permit required. Car hire companies require presentation of passport and generally impose age limits of 21-65 years. Drive on the right. Speed limit 60 k/hr in urban areas, 80 k/hr on motorways (highways).
Business hours Banks: 0930-1630 Mon-Fri, 0930-1330 Sat. Offices: Mar-Oct 0900-1800 Mon-Fri, 0900-1300 Sat, Nov-Feb (and Government offices) 0900-1700 Mon-Fri, 0900-1300 Sat. Shops: 1030-1930/2000 Mon-Sat, (Department stores 1030-2000 Tues-Sun).
Public holidays Jan 1; Mar 1; Apr. 5; May 5; June 6; July 17; Aug 15; Oct 3; Dec 25; also Lunar New Year, Buddha's Birthday and Ch'usok.

SPAIN

Capital Madrid
Language Spanish (Castillan), Catalan, Galician and Basque. English is fairly widely spoken in tourist-related industries in major cities and coastal areas.
Standard time GMT+2 (GMT+1 Oct-Mar)
Climate Summers hot and sunny, winters cooler with snow in central region.
Health No compulsory vaccinations. Tetanus immunisation recommended. Tap water safe to drink.
Passports and Visas Passports required for all except: Nationals of EU countries with valid National Identity Cards and nationals of Austria, Belgium, France, Luxembourg, The Netherlands, and Portugal whose passports expired less than 5 years. Nationals of Germany and the UK with passports expired less than 1 year. Nationals of Andorra, Iceland, Liechtenstein, Malta, Monaco, Netherland Antilles and Switzerland holding valid national ID cards or expired passports (maximum 5 years). Visas required by all except: Nationals of Aruba, Bolivia, Bonaire, Colombia, Costa Rica, Croatia, Curacao, Ecuador, El Salvador, Guatemala, Honduras, Kenya, Malaysia, Nicaragua, Panama, Paraguay, Singapore, Suriname and Venezuela for up to 3 months. Nationals who do not require a visa to visit a country which is a signatory to the Schengen agreement. Others should check. Non-EU nationals must hold onward or return tickets plus a minimum of GBP25 (sterling) per day of their intended stay, or a minimum of ESP50,000.
Customs regulations (inbound) Travellers from within EU countries need not complete Customs formalities. Goods bought outside the EU or in EU duty-free shops, persons aged 15+; 200 cigarettes or 50 cigars or 100 cigarillos or 250gm tobacco, 1 ltr spirits or 2 ltr sparkling or fortified wine, 2 ltr still table wine, 60ml perfume, 250ml toilet water, gifts to the value of ESP5,000.
Currency Peseta (ESP) = 100 Centimos

Postage Most post offices open 0800-1400 and 1700-1930. The larger ones offer a poste restante facility. Stamps can also be purchased from tobacconists. Postboxes are yellow with red stripes and over-seas mail should be put in the slot marked 'extranjero'.
Telephone codes Inward 34+ Barcelona 3, Bilbao 4, Cadiz 56, Torremolinos 5. The number for the international operator depends both on where you are calling from and where you are calling to. In Madrid 008 for Europe and 005 for all other continents. From elsewhere in Spain 9198 for Europe and 9191 for the other continents. National operator: 009, local operator: 003. Emergencies: Police 091 everywhere; Fire 080 in most towns, but can vary; Ambulance: numbers vary from place to place, so check locally.
Most of the ordinary public telephone booths take cash and have instructions in English. Many booths also take phonecards, obtainable from tobacconists. Bars also have pay telephones, but they are usually more expensive than the ordinary booths.
Thomas Cook Travellers' Cheque Toll-free Emergency number 900 99 4403
Mastercard Global Service Toll-free Emergency number 900 97 1231
Driving International Driving Permit (or official Spanish translation of national driving licence stamped by Spanish Consulate recommended). Drive on right. Insurance is required and a 'Green' card is strongly recommended.
Business hours Banks: Mon-Fri 0900-1400, Sat 0900-1300 (winter only). Mon-Fri 0830-1400 (summer). Offices: times vary considerably. Shops: Mon-Sat 0930/1000- 1400 and 1700-2000/2030, but major stores do not close for lunch and food shops often open on Sun.
Public Holidays 1, 6 Jan; several days at Easter; 1 May; Corpus Christi; 15 Aug; 12 Oct; 1 Nov; 6, 8 Dec and several days at Christmas. Not all of these are official holidays, but many places close anyway. In addition to national holidays, each region has at least four more, usually the local saints' days.

SRI LANKA

Capital Colombo (commercial), Jayawardanapura (administrative).
Language Sinhala, Tamil, English.
Standard time GMT+5½.
Climate Tropical, but cool in the hills. There are two monsoon periods: May-Sep with rain mainly in the south west May-July; Nov-Jan with rain mainly in the north east Dec-Jan. Humidity is high throughout the year, except in the Central Highlands. The coastal area are cooled by the sea winds.
Health Yellow Fever vaccination required by travellers over 1 year after leaving or transiting infected areas. Malaria risk exists all year outside Colombo. Precautions against Cholera, Malaria, Meningitis, Hepatitis A, Typhoid and Polio recommended. Tap water unsafe to drink without previously boiling.
Passports and visas Passports required by all. Passports must be valid for 3 months beyond date of intended stay. For tourist visits, nationals of the following countries will be issued a visa free of charge on arrival at Colombo airport: Nationals of EU countries for a maximum stay of 30 days (nationals of Finland and Sweden may stay up to 90 days). Nationals of Australia, Bangladesh, Malaysia, New Zealand, Philippines, and the USA for a maximum stay of 90 days. Nationals of Albania, Bahrain, Bosnia-Herzogovina, Bulgaria, Canada, CIS, Croatia, Cyprus, Czech Republic, Estonia, Hungary, Indonesia, Israel, Japan, Kuwait, Latvia, Lithuania, Maldives, Norway, Nepal, Oman, Pakistan, Poland, Qatar, Romania, Saudi Arabia, Singapore, Slovak Republic, Slovenia, S Korea, Switzerland, Thailand, Turkey, United Arab Emirates and Yugoslavia (Serbia and Montenegro) for a maximum stay of 30 days. Documentation: 1 photograph for visa. All passengers who visit for tourist purposes must be in possession of onward or return tickets, valid documentation for the next country to be visited, and sufficient funds for their stay.
Customs regulations (inbound) Persons aged 18+: 200 cigarettes or 50 cigars or 340gm tobacco, 2 bottles wine, 1.5 ltr spirits, perfume for personal use + 250ml toilet water. No free gifts. Declare valuable personal effects to ensure free export. Full tax payable on all electrical items.
Currency Sri Lankan Rupee (LKR) = 100 cents
Postage Postcard LKR20. Airmail letter LKR26 (up to 10 grams). Post boxes are red.
Telephone codes Inward 94 + Colombo 1, Kandy 8. Outward 00. Call boxes are red. Coin denominations required, or local phone cards.
Thomas Cook Travellers' Cheque Collect call Emergency number + 44 1733 318950
Mastercard Global Service Toll-free Emergency number 1 314 542 7111 (USA)
Driving International Permit required (obtain before departure to avoid lengthy red tape in Sri Lanka). Imported vehicles must be accompanied by a valid Carnet de Passage/Triptyque, and must be re-exported within 6 months. Third-party insurance is compulsory. Drive on the left. Speed limit 56 k/hr in Colombo, 72 k/hr elsewhere.
Business hours Banks: 0900-1300 Mon Sat, 0900-1500 Tue-Fri. Offices: 0900-1700 Mon-Fri. Shops: 0900-1730 Mon-Sat.
Public holidays Jan 14; Feb 4; May 1; Dec 25; also Ramazan Day, Maha Shiva Rathriya, Hajji Festival, Good Friday, day prior to Sinhala and Tamil New Year's Day, Sinhala and Tamil New Year's Day, day following Vesak Full Moon, Deepavali, Miladun-Nabi (Prophet's Birthday); also every 'Full Moon Day' (Poya Day).

SWEDEN

Capital Stockholm.
Language Swedish. Lapp and English are also spoken.
Standard time GMT+2 (GMT+1 Oct-Mar)
Climate Continental climate with wide temperature variation between winter and summer. Winters become colder and longer travelling northwards.
Health No compulsory vaccinations. Tetanus and polio immunisation recommended. Tapwater safe to drink.
Passports and Visas Passports required by all except: Nationals of Austria, Belgium, France, Germany, Greece, Ireland, Italy, Luxembourg, The Netherlands, Portugal, providing they hold a valid national identity card (for a stay of up to 3 months). Nationals of Denmark, Finland, Iceland, and Norway hoding travel documents issued for travel between these countries. Nationals of Liechtenstein and Switzerland providing they hold valid national ID cards (for a stay of up to 3 months). Visas required by all except: Nationals of Australia, Canada, USA, EU, and Japan. Nationals of Andorra, Argentina, Bahamas, Barbados, Belize, Bolivia, Botswana, Brazil, Brunei, Chile, Colombia, Costa Rica, Cyprus, Czech Republic, Dominica, Ecuador, El Salvador, Grenada, Guatemala, Honduras, Hong Kong, Hungary, Iceland, Israel, Jamaica, Kenya, Kiribati, Lesotho, Liechtenstein, Malaysia, Malta, Malawi, Mauritius, Mexico, Monaco, Namibia, New Zealand, Nicaragua, Norway, Panama, Paraguay, Poland, St Lucia, St Vincent & the Grenadines, San Marino, Seychelles, Singapore, Slovak Republic, Slovenia, Solomon Islands, S Korea, Swaziland, Switzerland, Trinidad & Tobago, Tuvali, Uruguay, Venezuela, and Zimbabwe.
Customs regulations (inbound) Goods bought outside the EU or in EU duty-free shops; 200 cigarettes or 50 cigars or 100 cigarillos or 250gm tobacco, 1 ltr spirits or 2 ltr sparkling or fortified wine , 2 ltr still table wine, 60ml perfume, 250ml toilet water. Travellers from EU countries: over 15 years 300 cigarettes, or 150 cigarillos, or 75 cigars, or 400gm tobacco; over 20 years, 1 ltr spirits, or 3 ltr strong wine and 5 ltr of wine and 15 ltr beer. Alcohol may be imported only by those aged 20+. Import of potatoes prohibited.
Currency Swedish Krona (SEK) = 100 re.

Postage Post offices (look for a posthorn on yellow or a yellow posthorn) generally open Mon-Fri 0900-1800, Sat 1000-1300, but there are variations. Stamps are available at newsagents and tobacconists. Postboxes for overseas mail are yellow.
Telephone codes Inward 46+ Stockholm 8, Helsingborg 42, Uppsala 18. Outward 009. Swedish directory 079 75. International operator 0018. International directory 079 77. All emergencies: 900 00 or 112. Public phones which take cash are decreasing in number, but most card phones accept both credit cards and Telia phonecards. There are English instructions and the panel displays the cost of the call. Local calls are half-price Mon-Fri 1800-0800 and weekends. International calls are cheapest Mon-Fri 2200-0800 (North America 2200-1000) and weekends.
Thomas Cook Travellers' Cheque Local Call Charge Emergency number 020 795 110
Mastercard Global Service Toll-free Emergency number 020 791 324
Driving National licence required. Vehicle registration document and 'Green' card insurance document recommended. Drive on right. Minimum driving age 18. Speed limit: motorways 110 k/hr, dual carriageways and other roads 90 k/hr, built up areas, 50 k/hr, other roads, 70 k/hr.
Business hours Banks: Mon-Fri 0930-1500 and Thur 1600-1730. Some, especially at transport terminals, have longer hours. Offices: flexible hours. Shops: Mon-Fri 0900/0930-1700/1800, Sat 0900/0930-1300/1600. Stores and malls often open until 2000/2200 and some open Sun 1200-1600.
Public holidays 1, 6 Jan; Good Fri; Easter Mon; 1 May; Ascension Day; Whit Mon; Midsummer Eve, Midsummer Day; All Saints' Day; 24, 25, 26, 31 Dec. Many places close early the previous day - or Fri if it's a long weekend.

SWITZERLAND

Capital Berne (Bern)
Language German, French, Italian and Romansch. Most Swiss people are at least bilingual and knowledge of English is widespread.
Standard time GMT+2 (GMT+1 Oct-Mar)
Climate Alpine peaks snow-covered whole year, lower levels have warmer, wetter summers.
Health No compulsory vaccinations. Tetanus and Polio immunisation recommended. Tapwater safe to drink.
Passports and Visas Passports valid for 6 months after intended period of stay required by all except: Nationals of Austria, Belgium, Finland, France, Germany, Greece, Italy, Luxembourg, The Netherlands, Portugal, and Spain, providing they hold a valid national identity card. Nationals of Cyprus, Liechtenstein, Malta, Monaco, and San Marino providing they hold valid national identity cards. Visas required by all except: Nationals of Australia, Canada, USA, EU, and Japan. Nationals of countries in South and Central America (except nationals of Belize and Peru who do need a visa). Nationals of Caribbean Island States (except nationals of the Dominican Republic and Haiti who do need a visa). Nationals of Andorra, Brunei, Cyprus, Czech Republic, Fiji, Hungary, Iceland, Israel, Kiribati, Liechtenstein, Malaysia, Malta, Monaco, New Zealand, Norway, Poland, San Marino, Singapore, Slovak Republic, Slovenia, Solomon Islands, S Africa, S Korea, Tuvali, and Vatican City. Nationals of Bosnia-Herzegovina, Croatia, Turkey, and Yogoslavia, providing they are resident in Canada, EU, USA, or EFTA countries. Return ticket required.
Customs regulations (inbound) Persons aged 17+: 200 cigarettes or 50 cigars or 250gm tobacco, 2 ltr alcohol up to 15% volume, and 1 ltr over 15% volume. Nationals living outside Europe are entitled to twice the tobacco allowance.
Currency Swiss Francs (CHF) = 100 Centimes (or Rappen)
Postage Post office opening times are usually Mon-Fri 0730-1200 and 1345-1830, Sat 0730-1100. In cities major branches usually stay open for much longer. Post boxes are yellow. Poste restante (Postlagernd) facilities are available at most post offices.
Telephone codes Inward 41+ Berne 31, Basle 61, Lucerne 41, Zurich 1. Outward 00. International enquiries and operators 114, national enquiries and operators 111. Emergencies: Police: 117; Fire: 118; Ambulance: 144 (most areas). The national network offices (in post offices) sell phonecards as do most rail stations. In the PTT offices you can pay for international calls when you have finished. Telephone boxes have instructions in English and operators speak English.
Thomas Cook Travellers' Cheque Toll-free Emergency number 0800 89 7092
Mastercard Global Service Toll-free Emergency number 0800 55 0130
Driving National licence required. 'Green' card is recommended. Drive on right. Minimum driving age 18. Speed limit motorways 120k/hr, cities 50 k/hr, other roads 80 k/hr.
Business hours Banks: Mon-Fri 0830-1630. Offices: 0800-1200, 1400-1700. Shops: Mon-Fri 0800-1830, Sat 0800-1600. Many close on Mon morning.
Public Holidays 1 Jan; Good Fri; Easter Mon; Ascension Day; Whit Mon; 1 August; 24 (pm only) 25, 26, 31 (pm only) Dec. 2 Jan, 1 May and Corpus Christi are public holidays in some areas.

TAIWAN (REPUBLIC OF CHINA)

Capital Taipei
Language Mandarin (Chinese), English and Japanese.
Standard time GMT+8.
Climate Sub-tropical, with long sultry summers. Rainy season occurs Oct-Mar in the north, Mar-Sep in the south. Rain can be very heavy and typhoons occur during the south-west monsoon (June-Sep).
Health Yellow Fever vaccination required if arriving from infected area. Precautions against Cholera, Hepatitis A, Typhoid and Polio recommended. Tap water should be boiled.
Passports and visas Passports required by all, and should be valid for at least 6 months from the date of entry. Holders of passports issued by the People's Rep. of China are prohibited at all times. Visas required by all except: Nationals of Australia, Austria, Belgium, Canada, France, Germany, Japan, Luxembourg, Netherlands, New Zealand, Portugal, Spain, Sweden, UK and USA, who can stay for a maximum of 14 days. A 30 day landing visa can be issued at CKS and Kaohsiung international Airports to nationals of the above countries and Czech Republic, Hungary, Italy, Poland, and Switzerland. (Fee TWD1500). Single Entry Visas allow one entry only and are valid for 3 months from date of issue. Business visas allow multiple entry and are valid 6 months. Both visas are initially valid for a stay of up to 60 days. Up to 2 extensions of 60 days each may be made during stay. Visitors should apply to a local police station and submit proof of reason for staying from an appropriate source. Application must be made in advance to a Taiwan R.O.C. Consulate, who will issue a letter of introduction in lieu of a visa. A fee of TWD1000 is charged for Visitor Visa; TWD2000 for Business Visa at Taipei Airport. Transit visas not required by passengers continuing their journey to a third country by the same or connecting aircraft on the same day, providing they hold confirmed onward tickets and do not leave the airport. Documentation: 2 photographs (1 for landing visa). Confirmed onward or return air ticket. Single entry visa applicants require document verifying purpose of visit. Business multiple-visa applicants require letter from their firm and must hold onward or return tickets. Passport must be valid for at least 6 months. Applicants must have a 'previous good record'.
Customs regulations (inbound) Persons aged 20+: 200 cigarettes or 25 cigars or 454gm tobacco, 1 bottle alcoholic beverage, one used camera. Articles for personal use if value less than TWD 20,000. Written declaration of baggage required.

Prohibited/restricted: Narcotics, toy pistols, games of chance or parts thereof, pornography, counterfeit money, communist propoganda, non-canned meat products.
Currency New Taiwan Dollar (TWD) = 100 cents
Postage Postcard TWD12 (approx.). Airmail letter TWD20 (approx.). Post boxes are green (domestic mail) or red (airmail).
Telephone codes Inward 886 + Taipei 2. Outward 002. Call boxes (internal calls only) are green. 1-Dollar coins required.
Thomas Cook Travellers' Cheque Collect call Emergency number + 44 1733 318950
Mastercard Global Service Toll-free Emergency number 0080 10 3400
Driving International Permit required. Drive on the right. Speed limit 90 k/hr max.
Business hours Banks: 0900-1530 Mon-Fri, 0900-1230 Sat. Offices: 0830-1730 Mon-Fri, 0830-1700 alternate Sats. Shops: 0900-2300 Mon-Sun.
Public holidays Jan 1; Mar 29; May 1; Sep 28; Oct 10, 25, 31; Nov 12; Dec 25; also Lunar New Year's Eve, Lunar New Year (Spring Festival - 3 days), Lantern Festival, Tomb Sweeping Day, Dragon Boat Festival, Mid-Autumn Festival.

THAILAND

Capital Bangkok
Language Thai. English widely understood in major tourist areas.
Standard time GMT+7
Climate Tropical, with a pronounced monsoon season, usually late May-mid Nov. In the southern peninsula the West Coast monsoon occurs late Apr-late Nov; the east Coast monsoon Aug-early Feb.
Health Yellow Fever vaccinations may be required if arriving from an endemic country. Precautions against Cholera, Malaria, Hepatitis A, Typhoid and Polio recommended. Tap water unsafe to drink. If within 14 days of arrival in Thailand you are ill with (1) Fever with rash (2) Fever with jaundice (3) Acute diarrhoea you are requested to contact the Health Office at the Ministry of Public Health, Samsen Road, Bangkok: 5918429 (0830 - 1630 Mon - Fri.) or Bamrasnaradun Infectious Disease Hospital, Nonthaburi,: 5883116 (24 hours).
Passports and visas Passports required by all and must be valid for at least 6 months beyond the date of intended departure from Thailand. Visas required by all except nationals of Algeria, Argentina, Australia, Austria, Bahrain, Belgium, Brazil, Brunei, Canada, Denmark, Djibouti, Egypt, Eire, Fiji, Finland, France, Germany, Greece, Iceland, Indonesia, Israel, Italy, Japan, Kenya, Korea Rep. (South)*, Kuwait, Luxembourg, Malaysia, Mauritania, Mexico, Morocco, Myanmar, Netherlands, New Zealand*, Norway, Oman, Papua New Guinea, Philippines, Portugal, Qatar, Samoa (Western), Saudi Arabia, Sénégal, Singapore, Solvenia, South Africa, Spain, Sweden, Switzerland, Tunisia, Turkey, UAE, UK, USA, Vanuatu and the Yemen provided their visit is for tourist purposes and their stay does not exceed 30 days (* 90 days). Nationals of Albania, Andorra, Antigua & Barbuda, Bahamas, Barbados, Belize, Bhutan, Bolivia, Botswana, Bulgaria, Burkina Faso, Burundi, Cameroon, Cape Verde, Central African Rep., Chad, Chile, Colombia, Comoros, Costa Rica, Côte d'Ivoire, Cyprus, Dominica, Dominican Rep., Ethiopia, Ecuador, Equatorial Guinea, Gabon, Gambia, Grenada, Guatemala, Guinea Bissau, Guinea Rep., Haiti, Honduras, India, Jamaica, Kiribati, Lesotho, Liberia, Liechtenstein, Malawi, Maldives, Mali, Malta, Mauritius, Monaco, Nauru, Niger, Panama, Paraguay, Peru, Rwanda, St. Kitts-Nevis, St. Lucia, St. Vincent and the Grenadines, San Marino, São Tomé & Príncipe, Seychelles, Sierra Leone, Solomon Is., Somalia, Suriname, Swaziland, Tanzania, Togo, Tonga, Trinidad & Tobago, Tuvalu, Uganda, Uruguay, Vatican, Venezuela, Re, Zambia and Zimbabwe can obtain a 15-day tourist visa on arrival at Don Muang, Chiang Mai, Phuket and Hat Yai Airports Immigration Office. Documentation: Passport must be valid at least 6 months longer than period of intended stay in Thailand. Tourist Visa: 1 application form per visitor (including infants); 2 recent photographs; pre-paid onward or return ticket valid for travel from Thailand within the 15-day validity of the visa. Non-Immigrant Visa: additionally require evidence substantiating purpose of visit; business visitors also require letter from their firm or business counterpart in Thailand.
Customs regulations (inbound) 200 cigarettes or 250gm cigars or tobacco, 1 ltr spirits and 1 ltr wine, goods to value THB3000. Prohibited/restricted: Arms and ammunition, narcotics, drugs, obscene literature, pictures or articles.
Currency Thai Baht (THB) = 100 Stangs
Postage Postcard to Europe THB8. Airletter THB10. Airmail letter from THB12. Post boxes are red.
Telephone codes Inward 66 + Bangkok 2, Pattaya 38, Phuket 76. Outward 001. Emergency Tourist Police 1699 or Bangkok 6521721. Call boxes are red (local calls) and blue (long-distance internal calls). New silvered metal boxes are being introduced. International calls cannot be made from payphones. 1-Baht coins required for local calls, 1- 5- or 10- Baht coins for long-distance.
Thomas Cook Travellers' Cheque Collect call Emergency number + 44 1733 318950
Mastercard Global Service Toll-free Emergency number 001 800 11 887 0663
Driving International Permit required. Drive on the left. Speed limit 60 k/hr in urban areas, 90 k/hr elsewhere.
Business hours Banks: 0830-1530 Mon-Fri. Offices: 0800-1700 Mon-Fri, Government offices 0830-1200, 1300-1630 Mon-Fri. Shops: 1000-2100 Mon-Sun.
Public holidays Jan 1; Apr 6, 12-14; May 1, 5; Aug 12; Oct 23; Dec 5, 10, 31; also Magha Puja (Feb 11), Ploughing Ceremony (May 8), Visakha Puja (May 10), Asalaha Puja (Jul 8), and Khao Phansa (Jul 9).

TURKEY

Capital Ankara.
Language Turkish; French, English and German are also spoken to some extent in Istanbul and coast resorts.
Standard time GMT+2 (+3 from 31 Mar to 27 Oct)
Climate Varies considerably according to region, ranging from Mediterranean climate with hot summers on the Marmara, Aegean and Mediterranean coasts, to severe winters in the Central Plateau and Eastern Anatolia.
Health No compulsory requirements. Precautions against Cholera, Malaria, Hepatitis A, Typhoid and Polio recommended. Note: Contagious diseases are on the increase in south east Turkey. Tap water generally safe to drink.
Passports and visas Passports required by all except nationals of France, Germany, Greece, Liechtenstein, Luxembourg, Malta, Netherlands, Portugal, Spain and Switzerland, who may enter with an official identity card. Visas required by all except nationals of Australia, Argentina, Bahamas, Bahrain, Barbados, Belize, Bolivia#, Bosnia*, Canada, Chile, Croatia*,Cyprus (Turkish), Denmark, Ecuador, Fiji, Finland, France, Germany, Greece, Grenada, Iceland, Indonesia*, Iran, Israel, Jamaica, Japan, Kazakhstan#, Kenya, Korea Rep. (South), Kuwait, Kyrgyzatan#, Liechtenstein, Luxembourg, FYR Macedonia*, Malaysia, Malta, Mauritius, Monaco, Morocco, New Zealand, Norway, Oman, Qatar, Romania*, St. Lucia, San Marino, Saudi Arabia, Seychelles, Singapore, Slovenia*, South Africa# , Sweden, Switzerland, Trinidad & Tobago, Tunisia, United Arab Emirates, and the Vatican. Nationals of the following countries obtain their visa at the point of entry ; Albania (15 days), Austria, Azerbaijan#, Belgium, Brazil, C.I.S#., Czech Rep#., Eire, Estonia#, Georgia#, Guatemala (15 days), Hungary#, Italy, Jordan (30 days), Latvia#, Lithuania#, Netherlands, Poland#, Portugal, Russia# , Slovakia#, Spain, Taiwan#, Turkenistan#, UK, USA. Austrian and UK nation-

als pay their visa in their national currencies, Eire Citizens in GBP, all others in US Dollars. Visits not to exceed 3 months except * 2 months and # 1 month. Transit visas not required by passengers continuing their journey to a third country by the same or first connecting aircraft, providing they hold confirmed onward tickets and do not leave the airport. Documentation: 1 photograph for visa.
Customs regulations (inbound) 200 cigarettes and 50 cigars or 200 gm tobacco, 5 x 100cc or 7 x 70cc bottles wine or spirits, 5 x 120 ml bottles perfume, personal effects in reasonable quantity. In addition the following may be purchased from Turkish Duty Free shops upon entering the country; 400 cigarettes, 100 cigars and 500gm pipe tobacco.
Currency Turkish Lira (TRL). On departure you can reconvert Lira into hard currencies only up to the value of 100 US dollars, so don't change more than necessary and keep exchange receipts
Postage Post offices have yellow PTT signs. The main offices are open 24 hrs daily, 0800-midnight in tourist centres. Smaller offices across the country open Mon-Fri 0830-1230 and 1330-1730. Postcard TL100,000. Airmail letter TL 100,000. Post boxes are yellow.
Telephone codes Inward 90 + Ankara 312, Bursa 224, Istanbul 212 (European side), 216 (Anatolian side), Izmir 232, Mersin 324. Call boxes are yellow. Special tokens are required: these are obtainable from post offices (PTT) in different values. Phone cards are also available. Emergency Numbers: Police 155, Traffic Police 154, Emergency 112.
Thomas Cook Travellers' Cheque Toll-free Emergency number 00 800 44 91 4895
Mastercard Global Service Toll-free Emergency number 00 800 13 887 0903
Driving International Permit required if taking own vehicle. National licence acceptable for car hire. Vehicles can be brought into Turkey for up to 6 months, vehicles should be accompanied by details of car ownership, a 'Green Card' endorsed for Turkish territory in both Europe and Asia. Alternatively, Turkish third-party insurance can be arranged on arrival at the frontier. A transit book is required for vehicles proceeding to the Middle East. Drive on the right. Speed limit 50 k/hr in urban areas; 90 k/hr on highways.
Business hours Banks: Mon-Fri 0830-1200 and 1330-1700. Shops: Mon-Sat 0930-1300 and 1400-1900. Shops in tourist areas often open until 2100 and also on Sun. The covered bazaar in Istanbul is open Mon-Sat 0800-1900.
Public holidays Jan 1; Apr. 23; May 19; Aug 30; Oct 29. Feast of Ramadan 3½ days, Feast of Sacrifice 4½ days.

UKRAINE

Capital Kiev (Kijiv)
Language Ukranian, Russian
Standard time GMT +3 (GMT +2 26 Oct- 28 Mar)
Climate Generally temperate summers and cool/cold winters with moderate rainfall. Towards the Black Sea coast, the weather is noticeably warmer and drier.
Health Precautions against Cholera, Diptheria & TB, Tick-borne Encephalitis, Rabies, Hepatitis A, Typhoid, Tetanus and Polio recommended. Tap water and some foods are unsafe.
Passports and visas Full passports valid for at least 3 months after date of departure are required by all. Visas are required by all. Note: Visa regulations are liable to change at short notice. Contact the Ukranian Embassy well in advance of travel.
Customs regulations (inbound) 200 gms of cigarettes, cigars or tobacco, 1 ltr spirits, 2 ltr wine, gifts up to a value of USD1,400.
Currency Ukrainian Hryvnia (UAH) = 100 Kopiyka
Postage Post offices open Mon-Fri 0900-2100, Sat 0900-1300. Stamps can also be purchased from kiosks and hotels. Post boxes are red for international mail and blue for local mail.
Telephone codes Inward 380 + Dneprpetrovsk 56, Donetsk 62, Kharkov 57, Kiev 44, Lvov 32, Odessa 48, Sevastopol 69, Simferopol 65, Yalta 654. Outward 810 or via operator. Telephone counters in city centre post offices are usually open 24 hours. Call boxes vary in colour and are for internal calls only. Emergency numbers: Police: 02; Fire: 01; Ambulance: 03.
Thomas Cook Travellers' Cheque Collect call Emergency number + 44 1733 318950
Mastercard Global Service Collect call Emergency number 1 314 542 7111 (USA)
Driving International Permit required. Drive on right. Speed limits: 90k/hr highways, 60-80 k/hr in urban areas. Note: petrol is hard to find - always carry spare petrol in cans.
Business hours Banks: Mon-Fri 0900-1730. Offices: Mon-Fri 0900-1800 with a lunch hour of at least 1.5 hours. Shops: Mon-Sat 0900-1900.
Public holidays 1 Jan; Orthodox Christmas; 8 Mar; 1, 2, 9 May; 7 Oct; 7, 8 Nov.

UNITED ARAB EMIRATES

(Abu Dhabi, Ajman, Dubai, Fujairah, Ras al Khaimah, Sharjah and Umm al Qawain)
Capital Abu Dhabi
Language Arabic, English.
Standard time GMT+4.
Climate Hot and humid in summer, slightly milder in winter. Rainfall is negligible.
Health Yellow Fever vaccination may be required if arriving from an endemic country. Precautions against Cholera, Malaria, Hepatitis A, Typhoid and Polio recommended. Tap water generally safe to drink.
Passports and visas Passports valid for at least 6 months from date of arrival required by all. Nationals of Israel, South Africa and holders of passports containing a valid visa for Israel or South Africa are prohibited at all times. Visas required by all except nationals of Bahrain, Kuwait, Oman, Qatar, Saudi Arabia and UK (30 days). Transit visas not required by passengers continuing their journey to a third country by the same or first connecting aircraft within 12 hours, providing they do not leave the airport, except nationals of Albania, Bulgaria, China (People's Rep.), Cuba, Czech Republic, Germany, Hungary, Kampuchea, Korea P D R (North), Laos, Mongolia, Poland, Romania, Russia, Viet Nam and Yugoslavia, who require a visa at all times. Documentation: 3 photographs for visa.
Customs regulations (inbound) 2000 cigarettes or 400 cigars or 2kg tobacco, 2 lt spirits and 2 lt wine, reasonable quantity of perfume. Prohibited/restricted: Natural or cultured unstrung pearls except for personal use, firearms and ammunition, drugs, wines and spirits, pork products, pornography.
Currency UAE Dirham (AED) = 100 Fils
Postage Most post boxes are at post offices.
Telephone codes Inward 971 + Abu Dhabi 2, Ajman 6, Dubai 4, Fujairah 9. Outward 0011 (Abu Dhabi) 010 (Dubai), 00 elsewhere.
Thomas Cook Travellers' Cheque Collect call Emergency number + 44 1733 318950
Mastercard Global Service Toll-free Emergency number 1 314 542 7111 (USA)
Driving International Permit or own national licence valid. Drive on the left. Speed limit 60 k/hr towns, 120 k/hr motorways.
Business hours Banks: 0800-1200 Sat-Wed, 0800-1100 Thur. Government Offices: 0700-1300 & 1600-1930 Sat-Wed, 0700-1200 Thur (closed Fri). Shops and Commercial offices: 0800-1300, 1600-1930 Sat-Thur.
Public holidays Jan 1; Aug 6 (Abu Dhabi), Dec 2, 3, 25; also Mawlid al-Nabi, Al-Isra'a Wal Meraj, Eid al-fitr (3 days), Eid al-Adha (4 days), Al Hijra.

✈ SECTION ONE • AIR TRAVEL FACTS   COUNTRY BY COUNTRY TRAVEL FACTS

UNITED KINGDOM

Capital London.
Language English
Standard time GMT+1 (GMT Oct-Mar)
Climate Temperate, cool to mild, warm summers. It is variable throughout the year and the country as a whole.
Health No compulsory vaccinations. Tetanus immunisation recommended. Tapwater safe to drink.
Passports and Visas Passports required by all except: Holders of EU National Identity Cards for tourist visits not exceeding 3 months. Nationals of Iceland, Leichtenstein, Monaco, Norway, and Switzerland with valid ID cards for tourist/social visits of not less than 6 months and in possession of a British Visitors guide (available from travel agents). Visas not required by EU nationals, and citizens of Australia, Canada, USA and Japan.
Customs regulations (inbound) Travellers from within EU countries need not complete Customs formalities. Goods bought outside the EU or in EU duty-free shops; 200 cigarettes or 50 cigars or 100 cigarillos or 250gm tobacco, 1 ltr spirits or 2 ltr sparkling or fortified wine, 2 ltr still table wine, 60ml perfume, 250ml toilet water, gifts to GBP145 in value (GBP 75 for gifts bought in the EU). Prohibited/restricted: drugs, firearms, flick knives, obscene videos and publications, meat, plants, fruit, animals, goods made from protected species (e,g, ivory, reptile leather).
Currency Pound Sterling (GBP) = 100 Pence
Postage Wide network of post offices and sub-post offices (logo: 'post office' in yellow on a red oval background). Opening hours are usually Mon-Fri 0930-1730, Sat 0930-1300. Smaller offices may shut for lunch and on Wed afternoon. Stamps are also sold by most people who sell postcards. Postboxes are red and usually free-standing.
Telephone codes Inward 44+ Inner London 171, Outer London 181, Birmingham 121, Edinburgh 131, Glasgow 141, Liverpool 151, Manchester 161. Outward 00, National operator 100, International operator 155, National directory 192, International directory 153. All emergencies 999. Public phone booths - traditionally red, but the glass type have replaced them in most towns. Some take only coins, others only cards, but the newer ones take both. Most card phones take credit cards as well as phonecards (on sale at newsagents).
There are two tarriffs for international calls and three for national. The most expensive: Mon-Fri 0800-1800, cheapest (for national calls) is all Sat and Sun. A number beginning '0800' or '0500' is free, a number beginning '0345' or '0645' is charged as if it were a local call.
Thomas Cook Travellers' Cheque Toll-free Emergency number 0800 622101
Mastercard Global Service Toll-free Emergency number 0800 96 4767
Driving National licence required. Drive on the left, Speed limits: 112k/hr motorways, 96k/hr major roads, 48k/hr urban areas. Front seat belts must be worn, and rear belts worn, if fitted.
Business hours Banks: Mon-Fri 0930-1700/1730. Some open Sat morning 0930-1200. Smaller branches Mon-Fri 0930-1530. Offices: Mon-Fri 0900-1700. Shops: Mon-Sat 0900-1730. Many open Sun (usually 1000-1600). Some have an early- and/or late-closing day and many small shops stay open very late.
Public holidays England and Wales: 1 Jan; Good Fri; Easter Mon; May Day (first Mon May, but this may change): Spring Bank Holiday (last Mon May); Summer Bank Holiday (last Mon Aug); 25, 26 Dec. There are variations in Scotland and Ireland.

UNITED STATES OF AMERICA

Capital Washington DC
Language English. Many other languages are also spoken.
Standard time: Eastern Zone GMT-5 (-4 from 6 Apr to 26 Oct); Indiana GMT-5; Central Zone GMT-6 (-5 from 6 Apr to 26 Oct); Mountain Zone GMT-7 (-6 from 6 Apr to 26 Oct); Arizona GMT-7; Pacific Zone GMT-8 (-7 from 6 Apr to 26 Oct); Alaska (Mainland and Eastern Aleutian Islands) GMT-9 (-8 from 6 Apr to 26 Oct); Alaska (Western Aleutian Islands) GMT-10 (-9 from 6 Apr to 26 Oct); Hawaii GMT-10.
Climate Varies greatly throughout the country with cold winters (severe inland) and warm summers in the north (hot and humid in the north east), mild wet winters and hot humid summers in the south east and mild winters and hot dry summers in the south west.
Health No compulsory requirements. Tap water safe to drink.
Passports and visas Passports required on entry by all except nationals of Canada arriving from anywhere in the Western hemishere with at least 1 proof of identity and residents of Canada or Bermuda who are arriving from North, Central or South America. Visas required by all except: Nationals of EU countries (except nationals of Greece and Portugal who do require visas) if not exceeding 90 days and with a valid passport, British subjects resident in the Cayman Islands or Turks & Caicos Islands who arrive directly from those islands. Nationals of Andorra, Brunei, Darussalem, Iceland, Japan, Liechtenstein, Monaco, New Zealand, Norway, San Marino, and Switzerland who have a valid passport and are not staying for more than 90 days. Note: it may be worthwhile to check with the relevant consular authority before finalising travel arrangements as visa/passport regulations may be subject to change at short notice. Documentation: 1 colour photograph for visa. Return ticket required.
Customs regulations (inbound) Non-US residents: Aged 21+ 200 cigarettes or 50 cigars or 2kg tobacco, 1 ltr (USA) alcoholic beverage; US residents: USD 400 worth of articles acquired abroad (USD 1200 US residents returning from American Samoa, Guam and Virgin Is.), 200 cigarettes, reasonable quantity tobacco, 100 cigars, 1 ltr (USA) alcoholic beverage. Prohibited/restricted: Meat and meat products, fish, vegetables, dairy products, some seeds, plants, fruits etc. All items purchased in Cuba, Iran, Iraq, Haiti, Libya, North Korea. Firearms and narcotics.
Currency U.S. Dollar (USD) = 100 Cents
Postage Airmail letter 46 cents per ounce Canada/Mexico, USD1 per ounce all other destinations. Post boxes are blue.
Telephone codes Inward 1 + Boston 617, Chicago 312, Fort Lauderdale 954, Honolulu 808, Los Angeles 213, Miami 305, New Orleans 504, NYC Bronx 718, NYC Brooklyn 718, NYC Manhattan 212, NYC Queens 718, NYC Staten Island 718, Richmond (Va.) 804, San Diego 619, San Francisco 415, Tampa 813, Washington (DC) 202. Outward 011 (Mainland), via operator (Alaska and Hawaii). Call boxes are blue. 5, 10, and 25 cent coins accepted.
Thomas Cook Travellers' Cheque Toll-free Emergency number 1 800 223 7373
Mastercard Global Service Toll-free Emergency number 1 800 307 7309
Driving International Permit or own national licence valid. Drive on the right. Speed limit signs shown in MPH. Speed limits vary from state to state but generally are 48km/h (30 mph) urban areas, 24 km/h (15mph) school zones, 64-72 km/h (40-45mph) bypass routes, 88km/h (55mph) non-interstate/ urban interstate highways, 105km/h (65mph) rural interstate highways.
Business hours Banks: 0900-1500 Mon-Fri. Offices: 0900-1730 Mon-Fri. Shops 0930-1800 Mon-Sat, 0930-2100 shopping centres.
Public holidays Jan 1; July 4; Nov 11; Dec 25; also Martin Luther King's Birthday (third Mon in Jan), Washington's Birthday (third

41

Mon in Feb), Memorial Day (last Mon in May), Labor Day (first Mon in Sep), Columbus Day (second Mon in Oct), and Thanksgiving Day (fourth Thurs in Nov); these apply to all states and territories. A large number of additional holidays are observed in various states and cities, especially Lincoln's Birthday, which is widely observed in the north and largely ignored in the south. Good Friday is also observed in most states. If a holiday falls on a Sunday, the following Monday is observed; if on a Saturday, the previous Friday.

VENEZUELA

Capital Caracas
Language Spanish. English, French, German and Portuguese.
Standard time GMT-4.
Climate Tropical, with high humidity, especially in coastal areas. However, there are considerable variations between day and night temperatures. Most pleasant time is form Jan-Apr. Raining season is May-Dec.
Health No compulsory requirements. Malaria risk exists all year. Precautions against Malaria, Bilharzia, Meningitis, Hepatitis A, Typhoid and Polio, also Yellow Fever (except infants under one year), recommended. Tap water unsafe to drink.
Passports and visas Passports required by all and must be valid for at least 6 months. Visas required by all except the following countries who do require a 90 day tourist card issued from an authorised sea or air carrier: Nationals of EU countries (except national of Greece and Portugal, who do require a visa). Nationals of Australia, Canada and the USA, Andorra, Antigua & Barbuda, Argentina, Barbados, Belize, Brazil, Chile, Costa Rica, Dominica, Grenada, Iceland, Jamaica, Leichtenstein, Lithuania, Mexico, Monaco, Netherland Antilles, New Zealand, Norway, San Marino, St Kitts & Nevis, St Lucia, St Vincent & the Grenadines, Switzerland, Taiwan (Republic of China) and Trinidad & Tobago. Documentation: Return ticket required. Requirements may change at short notice. Contact the embassy before departure.
Customs regulations (inbound) 200 cigarettes and 25 cigars, 2 ltr alcoholic beverages, 4 small bottles perfume. Prohibited/restricted: flowers, fruit, plants, pork products, Cuban and Dominican newsprint and magazines.
Currency Venezuelan Bolivar (VEB) = 100 Centimos
Postage Airmail letter and postcard VEB2.80 to Europe, but varies according to destination. Post boxes are yellow.
Telephone codes Inward 58 + Caracas 2, Maracaibo 61. Outward 00. Call boxes are silver and clear. Most call boxes now accept phonecards (available in bookshops and supermarkets).
Thomas Cook Travellers' Cheque Collect call Emergency number + 44 1733 318950
Mastercard Global Service Toll-free Emergency number 8001 2902
Driving International Permit required. Drive on the right. Speed limit 40 k/hr in urban areas, 60 k/hr (50 k/hr at night) elsewhere.
Business hours Banks: 0830-1130 & 1400-1630 Mon-Fri. Offices: 0830-1200, 1400-1730 Mon-Fri. Shops: 0900-1300 & 1500-1900 Mon-Sat. Some Sun opening in tourist areas (1000-1300).
Public holidays Jan 1; Feb 23, 24; Apr. 19; May 1; July 5, 24; Oct 12; Dec 25; also Holy Thursday and Good Friday.

ZIMBABWE

Capital Harare
Language English, Shona, Ndebele.
Standard time GMT+2.
Climate Temperate and pleasant throughout the year. Rainfall can occur at any time of year and averages 680 mm per year. Best time to visit is Apr-May and Aug-Sept.
Health Yellow Fever certificate required if arriving from an infected area (infants under one year exempt). Precautions against Cholera, Malaria, Rabies, Hepatitis A, Typhoid and Polio recommended. Bilharzia is a major health hazard; swimming in rivers and lakes should be avoided. Tap water generally safe to drink
Passports and visas Passports required by all and must be valid for at least 6 months beyond intended period of stay. Visas required by all except: Nationals of EU countries (except nationals of Finland, Portugal and Greece who do need a vsa). Nationals of Antigua & Barbuda, Bahamas, Barbados, Belize, Botswana, Brunei, Cyprus, Dominica, Fiji, French Overseas Territories, Gambia, Ghana, Grenada, Guyana, Iceland, Jamaica, Kenya, Kiribati, Lesotho, Liechtenstein, Malaysia, Maldive Is., Malta, Mauritius, Monaco, Namibia, Nauru, Nepal, New Caledonia, New Zealand, Norway, Papua New Guinea, St. Kitts-Nevis, San Marino, Senegal, Seychelles, Sierra Leone, Singapore, Solomon Is., South Africa, Swaziland, Switzerland, Tanzania, Tonga, Trinidad & Tobago, Tuvalu, Uganda, Vanuatu, Western Samoa, and Zambia. Note: Citizens of the former Yugslavia should contact the Zimbabwean diplomatic representation in order to obtain up to date information on visa requirements. Documentation: Return ticket required.
Customs regulations (inbound) Cigarettes and tobacco items for personal use but to be included in general goods allowance, new articles for personal use to total value ZWD2,000, Age 18+ 5 ltr alcoholic beverage of which no more than 2 ltr may be spirits. Prohibited/restricted: Agricultural products, animals and birds, drugs, firearms, flick and lockable knives, ammunition and explosives, indecent or obscene films and publications, radiocommunications equipment (permit issued on arrival).
Currency Zimbabwean Dollar (ZWD) = 100 Cents
Postage Postcard ZWD4. Airletter ZWD4. Post boxes are red.
Telephone codes Inward 263 + Bulawayo 9, Harare 4, Kariba 61, Victoria Falls 13. Outward 110. Call boxes are green. Phonecards and 10-, 20- and 50-Cent plus ZWD1 coins accepted.
Thomas Cook Travellers' Cheque Collect call Emergency number +44 1733 318950
Mastercard Global Service Toll-free Emergency number 1 314 542 7111 (USA)
Driving International Permit or national licence (for up to 90 days) if not in English must be accompanied by a certificate of authority or translation of text. Insurance for imported cars required. Minimum age 18 years. Drive on the left. Speed limit 60 k/hr.
Business hours Banks: 0800-1500 Mon-Tue & Thur-Fri, 0800-1300 Wed, 0800-1130 Sat. Offices: 0800-1630 Mon-Fri. Shops: 0800-1700 Mon-Fri. 0800-1300 Sat, larger centers open Sat & Sun until 1600.
Public holidays Jan 1; Apr. 18; May 25; Aug 11, 12; Dec 22, 25, 26; also Good Friday and Easter Monday.

THE A–Z OF AIR TRAVEL

AIRPASSES

If you are on the hop, planning to visit a number of locations in a country, check if any airpasses are available. These enable travellers to travel around an airline's domestic network, either on a single rover ticket offering unlimited travel within a given time period, or using a system of coupons which are exchanged for each leg of the flight. Airpasses usually have to be purchased before arrival in the country and in connection with the international ticket.

In practice, the advantage of an airpass depends on how closely the airline's network coincides with your travel plans. Two of the best for leisure travellers are Visit South Pacific Pass, covering several South Sea islands and Liat's, which scoops up 27 different islands in the Caribbean. Most Latin American airlines also offer airpasses (just as well considering some of the distances involved in flying around), including LAN Chile, Varig and Aerolineas Argentinas.

The main drawback to some airpasses is that you often have to return to the airline's hub to connect with your next destination. Another, and this is particularly true in the USA where there are so many good deals available, airpasses may work out more expensive than cut price fares between destinations.

AIRPORTS

What do you look for when choosing a holiday? A destination that is easy to reach? Somewhere with a decent hotel? Good shopping? A museum or two as well as organised excursions? A choice of restaurants, from ethnic and fancy to palatable fast food? The promise of a decent tan? A health club for keeping in shape? A round or two of golf? Look no further than the airport.

The simple function of providing a runway and a means of getting on and off an aircraft seems to be playing an almost secondary role in the design and function of today's airports. All the amenities and facilities listed above can be found in Amsterdam's Schiphol, the fourth busiest airport in Europe. You can even buy a duty-free car, just a ten minute shuttle bus ride from the terminal exit.

In the UK most airports, Heathrow and Gatwick included, make far more money from retailing than landing charges. On the whole the changing face of airports is good news for passengers. Anyone with a memory of draughty Nissen hut aerodromes, where 'customer care' was measured by a tea and coffee machine and a bony upright chair, will welcome the new shopping mall terminals with open arms. But where retail is king the consequences can also push airports to the other extreme of user friendliness. At some airports terminal confusion is almost as high as at a casino, where the last thing they want you to find is the way out. Come to think of it, Schiphol also has its own casino.

Another key measure of airport performance is how easy it is to reach from town by public transport. Many airports outside Europe are poorly served. So, at least until the new fast link to Paddington is fully operational, is Heathrow. Zürich, on the other hand, has not only train links every fifteen minutes or so to the city's main railway station but direct inter-city services originating at the airport and linking several major towns. You can even check in your luggage at one of a score of regional stations and next see it when you land at your home city. Brussels and Frankfurt both have excellent rail links to town while Amsterdam is also the hub of a rail network that not only regularly and frequently feeds the Dutch capital but offers services to three-quarters of all Dutch railway stations, as well as trains to other European cities.

One of the most sensational airports to open recently – after much delay caused by a revolutionary baggage transfer system that did not do the job it promised – is Denver International. Twice the size of Manhattan, ten times the size of Heathrow, it was the first to be built in the USA for 21 years. On the approach road from town, a no-traffic light, no-toll, 25 mile highway, the first sight of the $3 billion complex is a magnificent range of 34 white peaks mirroring the distant Rockies skyline. The roof is made of fibreglass coasted in non-stick Teflon to allow plenty of natural light to filter into the atrium-like interior. Some US $7.5 million was been spent on works of art – the concourse trains, for example, hurtle through a brightly lit gallery lined with banks of propellers turning in the wind.

The underlying approach has been to design an airport that can carry on expanding, adding module to module, concourse to concourse, in order to cope with an expected tripling of passengers by the year 2020, as well as the next generation of megaliners. There are, for example, currently five runways (three north south, two east west, making it the world's first 360 degrees airport) but there's room for a dozen. In thirty years time, the designers claim, it will still be the airport of the future. But they did say that before Dubai announced plans for its new $200 million concourse scheduled to open in 1999.

BAGGAGE

Luggage limits not only vary from country to country, but airline to airline and, in practice, even flight to flight. Many carriers impose weight restrictions (40 kilos for First Class, 30 for business and 20 for economy). On transatlantic and transpacific flights two pieces of checked luggage are allowed as long as their combined weight does not exceed 32 kilos; dimensions depend on class.

Excess charges, calculated as a percentage of first class fares, can be crippling, so read the small print on your ticket. Travellers can also expect airlines to become increasingly strict on hand baggage allowances, a move heralded by both British Airways and KLM.

With carry on baggage the theoretical limit – one small case in addition to a few other items needed on the flight – may be waived for business class travellers, who are invariably allowed garment bags in addition to briefcases. On other occasions a case which fits within the size restraints may be sent to the hold if it is deemed to heavy (on paper, anything weighing in at more than five kilos could be put in the hold).

CODE SHARING

You are about to board a flight, your ticket clearly coded with the initials of your chosen airline. But when the time comes to board you find that the aircraft and flight crew are sporting the livery of a completely different airline. How come?

Airlines spend huge sums of money telling us that they are the world's favourite or whatever. Yet when we are lured by the propaganda to fly them, we increasingly find the brand has been switched.

Code sharing, by which airlines collaborate rather than compete with their rivals, is a rapidly growing practice.

If you decide to buy a Ford from a garage you would not be amused to find they delivered a VW instead. But code sharing between airlines is perfectly legal and, in most cases, the marriage takes place between well-matched partners. Customers undoubtedly gain from better networks and frequencies. What is not acceptable is that passengers are not always made fully aware of the arrangements, which makes the choice of airline a rather meaningless exercise. It is always worth asking when you but your ticket, at the same time as checking on the routing (see below). In future we may well see the main alliance groupings, like United and Lufthansa, moving toward common branding.

CONSOLIDATION

A dirty word, and one mainly associated with charter flights to mass-market holiday destinations. Tour operators, who work to tight profit margins, have to fill the planes they charter in order to make a profit (with scheduled carriers the break even 'load factor' is much lower). Yet brochures have to be written a year or more ahead of the holidays they sell. If, several months down the line, a particular departure is not selling well the operator who chartered the aircraft cannot let it fly with spare capacity. Therefore, usually around March or April, operators may well change holiday flights, combining the passengers booked on one aircraft with those of another. Hopefully the changes will still mean a departure from the same airport and on the same day. For "Consolidators" see "Deals and Discounts."

COURIER FLIGHTS

One way to get a cheap fare is by acting as a courier, escorting either urgent packages or, more commonly, documents which relate to hold luggage which you never even see let alone have to carry. Somebody from the courier company will meet you at the check-in and another, at the other end will be on hand to process the paper work.

In return for a saving on the price of a ticket your own luggage allowance will be restricted. As well as travelling light (often with just cabin baggage so that the luggage allowance can be used by the company), most courier companies also require employees to dress smartly (no jeans or trainers). Although last minute flights are sometimes available, most require you to choose a date of travel two to three months in advance and invariably return within a specified period, usually four to six weeks.

DEALS AND DISCOUNTS

Once upon a time, not so long ago, the only place to buy a cheap airline seat was to seek out a bucket shop, often no more than a large broom cupboard up some seedy flight of stairs, pay your money and take your chances on finding your name in the airport computer at check in. The business was strictly against the rules.

Today the business of selling discounted tickets has come out of the closet, shifting from back street to high street, from unlicensed to a licensed and financially bonded agent. Although a few shady characters are still in business, the risks of losing your money have largely disappeared.

Not only have some of the specialist travel agents, who buy and sell enormous quantities of cut price tickets, become highly respectable but some of the principal sources of cheap airfares are now high street travel agencies.

With all facts at their fingertips, those who want to save the maximum amount of money can still choose a circuitous routing on one of the less popular Third World carriers, which have the poorest records for reliability, punctuality, legroom, in flight services and, above all, safety. Anyone wanting a non stop flight on a top carrier, say Qantas or Singapore Airlines, can also get a discounted seat, but usually at a higher price.

The official fares set by airlines, and approved by so-called bilateral agreements between governments, only account for a proportion of their business. As airlines are able to predict the sort of 'load factor' that a particular flight will carry, so they try and dispose of the unsold seats by the age old street market tactics of reducing the price. Rather than officially cutting their published fares they offer their leftovers to middle men known as 'consolidators.' Some deal directly with the public, others pass on their allocation to several smaller outlets.

Discounted seats on scheduled flights are mostly available to long haul destinations. Although these are normally associated with cheap seats at the back of the plane, both first and business class travel is also available on the cheap. Relatively speaking.

The Internet is rapidly gaining ground, especially in the USA, as a source of special offers. American Airlines, for example, has a mailing list of a million plus customers who subscribe to its 'NetSAAver' fares. Every Wednesday they are sent details of special offers for flights for the coming weekend. Currently special offers are now available from the US to Europe.

DENIED BOARDING COMPENSATION

Put yourself in this travel scenario. You arrive at the airport with bags of time for your flight. The information board shows no signs of a delay so you confidently join the queue at check in. You have a confirmed reservation and a valid ticket, a legally binding contract between you and the airline stamped with a big 'OK' beside the flight number. But when you present it, the agent at the desk tells you the flight is full. Although ruder verbs will no doubt spring to mind, in airline parlance you have been 'bumped'.

Most people can cope with the occasional bus turning up packed to the gills and having to wait at the stop for the next, but a flight is different. For one thing the pilot cannot lean out of the window with a chirpy 'standing room only' or a promise of 'another one along in a minute.'

For many travellers, a flight is a once or twice a year event, not a daily routine. And even for the frequent flying business traveller, the chances are that the flight has been chosen above all others because the departure time is important in a broader context of planned meetings and maybe other connections.

But overbooked scheduled flights are not some quirky, highly unfortunate circumstances but facts of flying life. Airlines deliberately accept more bookings – as high as 30 percent – for a flight than the aircraft could possible accommodate. Knowing that there will always be a proportion of passengers who fail to turn up, airlines overbook to avoid losing money by taking off with unfilled seats. If overbooking were to be outlawed, then fares would have to rise to make up this loss of revenue. This would not, argue the airlines, be in the best interests of passengers. In 1993 American Airlines alone recorded more then ten million no shows, worth more than $119 million in lost revenue. Had overbooking not been practised, it estimates that this figure would have been $238 million.

From a passenger point of view, this may seem a wholly unacceptable practice. But, retort the airlines, the finger of blame should really be pointed at those travellers who fail to honour their reservations, known in the business as 'no-shows.' Although some will have missed their flight for genuine reasons, such as being stuck in a traffic jam on the airport approaches, misreading the 24 hour ticket clock, or going to the wrong terminal, even the wrong airport, most no-showings are quite deliberate. Business travellers, needing to keep their travel timings flexible, often make two or more reservations on the same route to keep their options open and regularly fail to cancel those on flights which they have no hope of catching. Among the most famously overbooked flights are those leaving cities on a Friday afternoon, a time when working folk are anxious to get home for the weekend and cover their options by booking two or three flights rather than risk being stranded abroad. Airlines themselves are not without blame, occasionally accepting a late but lucrative block booking, for example, knowing that the flight is already full.

Rather than punish passengers by turfing them off flights, why do the airlines not introduce a scale of penalties for no shows, an obvious deterrent to holding a spread of reservations? The answer is simple. The only way airlines can justify the prices charged for business class and full fare economy tickets, their primary source of revenue, is by offering complete flexibility. No shows are simply an adverse side effect of such commercial strategies.

In the majority of cases, based on past experience and fancy computer footwork, airlines get their seat booking profiles right and flights overbooked on paper invariably end up with everyone who checks in getting a seat. Historically the level of denied boarding shows a downward trend. According to British Airways, current levels stand at around five per ten thousand.

But what are your rights if you find yourself among the bumped?

It all depends on where you are flying from and who is doing the bumping. The two places in the world which have laid down rules for compensation are the EC and the USA, irrespective of the nationality of the carrier or final destination. In all cases, compensation is only payable to passengers with valid tickets, confirmed reservations (i.e. not stand by, wait list or a ticket on a shuttle service) and who turn up at the airport at the requested check in time. Passengers denied boarding from EU airports are entitled to a cash payment, the amount depending on the distance they are travelling and the time of arrival of the next alternative flight. The airline may offer travel vouchers instead but you have a right to ask for cash, and in most cases you would be foolish to do otherwise since the vouchers will be limited to the one airline and may not be valid in exchange for a low fare ticket (although sometimes the voucher value is worth more than the cash). Normally airlines will first seek volunteers, but they also have the right to insist.

The sums involved are based on ECUs so the precise payment will depend on the prevailing exchange rate. The airline is also obliged to meet the cost of meals, any necessary overnight accommodation and getting a message to your final destination. If you are travelling on a package, then the compensation may be passed onto the tour operator who must then reimburse you. These rules do not apply to charter flights since overbooking is not practised by charter carriers; they have no need since they will have presold all seats to tour operators.

In the USA the level of compensation depends on the airfare as well as the length of delay. In practice, when a US flight is overbooked, you may well find the check-in or gate personnel conducting an impromptu auction. After announcing the need for so many passengers to give up their seats, as well as details of the next available flight they then propose a deal, sometimes cash, sometimes free seats on the airline's network. If they don't get the number of volunteers they need, the price goes up. I have seen this in action and believe me, the bumped come away with broader grins than those who travel, the latter often wishing their lives were not run on such inflexible schedules. According to American Airlines, some 97 percent of all passengers asked to give up their seat will volunteer in return for a suitable incentive – in 1993 to a tune of more than $30 million.

There are grey areas in both countries. When, for example, an airline substitutes a smaller plane for the one originally designated for the service, compensation may not be paid. Again, in the USA, planes holding fewer than 60 passengers are exempt from the Department of Transportation rulings.

But the real problem for the travellers arises when they fly from airports outside the EU and USA. Compensation is entirely at the discretion of the airline. While British Airways, for example, offer compensation worldwide, regardless of where passengers begin their journey, many airlines will bump without so much as a cheese sandwich to tide the passenger over to the next available flight, let alone a golden handshake. Although morally you have all the rights in the world, legally you might as well be on the moon. The only advice we can offer to avoid such dire consequences is to turn up on time and, when the 'No Vacancy' sign is hung on the tail fin, protest as loudly as you can.

FARES

In the 1950s a handful of airlines flew between the World's big cities. Now some 700 airlines serve 14,000 Airports. One of the consequences of the rise in popularity of flying and competition between carriers is a dramatic fall in airfares. Just before World War II it cost around £1,000 to fly from London to Bangkok and back, the equivalent of around £7,000 today. The same trip can now be done for as little as £400.

Ask each of the 400 or so passengers on a scheduled 747 how much they paid for their ticket and you will end up with almost as many different answers.

Example

London (Heathrow or Gatwick) – New York (JFK or Newark). Fares prevailing November 1 and valid until end of March, excluding Christmas period:

£305 Apex Book 21 days in advance Must stay 7 days and no more than 1 month Low season Midweek

£357 5 day break, 14 days book ahead

£375 Apex 14 days book ahead Minimum stay 7 days, maximum 1 month Low season Midweek

£450 Apex 14 days book ahead Minimum stay must include a Saturday, maximum 6 month

The above are for Midweek departures and incur charges for any changes or refunds. Those which follow are fully flexible and have no book ahead or minimum or maximum stay limits.

£844 Full Economy No advance purchase No minimum or maximum. Fully changeable and refundable but changes to routing incur charges.

£1402 Fully flexible economy fare.

£2414 Business Class.

£4984 First Class.

£5412 Concorde.

Airfares do not even have a cost-per-mile logic. A business class ticket from London to New York, for example, will cost twice as much per mile as one to less popular destinations, such as southern Africa or the Far East. And you pay a lot more per mile to fly within Europe than the USA.

As with most purchases, so with airline tickets: you get what you pay for. As you move up the price ladder, aside from creature comforts, you gain in flexibility. Once you begin to tell the airline what suits you – such as open dated returns, staying as long or as little as you like, travel on a weekend or at short notice, change, cancel or not show up without penalty, or make a one way trip or a ticket with a 12 month validity – so the fare goes up. With full fares you can, heaven forbid, even switch airlines.

The most flexible tickets of all, the full fare economy, business or first class, also permit unlimited stopovers are no extra cost as long as the itinerary does not add up to more than 25 percent of the total mileage between point of departure and final destination. The 'Maximum Permitted Mileage', for example, between Athens and Berlin is 1348, compared with the actual distance of 1124 miles. If the fare you buy allows stopovers, you could fly via Bucharest and Vienna – a total of 1326 miles – at no extra cost.

If, on the other hand, you don't need flexibility, think twice about paying for it. If you are prepared to accept certain restrictions on your ticket, paying in advance, staying for a minimum – and maximum – length of time at your destination (usually to include a Saturday night to make it unattractive to business travellers) and do not change your travel planes, you can make enormous savings by buying an excursion ticket, known as an Apex, Pex or Superpex, a Eurobudget or standby fare.

In addition to these official fares, airlines may also launch, usually at short notice and for a limited period of time, special promotional fares which not only serve to sharpen an airline's competitive edge but also provide a quick and subtle mechanism for responding to market trends, boosting demand in otherwise slack periods. Unlike Apex fares, which have to remain on offer until the aircraft is full – subject to the minimum book ahead requirement – the number of seats available on a promotional fare is limited. British Airways' 'World Offers' are the best known of these in the UK.

As well as varying according to the class of travel and the nature of the restrictions imposed on the ticket, fares also vary enormously according to season. An obvious way to cut travel costs, therefore, is to avoid the peaks. As a general rule of thumb, this tends to coincide with the Christmas, Easter and Summer holidays, as well as Thanksgiving, Memorial Day and Labor Day weekend in the US, although holiday patterns at the destinations may differ and affect the seasonality. Early July, for example, is a good time for low airfares to Australia when the weather is at its poorest. November tends to be a sluggish month for travel to the USA, hence the good transatlantic deals available at this time.

With charter flights the best deals are available at the shoulder season, just before and just after the summer holidays, when the airlines are already committed to running the peak season frequencies but the demand has not yet happened (or has already passed). The later you can leave the purchase the lower the chances of getting a seat but the better the odds of getting a bargain.

Check key seasonal dates before making a booking; you may find that shifting your flight by just one day can mean your journey falls within the less expensive low or shoulder (i.e. the middle) season.

When calculating the total costs of a trip bear in mind that the price curve of airfares does not always match with hotel rates at your destination. In the Caribbean, for example, the published 'rack rates' during the summer are at their lowest (when the weather in Europe and North America is at its sunniest) but airfares are high since aircraft are full with families on school holidays and people returning home to visit friends and relatives.

Competition exerts a key influence on airfares. Where two airlines have carved up all the business between two cities, fares tend to be high. When other carriers step into the marketplace airfares tend to tumble, showing just how much profit the first two made when they had the route to themselves. British Midland, for example, claims that on all routes in which it has been allowed to compete with flag carriers business, fares have tumbled. A recent study made by the EC showed that fares on routes with three or more carriers were significantly lower than on monopoly and duopoly routes. However, third carrier competition exists on only 7 percent of all European routes. With deregulation in the USA and Australia far more advanced than in Europe you find fares much more keenly priced than Europe.

With several airlines competing for transatlantic business, airfares to North America have never been as cheap. As a rule, the best deals are available on the non 'blue chip' airlines, the so-called Fifth Freedom carriers whose New York flights originate in a country other than the UK. Since neither Kuwait Airways nor Air India is the first airline that springs to mind when planning a visit to New York, both discount fares by wider margins than the American and British carriers.

FREEDOM OF THE SKIES

International aviation is still largely under the auspices of government control. Bilateral agreements, which determine who flies where, have their origin lying in the need for governments to protect their state-owned airlines. But as privatisation has increased, so has the call for deregulation, the precedent in Europe being set by the US in 1978 when President Carter deregulated the domestic industry with a single stroke of his pen.

Although airlines suffered, passengers gained enormously from cheap fares.

In Europe the process towards freedom of the skies began in 1993 and came to full fruition in April 97 when an airline of any one EU country was allowed to fly where it likes within any EU at whatever fares it chooses as long as they are neither too high, from the abuse of a monopolistic position, or too low, the result of predatory pricing designed to kill off competition as a prelude to then reinstating higher airfares.

Fares are falling but not without cost. More congestion, a risk of shoestring airlines having insufficient funds to keep their fleets well maintained and widespread liquidation all rank among the adverse side effects of freedom of the skies. Only two of more than thirty airlines that took off in the USA between 1978 and 1992 are still in business.

The other barrier to competition within Europe is the continued existence of government subsidies to national carriers, including Air France, Alitalia, Olympic and Iberia. Airlines wholly under private ownership rightly argue that, until the protection afforded these carriers from market forces is removed, the playing fields are not level and competition is unfair. According to Neil Kinnock, European Commissioner for Transport, the EU 'must ensure that government subsidies, and aids from public funds, do not distort competition.' But the fact of the matter is that they still do and the process towards full privatisation is likely to be a slow one and the huge restructuring needed to be carried out by several carriers likely to run well into the next millenium.

The current focus of attention regarding competition within the industry is on traffic between the US and Europe. British Airways, for example, would have liked the freedom to fly where it likes in the US, picking up passengers in say New York and taking them on to LA as well as serving both cities as non stop gateways. American carriers, on the other hand, want not only the same rights within Europe but access to precious slots or take off times, particularly at Heathrow where BA is so firmly entrenched. The USA already has an open skies deal with Germany : it may not be too long before a UK – USA deal is done.

FREQUENT FLYERS

Frequent flyer programmes have been the most successful marketing innovation in US airline history. Launched by American Airlines 15 years ago, when carriers were desperately seeking a commercial edge over their competitors in the wake of deregulation, their growth in popularity has been phenomenal. More than 50 million people belong to one or other programme which are now offered by airlines as far afield as China. American Airlines alone claim 30 million AAdvantage members, United some 18 million Mileage Plus members. Such is the popularity that in the US the concept has even spawned its own magazine, *Inside Flyer*.

Frequent flyers, particularly those who shuttle backwards and forwards across the Atlantic, are the airlines' favourite passengers. As US carriers stepped up their transatlantic services, particularly from Heathrow, so frequent flyer programmes have rapidly gained popularity with European carriers.

Members are enticed by a bouquet of incentives designed to generate customer loyalty. The more miles a passenger flies with a particular airline, the more credits he or she earns which can, in turn, be exchanged for free upgrades or free flights. On many schemes, travellers can also earn credits from airline partners (for example, American AAdvantage members can earn credits when flying with several other Airlines including Canadian, British Midland, South African, Cathay Pacific and with BA but not on transatlantic sectors and VV; similarly, United's Mileage Plus credits can be redeemed on British Midland, Lufthansa and SAS flights, JAL with partner Air France and so on.

Frequent flyer programmes are for passengers travelling on officially published, as distinct from discounted, fares. Some airlines – British Airways for example – restrict rewards to full fare payers, although most offer them to excursion fare payers and some, like American Airlines, extend mileage perks to all fares, including some consolidator tickets.

Some airlines put more emphasis on rewards other than mileage, on the grounds that the last thing a frequent flyer wants to do is get on another plane. Virgin Atlantic's Freeway programme, for example, offers hot air balloon rides, health club visits, flying lessons, golf tuition and photo safaris as well as free flights. British Airways also emphasise the broader 'service enhancement' advantages. Air Miles, incidentally, is a frequent buyer rather than a frequent flyer scheme – you can accumulate Air Miles when you fly in the same way as you would for spending money on a range of other products such as Hertz car rental, Travelex currency exchange, Hilton or Marriott hotels, Shell petrol, Sainsbury's groceries or everytime you use a NatWest credit card. The list of non-travel related participants is also growing within the US, even mortgages and investment funds produce mileage for members.

On most airlines, business class passengers can expect to earn 'points' or 'miles' in rough proportion to the distance flown (although there are discrepancies; crossing the Atlantic will probably earn more than flying to Australia). The rewards are also multiplied according to the class you travel.

Most have a two or three tier membership: the more frequently you travel, the higher up the tree you climb and the more 'generous' the rewards in the form of access to airport lounges, upgrades, guaranteed seats on 'full' planes, extra baggage allowances, priority on wait lists and at check-in, discounts on hotels or car rentals and holiday packages, even emergency cash loans, as well as free tickets.

You can join as many schemes as you like but it makes little sense to spread your allegiances, because you dilute the benefits. Decide which of the airline networks most closely coincides with your regular pattern of travel (those of the main carrier, its commuter subsidiaries and its cooperating partners). If your business interests take you mainly to and around the USA your most likely bet will be one of the US carriers; if your travel is more global, probably BA's network will be more suitable.

Frequent flyer schemes not only create brand loyalty but also identify airline passengers, 'distinguishing the chairman of a multinational from Aunty Flo on her annual pilgrimage to the relatives,' as one executive put it. As well as building up a database of high yield customers, the airlines can, by tinkering with the amount of rewards, use their frequent flyer programmes to stimulate business during an otherwise sluggish season or help promote new routes. While employees may be delighted with their frequent flyer perks, their employers may not be amused. Obsessed with upping their awards, businessmen tend to make more trips than they need in order to increase their rewards, by more than $5 billion a year in the US according to International Customer Loyalty Programmes Plc. In the words of one travel manager: 'A serious conflict of interests can occur if staff ignore the low corporate rate dictated by the travel policy and book a more expensive ticket that rewards them personally for their loyalty.'

GLOBAL COMMUNICATIONS

Ever since 1978, when Pan Am broke ranks with the world's airlines by selling a Round The World ticket at less than half the official IATA fare, such air tickets have been among the best bargains in travel. Not only do they allow you to circumnavigate the globe, but also enjoy a feast of stopovers along the way at no extra cost. What's more, you can buy such tickets for less than the price Pan Am was charging twenty years ago.

Since stopovers on ordinary, there-and-back, excursion fares are limited to one or two in each direction, even travellers to the other side of the world, from London to Auckland for example, would be well advised to consider a RTW ticket. The permutations are endless.

Only one airline flies completely around the world on its own: United. Flights UA1 and UA2 set off each day, east and westbound linking London, JFK, LAX, Hong Kong and Delhi in a 19500 mile circle. Other airlines put together RTW packages by cooperating with one or two partners, combining route networks in a single global fare. The British Airways/Qantas alliance, for example, means the option of twenty stopovers en route to Australia/New Zealand on one easy fare/ticket. In all more than forty airlines participate in schemes to produce almost two hundred ways of flying around the world linking as many as five hundred cities.

With so many choices you need to look at the airline networks – and their stopover options – to find which ones most closely fit your travel plans. The simplest way to do this is to pick up the timetables of two or three of the airlines that fly to where you want to go and simply study their routings.

The exact route must be described on your ticket (changes will incur a penalty charge), although the dates can be left open, other than the day of departure. You must also keep travelling in the same direction, eastbound or westbound. Tickets are valid for a year. Stick to the northern hemisphere and you'll pay less than if you dip south of the Equator.

If you can't find an off-the-peg routing that takes in the places you want to visit, turn to a tailor who can put together a customised routing, splicing a number of discount fares and coupling airlines other than the official marriage partners. The best tailors tend to be the agents who specialise in the sale of air tickets rather than the generalist travel agent whose prime role is the sale of holidays. Apart from being more flexible, they are generally less expensive than the official fares. But do check which airlines are being used; fares may be cheap because the carriers are inferior or because they fly circuitous routes, milk runs designed to pick up passengers but not necessarily landing in the places where you want to stopover.

Having decided to go around the world, which direction should you travel? The answer is: it all depends. On the time of year for one thing. In April, May and June, for example, it is less expensive to travel eastbound via Asia and back home across the Pacific. In November, January and February you will save money by flying out via the Pacific and returning across Asia. The airline industry is volatile and neither official or unofficial fares are etched in stone, so try to stay as flexible as you can, ready to take advantage of any special deals and discounts.

HOTELS

Airport hotels offer the ultimate in one night stands. Unlike those in more appealing urban or rural locations, their guests come not for pleasure but convenience. Nobody really wants to spend more time in them than they really have to, which must set a real challenge for a manager (even more for 'guest relations' personnel).

The two key occasions that airport hotels come into their own as are a stopping-off point for a night prior to a crack of dawn departure, or a place to collapse after a late arriving flight, especially before setting off in a hire car; trying to drive on unfamiliar roads, on the 'wrong' side' after a long day in the air can be hazardous to your health.

Airport hotels can also be a refuge when a flight is delayed (ideally paid for by the airline). Also, when executive time is at a premium, they can be ideal locations for meetings, drawing delegates from a variety of international routes without the additional time and hassle of getting to and from a city centre.

Airport hotels fall into two distinct camps. They are either located within the terminal building, a walk away from the check-in (sometimes with their own dedicated flight desks) or they lie close by. Or not so close by. You generally save money by choosing one 'off campus' but check whether the hotel operates its own (free?) courtesy bus service, the frequency of the service and the operating times, particularly if you are leaving early or arriving late. Another perk to look for is free parking for your own car while you are away. Some hotels will even drive you to the airport in your own vehicle and pick you up on return.

Some airports also offer day rooms, paid for by the hour, not for saucy intentions but just for a rest stop in between flights. The bad news is that your room may not have a window, which happens to suit most guests who just want to catch up on jet lag after their flight. At Miami guests can use the roof top swimming pool and health club, an ideal place to remind your body that it has other functions besides sitting down.

Although usually the exclusive domain of business travellers, there are also situations and circumstances when holidaymakers should give airport hotels serious consideration, especially when catching a wee hours charter flight. An overnight on site is far less demanding in both time and stress and also avoids such last minute packing panics or anxieties such as 'will the cab turn up on time' or 'what if they train is delayed'. If you're booked in a hotel the night before you can leave home when you are good and ready. With perhaps a swim and a sauna in the hotel leisure centre, followed by a leisurely dinner, the holiday mood will have already taken root before you even take off.

HUBS AND SPOKES

Born in the USA and now fast shaping the pattern of travel within Europe, hub and spoke networks make enormous sense for airlines, enabling then to link hundreds more cities via a single 'base' airport than they could possibly serve by direct services. It also enables the larger, international carriers to feed foreign travellers into their gateways and onto connecting flights on their network. In the USA, for example, Delta at Atlanta, American at Dallas/Fort Worth, TWA at St Louis and United at Chicago are each the dominant players in their respective airports.

Ever thought about going Dutch before flying to South America, or to Paris before winging your way to the Far East? Or flying from Manchester to Florence via Brussels, or Beijing via Copenhagen? Hub airports in Continental Europe are being used increasingly by British travellers as a convenient springboard to other European and worldwide destinations.

Since the range of destinations served by direct flights from UK regional airports is so limited, people living in the provinces usually fly, drive or train to London before flying to their final destination. But with the enormous growth of feeder services by European airlines, linking several British towns with fast-expanding Eurohub airports, you may be able to bypass London's congested airports. Indeed, one of the strongest arguments put forward by British carriers and BAA, the British Airports' Authority, for an additional terminal at Heathrow is that without the projected increase in capacity, passengers will be forced to favour Continental hubs.

Take Amsterdam. The city alone could never justify an airport the size of Schiphol. Almost half of the scheduled passengers are in fact just passing through, using the airport simply to catch a connecting flight to somewhere else while taking advantage of swift, hassle free, single terminal procedures, not to mention excellent shopping. Its significance lies in a far wider catchment of passengers. Billed as 'London's Third Airport', Schiphol now has more connections to UK regional airports than Heathrow.

Other airports in Europe developing their hub role are Brussels, a fitting growth given the city's role in Europolitics, and Frankfurt, situated at the commercial and geographical epicentre of Europe with a wide range of onward connections, particularly Lufthansa's flights to eastern Europe. Realising the reluctance of travellers to fly with eastern European airlines, Lufthansa developed an extensive East European network.

Paris-Charles de Gaulle has an extensive menu of flights to the UK provinces as well as a range of long haul services to destinations not always served from the UK. Different carriers have different strengths in different parts of the world, usually reflecting the country's colonial spread. Air France, for example, serves both Hanoi and Ho Chi Minh in Vietnam, BA doesn't serve either.

Charles de Gaulle has more room for expansion than any other major city airport – it occupies land the equivalent to a third of Paris proper – and now has a TGV/Eurostar station (it was the first airport in the world to integrate high speed trains and planes). Air France restructured its flight schedules so that virtually all flights fall into five distinct 'banks' of time, each one made up of a stack of both short and long haul arrivals followed by a stack of short and long haul departures. Aviation commentators no longer joke that Charles de Gaulle airport was merely a hub only for Parisians wanting to change from car to plane.

Being able to offer a range of connecting flights to a broad spread of scheduled destinations is one of the key factors in turning London's second airport, Gatwick, into a business as well as a leisure airport. More than a third of Gatwick's passengers do not even step out of the airport but simply switch planes. Billing itself as the 'hub without the hubbub', the British Airways' North Terminal has even managed to 'out Schiphol' Schiphol by offering minimum connecting times through the new Euro Lounge of twenty-six minutes, twenty minutes quicker than either its Dutch competitor or Paris Charles de Gaulle.

But the European growth of hubs and the importance of connections is overshadowed by the USA experience. Take Detroit, one of two key hubs for Northwest Airlines. The airline alone serves 450 destinations each day from this one airport. To take another example. The average American Airlines flight from Albuquerque to Dallas/Fort Worth carries 123 passengers. Only 43 of them are bound for Dallas. The rest fly on to 31 destinations, including London. In other words, 65% of passengers are bound for destinations beyond their hub, but they all fly in the same plane. The reverse is true of departing flights.

IN-FLIGHT ENTERTAINMENT

One of the fast growing elements in air travel has been the technological advances in in-flight entertainment. An increasing number of airlines are offering a choice of movies in all classes of travel, with those in the front of the plane having a comprehensive menu to choose from.

Interactive seat back videos, enabling you to play electronic games, make mail order purchases by scrolling through a catalogue then swiping your credit card, check out information on your destination, order a dozen red roses at 35,000 feet, play chess, tune in to real time news, follow the prices on Wall Street, gamble at cards or roulette, book a hire car or a table by the window in the best restaurant in town, and all without leaving your seat, are beginning to dawn.

For those who want to work on the hoof, Lauda-Air has already introduced Apple Powerbooks, several airlines now offer on board credit card telephones – often with a modem point – some able to communicate with a passenger on another flight - and faxes are appearing (on Singapore Airlines for example). American Airlines was the first transatlantic carrier to provide power points for business travellers, who need no longer worry about their batteries running out. And, for coping with post work fatigue, JAL have introduced massage machines.

J-CLASS

Eleven million passengers fly to North America every year – and that's not even counting those on countless charters, particularly to Florida. One million will be flying business class. 'J' is the mostly commonly found designator on the ticket coding, although you may also find 'C', which originated not on account of BA's Club Class but the original Pan Am Clipper Class, which was born in the 70s.

Business class travellers are the backbone of the airline industry. An airline flying between Heathrow and JFK can make a profit even if every single one of its economy seats is empty. Business class airfares cost around six times as much as economy. Yet no matter how generous the legroom the passengers do not gobble up six times the space as those at the back of the plane – which is why they are so passionately courted by the airlines.

Of all BA passengers for example, three quarters fly economy but generate only half the airline's international revenue. To Virgin Atlantic 'Upper Class' passengers are even more lucrative; 40 percent of the airline's revenue comes from this 10 to 15 percent quota.

A key advantage to paying a business class fare as distinct from a fully flexible economy fare is space. In recent months several airlines have been revamping the front cabins by extending the all important 'seat pitch', the distance between headrests. Steeper angles of recline, better lumber support, more effective footrests and flexible, head-supporting, wings have also been introduced.

Just twenty years ago only one airline, KLM, had a separate business class cabin for full fare paying passengers. Then came Pan Am's Clipper Class. Today's business class cabins are better than first class twenty years ago.

The pioneer of decent seating for its business class passengers was Virgin Atlantic, which promised its Upper Class passengers first class comfort for a business class fare. Continental followed with its BusinessFirst option replacing its previous first class cabin. And now several airlines have followed suit. Among those carriers with the most generous seat pitch are Air France, Cathay Pacific, BA, KLM, Singapore Airlines, Air Jamaica, American Airlines and Qantas, with 47 to 50 inches of legroom becoming the class norm. JAL 'Season' class is the latest, with a 50 inch pitch, an angle of recline between 127 and 140 degrees and a 6.4' video 8 channel video screen, the largest in the business.

In the intense competition between airlines for this lucrative market, business travellers are also showered with other perks. As well as superior in flight food served on decent china and fine wines, passengers are also offered more flexibility as to when they eat, more lighter fare options and non-stop larders for middle of the night snack attacks. Entertainment systems are more sophisticated, with a wider choice of options, even individual Sony video walkmans on American Airlines transatlantic. You can also expect a higher crew to passenger ratio and classier amenity kits.

The advantages of business class travel also extend to the ground, to free limo pick ups, dedicated check-in lines, and fast track channels through security and immigration. Emirates, for example, has a new service that enables business and first class passengers departing for Dubai with hand luggage only to check in from their free chauffeur drive car en route to the airport. The scheme operates from London, Manchester, Paris, Zürich, Rome, Hong Kong and Singapore.

Within Europe most business class fares have traditionally offered no more room than economy. The curtain, discreetly drawn across the cabin after take off, was rather like a conjurer's illusion, one which could be moved to suit the relative demand on an individual flight.

A business class ticket in Europe basically bought ticket flexibility but little else. But in recent months that is beginning to change, partly because of the threat from low cost, one class, no frills airlines. Lufthansa and Swissair were the first to offer a better seat after scrapping first class (the last to do so); now Air France, Alitalia, Swissair and Maersk are among the trendsetters. On domestic flights in the USA, carriers are also making the business travel experience more akin to long haul, with two, sometimes three classes.

KIDS

Travelling with the under-twos is a cinch. They cost little, weigh little and sleep a great deal. In fact, far from getting distraught and exhausted by the experience, first time parents can become very smug, dismissing all words of warning from those with well established litters as merely the sounding of duller and less adventurous spirits. It is the later years of childhood that make the parent-traveller's life tricky; meanwhile, with your under-two in tow, welcome to a lovely, rosy pink dawn. The only problem is that the dawn can come at any time, in the middle of the night if you leap across too many time zones.

All children need a ticket to fly. With scheduled carriers reckon on paying ten percent of the adult fare for an infant, be it an advance purchase ticket, a special promotional deal, a regular full fare, business or first class, even on Concorde. One infant has to be accompanied by one adult – having two laps or twins is no case for one adult claiming two infant fares. But pricing policies do vary, even between UK airlines and routes. Domestic sectors in the UK and the USA are generally free. But birthdays abroad may not be a cause for celebration; to qualify as an infant, a child must be under two on the date of its return flight, not the outbound leg. After that airfares take off from 10% to 50% or more of the adult fare.

Infant fares include neither a seat (unless there are some to spare) nor a baggage allowance, which can be a problem. The tiniest of offspring can generate more kit than a mogul emperor commuting between courts, what with a buggy, carry cot or car seat, changing bag, nappies, essential foods, enough cotton wool to stuff a sofa, bath toys and travel cot.

The best aircraft seats face a bulkhead, one of the internal walls with a fold down shelf for a skycot or bassinet, the most comfortable in-flight nest which frees the parental knees – vital on a long flight. But skycots are limited and need to be prebooked. Don't even hope for the extra legroom of an emergency row; children are not allowed to occupy the seats for fear of impeding an escape.

For take off, landings and turbulence you may – on British carriers for example – be issued with a 'belly belt' which is threaded onto the parent restraint. Carriers from other countries, including the USA, often rely on hands alone, not necessarily because of a cavalier attitude to safety but because of a genuine belief that belts can cause more injury than they prevent.

The safest approach is to use an airline-approved car seat, or fly with Virgin Atlantic who have specially designed seats for infants, but you will have to pay a child fare (either 50 percent of the full or 67 percent of a promotional fare).

Children matter even to the economics of the industry. Eight percent of all British Airways passengers are under 12 and they account for an amazing seven percent of revenue. The airlines also reckons that children are the fastest growing market segment. Yet from my experience, airlines differ significantly in the way they accommodate children. Some offer a handy (free) baby pack, for example, with disposable nappy, bib, baby wipes, talc and a deodorised plastic bag, some are reluctant to even warm a bottle of milk. Not all aircraft have a fold-down shelf in the toilet for changing nappies, which can be a disgusting prospect for someone in an adjacent seat.

Parents who don't give a second thought to piling their children in the back of a car and driving all the way from, say, London to the Scottish Highlands or across several states often think twice about a holiday that involves a long flight. But older children like flying. If it takes an hour before the 'when are we going to get there' sirens begin wailing from the back of the car, reckon on at least four or five in an plane. A flight, a relatively rare experience, is a treat, a car journey merely an extension of everyday routines. The closer the destination in terms of longitude, the easier the time you'll have when you arrive and, more important, the quicker the adjustment to home time on return. Studies show that children cope better with jetlag than parents, which is why families manage to survive even the hop to Australia, the mother of long hauls, a round-the-clock ride made all the more family affordable by charter flights.

Some airlines are more child friendly than others. The best – Virgin, Britannia and, more recently, BA – offer children's meals (or baby foods), dedicated entertainment channels, duffle bags or backpacks containing takeaway treats as well as in-flight colouring books, crayons, games, puzzles etc. Some US airlines, by comparison, tend to do either little or nothing at all for their fledgling flyers.

Children may occasionally need to fly alone, between colonial home and boarding school perhaps, between divorced parents, to visit grandparents or pen friends. Whatever the reasons, shop around before committing yourself to a particular airline since child minding prices vary. Some carriers levy a handling charge. Others will charge the full adult fare. Some, even more confusingly, charge the full adult fare for little children and child fares for older children on the grounds that they need less cosseting.

As a general rule, parents need to complete forms stating who will be taking the child to the airport, who will pick up, contact details and any special dietary or other needs. Airline staff will then escort the child through passport control, (giving the duty free shops a wide berth) and onto the plane where a crew member will have been designated to look after him or her. On arrival the reverse procedure takes place and the child is handed over to the person bearing proper identity. On some flights, to Hong Kong for example which has a high number of ex pat children travelling at the beginning and end of term, there is often a flying nanny on board.

LONG HAUL CHARTER FLIGHTS

Don't be a charter snob. A seat-only ticket on a holiday charter flight will not only save you money compared with a scheduled fare, but may also be the only non-stop approach to a destination. Charters fly their cargoes of holidaymakers straight to where they want to be, without having to change planes at some Clapham Junction of the airways.

As a rule, while scheduled flights serve cities, charters serve resorts, the sort of places we go to play rather than work. In recent years there has been an enormous growth in the number of long haul destinations on the charter menu, from the Maldives to Mexico, Mombasa to Montego Bay. One of the most popular destinations is Australia, with five times more capacity than when first launched eleven years ago, confounding those who prophesied that a 24 hour charter was doomed before it even took off.

There are, of course, still significant disadvantages to flying by charter. Whatever the airlines may tell you, they are not as comfortable as the best of scheduled carriers (although better than the worst). The essential way a charter airline makes money is by packing in people. You lose at least an inch, sometimes more, of the all important 'seat pitch' compared with an economy seat on the better scheduled carriers. Putting up with a charter flight when you are flying to the Mediterranean is one thing. But the prospect of being charter bound for endless hours at a stretch, or rather not at a stretch, is a more likely cause of angst than ardour.

Charter flights also operate to more restricted timetables, out and back on a weekly or fortnightly basis with no in-between options. But while scheduled carriers have comprehensive timetables, the cheaper the ticket you buy, the less you able you are to take advantage of such inherent flexibility, like changing your day of travel without penalty.

Charter flights are also more subject to delay than scheduled. Operating round the clock schedules, any planes that are delayed are likely to have a greater knock-on effect on later services. Also the destinations they serve, typically in Spain, Italy and Greece from the UK, lie at the end of airways which become notoriously congested during the peak summer months.

Another disadvantage is that charters cannot offer a true business class option. One or two offer improved seat pitch or a 'three-seats-for-two-passengers' deal, but none can match a properly designated cabin and superior service.

When it comes to price, the scheduled carriers are not a match for charters, which fly according to loads, not timetables, and do not have to maintain a chain of worldwide offices (often in the world's prime real estate sites). Nor do they spend huge sums of money telling us how good they are since we choose a holiday package on the strength of the tour operator not the airline it flies (or, more commonly nowadays, it owns).

LOUNGES

Ever since American Airlines opened the first for its top passengers in La Guardia in 1939, airport lounges, a natural extension to care in the air, have spread worldwide. American Airlines alone now has Check 45. Offering peaceful, comfortable oases away from the general airport hubbub, plus free drinks and snacks, sometimes showers and other body care services such as massage, shoeshine and hairdressing (all available at Virgin's Clubhouse at Heathrow), they are one of the perks of business and first class class travel – although some airlines restrict access to members of their executive clubs or frequent flyer programmes.

'Perks' is not meant to imply that lounges are pure leisure lairs. Most have work stations, usually a partitioned desk and a telephone although the number with power points for lap tops let alone modem points for sending material down the line are still few and far between. Again, there are usually fax and photocopy facilities and often one or more small conference rooms where meetings can be held in between flights (if airside) or before or after flights (if landside and accessible to non flyers).

Among those airlines with the most lounges, worldwide are Air New Zealand, American Airlines, British Airways, Emirates, KLM, Qantas, South African Airways and Singapore Airlines.

The newest brand is the arrivals lounge, where passengers can freshen up after a 'red eye', perfect for business men and women expected to make a slick presentation later that day.

Passengers flying at the back of the plane need not feel that the industry has overlooked them entirely. Some lounges can be accessed by all passengers on payment of a single usage fee. At Sydney airport economy passengers have their own transit lounge in the domestic terminal, the world's first.

MEGA AIRCRAFT AND AIRLINES

Flying giants will fill the skies in next century. Plans to create Hypersonic aircraft has been shelved in favour of the king size conventional jumbo capable of carrying around 600 or more passengers. They are already on the drawing boards, ready for take off within the next few months according to Airbus, whose A3XX, ready for delivery in 2003. They are gambling on the continued importance of mega hubs (currently around three-quarters of all air traffic operates between no more than thirty airports. Although Boeing has decided to shelve its plans and a whopper and consolidate its production on the hugely successful 747, on the grounds that the demand for more point to point services will make links between the major hubs less attractive to passengers. Both companies can be sure that the demand for air travel will rise enormously; the big debate is how.

For economy passengers the super jumbos will be like vast auditoriums, more like cinemas used to look before they became fragmented into multi-screen complexes. For business and first class passengers there is talk of in flight gyms, real business centres, flying secretaries, saunas and proper beds.

Aeronautics and engine power are not so much the constraint on growth but noise and exhaust emissions, especially as environmental controls get tighter. The airlines counter this by arguing that bigger planes will mean fewer journeys, landings and take offs, and less congestion in the air and on runways. But the real reason for fatter planes is to cope with demand. Long haul passenger numbers are expected to double early in the next century. Since runway and airport terminal capacity cannot keep up the pace, so the aircraft must grow to accommodate.

Not to be outdone by their hardware, airlines are also getting bigger. In the USA, three airlines dominate the skies, Delta, American and United. These, in turn have dovetailed services with foreign airlines to form global alliances – Delta with Swissair and Sabena for example, United with Lufthansa, SAS and others as well as Northwest with KLM. Airlines are also buying up sizeable morsels of their competitors (BA in Qantas, Alitalia in the Hungarian carrier Malev, Air France in the Czech airline CSA for instance) and franchising other smaller airlines to work within the system, benefiting from the giant's marketing and reservations clout and allowed to fly the flag in return for a sizeable fee. BA for example, has five such arrangements, with Maersk Air, City Flyer Express, Loganair, GB Airways, and British Mediterranean.

As I write, the Big Issue in aviation is the proposed merger between BA and American. Together they would control 70 percent of traffic between New York and London, and more than half the other transatlantic routes. Their combined fleet would total more than 800 aircraft, twice that number if all partner and franchise airlines are included, a monster force compared to, say, Virgin with fifteen. BA currently flies to 197 destinations in 83 countries, American to 263 in 39, including those within the US flown by its wholly owned subsidiary American Eagle. Together they would, through their gateway airports on both sides of the Atlantic, create a total of 36,000 city pairings. By the time this year's handbook reaches the bookstores (April) the deal, which is complicated by the question of open skies across the Atlantic and access of US airlines to slots at Heathrow, will either be ratified and taking shape or dispatched into the golden sidings. At the time of writing, United and American are the US carriers only have access to London's number one airport. Either way, it seems only a matter of time before the future of air travel becomes dominated by no more than half a dozen airlines.

At the same time as wanting to grow there is also a trend to disintegrate, to outsource much of the business, to subcontract the provision of meals, the handling of baggage, maintenance, cargo handling, reservation systems, even aircraft and crew on occasions. What the airline of tomorrow comprises may amount to little more than a brand, which can itself be sublet, a network of routes and slots and a management system. A vitual Airline, in other words.

MIDTOWN AIRPORTS

Centrally located 'secondary' airports have recently been enjoying a renaissance. Easy parking, shorter check-in times, expanding services and easy links to downtown has made them increasingly attractive to travellers. Belfast City Airport, the fastest growing airport in the UK, is a classic example. Just a seven minute drive to the middle of town, it has been poaching passengers from the more glamorous flagship airport, at Aldergrove, used by British Airways and British Midland but some 20 miles away from the city.

To go to Florence you used to have to fly to Pisa, 55 miles away, then catch a train or bus. Now several airlines are using Peretola, 15 minutes from the Uffizzi. Similarly, while Stockholm's main airport Arlanda lies 25 miles from town, Bromma, five miles from the centre, is beginning to steal some of the action, while in Berlin, Templehof airport is closer to downtown than Tegel.

With its Docklands location, fifteen or so minutes from the City (six miles, a third of the distance to Heathrow and less than a quarter to Gatwick), and with only 10-minute check-ins, London's City airport is a businessman's delight, especially since the extension of the runway to accommodate small jets (like the BAe 146) has also added to the (admittedly still limited) range of airports served.

In the USA some of the short haul, high frequency, point to point airlines are favouring smaller, old fashioned but less congested hubs. Love Field in Dallas, used by Southwest Airlines for example, is a 20 minute cab ride to town versus the gigantic Dallas/Fort Worth, a 45-minute or more ride away.

NO FRILLS

In an industry that has been on its knees, losing billions of dollars with several airlines going to the wall, Dallas-based Southwest Airlines has been a rip-roaring success. Some years, of course, have been better than others: 'We didn't make much in the beginning,' Chairman Herb Kelleher, the Branson of the American skies, told *Fortune* magazine, 'but it still felt like being the tallest guy in a tribe of dwarfs.'

Southwest is a short haul, high frequency, point to point airline. Unlike most US carriers, which tend to route their flights through a single hub, Southwest – now the seventh largest carrier operating within the US – concentrates on city pairings, mostly in the south and southwest of the US. Southwest Airlines is famous for its pit stop turnarounds; the average plane is on the ground for twenty minutes, a third of the industry norm. More than half are airborne within 15 minutes of arriving.

The intensive use of its aircraft is one of many reasons why Southwest's operating costs are the lowest in the business. The fleet of 161 aircraft comprises only Boeing 737s, the obvious advantages being standardised maintenance programmes, lower stocks of spares and efficient pilot training and deployment. Further savings have been achieved by refusing to link up with the costly computer systems used by travel agents; if they want to book a passenger they have to phone up like anyone else. Half the revenue comes from travellers calling the airline direct, a saving of around US $30 million a year in commission.

Running costs are also trimmed by a no frills approach to in-flight service, with no seat assignments, no movies, no meals and no free drinks. And although half the passengers are travelling on business, there is no business or first class option. Since the average flight is just 500 miles, no one seems to mind. In fact, Southwest has consistently topped the US Department of Transportation's statistics for the airline with the fewest customer complaints as well as the best baggage handling and the best on-time performance.

Another secret of Southwest's success is the friendliness of the cabin crews, all casually dressed in monogrammed sweat shirts, trousers (shorts in summer) and tennis shoes. They have been known to sing the safety regulations to the William Tell overture, hide in overhead luggage bins and pop out during passenger boarding, wear turkey outfits on Thanksgiving, antlers at Christmas.

But the biggest pull of all are the Southwest airfares, which are among the lowest in the business. Wherever the airline starts flying, fares come tumbling down and traffic soars. Within the US generally, fares between cities with competition from no frills carriers have fallen by 40 percent (US Department of Transportation figures). Such is the impact that other major carriers are having to cut costs so that, for example, the food offered on board US domestic flights varies considerably according to the length of the flight. On many flights over three hours outside normal meal times there is no food at all, so if this is an issue when flying check before choosing your airline or take sandwiches.

We have gone into detail about Southwest because it has become somewhat of a role model for other airlines, including Shuttle by United in the US and several European carriers. EasyJet is one of the latest in the field of 'peanut' carriers operating out of the UK. Flights – to Nice, Glasgow, Inverness, Aberdeen, Edinburgh, Amsterdam and Barcelona at the time of writing – operate out of London-Luton, unfashionable but reckoned to save at least £10 per passenger than Heathrow (with the added bonus of plenty of capacity, less congestion, cheaper parking and fast turnaround). Like Southwest, fares are kept to a minimum by passengers paying for what they consume; even a newspaper costs money. The airline also trims outgoings by minimal distribution costs, cutting out travel agents, loyalty schemes, interlining with other Airlines, CRS charges and eliminating printed tickets (passengers call the airline direct, pay by credit card and are issued with a boarding card at check in). Other airlines in the low/no frills Euro marketplace include Debonair, Ryanair and Virgin Express (which having bought Euro-Belgian Express) now operates from Brussels to Vienna, Rome, Milan, Barcelona and Nice at half the fares previous charged on these routes. It also recently announced a tie up with Sabena in order to feed UK passengers from Heathrow onto its services within Europe.

OPEN JAWS

The phrase 'open jaw' is one used by airlines as well as dentists. In essence it refers to a ticket routing that enables you to fly into one airport and home from another. Such tickets are ideal for fly drive holidays – or business travellers with meetings in two (or more) cities – although the often steep 'drop off' car hire charges need to be checked before you buy your air ticket.

Open jaws can be arranged for no additional cost, no matter whether they are full economy, business, first class or excursion fares. They are also easy to calculate; you simply take the return fares to both destinations – say London to New York and London to Miami – divide each one by half and add the two halves together.

PRIVATE CHARTERS

One of the boom areas in air travel is private charter. On a fare only comparison, it is much more expensive than flying by scheduled carrier. But such approaches may well prove cost effective when other factors, particularly executive time, are taken into account.

The main advantages of hiring a small aircraft or helicopter are twofold. In the first place, the aircraft departs and returns when its passengers are ready, not the other way round, thereby accommodating last minute changes of plan such as meetings which run later than expected.. There are also no queues for check in and no risk of the plane leaving while you are stuck in a traffic jam etc.

Secondly, since executive jets use smaller airfields than most commercial aircraft, sometimes not even an airfield, passengers can avoid lengthy transfers not to mention increasingly frequent delays because of congestion. You go where you want to go, not where schedules and networks dictate. And you can travel from airport to airport in a logical progression rather than be forced to return to hubs in order to make onward connections. Only ten percent of European airports, for example, are served by commercial flights from the UK.

Helicopters offer the greatest point-to-point flexibility, able to carry their customers to individual factory sites or the summit of office tower blocks. However, they are more expensive and less comfortable than fixed wing aircraft as well as being more prone to weather delays. They are also noisier, making in-flight business meetings next to impossible.

Any decision about whether or not to charter has to be based on individual circumstances. There are no hard and fast rules, beyond such obvious considerations as making sure the aircraft operates at, or as near to, optimum load as possible, and that it does a good deal

---

A cost comparison between scheduled services and private charter flights (source: Air London, July 96)

Heathrow to Frankfurt	
Six Club Class tickets @ £406 =	£2435
Six overnight hotel accommodation and dinners @ £200 =	£1200
Total Cost:	£3636
One day charter of 8-seater Learjet:	£3690

When you take into account, say, three hours of executive time, the company saves a further £8604 (worked out on the basis of £150,000 pa; cost to the company @ 2.4 times salary: £360,000; value to the company, @ 6 times salary: £900,000. This works out to £478 per working hour, so six executives hanging around airports would cost the employer £2872 an hour.

---

of flying rather than sitting on airport tarmacs.

Most countries have aircraft brokers, as well as air taxi and charter companies, who will do the shopping around on your behalf, adding their commission to the cost of the plane (though their knowledge may ultimately save you money).

Just one company, Air London, the world's largest business aircraft charter broker, has a client base that includes royalty, prime ministers, presidents and celebrities as well as air ambulance repatriates. Richard Dreyfuss, for example, flew recently from the US to Europe in a Gulfstream 3 chartered through the company to promote his movie 'Mr Holland's Opus' and to attend premieres in Rome, Hamburg, Paris and London before flying back to LA.

The cost depends on the destination, the length of time you need the aircraft, the number of passengers and the type of aircraft, all of which are interrelated. Prices in the UK start around £450 an hour for a four seater, relatively slow, short range prop, while a six seater Lear jet, capable of reaching North Africa non stop, costs three times as much. A 'Presidential', which can carry up to 18 people, with sleeper seats, hostess and full kitchen options, is priced twice as much again but it will fly you across the Atlantic faster than all commercial jets, barring Concorde. Which, incidentally, you can also charter.

QUEUES

Whether of people or planes, queues are a fact of modern day flying. Congested airports and overcrowded air corridors are likely to get worse as our seemingly insatiable demand for air travel continues to soar. Several airports are reaching saturation, air traffic controllers are juggling and should be an ever increasing number of movements, security procedures are tighter and lengthier, major routes are reaching their limits and airlines are losing millions of pounds each year on wasted fuel and idle assets. Such is the likelihood of delay that airlines have even built additional journey time into their schedules; in some instances jet planes now take 'longer' to reach their destinations than early turbo props.

Of all the above, air traffic control is the most commonly cited cause of delay, particularly in Europe where procedures are complicated by national boundaries. The USA, roughly a similar land mass to Europe, handles twelve times the number of flights.

Charter companies, whose planes are committed to more 'rotations', suffer more delays than scheduled and smaller airlines, without the spare 'back up' capacity when things go wrong, more than those with bigger fleets. On the other hand, smaller airports are less prone to delays than the mega hubs. And flights in parts of the world where the skies are empty – in the Pacific region for example – are rarely held up except by technical problems.

In the USA it is easy to find out which airlines have the worst record for delays and cancellations; recent performance history has to be published and in shown in the travel agents computer systems. In Europe there is no such requirement.

It is worth remembering that airlines are not legally obliged to offer even food, let alone accommodation, for serious delays. The only way to be sure of compensation is to take out travel insurance. One area in which we can look forward to saving time is at airports. Over the next few months we will see an increase in the number of airlines issuing automatic ticket and boarding passes which can simply be swiped through a machine, thereby eliminating the line up at check in – at least for those travelling with just hand baggage. Fast track is another innovation, designed to speed the passage of business travellers through passport and immigration controls in bound and out. And in the USA, at a limited number of airports, frequent travellers can have their palms read – not to tell their fortune but to speed their passage through US immigration, famously a nightmare of delay. Palm print technology works like this. The US Immigration and Naturalization Service (INS) has developed an automated system to expedite certain frequent travellers through the Immigration (but not Customs). It is not in lieu of proper documentation (passport and visa, if required). Citizens of twenty five countries – Andorra to the UK – who travel to the US for business three or more times a year can apply, completing a form obtainable from participating airlines or an INSPASS enrollment centre or US Immigration, then being interviewed after which fingerprints are taken and the card issued. To date the INSPASS facility is available at JFK and Newark.

REGIONAL ROUTINGS

Would you believe that, in this day and age of travel, you can actually hear the pilot of a scheduled international airline order the ground staff to 'chocks away?' Fly Suckling Airways from Cambridge to Amsterdam and, unless you're right at the back of the eight-row, 17 seater Dornier 228 aircraft, you will.

Named after Roy Suckling (MD and chief pilot) and his wife Merlyn (Sales and Marketing), the carrier is one of a number of small new airlines that have been quietly flourishing without fuss or fanfares while many of the world's major carriers have been struggling to keep out of the red.

One reason for the success of Suckling is the growing importance of Amsterdam as a convenient springboard to other European and worldwide destinations. But it is also symptomatic of a more widespread growth in regional or commuter airlines. The 55 mini carriers who belong to the European Regions' Airlines' Association reported an increase in traffic for 1995 in excess of thirteen percent, twice that for the airline industry as a whole. To pull out two examples of the many ERA member permutations, you can fly directly from Nantes in Britanny to Brussels on the French carrier Regional Airlines, and from Innsbruck in Austria to Frankfurt by Tyrolean Airways.

The big carriers are also having babies, either investing in smaller aircraft to feed smaller towns from the main international hubs, buying existing airlines and incorporating the fleet into their own or, when full parenthood would put too much strain on the finances, merging in order to get regional feed into the main network. Air France, for example, has handed over all its European services to sister carrier Air Inter, a low cost Airline which offers a more basic service and is more able to compete with the new breed of "peanut" airlines.

Backyard networking in a world of major carriers and congested hubs is the aviation equivalent of corner shop retailing in a market dominated by the supermarkets. By bringing planes to passengers rather than the other way round, thereby reducing travel times (only twenty percent of the average European 'flight' is actually spent in the air), regional airlines are clearly satisfying a need that business travellers have, to get to where they are going without having to change planes.

Some of the other lesser known routes from the UK to the continent include London City to Antwerp (with VLM), Newcastle to Oslo (Braethens), Birmingham to Basle (Crossair), Aberdeen to Esbjerg (Business Air), and Manchester to Eindhoven (BASE).

In Europe there are now scores of services between small regional airports, cutting out the main hubs altogether. Some examples include Crossair's flights between Lugano and both Venice and Nice.

The growth in regional airlines has had a knock-on effect on the fortunes of regional airports, which score over their larger relatives in their uncrowded terminals, minimal check-in (often 15 minutes before take off), less congested airways and fewer delays. A few years ago, 90 percent of the flights from Southampton Eastleigh for example were to the Channel islands. The airport now serves eleven domestic and Channel Islands destinations and five European towns.

ROUTES

Despite the implication of the word 'direct', such a routing is never as good as non-stop service since the time on the ground, to refuel and maybe take on passengers, even a fresh team of horses up front, coupled with the inevitable kink in the flight path, is bound to lengthen your journey. 'Direct' simply means that you will be carried to your final destination on the same plane.

A 'connecting' flight implies a change of aircraft but the timings are such that the arriving plane will be on the ground in time for passengers – and their luggage – to be transferred onto the onward flying aircraft. When you look up a route in, say, the OAG timetable it will list not only the non stop services but also the best connecting flights and the number of stops made along the way.

If you are buying a discounted ticket you should always find out the precise route and timings as well as the price of the ticket, since 'bargain' fares often involve circuitous routings and long layovers as well as Third World or East European airlines whose safety record, age of fleet and maintenance programmes are invariably poorer than those of the first. Or you might find the flight going through the airline's hub which involves a mighty dog leg from the route any sensible crow would fly.

Finding out an airline routing, the number of stops, the waits in between and the total journey time, is far more important than choosing an airline on the strength of its promises of superior service and finer food.

SAFETY

The statistics are reassuring. Air travel is the safest mode of transport, at least according to deaths per distance travelled as distinct from the number of journeys made (in which case motoring becomes the safer option). A single passenger, it is reckoned, would have to take a flight every day for the next 24,000 years before being involved in a fatal crash. And, in a worst case scenario, more than half the passengers on average involved in a major accident survive.

'A million spare parts flying in close formation' is how one expert defined the principles of aviation. Some aircraft are certainly safer than others. The track record of the Russian Tupolev is no match for a Boeing for example. And small airlines, although they account for no more than two percent of passenger movements, are responsible for forty percent of the disasters.

The best seat for survival? Arguably one in an exit row, on the aisle, and away from the engine. But the law says that only able bodies are allowed in emergency seats, so no gammy leg will get you a place, nor will children or elderly passengers who might otherwise impair the use of exists in an emergency. In the US FAA rules specifically exclude the 'feeble, obese, handicapped or those with full arm or leg casts' six footers should book early.

Safety does have its costs, which is why, for example, American airports have yet to install hand luggage scanners capable of detecting semtex and why British airports are only now beginning to screen all checked-in luggage. And why smoke hoods, which would undoubtedly save lives, have not been fitted under every seat (in lieu of life vests, perhaps), which have not saved a single life in recent years).

TIME ZONES

Over several years of air travel I have tried herbal pills, aroma therapy bath oils, metatonin (a synthetic version of the chemical secreted by the pineal gland to regulate the so-called circadian rhythms), amino acids and vitamin dietary supplements, worn a battery-powered medallion around my neck to generate a pulsating pattern of extra-low frequency magnetic waves, and munched sprouted wheat capsules containing anti-oxidant enzymes to mop up the excess of toxic chemical molecules called 'free radicals.' None of them would I class as a success. The only serious cure for jet lag is to stay at home.

The process of flying even within a single time zone, inhaling the same tired air and sedentary for an unhealthy length of time, is also exhausting. The longer the flight the more the fatigue. Flying in smoke-free cabins, I believe, makes a flight much less grim: although more and more airlines are banning the weed, flights to the Far East, eastern Europe and Latin America are unlikely to become smoke-free because of local demand.

But time zone changes are the killer. You need, it is generally agreed, a day to recover for every hour of time travel. The bad news is that few people can afford such luxury. Or else are back home before they have caught up with the first bout of jetlag. The least you can do is pamper your body with moisturisers and keep up the liquid intake – water and fruit juice rather than alcohol, tea or coffee – to combat dehydration, use ear plugs to reduce the debilitating effects of the plane engines, try a few 'flyrobics' which several airlines feature on their video systems and use a blindfold to help you sleep without distraction.

UPGRADES

There may be no such thing as a free lunch but there is, sometimes, a slim chance of a free upgrade. If the back of the plane has been overbooked, and before the question of denied boarding arises, a handful of economy passengers will find themselves being asked if they'd mind slumming it among the higher classes. Mind? No. Not this once.

Sure fire strategies on how to get chosen for elevated status are as numerous as they are ineffectual. They range from standing in the business class check in line in case they don't happen to notice that your ticket is economy, to turning up three hours before departure, dressed to go to a wedding and telling the check in clerk that you are the CEO's favourite nephew.

None of them works. Prospective candidates for the Big Seats are invariably drawn from the handful of full fare paying economy passengers, unless of course they happen to be clad in a grubby T short or accompanied by a screaming infant.

Frequent flyers, members of executive clubs (the higher the 'tier' the better the odds) and CIPs (commercially important passengers) who simply spend a lot of money on airline tickets are also likely candidates. Their names will show up on the screens at check in (frequent flyers who are entitled to an upgrade will not lose that entitlement if they get a discretionary one on a full flight).

You can fly business class at less than business class fares through discount ticket agents. Some of the best deals are available on holiday routes little used by businessmen. Since it is difficult to tinker with the configuration of a wide-bodied aircraft on a day to day, route to route basis, the airlines prefer to offer any excess of business class seats at reduced rates to wholesalers.

Other deals are on airlines which fly by a less convenient, or perceived as less convenient, routing (Gatwick to Newark rather than Heathrow to JFK for example – although both Newark and Gatwick can be quicker to their respective cities depending on where your final destination lies). Lesser known airlines, such as Air India or Kuwait Airways flying between the UK and USA are another source of cheaper business class seats.

There is some bad news. One of the key indices of the reversal of downward economic fortunes is the increased demand for fully paid-for business class travel. After years of cutbacks on travel budgets, more companies are once again prepared to indulge their flying executives with big seats, which means less spare capacity at the front so the chances of getting a surprise present at check-in will be even slimmer.

The next best thing to an upgrade is a decent seat in economy. Apart from the emergency exit rows, seat pitch does vary in other areas of the plane but the reservations and check in staff may not know the score. Seats to avoid are those near lavatories (too much to-ing and fro-ing), near the galleys (noisy), near babies (noisy; usually found in the bulkhead seats) and, if you don't want someone else's smoke, too near the back or too near the front where the rear row(s) of business class may be a puffing zone.

VIEWS

Who says looking out of a plane is boring, all sky blues and puffs of clouds with nothing to stir the emotions? Not I. Nor, I suspect, Richard Branson, even though he once declared that aircraft would fly better without their windows. Instead of hours of passing sky, he suggested that the window space could be more pleasurably filled with projected images of exotic destinations. But that was before Virgin Atlantic launched its service to Hong Kong.

Sit on the right hand side of the aircraft on its western approach to Kai Tak airport and you can almost reach out and snatch the laundry from the tower block washing lines. It is, in my experience, the best big plane white knuckle ride in the business. If you are the least bit squeamish, slip on the complimentary blindfold.

Sydney is another spectacular that can throw even the most jaded crew member off her stride. Early one morning, flying in from Singapore, one Qantas attendant who was dreamily peering through the door porthole as we glided over the magnificent harbour, the 'Coathanger' bridge and Opera House perfectly poised for inspection, took the microphone, welcomed everyone to Melbourne and wished us good afternoon.

Depending on the wind, passengers flying into LA are usually treated to the famous Hollywood sign on the hillside above the smog line. Chicago offers Great Lakes and sometimes skyscrapers, although in New York only domestic passengers arriving at La Guardia and those bound for Newark can get the full Manhattan skyline treat. Similarly, it's Washington's downtown National airport, just south of the Mall, not Dulles International, which exhibits the White House and the Lincoln Memorial. Again in Rio, it is the city centre Santos Dumont airport, the one where the Varig shuttle from São Paulo touches down, that reveals Sugar Loaf mountain and the spectacular bay and beaches, not the international.

Even at 30,000 or more feet there are amazing landscapes to behold. Like the frozen wilderness of Greenland on the Polar route to the US, which can enliven even the most routine of transatlantic flights, especially when the glaciers calve their brood of icebergs. Fly in the winter months with SAS to Tromso, some 200 miles within the Arctic Circle, and there's a fair chance of seeing the northern lights, while in midsummer the 21.50 non-stop flight from Heathrow lands at 2 am local time still in full daylight.

At 60,000 feet you can clearly see the curvature of the earth. Fly Concorde transatlantic and, despite the odd tiny windows, you can also enjoy two unique sightings not seen on any other plane. One is the sun rising in the west: in winter, the evening 7 pm plane bound for New York catches up with the sun which 'rises' on the wrong side. The other, on return flights, known to pilots as 'The Terminator', is the earth being obliterated by a fast moving disc of dark, as if the plug has been pulled on the light of existence. The best view is from the cockpit where the crew, according to a BA spokesman, 'respond favourably to requests to view.'

Even more impressive a mountain frieze than the Alps is the 350 – or more – mile parade of Himalayan peaks that accompany you on the last leg to Katmandu. Having whetted your appetite, Royal Nepal Airlines also arrange hour long flypasts of the summits, Mount Everest included, from both Katmandu and Pokhara. My single most vivid mountain memory was with KLM when the pilot not only flew within climber spotting range of the summit of Tanzania's Mount Kilimanjaro but did a complete circuit of the crater, just for the heck of it, before turning to roost at the nearby airport.

WHERE'S MY SUITCASE?

A couple of years ago a traveller, claiming the record for more miles flown than anyone else in the world, added that his grand total had only been beaten by his luggage. Breakfast in London, lunch in New York and luggage in Timbuctu is, claim the airlines, unfair comment. The vast majority of cases arriving safe and sound, just like their owners. According to IATA, seven in a thousand go astray, of which two never come back.

Before panicking, make sure your luggage is not on another carousel (at Gatwick, for example, some planes are off-loaded onto two different carousels). Next step is to report the loss to the baggage service desk or airline representative in the arrivals hall before you pass through customs, then complete a Property Irregularity Report. Some airlines insist that you follow this up with a written confirmation of the loss. Since each piece of checked-in luggage carries a bar-coded label, its individually numbered ID tag which can be logged into a computer, it is usually easy to trace.

Most of the world's major carriers subscribe to the computerised Bag Track/World Tracer system based in Atlanta, Georgia, so that anytime an item is reported lost, or turns up on a carousel without an owner, the two can swiftly be mated. In the meantime, if you happen to find yourself stranded without toothbrush, pyjamas and overnight wear etc, the airline staff are entitled to make an appropriate allowance to tide you over.

Compensation is laughable both for the ceiling amounts for lost luggage and for the time it takes for an airline to cough up. According to the Warsaw Convention, the limit is £13.63 a kilo which barely covers the cost of the suitcase let alone an Armani suit within. No airlines will fork out for the loss of valuables, which should be carried in hand luggage. Ordinary travel insurance is always a wise precaution.

Compensation can also be unbelievably slow, partly because the onus on tracing and paying up for a lost case is on the airline that bought you to the fateful carousel, but it may not be the one who misdirected the case in the first place. I have waited two years for a $100 claim for a toothbrush, a pair of undies and a pair of trousers and shirt (the day was baking and I was travelling only in T shirt and shorts but my overnight accommodation was Jamaica Inn, one of the poshest on the island with a strict dress code for dinner).

The best guarantee against losing your case is only to travel with hand luggage. Or fly only on non-stop flights. Other ways to help minimize the risks of losing luggage are: checking in on time, removing all previous tags, making sure your name and address is on each case, securely but not so that the address can be read by any prospective burglars (who are known to case airports to find empty houses) and by checking that the check in clerk tags your bag with the correct airport designator code. In addition, give your case a distinctive marking so that another passenger is unlikely to walk off with your by mistake, leaving you with their dirty laundry. And never overpack, otherwise your case may turn up but your smalls may be scattered all over the insides of the jumbo.

X-BORDER TICKETING

It may be cheaper to buy a ticket in a different country from home. As well as taking advantage of different rates of exchange you often find that airlines, which basically set fares according to what the market can stand, sell comparable journeys at vastly different prices. So, for example, you might save money by buying a ticket from Frankfurt to Singapore not in German Marks in Germany but Italian lire in Rome. Similarly, business travellers making frequent trips from, say, Paris and Madrid might be better off buying a one way ticket from Paris to Madrid and then travelling between the two cities on a series of round trips from Madrid to Paris.

YOUR TICKET EXPLAINED

An airline ticket is not an entirely self-explanatory document to those unfamiliar with its codes and layouts, but once deciphered it appears more logical and is easy to understand. On the next page a typical multi-sector ticket, in this case a British Midland flight from Glasgow to Paris, returning to London, is explained.

One of the major changes currently happening in air travel is the introduction of electronic ticketing, or more precisely ticketless travel, pioneered by United Airlines for domestic flights in the US. United maintains that more than forty percent of their domestic passengers now use E tickets and there are plans to introduce them internationally in the next few months. In Europe Lufthansa has already introduced it in the domestic German market. As well as its busiest international routes to Heathrow and Paris and British Airways on its domestic services as well as more than 90 percent of domestic routes flown by franchised airlines.

Passengers need only to turn up for their flight, obtain their boarding card with seat assignment by inserting a credit card into a machine and, if they are only carrying hand luggage, simply board their flight. Within the next few years ticket-less travel will be the norm.

Some questions and caveats: Is the ticket you bought the one you think you bought? Is the airline the one you chose, the dates of travel the ones you want, the flight times and the routing as you thought and the restrictions, if any, made clear? Does the little status box say OK or NK or KK, rather than WL for Wait Listed? If in doubt double-check with the airline to see if your reservation is logged in the system. Have you got the correct number of flight coupons, one for each sector of the journey? Have you actually been given a ticket before parting with any money? Is the agent fully bonded?

As long as the agent belongs to ABTA (in the UK) or IATA, and the ticket is written out correctly, it will be honoured by the airline. But if a scheduled carrier collapses you will not be protected unless you buy your ticket with a credit card (not a charge card or direct debit) directly from the airline.

Make sure that only the coupon needed for a particular sector is

A-Z OF AIR TRAVEL

SECTION ONE • AIR TRAVEL FACTS

YOUR TICKET EXPLAINED

1. Departure airport and terminal
2. Class of service (Euroclass is British Midland's Club Class). Any endorsements or ticket restrictions would also appear in this box.
3. Passenger name.
4. Routing, departure and destination airport. All BM tickets are issued as four coupons; if passenger is, as in this case, only travelling three sectors (in this case Glasgow-Paris-London-Paris), fourth sector is marked void).
5. Ticket fare, in the currency it was paid in (Sterling in this case).
6. UK departure tax.
7. French departure tax.
8. Total amount paid by passenger.
9. Ticket number. Shows airline code number and ticket serial number. Passenger should always make a separate note of it.
10. Breakdown of fare, detailing carrier for each sector abbreviated to two letters (BD is British Midland) and sometimes prices for each sector.
11. OK indicates a confirmed seat reservation; SA-space subject to availability; RQ-space requested but not confirmed; NS-infant not occupying seat; OPEN-reservation not requested.
12. Form of payment
13. Baggage allowance for each leg of the journey; 30kg in Business Class with British Midland, 20kg in Economy.
14. Date and place of issue.
15. Agency or airline stamp.
16. 'Issued in exchange for' box: if passenger decides to alter his route after ticket has been issued and he is part way through journey, he takes the ticket to the new departure airport where they issue a new coupon for the new sector and his original ticket number (236 4469 ...) will be put in this box.
17. Passenger booking reference.
18. Dates of travel, times and flight numbers.
19. C or J =Club Class; Y, M or B = Economy or Tourist Class; F = First Class, R = Supersonic (Concorde).

Ticket reproduced by kind permission of British Midland

removed at check-in. I once had two removed erroneously by one clerk in Nassau which caused a headache in Miami convincing the airline that its employee had made the mistake and nearly resulted in missing my flight home. And although it may look rather thin and flimsy, don't lose your ticket. Refunds take ages and the onus is usually on you to buy a replacement.

Zzzz (BEDS)

When businessmen were asked in an OAG survey what they preferred to do on a long-haul flight, four out of five said 'sleep.' And, when awake, half said 'work.' Most first class cabins throughout the industry are either being reduced in size or axed altogether on the grounds that the majority of passengers they carried had not paid a proper first class fare for the privilege (the cabins are often topped up with frequent flyers taking advantage of their free upgrade perks, pilots on repositioning flights, CIPs being treated and the like). Many airlines reason that revamped business class is almost as good at a fraction of the price.

In an ideal world planes flying at night would be completely different to planes flying by day. During the day the interior would be a compromise between a flying Quaglino's, the Reading Room of the British Museum and a private viewing theatre offering a degree of comfort normally reserved for film stars when watching their rushes. At night the plane would become a soft, silent bedroom, a boudoir for the business and first class passengers, dorms in the back in the style of Marilyn Monroe's 'Some Like It Hot' train ride. President Kennedy's did both. So did the old Pan Am Clipper flying machines. So did Philippine Airlines. But beds have gone. Even the Queen travelled in a commercial 747 of Air New Zealand (although she did take over the entire First Class cabin.)

One airline bucking-the-trend story is British Airways. Its new first class seats are more like private compartments, with five singles arranged down each side of the plane and two pairs of twins in the middle. Such is the flexibility that each unit can be a seat, a pair of seats which face each other across a desk or a flat sleeperette, the closest you can get to a boudoir in the skies.

The sleeper service is a simple idea that works.

ABERDEEN   ABZ

United Kingdom (see page 41)

National ✆ code: 44
Area ✆ code: 01224
Local time: Winter GMT, Summer GMT+1
Aberdeen Airport, Dyce, Aberdeen, AB21 7DU, Scotland
✆722331
Location: 8 miles NW of Aberdeen

TERMINALS AND TRANSFERS

Terminals
Main Terminal Airlines: All airlines.

Minimum transfer times
30 min

INFORMATION

Information enquiries
Airport ✆722331 ext 5312

EMERGENCIES

Police
Airport ✆722331 ext 5100

AIRPORT FACILITIES

Food and drink
Café/light meals Main Terminal
Restaurant Main Terminal
Bar Main Terminal

Luggage
Left luggage Main Terminal ⌀GBP1

Shopping
Gift Shops Main Terminal

DISABLED TRAVELLERS

Main Terminal Parking spaces

SMOKING POLICY

Main Terminal Smoking areas provided

SPECIAL PASSENGER LOUNGES

BA Executive Lounge Main Terminal
Servisair Executive Lounge Main Terminal

AIRPORT HOTELS

Airport Thistle ✆725252
Dyce Skean Dhu ✆723101
Speedbird ✆772884
Marriott ✆770011
Holiday Inn Crowne Plaza ✆409988

CAR RENTAL

Hertz ✆722373
Europcar ✆770770
Budget ✆771777
Avis ✆722282

TAXIS AND CHAUFFEUR-DRIVEN CARS

Taxis
City centre ✆725728 ⌀GBP10

PUBLIC TRANSPORT

City & suburbs
Aberdeen centre 🚌/🚆 Dyce-Link/Scotrail ⇒28 min.

Other towns and cities
Dundee 🚆 Scotrail ≫avg 1 hr ⇒1 hr 15 min
Elgin 🚆 Scotrail ≫5-8 per day ⇒1 hr 30 min
Inverness 🚆 Scotrail ≫5-8 per day ⇒2 hr 15 min

REGIONAL AIR CONNECTIONS

Dundee ✈ ≫daily ⇒30 min
Kirkwall ✈ ≫3 per day ⇒45 min
Shetland Isles ✈ ≫4 per day ⇒1 hr
Wick ✈ ≫2 per day ⇒45 min.

ABU DHABI — AUH

United Arab Emirates (see page 40)

National ✆ code: 971
Area ✆ code: 2
Local time: Winter GMT+4, Summer GMT+4
Abu Dhabi International Airport, PO Box 20, Abu Dhabi, United Arab Emirates
✆757500
🖷757205
Location: 38 km/23 miles E of Abu Dhabi

Terminals and Transfers

Terminals
International Terminal Airlines: All airlines. Layout: Crescent construction, 3 Levels. Ground Level: baggage systems, offices linked to 1200 space car park by pedestrian tunnels, First Floor Arrival/Departure, VIP & First Class Lounges, shops, Second Floor Administrative offices, Waiting areas, Snack bars, Cafeteria, Bank, Post Office, 5 Star Transit Hotel (Airside), Airside Circular Satellite linked by Corridor and Walkways, 2 Levels: Ground Level, shopping facilities, Cafeteria, Toilets, First Floor Level: Arrival, Departure and Central Transit Areas linked by Airbridges and Bus to Remote Stands.

Minimum transfer times
International: 1 hr
Domestic: 1 hr

Information

Flight enquiries
Airport ✆757611 🖷757205

Information and help desks
Airport & Tourist Information Desk International Terminal Ground Level ✆757611 ⏱24 hr *Airport information, Flights Hotel booking, Tourist information*

Emergencies

Police International Terminal throughout ⏱24 hr
Medical International Terminal First aid services via Information Desks ⏱24 hr
Lost Property International Terminal Handled by police ⏱24 hr

Airport Facilities

Money
ATM International Terminal ⏱24 hr
Bank International Terminal Central Transit Area ⏱24 hr

Food and drink
Restaurant International Terminal Central Transit Area ⏱24 hr
Restaurant International Terminal Satellite Building ⏱24 hr

Communications
Post office International Terminal Second Floor Main Building (Transit area)

Shopping
Duty free, arrival International Terminal Arrival Hall ⏱24 hr
Duty free, departure International Terminal Satellite Ground Level ⏱24 hr
Shopping mall International Terminal Satellite Ground Level ⏱24 hr

Luggage
Porters International Terminal Arrival/Departure areas ⏱24 hr
Trolleys/carts International Terminal Arrival/Departure areas ⏱24 hr

Disabled Travellers

International Terminal Adapted toilets; Lifts

Smoking Policy

International Terminal Smoking areas provided throughout

Special Passenger Lounges

All airlines Abu Dhabi Airport Services Lounge International Terminal Central Transit Area *First class passengers*
Gulf Air Lounge International Terminal Central Transit Area *First class passengers*

Conference and Business Facilities

Conference centre *Telephones*

Airport Hotels

Gulf Hotel ✆414777 🖷414537

Car Rental

Avis International Terminal Arrival Hall ✆757180 🖷757164
Budget International Terminal Arrival Hall ✆757188 🖷757178
EuropCar International Terminal Outside Arrival Hall

Car Parking

Long-stay Ground Level linked by pedestrian tunnels 1200 spaces ⊘Free (48 hr max)
Short-stay Outside Arrival Hall 1300 spaces ⊘Free (48 hr max)

Taxis and Chauffeur-driven Cars

Taxis
Outside Arrival Hall City centre ⟳30 min ⊘AED70

Chauffeur-driven cars
Outside Arrival Hall

Public Transport

City & suburbs
Abu Dhabi City centre 🚌 »30 min ⏱24 hr ⟳30 min ⊘AED3.

Regional Air Connections

Bahrain ✈ »Several per day ⟳60 min
Doha ✈ »Several per day ⟳50 min
Dubai ✈ »Several per week ⟳35 min
Muscat ✈ »Several per day ⟳55 min

Traveller's Notes

High-quality gold is the best-value and most popular duty free item. Wear natural fabrics and take a lightweight jacket for winter evenings. Always ask permission before photographing local people, especially women.

✆ Phone no.   🖷 Fax no.   ⏱ Hours of opening/operation   » Frequency of service   ⟳ Journey time   ⊘ Cost/one-way fare

SECTION TWO • AIRPORT DIRECTORY   ADELAIDE

ADELAIDE   ADL
Australia (see page 14)

National ✆ code: 61
Area ✆ code: 8
Local time: Winter GMT+9½,
Summer GMT+10½
Adelaide International Airport, No. 1 James Schofield Drive, South Australia 5950
✆: 308 9211
✉: 308 9311
Location: 6 km/4 miles W of Adelaide

TERMINALS AND TRANSFERS

Terminals
International Terminal Qantas, Singapore Airlines, Malaysia Airlines, Cathay Pacific Airways, Garuda Indonesia, Virgin Atlantic. Layout: One level.
Domestic Terminal Qantas, Ansett Australia, National Jet Systems. Layout: Two levels. Arrival and departures at ground level.

Minimum transfer times
Vehicle: 3 min. **Foot:** 10 min.
Transfer between terminals
Transit mini-buses ⇒ 30 minutes.

INFORMATION

Flight enquiries International Terminal Qantas ✆237 8541
Flight enquiries Domestic Terminal Qantas ✆407 2424, Ansett 131 515

Information and help desks
Tourist Information Desk International and Domestic Terminal Arrivals Tourist information.

EMERGENCIES

Medical Contact airport staff for first aid assistance at both terminals.

AIRPORT FACILITIES

Money
Thomas Cook Bureau de Change International Terminal, at entrance to Arrivals Hall ✆234 3320.
Bureau de Change Travelex, Domestic Terminal ✆234 4264.
ATM Domestic Terminal

Food and drink
Bar Ground floor, International Terminal. Departure lounge, Domestic Terminal.
Café/light meals Pump Deck Deli, departure lounge, Domestic Terminal. Ground floor, International Terminal.
Restaurant International Terminal, ground floor. Domestic Terminal, departure lounge.

Communications
Post Box At entrance to International Terminal. In Morgans Corner, Domestic Terminal.

Shopping
Duty free Departure lounge and arrivals hall of International Terminal ✆ 234 3294.
News, Stationery & Books Ground floor, International Terminal. Morgans Corner, Domestic Terminal. Newslink, departure lounge, Domestic Terminal.
Gift Shop Departure lounge, Domestic Terminal. Departure lounge, ground floor, International Terminal.

Luggage
Trolleys/carts Available in both terminals.

DISABLED TRAVELLERS

All Terminals Disabled parking bays in public car park adjacent to terminal entrances. Specially designed toilets and telephone facilities.

SPECIAL PASSENGER LOUNGES

Singapore Airlines Silver Kris Lounge Ground floor, International Terminal.
Qantas Captains Club Ground floor, International Terminal.
Qantas Club Departures lounge, Domestic Terminal.
Ansett Golden Wing Departures lounge, Domestic Terminal.

CAR RENTAL

Avis Departure lounge, ground floor, International Terminal. By entrance to Domestic Terminal.
Budget Departure lounge, ground floor, International Terminal. By entrance to Domestic Terminal.
Hertz Departure lounge, ground floor, International Terminal. By entrance to Domestic Terminal.
Thrifty Departure lounge, ground floor, International Terminal. By entrance to Domestic Terminal.

CAR PARKING

Long-stay Domestic Terminal AUD2 per first and second hr, AUD1 per hr thereafter. AUD12 per day
Off-airport International Terminal AUD2 per hr. AUD12 per day.

TAXIS AND CHAUFFEUR-DRIVEN CARS

Taxis
Outside both terminals City centre ⌀ AUD10.

PUBLIC TRANSPORT

Adelaide city centre
🚌 Public Transit ⌀ AUD6 (AUD2 children) ⇒ 30 min.

REGIONAL AIR CONNECTIONS

Alice Springs ✈ ⇒Several per day ⊃60 min
Broken Hill ✈ ⇒3 per day ⊃60 min
Port Augusta ✈ ⇒3 per day ⊃60 min
Port Lincoln ✈ ⇒Several per day ⊃50 min

✈ Air 🚆 Rail 🚌 Bus 🚘 Limousine Ⓜ Metro/subway 🚋 Tram 🚁 Helicopter ⛴ Water transport • For map symbols, see p. 9

ALICANTE (ALACANT)   ALC

Spain (see page 36)

National ✆ code: 34
Area ✆ code: 6
Local time: Winter GMT+1, Summer GMT+2
Aeropuerto de Alicante, 03071 Alicante, Spain.
✆: 568 27 71
🖷: 528 44 43

TERMINALS AND TRANSFERS

Terminals
Main Terminal Airlines: All airlines.
Layout: Three levels. Lower level, arrival lounge; level 1, check-in area and baggage claim; level 2, departure lounge.

INFORMATION

Flight enquiries
Iberia ✆ 69 19 196 SAS ✆ 568 25 30
Air Europa ✆ 568 23 64
KLM ✆ 568 24 10
Lufthansa ✆ 69 19 386
Monarch ✆ 69 19 314
Air Algerie ✆ 568 28 74

Information and help desks
Airport Information Desk Level 1, by check-in desks
Airport Information Desk Level 2, departure lounge
Tourist Information Desk Lower level, arrival lounge

EMERGENCIES

Police Lower level ✆ 514 95 00
Medical Level 1, check-in area.
Emergency services ✆ 524 76 00.
Red Cross ✆ 525 25 25
Lost Property Lower level and level 1, baggage claim

AIRPORT FACILITIES

Money
Bureau de Change Level 1, baggage claim ✆ 691 90 80
Bureau de Change Level 2, departure lounge ✆ 691 90 80
ATM Level 1, check-in area

Food and drink
Bar Level 2, public area
Bar Level 2, departure lounge
Café/light meals Level 1, check-in area
Café/light meals Level 2, departure lounge
Restaurant Level 2, public area
Restaurant Level 2, departure lounge

Shopping
Duty free Level 2, departure lounge ✆ 691 92 69
News, Stationery & Books Level 2, public area
Gift Shop Level 2, departure lounge
Pharmacy Lower level, arrival lounge

SPECIAL PASSENGER LOUNGES

VIP Lounge Level 2, departure lounge

CAR RENTAL

Avis Lower level, arrivals ✆ 568 65 79
Hertz Lower level, arrivals ✆ 691 91 25
Europcar Lower level, arrivals ✆ 691 91 27
Atesa Lower level, arrivals ✆ 568 25 26
Centauro Lower level, arrivals ✆ 691 92 41/2
Sol-Mar Lower level, arrivals ✆ 691 92 80

CAR PARKING

Long-stay 1200 spaces

TAXIS AND CHAUFFEUR-DRIVEN CARS

Taxis
At airport entrance Available 24 hr

PUBLIC TRANSPORT

City & suburbs
Alicante city centre 🚌 ≫ 60 min

Other towns and cities
Benidorm 🚆 Ferrocarrilis de la Generalitat Valenciana ≫1 hr ⟳1 hr 8 min

---

✆ Phone no. 🖷 Fax no. ⏲ Hours of opening/operation ≫ Frequency of service ⟳ Journey time ⊘ Cost/one-way fare

AMSTERDAM AMS

Netherlands (see page 30)

National ✆ code: 31
Area ✆ code: 020
Local time: Winter GMT+1, Summer GMT+2
Amsterdam Schiphol Airport, PO Box 7501, 1118 ZG, Netherlands
✆6019111
✆6041475
Internet e-mail: schiphol@xxlink.nl
WWW site: http://www.schiphol.nl/home.htm
Location: 14 km/9 miles SW of Amsterdam

TERMINALS AND TRANSFERS

Terminals
Main Terminal Airlines: All airlines. Layout: Departure (Upper) Level; Arrival (Lower) Level. Changes have recently been carried out to Main Central Area and there is a new conference and business facilities area

Minimum transfer times
International (outside Europe): 50 min
European and Domestic 40 min

INFORMATION

Flight enquiries
Airport ✆6010966

Information and help desks
Airport & Tourist Information Desks Main Terminal Arrival and Departure Levels (10 desks) ✆6012323 ⏲0600 until last flight *Airport information, Flights Hotel booking, Tourist information*
KLM Hotel Reservation Desk Main Terminal Arrival Hall after Baggage Reclaim ⏲0700–2300 *Hotel booking*

EMERGENCIES

Police Main Terminal Outside airport at Arrival Level ✆6038111 ⏲24 hr
Medical Main Terminal Medical/First aid Departure Level Lounge West ✆6012528/2527 ⏲24 hr
Lost Property Main Terminal Departure Level near passport control ✆6012325 ⏲0830–1630 Mon–Fri

AIRPORT FACILITIES

Money
ATM Main Terminal Arrival Level Lounge West/Departure Level Lounge South ⏲24 hr
Bank Main Terminal Schiphol Plaza Central Departure and Transit Hall ⏲0615–2400
Bureau de change Main Terminal Schiphol Plaza Central Departure and Transit Hall ⏲0600–2400

Food and drink
Bar Main Terminal Departure Level Lounge West ⏲24 hr
Café/light meals Main Terminal Departure Level Schiphol Plaza ⏲0730–2000
Café/light meals Main Terminal Departure Level Lounge South ⏲24 hr
Restaurant Main Terminal Departure Level Lounge South ⏲0630–2100
Restaurant Main Terminal Departure Level Schiphol Plaza Lounge ⏲0700–1900

Communications
Fax service Main Terminal Credit card operated, Lounges West/Central/South ⏲All flight times
Post office Main Terminal Lounge South/Central/West ⏲0600–until last flight

Shopping
Duty free, departure Main Terminal Schiphol Plaza ⏲All flight times
Shopping mall Main Terminal Schiphol Plaza ⏲All flight times

Luggage
Left Luggage Counter Main Terminal Basement Level below Schiphol Plaza ⏲0600–2245 ⌀NLG5 per item per day
Lockers Main Terminal Departure Level Lounge South; Arrival Level Lounge West ⏲24 hr ⌀NLG6 per day
Porters Main Terminal Baggage Service Desk in Baggage Reclaim Area ⌀NLG2 per item
Trolleys/carts Main Terminal throughout ⏲24 hr ⌀Free

DISABLED TRAVELLERS

Main Terminal Adapted toilets; Lifts Phones adapted for the deaf; Personal assistance ✆3161417

SMOKING POLICY

Main Terminal No-smoking areas available throughout Terminal

SPECIAL PASSENGER LOUNGES

All airlines Aero Ground Services Lounge Main Terminal Mezzanine Floor above Departure and Transit Level *First and*

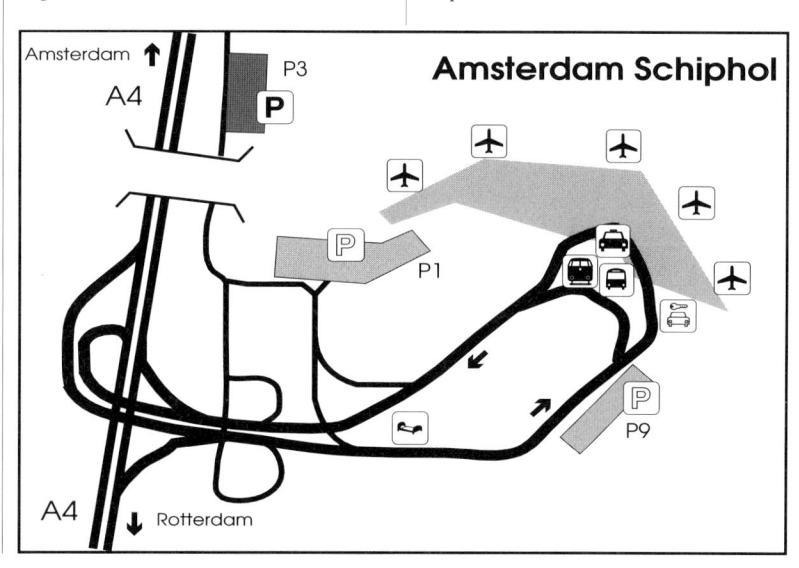

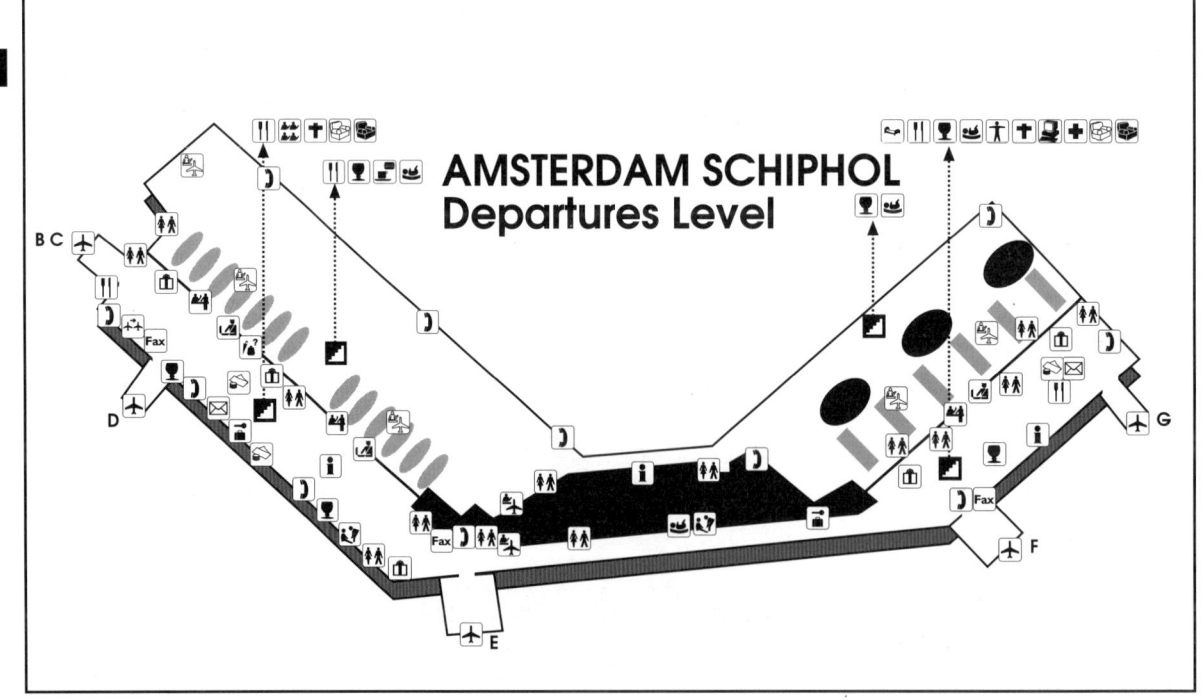

AMSTERDAM

SECTION TWO • AIRPORT DIRECTORY

AMSTERDAM SCHIPHOL
Arrivals Level

AMSTERDAM SCHIPHOL
Departures Level

Business class passengers
British Airways Executive Club Lounge Main Terminal Mezzanine Floor above Departure and Transit Level *Club members and First and Business class passengers*
KLM Van Gogh Lounge Main Terminal Mezzanine Floor above Departure and Transit Level *Club members and First and Business class passengers*

CONFERENCE AND BUSINESS FACILITIES

Business Centre Skyport, Departure Level

Lounge West ☏653 2480 ℻653 2566 ⏱0830–1730 Mon–Fri *Telephones, Fax service, Power points, Modem Points, Photocopier, Secretarial service, Translation/Interpretation service, Travel advice*

☏ Phone no. ℻ Fax no. ⏱ Hours of opening/operation ≫ Frequency of service ➲ Journey time ◇ Cost/one-way fare

SECTION TWO • AIRPORT DIRECTORY

AMSTERDAM

Airport Hotels

Hilton Schiphol ℂ603 4567 Ⓕ15186
Courtesy bus
Holiday Inn Crowne Plaza
Mercure Schiphol ℂ604 1339 Ⓕ655 0438

Car Rental

Avis Main Terminal Arrival Level ℂ601 5848
Budget Main Terminal Arrival Level ℂ604 1349
EuropCar Main Terminal Arrival Level ℂ604 1566
Hertz Main Terminal Arrival Level ℂ601 5416

Car Parking

Long-stay P3 open-air car park 2055 spaces ⬙NLG85 for 3 days; then NLG7.50 per day
Short-stay P1/P2 connected by covered way 9600 spaces ⬙Up to 3 hr, NLG3 per 30 min; then NLG3 per hr

Taxis and Chauffeur-driven Cars

Taxis
Outside Arrival Level City centre ⮕30 min ⬙NLG50

Public Transport

City & suburbs
Amsterdam city centre 🚌GBV ≫30 min ⓞ0615–2345 ⮕40 min ⬙NLG8.50.
Amsterdam city centre 🚆NS ≫Avg 15 min by day, 1 hr at night ⓞ24 hr ⮕17 min ⬙NLG4.50.

Other towns and cities
Amersfoort 🚆NS ≫avg 15 min to 1800/20 min to 0003 ⓞ0557–0003 ⮕39 min.
Antwerp 🚆NS ⮕1 hr 55 min.
Den Haag (The Hague) 🚆NS ≫Avg 15 min in day/avg 1 hr at night ⓞ24 hr 38 min.
Eindhoven 🚆NS ≫Avg 30 min ⓞ0653–2253 ⮕1 hr 24 min.
Hengelo 🚆NS ≫5 per day ⓞ0654–2222 ⮕3 hr. *Trains continue to Osnabrück, Hanover, Braunschweig and Berlin.*
Maastricht 🚆NS ≫Avg 30 min ⓞ0723–2153 ⮕2 hr 21 min.
Roosendaal 🚆NS ≫Avg 30 min ⓞ0646–2246 ⮕1 hr 23 min.
Rotterdam 🚆NS ≫Avg 30 min by day/1 hr at night ⓞ24 hr ⮕47 min.
Utrecht 🚆NS ≫Avg 30 min ⓞ0653–0009 ⮕22 min. *Faster and more frequent service via Duivendrecht with one change of train*

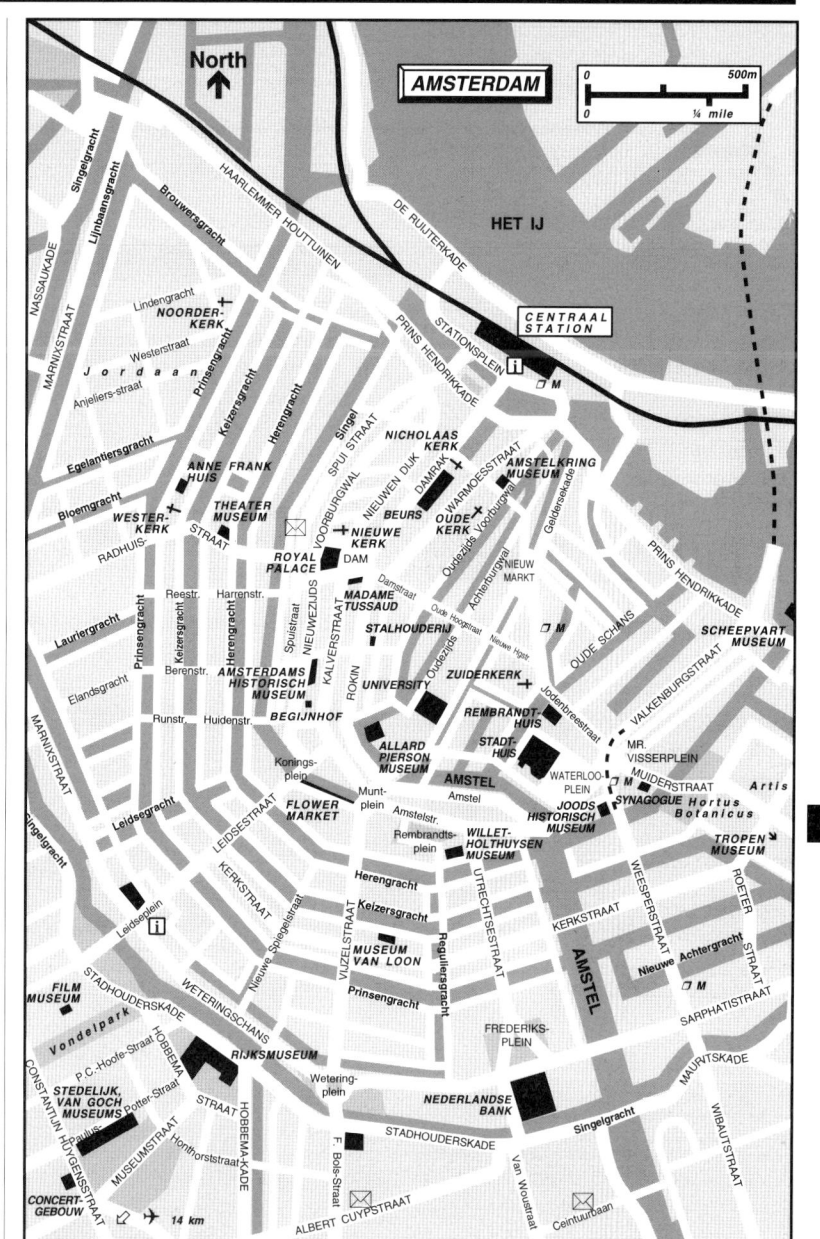

Zwolle 🚆NS ≫1 hr ⓞ0601–2327 ⮕1 hr 19 min.

Regional Air Connections

Antwerp ✈ ≫Several per day ⮕40 min
Bremen ✈ ≫Several per day ⮕1 hr
Brussels ✈ ≫Several per day ⮕50 min
Cambridge ✈ ≫At least daily ⮕1 hr
Cologne/Bonn ✈ ≫Several per day ⮕1 hr
Dortmund ✈ ≫Several per day ⮕50 min
Düsseldorf ✈ ≫Several per day ⮕50 min
Eindhoven ✈ ≫Several per day ⮕40 min
Enschede ✈ ≫At least daily ⮕30 min
Groningen ✈ ≫At least daily ⮕30 min
London ✈ ≫Several per week ⮕50–70 min
Luxembourg ✈ ≫Several per day ⮕1 hr 10 min
Maastricht ✈ ≫Several per day ⮕40 min
Norwich ✈ ≫Several per day ⮕1 hr
Paris ✈ ≫Several per day ⮕1 hr 5 min

Traveller's Notes

Schiphol rail station is linked to all stations in the Netherlands either directly or by short connecting journey to Amsterdam Centraal Station, and to many cities in neighbouring countries.

✈ Air 🚆 Rail 🚌 Bus 🚘 Limousine Ⓜ Metro/subway 🚊 Tram 🚁 Helicopter ⛴ Water transport • For map symbols, see p. 9

ANKARA ESB

Turkey (see page 39)

National ☎ code: 90
Area ☎ code: 0312
Local time: Winter GMT+2, Summer GMT+3
Esenboga Airport, Ankara 06970, Turkey
☎3980329/3980330
⊕3980345
Location: 35 km/22 miles N of Ankara

TERMINALS AND TRANSFERS

Terminals
Main Terminal Airlines: All airlines.

Minimum transfer times
International: 1 hr 30 min Domestic: 30 min

INFORMATION

Flight enquiries
Airport ☎3980328

EMERGENCIES

Medical Main Terminal Main Terminal ⓘ24 hr

AIRPORT FACILITIES

Money
Bank Main Terminal Departure and Arrival Area ⓘ24 hr
Bureau de change Main Terminal Departure and Arrival Area ⓘ24 hr

Food and drink
Café/light meals Main Terminal ⓘ24 hr
Restaurant Main Terminal ⓘ24 hr

Communications
Post office Main Terminal ⓘ24 hr

Shopping
Duty free, departure Main Terminal ⓘ24 hr
News, Stationery & Books Main Terminal Departure Area

Luggage
Left Luggage Counter Main Terminal ⓘ24 hr

SMOKING POLICY

Main Terminal No restrictions

SPECIAL PASSENGER LOUNGES

VIP Lounge Main Terminal

CAR RENTAL

Avis Main Terminal ☎3980315 ext. 1670
Hertz Main Terminal ☎3122820

TAXIS AND CHAUFFEUR-DRIVEN CARS

Taxis
Front of Terminal ⊘TRL50000

PUBLIC TRANSPORT

City & suburbs
Ankara city centre 🚌 ⤴30 min ⊘TRL7000.

REGIONAL AIR CONNECTIONS

Antalya ✈ »At least daily ⤴1 hr 5 min
Erzerum ✈ »Several per day ⤴1 hr 10 min
Gaziantep ✈ »At least daily ⤴1 hr 10 min
Istanbul ✈ »Several per day ⤴1 hr 5 min
Malatya ✈ »At least daily ⤴1 hr 10 min
Antalya ✈ »At least daily ⤴1 hr 5 min

☎ Phone no. ⊕ Fax no. ⓘ Hours of opening/operation » Frequency of service ⤴ Journey time ⊘ Cost/one-way fare

SECTION TWO • AIRPORT DIRECTORY   ATHENS

ATHENS (ATHINAI)   ATH
Greece (see page 23)

National ✆ code: 30
Area ✆ code: 01
Local time: Winter GMT+2, Summer GMT+3
Athens (Athinai) Airport, 16603 Hellinikon Athinai, Greece
✆ 969 91111
Location: 10 km/6 miles S of Athens

TERMINALS AND TRANSFERS

Terminals
East Terminal Airlines: All other airlines. Layout: Two Floors, one for Arrival, one for Departure
West Terminal Airlines: Olympic Airways (Except flight 8751). Layout: One Floor

Minimum transfer times
International: 1 hr–1 hr 30 min Domestic: 45 min

Transfer between terminals
Bus ≫35 min; East and West Terminals ⌀GRD160 (taxi 1000)

INFORMATION

Flight enquiries
Airport ✆969 9466; 969 9467
Aeroflot ✆322 0986 Air Algérie ✆323 5504 Air Canada ✆322 3206 Air France ✆323 0501 Air Malta ✆325 5533 Air Portugal TAP ✆324 9096 Air Seychelles ✆323 0434 Air Zimbabwe ✆323 9010 Alitalia ✆324 4383 Austrian Airlines ✆323 0844 Awood Air ✆324 4716 Balkan Bulgarian Airlines ✆322 6684 Biman Bangladesh Airlines ✆324 1116 British Airways ✆322 2521 CSA Czechoslovak ✆323 23 03 Cyprus Airlines ✆324 7801 Egyptair ✆323 3575 El Al Israel Airlines ✆323 0116 Ethiopian Airlines ✆323 4275 Finnair ✆325 5234 Gulf Air ✆322 6684 Iberia ✆323 4523 Iran Air ✆360 7611 Japan Airlines ✆323 0331 Kenya Airways ✆324 7000 KLM ✆322 6011 Kuwait Airways ✆323 4506 Lot Polish Airlines ✆322 11221 Lufthansa ✆369 2111 Luxair ✆923 9002 Malev Hungarian ✆324 1116 Middle East Airlines ✆322 6911 Olympic Airways ✆989 2111 Pakistan International Airlines ✆323 1931 Qantas Airways ✆360 7271 Royal Air Maroc ✆324 4302 Royal Jordanian Airlines ✆324 1377 Sabena World Airlines ✆323 6821 Saudia ✆324 4671 SAS ✆363 4444 Singapore Airlines ✆323 9111 South African Airways ✆322 9007 Swissair ✆323 1871 Syrian Arab Airlines ✆323 8711 Tarom Romanian Air ✆362 4808 Thai Airways ✆324 3241 Tunis Air ✆322 0104 Turkish Airlines ✆324 6024 TWA ✆323 6831

Information and help desks
Airport Information Desk East Terminal Arrival and Departure Hall ✆969 9530; 969 9466 ⏱24 hr *Airport information*
Airport Information Desk West Terminal Arrival and Departure Hall ✆969 9530; 969 9466 ⏱ *Airport information*
Tourist Information Desk West Terminal Arrival Hall ✆969 9523; 969 9500 ⏱24 hr *Tourist information*
Tourist Information Desk East Terminal Arrival Hall ✆969 9523; 969 9500 ⏱24 hr *Tourist information*

EMERGENCIES

Medical East Terminal ✆969 9533 ⏱24 hr
Medical West Terminal ✆969 9533 ⏱24 hr

AIRPORT FACILITIES

Money
Bank East Terminal 4, ⏱24 hr
Bank West Terminal 2, ⏱0700-2300; 0815–2030

Food and drink
Restaurant East Terminal Arrival Hall ⏱24 hr
Bar East Terminal Departure Hall, Arrival Hall, Transit Area, Charter Building ⏱24 hr
Bar West Terminal Int. and Domestic Departure Halls and Transit Area ⏱24 hr
Restaurant West Terminal Arrival Hall ⏱0700–2300

Communications
Post office East Terminal Departure Hall ⏱0730–2030
Post office West Terminal Departure Hall ⏱0730–2030

Shopping
Shopping mall East Terminal Arrival and Departure Areas ⏱24 hr
Duty free, departure East Terminal Transit Area ⏱24 hr
Shopping mall West Terminal Arrival and Departure ⏱24 hr
Duty free, departure West Terminal Transit Area ⏱0600–2300

Luggage
Trolleys/carts East Terminal ⌀GRD200
Trolleys/carts West Terminal ⌀GRD200

DISABLED TRAVELLERS

East Terminal Adapted toilets; Lifts; Special car parking; Phones at wheelchair height
West Terminal Adapted toilets; Lifts; Special car parking; Phones at wheelchair height

SMOKING POLICY

East Terminal Smoking permitted throughout
West Terminal Smoking permitted throughout

SPECIAL PASSENGER LOUNGES

VIP Lounge East Terminal Arrival Area

CAR RENTAL

Autorent East Terminal Arrival Hall ✆723 9396
Avis East Terminal Arrival Hall ✆322 4951
Budget East Terminal Arrival Hall ✆961 3634
Eurodollar East Terminal Arrival Hall ✆963 1672
EuropCar East Terminal Arrival Hall ✆961 3424
Hertz East Terminal Arrival Hall ✆961 3625

CAR PARKING

Short-stay East Terminal/West Terminal ⌀1 hr GDR 600; 2–8hr GDR 700; 9–24 hr GDR 1200

✈ Air 🚆 Rail 🚌 Bus 🚐 Limousine Ⓜ Metro/subway 🚋 Tram 🚁 Helicopter ⛴ Water transport • For map symbols, see p. 9

ATHENS

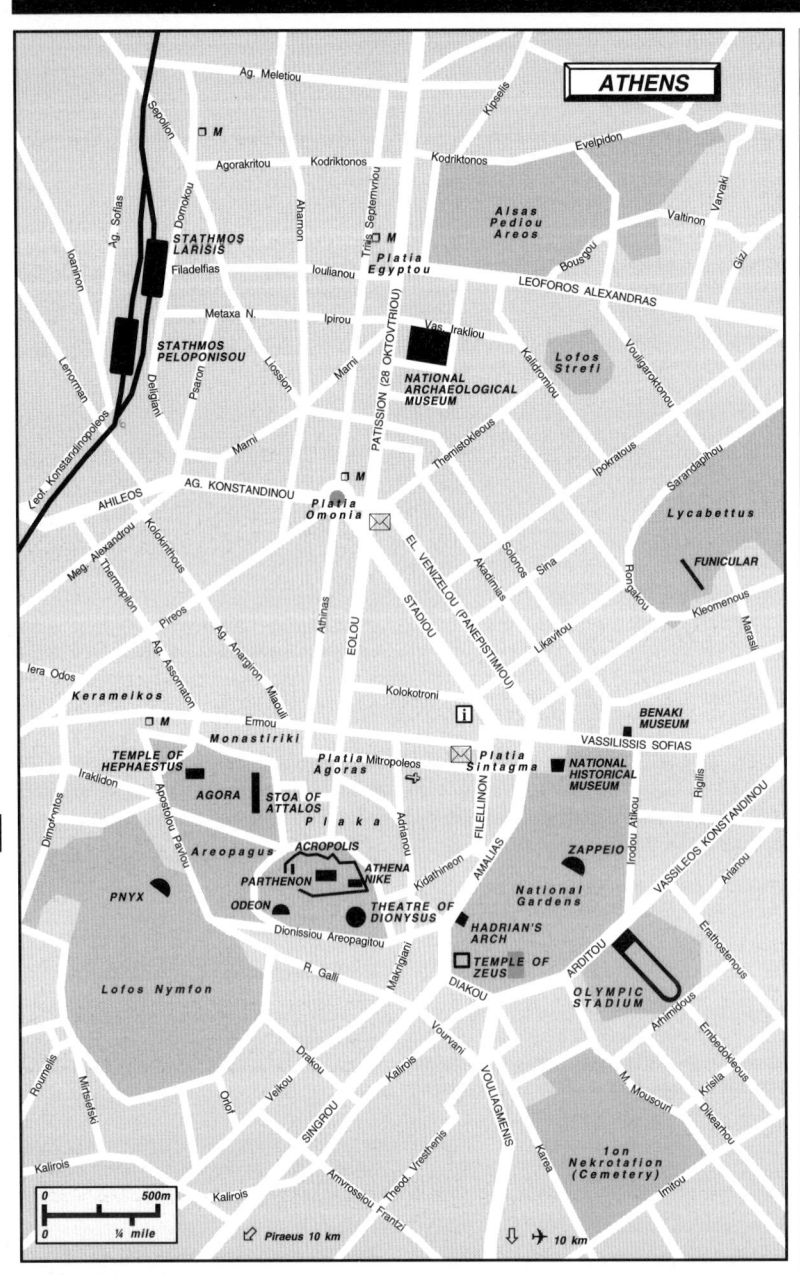

SECTION TWO • AIRPORT DIRECTORY

⊘GDR 160. Stops at both terminals. From Omonia Square metro to Piraeus. 20–30 min 0600–0200; 60 min 0200–0600
Athens city centre (Avenue Syngrou) 96
🚌Olympic Airways ⊃20 min
Athens city centre (Syntagma Square) Amalias Avenue 🚌Blue Bus »20–30 min
Piraeus 🚌Transport Enterprises (Yellow Bus no. 19) »Approx 60 min
⊕0600–0120 »30–40 min ⊘GDR 160. Stops: Akti Tzelepi, Karaiskaki Square

Regional Air Connections

Chania ✈ »Several times per day ⊃45 min
Chios ✈ »Several times per day ⊃50 min
Heraklion ✈ »Several times per day ⊃45–50 min
Ikaria ✈ »Several per week ⊃50 min
Izmir ✈ »Several per week ⊃55 min
Kalamata ✈ »At least daily ⊃50 min
Kavala ✈ »At least daily ⊃60–70 min
Kefallinia ✈ »Several per week ⊃1 hr
Kerkyra ✈ »Several per day ⊃50 min
Kithira ✈ »At least daily ⊃50 min
Kos ✈ »At least daily ⊃50 min
Lemnos ✈ »At least daily ⊃1 hr
Milos ✈ »Several per day ⊃45 min
Mykonos ✈ »Several per day ⊃45 min
Mytilene ✈ »Several per day ⊃45 min
Naxos ✈ »At least daily ⊃45 min
Paros ✈ »Several per day ⊃45 min
Preveza/Lefkas ✈ »At least daily ⊃1 hr
Rhodes ✈ »Several times per day ⊃55 min
Samos ✈ »Several times per day ⊃1 hr
Skiathos ✈ »Several times per day ⊃40 min
Skiros ✈ »At least daily ⊃45 min
Syros Island ✈ »Several times per day ⊃35 min
Thessaloniki ✈ »Several times per day ⊃50 min
Thira ✈ »Several times per day ⊃50 min
Zakinthos ✈ »Several times per day ⊃55 min

Traveller's Notes

Chauffeur-driven cars or taxis are more practical options than car rental. Taxis in the city may be difficult to find, so ask hotels to book them. When taking a taxi from the airport, ensure that the meter is on and number '1' illuminated; '2' should only be shown midnight–0600.

Taxis and Chauffeur-driven Cars

Taxis
Outside Arrival ⊃Approx 25 min
⊘GRD1500

Public Transport

City & suburbs
Athens city centre (Omonia Square)
🚌Transport Enterprises Express Buses A & B »20–30 min ⊕24 hr ⊃30 min

---

☏ Phone no. Ⓕ Fax no. ⊕ Hours of opening/operation » Frequency of service ⊃ Journey time ⊘ Cost/one-way fare

✈✈ SECTION TWO • AIRPORT DIRECTORY   ATLANTA

ATLANTA   ATL
USA (see page 41)

National & code: 1
Area & code: 404
Local time: Winter GMT-5,
Summer GMT-4
Hartsfield Atlanta International
Airport, 6000 N Terminal Parkway
Atlanta, GA 30320, USA
✆530 6600
530 6803
Location: 14 km/9 miles S of
Atlanta

TERMINALS AND TRANSFERS

Terminals
Main Terminal Airlines: All airlines.
Layout: Upper Level (Departure,
Concourses A (Gates A1–A34) B (Gates
B1–B36), C (Gates C1–C36), D (Gates
D1–D37), E (International) Gates
E1–E33) and T (Gates T1–T14); Lower
Level (Transportation Mall)

Minimum transfer times
International: 1 hr 30 min Domestic: 55
min

Transfer between terminals
People mover ≫2; All concourses ⌀Free

INFORMATION

Flight enquiries
Information and help desks
Information Center Main Terminal
Concourses A, B and T Airport, tourist
information
Atlanta Visitor Information Main
Terminal Atrium Tourist information
International Services Center Concourse E
Arrivals Area ✆530 2081; 530 2082
Airport, tourist information, translation
services
Traveller's Aid Main Terminal Atrium
Tourist information

Emergencies
Lost Property Main Terminal Lower
Level ✆530 2100

AIRPORT FACILITIES

Money
Bank Main Terminal Atrium
Thomas Cook Bureau de change Main
Terminal Concourse E near Gate E–26
⏲0700–2000
Thomas Cook Bureau de change Main
Terminal Concourse E (Mobile)
⏲1330–2000
Thomas Cook bureau de change Main
Terminal T ⏲0700–2000
ATM Main Terminal throughout

Food and drink
Bar Main Terminal throughout
Café/light meals Main Terminal throughout
Restaurant Main Terminal Atrium

Communications
Post office Main Terminal Atrium
Post box Main Terminal throughout
Fax Main Terminal Business Centers

Shopping
Duty free, Main Terminal Concourse E
Gift Shop Main Terminal throughout
News, Stationery & Books Main
Terminal throughout
Florist Main Terminal Concourse A and
C
Shopping mall Main Terminal Atrium

Luggage
Left Luggage Counter Main Terminal
Atrium ⏲0700–2300 ⌀USD5 per day
Lockers Main Terminal Concourses B, C
and T beyond security ⌀USD1 per day
Trolleys/carts Main Terminal ⏲24 hr
⌀USD1.50
Trolleys/carts Concourse E ⏲24 hr ⌀Free

DISABLED TRAVELLERS

Main Terminal Adapted toilets *throughout*. Lifts *throughout*. Phones at wheelchair height. Phones adapted for the deaf *throughout*. Personal assistance *Contact airlines*

SMOKING POLICY

Permitted in smoking lounges located in
Concourses B, C, E and T

SPECIAL PASSENGER LOUNGES

American Airlines Admirals Club Lounge
Main Terminal Concourse T Delta
Airlines Crown Room Main Terminal
Concourses A and B

CONFERENCE AND BUSINESS FACILITIES

Business Center, Main Terminal Atrium
✆761 0106 ⏲0600–2100
Business Center, self service, Main
Terminal Concourse C and E
Skytel Business Center, Main Terminal
Concourses A, B and T

CAR RENTAL

National Main Terminal Atrium ✆530
2800
Payless Main Terminal Atrium
Thrifty Main Terminal Atrium
Avis Main Terminal Atrium ✆530 2700
Budget Main Terminal Atrium ✆530
3000
Dollar Main Terminal Atrium ✆530 3100
Enterprise Main Terminal Atrium
Hertz Main Terminal Atrium ✆530 2900

CAR PARKING

Long-stay Next to Main Terminal spaces
⌀USD5 per day
Short-stay Next to Main Terminal spaces
⌀USD per 1 hr

TAXIS AND CHAUFFEUR-DRIVEN CARS

Taxis
Atlanta city centre ⌀USD18

PUBLIC TRANSPORT

City & suburbs
Atlanta (downtown hotels) 🚌 Atlanta
Airport Shuttle ≫20 min ⏲0700–2300
➲15 min ⌀USD8.
Atlanta city centre 🚌 Over 20 companies
at airport.
Atlanta city centre 🚊 MARTA ≫4–8 min
⏲0434–0016 ➲15 min ⌀USD1. 50.

Other towns and cities
Anniston AL 🚌 Alabama Limousine (205)
820 5990.
Auburn AL 🚌 Dixie Excursions (334)
887 6295. For Opelika and Tuskegee AL
Macon GA 🚌 Groome Transportation
(800) 537 7903. For Warner Robins GA
Rome GA 🚌 Shuttletran (800) 556 5466.
For Catersville and Dalton GA

67

✈ Air 🚆 Rail 🚌 Bus 🚐 Limousine 🚊 Metro/subway 🚋 Tram 🚁 Helicopter ⛴ Water transport • For map symbols, see p. 9

ATLANTA

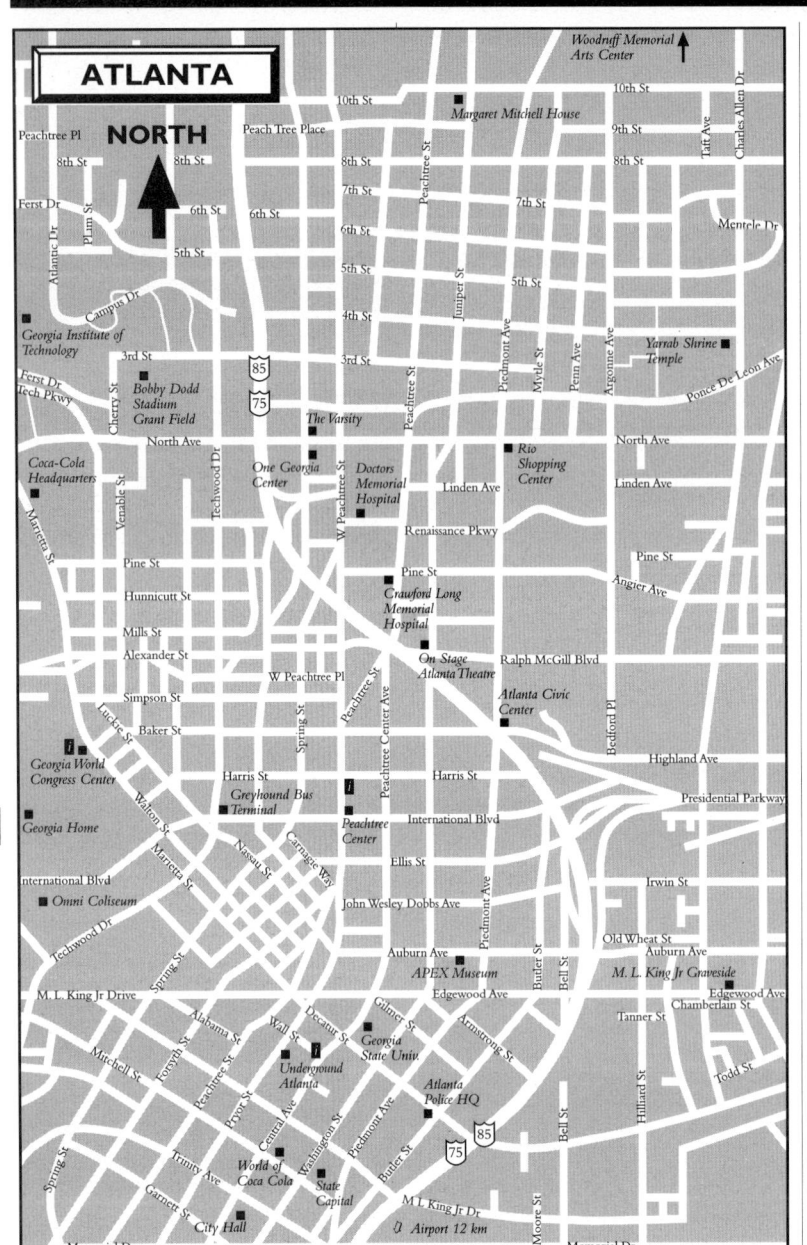

SECTION TWO • AIRPORT DIRECTORY ✈

REGIONAL AIR CONNECTIONS

Albany GA ✈ »Several per day ⊃55 min
Asheville NC ✈ »Several per day ⊃55 min
Augusta GA ✈ »Several per day ⊃50 min
Birmingham AL ✈ »Several per day ⊃45 min
Charleston SC ✈ »Several per day ⊃1 hr
Charlotte NC ✈ »Several per day ⊃1 hr
Chattanooga TN ✈ »Several per day ⊃50 min
Columbia SC ✈ »Several per day ⊃55 min
Columbus GA ✈ »Several per day ⊃40 min
Dothan AL ✈ »Several per day ⊃1 hr
Greenville/Spartanburg SC ✈ »Several per day ⊃1 hr
Huntsville/Decatur AL ✈ »Several per day ⊃50 min
Jacksonville FL ✈ »Several per day ⊃1 hr
Knoxville TN ✈ »Several per day ⊃55 min
Macon GA ✈ »Several per day ⊃35 min
Mobile AL ✈ »Several per day ⊃1 hr
Montgomery AL ✈ »Several per day ⊃50 min
Nashville TN ✈ »Several per day ⊃1 hr
Panama City FL ✈ »Several per day ⊃1 hr
Pensacola FL ✈ »Several per day ⊃1 hr
Savannah GA ✈ »Several per day ⊃1 hr
Tallahassee FL ✈ »Several per day ⊃1 hr
Valdosta GA ✈ »Several per day ⊃1 hr

TRAVELLER'S NOTES

Hartsfield Atlanta International Airport claims to be the second busiest airport in the world. Hartsfield's Concourse E is the largest, single international facility in the U.S. Atlanta has a first-class public transportation system, MARTA, with interlinked bus and rail systems. For information ℂ848 4711. A single fare of USD1.50 covers bus and rail with free transfer between the two.

ℂ Phone no. ℱ Fax no. ⏲ Hours of opening/operation » Frequency of service ⊃ Journey time ⊘ Cost/one-way fare

SECTION TWO • AIRPORT DIRECTORY

AUCKLAND — AKL

New Zealand (see page 30)

National ✆ code: 64
Area ✆ code: 09
Local time: Winter GMT+13, Summer GMT+12
Auckland International Airport, PO Box 73020 Auckland, New Zealand
✆2750789
✆2755835
Internet e-mail: admin@aial.co.nz
Location: 21 km/14 miles S of Auckland

Terminals
International Terminal Airlines: Aerolineas Argentinas, Air Caledonie International, Air Nauru, Air New Zealand, Air Pacific, Air Vanuatu, Ansett Australia, Britannia, British Airways, Canadian Airlines International, Cathay Pacific Airways, Eva Air, Garuda Indonesian Airlines, Great Barrier Air National, Japan Airlines, Korea Air, Lan Chile, Malaysian Airlines, Mandarin Airlines, Polynesian Airlines, Qantas Airways, Royal Tongan, Singapore Airlines, Thai Airways, United Airlines. Layout: Ground Floor (Arrival), First Floor (Departure)
Domestic Terminal Airlines: Air New Zealand, Air New Zealand Link. Layout: Ground Floor (check-in)
Ansett NZ Terminal Airlines:. Ansett New Zealand

Minimum transfer times
International: 55 min–1 hr 30 min
Domestic: 20–40 min

Transfer between terminals
Bus ≫20 min; Connects all terminals

INFORMATION

Information and help desks
Auckland Airport Visitors Centre Domestic Terminal Ground Floor ✆2757467 ✆2568942 ⊙0700–2200 *Airport information, Flights, Hotel booking, Tourist Information*
Tourism Auckland International Terminal Ground Floor ✆2756467 ✆2568942 ⊙0500 until last flight *Airport information, Flights, Weather, Hotel booking, Tourist Information*

EMERGENCIES
Lost Property Domestic Terminal Reception counter on Mezzanine Floor ✆2759046 International: Operations Building behind terminal.

AIRPORT FACILITIES

Money
ATM International Terminal Forecourt ⊙24 hr
Bank International Terminal First Floor ⊙0800–1600
ATM Domestic Terminal Ground Floor ⊙24 hr
Bank Domestic Terminal Ground Floor ⊙0800–1600
BNZ Building, Tom Pearce Drive.

Food and drink
Café/light meals International Terminal Airside
Café/light meals International Terminal First Floor
Café/light meals International Terminal Ground Floor
Restaurant/cafés International Terminal Second Floor
Café/light meals Domestic Terminal Ground Floor

Communications
Post box International Terminal First floor
Post box Domestic Terminal Ground Floor

Shopping
Duty free, departure International Terminal Departure Area
Florist International Terminal Departure Area
News, Stationery & Books International Terminal Departure Area
Duty free, departure Domestic Terminal Departure Area
Shopping Area (23) Airside

Luggage
Left Luggage Counter International Terminal Ground Floor
Lockers International Terminal Western Forecourt
Left Luggage Counter Domestic Terminal Johnston Desk

DISABLED TRAVELLERS
International Terminal Adapted toilets; Lifts; Special car parking; Phones at wheelchair height; Personal assistance *throughout terminal during flight times*
Domestic Terminal Adapted toilets; Lifts; Special car parking

SMOKING POLICY
International Terminal Restricted
Domestic Terminal Restricted

SPECIAL PASSENGER LOUNGES
Air New Zealand United Private Lounge International Terminal First Floor airside access to Second Floor lounge
Air Pacific Lounge International Terminal First Floor airside
British Airways VIP Lounge International Terminal First Floor airside
Cathay Pacific Airways First Class Lounge International Terminal First floor airside
Continental Airlines Business Class Lounge International Terminal First Floor airside
Diner's Club Lounge International Terminal Ground Floor airside
Qantas Captain's Club Lounge International Terminal First Floor airside access to second floor lounge
Singapore Airlines Silver Kris Lounge International Terminal First Floor airside
United Airlines Red Carpet Club Lounge International Terminal First Floor airside

CONFERENCE AND BUSINESS FACILITIES
Conference Room, International Terminal ⊙0600–last flight *Telephones, Fax service, Power points, Secretarial service*
The Clubhouse, Domestic Terminal ✆256 8660 ⊙0800–0430 *Telephones, Fax service, Power points, Secretarial service*

CAR RENTAL
Avis International Terminal ✆2568362
Budget International Terminal ✆2561792
Hertz International Terminal ✆2568686
Avis Domestic Terminal ✆2568362
Budget Domestic Terminal ✆2561792
Hertz Domestic Terminal ✆2568686

✈ Air ⎯ Rail ⎯ Bus ⎯ Limousine 🚇 Metro/subway ⎯ Tram ⎯ Helicopter ⎯ Water transport • For map symbols, see p. 9

AUCKLAND • BAHRAIN　　　　　　　　　　　SECTION TWO • AIRPORT DIRECTORY

National Car Rentals Domestic Terminal
☏2755918

Car Parking

Short-stay 2700 spaces ⊘NZD1 per hr; NZD11 per day

Taxis and Chauffeur-driven Cars

Taxis
Outside each terminal ⊃30 min ⊘NZD31

Public Transport

City & suburbs
Auckland city centre 🚌 Airporter bus ≫30 min ⊘NZD9.

Regional Air Connections

Hamilton ✈ ≫At least daily ⊃35 min
New Plymouth ✈ ≫At least daily ⊃50 min
Wanganui ✈ ≫At least daily ⊃1 hr
Wellington ✈ ≫Several per day ⊃1 hr
Whakatane ✈ ≫At least daily ⊃50 min
Whangarei ✈ ≫Several per day ⊃40 min

Airport Taxes

Airport departure tax of NZD20 is payable by all passengers taking international flights.

Traveller's Notes

Taxis to the city centre are expensive. Shuttle bus services pick up at the domestic and international terminals and drop off at city centre locations.

BAHRAIN　　　　　　　　　　　　　　　BAH

Bahrain (see page 16)

National ☏ code: 973
Area ☏ code: No code required
Local time: Winter GMT+3, Summer GMT+3
Bahrain International Airport, Manama, Bahrain
☏321155
🖷324096
Location: 3.3 km/2 miles N of Manama

Terminals and Transfers

Terminals
Main Terminal Airlines: All airlines. Layout: Four floors. Ground Floor, Customs, Arrivals, Public Concourse; First Floor, Immigration, Transfer; Second Floor, Check in, Departures, Duty Free, Transotel, Passenger lounges, Fourth Floor, Restaurant/Bar.

Minimum transfer times
International: 1 hr

Information

Flight enquiries
Airport ☏325555

Information and help desks
Airport & Tourist Information Desk Public Concourse, ☏321093 🖷321991 ⏰24 hr *Airport information, Flights Hotel booking, Tourist information*
Gulf Air Desks Main Terminal Departure Level (Second Floor) ⏰All flight times *Airport information, Flights Hotel booking*

Emergencies

Police Main Terminal Departure Level (Second Floor) ☏321604
Medical Main Terminal Arrivals Level (First Floor) ☏321690
Lost Property Arrivals Public Concourse (Ground Floor) ☏321429

Airport Facilities

Money
ATM Main Terminal Departure Level (Second Floor) and Arrivals Level (Ground Floor) ⏰24 hr
Bank Main Terminal Departure Level (Second Floor) and Arrivals Level (Ground Floor) ⏰24 hr
Bureau de change Arrivals (First floor) ⏰24 hr

Food and drink
Café/light meals Arrivals Public Concourse (Ground Floor) ⏰24 hr
Café/light meals Main Terminal Transit Area Level 2 near duty free shops ⏰24 hr
Fast Food Transit Area near gate 14 ⏰24 hr
Restaurant Fourth Floor ⏰24 hr

Communications
Fax service Main Terminal Transit Area ⏰24 hr
Post office Main Terminal Transit Area ⏰0700–1900

Shopping
Duty free Main Terminal Arrivals after Immigration (First Floor) ⏰All flight times
Duty free, departure Main Terminal Mezzanine Floor above Departures ⏰24 hr
Shopping mall Main Terminal Arrivals Public Concourse ⏰All Flight times

Luggage
Trolleys/carts Arrivals (Ground Floor) and Departures (Second Floor) ⏰24 hr ⊘Free
Baggage Services Arrivals Public Concourse (Ground Floor) ⏰24 hr

Disabled Travellers

Main Terminal Adapted toilets; Lifts, Special car parking, Wheelchairs available on request.

Smoking Policy

Main Terminal Not permitted except in area adjacent to Gate 11 Departures and café/restaurant

Special Passenger Lounges

Cathay Pacific Airways Business Class Lounge Main Terminal Transit Area Level 2 *First and Business class passengers*
Gulf Air Falcon Lounge Main Terminal Transit Area *First and Business class passengers*
Dilmuan Lounge Main Terminal Transit Area *First and Business class passengers*

Conference and Business Facilities

Al Dana Business Centre, ⏰0800–2400hr *Conference rooms, Secretarial facilities, Telephones, Fax service, Photocopier, Internet.*

☏ Phone no.　🖷 Fax no.　⏰ Hours of opening/operation　≫ Frequency of service　⊃ Journey time　⊘ Cost/one-way fare

Section Two • Airport Directory — Bahrain • Baltimore-Washington

Airport Hotels

Transotel For Transit passengers only ©321338
Diplomat ©531666 ©530843 *Courtesy bus*
Gulf ©713000 ©713040 *Courtesy bus*
Hilton ©535000 ©533097 *Courtesy bus*
Holiday Inn ©531122 ©530154 *Courtesy bus*
Meridien ©580000 ©580333 *Courtesy bus*
Ramada ©714921 ©742809 *Courtesy bus*
Regency ©231777 ©240028 *Courtesy bus*
Sheraton ©534055 ©534065 *Courtesy bus*

Car Rental

Avis Main Terminal Arrival Hall ©321239
Budget Main Terminal Arrival Hall ©321268
EuropCar Main Terminal Arrival Hall ©321999
Hertz Main Terminal Arrivals Hall ©321358
Eurodollar ©321264
Oscar ©321313

Car Parking

Long-stay Front of Arrival Hall 600 spaces ⌀BHD3.00 first day; BHD1.50 per day thereafter
Short-stay Front of Arrival Hall 600 spaces ⌀BHD0.20 first 7 hrs; BHD0.10 per hour thereafter

Taxis and Chauffeur-driven Cars

Taxis
Outside Arrival Hall City centre ⊃10 min ⌀BHD4

Chauffeur-driven cars
In front of Arrival Hall City centre ⊃10 min

Limousine service
To Kingdom of Saudi Arabia eastern province via Causeway ⊃1 hr

Regional Air Connections

Abu Dhabi ✈ »Several per day ⊃1 hr 5 min
Dhahran ✈ »Several per day ⊃25 min
Doha ✈ »Several per day ⊃40 min
Dubai ✈ »Several per day ⊃50 min
Kuwait ✈ »Several per day ⊃1 hr 5 min
Riyadh ✈ »Several per week ⊃1 hr 5 min

Baltimore Washington International — BWI
USA (see page 41)

National © code: 1
Area © code: 410
Local time: Winter GMT-5, Summer GMT-4
Baltimore–Washington International Airport, PO Box 8766, Baltimore, MD 21240, USA ©859 7111
WWW site: http://baltwashintlairport.com
Location: 16 km/10 miles S of Baltimore

Terminals and Transfers

Terminals
Main Terminal Airlines: All airlines.
Layout: Lower Level (Arrival, Baggage Claim, Car Rental, Ground Transportation), Upper Level (Departure), Pier A (Gates A1–A3), Pier B (Gates B1–B6), Pier C (Gates C1–C16), Pier D (Gates D1–D29), Pier D Extension (Commuter Terminal) (Gates D30–D37),

Minimum transfer times
International: 1 hr 30 min
Domestic: 35 min

Information

Flight enquiries
Air Aruba ©850 7374 Air Jamaica ©859 3866 Air Canada ©850 4766 Air Ontario ©850 4766 America West ©859 3222 British Airways ©993 4100 Continental Airlines ©850 0668 Delta Airlines ©859 3115 Icelandair ©850 4340 Northwest Airlines ©859 2737 Southwest Airlines ©859 0300 TWA ©859 2525 United Airlines ©859 2637 US Airways ©993 4976

Information and help desks
Information Desk Main Terminal Upper Level near Piers C and D Airport information, Tourist information
Traveller's Aid Main Terminal ©859 7207

Emergencies

Police Main Terminal Lower Level ©859 7040
Lost Property Main Terminal ©859 7387

Airport Facilities

Money
ATM Main Terminal Upper Level near Piers C and D
Bureau de change Main Terminal Upper Level between Piers C and D
Bureau de change Main Terminal Lower Level International Arrivals area

Food and drink
Bar Main Terminal Upper Level
Café/light meals Main Terminal Upper Level
Restaurant Main Terminal Upper Level

Communications
Post box Main Terminal Upper Level

Shopping
Duty free, Main Terminal Upper Level
Gift Shop Main Terminal throughout
News, Stationery & Books Main Terminal throughout

Luggage
Lockers Main Terminal Upper Level throughout
Trolleys/carts All Terminals throughout ⊙24 hr ⌀USD1.50

✈ Air ⎯ Rail ⎯ Bus ⎯ Limousine Ⓜ Metro/subway ⎯ Tram ⎯ Helicopter ⎯ Water transport • For map symbols, see p. 9

BALTIMORE-WASHINGTON — SECTION TWO • AIRPORT DIRECTORY

Disabled Travellers

Disabled services Main Terminal Lower Level

Special Passenger Lounges

Friendship Centre Main Terminal
US Airways Club Main Terminal Upper Level Pier D (near Gates 10 and 22)
United Airlines Red Carpet Room Main Terminal Upper Level

Conference and Business Facilities

Conference Rooms, Main Terminal
Conference Rooms, Sheraton International Hotel BWI

Airport Hotels

Sheraton International Hotel BWI (on airport grounds, free shuttle bus) 196 rooms ℗859 3300 ℱ859 0565

Car Rental

Alamo Main Terminal Lower Level ℗850 5011
Avis Main Terminal Lower Level ℗859 1680
Budget Main Terminal Lower Level ℗859 0850
Dollar Main Terminal Lower Level ℗684 3315
Hertz Main Terminal Lower Level ℗850 7400
National Main Terminal Lower Level ℗859 8860
Thrifty Main Terminal Lower Level ℗859 1136

Car Parking

Long-stay On airport perimeter (free shuttle bus) ⌀USD5 per day
Off-airport At airport Valet Parking ⌀USD32 per day, ⌀USD45 after 24 hrs
Short-stay Parking Garage ⌀USD4 per hr, USD20 per day (max)

Taxis and Chauffeur-driven Cars

Taxis
City centre ↻15 min ⌀USD18

Public Transport

City & suburbs
Baltimore (Penn Station) ⚌ Amtrak »25 day ⓗ0510–0035 ↻13 min ⌀USD5–8. Free airport shuttle bus »20 min to BWI rail stn
Baltimore (Penn Station) ⚌ MARC: Penn Line »20 day ⓗ0525–2215 Mon–Fri only ↻20 min ⌀USD3. Free airport shuttle bus »20 min to BWI rail stn
Baltimore city centre m MTA: Light Rail »115 min ⓗ0600–2300 Mon–Fri, 0800–2300 Sat, 1100–1900 Sun ↻40 min ⌀USD1.35
Baltimore city centre (downtown hotels) ⚌SuperShuttle »40 min ⓗ0545–0045 ↻30 min ⌀USD11.
Baltimore city centre ⚌Over 15 companies.
Baltimore (suburban hotels) ⚌SuperShuttle »2 hr ⓗ0700–0030 ⌀USD19.
For major hotels in Towson, Timonium, Hunt Valley and Pikesville MD

Other towns and cities
Annapolis MD ⚌SuperShuttle »2 hr ⓗ0700–2300 ⌀USD19. For Annapolis hotels and US Naval Academy
Philadelphia PA (30th St Stn) ⚌Amtrak »25 day ⓗ0510–0035 ↻1 hr 20 min ⌀USD33–63. Free airport shuttle bus »20 min to BWI rail stn.
Washington DC (Union Sta) ⚌Amtrak »25 day ⓗ0510–0035 ↻25 min ⌀USD12–21. Free airport shuttle bus »20 min to BWI rail stn. For New Carrollton MD (Metro stn).
Washington DC (Union Sta) ⚌MARC »20 day ⓗ0700–2045 Mon–Fri ↻35 min ⌀USD4.50 Free airport shuttle bus »20 min to BWI rail stn For New Carrollton MD (Metro stn).
Washington DC (Airport Shuttle Terminal) ⚌SuperShuttle »1 hr ⓗ0500–0030 ⌀USD21
Wilmington DE (Amtrak Stn) ⚌Amtrak »25 day ⓗ0510–0035 ↻1 hr ⌀USD30–49. Free airport shuttle bus »20 min to BWI rail stn

Regional Air Connections

Hagerstown MD ✈ »Several per day ↻50 min
Harrisburg PA ✈ »Several per day ↻35 min
Norfolk/Virginia Beach VA ✈ »Several per day ↻1 hr
Philadelphia ✈ »Several per day ↻40 min
Pittsburgh PA ✈ »Several per day ↻1 hr
Richmond VA ✈ »Several per day ↻40 min
Salisbury MD ✈ »Several per day ↻35 min
Washington DC (Dulles) ✈ »Several per day ↻30 min
Washington DC (National) ✈ »Several per day ↻30 min

Traveller's Notes

BWI serves both Baltimore and Washington metro areas and offers connections to Amtrak and MARC Northeast Corridor rail service. Observation Gallery, including aeronautical and educational exhibits, located in Main Terminal Upper Level between Piers B and C

Bangkok — BKK

Thailand (see page 39)

National ℗ code: 66
Area ℗ code: 02
Local time: Winter GMT+7, Summer GMT+7
Bangkok International Airport, 171 Vibhavadi Rangsit Road, Bangkok 10210, Thailand
℗535 1111
ℱ531 5559
Location: 22 km /14 miles N of Bangkok

Terminals and Transfers

Terminals
Terminal I Airlines: Yunnan Airlines, Air India, Biman Bangladesh Airlines, Royal Brunei Airlines, China Airlines, China Southern Airlines, Ethiopian Airlines, Japan Airlines, Druk-Air, Lot Polish

---

℗ Phone no. ℱ Fax no. ⓗ Hours of opening/operation » Frequency of service ↻ Journey time ⌀ Cost/one-way fare

Airlines, El Al Israel Airlines, Balkan Bulgarian Airlines, Malaysian Airlines, Egyptair, Air New Zealand, Olympic Airways, CSA Czechoslovak, Asiana Airlines, Pakistan International Airlines, Philippine Airlines, Qantas Airways, Lao Aviation, Varig Brazilian, Royal Jordanian Airlines, Tarom Romanian Air, South African Airways, SAS, Singapore Airlines, Swissair, Aeroflot, China Southwest, Thai Airways, Turkish Airlines, Myanmar Airways International, Air Lanka, Royal Air Cambodge, Vietnam Airlines. Layout: North section: VIP rooms and pier. Central block: Transit and Transfer Lounge. South section: main part serves Arrival and Departure
Terminal II Airlines: All other international flights. Layout: Ground Floor (First Floor) and Second Floor for Arrival, Third Floor for Departure. Transit Area including restaurants on Fourth Floor
Domestic Terminal Airlines: All domestic flights. Layout: First Floor Arrival, Second Floor Departure

Minimum transfer times
International: 1 hr 15 min–2 hr Domestic: 30 min

Transfer between terminals
Bus ≫ 15 min (0615–2330); All terminals ⊘ Free

INFORMATION

Flight enquiries
Airport ✆535 1254/1386 (Dep); 535 1301/1310 (Arr)
✆535 3486 ✆535 3974 ✆535 2444
Aeroflot ✆535 2111 **Air China** ✆535 4661 **Air France** ✆535 2112; 535 2113 **Air India** ✆535 2121; 535 2122 **Air Lanka** ✆535 2330; 535 2332 **Air Liberté** ✆535 2272 **Air New Zealand** ✆535 3981; 535 3982 **Alitalia** ✆535 2602 **All Nippon Airways** ✆535 2032 **Asiana Airlines** ✆535 3450 **Balkan Bulgarian Airlines** ✆535 3936 **Biman Bangladesh Airlines** ✆535 2151 **British Airways** ✆535 2143 **Canadian Airlines International** ✆535 2227 **Cathay Pacific Airways** ✆535 2155 **China Airlines** ✆535 2160 **China Eastern Airlines** ✆535 2354 **China Southern Airlines** ✆535 2355 **CSA Czechoslovak** ✆535 1866 **Delta Airlines** ✆535 2991 **Druk-Air** ✆535 1960 **Egyptair** ✆535 2348 **El Al Israel Airlines** ✆535 3566 **Emirates** ✆535 1946 **Ethiopian Airlines** ✆233 8951 **Eva Air** ✆535 3531 **Finnair** ✆535 2104 **Garuda Indonesian Airlines** ✆535 2170 **Gulf Air** ✆535 2313 **Japan Airlines** ✆535 2135 **KLM** ✆535 2190 **Korean Airlines** ✆535 2335 **Kuwait Airways** ✆535 2337 **Lao Aviation** ✆535 3591 **Lauda-Air** ✆535 2635 **Lot Polish Airlines** ✆535 2399 **LTU International Airways** ✆535 1930 **Lufthansa** ✆535 2210 **Malaysian Airlines** ✆535 2288 **Martinair Holland** ✆261 5031✆261 1047 **Myanmar Airways International** ✆535 2288 **Northwest Airlines** ✆535 2412 **Olympic Airways** ✆535 2058 **Pakistan International Airlines** ✆535 2127 **Philippine Airlines** ✆535 2312 **Qantas Airways** ✆535 2220 **Royal Air Cambodge** ✆535 3781 **Royal Brunei Airlines** ✆535 2626 **Royal Jordanian Airlines** ✆535 2152 **Royal Nepal Airlines** ✆535 2150 **Saudia** ✆535 2340 **SAS** ✆535 2322 **Singapore Airlines** ✆535 2260 **South African Airways** ✆535 4701 **Swissair** ✆535 2371 **Tarom Romanian Air** ✆253 1681 **Thai Airways** ✆535 2846 **Turkish Airlines** ✆535 2621 **United Airlines** ✆535 2232 **Uzbekistan Airways** ✆261 5084 **Varig Brazilian** ✆535 3784 **Vietnam Airlines** ✆535 2671 **Yunnan Airlines** ✆535 2354

Information and help desks
Airport Information Desk Terminal I Arrival Hall ✆535 1310, 535 1149 ⏱0530–0100 *Airport information*
Airport Information Desk Domestic Terminal Departure Hall ✆535 1192; 535 1277 ⏱0530–2130 *Airport information*
Airport Information Desk Domestic Terminal Arrival Hall ✆535 1253; 535 1305 ⏱0530–2200 *Airport information*
Airport Information Desk Terminal I Departure Hall ✆535 1254; 535 1123 ⏱24 hr *Airport information*

EMERGENCIES

Police Terminal I Arrival Hall ✆535 1641; 535 1388 ⏱24 hr
Medical Terminal I First Floor of Central Block, near Arrival Lobby ✆535 1113; 535 1755 ⏱24 hr
Lost Property Terminal I Baggage Service Counter, Arrival Lounge ✆535 2173; 535 2811 ⏱24 hr

AIRPORT FACILITIES

Money
Bureau de change Terminal I Departure Hall and Arrival Hall ⏱24 hr
ATM Terminal I Arrival Hall and Departure Hall ⏱0530–2200
Bureau de change Terminal II Arrival Hall and Departure Hall ⏱24 hr
ATM Terminal II Arrival Hall and Departure Hall ⏱0530–2200
Bureau de change Domestic Terminal Arrival Hall and Departure Hall ⏱0600–2200
ATM Domestic Terminal Arrival Hall and Departure Hall ⏱0530–2200

Food and drink
Bar Terminal I Departure and Arrival Halls ⏱24 hr
Café/light meals Terminal I Departure and Arrival Halls ⏱24 hr
Café/light meals Terminal II Several locations ⏱24 hr
Café/light meals Domestic Terminal Ground Floor ⏱0600–2130
Restaurant Terminal I Fourth Floor ⏱0600–2300
Restaurant Terminal I Second Floor ⏱0630–2315
Restaurant Terminal II Second Floor ⏱0700–2300

Communications
Post office Terminal I Arrival Hall, Departure Lobby, Transit Lounge ⏱Arrival Hall 0830–1630; others 24 hr
Post office Terminal II Ground Floor

Shopping
Florist Terminal I Departure Lounge (3 shops) ⏱0600–0100
Duty free, arrival Terminal I Arrival Lounge ⏱24 hr
Shopping mall Terminal I Departure Lounge and throughout ⏱24 hr
Hairdresser Terminal I Transit Lounge, Central Block; Departure Hall ⏱0700–2100
Duty free, departure Terminal I Departure and Transit Lounges ⏱24 hr
Duty free, departure Terminal II Third Floor
Florist Terminal II Third Floor
Duty free, arrival Terminal II Arrival Lounge, Ground Floor ⏱24 hr
Shopping mall Terminal II throughout ⏱24 hr
Hairdresser Terminal II Departure Hall ⏱0700–2100

Luggage
Left luggage counter Terminal I Departure Hall ⏱24 hr ⊘THB20 per item per day
Trolleys/carts Terminal I Departure Hall ⏱24 hr ⊘Free
Left luggage counter Terminal I Arrival Hall ⏱24 hr ⊘THB20 per item per day
Trolleys/carts Terminal I Arrival Hall ⏱24 hr ⊘Free
Left luggage counter Terminal II Ground and Third Floors ⏱24 hr ⊘THB20 per item per day
Left luggage counter Domestic Terminal Ground and Second Floor ⏱0600–2200 ⊘THB20 per item per day

DISABLED TRAVELLERS

Terminal I Adapted toilets; Lifts; Personal assistance.

BANGKOK

SMOKING POLICY

Terminal I Restricted (smoking areas provided)

SPECIAL PASSENGER LOUNGES

Special VIP Lounge Terminal II Third Floor *First Class 1 hr 30 min THB3000 per room, next hr THB1000*
VIP Lounge Terminal II Third Floor *First/Business Class THB300–500 per 2 hr*
VIP Lounge Terminal I Third Floor *First Class THB500 per 2 hr, Business Class THB300 per 2 hr*
Special VIP Lounge Terminal I Third Floor *First Class 1 hr 30 min THB3000 per room, next hr THB1000*
Thai Airways Business Class Terminal I *Also NZ, KB, LO, MH, IC, RJ, VJ, RG*
Thai Airways Louis Tavern CIP Lounge Terminal I *Also JL, KL, RA, SA, SR, RO, OA, NW, UB, BI, TK, VN Also UL, CA, OZ, 3Q, OK, MS, EK, LY, MH, KU, ET, AY, GA, GF*
Air France Lounge Terminal I
Air India Maharajah Lounge Terminal I
Alitalia Lounge Terminal I
All Nippon Airways Fuji Lounge Terminal I
Biman Bangladesh Airlines Maslin Lounge Terminal I
British Airways Executive Lounge Terminal I
Canadian Airlines International Empress Lounge Terminal I
Cathay Pacific Airways Marco Polo Lounge Terminal I
China Airlines Dynasty Lounge Terminal I
China Eastern Airlines First Class Lounge Terminal I *Also MA*
China Southern Airlines Lounge Terminal I
Eva Air Evergreen Lounge Terminal I
Japan Airlines Sakura Lounge Terminal I
Korean Airlines Morning Calm Lounge Terminal I
Lauda-Air Lounge Terminal I
Lufthansa Senator Lounge Terminal I
Pakistan International Airlines Shalimar Lounge Terminal I
Philippine Airlines Mabuhay Lounge Terminal I
Qantas Airways Club Lounge Terminal I
Saudia Alfursan Lounge Terminal I
SAS Euro Class Lounge Terminal I
Singapore Airlines Silver Kris Lounge Terminal I
Thai Airways Royal First Class Lounge Terminal I
Thai Airways Royal Orchid Lounge Terminal I
United Airlines Red Carpet Club Lounge Terminal I

CONFERENCE AND BUSINESS FACILITIES

Cellular phone rental counter, Arrival Lounge, Terminals I and II ℂ535 3598 *Telephones*

AIRPORT HOTELS

Amari Airport ℂ566 1020 ℱ566 1941

CAR RENTAL

Avis Terminal II Ground Floor ℂ535 4031
Hertz Domestic Terminal Ground Floor ℂ535 3004

CAR PARKING

Long-stay Terminal I and main car park 4000 spaces ⊘THB10–15 per hr, THB150 for 7–24 hr
Short-stay Domestic Terminal ⊘THB10–20 per hr, THB150 per 7–24 hr

TAXIS AND CHAUFFEUR-DRIVEN CARS

Taxis
Arrival Hall, Ground Floor, all terminals Thai Limousine ℂ535 2801 City centre ⊃45–90 min ⊘THB650
Arrival Hall all terminals Public taxis ℂ535 1247 City centre ⊃45–90 min ⊘Approx THB500 or according to meter

PUBLIC TRANSPORT

City & suburbs
Bang Pakaew 🚌 Air-conditioned bus, line 10. *Via Rama Gardens Hotel and Central Plaza Hotel*
Bangkok city centre 🚌 Airport Bus ⊘THB70. *Route A1 (South) to Silom; Route A2 (West) to Sanam Luang (Grand Palace); Route A3 (East) Prakanong.*
Bangkok Emerald Buddha Temple (Snam Luang) 🚌Public bus line 59. *Via Central Plaza Hotel and Royal Hotel*
Bangkok (rail stn) 🚌 Public buses, line 29 ⊃1 hr ⊘THB3.50. *Air-conditioned bus also available on line 29, cost THB 16*
Bangkok, Klong Toey 🚌 Public bus, line 95. *Via Hua Mark*
Bangrak 🚌Air-conditioned bus, line 4. *Via following hotels: Rama Gardens, Central Plaza, Indra regent, Regent, Dusit Thani and Narai*
Samrong 🚌Air-conditioned bus, line 13. *Via following hotels: Rama Gardens, Central Plaza, Indra Regent, Le Meridien President, Ambassador*
Bangkok (Hualampong rail stn) 🚆State Railway of Thailand ≫13 per day ⏱0341–2144 ⊃45 min ⊘THB10. *Express service 35 min*

Other towns and cities
Chiang Mai 🚆State Railway of Thailand ≫6 per day ⏱0727–2247 ⊃12–13 hr ⊘Approx THB250.
Nong Khai 🚆State Railway of Thailand ≫3 per day ⏱0654–2112 ⊃10–11 hrs ⊘Approx THB200.
Phitsanulok 🚆State Railway of Thailand ≫11 per day ⏱0727–2349 ⊃4 hr 40 min– 6 hr 50 min ⊘Approx THB140.
Ubon Ratchathani 🚆State Railway of Thailand ≫6 per day ⏱0739–0014 ⊃9–12 hr ⊘Approx THB180.

REGIONAL AIR CONNECTIONS

Hua Hin ✈ ≫At least daily ⊃30 min
Khon Kaen ✈ ≫Several per day ⊃55 min
Nakhon Ratchasima ✈ ≫At least daily ⊃45 min
Phitsanulok ✈ ≫Several per day ⊃55 min
Vientiane ✈ ≫At least daily ⊃1 hr
Yangon ✈ ≫Several per day ⊃45 min

AIRPORT TAXES

Airport departure tax is THB200.

TRAVELLER'S NOTES

Use a registered taxi to reach central Bangkok; their drivers wait in the lobby in the arrivals hall. Be wary of touts offering to take you to your hotel. Photography is prohibited at the airport and any military installations.

ℂ Phone no. ℱ Fax no. ⏱ Hours of opening/operation ≫ Frequency of service ⊃ Journey time ⊘ Cost/one-way fare

BARCELONA

BCN

Spain (see page 36)

National ✆ code: 34
Area ✆ code: 03
Local time: Winter GMT+1, Summer GMT+2
Barcelona Airport, Edificio Bloque Tecnico, 08820 El Prat de Llobregat, Barcelona, Spain
✆ 298 38 38
🅕298 37 37
Location: 10 km/6 miles SW of Barcelona

TERMINALS AND TRANSFERS

Terminals
Terminal A Airlines: All international flights. Layout: Two floors. Check-in desks on Ground Floor
Terminal B Airlines: All domestic flights. Layout: Two floors. Check-in desks on Ground Floor
Terminal C Airlines: Iberia (Barcelona–Madrid Air Shuttle). Layout: Two floors. Check-in desks on Ground Floor

Minimum transfer times
International: 45 min **Domestic:** 30 min

INFORMATION

Flight enquiries
Airport ✆298 38 38
Adria Airways ✆280 48 90 🅕280 54 20
Air Algérie ✆370 84 01 🅕487 46 27 Air France ✆487 24 24 🅕478 04 24 Air Malta ✆416 01 35 🅕301 38 93 Air Portugal TAP ✆215 65 65 🅕370 30 52 Alitalia ✆416 04 24 🅕415 83 79 Austrian Airlines ✆487 21 73 🅕487 07 84 Balkan Bulgarian Airlines ✆370 05 54 🅕370 05 54 British Airways ✆902 111 333 🅕215 66 58 Delta Airlines ✆412 43 33 🅕412 33 39 Egyptair ✆301 73 12 🅕301 71 90 El Al Israel Airlines ✆1 541 20 05 🅕1 542 24 95 Finnair ✆478 69 56 🅕478 33 93 Iberia ✆902 400 500 🅕401 33 62 KLM ✆379 54 58 🅕370 25 53 Lauda-Air ✆487 03 00 🅕487 28 89 Lufthansa ✆487 03 00 🅕487 28 89 Luxair ✆379 25 00 Malev Hungarian ✆487 65 75 🅕487 76 91 Meridiana ✆487 41 41 🅕488 01 21 Olympic Airways ✆478 26 01 🅕478 24 22 Royal Air Maroc ✆301 84 74 🅕318 90 85 Sabena World Airlines ✆487 47 79 🅕478 04 24 SAS ✆379 27 08 🅕370 90 58 Swissair ✆215 91 50 🅕488 26 99 Tarom Romanian Air ✆301 17 82 🅕301 10 63 Thai Airways ✆318 30 05 🅕317 46 11 Tunis Air ✆488 10 05 🅕487 66 98 TWA ✆379 51 12 🅕370 10 53 Varig Brazilian ✆215 34 24 🅕215 58 30 VASP ✆487 11 38 🅕487 65 90 Virgin ✆900 993 276

Information and help desks
Airport Information Desk Terminal B Transit Lobby ✆298 38 38 🅕🕒0630–2230 Airport information, Flights
Airport Information Desk Terminal B Terminal Hall ✆298 38 38 🅕🕒0630–2230 Airport information, Flights
Airport Information Desk Terminal A Terminal Hall ✆298 38 38 🅕🕒0630–2230 Airport information, Flights
Tourist Information Desk Terminal A Terminal Hall ✆478 47 04 🅕478 47 36 🕒0930–2000, Tourist Information
Tourist Information Desk Terminal B Terminal Hall ✆478 47 04 🅕478 47 36 🕒0930–2000, Tourist Information

Emergencies
Police Terminal A Next to passport control ✆379 15 84; 379 10 16 🕒24 hr
Medical Terminal A Bloque Tecnico ✆298 38 00 🕒24 hr
Lost Property Terminal A Airport Information Desk ✆298 38 38 🕒24 hr

AIRPORT FACILITIES

Money
Bureau de change Terminal A Transit Hall 🕒0715–2245
Bank Terminal A Banco Exterior de España 🕒0900–1400 Mon–Sat
ATM Terminal A throughout 🕒24 hr
ATM Terminal B throughout 🕒24 hr
ATM Terminal C throughout 🕒24 hr

Food and drink
Bar Terminal A Transit Hall 🕒0700–2300
Café/light meals Terminal A Transit Lobby 🕒0400–2200
Bar Terminal B Transit Hall 🕒0700–2300
Bar Terminal B Transit Lobby 🕒24 hr
Café/light meals Terminal B Transit Lobby 🕒0700–2200
Café/light meals Terminal C First Floor 🕒0600–2300
Restaurant Terminal C First Floor 🕒0700–2300

Shopping
Duty free, departure Terminal A First Floor 🕒0700–2000
Gift Shop Terminal A Transit Hall 🕒0700–2200
News, Stationery & Books Terminal A Transit Hall 🕒0700–2200

DISABLED TRAVELLERS

Terminal A Adapted toilets; Lifts; Special car parking; Phones at wheelchair height.
Terminal B Adapted toilets; Lifts; Special car parking; Phones at wheelchair height.
Terminal C Adapted toilets; Lifts; Special car parking; Phones at wheelchair height.

SMOKING POLICY

Terminal A Restricted
Terminal B Restricted
Terminal C Restricted

SPECIAL PASSENGER LOUNGES

Air France Lounge Terminal A
All airlines Canudas Airport Lounge Terminal B
All airlines Barcelona Airport Lounge Terminal A
British Airways Lounge Terminal B Transit Lobby
Iberia Lounge Terminal C
Iberia Gaudi Lounge Terminal B

CONFERENCE AND BUSINESS FACILITIES

Business Centre, Terminal B ✆478 67 99 🅕478 67 05 🕒0830–2030 Mon–Fri

AIRPORT HOTELS

Alfa Aeropuerto ✆336 25 64 🅕

CAR RENTAL

Atesa Terminal A ✆302 28 32
Avis Terminal A ✆379 40 26
EuropCar Terminal A ✆478 52 94
Hertz Terminal A ✆370 57 52

BARCELONA

SECTION TWO • AIRPORT DIRECTORY

Avis Terminal B ℅478 74 19
EuropCar Terminal B ℅478 31 78
Hertz Terminal B ℅478 78 57
Avis Terminal C ℅379 40 26
EuropCar Terminal C ℅478 31 78
Hertz Terminal C ℅370 58 11
Budget ℅298 3500/1/2/3

CAR PARKING

Short-stay 6200 spaces ⌀ESP200 per hr; ESP1200 per day

TAXIS AND CHAUFFEUR-DRIVEN CARS

Taxis
Outside terminal buildings ➲25 min ⌀ESP2200

PUBLIC TRANSPORT

City & suburbs
Barcelona city centre (Plaza Cataluña) 🚌
Transports Ciutat Comtal, SA: Aerobus
≫15 min ⏰0600–2300 ➲35 min ⌀ESP450.
Barcelona city centre (Plaza España) 🚌
SPM: Service Code EN ≫1 hr 20 min
⏰0620–2100 ➲40 min ⌀ESP130.
Barcelona city centre (Sants rail stn) 🚌
RENFE ≫30 min ⏰0613–2213 ➲23 min ⌀ESP300.

REGIONAL AIR CONNECTIONS

Alicante ✈ ≫Several per day ➲55 min
Bilbao ✈ ≫Several per day ➲1 hr
Ibiza ✈ ≫Several per day ➲40 min
Lisbon ✈ ≫Several per day ➲50 min
Madrid ✈ ≫Several per day ➲1 hr
Menorca ✈ ≫Several per day ➲45 min
Palma, Mallorca ✈ ≫Several per day ➲40 min
Pamplona ✈ ≫Several per week ➲55 min
Valencia ✈ ≫Several per day ➲1 hr

TRAVELLER'S NOTES

The people of Barcelona and the surrounding region speak Catalan, a separate language and not a dialect of Spanish. Signs and notices are usually in both languages.

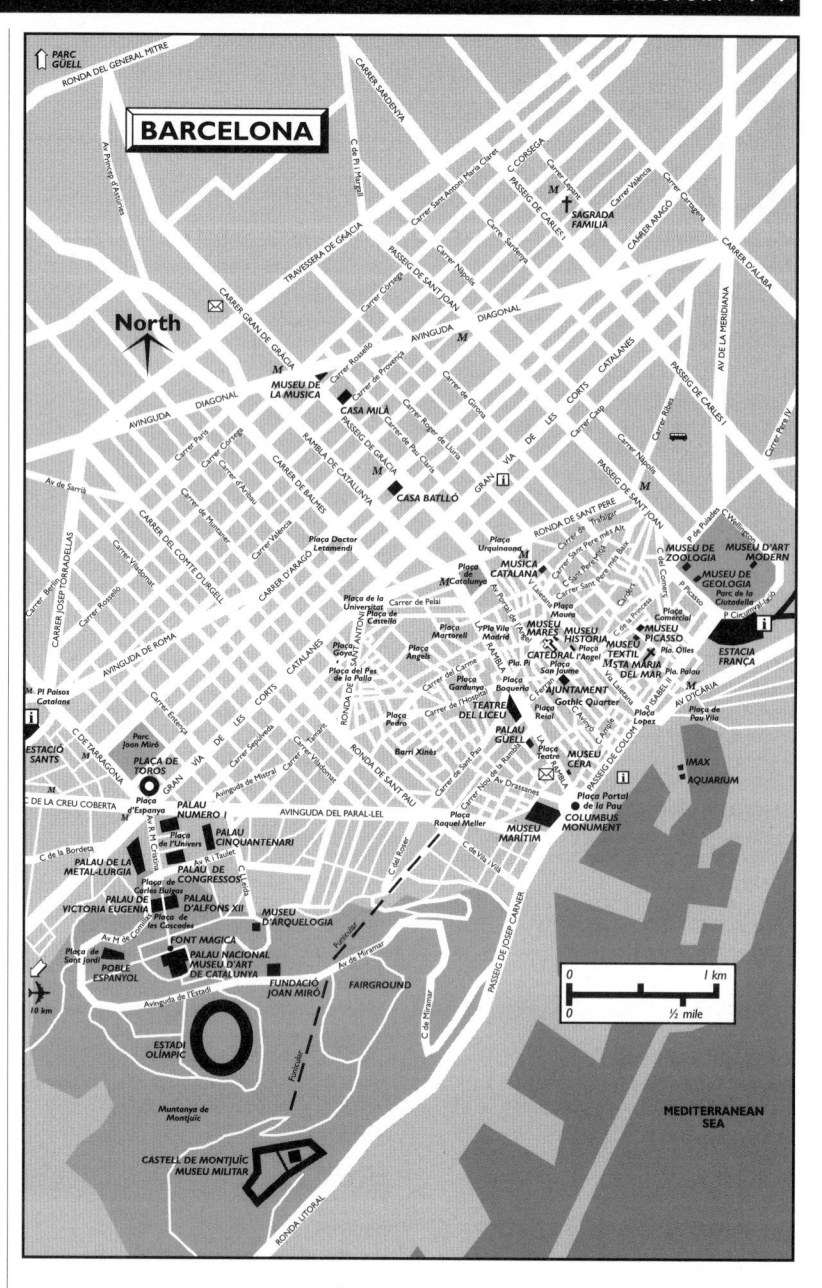

℅ Phone no. Ⓕ Fax no. ⏰ Hours of opening/operation ≫ Frequency of service ➲ Journey time ⌀ Cost/one-way fare

BEIJING

PEK

China (People's Republic) (see page 19)

National ✆ code: 86
Area ✆ code: 01
Local time: Winter GMT+8, Summer GMT+8
Beijing Capital International Airport, Beijing, People's Republic of China
✆456 2233
℻456 4224
Location: 28 km/16 miles NE of Beijing

TERMINALS AND TRANSFERS

Terminals
Main Terminal Airlines: All international flights.
Domestic Terminal Airlines: All domestic flights.

Minimum transfer times
International: 1 hr 30 min Domestic: 1 hr 30 min–2 hr

INFORMATION

Flight enquiries
Airport ✆552 515, 555 402, 456 3604, 456 3605

Information and help desks
Airport Information Desk Main Terminal Second Floor of Departure Level ✆456 3606 ⏱0600–last flight arrival *Airport information*
Tourist Information Desk Main Terminal First Floor of Arrival Lounge ✆456 2233 ⏱0830–last flight arrival *Tourist information*

EMERGENCIES

Lost Property Main Terminal Arrival Hall ✆456 3572 ⏱Until last flight

AIRPORT FACILITIES

Money
Bureau de change Main Terminal Arrival and Departure Halls (2) ⏱0630–last flight

Food and drink
Café/light meals Main Terminal 2, ⏱0700–2100

Restaurant Main Terminal 2, ⏱1100–1400, 1700–2000

Communications
Post office Main Terminal ⏱0700–2000
Post office Domestic Terminal ⏱0700–2000

Shopping
Duty free, departure Main Terminal International Departure Lounge
Shopping mall Main Terminal

Luggage
Left luggage counter Main Terminal Outside building ⏱0730–2200 ◇CNY1–3 per item/day

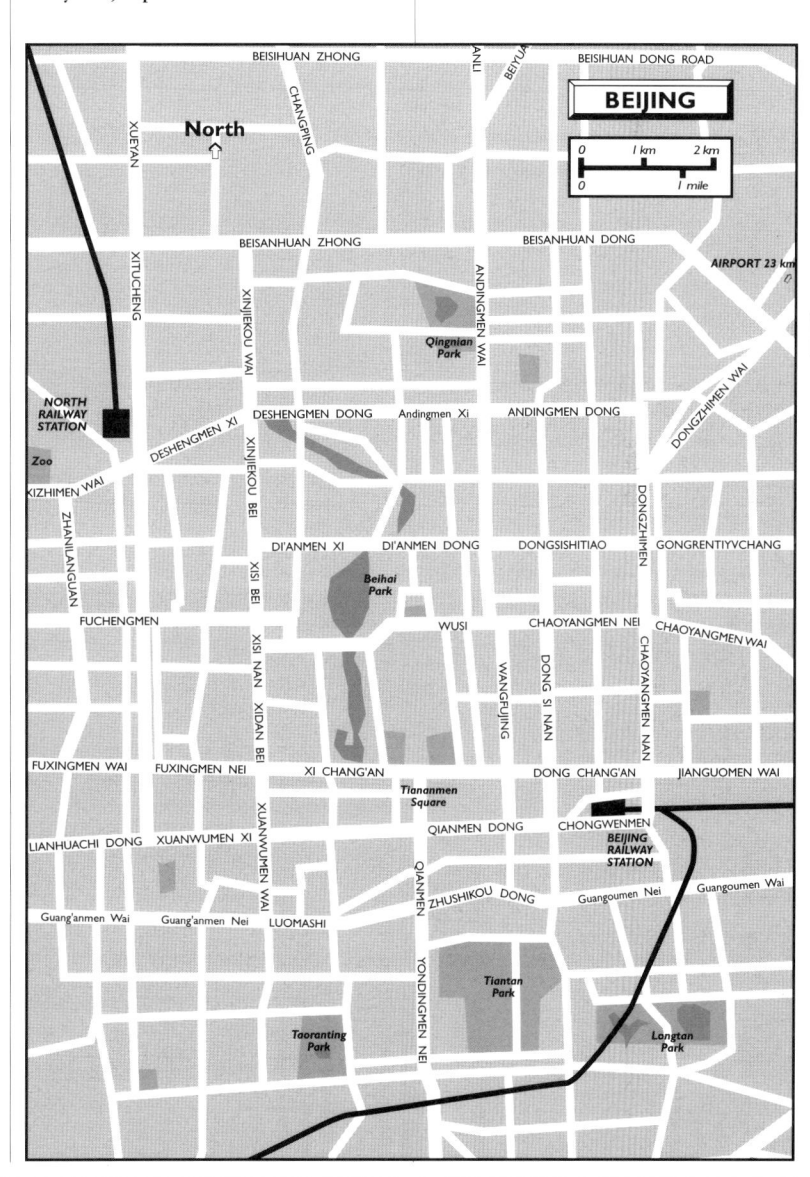

BEIJING • BELFAST   SECTION TWO • AIRPORT DIRECTORY

DISABLED TRAVELLERS
Main Terminal Lifts

CAR PARKING
Long-stay ⊘CNY40 per day

TAXIS AND CHAUFFEUR-DRIVEN CARS
Taxis
City centre ⊃Approx 40 min ⊘Approx CNY70

PUBLIC TRANSPORT
City & suburbs
Beijing city centre 🚌 »30 min ⏲0500–1800 ⊃Approx 45 min ⊘CNY8.

REGIONAL AIR CONNECTIONS
Jinan ✈ »Several per day ⊃45–60 min
Weihai ✈ »Several per week ⊃1 hr
Yantai ✈ »Several per day ⊃60–75 min
Zhengzhou ✈ »At least daily ⊃60–75 min

TRAVELLER'S NOTES
Car rental exists only on a minimal basis; it is easier to take a taxi or bus. Hotel taxis are more expensive than those hailed in the streets. Airport tax is payable at a special counter before departure.

BELFAST-INTERNATIONAL — BFS
United Kingdom (see page 41)

National ✆ code: 44
Area ✆ code: 01849
Local time: Winter GMT, Summer GMT+1
Belfast International, Belfast, BT29 4AB, Northern Ireland, United Kingdom
✆422888
🖷452096
WWW site: www.bial.co.uk
Location: 22 km/14 miles NW of Belfast

TERMINALS AND TRANSFERS
Terminals
Main Terminal Airlines: All airlines. Layout: Departure and Arrival Halls

Minimum transfer times
International: 45–55 min Domestic: 20 min

INFORMATION
Flight enquiries
Airport ✆422888
Air UK ✆422888 British Midland Airways ✆422888

Information and help desks
Information Desk Main Terminal Arrival Hall ✆422888 ext. 2300 ⏲All flight times
Airport information Hotel booking, Tourist information

Emergencies
Police Main Terminal throughout ✆422888 ext. 2226 ⏲All flight times
Medical Main Terminal Information Desk ✆422888] ⏲24 hr
Lost Property Main Terminal Airline or Information Desk ✆422888 ⏲All flight times

AIRPORT FACILITIES
Money
ATM Main Terminal Departure Hall/Entrance Hall ⏲24 hr
Bank Main Terminal Departure Hall/Entrance Hall
Thomas Cook bureau de change Main Terminal Departure Concourse ⏲0630–2000 Mon–Fri; 0630–2200 Sat, Sun. Main Terminal Arrivals Concourse.

Food and drink
Bar Main Terminal Departure and Arrival Halls ⏲0630–last flight
Café/light meals Main Terminal Departure and Arrival Halls ⏲0630–2130
Restaurant Main Terminal Departure Concourse ⏲0630–last flight

Communications
Fax service Main Terminal Business

✆ Phone no. 🖷 Fax no. ⏲ Hours of opening/operation » Frequency of service ⊃ Journey time ⊘ Cost/one-way fare

SECTION TWO • AIRPORT DIRECTORY — BELFAST

Centre ⓘAll flight times
Post box Main Terminal Departures Concourse ⓘAll flight times

Shopping
Duty free, departure Main Terminal Departure Concourse ⓘAll flight times
Shopping mall Main Terminal Departure Concourse ⓘAll flight times

Luggage
Porters Main Terminal Information Desk ⓘAll flight times
Trolleys/carts Main Terminal Information Desk ⓘAll flight times ⊘Free

Disabled Travellers
Main Terminal Adapted toilets; Lifts; Phones at wheelchair height; Car parking facilities; Personal assistance at Information Desk

Smoking Policy
Main Terminal Smoking areas available

Special Passenger Lounges
British Airways Executive Club Lounge Main Terminal Near Departure Gate 9 Club members
British Midland Airways Diamond Club Lounge Main Terminal Near Departure Gate 18 Club members

Conference and Business Facilities
Aldergrove Airport Hotel ℂ422033 ⒻF 423500 Telephones, Fax service, Photocopier, Secretarial service, Conference and meeting rooms

Airport Hotels
Aldergrove Airport Hotel ℂ422033 Ⓕ 423500

Car Rental
Avis Main Terminal Arrival Hall ℂ422333
EuropCar Main Terminal Arrival Hall ℂ423444
Hertz Main Terminal Arrival Hall ℂ422533

Car Parking
Long-stay 980 spaces ⊘GBP0.70 per hr; GBP2 per day
Off-airport 2000 spaces ⊘GBP1.50 per day; GBP6 per week
Short-stay 168 spaces ⊘GBP1.60 per hr; GBP15.60 per week

Taxis and Chauffeur-driven Cars

Taxis
Outside terminal building City centre ⊃30 min ⊘GBP16

Chauffeur-driven cars
Outside terminal building

Public Transport

City & suburbs
Belfast city centre 🚌Ulsterbus »30 min (»60min Sun) ⓘ0645–2250 Mon–Sat ⊃30–40 min ⊘GBP3.50.

Other towns and cities
Dublin 🚌Ulsterbus qavg 3 hr ⓘ0800–1800 ⊃3 hr ⊘GBP9.50.

Regional Air Connections
Birmingham (UK) ✈ »Several per day ⊃1hr 05 min
Blackpool ✈ »Several per day ⊃50 min
Cardiff ✈ »At least daily ⊃1hr 10 min
Cork ✈ »Several per day ⊃1hr 15 min
East Midlands ✈ »Several per day ⊃1hr 05 min
Edinburgh ✈ »At least daily ⊃50 min
Glasgow ✈ »Several per day ⊃45 min
Isle of Man ✈ »Several per day ⊃35 min
Leeds/Bradford ✈ »Several per day ⊃1hr 05 min
Liverpool ✈ »Several per day ⊃50 min
Londonderry ✈ »At least daily ⊃30 min
Manchester (UK) ✈ »Several per day ⊃1hr
Newcastle (UK) ✈ »Several per day ⊃55 min
Shannon ✈ »Several per week ⊃1 hr

✈ Air 🚆 Rail 🚌 Bus 🚙 Limousine Ⓜ Metro/subway 🚊 Tram 🚁 Helicopter ⛴ Water transport • For map symbols, see p. 9

BERLIN-TEGEL

TXL

Germany (see page 22)

National ☏ code: 49
Area ☏ code: 030
Local time: Winter GMT+1, Summer GMT+2
Flughafen Berlin-Tegel, D-13405 Berlin, Germany
☏4101 1
🖷4101 2111
Location: 8 km/5 miles NW of Berlin

TERMINALS AND TRANSFERS

Terminals
Main Terminal Airlines: All airlines.
Layout: Five Levels

Minimum transfer times
International: 30 min Domestic: 30 min

INFORMATION

Flight enquiries
Airport ☏4101 2306/2307
Air France ☏4104 2715 Alitalia ☏4101 2650 Austrian Airlines ☏4101 2615 British Airways ☏4101 2647 Delta Airlines ☏4101 3445 Finnair ☏4101 3499 Iberia ☏4101 2698 KLM ☏4101 3844 Lufthansa ☏8875 6333 Olympic Airways ☏4101 2645 Swissair ☏4101 2615 TAP Air Portugal ☏2611687 Turkish Airlines ☏4101 3413

Information and help desks
Airport Information Desk Main Terminal Main Hall ☏4101 2306 ⏰0500–2300 Airport information, Flights
Berlin Tourist Desk Main Terminal Main Hall ☏4101 3145 ⏰0800–2300 Hotel booking, Tourist information
Hotel Reservations Desk Main Terminal Near Gates 7/8 Hotel booking

EMERGENCIES

Police Main Terminal Third Floor & near Left Luggage ☏4101 3100
Medical Main Terminal First aid below Main Hall ☏4101 2320 ⏰24 hr
Lost Property / Baggage Storage Service Main Terminal At left luggage near Gate 1 ⏰0500–2230 ☏4101 2315

AIRPORT FACILITIES

Money
ATM Main Terminal Near Gates 4 & 10 ⏰24 hr
Bank Main Terminal Gallery ⏰0830–1330 Mon–Fri, 1500–1800 Tue and Thur.
Bureau de change Main Terminal Main Hall ⏰0800–2200 ☏ 417 85 40

Food and drink
Bar Main Terminal ⏰0600–2200 ☏ 4101 3302
Café/light meals Main Terminal ⏰0515–2045 ☏ 4101 3337
Café/light meals Main Terminal ⏰0745–2300 ☏ 4101 3336
Restaurant Main Terminal Third Floor ⏰0700–2100 ☏ 4101 3338

Communications
Post office Main Terminal First Floor Gallery ⏰0700–2100 Mon–Fri; ⏰0800–2000 Sat and Sun. ☏ 4 17 84 90
Fax service In Post Office 🖷 4 12 80 89

Shopping
Duty free, departure Main Terminal International Departures ⏰All flights
Shopping mall Main Terminal Main Hall ⏰0600–2200

Luggage
Left Luggage Counter Main Terminal Between Gate No1 & Main Hall ⏰0500–2230 ⊘ DEM5 per day ☏ 4101 2315
Porters Main Terminal Information Desk ⏰All flight times
Trolleys/carts Main Terminal throughout ⏰24 hr ⊘Free

DISABLED TRAVELLERS

Main Terminal Adapted toilets; Lifts Special car parking

SMOKING POLICY

Main Terminal Smoking permitted throughout

SPECIAL PASSENGER LOUNGES

Diners Club Lounge Main Terminal First Floor Gallery ☏ 4101 2865 Diners Club cardholders and guests
British Airways Executive Club Lounge Main Terminal First Floor Gallery ☏ 4101 6235 Club members
Lufthansa Frequent Traveller Lounge Main Terminal First Floor Gallery ☏ 8875 6334
Lufthansa Senator Lounge Main Terminal First Floor Gallery ☏ 8875 6370 All other international flights **Otto-Lilienthal Lounge** Main Terminal First Floor Gallery ☏ 8875 6220 Airline club members

CONFERENCE AND BUSINESS FACILITIES

Novotel Hotel ☏4101 60 🖷381 94 03 Telephones, Fax service, Photocopier, Secretarial service

AIRPORT HOTELS

Novotel ☏4106 0 🖷4106 700

CAR RENTAL

Avis Main Terminal P2 Building near Gate No 18 ☏4101 3148
EuropCar Main Terminal P2 Building near Gate No 18 ☏4101 3323
Hertz Main Terminal P2 Building near Gate No 18 ☏4101 3315
Alamo Main Terminal P2 Building near Gate 18 ☏4101 3383
Sixt Main Terminal P2 Building near Gate 18 ☏4101 2886
Westfehling Main Terminal P2 Building near Gate 18 ☏4101 3364

CAR PARKING

Long-stay 1900 spaces ⊘DEM3 per hr; DEM6 per 2 hr; DEM15–18 per day
Short-stay 230 spaces ⊘20 min free/DEM2 per 20 min/DEM4 first hr; DEM142 per day

TAXIS AND CHAUFFEUR-DRIVEN CARS

Taxis
In Front Main Hall near Gate No 8/9 City centre ➲30 min ⊘DEM 25

Chauffeur-driven cars
Front of Main Hall

☏ Phone no. 🖷 Fax no. ⏰ Hours of opening/operation » Frequency of service ➲ Journey time ⊘ Cost/one-way fare

SECTION TWO • AIRPORT DIRECTORY

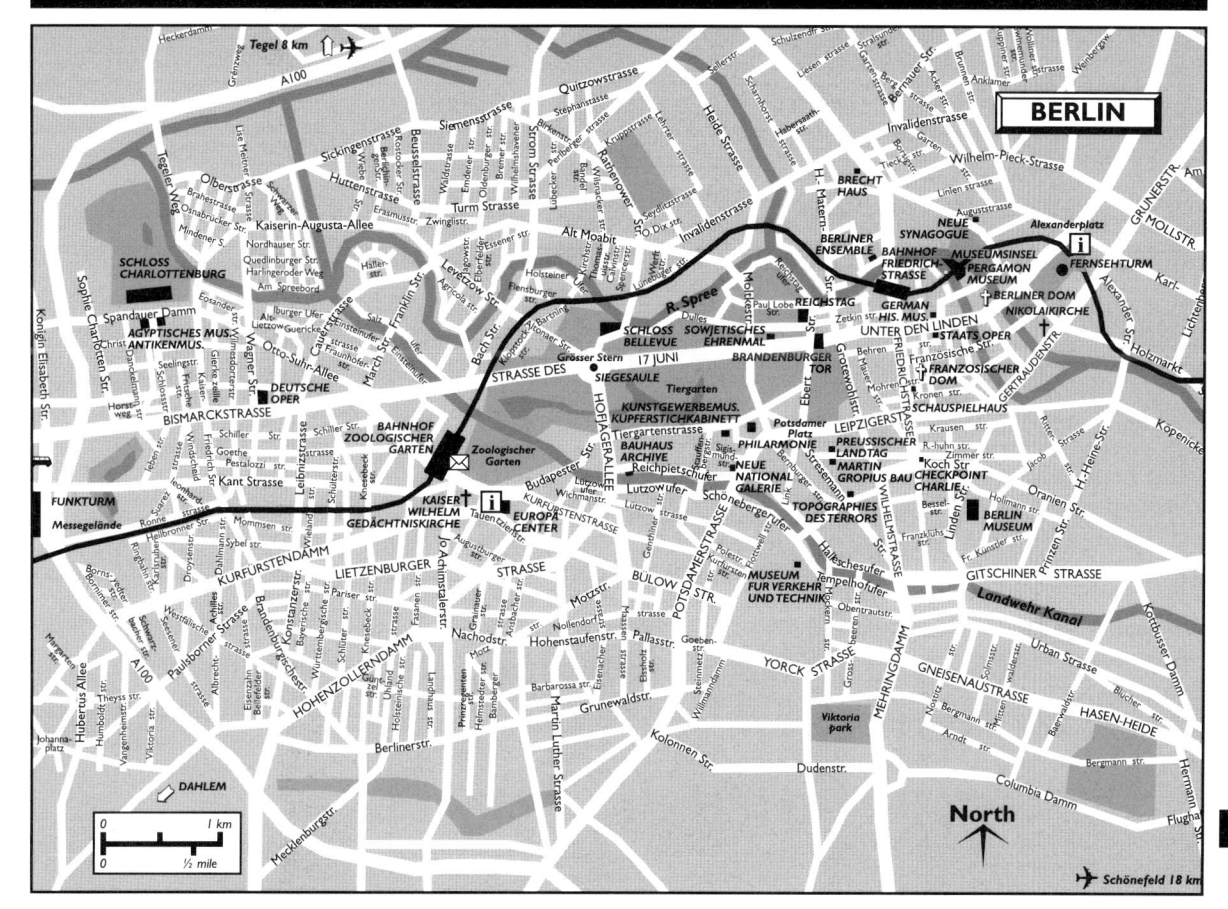

BERLIN-TEGEL

PUBLIC TRANSPORT

City & suburbs
Berlin (Zoo rail stn) BVG Service 109 and X9 »approx 10 min ⓒ0454–0014 ↻25 min ⌀DEM3.

REGIONAL AIR CONNECTIONS

Bremen ✈ »Several pr day ↻1 hr

Cologne/Bonn ✈ »Several per day ↻1 hr 5 min
Düsseldorf ✈ »Several per day ↻1 hr
Frankfurt ✈ »Several per day ↻1 hr 5 min
Hamburg ✈ »Several per day ↻1 hr
Munich ✈ »Several per day ↻1 hr 10 min
Münster ✈ »Several per day ↻1 hr 5 min

Nuremberg ✈ »At least daily ↻1 hr 10 min
Salzburg ✈ »Several per week ↻1 hr
Stuttgart ✈ »Several per day ↻1 hr 10 min

TRAVELLER'S NOTES

New rail link to city centre under construction.

✈ Air ⇌ Rail ⇌ Bus ⇌ Limousine Ⓜ Metro/subway ⇌ Tram ⇌ Helicopter ⇌ Water transport • For map symbols, see p. 9

BIRMINGHAM   BHX

United Kingdom (see page 41)

National ☎ code: 44
Area ☎ code: 0121
Local time: Winter GMT, Summer GMT+1
Birmingham International Airport, Birmingham B26 3QJ, United Kingdom
☎767 5511
📠782 8802
Internet e-mail: joanneg@bhx.co.uk
WWW site: http://www.bhx.co.uk
Location: 13 km/8 miles SE of Birmingham

TERMINALS AND TRANSFERS

Terminals
Main Terminal Airlines: Aer Lingus, Air Malta, Air UK, Air 2000, American Airlines, BASE Regional Airlines, British Midland, Continental Airlines, Crossair, Cyprus Airways, Jersey European, Lufthansa, Manx Airlines, Newair, Ryanair, Turkmenistan. Layout: Ground Floor, First Floor and Departure Lounges
Eurohub Airlines: British Airways. Layout: Ground Floor, First Floor and Departure Lounges

Minimum transfer times
International: 45 min Domestic: 30 min

Transfer between terminals
Bus ≫10 min; Both terminals, Birmingham International rail station and National Exhibition Centre ⊘Free

INFORMATION

Flight enquiries
Airport ☎767 7798/9
Aer Lingus ☎(0645) 737747 Air Malta ☎(0345) 581195 Air UK ☎(0345) 666777 Air 2000 ☎(0161)745 4644 American Airlines ☎(0345) 789789 BASE Regional Airlines ☎(01293) 538717 British Airways ☎(0345) 222111 British Midland Airways ☎(0345) 554554 Continental Airlines ☎(0800) 776464 Crossair ☎(0345) 581333 Cyprus Airlines ☎(0171) 388 5411 Jersey European Airlines ☎(0345) 676676 Lufthansa ☎(0345) 737747 Manx Airlines ☎(0345) 256256 Newair ☎(0161) 489 2802 Ryanair ☎(0171) 435 7101 Turkmenistan ☎(0181) 746 3080

Information and help desks
Information desk Eurohub Ground Floor, Main Concourse ☎767 7502 📠782 2001 ⏱0600–2300 Airport information, Flights, Tourist information
Information Desk Main Terminal Ground Floor ☎767 5511 📠782 8802 ⏱24 hr Airport information, Flights, Tourist information

EMERGENCIES

Police Main Terminal Adjacent to terminal ☎712 6169 ⏱24 hr
Medical Main Terminal Ground Floor ☎767 7137 ⏱24 hr

AIRPORT FACILITIES

Money
Bureau de change Main Terminal Ground Floor ⏱0530–2300 May–Sept; 0530–2200 Oct–Apr
Bureau de change Main Terminal International Baggage Reclaim Hall ⏱0530–2300 May–Sept; 0530–2200 Oct–Apr
ATM Main Terminal First and Ground Floors ⏱24 hr
Bureau de change Eurohub First Floor ⏱0530–2200 Mon–Fri, 0600–2200 Sat–Sun
Bureau de change Eurohub International Baggage Reclaim Hall ⏱0530–2200 Mon–Fri, 0600–2200 Sat–Sun

Food and drink
Café/light meals Main Terminal Ground Floor ⏱Summer 24 hr; winter 0700–2200 Mon–Fri, 0900–2200 Sat, 0930–2200 Sun
Restaurant Main Terminal First Floor ⏱24 hr
Café/light meals Main Terminal First Floor ⏱Until last flight departure
Bar Main Terminal First Floor ⏱normal licensing hours
Café/light meals Main Terminal Departure Lounge ⏱24 hr
Bar Eurohub Ground Floor ⏱0530–2200
Bar Eurohub First Floor (Departure Lounges) ⏱0530–2200

Communications
Post box Main Terminal Main Concourse, Ground Floor (by information desk)

Shopping
News, Stationery & Books Main Terminal Ground Floor ⏱Summer 0600–2300; winter 0600–1900
News, Stationery & Books Main Terminal First Floor ⏱Summer 24 hr; winter 0500–2300
Pharmacy Main Terminal First Floor ⏱Summer 0530–2200; winter 0530–1900 (Mon–Fri); 0600–1900 (Sat–Sun)
News, Stationery & Books Eurohub Ground Floor ⏱0530–2200
News, Stationery & Books Eurohub Departure Lounge ⏱0530–2100 (domestic lounge); 0530–1930 (International lounge)
Duty free Main Terminal Departure Lounge ⏱24 hr
Duty free, departure Eurohub International departure Lounge ⏱ for all departing international flights.

Luggage
Trolleys/carts Main Terminal Main entrance ⏱24 hr
Trolleys/carts Main Terminal Baggage Reclaim Halls ⏱24 hr
Left luggage counter Main Terminal Main Concourse Arrival Hall, Ground Floor (by check-in desks) ⏱0700–1900
Trolleys/carts Eurohub Baggage Reclaim Halls ⏱24 hr

DISABLED TRAVELLERS

Main Terminal Adapted toilets; throughout terminal and in multi-storey car park Lifts; Ground and First Floors Special car parking; Short-stay car park; ground floor of multi-storey car park Phones adapted for the deaf; Information Desk. Minicom ☎(0121) 782 0158 Personal assistance Airport Information Desk 24 hr.
Eurohub Adapted toilets; throughout terminal and in multi-storey car park Lifts; Ground and First Floors Special car parking; Short-stay car park; ground floor of multi-storey car park Phones adapted for the deaf; Personal assistance Staff on the information desk can sign.

SMOKING POLICY

Main Terminal Permitted on First Floor, adjacent to pub
Main Terminal Permitted in Granary Buffet area

SECTION TWO • AIRPORT DIRECTORY — BIRMINGHAM

Main Terminal Permitted in Departure Lounges where marked
Eurohub Permitted in Departure Lounges and Main Concourse

SPECIAL PASSENGER LOUNGES

Executive Lounges Main Terminal Departure Lounge
British Airways Executive Club Lounge Eurohub Departure Lounges

CONFERENCE AND BUSINESS FACILITIES

Business Centre, Eurohub ℂ ℻780 3622 ⏲ Telephones, Fax service, Power points, Photocopier, Secretarial service.

AIRPORT HOTELS

Forte Posthouse Birmingham Airport ℂ782 8141 ℻782 2476
Novotel Birmingham Airport ℂ782 7000 ℻782 0445

CAR RENTAL

Alamo Main Terminal Ground Floor Main Concourse Arrival Hall ℂ767 8130
Avis Main Terminal Ground Floor Main Concourse Arrival Hall ℂ782 6183
EuroDollar Main Terminal Ground Floor Main Concourse Arrival Hall ℂ782 5481
EuropCar Main Terminal Ground Floor Main Concourse Arrival Hall ℂ782 6507
Hertz Main Terminal Ground Floor Main Concourse Arrival Hall ℂ782 5158
Avis Eurohub Ground Floor Main Concourse Arrival Hall ℂ782 6183
EuropCar Eurohub Ground Floor Main Concourse Arrival Hall ℂ782 6507
Hertz Eurohub Ground Floor Main Concourse Arrival Hall ℂ782 5158

CAR PARKING

Long-stay Multi-storey car park 1989 spaces ⌀GBP1.20 per hr; GBP5.50 per 24 hr
Off-airport Adjacent to Eurohub Terminal NCP Ltd 3997 spaces ⌀GBP2.10 per 8 hr; GBP4.00 per 24 hr
Short-stay Opposite terminal building 357 spaces ⌀GBP1.20 per hr; GBP20.00 per 24 hr

TAXIS AND CHAUFFEUR-DRIVEN CARS

Taxis
At entrance to both terminals ℂ782 3744 City centre ⏱20 min ⌀GBP11

PUBLIC TRANSPORT

Airport to airport
London-Gatwick Airport 🚌National Express 225. For information ℂ0990 808080
London-Heathrow Airport 🚌National Express 225. For information ℂ0990 808080
London-Luton Airport 🚌National Express 325. For information ℂ0990 808080
Manchester Airport 🚌National Express 325. For information ℂ0990 808080

City & suburbs
Birmingham (UK) city centre (St Martin's Circus) 🚌West Midlands Travel 900 »20 min ⏲0453–0003 Mon–Sat; 0759–0003 Sun ⏱30 min. For information ℂ (0121) 200 2700

Other towns and cities

Coventry 🚌West Midland Travel: 900 »20 min ⏲0555–0100 Mon–Sat; 0655–0100 Sun ⏱30 min. For information ℂ (0121) 200 2700
Coventry 🚆 »1 hr ⏲0716–2052 Mon–Sat; 1623–1921 Sun ⏱15 min
Leicester 🚆Leicesterline X66 »2 hr (3 hr Sun) ⏲0840–1948 Mon–Sat; 1120–2020 Sun ⏱1 hr 30 min. For information ℂ (0116) 251 1411
London 🚆InterCity »30 min ⏲0555–2300 Mon–Sat; 1611–2300 Sun ⏱85 min
Manchester (UK) 🚆North West Regional Railways »Approx. every 40 min ⏲0555–2300 Mon–Sat; 1611–2300 Sun ⏱Approx. 2 hr
Sheffield city centre 🚆 »Twice daily; once only Sun ⏲1243 and 1525 Mon–Sat; 1640 Sun ⏱2 hr
Walsall 🚌West Midland Travel: 966 »30 min Mon–Sat; 1 hr Sun ⏲0630–2300 Mon–Sat; 1000–2300 Sun ⏱1 hr 20 min
Wolverhampton city centre 🚆 »1 hr ⏲0808–0119 Mon–Sat; 1634–0120 Sun ⏱40 min
York (UK) 🚆 »Twice daily; once only Sun ⏲1243 and 1525 Mon–Sat; 1640 Sun ⏱2 hr 30 min

REGIONAL AIR CONNECTIONS

Belfast ✈ »Several per day ⏱55 min
Dublin ✈ »Several per day ⏱1 hr
Edinburgh ✈ »Several per day ⏱1 hr
Jersey ✈ »At least daily ⏱55 min

TRAVELLER'S NOTES

It may be hard to find accommodation in the city during major events at the National Exhibition Centre.

✈ Air 🚆 Rail 🚌 Bus 🚐 Limousine 🚇 Metro/subway 🚋 Tram 🚁 Helicopter ⛴ Water transport • For map symbols, see p. 9

BOGOTA   BOG

Colombia (see p. 20)

National ✆ code: 57
Area ✆ code: 01
Local time: Winter GMT-5, Summer GMT-5
Bogota International Airport, Bogota, Colombia
✆266 9200
🖷263 9645
Location: 11 km/6½ miles NW of Bogota

TERMINALS AND TRANSFERS

Terminals
Main Terminal Airlines: All airlines

Minimum transfer times
International: 1 hr 30 min Domestic: 20 min

INFORMATION

Information and help desks
ANATO Main Terminal First floor ✆413 8972 🖷 ⏱0700–2000 Mon–Sat, *Tourist Information*
Corporacion Nacional de Turismo Main Terminal Second floor ✆413 8093/413 9202 ⏱0700–2000 Mon–Fri; 0700–1430 Sat–Sun, *Tourist Information*
Instituto Distrital de Cultura y Turismo Main Terminal First floor ✆413 9063 ⏱0700–1800, *Tourist Information*

AIRPORT FACILITIES

Money
Bank Main Terminal First Floor
⏱0700–1800

Food and drink
Bar Main Terminal Second Floor
⏱1200–2100
Café/light meals Main Terminal Second Floor ⏱0900–2130 Mon–Sat; 1000–1800 Sun
Restaurant Main Terminal ⏱0500–2200
Restaurant Main Terminal Second Floor ⏱0700–2000 Mon–Sat; 0800–1500 Sun

Communications
Post office Main Terminal Puente Aereo ⏱0700–2100 Mon–Fri; 0700–1900 Sat

Shopping
Duty free, departure Main Terminal International platform ⏱0730–2000

Luggage
Left Luggage Counter Main Terminal First Floor ⏱24 hr

DISABLED TRAVELLERS
Main Terminal Adapted toilets *First and Second Floors*

SPECIAL PASSENGER LOUNGES
American Airlines Lounge Main Terminal
Avianca Colombian Airlines Lounge Main Terminal
Lufthansa Lounge Main Terminal

CAR RENTAL
Avis Main Terminal
Dollar Main Terminal
Hertz Main Terminal
National Main Terminal

CAR PARKING
Long-stay ◇COP34;100 per week
Off-airport ◇COP200 per hr plus COP500 for service
Short-stay ◇COP200 per hr; COP5300 per day

TAXIS AND CHAUFFEUR-DRIVEN CARS

Taxis
Exit 6 International Terminal ✆413 8726/413 9528 City centre ◇COP18

PUBLIC TRANSPORT

City & suburbs
Bogota city centre 🚆 »15 min
⏱0520–2200 ⊃30 min ◇COP150 (day); COP160 (night).

REGIONAL AIR CONNECTIONS
Armenia (Colombia) ✈ »Several per week ⊃50 min
Barrabermeja ✈ »At least daily ⊃57 min
Bucaramanga ✈ »At least daily ⊃1 hr
Cali ✈ »Several per day ⊃50 min
El Yopal ✈ »Several per week ⊃50 min
Ibague ✈ »Several per week ⊃30 min
Neiva ✈ »Several per week ⊃50 min
Pereira ✈ »Several per week ⊃50 min

TRAVELLER'S NOTES
A tax of USD20 is payable for all departures. Avoid unofficial taxis. Registered taxis are found at the left side of the main terminal: a policeman notes the number and gives out a paper stating the fare. Be cautious if out in the city centre in the evening.

✆ Phone no. 🖷 Fax no. ⏱ Hours of opening/operation » Frequency of service ⊃ Journey time ◇ Cost/one-way fare

✈ SECTION TWO • AIRPORT DIRECTORY   BOSTON

BOSTON   BOS

USA (see page 41)

National ✆ code: 1
Area ✆ code: 617
Local time: Winter GMT-5, Summer GMT-4
Boston/Logan International Airport, East Boston, MA 02128, USA
✆561 1800
📠561 1830
Internet e-mail: massport.com
WWW site: http//www.massport.com/logan
Location: 5 km/3 miles NE of Boston

TERMINALS AND TRANSFERS

Terminals
Terminal A Airlines: Cape Air, Colgan Air, Continental Airlines, Frontier Airlines, Midwest Express, Spirit Airlines, US Airways Shuttle (La Guardia, N.Y. only). Layout: Upper Level: Gates 1–12, A, B; Lower Level: baggage reclaim, car rental, ground transportation
Terminal B Airlines: America West Airlines, American Airlines (Except international arrivals), American Eagle, Canadian Airlines, Delta Shuttle (La Guardia, N.Y. only), Midway Airlines, Qantas, US Airways (except international arrivals), US Airways Express, Virgin Atlantic (departures only). Layout: Upper Level: Gates 1–27; Lower Level: baggage reclaim, car rental, ground transportation
Terminal C Airlines: Business Express/Delta Connection, Comair, Delta Airlines, Delta Express, Sabena World Airlines (departures only), TW Express, TWA, United Airlines, United Express. Layout: Upper Level: Gates 11–21, 25–36, 40–43; Lower Level: baggage reclaim, car rental, ground transportation
Terminal D Airlines: All charter flights, Air Trans, Alitalia (departures only). Layout: Upper Level: boarding gates; Lower Level: baggage reclaim, car rental, ground transportation
Terminal E Airlines: Aer Lingus, Air Alliance, Air Atlantic, Air Canada, Air Nova, Alitalia (International arrivals only), American (International arrivals only), ATA, British Airways, Icelandair, KLM, Korean Air, Lufthansa, Northwest, Olympic, Sabena (International arrivals only), Swissair, TAP Air Portugal, US Airways (International arrivals only), Virgin Atlantic (International arrivals only). Layout: Upper Level: Customs, Gates 1–8; Lower Level: immigration, baggage reclaim, car rental, ground transportation

Minimum transfer times
International: 1 hr 30 min Domestic: 30 min - 1hr

Transfer between terminals
Bus 》8–12 min ⓘ0530-0100; All terminals and airport subway station (Bus 11 does not serve the Airport 🚇MBTA: Blue Line station) ⌀Free

INFORMATION

Information and help desks
Information Desk Terminal A Lower Level ⓘ0730–2300 Airport, Tourist Information
Information Desk Terminal C Lower Level ⓘ0730–2300 Airport, Tourist Information
Information Desk Terminal E Lower Level ⓘ1000–2130 (Winter season), ⓘ0730–2300 or until last international arrival (Summer peak season) Airport, Tourist Information
Meegan Services Terminal C ✆569 3800 Hotel booking
Meegan Services Terminal E ✆569 3800 Hotel booking

EMERGENCIES

Lost Property ✆561 1714
Medical Logan Office Center

AIRPORT FACILITIES

Money
ATM All Terminals throughout
Bank Terminal D Lower Level ⓘ1000–1600 Mon–Fri
Bureau de change Terminal B Lower Level ⓘ0730–0930, 1430–2030 (depending on flight activity)
Bureau de change Terminal C Lower Level ⓘ0800–1900
Bureau de change Terminal E Lower Level ⓘ0800–2130 Mon–Fri; 1130–2130 Sat, Sun

Food and drink
Bar Terminal A Upper Level
Bar Terminal E Upper Level
Café/light meals All Terminals Upper Level
Restaurant Terminal B Upper Level
Restaurant Terminal C Upper Level
Restaurant Terminal E Upper Level

Communications
Fax All Terminals throughout
Post box All Terminals throughout

Shopping
Duty free, departure Terminal C Upper Level
Duty free, departure Terminal E Upper Level
Gift Shop All Terminals Upper Level
Hairdresser Terminal C Upper Level
News, Stationery & Books All Terminals Upper Level
Shopping Mall Terminal C

Luggage
Left Luggage Counter All Terminals Airline baggage offices
Lockers All Terminals Beyond security control
Trolleys/carts Terminal E Customs Area ⌀Free

DISABLED TRAVELLERS

All Terminals Adapted toilets; Lifts; Phones adapted for the deaf.

SMOKING POLICY

All Terminals No Smoking except in designated areas outside of terminals.

SPECIAL PASSENGER LOUNGES

Aer Lingus Gold Circle Club Lounge Terminal E, above Aer Lingus ticket counter
American Airlines Admirals Club Lounge Terminal B Upper Level
British Airways Executive Club Lounge Terminal E
British Airways First Class Lounge Terminal E
Continental Airlines President's Club Lounge Terminal A, near gates 3–6
Delta Airlines Crown Room Terminal C, near gate 26
Delta Shuttle Business Club Terminal C
Lufthansa Lounge Terminal E, above British Airways ticket counter

BOSTON

SECTION TWO • AIRPORT DIRECTORY

Boston Logan International

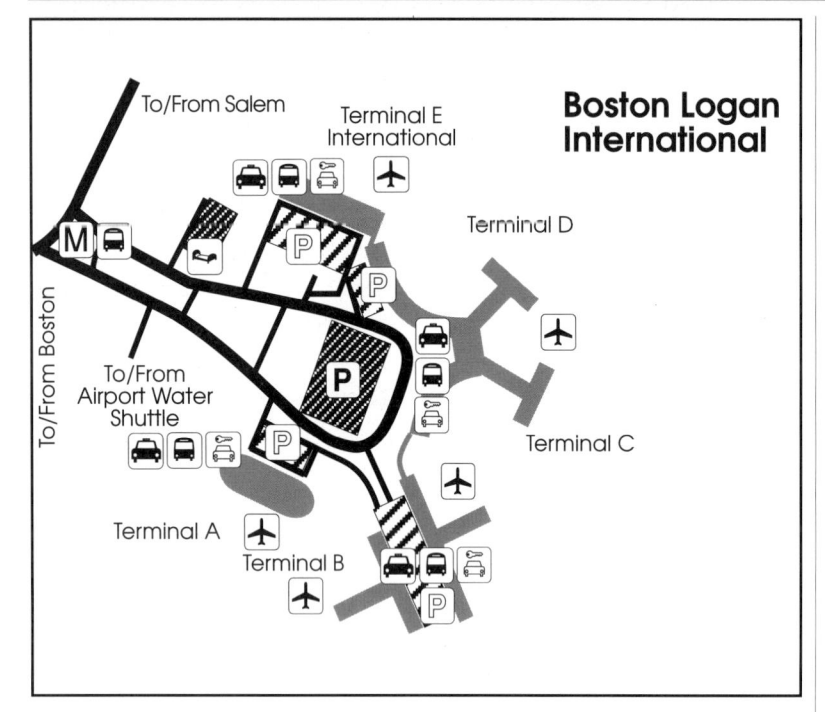

(Map showing terminals A, B, C, D, E; To/From Salem; To/From Boston; To/From Airport Water Shuttle; parking areas marked P)

Northwest Airlines World Club Terminal E near gates 1–3
Swissair Lounge Terminal E
TWA Ambassador Club Terminal C, pier B
United Airlines Red Carpet Room Terminal C, near gates 40–41
US Airways Club Terminal B, near gates 1–3
Virgin Atlantic Upper Class Lounge Terminal B, near gates 41–42

CONFERENCE AND BUSINESS FACILITIES

Airport Hotels
Harborside Hyatt ℂ568 1234 ℱ567 8856 270 rooms Courtesy bus
Holiday Inn ℂ569 5250 ℱ569 5159 351 rooms Courtesy bus
Logan Airport Ramada ℂ569 9300 ℱ569 3981 542 rooms Courtesy bus

CAR RENTAL

Alamo All Terminals Lower Level ℂ561 4101
Avis All Terminals Lower Level ℂ561 3517
Dollar All Terminals Lower Level ℂ569 5300
Hertz All Terminals Lower Level ℂ569 7272
National All Terminals Lower Level ℂ569 7070
Thrifty All Terminals Lower Level ℂ634 7355

CAR PARKING

Long-stay Central Parking Garage ⊘USD 18 per day; USD 18 per day thereafter; USD 70 per week max
Long-stay Satellite Lots Free shuttle bus ≫10 min ⊘USD12 day; USD50 per week max
Short-stay Next to all terminals ⊘USD4 per hr; USD2 per hr thereafter

TAXIS AND CHAUFFEUR-DRIVEN CARS

Taxis
Outside all terminals City centre ↻20–25 min ⊘USD10–18

PUBLIC TRANSPORT

City & suburbs
Boston (downtown hotels) ⇌ City Transportation ≫30 min ⊕0715–2115 ⊘USD7.50.
Boston city centre ⌥MBTA: Blue Line ≫4–12 min ⊕0530–0030 ↻7 min ⊘USD0.85. Free Massport shuttle buses connect all terminals with Airport station every 8–12 min 0530–0100
Boston city centre (South rail stn) ⇌ Logan Link: ≫15 min ⊕0555–2315 ↻15–30 min ⊘USD6. For Amtrak and southside MBTA commuter rail, Bonanza Bus Lines, C & J Trailways, Concord Trailways, Peter Pan Trailways, Plymouth & Brockton and Vermont Transit buses. Board at bus stops at lower level of all terminals. Look for "South Station" card in bus window.
Boston city centre (North rail stn) ⌥ MBTA: Blue Line ≫4–8 min ⊕0530–0030 ↻15 min ⊘USD0.85. For northside MBTA commuter rail. Transfer to Orange Line at State.
Boston city centre (Rowes Wharf) w Airport Water Shuttle ≫15–30 min ⊕0600–2000 Mon–Thurs, ⊕0600–2300 Fri, ⊕1000–2300 Sat, 1000–2000 Sun j7 min ⊘USD8. Free shuttle buses operate between the airport ferry dock and all airport terminals.
Boston city centre (more than 10 landings in Boston Harbor) ⛵ Airport Water Taxi ℂ422 0392 ⊘USD10. Free shuttle buses operate between the airport ferry dock and all airport terminals. For World Trade Center, Anthony's Pier 4, Museum Wharf, Long Wharf, Burrough's Wharf in the North End, Pier 4 in Charlestown, and North Station pier at Beverly Street. Free shuttle buses operate between the airport ferry dock and all airport terminals.
Boston city centre ⇌ Over 30 companies at airport.

Other towns and cities
Andover MA ⇌ Flight Line ≫ On-call ⊕24 hr ⊘USD22–24. For Chelmsford, Haverhill, Lawrence, Lowell, Methuen and Tewksbury MA
Bangor ME ⇌ Concord Trailways ≫3 day ⊕0915; 1315;1715 ↻5 hr 15 min. For Portland ME
Bangor ME (Maine Coast) ⇌ Concord Trailways ≫2 day ⊕1115; 1515 ↻7 hr. For Portland, Brunswick, Bath, Wiscasset, Damariscotta, Waldboro, Rockland, Camden/Rockport, Lincolnville, Belfast and Searsport ME
Bedford MA ⇌ M and L Transportation ≫ On-call ⊘USD15–18. For Burlington, Chelmsford, Lowell and Woburn MA
Berlin NH ⇌ Concord Trailways ≫1 day ⊕1615 ↻5 hr 10 min.
Braintree MA (MBTA Red Line Stn) ⇌ Logan Express ≫30 min ⊕0630–2400 ⊘USD6-8.
Concord NH ⇌ Concord Trailways ≫1–2 hr ⊕0715–2130 ↻2 hr 15 min. For Manchester NH
Conway NH ⇌ Concord Trailways ≫2 day ⊕0915; 1615 ↻4 hr 10 min. For Meredith NH
Dover NH ⇌ C & J Trailways ≫1–2 hr ⊕0730–2245 ↻1 hr 45 min ⊘USD17. For Newburyport MA and Portsmouth NH
Durham NH ⇌ C & J Trailways ≫3 day ⊕0915; 1315; 2015 ↻2 hr ⊘USD17.
Framingham MA ⇌ Logan Express ≫30 min ⊕0630–2400 ⊘USD6-8
Hyannis MA ⇌ Plymouth & Brockton ≫1 hr ⊕0745–2315 ↻2 hr For Plymouth,

---

ℂ Phone no. ℱ Fax no. ⊕ Hours of opening/operation ≫ Frequency of service ↻ Journey time ⊘ Cost/one-way fare

✈ **SECTION TWO • AIRPORT DIRECTORY**   **BOSTON**

Barnstable MA and Steamship Authority Docks
Laconia NH 🚌 Concord Trailways ≫2–3 day ⏱0915; 1215; 1930 (Fri and Sun only) ➲3 hr
Littleton NH 🚌 Concord Trailways ≫1 day ⏱1515 ➲4 hr 15 min. For Franconia and Lincoln NH
Manchester NH l Flight Line ≫ On-call ⏱24 hr ⊘USD22–26. For Merrimack, Nashua and Salem NH
Nashua NH l M and L Transportation ≫ On-call ⊘USD21–22. For Merrimack NH
Portland ME 🚌 Concord Trailways ≫2 hr ⏱0715–2130 ➲2 hr 45 min
Plymouth NH 🚌 Concord Trailways ≫2 day ⏱1015; 1515 ➲3 hr 15 min.
Provincetown MA 🚌 Plymouth & Brockton ≫3 per day ⏱0845; 1145; 1445; 1645 (Sat only) ➲4 hr. For Orleans MA
Providence RI 🚌 Bonanza Bus Lines ≫2 hr ⏱0730–2400 ➲1 hr 30 min
For Foxboro MA and Pawtucket RI
Woburn MA 🚌 Logan Express ≫30 min ⏱0630–2400 ⊘USD6.
Woods Hole MA 🚌 Bonanza Bus Lines ≫2–3 hr ⏱0715–2130 ➲2 hr 20 min
For Bourne, Otis Air Force Base and Falmouth MA and Steamship Authority

REGIONAL AIR CONNECTIONS

Albany NY ✈ ≫Several per day ➲50 min
Augusta ME ✈ ≫Several per day ➲50 min
Bangor ME ✈ ≫Several per day ➲1 hr
Burlington VT ✈ ≫Several per day ➲1 hr
Halifax NS ✈ ≫Several per day ➲1 hr
Hartford CT ✈ ≫Several per day ➲45 min
Hyannis MA ✈ ≫Several per day ➲35 min
Lebanon NH ✈ ≫Several per day ➲50 min
Long Island, NY ✈ ≫Several per day ➲55 min
Manchester, NH ✈ ≫Several per day ➲30 min
Martha's Vineyard, MA ✈ ≫Several per day ➲35 min
Nantucket MA ✈ ≫Several per day ➲45 min
Newburgh NY ✈ ≫Several per day ➲1 hr
Portland ME ✈ ≫Several per day ➲40 min
Provincetown MA ✈ ≫Several per day ➲35 min
Rockland ME ✈ ≫Several per day ➲55 min
St John NB ✈ ≫Several per day ➲j25 min
Westchester County NY ✈ ≫Several per day ➲1 hr

TRAVELLER'S NOTES

Located just 5 km/3 miles from the city centre, Logan is just minutes away from Boston's historic landmarks. Logan's five terminals are connected via walkways and a free intra-terminal bus system. The quickest way to the city centre is via intra-terminal bus to the mMBTA Blue Line or water shuttles; taxis/cars can take a great deal longer if traffic is heavy.

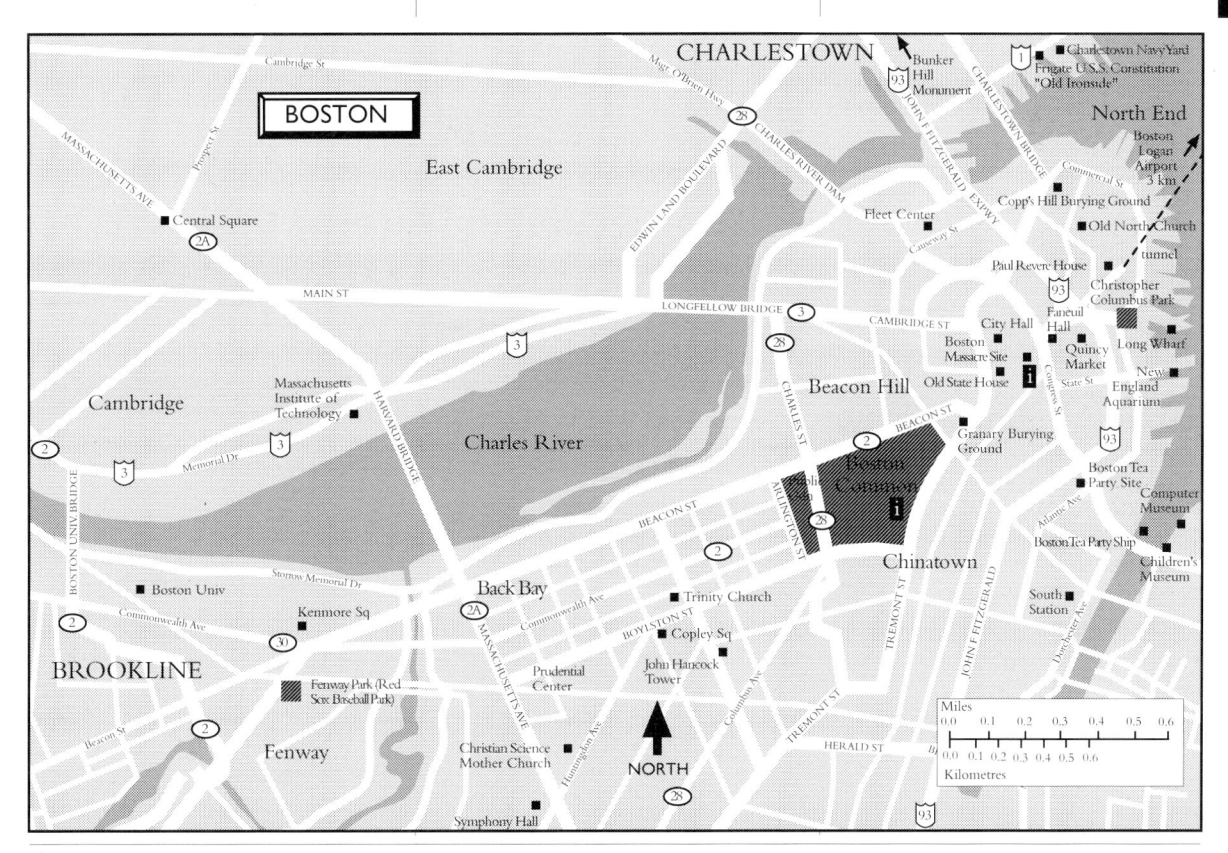

✈ Air 🚆 Rail 🚌 Bus 🚘 Limousine Ⓜ Metro/subway 🚋 Tram 🚁 Helicopter ⛴ Water transport • For map symbols, see p. 9

BRIDGETOWN   BGI

Barbados (see page 16)

National ☎ code: 1
Area ☎ code: 809
Local time: Winter GMT-4,
Summer GMT-4
Grantley Adams International
Airport, Christ Church, Barbados
☎ 428 7101
📠 420 7069
Internet e-mail:
adamsair@sunbeachnet
Location: 14 km/8½ miles E of
Bridgetown

TERMINALS AND TRANSFERS

Terminals
Main Terminal Airlines: All airlines. Layout: First Floor Arrivals, Ground Floor Departures

Minimum transfer times
International: 1 hr–1 hr 15 min Domestic: 20 min

INFORMATION

Flight enquiries
Airport ☎428 7107 ext 4605 (0800-2000)

Information and help desks
Tourist Information Desk Main Terminal Departure and Arrival Halls (2 desks) ☎428 7101 ext 4636 ☎428 0937 ⏰0800–last flight *Tourist information*

EMERGENCIES

Police Main Terminal ☎428 0929
Medical Main Terminal ☎428 0918

Money
Bank Main Terminal Departure lounge ⏰0800–last flight

Food and drink
Bar Main Terminal throughout ⏰Until last flight departure
Café/light meals Main Terminal throughout ⏰Until last flight departure
Restaurant Main Terminal ⏰Until last flight departure

Communications
Post office Main Terminal Mezzanine Level ⏰0800–1500 Mon–Fri

Shopping
Duty free, arrival Main Terminal Arrival Hall
Duty free, departure Main Terminal Departure Hall
Shopping mall Main Terminal Departure Hall ⏰Until last flight departure
Pharmacy Main Terminal Departure Hall ⏰0730–1100

DISABLED TRAVELLERS

Main Terminal Adapted toilets; Lifts

Main Terminal Restricted

SPECIAL PASSENGER LOUNGES

British Airways Club Caribbean Lounge Main Terminal
British Airways Executive Club Lounge Main Terminal
BWIA International BWA Lounge Main Terminal

CONFERENCE AND BUSINESS FACILITIES

Conference Room Main Terminal, Mezzanine Floor ⏰Open on request ☎428 8339/0982 📠420 7069

CAR RENTAL

Barbados Rent A Car Main Terminal ☎428 0960

Courtesy Rent-a-car Main Terminal North of Arrivals Hall ☎420 7153

CAR PARKING

Long-stay North of Main terminal spaces ⊘BBD4.50
Short-stay North of Main Terminal spaces ⊘BBD0.75 per hr; BBD4.50 per day

TAXIS AND CHAUFFEUR-DRIVEN CARS

Taxis
☎428 7101 City centre ➔Approx 30 min ⊘BBD28

PUBLIC TRANSPORT

City & suburbs
Bridgetown centre 🚌 » ⏰0500–2300 ➔45 min ⊘BBD1.50.

REGIONAL AIR CONNECTIONS

Dominica Cane Field ✈ »Several per week ➔55 min
Grenada ✈ »Several per day ➔50 min
Port of Spain ✈ »Several per day ➔55 min
St Lucia Vigie Apt ✈ »Several per day ➔35–45 min
St Vincent ✈ »Several per day ➔40 min

AIRPORT TAXES

A tax of BBD25 is payable upon departure.

TRAVELLER'S NOTES

If travelling onward to the smaller Caribbean Islands, reconfirm the journey as soon as possible. For souvenirs, there are duty-free shops centred around Broad Street in Bridgetown.

☎ Phone no. 📠 Fax no. ⏰ Hours of opening/operation » Frequency of service ➔ Journey time ⊘ Cost/one-way fare

SECTION TWO • AIRPORT DIRECTORY   BRISTOL

BRISTOL   BRS

United Kingdom (see page 41)

National ☎ code: 44
Area ☎ code: 01275
Local time: Winter GMT, Summer GMT+1
Address: Bristol International Airport, Bristol, BS19 3DY
☎: 474444
℻: 474800
Location: 13 km/8 miles S of Bristol

Terminals and Transfers

Terminals
Main Terminal British Airways, Aer Lingus, Ryanair, Isle of Scilly Skybus, Jersey European Airways, KLM, Sabena Airways

Information

Information and help desks
Airport and Tourist Information Desk ☎ 474444
Airport information, tourist information, hotel booking, travel information

Airport Facilities

Money
Thomas Cook Bureau de Change Main concourse ☎ 474535
Thomas Cook Bureau de Change Departure lounge ☎ 474535
ATM Main concourse

Food and drink
Bar First floor. ⏰ vary daily
Café/light meals Domestic and international departure lounges
Restaurant First floor. ⏰ vary daily

Communications
Post office Stamps are available from the information desk
Post box Outside terminal building
Fax service Airport and tourist information desk

Shopping
Duty free International departure lounge
News, Stationery & Books International departure lounge
Gift Shop International departure lounge

Luggage
Trolleys/carts

Disabled Travellers
Special car parking; wheelchairs; low-level telephones; lift; disabled toilet facilities.

Special Passenger Lounges
Brunel Executive Lounge International departure lounge

Car Rental
Avis Arrivals concourse ☎ 472613
Hertz Arrivals concourse ☎ 9779777/472807
Europcar Arrivals concourse ☎ 474623

Car Parking
Long-stay ⌀ GBP2.80 per day
Short-stay ⌀ GBP1 per 2 hr; GBP3 per 2–5 hr; GBP5 per 5–12 hr; GBP6 per 12–24 hr

Taxis and Chauffeur-driven Cars
Taxis
☎ 474812. City centre ⌀ GBP12

Public Transport
City & suburbs
(Bristol Marlborough Street Bus and Coach Station)
🚌 »Frequent service ⟳ 20 min

Regional Air Connections
Plymouth ✈ »4 per week ⟳ 35 min

89

✈ Air ⛴ Rail 🚌 Bus 🚘 Limousine 🚇 Metro/subway 🚋 Tram 🚁 Helicopter 🚢 Water transport • For map symbols, see p. 9

BRUSSELS (BRUXELLES/BRUSSEL) BRU

Belgium (see page 16)

National ✆ code: 32
Area ✆ code: 02
Local time: Winter GMT+1, Summer GMT+2
Brussels National Airport, Zaventem, Belgium
WWW site: http://www.brusselsairport.be
✆753 39 13
℻753 68 92
Location: 13 km/8 miles NE of Brussels

Terminals and Transfers

Terminals
Main Terminal Airlines: All airlines.

Layout: Four Levels. Underground Level, rail station; Ground Level, Arrival/Departure; Level 1, Transit Area with shops and airport lounges; Level 2, restaurants.

Minimum transfer times
International (outside Europe): 50 min
European flights: 40 min

Transfer between terminals
Bus ≫10 min; Terminals A and B ⊘Free

Information

Flight enquiries
Airport ✆753 39 13
Aer Lingus ✆723 36 52 Air Algérie ✆720 94 17 Air Canada ✆725 39 40 Air France ✆720 71 58 Air Lanka ✆722 31 32 Air Malta ✆723 06 66 Air Portugal TAP ✆720 02 03 Air UK ✆720 71 43 Alitalia ✆720 44 12 All Nippon Airways ✆722 30 10 American Airlines ✆725 35 50 Austrian Airlines ✆722 30 64 Balkan Bulgarian Airlines ✆720 39 37 British Airways ✆723 03 11 British Midland Airways ✆722 38 31 China Airlines ✆722 36 72 CSA Czechoslovak ✆721 12 64 Delta Airlines ✆722 38 02 Egyptair ✆722 30 69 El Al Israel Airlines ✆722 31 54 Finnair ✆725 08 80 Garuda Indonesian Airlines ✆721 18 40 Iberia ✆720 21 06 Jat Yugoslav Airlines ✆722 38 72 KLM ✆720 71 43 Lot Polish Airlines ✆751 89 57 Lufthansa ✆720 22 26 Malaysian

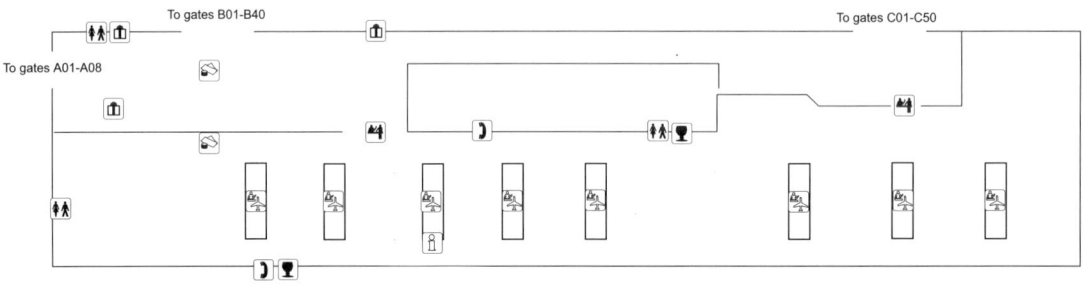

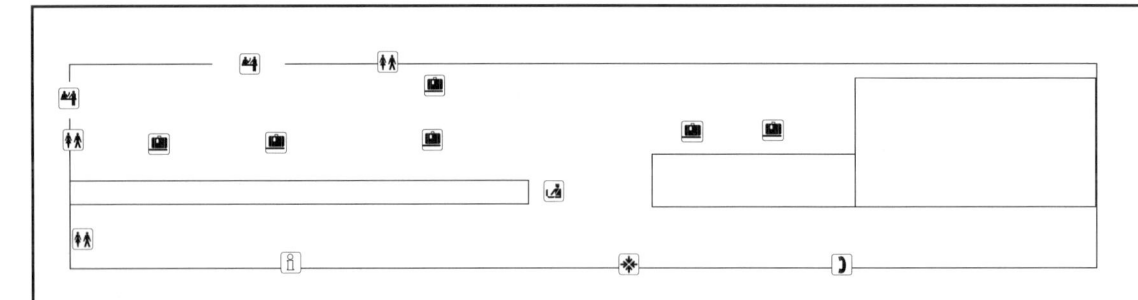

BRUSSELS NATIONAL AIRPORT — Departures Level

To gates A01-A08 | To gates B01-B40 | To gates C01-C50

BRUSSELS NATIONAL AIRPORT — Arrivals Level

✆ Phone no. ℻ Fax no. ⊕ Hours of opening/operation ≫ Frequency of service ↻ Journey time ⊘ Cost/one-way fare

SECTION TWO • AIRPORT DIRECTORY — BRUSSELS

Airlines ✆722 36 16 Malev Hungarian ✆722 30 09 Meridiana ✆723 60 28 Olympic Airways ✆722 30 21 Royal Air Maroc ✆722 31 14 Royal Jordanian Airlines ✆720 91 08 Sabena ✆723 60 28 Saudia ✆722 36 57 Singapore Airlines ✆722 35 75 Swissair ✆720 91 26 Tarom Romanian Air ✆723 33 31 Thai Airways ✆725 98 33 Tunis Air ✆720 36 78 Turkish Airlines ✆722 31 95 United Airlines ✆722 46 43

Information and help desks
Information Desk Main Terminal Departures Hall
Belgium Tourist Board Main Terminal Arrivals Hall ⏰All flight times Hotel booking, Tourist information

EMERGENCIES
Police ✆753 70 00 ⏰24 hr
Medical Contact airport staff

AIRPORT FACILITIES

Money
Bank Main Terminal ✆720 74 72
Bank Main Terminal ✆753 23 70
Bank Main Terminal ✆720 16 82
ATM Main Terminal Arrivals Hall

Food and drink
Bar Main Terminal throughout ⏰ all flight times
Café/light meals Main Terminal throughout ⏰ all flight times
Restaurant Main Terminal throughout ⏰ all flight times

Communications
Post box Main Terminal Arrivals Hall ⏰0900–1700 Mon-Fri
Fax/Internet Service Airport Forum Arrivals Hall ✆ 753 20 47

Shopping
Duty free Main Terminal ⏰ All flight times
Shopping mall Main Terminal airside ⏰ All flight times
Shopping mall Main Terminal transit area ⏰All flight times

Luggage
Lockers Level 0
Trolleys/carts ⏰24 hr ◇ free

DISABLED TRAVELLERS
Adapted toilets; Lifts; Special car parking

SPECIAL PASSENGER LOUNGES
Diners Club Lounge Above Satellite Pier Diners Club cardholders and guests
American Airlines Admiral's Club Lounge Above Satellite Pier Club members, First and Business class passengers
British Airways Executive Club Lounge Along corridor towards Gates B1–40 Club members, First and Business class passengers
British Airways Executive Club Lounge Above Satellite Pier Club members, First and Business class passengers
Sabena Lounge Club members, First class/Business class passengers
Sabena Lounge Level 1 between main Transit Area and Satellite First class passengers and Business class passengers
SAS Lounge Above Satellite Pier Royal Viking Club members, First and Euroclass passengers
Swissair Lounge Above Satellite Pier Club members, First and Business class passengers

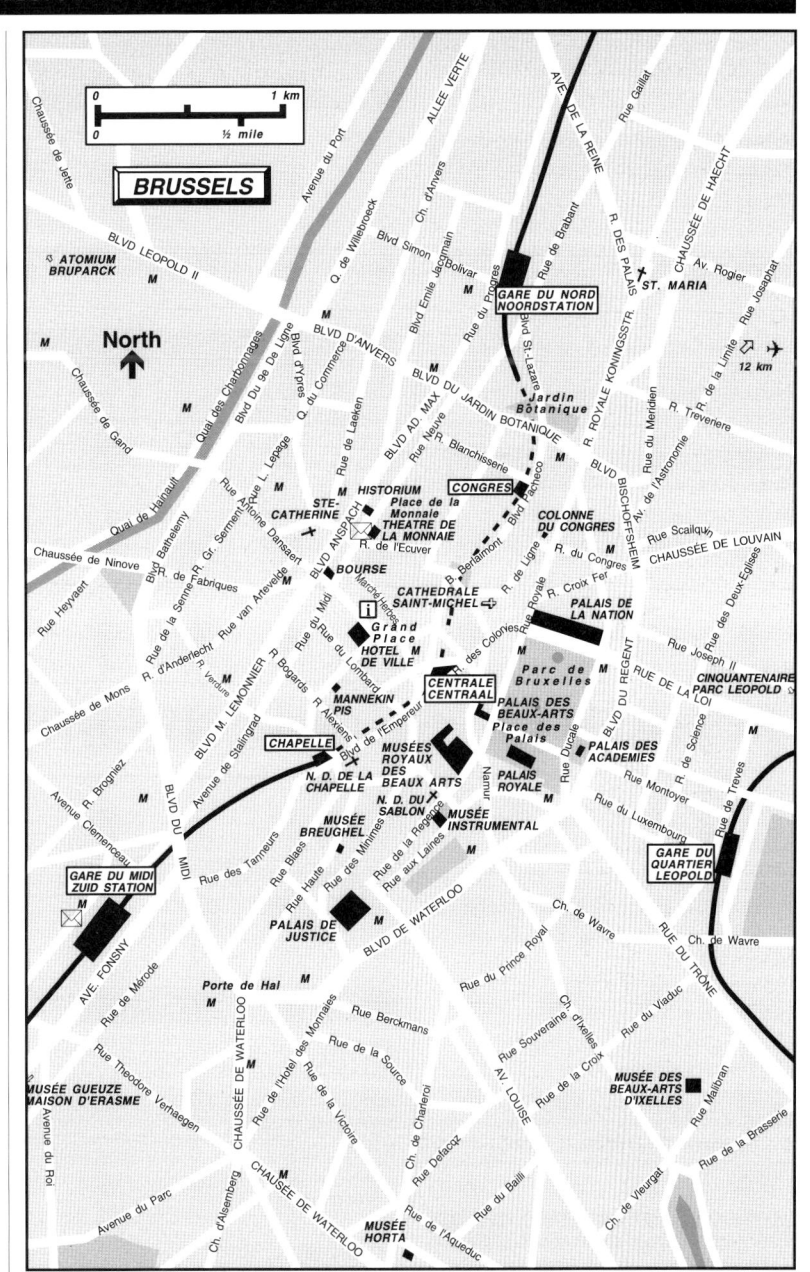

CONFERENCE AND BUSINESS FACILITIES
Skyport Corporate Meeting Centre, Promenade/landside of Shopping Mall, ✆714 02 00 ℻714 02 01 ⏰All flight times Telephones, Fax service, Photocopier

---
✈ Air 🚆 Rail 🚌 Bus 🚐 Limousine Ⓜ Metro/subway 🚋 Tram 🚁 Helicopter ⛴ Water transport • For map symbols, see p. 9

BRUSSELS • BUCHAREST   SECTION TWO • AIRPORT DIRECTORY

AIRPORT HOTELS
Sheraton ℂ 725 10 00 ℱ 725 11 55

CAR RENTAL
Alamo Ground Level Arrival Hall ℂ753 20 60
Avis Ground Level Arrival Hall ℂ720 09 44
Budget Ground Level Arrival Hall ℂ753 21 70
EuropCar Ground Level Arrival Hall ℂ721 05 92
Hertz Ground Level Arrival Hall ℂ 720 60 44

CAR PARKING
Long-stay Outside Departure Hall ⊘BEF370 per 24 hr

TAXIS AND CHAUFFEUR-DRIVEN CARS
Taxis
Ground Level Arrival Hall City centre ⊃20min ⊘BEF1000

Chauffeur-driven cars
Ground Level Arrival Hall ℂ 725 13 13
Public Transport

PUBLIC TRANSPORT
City & suburbs
Brussels (Nord/Noord rail stn) 🚌 De Lijn ≫ 1 hr ⊕0620–2305 ⊃35 min ⊘BEF65.
Brussels (Centrale/Centraal rail stn) 🚌 SNCB ≫30 min ⊕0542–2356 ⊃15 min ⊘BEF85.

Other towns and cities
Antwerp 🚌 Sabena ≫1 hr ⊕0700–2300 ⊃50 min ⊘BEF220.

REGIONAL AIR CONNECTIONS
Amsterdam ✈ ≫Several per day ⊃40 min
Düsseldorf ✈ ≫Several per day ⊃40 min
Frankfurt ✈ ≫Several per day ⊃1 hr
Le Havre ✈ ≫Several per week ⊃1 hr 5 min
London ✈ ≫Several per week ⊃1 hr–1 hr 10 min
Luxembourg ✈ ≫Several per day ⊃45 min
Paris ✈ ≫Several per week ⊃35 min–1 hr
Southampton ✈ ≫Several per week ⊃1 hr 5 min
Strasbourg ✈ ≫At least daily ⊃1 hr 5 min

TRAVELLER'S NOTES
Airport rail station is Nationaal (do not alight at Zaventem station). Use only metered taxis; the tip is included in the fare. If buying Belgian lace, check its origin: much of the lace on sale is made in the Far East.

BUCHAREST (BUCURESTI) OTP
Romania (see page 34)

National ℂ code: 40 Area ℂ code: 1
Local time: Winter GMT+2, Summer GMT +3
Address: Bucharest Otopeni International Airport, Sos. Bucuresti-Ploiesti Km. 16, 5, Bucharest, Romania.
ℂ: 230 45 42
ℱ: 312 27 44
Location: 17km/11 mile N of Bucharest

TERMINALS AND TRANSFERS
Terminals
Main Terminal Airlines: All airlines.
Layout: Arrivals ground floor, departures first floor.

Minimum transfer times
45 min

INFORMATION
Flight enquiries
ℂ 230 16 02

Information and help desks
ℂ 230 16 02

Emergencies
Police ℂ 230 00 22
Lost Property ℂ 230 26 12

AIRPORT FACILITIES
Money
Bureau de Change Available

Food and drink
Bar Available
Café/light meals Available
Restaurant Available

Shopping
Duty free Available

Luggage
Trolleys/carts Available

DISABLED TRAVELLERS
Special toilets; buses have wheelchair access

SPECIAL PASSENGER LOUNGES
Business Class Lounge
VIP Lounge

CAR RENTAL
Rent a Car

CAR PARKING
Long-stay Available

TAXIS AND CHAUFFEUR-DRIVEN CARS
Taxis
Available

PUBLIC TRANSPORT
City & suburbs
Bucharest 🚌 ≫ 15 min ⊃30 min.

REGIONAL AIR CONNECTIONS
Arad ✈ ≫2 per day ⊃2 hr
Cluj ✈ ≫4 per day ⊃1 hr
Timisoara ✈ ≫4 per day ⊃1 hr

ℂ Phone no. ℱ Fax no. ⊕ Hours of opening/operation ≫ Frequency of service ⊃ Journey time ⊘ Cost/one-way fare

BUDAPEST   BUD

Hungary (see page 24)

National ✆ code: 36
Area ✆ code: 01
Local time: Winter GMT+1,
Summer GMT+2
Budapest Ferihegy Airport, PO Box 53, 1675 Budapest, Hungary
✆296 6300
🖷296 6982
Location: 16 km/10 miles SE of Budapest

TERMINALS AND TRANSFERS

Terminals
Terminal 1 Airlines: British Airways, Sabena, El Al, Austrian Airlines, Tunis Air, Moldavian Airlines, Air Lithuania, Aeroflot, Air Ukraine, Olympic Airways, KLM, Finnair, Air Malta, Kazakhstan Airlines, LOT, Balkan Airlines, Egypt Air, Tarom, Scandinavian Airlines, Turkish Airlines. Layout: Older terminal with all facilities on Ground Level
Terminal 2 Airlines: Malév, Swissair, Delta, Lufthansa, Air France, Czech Airlines. Layout: Modern terminal with facilities on 3 Levels and with more facilities than Terminal 1

Minimum transfer times
International: 35–45 min (2 hr El Al flights)

Transfer between terminals
Bus Terminals 1 and 2 ⌀HUF 400 Transfer charge between terminals HUF 500.

INFORMATION

Flight enquiries
Airport ✆296–9696
Aeroflot ✆ 118–5892 Air Algérie ✆ 296–8770 Air France ✆ 118 0411 Alitalia ✆ 118–6898 Austrian Airlines ✆117–1550 Balkan Bulgarian Airlines ✆117–1818 British Airways ✆118–3299 CSA Czechoslovak ✆118–3045 Delta Airlines ✆266–1400 El Al Israel Airlines ✆266–2970 Finnair ✆117 4022 Iberia ✆117 4228 KLM ✆117–4522 Lot Polish Airlines ✆117 2444 Lufthansa ✆266–4511 Malev Hungarian ✆266–5913/296–7554 Sabena World Airlines ✆118 4111 SAS ✆266–2633 Swissair ✆267–2500 Syrian Arab Airlines ✆117 9596 Tarom Romanian Air ✆166 9684

Information and help desks
Budapest Tourist Office Terminal 2 ⏱0800–1900 Hotel booking, Tourist information
Budapest Tourist Office Terminal 1 ✆296–8670/8680 ⏱0800–1900 Hotel booking, Tourist information
IBUSZ Terminal 2 ✆296–8470 ⏱0700–2100 Airport information, Flights Hotel booking, Tourist information
IBUSZ Terminal 1 ✆296–8657 ⏱0700–2100 Hotel booking, Tourist information
LRI/APS Terminal 2 ✆296–6368 ⏱24 hr Airport information Hotel booking, Tourist information
LRI/APS Terminal 1 ✆296–8555 ⏱24 hr Airport information Hotel booking, Tourist information
Malev Desk Terminal 1 ✆296–7554 ⏱24 hr Airport information, Flights
Malev Desk Terminal 2 ✆296–8406/7831/8768 ⏱24 hr Airport information, Flights

Emergencies
Police Terminal 1 Office adjacent to terminal ✆296–9696 extension 6364
Police Terminal 2 At Terminal 1 ✆296–9696 extension 8934
Medical Terminal 1 ✆296–6160
Lost Property Terminal 1 ✆296–7690 ⏱0700–2300
Lost Property Terminal 2 Desk ✆296–8108 ⏱24 hr

AIRPORT FACILITIES

Money
Bank Terminal 1 ⏱0600–2300
Bureau de change Terminal 1 Budapest Tourist Desk ⏱0600–2300
Bank Terminal 2 ⏱24 hr
Bureau de change Terminal 2 ⏱24 hr

Food and drink
Bar Terminal 1 Transit Area ⏱0700–1900
Café/light meals Terminal 1 Transit Area ⏱0700–1900
Restaurant Terminal 1 Transit Area ⏱0700–2200
Bar Terminal 2 Transit Area ⏱0630–2200
Café/light meals Terminal 2 Transit Area ⏱0630–2200
Restaurant Terminal 2 Transit Area ⏱0630–2200

Communications
Post office Terminal 1 ⏱0815–1530 Mon-Fri
Post office Terminal 2 ⏱0815–1530 Mon-Fri
Fax service Terminal 2 Post Office ⏱0815–1530

Shopping
Duty free, arrival Terminal 1 Arrival Hall ⏱0730–1800
Duty free, departure Terminal 1 Transit Area ⏱All flight times
Duty free, arrival Terminal 2 Arrival Hall ⏱0615–2100
Duty free, departure Terminal 2 Transit Area ⏱0615–2100
Florist Terminal 1 Transit Area ⏱0700–1900
Florist Terminal 2 Transit Area ⏱0700–1900
Gift Shop Terminal 1 Transit Area ⏱0700–1900
Gift Shop Terminal 2 Transit Area ⏱0700–1900
News, Stationery & Books Terminal 1 Transit Area ⏱0700–1900
News, Stationery & Books Terminal 2 Transit Area ⏱0700-1900

Luggage
Left Luggage Counter Terminal 1
Left Luggage Counter Terminal 2
Trolleys/carts Terminal 1
Trolleys/carts Terminal 2

DISABLED TRAVELLERS

Terminal 2 Adapted toilets; Lifts Personal assistance Via Service Desks

SMOKING POLICY

Terminal 1 Smoking permitted throughout
Terminal 2 Smoking permitted throughout

SPECIAL PASSENGER LOUNGES

Air France Lounge Terminal 2 Upper Level Transit Area Club members, First

BUDAPEST

SECTION TWO • AIRPORT DIRECTORY

Telephones, Fax service, Photocopier, Secretarial service, Translation/Interpretation service, Travel advice

AIRPORT HOTELS

None

CAR RENTAL

EuropCar Terminal 1 ⓟ296–6680 Terminal 2 ⓟ296 6610
Hertz Terminal 1 ⓟ296 8280 Terminal 2 ⓟ296–6988
LRI Rent a Car ⓟ296–7170

CAR PARKING

Long-stay 836 spaces ⊘HUF80 per hr; HUF560 per day
Short-stay 97 spaces ⊘HUF20 per 15 min

TAXIS AND CHAUFFEUR-DRIVEN CARS

Taxis
Outside terminals City centre ⊃15 min ⊘HUF1500–3000

Chauffeur-driven cars
Outside terminals

PUBLIC TRANSPORT

City & suburbs
Budapest city centre 🚌Centrum ≫30 min ⓞ0600–2200 ⊃15 min ⊘HUF 600.
LRI Airport Minibus, door to door, 24 hour service ⊃15 min, HUF1200.
Budapest city centre 🚇Metro. Bus no 93 to Metro Line 3 from Terminals 1/2

REGIONAL AIR CONNECTIONS

Munich ✈ ≫Several per day ⊃1hr 10 min
Prague ✈ ≫Several per day ⊃1 hr
Vienna ✈ ≫Several per day ⊃1 hr
Warsaw ✈ ≫Several per day ⊃1 hr 15 min

TRAVELLER'S NOTES

Taxis from the airport generally overcharge; take a bus instead. If using taxis in the city, have the destination written down and ensure the meter is running. Accommodation can be hardest to find mid-summer and around Christmas.

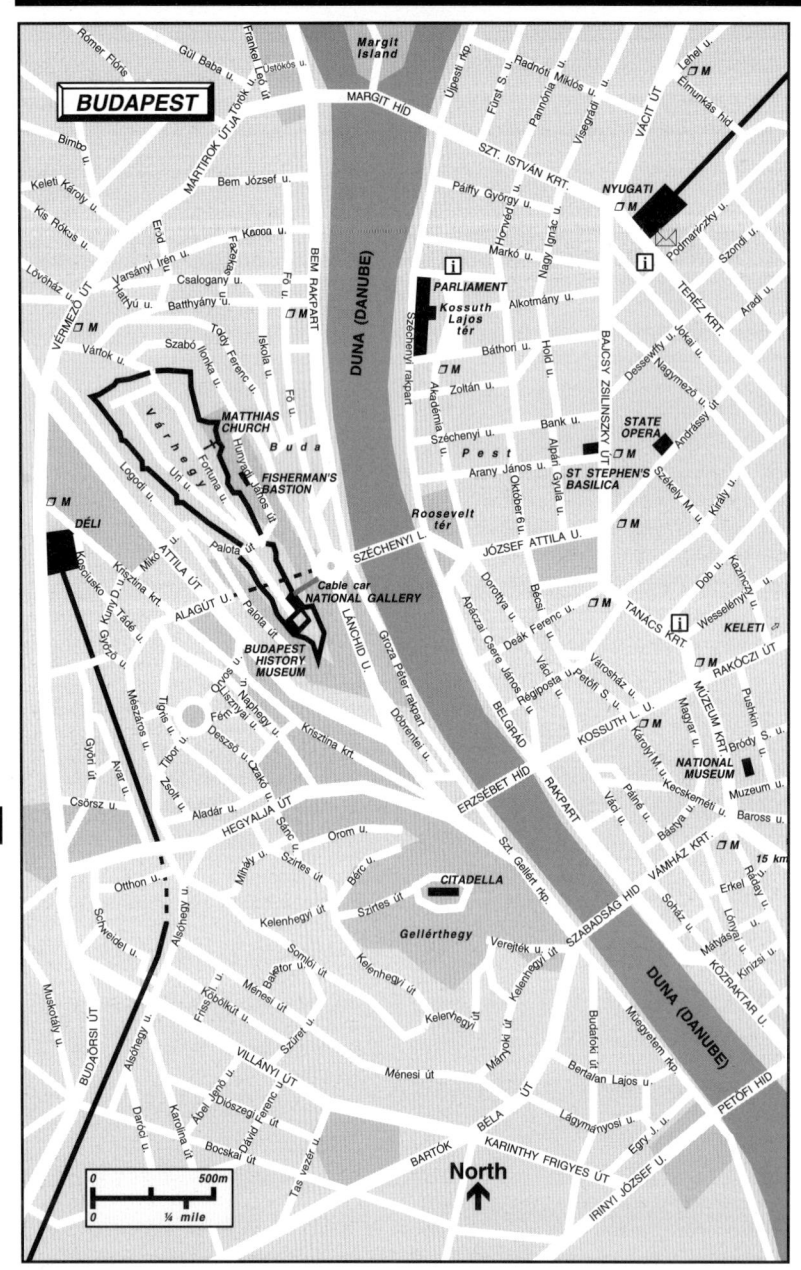

and Business class passengers
British Airways Executive Club Lounge Terminal 1 Main Transit Area Club members, First and Business class passengers
Lufthansa Senator Club Lounge Terminal 2 Upper Level Transit Area Club members, First and Business class passengers
Malev Hungarian Lounge Terminal 2 Upper Level Transit Area
SAS Lounge Terminal 1 Main Transit Area Club members, First and Business class passengers
Swissair Lounge Terminal 1 Main Transit Area Club members, First and Business class passengers

CONFERENCE AND BUSINESS FACILITIES

Airport Program Office, Terminal 1 ⓟ296 7357 Terminal 2 ⓟ296 8706

ⓟ Phone no. ⓕ Fax no. ⓞ Hours of opening/operation ≫ Frequency of service ⊃ Journey time ⊘ Cost/one-way fare

Buenos Aires

EZE

Argentina (see page 14)

National ✆ code: 54
Area ✆ code: 01
Local time: Winter GMT-3,
Summer GMT-3
Ministro Pistarini (Ezeiza)
International Airport, Buenos Aires,
Argentina
✆620 0011
✆620 0479
Location: 30 km/18 miles SW of
Buenos Aires

Terminals and Transfers

Terminals
Main Terminal Airlines: All airlines.
Layout: Ground floor: check-in desks

Minimum transfer times
International: 1 hr Domestic: 1 hr

Information

Flight enquiries
Airport ✆620 0217

Information and help desks
Tourist Information Desk Main Terminal
Ground floor ⏱0830–1930, Tourist
Information

Airport Facilities

Money
Bureau de change Main Terminal Ground
floor ⏱0800–2400

Food and drink
Bar Main Terminal ⏱0700–2200
Café/light meals Main Terminal
⏱0600–2300
Restaurant Main Terminal ⏱0700–2200

Communications
Post office Main Terminal ⏱0800–2000

Shopping
Duty free, departure Main Terminal
Departure Lounge ⏱0700–2000
Duty free, arrival Main Terminal
Departure Lounge ⏱0700–2000
News, Stationery & Books Main
Terminal Ground Floor ⏱0800–2200
Gift Shop Main Terminal Ground Floor
⏱0800–2200

Disabled Travellers

Main Terminal Lifts

Special Passenger Lounges

VIP Lounge Main Terminal Upper Floor

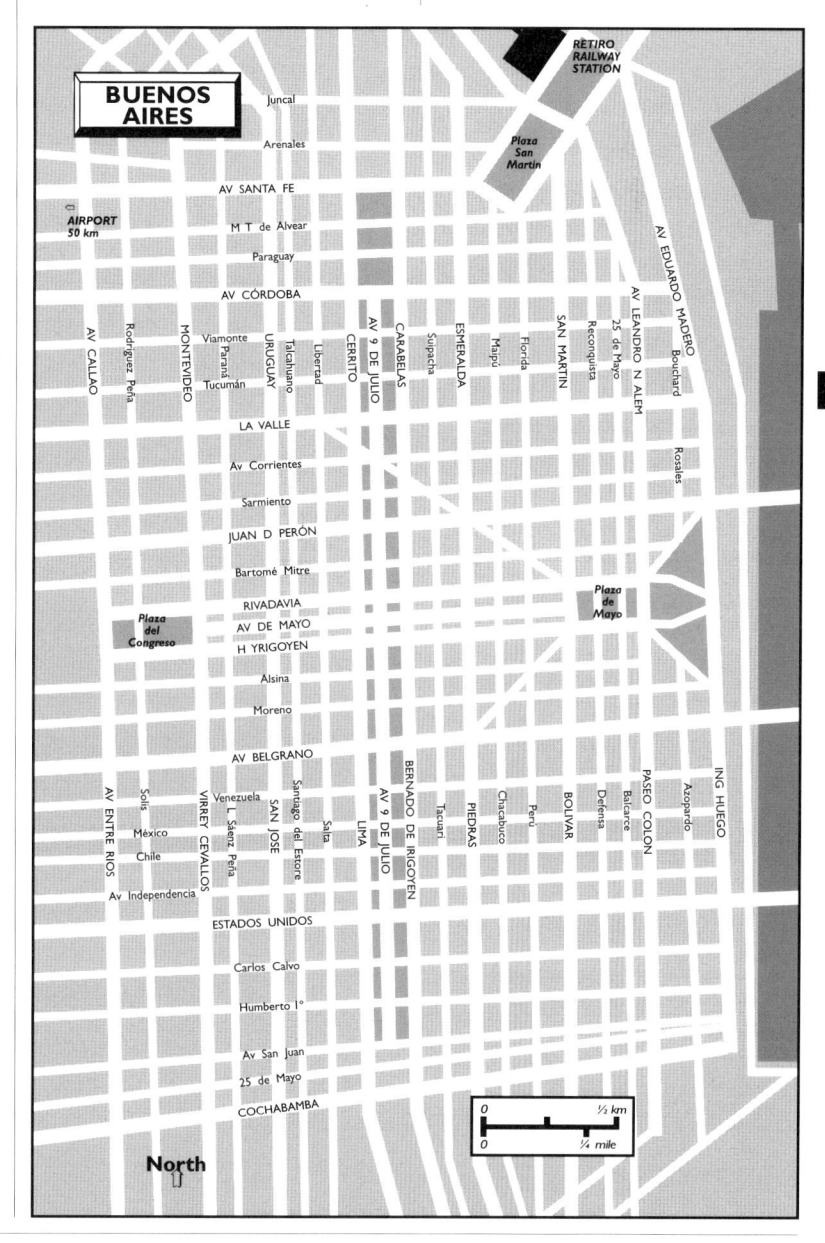

CONFERENCE AND BUSINESS FACILITIES

Conference room

CAR RENTAL

Avis Main Terminal ℂ311 3899/8055/8882
Hertz Main Terminal ℂ312 1317; 311 9323

CAR PARKING

Short-stay 2000 spaces ⌀ARS2. 50 per hr; ARS12. 50 per day

TAXIS AND CHAUFFEUR-DRIVEN CARS

Taxis
City centre ⌀ARS26

PUBLIC TRANSPORT

City & suburbs
Buenos Aires city centre (Hotel Gran Colon) 🚌 Manuel Tienda Leon Co. »15 min (0900–1800); 30 min (1800–2000) ⏱0900–2000 ⊃35 min ⌀ARS12.

REGIONAL AIR CONNECTIONS

Asuncion ✈ »Several per day ⊃50 min
Colonia ✈ »Several per week ⊃18 min
Montevideo ✈ »Several per day ⊃45 min
Punta D'Este ✈ »Several per week ⊃50 min
Santa Fe (Argentina) ✈ »Several per week ⊃1 hr

AIRPORT TAXES

There is a departure tax of USD13.

TRAVELLER'S NOTES

Tickets for the shuttle bus can be bought at the transport desk in the Arrival Hall.

CAIRNS — CNS

Australia (see page 14)

National ℂ code: 61
Area ℂ code: 070
Local time: Winter and Summer GMT +10
Address: Cairns International Airport, Airport Avenue, Aeroglen, QLD 4870.
ℂ: 4052 3888
ℱ: 4035 9106
Location: 8km/6 mile N of Cairns

TERMINALS AND TRANSFERS

Terminals
International and Domestic Terminals

Minimum transfer times
International 1 hr
Domestic 30 min

INFORMATION

Emergencies
Police ℂ 4035 9797
Lost Property ℂ 4052 3888

AIRPORT FACILITIES

Money
Bureau de Change International departure lounge, International baggage reclaim, International arrivals hall, Domestic departure hall.

Food and drink
Bar Available
Café/light meals Available
Restaurant Available

Shopping
Duty free Available

Luggage
Trolleys/carts Available free
Lockers ⌀AUD4-8

DISABLED TRAVELLERS

Special toilets; lowered telephones, parking places

SMOKING POLICY

Designated areas only

SPECIAL PASSENGER LOUNGES

Ansett Golden Wing Lounge
Qantas Captains Club
Air Nuigini Paradise Lounge

CAR RENTAL

Avis
Hertz
Thrifty

CAR PARKING

Long-stay Available

TAXIS AND CHAUFFEUR-DRIVEN CARS

Taxis
Available to town centre ⌀AUD10

Chauffeur-driven Cars
Cairns Limousines and Acacia Luxury Transport

PUBLIC TRANSPORT

City & suburbs
Cairns city centre (hotels) 🚌 »1 hr.

REGIONAL AIR CONNECTIONS

Hayman Island ✈ »daily ⊃1 hr 30 min
Mackay ✈ »Several per day ⊃2 hr
Townsville ✈ »Several per day ⊃50 min

AIRPORT TAXES

Included in ticket price

ℂ Phone no. ℱ Fax no. ⏱ Hours of opening/operation » Frequency of service ⊃ Journey time ⌀ Cost/one-way fare

CAIRO

CAI

EGYPT (see page 21)

National ✆ code: 20
Area ✆ code: 02
Local time: Winter GMT+2, Summer GMT+3
Cairo International Airport, Cairo, Egypt
✆666688, 667711, 2914255, 2914266
🖶2432522, 2437132
Location: 25 km/15 miles NE of Cairo

TERMINALS AND TRANSFERS

Terminals
Terminal 1 Airlines: Air Algérie, Royal Air Maroc, Finnair, Cyprus Airlines, Ethiopian Airlines, Yemen Airways, Air Malta, Kenya Airways, Lot Polish Airlines, El Al Israel Airlines, Balkan Bulgarian Airlines, Malev Hungarian, Middle East Airlines, Egyptair, CSA Czechoslovak, Royal Jordanian Airlines, Tarom Romanian Air, Sudan Airways, Aeroflot, Tunis Air. Layout: Departure and Arrival Halls
Terminal 2 Airlines: Air France, Alitalia, British Airways, China Airlines, Emirates, Garuda Indonesian Airlines, Gulf Air, Iberia, Jat Yugoslav Airlines, KLM, Kuwait Airways, Lufthansa, Olympic Airways, Austrian Airlines, Pakistan International Airlines, Singapore Airlines, Swissair, Saudia, Thai Airways. Layout: Departure and Arrival Halls

Minimum transfer times
International: 2hr, Domestic: 1hr, El Al: 3hr

Transfer between terminals
Taxi ≫15 min; Terminals 1 and 2 ⊘Free

INFORMATION

Flight enquiries
Airport ✆2448566, 2436959

Information and help desks
Information Desk Terminal 1 ✆2914255 ext 3414 ⓒ24 hr *Airport, Tourist Information*
Information Desk Terminal 2 ✆2914255 ext 2222 ⓒ24 hr *Airport, Tourist Information*

AIRPORT FACILITIES

Money
Thomas Cook bureau de change Terminal 1 and 2

Food and drink
Bar Terminal 1 Departure Hall ⓒ24 hr
Café/light meals Terminal 1 Arrival Hall ⓒ24 hr
Café/light meals Terminal 1 Departure Hall ⓒ24 hr
Restaurant Terminal 1 Departure Hall ⓒ24 hr
Café Terminal 2 Departure Hall ⓒ24 hr
Café/light meals Terminal 2 Arrival Hall ⓒ24 hr
Café/light meals Terminal 2 Departure Hall ⓒ24 hr
Restaurant Terminal 2 Departure Hall ⓒ24 hr

Communications
Post office Terminal 1 Departure Hall ⓒ24 hr
Post office Terminal 2 Departure Hall ⓒ24 hr

Shopping
Duty free, departure Terminal 1 Departure Hall
Duty free, arrival Terminal 1 Arrival Hall
Duty free, arrival Terminal 2 Arrival Hall
Duty free, departure Terminal 2 Departure Hall

Luggage
Left Luggage Counter Terminal 1 Basement and Terminal 2

DISABLED TRAVELLERS
Terminal 1 Lifts
Terminal 2 Lifts

CONFERENCE AND BUSINESS FACILITIES
Conference centre, Mövenpick Hotel

AIRPORT HOTELS
Mövenpick ✆679787 🖶667374
Novotel ✆2918577 🖶2914794
Sheraton Heliopolis ✆2902027 🖶2904061

CAR RENTAL
Alexandria Limousine Terminal 2
Avis Terminal 2
Budget Terminal 2
Hertz Terminal 2
G Car Terminal 2
Misr Travel Terminal 1
Nasser Bank Co. Terminal 1
Rhodes Terminal 2
Target Terminal 2

CAR PARKING
Short-stay 8000 spaces ⊘EGP2 per hr

TAXIS AND CHAUFFEUR-DRIVEN CARS

Taxis
City centre ➲40 min ⊘EGP40

PUBLIC TRANSPORT

City & suburbs
Cairo city centre (Atabah Sq.) 🚌 Public bus: 410 ≫1 hr ⓒ24 hr ➲1 hr ⊘EGP0.50. Departs from Terminal 1 car park
Cairo city centre (Tahrir Sq.) 🚌 Public bus: 400 ≫1 hr ⓒ24 hr ➲1 hr ⊘EGP0.50. Departs from Terminal 1 car park
Cairo city centre (Tahrir Sq.) 🚌 Air conditioned bus: ≫1 hr ⓒ24 hr ➲1 hr ⊘EGP2; cases EGP0.50.

REGIONAL AIR CONNECTIONS
Alexandria (Egypt) ✈ ≫Several per day ➲30–50 min
Tel Aviv ✈ ≫Several per day (not Sat) ➲1 hr 10 min

TRAVELLER'S NOTES
Visas can be obtained on arrival, at one of the banks near the immigration barrier. Confirm flights 72 hrs before departure. The most practical method of travelling into the city is by taxi or limousine (found outside the exit) but always agree a price beforehand.

CALGARY

Canada (see page 18)

National ✆ code: 1
Area ✆ code: 403
Local time: Winter GMT-7, Summer GMT-6
Calgary International Airport, 2000 Airport Rd, Calgary AB T2E 6W5, Canada
✆735 1372
Email: airport@agt.net
WWW site: http://www.airport.calgary.ab.ca
Location: 14 km/9 miles NE of Calgary

Terminals and Transfers

Terminals
Main Terminal Airlines: All airlines. Layout: Arrivals Level 1 (Arrivals, Baggage Claim, Car Rental, Ground Transportation), Departures Level 2 (Departures), Concourse A (Gates 1–12), Concourse B (Gates 20–25), Concourse C (Gates 26–29), Concourse D (Gates 31–40), Mezzanine Level 3 (Food Court)

Minimum transfer times
International: 1 hr 30 min **Domestic:** 45 min

Information

Flight enquiries
Air BC ✆265 9555 Air Canada ✆265 9555 Air Transat ✆250 5042 Canada 3000 Airlines ✆221 1870 Canadian Airlines International ✆235 1161 Cathay Pacific ✆269 8900 Continental Airlines ✆265 9555 Delta Airlines ✆265 7610 Japan Airlines ✆233 2488 KLM ✆236 2600 NWT Air ✆265 9555 Westjet ✆266 8086

Information and help desks
Information Desk Main Terminal Arrivals Level 1 ⊕0100–2200 Airport information, Tourist information
Information Desk Main Terminal Departures Level 2 ⊕0700–2300 Airport information, Tourist information

Emergencies
Police Main Terminal Arrivals Level 1 ✆737 7400

Lost Property Main Terminal Departures Level 2 ⊕0700–2300 ✆292 8709

Airport Facilities

Money
ATM Main Terminal Departures Level
Thomas Cook Bureau de change Main Terminal Departures Level 2 near Meeting Place B and adjacent to US departures area
Thomas Cook Bureau de change Main Terminal Arrival Level 1 outside Canada Customs

Food and drink
Bar Main Terminal throughout
Bar Main Calgary Airport Hotel
Café/light meals Main Terminal throughout (Food Court Mezzanine Level 3)
Restaurant Main Terminal Departures Level 2
Restaurant Calgary Airport Hotel

Communications
Post office Main Terminal Departures Level 2 adjacent to US departures area
Fax Main Terminal Departures Level 2 adjacent to US departures area

Shopping
Duty free, departure, Main Terminal Departures Level 2 Concourses A, B and C
Gift Shop Main Terminal throughout
News, Stationery & Books Main Terminal throughout

Luggage
Left Luggage/Lockers Main Terminal Departures Level 2 ⊕0700–2300 ✆292 8709
Lockers Main Terminal Upper Level throughout
Trolleys/carts All Terminals throughout ◊Free

Disabled Travellers
Adapted toilets; Lifts; Special Car Parking (Arrivals Level 1 metered parking area, Parkade Levels 3 and 4); Phones at wheelchair height; Phones adapted for the deaf; Personal assistance ✆735 1250

Smoking Policy
Allowed only in smoking lounges Main Terminal Departures Level Concourses B, C and D

Special Passenger Lounges
Air Canada Maple Leaf Lounge Main Terminal Departures Level 2 Concourse A
Canadian Airlines International Empress Lounge Main Terminal Departures Level 2 Concourse B
Canadian Airlines International Empress Lounge Main Terminal Departures Level 2 Concourse D
Delta Airlines Crown Club Room Main Terminal Departures Level 2 Concourse C

Conference and Business Facilities
Conference Rooms, Calgary Airport Hotel
Calgary Airport Hotel 288 rooms ✆291 2600 ℻250 8722 connected to Main Terminal by skywalk from Mezzanine Level 3

Car Rental
Avis Main Terminal Arrivals Level 1
Budget Main Terminal Arrivals Level 1
Dollar Main Terminal Arrivals Level 1
Hertz Main Terminal Arrivals Level 1
Thrifty Main Terminal Arrivals Level 1
Tilden Main Terminal Arrivals Level 1

Car Parking
Long-stay Park 'n Fly (free shuttle bus from Arrivals Level Bus Bay 2) ◊CAD6.95 per day
Long-stay Park 'n Jet (free shuttle bus from Arrivals Level Bus Bay 2) ◊CAD5.95 per day
Short-stay Parkade ◊CAD1.25 30 min, CAD10 per day (max)

Taxis and Chauffeur-driven Cars

Taxis
City centre ➲20 min ◊CAD20

✆ Phone no. ℻ Fax no. ⊕ Hours of opening/operation ≫ Frequency of service ➲ Journey time ◊ Cost/one-way fare

✈ SECTION TWO • AIRPORT DIRECTORY   CALGARY • CAPE TOWN

PUBLIC TRANSPORT

City & suburbs
Calgary (city centre hotels) 🚌 Cardinal Airporter ≫30 min ⓘ0630–2330 ⌚30 min ⊘CAD8.50
Calgary (Whitehorn C-Train stn) 🚇 Calgary Transit: 57 ≫30 min ⓘ0530–2325 (no service 1705–2125) Mon–Sat; ≫30 min ⓘ0630–0810, 1425–1705 and 2125–2325 ⌚30 min ⊘CAD1.60

Other towns and cities
Banff/Lake Louise AB 🚌 Brewster Airport Express ≫2 day ⓘ1230; 1800 ⌚3hr 45 min ⊘CAD39. For Kananaskis Village, Canmore, Banff Springs Hotel, Chateau Lake Louise AB
Banff AB 🚌 Laidlaw ≫2 day ⓘ1200; 1500 ⌚2hr ⊘CAD32. Service may continue to Lake Louise
Edmonton AB 🚌 Greyhound ≫1 day ⓘ1320; 0040 ⌚3 hrs 35 min ⊘CAD33. For Red Deer AB
Kelowna BC 🚌 Greyhound ≫1 day ⓘ1215 ⌚11 hr. For Canmore AB, Banff, Lake Louise, Field, Golden, Rogers Pass, Revelstoke, Sicamous, Salmon Arm, Enderby, Armstrong, Vernon and Winfield BC
Vancouver BC 🚌 Greyhound ≫1 day ⓘ1700 ⌚15 hr. For Canmore AB, Banff, Lake Louise, Field, Golden, Rogers Pass, Revelstoke, Sicamous, Salmon Arm, Chase, Kamloops, Chilliwack and Abbotsford BC

REGIONAL AIR CONNECTIONS
Castlegar BC ✈ ≫Several per day ⌚1 hr
Cranbrook BC ✈ ≫Several per day ⌚40 min
Edmonton AB ✈ ≫Several per day ⌚40 min
Kelowna BC ✈ ≫Several per day ⌚1 hr
Lethbridge AB ✈ ≫Several per day ⌚40 min
Medicine Hat AB ✈ ≫Several per day ⌚50 min

TRAVELLER'S NOTES
White Hat hosts are available throughout the terminal to offer a helping hand to travellers. These volunteers can be recognised by their distinctive white Stetsons and red vests.

CAPE TOWN   CPT
South Africa (see page 35)

National ℡ code: 27
Area ℡ code: 021
Local time: Winter GMT+2, Summer GMT+2
D. F. Malan Airport, Cape Town, South Africa
℡937 1200
📠934 0932
Internet address: www.airports.co.za
Location: 23 km/14 miles E of Cape Town

TERMINALS AND TRANSFERS

Terminals
Domestic Terminal Airlines: All domestic flights.
International Terminal Airlines: All international flights.

Minimum transfer times
International: 1 hr Domestic: 30 min

INFORMATION

Flight enquiries
Airport ℡937 1200

Information and help desks
Tourist Information Desk International and Domestic Terminals. Arrival Lounge ℡937 1276 📠934 0932 ⓘ0600–2200 Airport information, Flights

EMERGENCIES
Lost Property Domestic Terminal Arrival Lounge ℡ⓘOpen daily
Lost Property International Terminal Arrival Lounge
Police ℡937 1263
Doctor ℡934 2246

AIRPORT FACILITIES

Money
Bank Domestic Terminal Departure Lounge ⓘ0900–1530 Mon–Fri; 0830–1030 Sat
Bank International Terminal Arrival and Departure Hall ⓘAll flight times
ATM Domestic Arrivals
ATM Domeatic Departures

Food and drink
Bar Domestic Terminal Arrival Lounge ⓘ0600–2200
Bar Domestic Terminal Departure Lounge ⓘ0600–2300
Restaurant Domestic Terminal Arrival Lounge ⓘ0600–2200
Restaurant Domestic Terminal Departure Lounge ⓘ0600–2300
Bar International Terminal Departure Lounge ⓘAll flight times
Café/light meals International Terminal Arrival Lounge ⓘAll flight times
Café/light meals International Terminal Departure Lounge ⓘAll flight times

Communications
Post office Domestic Terminal Arrival Lounge ⓘ0830–1630 Mon–Fri

Shopping
Duty free, departure International Terminal Departure Lounge ⓘAll flight times

Luggage
Lockers Domestic Terminal Arrival Lounge ⓘ24 hr

DISABLED TRAVELLERS
Passenger Aid Unit to assist physically challenged passengers
Domestic Terminal Adapted toilets
International Terminal Adapted toilets

SMOKING
Restricted areas

SPECIAL PASSENGER LOUNGES
South African Airways VIP Lounge

✈ Air 🚆 Rail 🚌 Bus 🚘 Limousine Ⓜ Metro/subway 🚋 Tram 🚁 Helicopter ⛴ Water transport • For map symbols, see p. 9

CAPE TOWN

SECTION TWO • AIRPORT DIRECTORY

Domestic Terminal Departure Lounge
South African Airways VIP Lounge
International Terminal Departure Lounge
British Airways Lounge International Departures
Rennies Premier Club lounge Domestic Departures.

CONFERENCE AND BUSINESS FACILITIES

Conference room and Boardroom, Domestic Departures building
Press room, Departure Lounge, International Terminal
Training Center next to Control Tower

CAR RENTAL

Avis Domestic and International Terminal
Budget Domestic and International Terminal
Campell Domestic Terminal
Europ Domestic and International Terminal
Hertz Domestic and International Terminal
Imperial Domestic and International Terminal
Khaya Domestic Terminal
Levitt's Domestic Terminal
Tempest Domestic and International Terminal

CAR PARKING

Short-stay 2113 spaces ⌀ZAR1. 30 per hr; ZAR4. 40 per 12 hr; ZAR6. 60 per 24 hr

TAXIS AND CHAUFFEUR-DRIVEN CARS

Taxis
City centre ⊃20 min ⌀ZAR80

Chauffeur-driven cars
⌀ZAR26–36 per hr

REGIONAL AIR CONNECTIONS

George ✈ »At least daily ⊃1 hr
Walvis Bay ✈ »Several per week ⊃1 hr

AIRPORT TAXES

Domestic flights ZAR19
International flights ZAR61

TRAVELLER'S NOTES

Airport is in the process of being renovated and enlarged. Avoid the townships unless travelling in a escorted tour. Taxis in the city are more reliable and safer than minibus taxis, but have to be pre-booked.

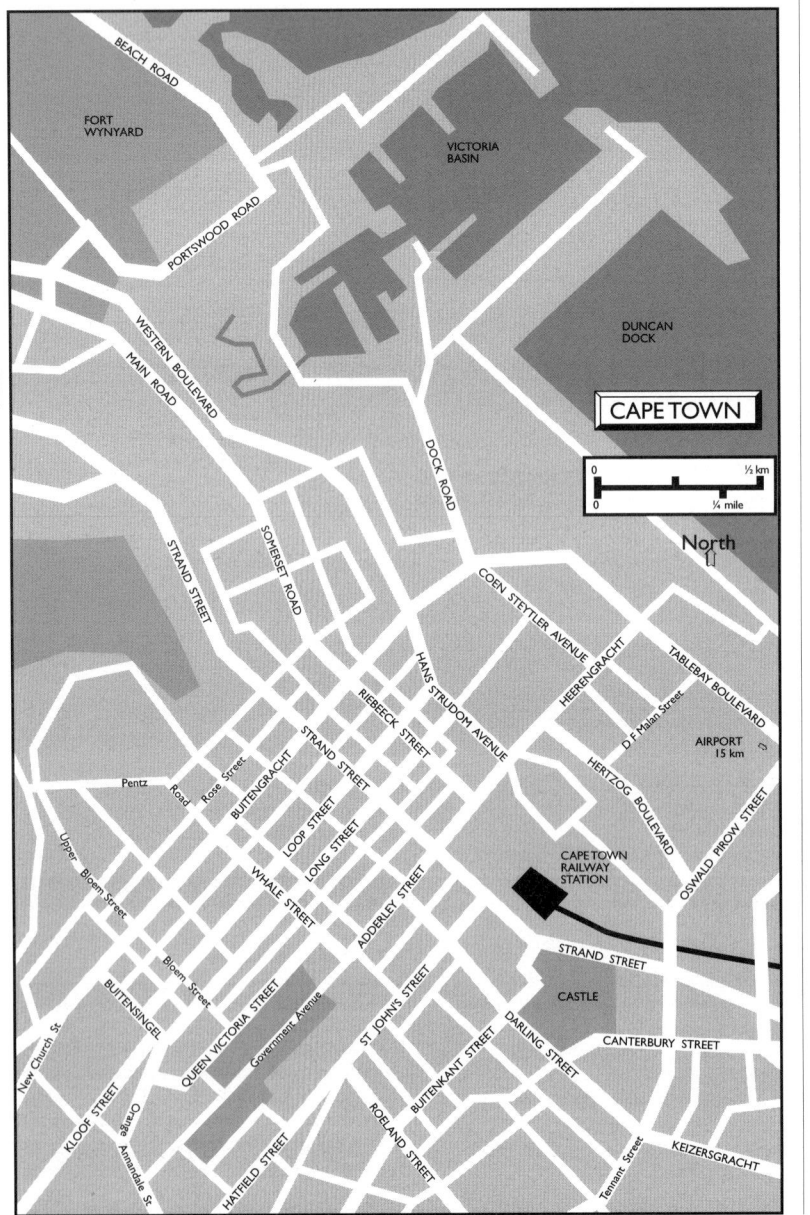

ⓒ Phone no. ⓕ Fax no. ⓞ Hours of opening/operation » Frequency of service ⊃ Journey time ⌀ Cost/one-way fare

ADVERTISEMENT

ESSENTIAL GUIDES FOR THE INTERNATIONAL TRAVELLER FROM THOMAS COOK PUBLISHING

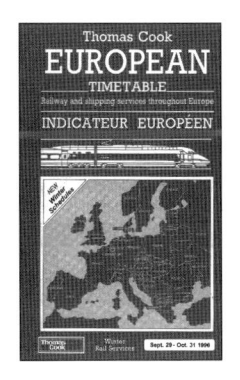

THOMAS COOK EUROPEAN TIMETABLE

First choice amongst rail travellers, and now in its 124th year. Covers 50,000 rail and ferry services across 35 countries and published monthly to ensure constant accuracy. An essential complement to the International Air Travel Handbook.
Published monthly. Price £8.40

THOMAS COOK OVERSEAS TIMETABLE

The widest-ranging guide to rail and bus services in every country outside Europe. Clear and accurate timetables are accompanied by general advice on public transport options. Ideal for advance planning and en route reference.
Published bi-monthly. Price £8.40

THOMAS COOK GUIDE TO EUROPEAN NIGHT TRAINS

Accurate and up-to-date timetables for national and international sleeping car and couchette services throughout the Continent, as well as a guide to travelling by sleeper. Motorail services and booking information have also been included.
Published in May and October. Price £7.95

These publications are available from bookshops and Thomas Cook shops, or direct from Thomas Cook Publishing, (Dept IATH), PO Box 227, Thorpe Wood, Peterborough, PE3 6PU, UK, telephone 01733 (+44 1733) 503571/2 (extra for postage and packing).

CARACAS   CCS

Venezuela (see page 42)

National ✆ code: 58
Area ✆ code: 02
Local time: Winter GMT-4, Summer GMT-4
Maiquetia (Simon Bolivar) International Airport, Apartado 146, La Guaira Caracas, Venezuela
✆27910; 23213; 26127
🖷523986
Location: 22 km/13 miles N of Caracas

TERMINALS AND TRANSFERS

Terminals
International Terminal Airlines: Air France, Aerolineas Argentinas, Avianca Colombian Airlines, Alitalia, Iberia, KLM, Lufthansa, Varig Brazilian, Air Portugal TAP, VIASA Venezuelan.
Domestic Terminal Airlines: All domestic flights.

Minimum transfer times
International: 1 hr–2 hr Domestic: 30 min–1 hr

INFORMATION

Information and help desks
Tourist Information Desk International Terminal ✆552747 ⏲0700–2400 *Tourist Information*
Tourist Information Desk Domestic Terminal ✆552747 ⏲0700–2100 *Tourist Information*

AIRPORT FACILITIES

Money
ATM International Terminal throughout the terminal ⏲24 hr
Bank International Terminal ⏲0800–1200, 1330–1600 Mon–Fri
Bureau de change International Terminal ⏲0800–1830
ATM Domestic Terminal throughout the terminal ⏲24 hr

Food and drink
Café/light meals International Terminal ⏲0800–2200
Restaurant International Terminal ⏲0800–2200

Communications
Post office International Terminal ⏲0800–1700

Shopping
Duty free, departure International Terminal Departure Lounge

DISABLED TRAVELLERS

International Terminal Adapted toilets; Phones at wheelchair height.
Domestic Terminal Adapted toilets; Phones at wheelchair height.

SMOKING POLICY

International Terminal No restrictions
Domestic Terminal No restrictions

CAR RENTAL

Budget International Terminal
Hertz International Terminal
National International Terminal
Progreso International Terminal

CAR PARKING

Short-stay Domestic and International Terminals 7650 spaces ⊘BEV5. 50 per hr; BEV90 per day

TAXIS AND CHAUFFEUR-DRIVEN CARS

Taxis
City centre ➲45 min ⊘BEV10

PUBLIC TRANSPORT

City & suburbs
Caracas city centre 🚌 »20 min ➲30 min ⊘BEV40.

REGIONAL AIR CONNECTIONS

Barquisimeto ✈ »Several per week ➲40 min
Bonaire ✈ »Several per week ➲50 min
Curacao ✈ »Several per week ➲50 min
Las Piedras ✈ »Several per day ➲40 min
Maturin ✈ »Several per week ➲50 min
Porlamar ✈ »Several per day ➲40 min
Puerto Ordaz ✈ »Several per day ➲1 hr

TRAVELLER'S NOTES

Taxi is usually the best form of transport to the city centre. Fares should be flat rate: get a ticket from the taxi office at the airport and check the fare with the driver.

CARDIFF

United Kingdom (see page 41)

National ✆ code: 44
Area ✆ code: 01446
Local time: Winter GMT, Summer GMT+1
Address: Cardiff International Airport, South Glamorgan, CF62 3BD.
✆: 711111
℻: 711675
Location: 19 km/12 miles W of Cardiff.

TERMINALS AND TRANSFERS

Terminals
Main Terminal All airlines Layout:

Information
Information and help desks
First floor. ✆ 711111. Tourist information, hotel accommodation

Emergencies
Lost Property Contact information desk ✆ 711111

AIRPORT FACILITIES

Money
Bank First floor ⊕ 24 hr May–October; 0500–2100 November–April. ✆ 712283
Bureau de Change First floor ⊕ 24 hr May–October; 0500–2100 November–April. ✆ 712283
ATM Terminal entrance

Food and drink
Bar First floor
Bar International departure lounge ✆ 710514
Café/light meals First floor
Café/light meals International departure lounge ✆ 710514
Restaurant First floor

Communications
Post Box
Post Office
Fax Service Available from information desk

Shopping
Duty free International departure lounge ✆ 711663
News, Stationery & Books First floor ✆ 712603
News, Stationery & Books International departure lounge ✆ 712603
News, Stationery & Books Arrivals hall ✆ 712603
Gift Shop International departure lounge

Luggage
Trolleys/carts

DISABLED TRAVELLERS

Lifts; adapted toilets; accessible telephones; wheelchairs; car parking facilities. A mini-com telephone for the deaf is available at the information desk.

SPECIAL PASSENGER LOUNGES

British Airways Executive Lounge Enquire at British Airways check-in desk

CONFERENCE AND BUSINESS FACILITIES

Conference room ✆ 712671 ⊕ 7 days. Catering; audio-visual equipment

CAR RENTAL

Hertz Ground floor international arrivals lounge ✆ 711722
Europcar Ground floor international arrivals lounge ✆ 711924

CAR PARKING

Long-stay ⌀ GBP4 per day (cheaper if booked in advance ✆ 0800 128128)
Short-stay Opposite terminal building ⌀ GBP0.50 per 30 min; GBP1 per 1 hr. Max. stay 1 hr
Short-stay Adjacent to long-stay facility ⌀ GBP1 per 1 hr; GBP2.50 per 3 hr. Max. stay 3 hr

TAXIS AND CHAUFFEUR-DRIVEN CARS

Taxis
Taxi desk ground floor international arrivals hall. City centre ⌀ GBP14. ✆ 710693

PUBLIC TRANSPORT

City & suburbs
Cardiff city centre (Central Station) ⇌ ✆ (01222) 228000
Cardiff city centre ⇌ Brewers Air Shuttle ⊕ Mon–Sat 0700–1800; Sun 0900–1800 ⌀ GBP2.10 single; GBP2.50 return » 1 hr
Cardiff city centre ⇌ Brewers Service X5 ⊕ Mon–Sat 0700–2300; Sun 0930–2200 ⌀ GBP2.10 single; GBP2.50 return » 1 hr
Cardiff city centre ⇌ Cardiff Bus Service X91/X92 ⊕ Mon–Sat 0630–1830 ⌀ GBP2.10 single; GBP2.70 return » 1 hr
Swansea city centre ⇌ South Wales Transport Flight Path ⊕ Mon–Sun 24 hr ⌀ GBP8 single; GBP14 return » 1 hr 30 min.

Other towns and cities
Newport ⇌ » 30 min ⇌ 30 min
Swansea ⇌ » 30 min ⇌ 1 hr

CASABLANCA   CMN
Morocco (see page 30)

National ✆ code: 212
Area ✆ code: 02
Local time: Winter GMT, Summer GMT
Mohammed V Airport, BP 8101
Casablanca-Oasis, Morocco
✆33 90 40; 33 91 40
℻33 99 01
Internet e-mail: ondaamv@atlas.net.ma
WWW site: www.onda.org.ma
Location: 30 km/18 miles S of Casablanca

TERMINALS AND TRANSFERS

Terminals
Main Terminal Airlines: All international flights. Layout: Departures on levels 0, 1 and 2; Arrivals on levels 0 and 1.

Minimum transfer times
International: 50 min Domestic: 50 min

INFORMATION

Flight enquiries
Airport ✆33 90 40
Information and help desks
Hotel Reservation Desk Main Terminal ✆33 87 73 ⏲0600–2300, Hotel booking
Tourist Information Desk Main Terminal Arrival Lounge ✆33 90 40 ⏲0830–1800 Airport, Tourist Information

AIRPORT FACILITIES

Money
Bank Main Terminal Arrivals Hall ⏲0830–1500 Mon–Fri
Bureau de change Main Terminal Arrivals Hall ⏲24 hr
Bureau de change Main Terminal Departures Hall ⏲24 hr

Food and drink
Bar Main Terminal Departures Hall Level 2
Bar Main Terminal Departures Hall Level 1
Bar Main Terminal Arrivals Hall Level 1
Café/light meals Main Terminal Arrivals Hall Level 0
Café/light meals Main Terminal Arrivals Hall Level 1
Café/light meals Main Terminal Departures Hall Level 1
Restaurant Main Terminal Departures Hall Level 0
Restaurant Main Terminal Departures Hall Level 2

Communications
Post office Main Terminal Departures Hall Level 0

Shopping
Duty free Arrivals Hall
Duty free Departures Hall
Shopping Mall Between Departures Hall and Arrivals Hall

Luggage
Left Luggage Counter Main Terminal Arrival Lounge ⏲24 hr ⊘MAD5 per bag

SMOKING POLICY
Main Terminal No restrictions

CAR RENTAL
RenCar Parking
Renaissance Car
Express
Hertz
Citer
Jet Car
First Car
Visa Car
Budget
SAFLOC
Europe Car
Nova Tour
Tourist Car
Avis
Janoub Tour

CAR PARKING
Short-stay 1600 spaces ⊘MAD3 per hr; MAD10 per day

TAXIS AND CHAUFFEUR-DRIVEN CARS

Taxis
City centre ➲30 min ⊘MAD150

PUBLIC TRANSPORT

City & suburbs
Casablanca city centre 🚌 ➲30 min ⊘MAD20.

REGIONAL AIR CONNECTIONS
Agadir ✈ »At least daily ➲1 hr
Fez ✈ »Several per week ➲50 min
Marrakech ✈ »Several per day ➲40 min
Tangier ✈ »At least daily ➲55 min

TRAVELLER'S NOTES
Car hire is expensive. It is cheaper to arrange overseas, and pay for in your local currency, before leaving home. If travelling in a taxi, always insist that the meter is turned on.

✈✈ SECTION TWO • AIRPORT DIRECTORY   CHICAGO-MIDWAY

CHICAGO-MIDWAY   MDW

USA (see page 41)

National ✆ code: 1
Area ✆ code: 773
Local time: Winter GMT-6, Summer GMT-5
Chicago Midway Airport, 5700 South Cicero Avenue, Chicago IL 6038, USA
✆767 0500
Internet e-mail: ci.chi.il.us
WWW site: http//www.ci.chi.il.us/WorksMart/Aviation/Midway
Location: 18 km/11 miles SW of Chicago

TERMINALS AND TRANSFERS

Terminals
Main Terminal: All Airlines Layout: Arrivals, Departures, Concourses A (Gates A1–A16), B (Gates B1–B14) and C (Gates C1–C5)

Minimum Transfer Times
International: 1 hr Domestic: 25 min

Transfer between terminals
Information and help desks
Airport Information Main Terminal South End ⓒ0600–2300 ✆767 0500
Airport, Tourist Information

Emergencies
Police Main Terminal North End ✆735 7773 ⓒ24 hr
Lost Property Main Terminal North End

AIRPORT FACILITIES

Money
ATM Main Terminal throughout

Food and drink
Bar Main Terminal throughout
Café/light Main Terminal throughout
Restaurant Main Terminal, near entrance to Concourse A and C

Communications
Post box All Terminals throughout

Shopping
News, Stationery & Books Main Terminal throughout
Gift Shop Main Terminal throughout

Luggage
Lockers
Trolleys/carts

DISABLED TRAVELLERS

Main Terminal Adapted toilets throughout; Phones at wheelchair height; Phones adapted for the deaf throughout

CAR RENTAL

Avis Main Terminal North End
Budget Main Terminal North End
Dollar Main Terminal North End
Hertz Main Terminal North End
National Main Terminal North End

CAR PARKING

Long-stay Long Term Lot on airport perimeter ⌀USD10 day Free shuttle bus from Main Terminal ≫15
Long-stay Economy Lot on airport perimeter ⌀USD6 day Free shuttle bus from Main Terminal ≫15
Short-stay Hourly Lot across from Main Terminal ⌀USD3 hr and the USD2 hr thereafter USD49 day max
Short-stay Daily Lot ⌀USD3 hr and the USD4 4 hr USD20 day max

TAXIS AND CHAUFFEUR-DRIVEN CARS

Taxis
Main Terminal kerbside City centre ⊃20 min ⌀USD20

PUBLIC TRANSPORT

Airport to airport
Chicago (O'Hare Airport) 🚌 Tri-State Coach ≫1 hr ⓒ0650–2050 1 hr 25 min ⌀USD12.

City & suburbs
Chicago city centre 🚇 CTA: Orange Line ≫6–12 min ⓒ0500–2330 ⊃30 min ⌀USD1. 50. Access CTA station via Pedestrian Bridge from Main Terminal.
Chicago metro area 🚐 Over 50 companies at airport
Chicago (suburbs) IL 🚌 Airport Express ≫5–10 min ⓒ0600–2330 ⊃45–60 min ⌀USD14. For Oak Brook, North Shore, Rosemont Hotels and Great Lakes Naval Station IL
Chicago downtown hotels 🚌 Airport Express ≫15 min ⓒ0600–2330 ⊃30–45 min ⌀USD11.

Other towns and cities
Merrillville IN 🚌 Tri-State Coach ≫1 hr ⓒ0650–2240 ⊃1hr 50 min ⌀USD16. For For Crestwood/Alsip, Harvey, Matteson IL, Hammond/Highland, Glen Park, Merrilville and Portage IN

REGIONAL AIR CONNECTIONS

Columbus OH ✈ ≫Several per day ⊃1 hr
Detroit MI ✈ ≫Several per day ⊃1 hr
Grand Rapids, MI ✈ ≫Several per day ⊃55 min
Indianapolis, IN ✈ ≫Several per day ⊃45 min
Louisville, KY ✈ ≫Several per day ⊃55 min
Milwaukee WI ✈ ≫Several per day ⊃45 min

TRAVELLER'S NOTES

Once the world's busiest airport, before O'Hare, serving 10 million passengers in 1959.

✈ Air 🚆 Rail 🚌 Bus 🚐 Limousine 🚇 Metro/subway 🚋 Tram 🚁 Helicopter 🚤 Water transport • For map symbols, see p. 9

CHICAGO-O'HARE · SECTION TWO • AIRPORT DIRECTORY

CHICAGO-O'HARE · ORD

USA (see page 41)

National ☏ code: 1
Area ☏ code: 773
Local time: Winter GMT-6, Summer GMT-5
Chicago O'Hare International Airport, PO Box 66142 Chicago, IL 60666, USA
☏686 2200
📠686 4980
Internet e-mail: ci.chi.il.us
WWW site: http//www.ci.chi.il.us/WorksMart/Aviation/OHare
Location: 29 km/18 miles NW of Chicago

Terminals and Transfers

Terminals
Terminal 1 Airlines: Lufthansa, United Airlines, United Express. Layout: Upper Level (Concourses B and C); Lower Level (airport transit system, baggage reclaim, car rental, ground transportation)
Terminal 2 Airlines: Air Jamaica, America West Airlines, Continental Airlines, Great Lakes, Northwest Airlines, TWA, United Airlines, United express, US Airways. Layout: Upper Level (Concourses E and F); Lower Level (airport transit system, baggage reclaim, car rental, ground transportation)
Terminal 3 Airlines: Air Canada, American Airlines, American Eagle, Canadian Airlines International, Delta Airlines, Qantas, Reno Air, Sun Country, Transmeridian. Layout: Upper Level (Concourses G, H, K and L); Lower Level (airport transit system, baggage reclaim, car rental, ground transportation)
Terminal 5-International Airlines: Aer Lingus, Aeroflot, Air France, Air Ukraine, Air India, Alitalia, American (international arrivals), American Trans Air, British Airways, China Eastern Airlines, Czechoslovak, Taesa, Japan Airlines, KLM, Korean Airlines, Kuwait Airways, Lot Polish Airlines, Lufthansa (international arrivals), Mexicana, NACA (Charters), Northwest (international arrivals), Qantas, (international arrivals), Royal Jordanian Airlines, Sabena World Airlines, SAS, Swissair, Taesa, Tarom Romanian Air, Transmeridian (international arrivals), United (international arrivals), Varig Brazilian Airlines. Layout: Upper Level (Gates M1–M21); Lower Level (airport transit system, baggage reclaim, car rental, customs, immigration)

Minimum transfer times
International: 1 hr 30 min Domestic: 50 min

Transfer between terminals
Bus » Frequent; Lot F and People Mover Terminal in Lot E

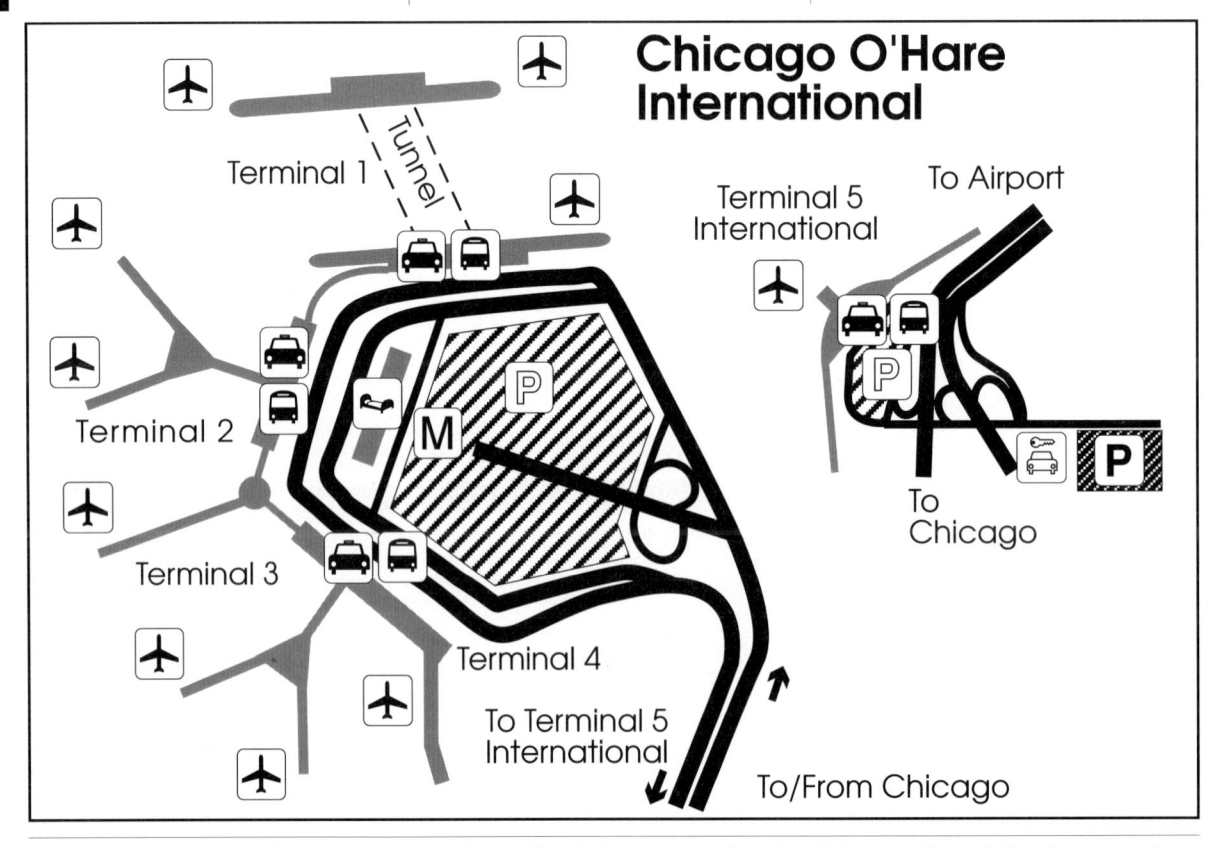

106

Chicago O'Hare International

Terminal 1
Tunnel
Terminal 2
Terminal 3
Terminal 4
To Terminal 5 International
Terminal 5 International
To Airport
To Chicago
To/From Chicago

☏ Phone no. 📠 Fax no. ⏱ Hours of opening/operation » Frequency of service ➔ Journey time ◯ Cost/one-way fare

SECTION TWO • AIRPORT DIRECTORY

CHICAGO-O'HARE

People mover》 Frequent; All terminals and long-stay parking

INFORMATION

Flight enquiries
Aeroflot ✆819 2350

Information and help desks
Airport Information Terminal 5-International Upper and lower levels ✆686 2304 ⌚0815-2000

Airport, Tourist Information
Airport Information Terminal 1 Lower Level ✆686 2304 ⌚0815–2000 Airport, Tourist Information
Airport Information Terminal 2 Lower Level ✆686 2304 ⌚0815–2000 Airport, Tourist Information
Airport Information Terminal 3 Lower Level ✆686 2304 ⌚0815–2000 Airport, Tourist Information
Traveller's Aid Terminal 3 Upper Level, across from gate K1 ✆894 2427 ⌚ 0800-1700 Mon-Fri

EMERGENCIES

Police Terminal 2 Mezzanine Level ✆686 2230 ⌚24 hr
Medical UIC Medical Center Terminal 2 Upper Level ✆894 5100 ⌚0600-2400
Lost Property All Terminals throughout ✆686 2385 ⌚24 hr

AIRPORT FACILITIES

Money
Bureau de change Terminal 3 Upper Level, across from Gate K11 ✆686 7965 ⌚1000-1930
Bureau de change Terminal 5-International Lower Level, near McDonald's and meeter/greeter area ✆686 7965 ⌚0900-2000
Bureau de change Terminal 5-International Upper Level, past security, across from Gate M9 ✆686 7965 ⌚0800-1600
ATM Terminal 1 Upper Level ⌚24 hr
ATM Terminal 2 Upper Level ⌚24 hr
ATM Terminal 3 Upper Level ⌚24 hr
ATM Terminal 5 Upper Level ⌚24 hr
ATM Terminal 5 Lower Level ⌚24 hr

Food and drink
Bar All Terminals throughout
Café/light meals All Terminals throughout
Restaurant All Terminals Throughout

Communications
Post office Terminal 2 Upper Level ✆686 6980 ⌚0700–1900 Mon–Fri
Post box All Terminals throughout

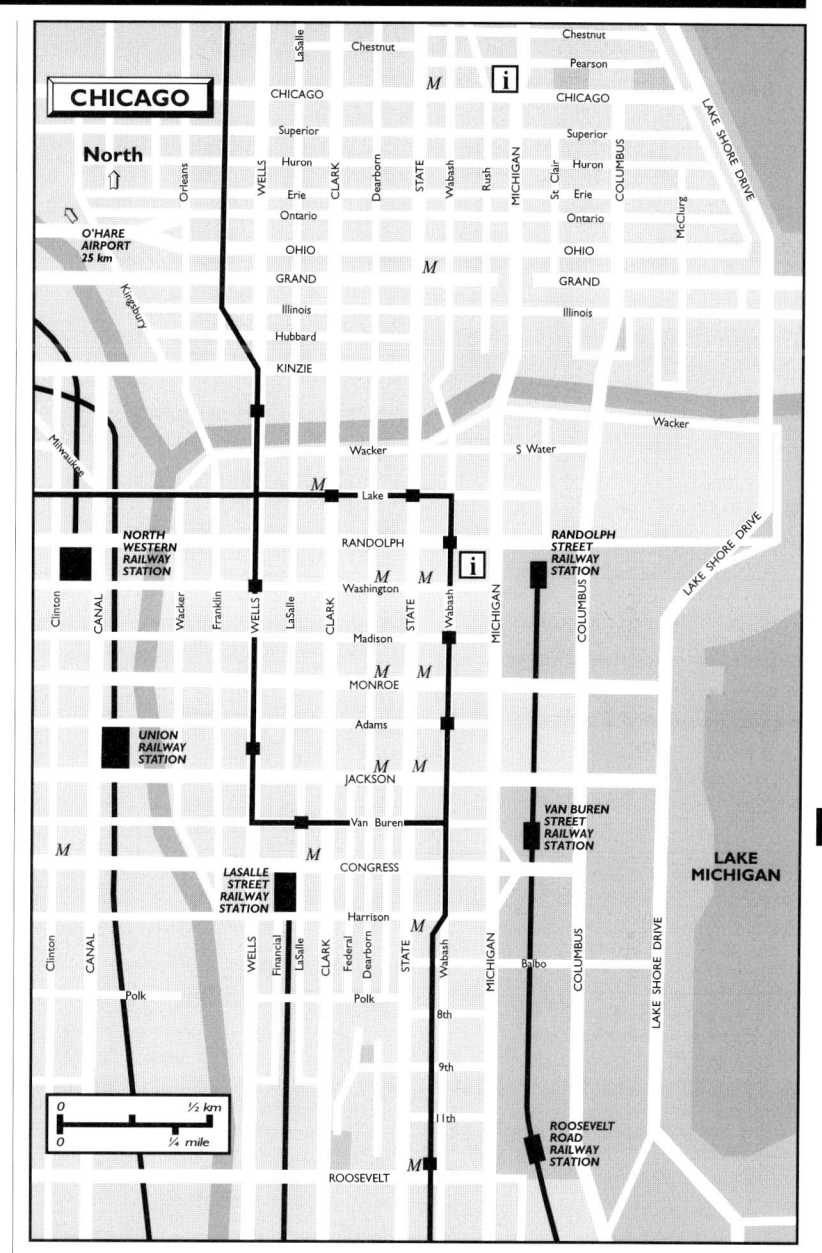

Shopping
Duty free, departure Terminal 1 Upper Level, near gate C18
Duty free, departure Terminal 3 Upper Level, across from gate K11
Duty free, departure Terminal 5-International Upper Level ✆894 3580 ⌚0700-2000
News, Stationery & Books All Terminals throughout
Gift Shop All Terminals throughout

Luggage
Lockers Terminal 2 Upper Level, Concourses E and F
Lockers Terminal 3 Upper Level, Concourses H and K
Trolleys/carts All Terminals throughout ⌀USD1.25 (free of charge to international passengers arriving at Terminal 5, the international terminal)

DISABLED TRAVELLERS

All Terminals Adapted toilets throughout; Lifts throughout; Phones at wheelchair height; Phones adapted for the deaf throughout

SPECIAL PASSENGER LOUNGES

American Airlines Admiral's Club Lounge

✈ Air ➥ Rail ➥ Bus ➥ Limousine Ⓜ Metro/subway ➥ Tram ➥ Helicopter ➥ Water transport • For map symbols, see p. 9

CHICAGO-O'HARE

SECTION TWO • AIRPORT DIRECTORY

Terminal 3 Upper Level, Concourse H
Continental Airlines Presidents Club Lounge Terminal 2 Upper Level, Concourse F
Delta Airlines Crown Room Terminal 3 Upper Level, Concourse L
Northwest Airlines World Club Lounge Terminal 2 Upper Level, Concourse E
United Airlines Red Carpet Club Lounge Terminal 1 Upper Level, Concourses B and C

CONFERENCE AND BUSINESS FACILITIES

Conference and business rooms, O'Hare Hilton Hotel ⓒ686 8000 f601 2873 Fax service, Photocopier
Skybird Meeting Center, Rotunda, between Terminal 2 and Terminal 3 ⓒ686 6101
Business Center, Terminal 3, Concourse H

AIRPORT HOTELS

O'Hare Hilton across from Terminal 2, reached by lower level pedestrian tunnels ⓒ686 8000 ⒻF601 2873 858 guests courtesy bus

CAR RENTAL

Alamo All Terminals (except 5) Lower Level
Avis All Terminals (except 5) Lower Level
Budget All Terminals (except 5) Lower Level
Dollar All Terminals (except 5) Lower Level
Hertz All Terminals (except 5) Lower Level
National All Terminals (except 5) Lower Level

CAR PARKING

Long-stay Economy Lots E and F 5300 spaces ⌀USD6–9 day
Short-stay Main Garage Lots A, B, C and International Lot D 10237 spaces ⌀USD3 hr

TAXIS AND CHAUFFEUR-DRIVEN CARS

Taxis
All Terminals, Lower Level City centre ⊃50 min ⌀USD30

PUBLIC TRANSPORT

Airport to airport
Chicago (Midway Airport) 🚌 Tri-State Coach »1 hr ⊙0545–1945 1 hr 25 min ⌀USD12.
South Bend Michiana Regional Airport IN 🚌 United Limo »1–2 hr ⊙0715–2300 ⊃2 hr 20 min ⌀USD28.
Milwaukee Mitchell International Airport WI 🚌 United Limo »1–2 hrs ⊙0700–2330 ⊃1 hr 50 min⌀USD18.

City & suburbs
Chicago city centre m CTA: Blue Line »5–15 min ⊙24 hr⊃35 min ⌀USD1.50. Lower level of Terminals 1, 2 and 3. From Terminal 5 take ATS People Mover to Terminal 3.
Chicago metro area l Over 50 companies at airport From all terminals, Lower Level.
Chicago (downtown hotels) 🚌 Continental Air Transport »5–10 min ⊙0600–2330 ⊃45–60 min ⌀USD15
Chicago (suburbs) IL 🚌 Airport Express »5–10 min ⊙0600–2330 ⊃45–60 min ⌀USD14. For Oak Brook, North Shore, Rosemont Hotels and Great Lakes Naval Station IL
Chicago downtown hotels 🚌 Airport

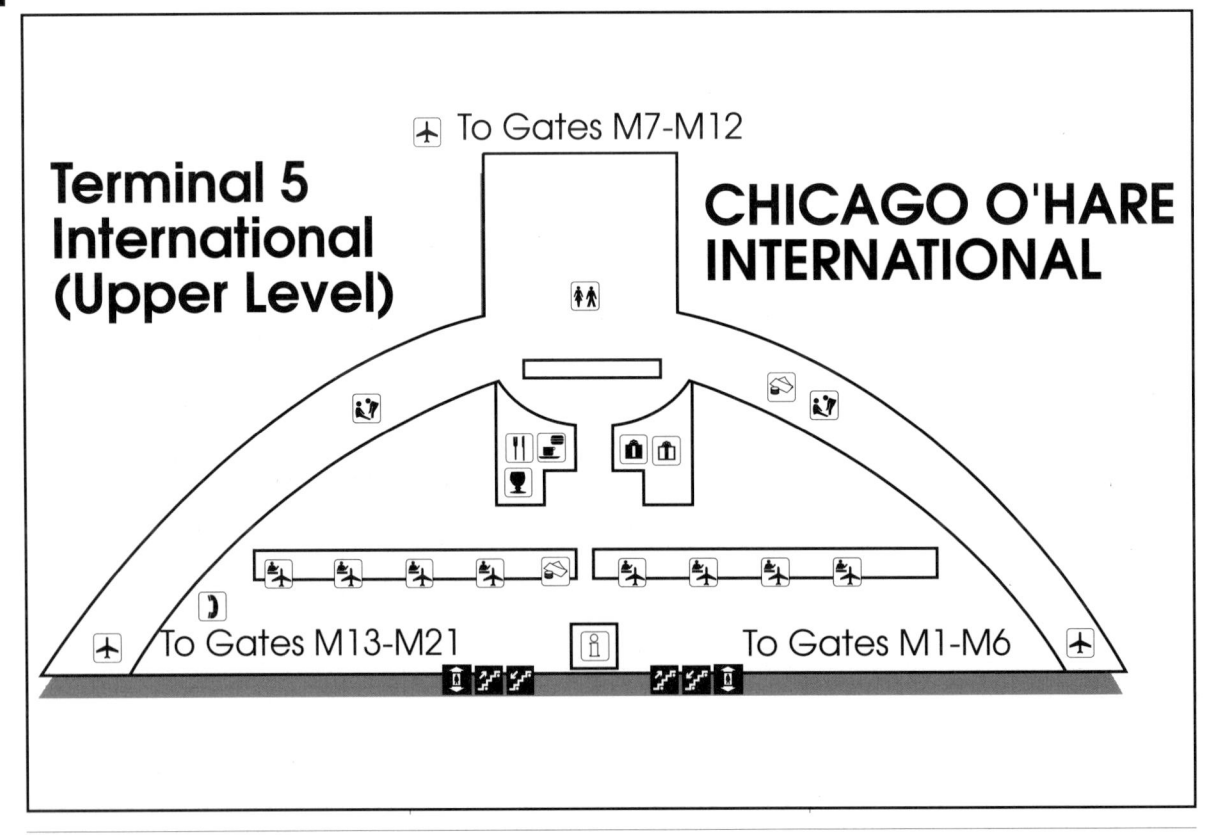

Terminal 5 International (Upper Level)

CHICAGO O'HARE INTERNATIONAL

To Gates M7–M12

To Gates M13–M21

To Gates M1–M6

ⓒ Phone no. Ⓕ Fax no. ⊙ Hours of opening/operation » Frequency of service ⊃ Journey time ⌀ Cost/one-way fare

SECTION TWO • AIRPORT DIRECTORY — CHICAGO-O'HARE

Express »5–10 min ⊕0600–2330 ↻45–60 min ⌀USD14.

OTHER TOWNS AND CITIES

Elkhart IN 🚌United Limo »1–2 hr ⊕0720–2245 ↻3 hr 25 min ⌀USD31. For Portage, Michigan City, La Porte, South Bend, Notre Dame and Mishawaka IN

Madison WI 🚌Van Galder »1–2 hr ⊕0630–2300 ↻3hr 5 min ⌀USD18. For Rockford IL, South Beloit WI, Janesville WI and University of Wisconsin

Milwaukee WI 🚌 United Limo »1–2 hrs ⊕0700–2330 ↻2 hr ⌀USD18. For Gurnee IL, Kenosha and WI

Peoria IL 🚌Illinois Valley Coaches. For LaSalle, Morris and Ottawa IL

Rockford IL 🚌Peoria-Rockford Bus

Merrillville IN 🚌Tri-State Coach»1 hr ⊕0525–2340 ↻2 hr ⌀USD16. For Crestwood/Alsip, Harvey, Matteson IL, Hammond/Highland and Glen Park IN

Regional Air Connections

Appleton, WI ✈ »Several per day ↻50 min
Bloomington-Normal, IL ✈ »Several per day ↻50 min
Burlington, IA ✈ »Several per day ↻55 min
Cedar Rapids, IA ✈»Several per day ↻50 min
Champaign, IL ✈ »Several per day ↻55 min
Danville, IL ✈ »At least daily ↻50 min
Columbus OH ✈»Several per day ↻1 hr
Dayton OH ✈»Several per day ↻1 hr
Decatur, IL ✈ »At least daily ↻50 min
Dubuque, IA ✈»Several per day ↻45 min
Fort Wayne IN ✈ »Several per day ↻1 hr
Grand Rapids, MI ✈ »Several per day ↻1 hr
Green Bay, WI ✈ »Several per day ↻1 hr
Indianapolis, IN ✈ »Several per day ↻50 min
Kalamazoo, MI ✈»Several per day ↻50 min
Lafayette, IN ✈ »At least daily ↻45 min
Lansing, MI ✈ »Several per day ↻1 hr
Louisville, KY ✈ »Several per day ↻j1 hr
Madison, WI ✈ »Several per day ↻45 min
Milwaukee WI ✈ »Several per day ↻45 min
Moline, IL ✈ »Several per day ↻45 min
Oshkosh, WI ✈ »Several per day ↻50 min
Peoria, IL ✈ »Several per day ↻55 min
Rochester, MN ✈ »Several per day ↻1 hr
Saginaw, MI ✈ »Several per day ↻55 min
South Bend, IN ✈ »Several per day ↻40 min
Springfield, IL ✈»Several per day ↻55 min
Wausau, WI ✈ »Several per day ↻55 min

TRAVELLER'S NOTES

The world's busiest airport, with over 60 million passengers a year (but only 10% are international).

✈ Air   🚋 Rail   🚌 Bus   🚐 Limousine   Ⓜ Metro/subway   🚊 Tram   🚁 Helicopter   ⛴ Water transport   • For map symbols, see p. 9

COLOMBO | SECTION TWO • AIRPORT DIRECTORY

COLOMBO · CMB

Sri Lanka (see page 37)

National ✆ code: 94
Area ✆ code: 01
Local time: Winter GMT+5½,
Summer GMT+5½
Bandaranaike International Airport,
Katunayake, Colombo, Sri Lanka
✆ 252861
⒡ 253187
Location: 32 km/19 miles N of
Colombo

TERMINALS AND TRANSFERS

Terminals
Arrival Terminal Airlines: All airlines.
Departure Terminal Airlines: All airlines.

Minimum transfer times
International: 1 hr–1 hr 30 min

INFORMATION

Flight enquiries
Airport ✆ 073 5555 ext. 2730
Information and help desks
Ceylon Tourist Board Arrival Terminal &
252411 ⏱24 hr Tourist Information

Emergencies
Lost Property Departure Terminal Airport
security offices ⏱0845–1700 Mon–Fri

AIRPORT FACILITIES

Money
Bank Arrival Terminal ⏱24 hr
Bank Departure Terminal ⏱24 hr

Food and drink
Restaurant Arrival Terminal ⏱24 hr
Restaurant Departure Terminal ⏱24 hr

Communications
Post office Arrival Terminal, outer porch
and transit area ⏱24 hr

Shopping
Duty free, arrival Arrival Terminal
Gift Shop Arrival Terminal
Duty free, departure Departure Terminal
Gift Shop Departure Terminal

Luggage
Left Luggage Counter Departure outer
porch ⏱24 hr ⌀LKR60

DISABLED TRAVELLERS

Arrival Terminal Adapted toilets; Personal assistance.
Departure Terminal Adapted toilets; Personal assistance.

SMOKING POLICY

Arrival Terminal Restricted
Departure Terminal Restricted

SPECIAL PASSENGER LOUNGES

Business Class Anthurium Lounge
Departure Terminal Holders of Business
class tickets with any airline
First Class Lotus Lounge Departure
Terminal Holders of First class tickets
with any airline
Air Lanka Peacock Lounge Departure
Terminal Holders of Business class tickets

CAR RENTAL

EuropCar Arrival Terminal
Rent a Car Arrival Terminal

CAR PARKING

Short-stay ⌀LKR50 per day
Off-airport ⌀ LKR30 per day

TAXIS AND CHAUFFEUR-DRIVEN CARS

Taxis
City centre ➲1 hr ⌀LKR670 (LKR737
with air conditioning)

PUBLIC TRANSPORT

City & suburbs
Colombo city centre 🚌 Central
Transport Board »Avg 30 min ➲1 hr
⌀LKR8.
Colombo city centre (Fort Station) 🚆
»Twice daily ⏱0740 and 1800 ➲1 hr
⌀LRK9.

REGIONAL AIR CONNECTIONS

Madras ✈ »Daily ➲1 hr

AIRPORT TAXES

A departure tax of LKR500 is levied.

TRAVELLER'S NOTES

Passenger Assistance staff can guide travellers through baggage reclaim and immigration. Part II of the Immigration Card should be retained until departure.

✆ Phone no. ⒡ Fax no. ⏱ Hours of opening/operation » Frequency of service ➲ Journey time ⌀ Cost/one-way fare

SECTION TWO • AIRPORT DIRECTORY COPENHAGEN

COPENHAGEN (KØBENHAVN) CPH

Denmark (see page 20)

National ✆ code: 45
Area ✆ code: No code required
Local time: Winter GMT+1, Summer GMT+2
Copenhagen International Airport, PO Box 74, DK2770 Kastrup, Denmark
✆32 31 32 31
📠32 31 31 33
Internet e-mail: info-dept@cph.dk
Location: 9 km/5½ miles SE of Copenhagen

TERMINALS AND TRANSFERS

Terminals
International Terminal Airlines: All international flights. Layout: Three Levels: Ground Level, Arrival and Departure; Level 1, Transit Area, Shopping Malls and Arrival/Departure Piers; Level 2, airline lounges, restaurants
Domestic Terminal Airlines: All domestic flights. Layout: One Level for Arrival, Departure and service facilities.

Minimum transfer times
International: 45 min Domestic: 30 min

Transfer between terminals
Bus »5 min; Domestic and International Terminals ⊘Free

INFORMATION

Flight enquiries
Airport ✆32 47 47 47

Information and help desks
SAS Arrivals Desk International Terminal Arrival Area ✆32320000 ⏰All flight times *Hotel booking, Tourist information*
Service Centres International Terminal A,B,C,D, Pier Areas (4 desks) ✆32320000 📠31 51 11 33 ⏰All flight times *Airport information, Flights*
Service Centres Domestic Terminal ✆32474747 ⏰All flight times *Airport information, Flights*

EMERGENCIES

Police International Terminal Ground Level between International Terminal/Domestic Terminal ✆32 45 14

48 ⏰24 hr
Medical Domestic Terminal
Medical International Terminal SAS and airport staff first aid-trained ✆01 ⏰24 hr
Lost Property International Terminal Terminal Arrival Desk ✆01 ⏰0800–2300
Lost Property Domestic Terminal ✆32 31 32 31 ⏰All flight times

AIRPORT FACILITIES

Money
ATM International Terminal Arrival Hall ⏰24 hr
ATM Domestic Terminal Arrival Hall ⏰24 hr
Bank International Terminal Level 1 Central Transit Area ⏰0630–2200
Bank Domestic Terminal
Bureau de change International Terminal Ground Level Arrival Hall ⏰0630–2200
Bureau de change Domestic Terminal

Food and drink
Bar International Terminal Central Transit Area & A,B,D Piers ⏰0630–2300 hr
Bar Domestic Terminal Hall 6 ⏰0700–2200
Café/light meals International Terminal Central Transit Area First/Second Level ⏰0630–2300
Café/light meals Domestic Terminal Halls 3 and 6 ⏰0700–2200
Restaurant International Terminal Central Transit Area Second Level ⏰0630–2200 hr
Restaurant Domestic Terminal

Communications
Fax service International Terminal Transit Area Central Level 1 ⏰All flight times
Fax service Domestic Terminal
Post office International Terminal Arrival Hall Ground Level ⏰0900–1730 Mon–Fri; 0900–1730 Sat
Post office International Terminal Transit Hall, Post and telecom only ⏰0630–2200
Post box Domestic Terminal

Shopping
Shopping mall International Terminal Central Transit Area ⏰0700–2200
Hairdresser International Terminal Hotel Area Transit Hall ⏰0900–1900
Duty free, departure International Terminal Main Departures concourse

First Level ⏰all Flight hours
Shopping mall Domestic Terminal

Luggage
Left Luggage Counter International Terminal Arrival Hall Ground Level ⏰0600–2300 Mon-Sat
Trolleys/carts International Terminal Arrival Hall Baggage reclaim ⏰24 hr ⊘Free
Trolleys/carts International Terminal Central Transit Area ⏰24 hr ⊘Free
Left Luggage Counter Domestic Terminal International Terminal Terminal Arrivals Hall ⏰0600–2300 Mon-Sat
Trolleys/carts Domestic Terminal Halls 0-6 ⏰24 hr ⊘Free

DISABLED TRAVELLERS

International Terminal Adapted toilets *Transit Area Central*; Lifts *Departure Hall to Transit Area*; Personal assistance *Information Desk Transit Area All flight times*

SMOKING POLICY

International Terminal Smoking alllowed in designated areas
Domestic Terminal Smoking allowed in designated areas

SPECIAL PASSENGER LOUNGES

British Airways Executive Club Lounge International Terminal Transit Area First Level *Club members, First and Business class passengers*
SAS Royal Viking Club Lounge International Terminal Transit Area Upper Level *Club members*
SAS Euro Class Lounge International Terminal Transit Area opposite Central Service Desks *Euro Class Passengers*
All other airlines Mermaid Lounge International Terminal Transit Area Upper Level *Business class passengers*
All other airlines Novia Lounge International Terminal Transit area, Upper Level

CONFERENCE AND BUSINESS FACILITIES

Conference centre, Within SAS Euroclass Lounge ✆32 32 46 42 📠31 50 40 73

111

✈ Air 🚆 Rail 🚌 Bus 🚗 Limousine Ⓜ Metro/subway 🚋 Tram 🚁 Helicopter ⛴ Water transport • For map symbols, see p. 9

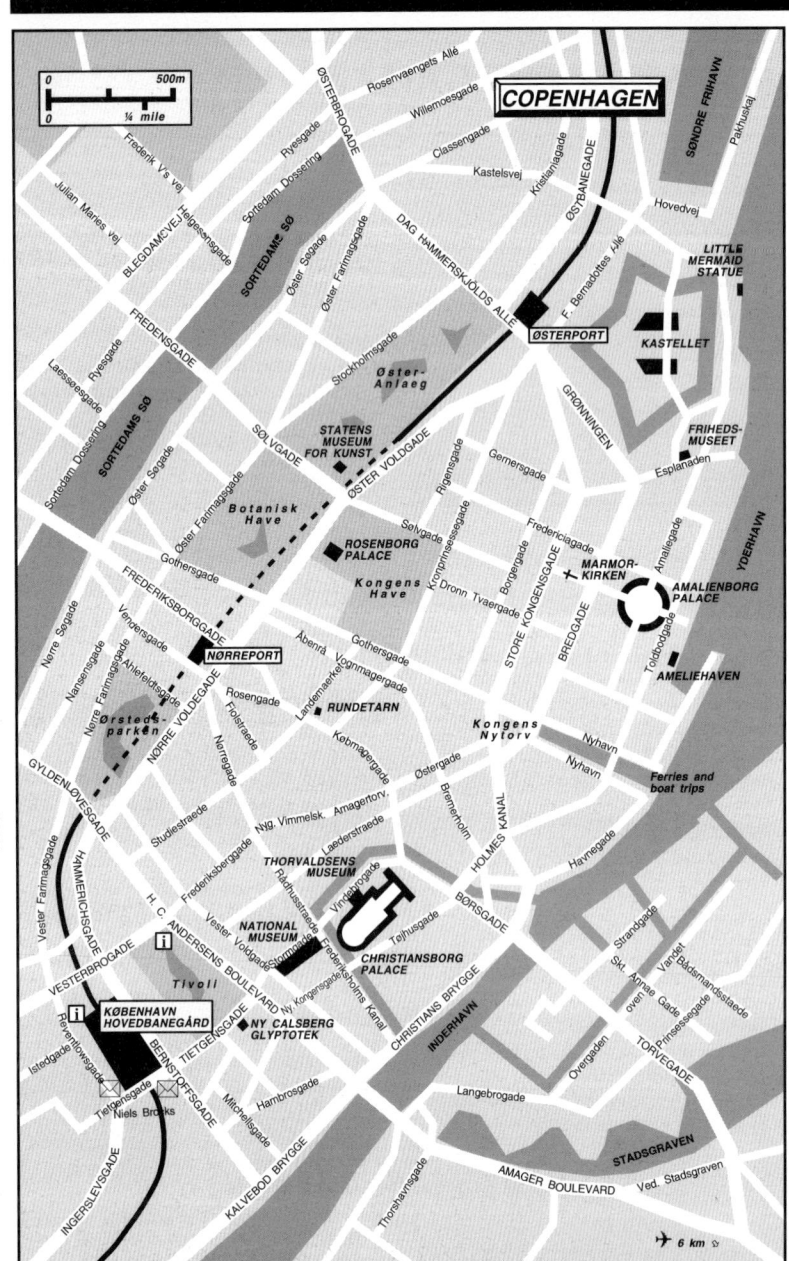

COPENHAGEN

SECTION TWO • AIRPORT DIRECTORY

Car Parking

Long-stay Domestic and International Terminals 1450 spaces ⌀DKK15 per hr; DKK45–65 per day
Short-stay Domestic and International Terminals 3370 spaces ⌀DKK25 per hr; DKK65 per day

Taxis and Chauffeur-driven Cars

Taxis
Outside Arrival Hall City centre ⤳20 min ⌀DKK 120

Chauffeur-driven cars
Outside Arrival Hall

Public Transport

City & suburbs
Copenhagen city centre 🚌SAS »10–15 min ⏱0542–2100 ⤳20–30 min ⌀DKK35.
Copenhagen city centre 🚌City transport »30 min ⤳20–30 min ⌀DKK15

Other towns and cities
Malmö 🚢SAS »1 hr ⏱0730–2225 ⤳35 min ⌀DKK 695. *Hovercraft and high-speed ferries*

Regional Air Connections

Aalborg ✈ »Several per day ⤳45 min
Århus ✈ »Several per day ⤳35 min
Billund ✈ »Several per day ⤳35 min
Bornholm ✈ »Several per day ⤳35 min
Esbjerg ✈ »Several per day ⤳50 min
Gothenburg ✈ »Several per day ⤳55 min
Hamburg ✈ »Several per day ⤳50 min
Helsingborg H/P ✈ »Several per day ⤳15 min
Jonköping ✈ »Several per day ⤳55 min
Kalmar ✈ »Several per day ⤳50 min
Karup ✈ »Several per day ⤳45 min
Kristianstad ✈ »Several per week ⤳35 min
Malmö ✈ »Several per day ⤳35 min
Odense ✈ »Several per day ⤳35 min
Oslo ✈ »Several per day ⤳1 hr 5 min
Sonderborg ✈ »Several per day ⤳40 min
Stockholm ✈ »Several per day ⤳1 hr 10 min

Traveller's Notes

Knitwear, furs and silverwork are typical souvenirs bought from shops along the Strøget, the pedestrianised streets in the city.

⏱All flight times *Telephones, Fax service, Photocopier, Travel advice*

Airport Hotels

Sara Dan ☏32 52 14 00 *Courtesy bus*
Scandic ☏31 51 30 33
Transfer Hotel (Airport) ☏32 31 32 31 ℻32 31 31 09 16 guest cabins

Car Rental

Avis International Terminal Arrival Hall ☏32 51 22 99
Budget International Terminal Arivals Hall ☏32 52 39 00
EuropCar International Terminal Arrival Hall ☏32 50 30 90
Hertz International Terminal Arrival Hall ☏32 50 93 00

☏ Phone no. ℻ Fax no. ⏱ Hours of opening/operation » Frequency of service ⤳ Journey time ⌀ Cost/one-way fare

✈✈ SECTION TWO • AIRPORT DIRECTORY   DALLAS/FORT WORTH

DALLAS/FORT WORTH   DFW
USA (see page 41)

National ✆ code: 1
Area✆ code: 972
Local time: Winter GMT-6,
Summer GMT-5
Dallas Fort Worth International
Airport, PO Box 619428, DFW
Airport, TX 75261, USA
✆574 6000
🖷574 8544
WWW site: http://www.dfwair-port.com/
Location: 27 km/17 miles NW of
Dallas and E of Fort Worth

TERMINALS AND TRANSFERS

Terminals
Terminal 2E Airlines: American Airlines, American Eagle, Canadian Airlines International. Layout: Upper Level (Gates 1–23), Lower Level (Ground Transportation)
Terminal 2W Airlines: Air Canada, America West, Aspen Mountain Air, British Airways, Continental Airlines, Korean Air, Lufthansa, Mesa Airlines, Midwest Express, Northwest Airlines, Sun Country, TWA, United Airlines, US Airways, ValuJet/Air Tran Airways, Vanguard, Western Pacific. Layout: Upper Level (Gates 1-24), Lower Level (Ground Transportation)
Terminal 3E Airlines: American Airlines. Layout: Upper Level (Gates 24–44), Lower Level (Ground Transportation)
Terminal 4E Airlines: Aeromexico, Atlantic Southeast, Delta Airlines. Layout: Upper Level (Gates 1-38), Lower Level (Ground Transportation)

Minimum transfer times
International: 50 min–1 hr 10 min
Domestic: 50 min

Transfer between terminals
People mover ⇉8 min ⏰24 hr; All terminals, long stay parking areas and hotel ◇Free

INFORMATION

Flight enquiries
Air Canada ✆(800) 869 9000
Aeromexico ✆(800) 237 6639 America West ✆(800) 235 9292
American/American Eagle Airlines

✆(214)267 1151 Atlantic Southeast
✆(214) 630 3200 British Airways✆ (800) 247 9297 Canadian Airlines International
✆(800) 426 7000 Continental Airlines
✆263 0523 Delta Airlines ✆(214) 630 3200 Korean Air ✆(800) 438 5000 Lone Star /Aspen Airlines ✆(817) 626 3932 Lufthansa ✆(800) 645 3880 Mesa Airlines ✆(800) 637 2247 Midwest Express ✆(800) 452 2022 Northwest Airlines ✆(800) 225 2525 Sun Country ✆(800) 752 1218 TWA✆(214) 741 6741 United Air Lines ✆(800) 241 6522 US Airways ✆(800) 428 4322
ValuJet/AirTran Airways ✆(800) 825 8538 Vanguard ✆(800) 826 4827 Western Pacific ✆(800) 930 3030

Information and help desks
Airport Assistance Center Terminal 2W

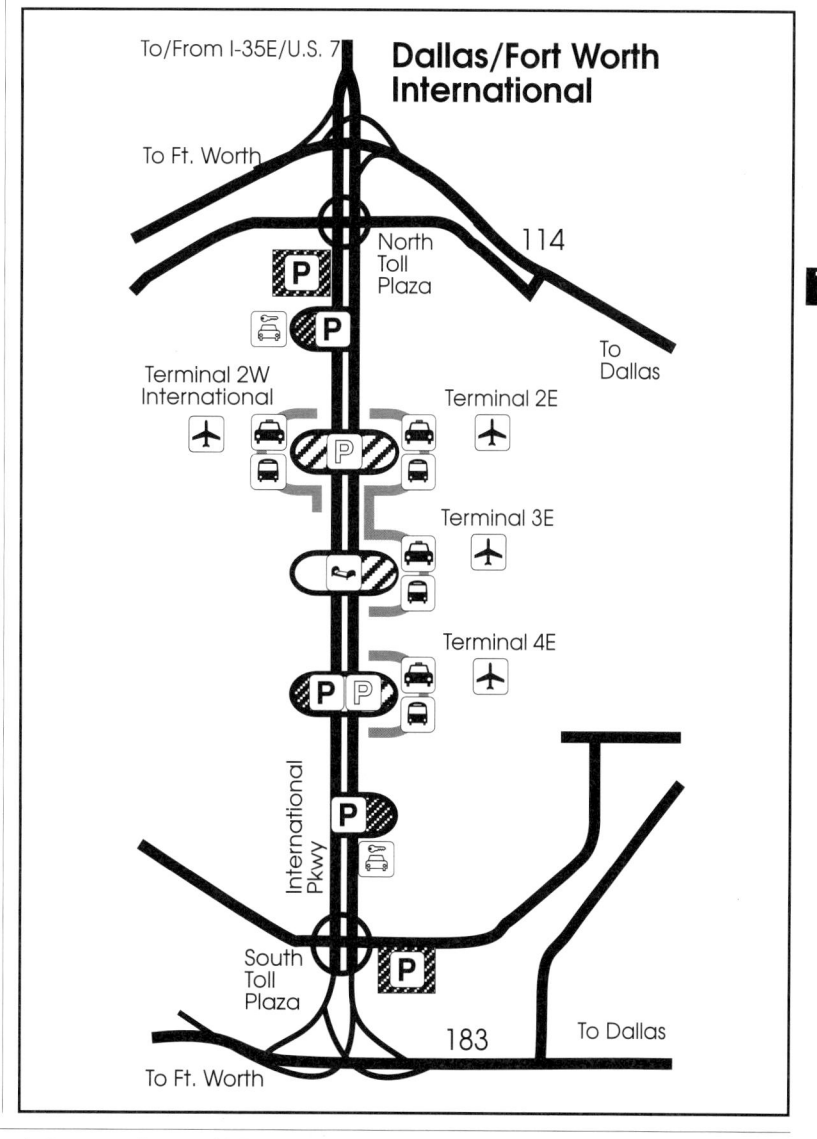

Dallas/Fort Worth International

✈ Air 🚊 Rail 🚌 Bus 🚖 Limousine Ⓜ Metro/subway 🚋 Tram 🚁 Helicopter ⛴ Water transport • For map symbols, see p. 9

DALLAS/FORT WORTH

SECTION TWO • AIRPORT DIRECTORY

Gate 4 ℗574 4420 ⓗ24 hr Airport, Tourist Information

Emergencies

Police All Terminals throughout ℗574 4454
Lost Property All Terminals No Location ℗574 4454

Airport Facilities

Money
ATM Terminal 2E Gates 4, 11, and 21
ATM Terminal 2W Gates 6, 13 and 18
ATM Terminal 3E Gates 28, 34 and 39
ATM Terminal 4E Gates 8, 14 and 31
Thomas Cook bureau de change Terminal 2E Gate 18 (Main office) ⓗ0830–2130
Thomas Cook bureau de change Terminal 2E Gate 21 (Near Customs) ⓗ09300–1900
Thomas Cook bureau de change Terminal 4E Gate 34 ⓗ0930–1900
ATM Terminal 2W Gate 11
Thomas Cook bureau de change Terminal 2W Gates 20 and 23 ⓗ1300–1900 Mon–Sat

Food and drink
Bar All Terminals Upper Level ⓗ0600 (1200 Sun)–2300
Café/light meals All Terminals Upper Level
Restaurant All Terminals Upper Level ⓗ0530–2100

Communications
Fax service Terminal 3E American Admiral's Club Gate 33
Fax service Terminal 4E Delta Crown Rooms Gates 14, 17, 21, 31 and 32
Internet Terminal 2W Gate 7
Internet Terminal 2E Gates 3, 6 and 11
Internet Terminal 3E Gates 28, 32 and 33
Internet Terminal 4E Gates 5, 14, 31
Post box All Terminals throughout

Shopping
Duty free, departure Terminal 2E Gates 18 and 20
Duty free, departure Terminal 4E Gate 34
Hairdresser Terminal 4E Gate 12
Duty free, departure Terminal 2W Gate 23
Hairdresser Terminal 2W Gate 14
Shopping mall All Terminals Upper Level

Luggage
Lockers Terminal 2E Gates 3, 4, 17 and 19
Lockers Terminal 3E Gates 28, 29, 32, 35 and 39
Lockers Terminal 4E Gates 4, 14, 31 and 32
Lockers Terminal 2W Gates 5, 14, and 20

Disabled Travellers

All Terminals Adapted toilets; Lifts; Phones at wheelchair height; Phones adapted for the deaf; Personal assistance In Terminal 2W

Special Passenger Lounges

American Airlines Admiral's Club Lounge Terminal 2E Gate 21
American Airlines Admiral's Club Lounge Terminal 3E Gate 33
Delta Airlines Crown Room Terminal 4E Gates 10, 34, satellite

Conference and Business Facilities

DFW Hyatt Regency Hotel, Across from Terminal 3E ℗453 1234 ⓕ456 8668

Airport Hotels

DFW Hyatt Regency ℗453 1234 ⓕ456 8668 1400 rooms

Car Rental

Avis All Terminals Lower Level ℗574 4130
Budget All Terminals Lower Level ℗574 2115
Hertz All Terminals Lower Level ℗453 0370
National All Terminals Lower Level ℗574 3400

Car Parking

Long-stay Shuttle Parking spaces ⓒUSD0.50 hr; USD5-7 day max
Short-stay At each terminal spaces ⓒUSD0.50 hr; USD9–12 day max

Taxis and Chauffeur-driven Cars

Taxis All Terminals Upper Level
Dallas city centre ⟶25 min ⓒUSD25

Public Transport

City & suburbs
Dallas city centre 🚌 Airporter ⟫30 min ⓗ0500–2400 ⓒUSD8.
Fort Worth city centre 🚌 Airporter ⟫30 min ⓗ0500–2400 ⓒUSD8.
Dallas (suburbs) 🚌 DART 409 ⟫30 min - 1 hr ⓗ0545-2400 ⓒUSD
For King Center, Fair Park, Parkland Medical Center, South Irving Transit Centre
Plano 🚌 DART: 700 ⟫1 hr ⓗ0500-2400 ⓒUSD
For Richardson and North Irving TX
Dallas–Fort Worth Metro Area 🚗 Over 30 companies at airport.

Other towns and cities
Waco TX 🚌 Waco Streak. For Hillsboro, Killeen and Temple TX
Wichita Falls TX 🚌 Skylark Van Service. For Sheppard AFB TX

Regional Air Connections

Abilene TX ✈ ⟫Several per day ⟶1 hr
Austin TX ✈ ⟫Several per day ⟶50 min
Brownwood TX ✈ ⟫At least daily ⟶45 min
College Station TX ✈ ⟫Several per day ⟶1 hr
Houston TX ✈ ⟫Several per day ⟶1 hr
Killeen TX ✈ ⟫Several per day ⟶50 min
Lawton OK ✈ ⟫Several per day ⟶50 min
Longview TX ✈ ⟫Several per day ⟶55 min
Oklahoma City OK ✈ ⟫Several per day ⟶1 hr
San Antonio TX ✈ ⟫Several per day ⟶1 hr
Shreveport LA ✈ ⟫Several per day ⟶1 hr
Texarkana AR ✈ ⟫Several per day ⟶1 hr
Tyler TX ✈ ⟫Several per day ⟶50 min
Waco TX ✈ ⟫Several per day ⟶50 min
Wichita Falls TX ✈ ⟫Several per day ⟶50 min

Traveller's Notes

Located on a stretch of prairie the size of Manhattan, Dallas/Fort Worth International is one of the busiest airports in the world, with over 50 million passengers per year, of whom approx. 3 million are on international flights.

℗ Phone no.   ⓕ Fax no.   ⓗ Hours of opening/operation   ⟫ Frequency of service   ⟶ Journey time   ⓒ Cost/one-way fare

DARWIN DRW

Australia (see page 14)

National ✆ code: 61
Area ✆ code: 89
Local time: Winter GMT+9½, Summer GMT+9½
Address: Federal Airports Corporation, FAC Airport Management Centre, Fenton Court, Marrara NT 0812
✆: 20 1811
🖷: 20 1800
Location: 13 km/8 miles N of Darwin

TERMINALS AND TRANSFERS

Terminals
Main Terminal Layout: Two floors
Information Information and help desks
Darwin Regional Tourism Association Main terminal Tourist information

Emergencies
Lost Property FAC Terminal Control Office adjacent to gate 6 on the ground floor

AIRPORT FACILITIES

Money
Thomas Cook Bureau de Change Ground floor opposite baggage reclaim area
ATM Ground floor near the escalator

Food and drink
Bar International departure lounge
Café/light meals First floor opposite the domestic departure lounge
Café/light meals Ground floor
Restaurant First floor opposite the domestic departure lounge

Communications
Post Box

Shopping
Duty free First floor shopping mall
Duty free International departure lounge
News, Stationery & Books First floor shopping mall
Gift Shop First floor shopping mall

Luggage
Lockers Next to gate 6
Trolleys/carts Throughout the terminal building ⌀ AUD Free

SPECIAL PASSENGER LOUNGES

Ansett Golden Wing First floor
Qantas Club First floor

CAR RENTAL

Avis Ground floor near baggage reclaim area
Budget Ground floor near baggage reclaim area
Hertz Ground floor near baggage reclaim area
Thrifty Ground floor near baggage reclaim area
Territory Rent-a-car Ground floor near baggage reclaim area
Dasfleet Ground floor near baggage reclaim area

CAR PARKING

Long-stay
Off-airport

TAXIS AND CHAUFFEUR-DRIVEN CARS

Taxis
City centre ⌀ AUD13 by day; AUD15 by night and at weekends

PUBLIC TRANSPORT

City & suburbs (calling at major hotels) 🚌 ⌀ AUD6 one way; AUD10 return ✆ 1 800 358 945

REGIONAL AIR CONNECTIONS

Bathurst Island ✈ ⟫2 per day ⟳30 min
Katherine ✈ ⟫2 per day ⟳50 min

DELHI   DEL

India (see page 25)

National ✆ code: 91
Area ✆ code: 11
Local time: Winter GMT+5½,
Summer GMT+5½
Indira Gandhi International
Airport, New Delhi 110010, India
✆5484021
⨍3295444; 5452444
Location: 22 km/13 miles SW of
New Delhi

TERMINALS AND TRANSFERS

Terminals
International Terminal Airlines: Air France, Air India, Alitalia, British Airways, Delta Airlines, Emirates (`), Gulf Air, Japan Airlines, KLM, Kuwait Airways, Lufthansa, Lot Polish Airlines, Malaysian Airlines, Pakistan International Airlines, Royal Nepal Airlines, Royal Jordanian Airlines, Singapore Airlines, Swissair, Saudia, Thai Airways.
Domestic Terminal Airlines: All domestic flights.

Minimum transfer times
International: 1 hr 30 min–3 hr Domestic: 1 hr 30 min

Transfer between terminals
Bus ⌀Free

INFORMATION

Flight enquiries
Airport ✆5452011 International;
5452126 Domestic

Information and help desks
Tourist Information Desk International Terminal (2 desks) *Tourist Information*

EMERGENCIES

Lost Property International Terminal Airport Manager's office

Money
Bank International Terminal International Terminal ⏱24 hr
Bank Domestic Terminal Domestic Terminal ⏱0600–2000 Mon–Fri; 1000–1700 Sat

Food and drink
Bar International Terminal Departure Lounge
Café/light meals International Terminal Arrival Lounge
Café/light meals International Terminal Departure Lounge
Café/light meals International Terminal Transit Area
Restaurant International Terminal

New Delhi Airport

✆ Phone no.   ⨍ Fax no.   ⏱ Hours of opening/operation   ≫ Frequency of service   ⊃ Journey time   ⌀ Cost/one-way fare

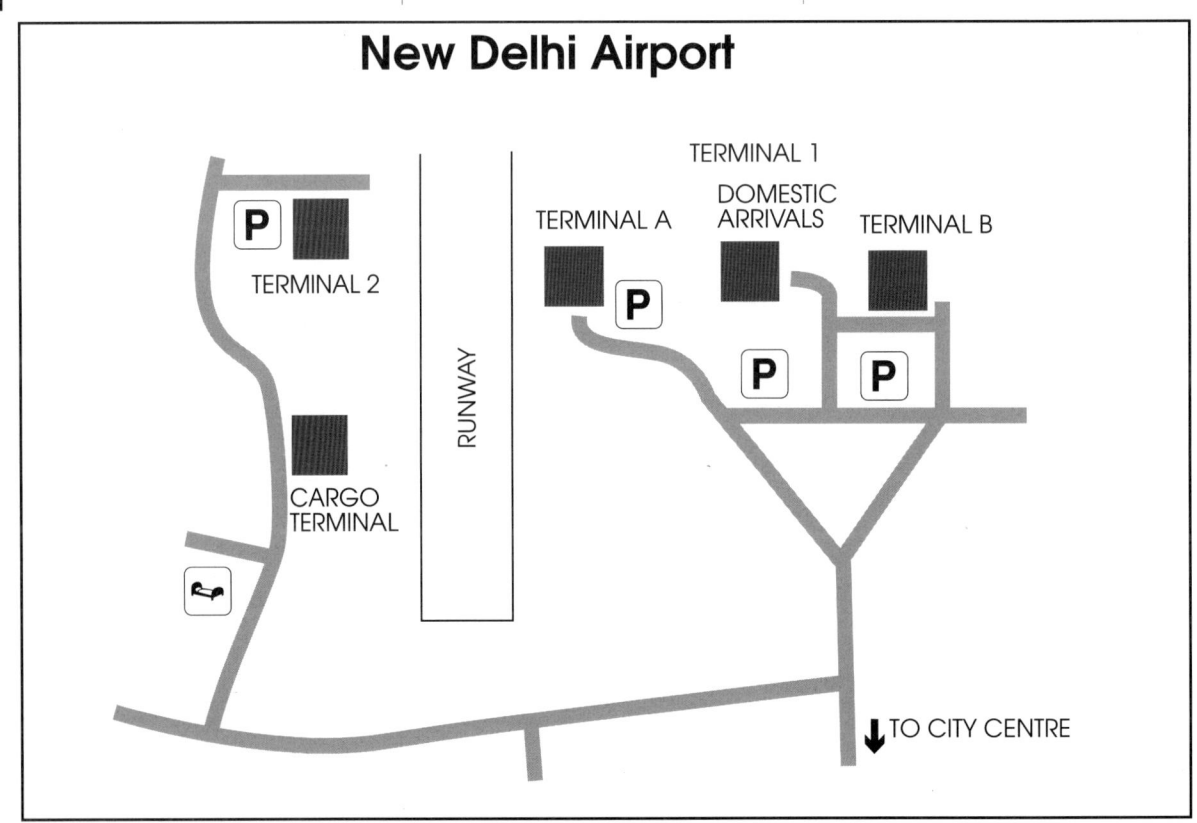

SECTION TWO • AIRPORT DIRECTORY — DELHI

Departure Lounge ⏰24 hr
Restaurant International Terminal Transit Area ⏰24 hr
Café/light meals Domestic Terminal Arrival Lounge
Café/light meals Domestic Terminal Departure Lounge
Café/light meals Domestic Terminal Transit Area

Communications
Post office International Terminal Departure Lounge ⏰24 hr

Shopping
Duty free, arrival International Terminal Arrival Lounge
Duty free, departure International Terminal Departure Lounge
Gift Shop International Terminal Departure Lounge

Luggage
Left Luggage Counter International Terminal Car park ⏰24 hr
Left Luggage Counter Domestic Terminal Car park ⏰24 hr

International Terminal Adapted toilets
Domestic Terminal Adapted toilets

SMOKING POLICY
International Terminal No restrictions
Domestic Terminal No restrictions

SPECIAL PASSENGER LOUNGES
Air India Maharaja Lounge International Terminal Departure Area
All airlines Maurya Business Lounge International Terminal Departure Area

CONFERENCE AND BUSINESS FACILITIES
Airport business centre
Conference room

CAR RENTAL
Nitin Transport International Terminal
EuropCar International Terminal

CAR PARKING
Short-stay 100 spaces ⊘INR5 per 6 hr; INR20 per day

TAXIS AND CHAUFFEUR-DRIVEN CARS
Taxis
City centre ➲30 min ⊘INR180

PUBLIC TRANSPORT
City & suburbs
Delhi city centre 🚌 Delhi Transport Corporation: 780 ➲45 min ⊘INR5.

REGIONAL AIR CONNECTIONS
Jaipur ✈ »Several per week ➲50 min

AIRPORT TAXES
Departure tax (INR50–300 in local currency only) must be paid before check-in.

TRAVELLER'S NOTES
Terminals are widely separated. Domestic Terminal is only 15 km/9 miles from Delhi. Pre-paid taxi journeys are the easiest way of reaching the city centre: buy tickets from the kiosk in the Arrival Hall. Reconfirm international flights 72 hrs before departure.

DENVER | SECTION TWO • AIRPORT DIRECTORY

DENVER
DEN
USA (see page 41)

National ✆ code: 1
Area ✆ code: 303
Local time: Winter GMT-7, Summer GMT-6
Denver International Airport, 8500 Peña Blvd, Denver CO 80249, USA
✆342 2000

Internet e-mail: aviation@infodenver.denver.co.us
WWW site: http// infodenver.denver.co.us/~aviation/
Location: 37 km/23 miles NE of Denver

TERMINALS AND TRANSFERS

Terminals
Jeppesen Terminal Airlines: All airlines.
Layout: Jeppesen Terminal: Level 4 (Passenger Pick-up), Level 5 (Baggage Claim/Ground Transportation), Level 6 (Check-in/Ticketing); Concourses A, B and C: Level 1 (Train Station), Level 2 (Gates), Level 3 (Mezzanine) and Level 4 (Bridge to Jeppesen Terminal–Concourse A only)
Concourses A, B and C

Minimum transfer times
International: 1 hr Domestic: 50 min

Transfer between terminals
People mover ≫2 min; Terminal and all concourses ⌀Free

INFORMATION

Flight enquiries
Airport ✆342 2000

Information and help desks
DIA Information Jeppesen Terminal throughout Airport Information
Tourist Information Jeppesen Terminal Level 5 and Concourse B Tourist Information

EMERGENCIES

Medical Jeppesen Terminal Level 6 and Concourse B
Lost Property Jeppesen Terminal Level 5

AIRPORT FACILITIES

Money
ATM Jeppesen Terminal Level 5 and Concourses A, B and C
Bureau de change Jeppesen Terminal Level 5 and Concourses A and B

Food and drink
Bar Jeppesen Terminal and Concourses throughout
Café/light meals Jeppesen Terminal and Concourses throughout
Restaurant Jeppesen Terminal and Concourses throughout

Communications
Post box Jeppesen Terminal and Concourses throughout
Post office Jeppesen Terminal Level 6

Shopping
News, Stationery & Books Jeppesen Terminal and Concourses throughout
Gift Shop Jeppesen Terminal and Concourses throughout

Luggage
Lockers Concourses A, B and C ⏰24 hr
Left luggage counter Jeppesen Terminal Level 5 ⏰0630–2330 ⌀USD2–8

DISABLED TRAVELLERS

Jeppesen Terminal Adapted toilets; Lifts; Special car parking; Phones at wheelchair height; Phones adapted for the deaf; Personal assistance.
Concourses Adapted toilets; Lifts; Special car parking; Phones at wheelchair height; Phones adapted for the deaf; Personal assistance.

SMOKING POLICY

Jeppesen Terminal Permitted only in the Aviator's Club (on minimum purchase of one drink)
Concourses Concourse B Permitted only in the Aviator's Club (on minimum purchase of one drink)

SPECIAL PASSENGER LOUNGES

American Airlines Admiral's Club Lounge Concourses Concourse C

Continental Airlines Presidents Club Lounge Concourses Concourse A
Delta Airlines Crown Room Concourses Concourse C
United Airlines Red Carpet Club Lounge Concourses Concourse B

CAR RENTAL

Alamo Jeppesen Terminal Level 5 ✆342 7373
Avis Jeppesen Terminal Level 5 ✆342 5500
Budget Jeppesen Terminal Level 5 ✆341 2277
Dollar Jeppesen Terminal Level 5 ✆342 9099
Enterprise Jeppesen Terminal Level 5 ✆342 7350
Hertz Jeppesen Terminal Level 5 ✆342 3800
National Jeppesen Terminal Level 5 ✆342 0717
Payless Jeppesen Terminal Level 5 ✆342 9444
Resort Jeppesen Terminal Level 5 ✆342 3444
Thrifty Jeppesen Terminal Level 5 ✆342 9400
USA Jeppesen Terminal Level 5 ✆555 1955
Value Jeppesen Terminal Level 5 ✆342 0650

CAR PARKING

Long-stay Jeppesen Terminal Surface Lots ⌀USD1 hr; USD5 day Free Shuttle bus
Short-stay Jeppesen Terminal Garage Spaces ⌀USD2 hr; USD10 day

TAXIS AND CHAUFFEUR-DRIVEN CARS

Taxis
Jeppesen Terminal Level 5 City centre ⌛45 min ⌀USD35

PUBLIC TRANSPORT

City & suburbs
Arvada CO 🚌 RTD SkyRide: AA ≫1 hr ⏰0325–2310 ⌛1 hr 10 min ⌀USD8.
Boulder CO 🚌 RTD: SkyRide AB ≫1 hr ⏰0425–2245 ⌛1 hr 30 min ⌀USD8. Also serves Stapleton Transfer Station

---

✆ Phone no. ℱ Fax no. ⏰ Hours of opening/operation ≫ Frequency of service ⌛ Journey time ⌀ Cost/one-way fare

SECTION TWO • AIRPORT DIRECTORY — DENVER • DUBAI

Boulder CO → Airporter »1 hr ⏱0800–2300.
Lakewood CO → RTD SkyRide: AF At airport »1 hr ⏱0330–0045»1 hr 15 min ⌀USD8. Also serves Stapleton Transfer Station, Denver city centre (Denver Bus Center and Market Street Station)
Littleton CO → RTD: SkyRide: AT »1 hr ⏱0330–2305 »1 hr 20 min ⌀USD8. Also serves Denver Tech Centre
Stapleton Transfer Station CO → RTD SkyRide: AS »30 min–1 hr ⏱0335–2400 »40 min ⌀USD4. Stapleton Transfer Station also served by SkyRide buses AB and AF
Denver city centre → Airporter »1 hr ⏱0800–2300.
Denver Metro Area → Golden West Shuttle »30 min–1 hr ⏱0730–2300.
Denver Metro Area (hotels) → Super Shuttle »15 min ⏱0630–2400.

Other towns and cities
Aspen/Snowmass →Colorado Mountain Express ✆(800) 525 6363
Front Range Cities →Airport Express ✆933 0505. For Castle Rock, Colorado Springs, Fort Collins, Longmont, Loveland CO
Golden lGolden West Shuttle ✆342 9300
Northeast CO →Dashabout Roadrunner ✆(800) 720-3274. For Fort Morgan, Julesburg, Sterling CO
Ski Areas CO → Resort Express ✆(800) 334 7433 For Breckenridge, Copper Mountain, Dillon, Frisco, Keystone and Vail CO
Wyoming →Airport Express ✆(970) 482 0505. For Cheyenne and Laramie WY

Regional Air Connections
Aspen CO ✈ »Several per day ⏱40 min
Cheyenne WY ✈ »Several per day ⏱40 min
Colorado Springs CO ✈ »Several per day ⏱35 min
Fort Collins/Loveland CO ✈ »Several per day ⏱30 min
Grand Junction CO ✈ »Several per week ⏱1 hr
Gunnison CO ✈ »Several per day ⏱50 min
Laramie WY ✈ »Several per day ⏱40 min
Montrose CO ✈ »Several per day ⏱1 hr
Pueblo CO ✈ »Several per day ⏱40 min
Scottsbluff NE ✈ »Several per day ⏱50 min
Steamboat Springs CO ✈ »Several per day ⏱50 min
Telluride CO ✈ »Several per day ⏱1 hr
Vail CO ✈ »At least daily ⏱45 min

Traveller's Notes
Denver International Airport is the newest major airport in the USA. It is a major hub for domestic flights.

DUBAI DXB
United Arab Emirates (see page 40)

National ✆ code: 971
Area ✆ code: 04
Local time: Winter GMT+4, Summer GMT+4
Dubai International Airport, Dubai, United Arab Emirates
✆245555/245333
℻244074
Location: 4 km/2½ miles SE of Dubai

TERMINALS AND TRANSFERS

Terminals
Arrival Terminal Airlines: All arrivals.
Departure Terminal Airlines: All departures.

Minimum transfer times
International: 1–2 hr

INFORMATION

Flight enquiries
Airport ✆245777 ℻244387

Information and help desks
Dubai Commerce & Tourism Promotion Board Arrival Terminal ✆245252 ℻245161 Hotel booking, Tourist information
Information Desk Arrival Terminal ✆ 2062032 ℻ 245161 ⏱24 hr Airport information, Flight information, Hotel booking
Information Desk Departure Terminal ✆ 2062047 ℻ 245161 ⏱24 hr Airport information, Flight information, Hotel booking, Tourist information

Emergencies
Police Departure Terminal
Police Arrival Terminal
Medical Departure Terminal ⏱24 hr
Medical Arrival Terminal ⏱24 hr
Lost Property Arrival Terminal Ground Level of Arrival Hall ✆245383 ⏱24 hr
Lost Property Departure Terminal Ground Level of Arrival Hall ✆245383 ⏱24 hr

AIRPORT FACILITIES

Money
ATM Arrival Terminal ⏱24 hr
ATM Departure Terminal ⏱24 hr
Bank Arrival Terminal ⏱24 hr
Bank Departure Terminal ⏱24 hr

Food and drink
Café/light meals Arrival Terminal ⏱24 hr
Café/light meals Departure Terminal ⏱24 hr
Restaurant Arrival Terminal Upper Level of Departure Terminal ⏱24 hr
Restaurant Departure Terminal Upper Level Transit Area ⏱24 hr

Shopping
Duty free, arrival Arrival Terminal ⏱24 hr
Duty free, departure Departure Terminal Ground Level in Shopping Mall ⏱24 hr
Shopping mall Departure Terminal Ground Level ⏱24 hr

Luggage
Trolleys/carts Arrival Terminal through-

✈ Air → Rail → Bus → Limousine 🚇 Metro/subway → Tram → Helicopter → Water transport • For map symbols, see p. 9

DUBAI • DUBLIN   SECTION TWO • AIRPORT DIRECTORY

out ⓣ24 hr ⓒFree
Trolleys/carts Departure Terminal throughout ⓣ24 hr ⓒFree

DISABLED TRAVELLERS

Arrival Terminal Adapted toilets; Lifts Personal assistance Medical Centre 24 hr
Departure Terminal Adapted toilets; Lifts Personal assistance Medical Centre 24 hr

SMOKING POLICY

Arrival Terminal Smoking areas provided throughout
Departure Terminal Smoking areas provided throughout

SPECIAL PASSENGER LOUNGES

All airlines Airport Executive Lounge Arrival Terminal Club members and Business class passengers

CONFERENCE AND BUSINESS FACILITIES

Conference centre Telephones, Fax service, Photocopier

AIRPORT HOTELS

Forte Grand Dubai ⓟ824040 ⓕ825540 384 Courtesy bus
Transit rooms 6 rooms

CAR RENTAL

Avis Arrival Terminal ⓟ 245219 ⓕ 244150
Budget Arrival Terminal ⓟ 245192 ⓕ 245987
EuropCar Arrival Terminal ⓟ 245240 ⓕ 244440
Hertz Arrival Terminal ⓟ 245222 ⓕ 244288
Interrent Arrival Terminal ⓟ 245044 ⓕ 244692
Thrifty Arrival Terminal ⓟ 245404 ⓕ 245418

CAR PARKING

Long-stay In front of Arrival/Departure Terminals 734 spaces ⓒAED5 per hr; AED10 per day after 24 hr
Off-airport 300 m E of Departure Terminal

TAXIS AND CHAUFFEUR-DRIVEN CARS

Taxis
Arrival Hall City centre ⤷15–20min ⓒAED35

Chauffeur-driven cars
Arrival Hall

REGIONAL AIR CONNECTIONS

Abu Dhabi ✈ »Several per week ⤷35 min
Bahrain ✈ »Several per day ⤷1 hr
Doha ✈ »Several per day ⤷1 hr
Muscat ✈ »Several per day ⤷50 min

TRAVELLER'S NOTES

The new terminal features the world's first bulk, and regular, duty-free shopping, including a purpose-built conveyor to transport duty-free goods straight to the aircraft.

DUBLIN   DUB

Republic of Ireland (see page 26)

National ⓟ code: 353
Area ⓟ code: 01
Local time: Winter GMT, Summer GMT+1
Aer Rianta Dublin Airport, Cloghran, County Dublin, Republic of Ireland
ⓟ8444900
ⓕ7044614
Location: 9 km/5½ miles N of Dublin

TERMINALS AND TRANSFERS

Terminals
Main Terminal Airlines: All airlines.
Layout: One Terminal: three Levels and 2 Piers (third pier and terminal extension under construction)

Minimum transfer times
International: 40 min Domestic: 40 min

INFORMATION

Flight enquiries
Aer Lingus ⓟ7056705 ⓕ7053884 Air France ⓟ8445653 ⓕ8446417 Air Portugal TAP ⓟ6798844 ⓕ6798810 Alitalia ⓟ8446035 ⓕ8446035 British Midland Airways ⓟ7044259 ⓕ8446556 CityJet ⓟ 8445577 Crossair ⓟ 704 4946 Delta Airlines ⓟ8444166 ⓕ8444171 Finnair ⓟ 8446565 Iberia ⓟ8444939 ⓕ8444939 Jersey European Airlines ⓟ7044946 Lufthansa ⓟ7044756 ⓟ8445944 Manx Airlines ⓟ7044259 ⓕ8446556 Ryanair ⓟ1550 200200 Sabena ⓟ8445454 ⓕ8445400 SAS ⓟ8445440 ⓕ8445414
Information and help desks
Airport Information Desk Main Terminal Arrival Hall ⓟ704 4222 ⓣ0600–2300 Airport information
Tourist Desk Main Terminal Arrival Hall ⓣ0630–2300 Hotel booking, Tourist information

Emergencies
Police Main Terminal Police station on arrival road ⓟ704 4300 ⓣ24 hr
Medical Main Terminal Contact via airport police ⓟ704 4300 ⓣ24 hr
Lost Property Main Terminal Contact airport police station on arrival road ⓟ7044481 ⓣ24 hr

AIRPORT FACILITIES

Money
ATM Main Terminal Arrival Hall/Departure Hall ⓣ24 hr
Bank Main Terminal Departure Concourse ⓣ1000–1600

ⓟ Phone no. ⓕ Fax no. ⓣ Hours of opening/operation » Frequency of service ⤷ Journey time ⓒ Cost/one-way fare

SECTION TWO • AIRPORT DIRECTORY — DUBLIN

Bureau de change Main Terminal Customs Hall ℗ Departure Hall ⓘ0615–2200

Food and drink
Bar Main Terminal Arrivals Level, Departures Level, Mezzanine Level
Café/light meals Main Terminal Arrivals Level, Departures Level, Mezzanine Level
Restaurant Main Terminal Mezzanine Level ⓘ1200–1500

Communications
Post office Main Terminal Car Park atrium ⓘ0900–1700
Fax service Main Terminal Business Centre in arrivals Hall cearly a/m to late p/m

Shopping
Duty free, departure Main Terminal Departure Pier A & Pier B ⓘAll departure times
Shopping mall Main Terminal Departure Pier Area A & B ⓘAll departure times

Luggage
Porters Main Terminal Departure/Arrival Halls ⓘAll flight times ℗ 704 4633
Trolleys/carts Main Terminal Arrival/Departure Halls ⓘAll flight times ⌀Free
Left Luggage Counter Main Terminal Car Park Atrium ⓘ0600–2200 ℗ 704 4633

DISABLED TRAVELLERS
Main Terminal Adapted toilets; Lifts Special car parking Ground Level multi-storey car park Phones at wheelchair height; Phones adapted for the deaf; Personal assistance Medical staff via Police Station 24 hr

SMOKING POLICY
Main Terminal Restricted

SPECIAL PASSENGER LOUNGES
Aer Lingus Gold Circle Club Main Terminal Pavilion area Pier A Club members and First class passengers
British Midland Diamond Club Lounge Main Terminal Pavilion area Club members
Delta Airlines Lounge Main Terminal Pavilion area Club members and First class passengers
Anna Livia Lounge Main Terminal Pavilion area Club members and designated passengers; all Diners Card holders.

CONFERENCE AND BUSINESS FACILITIES
Business Centre Arrivals Level ℗704 4836 ⓘ0900–1700 Telephones, Fax service, Power points, Modem Points, Photocopier, Secretarial service

AIRPORT HOTELS
Forte Crest International Airport ℗8444211 ℗8425874. 169 rooms Courtesy bus

CAR RENTAL
Avis Main Terminal Arrival Concourse ℗8445204
Budget Main Terminal Arrival Concourse ℗8420793
EuropCar Main Terminal Arrival Concourse ℗8444179
Hertz Main Terminal Arrival Concourse

CAR PARKING
Long-stay In front of airport Car Park 2 1800 spaces ⌀IEP4 per day; IEP20 per week
Park & Ride Entrance to airport ⌀IEP12 per wk

TAXIS AND CHAUFFEUR-DRIVEN CARS

Taxis
Arrival road outside Terminal City centre ➲30 min ⌀IEP10

Chauffeur-driven cars
Arrival roadway outside Terminal ECL ℗7044062

PUBLIC TRANSPORT

City & suburbs
Dublin city centre 🚌 qavg 15 min ⓘ0600–2330 ➲30 min ⌀IEP 1.10.
Dublin city centre (bus and Heuston rail stns) 🚌 Dublin Bus (Airlink) qavg 15 min ⓘ0640–2300 ➲25 min ⌀IEP2.50.

REGIONAL AIR CONNECTIONS
Birmingham ✈ »Several times daily ➲55 min
Bournemouth ✈ »Daily ➲60min
Bristol ✈ »Several per day ➲1 hr
Cardiff ✈ »At least daily ➲45 min
Cork ✈ »Several per day ➲45 min
Donegal ✈ »Daily ➲50 min
East Midland ✈ »Daily ➲65 min
Edinburgh ✈ »Several per day ➲70 min
Galway ✈ »At least daily ➲1 hr
Glasgow ✈ »Several Daily ➲1 hr
Isle of Man ✈ »At least daily ➲35 min
Kerry ✈ »At least daily ➲50 min
Leeds/Bradford ✈ »Several per day ➲1 hr
Liverpool ✈ »Several per day ➲45 min
All five London Airports ✈ »Hourly ➲65–70 min
Manchester ✈ »Several per day ➲1 hr
Plymouth ✈ »Daily ➲80 min
Shannon ✈ »Several per day ➲45 min

TRAVELLER'S NOTES
The airport is currently undergoing a considerable programme of expansion. This will include additional departure gates, check-in facilities and car parking spaces.

✈ Air 🚋 Rail 🚌 Bus 🚐 Limousine Ⓜ Metro/subway 🚊 Tram 🚁 Helicopter 🚢 Water transport • For map symbols, see p. 9

DUSSELDORF

DUS

Germany (see page 22)

National ☎ code: 49
Area ☎ code: 0211
Local time: Winter GMT+1, Summer GMT+2
Rhein-Ruhr Flughafen Düsseldorf, Postfach 300363, Düsseldorf, Germany
☎421 0
🖷421 6666
Location: 7 km/4 miles N of Düsseldorf

TERMINALS AND TRANSFERS

Terminals
Terminal A Airlines: Augsburg Airways, Finnair, Lauda Air, Lufthansa, Malev, SAS, United Airlines. Terminal C Airlines: Aer Lingus, Aeroflot, Air Canada, Air France, Air UK, Alitalia, Austrian Airlines, Brit Air, British Airways, Brymon Airways, City Flyer, Continental Airlines, Croatia Airlines, Crossair, CSA Czech Airlines, Deutsche BA, Donavia Airlines, Egypt Air, El Al, Eurowings, Ghana Airways, Gillair, Iberia, KLM, LOT, Lufthansa, Olympic Airways, OLT, RAS, Regional Airlines, Royal Air Maroc, Sabena, Swissair, Tarom, Tunis Air, Turkish Airlines, Tyrolean Airways, Yugoslav Airlines. Terminal D Airlines: Aero Lloyd, Canada 3000, Condor, Croatia Airlines, Cronus Airlines, Eurocypria, Eurowings, Germania, GTI Airlines, Hapag-Lloyd, Istanbul Airlines, Onur Air, Ratioflug, Shorouk Air, Sun Express, Taesa, Tunis Air, Turkish Airlines. Terminal E Airlines: Air Alfa, Air Berlin, Air Europa, Air Malta, Air Via Bulgarian, Air Yugoslavia, American Trans Air, Aviogenex, Avioimpex, Balkan Bulgarian, Eurobelgian Airlines, Futura, Jaro International, Kibris Turkish Airlines, LTU, Macedonian Airlines, Nordic East Airways, Nouvelair Tunisie, Oasis International, Pegasus, San Kazakhstan, Spanair, Sunways Airlines, Sunways Intersun, Tarom, Top Air, Transavia Holland, Viva Air.

INFORMATION

Flight enquiries
Airport ☎421 2223
Air Berlin ☎9418 888, Air France ☎421 6322, Royal Air Maroc ☎421 6322, Avioimpex ☎421 6510, Finnair ☎86 86 86, Alitalia ☎421 6322, British Airways ☎421 6686, Brymon Air ☎421 6686, Canada 3000 ☎421 6698, Continental Airlines ☎421 2173, Cronus Airlines ☎421 2173, Condor ☎86 86 86, Deutsche BA ☎421 6686, Donavia Airlines ☎421 6510, Eurobelgian Airlines ☎421 6510, Eurocypria Airlines ☎421 6322, Aer Lingus ☎421 6211, Eurowings ☎421 6275, Futura International Airways ☎421 6510, Viva Air ☎421 6510, Ghana Airways ☎421 6510, GTI Airlines ☎421 2173, Hapag-Lloyd ☎421 6698, Iberia ☎421 6698, Istanbul Airlines ☎421 6426, Macedonian Airlines ☎421 6322, Augsburg Airways ☎86 86 86, JAT ☎421 6211, KLM ☎421 6275, Air Malta ☎421 6322, Nouvelair Tunisie ☎421 6510, Air Alfa ☎421 7748, Lufthansa ☎86 86 86, LOT ☎421 6322, LTU ☎9418 888, Crossair ☎421 6291, El Al ☎421 6322, Balkan Bulgarian Airlines ☎421 6510, Malev ☎86 86 86, Egypt Air ☎421 6340, Lauda Air ☎86 86 86, Olympic Airways ☎421 6698, Onur Air ☎421 2173, CSA Czech Airlines ☎421 6322, Austrian Airlines ☎421 6524, Croatia Airlines ☎421 6322, Pegasus ☎421 6510, TAROM ☎421 6322, RAS Fluggesellschaft ☎9418 888, South African Airways ☎86 86 86, SAS ☎86 86 86, Sabena ☎421 6322, Spanair ☎421 6510, Swissair ☎421 6291, Germania ☎421 2173, Aeroflot ☎421 6510, Turkish Airlines ☎421 6510, Top Air ☎421 6510, Transavia ☎421 6322, Tunis Air ☎421 6322, United Airlines ☎421 2173, Air UK ☎421 6275, VLM ☎(02161) 699 99 22, Air Via Bulgarian Airways ☎421 6510, Regional Airlines ☎421 6211, Tyrolean Airlines ☎421 6524, SunExpress ☎421 6510, Aero Lloyd ☎421 6322, Air Yugoslavia ☎421 6211, Debonair ☎421 7748.

Information and help desks
Airport information Terminal C, Arrival Level and Departure Levels of all other terminals ☎421 22 23 Airport information, flights

EMERGENCIES
Police Terminals A, B and C
Medical Terminals A, C, D and E Departure Levels ☎421 2597
Lost Property Terminal C

AIRPORT FACILITIES

Money
Bank Departures Level Terminals A and C

Food and drink
Restaurant Terminal A Departures Level ⏱0600–2130
Café/light meals Terminal C Departures Level ⏱0430–0030
Restaurant Terminal C Departures Level ⏱0430–0030
Restaurant Terminal D Departures Level 0330–2130
Restaurant Terminal E Departures Level 0430–2115

Communications
Fax service Terminal C Departure Level and in the Arrivals Terminal ⏱24 hr
Post office Between Terminals C and D ⏱0800–1800 Mon–Fri; 0800–1400 Sat

Shopping
Duty free Departure Levels of all terminals
Gift Shop Departure Levels of all terminals
News, Stationery & Books Departure Levels of all terminals

Luggage
Left Luggage Counter Arrival Terminal ⏱24 hr ⊘DM3.50 per day
Trolleys/carts Departure Levels of all terminals ⏱24 hr ⊘DM2

DISABLED TRAVELLERS
Main Terminal Adapted toilets; Lifts Personal assistance Via Johanniter Terminal B Departure Level

SMOKING POLICY
Terminals A, C, D, E Permitted throughout

SPECIAL PASSENGER LOUNGES
Diners Club Terminal A Departures Level Room 6022 Diners Club cardholders and guests
British Airways Executive Club Lounge Terminal C Departures Level Club members, First and Business class passengers

SECTION TWO • AIRPORT DIRECTORY

DUSSELDORF

Lufthansa Business Suite Terminal A Departures Level Club members and First class passengers

CONFERENCE AND BUSINESS FACILITIES

Arabella Airport Hotel, on the roof of car park 3 ✆41 730 Telephones, Fax service, Photocopier, Secretarial service, conference rooms

AIRPORT HOTELS

Arabella ✆41 730

CAR RENTAL

Alamo Ground floor of car park 3 ✆42 77 70
Avis Ground floor of car park 3 ✆421 67 48
EuropCar Ground floor of car park 3 ✆421 64 95
Hertz Ground floor of car park 3 ✆421 64 48
Sixt Ground floor of car park 3 ✆421 64 99

CAR PARKING

Long-stay Car park 4 ⊘DEM1 per 30 min; DEM1 per hr; DEM13 per 1st week; DEM11 per 2nd week; DEM9 per 3rd week
Short-stay Car park 1 ⊘DEM2 per 30 min; DEM4 per hr
Short-stay Car park 2 ⊘DEM2 per 30 min; DEM4 per hr; DEM21 per day
Short-stay Car park 3 ⊘DEM2 per 30 min; DEM4 per hr; DEM21 per day (DEM35 per day in protected parking lots)

TAXIS AND CHAUFFEUR-DRIVEN CARS

Taxis
Outside Main Terminal Building City centre ➲15 min ⊘DM25

PUBLIC TRANSPORT

City & suburbs
Düsseldorf city centre ➾RB »20 min ⓞ0521–0027 ➲26 min ⊘DEM2.60.
Düsseldorf city centre (Hbf – central rail stn) ➾ DB »10 min ⓞ0525–0035 ➲11 min ⊘DEM2.60.
Eller ➾ S-Bahn S7 »Avg 20 min ⓞ0500–0030 ➲21 min.

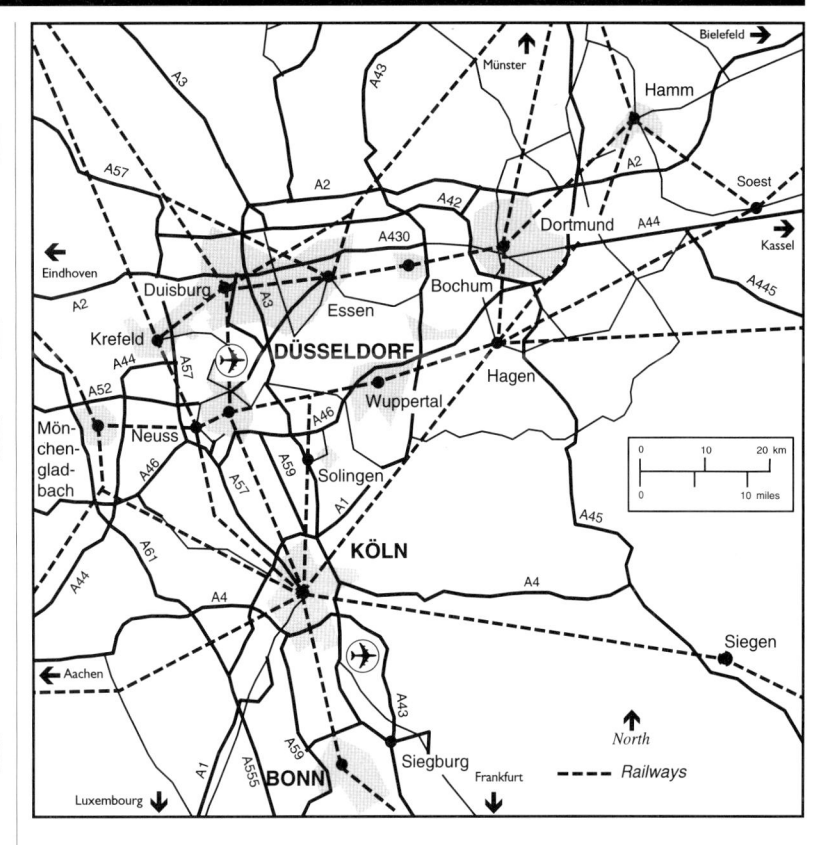

Other towns and cities
Bielefeld ➾DB »Avg 20 min ⓞ0505–0037 ➲1 hr 55 min.
Bonn ➾DB »Avg 20 min ⓞ0645–0100 ➲1 hr 07 min.
Cologne ➾DB »Avg 20 min ⓞ0645–0100 ➲1 hr 07 min.
Dortmund ➾DB »Avg 30 min ⓞ0539–2337 ➲1 hr 15 min.
Essen ➾DB »Avg 30 min ⓞ0539–2337 ➲39 min.
Frankfurt ➾Lufthansa/DB »4 per day ⓞ0600–1800 ➲2hr 30min ⊘Free.
Lufthansa Express free for Lufthansa passengers
Krefeld ➾DB »Avg 20 min ⓞ0525–2305 ➲51 min.
Mönchengladbach ➾DB »20 min ⓞ)505–0035 ➲45 min.
Münster ➾DB »Avg 20 min ⓞ0547–0005 ➲1 hr 45 min.
Ratingen ➾Busline 760 »avg 20 min ⓞ0522–2215 ➲35 min.

REGIONAL AIR CONNECTIONS

Amsterdam ✈ »Several per day ➲50 min
Berlin ✈ »Several per day ➲1 hr 5 min
Brussels ✈ »Several per day ➲50 min
Dresden ✈ »Several per day ➲1 hr 10 min
Erfurt ✈ »Several per week ➲1 hr 10 min
Frankfurt ✈ »Several per day ➲1 hr
Hamburg ✈ »Several per day ➲1 hr
Leipzig ✈ »Several per week ➲1 hr 5 min
Munich ✈ »Several per day ➲1 hr 5 min
Nuremberg ✈ »Several per week ➲1 hr
Paris ✈ »Several per day ➲1 hr 5 min
Saarbrücken ✈ »Several per week ➲50 min
Stuttgart ✈ »Several per day ➲1 hr

TRAVELLER'S NOTES

The new Express Airport at Mönchengladbach has services to London City, London-Luton, Westerland, Paris

✈ Air ➾ Rail ➾ Bus ➾ Limousine Ⓡ Metro/subway ➾ Tram ➾ Helicopter ➾ Water transport • For map symbols, see p. 9

EAST MIDLANDS   EMA

United Kingdom (see page 41)

National ✆ code: 44
Area ✆ code: 01332
Local time: Winter GMT, Summer GMT+1
East Midlands Airport, Castle Donington Derby DE74 2SA, United Kingdom
✆852852
🖷850393
Location: 19 km/12 miles SE of Derby

TERMINALS AND TRANSFERS

Terminals
Main Terminal Airlines: All airlines.

Minimum transfer times
International: 30 min Domestic: 30 min

INFORMATION

Flight enquiries
Airport ✆852852

Information and help desks
Information desk Main Terminal Concourse ✆852852 ⓗAll flight departures Airport, Tourist information

EMERGENCIES

Police Main Terminal Information Desk ✆852852
Medical Main Terminal Information Desk ✆852852
Lost Property Main Terminal Information Desk ✆852852

AIRPORT FACILITIES

Money
Bureau de change Main Terminal Opposite Information Desk ⓗAll flight departures
Bureau de change Main Terminal Departures hall ⓗAll flight departures

Food and drink
Café/light meals Main Terminal First Floor ⓗAll flight departures
Café/light meals Main Terminal International departure lounge ⓗAll flight departures
Bar Main Terminal International departure lounge ⓗAll flight departures
Bar Main Terminal first floor

Shopping
Duty free, departure Main Terminal International Departure Lounge ⓗAll flight departures
News, Stationery & Books Main Terminal Main entrance ⓗAll flight departures
Gift Shop Main Terminal Main Concourse ⓗAll flight departures

DISABLED TRAVELLERS

Main Terminal Adapted toilets; Lifts; Phones at wheelchair height

SMOKING POLICY

Main Terminal Restricted

SPECIAL PASSENGER LOUNGES

Euroclass Lounge Main Terminal International Departure Lounge
British Midland Airways Diamond Club Lounge Main Terminal Airside access

CONFERENCE AND BUSINESS FACILITIES

Britannia Conference Suites, 🖷812469 ⓗ0900–1700

AIRPORT HOTELS

Donnington Thistle ✆850700 Courtesy bus

CAR RENTAL

Alamo Main Terminal Main Concourse ✆853551
Avis Main Terminal Main Concourse ✆811403
EuropCar Main Terminal Main Concourse ✆853679
Hertz Main Terminal Main Concourse ✆811726

CAR PARKING

Short-stay ⊘GBP1.30 per hr, ⊘GBP2.10 per 2 hr, ⊘GBP3 per 3 hr, ⊘GBP3.70 per 4 hr, ⊘GBP5 per 24 hr ✆0800 128128
Long-stay 4000 spaces ⊘GBP3.20 per day (up to 6 days), GBP3 per day (over 6 days) ✆0800 128128

TAXIS AND CHAUFFEUR-DRIVEN CARS

Taxis
Main entrance Derby city centre ⤴20 min ⊘GBP12 ✆814225

PUBLIC TRANSPORT

Airport to Airport
Gatwick 🚌National Express ✆ 0990 757747
Heathrow 🚌National Express ✆ 0990 757747

City & suburbs
Derby 🚌Midland Fox ⓗ0805–1730 ⤴30 min ⊘GBP2.

Other towns and cities
Leicester 🚌Midland Fox 121–124 »1 hr peak times, slower off-peak ⓗ0715–1745 ⤴1 hr–1 hr 15 min ⊘GBP1.80.
Nottingham 🚌Barton Transport 3 »Approx. 1 hr ⓗ0720–2140 ⤴1 hr ⊘GBP1.90. ✆(01602) 255292

REGIONAL AIR CONNECTIONS

Edinburgh ✈ »Several per day ⤴55 min
Glasgow ✈ »At least daily ⤴55 min
Jersey ✈ »At least daily ⤴1 hr

✆ Phone no. 🖷 Fax no. ⓗ Hours of opening/operation » Frequency of service ⤴ Journey time ⊘ Cost/one-way fare

SECTION TWO • AIRPORT DIRECTORY   EDMONTON

EDMONTON   YEG
Canada (see page 18)

National ⌀ code: 1
Area ⌀ code: 403
Local time: Winter GMT-7,
Summer GMT-6
Edmonton International Airport,
PO Box 9860, Edmonton AB T5J
2T2, Canada
⌀890 8900
WWW site: http://www.edmonton-airports.com
Location: 30 km/19 miles S of Edmonton

TERMINALS AND TRANSFERS

Terminals
Main Terminal Airlines: All airlines.
Layout: Arrivals Level 1 (Arrivals, Baggage Claim, Car Rental, Ground Transportation), Departures Level 2 (Departures), Gates 1–40, Mezzanine Level 3

Minimum transfer times
International: 1 hr 30 min Domestic: 45 min

INFORMATION

Flight enquiries
Air Canada ⌀423 1101 Canada 3000
⌀890 4592 Canadian Airlines ⌀890 4290
Westjet ⌀890 8040

Information and help desks
Information Desk Main Terminal Arrivals Level 1 ⌀0730–2330 ⌀890 8382 Airport information, Tourist information

Emergencies
Police (Security) Main Terminal Arrivals Level 1 ⌀890 2354
Medical
First Aid Main Terminal Departures Level 2
Lost Property Main Terminal Arrivals Level 1 (at Information desk)
⌀0700–2330

AIRPORT FACILITIES

Money
ATM Main Terminal Departures Level 2
Bureau de change Main Terminal Departures Level 2

Food and drink
Bar Main Terminal Departures Level 2
Café/light meals Main Terminal throughout

Communications
Fax Main Mutual of Omaha/Travel Extra Foreign Exchange Main Terminal Departures Level 2
Internet Nettime kiosk Main Terminal Departures Level 2 near escalator
Modems Main Terminal Mezzanine Level 3

Shopping
Duty free, departure, Main Terminal Departures Level 2
Gift Shop Main Terminal Departures Level 2 across from escalator
News, Stationery & Books Main Terminal Departures Level 2

Luggage
Left Luggage/Lockers Ground Transportation Office Main Terminal Arrivals Level 1 ⌀890 8553
Trolleys/carts All Terminals throughout ⌀Free

DISABLED TRAVELLERS
Adapted toilets; Lifts; Special Car Parking; Phones at wheelchair height; Phones adapted for the deaf; Personal assistance ⌀890 8382

SPECIAL PASSENGER LOUNGES
Air Canada Maple Leaf Lounge Main Terminal Departures Level 2 near Gates 1–16
Canadian Airlines Empress Lounge Main Terminal Departures Level 2 near Gates 19–40

CONFERENCE AND BUSINESS FACILITIES
Business Centre Mutual of Omaha/Travel Extra Foreign Exchange Main Terminal Departures Level 2 fax, photocopying
Conference Rooms, Main Terminal

CAR RENTAL
Avis Main Terminal Arrivals Level 1 ⌀890 7596

Budget Main Terminal Arrivals Level 1 ⌀448 2000
Hertz Main Terminal Arrivals Level 1 ⌀890 4435
National/Tilden Main Terminal Arrivals Level 1 ⌀890 7232
Thrifty Main Terminal Arrivals Level 1 ⌀428 8555

CAR PARKING
Long-stay Long Term Parking Lot ⌀CAD7 per day
Short-stay Hourly Parking Lot across from Main Terminal ⌀CAD1 30 min, CAD10 per day (max)

TAXIS AND CHAUFFEUR-DRIVEN CARS

Taxis
City centre ⌾30 min ⌀CAD29

PUBLIC TRANSPORT

City & suburbs
Edmonton (city centre hotels) 🚌 Sky Shuttle ⌾20 min ⌚0415–0025 ⌾1 hr ⌀CAD11. For Greyhound Bus Stn
Edmonton (West End hotels) 🚌 Sky Shuttle ⌾45 min ⌚0405–0045 ⌾45 min ⌀CAD11
Edmonton (University and hotels) 🚌 Sky Shuttle ⌾45 min ⌚0420–2400 ⌾45 ⌾1 hr ⌀CAD11. For University and South End Greyhound Bus Stn

REGIONAL AIR CONNECTIONS
Calgary AB ✈ »Several per day ⌾40 min
Fort McMurray AB ✈ »Several per day ⌾1 hr
Grand Prairie AB ✈ »Several per day ⌾1 hr
Peace River AB ✈ »At Least daily ⌾1 hr

TRAVELLER'S NOTES
Edmonton is gateway to Canada's North. Volunteer Airport Ambassadors are available throughout the terminal to offer a helping hand to traveller's.

125

✈ Air 🚆 Rail 🚌 Bus 🚐 Limousine Ⓜ Metro/subway 🚊 Tram 🚁 Helicopter 🚢 Water transport • For map symbols, see p. 9

FRANKFURT — FRA

Germany (see page 22)

National & code: 49
Area & code: 069
Local time: Winter GMT+1, Summer GMT+2
Frankfurt Main International Airport, D-6000 Frankfurt am Main 75, Germany
✆ 690 1
🖷 690 790081
Internet e-mail: frankfurt@xxx.com
WWW site: htp\ \ www.frankfurt.com
Location: 9 km/5½ miles SW of Frankfurt

TERMINALS AND TRANSFERS

Terminals

Terminal 1 Airlines: All charter flights (From Pier C), Palair Macedonian Airlines (Terminal Area B/C), Air Algérie (Terminal Area B), Air India (Terminal Area C), Aerolineas Argentinas (Terminal Area B), Royal Air Maroc (Terminal Area B), Avianca Colombian Airlines (Terminal Area B), Finnair (Terminal Area B), Alitalia (Terminal Area B), British Midland Airways (Terminal Area B), Biman Bangladesh Airlines (Terminal area C), Royal Brunei Airlines (Terminal Area C), Air Baltic (Terminal Area B), Air China (Terminal Area B), China Airlines (Terminal Area C), Canadian Airlines International (Terminal Area A), Cubana (Terminal Area C), Cyprus Airlines (Terminal Area B), Condor (Terminal Area B), Maersk Air (Terminal Area B), Emirates (Terminal Area C), Ethiopian Airlines (Terminal Area C), Viva Air (Terminal Area B), Garuda Indonesian Airlines (Terminal Area C), Gulf Air (Terminal Area C), Hapag Lloyd (Terminal Area B), Air Seychelles (Terminal Area C), Uzbekistan Airways (Terminal area C), Iberia (Terminal Area B), Meridiana (Terminal Area b), Business Air (Terminal Area A), TAT European Airlines (Terminal Area C), Istanbul Airlines (Terminal Area C), Iran Air (Terminal Area C), Yemen Airways (Terminal Area C), Arkia Israeli Arlines (Terminal Area C), Spanair (Terminal Area B/C), Adria Airways (Terminal Area A), Jat Yugoslav Airlines (Terminal Area B), Kazakhstan Airlines (Terminal Area B), Korean Airlines (Terminal Area B), Kenya Airways (Terminal Area B), Kuwait Airways (Terminal Area B), Luxair (Terminal Area A), Lufthansa (A mainly short-haul & domestic, B mainly long-haul), LTU International Airways (Terminal Area B/C), Crossair (Terminal Area B), El Al Israel Airlines (Terminal Area C), Balkan Bulgarian Airlines (Terminal Area B/C), Malev Hungarian (Terminal Area B), Air Madagascar (Terminal Area B), Middle East Airlines (Terminal Area B), Malaysian Airlines (Terminal Area C), Air Mauritius (Terminal Area B), Egyptair (Terminal Area B), Lauda-Air (Terminal Area A), Eurowings (Terminal Area B), Olympic Airways (Terminal Area B), Austrian Airlines (Terminal Area B), Croatia Airlines (Terminal Area B), Estonian Air (Terminal Area C), Pakistan International Airlines (Terminal Area B), Philippine Airlines (Terminal Area C), Royal Nepal

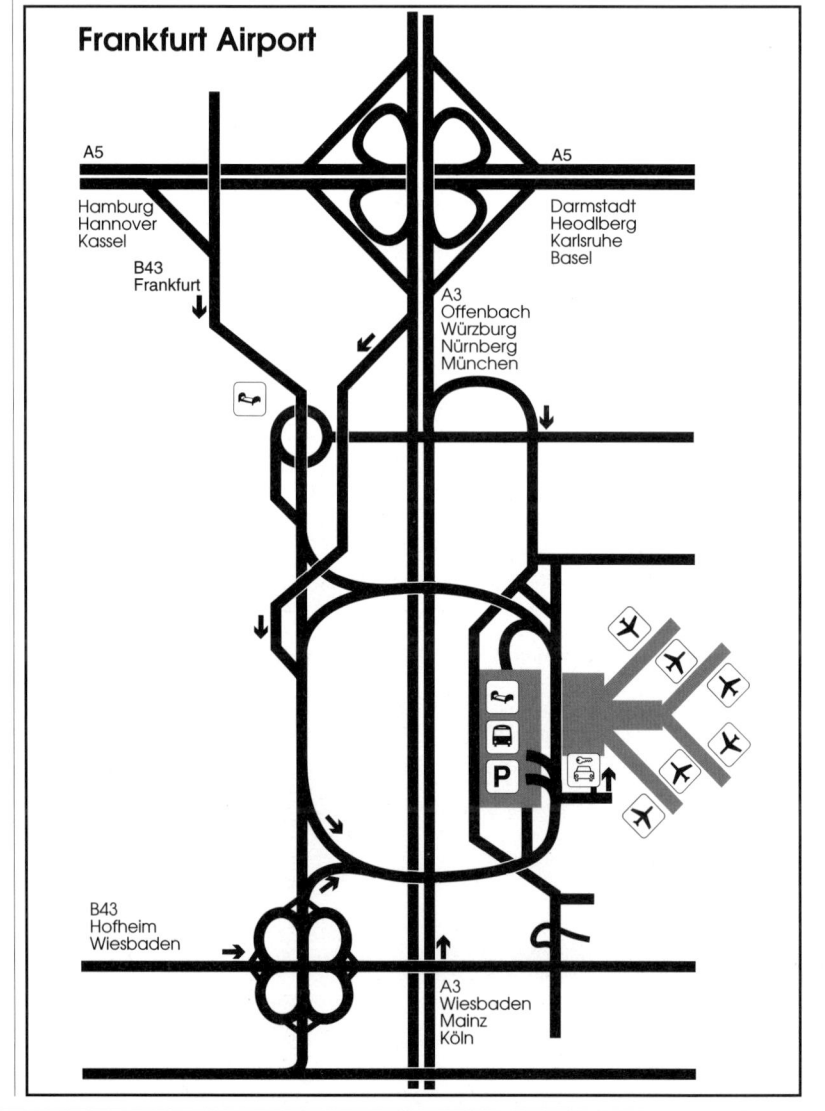

✆ Phone no. 🖷 Fax no. ◷ Hours of opening/operation ⇉ Frequency of service ➲ Journey time ⊘ Cost/one-way fare

SECTION TWO • AIRPORT DIRECTORY — FRANKFURT

FRANKFURT TERMINAL 1
Arrivals Level

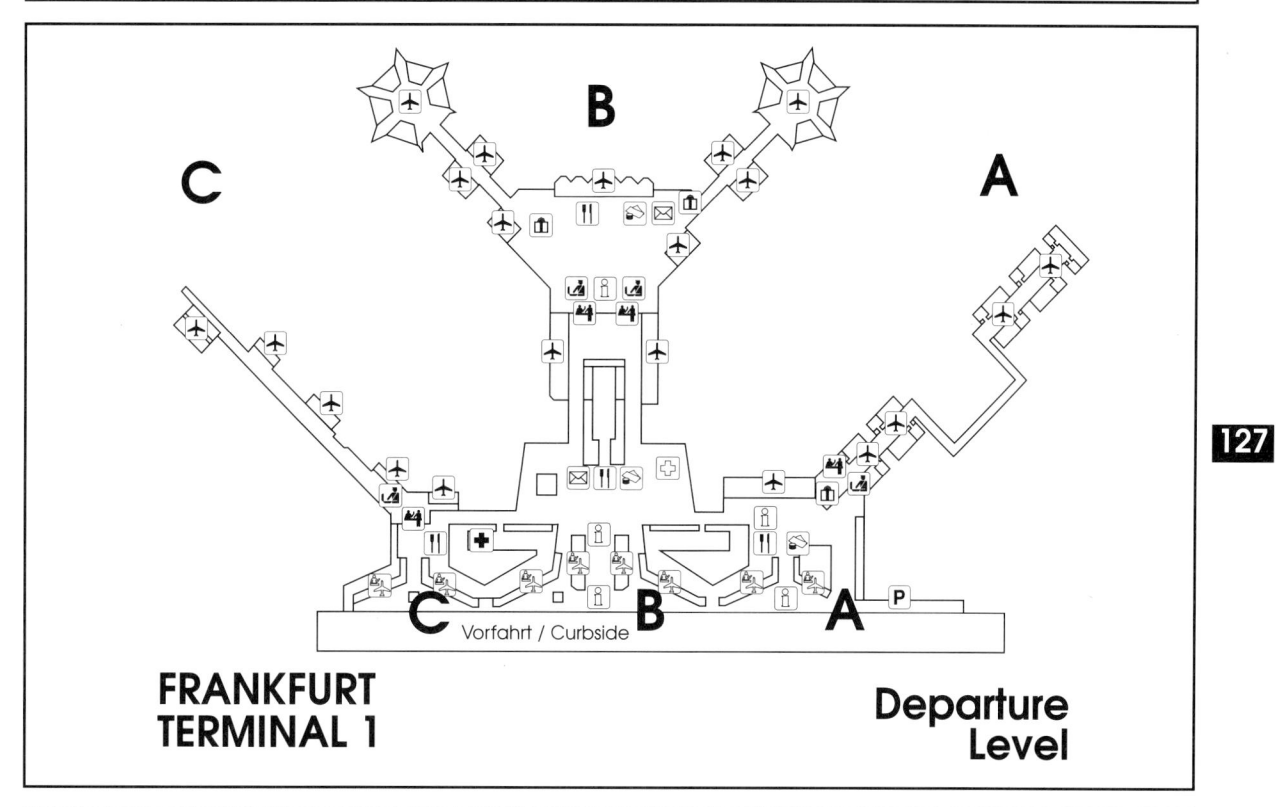

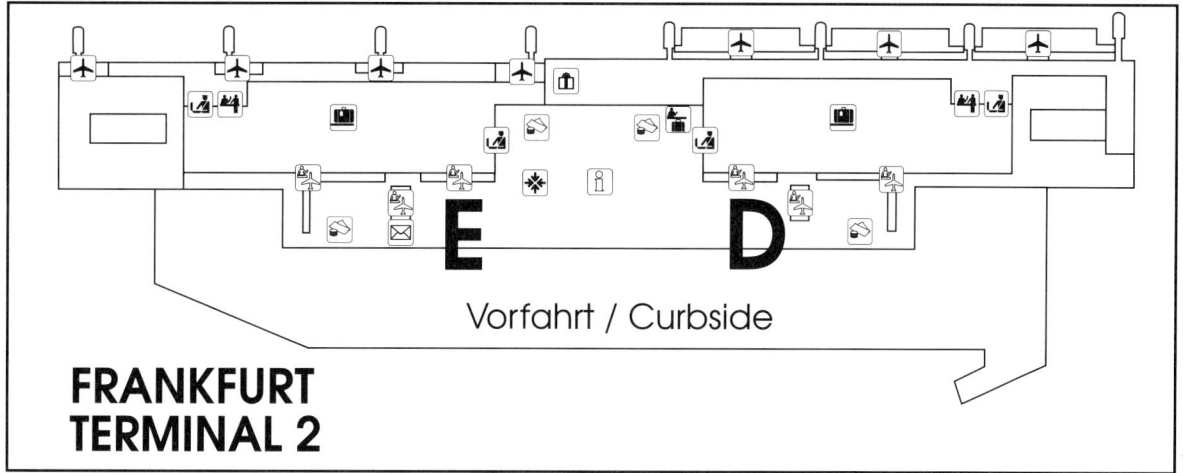

C Vorfahrt / Curbside B   A

FRANKFURT TERMINAL 1
Departure Level

C Vorfahrt / Curbside B   A

FRANKFURT TERMINAL 2

E   D

Vorfahrt / Curbside

✈ Air · Rail · Bus · Limousine · Metro/subway · Tram · Helicopter · Water transport • For map symbols, see p. 9

FRANKFURT

Airlines (Terminal Area B), Syrian Arab Airlines (Terminal Area B), Varig Brazilian (Terminal Area B), Royal Jordanian Airlines (Terminal Area B), Tarom Romanian Air (Terminal Area B), South African Airways (Terminal Area B), Sudan Airways (Terminal Area C), SAS (Terminal Area A), Singapore Airlines (Terminal Area B/C), Swissair (Terminal Area B), Aeroflot (Terminal Area B), Saudia (Terminal Area C), Air Namibia (Terminal Area B), Thai Airways (Terminal Area B), Turkish Airlines (Terminal Area B), Air Portugal TAP (Terminal Area B), Tunis Air (Terminal Area B), TWA (Terminal Area B), American Trans Air (Terminal Area B/C), United Airlines (Terminal Area B/C), Air Lanka (Terminal Area C), Air Zimbabwe (Terminal Area B), Transaero Airlines (Terminal Area B/C), Air Europa (Terminal Area B/C), VIASA Venezuelan (Terminal Area B), Tyrolean Airways (Terminal Area B), Aero Lloyd (Terminal Area C). Layout: OlderTerminal divided into three areas: A, mainly short haul and mainly Lufthansa; B, long haul; C, mainly charter. each area on five Levels, inc. rail station at basement Level

Terminal 2 Airlines: Air France (Terminal Area D), Belavia (Terminal Area D), British Airways (Terminal Area E), BWIA International (Terminal Area E), Continental Airlines (Terminal Area E), Cathay Pacific Airways (Terminal Area D), Delta Airlines (Terminal Area D), Aer Lingus (Terminal Area D), Icelandair (Terminal Area D), Japan Airlines (Terminal Area D), KLM (Terminal Area 2), Air Malta (Terminal Area E), Lot Polish Airlines (Terminal Area E), Malev Hungarian (Terminal area D), All Nippon Airways (Terminal Area E), Northwest Airlines (Terminal Area E), Air New Zealand (Terminal Area D), CSA Czechoslovak (Terminal Area D), Ukraine International Airlines (Terminal Area D), Qantas Airways (Terminal Area E), Air Engadiana (Terminal Area D), Sabena World Airlines (Terminal Area D), Lithuanian Airlines (Terminal Area D), Air UK (Terminal Area E), USAir (Terminal Area E), World Airways (Terminal Area D). Layout: New Terminal on 3 Levels 2 Departure Areas D & E. Access only from Terminal 1 for departing passengers

Minimum transfer times
International: 45 min (some longer - check with airline) **Domestic:** 45 min

Transfer between terminals
Monorail ≫2–3 min; Terminals 1 and 2 ⊘Free

INFORMATION

Flight enquiries
Airport ☏690 305 11

Information and help desks
Airport Information Desk Terminal 2 Centre Arrival Hall ⊙0630–2200 Airport information, Flights
Airport Information Desk Terminal 1 Arrival B Pier Area (2 desks) ☏690 704 02 ⊙0630–2200 Airport information, Flights Hotel booking, Tourist information
Community Service Desk Terminal 1 Arrival Area centre of B Pier ☏690 50 20 ⊙0800–1800 Airport information Hotel booking, Tourist information
Information Desk Terminal 2 E Pier Area ☏690 70402 ⊙0800–1800 Airport information Hotel booking, Tourist information
Lufthansa Information Desk Terminal 2 Arrival Area ☏ ⊙0600–2300 Airport information, Flights
Lufthansa Information Desks Terminal 1 Pier A Departure Area ☏ Pier B Departure Area (2 desks) ☏690 712 22 ⊙0600–2300 Airport information, Flights

EMERGENCIES
Police Terminal 1 throughout ⊙24 hr
Police Terminal 2 throughout ⊙24 hr
Medical Terminal 1 Arrival Level Piers B/C ☏690 667 67 ⊙24 hr
Medical Terminal 2 First aid in Pier E ⊙24 hr
Lost Property Terminal 1 Pier B Arrival Level ☏690 663 59 ⊙0700–1900

AIRPORT FACILITIES

Money
ATM Terminal 1 A pier ⊙24 hr
Bank Terminal 1 Departure B Pier Skyline Arcade ⊙0700–2130
Bank Terminal 1 Arrival Area B Pier ⊙0715–2100 Mon-Sat; 0715–1500 Sun
Bank Terminal 1 Departure Area B Pier Dom ⊙0700–2130
Bank Terminal 1 Departure Area B Pier Int ⊙0700–2130
Bank Terminal 1 Arrival A Pier ⊙0600–2300
Bank Terminal 2 Departure Area ⊙0600–2300 Mon–Fri; 1000–1800 Sat, Sun
Bank Terminal 2 Arrival Area
Bureau de change Terminal 1 Pier B ⊙0700–2130 Mon–Sat

Food and drink
Bar Terminal 1 Central Transit Area ⊙0800–2300
Café/light meals Terminal 1 Departure Area A/B Pier ⊙24 hr
Restaurant Terminal 1 Departure Piers A/B ⊙24 hr
Restaurant Terminal 2 D pier Departure Area ⊙0600–2345

Communications
Post office Terminal 1 B Pier ⊙0600–2200
Post office Terminal 2 Arrival Area

Shopping
Duty free, departure Terminal 1 A/B/C/Departure Areas ⊙All flight times
Duty free, departure Terminal 2 Main Departure/Transit Area ⊙All flight times
Hairdresser Terminal 1 A Pier Area ⊙0800–2200
Hairdresser Terminal 2 D Pier Departure/Transit ⊙0900–2300
Pharmacy Terminal 1 A Pier Area ⊙24 hr
Shopping mall Terminal 1 Sky Line Arcade ⊙All flight times
Shopping mall Terminal 2 Central/Departure Area ⊙All flight times

Luggage
Left Luggage Counter Terminal 1 A Pier/B Pier Arrival ⊙24 hr
Left Luggage Counter Terminal 2 D Pier Arrival Area ⊙24 hr
Porters Terminal 1 throughout ⊙All flight times
Porters Terminal 2 throughout ⊙All flight times
Trolleys/carts Terminal 1 throughout ⊙24 hr ⊘Free
Trolleys/carts Terminal 2 throughout ⊙24 hr ⊘Free

DISABLED TRAVELLERS
Terminal 1 Adapted toilets; Lifts Special car parking Via Departure Level; Personal assistance
Terminal 2 Adapted toilets; Lifts Special car parking Underground garage; Personal assistance

SMOKING POLICY
Terminal 1 Permitted throughout except boarding gates
Terminal 2 Permitted throughout except boarding gates

SPECIAL PASSENGER LOUNGES
American Express Lounge Terminal 1
Air Canada Maple Leaf Lounge Terminal 1 B Pier Departure Area Gallery
American Airlines Admiral's Club Lounge Terminal 1 B Pier Departure Area
British Airways Executive Club Lounge Terminal 1
Cathay Pacific Lounge Terminal 1 First

☏ Phone no. ⊠ Fax no. ⊙ Hours of opening/operation ≫ Frequency of service ⊃ Journey time ⊘ Cost/one-way fare

SECTION TWO • AIRPORT DIRECTORY — FRANKFURT

class passengers
Delta Airlines Delta Lounge Terminal 1 First class passengers
Diners Club Lounge Terminal 1 Diners Club cardholders and guests
Lufthansa Senator Club Lounge Terminal 1 Departure Level A Pier and Departure Level B Pier Club members
Lufthansa Frequent Traveller Lounge Terminal 1 Departure Level A Pier First and Business class passengers
Qantas Airways Captains Club Lounge Terminal 1
TWA Ambassadors Club Lounge Terminal 1 Departure Level Pier B
All other airlines Europe City Club Lounge Terminal 1

CONFERENCE AND BUSINESS FACILITIES

Airport Conference Centre, Across railway line ℅690 70503 ℅690 71618 ⏰0700–2130 Mon–Sat Telephones, Fax service, Power points, Modem Points, Photocopier, Secretarial service, Translation/Interpretation service, Travel advice

AIRPORT HOTELS

Sheraton ℅696 9770 ℅696 9771. 300 rooms Courtesy bus

CAR RENTAL

Alamo Terminal 1 Arrival Area
Avis Terminal 1 Arrival Area ℅690 2777
EuropCar Terminal 1 Arrival Area ℅690 5464
Hertz Terminal 1 Arrival Area

CAR PARKING

Short-stay Multi-storey/underground Terminal 1 12000 spaces ⊘DEM4 first hr; DEM5–24 per day

TAXIS AND CHAUFFEUR-DRIVEN CARS

Taxis
In front of Terminal Building 1 City centre ➲20 min ⊘DEM35

PUBLIC TRANSPORT

City & suburbs
Frankfurt city centre (Hbf – central rail stn) 🚆 S-Bahn: Line S1 »20 min ⏰0500–2230 ➲12 min ⊘DEM3.80. S-Bahn connects at Frankfurt Hbf to extensive system of S-Bahn and U-Bahn (subway) lines to all suburbs and city centre stops.

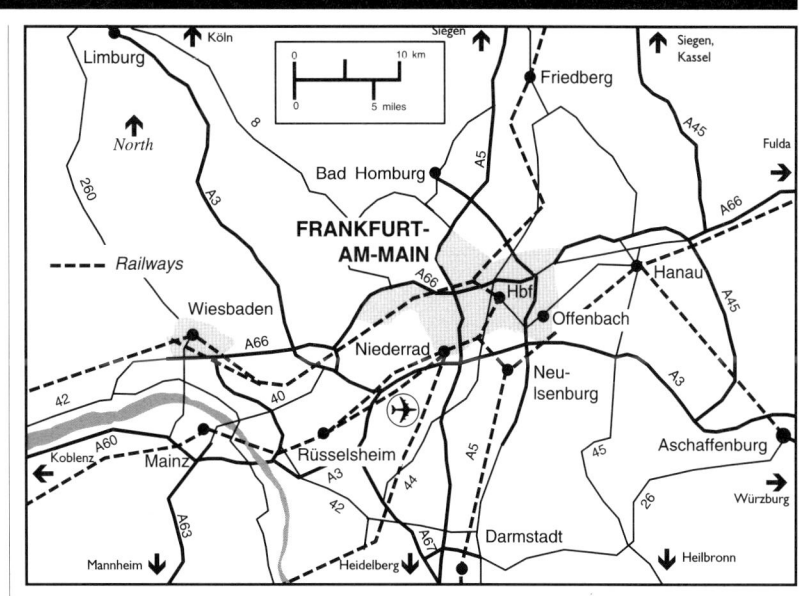

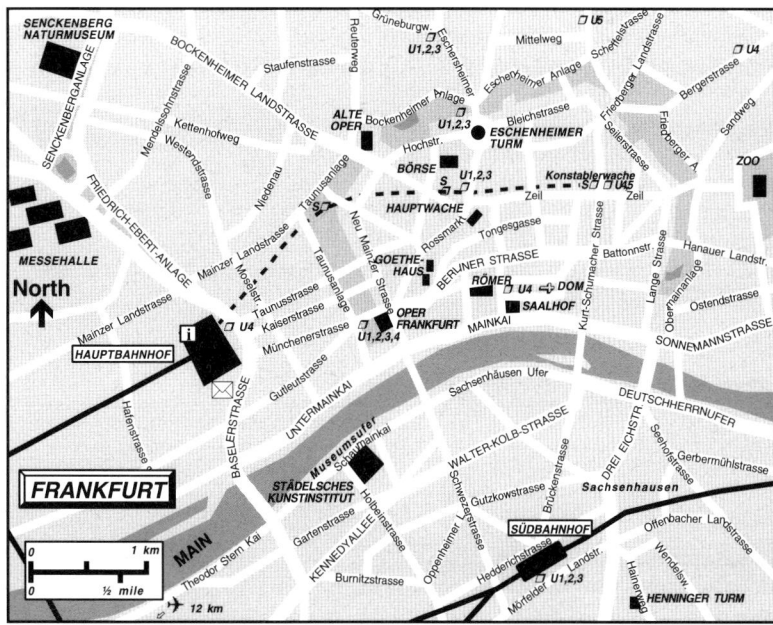

Other towns and cities
Bonn 🚆DB »avg 1 hr (day), 2 hr (night) ⏰24 hr ➲1 hr 41 min.
Bremen 🚆DB »avg 1 hr ⏰0603–1804 ➲5 hr 11 min.
Cologne 🚆DB »avg 1 hr Day/2 hr night ⏰24 hr ➲2 hr.
Dortmund 🚆DB »avg 1 hr ⏰0603–1804 ➲3 hr 15 min.
Düsseldorf 🚆DB »avg 1 hr (day), 2 hr (night) ⏰24 hr ➲2 hr 29 min.
Hamburg 🚆DB »avg 1 hr ⏰0603–1804 ➲6 hr.
Mainz 🚆S-Bahn Lines S1, S8 »20–30 min ⏰0500–2330 ➲29 min.
Wiesbaden 🚆S-Bahn Lines S1, S8 »20–30 min ⏰0500–2330 ➲41 min.

REGIONAL AIR CONNECTIONS

Cologne/Bonn ✈ »Several per day ➲45 min
Dresden ✈ »Several per day ➲1 hr
Düsseldorf ✈ »Several per day ➲50 min
Friedrichshafen ✈ »Several per day ➲50 min
Leipzig ✈ »Several per day ➲55 min
Munich ✈ »Several per day ➲55 min
Münster ✈ »Several per day ➲1 hr
Nuremberg ✈ »Several per day ➲45 min
Stuttgart ✈ »Several per day ➲45 min

✈ Air 🚆 Rail 🚌 Bus 🚘 Limousine Ⓜ Metro/subway 🚋 Tram 🚁 Helicopter ⛴ Water transport • For map symbols, see p. 9

GENEVA GVA
Switzerland (see page 38)

National ☏ code: 41
Area ☏ code: 22
Local time: Winter GMT+1, Summer GMT+2
Address: Aéroport International de Genève, Case postale 100, 1215 Genève 15, Switzerland
☏: 717 71 11
📠: 798 43 77
Location: 5km/3mls N of Geneva.

Terminals and Transfers
Main Terminal Layout: Three levels. Level -1 arrivals and train station; Level 0 check-in; Level 1 departures; Level 2 restaurants and lounges.

Information
Flight enquiries
☏ 157 15 00
Airport ☏ 717 71 11 Level -1

Information and help desks
Tourist Information ☏ 717 80 83 Level -1
Hotel Reservations ☏ 788 05 58 Level -1

Emergencies
Police ☏ 788 22 26 Level -1
Medical ☏ 717 71 90 Level 0
Lost Property ☏ 799 33 35/788 22 26 Level -1

Airport Facilities
Money
Bureau de Change ⏱ 0600–2100 ☏ 798 04 21 Level 1
Bureau de Change ⏱ 0800–2300 ☏ 798 21 80 Level -1

Food and drink
Bar ⏱ 1000–0100 ☏ 717 76 76 Level -1
Bar ⏱ 0600–last flight ☏ 717 76 76 Transit area
Café/light meals ⏱ 0800–2100 ☏ 717 76 76 Level 2
Café/light meals ⏱ 0600–2300 ☏ 717 76 76 Level -1
Café/light meals ⏱ 0600–2130 ☏ 717 76 76 Level -1
Café/light meals ⏱ 0630–2000 ☏ 717 76 76 Level -1
Café/light meals ⏱ 0600–1930 ☏ 717 76 76 Level 1
Restaurant ⏱ 1130–1430; 1900–2230 Mon–Fri ☏ 717 76 76 Level 2
Restaurant ⏱ 1130–1500; 1800–2230 Mon–Fri. 1100–2230 Sat–Sun ☏ 717 76 76 Level 2
Restaurant ⏱ 1100–2100 ☏ 717 76 76 Transit area
Restaurant ⏱ 1030–1930 ☏ 717 76 76 Transit area
Restaurant ⏱ 0800–2300 ☏ 798 11 30 Train station mall
Restaurant ⏱ 1115–2200 ☏ 798 63 77 Train station mall

Communications
Post office ⏱ 0730–1800 Mon–Fri; 0800–1100 Sat ☏ 798 11 55 Level -1
Fax Service ⏱ 0700–2200 Mon–Sun ☏ 791 03 33 Level 1

Shopping
Duty free ☏ 799 33 80 Transit area
News, Stationery & Books ☏ 798 25 51 Level -1
News, Stationery & Books ☏ 798 57 81 Level 1
News, Stationery & Books ☏ 798 34 70 Train station mall
Gift Shop Shopping mall Level 1
Gift Shop Shopping mall Level -1

Luggage
Trolleys/carts

Disabled Travellers
Assistance for disabled available on Level 0 ☏ 799 33 45

Special Passenger Lounges
Swissair Level 2 ☏ 799 33 42
British Airways Level 2 ☏ 798 79 23
Air France Level 1 ☏ 717 82 55
Lufthansa Level 2 ☏ 798 78 25

Conference and Business Facilities
SKYCOM Level 1 ☏ 788 14 30 private offices with PC, fax and modem facilities; 11 conference rooms; secretarial and translation services; catering service.

Car Rental
Alamo Level -1 ☏ 788 24 34
Avis Level -1 ☏ 798 23 00
Avis France (French sector Level 0) ☏ 798 33 21

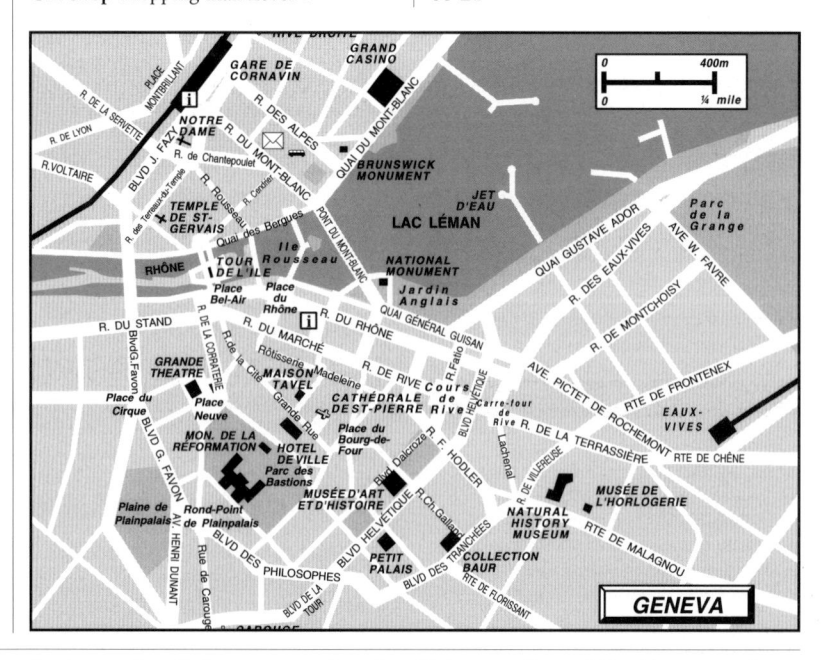

☏ Phone no. 📠 Fax no. ⏱ Hours of opening/operation ≫ Frequency of service ⊃ Journey time ⊘ Cost/one-way fare

Budget Level -1 ✆ 798 22 53
Budget/Léman Voyages (French sector Level 0) ✆ 798 14 84
Europcar Level -1 ✆ 798 11 10
Europcar France (French sector Level 0) ✆ 798 11 25
Hertz Level -1 ✆ 798 22 02
Hertz France (French sector Level 0) ✆ 798 17 71

Car Parking

Short-stay P1 Underground car park ⊘ free per first 10 min; CHF1 per hr; CHF25 per 24 hr
Short-stay P2 Car park at arrival level ⊘ free per first 10 min; CHF1 per first 30 min; CHF2 per 30–60 min; CHF4 per 60–90 min; CHF5 per 30 min after first 90 min
Short-stay P3 Car park at departure level ⊘ free per first 10 min; CHF1 per 10–20 min; CHF2 per 20–30 min; CHF3 per 30–60 min; CHF5 per 30 min after first 60 min
Long-stay P5 8 min walk from terminal ⊘ free per first 10 min; CHF1 per first 8 hr; CHF9 from 8 to 9 hr; CHF15 for 24 hr

Taxis and Chauffeur-driven Cars

Outside arrival level. In the French sector ask at the Léman desk.

Public Transport

City & suburbs
🚌 Geneva Public Transportation No 10 »10 min. Level 0
🚌 Hotel Courtesy Buses (Penta, Holiday Inn, Mövenpick ICC Center, Mövenpick Cadett) p 20 min ⏲ from 0600 ⊘ free

Other towns and cities
Aigle 🚆 SBB » 1hr ⊃ 1hr 20min
Bern 🚆 SBB » 1hr ⊃ 2hr
Biel 🚆 SBB » 1hr ⊃ 1hr 40min
Chambéry Gare SNCF 🚌 ⏲ 0915, 1315, 1900, 2115 (Sat and Sun 0915 and 1900 only) ⊃ 1hr
Fribourg 🚆 SBB » 1hr ⊃ 1hr 30min
Grenoble Pl. Verdun 🚌 ⏲ 0915, 1315, 1900, 2115 (Sat and Sun 0915 and 1900 only) ⊃ 1hr 45 min
Lausanne 🚆 SBB » 30min ⊃ 50min
Martigny 🚆 SBB » 1hr ⊃ 1hr 50min
Montreux 🚆 SBB » 1hr ⊃ 1hr 15min
Neuchâtel 🚆 SBB » 1hr ⊃ 1hr 20min
Nyon 🚆 SBB » 30min ⊃ 25min

Regional Air Connections

Basel ✈ »5 per day ⊃45 min
Bern ✈ »16 per day ⊃2hr
Zurich ✈ »20 per day ⊃50 min

GLASGOW GLA
UK (see page 41)

National ✆ code: 44
Area ✆ code: 0141
Local time: Winter GMT, Summer GMT+1
Glasgow Airport, Paisley, PA3 2ST, Scotland, United Kingdom
✆887 1111
☏848 4586
Location: 16 km/10 miles W of Glasgow

Terminals and Transfers

Terminals
Main Terminal Airlines: All airlines.
Layout: Ground Level, Level 1 and Level 2

Minimum transfer times
International: 45 min Domestic: 30 min

Information

Flight enquiries
Airport ✆887 1111

Information and help desks
Glasgow Tourist Board Main Terminal International Arrival Hall ✆848 4440 ⏲0800–2000 Hotel booking, Tourist information

Emergencies

Police Main Terminal A Block ✆848 4515 ⏲24 hr
Medical Main Terminal Information Desk ✆ext 4552 ⏲24 hr
Lost Property Main Terminal Level 1, Information Desk

Airport Facilities

Money
ATM Main Terminal Level 1 ⏲24 hr
Bureau de change Main Terminal Main Terminal Level 1 ⏲Summer 0530–2300
Bureau de change Main Terminal Domestic Pier Level 1 ⏲Summer 0530–2300
Thomas Cook bureau de change Main Terminal International Arrival Hall ⏲Summer 0600–2300; winter 0730–1400
Thomas Cook bureau de change Main Terminal Level 1 ⏲0800–2000 Mon–Sat; 0800–1800 Sun
Thomas Cook bureau de change Main Terminal International Departure Lounge ⏲Summer 0600–2200; winter 0700–1700

Food and drink
Bar Main Terminal Level 1 ⏲1000–2300;

GLASGOW

Fri 1230–2300
Café/light meals Main Terminal Ground Level, Level 1 and International Departure ⓗ0600–2200
Restaurant Main Terminal Level 1 ⓗ24hr
Restaurant Main Terminal Level 2 ⓗ0800–2300;Sat 0800–2345

Communications
Post office Main Terminal Level 1 ⓗ0900–1730 Mon–Sat

Shopping
Duty free, departure Main Terminal International Departure Lounge ⓗAll flight times
Gift Shop Main Terminal Level 1 ⓗAll flight times
News, Stationery & Books Main Terminal Level 1 ⓗAll flight times
Pharmacy Main Terminal Level 1 ⓗAll flight times

Luggage
Left luggage counter Main Terminal ⓗ0700–2330
Trolleys/carts Main Terminal throughout ⓗAll flight times⊘Free

DISABLED TRAVELLERS
Main Terminal Adapted toilets; Lifts; Personal assistance *Via Information Desk* ⓒext 4552 24 hr

SMOKING POLICY
Main Terminal No-smoking areas marked

SPECIAL PASSENGER LOUNGES
Servisair CIP Lounge Main Terminal Second Floor
British Airways Executive Club Lounge Main Terminal Domestic Pier *Club members, First and Business class passengers*
British Midland Airways Diamond Club Lounge Main Terminal Domestic Pier *Club members, First and Business class passengers*

AIRPORT HOTELS
Forte Crest ⓒ887 1212 ⒻAX 887 3738 *Courtesy bus*

CAR RENTAL
Alamo Main Terminal Ground Level Domestic Baggage recla im ⓒ848–6488
Avis Main Terminal Ground Level Domestic Baggage Reclaim ⓒ887 2261
EuropCar Main Terminal Ground Level Domestic Baggage Reclaim ⓒ887 0414
Hertz Main Terminal Ground Level Domestic Baggage Reclaim ⓒ887 2451

CAR PARKING
Long-stay 1920 spaces ⊘GBP1.30 per hr; GBP3.90 per day
Off-airport 4 km/2 miles from Airport Airpark; Skyport ⊘GBP2.50 per day; GBP18 per week
Short-stay 80 spaces ⊘GBP0.40 per 20 min; GBP0.80 per 45 min

TAXIS AND CHAUFFEUR-DRIVEN CARS
Taxis
Taxi rank terminal forecourt City centre ⏲15 min ⊘GBP11

PUBLIC TRANSPORT
Airport to airport
London-Gatwick Airport 🚌Citylink »1 per day ⓗ2100 ⏲9 hr 45 min ⊘GBP32.50.
London-Heathrow Airport 🚌Citylink »1 per day ⓗ2100 ⏲8 hr 30 min ⊘GBP30.

City & suburbs
Glasgow city centre 🚌Scottish Citylink »15–20 min ⓗ0550–0020 Mon-Sat ⏲25 min ⊘GBP2.0.

Other towns and cities
Ayr 🚆 Scotrail » 30min ⏲ 1hr
Dumfries 🚆 Scotrail » 7 per day ⏲ 1hr 50 min
Dundee 🚆 Scotrail » 30min ⏲ 1hr
Edinburgh 🚆 Scotrail » 30min ⏲ 1hr
Edinburgh 🚌Scottish Citylink »avg 1 hr ⓗ0655–2255 Mon-Sat ⏲1 hr 45 min ⊘GBP5.
Kilmarnock 🚆 Scotrail » 7 per day ⏲ 40min
Perth 🚆 Scotrail » 30min ⏲ 1hr
Stirling 🚆 Scotrail » 30min ⏲ 1hr

REGIONAL AIR CONNECTIONS
Aberdeen ✈ »Several per day ⏲55 min
Barra ✈ »Several per week ⏲1hr 05 min
Belfast ✈ »Several per day ⏲45 min
Birmingham (UK) ✈ »Several per day ⏲1hr
Campbeltown ✈ »Several per week ⏲40 min
Dublin ✈ »Several per day ⏲45 min
East Midlands ✈ »At least daily ⏲1hr 5 min
Inverness ✈ »Several per week ⏲40 min
Islay ✈ »Several per week ⏲45 min
Isle of Man ✈ »At least daily ⏲55 min
Kirkwall ✈ »Several per week ⏲1hr 10 min
Leeds/Bradford ✈ »Several per week ⏲1hr
Londonderry ✈ »At least daily ⏲55 min
Manchester (UK) ✈ »At least daily ⏲1hr
Stornaway ✈ »Several per week ⏲1hr

ⓒ Phone no. Ⓕ Fax no. ⓗ Hours of opening/operation » Frequency of service ⏲ Journey time ⊘ Cost/one-way fare

SECTION TWO • AIRPORT DIRECTORY   GOTHENBURG

GOTHENBURG   GOT
Sweden (see page 37)

National ☎ code: 46
Area ☎ code: 31
Local time: Winter GMT+1, Summer GMT+2
Address: Göteborg-Landvetter Airport, S-438 80 Landvetter, Sweden
☎: 94 10 00
Location: 24km/15mls E of Gothenburg

INFORMATION

Flight enquiries
Information and help desks
Information desk In both terminals ⓘ all arrivals and departures ☎94 11 00 ℻94 11 89 Flight and general airport information

EMERGENCIES

Police ☎94 13 54 ℻94 60 74
Medical Information desk, International Terminal ☎94 11 00
Lost Property Information desk, International Terminal ☎94 11 00

AIRPORT FACILITIES

Money
Bank International Terminal ☎94 11 94 ℻94 64 71
Bureau de Change International Terminal landside ☎94 65 41
Bureau de Change International Terminal landside ☎94 11 94
Bureau de Change International Terminal airside ☎94 65 41
ATM Domestic and International Terminals

Food and drink
Bar Domestic Terminal landside ☎94 16 80
Bar International Terminal landside ☎94 16 82
Bar International departure lounge airside ☎94 16 87
Café/light meals International Terminal landside 94 16 83

Café/light meals International Terminal landside 94 16 82
Café/light meals International Terminal landside ☎94 16 63
Restaurant Domestic Terminal landside ☎94 16 83
Restaurant International Terminal landside ☎94 16 82
Restaurant International departure lounge airside ☎94 16 84

Communications
Fax service Information desk, International Terminal ☎94 11 89

Shopping
Duty free International departure lounge airside ☎94 11 95
Duty free International departure lounge airside ☎94 20 91
Duty free International departure lounge airside ☎94 11 87
News, Stationery & Books International Terminal landside ☎94 62 05
News, Stationery & Books Domestic Terminal landside ☎94 66 00
Gift Shop International Terminal landside ☎94 12 25
Gift Shop International Terminal landside ☎94 63 00
Gift Shop International departure lounge airside ☎94 20 40
Gift Shop International departure lounge airside ☎94 10 78

Luggage
Lockers In the corridor between the Domestic and the International Terminals. Luggage can also be left at the information desk in the International Terminal.

DISABLED TRAVELLERS
Lifts, resting areas, disabled toilets. For assistance with transport ☎94 16 01

CONFERENCE AND BUSINESS FACILITIES
Conference Room Located on the first floor between the Domestic and the International Terminal ☎94 11 00 ℻94 19 91
Office services Multi-storey building directly in front of Domestic Terminal Postal service, photocopying service

CAR RENTAL
Avis ☎94 60 30 ℻94 18 26
Budget ☎94 60 55 ℻94 63 82
Hertz ☎94 60 20 ℻94 17 97
Europcar Interrent ☎94 71 00 ℻94 64 86

CAR PARKING
Long-stay ⊘SEK10 per hr; SEK40 per day for the first 3 days; SEK15 per day from day 4 onwards
Short-stay Domestic ⊘SEK20 per hr; SEK70 per day for the first 7 days; SEK45 per day from day 8 onwards
Short-stay International ⊘SEK20 per hr; SEK70 per day for the first 7 days; SEK45 per day from day 8 onwards
Short-stay Multi-storey ⊘SEK25 per hr; SEK90 per day for the first 7 days; SEK50 per day from day 8 onwards

TAXIS AND CHAUFFEUR-DRIVEN CARS
Taxis
City centre ⊘SEK230.

PUBLIC TRANSPORT
City & suburbs
Göteburg city centre 🚌 ⊘SEK50 » 15 min ➲ 25 min

Other towns and cities
Borås city centre 🚌 ⊘SEK70 » 1 hr ➲ 35 min
Karlstad 🚆 » 6 per day ➲ 3 hr

REGIONAL AIR CONNECTIONS
Linkoping ✈ » 2 per day ➲ 40 min
Malmo ✈ » 5 per day ➲ 35 min
Norrkoping ✈ » 2 per day ➲ 1 hr
Sundsvall ✈ » 6 per day ➲ 1 hr 10 min

✈ Air 🚆 Rail 🚌 Bus 🚐 Limousine Ⓜ Metro/subway 🚋 Tram 🚁 Helicopter ⛴ Water transport • For map symbols, see p.9

Halifax   YHZ

Canada (see page 18)

National ✆ code: 1
Area ✆ code: 902
Local time: Winter GMT-4, Summer GMT-3
Halifax International Airport, PO Box 40, Elmsdale NS B0N 1M0, Canada
✆890 8900
WWW site:
http://home.istar.ca/~tc_yhz1
Location: 42 km/26 miles NE of Halifax

Terminals and Transfers

Terminals
Main Terminal Airlines: All airlines. Layout: Lower Lobby (Lost Property), Main Level (Arrivals, Baggage Claim, Car Rental, Ground Transportation), Second Level (Departures), Gates 1–50

Minimum transfer times
International: 1 hr 15 min Domestic: 45 min

Information

Flight enquiries
Air Canada ✆429 7980 Air Nova ✆429 7980 Canadian ✆873 5345 Air Atlantic ✆873 5345 Icelandair ✆223 5500 Air St. Pierre ✆873 3566 Air Transat ✆873 3884 Royal Airlines ✆873 3884 Canada 3000 ✆873 3555

Information and help desks
Information Booth Main Terminal Main Level ⏲0900–2100 ✆873 1223 Airport information, Tourist information

Emergencies
Police RCMP Main Terminal Main Level ⏲24 hr ✆873 1300
First Aid Main Terminal Main Level ⏲24 hr ✆873 1216
Lost Property Main Terminal Lower Lobby ✆873 3057

Airport Facilities

Money
ATM Main Terminal Throughout
Bureau de change Main Terminal Main Level

Food
Bar Main Terminal throughout
Café/light meals Main Terminal throughout
Restaurant Main Terminal Main Level

Communications
Post Box Main Terminal throughout

Shopping
Duty free, departure, Main Terminal Second Level, across from Gate 20
Gift Shop Main Terminal throughout
News, Stationery & Books Main Terminal throughout

Disabled Travellers

Adapted toilets; Lifts; Special Car Parking; Phones at wheelchair height; Phones adapted for the deaf; Personal assistance

Special Passenger Lounges

Air Canada Maple Leaf Lounge Main Terminal ✆873 2338
Canadian Airlines Empress Lounge Main Terminal ✆873 5100

Car Rental

Avis Main Terminal Main Level ✆873 3522
Budget Main Terminal Main Level ✆492 7551
Dollar Main Terminal Main Level ✆860 0203
Hertz Main Terminal Main Level ✆873 2273
Tilden Main Terminal Main Level ✆873 3921
Thrifty Main Terminal Main Level ✆873 3527

Car Parking

Long-stay Main Parking Lot across from Main Terminal ⊘CAD7.50 day
Short-stay Main Parking Lot across from Main Terminal ⊘CAD1.35 hr

Taxis and Chauffeur-driven Cars

Taxis
City centre ➲30 min ⊘CAD35

Public Transport

City & suburbs
Halifax (city centre hotels) 🚌 Airbus ≫30 min–1 hr ⏲0745–2315 ➲45 min ⊘CAD11.

Other towns & cities
Moncton NB 🚌 Acadian Lines ≫3 day; 0730, 1315, 1625 ➲3 hr 30 min. For Truro, Amherst NS and Sackville NB
Sydney NS 🚌 Acadian Lines ≫4 day ⏲0845; 1315; 1625; 1900 (New Glasgow only) ➲6 hrs. For Truro, New Glasgow, Antigonish, Port Hastings NS

Regional Air Connections

Charlottetown PEI ✈ ≫Several per day ➲35 min
Fredericton NB ✈ ≫Several per day ➲45 min
Moncton NB ✈ ≫Several per day ➲35 min
St John NB ✈ ≫Several per day ➲35 min
Sydney NS ✈ ≫Several per day ➲1 hr
Yarmouth NS ✈ ≫At least daily ➲40 min

Traveller's Notes

Halifax is gateway to Atlantic Canada

✆ Phone no. ℻ Fax no. ⏲ Hours of opening/operation ≫ Frequency of service ➲ Journey time ⊘ Cost/one-way fare

HAMBURG

HAM

Germany (see page 22)

National ✆ code: 49
Area ✆ code: 040
Local time: Winter GMT+1, Summer GMT+2
Flughafen Hamburg, D-22331 Hamburg, Germany
✆50 75 0
⊕50 75 12 34
Internet e-mail: fhg@ham.airport.de
WWW site: From 1 Jan 97 (details unknown)
Location: 8 km/5 miles N of Hamburg

Terminals and Transfers

Terminals
Terminal 1 Airlines: Aero Lloyd, Air Alfa, Air Europa, Arkia Israeli Airlines, Aviogenex, Avioimpex, Balkan Bulgarian Airlines, Croatia Airlines, Egypt Air, Eurobelgian Airlines, GTI Airlines, Hapag-Lloyd Flug, Holiday Air, Istanbul Airlines, Kibris Turkish Airlines, Lithuanian Airlines, Macedonian Airlines, Nouvelair Tunisie, Olympic Airways, Palair Macedonian, Pegasus Air, Portugalia, Spanair, Sunexpress, Sunway, Transavia Airlines, Via Bulgarian Airways, Viva Air. Layout: One level including both departures and arrivals
Terminal 3 Airlines: Canada 3000, LTU, Onur Air, Tunis Air. Layout: Arrival and Departure Areas
Terminal 4 Airlines: All other airlines. Layout: Four levels, arrival and departure Areas

Minimum transfer times
International: 35 min Domestic: 40 min

Information

Flight enquiries
Airport ✆50 75 25 56
Aer Lingus ✆(0211) 323 0231 Aero Lloyd ✆4 10 18 00 Aeroflot ✆374 28 83 Air France ✆30 20 66 55 Air India ✆33 19 99 Air Lithuania ✆(0180) 325 03 25 Air Malta ✆(069) 23 90 76 Air UK ✆(01805) 21 42 01 Alitalia ✆50 05 680 Austrian Airlines ✆(01805) 25 85 76 Base Regional Airlines ✆(01805) 21 42 01 British Airways ✆(01803) 34 03 40 Canada 3000 ✆(0130) 81 42 05 China Airlines ✆3 50 85 23 Condor ✆(06107) 93 98 80 Crossair ✆(01805) 25 85 75 CSA Czechoslovak ✆3 39 35 45 Cyprus Airlines ✆(069) 69 58 93 20 Delta Airlines ✆(01803) 33 78 80 Deutsche BA ✆(01803) 34 03 40 Deutsche Lufthansa ✆35 92 55 Estonian Air ✆(06105) 20 60 70 Eurowings ✆(0231) 9 24 53 33 Finnair ✆32 35 13 Friesenflug ✆(04651) 12 11 Hamburg Airlines ✆(01803) 25 03 25 Hapag-Lloyd-Flug ✆50 75 23 25 Helgoland Airlines ✆(04 421) 9 26 00 Iberia ✆34 08 15 Icelandair ✆(069) 29 99 78 Iran Air ✆24 55 00 Japan Airlines ✆(01802) 22 87 00 JAT ✆32 34 16 KLM ✆(01805) 21 42 01 Korean Airlines ✆34 38 43 Lot Polish Airlines ✆24 47 47 LTU International Airways ✆50 75 11 49 Luftfahrtges Walter ✆50 75 31 78 Lufthansa ✆35 92 55 Luxair ✆35 92 55 Malaysian Airlines ✆35 29 30 Malev Hungarian ✆34 14 97 Northwest Airlines ✆(01805) 2 54 65 Olympic Airways ✆33 88 13 Palair Macedonian Airlines ✆5 00 79 12 Sabena World Airlines ✆50 05 76 10 SAS ✆59 19 51 South African Airways ✆32 17 71 Swissair ✆(01805) 25 85 75 TAP Air Portugal ✆34 04 34 Thai Airways ✆(0 69) 6 30 00 40 Trans Travel Airlines ✆(01803) 25 03 25 Tunis Air ✆32 30 41 Turkish Airlines ✆3 25 80 50 Tyrolean Airways ✆35 92 55 United Airlines ✆(0 69) 60 50 20 Varig Brazilian ✆(01805) 33 43

Information and help desks
Information Desk Terminal 4 Departure hall ✆50 75 25 56 ⊕50 75 12 34 ⓘ0500–2300 Airport information.
Hotel reservations ✆30 05 13 00 ⓘ0800–2000
Tourist Information ✆30 05 13 00 ⓘ0800–2000
Police Terminal 4 Departure Hall ✆110 ⓘ0600–2300
Medical Terminal 4 Departure Hall ✆112 ⓘ0600–2200
Lost Property Terminal 4 Enquire at Information Desk ✆50 752 556 ⓘAirport operating hours

Airport Facilities

Money
ATM Terminal 4 Various locations (4)
Bureau de change Terminal 4 Arrival area ⓘ0600–2200
Bank Terminal 4 Arrival area ⓘ0900–1300, 1430–1600/1800 M-F. Change 0630–2030

Food and drink
Café/light meals Terminal 1 Observation terrace, between Terminals 1 and 2 ⓘ0700/0800–2000
Bar Terminal 1 Arrival and Departure Areas (various locations)
Café/light meals Terminal 3 Passage Level 0, between Terminals 3 and 4 ⓘ0500–2100
Café/light meals Terminal 4 Gallery Level ⓘ0500–2040
Café/light meals Terminal 4 Arrival Area ⓘ0700–2300
Café/light meals Terminal 4 Gate Area (2 locations) ⓘ0430–2100
Bar Terminal 4 Gate area
Restaurant Terminal 4 Gallery Level (3 locations) ⓘ0800–2200

Communications
Post office Terminal 4 Arrival Area ⓘ0630–2100 Mon–Fri, 0700-2100 Sat, 0900–2000 Sun ✆5 00 04 85

Shopping
Duty free, departure Terminal 1 Departure Lounge
Duty free, arrival Terminal 1 Arrival Hall
Travel agency Terminal 1
Travel agency Terminal 3
Shopping mall Terminal 4 Lower Level ⓘDawn–last flight
Duty free, departure Terminal 4 Departure lounge
Travel agency Terminal 4 Lower Level ⓘUntil last flight
Hairdresser Terminal 4 Lower Level ⓘ0800–2000
Duty free, arrival Terminal 4 Arrivals Hall
Luggage
Trolleys/carts Terminal 1 Inside and in front of terminal ⌀DEM 2.50
Porters Terminal 1 On request; ✆2557
Left luggage counter Terminal 1 Arrival area ⓘ0400–2400
Porters Terminal 3 Location ⓘOn request, ✆2557
Trolleys/carts Terminal 3 Inside and in front of terminal ⌀DEM 2.50
Left luggage counter Terminal 4 Arrivals area ⓘ0400–2400
Porters Terminal 4 On request, ✆2557

HAMBURG

SECTION TWO • AIRPORT DIRECTORY

Trolleys/carts Terminal 4 Inside and in front of terminal ⌀DEM 2.50

Disabled Travellers

Terminal 1 Adapted toilets; Special car parking; Phones at wheelchair height
Terminal 3 Adapted toilets; Special car parking; Phones at wheelchair height
Terminal 4 Adapted toilets; Special car parking; Phones at wheelchair height

Smoking Policy

Terminal 1 "European standard" smoking policy – all terminals

Special Passenger Lounges

Diners Club Terminal 4 Gallery Level Diners Club cardholders
Hanseatic Lounge Terminal 4 Gallery Level Entrance DEM30, open all passengers paying by credit card
Hapag Lloyd Lounge Terminal 1
British Airways Executive Club Terminal 4 Gallery Level Club members
Lufthansa Senator Lounge Terminal 4 Gallery Level HON Club, Senator Card holders, frequent flyers

Conference and Business Facilities

Hanseatic Conference and Banquet Centre, Terminal 4 ✆5075 3338 Fax service, Photocopier, Secretarial service, Translation/Interpretation service.

Airport Hotels

Airport Hotel ✆531 020 ℻531 02 22 63 rooms, 95 suites Courtesy bus
Alsterkrug ✆51 30 30 ℻51 30 3-403 52 rooms, 98 suites
Dorint ✆532 09-0 ℻532 09-600 16 rooms, 129 suites

Car Rental

ADAC Terminal 4 Arrival Area (also Terminal 1 Arrival Area) ✆59 81 87
Alamo Terminal 4 Arrival Area (also Terminal 1 Arrival Area) ✆50 752 301
Avis Terminal 4 Arrival Area (also Terminal 1 Arrival Area) ✆50 752 314
EuropCar Terminal 4 Arrivals area (also Terminal 1 Arrival Area) ✆50 02 17 0
Hertz Terminal 4 Arrival Area (also Terminal 1 Arrival Area) ✆50 752 302
MBnz Terminal 4 Arrival Area (also Terminal 1 Arrival Area) ✆50 751 937
Sixt Terminal 4 Arrival Area (Terminal 1 Arrival Area) ✆50 752 305

Car Parking

Long-stay On airport perimeter P6 5138 spaces ⌀DEM9 per day, DEM50 per week, DEM79 per 2 weeks
Short-stay P2a, P2b, P2c 768 spaces ⌀DEM 7–8 per 6 hrs, DEM 12–15 per 6–24 hrs and each extra day
Short-stay Beside terminals P3, P4, P4a, P5 768 spaces ⌀DEM2.50 per hr up to 4 hr, DEM25–40 for 4–24 hr and each extra day

Taxis and Chauffeur-driven Cars

Taxis

Front of each terminal ✆411 411 City centre ⊃Approx 30 min ⌀DEM30

Public Transport

City & suburbs

Hamburg (Hbf–main rail stn) 🚌 Airport-City-Bus/Jasper »20 min ⊃30 min ⊕0622–2252 ⌀DEM8. Stops outside Terminals 1 and 4. ✆22 71 06 11.
Hamburg city centre 🚌 HVV-Airport-Express (via Ohlsdorf U-Bahn/S-Bahn) Linie 110 »10 min ⊃approx 30 min ⊕0543–2254 then at 2314, 2344, 0014 and 0044 ⌀DEM4.10. Stops in front of Terminals 1 and 4. ✆1 94 49

Other towns and cities

Kiel 🚌 Autokraft Kielius »2 hr ⊕0427–0025 ⊃1 hr ⌀DEM 22. Stops in front of Terminals 1 and 4; ✆0431 71 070
Neumünster 🚌 Autokraft Kielius »2 hr ⊕0427–0025 ⊃1 hr ⌀DEM 17.

Regional Air Connections

Amsterdam ✈ »Several per day ⊃60–65 min
Berlin ✈ »Several per day ⊃1 hr
Cologne/Bonn ✈ »Several per day ⊃55–75 min
Copenhagen ✈ »Several per day ⊃55–60 min
Dortmund ✈ »Several per week ⊃55 min
Dresden ✈ »Several per day ⊃55–70 min
Düsseldorf ✈ »Several per day ⊃55 min
Helgoland ✈ »Several per week ⊃45–60 min
Leipzig ✈ »Several per week ⊃55–70 min

✆ Phone no. ℻ Fax no. ⊕ Hours of opening/operation » Frequency of service ⊃ Journey time ⌀ Cost/one-way fare

✈✈ SECTION TWO • AIRPORT DIRECTORY   HARARE • HELSINKI

HARARE   HRE
Zimbabwe (see page 42)

National ✆ code: 263
Area ✆ code: 04
Local time: Winter GMT+2,
Summer GMT+2
Harare Airport, Harare, Zimbabwe
✆0 50422
✆728110
Location: 13 km/8 miles from
Harare

TERMINALS AND TRANSFERS

Terminals
Main Terminal Airlines: All airlines

Minimum transfer times
International: 45 min–1 hr 20 min
Domestic: 30 min

INFORMATION

Information and help desks
Air Zimbabwe Information Desk Main
Terminal Main Terminal ✆737011
✆731444 ⏲All flight times *Flights*

EMERGENCIES

Lost Property Main Terminal ⏲According to flights

AIRPORT FACILITIES

Money
Bank Main Terminal Main Terminal
⏲Flight times

Food and drink
Restaurant Main Terminal Main Terminal
⏲0600–2230

Communications
Post office Main Terminal Main Terminal
⏲0800–1600

Shopping
Duty free, departure Main Terminal
Departure Lounge

DISABLED TRAVELLERS

Main Terminal Personal assistance

SMOKING POLICY

Main Terminal No restrictions

SPECIAL PASSENGER LOUNGES

First Class Lounge Main Terminal
Business Class Lounge Main Terminal

CAR RENTAL

Avis Main Terminal
Hertz Main Terminal

CAR PARKING

Short-stay 300 spaces ⌀Free

TAXIS AND CHAUFFEUR-DRIVEN CARS

Taxis
City centre ➲10–15 min ⌀ZWD40

PUBLIC TRANSPORT

City & suburbs
Harare city centre 🚌 Air Zimbabwe
coach »1 hr ⏲0600–2200 ➲15 min
⌀ZWD15.

REGIONAL AIR CONNECTIONS

Bulawayo ✈ »Several per day ➲50 min
Kariba ✈ »Several per day ➲45 min
Lilongwe ✈ »Several per week ➲1 hr 5 min
Lusaka ✈ »Several per week ➲55 min
Victoria Falls ✈ »Several per day ➲1 hr

AIRPORT TAX

There is a departure tax of USD20 for non-residents.

137

HELSINKI   HEL
Finland (see page.21)

National ✆ code: 358
Area ✆ code: 090
Local time: Winter GMT+2,
Summer GMT+3
Helsinki-Vantaa Airport, PO Box
29, 01531 Vantaa, Finland
✆82 77 1
✆82 77 30 39
Location: 20 km/12 miles N of
Helsinki

TERMINALS AND TRANSFERS

Terminals
International Terminal Airlines: All international flights.
Domestic Terminal Airlines: All domestic flights, Finnair.
Gateway Terminal

Minimum transfer times
International: 30–40 min Domestic: 20 min

Transfer between terminals
Bus »Shuttle; International and Domestic
Terminals ⌀Free

INFORMATION

Flight enquiries
Airport ✆600 8100 ⏲24 hr
Aeroflot ✆818 5734 Air Botnia ✆870
2530 Air France ✆821 068 Air Lithuania
✆818 81 Austrian Airlines ✆171 311
Balkan Bulgarian Airlines ✆647 752

✈ Air 🚆 Rail 🚌 Bus 🚘 Limousine 🚇 Metro/subway 🚋 Tram 🚁 Helicopter ⛴ Water transport • For map symbols, see p .9

HELSINKI

SECTION TWO • AIRPORT DIRECTORY

British Airways ⓒ6151 3939 Cyprus Airways ⓒ818 81 CSA Czechoslovak ⓒ622 3577 Delta Airlines ⓒ822 040 El Al ⓒ6151 3948 Estonain Air ⓒ6151 3900 Finnair ⓒ818 81 KLM ⓒ870 1747 Lot Polish Airlines ⓒ6151 3823 Lufthansa ⓒ348 110 Malev Hungarian ⓒ6151 3940 Northwest Airlines ⓒ870 1722 Sabena World Airlines ⓒ870 3113 SAS ⓒ2280 2277 Swissair ⓒ870 3373 Thai Airways ⓒ133 840.

Information and help desks
Airport Information ⓞ24 hr ⓒ600 8100
Information Desk International Terminal, Departures Hall ⓞfor departing flights Airport information, flights, public transport, hotel reservations
Information Desk International Terminal, Arrivals Hall ⓞ24 hr Airport information, flights, public transport, hotel reservations
Information Desk Domestic Terminal, Arrivals Hall ⓞ0500–2330 Airport information, Flights

EMERGENCIES

Police ⓒ8388 3700
Medical First aid rooms are available in both terminals. Ask at the information desks for assistance.
Lost Property International Terminal, Arrivals Floor ⓒ818 5324 ⓞ0815–1515

AIRPORT FACILITIES

Money
ATM International Terminal, Arrivals, Departures and Ground floors. Also in transit area. ⓞ24 hr
ATM Domestic Terminal, both floors.
Bank International Terminal, Departures floor ⓞ0630–1930 daily
Bank International Terminal, transit area ⓞ0630–2300
Bank International Terminal, Ground floor ⓞ0915–1615 Mon–Fri
Thomas Cook Bureau de change International Terminal, Arrivals floor ⓞ0630–0045 Mon–Thurs; 0630–2200 Fri; 0830–2200 Sat; 0830–0045 Sun. ⓒ6151 3852/6151 3853.

Food and drink
Bar International Terminal near gate 30
Bar Gateway Terminal
Café/light meals International Terminal, Departures floor Hall 3 ⓞ24 hr ⓒ818 3753
Café/light meals International Terminal near gate 28 ⓞflight departure times ⓒ818 3746
Café/light meals Domestic Terminal, airside ⓒ818 3774
Café/light meals Gateway Terminal
Restaurant International Terminal, Hall 3 ⓒ818 3750

Restaurant International Terminal, ground floor ⓒ818 3750
Restaurant International Terminal opposite gate 29 ⓞ1000–2000 Mon–Weds; 1000–2200 Thurs–Sun ⓒ818 3742.
Restaurant Domestic Terminal, Departures floor ⓒ818 3772
Restaurant Gateway Terminal, Gateway Hall ⓞ1200–2000 Mon–Weds; 1200–2100 Thurs–Sun ⓒ818 3760.

Communications
Post office International Terminal, Ground floor ⓞ0700–1900 Mon–Fri; 1000–1800 Sat–Sun. ⓒ826 178.
Post Office Domestic Terminal, Departures floor ⓞ0700–1200 and 1400–1900 Mon–Fri. ⓒ827 5738.

Shopping
Gift Shop Domestic Terminal, Arrivals floor
News, Stationery & Books International Terminal, Departures floor Hall 3 ⓒ826 694
News, Stationery & Books Domestic Terminal, Arrivals floor ⓒ822 339
Pharmacy International Terminal, ground floor ⓞ0800–2000 Mon–Fri; 0800–1800 Sat–Sun ⓒ270 907 72.
Shopping Mall International Terminal, Transit area
Shopping Mall Gateway Terminal

Luggage
Left Luggage Counter International Terminal, Arrivals floor Arrival Services Ltd ⓞ24 hr
Lockers International Terminal, Ground floor
Lockers Domestic Terminal, Arrivals floor
Porters International Terminal, Arrivals floor Arrival Services Ltd ⓞ24 hr
Trolleys/carts Throughout the airport ⓞ24 hr ⓒFree

DISABLED TRAVELLERS

International Terminal Adapted toilets; Lifts
Domestic Terminal Adapted toilets; Lifts

SMOKING POLICY

International Terminal Restricted
Domestic Terminal Restricted

SPECIAL PASSENGER LOUNGES

Finnair CIP Lounge Domestic Terminal
Finnair Business Class Lounge International Terminal Business class passengers
Finnair First Class Lounge International Terminal First class passengers

CONFERENCE AND BUSINESS FACILITIES

VIP/Press/Conference Room Domestic Terminal, Departures floor ⓒ8277 3117 Telephones, Photocopier

AIRPORT HOTELS

Cumulus ⓒ870 600
Holiday Inn Garden Court ⓒ870 900 ⓕ870 901 01
Rantasipi ⓒ87051

CAR RENTAL

Avis International Terminal Arrival Level ⓒ822 833
Budget International Terminal Arrival Level ⓒ870 1606
Europcar International Terminal Arrival Level ⓒ7515 5700. Domestic Terminal ⓒ7515 5720
Hertz International Terminal Arrival Level ⓒ1667 1300. Domestic Terminal ⓒ1667 1400.

CAR PARKING

Long-stay P2 ⓒFIM70 per day ⓒ8277 3200
Long-stay P3, P4 ⓒFIM50 per day ⓒ8277 3200
Off-Airport ⓒFIM25 per day ⓒ870 2187
Short-stay 230 spaces ⓒFIM5 per 20 min (minimum charge ⓒf FIM10) ⓒ8277 3200

TAXIS AND CHAUFFEUR-DRIVEN CARS

Taxis
Terminal forecourts City centre ⓞ20–30 min ⓒFIM110

PUBLIC TRANSPORT

City & suburbs
Helsinki city centre 🚌Finnair »20 min ⓞ0500–0110 ⓞ25–30 min ⓒFIM24.

Other towns and cities
Joensuu 🚌Pohjolan Liikenne »0900 ⓞ0900 ⓞ8 hr ⓒFIM170.
Lahti 🚌Finnair »avg 1 hr ⓞ0100–2400 ⓞ1 hr 20 min ⓒFIM59.
Turku 🚌Pohjolan Liikenne »avg 1 hr ⓞ0100–2310 ⓞ2 hr 30 min ⓒFIM60.

REGIONAL AIR CONNECTIONS

Riga ✈ »Several per day ⓞ55 min
Stockholm ✈ »Several per day ⓞ55 min
Tallinn ✈ »Several per day ⓞ35 min
Turku ✈ »Several per day ⓞ35 min

ⓒ Phone no. ⓕ Fax no. ⓞ Hours of opening/operation » Frequency of service ⓞ Journey time ⓒ Cost/one-way fare

HONG KONG   HKG

Hong Kong (see page 23)

National ✆ code: 852
Area ✆ code: No code required
Local time: Winter GMT+8,
Summer GMT+8
Hong Kong International Airport,
Hong Kong
✆2769 7531
📠2764 9656
Location: 4.5 km/3 miles NE
Kowloon, Star Ferry Pier

TERMINALS AND TRANSFERS

Terminals
Main Terminal Airlines: All airlines.

Minimum transfer times
International: 1 hr– 2 hr

INFORMATION

Flight enquiries
Airport ✆2769 7531; 2769 6360; 2769 6258

Information and help desks
Honk Kong Tourist Association Main Terminal Buffer Hall, B4 and B17 (2 desks) ✆2769 7765 ⓘ0800–2230 (B4);1300–1900 (B17) Tourist information

EMERGENCIES

Lost Property Main Terminal Arrival Greeting Hall (Neighbrhd Police office) ⓘ24 hr

AIRPORT FACILITIES

Money
Bank Main Terminal, ⓘ0900–1700
ATM Main Terminal
Bureau de change Main Terminal

Food and drink
Restaurant Main Terminal Eastern and Western Departure Halls ⓘSee notes
Café/light meals Main Terminal Eastern restricted Area of Departure Hall ⓘSee notes

Communications
Post office Main Terminal Departure Hall ⓘ0930–1800 Mon–Fri; 0930–1300 Sat

Shopping
Duty free, departure Main Terminal Departure Hall

Luggage
Left luggage counter Main Terminal

Buffer Hall and landside Departure Hall ⓘ0630–0100 (both)

DISABLED TRAVELLERS

Main Terminal Adapted toilets; Lifts; Phones at wheelchair height

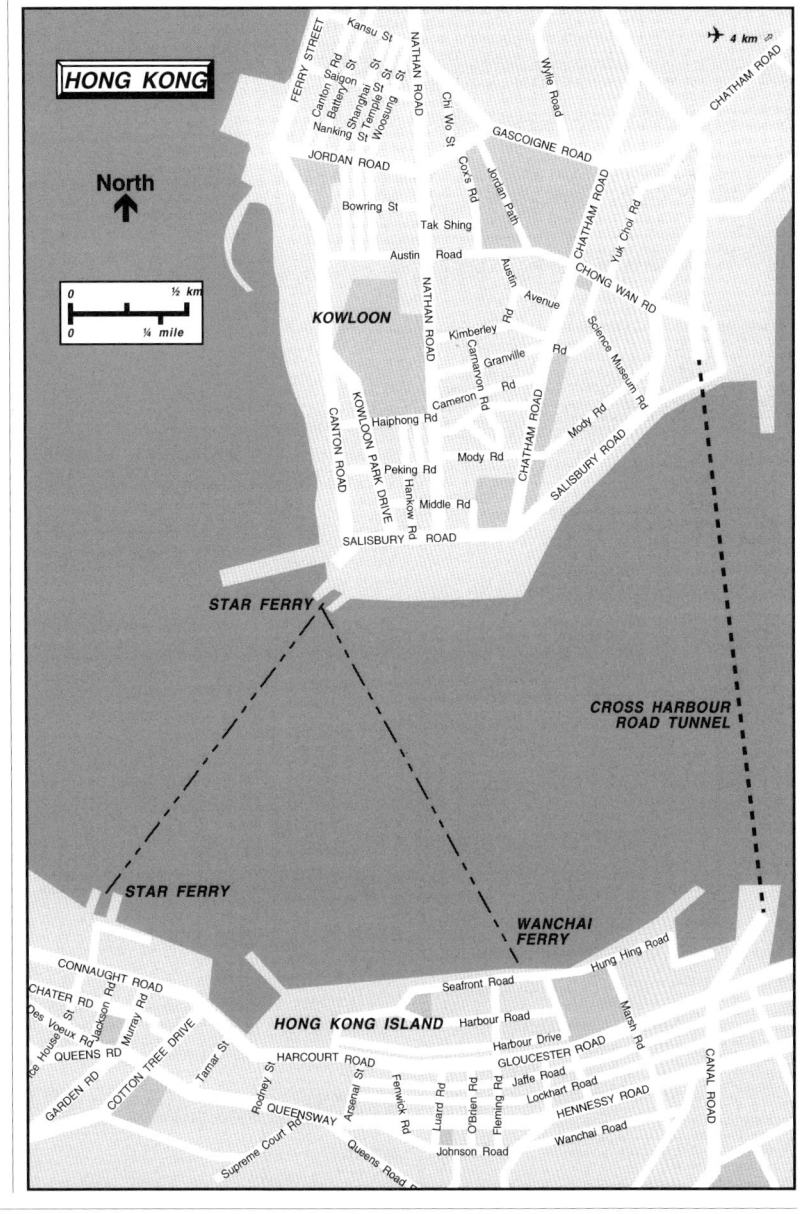

HONG KONG • HONOLULU   SECTION TWO • AIRPORT DIRECTORY

SPECIAL PASSENGER LOUNGES
Most airlines have First Class Lounges in the Main Terminal

CONFERENCE AND BUSINESS FACILITIES
Airport Business and Conference Centre, Regal Airport Hotel

AIRPORT HOTELS
Regal Airport 5-min walk from airport

CAR PARKING
Short-stay 1026 spaces ⌀HKD9.50 first 4.5 hr, then HKD38 per hr

TAXIS AND CHAUFFEUR-DRIVEN CARS
Taxis
Kowloon ⌀HKD48–63
New Territories ⌀HKD98–258
Hong Kong Island ⌀HKD116–158

PUBLIC TRANSPORT
City & suburbs
Hong Kong Island, Central/Wan Chai 🚌 Kowloon Motor Bus Co Airbus A2/A20 ⌀HKD19
Hong Kong Island, Causeway Bay 🚌 Kowloon Motor Bus Co Airbus A3 ⌀HKD19
Hong Kong Island, Quarry Bay/North Point 🚌 Kowloon Motor Bus Co Airbus A5 ⌀HKD19
Hong Kong Central (Macau Ferry) Area 🚌 Kowloon Motor Bus Co A2 ⟫12–15 min ⏱0650-2400 ⌀HKD 19.
Kowloon, Tong MTRstn 🚌 Kowloon Motor Bus Co Airbus A7 ⌀HKD6.70. For Mass Transit Railway to many parts of Hong Kong
Kowloon, Tsim Sha Tsui 🚌 Kowloon Motor Bus Co Airbus A1 ⌀HKD12.30.

REGIONAL AIR CONNECTIONS
Haikou ✈ ⟫Several times per week ↻60–70 min
Shantou ✈ ⟫Several times per day ↻50–60 min

TRAVELLER'S NOTES
Taxi fares vary widely depending on the actual destination, and from the airport include cross-harbour tunnel fees for the driver's return journey. Car rental is inadvisable, but cars with chauffeurs are popular and can be rented at most hotels. Public transport is excellent and widely used by visitors. On 1 July 1997 the sovereignty of Hong Kong reverted to China, but local administration, law and border controls remain in place.

HONOLULU   HNL
USA (see page 41)

National ☎ code: 1
Area ☎ code: 808
Local time: Winter GMT-10, Summer GMT-10
Honolulu International Airport, 300 Rogers Blvd, Honolulu, HI 96819, USA
☎836 6411
🖷836 6682
WWW site:
http//kumu.icsd.hawaii.gov/dot/hono.htm
Location: 6 km/4 miles W of Honolulu

TERMINALS AND TRANSFERS
Terminals
Main Overseas Terminal Airlines: All other airlines. Layout: Ground Level (Baggage Claim, Car Rental, Customs); Second Level (Diamond Head Gull Wing, Central and Ewa Concourses), Third Level (Shops and Restaurants)
Inter-Island Terminal Airlines: Mahalo Air, Aloha Airlines, Hawaiian Airlines, Island Air, Trans Air. Layout: Single level

Minimum transfer times
International: 2 hr Domestic: 1 hr 15 min

Transfer between terminals
Bus ⟫15 min; Main Terminal lobby and outlying gates ⌀Free

INFORMATION
Flight enquiries
Airport ☎836 6413

Information and help desks
Visitor Information Main Overseas Terminal throughout ☎836 6413 f836 6689 ⏱24 hr, Tourist Information

EMERGENCIES
Police Main Overseas Terminal Second Level, Tower Lobby ☎836 6606 ⏱24 hrs
Medical Main Overseas Terminal First Level, Garden Court ☎836 6643 ⏱24 hrs
Lost Property Main Overseas Terminal First Level, Parking Garage ☎836 6547

AIRPORT FACILITIES
Money
ATM Main Overseas Terminal Central Concourse ⏱24 hr
Bank Main Overseas Terminal First Level Parking Garage ⏱0830–1500 Mon–Thu; 0830–1800 Fri
Thomas Cook bureau de change Main Overseas Terminal Diamond Head Concourse ⏱0600–1330
Thomas Cook bureau de change Main Overseas Terminal International Arrivals Area ⏱0530–1330 (or last foreign arrival flight)
Thomas Cook bureau de change Main Overseas Terminal International Tour Group Arrivals (2nd level) ⏱0530–1200 (depending on flights)
Thomas Cook bureau de change Main Overseas Terminal Central Concourse ⏱0830–1630
Thomas Cook bureau de change Main Overseas Terminal Ewa Concourse ⏱0630–1400 and 2000–0330

Food and drink
Bar Main Overseas Terminal throughout ⏱0600–0100
Café/light meals Main Overseas Terminal throughout ⏱0600–0130
Restaurant Main Overseas Terminal throughout ⏱0600–0100
Bar Inter-Island Terminal throughout
Café/light meals Inter-Island Terminal

☎ Phone no. 🖷 Fax no. ⏱ Hours of opening/operation ⟫ Frequency of service ↻ Journey time ⌀ Cost/one-way fare

throughout
Restaurant Inter-Island Terminal throughout

Communications
Post box Main Overseas Terminal throughout ⊙24 hr

Shopping
Duty free, departure Main Overseas Terminal throughout ⊙ according to International Departures
Florist Main Overseas Terminal throughout ⊙0700–2300
Hairdresser Main Overseas Terminal Central Concourse ⊙0830–1930
Gift Shop Main Overseas Terminal throughout ⊙ according to flight departures
News, Stationery & Books Main Overseas Terminal throughout ⊙24 hr
News, Stationery & Books Inter-Island Terminal throughout
Gift Shop Inter-Island Terminal throughout

Luggage
Lockers Main Overseas Terminal Ground Level Parking Garage ⊙24 hr ⌀USD4–6 day
Left Luggage Counter Main Overseas Terminal Ground Level Parking Garage ⊙24 hr ⌀USD3–10 per day
Lockers Main Overseas Terminal Opposite Gates 12, 13, 14, 23 and 24 ⊙24 hr ⌀USD0.50 hr, ⌀USD3 max

Disabled Travellers
Main Overseas Terminal Adapted toilets; Lifts; Special car parking; Phones adapted for the deaf Main Lobby, between Lobbies 4–5 and in Lobby 7; Personal assistance Contact airlines

Smoking Policy
Main Overseas Terminal Permitted in designated areas in restaurants and open air areas

Special Passenger Lounges
Air New Zealand First Class Lounge Main Overseas Terminal Ground Level (Garden Conference Area)
Aloha Airlines Suite 737 Inter-Island Terminal Second Level
American Airlines Admiral's Club Lounge Main Overseas Terminal Ground Level (Garden Conference Area)
Canadian Airlines International Empress Lounge Main Overseas Terminal Ground Level (Garden Conference Area)
China Airlines Dynasty Lounge Main Overseas Terminal Ground Level (Garden Conference Area)
Continental Airlines President's Club Main Overseas Terminal Second Level (Opposite Gate 13)
Delta Airlines Crown Room Lounge Main Overseas Terminal Ground Level (Garden Conference Area)
Hawaiian Airlines Premier Lounge Inter-Island Terminal Third Level
Japan Airlines Sakura Lounge Main Overseas Terminal Ground Level (Garden Conference Area)
Korean Airlines Morning Calm Lounge Main Overseas Terminal Ground Level (Garden Conference Area)
Northwest Airlines World Club Main Overseas Terminal Second Level (Opposite Gate 13)
Philippine Airlines Mabuhay Lounge Main Overseas Terminal Ground Level (Garden Conference Area)
Qantas Airways Captain's Club Main Overseas Terminal Third Level (Above Gate 26)
United Airlines Red Carpet Room Main Overseas Terminal Third Level (Above Gate 10)

Conference and Business Facilities
Business Center Main Overseas Terminal, Central Lobby ✆831 3600 ⊙0800–1700 Telephones, Fax service, Photocopier
Conference Center Main Overseas Terminal Ground Level (Garden Area) ⌀836 6459
Conference Inter-Island Terminal ⌀836 6459

Airport Hotels
Airport Mini Hotel ✆836 3044 ℻834 8985

Car Rental
Alamo Main Overseas Terminal Ground Level ✆833 4585
Avis Main Overseas Terminal Ground Level ✆834 5536
Budget Main Overseas Terminal Ground Level ✆537 3600
Dollar Main Overseas Terminal Ground Level ✆831 2331
Hertz Main Overseas Terminal Ground Level ✆831 3500
National Main Overseas Terminal Ground Level ✆831 3800
Thrifty Main Overseas Terminal Ground Level ✆833 0046

Car Parking
Long-stay Across from Main Terminal 3178 spaces ⌀USD10 per day
Short-stay Across from Main Terminal AMPCO Inc 3178 spaces ⌀USD1 per 30 min and USD1 hr thereafter, USD10 per day, USD100 per month

Taxis and Chauffeur-driven Cars
Taxis
Ground Level (kerbside) City centre ⊃30 min ⌀USD25

Public Transport
City & suburbs
Honolulu city centre 🚌 The Bus: 19, 20 ≫20-30 min ⊙0510–0125 ⌀USD1. Various stops east- and west-bound. ✆848 5555 for information.
Honolulu (all downtown hotels) 🚌 Airport Motorcoach ≫20 min ⊙24 hr ⌀USD8
Honolulu Metro Area l Over 15 companies at airport.

Regional Air Connections
Hilo, HI ✈ ≫Several per day ⊃50 min
Kahului, HI ✈ ≫Several per day ⊃35 min
Kalaupapa, HI ✈ ≫Several per day ⊃55 min
Kamuela, HI ✈ ≫At least daily ⊃55 min
Kapalua, HI ✈ ≫Several per day ⊃35 min
Lihue, HI ✈ ≫Several per day ⊃35 min
Kona, HI ✈ ≫Several per day ⊃40 min
Lanai City, HI ✈ ≫Several per day ⊃30 min
Molokai/Hoolehua, HI ✈ ≫Several per day ⊃30 min

Traveller's Notes
Pacific Aerospace Museum (✆836 0777) located at airport. Open 0900–1800 daily. Admission ⌀USD3

HOUSTON

IAH

USA (see page 41)

National ✆ code: 1
Area ✆ code: 281
Local time: Winter GMT-6,
Summer GMT-5
Bush Intercontinental Airport, PO
Box 60106, Houston, TX 77205,
USA
✆230 3100
⒡230 2874
WWW site:
http://www.ci.houston.tx.us/depart
me/aviation/iah/
Location: 32 km/20 miles N of
Houston

Terminals and Transfers

Terminals
Terminal A Airlines: Delta Airlines, United Airlines, US Airways, Western Pacific Airlines, Southwest. Layout: Lower Level (Underground Walkway, Inter-terminal train service), First Level (Baggage Claim, Car Rental, Ground Transportation), Second Level (Flight Station 1, 2, 3, 4)
Terminal B Airlines: American Airlines, Continental Express. Layout: Lower Level (Underground Walkway, Inter-terminal train), First Level (Baggage Claim, Car Rental, Ground Transportation), Second Level (Flight Station 5, 6, 7, 8)
Terminal C Airlines: Continental Airlines, America West Airlines. Layout: Lower Level (Underground Walkway, Inter-terminal train), First Level (Baggage Claim, Car Rental, Ground Transportation), Second Level (North Concourse, South Concourse)
Mickey Leland International Airlines Building (IAB) Airlines: Air Canada, Air France, Aeromexico, British Airways, Continental Airlines (International), Aviateca, KLM, Cayman Airways, Lufthansa, TACA International Airlines. Layout: Arrival Level (Immigration), Main Lobby Level (Baggage Claim, Car Rental, Customs, Ground Transportation), Departure Level (Gates)

Minimum transfer times
International: 1 hr 15 min Domestic: 45 min

Transfer between terminals
People mover ≫3 min; All terminals, parking area 2 and hotel ⊘Free

Information

Information and help desks
Info Center All Terminals First Level Airport information, Tourist information
Tourist Information Desk Terminal C Second Level (3 desks) ✆233 3818 ⊙0700–2230 Tourist information
Tourist Information Desk International Airlines Building Main Lobby Level (3 desks) ✆233 3819 ⊙1000–2230 Tourist information
Tourist Information Desk Terminal B Second Level (2 desks) ✆2333 3817 ⊙1000–1900 Tourist information
Tourist Information Desk Terminal A Second Level (2 desks) ✆233 3816 ⊙1000–1900 Tourist information

Emergencies

Police All Terminals ✆230 3111
Medical All Terminals ✆230 3111
Lost Property All Terminals ✆230 3111

Airport Facilities

Money
ATM Terminal A Second Level
ATM Terminal B Second Level
Bureau de change Terminal C Second Level ⊙0630–2400
Bureau de change IAB Departure Level ⊙0900–1900
Bureau de change IAB Arrival Level ⊙1030–2030

Food and drink
Bar All Terminals Upper Level
Café/light meals All Terminals Second Level
Restaurant IAB Second Level

Communications
Fax service Terminal A Second Level
Fax service Terminal B Second Level
Fax service Terminal C Second Level
Post box All Terminals throughout

Shopping
Duty free, departure Terminal C Second Level ⊙0530–2400
Duty free, arrival International Airlines Building Arrival Level ⊙0600–last flight arrival
Duty free, departure IAB Departure Level ⊙0600–last flight
Gift Shop All Terminals Second Level
News, Stationery & Books All Terminals Second Level

Luggage
Left luggage counter Terminal A Second Level ⊙24 hr ⊘USD1 per day
Left luggage counter Terminal B Second Level ⊙24 hr ⊘USD1 per day
Left luggage counter Terminal C Main Lobby Level ⊙24 hr ⊘USD1 per day

Disabled Travellers

All Terminals Adapted toilets; Special car parking; Phones adapted for the deaf

Special Passenger Lounges

Air France First Class Lounge IAB Departure Level
British Airways Speedwing Lounge IAB Departure Level
Continental Airlines Presidents Club Terminal C Mezzanine Level
Delta Airlines Crown Lounge Terminal B Mezzanine Level
KLM Club Rembrandt Room IAB Departure Level
Lufthansa Senator Lounge IAB Departure Level

Airport Hotels

Mariott Houston Airport ✆443 2310 ⒡443 5271. 566 rooms

Car Rental

Advantage All Terminals First Level (Main Level IAB)
Alamo All Terminals First Level (Main Level IAB)
Avis All Terminals First Level (Main Level IAB)
Budget All Terminals First Level (Main Level IAB)
Dollar All Terminals First Level (Main Lobby IAB)
Hertz All Terminals First Level (Main Level IAB)
National All Terminals First Level (Main Level IAB)

✆ Phone no. ⒡ Fax no. ⊙ Hours of opening/operation ≫ Frequency of service ⊃ Journey time ⊘ Cost/one-way fare

SECTION TWO • AIRPORT DIRECTORY   HOUSTON • ISTANBUL

Thrifty All Terminals First Level (Main Lobby IAB)

Car Parking

Long-stay Take shuttle bus ⌀USD4 day
Short-stay Terminals ⌀USD 2 hr, USD9 day (max)
Short-stay Terminal C ⌀USD2 hr, USD30 day (max)

Taxis and Chauffeur-driven Cars

Taxis
City centre ⊃25 min ⌀USD32

Public Transport

Airport to airport
Hobby Airport 🚌Airport Express »30 min ⓘ0730–2330 ⌀USD17.

City and suburbs
Houston (city centre) 🚌Airport Express »30 min ⓘ0715–2315 ⊃45 min
⌀USD16. For Medical Center, Astrodome, Galleria, Greenway Plaza and Westside.
Houston (city centre) 🚇METRO: 102 »30 min–1 hr 102 ⓘ0600–2400 Mon–Fri only ⊃50 min ⌀USD1.50. From south side of Terminals A, B and C and the west end of the International Airlines Building.

Other towns and cities
Galveston TX 🚌Galveston Limo »1 hr 30 min ⓘ0700–2200 ⌀USD26. For League City and Texas City.

Regional Air Connections

Alexandria LA ✈ »Several per day ⊃1 hr
Austin TX ✈ »Several per day ⊃45 min
Beaumont/Port Arthur TX ✈ »Several per day ⊃30 min
College Station TX ✈ »Several per day ⊃30 min
Corpus Christi TX ✈ »Several per day ⊃1 hr
Dallas/Fort Worth TX ✈ »Several per day ⊃1 hr
Houston Ellington Field TX ✈ »Several per day ⊃25 min
Houston Hobby Apt TX ✈ »Several per day ⊃25 min
Killeen TX a »At least daily ⊃50 min
Lafayette LA ✈ »Several per day ⊃1 hr
Lake Charles LA ✈ »Several per day ⊃45 min
San Antonio TX ✈ »Several per day ⊃50 min
Shreveport LA ✈ »Several per day ⊃1 hr
Tyler TX ✈ »Several per day ⊃50 min
Victoria TX ✈ »Several per day ⊃45 min
Waco TX ✈ »Several per day ⊃50 min

Traveller's Notes

While Houston is the fourth largest city in the U.S., its sprawling nature suggests Los Angeles more than New York or Chicago. Public (bus) transportation is available, but given the sprawling nature of the city, renting a car for the duration of your stay may be the best solution.

143

ISTANBUL   IST

Turkey (see p. 39)

National ✆ code: 90
Area ✆ code: 0216
Local time: Winter GMT+2, Summer GMT+3
Istanbul Airport, Ataturk Havalimani Yesilkoy 34830, Turkey
✆5737240
✆5744148
Location: 24 km/15 miles SW of Istanbul

Terminals and Transfers

Terminals
International Terminal Airlines: Air France, Alitalia, British Airways, China Airlines, Delta Airlines, Emirates, Gulf Air, Iberia, Iran Air, KLM, Kuwait Airways, Lufthansa, Lot Polish Airlines, El Al Israel Airlines, Balkan Bulgarian Airlines, Malev Hungarian, Malaysian Airlines, Egyptair, Olympic Airways, Austrian Airlines, Syrian Arab Airlines, Royal Jordanian Airlines, SAS, Sabena, Singapore Airlines, Swissair, Saudia.
Domestic Terminal Airlines: Turkish Airlines.

Minimum transfer times
International: 1 hr 30 min Domestic: 30 min

Information

Flight enquiries
Airport ✆5748300
Air France ✆1543193 Alitalia ✆1313391 Austrian Airlines ✆1322200 Balkan Bulgarian Airlines ✆1452456 British Airways ✆1341300 China Airlines ✆1327111 Delta Airlines ✆1312339 Egyptair ✆1311126 El Al Israel Airlines ✆1465303 Emirates ✆1323216 GulfAir ✆1313450 Iberia ✆1551968 Iran Air ✆1411916 KLM ✆1300311 Kuwait Airways ✆1404081 Lot Polish Airlines ✆1407927 Lufthansa ✆1517180 Malaysian Airlines ✆1306431 Malev Hungarian ✆1488153 OlympicAirways ✆1473701 Royal Jordanian Airlines ✆1330744 Sabena World Airlines ✆1547254 Saudia ✆1564800 SAS ✆1466078 Singapore Airlines ✆1323706 Swissair ✆1312849 Syrian Arab Airlines ✆1461781 Turkish Airlines ✆5747300

Information and help desks
Information Desk International Terminal Arrival Lounge ✆5748300 ext. 2424
Airport, Flights, Tourist Information
Information Desk International Terminal Departure Lounge ✆5748300 ext. 2324
ⓘ24 hr *Airport, Flights, Tourist*

✈ Air 🚂 Rail 🚌 Bus 🚐 Limousine 🚇 Metro/subway 🚊 Tram 🚁 Helicopter ⛴ Water transport • For map symbols, see p. 9

Istanbul

SECTION TWO • AIRPORT DIRECTORY

Information
Tourist Information Desk International Terminal Arrival Lounge
ⓒ5737399/5734136 ⓘ0830–2100
Tourist Information

Emergencies

Medical Domestic Terminal Departure Lounge ⓒ5748300
Medical International Terminal Departure Lounge ⓒ5748300
Lost Property International Terminal Arrival Lounge (Airport Duty Manager) ⓒ5737867

Airport Facilities

Money
ATM International Terminal Arrival Lounge ⓘ24 hr
ATM International Terminal Departure Lounge ⓘ24 hr
Bank International Terminal Arrival Lounge ⓘ24 hr
Bank International Terminal Departure Lounge ⓘ24 hr
Bureau de change International Terminal Arrival Lounge ⓘ24 hr
Bureau de change International Terminal Departure Lounge ⓘ24 hr

Food and drink
Bar International Terminal Arrival Lounge ⓘ24 hr
Bar International Terminal Mezzanine Level ⓘ24 hr
Café/light meals International Terminal Arrival Lounge ⓘ24 hr
Café/light meals International Terminal Departure Lounge ⓘ24 hr

Communications
Post office International Terminal ⓘ24 hr
Post office Domestic Terminal ⓘ24 hr

Shopping
News, Stationery & Books International Terminal ⓘ24 hr
Gift Shop International Terminal ⓘ24 hr
Duty free, departure International Terminal Departure Lounge ⓘ24 hr

Luggage
Left Luggage Counter International Terminal ⓘ24 hr

Disabled Travellers

International Terminal Adapted toilets; Lifts
Domestic Terminal Adapted toilets; Lifts

Smoking Policy

International Terminal No restrictions
Domestic Terminal No restrictions

Special Passenger Lounges

VIP Lounge International Terminal Mezzanine Level
VIP Lounge Domestic Terminal Apron Level

Conference and Business Facilities

Conference Hall, International Terminal ⓒ5737240

Car Rental

Avis International Terminal ⓒ5736445/5734660
Avis Domestic Terminal ⓒ5731452/5733870
Budget Domestic Terminal ⓒ5735987/5746010
EuropCar Domestic Terminal ⓒ5737024
Hertz Domestic Terminal ⓒ5735987/5746948
Interrent Domestic Terminal ⓒ5741908

Car Parking

Long-stay 1160 spaces ⌀USD1.50 per hr; USD7.50 per day
Off-airport spaces ⌀TRL25000 per hr; TRL50000 per day
Short-stay 1160 spaces ⌀USD1 per hr; USD5 per day

Taxis and Chauffeur-driven Cars

Taxis
City centre ⤳30 min ⌀TRL45000

Public Transport

City & suburbs
Istanbul city bus terminal (Sishane) 🚌
HAVAS ⪢Approx. 1 hr ⓘ0600–2300
⤳30 min ⌀TRL15000.

Regional Air Connections

Ankara ✈ ⪢Several per day ⤳1 hr
Budapest ✈ ⪢Several per week ⤳1 hr
Pristina ✈ ⪢Several per week ⤳20 min
Tirana ✈ ⪢Several per week ⤳45 min

ⓒ Phone no. ⓕ Fax no. ⓘ Hours of opening/operation ⪢ Frequency of service ⤳ Journey time ⌀ Cost/one-way fare

SECTION TWO • AIRPORT DIRECTORY

JAKARTA   JKT

Indonesia (see page 25)

National ☏ code: 62
Area ☏ code: 021
Local time: Winter GMT+7, Summer GMT+7
Jakarta Soekarno-Hatta International Airport, Tangerang, Jakarta, Indonesia
☏ 550 5964
℻ 550 1684
Location: 20 km/12 miles NW of Jakarta

TERMINALS AND TRANSFERS

Terminals
Terminal A Airlines: Sempati Air.
Terminal B Airlines: Merpati Nusantara Airlines.
Terminal C Airlines: Bouraq Indonesia Airlines, Mandala Airlines.
Terminal D Airlines: All international flights (Except Garuda).
Terminal E Airlines: Garuda Indonesian Airlines (International flights only).
Terminal F Airlines: Garuda Indonesian Airlines (Domestic flights only).

Minimum transfer times
International: 2 hr Domestic: 1 hr

Transfer between terminals
Bus   All terminals ⌀IDR500

INFORMATION

Flight enquiries
Airport ☏550 5307; 550 5308; 550 5309 Bouraq Indonesia Airlines ☏550 1708, 550 7404 Garuda Indonesian Airlines ☏550 6089, 550 6091 Mandala Airlines ☏550 5198, 550 7911 Merpati Nusantara Airlines ☏550 7425, 550 7156 Sempati Air ☏550 7448, 550 7009

Information and help desks
Airport Information Desk Terminal A ☏550 5307; 550 5308 ⓗ24 hr *Airport information*
Tourist Information Desk Terminal A ☏550 7088 ⓗAll flights *Tourist information*
Tourist Information Desk Terminal B ☏550 7180 ⓗAll flights *Tourist information*
Tourist Information Desk Terminal C ☏550 7181 ⓗAll flights *Tourist information*
Tourist Information Desk Terminal D ☏550 0443 ⓗAll flights *Tourist information*
Tourist Information Desk Terminal E ☏550 6451 ⓗAll flights *Tourist information*
Tourist Information Desk Terminal F ☏550 7179 ⓗAll flights *Tourist information*

EMERGENCIES

Medical Terminal A ☏550 5238, 550 5239
Fire Terminal A ☏550 5513

Money
Bank Terminal A throughout ⓗ1 hr before–1 hr after flights
Bureau de change Terminal A throughout ⓗ1 hr before–1 hr after flights
Bank Terminal B
Bank Terminal C
Bank Terminal D
Bank Terminal E
Bank Terminal F

Food and drink
Café/light meals Terminal A throughout ⓗDuring flight times
Restaurant Terminal A throughout ⓗDuring flight times

Communications
Post office Terminal A ⓗ0800–1700 Sat, Sun
Post office Terminal A Transit Room ⓗ0900–1700 Mon–Fri
Post office Terminal B ⓗ0800–1700 Sat, Sun

Shopping
Duty free, departure Terminal D Departure Hall
Duty free, departure Terminal E Departure Hall

Luggage
Left luggage counter Terminal A ⌀IDR 1850

DISABLED TRAVELLERS
Terminal A Adapted toilets; Lifts

AIRPORT HOTELS
Chengkareng Airport ☏811 954

CAR RENTAL
Hertz Terminal A

CAR PARKING
Short-stay 5100 spaces ⌀IDR600 per hr; after first 12 hr IDR200 per hr

TAXIS AND CHAUFFEUR-DRIVEN CARS

Taxis
City centre ⌀IDR12000

PUBLIC TRANSPORT

City & suburbs
Jakarta city centre 🚌 »30 min ⓗ0400–2100 ⤴45–60 min ⌀IDR 3000.

REGIONAL AIR CONNECTIONS
Bandar Lampung ✈ »Several per day ⤴55 min
Bandung ✈ »Several per day ⤴40 min
Palembang ✈ »Several per day ⤴1 hr
Semarang ✈ »Several per day ⤴1 hr

145

JEDDAH   JED

Saudi Arabia (see page 34)

National ✆ code: 966
Area ✆ code: 02
Local time: Winter GMT+3, Summer GMT+3
King Abdulaziz International Airport, Jeddah, Saudi Arabia
✆685 5527
℻685 4985

Location: 19 km/11½ miles N of Jeddah

TERMINALS AND TRANSFERS

Terminals
North Terminal Airlines: All other airlines.
South Terminal Airlines: Saudia.

Minimum transfer times
International: 1 hr 30 min–2 hr 30 min
Domestic: 1 hr 15 min

INFORMATION

Flight enquiries
Airport ✆685 5526/5527

Information and help desks
Bi lingual aides North Terminal Centre of Arrival lobby ⏲All flight times *Airport information, Flights*
Bilingual aides South Terminal Centre of Arrival Lobby ⏲All flight times *Airport information, Flights*
Information Desk South Terminal Near Domestic Departure ⏲24 hr *Airport information, Flights Hotel booking, Tourist information*

AIRPORT FACILITIES

Money
ATM North Terminal Centre of Arrival Lobby ⏲24 hr
Bank North Terminal Centre of Arrival Lobby
Bank South Terminal Centre of Arrival Lobby

Food and drink
Café/light meals North Terminal Within Restaurants
Café/light meals South Terminal Arrival Lobby
Restaurant North Terminal East end of Terminal pre Departure
Restaurant South Terminal Above Departure Level

Communications
Post box North Terminal Arrival Lobby ⏲Normal business hours
Fax service North Terminal King Abdulaziz Hotel
Post box South Terminal Arrival Lobby ⏲Normal business hours
Fax service South Terminal King Abdulaziz Hotel

Shopping
Gift Shop North Terminal Departure Lounge ⏲All flight times
Gift Shop South Terminal Departure Lounge ⏲All flight times
News, Stationery & Books North Terminal Departure Lounge ⏲All flight times
News, Stationery & Books South Terminal Departure Lounges ⏲All flight times

DISABLED TRAVELLERS

North Terminal Adapted toilets; Lifts Medical Lift Lounge Phones at wheelchair height
South Terminal Adapted toilets; Lifts Medical Lift Lounge Phones at wheelchair height

SMOKING POLICY

North Terminal Smoking areas provided
South Terminal Smoking areas provided

SPECIAL PASSENGER LOUNGES

VIP Lounges North Terminal Mezzanine Level of Departure Lounges *Holders of VIP Lounge admission cards*
VIP Lounge South Terminal Mezzanine Level of Departure Lounges *Holders of VIP Lounge Admission cards*
Saudia Government VIP Lounge South Terminal Near Check in facilities at Arrivals Level *Government VIPs*

CONFERENCE AND BUSINESS FACILITIES

Conference facilities, King Abdulaziz Hotel in East Wing of South Terminal ⏲24 hr *Telephones, Fax service, Secretarial service*

AIRPORT HOTELS

King Abdulaziz

CAR RENTAL

North Terminal Car Rental counter near SAPTCO and Hotel Desks in Arrival Hall
South Terminal Car Rentals Counter near SAPTCO and Hotel desks in Arrival Hall

TAXIS AND CHAUFFEUR-DRIVEN CARS

Taxis
City centre ⌀SAR50

PUBLIC TRANSPORT

City & suburbs
Jeddah centre 🚌SAPTCO ⟳40 min.

Other towns and cities
Mecca 🚌SAPTCO.
Medina 🚌SAPTCO.
Taif 🚌SAPTCO.

REGIONAL AIR CONNECTIONS

Amman ✈ »Several per week ⟳1 hr
Bisha ✈ »At least daily ⟳1 hr
Cairo ✈ »Several per day ⟳1 hr
Madinah ✈ »Several per day ⟳50 min
Riyadh ✈ »Several per day ⟳1 hr 30 min

TRAVELLER'S NOTES

Always ask permission before photographing local people.

✆ Phone no.   ℻ Fax no.   ⏲ Hours of opening/operation   » Frequency of service   ⟳ Journey time   ⌀ Cost/one-way fare

JOHANNESBURG JNB

South Africa (see page 35)

National ✆ code: 27
Area ✆ code: 011
Local time: Winter GMT+2,
Summer GMT+2
Johannesburg International Airport,
Johannesburg, South Africa
✆921 6911
📠394 7236
Location: 24 km/14 miles W of
Johannesburg

TERMINALS AND TRANSFERS

Terminals
International Terminal Airlines: Aeroflot, Aero Zambia, Air Afrique, Air Austria, Air Botswana, Air France, Air Madagascar, Air Malawi, Air Namibia, Air Seychelles, Air Tanzania, Cathay Pacific, Egypt Air, Emirates, Ghana Airways, Qantas Airways, Singapore Airlines.
Domestic Arrival Terminal Airlines: All domestic arrivals.
Domestic Departure Terminal Airlines: All domestic departures.
Feeder Services Terminal.

Minimum transfer times
International: 1 hr Domestic: 30 min

INFORMATION

Flight enquiries
Airport ✆390 1420

Information and help desks
Information Desk Domestic Arrival Terminal Arrival Lounge ⏰24 hr
Information Desk International Arrival Terminal Arrival Lounge ⏰24 hr
South African Tourist Board International Arrival Terminal Arrival Lounge ⏰24 hr Tourist Information

EMERGENCIES

Lost Property Domestic Departure and Arrival Terminal

AIRPORT FACILITIES

Money
ATM International Arrival Terminal ⏰24 hr
ATM Domestic Arrival Terminal ⏰24 hr
Bank International Departure Terminal ⏰24 hr
Thomas Cook bureau de change International Arrival Terminal ⏰0500–2100

Food and drink
Restaurant International Arrival Terminal
Restaurant Domestic Arrival Terminal ⏰24 hr
Restaurant Domestic Departure Terminal

Communications
Post office International Arrival Terminal Between International Arrival and Domestic Arrival Terminals ⏰0700–2100

Shopping
Duty free, departure International Departure Terminal ⏰0600–2000
News, Stationery & Books International Departure Terminal
Gift Shop International Departure Terminal

Luggage
Lockers International Departure Terminal Upper Level of the undercover parking Area ⊘ZAR0.50

DISABLED TRAVELLERS

International Arrival Terminal Special car parking; Phones at wheelchair height
International Departure Terminal Special car parking; Phones at wheelchair height
Domestic Arrival Terminal Special car parking; Phones at wheelchair height
Domestic Departure Terminal Special car parking; Phones at wheelchair height

SPECIAL PASSENGER LOUNGES

Domestic Lounge Domestic Departure Terminal
British Airways Executive Club Lounge International Departure Terminal
Lufthansa Lounge International Departure Terminal

CONFERENCE AND BUSINESS FACILITIES

Conference Room
Committee Room

CAR RENTAL

Avis Domestic Arrival Terminal ✆394 5433
Budget Domestic Arrival Terminal ✆394 2905
Imperial Domestic Arrival Terminal ✆975 6736

CAR PARKING

Short-stay ⊘ZAR4 per hr; ZAR5.50 per 2 hr; ZAR6.50 per 2–3 hr; ZAR11 per 3–4 hr (thereafter ZAR10 for every additional 12 hr). Minimum charge of ZAR4.
Long-stay 1 & 2 ⊘ZAR17 per 12 hr; ZAR19 per 12–16 hr; ZAR21 per 16–20 hr; ZAR25 per 20–24 hr (thereafter ZAR14 for every additional 12 hr). Minimum charge of ZAR17. ✆975 6400.
Long-stay 3 ⊘ZAR17 per 12 hr. Minimum charge of ZAR17 must be paid on entry. ✆975 6400.
Off-airport ⊘ZAR4 per hr; ZAR5.50 per 1–2 hr; ZAR6.50 per 2–3 hr; ZAR11 per 3–8 hr; ZAR17 per 12 hr; ZAR19 per 12–16 hr; ZAR21 per 16–20 hr; ZAR25 per 20–24 hr (thereafter ZAR14 for every additional 12 hr). Minimum charge of ZAR4.

TAXIS AND CHAUFFEUR-DRIVEN CARS

Taxis
Outside International and Domestic Arrival City centre ⤳30 min ⊘ZAR40

Chauffeur-driven cars
Airport Link ✆803 9474; 803 0204 (Book in advance) City centre ⤳30 min ⊘ZAR80 per passenger

JOHANNESBURG • KARACHI   SECTION TWO • AIRPORT DIRECTORY

Public Transport

City & suburbs
Johannesburg city centre 🚌 Airport bus
≫30 min ⏱0500–2300.

Regional Air Connections

Bloemfontein ✈ ≫Several per day ⏲55 min
Durban ✈ ≫Several per day ⏲1 hr
Maputo ✈ ≫At least daily ⏲55 min

Traveller's Notes

Mugging is a problem in Johannesburg city centre, even during the day, so exercise caution.

KARACHI   KHI

Pakistan (see p. 32)

National ☎ code: 92
Area ☎ code: 021
Local time: Winter GMT+5,
Summer GMT+5
Karachi Airport, Karachi, Pakistan
☎485081
Location: 14 km/8½ miles NE of Karachi

Terminals and Transfers

Terminals
Terminal 1 Airlines: Gulf Air, Iran Air, Japan Airlines, KLM, Kuwait Airways, Lufthansa, Malaysian Airlines, Philippine Airlines, Royal Nepal Airlines, Royal Jordanian Airlines, Tarom Romanian Air, Singapore Airlines, Swissair, Saudia, Thai Airways. (All arrival only)
Terminal 2 Airlines: British Airways, Emirates, Egyptair. (All arrival only)
Terminal 3 Airlines: All international departures.

Minimum transfer times
International: 1 hr 30 min Domestic: 30 min

Information

Flight enquiries
Airport ☎482221

Information and help desks
Tourist Information Desk Terminal 1
Airport, Tourist Information
Tourist Information Desk Terminal 2
Airport, Tourist Information

Airport Facilities

Money
Bank Terminal 1 ⏱24 hr
Bank Terminal 2 ⏱24 hr
Bank Terminal 3 ⏱24 hr

Food and drink
Café/light meals Terminal 1 ⏱24 hr
Restaurant Terminal 1 ⏱24 hr
Café/light meals Terminal 2 ⏱24 hr
Restaurant Terminal 2 ⏱24 hr
Café/light meals Terminal 3 ⏱24 hr
Restaurant Terminal 3 ⏱24 hr

Communications
Post office Terminal 1 ⏱24 hr

Shopping
Duty free, arrival Terminal 1 ⏱24 hr
Duty free, arrival Terminal 2 ⏱24 hr
Duty free, departure Terminal 3 ⏱24 hr

Luggage
Left Luggage Counter Terminal 1 CAA supply store ⏱0745–1425 Sun–Thur ⊘PKR16 per item

Disabled Travellers

Terminal 1 Special car parking
Terminal 2 Special car parking
Terminal 3 Special car parking

Conference and Business Facilities

Conference centre, Terminal 1
Midway House Hotel

Car Parking

Short-stay 2000 spaces

Taxis and Chauffeur-driven Cars

Taxis
City centre ⏲20 min ⊘PKR2

Public Transport

City & suburbs
Karachi city centre 🚌 ≫30 min ⏱24 hr
⏲30 min ⊘PKR2.

Regional Air Connections

Hyderabad ✈ ≫Several per week ⏲45 min
Islamabad ✈ ≫Several per week ⏲2 hr
Lahore ✈ ≫Several per week ⏲1 hr 45 min
Nawabshah ✈ ≫Several per week ⏲55 min

☎ Phone no. ⓕ Fax no. ⏱ Hours of opening/operation ≫ Frequency of service ⏲ Journey time ⊘ Cost/one-way fare

KIEV — KBP

Ukraine (see page 40)

National ✆ code: 380
Area ✆ code: 44
Local time: Winter GMT+2, Summer GMT+3
Address: International Airport Boryspil, Airport Boryspil, Boryspil-7, Kyiv Region, Ukraine 256 300
✆: 296 7244/224 4131
℻: 295 8996
Location: 38km/24mls E of Kiev

Terminals and Transfers

Terminals
Terminal A Domestic flights
Terminal B International flights

Minimum transfer times
Transfer between terminals 3 mins

Information

Flight enquiries
Airport ⏱24 hr

Information and help desks
Tourist information desk ✆290 7439/225 3051/210 4267/263 4376 ⏱24 hr
Hotel Reservations Desk ✆219 1449

Emergencies

Medical ⏱24 hr

Airport Facilities

Food and drink
Bar ⏱24 hr
Restaurant ⏱24 hr

Shopping
Duty free ⏱24 hr ✆295 6763/296 7241 ⏱24 hr

Special Passenger Lounges

VIP Lounge ✆296 6139

Airport Hotels

✆296 7206/296 7105

Taxis and Chauffeur-driven Cars

Taxis
City centre ➔10 min

Public Transport

City & suburbs
🚌 Airport Bus »60 min ➔70 min

Regional Air Connections

Kharkov ✈ »Several per week ➔1 hr 15 min
Kishinev ✈ »Several per week ➔1 hr 20 min
Lvov ✈ »Several per day ➔1 hr 30 min

KINGSTON — KIN

Jamaica (see page 27)

National ✆ code: 1
Area ✆ code: 876
Local time: Winter GMT-5,
Summer GMT-5
Norman Manley International Airport, Palisadoes, Kingston, Jamaica
✆924 8452 6
⊕924 8566
Location: 21 km/12½ miles SE of Kingston

TERMINALS AND TRANSFERS

Terminals
Main Terminal Airlines: All international flights.

Minimum transfer times
1 hr 15 min

INFORMATION

Flight enquiries
Air Canada ✆924 8211 3 Air Jamaica ✆924 8231 American Airlines ✆924 8249 British Airways ✆924 8182

Information and help desks
Phone line ✆924 8024/8673 Airport, Tourist Information

EMERGENCIES

Police ✆926 8002
Medical ✆924 8856

AIRPORT FACILITIES

Money
Bureau de change By customs
Bureau de change Main Terminal cAll flight times

Food and drink
Bar Main Terminal throughout ⊕0900–1900 daily
Restaurant Main Terminal throughout ⊕0900–1900 daily

Communications
Post office Main Terminal ⊕0600–1600

Shopping
Duty free, departure Main Terminal Departure Hall

DISABLED TRAVELLERS

Main Terminal Adapted toilets; Special car parking

SPECIAL PASSENGER LOUNGES

Air Jamaica Lounge Main Terminal First class passengers
British Airways Lounge Main Terminal First class passengers
American Airlines Main Terminal First class passengers

CONFERENCE AND BUSINESS FACILITIES

Airports Authority of Jamaica Conference Room.

CAR RENTAL

Budget Main Terminal
Island Main Terminal
Jamaica Main Terminal
Avis Main Terminal
Gemini Main Terminal

CAR PARKING

TAXIS AND CHAUFFEUR-DRIVEN CARS

Taxis
City centre ⌲40 min

PUBLIC TRANSPORT

City & suburbs
Kingston city centre 🚌 SR8 ⌲30 min

REGIONAL AIR CONNECTIONS

Montego Bay ✈ »Several per day ⌲30–40 min
Negril ✈ »At least daily ⌲45 min
Port Antonio ✈ »At least daily ⌲15 min

AIRPORT TAX

Airport tax of JMD4 payable on departure.

TRAVELLER'S NOTES

The distance from the aircraft to immigration hall involves a long walk.

✆ Phone no. ⊕ Fax no. ⊕ Hours of opening/operation » Frequency of service ⌲ Journey time ⊘ Cost/one-way fare

SECTION TWO • AIRPORT DIRECTORY   KUALA LUMPUR

KUALA LUMPUR   KUL

Malaysia (see page 29)

National ✆ code: 60
Area ✆ code: 3
Local time: Winter GMT+8, Summer GMT+8
Sultan Abdul Aziz Shah International Airport, Subang, 47200 Subang Selangor Darul Ehsan, Malaysia
✆746 1833
📠746 3679
Internet e-mail: airport@po.jaring.my
WWW site: http://www.jaring.my/airport
Location: 22 km/14 miles SW of Kuala Lumpur

TERMINALS AND TRANSFERS

Terminals
Terminal 1 Airlines: All international flights. Layout: Ground Floor, Mezzanine Floor, First Floor
Terminal 2 Airlines: All domestic flights. Layout: Departures and arrivals on Ground Floor; Mezzanine Concourse.
Terminal 3 Airlines: All domestic flights. Layout: Departures and arrivals on Ground Floor; Mezzanine Concourse.

Minimum transfer times
International: 1 hr–1 hr 30 min Domestic: 45 min

Transfer between terminals
Bus ≫20 min; Terminals 1, 2, 3 ⊘Free

INFORMATION

Flight enquiries
Airport ✆ 746 1235, 746 1014 Terminal 1; 746 7807 Terminal 2; 746 4646 Terminal 3
Aeroflot ✆746 5578 **Air France** ✆746 2287 **Air India** ✆746 4805 **Air Lanka** ✆746 4500 **Air Mauritius** ✆242 9161 **Air New Zealand** ✆242 5577 **All Nippon Airways** ✆746 3368 **Ansett Australia** ✆746 7911 **Balkan Bulgarian Airlines** ✆241 9245 **Biman Bangladesh Airlines** ✆746 1118 **Bouraq Indonesia Airlines** ✆629 5364 **British Airways** ✆746 1175 **Cathay Pacific Airways** ✆746 3550 **China Airlines** ✆746 5885 **China Southern Airlines** ✆746 8918 **Eva Air** ✆746 4012; 746 4013 **Garuda Indonesian Airlines** ✆746 2627 **Gulf Air** ✆746 9919; 746 9920 **Indian Airlines** ✆294 5055 **Iran Air** ✆740 5699 **Japan Airlines** ✆746 5554 **KLM** ✆746 2663 **Korean Airlines** ✆746 4745 **Kuwait Airways** ✆201 8343 **Lufthansa** ✆746 4433 **Malaysian Airlines** ✆746 4555 **Myanmar Airways International** ✆264 3288 **Pakistan International Airlines** ✆746 4809 **Pelangi Air** ✆262 4448; 2624453 **Philippine Airlines** ✆746 1760 **Qantas Airways** ✆746 2557; 746 2530 **Royal Air Cambodge** ✆746 4555 **Royal Brunei Airlines** ✆746 2872 **Royal Jordanian Airlines** ✆746 36 5 **Saudia** ✆746 3153 **Sempati Air** ✆746 5878 **Silk Air** ✆542 8111 **Singapore Airlines** ✆746 3824; 746 3866 **Thai Airways** ✆746 5287 **Uzbekistan Airways** ✆244 8994 **Vietnam Airlines** ✆241 2416; 241 3288

Information and help desks
Malysia Airports Information Counter Terminal 1 Public Councourse, Level 1 ✆746 1235; 746 1014 *Airport information.*
Malaysian Tourist Board Terminal 1 Arrival Hall ✆746 5707 ⊙0900–2200 *Tourist information*
MAB Information Counter Terminal 2 Departure Area ✆746 7807; 746 7808 *Airport information.*
Malaysia Airports Information Counter Terminal 3 Ground Floor ✆746 4646; 746 2087 *Airport information.*

EMERGENCIES

Police Terminal 1 Ground Level ✆746 2222
Police Terminal 2 Concourse ✆746 2222
Police Terminal 3 Ground Floor ✆746 2222
Medical Terminal 1 Level 1, near departure gate A ✆746 2432
Medical Terminal 2 Baggage claim area
Lost Property Terminal 2 Baggage claim area ✆746 2222 (Airport police)
Lost Property Terminal 1 Airport Police Station, Ground level ✆746 2222
Lost Property Terminal 3 Ground Floor ✆746 2222 (Airport police)

AIRPORT FACILITIES

Money
ATM Terminal 1 throughout
ATM Terminal 2 throughout
Bank Terminal 1 Departure Hall ⊙24 hr
Bureau de change Terminal 1 Departure and Arrival Halls ⊙0800–2300
Bureau de change Terminal 2 Departure Public Concourse ⊙0600–2400
ATM Terminal 3 throughout
Bank Terminal 3 Public Concourse (2 locations)
Bureau de change Terminal 3 Public concourse ⊙Office hours

Food and drink
Restaurant Terminal 1 Departure Hall, Mezzanine Floor, First Floor ⊙24 hr (1st floor 0900–2200)
Café/light meals Terminal 1 Arrivals and departure area ⊙24 hr
Restaurant Terminal 2 Departure Hall ⊙24 hrs
Café/light meals Terminal 2 Departure Area
Restaurant Terminal 3 Departure Hall ⊙24 hr
Café/light meals Terminal 3 Departure Hall ⊙24 hr

Communications
Post office Terminal 1 Departure Hall ⊙0800–1700
Fax Terminal 1 Business Centre, near Gate 6.

Shopping
Duty free, departure Terminal 1 North wing and south wing
Pharmacy Terminal 1
Shopping mall Terminal 1
Duty free, departure Terminal 2 Departure and Arrival Halls
Duty free, arrival Terminal 2 Arrival Hall
Shopping mall Terminal 3 Departure Hall

Luggage
Left luggage counter Terminal 1 Outside Arrival Hall, across road to left of term ⊙24hr⊘MYR4 per item per day
Left luggage counter Terminal 2 Outside Arrival Hall, on the right ⊙24 hr⊘MYR4 per item per day
Left luggage counter Terminal 3 Outside Arrival Hall, on the right ⊙24 hr⊘MYR4 per item per day

DISABLED TRAVELLERS

Terminal 1 Adapted toilets; *Arrrival and*

✈ Air 🚆 Rail 🚌 Bus 🚘 Limousine Ⓜ Metro/subway 🚋 Tram 🚁 Helicopter ⛴ Water transport • For map symbols, see p.9

Kuala Lumpur

SECTION TWO • AIRPORT DIRECTORY

Departure Halls Lifts; *Arrival and Departure Halls* Phones at wheelchair height; Personal assistance
Terminal 2 Adapted toilets; *Public, Arrivals, Departures* Lifts; *Public, Arrivals, Departures* Personal assistance
Terminal 3 Adapted toilets; *Public, arrival, departure* Lifts; Personal assistance

Special Passenger Lounges

CIP Lounges Terminal 1 Near Gate 8 *MYR 32.50 per person*
Cathay Pacific Airways Lounge Terminal 1 First Floor, Subang Airport Hotel *First class and Marco Polo club members*
Malaysian Airlines Golden Lounge Terminal 2 Departure Hall, after security checkpoint *First and Club class passengers*
Malaysian Airlines Golden Lounge Terminal 1 Mezzanine Floor, near Immigration Departure Hall A *First and Club class passengers*
Malaysian Airlines Golden Lounge Terminal 3 Near Departure Hall (airside) next to Gate 31 *First and Club class passengers*
Singapore Airlines Silver Kris Lounge Terminal 2 Departure Hall *First and Business class passengers*

Conference and Business Facilities

Business Centre, Terminal 1 Near Gate 6.

Airport Hotels

Subang Airport ℂ746 2122 Ⓕ746 1097 157 rooms *Courtesy bus*

Car Rental

Mayflower Terminal 1 Outside Arrival Hall
National Terminal 1 Outside Arrival Hall
Orix Terminal 1 Outside Arrival Hall
SMAS Terminal 1 Outside Arrival Hall
Thrifty Terminal 1 Outside Arrival Hall
Toyota Terminal 1 Outside Arrivasl Hall
U-Drive Terminal 1 Outside Arrival Hall
Avis Terminal 1 Outside Arrival Hall
Budget Terminal 1 Outside Arrival Hall
Hertz Terminal 1 Outside Arrival Hall

Car Parking

Short-stay 760 spaces ⌀MYR1.68–3 per hr; MYR10-25 per day; MYR130–180 per month

Taxis and Chauffeur-driven Cars

Taxis
Outside Arrival Hall ℂ746 8954; 746 9135; 746 5705 City centre ⟶30 min ⌀MYR30

Public Transport

City & suburbs
Kuala Lumpur city centre 🚌 Sri Jaya Transport Company ≫15 min ⏱0600–2400 ⟶60 min ⌀MYR2.

Regional Air Connections

Alor Settar ✈ ≫Several pcr day ⟶50 min
Bangkok ✈ ≫Several per day ⟶1 hr
Ho Chi Minh City ✈ ≫At least daily ⟶45–55 min
Ipoh ✈ ≫Several per day ⟶35 min
Jakarta ✈ ≫Several per day ⟶1hr
Johor Bahru ✈ ≫Several per day ⟶45 min
Kerteh ✈ ≫Several per day ⟶55 min
Kota Bharu ✈ ≫Several per day ⟶50 min
Kuala Terengg ✈ ≫Several per week ⟶45 min
Kuantan ✈ ≫Several per day ⟶40 min
Langkawi ✈ ≫Several per day ⟶50–70 min
Padang ✈ ≫Several per day ⟶25 min
Penang ✈ ≫Several per day ⟶45 min
Phnom Penh ✈ ≫At least daily ⟶45 min
Phuket ✈ ≫At least daily ⟶15–20 min
Singapore ✈ ≫Several per day ⟶55 min
Tioman ✈ ≫Several per day ⟶60 min
Yangon ✈ ≫Several per week ⟶1 hr

Traveller's Notes

Taxis from the airport operate a coupon system, purchased from a booth at the airport. It is designed to eliminate fare cheating.

ℂ Phone no. Ⓕ Fax no. ⏱ Hours of opening/operation ≫ Frequency of service ⟶ Journey time ⌀ Cost/one-way fare

LAGOS   LOS

Nigeria (see page 31)

National ✆ code: 234
Area ✆ code: 01
Local time: Winter GMT+1, Summer GMT+1
Murtala Muhammed International Airport, PO Box 4532, P.M.B. 21607, Ikeja Lagos, Nigeria
✆4970339, 4528651
Location: 28 km/16 miles NW of Lagos

TERMINALS AND TRANSFERS

Terminals
International Terminal: Domestic Terminal I: Domestic Terminal II

Minimum transfer times
International: 1 hr 15 min–2 hr 15 min
Domestic: 1 hr

INFORMATION

Flight enquiries
Airport ✆4970339; 4528651 ext 5029
Information and help desks
Nigerian Tourist Board International Terminal ⊙0700–2000 Tourist Information

AIRPORT FACILITIES

Money
Bank International Terminal ⊙24 hr
Bureau de change International Terminal Arrival Lounge ⊙24 hr
Bureau de change International Terminal Departure Lounge ⊙24 hr

Food and drink
Bar International Terminal Arrival Lounge ⊙24 hr
Bar International Terminal Departure Lounge ⊙24 hr
Café/light meals International Terminal Departure Lounge ⊙24 hr
Restaurant International Terminal Arrival Lounge ⊙24 hr
Restaurant International Terminal Departure Lounge ⊙24 hr

Communications
Post office International Terminal Ground Floor Arrival Lounge ⊙0800–1630 Mon–Fri; 0900–1300 Sat; 0900–1200 Sun

Shopping
Duty free, departure International Terminal
Gift Shop International Terminal

Luggage
Left Luggage Counter International Terminal ⊙24 hr

DISABLED TRAVELLERS
International Terminal Adapted toilets

SMOKING POLICY
International Terminal No smoking throughout

SPECIAL PASSENGER LOUNGES
Nigeria Airways Lounge International Terminal
British Airways Lounge International Terminal

CONFERENCE AND BUSINESS FACILITIES
Press centre

AIRPORT HOTELS
Lagos Airport

CAR RENTAL
Avis Rent-A-Car
Coastal Services International Terminal
Safelink Venture International Terminal

CAR PARKING
Short-stay 750 spaces ⌀NGN30 per day; NGN100 per 24 hr

TAXIS AND CHAUFFEUR-DRIVEN CARS

Taxis
City centre ➲30 min ⌀NGN800

PUBLIC TRANSPORT

City & suburbs
Lagos city centre 🚆 Nigerian Airways ➲40 min. Buses and coach services to major hotels and the city centre available by prior arrangement

REGIONAL AIR CONNECTIONS
Accra ✈ »Several per day ➲50 min
Lome ✈ »Several per week ➲40 min
Port Harcourt ✈ »Several per week ➲1 hr

LAS VEGAS
USA (see page 41)

LAS

National © code: 1
Area © code: 702
Local time: Winter GMT-8, Summer GMT-7 McCarran International Airport, PO Box 11005, Las Vegas NV 89111, USA
©261 5100
WWW site: http://www.mccarran.com Location: 11 km/7 miles S of Las Vegas

TERMINALS AND TRANSFERS

Terminals
Terminal 1 Airlines: Alaska Airlines, America West, American Airlines, American Eagle, Canadian Airlines, Continental Airlines, Delta Airlines, Frontier Airlines, Hawaiian Air, Midwest Express, Northwest Airlines, Reno Air, Skywest, Southwest Airlines, Sun Country, TWA, United Airlines, US Airways, Vanguard. Layout: Level 1 (Arrivals, Baggage Claim, Car Rental, Ground Transportation), Level 2 (Departures), Concourse A (Gates A1–A24), Concourse B (Gates B1–B24), Concourse C (Gates C1–C27).
Terminal 2 (International) Aeroexo, Aero Mexico, Air Canada, Air France, Airtours International, Air Transat, America West, American Trans Air, Canada 3000, Canadian, Condor, German Air Force, Hawaiian Airlines, Mexicana, Monarch, Royal Airlines, Skyservice, Sobel Air, Sun Country, Trans Aero.

Minimum transfer times
International: 1 hr **Domestic:** 35 min
Information Flight enquiries ©261 4636 Information and help desks
Information Desk Terminal 1 Level 2
Airport information, Tourist information ©261 5733
Information Desk Terminal 2

Emergencies
Police Terminal 1 Level 2 behind ticket counter south
Medical First Aid Terminal 1 Level 2 behind ticket counter south
Medical First Aid Terminal 2

Lost Property
Terminal 1 Level 2 behind ticket counter north

Money
ATM Terminal 1 Level 2
ATM Terminal 2
Bureau de change

Food and drink
Bar Terminal 1 throughout
Café/light meals All Terminals throughout

Communications
Fax Business Service Center Terminal 1 Level 2 between north and south ticket counters

Shopping
Duty free, departure, Terminal 2
Gift Shop All Terminals throughout
News, Stationery & Books All Terminals throughout

Baggage
Lockers Terminal 1 Level 2 Concourse A, B and C beyond security
Lockers Terminal 2
Trolleys/carts All Terminals throughout

DISABLED TRAVELLERS
Special Parking all lots; Personal assistance

SMOKING POLICY
Permitted in Smoking Lounges Terminal 1 Concourses A, B and C
Permitted in Smoking Lounge Terminal 2

SPECIAL PASSENGER LOUNGE
Delta Crown Room Terminal 1 Level 2

CONFERENCE AND BUSINESS FACILITIES
Business Service Center Terminal 1 Level 2 fax, photocopying
Conference Rooms

CAR RENTAL
Alamo Terminal 1 Level 1
Allstate Terminal 1 Level 1
Avis Terminal 1 Level 1
Budget Terminal 1 Level 1
Dollar Terminal 1 Level 1
Hertz Terminal 1 Level 1
National Terminal 1 Level 1
Thrifty Terminal 1 Level 1

CAR PARKING
Long-stay Gold and Silver garages ⊘USD6 day
Long-stay Uncovered ⊘USD4 day
Short-stay Gold and Silver garages ⊘USD1 hr

TAXIS AND CHAUFFEUR-DRIVEN CARS
Taxis
City centre ⊃20 min ⊘USD16

PUBLIC TRANSPORT
City & suburbs
Las Vegas (city centre) CAT: 109 »15 min ⊕0530–0158 ⊃35 min ⊘USD1. For Downtown Transportation Center
Las Vegas (downtown hotels) Bell Trans Shuttle Bus ⊘USD4.75
Las Vegas (downtown hotels) Greyline ⊘USD4.75
Las Vegas (downtown hotels) Lucky 7 ⊘USD5
Las Vegas (downtown hotels) Ray and Ross ⊘USD4.50
Las Vegas (Strip) CAT: 108 »30 min ⊕0550–0120 ⊃20 min ⊘USD1.
Las Vegas (Strip hotels) Bell Trans Shuttle Bus ⊘USD3.50
Las Vegas (Strip hotels) Greyline ⊘USD3.75
Las Vegas (Strip hotels) Lucky 7 ⊘USD4
Las Vegas (Strip hotels) Ray and Ross ⊘USD3.50
Las Vegas (metro area) Over 10 companies at airport

Other towns and cities
Bullhead City AZ Best way
Laughlin NV Best Way

REGIONAL AIR CONNECTIONS
Burbank CA ✈ »Several per day ⊃55 min
Grand Canyon AZ ✈ »Several per day ⊃1 hr
Los Angeles CA ✈ »Several per day ⊃1 hr

© Phone no. ® Fax no. ⊕ Hours of opening/operation » Frequency of service ⊃ Journey time ⊘ Cost/one-way fare

✈︎ SECTION TWO • AIRPORT DIRECTORY   LAS VEGAS • LEEDS/BRADFORD

Ontario CA ✈ »Several per day ⊃50 min
Orange County CA ✈ »Several per day ⊃55 min
Palm Springs CA ✈ »Several per day ⊃50 min
Phoenix AZ ✈ »Several per day ⊃1 hr
St George UT ✈ »Several per day ⊃40 min
San Diego CA ✈ »Several per day ⊃1 hr

TRAVELLER'S NOTES
Aviation Museum Terminal 1 Level 2

LEEDS/BRADFORD LBA
United Kingdom (see page 41)

National ℗ code: 44
Area ℗ code: 0113
Local time: Winter GMT, Summer GMT+1
Address: Leeds Bradford International Airport, Leeds LS19 7TU
℃: 250 9696
℗: 250 5426
Location: 14 km/9 miles NW of Leeds

TERMINALS AND TRANSFERS
Terminals
Main Terminal Airlines: Aer Lingus, Air UK, British Airways Express, British Midland, Gill Airways, Jersey European, Manx Airlines, Ryanair, Sabena. Layout:

INFORMATION
Flight enquiries
Airport ℗ 250 9696
Aer Lingus ℗ 250 8194 Air UK ℗ 250 3251 British Airways Express ℗ 250 3251 British Midland ℗ 250 8194 Gill Airways ℗ 250 3251 Jersey European ℗ 250 3251 Manx Airlines ℗ 250 3251 Ryanair ℗ 250 3251 Sabena ℗ 250 3251

AIRPORT FACILITIES
Money
Thomas Cook Bureau de Change Main departures concourse ℗ 250 0682
Thomas Cook Bureau de Change Arrivals areal ℗ 250 5950

Food and drink
Bar Domestic departure lounge
Bar International departure lounge
Bar First floor, landside, main terminal building
Café/light meals International departure lounge
Café/light meals First floor, landside, main terminal building

Shopping
Duty free International departure lounge
News, Stationery & Books International departure lounge

DISABLED TRAVELLERS
Lift, ramps, parking, special needs area, toilets, wheelchairs

SPECIAL PASSENGER LOUNGES
British Midland Diamond Club Lounge
Servisair Executive Lounge
Yorkshire Executive Club full bar service, complimentary newspapers, fax machine, telephone ℗ 239 1455

CAR RENTAL
Avis ℗ 250 3880
Hertz ℗ 250 4811
Europcar ℗ 250 9066

CAR PARKING
Long-stay ⌀ GBP6 for 2 days; GBP3 per day thereafter; GBP22 per 8 days; GBP42 per 15 days
Short-term ⌀ free for first 20 min; GBP1 20min–1hr; GBP2 1–2 hr; GBP4 2–4 hr; GBP5 per 12 hr; GBP6 per 24 hr
Off-airport Sentinel (Security car park) ℗ 250 2255

TAXIS AND CHAUFFEUR-DRIVEN CARS
Taxis
Taxis available to city centre

PUBLIC TRANSPORT
City & suburbs
Leeds city centre (city bus station) 🚌
LBA Airlink 757 ⌀GBP1 »11 per day ⊕ 0620–2215 Sun-Fri (last service 2150 Sat) ⊃30 min ℗ 245 7676

Other towns and cities
Bradford 🚆 » Frequent ⊃ 25 min
Harrogate 🚆 » Frequent ⊃ 40 min
Huddersfield 🚆 » Frequent ⊃ 25 min
Hull 🚆 » 1 hr ⊃ 1 hr
Sheffield 🚆 » Frequent ⊃ 1 hr 20 min
York 🚆 » Frequent ⊃ 30 min

155

✈ Air 🚆 Rail 🚌 Bus 🚐 Limousine Ⓜ Metro/subway 🚋 Tram 🚁 Helicopter ⛴ Water transport • For map symbols, see p. 9

LISBON (LISBOA)   LIS

Portugal (see page 33)

National ✆ code: 351
Area ✆ code: 01
Local time: Winter GMT, Summer GMT+1
Lisbon Airport, ANA EP, Alameda das Comunidades Portuguesas, Aeropuerto 1700, Lisboa, Portugal
✆808044; 8481101
🅕801837
Location: 7 km/4½ miles N of Lisbon

TERMINALS AND TRANSFERS

Terminals
Main Terminal Airlines: All airlines.

Minimum transfer times
International: 1 hr Domestic: 45 min

INFORMATION

Flight enquiries
Airport ✆802060
Air France ✆562171 Air Portugal TAP ✆8489181 Alitalia ✆8491421 Austrian Airlines ✆7932207 British Airways ✆8486482 Delta Airlines ✆8489266 El Al Israel Airlines ✆804542 Finnair ✆802413 Iberia ✆8493693 KLM ✆579110 Lufthansa ✆573852 Royal Air Maroc✆3521659 Sabena World Airlines ✆8485605 SAS ✆8481223 South African Airways ✆8489181 Swissair ✆371111 Tarom Romanian Air 🅕3960866 TWA ✆8490644 Varig Brazilian 🅕8489176 f

Information and help desks
Information Desk Main Terminal Upper Level, Departure Lounge ✆8494323; 8493689 ⏲24 hr Airport, Flights, Hotel booking, Tourist Information
Information Desk Main Terminal Lower Level, Arrival Lounge ✆8494323; 8493689 ⏲24 hr Airport, Flights, Hotel booking, Tourist Information

EMERGENCIES

Police Main Terminal ✆8496132
Medical Main Terminal ⏲24 hr

AIRPORT FACILITIES

Money
Bank Main Terminal Lower Level, Arrival Lounge ⏲0830–1500
Bureau de change Main Terminal Lower Level, Arrival Lounge ⏲24 hr
Bureau de change Main Terminal Departure Lounge ⏲24 hr
ATM Main Terminal throughout ⏲24 hr

Food and drink
Bar Main Terminal Transit Area ⏲0800–2400
Café/light meals Main Terminal Domestic Departure Lounge ⏲0700–2400
Café/light meals Main Terminal International Departure Lounge ⏲0700–2400
Café/light meals Main Terminal ⏲0700–2400
Café/light meals Main Terminal Transit Area ⏲0700–2400
Restaurant Main Terminal International Departure Lounge ⏲24 hr
Restaurant Main Terminal ⏲1000–1500 and 1900–0200
Restaurant Main Terminal Transit Area ⏲24 hr

Communications
Post office Main Terminal First Floor ⏲24 hr
Post office Main Terminal Next to the terminal building ⏲24 hr

Shopping
Duty free, departure Main Terminal Transit Area ⏲0700–2400
News, Stationery & Books Main Terminal Transit Area ⏲0700–2400
News, Stationery & Books Main Terminal International Arrival Lounge ⏲0700–2400
Gift Shop Main Terminal Transit Area ⏲0700–2400

Luggage
Left Luggage Counter Main Terminal Adjacent to the International Arrival Lounge ⏲24 hr ✍PTE200

DISABLED TRAVELLERS

Main Terminal Adapted toilets Lifts

SMOKING POLICY

Main Terminal No restrictions

SPECIAL PASSENGER LOUNGES

Air Portugal TAP Navigator Lounge Main Terminal First Floor

CAR RENTAL

Avis Main Terminal International Arrival Lounge ✆8494836
Budget Main Terminal International Arrival Lounge ✆803686
EuropCar Main Terminal International Arrival Lounge ✆801163
Hertz Main Terminal International Arrival Lounge ✆8492722
Interrent Main Terminal International Arrival Lounge ✆8486191
RN Tours Main Terminal International Arrival Lounge ✆801704
Viata Main Terminal International Arrival Lounge ✆809199

CAR PARKING

Long-stay 300 spaces ✍PTE60 per hr; PTE750 per day; PTE8850 per week
Short-stay 2030 spaces ✍PTE250 per hr; PTE3750 per day; PTE25900 per week

TAXIS AND CHAUFFEUR-DRIVEN CARS

Taxis
International Arrival, Domestic Departures and Arrival City centre ➲25 min ✍PTE1500

PUBLIC TRANSPORT

City & suburbs
Lisbon city centre (Cais do Sodre rail stn) 🚆 Companhia Carris de Ferro de Lisboa: Service 44.
Lisbon city centre (Santa Apolonia rail stn) 🚆 Companhia Carris de Ferro de Lisboa: Ligne Verte »15–20 min ⏲0730–2120 ➲30 min ✍PTE270.

REGIONAL AIR CONNECTIONS

Faro ✈ »Several per day ➲40 min
Porto ✈ »Several per day ➲45 min

✆ Phone no. 🅕 Fax no. ⏲ Hours of opening/operation » Frequency of service ➲ Journey time ✍ Cost/one-way fare

SECTION TWO • AIRPORT DIRECTORY   LIVERPOOL • LONDON CITY

LIVERPOOL   LPL

United Kingdom (see page 41)

National ☎: 44
Area ☎ code: 0151
Local time: Winter GMT, Summer GMT+1
Address: Liverpool Airport plc, Liverpool L24 1YD
☎: 486 8877
🖷: 486 3339
Location: 11 km/7 miles SE of Liverpool

TERMINALS AND TRANSFERS

Terminals
Main Terminal British Airways Express, British Midland, Manx Airlines, Emerald Airways, Ryanair.
Layout: Ground floor international and domestic arrivals and departures; first floor BA Exec lounge, catering facilities.

INFORMATION

Flight enquiries
Airport ☎ 486 8877
British Airways Express ☎ (0345) 222 111
British Midland ☎ (0345) 554 554 Manx Airlines ☎ (03450) 256 256 Emerald Airways ☎ (0500) 600 748 Ryanair ☎ (0541) 569 569

Information and help desks
Information Desk International arrivals, by Servisair desk

AIRPORT FACILITIES

Money
Thomas Cook Bureau de Change Main concourse ⊕ daily for all international flights

Food and drink
Bar First floor
Bar Ground floor, departure lounge
Restaurant First floor
Restaurant Ground floor, departure lounge

Shopping
Duty free Ground floor, departure lounge
News, Stationery & Books Main concourse

DISABLED TRAVELLERS

Ambulift, wheelchairs, special car parking, lift, disabled toilet.

SPECIAL PASSENGER LOUNGES

British Airways Executive Lounge First floor, before restaurant and bar areas.
British Airways Executive Club and Manx Sovereign Club.

CAR RENTAL

Avis ☎ 486 6686

Europcar ☎ 448 0020
Hertz ☎ 486 7111

CAR PARKING

Long-stay ⊘ GBP1 per 45 min; GBP1.90 per 3 hr; GBP2.90 per 12 hr; GBP3.90 per 24 hr
Short-stay ⊘ GBP1 per 45 min; GBP1.90 per 3 hr; GBP2.90 per 12 hr; GBP3.90 per 24 hr

TAXIS AND CHAUFFEUR-DRIVEN CARS

Taxis
City centre ⊃ 20 min. Pick-up directly outside entrance to terminal building

PUBLIC TRANSPORT

City & suburbs
Liverpool city centre 🚌 Merseybus No. 80 ⟫ 30 min Mon–Sat (No. 180 Sun) ☎ 236 7676

Other towns and cities
Chester 🚆 ⟫ 30 min ⊃ 40 min
Preston 🚆 ⟫ 1 hr ⊃ 1 hr
Southport 🚆 ⟫ Frequent ⊃ 45 min
Warrington 🚆 ⟫ Frequent ⊃ 25 min
Wigan 🚆 ⟫ Frequent ⊃ 45 min

LONDON-CITY   LCY

United Kingdom (see page 41)

National ☎ code: 44
Area ☎ code: 0171
Local time: Winter GMT, Summer GMT+1
London City Airport, Royal Docks, London E16 2PX, United Kingdom

☎646 0000/(0800) 834 163 (freephone)
🖷511 1040
Location: 13 km/8 miles E of central London

TERMINALS AND TRANSFERS

Terminals
Main Terminal Airlines: All airlines.
Layout: Ground Floor for most facilities and services, Departure Lounges on First Floor

---

✈ Air 🚆 Rail 🚌 Bus 🚗 Limousine Ⓜ Metro/subway 🚊 Tram 🚁 Helicopter ⛴ Water transport • For map symbols, see p. 9

London City

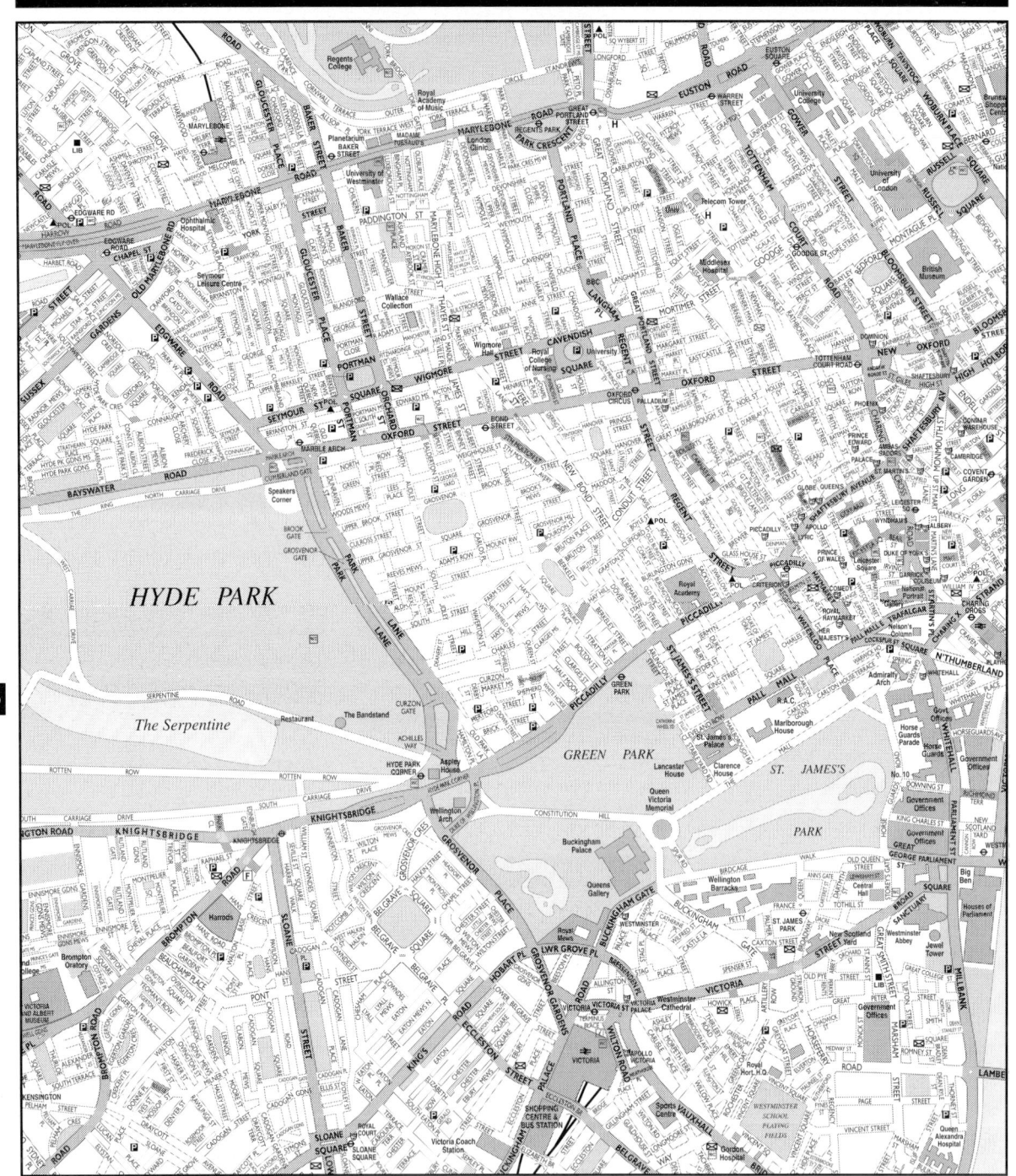

SECTION TWO • AIRPORT DIRECTORY

Minimum transfer times
International: 30 min **Domestic:** 30 min

Information

Flight enquiries
Airport ✆646 0088
Air Engiadina ✆(0345) 666777 Air France ✆(0181) 742 6600 Air Jet ✆476 6000 Air UK ✆(0345) 666777 Azzurra Air ✆(0181) 785 3177 City Jet ✆(0345) 445588 Crossair ✆434 7300 Lufthansa ✆(0345) 737747 Malmö Aviation ✆(01293) 530839 Sabena ✆(0181) 780 1444 VLM ✆476 6677. London Executive Aviation (private charter) ✆646 0667/0668

Information and help desks
Infomation Desk Main Terminal Left, just inside terminal ✆646 0088 ⨏511 1040 Airport information, Flights, Hotel booking, Tourist information.

Emergencies

Lost Property Main Terminal Ground Floor, beside Information desk

---

✆ Phone no. ⨏ Fax no. ⏲ Hours of opening/operation ≫ Frequency of service ⮎ Journey time ◇ Cost/one-way fare

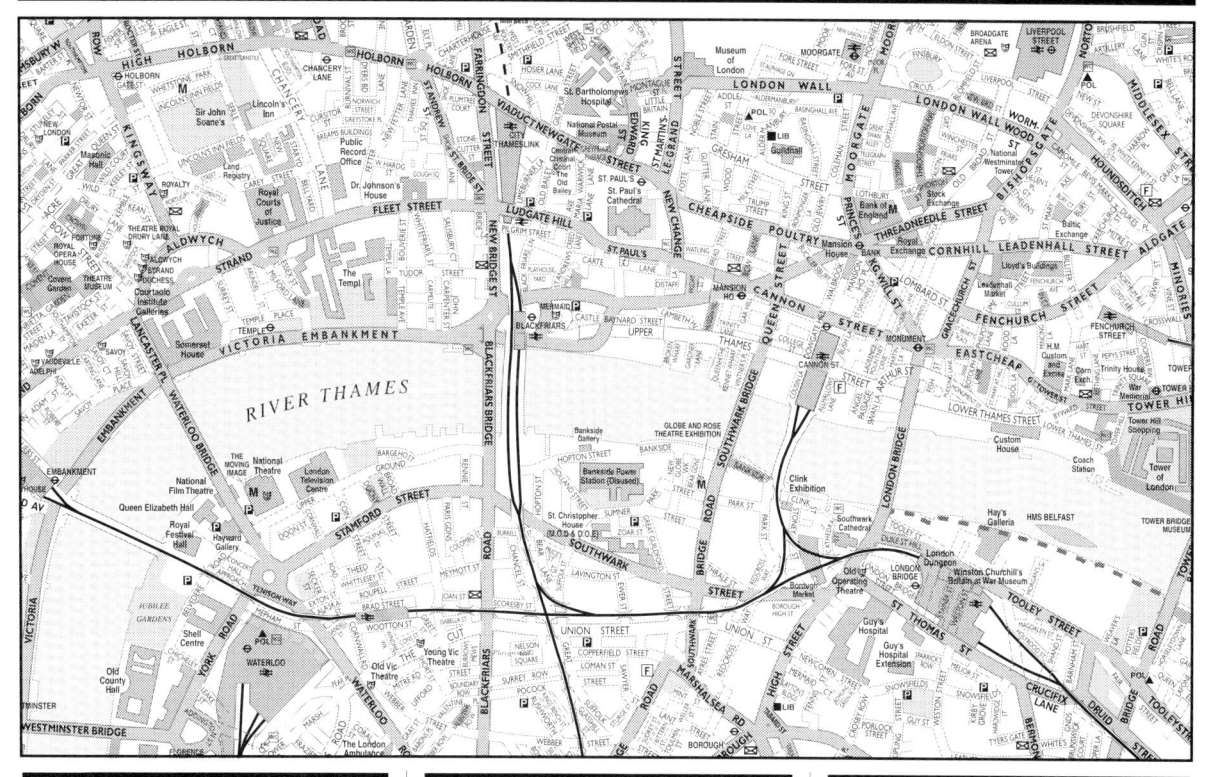

SECTION TWO • AIRPORT DIRECTORY

LONDON CITY

Airport Facilities

Money
ATM Main Terminal Ground Floor
Bureau de change Main Terminal Ground Floor

Food and drink
Restaurant Main Terminal First Floor
Bar Main Terminal First Floor and departure lounges

Communications
Post box Main Terminal Ground Floor, at terminal entrance
Fax service Main Terminal International Departure Lounge, First Floor

Shopping
News, Stationery & Books Main Terminal Ground Floor
Duty free, departure Main Terminal First Floor

Luggage
Left luggage counter Main Terminal Ground Floor, beside Information Desk

Disabled Travellers

Allocated parking spaces in main stay car park; lifts in terminal building; disabled facilities on the airport shuttle bus; special assistance available upon request.

Smoking Policy

Main Terminal Restricted

Special Passenger Lounges

Air France Lounge Main Terminal First Floor

Conference and Business Facilities

Business and Conference Centre, Ground Floor ℭ646 0900 ℱ476 3727
⊙0830–1730 Mon–Fri Telephones, Fax service, Photocopier, Secretarial service.

Car Rental

EuropCar Main Terminal Ground Floor ℭ476 0309
Avis Main Terminal Ground Floor ℭ476 7151

Car Parking

Main-stay 2-min walk from terminal
⌀GBP1 per 2 hr, then GBP1 per hr, then GBP 3.50 per 12 hr

Taxis and Chauffeur-driven Cars

Taxis
Front of terminal ℭ646 0850 City centre ⟳20–30 min

Public Transport

City & suburbs
London, City (Liverpool St rail stn) Airport Shuttlebus ≫10 min ⊙Airport operating hours ⟳25 min ⌀GBP4. Also links to Docklands Light Railway, Bank and Tower Gateway stns (City of London).
London (Canary Wharf) 🚌Airport Shuttlebus ≫10 min ⊙Airport operating hrs ⟳10 min ⌀GBP2.

Regional Air Connections

Amsterdam ✈ ≫Several per day ⟳50 min
Antwerp ✈ ≫Several per day ⟳1 hr
Brussels ✈ ≫Several per day ⟳1 hr
Dublin ✈ ≫Several per day ⟳1 hr 5 min
Paris ✈ ≫Several per day ⟳1 hr
Rotterdam ✈ ≫Several per day ⟳1 hr

Traveller's Notes

Fastest check-in (10 min) and arrival (5 min) procedures in Europe.

✈ Air 🚆 Rail 🚌 Bus 🚘 Limousine Ⓜ Metro/subway 🚋 Tram 🚁 Helicopter ⛴ Water transport • For map symbols, see p. 9

LONDON-GATWICK LGW

UK (see page 41)

National ℗ code: 44
Area ℗ code: 01293
Local time: Winter GMT, Summer GMT+1
London Gatwick Airport, West Sussex, RH6 0NP, United Kingdom
℗535353
Location: 43 km/28 miles S of central London

TERMINALS AND TRANSFERS

Terminals
North Terminal Airlines: British Airways, Brit Air, Brymon Airways, Deutsche BA, Delta Airlines, Maersk Air, Air 2000, Emirates, GB Airways, TAT European Airlines, Caledonian, Royal Nepal Airlines, Air Zimbabwe. Layout: 3 Levels
South Terminal Airlines: All other airlines. Layout: Most passenger services on 3 Levels; Level 3 includes Gatwick Village shopping area

Minimum transfer times
International: 45 min–1 hr **Domestic:** 40–45 min

Transfer between terminals
Monorail ≫3 min; North and South Terminals ⌀Free

INFORMATION

Flight enquiries
Airport ℗535353
Air 2000 ℗535353 Air Afrique ℗535353 Air Baltic ℗535353 Air Europa ℗535353 Air Liberté ℗535353 Air Malta ℗535353 Air Seychelles ℗535353 Air UK ℗535353 Air Zimbabwe ℗535353 Airtours ℗535353 Alitalia ℗(0181) 745 8201 American Airlines ℗535353 BASE Regional Airlines ℗535353 Belavia ℗535353 Braathens S.A.F.E. ℗535353 Brit Air ℗535353 British Airways ℗(0181) 759 2525 British Midland Airways ℗535353 Brymon Airways ℗535353 Caledonian ℗535353 Cameroon Airlines ℗535353 Continental Airlines ℗535353 Cyprus Airlines ℗535353 Delta Airlines ℗535353 Emirates ℗535353 Estonian Air ℗535353 Finnair ℗535353 Garuda Indonesian Airlines ℗535353 GB Airways ℗535353 Iberia ℗535353 Jersey European Airlines ℗535353 Lauda-Air ℗(0171) 630 5924 Lufthansa ℗535353 Maersk Air ℗(0181) 759 1818 Meridiana ℗535353 Northwest Airlines ℗535353 Philippine Airlines ℗535353 Qatar Airlines ℗535353 Royal Nepal Airlines ℗(0181) 759 1818 Ryanair ℗535353 Transavia ℗535353 Transwede Airways ℗535353 TWA ℗535353 Ukraine International Airlines ℗535353 Virgin Atlantic ℗535353 Yemen Airways ℗535353

Information and help desks
Information North Terminal Arrival Concourse ℗535353 ⏰24 hr Airport information Hotel booking, Tourist information
Information Desk South Terminal Arrival Concourse ℗535353 ⏰24 hr Airport information Hotel booking, Tourist information
Coach and Bus Information Desk North and South Terminal ℗0990 747777 ⏰0800–2000

EMERGENCIES
Police North Terminal Perimeter road between terminals ℗531122 ⏰24 hr
Police South Terminal Station on North Perimeter Road ℗531122 ⏰24 hr
Medical South Terminal Adjacent to terminal building ℗507400 ⏰0700–2300
Lost Property South Terminal Departure Concourse ℗503463 ⏰0800–1630
Lost Property North Terminal South Terminal Departure Concourse ℗Information Desk ⏰24 hr

AIRPORT FACILITIES

Money
ATM North Terminal Level 1, Transit and International Departure Lounges ⏰24 hr
ATM South Terminal International Departure Lounge, check-in area ⏰24 hr
Thomas Cook bureau de change North Terminal Arrival Area, airside ⏰0500–2400
Thomas Cook bureau de change North Terminal Arrival Area, landside ⏰Summer 0500–2100; winter 0600–2100
Thomas Cook bureau de change North Terminal Check-in ⏰24 hr
Thomas Cook bureau de change North Terminal Interchange Area ⏰0600–2200
Thomas Cook bureau de change South Terminal Level 3, Gatwick Village ⏰0600–2100
Thomas Cook bureau de change South Terminal at Thomas Cook Travel Shop ⏰0600–2300
Thomas Cook bureau de change South Terminal Departure Area, airside ⏰0600–2100
Thomas Cook bureau de change South Terminal Departure Area, Check-in ⏰24 hr

Food and drink
Restaurant North Terminal Before and after passport control ⏰All flight times
Bar North Terminal Before and after passport control ⏰All flight times
Café/light meals North Terminal Before and after passport control ⏰All flight times
Restaurant South Terminal Before and after passport control ⏰All flight times
Bar South Terminal Before and after passport control ⏰All flight times
Café/light meals South Terminal Before and after passport control ⏰All flight times

Communications
Post box North Terminal throughout ⏰24 hr
Post box South Terminal throughout ⏰24 hr
Post office South Terminal Level 3, Gatwick Village ⏰0700–1900

Shopping
Duty free, departure North Terminal International Departure Lounge ⏰24 hr
Shopping mall North Terminal Departure Hall pre passport control ⏰Some 24hr
Duty free, departure South Terminal International Departure Lounge and Departure Pier ⏰24 hr
Shopping mall South Terminal Gatwick Village Level 3 ⏰Some shops 24 hr
Thomas Cook travel agency South Terminal ⏰0600–2300

Luggage
Left luggage counter North Terminal Check-in Concourse 0600–2200 ⌀GBP2 per item per 12 hr
Left luggage counter South Terminal Arrival Concourse ⏰0500–2300 ⌀GBP2 per item per 12 hr
Porters North Terminal Arrival and

LONDON GATWICK

Departure Levels ⓘAll flight times ⊘Free
Porters South Terminal Arrival and Departure Levels ⓘAll flight times ⊘Free
Trolleys/carts North Terminal throughout ⓘ24 hr ⊘Free
Trolleys/carts South Terminal throughout ⓘ24 hr ⊘Free

DISABLED TRAVELLERS

North Terminal Adapted toilets; Lifts All Levels; Special car parking within multi-storey car parks; Phones at wheelchair height; Phones adapted for the deaf; Personal assistance via Medical Centre and airport staff All flight times
South Terminal Adapted toilets; Lifts All Levels; Special car parking Special areas of multi-storey car parks; Phones at wheelchair height; Phones adapted for the deaf; Personal assistance via Medical Centre and airport staff All flight times

SMOKING POLICY

North Terminal Smoking areas marked throughout
South Terminal Smoking areas marked throughout

SPECIAL PASSENGER LOUNGES

Servisair Lounge South Terminal Departure Area First and Business class passengers of RK, UK, KM, J2, CY, NG and JY
All airlines Premier Lounge South Terminal Departure Area Gates 12/14, run by Air Navigation Open on payment of small fee
Gatwick Handling South Terminal Departure Area First and Business class passengers of HM, BT, 5E, VS, AY and NW
American Airlines Admirals Club Lounge South Terminal Arrival Lounge, London Gatwick Hilton Hotel Club members and First and Business class passengers
British Airways Arrival Lounge North Terminal Forte Crest Hotel First/Club, Premier/Gold Executive Card holders
British Airways Executive Club Lounge North Terminal Business Pavilion Lounge Club members and UM, DM, RA and EK First and Business class passengers
British Airways Club World/Europe Lounge North Terminal **Business Pavilion Lounge** Club World/Club Europe, DI and IJ passengers
British Airways Lounge North Terminal **Business Pavilion Lounge** First class passengers of BA and UM
Continental Airlines Presidents Club Lounge South Terminal Departure Area Club members and First and Business class passengers
Delta Airlines Lounge North Terminal Departure Area Pavilion Level 1 First and Business class passengers and American Express cardholders

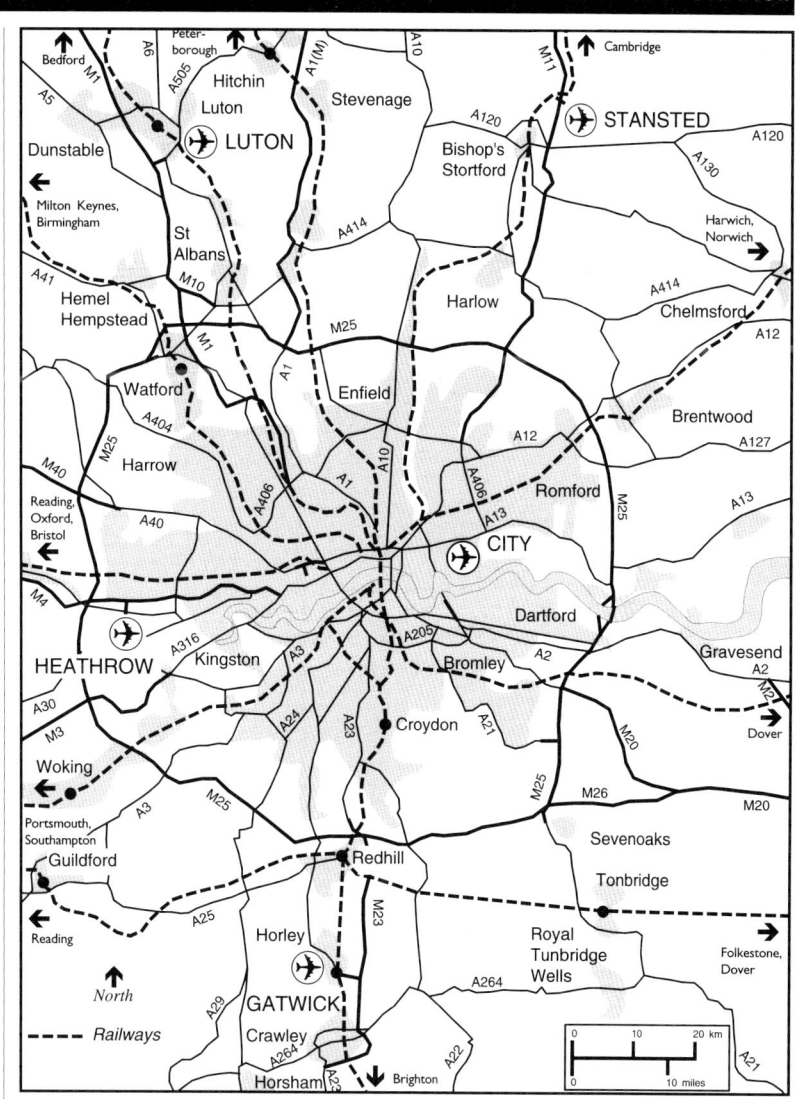

CONFERENCE AND BUSINESS FACILITIES

Business Centre, South Terminal, and Airport Hotels ✆505333 ⓘAll flight times Telephones, Fax service, Secretarial service, Travel advice

AIRPORT HOTELS

Meridiana Gatwick ✆567070 ✆567739
London Gatwick Hilton ✆518080 ✆526980

CAR RENTAL

Alamo North Terminal Rental Building, lower forecourt road ✆(0800) 272300
Alamo South Terminal Rental Building, lower forecourt road ✆(0800) 272300
Avis North Terminal Rental Building, lower forecourt road ✆529721
Avis South Terminal Rental Building, lower forecourt road ✆529721
Budget North Terminal Rental Building, lower forecourt road ✆(0800) 626063
Budget South Terminal Rental Building, lower forecourt road ✆(0800) 626063
Eurodollar North Terminal Rental Building, lower forecourt road ✆619368
Eurodollar South Terminal Rental Building, lower forecourt road ✆619368
EuropCar North Terminal Rental Building, lower forecourt road ✆531062
EuropCar South Terminal Rental Building, lower forecourt road ✆531062
Hertz North Terminal Rental Building, lower forecourt road ✆530555
Hertz South Terminal Rental Building, lower forecourt road ✆530555

London Gatwick

Car Parking

Long-stay Short bus ride from terminals 18882 spaces ⌀GBP4.50 per 24 hr
Short-stay Next to terminals 4128 spaces ⌀GBP0.80 first 30 min; thereafter GBP1.50 per hr

Taxis and Chauffeur-driven Cars

Taxis
Front of terminal City centre ➲1 hr 30 min–1 hr 50 min

Chauffeur-driven cars
Front of terminal Airport Cars/Goldline Cars ✆562291, 568468

Public Transport

Airport to airport
Birmingham Apt 🚌National Express »avg 3 hr ⏱0740–2155 ➲4 hr 30 min ⌀GBP22.
London-Heathrow Apt 🚌Speedlink »15 min a.m.; 30 min p.m. ⏱0615–2200 ➲1 hr ⌀GBP13.50.
London-Heathrow Apt 🚌Jetlink 747 »avg 30 min ⏱0530–2145 ➲1 hr ⌀GBP11.
London-Luton Apt 🚌Jetlink 747 »avg 1 hr 25 min ⏱0530–2145 ➲3 hr ⌀GBP11.
London-Stansted Apt 🚌Jetlink 747 »avg 1 hr 30 min ⏱0530–1545 ➲4 hr 30 min ⌀GBP13.

Manchester Apt 🚌National Express »avg 3 hr ⏱0740–2155 ➲8 hr 30 min ⌀GBP27.

City & suburbs
London city centre (Victoria Coach Stn) 🚌Flightline »avg 1 hr ⏱0515–2152 ➲1 hr–1 hr 10 min ⌀GBP6.50.
London city centre (Victoria rail stn) 🚆Connex South Central »avg 20 min ⏱24 hr ➲35 min.
London city centre (Victoria rail stn) 🚆Gatwick Express »15 min (day); 30 min–1 hr (after 2100) ⏱24 hr ➲30 min ⌀GBP8.90.
London (City of London) 🚆Thameslink »avg 15 min ⏱24 hr ➲30–45 min ⌀GBP8.90. Continues to Kings Cross rail stn for connections to northern England, Scotland

Other towns and cities
Bedford 🚆Thameslink »avg 20 min ⏱24 hr ➲37 min.
Brighton 🚌Jetlink 747 »avg 30 min ⏱0605–2335 ➲45 min.
Brighton 🚆Connex South Central, Thameslink »avg 20 min ⏱24 hr ➲37 min. Many other connections to destinations in southern England: ✆01273 206755 for information.
Bristol 🚌National Express »2 hr ⏱0735–2235 ➲3 hr ⌀GBP20.
Cambridge (UK) 🚌Cambridge Coach »1 hr ⏱0600–0000 ➲3 hr ⌀GBP14.
Norwich 🚌Jetlink 747 »avg 2 hr ⏱0130–2130 ➲4 hr 30 min. ⌀GBP22.

Oxford 🚌Oxford Citylink X70/X80 »avg 2 hr 30 min ⏱0200–2300 ➲2 hr ⌀GBP13.

Regional Air Connections

Amsterdam ✈ »Several per day ➲1 hr 5 min
Antwerp ✈ »Several per day ➲1 hr 10 min
Belfast ✈ »Several per day ➲1 hr 20 min
Birmingham (UK) ✈ »Several per week ➲55 min
Brussels ✈ »Several per day ➲1 hr 05min
Guernsey ✈ »Several per day ➲50 min
Jersey ✈ »Several per day ➲1 hr
Le Havre ✈ »Several per week ➲45 min
Leeds/Bradford ✈ »Several per week ➲1 hr 15 min
Manchester (UK) ✈ »Several per day ➲1 hr
Paris ✈ »Several per day ➲1 hr
Rotterdam ✈ »Several per day ➲1 hr 10 min

Traveller's Notes

Although Gatwick is further from central London than Heathrow, connections to the city are generally quicker and easier. Many destinations in southern England can be reached by rail from the airport.

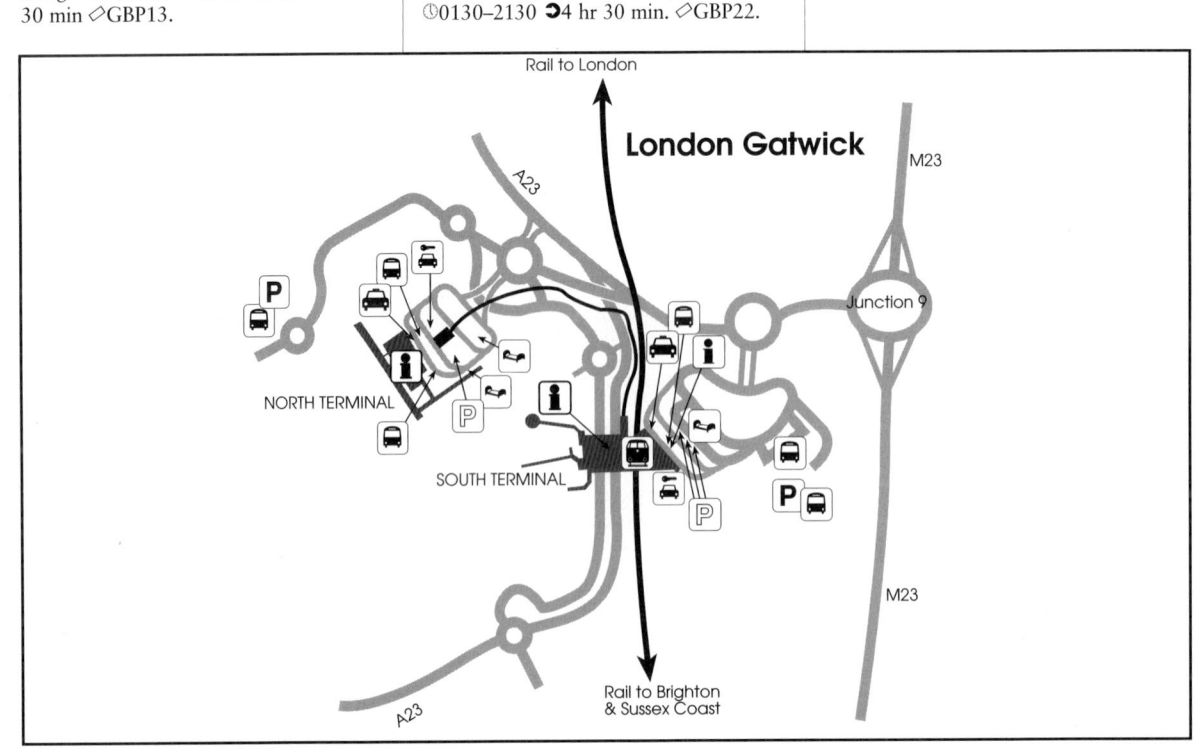

✆ Phone no. 🖷 Fax no. ⏱ Hours of opening/operation » Frequency of service ➲ Journey time ⌀ Cost/one-way fare

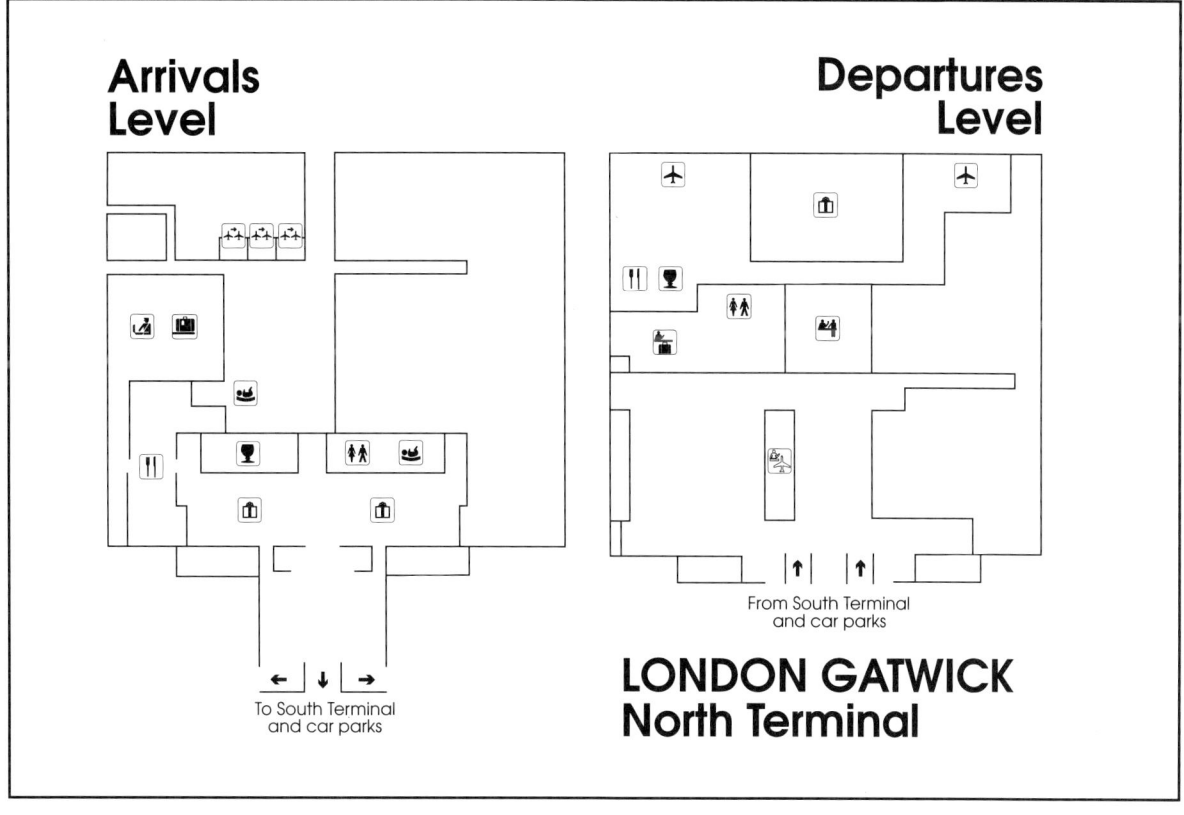

SECTION TWO • AIRPORT DIRECTORY — LONDON GATWICK

Arrivals Level

Departures Level

To South Terminal and car parks

From South Terminal and car parks

LONDON GATWICK
North Terminal

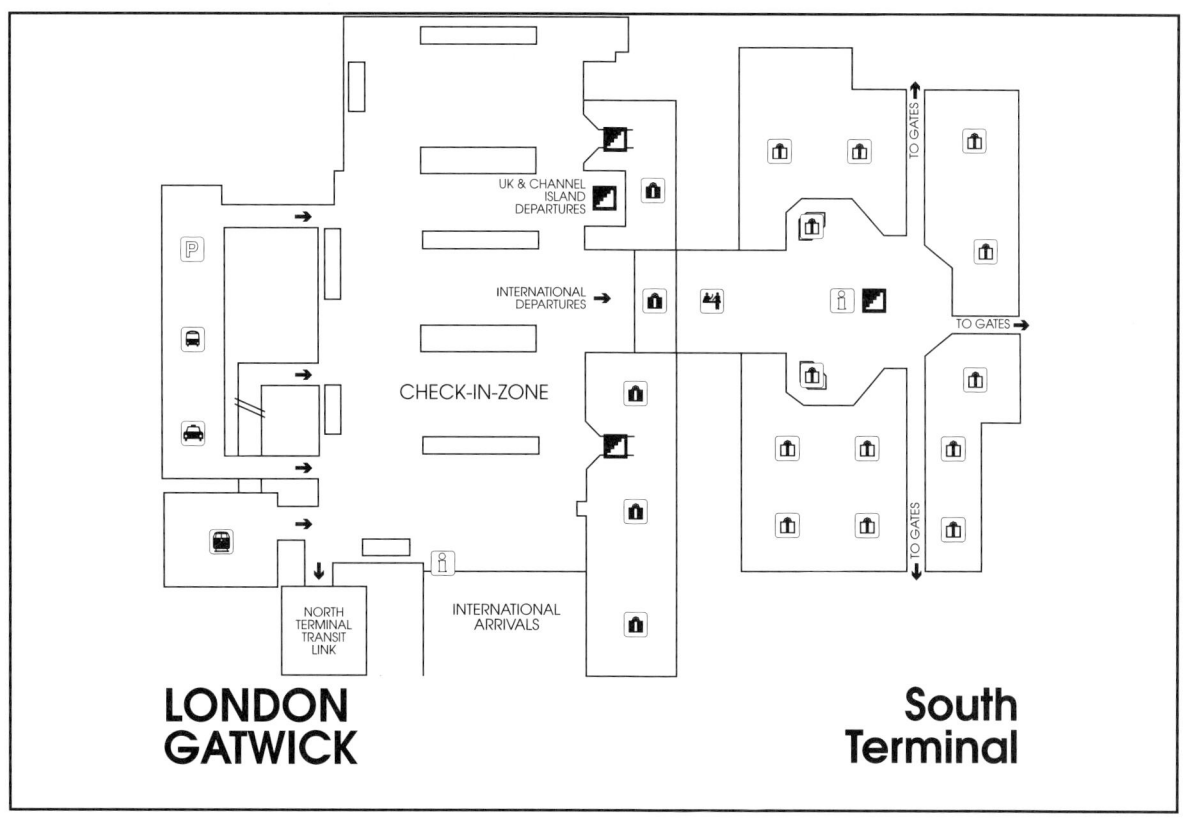

UK & CHANNEL ISLAND DEPARTURES

INTERNATIONAL DEPARTURES →

CHECK-IN-ZONE

TO GATES

NORTH TERMINAL TRANSIT LINK

INTERNATIONAL ARRIVALS

LONDON GATWICK

South Terminal

✈ Air   Rail   Bus   Limousine   Metro/subway   Tram   Helicopter   Water transport   • For map symbols, see p. 9

LONDON HEATHROW — SECTION TWO • AIRPORT DIRECTORY

LONDON-HEATHROW   LHR

United Kingdom (see page 41)

National ✆ code: 44
Area ✆ code: 0181
Local time: Winter GMT, Summer GMT+1
London Heathrow Airport, 234 Bath Road, Harlington, Middlesex, UB3 5AP, United Kingdom
✆759 4321
⒡745 4290
WWW site: http://www.murray.org/travel/heathrow.htm#terms
Location: 24 km/15 miles W of central London

Terminals and Transfers

Terminals
Terminal 1 Airlines: Brymon Airways, Finnair, British Airways (Domestic, Ireland and other short-haul European), British Midland Airways, Cyprus Airlines, Aer Lingus, Alliance, Icelandair, GB Airways, Manx Airlines, El Al Israel Airlines, South African Airways, Sabena World Airlines, Air UK, Virgin Express.
Layout: 3 Levels, Arrivals on Ground Level, Departures on First Level, Catering and Offices on Upper Level.
Terminal 2 Airlines: Air France, Air Algérie, Royal Air Maroc, Alitalia, Aviance, Uzbekistan Airways, Iberia, Istanbul Airlines, Air Inter, Adria Airways, Jat Yugoslav Airlines, Luxair, Lufthansa, Lot Polish Airlines, Crossair, Balkan Bulgarian Airlines, Malev Hungarian, Olympic Airways, CSA Czechoslovak, Austrian Airlines, Croatia Airlines, Tarom Romanian Air, Swissair, Syrian Arab, Aeroflot, Air Portugal TAP, Tunis Air.
Layout: 3 Levels, recently internally reconstructed. Ground Level Check in, First Level Departures and Arrivals, Second Level Catering and Offices.
Terminal 3 Airlines: American Airlines, Air Canada, Air India, Aerolineas Argentinas, Biman Bangladesh Airlines, Royal Brunei Airlines, Eva Air, Air Baltic, BWIA International, Air China, Cathay Pacific Airways, Emirates, Ethiopian Airlines, Gulf Air, Ghana Airways, Iran Air, Japan Airlines, Air Jamaica, Korean Airlines, Kuwait Airways, Middle East Airlines, Malaysian Airlines, Air Mauritius, Egyptair, All Nippon Airways, Air New Zealand, Pakistan International Airlines, Philippine Airlines, Qantas Airways, Qatar, Varig Brazilian, Royal Jordanian Airlines, Sudan Airways, SAS, Singapore Airlines, Saudia, Air Namibia, Turkmenistan, Lithuanian Airlines, Thai Airways, Turkish Airlines, United Airlines, Virgin Atlantic, Nigeria Airways, Yemenia.
Layout: 4 Levels. West facing Ground Level check in, North facing Ground Level arrivals, West facing First Level Departures, North facing First Level Catering & Offices, other Levels Administrative.

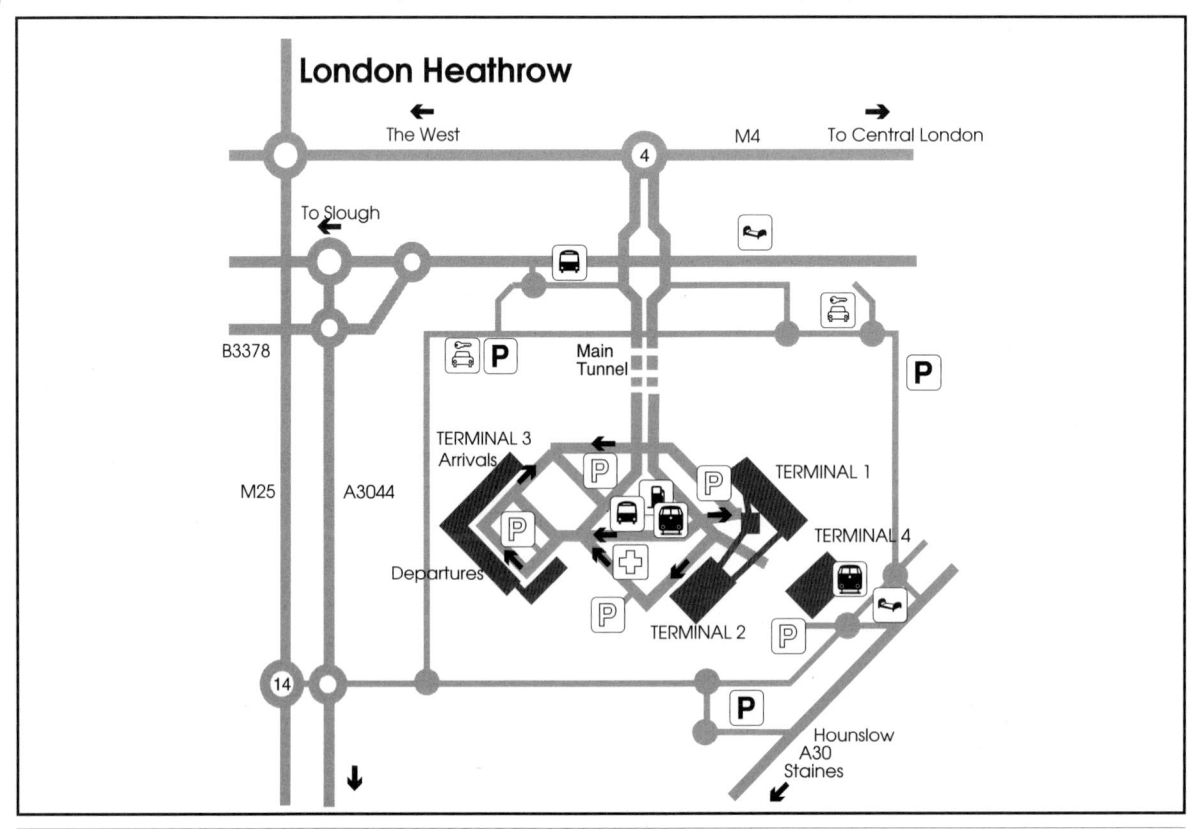

✆ Phone no. ⒡ Fax no. ⓧ Hours of opening/operation » Frequency of service ⤴ Journey time ◊ Cost/one-way fare

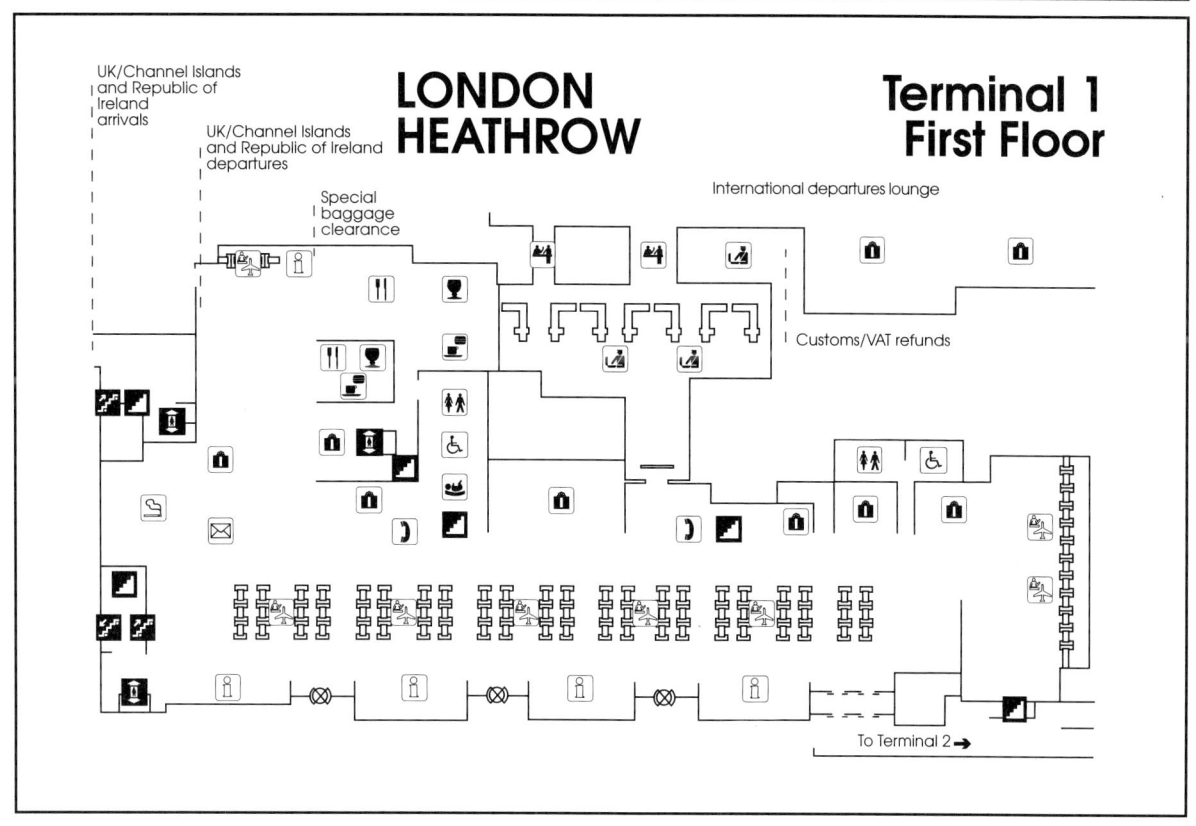

SECTION TWO • AIRPORT DIRECTORY

LONDON HEATHROW

LONDON HEATHROW

Terminal 1 First Floor

UK/Channel Islands and Republic of Ireland arrivals

UK/Channel Islands and Republic of Ireland departures

Special baggage clearance

International departures lounge

Customs/VAT refunds

To Terminal 2 →

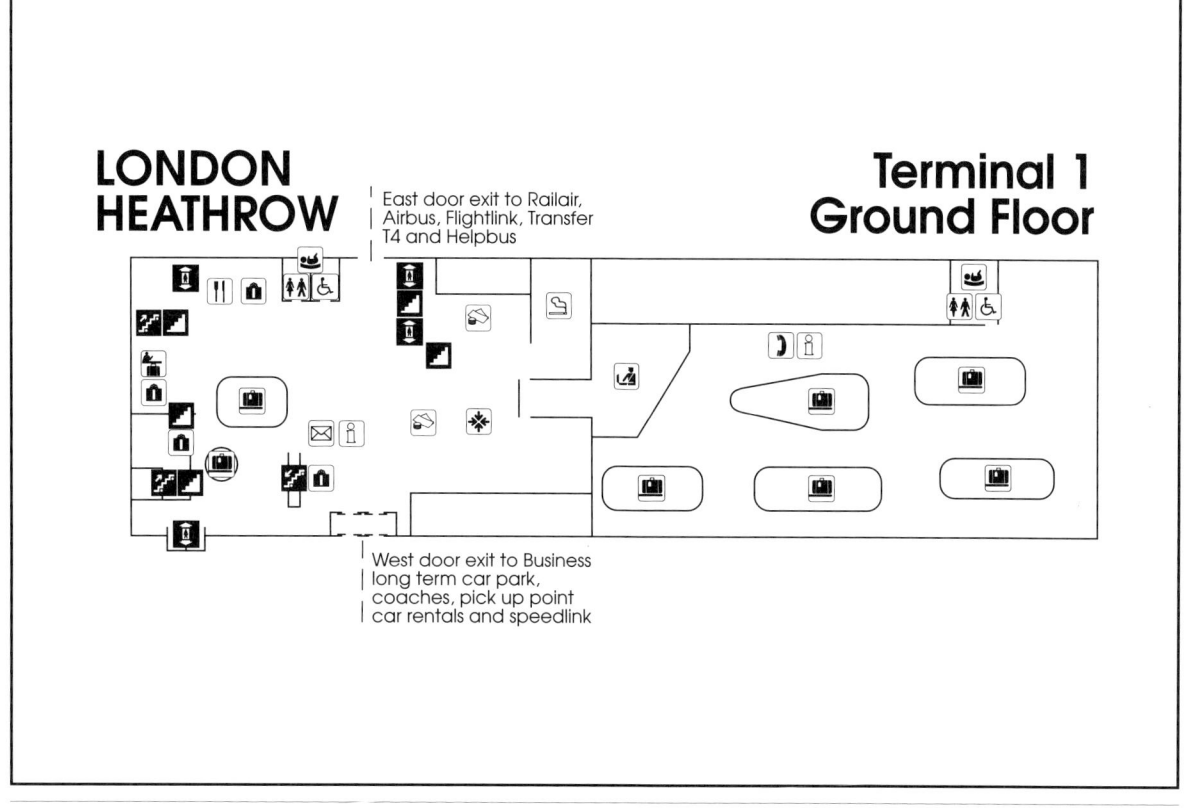

LONDON HEATHROW

Terminal 1 Ground Floor

East door exit to Railair, Airbus, Flightlink, Transfer T4 and Helpbus

West door exit to Business long term car park, coaches, pick up point car rentals and speedlink

✈ Air • Rail • Bus • Limousine • Metro/subway • Tram • Helicopter • Water transport • For map symbols, see p. 9

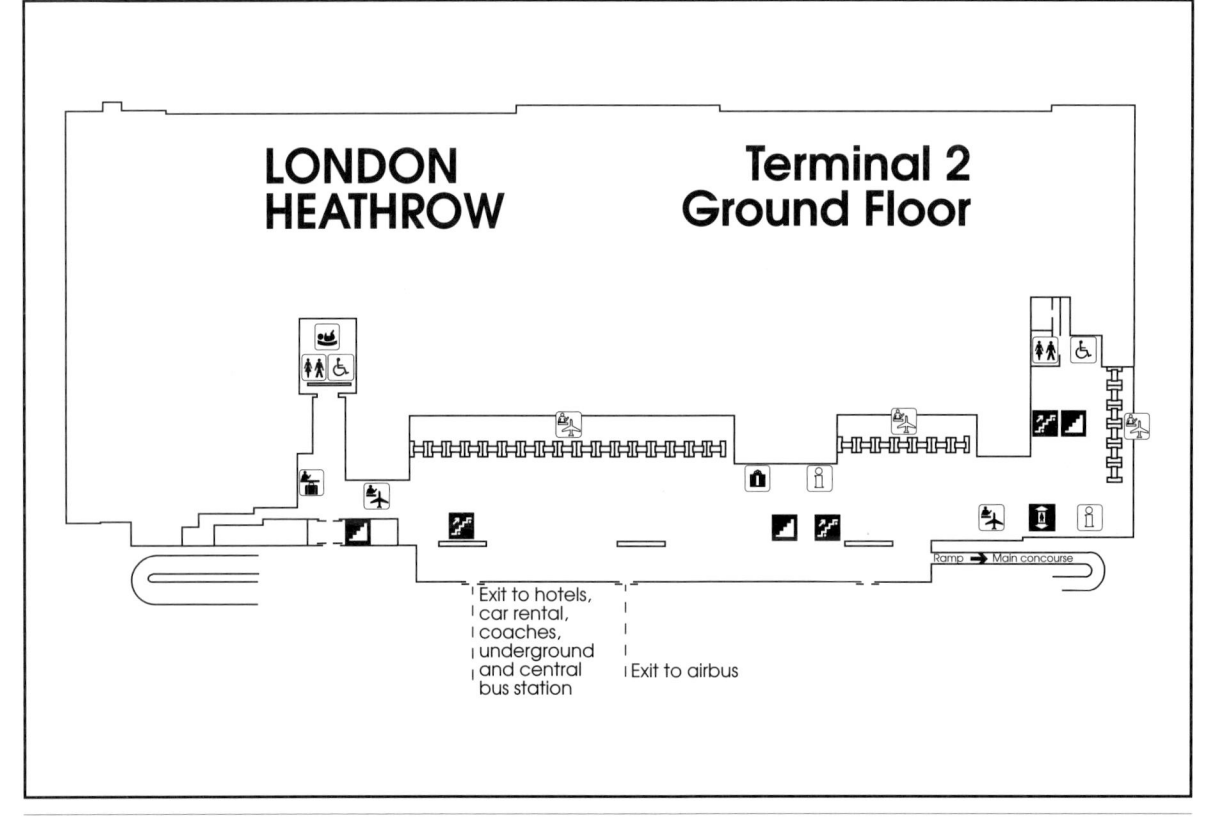

LONDON HEATHROW • SECTION TWO • AIRPORT DIRECTORY

LONDON HEATHROW
Terminal 2 First Floor

Custom's VAT desk

Departure lounge

Mezzanine

Ramp → Car Park
Ramp → Check-in

Walkway to terminal 1

International arrivals

LONDON HEATHROW
Terminal 2 Ground Floor

Ramp → Main concourse

Exit to hotels, car rental, coaches, underground and central bus station

Exit to airbus

☏ Phone no. ℱ Fax no. ⏲ Hours of opening/operation » Frequency of service ⤳ Journey time ◇ Cost/one-way fare

SECTION TWO • AIRPORT DIRECTORY — LONDON HEATHROW

Terminal 4 Airlines: British Airways (Long-haul flights and Paris flights), Canadian Airlines International, TAT European Airlines, British Mediterranean, KLM, Kenya Airways, Air Malta, Air Lanka.

Layout: 4 Levels, Underground Level for Underground Station, Ground Level for Arrivals and Road Arrivals and Departures, First Level Departures, other Levels Administrative.

Minimum transfer times
International: 1 hr (longer if changing terminals) **Domestic:** 45 min

Transfer between terminals
Bus ⟫Frequent; All terminals ⊘Free

INFORMATION

Flight enquiries
Airport ✆0839 222222
Adria Airways ✆759 2311 Aer Lingus ✆745 4848 Aeroflot ✆(0990) 111666 Aerolineas Argentinas ✆897 7941 Air Algérie ✆745 5099 Air Baltic ✆(01426) 931301 Air Canada ✆(0990) 247226 Air China ✆(0990) 111666 Air France ✆759 2311 Air India ✆745 1000 Air Inter ✆759 2311 Air Jamaica ✆745 1224 Air Lanka ✆(0990) 111666 Air Malta ✆745 4133 Air Mauritius ✆759 8636 Air Namibia ✆750 1049 Air New Zealand ✆(0990) 111666 Air Portugal TAP ✆759 2311 Air UK ✆745 7321 Alliance ✆745 4848 Alitalia ✆745 8468 All Nippon Airways ✆(0990) 111666 American Airlines ✆572 5555 Austrian Airlines ✆754 8594 Balkan Bulgarian Airlines ✆759 2311 Biman Bangladesh Airlines ✆(0990) 111666 British Airways ✆(0990)111666 British Mediterranean ✆(0990) 111666 British Midland Airways ✆745 7321 Brymon Airways ✆(0990) 444000 BWIA International ✆(01426) 925560 Canadian Airlines International ✆(0990) 111666 Cathay Pacific Airways ✆759 8636 Croatia Airlines ✆(0990) 111666 Crossair ✆754 8594 CSA Czechoslovak ✆759 2311 Cyprus Airlines ✆745 7321 Egyptair ✆745 5495 El Al Israel Airlines ✆(0171) 957 4100 Emirates ✆759 3303 Ethiopian Airlines ✆(0990) 111666 Eva Air ✆745 7779 Finnair ✆745 4848 GB Airways ✆(0990) 111666 Ghana Airways ✆(0990) 111666 Gulf Air ✆897 0402 Iberia ✆897 7941 Icelandair ✆745 4860 Iran Air ✆564 9806 Istanbul Airlines ✆(0345) 737747 Japan Airlines ✆(0171) 408 1000 Jat Yugoslav Airlines ✆759 2311 Kenya Airways ✆(0171) 409 0277 KLM ✆750 9820 Korean Airlines ✆(0990) 111666 Kuwait Airways ✆745 4860 Lithuanian Airlines ✆(0990) 111666 Lot Polish Airlines ✆759 2311 Lufthansa ✆750 3300 Luxair ✆759 2311 Malaysian Airlines ✆745 4860 Malev Hungarian ✆(0990) 111666 Manx Airlines ✆745 7321 Middle East Airlines ✆759 9211 Nigeria Airways ✆(0990) 111666 Olympic Airways ✆745 4908 Pakistan International Airlines ✆(0990) 111666 Philippine Airlines ✆897 1331 Qantas Airways ✆(01426) 910 020 Royal Air Maroc ✆759 2311 Royal Brunei Airlines ✆(0990) 111666 Royal Jordanian Airlines ✆897 8319 Sabena World Airlines ✆745 4848 Saudia ✆759 7634 SAS ✆(01426) 931 301 Singapore Airlines ✆(0990) 111666 South African Airways ✆(0990) 111666 Sudan Airways ✆(0990) 111666 Swissair ✆754 8594 Syrian Arab Airlines ✆(0990) 111666 Tarom Romanian Air ✆759 2311 TAT European Airlines ✆(0990) 444000 Thai Airways ✆759 8636 Tunis Air ✆759 2311 Turkish Airlines ✆(0990) 111666 Turkmenistan ✆893 5565 United Airlines ✆(01426) 915 500 Uzbekistan Airways ✆(0990) 111666 Varig Brazilian ✆01426 931 301 Virgin Atlantic ✆(01293) 511 581 Virgin Express ✆745 4848 Yemenia ✆897 1331

Information and help desks
Airport Information Terminal 3 Departure Level ✆745 7412 ⓘ0700–2130 Airport information Hotel booking, Tourist information
Airport Information Terminal 4 Level 1, Ground Level (2 desks) ✆745 4540 ⓘ0500–2230 (0530 winter) Airport information Hotel booking, Tourist information
Airport Information Terminal 3 Ground Level ✆745 7412 ⓘ0530–2230 Airport information Hotel booking, Tourist information
Airport Information Terminal 2 Ground Level & First Level (2 desks) ✆745 7115 ⓘ0600–2300 Airport information Hotel booking, Tourist information
Airport Information Terminal 1 Ground Level Arrival Concourse ✆745 7702 ⓘ0630–2300 Airport information Hotel booking, Tourist information

EMERGENCIES

Police Terminal 4 North Perimeter Road ✆897 7373 ⓘ24 hr
Police Terminal 2 North Perimeter Road ✆897 7373 ⓘ24 hr
Police Terminal 3 North Perimeter Road ✆897 7373 ⓘ24hr
Police Terminal 1 North Perimeter Road ✆897 7373 ⓘ24 hr
Medical Terminal 2 Queens Building, between Terminals 1 and 2 ✆562 7070
Medical Terminal 3 Queens Building, between Terminals 1 and 2 ✆562 7070
Medical Terminal 4 Queens Building, between Terminals 1 and 2 ✆562 7070
Medical Terminal 1 Queens Building, between Terminals 1 and 2 ✆562 7070
Lost Property ✆745 7727 ⓘ0800–1700 Mon–Fri; 0800–1600 Sat–Sun

AIRPORT FACILITIES

Money
ATM Terminal 1 Ground Level outside Arrival exit ⓘ24 hr
ATM Terminal 2 Level 1 Arrivals/Departures area ⓘ24 hr
ATM Terminal 3 Arrival and Departure Areas ⓘ24 hr
ATM Terminal 4 Arrival and Departure Areas ⓘ24 hr
Bureau de change Terminal 1 Departures Level 1, Central Area ⓘ0600–2100
Bureau de change Terminal 1 Arrival Area ⓘ0700–2300
Bureau de change Terminal 2 Level 1 Departures area ⓘ0600–2100
Bureau de change Terminal 2 Arrivals area ⓘ0630–2300
Bureau de change Terminal 3 Ground Level, Arrival Area ⓘ0515–2130
Bureau de change Terminal 3 Arrivals area ⓘ24 hr
Bureau de change Terminal 4 Ground Level ⓘ24 hr
Bureau de change Terminal 4 Arrivals area ⓘ0515–2100
Thomas Cook bureau de change Terminal 1 Ground Level, outside Arrival exit ⓘ24 hr
Thomas Cook bureau de change Terminal 1 Departure Area, landside ⓘ0600–2130
Thomas Cook bureau de change Terminal 1 Departure Lounge, airside ⓘ0530–2200
Thomas Cook bureau de change Terminal 1 Domestic Pier ⓘ0700–2130
Thomas Cook bureau de change Terminal 1 Irish Pier ⓘ0700–2100
Thomas Cook bureau de change Terminal 1 Transit Area ⓘ0630–2230
Thomas Cook bureau de change Terminal 1 Underground stn ⓘ0630–2130
Thomas Cook bureau de change Terminal 2 Departure Area, airside ⓘ0600–2130
Thomas Cook bureau de change Terminal 3 Arrival Area, airside ⓘ0530–2130
Thomas Cook bureau de change Terminal 3 Arrival Area, landside ⓘ0530–2230
Thomas Cook bureau de change Terminal 3 Departure Area, airside ⓘ0600–2200
Thomas Cook bureau de change Terminal 3 Departure Area, landside ⓘ0530–2200
Thomas Cook bureau de change Terminal 4 Departure Area, airside ⓘ0600–2200
Thomas Cook bureau de change Terminal 4 Departure Area, landside ⓘ0515–2215
Thomas Cook bureau de change Terminal 4 Arrival Area, landside ⓘ24 hr
Thomas Cook bureau de change Terminal 4 Arrival Area, airside ⓘ0600–2100
Thomas Cook bureau de change Terminal 4 Central Area ⓘ0600–2100

✈ Air ⬛ Rail ⬛ Bus ⬛ Limousine Ⓜ Metro/subway ⬛ Tram ⬛ Helicopter ⬛ Water transport • For map symbols, see p. 9

LONDON HEATHROW — SECTION TWO • AIRPORT DIRECTORY

LONDON HEATHROW
Terminal 3 First Floor

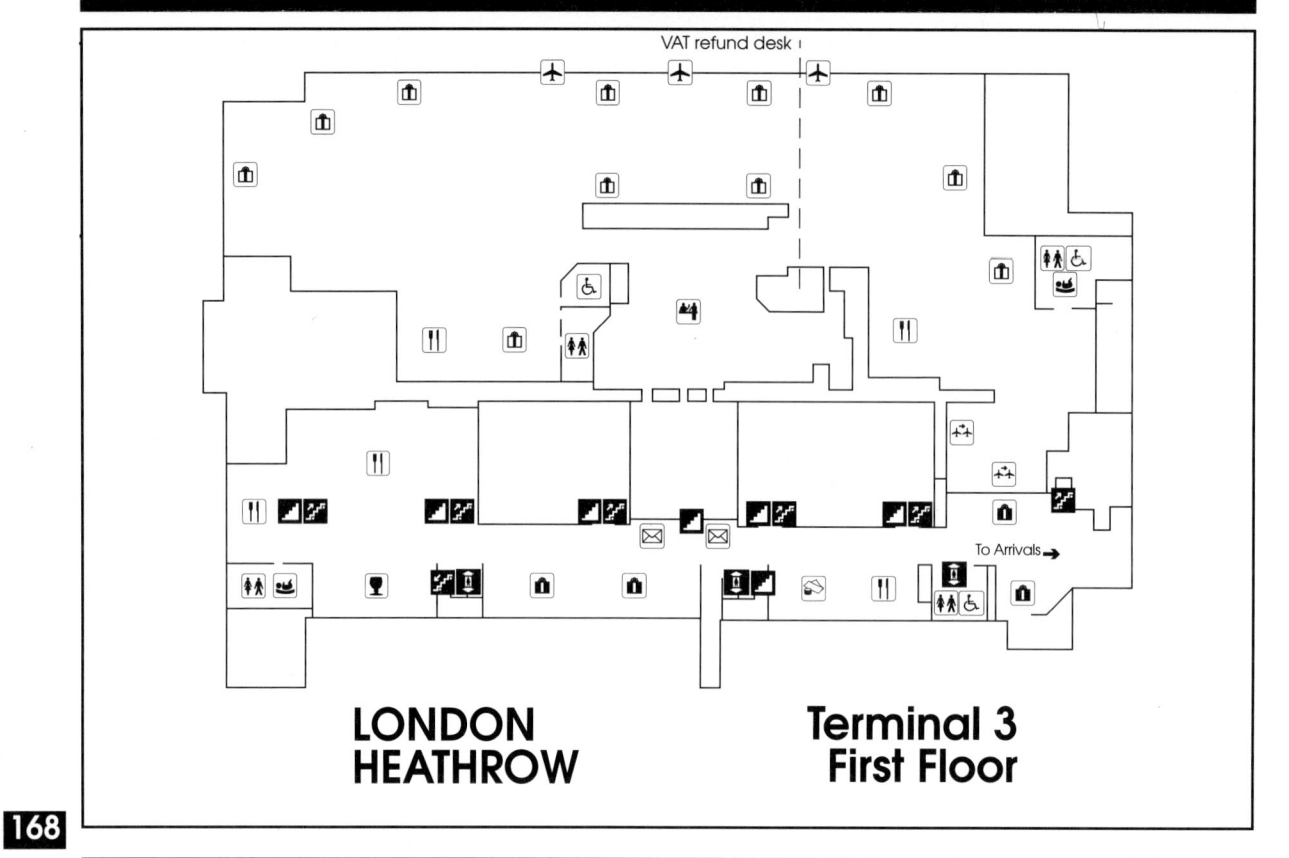

LONDON HEATHROW
Terminal 3 Ground Floor Departures

☏ Phone no. ℻ Fax no. ⏱ Hours of opening/operation » Frequency of service ➲ Journey time ◊ Cost/one-way fare

Food and drink

Bar Terminal 1 Level 1, airside and landside ⓘAll flight times
Bar Terminal 2 Level 1, airside and landside ⓘAll flight times
Bar Terminal 3 Level 1, airside and landside ⓘAll flight times
Bar Terminal 4 Level 1, airside and landside ⓘAll flight times
Café/light meals Terminal 1 Ground Level and Level 1, airside and landside ⓘAll flight times
Café/light meals Terminal 2 Level 1, airside and landside ⓘAll flight times
Café/light meals Terminal 3 Level 1, airside and landside ⓘAll flight times
Café/light meals Terminal 4 Level 1, airside and landside ⓘAll flight times
Restaurant Terminal 1 Level 1 Departure Concourse, airside and landside ⓘAll flight times
Restaurant Terminal 2 Level 1, airside and landside ⓘAll flight times
Restaurant Terminal 3 Level 1, airside and landside ⓘAll flight times
Restaurant Terminal 4 Level 1, airside and landside ⓘAll flight times

Communications

Post box Terminal 1 Level 1 West side Departures Hall ⓘ24 hr
Post office Terminal 2 Level 1, Main Concourse, Arrival and Departure Areas ⓘ0830–1730 Mon–Sat; 0900–1300 Sun
Post box Terminal 3 Level 1, centre of Departure Concourse pre Passport control ⓘ24 hr
Post office Terminal 4 Ground Level, south side ⓘ0900–1730 Mon–Sat; 0900–1300 Sun
Post box Terminal 4 Airside Departure Area ⓘ24 hr

Shopping

Duty free, departure Terminal 1 Departure Concourse Level 1 ⓘAll flight times
Duty free, departure Terminal 2 Departure Concourse Level 1 ⓘAll flight times
Duty free, departure Terminal 3 Departure Concourse Level 1 ⓘAll flight times
Duty free, departure Terminal 4 Departure Concourse Level 1 ⓘAll flight times
Shopping mall Terminal 1 Departure Concourse Level 1 ⓘAll flight times
Shopping mall Terminal 2 Departure Concourse Level 1 ⓘAll flight times
Shopping mall Terminal 3 Departure Concourse Level 1 ⓘAll flight times
Shopping mall Terminal 4 Departure Concourse Level 1 ⓘAll flight times

Thomas Cook travel agency Terminal 1 Departure Concourse Level 1 ⓘ0600–2130

Luggage

Left luggage counter Terminal 1 Mezzanine Floor ⓘ0600–2300 ⊘GBP2 per item per 12 hr, £3 for 12–24hr
Left luggage counter Terminal 2 adjacent to T2 and The Queens Building ⓘ0600–2230 ⊘GBP2 per item per 12 hr, GBP3 for12–24hr
Left luggage counter Terminal 3 Ground Level ⓘ0530–2230 ⊘GBP2 per item per 12hr, GBP3 for 12–24hr
Left luggage counter Terminal 4 Ground Level ⓘ0530–2230 ⊘GBP2 per item per 12hr, GBP3 for 12/24hr
Porters Terminal 2 Arrival and Departure Areas ⓘAll flight times ⊘GBP5 per item
Porters Terminal 3 Arrival and Departure Areas ⓘAll flight times ⊘GBP5 per item
Porters Terminal 1 Arrival and Departure Areas ⓘall flight times ⊘GBP5 per item
Porters Terminal 4 Arrival and Departure Areas ⓘAll flight times ⊘GBP5 per item
Trolleys/carts Terminal 2 Arrival and Departure Areas ⓘ24 hr ⊘Free
Trolleys/carts Terminal 3 Arrival and Departure Areas ⓘ24 hr ⊘Free
Trolleys/carts Terminal 1 Arrival and Departure Areas ⓘ24 hr ⊘Free

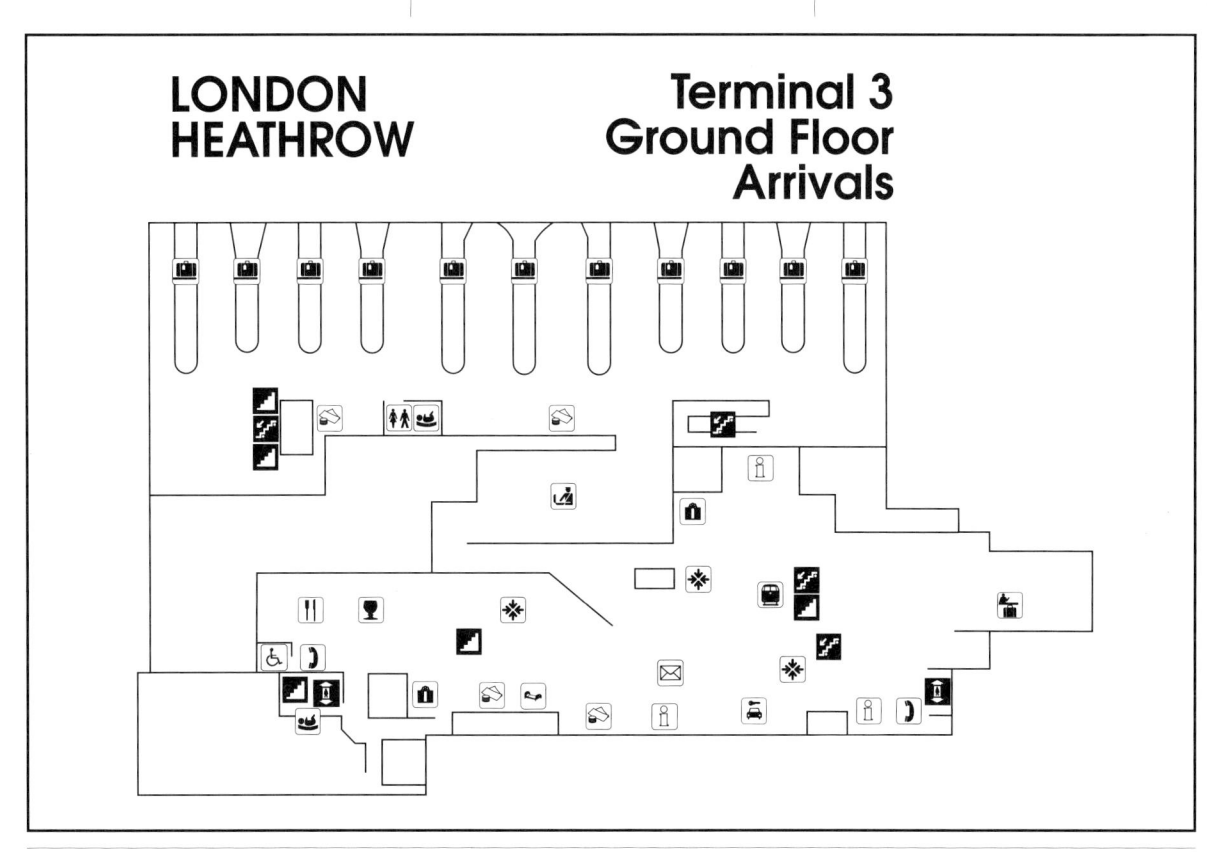

LONDON HEATHROW
Terminal 3 Ground Floor Arrivals

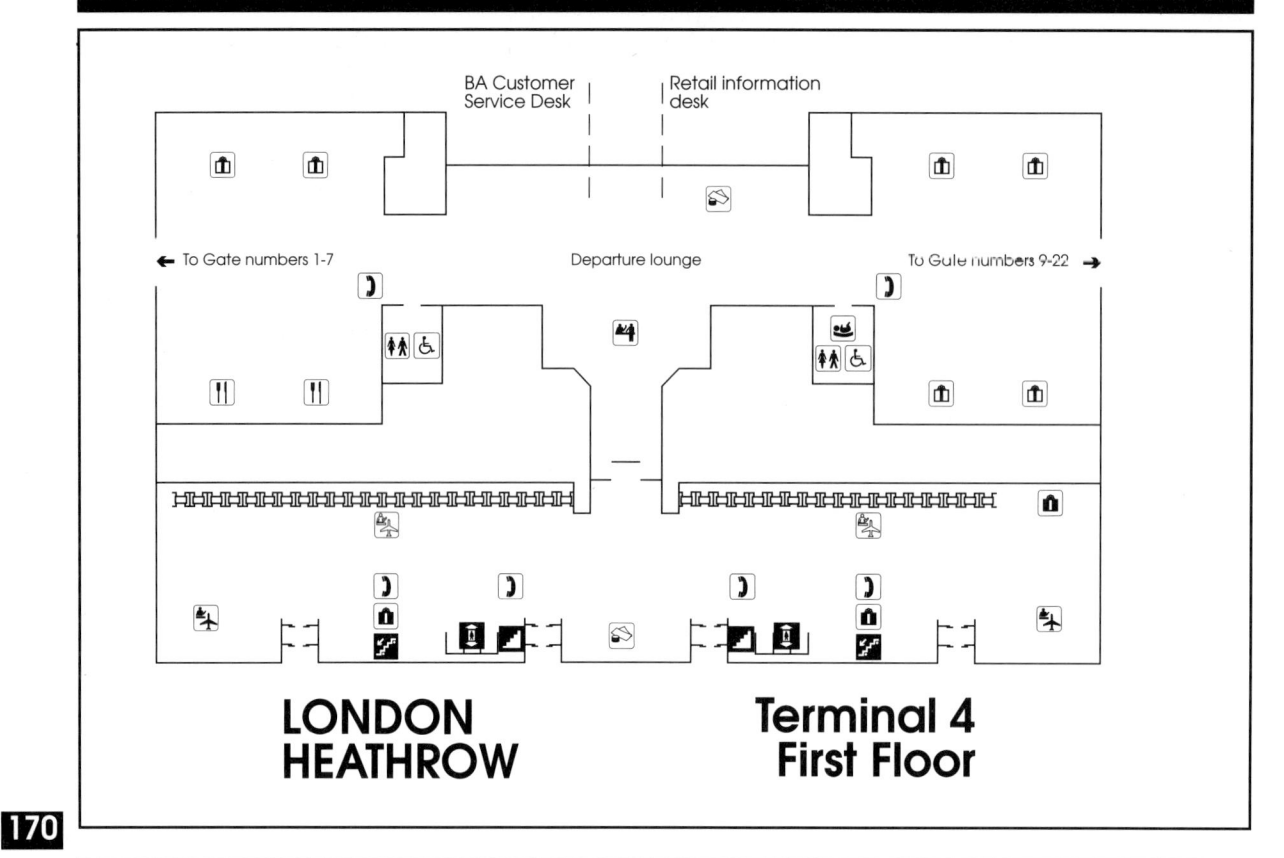

LONDON HEATHROW SECTION TWO • AIRPORT DIRECTORY

LONDON HEATHROW — Terminal 4 First Floor

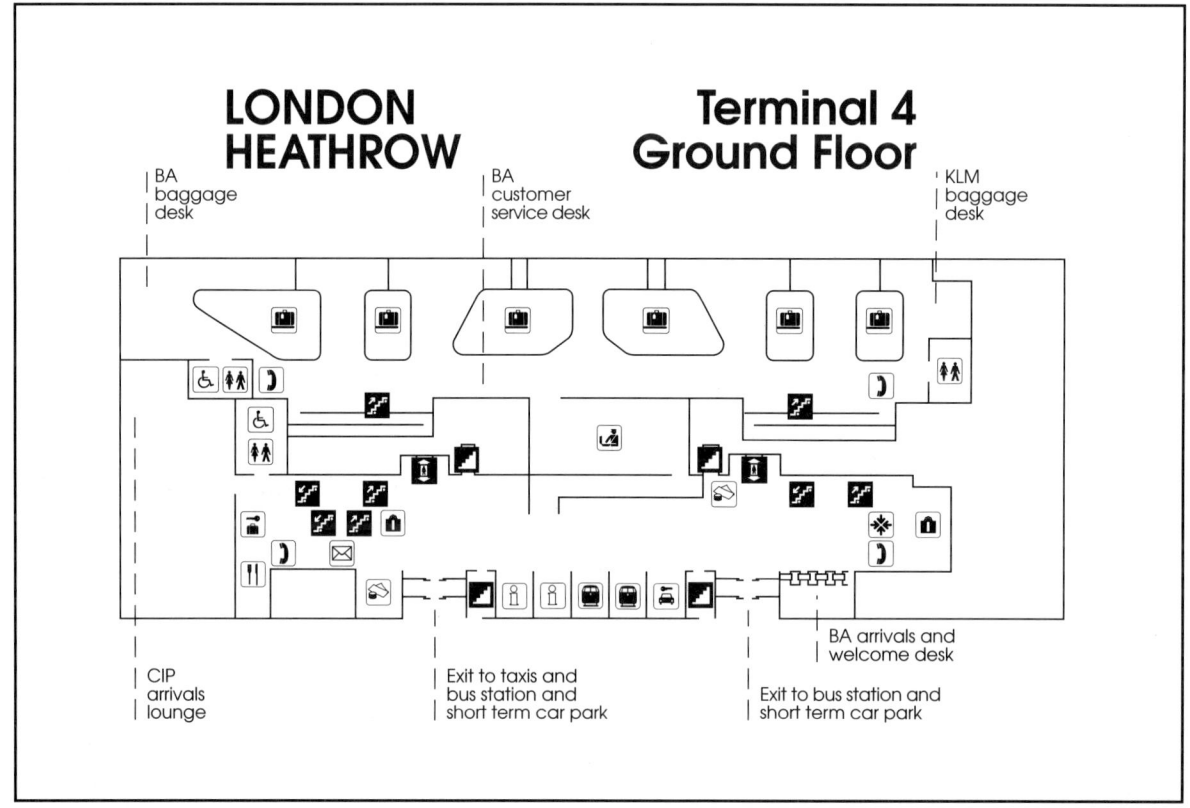

- BA Customer Service Desk
- Retail information desk
- ← To Gate numbers 1–7
- Departure lounge
- To Gate numbers 9–22 →

LONDON HEATHROW — Terminal 4 Ground Floor

- BA baggage desk
- BA customer service desk
- KLM baggage desk
- CIP arrivals lounge
- Exit to taxis and bus station and short term car park
- BA arrivals and welcome desk
- Exit to bus station and short term car park

☏ Phone no.   ℻ Fax no.   ⓞ Hours of opening/operation   ≫ Frequency of service   ↻ Journey time   ◇ Cost/one-way fare

Trolleys/carts Terminal 4 Arrival and Departure Areas ⓘ24 hr ⊘Free

DISABLED TRAVELLERS

Terminal 1 Adapted toilets All toilet areas; Lifts West side of terminal; Special car parking Orange areas in all short-stay car parks; Phones at wheelchair height; Phones adapted for the deaf All phone areas; Personal assistance Via Information Desks 0630–2300
Terminal 2 Adapted toilets Ground Level, next to main toilets; Lifts Ramp and lifts south side of terminal; Special car parking Orange areas in all short-stay car parks; Phones at wheelchair height; Phones adapted for the deaf All phone areas; Personal assistance Via Information Desks 0600–2300
Terminal 3 Adapted toilets All toilet areas; Lifts Central Departure Level; Special car parking Orange areas in all short-stay car parks; Phones at wheelchair height; Phones adapted for the deaf All phone areas; Personal assistance Via Information Desks 0530–2130
Terminal 4 Adapted toilets Most toilet areas; Lifts Centre of Arrival/Departure Concourse; Special car parking Orange areas in all short-stay car parks; Phones at wheelchair height; Phones adapted for the deaf All phone areas; Personal assistance Via Information Desks 0530–2230

SMOKING POLICY

Terminal 1 Smoking only in marked areas
Terminal 2 Smoking only in marked areas
Terminal 3 Smoking only in marked areas
Terminal 4 Smoking only in marked areas

SPECIAL PASSENGER LOUNGES

Aer Lingus Gold Circle Lounge Terminal 1 Club Members, First and Business class passengers
Air Canada Maple Leaf Lounge Terminal 3 Near Departure Piers after Departure Concourse Club members, First and Business class passengers
Air France VIP Lounge Terminal 2 Near West Departure Pier AF and LH Club Members and First and Business class passengers
Air India Maharaja Lounge Terminal 3 Near Departure Piers after Departure Concourse Club members, First and Business class passengers
Servisair Executive Lounge Terminal 2 In corridor after Departure Lounge First and Business class passengers of AZ, OS, LX, IB, MH, OA, TP, SR and FV
All Nippon Airways Fuji and ANA Lounges Terminal 3 Near Departure Piers after Departure concourse Fuji First class, Anna Business/Club members

American Airlines Admirals Club Lounge Terminal 3 Near Departure Piers after Departure Concourse Club members, First and Business class passengers
British Airways Executive/Club Europe Lounge Terminal 1 Departure Lounge Level 2 Club members, First and Business class passengers
British Airways Executive Club Lounge Terminal 4 North side of Main Departure Concourse Club members, First and Business class passengers
British Airways St George's Club Lounge Terminal 3 Club members, First and Business class passengers and passengers travelling on flights handled by this airline
British Midland Airways Diamond Club Lounge Terminal 1 Club members, First and Business class passengers
Cathay Pacific Airways First Lounge Terminal 3 Near Departure Piers after Departure Concourse First class Passengers
El Al Israel Airlines King David Lounge Terminal 1 Near entrance to Departure Piers First and Business class passengers
Japan Airlines Sakura Lounge Terminal 3 Near Departure Piers after Departure Concourse First and Business class passengers
KLM Lounge Terminal 4 Club members, First and Business class passengers
Korean Airlines Morning Calm Lounge Terminal 3 Near Departure Piers after Departure Concourse First and Business class passengers
Malaysian Airlines MAS Golden Lounge Terminal 3 Near Departure Piers after Departure Concourse First and Business class passengers
Pakistan International Airlines Shalimar Lounge Terminal 3 Near Departure Piers after Departure Concourse First and Business class passengers
Qantas Airways Captains Club Lounge Terminal 3 Near Departure Piers after Departure concourse First and Business class passengers
Saudia Al-Furzan Lounge Terminal 3 Near Departure Piers after Departure Concourse First and Business class passengers
SAS Euroclass Lounge Terminal 3 Near Departure Piers after Departure Concourse RVC Club members, First and Business class passengers
Singapore Airlines Silver Kris Lounge Terminal 3 Near Departure Piers after Departure Concourse First and Business class passengers
South African Airways Servisair Business Lounge Terminal 1 Near entrance to Departure Piers SAA/Finnair/Alliance Club members, First and Business class passengers
Thai Airways Royal Orchid Lounge Terminal 3 Near Departure Piers after

Departure Concourse First and Business class passengers
United Airlines Red Carpet Club Lounge Terminal 3 Near Departure Piers after Departure Concourse First and business class passengers
Virgin Atlantic Virgin Clubhouse Terminal 3 Near Departure Piers after Departure Concourse First and Business class passengers

CONFERENCE AND BUSINESS FACILITIES

The Business Centre, Queens Building, between Terminals 1 and 2 ⓒ759 2434 ⓕ759 1797 ⓘ0700–2100 Mon–Fri Telephones, Fax service, Power points, Modem Points, Photocopier, Secretarial service, Shower and washroom facilities

AIRPORT HOTELS

Arlington ⓒ573 6162. 80 rooms Courtesy bus
Edwardian ⓒ759 6311. 450 rooms Courtesy bus
Excelsior Forte ⓒ759 6611 Courtesy bus
Forte Crest ⓒ759 2323. 574 rooms Courtesy bus
Forte Posthouse ⓒ759 2552. 186 rooms Courtesy bus
Heathrow Marriot ⓒ(01753) 544 244. 350 rooms Courtesy bus
Heathrow Park ⓒ759 2400. 303 rooms Courtesy bus
Hilton ⓒ759 7755. 400 rooms Courtesy bus
Holiday Inn Crowne Plaza ⓒ(01895) 445555. 374 rooms Courtesy bus
Ibis Heathrow ⓒ759 4888. 354 rooms Courtesy bus
Jarvis ⓒ897 2121. 73 rooms Courtesy bus
Master Brewer ⓒ(01895) 251199. 106 rooms
Novotel Heathrow ⓒ(01895) 431431. 178 rooms Courtesy bus
Ramada ⓒ897 6363 Courtesy bus
Sheraton Heathrow ⓒ759 2424. 431 rooms Courtesy bus
Sheraton Skyline Hotel ⓒ759 2535. 352 rooms Courtesy bus

CAR RENTAL

Alamo Terminal 1 Pick up point Ground Level Arrivals Hall ⓒ(0800) 272 300
Alamo Terminal 2 Level 1, Main Concourse, near Arrival exit ⓒ(0800) 272 300
Alamo Terminal 3 Ground Level, Main Concourse near Arrival exit ⓒ(0800) 272 300
Alamo Terminal 4 Ground Level, Main Concourse near Arrival exit ⓒ(0800) 272 300
Avis Terminal 1 Pick up point Ground

London Heathrow

Section Two • Airport Directory

Level Arrivals Hall ℡899 1000
Avis Terminal 2 Level 1, Main Concourse, near Arrival exit ℡899 1000
Avis Terminal 3 Ground Level, Main Concourse near Arrival exit ℡899 1000
Avis Terminal 4 Ground Level, Main Concourse near Arrival exit ℡899 1000
Budget Terminal 1 Pick up point Ground Level Arrivals Hall ℡759 2216
Budget Terminal 2 Level 1, Main Concourse, near Arrival exit ℡759 2216
Budget Terminal 3 Ground Level, Main Concourse near Arrival exit ℡759 2216
Budget Terminal 4 Ground Level, Main Concourse near Arrival exit ℡759 2216
Eurodollar Terminal 1 Ground Level, Arrivals ℡897 3232
Eurodollar Terminal 2 Ground Level, Departures ℡897 3232
Eurodollar Terminal 3 Ground Level, Arrivals ℡897 3232
Eurodollar Terminal 4 Ground Level, Arrivals ℡897 3232
EuropCar Terminal 1 Pick up point Ground Level Arrivals Hall ℡897 0811
EuropCar Terminal 2 Level 1, Main Concourse, near Arrival exit ℡897 0811
EuropCar Terminal 3 Ground Level, Main Concourse near Arrival exit ℡897 0811
EuropCar Terminal 4 Ground Level, Main Concourse near Arrival exit ℡897 0811
Hertz Terminal 1 Pick up point Ground Level Arrivals Hall ℡897 2072
Hertz Terminal 2 Level 1, Main Concourse, near Arrival exit ℡897 2072
Hertz Terminal 3 Ground Level, Main Concourse near Arrival exit ℡897 2072
Hertz Terminal 4 Ground Level, Main Concourse near Arrival exit ℡897 2072

Car Parking

Long-stay Eastern Perimeter Road 4450 spaces ⌀GBP4.50 per 12 hr, GBP8.20 per 24 hr
Short-stay Next to Terminal 1 Central Parking ⌀GBP1.0 per 30 min up to 4 hr; then GBP2 per hr

Taxis and Chauffeur-driven Cars

Taxis
Terminal forecourts ℡745 7302/ 4655/ 5408/ 7487
City centre ⌚1 hr ⌀GBP35

Public Transport

Airport to airport
Birmingham (UK) Apt 🚌National Express »avg 2 hr ⌚0905–2335 ⌚2 hr 45 min ⌀GBP19.
London-Gatwick Apt 🚌Jetlink 747 »avg 30 min ⌚0630–2225 ⌚1 hr ⌀GBP9.
London-Gatwick Apt 🚌 Speedlink at »15–20 min ⌚1 hr ⌀GBP13.50 Depart from Terminal 1
London-Luton Apt 🚌National Express »avg 2 hr ⌚0905–2335 ⌚50 min ⌀GBP9.
London-Stansted Apt 🚌Jetlink »avg 2 hr ⌚0630–1805 ⌚1 hr 40 min ⌀GBP11
Manchester (UK) Apt 🚌National Express »avg 2 hr ⌚0905–2155 ⌚5 hr 45 min ⌀GBP21.50.

City & suburbs
London city centre (Euston and King's Cross rail stns) 🚌London Buses: A2 »20–30 min ⌚0610–2130 ⌚1 hr–1 hr 25 min ⌀GBP5. Via Oxford Street
London city centre (Victoria rail stn) 🚌London Buses: A1 »20–30 min ⌚0620–2015 ⌚1 hr–1 hr 10 min ⌀GBP5.
London city centre (Paddington rail stn) 🚂 ⌚0510–2240 ⌚30 min. Via coach link to each terminal
London city centre (Piccadilly Circus) 🚇 London Underground: Piccadilly Line »5–9 min ⌚0508–2349 ⌚47 min ⌀GBP3. Leaves from separate stations at Terminal 4 and Terminals 1/2/3. Connects to many central and outlying destinations on London Underground system.

Other towns and cities
Brighton 🚌Jetlink 747 »avg 2 hr ⌚0500–2100 ⌚1 hr 55 min.
Bristol 🚌National Express »avg 1 hr ⌚0845–2345 ⌚2 hr ⌀GBP15.
Cambridge (UK) 🚌Cambridge Coach »1 hr ⌚0700–0100 ⌚2 hr 10 min ⌀GBP9.
Norwich 🚌Jetlink 747 »Day avg 2 hr ⌚0130–2130 ⌚3 hr 15 min.
Oxford 🚌City Link X70/X80 »avg 30 min ⌚0615–2230 ⌚1 hr 25 min ⌀GBP6.
Poole 🚌Excelsior Coaches »1 hr 45 min ⌚0755–1950 Fri–Sun ⌚2 hr 10 min ⌀GBP12.
Reading 🚌 »avg 30 min ⌚0635–2250 ⌚45–70 min. To Reading rail stn for fast rail services to western England and Wales
Woking 🚌Network South East »30 min ⌚0630–2000 ⌚50 min. To Woking rail stn for fast rail services to south-western England

Regional Air Connections

Amsterdam ✈ »Several per day ⌚1 hr 5 min
Antwerp ✈ »Several per week ⌚1 hr 10 min
Belfast ✈ »Several per day ⌚1 hr 15 min
Brussels ✈ »Several per day ⌚1 hr
Edinburgh ✈ »Several per day ⌚1 hr 15 min
Glasgow ✈ »Several per day ⌚1 hr 15 min
Guernsey ✈ »Several per day ⌚1 hr 5 min
Isle of Man ✈ »Several per day ⌚1 hr 10 min
Jersey ✈ »Several per day ⌚55 min
Leeds/Bradford ✈ »Several per day ⌚55 min
Luxembourg ✈ »Several per day ⌚1 hr 10 min
Manchester (UK) ✈ »Several per day ⌚50 min
Newcastle (UK) ✈ »Several per day ⌚1 hr 5 min
Paris ✈ »Several per day ⌚1 hr
Plymouth (UK) ✈ »Several per day ⌚1 hr 5 min
Rotterdam ✈ »Several per day ⌚1 hr 10 min
Teesside ✈ »Several per day ⌚1 hr 10 min

Traveller's Notes

Heathrow remains the world's busiest international airport: over 90% of its 50 million passengers are travelling overseas.

℡ Phone no. ℻ Fax no. ⌚ Hours of opening/operation » Frequency of service ⌚ Journey time ⌀ Cost/one-way fare

LONDON STANSTED — STN

United Kingdom (see page 41)

National ☏ code: 44
Area ☏ code: 01279
Local time: Winter GMT, Summer GMT+1
London Stansted Airport, Essex, CM24 1QW, United Kingdom
☏680500
☏662066
Location: 50 km/30 miles NE of London

TERMINALS AND TRANSFERS

Terminals
Main Terminal Airlines: All airlines. Layout: Main Concourse, Arrival, Departure and most facilities; Basement, rail station; Satellite building for international departures, connected by monorail to Main Terminal; Satellite for domestic departures, accessed directly from Main Terminal.

Minimum transfer times
International: 45 min Domestic: 45 min

INFORMATION

Flight enquiries
Airport ☏680500
Aer Lingus ☏(0181) 899 4747 Air Exel ☏(0345) 666777 Air One ☏(0171) 434 7321 Air UK ☏(0345) 666777 British Airways ☏(0345) 222111 CSA Czech Airlines ☏(0171) 255 1898/1366 Cyprus Airways ☏(0171) 388 5411 El Al Israel Airlines ☏(0345) 125725 Jersey European Airlines ☏(0345) 676676 Luxair ☏(0181) 745 4254 Ryanair ☏(0171) 435 7101

Information and help desks
Information Desk Main Terminal International Arrival Concourse ☏(01279) 680500 ⓣ24 hr Airport information, Flights, Hotel booking

EMERGENCIES

Police Main Terminal Police Station in Airport ☏680298 ⓣ24 hr
Medical Main Terminal Information Desk ☏680500 ⓣ24 hr
Lost Property Main Terminal Information Desk ☏680500 ⓣ24 hr

AIRPORT FACILITIES

Money
ATM Main Terminal Main Concourse, Departures Area ⓣ24 hr
Thomas Cook bureau de change Main Terminal Arrival Lounge, airside ⓣAll international flight arrivals ☏681113.
Bureau de change Main Terminal Departure Lounge, International Satellite ⓣ0530–last flight departure ☏680921.
Bureau de change Between the departures and international arrivals concourses at both ends of the check-in desks ☏680921.

Food and drink
Bar Main Terminal Main Concourse ⓣ0700–2300
Café/light meals Main Terminal Main Concourse ⓣ24 hr
Restaurant Main Terminal Main Concourse ⓣ24 hr

Communications
Post box Main Terminal Arrivals Area ⓣ24 hr
Post box Main Terminal Departure Area ⓣ24 hr
Fax service Main Terminal Near Airport Information Desk ⓣ24 hr

Shopping
Duty free, Main Terminal Departure Area ⓣ0530–2300
Duty free, Main Terminal Airside Satellite ⓣ0530–2300
Gift Shop Main Terminal Departure Concourse ⓣ0600–2300
News, Stationery & Books Main Terminal Main Concourse, landside and International Satellite ⓣ0600–2300
Pharmacy Main Terminal Main Concourse landside ⓣ0600–2300
Shopping mall Main Terminal Main Concourse landside ⓣ0600–2300

Luggage
Porters Main Terminal ⓣAll flight times ⊘Free
Trolleys/carts Main Terminal ⓣ24 hr ⊘Free

DISABLED TRAVELLERS

Main Terminal Adapted toilets 3 in Main Concourse, 2 in International Satellite; Lifts At entrance; Special car parking Long- and short-stay car parks; Phones at wheelchair height; Personal assistance Via Information Desk ☏680500 24 hr

SMOKING POLICY

Main Terminal Smoking only in marked areas

SPECIAL PASSENGER LOUNGES

Air UK Lounge Satellite 1 Club members and First class passengers

CONFERENCE AND BUSINESS FACILITIES

Fulton Room, ☏680500 Telephones, Photocopier, Secretarial service

AIRPORT HOTELS

Hilton National ☏680800 ☏680828. 238 rooms Courtesy bus

CAR RENTAL

Avis Main Terminal Main Concourse International Arrival Area ☏663030
Budget Main Terminal Main Concourse International Arrival Area ☏681194
EuropCar Main Terminal Main Concourse International Arrival Area ☏680240
Hertz Main Terminal Main Concourse International Arrival Area ☏680154

CAR PARKING

Long-stay Behind airport; free shuttle bus. 7763 spaces ⊘GBP4.80 per day
Short-stay In front of terminal. 1860 spaces ⊘GBP0.80 per 30 min; GBP9.00 per day

TAXIS AND CHAUFFEUR-DRIVEN CARS

Taxis
Booking desk in International Arrival area Stansted Airport Cars ☏662444 London city centre ⊃1 hr–1 hr 30 min ⊘GBP60

LONDON STANSTED • LOS ANGELES SECTION TWO • AIRPORT DIRECTORY

Public Transport

Airport to airport
London-Heathrow Apt ⇌ Jetlink » avg 2 hr 30 min ⓗ 0820–2005 ⤳ 1 hr 20 min ⌀ GBP11.
London-Gatwick Apt ⇌ Jetlink » avg 2 hr 30 min ⓗ 0820–2005 ⤳ 2 hr 30 min ⌀ GBP13.

City & suburbs
London (Liverpool Street rail stn) ⇌ WAGN » 30 min ⓗ 0541–2359 ⤳ 41 min ⌀ GBP9.80.

Other towns and cities
Brighton ⇌ Jetlink 747 » avg 2 hr ⓗ 0335–2335 ⤳ 3 hr 20 min.
Cambridge ⇌ Cambridge Coach » avg 2 hr 30 min ⓗ 0815–0015 ⤳ 50 min ⌀ GBP10.
Edinburgh ⇌ National Express » 1 per day ⓗ 0915 ⤳ 12 hr ⌀ GBP26.50.
Norwich ⇌ Cambridge Coach, Jetlink » avg 2 hr ⓗ 0250–2250 ⤳ 2 hr ⌀ GBP14.
Oxford ⇌ Cambridge Coach » avg 2 hr ⓗ 0345–1945 ⤳ 2 hr ⌀ GBP11.

Regional Air Connections

Amsterdam ✈ » Several per day ⤳ 1 hr
Belfast ✈ » Several per day ⤳ 1 hr 15 min
Brussels ✈ » At least daily ⤳ 1 hr
Cork ✈ » Several per day ⤳ 1 hr 20 min
Dublin ✈ » Several per day ⤳ 1 hr 10 min
Edinburgh ✈ » At least daily ⤳ 1 hr 20 min
Glasgow ✈ » Several per day ⤳ 1 hr 15 min
Guernsey ✈ » At least daily ⤳ 1 hr 10 min
Jersey ✈ » At least daily ⤳ 1 hr 10 min
Maastricht ✈ » Several per day ⤳ 1 hr
Manchester (UK) ✈ » Several per week ⤳ 1 hr
Newcastle (UK) ✈ » Several per week ⤳ 1 hr 15 min
Paris ✈ » Several per day ⤳ 1 hr 15 min
Rotterdam ✈ » Several per week ⤳ 1 hr

LOS ANGELES   LAX
USA (see page 41)

National ☎ code: 1
Area ☎ code: 310
Local time: Winter GMT-8, Summer GMT-7
Los Angeles International Airport, 1 World Way, PO Box 92216, Los Angeles, CA 90009-2216, USA
☎ 646 5252
℻ 646 0523
Location: 27 km/17 miles SW of Los Angeles

Terminals and Transfers

Terminals
Terminal 1 Airlines: America West Airlines, Southwest, US Airways, US Airways Express (Trans States). Layout: Lower Level (Arrivals, Baggage Claim, Car Rental, Ground Transportation), Upper Level (Departures, Gates 1–14).
Terminal 2 Airlines: Air Canada, Air China, Air Mobility Command, Air New Zealand, Allegro, American Trans Air, Asiana Airlines, Avianca Colombian Airlines, Caledonian, CityBird, Hawaiian Airlines, KLM, Miami Air, Northwest Airlines, Pan Am, Sun Country, VASP, Virgin Atlantic. Layout: Lower Level (Arrivals, Baggage Claim, Car Rental, Ground Transportation), Upper Level (Customs, Departures, Gates 20–29).
Terminal 3 Airlines: Alaska Airlines, Express One, Midwest Express, Reno Air, TWA, TW Express, Western Pacific Airlines. Layout: Lower Level (Arrivals, Baggage Claim, Car Rental, Ground Transportation), Upper Level (Departures, Gates 30–39).
Tom Bradley International Terminal Airlines: Aero California, Aeroflot, Aerolineas Argentinas, Aeroperu, Air France, Air Pacific, Alitalia, ANA All Nippon, AOM French Airlines, British Airways, Canada 3000, Carnival/Iberia, Cathay Pacific, China Airlines, China Eastern, CORSAIR International, Egyptair, El Al Israel, EVA Air, Garuda Indonesian, Japan Airlines, LACSA, Lan Chile, LTU, Malaysia, Martinair Holland, Mexicana, Philippine Airlines, Qantas, Singapore Airlines, Sobel/Bal Air, Swissair, TACA, Thai, Tower Air, Transaero, Varig, World. Layout: Lower Level (Arrivals, Baggage Claim, Car Rental, Ground Transportation), Upper Level (Customs, Departures, Gates 101–123, 107–118).
Terminal 4 Airlines: American Airlines, American Eagle, Canadian Airlines International, Sun Country, Transaero Airlines. Layout: Lower Level (Arrivals, Baggage Claim, Car Rental, Ground Transportation), Upper Level (Departures, Gates 40–49).
Terminal 5 Airlines: Aeromexico, China Southern, Delta Airlines, Vanguard. Layout: Lower Level (Arrivals, Baggage Claim, Car Rental, Ground Transportation), Upper Level (Customs, Departures, Gates 50–59).
Terminal 6 Airlines: Air Jamaica, Continental Airlines, Frontier Airlines, Lufthansa, Skywest, United Airlines (International flights). Layout: Lower Level (Arrivals, Baggage Claim, Car Rental, Ground Transportation), Upper Level (Departures, Gates 60–69).
Terminal 7 Airlines: United Airlines, United Express. Layout: Lower Level (Arrivals, Baggage Claim, Car Rental, Ground Transportation), Upper Level (Departures, Gates 70–77), Satellite Building 8 (Gates 80–84)
Imperial Terminal Airlines: All charter flights. Layout: All facilities on Main Level

Minimum transfer times
International: 2 hr **Domestic:** 20 min–1 hr 30 min

Transfer between terminals
Bus » Frequent; All terminals ⌀ Free

Information

Information and help desks
Information Center Tom Bradley International Terminal Lower Level Airport Information
Traveller's Aid All Terminals Lower Level ☎ 646 2270 ⓗ 0700–2200 Tourist information

Emergencies

Police All Terminals throughout ☎ 646 7911
Medical Tom Bradley International Terminal Upper Level ☎ 215 6000 ⓗ 0700–2300
Lost Property All Terminals For lost luggage, contact airlines ☎ 417 0440

☎ Phone no. ℻ Fax no. ⓗ Hours of opening/operation » Frequency of service ⤳ Journey time ⌀ Cost/one-way fare

SECTION TWO • AIRPORT DIRECTORY — LOS ANGELES

Airport Facilities

Money
ATM Terminal 1 Upper Level
AMT Terminal 4 Upper Level
ATM Terminal 5 Upper Level
ATM Terminal 7 Upper Level
ATM Tom Bradley International Terminal Upper and Lower Levels
Bureau de change All Terminals Upper Level

Food and drink
Bar All Terminals throughout
Café/light meals All Terminals throughout
Restaurant All Terminals throughout
Restaurant Theme Building (centre of airport) ⏲1100–2200

Communications
Fax service Terminal 1 Business Center
Fax service Terminal 3 Business Center
Fax service Terminal 7 Business Center
Post office Tom Bradley International Terminal Upper Level ⏲0900–1700
Post box All Terminals throughout

Shopping
Duty free, departure Terminal 2 Upper Level
Duty free, departure Terminal 3 Upper Level
Duty free, departure Tom Bradley International Terminal Upper Level
Duty free, departure Terminal 4 Upper Level
Duty free, departure Terminal 5 Upper Level
Duty free, departure Terminal 6 Upper Level
Duty free, departure Terminal 7 Upper Level
Gift Shop All Terminals throughout
News, Stationery & Books All Terminals throughout

Luggage
Left luggage counter Terminal 1 Business Center, Upper Level
Left luggage counter Terminal 3 Business Center, Upper Level
Left luggage counter Terminal 7 Business Center, Upper Level
Left luggage counter Tom Bradley International Terminal Upper Level
Trolleys/Carts All Terminals ⌀USD1.50
Trolleys/Carts Tom Bradley International Terminal ⌀Free for international arriving passengers

Disabled Travellers

All Terminals Adapted toilets; Lifts Phones at wheelchair height; Phones adapted for the deaf, special parking, assistance available from airlines upon request

Smoking Policy

All Terminals Smoking atriums only

Special Passenger Lounges

All Airlines Lounges International Terminal beyond security, All Lounges on Fourth or Fifth Floor
Air Canada Maple Leaf Lounge Terminal 2 Upper Level, Gates 23–28
Air New Zealand First Class Lounge Terminal 2 Upper Level, Gates 23–28
American Airlines Admirals Club Terminal 4 Upper Level, Gate 43B
Asiana Airlines VIP Lounge Terminal 2 Upper Level, Gates 23–28
Continental Airlines Presidents Club Terminal 5 Upper Level, Gate 63
Delta Airlines Crown Room Terminal 5 Upper Level, Gates 54–59
Hawaiian Airlines Premier Club Terminal 2 Upper Level, Gates 23–28
KLM World Business Class Terminal 2 Upper Level, Gates 23–28
Northwest Airlines World Club Terminal 2 Upper Level, Gates 23–28
TWA Ambassadors Club Terminal 3

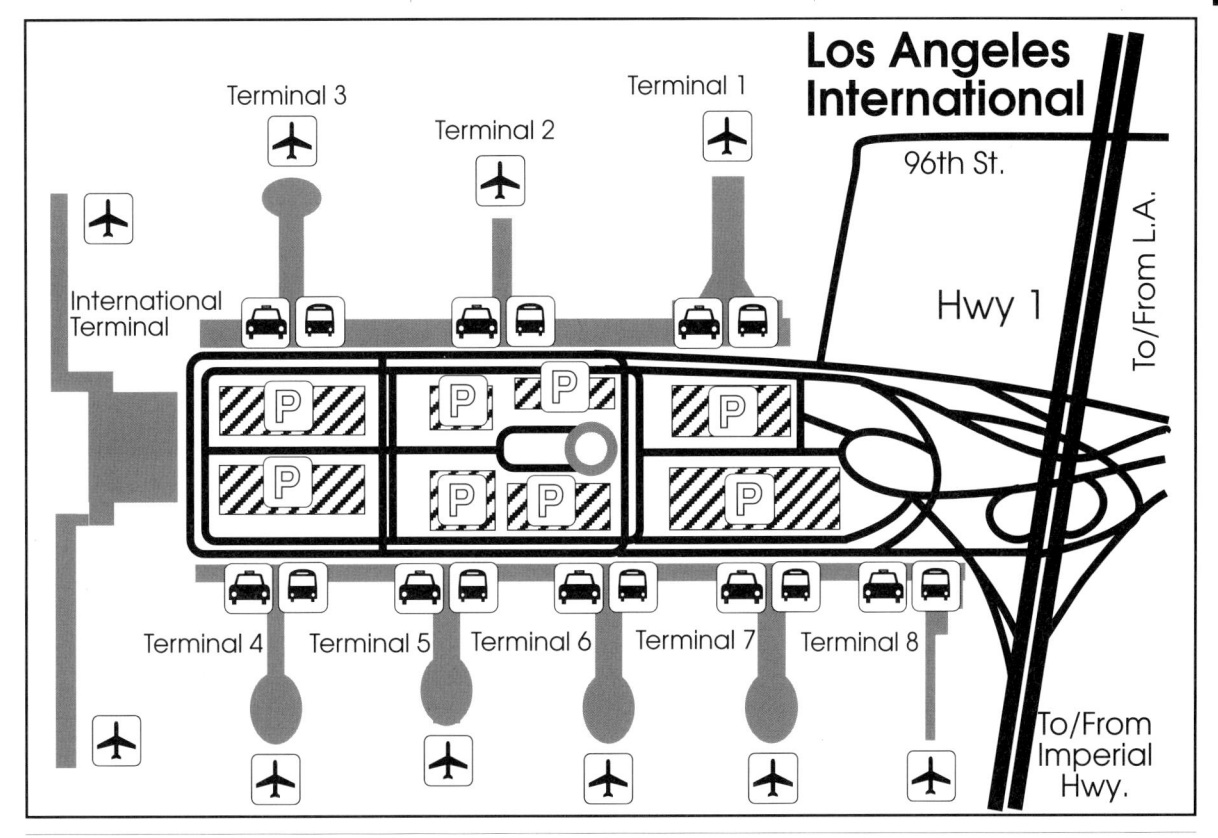

LOS ANGELES

SECTION TWO • AIRPORT DIRECTORY

Upper Level, Gates 35 and 31A
United Airlines Red Carpet Club
Terminal 7 Upper Level, Past Security
US Airways Club Terminal 1 Upper Level, Gate 2
Virgin Atlantic Upper Class Lounge
Terminal 2 Upper Level, Gates 23–28

CONFERENCE AND BUSINESS FACILITIES

Business Centers, Terminals 1, 3, 7 and Tom Bradley International Terminal Telephones, Fax, Photocopier

CAR RENTAL

Alamo All Terminals Lower Level
Avis All Terminals Lower Level
Budget All Terminals Lower Level
Dollar All Terminals Lower Level
Hertz All Terminals Lower Level
National All Terminals Lower Level

CAR PARKING

Long-stay 1km/½ mile (take free LAX Lot 'B' and 'C' bus) 16400 spaces ⌀Free first 2 hr, then USD2 per 2 hr, USD5–7 per day max

Off-airport 2 km/1 mile Five companies
Short-stay Central Terminal Lots 1–7, 8850 spaces ⌀USD3 per 2 hr, then USD1 hr thereafter, USD16 per day (max)

TAXIS AND CHAUFFEUR-DRIVEN CARS

Taxis
Lower Level, outside baggage claim City centre ⤴30–45 min ⌀USD25

PUBLIC TRANSPORT

Airport to airport
Orange County Airport ⇌Airport Coach »30 min ⓗ0530–2000 ⤴1 hr 50 min ⌀USD20. Transfer at Disneyland Hotel City & suburbs
Disneyland CA ⇌Airport Coach »30 min, 60 min overnight ⓗ24 hr ⤴50 min ⌀USD14.
Buena Park (Knott's Berry Farm Theme Park) ⇌Airport Coach »1 hr ⓗ0700–2200 ⤴50 min ⌀USD14.
Los Angeles (Union Station) ⇌Metro: 439 »30–60 min ⓗ0511–2145 ⤴1 hr ⌀USD1.35. From City Bus Center (take LAX Shuttle 'C' from Lower Level of all terminals)

Los Angeles city centre ⇌MTA: 439 »30–60 min ⓗ0511–2145 ⤴1 hr ⌀USD1.35. From City Bus Center (take LAX Shuttle 'C' from Lower Level of all terminals)
Los Angeles (Metro Area) ⇌ Over 50 companies at Airport.
Los Angeles city centre m Metro: Green Line »7–20 min ⓗ0430–2330 ⤴45 min–1 hr ⌀USD1.60. Take LAX Shuttle 'G' from Lower Level of all terminals. Transfer to Blue Line at Imperial/Wilmington
Oxnard/Ventura CA ⇌Ventura County Airporter »7 day ⓗ0645–2100 (1830 Sat ⤴1 hr 30 min ⌀USD20.
Palmdale/Lancaster CA ⇌Antelope Valley Airport Express »7 per day ⓗ0730–2200 ⤴2 hr ⌀USD28.
Pasadena CA bAirport Coach »60 min ⓗ0615–2315 ⤴1 hr ⌀USD12.
Santa Monica CA ⇌Big Blue Bus: 3 »20–60 min ⓗ0735–2315 ⤴35 min ⌀USD0.50. From City Bus Center (take LAX Shuttle 'C' from Lower Level of all terminals)
Torrance CA ⇌Torrance Transit: 8 »20–60 min ⓗ0600–2230 Mon–Fri ⤴45 min ⌀USD0.50. From City Bus Center (take LAX Shuttle 'C' from Lower Level of all terminals)
Van Nuys CA ⇌FlyAway Van Nuys »30 min ⓗ24 hr ⤴1 hr ⌀USD3.
Ventura CA ⇌Great American Stageline »7 per day ⓗ0615–2150 ⤴45 min-2 hr ⌀USD12-22. Service to Woodland Hills, Thousand Oaks, Westlake Village, Camarillo and Oxnard
Ventura County CA ⇨Ventura County Shuttle (805) 382 8300 .
Westwood (UCLA) CA ⇌Culver CityBus: 6 »12 min, 60 min evenings ⓗ0540–2200 ⤴50 min ⌀USD0.50. From City Bus Center (take LAX Shuttle 'C' from Lower Level of all terminals)

Other towns and cities
Bakersfield CA ⇌Airport Bus of Bakersfield »8 day ⓗ0900–0030 ⤴2 hr 30 min ⌀USD25.
Santa Barbara CA ⇌Santa Barbara Airbus »7 day ⓗ0800–2300 ⤴2 hr 30 min ⌀USD35. Service to Carpinteria and Goleta CA
Palm Springs CA ⇨Palm Springs Limousine (619) 320 0044.

REGIONAL AIR CONNECTIONS

Bakersfield CA ✈ »Several per day ⤴45 min
Carlsbad CA ✈ »Several per day ⤴45 min
El Centro/Imperial CA ✈ »Several per day ⤴1 hr
Fresno CA ✈ »Several per day ⤴1 hr

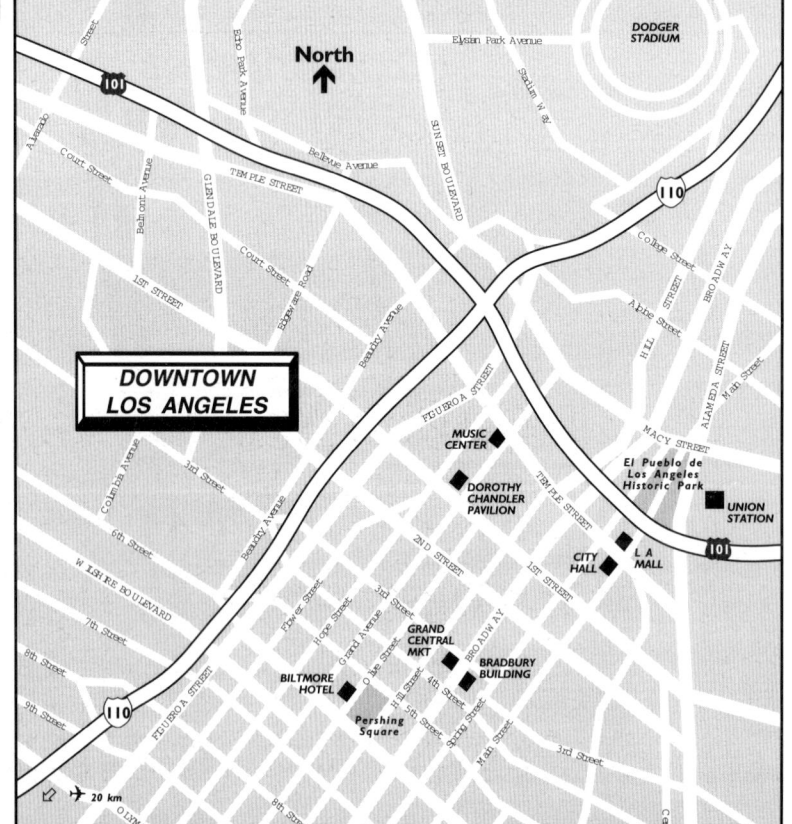

ⓒ Phone no. ⓕ Fax no. ⓗ Hours of opening/operation » Frequency of service ⤴ Journey time ⌀ Cost/one-way fare

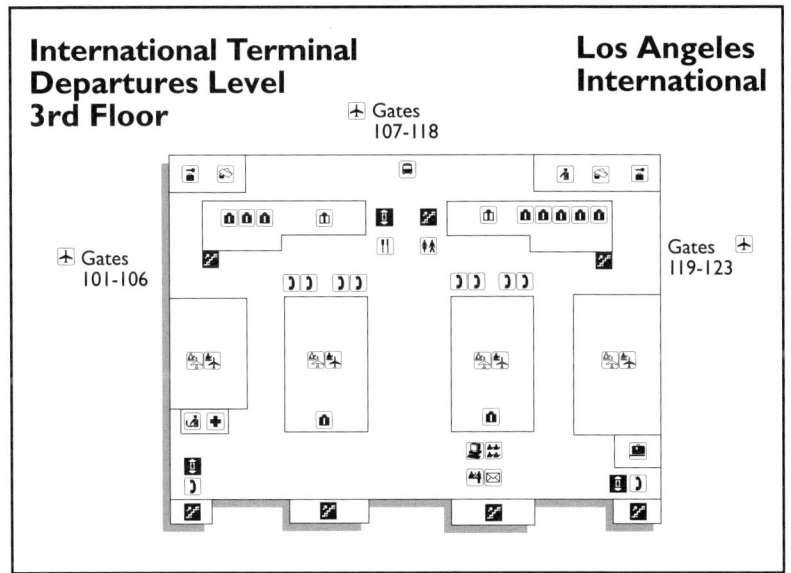

✈ ✈ SECTION TWO • AIRPORT DIRECTORY   LOS ANGELES

International Terminal Departures Level 3rd Floor

Los Angeles International

Gates 107-118
Gates 101-106
Gates 119-123

Palm Springs CA ✈ »Several per day ↻40 min
Palmdale/Lancaster CA ✈ »Several per day ↻35 min
Phoenix AZ ✈ »Several per day ↻1 hr \
San Diego CA ✈ »Several per day ↻45 min
San Jose CA ✈ »Several per day ↻1 hr
San Luis Obispo CA ✈ »Several per day ↻50 min
Santa Barbara CA ✈ »Several per day ↻40 min
Santa Maria CA ✈ »Several per day ↻50 min

TRAVELLER'S NOTES

The extent of public transportation belies Los Angeles' reputation as an automobile-dominated city. Walking is out of the question, however, both because of the distances and for safety reasons. While there are relatively few attractions in the city centre, it does make a good base for those who would rather not experience the legendary freeway traffic. Los Angeles Union Station is served by the Metro Red Line subway, Amtrak and Metrolink trains serving much of Southern California.

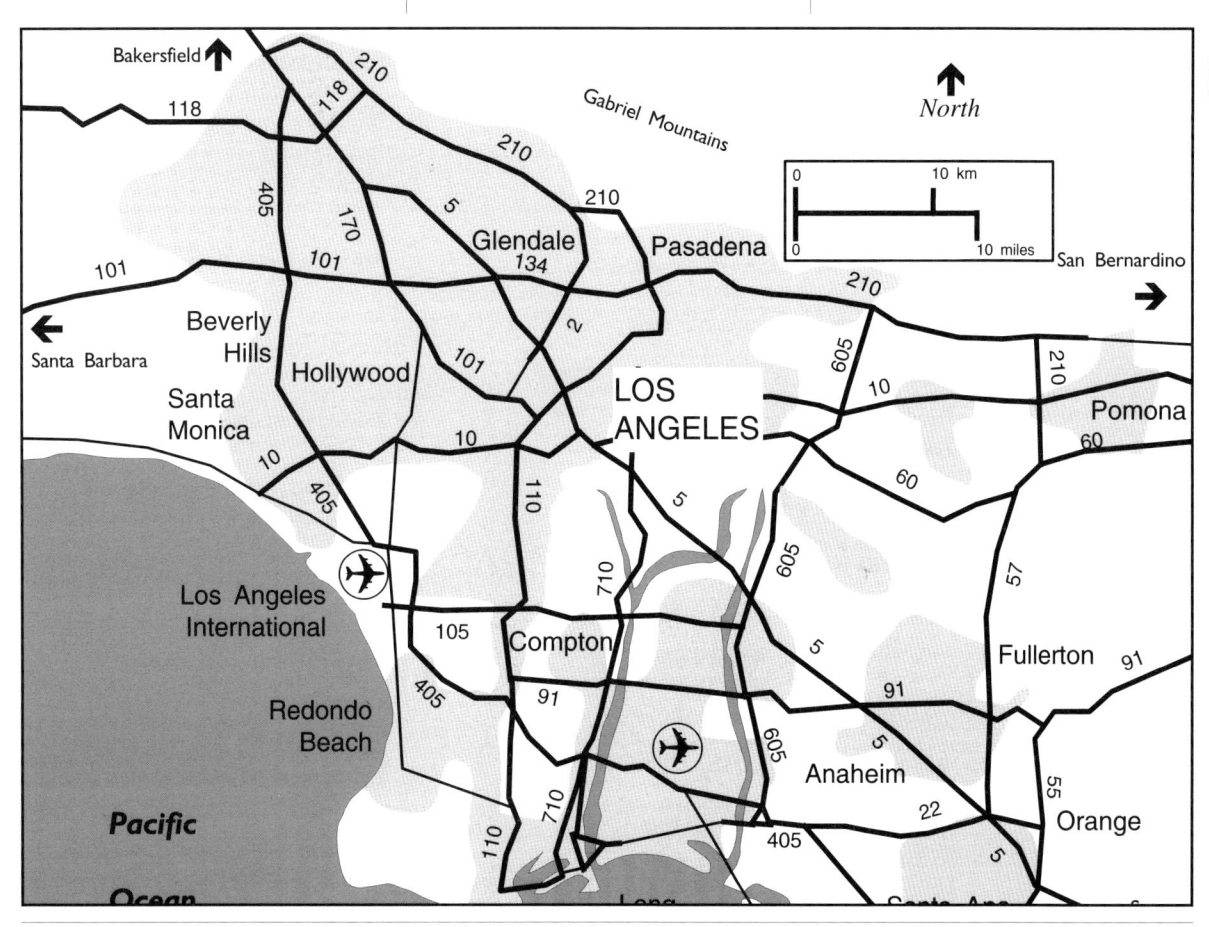

Inyokern CA ✈ »Several per day ↻50 min
Las Vegas NV ✈ »Several per day ↻55 min
Oakland CA ✈ »Several per day ↻1 hr
Ontario CA ✈ »Several per day ↻35 min
Orange County CA ✈ »Several per day ↻30 min
Oxnard CA ✈ »Several per day ↻35 min

177

✈ Air ⇌ Rail ⇌ Bus ⇌ Limousine Ⓜ Metro/subway ⇌ Tram ⇌ Helicopter ⇌ Water transport • For map symbols, see p. 9

LYON — LYS

France (see p. 21)

National ℡ code: 33
Area ℡ code: 04
Local time: Winter GMT+1, Summer GMT+2
Aéroport Lyon-Satolas, BP 113, 69125 Satolas, Lyon, France
℡ 72 22 72 21
℻ 72 22 74 71
Location: 32 km /20 miles E of Lyon

Terminals and Transfers

Terminals
Terminal 1 Airlines: All international flights. Layout: Divided into Blocs 2, 4, 6, 8 and 9. International flights
Terminal 2 Airlines: All domestic flights. Layout: Divided into Blocs 1, 3 and 5. Domestic and regional flights.
Halle Central Airlines:. Layout: Central Reception/Entrance Area split into Level 1 and Level 2

Minimum transfer times
International: 45 min Domestic: 35 min

Information

Flight enquiries
Airport ℡72 22 72 21
Air Algérie ℡78 42 64 95 Air France ℡75 56 22 20 Air Liberté ℡(01) 49 79 09 Air Malta ℡(01) 44 86 08 40 Air Portugal TAP ℡93 21 34 35 Alitalia ℡73 37 77 38 All domestic flights ℡72 22 77 07 AOM French Airlines ℡72 56 24 20 British Airways ℡05 12 51 25 Eurowings ℡(01) 48 62 79 38 KLM ℡(01) 44 56 18 13 Lot Polish Airlines ℡78 42 27 10 Lufthansa ℡05 46 98 41 Royal Air Maroc ℡78 37 17 46 Sabena World Airlines ℡72 22 82 85 SAS ℡72 22 84 32 Swissair ℡72 35 03 31 TAT European Airlines ℡05 05 50 05 Tunis Air ℡72 77 37 37 Turkish Airlines ℡78 24 13 24

Information and help desks
Information Desk Halle Central Level 1 ℡72 22 72 21 ℻72 22 74 71 Airport, Flights Tourist information

Emergencies
Police Terminal 1 Bloc 8 ℡72 22 74 40

Medical Halle Central Ground level of Arc bldg ℡72 22 73 69 ⏰24 hr
Lost Property Terminal 1 Bloc 4 ℡72 22 74 28 ⏰0800–2000

Airport Facilities

Money
ATM Terminal 1 Bloc 4
ATM Terminal 1 Arrival Gate B between Bloc 2 and Bloc 4
ATM Terminal 2 Arrival Hall between Bloc 1 and Bloc 3
Bureau de change Halle Central Near information desk ⏰0630–2230 Mon–Fri; 0800–1200 Sat
Bureau de change Halle Central Post office, Main Concourse ⏰0800-2000 Mon-Fri; 0800–1200 Sat

Food and drink
Bar Terminal 1 Bloc 6 and Duty-free lounge
Bar Terminal 2 Bloc 7
Bar Terminal 2 Bloc 3
Bar Terminal 2 Gates 3–5
Bar Halle Central Upper Level
Restaurant Halle Central Upper Level

Communications
Post office Halle Central Main Concourse ⏰0800–2000 Mon–Fri; 0800–1200 Sat
Fax service Halle Central Main Concourse, near Post Office

Shopping
Shopping mall Terminal 1
Duty free, departure Terminal 1 Blocs 2, 4, 6, 8

Luggage
Left luggage counter Terminal 1 Arrivals B (Bloc 2/4) ⏰24 hr ⌀FFR10–20 per day

Disabled Travellers
Halle Central Adapted toilets; *Main Concourse* Lifts; *Main Concourse* in covered car park (P0), next to Gare TGV

Smoking Policy
Terminal 1 Permitted near Bloc 2
Terminal 2 Permitted in Bloc 7

Special Passenger Lounges
Mont-Blanc Room Terminal 1 *Business class, by res.ervation,* ℡72 22 73 43
VIP Lounge Halle Central *VIPs, by reservation,* ℡72 22 72 88

Conference and Business Facilities
Business Centre, Arc Building, by Central Hall ℡72 22 82 66 ℻72 22 74 71 *Secretarial service.*

Airport Hotels
Climat ℡72 23 90 90 ℻72 23 80 32; 84 rooms
Sofitel ℡72 23 38 00 ℻72 23 98 00

Car Rental
Avis Halle Central Ground Level ℡72 22 75 25
Budget Halle Central Ground Floor ℡72 22 74 74
Eurodollar-Citer Halle Central Ground Floor ℡72 22 74 87
EuropCar Halle Central Ground Floor ℡72 2275 27
Eurorent Halle Central Ground Floor ℡72 22 75 59
Hertz Halle Central Ground Floor ℡72 22 74 49
Mattei Halle Central Ground Floor ℡72 22 74 92

Car Parking
Long-stay Next to rail station (Gare de Satolas TGV) ⌀FRF10–30 per day after first day
Short-stay Near Terminal 1 (P4), near Terminal 2 (P3) ⌀FRF30 per 8 hr, FRF45 per day

Taxis and Chauffeur-driven Cars

Taxis
In front of both terminals City centre ⤳30–50 min ⌀FRF210

℡ Phone no. ℻ Fax no. ⏰ Hours of opening/operation ⤳ Frequency of service ⤳ Journey time ⌀ Cost/one-way fare

Public Transport

Airport to airport
Geneva Apt 🚌 Intercars »4–5 per day ⏱0600–2100 ➲1hr 40 min ⊘FRF175. *For information ✆78 37 20 80*
Paris-Charles de Gaulle Apt 🚆 SNCF »1 per day ⏱1547 ➲2 hr 5 min. *For information, ✆36 35 35 35*

City & suburbs
Lyon (Lyon-Perrache rail stn) 🚌 Satobus »20 min ⏱0500–2100 ➲40 min ⊘FRF46. Via Part Dieu rail stn. *For information ✆72 22 72 21/78 67 09 10*

Other towns and cities
Aix-les-Bains 🚌 Satobus »5 perday M-Fr, 1 S, S ⏱0600-1900 ➲1 hr 25 min ⊘FRF125. *Information, ✆79 35 33 97*
Annecy 🚌 Satobus »according to demand ⊘FRF260. *For information, ✆50 51 20 08*
Avignon 🚆SNCF »1 per day ⏱1512 ➲1hr 30 min. *For information ✆36 35 35 35*
Bourgoin 🚌Cars Faure »4 per day ⏱0610–1720 ➲40 min ⊘FRF22.50. *For information, ✆78 96 11 44*
Chambery 🚆SNCF »1 per day exc Sat ⏱1910 ➲1 hr. *For information, ✆36 35 35 35*
Chambery 🚌Satobus »5 /day M-F, 1/St 1/S ⏱0625–1925 ➲1 hr ⊘125 FRF.
Grenoble 🚆 SNCF »2 per day ⏱1147, 1639 ➲1 hr 7 min. *For information, ✆36 35 35 35*
Grenoble 🚌 Satobus/ Cars Faure »9–13 per day ⏱0500–1915 ➲1 hr 5 min ⊘FRF130. *For information, ✆72 22 72 21/78 96 11 44*
Lille Europe 🚆 SNCF »1 per day ⏱Departs 1547 ➲3 hr 20 min. *For Eurostar connections.*
L'Isle-D'Abeau 🚌 Cars Faure »3 per day ⏱0617–1727 ➲33 min ⊘FRF16.50. *For information, ✆78 96 11 44*
Marseille 🚆 SNCF »1 per day ⏱1512 ➲2 hr 35 min. *For information, ✆36 35 35 35*
Paris (Gare de Lyon rail stn) 🚆 SNCF »3 per day ⏱0705–1518 ➲2hr 3 min. *For information, ✆36 35 35 35*
Saint-Etienne 🚌 Satobus »5–6 per day ⏱0500–2035 ➲1 hr 10 min–1 hr 25 min ⊘FRF95. *Via Saint-Chamond, Rive-de-Gier, Givors. For information, ✆77 25 97 79*
Valence 🚆 SNCF »1 per day ⏱1512 ➲30 min. *For information, ✆36 35 35 35*
Valence 🚌 Satobus »2 per day ⏱0630–1630 ➲1 hr 20 min ⊘FRF140. *Reservations required on Sun and Bank Hols. For information, ✆07 34 44 49*
Vienne 🚌 Satobus »2 per day ⏱0710–1710 ➲40 min ⊘FRF60. *Reservations required on Sun and Bank Hols. For information, ✆07 34 44 49*
Villefontaine 🚌 Cars Faure »3 per day ⏱0625–1735 ➲25 min ⊘FRF16.50. *For information, ✆78 96 11 44*

Regional Air Connections

Annaba ✈ »Several per week ➲45 min
Bastia ✈ »Several per week ➲60–65 min
Bejaia ✈ »Several per week ➲45 min
Bordeaux ✈ »Several per day ➲60 min
Clermont-Ferrand ✈ »Several per week ➲30-35 min
Constantine ✈ »Several per day ➲35–40 min
Limoges ✈ »Several per week ➲60 min
Marseille ✈ »Several per day ➲50 min
Milan ✈ »Several per week ➲55–65 min
Montpelier ✈ »Several per week ➲1 hr
Mulhouse/Basel ✈ »Several per week ➲55 min
Nice ✈ »Several per day ➲50 min
Paris ✈ »Several per day ➲50–60 min
Rodez ✈ »Several per week ➲50 min
Strasbourg ✈ »Several per week ➲55 min
Toulouse ✈ »Several per day ➲50–55 min
Zürich ✈ »Several per day ➲60–70 min

MADRID   MAD

Spain (see page 36)

National ✆ code: 34
Area ✆ code: 01
Local time: Winter GMT+1, Summer GMT+2
Aeropuerto de Madrid/Barajas, 28042 Barajas, Madrid, Spain
✆393 60 00
⊕393 62 00
Location: 13 km/8 miles NE of Madrid

TERMINALS AND TRANSFERS

Terminals
International Terminal Airlines: All international flights.
Domestic Terminal Airlines: All domestic flights.

Minimum transfer times
International: 45 min–1 hr **Domestic:** 45 min

INFORMATION

Flight enquiries
Airport ✆305 83 43/4/5/6
Aer Lingus ✆541 42 16 Aerolineas Argentinas ✆305 87 31 Air Algérie ✆305 86 80 Air France ✆305 84 47 Air Portugal TAP ✆305 42 37 Alitalia ✆305 43 36 American Airlines ✆305 83 47 Austrian Airlines ✆305 83 75 Avianca Colombian Airlines ✆305 42 10 Balkan Bulgarian Airlines ✆305 84 30 British Airways ✆305 40 08 Continental Airlines ✆305 80 46 Delta Airlines ✆305 82 75 Egyptair ✆305 55 83 El Al Israel Airlines ✆305 43 67 Finnair ✆305 89 80 Iberia ✆305 42 18 Iran Air ✆305 52 43 Japan Airlines ✆305 58 11 KLM ✆305 43 37 Kuwait Airways ✆305 88 38 Lot Polish Airlines ✆305 42 40 Lufthansa ✆305 42 40 Meridiana ✆305 84 09 Middle East Airlines ✆305 86 68 OlympicAirways ✆305 48 53 Royal Air Maroc&305 59 22 Royal Jordanian Airlines ✆305 84 46 Sabena World Airlines ✆305 40 40 Saudia ✆305 53 41 SAS ✆305 42 14 Singapore Airlines ✆305 54 46 Swissair ✆305 51 46 Tarom Romanian Air ✆305 50 78 Thai Airways ✆305 58 47 Tunis Air ✆305 63 58 Turkish Airlines ✆305 53 84 TWA ✆305 42 91 United Airlines ✆305 61 04 Varig Brazilian ✆305 41 47 VIASA Venezuelan ✆305 43 21

Information and help desks
Airport Information Desk Domestic Terminal First floor ✆322 11 65 ext. 1137 ⓞ24 hr Airport information
Airport Information Desk Domestic Terminal Second Floor ✆322 11 65 ext. 1089 Airport information
Information Desk International Terminal Arrival Lounge ✆322 11 65 ext. 2756 ⓞ24 hr Airport information, Flights
Tourist Information Desk International Terminal Arrival Lounge ✆322 11 65 ext. 2254 ⓞ0800–2000 Tourist Information
Hotel Reservation Desk International Terminal Arrivals Lounge, facing Halls 1 and 2 ✆305 4224/305 8419 ⓞ0700–1200

EMERGENCIES

Police Domestic Terminal ✆305 43 81
Police International Terminal ✆305 42 49
Medical International Terminal ✆322 11 65 ext. 1025
Lost Property International Terminal ✆322 11 65 ext. 1010
Lost Property Domestic Terminal ✆322 11 65 ext. 1082

AIRPORT FACILITIES

Money
Bank International Terminal, 2nd floor, next to restaurant ⓞ0815–1430.
Bureau de change International Terminal Transit Area ⓞ24 hr
Bureau de change International Arrivals Halls 1 and 2 ⓞ24 hr
ATM International Terminal throughout ⓞ24 hr
Bank Domestic Terminal, next to check-in desks ⓞ0815–1430.
Bureau de change Domestic Terminal check-in hall ⓞ24 hr.
ATM Domestic Terminal throughout ⓞ24 hr.

Food and drink
Café/light meals International Terminal First Floor Transit Area ⓞ24 hr
Café/light meals International Terminal Ground Floor Arrival Lounge ⓞ24 hr
Restaurant International Terminal Second Floor Transit Area ⓞ1230–2400
Café/light meals Domestic Terminal First Floor Departure Lounge ⓞ24 hr
Café/light meals Domestic Terminal Ground Floor Arrivals Lounge ⓞ0800–2400
Café/light meals Domestic Terminal Second Floor Departure Lounge ⓞ0700–2400.
Restaurant Domestic Terminal Second Floor Departures Lounge ⓞ1230–1800, 2000–2400.

Communications
Post office International Terminal Arrivals Lounge ⓞ0800–2000 Mon–Fri; 0800–1300 Sat ✆305 8657

Shopping
Shopping mall International Terminal First Floor Transit Area ⓞ0700–2300
Hairdresser First Floor Domestic Terminal ⓞ0800–2000 Mon–Sat ✆305 4770.
Pharmacy International Terminal Ground Floor Arrivals Lounge
Pharmacy Domestic Terminal Second Floor Transit Area ⓞ0800–2400
News, Stationery & Books Domestic Terminal ⓞ0800–2400

Luggage
Left Luggage Counter International Terminal ⌀Free ⓞ0700–0000 daily.
Lockers International Terminal ⌀Free

DISABLED TRAVELLERS

International Terminal Adapted toilets; Lifts; Special car parking
Domestic Terminal Adapted toilets; Lifts; Special car parking

SMOKING POLICY

International Terminal Restricted
Domestic Terminal Restricted

SPECIAL PASSENGER LOUNGES

VIP Lounge International Terminal Ground Floor Departure Lounge
Sala Madrid International Terminal First Floor Departure Lounge
Sala Plaza Oriente International Terminal First Floor Departure Lounge
Iberia Sala Prado International Terminal First Floor Departure Lounge
Iberia VIP Lounge Domestic Terminal First Floor Departure Lounge

SECTION TWO • AIRPORT DIRECTORY   MADRID

CONFERENCE AND BUSINESS FACILITIES

Conference facilities, Domestic Terminal
ⓒ305 61 02 ⓢ24 hr
Conference room, International Terminal
ⓒ305 88 07 ⓕ305 88 08 ⓢ0800–2100

CAR RENTAL

Atesa International Terminal Arrival Lounge ⓒ305 86 60
Avis International Terminal Ground Floor ⓒ305 42 73
EuropCar International Terminal Ground Floor ⓒ305 52 36
Hertz International Terminal Ground Floor ⓒ305 48 55
Atesa Domestic Terminal Ground Floor ⓒ305 86 60
Avis Domestic Terminal Ground Floor ⓒ305 42 73
EuropCar Domestic Terminal Ground Floor ⓒ305 44 20
Hertz Domestic Terminal Ground Floor ⓒ305 84 52

CAR PARKING

Short-stay 6530 spaces ◇ESP200 per hr; ESP1750 per 24 hr.

TAXIS AND CHAUFFEUR-DRIVEN CARS

Taxis
Front of each terminal building ⓒCourtesy phones (by Customs, International Terminal.). City centre ↻20 min ◇ESP1500 approx. plus ESP50 per bag

PUBLIC TRANSPORT

City & suburbs
Madrid city centre (Terminal Colon) 🚌 Empresa Municipal de Transportes de Madrid »12 min ⓢ0445–0200 ↻30 min ◇ESP360.

REGIONAL AIR CONNECTIONS

Alicante ✈ »Several per day ↻55 min
Asturias ✈ »Several per day ↻1 hr
Barcelona ✈ »Several per day ↻1 hr
Bilbao ✈ »Several per day ↻50 min
Ibiza ✈ »Several per day ↻1 hr
Jerez de la Frontera ✈ »Several per day ↻55 min
La Coruña ✈ »Several per day ↻1 hr
Lisbon ✈ »Several per day ↻1 hr 10 min
Malaga ✈ »Several per day ↻50 min
Porto ✈ »Several per day ↻30 min
Seville ✈ »Several per day ↻55 min
Valencia ✈ »Several per day ↻50 min
Vigo ✈ »Several per day ↻1 hr

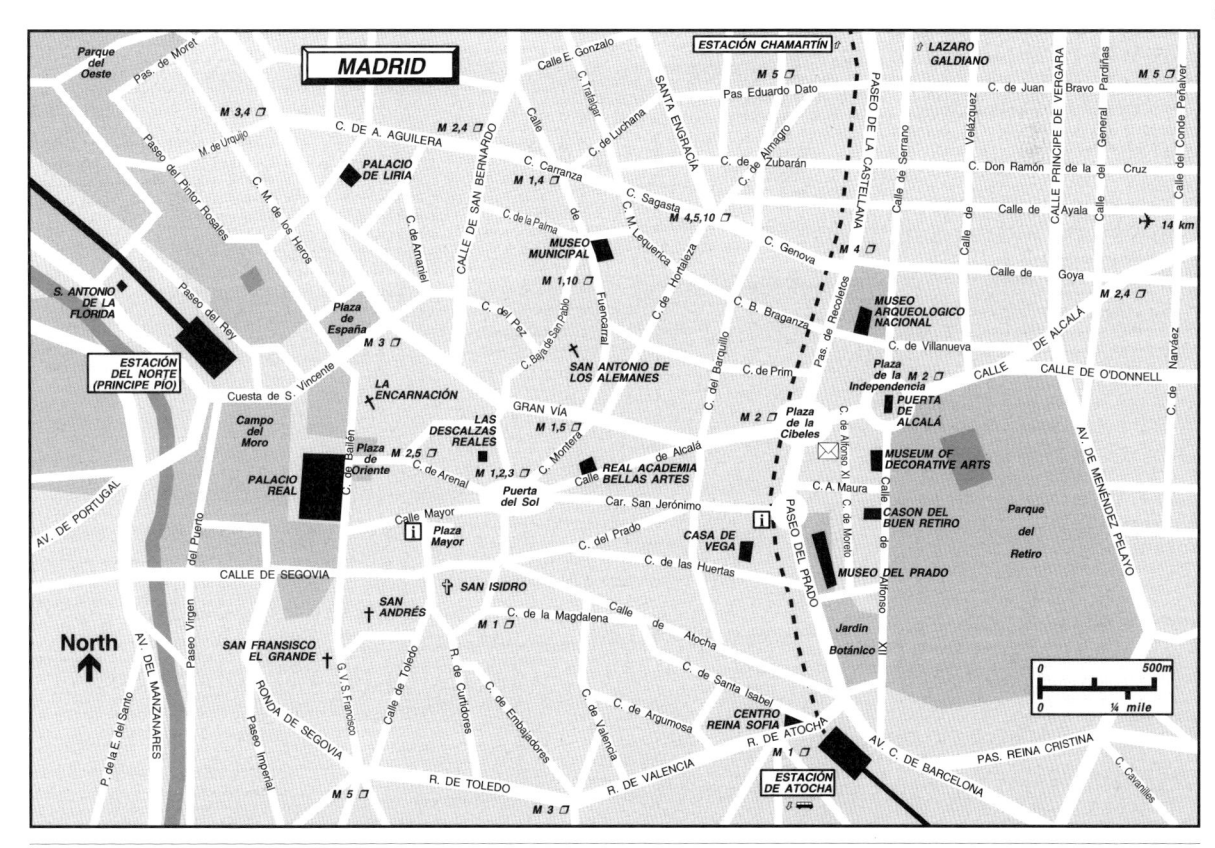

181

✈ Air 🚆 Rail 🚌 Bus 🚘 Limousine Ⓜ Metro/subway 🚊 Tram 🚁 Helicopter ⛴ Water transport • For map symbols, see p. 9

MALTA
Malta

MLA

National ℂ code: 356
Local time: Winter GMT+1, Summer GMT+2
Address: Malta International Airport Ltd, Luqa LQA 05, Malta
ℂ: 697800/249600
ℱ: 249563
Location: 5kms/3mls from Valletta

TERMINALS AND TRANSFERS
Main Terminal Airlines: Alitalia, British Airways, Lufthansa, Austrian/Swissair, Transavia, Britannia, Air 2000, Tuninter, Aeroflot, Condorflug, Airtours, Caledonian. Layout: first floor departure and arrival lounges; second floor check-in hall and Welcomer's hall

INFORMATION
Flight enquiries
Alitalia ℂ 6999 ext. 6311, British Airways ℂ 6999 ext. 6053, Lufthansa ℂ 6999 ext. 6286, Austrian/Swissair ℂ 6999 ext. 6305, Transavia, Britannia, and Air 2000 ℂ 6999 ext. 6313, Tuninter ℂ 6999 ext. 6283, Aeroflot ℂ 6999 ext. 6309, Condorflug, Airtours, and Caledonian ℂ 6999 ext. 6316.

Information and help desks
Customer service desk check-in hall flight information, wheelchair requests, left luggage ℂ 69997002 ⓞ 24 hr
Tourist information desk far end of the Welcomer's hall Tourist information, hotel reservations

Emergencies
Police ℂ 6999 ext. 6399
Medical Customer service centre ℂ 69997002
Lost Property Welcomer's hall and baggage reclaim area ℂ 69996063/69996064

AIRPORT FACILITIES
Money
Bureau de Change Baggage reclaim hall
Bureau de Change Welcomer's hall
Bank Welcomer's hall

Food and drink
Café/light meals Departures lounge ⓞ 24 hr
Café/light meals Welcomers' hall ⓞ 24 hr
Café/light meals Check-in hall ⓞ 24 hr
Restaurant Car park level ⓞ 24 hr

Communications
Post Box Check-in hall

Shopping
Duty free Departures lounge ℂ 0800 77 6688
Duty free Arrivals lounge ℂ 0800 77 6688
News, Stationery & Books Check-in hall ℂ 0800 77 6688

Luggage
Lockers Customer service desk ℂ 2496000 ⓞ 24 hr

DISABLED TRAVELLERS
Special parking, disabled toilets, low-level telephones, wheelchairs ℂ 69997002

CAR RENTAL
Avis Welcomers' hall
Budget Welcomers' hall
Eurodollar Welcomers' hall
Europcar Welcomers' hall
Hertz Welcomers' hall
Holiday Autos Welcomers' hall
Thrifty Welcomers' hall

CAR PARKING
Long-stay ⌀ 20 per hr; 30 per 1–4 hr; 60 per 4–13 hr; 90 per 13–24 hr

TAXIS AND CHAUFFEUR-DRIVEN CARS
Taxis
City centre ⌀ Public Transport City & suburbs
Valletta city centre 🚌 Route bus 8

ℂ Phone no. ℱ Fax no. ⓞ Hours of opening/operation » Frequency of service ↪ Journey time ⌀ Cost/one-way fare

MANCHESTER   MAN

United Kingdom (see page 41)

National ✆ code: 44
Area ✆ code: 0161
Local time: Winter GMT, summer GMT+1
Manchester Airport plc, Manchester M90 1QX, United Kingdom
✆489 3000
📠489 3813/3647
WWW site: http://www.manairport.co.uk
Location: 16 km/9½ miles S of Manchester

TERMINALS AND TRANSFERS

Terminals
Terminal 1 Domestic Airlines: Air South West, British Airways, Business Air, Cityflyer Express, European Airways, Manx Airlines, Suckling Airways. Layout: Arrival and Departure Levels.
Terminal 1 International Airlines: Aer Lingus, Air Engiadina, Air France, Air UK, BASE Regional Airlines, British Airways, Crossair, CSA Czech Airlines, Cyprus Airways, El Al Israel Airlines, Emirates, Finnair, Iberia, Icelandair, Lauda Air, LOT Polish Airlines, Lufthansa, Luxair, Newair, PGA Portugalia, Sabena, SAS Scandinavian Airlines, Swissair, Turkish Airways. Layout: Arrival and Departure Levels.
Terminal 2 Airlines: Adria Airways, Aeroflot, Air 2000, Air Canada, Air India, Air Malta, Air Mauritius, American Airlines, Cathay Pacific Airlines, Continental Airlines, Delta Air Lines, Laker Airways, Pakistan International Airlines, Ryanair, Singapore Airlines, Uzbekistan Airways, Virgin Atlantic Airways. Layout: Arrival and Departure Levels.

Minimum transfer times
Domestic to Domestic: 30 mins.
Domestic to International: 30 min–1 hr.
International to Domestic: 30 min–1 hr.

Transfer between Terminals
Skywalk covered walkway with travellators between Terminal 1 and Terminal 2.

INFORMATION

Flight enquiries
Airport ✆489 8000

Adria Airways ✆489 8042, Aer Lingus ✆489 8029, Aeroflot ✆489 8073, Air 2000 ✆489 8011, Air Canada ✆489 8006, Air Engiadina ✆489 8057, Air France ✆489 8008, Air India ✆489 8125, Air Malta ✆489 8045, Air Mauritius ✆489 8129, Air South West ✆489 8003, Air UK ✆489 8082, American Airlines ✆489 8004, BASE Regional Airlines ✆489 8089, British Airways ✆489 8015, Business Air ✆489 8039, Cathay Pacific Airlines ✆489 8025, Cityflyer Express ✆489 8116, Continental Airlines ✆489 8115, Crossair ✆489 8124, CSA Czech Airlines ✆489 8058, Cyprus Airways ✆489 8026, Delta Airlines ✆489 8027, El Al Israel Airlines ✆489 8054, Emirates ✆489 8030, European Airways ✆489 8024, Finnair ✆489 8014, Iberia ✆489 8038, Icelandair ✆489 8046, Laker Airways ✆489 2988, Lauda Air ✆489 8048, LOT Polish Airlines ✆489 8047, Lufthansa ✆489 8050, Luxair ✆489 8119, Manx Airlines ✆489 8041, Newair ✆489 8087, Pakistan International Airlines ✆489 8061, PGA Portugalia ✆489 8051, Ryanair ✆489 8101, Sabena ✆489 8069, SAS ✆489 8068, Singapore Airlines ✆489 8071, Suckling Airways ✆489 8019, Swissair ✆489 8072, Turkish Airways ✆489 8067, Uzbekistan Airways ✆489 8108, Virgin Atlantic Airways ✆489 8130.

Information and help desks
Information Desk Terminal 1 International Arrivals Area ✆489 3000 🕐24 hr Airport information
Tourist Information Desk Terminal 1 International Arrivals Area ✆436 3344 🕐0800–2100
Thomas Cook Hotel Reservations Desk Terminal 1 International Arrivals Area 🕐0800–2300 ✆489 2063/499 0284
Information Point Terminal 1 Domestic Airport Information Desk Terminal 2, Arrivals Area 🕐24 hr ✆489 3000 Airport information.
Tourist Information Desk Terminal 2, Arrivals Area 🕐0730–1430 ✆489 6412

EMERGENCIES

Police Airport Police Station ✆856 0232/0233/0235 🕐24 hr
Medical Non-emergencies Terminal 1 🕐0800–1600

Medical Emergencies Fire Station 🕐24 hr
Lost Property Terminal 1 International Arrivals Area 🕐24 hr ✆489 3463
Lost Property Terminal 1 Domestic Arrivals Area 🕐0600–2200 ✆489 3464
Lost Property Terminal 2 Arrivals Area 🕐0600–2200 ✆489 6031

AIRPORT FACILITIES

Money
ATM Terminal 1 Domestic Arrivals Area 🕐24 hr
ATM Terminal 1 International Arrivals Area 🕐24 hr
ATM Terminal 2 throughout 🕐24 hr
Bank Terminal 1 Domestic Arrivals Area 🕐0700–1900
Bureau de Change Terminal 1 Domestic Arrivals Area 🕐0700–1900
Thomas Cook bureau de change Terminal 1 International Departures Area 🕐summer 24 hr; winter 0530–2200
Thomas Cook bureau de change Terminal 1 Arrivals Area 🕐summer 0630–2200; winter 0630–2200
Bureau de Change Terminal 1 Arrivals Area and Terminal 1 Departures Area after passport control 🕐summer 0500–2400; winter 0530–2200
Thomas Cook bureau de change Terminal 2 Arrivals Area 🕐0530–2200
Thomas Cook bureau de change Terminal 2 Departure Area after passport control 🕐summer 0530–2400; winter 0600–2000
Bureau de Change Terminal 2 Departure Area 🕐summer 0500–2400; winter 0530–2200

Food and drink
Café/light meals Terminal 1 Domestic Arrivals Area 🕐0600–2230
Café/light meals Terminal 1 Domestic departure lounge 🕐0530–2000
Restaurant Terminal 1 International Main Concourse 🕐24 hr
Café/light meals Terminal 1 International Main Concourse 🕐summer 0530–2200 Mon–Thurs, 24 hr Fri, Sat and Sun; winter 0600–1800
Café/light meals Terminal 1 International Departure Lounge 🕐24 hr
Café/light meals Terminal 1 International Arrivals Area 🕐0600–2400 Mon–Thurs, 24 hr Fri, Sat and Sun
Bar Terminal 1 International Main Concourse 🕐1100–2300 Mon–Sat; 1200–2230 Sun

MANCHESTER

SECTION TWO • AIRPORT DIRECTORY

Bar Terminal 1 International Departure Lounge ⊕24 hr
Bar Terminal 1 International Arrivals Area ⊕1100–2300 Mon–Sat; 1200–2230 Sun
Restaurant Terminal 2 Main Concourse ⊕0700–2200
Café/light meals Terminal 2 Main Concourse ⊕24 hr
Café/light meals Terminal 2 Departure Lounge ⊕24 hr
Café/light meals Terminal 2 Arrivals Area ⊕24 hr
Bar Terminal 2 Main Concourse ⊕1100–2300 Mon–Sat; 1200–2230 Sun
Bar Terminal 2 Departure Lounge ⊕24 hr
Bar Terminal 2 Arrivals Area ⊕1100–2300 Mon–Sat; 1200–2230 Sun

Communications

Post office Terminal 1 International International Arrivals Area ⊕0800–1800
Post boxes Terminal 1 International and Terminal 2

Shopping

News, Stationery & Books Terminal 1 Domestic Departure Area ⊕summer 24 hr; winter 0600–variable closing times
Hairdresser Terminal 1 Domestic Arrivals Area ⊕0600–variable closing times
News, Stationery & Books Terminal 1 International Main Concourse ⊕summer 24 hr; winter 0600–variable closing times
Shopping Mall Terminal 1 International Main Concourse ⊕0600–variable closing times
Pharmacy Terminal 1 Main Concourse ⊕0600–variable closing times
News, Stationery & Books Terminal 1 International Departure Lounge ⊕all flight times
Duty free, departure Terminal 1 International Departure Lounge ⊕all flight times
News, Stationery & Books Terminal 2 Main Concourse ⊕summer 24 hr; winter 0600–variable closing times
Shopping Mall Terminal 2 Main Concourse ⊕0600–variable closing times
Pharmacy Terminal 2 Main Concourse ⊕0600–variable closing times
News, Stationery & Books Terminal 2 Departure Lounge ⊕all flight times
Duty free, departure Terminal 2 Departure Lounge ⊕all flight times

Luggage

Left luggage counter Terminal 1 Domestic Arrivals Area ⊕0600–2200 ℅489 3464
Left luggage counter Terminal 1 International Arrivals Area ⊕24 hr ℅489 3463
Left luggage counter Terminal 2 Arrivals Area ⊕0600–2200 ℅489 6031

DISABLED TRAVELLERS

Terminal 1 Domestic Adapted toilets; Lifts; Special car parking; Telephones at wheelchair height; Adapted telephones; Personal or wheelchair assistance
Terminal 1 International Adapted toilets; Lifts; Special car parking; Telephones at wheelchair height; Adapted telephones; Personal or wheelchair assistance
Terminal 2 Adapted toilets; Lifts; Special car parking; Telephones at wheelchair height; Adapted telephones; Personal or wheelchair assistance

SMOKING POLICY

Terminal 1 Domestic Restricted
Terminal 1 International Restricted
Terminal 2 Restricted

SPECIAL PASSENGER LOUNGES

Lakeland Lounge Terminal 1 Domestic Departure Area
Manchester Handling Executive Lounge Terminal 1 International Departure Area
Servisair Executive Lounge Terminal 1 International Departure Area
British Airways Ringway Lounge Terminal 1 International Departure Area
Sigma Aviation Executive Lounge Terminal 1 International Departure Area
Marco Polo Lounge Terminal 2 Departure Area
Servisair Executive Lounge Terminal 2 Departure Area

CONFERENCE AND BUSINESS FACILITIES

Atlantic Suite, Terminal 2 ℅489 6182 ⊕24 hr Telephones, Fax service, Power points, Photocopier, Secretarial service; Meeting room hire
Manchester TEC Business Centre Terminal 1 Domestic ℅437 8787 ⊕0830–1700 Mon–Fri Private workstations with telephone, Fax service, Photocopying, Meeting room hire, Message taking, Flight information and booking service, Video conferencing.

AIRPORT HOTELS

Forte Posthouse ℅437 5811 ℻436 2340
Hilton ℅435 3000 ℻435 3040
Holiday Inn Garden Court ℅498 0111/0333 ℻498 0222

CAR RENTAL

Each car hire company is located at Terminal 1 Domestic adjacent to the Arrivals Area on the ground floor of the short-stay car park; Terminal 1 International Arrivals Area; Terminal 2 adjacent to the Arrivals Area on the ground floor of the multi-storey car park.
Avis ℅436 2020
Alamo ℅489 8857/8858
Budget ℅489 5749
Eurodollar ℅499 3320
EuropCar InterRent ℅499 2200
Hertz Terminal 1 ℅437 8208; Terminal 2 ℅490 8134

CAR PARKING

Long-stay ⌀GBP4.10 per day
Short-stay ⌀GBP1.00 up to 30 min; GBP1.40 up to 1 hr; staggered rate up to GBP16.00 per day
℅489 3723

TAXIS AND CHAUFFEUR-DRIVEN CARS

Taxis
Arrivals Area of each terminal City centre ⊃30 min ⌀GBP12–15

Chauffeur-driven Cars
Airport Executive Cars ℅499 3322

PUBLIC TRANSPORT

Airport to airport
London-Gatwick Airport 🚌Flightlink Services 212 ℅0990 757747.
London-Heathrow Airport 🚌Flightlink Services 212 ℅0990 757747.
Birmingham Airport 🚌Flightlink Services 212 ℅0990 757747.

City & suburbs
Manchester city centre (Piccadilly rail stn) 🚌 »10–15 min ⊃15–20 min ⌀GBP2.45 ℅0345 48 49 50

Other towns and cities
Birmingham 🚌Flightlink 211/212 ℅ National Express 325 »Every 1–2 hr 0020–2020 ⊃2 hr ℅(0990) 808080/(0990) 757747
Buxton 🚌Trent: 198/199 »Approx. every 30 min ⊕0610–1915 and 2215 ⊃1 hr 30 min. For information ℅01298 23098
Chester 🚌Starline: X3 »Approx. 2 hr ⊕0749–2019 Mon–Sat ℅945 0055
Crewe 🚆North-West Regional Railways »Approx. 1 per hr ⊕0652–0136 ⊃25 min
Leeds 🚆Regional Railways North East »1 per hr ⊕0128–2328 daily ⊃1 hr 30 min ℅0345 484950
Liverpool 🚌National Express »Approx. 6 daily 0420–2120 ⊃50 min ℅0990 808080
Liverpool 🚆North Western »Approx.

℅ Phone no. ℻ Fax no. ⊕ Hours of opening/operation » Frequency of service ⊃ Journey time ⌀ Cost/one-way fare

Hourly 0715–2259 ⏱1hr 40 min ✆0345 484950
London 🚌 National Express 540 »4 per day ⏰0805, 1305, 1805, 0025 ⏱3 hr 30 min ⊘GBP19.50.
Stockport 🚌 Trent 198/199 »30 min ⏰0610–1915 and 2215 ⏱15 min

Sheffield 🚆 Regional Railways North-East »Approx. every hourly ⏰0155–2350 ⏱1 hr 25 min ✆(0345) 484950

Regional Air Connections

Belfast ✈ »Several per day ⏱1 hr

Cardiff ✈ »Twice daily ⏱55 min
Dublin ✈ »Several per day ⏱50 min
Edinburgh ✈ »Several per day ⏱1 hr
Glasgow ✈ »Several per day ⏱1 hr
Isle of Man ✈ »Several per day ⏱40 min
London ✈ »Several per day ⏱55 min
Newcastle ✈ »Twice daily ⏱45 min
Norwich ✈ »Twice daily ⏱50 min
Southampton ✈ »Several per day ⏱1 hr

MANILA — MNL
Philippines (see page 32)

National ✆ code: 63
Area ✆ code: 02
Local time: Winter GMT+8, Summer GMT+8
Ninoy Aquino International Airport, Metro Manila, Philippines ✆ 832 1961; 832 1962/9
Location: 12 km/ 7 miles S of Manila

Terminals and Transfers

Terminals
Main Terminal Airlines: All airlines.
Layout: Departure Area, Upper Level; Arrival Area, Lower Level

Minimum transfer times
International: 1–2 hr **Domestic:** 45 min

Information

Flight enquiries
Airport ✆832 1961
Air France ✆831 2226; 832 3015 Air Niugini ✆831 4738 Alitalia ✆804 0767 Asiana Airlines ✆891 6126 British Airways ✆831 7131 Cathay Pacific ✆831 1492; 832 1412 China Airlines ✆832 3008 China Southern Airlines ✆832 1961; local 3593 Egyptair ✆831 0661 Emirates ✆832 5350 Eva Air ✆831 0661; 831 4009 Garuda Indonesian Airlines ✆862 458; 818 1737 Gulf Air ✆831 9655 Japan Airlines ✆831 0718 KLM ✆832 1756; 831 2295 Korean Airlines ✆832 5974; 831 3729 Kuwait Airways ✆831 3664; 831 3662 Lufthansa ✆831 2927 Malaysian Airlines ✆831 0709 Northwest Airlines ✆831 4817 Pakistan International Airlines ✆832 2973 Philippine Airlines ✆833 9923 Qantas ✆832 2978 Royal Brunei Airlines ✆817 1631; 817 1632 Saudia ✆833 2753; 833 2868 Singapore Airlines ✆831 1793 Swissair ✆834 0849 Thai Airways ✆832 5349 United Airlines ✆832 2984 Vietnam Airlines ✆816 4865; 816 4866

Information and help desks
Information Desk Main Terminal Arrival and Departure Lobbies ✆833 5998; 832 1961 Airport information.
Tourist Information Desk Main Terminal Immediately on exit from Immigration, Lower Level ⏰ Tourist information

Emergencies

Medical Main Terminal Apron Level and Arrival (Lower Level) ⏰24 hr

Airport Facilities

Money
Bank Main Terminal Arrival and Departure ⏰All flight times.

Food and drink
Restaurant Main Terminal Arrival, Lower Level
Café/light meals Main Terminal Arrival, Lower Level

Communications
Post office Main Terminal Arrival (Lower Level) extension area ⏰24 hr Mon–Fri; 0800–2000 Sat

Shopping
Duty free, arrival Main Terminal Arrival (Lower Level)
Duty free, departure Main Terminal Departure (upper level)

Luggage
Trolleys/carts Main Terminal Arrivals (Lower Level) outside immigration exit ⊘PHP30
Porters Main Terminal Arrivals Lobby (Lower Level) ⊘Free

✈ Air 🚆 Rail 🚌 Bus 🚐 Limousine 🚇 Metro/subway 🚋 Tram 🚁 Helicopter ⛴ Water transport • For map symbols, see p. 9

MANILA • MELBOURNE   SECTION TWO • AIRPORT DIRECTORY

DISABLED TRAVELLERS
Main Terminal Adapted toilets; Lifts; Personal assistance

SMOKING POLICY
Main Terminal No-smoking throughout

SPECIAL PASSENGER LOUNGES
Cathay Pacific Airways Club Manila Main Terminal
Lufthansa Senator Lounge Main Terminal
Malaysian Airlines Golden Lounge Main Terminal
Philippine Airlines Mabuhay and Sampaguita Lounges Main Terminal
Qantas Airways Captain's Lounge Main Terminal
Singapore Airlines Silver Kris Lounge Main Terminal
Thai Airways Royal Orchid Lounge Main Terminal

CONFERENCE AND BUSINESS FACILITIES
Airport Authority Conference Room/VIP Lounge.

AIRPORT HOTELS
Mercure Philippine Village Airport Hotel

CAR RENTAL
Avis Main Terminal
Hertz Main Terminal
Nissan Main Terminal

CAR PARKING
Short-stay In front of terminal 650 spaces

TAXIS AND CHAUFFEUR-DRIVEN CARS

Taxis
Exit left from Arrival lobby City centre ⊃Approx 20 min ⊘Pre-paid at Arrival

PUBLIC TRANSPORT
City & suburbs
Pasay City, Makati City, Manila, Mandaluyong City, Pasig City, Quezon City and Caloocan City 🚌Public utility bus ⊃Approx 30 min

REGIONAL AIR CONNECTIONS
Baguio ✈ »At least daily ⊃40–50 min
Caticlan ✈ »At least daily ⊃1 hr
Cebu ✈ »At least daily ⊃1 hr
Iloilo ✈ »At least daily ⊃1 hr
Kalibo ✈ »Several per day ⊃55 min

TRAVELLER'S NOTES
The airport is particularly security-conscious: expect to be pretty thoroughly examined. Taxi fares are comparatively low.

186

MELBOURNE   MEL
Australia (see page 14)

National ✆ code: 61
Area ✆ code: 03
Local time: Winter GMT+11, Summer GMT+10
Melbourne Airport, Locked Bag 116, Tullamarine Vic 3043, Australia
✆9297 1600
🖷9297 1886
WWW site: www.melair.com.au
Location: 20 km/12 miles NW of Melbourne

TERMINALS AND TRANSFERS
Terminals
International Terminal Airlines: All international flights. Layout: First Floor, Departures; Ground Floor, Arrivals
Domestic Terminal Airlines: All domestic flights.

Minimum transfer times
International: 90 min **Domestic:** 30 min

INFORMATION
Flight enquiries
Airport ✆9297 1600

Information and help desks
Information Desk International Terminal, first floor ✆9297 1600 Airport information.
Tourist Information Desk International Terminal, ground floor ✆9297 1805 🖷9297 1051 call flight times Tourist information; Hotel reservations

EMERGENCIES
Medical First floor, International Terminal ✆000 for emergencies
Lost Property Domestic Terminal Baggage claim desk
Lost Property International Terminal Information desk, ground floor

AIRPORT FACILITIES
Money
Bank International Terminal ⊙All international flight times
Bureau de change Thomas Cook Bureau de Change located throughout the International Terminal ✆9335 5455
ATM International Terminal, departures level

Food and drink
Restaurant International Terminal, first floor ⊙0600–2400
Café/light meals International Terminal, first floor ⊙24 hr Sat–Sun; extended hrs Mon–Fri
Bar International Terminal, first floor

✆ Phone no. 🖷 Fax no. ⊙ Hours of opening/operation » Frequency of service ⊃ Journey time ⊘ Cost/one-way fare

✈✈ SECTION TWO • AIRPORT DIRECTORY   MELBOURNE • MEXICO

Communications
Post office International Terminal, first floor
Fax Service Throughout the airport
E-Mail Sites Throughout the airport

Shopping
Duty free, departure International Terminal, first floor
Duty free, arrivals International Terminal, ground floor, before baggage reclaim.
Shopping Mall International Terminal, Departure Lounge

Luggage
Lockers International Terminal ⓒ24 hr

DISABLED TRAVELLERS
International Terminal Adapted toilets; Lifts; Special car parking; Phones at wheelchair height
Domestic Terminal Adapted toilets; Lifts; Special car parking; Phones at wheelchair height

SPECIAL PASSENGER LOUNGES
British Airways Executive Club International Terminal
Cathay Pacific Airways Marco Polo Club International Terminal
Qantas Airways Captain's Lounge International Terminal
Singapore Airlines Silver Kris Room International Terminal

CONFERENCE AND BUSINESS FACILITIES
Melbourne Airport Travelodge ⓒ9338 2322

AIRPORT HOTELS
Melbourne Airport Travelodge ⓒ9338 2322

CAR RENTAL
Avis International Terminal, ground floor ⓒ9338 1800
Budget International Terminal, ground floor ⓒ9338 6955
Hertz International Terminal, ground floor ⓒ9338 4044
Thrifty International Terminal, ground floor ⓒ9330 1522

CAR PARKING
Long-stay ⌀AUD7 per day, AUD42 per week
Off-airport Tullamarine Jetport Security Parking
Short-stay 1800 spaces ⌀AUD2 per hr ⓒ9338 8398

TAXIS AND CHAUFFEUR-DRIVEN CARS
Taxis
City centre ➲30 min ⌀AUD25–30

PUBLIC TRANSPORT
City & suburbs
Melbourne city centre (Franklin Street) 🚌Skybus »30 min ➲30 min ⌀AUD9 ⓒ9335 3066

REGIONAL AIR CONNECTIONS
Adelaide, SA ✈ »Several per day ➲45 min
Albury, NS ✈ »Several per day ➲45 min
Canberra, ACT ✈ »Several per day ➲55 min
King Island, TS ✈ »At least daily ➲45 min
Launceston, TS ✈ »Several per day ➲55 min
Portland, VIC ✈ »Several per day ➲50–55 min

MEXICO CITY   MEX
Mexico (see page 29)

National ⓒ code: 52
Area ⓒ code: 05
Local time: Winter GMT-6, Summer GMT-6
Mexico City-Benito Juarez International Airport, Mexico City, Mexico
ⓒ 571 4545; 571 4941; 571 6396
Location: 7 km/4 miles E of Mexico City

TERMINALS AND TRANSFERS
Terminals
Terminal 1 Airlines: All domestic flights. Layout: Two Floors
Terminal 2 Airlines: All international flights.

Minimum transfer times
International: 1 hr 30 Domestic: 45 min

INFORMATION
Information and help desks
Hotel Association Office Terminal 2 Baggage Claim Area, *Hotel booking Tourist information*
Visitor Information Centre Terminal 2 ⓒ784 2040; 571 3469 *Airport, Hotel booking Tourist information*

AIRPORT FACILITIES
Money
Bureau de change Terminal 2 throughout ⓒ24 hr

Food and drink
Bar Terminal 2 throughout ⓒ24 hr
Café/light meals Terminal 2 throughout ⓒ24 hr
Restaurant Terminal 2

Communications
Post office Terminal 2 ⓒ0900–1700

Shopping
Shopping mall Terminal 2
Duty free, departure Terminal 2 Departure Hall
Florist Terminal 2 Departure Hall
Pharmacy Terminal 2 Departure Hall

Luggage
Lockers Terminal 2 ⓒ24 hr ⌀USD1.50

SPECIAL PASSENGER LOUNGES
Amex Lounge Terminal 2 *American Express card holders*
Aeromexico Lounge Terminal 2

✈ Air 🚂 Rail 🚌 Bus 🚗 Limousine Ⓜ Metro/subway 🚋 Tram 🚁 Helicopter ⛴ Water transport • For map symbols, see p. 9

MEXICO

SECTION TWO • AIRPORT DIRECTORY

Air France Lounge Terminal 2
Japan Airlines Lounge Terminal 2
Mexicana Lounge Terminal 2
Varig Brazilian Lounge Terminal 2

CONFERENCE AND BUSINESS FACILITIES

Conference rooms

AIRPORT HOTELS

Fiesta Americana ⓟ762 0199 ⓕ785 1034
Holiday Inn ⓟ(212) 949 7250

CAR RENTAL

Arrendadora Metro. Terminal 2
Autos Alfil Terminal 2
AVA Terminal 2
Avis Terminal 2
Budget Terminal 2
Econo Rent a Car Terminal 2
Promociones Pegaso Terminal 2

TAXIS AND CHAUFFEUR-DRIVEN CARS

Taxis
City centre ⌀USD10

PUBLIC TRANSPORT

City & suburbs
Mexico City centre 🚇 STC Metro: Line 5. ⓘ0600–2400 Mon–Fri; 0600–2030 Sat; 0700–2030 Sun, Pub Hol. »4–8 min ⌀approx. MXN0.70 *From Terminal Aerea stn at the airport, which is some way on foot from the international terminal.*

REGIONAL AIR CONNECTIONS

Acapulco ✈ »Several per day ⟳50 min
Aguascalientes ✈ »Several per day ⟳55–60 min
Culiacan ✈ »Several per day ⟳45–50 min
Guatemala City ✈ »At least daily ⟳45–55 min
Ixtapa/Zihuatanejo ✈ »Several per day ⟳50–55 min
Leon/Guanajuato ✈ »Several per day ⟳50 min
Mazatlan ✈ »Several per day ⟳25–35 min
Minatitlan ✈ »Several per day ⟳60–65 min
Morelia ✈ »Several per day ⟳50–55 min
Oaxaca ✈ »Several per day ⟳50–55 min
Poza Rica ✈ »Several per week ⟳50 min
Puebla ✈ »Several per week ⟳35 min
Puerto Escondido ✈ »At least daily ⟳55–60 min
Queretaro ✈ »Several per week ⟳50 min
San Jose Cabo ✈ »At least daily ⟳1 hr
San Luis Potosi ✈ »Several times per day ⟳45–75 min
San Pedro Sula ✈ »Several per week ⟳1 hr
Tampico ✈ »Several per day ⟳55 min
Tepic ✈ »Several per day ⟳15 min
Veracruz ✈ »Several per day ⟳50 min
Zacatecas ✈ »Several per day ⟳60–65 min

TRAVELLER'S NOTES

Purchase taxi-coupons from the booth at the airport; ignore touts offering private transport. There is a departure tax both on international and some domestic flights.

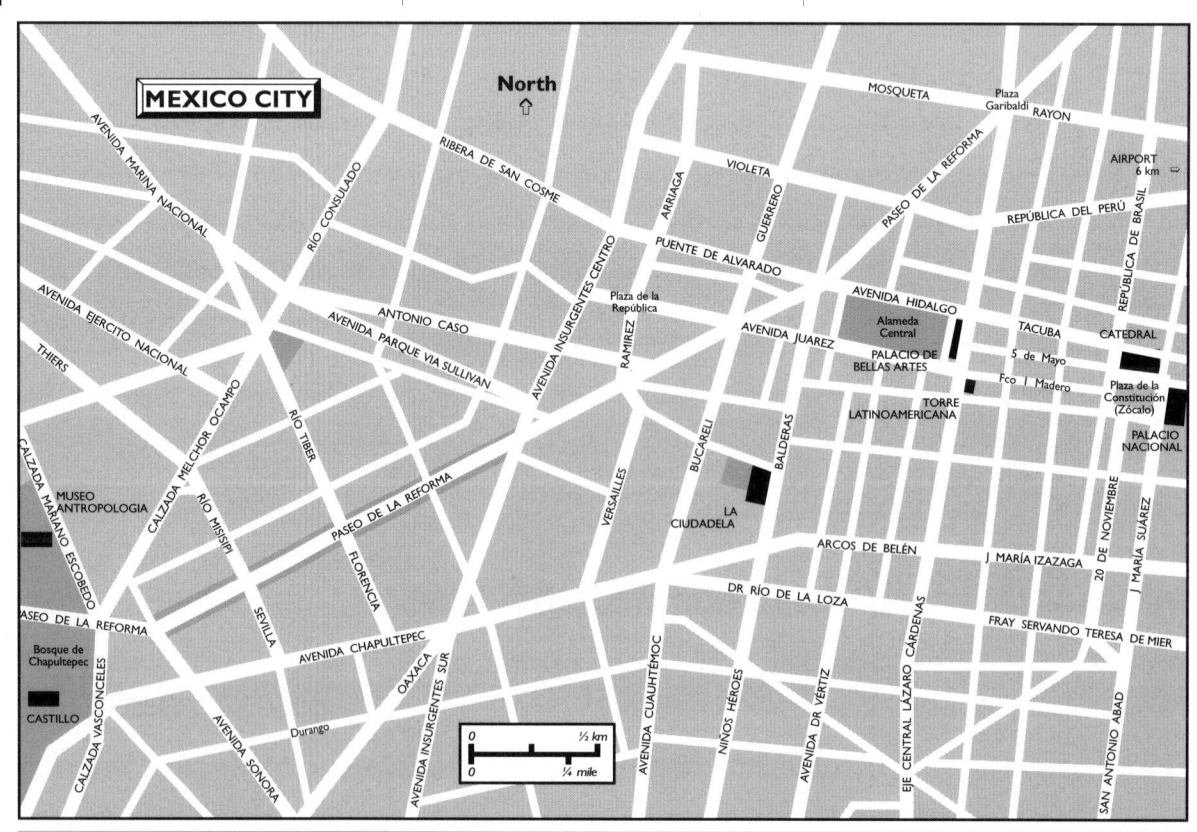

188

ⓟ Phone no. ⓕ Fax no. ⓘ Hours of opening/operation » Frequency of service ⟳ Journey time ⌀ Cost/one-way fare

Miami   MIA

USA (see page 41)

National ✆ code: 1
Area ✆ code: 305
Local time: Winter GMT-5, Summer GMT-4
Miami International Airport, PO Box 592075, Miami, FL 33159, USA
✆876 7000
📠876 0819
WWW site: http://www.miami-airport.com/
Location: 11 km/7 miles NW of Miami

Terminals and Transfers

Terminals
Main Terminal Airlines: All airlines. Layout: Level 1 (Arrivals, baggage claim, car rental, ground transportation); Level 2 (Departures, Concourse A (Gates A3–A18), B (Gates B1–B15), C (Gates C1–C15), D (Gates D1–D20), E (International Gates E1–E35), F (Gates F1–F23), G (Gates G1–G19), H (Gates H1–H18); Level 3 (Moving Walkways)

Minimum transfer times
International: 1 hr 30 min Domestic: 1 hr

Transfer between terminals
Bus Q Frequent; Main Terminal and Commuter Satellite ⌀Free

Information

Flight enquiries
Avianca Colombian Airlines ✆883 5151 BWIA International ✆371 2942 Continental Airlines ✆871 1400 Delta Airlines ✆448 7000 SAETA ✆477 3947 Eucatoriana ✆372 1918 Guyana Airways ✆871 8480 Airways International ✆526 2000 Cayman Airways ✆266 4141 Lan Chile ✆670 9999 Lloyd Aero Boliviano ✆374 4600 ALM Antillean Airlines ✆477 0955 LTU International Airways ✆530 2208 Air Atlantic Dominica ✆592 5795 Aero Costa Rica ✆888 2727 Zuliana De Aviacion ✆597 8780 Aeroperu ✆448 1947 Surinam Airways ✆262 9792 Aeroflot ✆577 8500 Sun Country ✆754 3255 Transbrasil ✆591 8322 TWA ✆371 7471 Air Europa ✆372 8880 Servivensa ✆381 8001 Avensa ✆381 8001 Aces ✆265 1272 Halisa ✆477 2400

Information and help desks
Tourist/Information Center Main Terminal Level 2, Concourse E (across from the Hotel) ✆876 7579 ⏱24 hr (Concourse E) Airport information, Tourist information

Emergencies

Police Main Terminal Level 1, Parking Garage 2 ✆876 7373
Lost Property Main Terminal Level 2, Concourse E ✆876 7377 ⏱1000–1800 Mon–Sat; 0900–1700 Sun

Airport Facilities

Money
ATM Main Terminal Level 2, between Concourse B and C
ATM Main Terminal Level 2, between Concourse G and H
Bank Main Terminal Level 4, Concourse B ⏱ Mon–Fri
Bank Main Terminal Level 2, Concourse C
Bureau de change Main Terminal throughout ⏱24 hr (Concourse E)

Food and drink
Bar Main Terminal throughout
Café/light meals Main Terminal throughout
Restaurant Main Terminal throughout

Communications
Post box Main Terminal throughout
Post office Main Terminal Level 4, Concourse B
Fax service Main Terminal Level 2, throughout

Shopping
Duty free, departure Main Terminal throughout ⏱24 hr (Concourse E)
Gift Shop Main Terminal throughout
News, Stationery & Books Main Terminal Level 2, throughout
Hairdresser Main Terminal Level 2, Concourse E
Pharmacy Main Terminal Level 2, Concourse F ⏱24 hr

Luggage
Left luggage counter Main Terminal Level 2, Concourse B, Level 1 Concourse G ⏱24 hr (0800–2100 Concourse B)⌀USD4 day
Lockers Main Terminal throughout ⏱24 hr ⌀USD4 per day

Disabled Travellers

Main Terminal Adapted toilets; Lifts Special car parking Level 3 of all parking garages; Phones at wheelchair height; Phones adapted for the deaf Concourse C, E (Information)

Smoking Policy

Main Terminal No-smoking throughout

Special Passenger Lounges

American Airlines Admirals Club Main Terminal Concourse D
Delta Airlines Crown Room Main Terminal Concourse H
United Airlines Red Carpet Club Main Terminal Concourse F

Conference and Business Facilities

Airport Executive Conference Center, Miami International Airport Hotel Main Terminal Concourse E ✆871 4100

Airport Hotels

Miami International Airport ✆871 4100 📠871 0800 260

Car Rental

Avis Main Terminal Level 1 ✆637 4900
Budget Main Terminal Level 1 ✆871 3053
Dollar Main Terminal Level 1 ✆887 6000
Hertz Main Terminal Level 1 ✆871 0300
National Main Terminal Level 1 ✆638 1026
Value Main Terminal Level 1 ✆871 6760

Car Parking

Long-stay Centre of airport 6158 spaces ⌀USD3 per hr, USD8 per day (max)
Short-stay Centre of airport 200 spaces

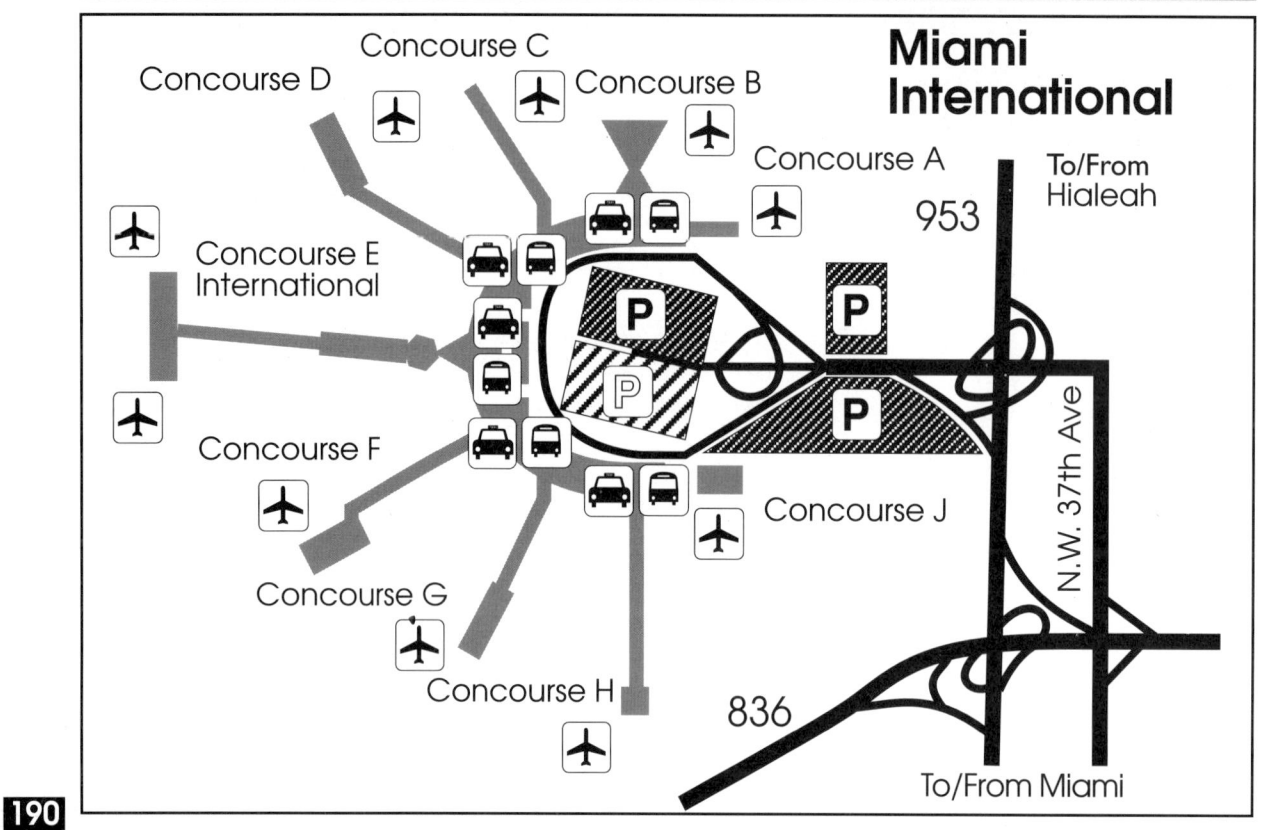

MIAMI — SECTION TWO • AIRPORT DIRECTORY

Miami International

- Concourse D
- Concourse C
- Concourse B
- Concourse A
- Concourse E International
- Concourse F
- Concourse G
- Concourse H
- Concourse J

To/From Hialeah — 953
N.W. 37th Ave
836 — To/From Miami

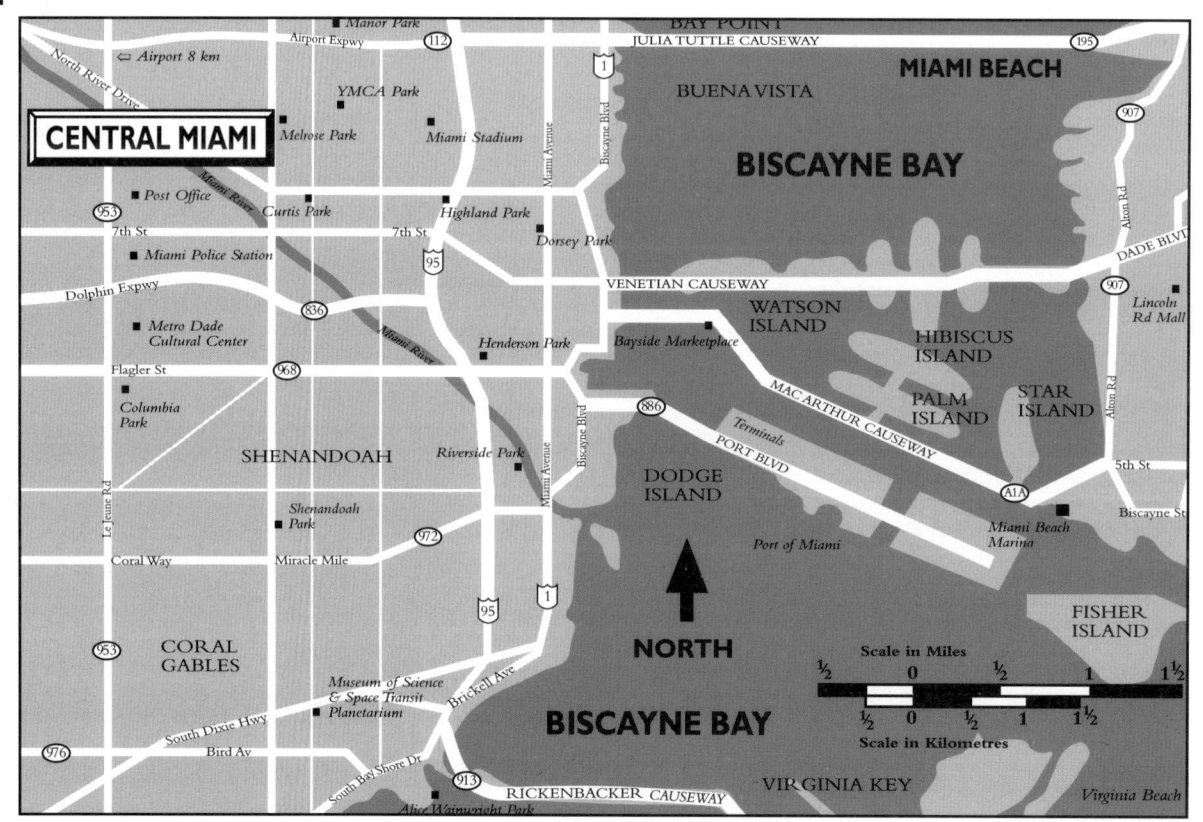

CENTRAL MIAMI

Manor Park, Airport Expwy, 112, Julia Tuttle Causeway, 1, 195, MIAMI BEACH, 907, BAY POINT, BUENA VISTA, BISCAYNE BAY, North River Drive, Airport 8 km, YMCA Park, Melrose Park, Miami Stadium, Miami Avenue, Biscayne Blvd, 953, Post Office, Miami River, Curtis Park, Highland Park, 7th St, 7th St, Dorsey Park, Dade Blvd, Miami Police Station, 95, 907, Dolphin Expwy, Venetian Causeway, Alton Rd, Lincoln Rd Mall, 836, Metro Dade Cultural Center, Henderson Park, Watson Island, Hibiscus Island, Bayside Marketplace, Flagler St, 968, Palm Island, Star Island, Columbia Park, Terminals, MacArthur Causeway, 5th St, A1A, SHENANDOAH, Riverside Park, Biscayne Blvd, 886, Port Blvd, Miami Beach Marina, Biscayne St, Shenandoah Park, Dodge Island, 972, Coral Way, Miracle Mile, Port of Miami, FISHER ISLAND, 953, CORAL GABLES, 95, 1, NORTH, Museum of Science & Space Transit Planetarium, Brickell Ave, Scale in Miles, Scale in Kilometres, 976, South Dixie Hwy, Bird Av, South Bay Shore Dr, 913, Alice Wainwright Park, RICKENBACKER CAUSEWAY, VIRGINIA KEY, Virginia Beach, BISCAYNE BAY

ⓒ Phone no. ⓕ Fax no. ⓗ Hours of opening/operation ≫ Frequency of service ↪ Journey time ◊ Cost/one-way fare

⌀USD2 per 30 min, USD24 per day (max)

TAXIS AND CHAUFFEUR-DRIVEN CARS

Taxis
Outside Level 1 of Main Terminal City centre ➲20 min ⌀USD16

PUBLIC TRANSPORT

City & suburbs
Miami (city centre) 🚌Greyhound ≫3 day ⏱1140; 1525; 2140 ➲15 min. For Miami Bayside Bus Station
Miami city centre 🚌Metrobus: 7 ≫40 min ⏱0525–2105 ➲35 min ⌀USD1.25.
Miami city centre 🚘 Over 30 companies at airport.
Miami (Tri-Rail Station) 🚆Tri-Rail Shuttle ≫1-2 hr ⏱0505–0005 ➲15–20 min ⌀Free. For commuter rail service to Hialeah Metro Rail, Ft Lauderdale, Palm Beach and West Palm Beach

Other towns and cities
Florida Keys FL 🚌Airporter 852 3413.
Key West FL 🚌Greyhound ≫3 per day ⏱0710; 1210; 1955 ➲4 hr 45 min. For Homestead, Key Largo, Islamorada, Marathon, Marathon Airport and Ramrod Key FL

REGIONAL AIR CONNECTIONS

Bimini ✈ ≫Several per day ➲30 min
Fort Lauderdale FL ✈ ≫Several per day ➲30 min
Fort Myers FL ✈ ≫Several per day ➲40 min
Freeport ✈ ≫Several per day ➲45 min
Key West FL ✈ ≫Several per day ➲45 min
Kingston ✈ ≫Several per day ➲45 min
Marathon FL ✈ ≫At least daily ➲40 min
Montego Bay ✈ ≫Several per day ➲45 min
Naples FL ✈ ≫Several per day ➲40 min
Nassau ✈ ≫Several per day ➲1 hr
Sarasota/Bradenton FL ✈ ≫Several per day ➲1 hr
West Palm Beach FL ✈ ≫Several per day ➲35 min

TRAVELLER'S NOTES

Miami has become notorious in Europe because of well-publicised incidents of car hi-jacking involving visitors. As a result, the city has marked preferred routes to downtown from the airport with blue signs carrying an orange sun. Hire cars no longer have identifying markings.

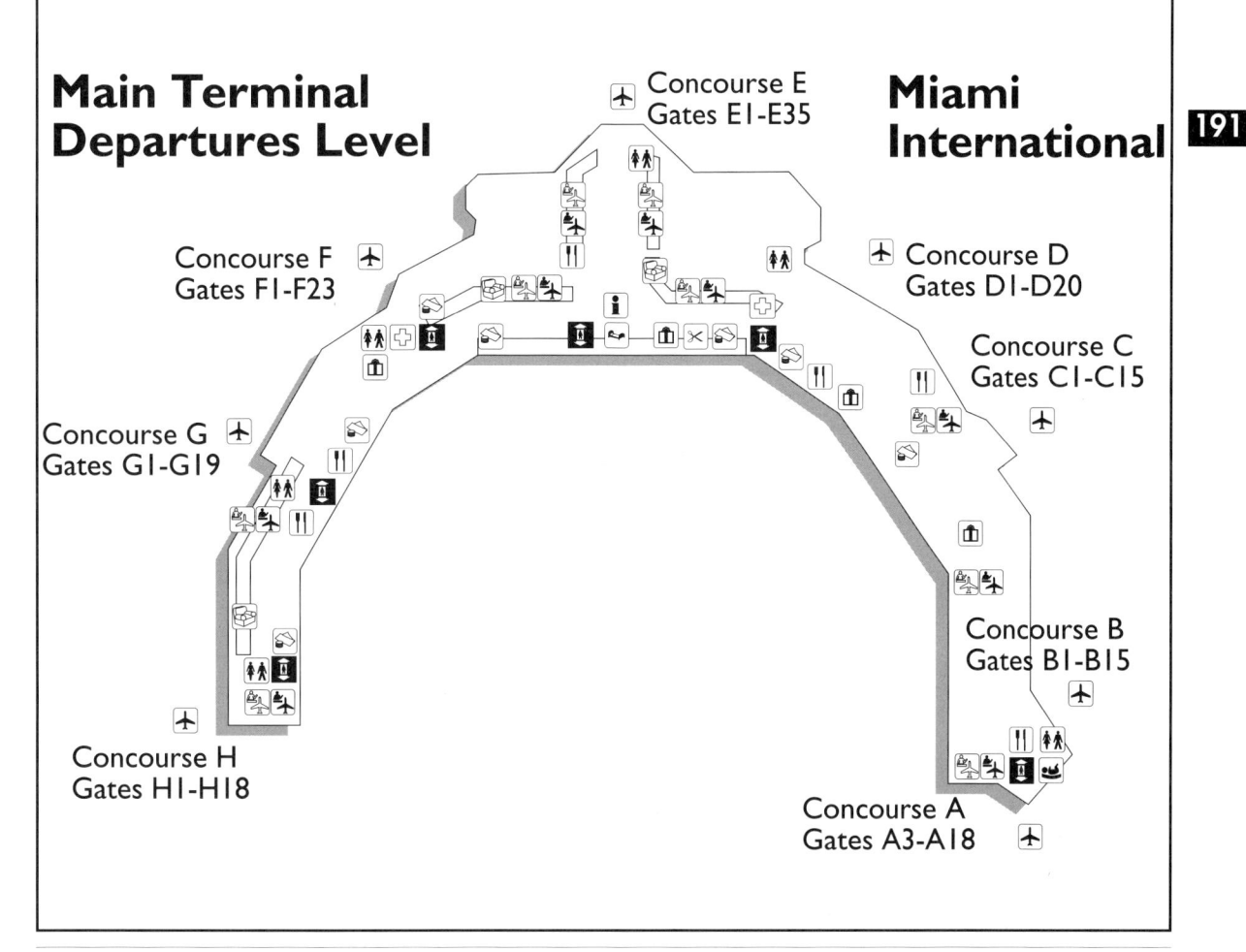

Main Terminal Departures Level

Miami International

- Concourse E — Gates E1-E35
- Concourse F — Gates F1-F23
- Concourse D — Gates D1-D20
- Concourse C — Gates C1-C15
- Concourse G — Gates G1-G19
- Concourse B — Gates B1-B15
- Concourse H — Gates H1-H18
- Concourse A — Gates A3-A18

✈ Air 🚆 Rail 🚌 Bus 🚘 Limousine 🚇 Metro/subway 🚋 Tram 🚁 Helicopter ⛴ Water transport • For map symbols, see p. 9

MILAN-LINATE | SECTION TWO • AIRPORT DIRECTORY

MILAN-LINATE (MILANO)   LIN
Italy (see page 27)

National ☏ code: 39
Area ☏ code: 02
Local time: Winter GMT+1, Summer GMT+2
Milan-Linate Airport, Societa Esercizi Aeroportuali, Direzione Generale, 20090 Milano Linate, Italy
☏74852200
℻74852010
Location: 8 km/5 miles E of Milan

TERMINALS AND TRANSFERS

Terminals
Main Terminal Airlines: All airlines. Layout: Ground Floor, Arrival; First Floor, Departure

Minimum transfer times
International: 40–45 min **Domestic:** 40 min

INFORMATION

Flight enquiries
Airport ☏28106324 (Intnatl Dep); 28106300 (Domestic Dep); 28106310 (Intnatl Arr); 28106282 (Domestic Arr)

Information and help desks
Help Desk Main Terminal Arrival Area ⏰0800–2000 Airport, Tourist information
Help Desk Main Terminal Departure Area ⏰0800–2000 Airport, Tourist information
Tourist Information Desk Main Terminal Arrival Area ⏰0800–2000 Tourist information

EMERGENCIES

Police Main Terminal Main Concourse ☏7384426
Medical Main Terminal Outside International Arrival Area ☏74852222
Lost Property Main Terminal Left luggage office ☏70124451 ⏰0800–1800

AIRPORT FACILITIES

Money
ATM Main Terminal Domestic Arrival ⏰24 hr
ATM Main Terminal Main Concourse ⏰24 hr
Bureau de change Main Terminal International Arrival ⏰0800–2100
Bureau de change Main Terminal International Departure ⏰0800–2100

Food and drink
Restaurant Main Terminal Second Floor ⏰1140–1530, 1830–2200 Mon–Fri; 1900–2230 Sat
Café/light meals Main Terminal Second Floor ⏰0930–2200
Café/light meals Main Terminal First Floor, Departure Lounge ⏰0930–2200
Bar Main Terminal International Departure Lounge
Bar Main Terminal International Arrival Lounge
Bar Main Terminal Domestic Arrival Lounge
Bar Main Terminal International Transfer Lounge
Bar Main Terminal Domestic Transfer Lounge

Communications
Post office Main Terminal Arrivals Area ⏰0815–1900

Shopping
Shopping mall Main Terminal First Floor, International Departure Area
Gift Shop Main Terminal First Floor, Domestic Transfer Area
Gift Shop Main Terminal First Floor, International Transfer Area
News, Stationery & Books Main Terminal First Floor, International Transfer Area
Pharmacy Main Terminal Domestic Arrival Area ⏰0800–2000 daily
News, Stationery & Books Main Terminal First Floor, International Departure Area
Shopping mall Main Terminal First Floor, International Transfer Area
Duty-free, departure Main Terminal First Floor, International Transfer Area
News, Stationery & Books Main Terminal First Floor, Domestic Transfer Area

Luggage
Left luggage counter Main Terminal Ground Floor Arrival Area (near post office)

DISABLED TRAVELLERS

Main Terminal Adapted toilets; Lifts; Phones at wheelchair height

SMOKING POLICY

Main Terminal Restricted only at the departure gates

SPECIAL PASSENGER LOUNGES

Air France Lounge Main Terminal First Floor
Alitalia Domestic VIP Lounge Main Terminal Ground Floor
Alitalia Lounge Main Terminal First Floor
British Airways Lounge Main Terminal Ground Floor
Lufthansa Lounge Main Terminal First Floor

CONFERENCE AND BUSINESS FACILITIES

Air Business Centre, Arrival Area ☏70200165 ℻70200189 ⏰ Telephones, Fax service, Photocopier, Secretarial service, Translation/Interpretation service. Conference Room ☏ 7383741/3

AIRPORT HOTELS

Novotel Milano Est Aeroporto Courtesy bus
Country Hotel Borromeo Courtesy bus

CAR RENTAL

Avis Main Terminal Arrival Area ☏717214
Budget Main Terminal Arrival Area ☏76110234
Eurodollar Main Terminal Arrival Area ☏70200268
EuropCar Main Terminal Arrival Area ☏76110258
Hertz Main Terminal Arrival Area ☏70200256
Maggiore Main Terminal Arrival Area ☏717210
Tirreno Main Terminal Arrival Area ☏70200238

☏ Phone no. ℻ Fax no. ⏰ Hours of opening/operation ≫ Frequency of service ➲ Journey time ⬦ Cost/one-way fare

✈✈ SECTION TWO • AIRPORT DIRECTORY   MILAN-LINATE

CAR PARKING

Short-stay 4643 spaces ⊘LIT5000 first hr; LIT7000 per 6 hr; LIT24000 per 24 hr

TAXIS AND CHAUFFEUR-DRIVEN CARS

Taxis
Outside International Arrival Area City centre ⊃15 min ⊘LIT20000

PUBLIC TRANSPORT

Airport to airport
Milan-Malpensa Airport 🚌Bus Air Pullman »4 daily ⊕0915, 1045, 1215, 1545 ⊃75 min ⊘LIT18000.

City & suburbs
Milan city centre (Piazza S. Babila) 🚌ATM Bus 73 »15 min ⊕0600–0057 ⊃25 min ⊘LIT1500.
Milan city centre (Stazione Centrale) 🚌 »0600–1900 ⊕30 min ⊃20 min ⊘LIT4500.

REGIONAL AIR CONNECTIONS

Bologna ✈ »Several per day ⊃45 min
Florence ✈ »At least daily ⊃55 min
London ✈ »At least daily ⊃55 min–1 hr
Munich ✈ »At least daily ⊃1 hr
Olbia ✈ »At least daily ⊃1 hr
Pisa ✈ »Several per day ⊃50 min
Strasbourg ✈ »At least daily ⊃55 min
Venice ✈ »Several per day ⊃55 min
Zürich ✈ »Several per day ⊃55 min

TRAVELLER'S NOTES

Airport planned to transfer most of its current traffic to Malpensa Airport during 1998. See notes on Malpensa.

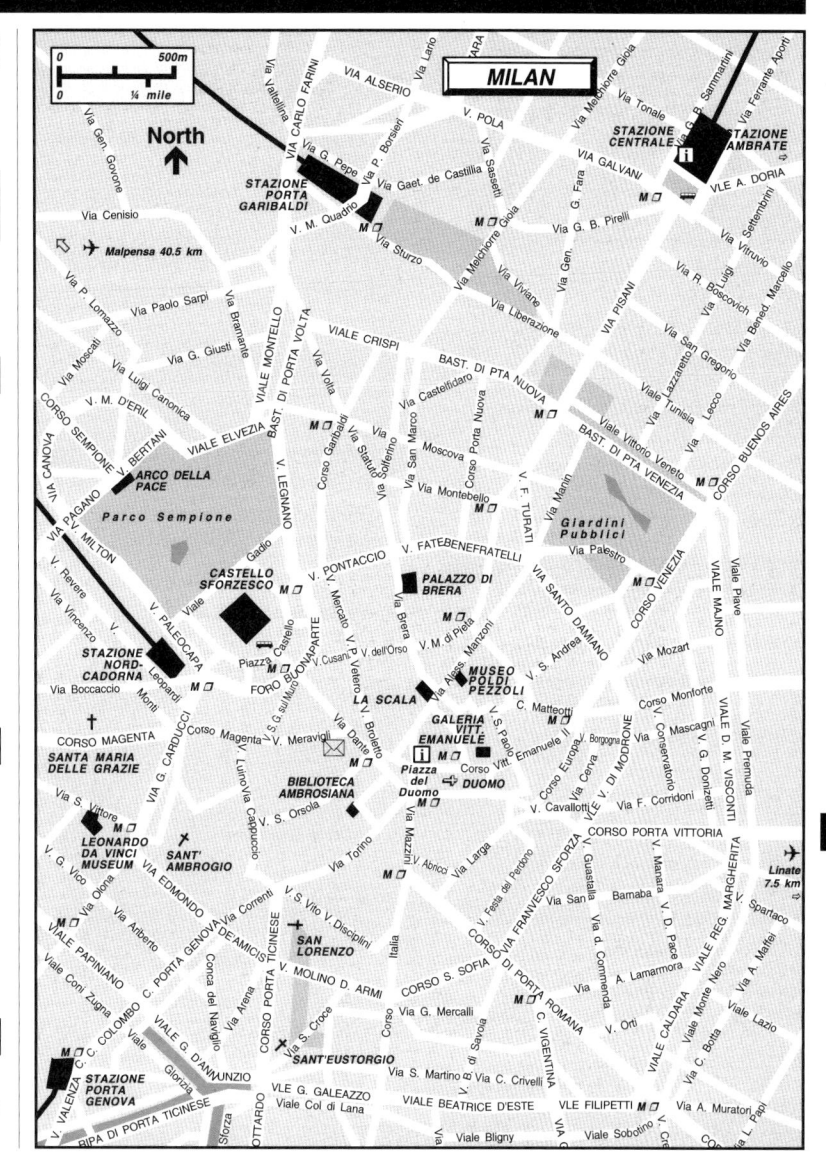

✈ Air 🚆 Rail 🚌 Bus 🚐 Limousine Ⓜ Metro/subway 🚋 Tram 🚁 Helicopter ⛴ Water transport • For map symbols, see p. 9

MILAN-MALPENSA (MILANO) — MXP

Italy (see page 27)

National ✆ code: 39
Area ✆ code: 02
Local time: Winter GMT+1, Summer GMT+2
Milan-Malpensa Airport, 21010 Malpensa Varese, Milano, Italy
✆74852200
📠74854010
Location: 45 km/29 miles NW of Milan

Terminals and Transfers

Terminals
Main Terminal Airlines: All airlines.

Layout: Departure and Arrival Areas are both on the Ground Floor in separate halls

Minimum transfer times
International: 50 min–1 hr **Domestic:** 40 min

Information

Flight enquiries
Airport ✆26800627 (Intnatl Dep); 26800606 (Domestic Dep); 26800619 (Intnatl Arr); 26800463 (Domestic Arr)
Information and help desks
Italiatour Desk Main Terminal Arrival Lounge ✆74854768 ⏱0900–1700 Hotel booking, Tourist information

Emergencies

Police Main Terminal Arrival Area ✆40099736
Medical Main Terminal Outside International Arrival Area ✆74854444
Lost Property Main Terminal ✆74854215

Airport Facilities

Money
Bureau de change Main Terminal Departure Area ⏱0830–1330, 1445–1545 Mon-Fri
Bureau de change Main Terminal Arrival Area ⏱0800–2000

Food and drink
Restaurant Main Terminal First floor ⏱1130–2200
Bar Main Terminal First Floor ⏱0830–1700
Bar Main Terminal International Departure Area
Bar Main Terminal Domestic Departure Area
Bar Main Terminal Arrival Area
Bar Main Terminal International transfer Area
Restaurant Main Terminal International transfer Area
Restaurant Main Terminal Ground floor

Communications
Post office Main Terminal ⏱0810–1810

Shopping
News, Stationery & Books Main Terminal Arrival Area
News, Stationery & Books Main Terminal Departure Area
Gift Shop Main Terminal International Transfer Area
Duty free, departure Main Terminal International Transfer Area
Pharmacy Main Terminal Ground floor, Departure Area ⏱0800–2000

Luggage
Left luggage counter Main Terminal Arrival Area ⏱0800–1800 💲ITL2850 per item

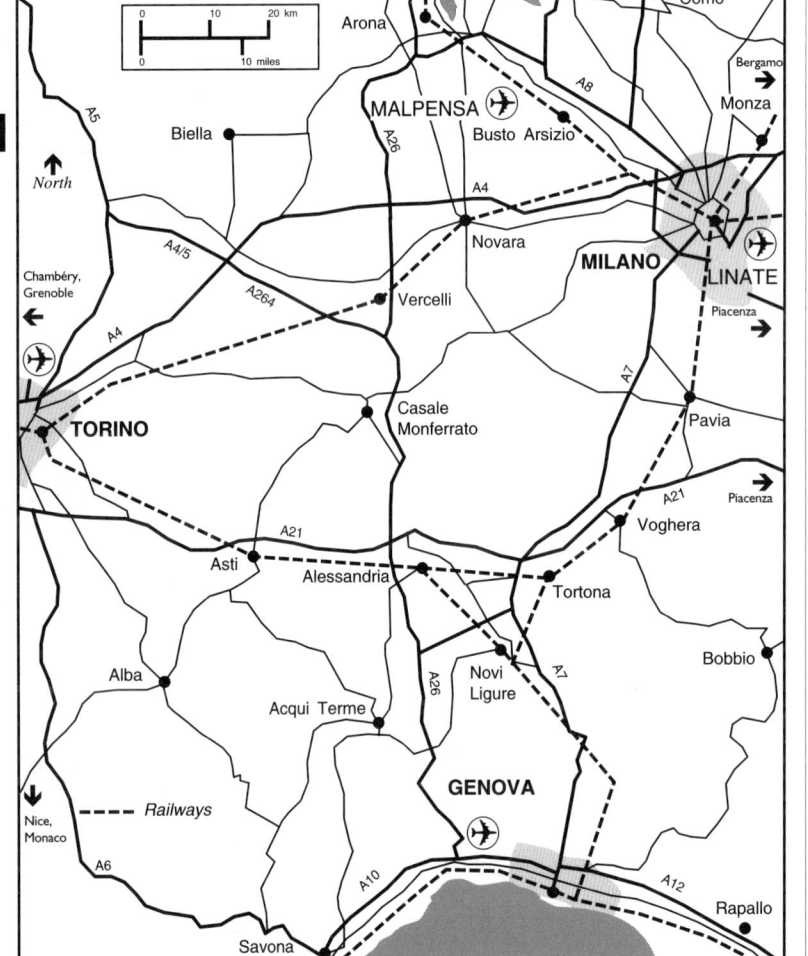

✆ Phone no. 📠 Fax no. ⏱ Hours of opening/operation ≫ Frequency of service ➲ Journey time 💲 Cost/one-way fare

Disabled Travellers

Main Terminal Adapted toilets; Lifts; Phones at wheelchair height

Smoking Policy

Main Terminal Smoking permitted everywhere except within the departure gates

Special Passenger Lounges

Le Cascate Lounge Main Terminal First floor
Puccini Lounge Main Terminal check-in area
Rossini Lounge Main Terminal Arrivals area
SEA Club First Class Lounge Main Terminal
Verdi Lounge Transit Hall

Airport Hotels

Airport Hotel

Car Rental

Hertz Main Terminal Arrival Area ✆40099000
Maggiore Main Terminal Arrival Area ✆40099330
Tirreno Main Terminal Arrival Area ✆40099387
AVIS Main Terminal Arrival Area ✆40099375
Budget Main Terminal Arrival Area ✆40099234
Eurodollar Main Terminal Arrival Area ✆40099481
EuropCar Main Terminal Arrival Area ✆40099351

Car Parking

LIT5000 per first 2 hr; LIT25000 per day; LIT35000 per 2 days; LIT40000 per 3 days

Taxis and Chauffeur-driven Cars

Taxis
Outside Arrival Area City centre ➔45 min

Public Transport

Airport to airport
Milan-Linate Airport Bus Malpensa Shuttle »4 daily 0945–1600 ➔75 min LIT18000.

City & suburbs
Lampugnano Bus Malpensa Shuttle »1 hr 0930–1900 ➔30 min LIT13000.
Milan city centre (Stazione Centrale) Bus Malpensa Shuttle »30 min 0800–2100 ➔1 hr LIT13000.

Regional Air Connections

Basel ✈ »At least daily ➔1 hr
Venice ✈ »Several per day ➔45 min

Traveller's Notes

A new airport, Malpensa 2000, is being constructed at this site and is planned to open during 1998.

MINNEAPOLIS/ST PAUL MSP 195

USA (see page 41)

National ✆ code: 1
Area ✆ code: 612
Local time: Winter GMT-6, Summer GMT-5
Minneapolis–St Paul International Airport, Charles A Lindbergh Terminal, Room 325, St Paul, MN 55111, USA
✆726 5555
📠726 5527
Internet e-mail: @macavsat.org
WWW site: http://www.macavsat.org/
Location: 16 km/10 miles S of Minneapolis; 12 km/7 miles SW of St Paul

Terminals and Transfers

Terminals
Lindbergh Terminal Airlines: All airlines (International departures). Layout: Ground Transportation Center (Car Rental, Ground Transportation, Parking Ramps); Baggage Level (Baggage Claim), Ticket Level (Departure, Gates) Concourses: Gold (Gates 1–19), Red (Gates 21–40), Blue (Gates 41–60) and Green (Gates 61–86)
Hubert H. Humphrey Terminal Airlines: All international flights (International arrivals). Layout: Gates 1–3
Regional Terminal Airlines: All other airlines. Layout: Gates 87–90

Minimum transfer times
International: 1 hr–1 hr 30 Domestic: 40–50 min

Transfer between terminals
Bus »10 min; Lindbergh and Hubert H Humphrey Terminals Free

Information

Flight enquiries
Continental Airlines ✆332 1471 Delta Airlines ✆339 7477 Northwest Airlines ✆726 1234 TWA ✆333 6543 United Airlines ✆339 3671

Information and help desks
Traveller's Assistance Lindbergh Terminal Ticket Level Door 3 ✆726 5500 Airport information, Tourist information
Travellers Assistance Lindbergh Terminal Ticket Level ✆726 5500 Airport information

Emergencies

Police All Terminals throughout ✆726 5577
Medical Lindbergh Terminal Baggage Level
Medical Hubert H. Humphrey Terminal International Arrival waiting area
Lost Property Lindbergh Terminal Baggage Level ✆726 5141

Airport Facilities

Money
ATM All Terminals throughout
Bank Main Lindbergh Terminal Ticket Level 0730–1800 Mon–Fri
Bureau de change Lindbergh Terminal

MINNEAPOLIS/ST PAUL

SECTION TWO • AIRPORT DIRECTORY

Ticket Level
Bureau de change Hubert H. Humphrey Terminal International Arrival waiting area

Food and drink
Bar Lindbergh Terminal throughout
Bar Hubert H. Humphrey Terminal Across from International Arrival
Café/light meals Lindbergh Terminal throughout
Café/light meals Hubert H. Humphrey Terminal Near Customs
Restaurant Lindbergh Terminal throughout
Restaurant Hubert H. Humphrey Terminal Near Customs

Communications
Post box All Terminals throughout

Shopping
Duty free, departure Lindbergh Terminal Ticket Level, Gold Concourse (across from Gate 4) ⓘ 0730–1930
Florist Lindbergh Terminal Ticket Level (near Red Concourse)
Gift Shop Lindbergh Terminal throughout
Gift Shop Hubert H. Humphrey Terminal International Arrival
Hairdresser Lindbergh Terminal Ticket Level

Luggage
Left luggage counter All Terminals Contact airlines
Lockers Lindbergh Terminal throughout
Trolleys/carts Lindbergh Terminal throughout
Trolleys/carts Hubert H. Humphrey Terminal throughout

DISABLED TRAVELLERS
All Terminals Adapted toilets; Lifts Special car parking; Phones at wheelchair height; Phones adapted for the deaf; Personal assistance Traveller's Assistance Lindbergh Terminal Ticket Level

SMOKING POLICY
All Terminals No-smoking throughout

SPECIAL PASSENGER LOUNGES
Delta Airlines Crown Room Lindbergh Terminal Ticket Level, Blue Concourse
Northwest Airlines World Club Lindbergh Terminal Ticket Level, Gold, Red and Green Concourses

CONFERENCE AND BUSINESS FACILITIES
Business Service Center, Lindbergh

Terminal (Ticket Level near Traveller's Assistance and near Gates 21 (Red Concourse) and 42 (Blue Concourse) Fax service, Photocopier

CAR RENTAL
Alamo Lindbergh Terminal Ground Transportation Center ⓒ 726 5323
Avis Lindbergh Terminal Ground Transportation Center ⓒ 726 5220
Budget Lindbergh Terminal Ground Transportation Center ⓒ 726 9258
Dollar Lindbergh Terminal Ground Transportation Center ⓒ 725 0838
Hertz Lindbergh Terminal Ground Transportation Center ⓒ 726 1600
National Lindbergh Terminal Ground Transportation Center ⓒ 726 5222

CAR PARKING
Long-Stay Humphrey Terminal Econo-Lot ⌀ USD1 per hr, USD6 per day (max) Free shuttle bus
Short-stay Lindbergh Terminal 400 spaces ⌀ USD1 per hr

TAXIS AND CHAUFFEUR-DRIVEN CARS
Taxis
Lindbergh Terminal Ground Transportation Center Minneapolis city centre ➲ 20 min ⌀ USD25
Lindbergh Terminal Ground Transportation Center St Paul city centre ➲ 15 min ⌀ USD14

PUBLIC TRANSPORT
City & suburbs
Minneapolis/St Paul metro Area Airport Express.
Minneapolis (Mall of America) 🚌 Jefferson Lines » 20 min ➲ 10 min.
Minneapolis city centre 🚌 MTC: 7 ➲ 30 min ⌀ USD0.85.
Minneapolis city centre 🚕 Over 20 companies at airport.
St Paul MN 🚌 MTC 15. 62.
St Paul MN 🚕 Premier Transportation 331 7433.

Other towns and cities
Alexandria MN 🚕 Twin City Passenger Service 762 1544.
For Ridgedale Center MN Sauk Center MN
Ames IA 🚌 Jefferson Lines » 2 per day ⓘ 1220; 1915 ➲ 5 hr.
Brainerd MN 🚕 Executive Express 253 2226.
Cannon Falls MN 🚌 Jefferson Lines » 2 per day ⓘ 0800; 1815 ➲ 45 min.
Decorah IA 🚌 Rochester Express.

Des Moines IA 🚌 Jefferson Lines » 2 per day ⓘ 1220; 1915 ➲ 5 hr 30 min.
For Northfield, Faribault, Owatonna, Albert Lee MN, Mason City and Ames IA Eau Claire WI lEau Claire Passenger Service (715) 835 0399.
For Hudson WI Baldwin WI Menomonie WI
La Crosse WI 🚌 Jefferson Lines » 2 per day ⓘ 0800; 1240 ➲ 3 hr 45 min.
For Winona MN
Mankato, MN 🚕 Mankato Land to Air » 4 per day ⓘ 1030; 1315; 1600; 1915 ➲ 1 hr 30 min ⌀ USD22. For St. Peter MN
New Ulm MN 🚕 New Ulm Mini-Bus (800) 642 5445.
Rochester MN 🚕 Rochester Direct 725 0303
Rochester MN 🚕 Rochester Express (800) 479 7824. For Decorah IA
Rochester MN 🚌 Jefferson Lines » 3 per day ⓘ 0800; 1240; 1815 ➲ 1 hr 45 min.
St Cloud MN 🚕 Executive Express 253 2226.
Tomah WI 🚌 Jefferson Lines » 1 per day ⓘ 1240 ➲ 4 hr 25 min.
Willmar MN 🚕 Executive Express 253 2226.
Zumbrota MN 🚌 Jefferson Lines » 2 per day ⓘ 0800; 1815 ➲ 1 hr 10 min.

REGIONAL AIR CONNECTIONS
Brainerd MN ✈ » Several per day ➲ 50 min
Des Moines IA ✈ » Several per day ➲ 1 hr
Duluth MN ✈ » Several per day ➲ 55 min
Eau Claire WI ✈ » Several per day ➲ 40 min
Fairmont MN ✈ » Several per week ➲ 45 min
Fargo ND ✈ » Several per day ➲ 1 hr
Grand Rapids MN ✈ » Several per day ➲ 1 hr
Ironwood MN ✈ » At least daily ➲ 55 min
La Crosse WI ✈ » Several per day ➲ 55 min
Madison WI ✈ » Several per day ➲ 1 hr
Mason City IA ✈ » Several per day ➲ 50 min
Rochester MN ✈ » Several per day ➲ 40 min
Saint Cloud MN ✈ » Several per day ➲ 45 min
Sioux Falls SD ✈ » Several per day ➲ 1 hr

TRAVELLER'S NOTES
If you intend to drive in the metro area, its size makes an unlimited mileage option advisable. A major attraction is the enormous Mall of America shopping complex.

ⓒ Phone no.   ⓕ Fax no.   ⓘ Hours of opening/operation   » Frequency of service   ➲ Journey time   ⌀ Cost/one-way fare

SECTION TWO • AIRPORT DIRECTORY   MONTRÉAL-DORVAL

MONTRÉAL-DORVAL
Canada (see page 18)

National ✆ code: 1
Area ✆ code: 514
Local time: Winter GMT-5,
Summer GMT-4
Montréal Mirabel International
Airport, 12655 Rue Commerce A4,
Montréal PQ, JN7 1E1, Canada ✆
633 3105
🖷476 3178
WWW site: http://www.admtl.com
Location: 22 km/14 miles W of
Montréal

TERMINALS AND TRANSFERS

Terminals
Main Terminal Airlines: All airlines.
Layout: Ground Floor (Arrivals, Baggage
Claim, Car Rental and Ground
Transportation), First Floor (Departures,
Domestic Finger (Gates 1–12),
Transborder Finger (Gates 14–24),
Aeroquai (Gates 27–46)

Minimum transfer times
International: 1 hr Domestic: 30 min

INFORMATION

Flight enquiries
Airport ✆633 3105 Aeroflot ✆288 2125
Aerolineas Argentinas ✆282 1078 Air
Alliance ✆393 3333 Air Alma ✆636 5889
Air Atlantic ✆847 2211 Air Canada ✆393
3333 Air France ✆847 1106 Air Inuit
✆633 6787 Air Nova ✆393 3333 Air
Ontario ✆393 3333 Air Saint-Pierre ✆847
2211 American Airlines ✆397 9635
British Airways ✆287 9161 Business
Express ✆337 5520 Canadian ✆847 2211
Canadien Regional ✆847 2211 Comair
✆337 5520 CSA Czech Airlines ✆844
4200 Delta Airlines ✆337 5520 El Al
Israel ✆875 8900 Inter Canadien ✆636
3890 KLM ✆939 4040 Olympic Airways
✆878 9691 Royal Air Maroc ✆285 1435
Royal Jordanian Airlines ✆288 1647
Swissair ✆879 9154

Information and help desks
Aeroports de Montréal Information Main
Terminal First Floor, across from main
elevators ✆633 3105
Airport information, Tourist information

Emergencies
Police ✆633 3354
Lost Property ✆633 3094

AIRPORT FACILITIES

Money
ATM Main Terminal throughout
Thomas Cook Bureau de change Main
Terminal First Floor, across from infor-
mation counter
Thomas Cook Bureau de change Main
Terminal Ground Floor, outside baggage
claim

Food and drink
Bar Main Terminal throughout
Café/light meals Main Terminal through-
out
Restaurant Main Terminal First Floor

Communications
Post box Main Terminal throughout

Shopping
Duty free, departure Main Terminal First
Floor
Gift Shop Main Terminal First Floor
News, Stationery & Books Main
Terminal First Floor

Luggage
Left luggage counter Main Terminal
Ground Floor

SPECIAL PASSENGER LOUNGES

Air Canada Maple Leaf Lounge Main
Terminal First Floor Domestic Finger,
between gates 3 and 4
Air France Salon Première Classe Lounge
Main Terminal up escalator from First
Floor
Canadian Airlines Empress Lounge Main
Terminal First Floor, across from Gates 1
and 2

CAR RENTAL

Alamo Main Terminal Ground Floor
✆633 1222
Avis Main Terminal Ground Floor ✆636
1902
Budget Main Terminal Ground Floor
✆636 0052
Hertz Main Terminal Ground Floor
✆636 9530
National Tilden Main Terminal Ground
Floor ✆636 9030
Thrifty Main Terminal Ground Floor
✆631 5567

CAR PARKING

Long-stay Airport Perimeter 🚌Shuttle
»10 min ⌀CAD45 per week
Short-stay Garage ⌀CAD5 hr, CAD9.50
per day (max)
Short-stay Adjacent to Terminal ⌀CAD6
hr, CAD15 per day (max) Valet ⌀CAD9
plus CAD9.75 day

TAXIS AND CHAUFFEUR-DRIVEN CARS

Taxis
Montréal city centre ➲25 min
⌀CAD25 Mirabel Airport ⌀CAD55

PUBLIC TRANSPORT

Airport to airport
Montréal International-Dorval
🚌Connaisseur »30 min–1 hr
◷0930–2330 ➲35 min ⌀CAD12.50.
Free to in-transit passengers with less than
15 hrs between connections

City & suburbs
Montréal (City Centre Air Terminal)
🚌Connaisseur »20–30 min
◷0510–0100 ➲40 min ⌀CAD9
Montréal metro area 🚌7 companies at
Airport.

✈ Air 🚋 Rail 🚌 Bus 🚐 Limousine Ⓜ Metro/subway 🚊 Tram 🚁 Helicopter ⛴ Water transport • For map symbols, see p. 9

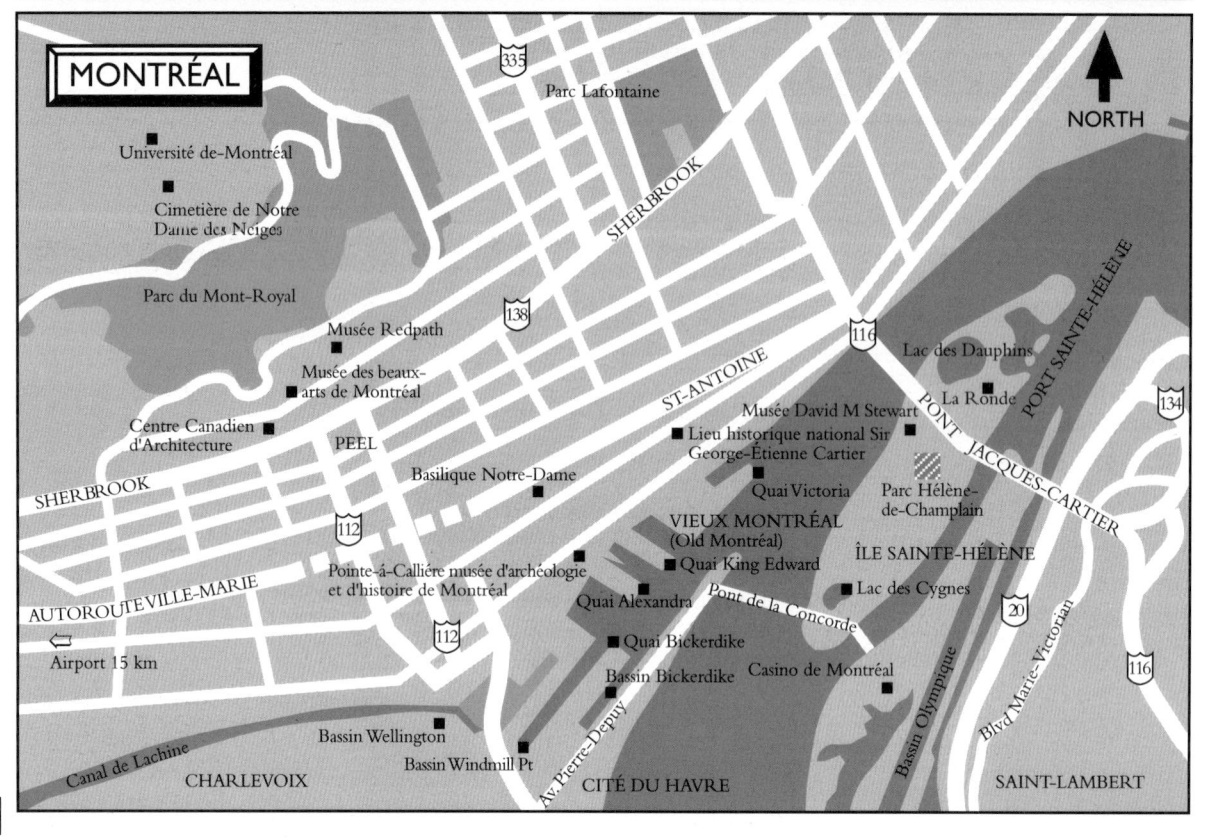

MONTRÉAL DORVAL

SECTION TWO • AIRPORT DIRECTORY

Other towns and cities
Dorval (Gare Dorval) STCUM: 204 »30 min–1 hr ⏱0510–0100 ⟳10 min ⌀CAD1.85. For VIA Rail services **Cap-de-la-Madeleine PQ** La Québecoise »2 per day ⏱1600; 1900 ⌀CAD35.
Laval (Sheraton Centre) Connaisseur Q On-demand ⌀CAD9.

Ottawa ON Voyageur »5 per day ⏱1200; 1400; 1540; 1800; 1940 ⟳1 hr 40 min ⌀CAD23. For Hull PQ **Quebec PQ** Voyageur »4 per day ⏱0930; 1300; 1645; 2000; ⟳3 hr 45 min. For Cap-de-la-Madeleine
Sherbrooke PQ »1 day ⏱2020 ⌀CAD38. For Magog and Granby

REGIONAL AIR CONNECTIONS
Boston MA ✈ »Several per day ⟳1 hr
Ottawa ON ✈ »Several per day ⟳40 min
Québec PQ ✈ »At least daily ⟳45 min

☏ Phone no. ⊕ Fax no. ⏱ Hours of opening/operation » Frequency of service ⟳ Journey time ⌀ Cost/one-way fare

MONTRÉAL-MIRABEL   YMX

Canada (see page 18)

National © code: 1 Area & code: 514
Local time: Winter GMT-5, Summer GMT-4
Montréal Mirabel International Airport, 12655 Rue Commerce A4, Montréal PQ, JN7 1E1, Canada
©476 3010
®476 3178 WWW site: http://www.dmtl.com
Location: 53 km/33 miles NW of Montréal

TERMINALS AND TRANSFERS

Terminals
Main Terminal Airlines: All airlines. Layout: Main Floor (Arrival, Departure, Baggage Claim, Car Rental and Ground Transportation), Promenade (Shopping and Restaurants)

Minimum transfer times
1 hr 30 min

INFORMATION

Flight enquiries
Airport ©476 3010 Air Transat ©476 1118 Air Charter ©847 1106 Canada 3000 ©476 9500 Corsair ©476 9572 Cubana ©871 1222 Jaro International ©476 3429 Royal Aviation/Conifair Aviation ©476 9572 TACA ©476 9572 TAP Air Portugal ©476 3429

Information and help desks
Aeroports de Montréal Information Main Terminal Main Floor ©476 3010 Airport information, Tourist information

Emergencies
Police Main Terminal Main Floor ©476 9900 ⓒ24 hr
Lost Property Main Terminal Main Floor, next to Information ©476 3010 ⓒ0800–2300

AIRPORT FACILITIES

Money
ATM Main Terminal Main Floor and Promenade Level
Bureau de change Main Terminal Main Floor

Food and drink
Bar Main Terminal Promenade
Café/light meals Main Terminal throughout
Restaurant Main Terminal Promenade

Communications
Post box Main Terminal throughout

Shopping
Duty free, departure Main Terminal throughout
Gift Shop Main Terminal Promenade
News, Stationery & Books Main Terminal throughout
Hairdresser Main Terminal Promenade

Luggage
Left luggage counter Main Terminal Main Floor

DISABLED TRAVELLERS

Main Terminal Adapted toilets; Lifts Phones at wheelchair height; Phones adapted for the deaf

SMOKING POLICY

Main Terminal Permitted in designated areas on Main Floor and Promenade

SPECIAL PASSENGER LOUNGE

Main Terminal Main Floor

CONFERENCE AND BUSINESS FACILITIES

Press Room, Main Terminal ©476 3060

AIRPORT HOTEL

Château Mirabel ©476 1611 ®476 0873 351

CAR RENTAL

Avis Main Terminal Main Floor ©476 3481
Budget Main Terminal Main Floor ©476 2687
Hertz Main Terminal Main Floor ©476 3385
National Tilden ©476 3460
Thrifty Main Terminal Main Floor ©476 0496

CAR PARKING

Long-stay Adjacent to terminal ⊘CAD31.50 per week
Short-stay Adjacent to terminal ⊘CAD4 hr, CAD9 per day (max)

TAXIS AND CHAUFFEUR-DRIVEN CARS

Taxis
Main Terminal Montréal city centre ⊃45 min ⊘CAD58
Main Terminal Dorval Airport ⊘CAD55

PUBLIC TRANSPORT

Airport to airport
Montréal International-Dorval
🚌Connaisseur »30 min–1 hr ⓒ0930–2330 ⊃35 min ⊘CAD12.50. Free to in-transit passengers with less than 15 hrs between connections

City & suburbs
Montréal city centre (City Centre Air Terminal) 🚌Connaisseur »30 min–1 hr ⓒ0500–0100 ⊃1 hr ⊘CAD7.25
Montréal metro area l7 companies at Airport.

Other towns and cities
Quebec City PQ 🚌La Québécoise »2 per day ⓒ1630; 1945 ⊘CAD40. For Cap-de-la-Madeleine and Ste-Foy
Laval (Sheraton Centre) 🚌Connaisseur »On-demand ⊘CAD10.
Mont-Tremblant 🚌Mont-Tremblant Shuttle Service
Sherbrooke PQ »daily ⊘CAD38. For Magog and Granby

MOSCOW-SHEREMETYEVO
(MOSKVA) Russia (see p. 34)

SVO

National ✆ code: 7
Area ✆ code: 095
Local time: Winter GMT+3, Summer GMT+4
Moscow-Sheremetyevo Airport, Moskva 103304, Russia
✆57876631/5785753
⑤Telex SVO 411916
Location: 29 km/18 miles NW of Moscow

TERMINALS AND TRANSFERS

Terminals
Terminal 1 Airlines: All domestic flights, El Al Israel Airlines, Turkish Airlines. Layout: Older terminal with limited facilities, on three Levels
Terminal 2 Airlines: All other international flights. Layout: Modern Terminal with passenger facilities on two Levels

Minimum transfer times
International: 1 hr Domestic: 2 hr 30 min–4 hr

Transfer between terminals
Bus Terminals 1 and 2

INFORMATION

Flight enquiries
Airport ✆5782356

Information and help desks
Airport Information Desk Terminal 2 Arrival/Departure Halls (2 desks) *Airport information, Flights*
Intourist Terminal 2 Ground Level Arrival Hall (2 desks) *Hotel booking, Tourist information*

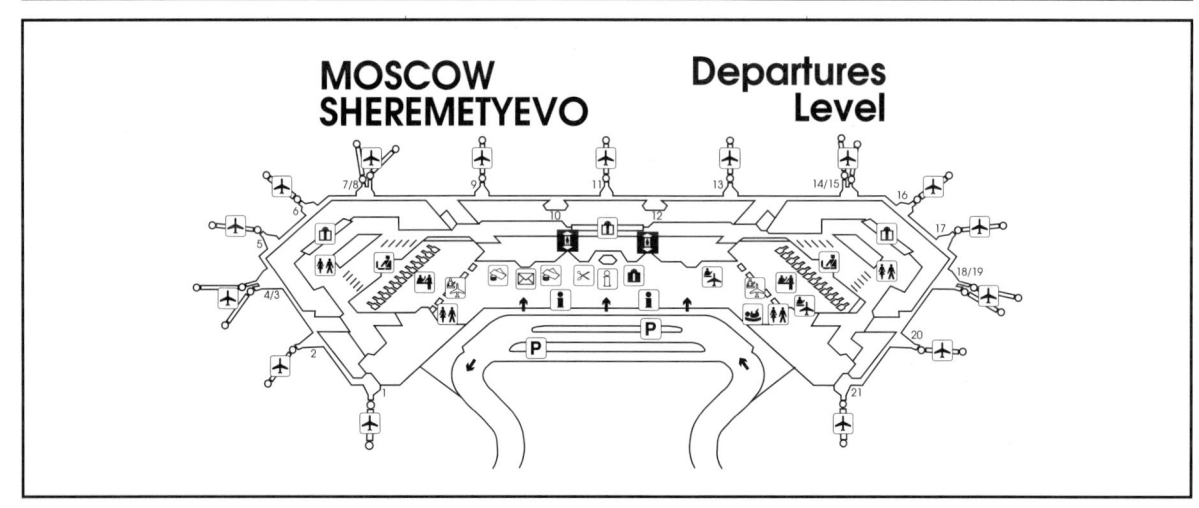

MOSCOW SHEREMETYEVO — Arrivals Level

MOSCOW SHEREMETYEVO — Departures Level

✆ Phone no. ⑤ Fax no. ⏱ Hours of opening/operation ≫ Frequency of service ➲ Journey time ◊ Cost/one-way fare

SECTION TWO • AIRPORT DIRECTORY

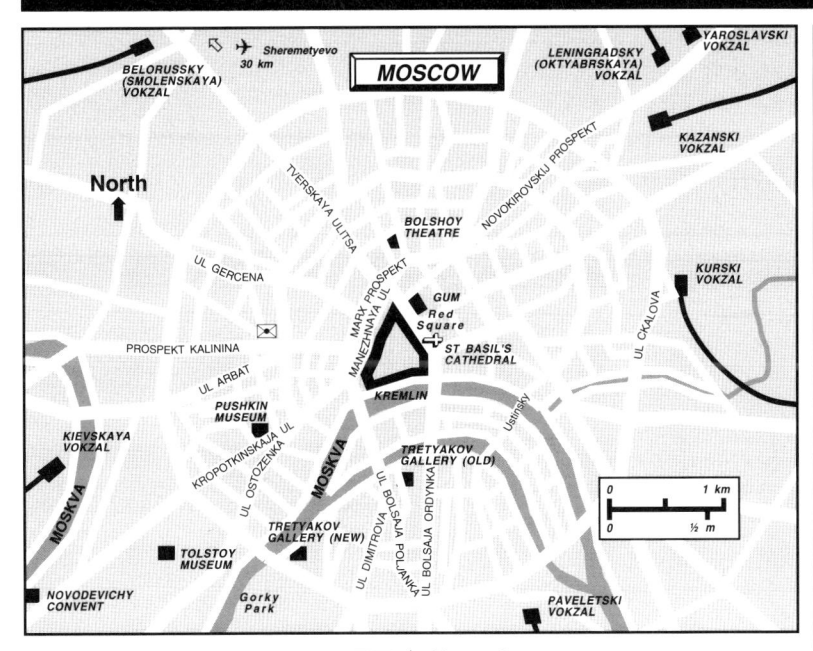

MOSCOW

SPECIAL PASSENGER LOUNGES

All international flights VIP Lounge Terminal 2

AIRPORT HOTELS

Sheremetyevo ℂ5789401/08 ℉5872794

CAR RENTAL

Avis Terminal 2

CAR PARKING

Long-stay Opposite Terminal entrance
Short-stay Opposite Terminal entrance

TAXIS AND CHAUFFEUR-DRIVEN CARS

Taxis
Outside Terminal Building City centre ⊃40 min ⌀RUR25

PUBLIC TRANSPORT

City & suburbs
Moscow city centre 🚌 »1 hr. *Not a reliable service*

REGIONAL AIR CONNECTIONS

Helsinki ✈ »Several per day ⊃1 hr 50 min
Kiev ✈ »Several per day ⊃1 hr 45 min
Minsk ✈ »Several per day ⊃1 hr 30 min
Vilnius ✈ »At least daily ⊃1 hr 45 min

TRAVELLER'S NOTES

Helpful if you can find own-language speaker who also speaks Russian. Most flight announcements made in Russian, some in German. Taxis are the best way to reach the city centre; many are private vehicles. Be prepared to bargain hard.

EMERGENCIES

Police Terminal 2 throughout Airport
Medical Terminal 2 Departure/Arrival Halls
Lost Property Terminal 2 Near Left Luggage, Arrival Hall Ground Level
Lost Property Terminal 2 Contact Aeroflot Desk

AIRPORT FACILITIES

Money
Bank Terminal 2 Departure Hall ⓒ24 hr
Bureau de change Terminal 2 Arrival Hall

Food and drink
Bar Terminal 2 Departure Area & Arrival Hall
Café/light meals Terminal 2 Irish pub
Restaurant Terminal 2 Departure Area Levels 1 and 4

Communications
Post office Terminal 2 Ground Level Departure Hall ⓒ0800–2000

Shopping

Duty free, arrival Terminal 2 Arrival Hall ⓒAll flight times
Duty free, departure Terminal 2 Departure Area Level 1 ⓒAll flight times
Shopping mall Terminal 2 Departure Area Level 1 ⓒAll flight times

Luggage

Left Luggage Counter Terminal 2 Arrival Hall, Ground Level
Porters Terminal 2 Arrival and Departure Areas ⌀Variable
Trolleys/carts Terminal 2 Arrival Hall ⓒ24 hr ⌀USD1 per trolley

DISABLED TRAVELLERS

Terminal 2 Lifts

SMOKING POLICY

Terminal 1 Smoking permitted throughout
Terminal 2 Smoking permitted throughout

✈ Air ⎯ Rail 🚌 Bus ⎯ Limousine 🚇 Metro/subway ⎯ Tram 🚁 Helicopter ⎯ Water transport • For map symbols, see p. 9

MUMBAI (BOMBAY) — BOM

India (see page 25)

National ☏ code: 91
Area ☏ code: 022
Local time: Winter GMT+5½, Summer GMT+5½
Mumbai/Bombay Sahar International Airport, Mumbai, India
☏6366700; 6329090; 6366767

Location: 29 km/17½ miles N of Mumbai

TERMINALS AND TRANSFERS

Terminals
Terminal I Airlines: Air France, Alitalia, British Airways, Cathay Pacific Airways, Delta Airlines, Emirates, Gulf Air, Kuwait Airways, Lufthansa, Saudia, Air Lanka.
Terminal II Airlines: Air India, Ethiopian Airlines, Iran Air, Yemen Airways, Kenya Airways, Air Mauritius, Egyptair, Syrian Arab Airlines, Singapore Airlines, Turkish Airlines.

Minimum transfer times
International: 1 hr 30 min– 2 hr 30 min
Domestic: 30 min–2 hr

Transfer between terminals
Bus Terminals I and II ⊘INR14

INFORMATION

Flight enquiries
Airport ☏5452011; 5452021

Information and help desks
Tourist Information Desk Terminal II Arrival Lounge ☏6366767 ⏱24 hr, *Tourist Information*
Tourist Information Desk Terminal I Arrival Lounge ☏6366767 ⏱24 hr, *Tourist Information*

EMERGENCIES

Lost Property Terminal I Airport police authorities ⏱24 hr
Lost Property Terminal II Airport police authorities ⏱24 hr

AIRPORT FACILITIES

Money
Bank Terminal I Arrival and Departure Lounges ⏱24 hr
Bank Terminal II Arrival and Departure Lounges ⏱24 hr
Thomas Cook bureau de change Terminal II Arrival Lounge ⏱24 hr
Thomas Cook bureau de change Terminal II Departure Lounge ⏱24 hr

Food and drink
Café/light meals Terminal I Arrival and Departure Lounge
Restaurant Terminal I Arrival and Departure Lounges
Café/light meals Terminal II Arrival and Departure Lounges
Restaurant Terminal II Arrival and Departure Lounges

Communications
Post office Terminal I Departure Lounge ⏱24 hr

Shopping
Duty free, departure Terminal I Departure Lounge
Gift Shop Terminal I Departure Lounge
Duty free, departure Terminal II Departure Lounge
Gift Shop Terminal II Departure Lounge

Luggage
Left Luggage Counter Terminal I Car parking Area ⏱24 hr

DISABLED TRAVELLERS

Terminal I Adapted toilets
Terminal II Adapted toilets

SPECIAL PASSENGER LOUNGES

Air India Executive Class Lounge Terminal II *Business class ticket holders only*
Air India Unaccompanied Minors Lounge Terminal II *Unaccompanied minors only*
Air India Maharaja Lounge Terminal II *First class ticket holders only*

CAR RENTAL

Mackson Pvt. Ltd Terminal I

CAR PARKING

Short-stay ⊘INR5 per 6 hr

TAXIS AND CHAUFFEUR-DRIVEN CARS

Taxis
Counter in Terminal I City centre ⤳1 hr 30 min
Counter in Terminal II City centre ⤳1 hr 30 min

PUBLIC TRANSPORT

Airport to airport
Mumbai Domestic Airports 🚌 International Airport Authority of India »45 min (day); 2 hr (night). *Picks up outside the arrival hall of Terminal I*

City & suburbs
Mumbai city centre 🚌 Ex-Serviceman's Airlink Transport Services Ltd »30 min ⏱0500–0100 ⊘INR35.
Mumbai city centre (SEEPZ bus terminal) 🚌 Bombay Electric Supply and Transport Undertaking: Route 338 »13 min ⏱0545–2230 ⊘INR2.

REGIONAL AIR CONNECTIONS

Muscat ✈ »Several per week ⤳50 min
Rajkot ✈ »Several per week ⤳50 min

AIRPORT TAX

A departure tax (from INR50–300, depending on destination) is levied.

TRAVELLER'S NOTES

Prepaid taxi is the most practical transport into the city; retain the receipt and give to driver at the end of the journey.

Munich (München) MUC

Germany (see page 22)

National ✆ code: 49
Area ✆ code: 089
Local time: Winter GMT+1, Summer GMT+2
Flughafen München GmbH, Postfach 23 17 55, D-85326 München, Germany
✆975 00
🅕975 57906
Location: 28 km/17 miles NE of Munich

Terminals and Transfers

Terminals
Main Terminal Airlines: All other airlines. Layout: Departure & Arrival Areas A, B, C, D and E. Departure Level 4, Arrivals Level 4
Terminal F Airlines: Condor, Arkia Israeli Airlines, Lufthansa, El Al Israel Airlines, Aero Lloyd. Layout: Separate Terminal for special flights, particularly to Israel. Departure & Arrivals Area F. Departure Level 3, Arrivals Level 3

Minimum transfer times
International: 35 min **Domestic:** 35 min

Information

Flight enquiries
Airport ✆975 21313
Adria Airways ✆(0 18 03) 80 38 03 Aero Lloyd ✆975 92233 Aeroflot ✆975 92233 Air Alfa ✆975 92233 Air Atlanta Iceland ✆(0 18 03) 80 38 03 Air Bosnia ✆975 92233 Air Dolomiti ✆(0 18 03) 80 38 03 Air Engadiana ✆975 92350 Air Europa ✆975 92350 Air France ✆975 91100 Air Madagascar ✆975 92233 Air Malta ✆975 91888 Air Mauritius ✆975 92233 Air UK ✆975 91888 Air Via ✆975 92233 Air Yugoslavia ✆975 92233 Alitalia ✆975 91150 Arkia Israeli Airlines ✆975 92233 Austrian Airlines ✆975 92233 Balkan Bulgarian Airlines ✆(0 18 03) 80 38 03 British Airways ✆975 91320 Canada 3000 Airlines ✆975 92233 China Airlines ✆975 92233 Condor ✆(0 18 03) 80 38 03 Croatia Airlines ✆975 92233 Cronus Air ✆975 92233 Crossair ✆975 92233 CSA Czechoslovak ✆(0 18 03) 80 38 03 Dac Air ✆975 92678 Debonair ✆975 92680 Delta Airlines ✆975 91602 Deutsche BA ✆975 91320 Eagle Airlines ✆975 92350 Egyptair ✆975 92233 El Al Israel Airlines ✆975 92233 Eurocypria Airlines ✆975 92232 European Aircharter ✆975 92233 Eurowings ✆975 92350 Finnair ✆(0 18 03) 80 38 03 Futura ✆975 9 19 00 Germania ✆975 9 19 00 GTI Airlines ✆975 9 22 33 Hamburg Airlines ✆(0 18 03) 80 38 03 Hapag Lloyd ✆975 91750 Iberia ✆975 9 18 00 Istanbul Airlines ✆975 92396 Kibris Turkish Airlines ✆975 9 22 33 KLM ✆975 91888 Kuwait Airways ✆(0 18 03) 80 38 03 Lauda-Air ✆(0 18 03) 80 38 03 Lineas Aereas Navarras ✆975 9 22 33 Lot Polish Airlines ✆975 92233 LTU International Airways ✆975 9 19 00 Lufthansa ✆(0 18 03) 80 38 03 Luxair ✆(0 18 03) 80 38 03 Macedonian Airlines ✆975 9 22 33 Malaysia Airlines ✆975 92233 Malev Hungarian ✆975 9 21 90 Olympic Airways ✆975 92233 Onur Air ✆975 9 19 00 Pegasus Airlines ✆975 9 22 33 Rheintalflug ✆975 9 23 50 Royal Aviation ✆975 9 22 33 Sabena World Airlines ✆975 92520 SAS ✆(0 18 03) 80 38 03 Shorouk Air ✆975 9 22 33 SunExpress ✆(0 18 03) 80 38 03 Sunways Airlines ✆975 9 22 33 Sunways Intersun ✆975 9 22 33 Swissair ✆975 92600 Syrianair ✆975 92640 TAP Air Portugal ✆975 9 22 33 Tarom ✆975 9 22 33 Thai Airways ✆975 9 26 70 Transavia ✆975 9 22 33 Tunis Air ✆(0 18 03) 80 38 03 Turkish Airlines ✆975 92700 Tyrolean Airways ✆(0 18 03) 80 38 03 Ukraine International Airlines ✆975 92233 US Airways ✆975 92103/4

Information and help desks
Central Information Desk Main Terminal, immediately beside the escalators to the rapid transit train ⏰All flight times Airport information, Flights Hotel booking, Tourist information ✆975 21390
Information Desks Main Terminal A/B/C/D/E Central Departure Areas (4 desks) ⏰All flight times Airport information, Flights Hotel booking
Lufthansa Information desks Main Terminal Central Arrival Hall ✆ A/B Departure areas ✆54 55 99 ⏰All flight hours Airport information, Flights
Tourist Information Main Terminal Central arrival Hall ⏰All flight hours Tourist information

Emergencies
Police Main Terminal Central Departure Area Level 3 ✆Ext 110
Medical Main Terminal Level 3 Terminal E Departure Area ✆975 63344
Lost Property Main Terminal Level 3 Central Area ✆975 21370 ⏰24 hr

Airport Facilities

Money
Bank Main Terminal Central Departure Area Level 3 ⏰0830–1230, 1330–1730 Mon; 0830–1230, 1330–1600 Tue–Fri ✆975 99380/973000
Bureau de Change Main Terminal Central Departure Area Level 3 ⏰0700–2130 daily ✆975 99380/973000
Bureau de Change Main Terminal Central Departure Area Level 3 ⏰0615–2200 daily ✆9701721

Food and drink
Café/light meals Main Terminal Central Area Level 3 ⏰24 hr ✆975 92869
Restaurant Main Terminal Area B Level 7 ⏰1100–2300 ✆975 92870
Restaurant Main Terminal Area B Level 6 ⏰1100–2300 ✆975 92870
Restaurant Main Terminal Central Area Level 4 ⏰0800–1800 975 92860
Restaurant Main Terminal Central Area Level 4 ⏰1100–2100 975 92860

Communications
Post Office Main Terminal Central Area Level 3 ⏰0800–2000 Mon-Fri; 0800–1800 Sat; 1000–1800 Sun and holidays ✆9701460
Fax service Fax machines are located throughout airport

Shopping
Duty free, departure Main Terminal Departure Areas B, C, D and F, Level 4 ⏰All flight times
News, Stationery & Books Main Terminal Central Area Level 3 and Departure A, B, C and D Level 4
Shopping Mall Main Terminal Central Area Level 3
Pharmacy Main Terminal Central Area Level 4 ⏰0700–2100 daily ✆975 92950

Luggage
Porters Main Terminal throughout ✆975

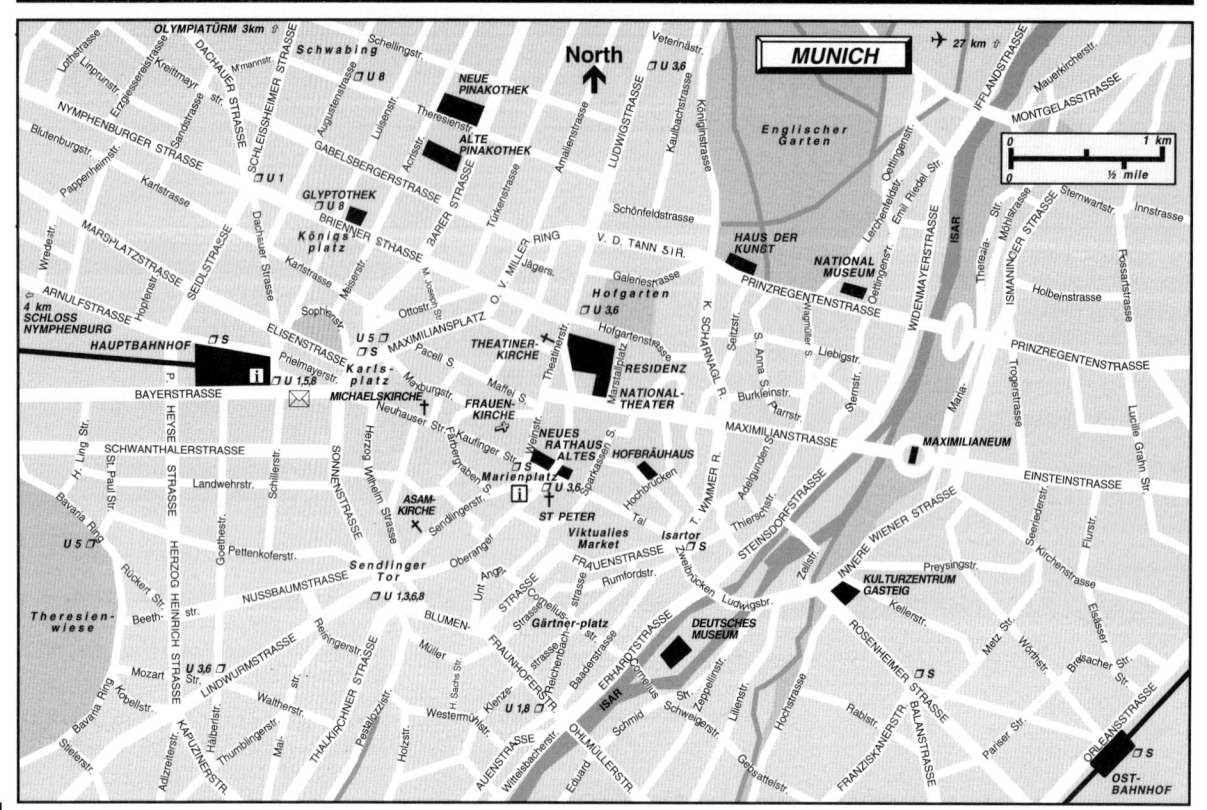

MUNICH

SECTION TWO • AIRPORT DIRECTORY

99795
Trolleys/carts Main Terminal Central Area/Area F/car parks ⌀DEM2
Left Luggage Counter Main Terminal Central Area Level 3 ⓣ24 hr ⌀DEM4 per item per day

Disabled Travellers

Main Terminal Adapted toilets; Lifts; Personal assistance Medical Centre ⓟ975 63333

Smoking Policy

Main Terminal Designated smoking areas in Departure Lounges

Special Passenger Lounges

Air France Lounge Main Terminal Departure Area D Level 5 Club members and First class passengers
All airlines Atlantik Lounge Main Terminal Departure Area C Level 5 First and Business class passengers
All airlines Europa Lounge Main Terminal Departure Area B Level 5 First and Business class passengers
Austrian Airlines Lounge Main Terminal Departure Area D Level 5 Club members and First class passengers
British Airways Executive Club Lounge Main Terminal Departure Area D Level 5 Club members and First/Business class
Delta Airlines Lounge Main Terminal Departure Area C Level 5 Club members and First class passengers
Lufthansa Business Class Lounge Main Terminal Departure Area B Level 5 Business class passengers
Lufthansa Senator Club Lounge Main Terminal Departure Area B Level 5 Club members

Conference and Business Facilities

Business Service Centre, near multi-storey car park P8 ⓟ975 90999 ⓣ0800–1900 Mon–Fri, 0900–1300 Sat (or by arrangement) Telephones, Fax service, Photocopier, Secretarial service, Translation/Interpretation service

Airport Hotels

Kempinski ⓟ0130 3333 (toll-free)

Car Rental

Alamo Main Terminal Car Rental Centre opposite Main Terminal Departure Area A ⓟ975 97680
Avis Main Terminal Car Rental Centre opposite Main Terminal Departure Area A ⓟ975 97600
EuropCar Main Terminal Car Rental Centre opposite Main Terminal Departure Area A ⓟ975 97001
Hertz Main Terminal Car Rental Centre opposite Main Terminal Departure Area A ⓟ978860
Sixt Main Terminal Car Rental Centre opposite Main Terminal Departure Area A ⓟ975 96666

Car Parking

Long-stay 2 multi-storey and 2 covered garages 10000 spaces (P6–P8/P26/P24) ⌀DEM4 per hr; DEM25 per day; DEM175 per week
Off-airport Nord Allee area direction Autobahn Munich ⌀DEM50 per week
Short-stay 1 multi-storey and 2 covered garages 10000 spaces (P1–P4/P9) ⌀DEM2 per 30 min; DEM25 per day

Taxis and Chauffeur-driven Cars

Taxis
Front of Arrival/Departures ⓟ77 30 43
City centre ⤳20 min ⌀DEM85

ⓟ Phone no. ⓕ Fax no. ⓣ Hours of opening/operation » Frequency of service ⤳ Journey time ⌀ Cost/one-way fare

SECTION TWO • AIRPORT DIRECTORY — MUNICH • NAIROBI

PUBLIC TRANSPORT

City & suburbs
Munich city centre (Hbf – central rail stn) S-Bahn »20 min ⓘ0355–0055 ⊃38 min ⌀DEM 10. Hbf is major departure point for national and international trains

Other towns and cities
Other cities MVV »20 min ⓘ0520–3212 ⊃15 min ⌀DEM1.40. Bus to Freising rail stn to connect with trains to other cities

REGIONAL AIR CONNECTIONS

Berlin ✈ »Several per day ⊃1 hr 10 min
Berne ✈ »At least daily ⊃55 min
Bratislava ✈ »At least daily ⊃1 hr
Cologne/Bonn ✈ »Several per day ⊃1hr 5 min
Dresden ✈ »Several per day ⊃1 hr
Düsseldorf ✈ »Several per day ⊃1 hr 10 min
Erfurt ✈ »Several per week ⊃55 min
Frankfurt ✈ »Several per day ⊃1 hr 5 min
Graz ✈ »Several per week ⊃1 hr
Hanover ✈ »Several per day ⊃1 hr 10 min
Leipzig ✈ »Several per day ⊃1 hr
Prague ✈ »Several per week ⊃1 hr
Saarbrücken ✈ »At least daily ⊃1 hr 10 min
Strasbourg ✈ »Several per week ⊃1 hr 5 min
Stuttgart ✈ »Several per day ⊃55 min
Vienna ✈ »Several per day ⊃1 hr
Zürich ✈ »Several per day ⊃1 hr

TRAVELLER'S NOTES

Munich is an excellent shopping and cultural centre, with world-class museums and galleries. Technology buffs and children of all ages should not miss the Deutsches Museum on the east of the city centre.

NAIROBI — NBO

Kenya (see page 28)

National ☎ code: 254
Area ☎ code: 02
Local time: Winter GMT+3, Summer GMT+3
Jomo Kenyatta International Airport, PO Box 19187, Embakasi, Nairobi, Kenya
☎ 822111
Location: 18 km/11 miles SE of Nairobi

TERMINALS AND TRANSFERS

Terminals
Main Terminal Airlines: Air France (Departs from Unit 1), Air India (Departs from Unit 1), Alitalia (Departs from Unit 1), British Airways (Departs from Unit 1), Gulf Air (Departs from Unit 1), KLM (Departs from Unit 2), Kenya Airways (Departs from Unit 3), Lufthansa (Departs from Unit 1), El Al Israel Airlines (Departs from Unit 3), Balkan Bulgarian Airlines (Departs from Unit 2), Olympic Airways (Departs from Unit 1), Austrian Airlines (Departs from Unit 2), Pakistan International Airlines (Departs from Unit 2), Sabena World Airlines (Departs from Unit 2), Swissair (Departs from Unit 2), Saudia (Departs from Unit 2). Layout: Divided into Units 1, 2 and 3

Minimum transfer times
International: 1 hr Domestic: 30 min

INFORMATION

Information and help desks
Tourist Information Desk Main Terminal
Hertz car rental desk ☎822339 ⓘ24 hr Tourist Information

EMERGENCIES

Lost Property Main Terminal

AIRPORT FACILITIES

Money
Bank Main Terminal ⓘ24 hr
Bank Main Terminal ⓘ0600–2400

Food and Drink
Bar Main Terminal Arrival Lounge ⓘ24 hr
Bar Main Terminal Units 1, 2 and 3 ⓘ24 hr
Café/light meals Main Terminal Arrival Lounge ⓘ24 hr
Café/light meals Main Terminal Units 1, 2 and 3 ⓘ24 hr
Restaurant Main Terminal Fifth Floor, Central Building

Communications
Post office Main Terminal International Arrival Lounge ⓘ0800–1700

Shopping
Duty free, arrival and departure Main Terminal Departure Lounge ⓘ24 hr

DISABLED TRAVELLERS

Main Terminal Personal assistance

SMOKING POLICY

Main Terminal No restrictions

SPECIAL PASSENGER LOUNGES

Kenya Airways Lounge Main Terminal

CAR RENTAL

Avis Main Terminal
EuropCar Main Terminal
Glory Main Terminal
Hertz Main Terminal
NAZ Main Terminal
Payless Main Terminal

CAR PARKING

Long-stay 260 spaces
Short-stay 960 spaces

TAXIS AND CHAUFFEUR-DRIVEN CARS

Taxis
City centre ⊃20 min ⌀KES300–360

PUBLIC TRANSPORT

City & suburbs
Nairobi city centre Kenya Bus

✈ Air Rail Bus Limousine Metro/subway Tram Helicopter Water transport • For map symbols, see p. 9

NAIROBI • NASSAU — SECTION TWO • AIRPORT DIRECTORY

Services: 34 » Approx. 30 min
0705–2020 Mon–Sat; 0745–2045 Sun, Pub Hol ⊃35–40 min ⌀KES7. 50.

Regional Air Connections

Bujumbura ✈ »Several per week ⊃35 min

Kigali ✈ »Several per week ⊃30 min
Kisumu ✈ »Several per week ⊃1 hr
Mara Lodges ✈ »Several per week ⊃45 min
Nayuki ✈ »Several per week ⊃45 min

Airport Taxes

International flights: USD20
Domestic flights: KES100

Traveller's Notes

Excellent duty-free shops in both departure and arrivals halls. The small departure tax (even on domestic flights) must be paid in currency cash – traveller's cheques are not accepted.

NASSAU — NAS

Bahamas (see page 15)

National ✆ code: 1
Area ✆ code: 242
Local time: Winter GMT-5, Summer GMT-4
Nassau International Airport, Box N-975 Nassau, Bahamas
✆32 76755
Ⓕ32 77281, 32 82220
Location: 19 km/12 miles W of Nassau

Terminals and Transfers

Terminals
Domestic Terminal Airlines: Bahamasair.
International Terminal Airlines: All international flights.

Minimum transfer times
International: 1 hr–1 hr 30 min Domestic: 1 hr

Information

Flight enquiries
Airport ✆32 77116

Information and help desks
Tourist Information Desks International Terminal Outside bookshop; Immigration Arrivals Hall (2 desks) ✆32 76806; 32 76782 0830–2400 Airport, Flights, Hotel booking, Tourist Information

Emergencies

Lost Property International Terminal Contact airport police

Airport Facilities

Money
Bank International Terminal 0930–1500

Food and Drink
Bar International Terminal throughout 0900–2000
Café/light meals International Terminal throughout 0700–1900
Restaurant International Terminal Second Floor 0700–2200

Communications
Post office International Terminal Next to terminal building 0900–1600

Shopping
Duty free, departure International Terminal Departure Area
News, Stationery & Books International Terminal

Luggage
Left luggage counter International Terminal Handled by airlines

Disabled Travellers

International Terminal Adapted toilets

Conference and Business Facilities

Airport boardroom

Airport Hotels

Orange Hill Beach Inn ✆77157

Car Rental

Avis International Terminal
Budget International Terminal
Hertz International Terminal
National International Terminal

Car Parking

Long-stay ⌀BSD24 per week
Short-stay ⌀BSD2 per hr

Taxis and Chauffeur-driven Cars

Taxis
City centre ⊃20–25 min ⌀BSD15

Public Transport

City & suburbs
Nassau city centre 🚌City bus ⊃30 min.

Regional Air Connections

Fort Lauderdale FL ✈ »Several per day

✆ Phone no. Ⓕ Fax no. Hours of opening/operation » Frequency of service ⊃ Journey time ⌀ Cost/one-way fare

○55–60 min
Freeport NY ✈ »Several per day ○40 min
George Town (Cayman Is) ✈ »At least daily ○40 min
Mangrove Cay ✈ »Several per day ○20 min
Marsh Harbour ✈ »Several per day ○1 hr 5 min

Miami FL ✈ »Several per day ○1 hr 5 min
Rock Sound ✈ »At least daily ○1 hr
San Andros ✈ »Several per day ○1 hr
San Salvador (Bahamas) ✈ »Several per week ○1 hr
South Andros ✈ »Several per day ○40 min
Stella Maris ✈ »Several per week ○45 min

The Bight ✈ »Several per week ○55 min
Treasure Cay ✈ »Several per day ○35 min

TRAVELLER'S NOTES

Reputedly one of the best places in the world to buy watches. Other duty-free bargains include jewellery, crystal, china and leather.

NEWCASTLE

United Kingdom (see page 41)

National ✆ code: 44
Area ✆ code: 0191
Local time: Winter GMT, Summer GMT+1
Address: Newcastle International Airport Ltd, Woolsington, Newcastle upon Tyne, NE13 8BZ
✆: 286 0966
℻: 271 6080
WWW site: www.newcastleairport.com
Location: 4km/6 miles

TERMINALS AND TRANSFERS

Terminals
Main Terminal Airlines: Air France, Aer Lingus, Air UK, Braathens, British Airways, Brymon, British Airways Express, Cimber Air, European Airways, Gill Airways, KLM, Maersk Air, Sabena, SAS Layout: Four Levels

INFORMATION

Flight enquiries
Airport ✆214 4444
Air France ✆286 0966 ext.4224, Aer Lingus ✆286 0966 ext.4271, Air UK ✆286 0966 ext.4271, Braathens ✆286 0966 ext.4224, British Airways ✆286 0966 ext.4224, Brymon ✆286 0966 ext.4224, British Airways Express ✆286 0966 ext.4224, Cimber Air ✆286 0966 ext.4271, European Airways ✆286 0966 ext.4224, Gill Airways ✆286 0966 ext.4224, KLM ✆286 0966 ext.4271, Maersk Air ✆286 0966 ext.4224, Sabena ✆286 0966 ext.4401, SAS ✆286 0966 ext.4271

Information and help desks
Information Desk Centre of Main Terminal ✆214 3334 Flight information

Tourist Information Desk Centre of Main Terminal ✆214 4422 Tourist information, Hotel reservations

EMERGENCIES

Medical Contact airport staff
Lost Property Airport security office, Level 0

AIRPORT FACILITIES

Money
Bank Main Terminal ⏰0600–1900 Mon–Fri; 0900–1500 Sat–Sun
Bureau de Change Travel agency, Main Terminal ⏰0530–2130 Mon–Fri; 0530–2000 Sat; 0530–2030 Sun

Food and drink
Bar Level 1, Main Terminal
Café/light meals Level 1, above International Arrivals area
Restaurant Level 1, Main Terminal

Communications
Post Box Next to lift, Level 1

Shopping
Duty free International Departure Lounge, Level 1
News, Stationery & Books International Departure Lounge, Level 1
Gift Shop International Departure Lounge, Level 1

Luggage
Left Luggage Counter Security Desk, Domestic Arrivals meeting point, Level 1
Trolleys/carts Throughout terminal ⌀Free

DISABLED TRAVELLERS

Special car parking bays at front of terminal, disabled toilets, minicom telephone at information desk, pay text phone on main concourse opposite information desk, assistance available on request

CAR RENTAL

Alamo Opposite International Arrivals, Level 1
Avis Opposite International Arrivals, Level 1
Europcar Opposite International Arrivals, Level 1
Hertz Opposite International Arrivals, Level 1

CAR PARKING

Long-stay ✆286 0966 ext.4341
Short-stay ✆286 0966 ext.4341

TAXIS AND CHAUFFEUR-DRIVEN CARS

Taxis
City centre ○15–20 min.

PUBLIC TRANSPORT

City & suburbs
Newcastle, city centre 🚆Metro rail link »7 min ⌀GBP1.60 ✆232 5325
Newcastle, city centre (Eldon Square Bus Concourse) 🚌78 »20 ⏰0605–2300 (0730 Sun) ⌀GBP1.10 ✆232 5325

Other towns and cities
Carlisle 🚆 » 1 hr ○1 hr 30 min
Durham 🚆 » 30 min ○15 min
Middlesbrough 🚆 » 1 hr ○1 hr 15 min
Sunderland 🚆 » Frequent ○30 min

✈ Air 🚆 Rail 🚌 Bus 🚐 Limousine Ⓜ Metro/subway 🚋 Tram 🚁 Helicopter 🚢 Water transport • For map symbols, see p. 9

NEW ORLEANS | SECTION TWO • AIRPORT DIRECTORY

NEW ORLEANS
USA (see page 41)

National ✆ code: 1
Area ✆ code: 504
Local time: Winter GMT-6, Summer GMT-5
Chicago Midway Airport, PO Box 20007, New Orleans LA, 70141, USA
✆464 3547
🅕465 2303
WWW site: http//gnofn.org/~airport
Location: 16 km/10 miles NW of New Orleans

TERMINALS AND TRANSFERS

Terminals
Main Terminal: All Airlines Layout: Lower Level (Arrivals, Baggage Claim, Ground Transportation), Upper Level (Departures), Concourses A, B, C and D

Minimum Transfer Times
International: 1 hr 30 min Domestic: 30 min

Transfer between terminals
Information and help desks
Visitor Information Services Main Terminal Upper Level West Lobby ⏰0800–2100 ✆464 2752 Airport, Tourist Information
Visitor Information Services Main Terminal Upper Level East Lobby ⏰0800–2100 ✆464 2752 Airport, Tourist Information
Visitor Information Services Main Terminal Lower Level West Baggage Claim ⏰0800–2100 ✆463 1020 Airport, Tourist Information
Visitor Information Services Main Terminal Lower Level East Baggage Claim ⏰0800–2100 ✆463 1006 Airport, Tourist Information
Traveller's Aid Main Terminal Upper Level East Lobby ✆464 3522 Tourist information

Emergencies
Police Main Terminal Lower Level
Medical
Lost Property Main Terminal Lower Level West End (Airport Operations Office) ⏰24 hr ✆464 2672; 464 0831

AIRPORT FACILITIES

Money
ATM Main Terminal Upper Level East Lobby near entrance to Concourse B
ATM Main Terminal Upper Level West Lobby near bank
ATM Main Terminal Lower Level West Baggage Claim area near rental car agencies
Bank Main Terminal Upper Level across from Delta ticket counter ⏰0830–1500 (1730 Fri)
Bureau de change Main Terminal Upper Level (Bank)
Bureau de change Main Terminal Upper Level West Lobby (Mutual of Omaha Business Service Center)

Food and drink
Bar Main Terminal Upper Level throughout
Café/light Main Terminal Upper Level throughout
Restaurant Main Terminal, Upper Level throughout

Communications
Post office Main Terminal Upper Level West Lobby across from Delta ticket counter ⏰24 hr
Post box Main Terminal Upper Level East Lobby near water fountain ⏰24 hr

Shopping
Duty free, departure, Main Terminal Upper Level near Gate C–1
News, Stationery & Books Main Terminal Upper Level
Gift Shop Main Terminal Upper Level

Luggage
Lockers Main Terminal Upper Level past security in all concourses ⏰24 hr ⊘USD0.50
Trolleys/carts

DISABLED TRAVELLERS
Main Terminal Adapted toilets throughout; Lifts; Phones adapted for the deaf throughout; Special Parking close to lifts in parking garage

SPECIAL PASSENGER LOUNGES
Delta Crown Room Main Terminal Upper Level Concourse D near Gate 4

CONFERENCE AND BUSINESS FACILITIES
Business Service Center (Mutual of Omaha) Main Terminal Upper Level West Lobby ⏰0600–1900 Currency Exchange, Fax, Photocopies, travel advice
Meeting Rooms Main Terminal Upper Level ✆464 3547

CAR RENTAL
Alamo Main Terminal Lower Level West Baggage Claim ✆469 0532
Avis Main Terminal Lower Level West Baggage Claim ✆464 9511
Budget Main Terminal Lower Level West Baggage Claim ✆467 2277
Hertz Main Terminal Lower Level West Baggage Claim ✆468 3695
National Main Terminal Lower Level West Baggage Claim ✆466 4335
Payless Main Terminal Lower Level West Baggage Claim ✆441 5700
Thrifty Main Terminal Lower Level West Baggage Claim ✆467 8796

CAR PARKING
Long-stay Parking Garage across from Main Terminal ⊘USD7 day
Short-stay Parking Garage across from Main Terminal ⊘USD2.50 hr and USD1.50 hr thereafter USD7 day max
Off-airport Park and Fly ⊘USD6.40 day Courtesy transport
Off-airport US Park ⊘USD5 day Courtesy transport

TAXIS AND CHAUFFEUR-DRIVEN CARS
Taxis
Main Terminal kerbside City centre ➲20 min ⊘USD21

PUBLIC TRANSPORT
City & suburbs
New Orleans city centre 🚌 Airport Shuttle Service from Main Terminal Upper Level outside of Entrance #5 »15

✆ Phone no. 🅕 Fax no. ⏰ Hours of opening/operation » Frequency of service ➲ Journey time ⊘ Cost/one-way fare

min ⏱45 min–1 hr ⊘USD10
New Orleans city centre 🚌 Jefferson Transit from Main Terminal Lower Level ⟫15–30 min ⏱0600–1830 ⏱45 min–1 hr ⊘USD1.50
New Orleans metro area 🚗 Over 20 companies at airport

Other towns and cities
Houston TX 🚌Greyhound ⟫2 day ⏱0945; 1615 ⏱8 hr 15 min. For Baton Rouge, Lafayette and Lake Charles LA
Lafayette LA 🚌Greyhound ⟫4 day

⏱0945; 1300; 1615; 2000 ⏱3 hr. For Baton Rouge LA and Louisiana State University
Mobile AL 🚌Greyhound ⟫2 day ⏱1410; 1815 ⏱30 hr 30 min.
Pascagoula MS 🚌Coastliner/Mississippi Gulf Service ⟫9 day ⏱0800–2330 ⊘USD44. For Slidell LA and Bay St Louis MS
Lafayette LA 🚌Greyhound ⟫4 day ⏱0945; 1300; 1615; 2000 ⏱3 hr. For Baton Rouge LA
Shreveport LA 🚌Greyhound ⟫2 day

⏱1300, 2000 ⏱8 hr. Baton Rouge, Lafayette, Opelousas and Alexandria LA

REGIONAL AIR CONNECTIONS
Baton Rouge LA ✈ ⟫At least daily ⏱30 min
Beaumont/Port Arthur TX ✈ ⟫At least daily ⏱1 hr
Birmingham AL ✈ ⟫Several per day ⏱1 hr
Houston TX ✈ ⟫Several per day ⏱1 hr
Jackson MS ✈ ⟫At least daily ⏱50 min

NEW YORK-JFK
JFK 209
USA (see page 41)

National ⊙ code: 1
Area ⊙ code: 718
Local time: Winter GMT-5, Summer GMT-4
New York–John F Kennedy International Airport, Port Authority of New York and New Jersey, One World Trade Center, New York, NY 10048, USA
⊙244 4444
WWW site: http://www.panynyj.gov/
Location: 24 km/14 miles SE of New York City

TERMINALS AND TRANSFERS
Terminals
Terminal 2 Airlines: Aeromexico, America West Airlines, American Trans Air, Continental Express, Finnair, LACSA, Saudia, TACA International Airlines (Departures), American Trans Air, Varig, Virgin Atlantic (Departures). Layout: Lower Level (Baggage Claim, Car Rental, Ground Transportation), Upper Level (Departure, Gates 19–30)
Terminal 3 Airlines: Aeroflot, Air China, Air Ukraine, All Nippon Airways, Austrian Airlines, Avianca Colombian Airlines, Cathay Pacific, China Airlines, Delta Airlines, Delta Connection, Malev Hungarian, Sabena World Airlines, Singapore Airlines, Swissair, TAP Air Portugal, Tarom Romanian, Virgin Atlantic (arrivals). Layout: Lower Level (Baggage Claim, Car Rental, Ground Transportation), Upper Level (Departure, Gates 1–18)
Terminal 4E Airlines: Aer Lingus, Aerolineas Argentinas, Aeroperu, APA Dominicana, Balkan Bulgarian, Carnival Airlines, Ecuatoriana, Eva Airways, Guyana, Iberia, Icelandair, Japan Airlines, KLM, Kuwait Airlines, LTU, Lufthansa, Northwest, Olympic International, Pan Am, Rich International, Royal Air Maroc, Royal Jordanian. Layout: Lower Level (Baggage Claim, Car Rental, Ground Transportation), Upper Level (Gates 9–21), Third Floor (Airline Lounges)
Terminal 4W Airlines: Air Afrique, Air France, Air India, Air Jamaica, Air South, Alitalia, Allegro Airlines, Aviacsa, Biman Bangladesh, Corsair, Egypt Air, El Al Israel, Ghana Airways, Korean Airlines, Kras Air, Mexicana, Miami Air, Oaisis, Pakistan, Servivensa, Spanair, Taesa, Transbrasil, Turkish Airlines, Uzbekistan Airways, Vasp. Layout: Lower Level (Baggage Claim, Car Rental, Ground Transportation), Upper Level (Gates 24–35), Third Floor (Airline Lounges)
Terminal 5 Airlines: North American, TW Express, TWA (International). Layout: Lower Level (Baggage Claim, Car Rental, Ground Transportation), Upper Level (Departure, Gates 21–45)
Terminal 6 Airlines: Sun Country, TWA (Domestic). Layout: Lower Level (Baggage Claim, Car Rental, Ground Transportation), Upper Level (Departure, Domestic Gates 1–17)
Terminal 7 Airlines: British Airways, Lan Chile, Saeta Ecuador, SAS, United Airlines, United Express, US Airways, US Airways Express. Layout: Lower Level (Baggage Claim, Car Rental, Ground Transportation), Upper Level (Departure, Gates 1–12)

New York-JFK

Terminal 8 Airlines: Air Europa, American Airlines (International and Caribbean), BWIA International, Lot Polish Airlines, South African Airways. Layout: Lower Level (Baggage Claim, Car Rental, Ground Transportation), Upper Level (Departure, Concourses A and B, Gates 2–16).
Terminal 9 Airlines: American Airlines (Domestic and Puerto Rico), American Eagle, Canadian Airlines International, Qantas Airways. Layout: Lower Level (Baggage Claim, Car Rental, Ground Transportation), Upper Level (Departure, Concourses C and D, Gates 30–49)
Tower Air Terminal Airlines: Tower Air. Layout: Lower Level (Baggage Claim, Car Rental, Ground Transportation) Upper Level (Departure)

Minimum transfer times
International: 2 hr–2 hr 45 Domestic: 1 hr

Transfer between terminals
Bus ≫5–15 min; All terminals ⌀Free

INFORMATION

Flight enquiries
Airport ✆656 4520
Aer Lingus ✆(212) 557 1110 Air Afrique ✆(212) 586 5908 Air China ✆(212) 371 9898 Air India ✆(212) 751 6200 Asiana Airlines ✆(212) 371 9000 Aviacsa ✆656 3018 Balkan Bulgarian Airlines ✆(212) 573 5530 Biman Bangladesh Airlines ✆(212) 808 4477 Corsair ✆(212) 779 0600 Guyana Airways ✆693 8000 Malev Hungarian ✆(212) 757 6480 North American ✆656 2650 Olympic Airways ✆(212) 838 3600 Pakistan International Airlines ✆(212) 370 9158 Royal Air Maroc ✆(212) 750 6071 Royal Jordanian Airlines ✆(212) 949 0050 Saudia ✆(212) 751 7117 Servivensa ✆244 6744 TAESA ✆6563018 Tarom Romanian Air ✆(212) 687 6013 Tower Air ✆553 8500 Turkish Airlines ✆(212) 339 9650 Uzebkistan Airways ✆(212) 489 3954

Information and help desks
Airport Hotel Services Terminal 5 Upper Level ✆244 6194 Hotel booking ⌀USD5 service charge
Concordia Worldwide Hotel Reservations Terminal 4E Upper Level ✆(800) 347 2659 Hotel booking
Concordia Worldwide Hotel Reservations Terminal 4W Upper Level ✆(800) 347 2659 Hotel booking
EJM Rservations Terminal 3 Upper Level Hotel booking
Information Desk All Terminals Upper Level ✆244 7990; 244 4520 Airport information, Tourist information
Meegan Services Terminal 7 Upper Level ✆(800) 441 1115 Hotel booking ⌀USD5 service charge
Meegan Services Terminal 8 Upper Level ✆(800) 441 1115 Hotel booking ⌀USD5 service charge

EMERGENCIES

Police All Terminals throughout ✆244 4225; 244 4226
Medical All Terminals throughout ✆656 5344
Dental Services ✆656 4747
Lost Property All Terminals throughout ✆244 4225; 244 4226

AIRPORT FACILITIES

Money
ATM Terminal 4W Upper Level
ATM Terminal 8 throughout
ATM Terminal 9 throughout
Bank Terminal 8 Upper Level
Bank Terminal 2 Upper Level
Bank Terminal 4E Upper Level
Bureau de change All Terminals throughout

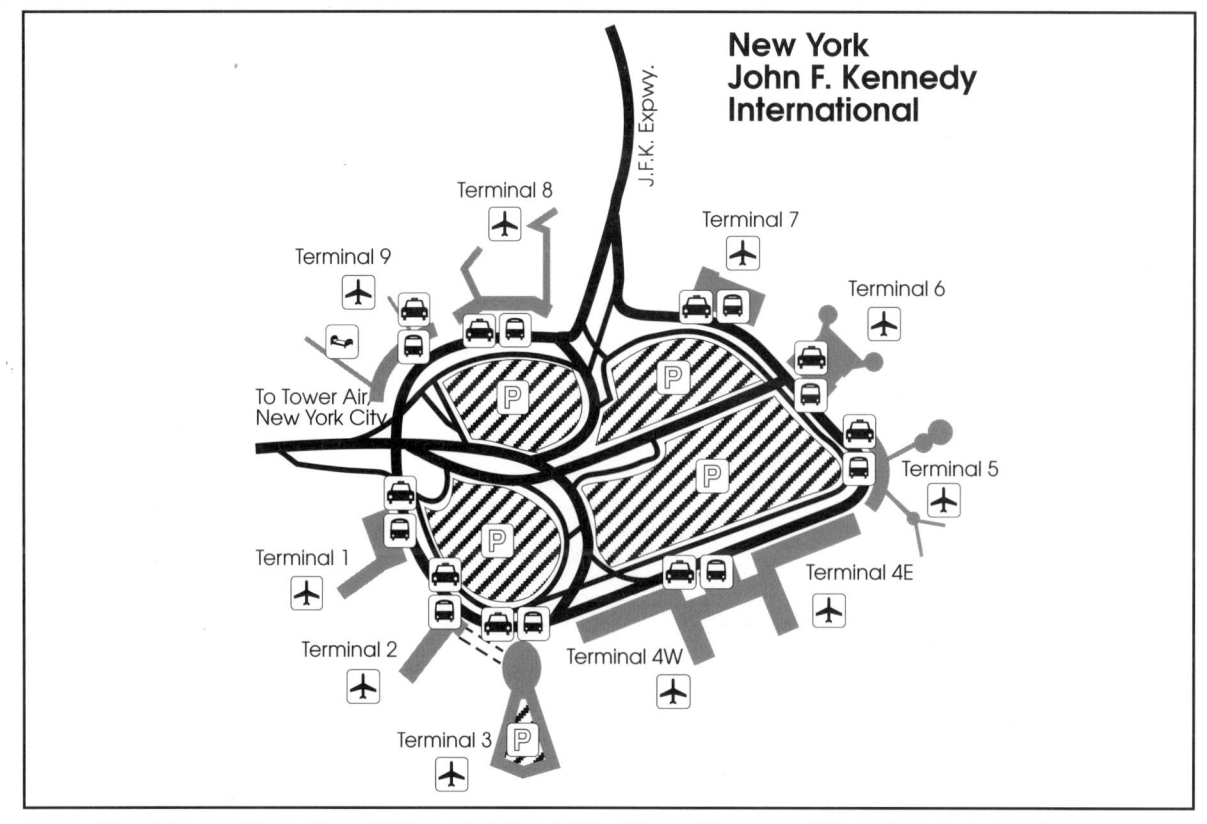

New York John F. Kennedy International

✆ Phone no. ℱ Fax no. ⓗ Hours of opening/operation ≫ Frequency of service ⊃ Journey time ⌀ Cost/one-way fare

Terminal 4 International

NEW YORK JOHN F. KENNEDY INTERNATIONAL

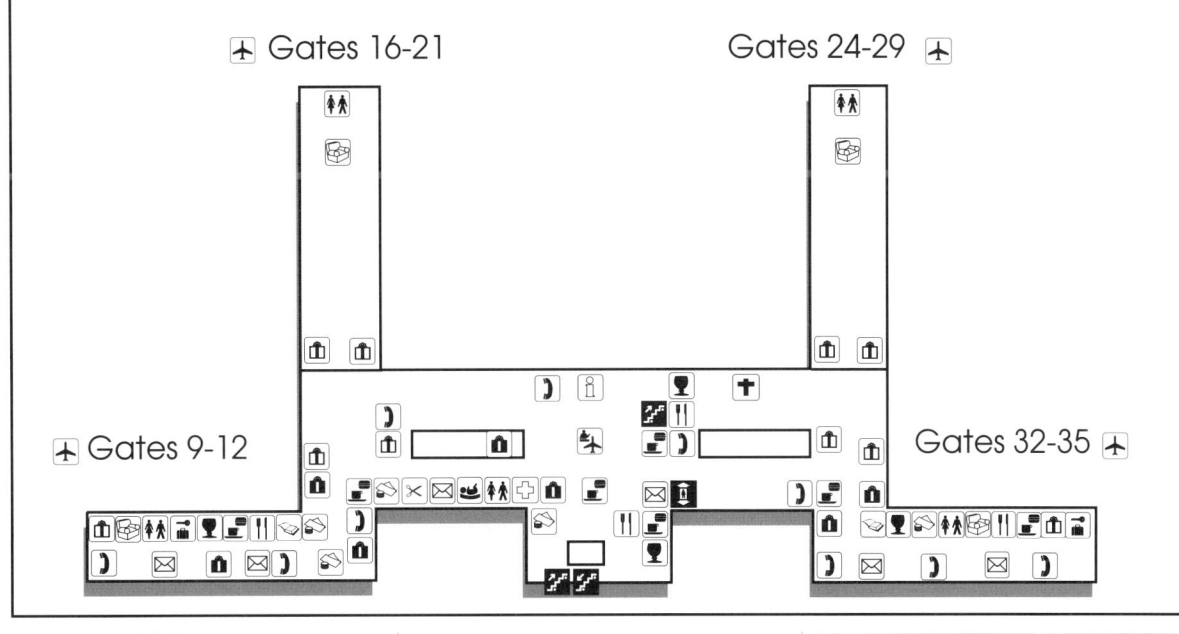

✈ Gates 16-21   Gates 24-29 ✈

✈ Gates 9-12   Gates 32-35 ✈

Food and drink
Bar All Terminals throughout
Café/light meals All Terminals throughout
Restaurant All Terminals throughout

Communications
Post office Terminal 4W Lower Level Lobby
Post office Terminal 4E Upper Level
Post office Terminal 4W Upper Level

Shopping
Duty free, departure All Terminals
Gift Shop All Terminals Upper Level
Hairdresser Terminal 4E Upper Level
Hairdresser Terminal 4W Upper Level
News, Stationery & Books All Terminals Upper Level
Pharmacy Terminal 4E Upper Level
Pharmacy Terminal 4W Upper Level

Luggage
Left luggage counter Terminal 4E Upper Level between Gates 10 and 11
⏰0700–2300 💰USD1.50–5 per day
Left luggage counter Terminal 4W Upper Level between Gates 33 and 34
⏰0700–2300 💰USD1.50–5 per day
Trolleys/carts All Terminals throughout
⏰24 hr 💰USD1.50
Left luggage counter Terminal 4E Upper Level between Gates 10 and 11
⏰0700–2300 💰USD1.50–5 per day

DISABLED TRAVELLERS

All Terminals Adapted toilets; Lifts Special car parking; Phones at wheelchair height; Phones adapted for the deaf; Personal assistance

SMOKING POLICY

All Terminals No-smoking throughout

SPECIAL PASSENGER LOUNGES

American Airlines Admirals Club Terminal 8 Upper Level
American Airlines Admirals Club Terminal 9 Upper Level
British Airways Club Terminal 7 Upper Level
Delta Airlines Crown Room Terminal 2 Upper Level
TWA Ambassadors Club Terminal 5 Upper Level
TWA Ambassadors Club Terminal 6 Upper Level
United Airlines Red Carpet Club Terminal 7 Upper Level

CONFERENCE AND BUSINESS FACILITIES

Business Services
Business Services, Mutual of Omaha, Terminal 4E Upper Level
Business Services, Mutual of Omaha, Terminal 4W Upper Level
Business Services, Terminal 6
Business Services, Terminal 8
Conference Rooms, Terminal 2
Conference Rooms, Terminal 4E
Conference Rooms, Terminal 4W
Conference Rooms, Terminal 7
Conference Rooms, Terminal 8

AIRPORT HOTELS

Ramada Plaza ✆995 9000 Courtesy bus

CAR RENTAL

Avis All Terminals Lower Level ✆244 5400
Budget All Terminals Lower Level ✆656 6010
Dollar All Terminals Lower Level ✆656 2400
Hertz All Terminals Lower Level ✆656 7600
National All Terminals Lower Level ✆632 8300

✈ Air • Rail • Bus • Limousine • Metro/subway • Tram • Helicopter • Water transport • For map symbols, see p. 9

NEW YORK-JFK

SECTION TWO • AIRPORT DIRECTORY

Car Parking

Long-stay 4 km/2.5 miles from terminals (24 hr shuttle bus) ⌀USD6 day
Short-stay Central Terminal Parking Area Lots ⌀USD4 first 4 hrs or part, and USD4 hr thereafter, USD24 day max

Taxis and Chauffeur-driven Cars

Taxis
All terminals New York City (Manhattan) ⌁45 min ⌀USD30 plus tolls

Public Transport

Airport to airport
New York-La Guardia Apt 🚌Carey Coach Express »30 min ⌚0530–2300 ⌁45 min ⌀USD11.
New York-Newark International Apt 🚌Princeton Airporter »1–2 hr ⌚0900–2200 ⌁1 hr 15 min ⌀USD19.

City & suburbs
Bronx 🚌Marc 1 Q On-demand ⌀USD25.
Brooklyn 🚌Carey Coach Express »2 hr ⌚1000–2000 ⌁1 hr–1hr 15 min ⌀USD9.50.
Brooklyn 🚌TA: B15 »30 min ⌚0500–0100 ⌀USD1.50. For subway trains 3, 4 at New Lots and Livonia Ave
Brooklyn 🚇TA: A Train »15 min ⌚24 hr ⌀USD1.50. Take free yellow, white and blue long-stay parking lot bus (15 min frequency) to Howard Beach/JFK Airport Station
New York (metro area/Tri-State Area) 🚕Over 80 companies at Airport.
New York (Grand Central rail stn) 🚌Carey Coach Express »30 min ⌚0600–2400 ⌁1 hr ⌀USD13. For Metro–North Railroad
New York (Manhattan) 🚇TA: A Train »15 min ⌚24 hr ⌁60–75 min ⌀USD1.50. Take free yellow, white and blue long-stay parking lot bus (15 min frequency) to Howard Beach/JFK Airport Station
New York (Pennsylvania rail stn) 🚌Carey Coach Express »60 min ⌚0600–2400 ⌁1 hr ⌀USD13. For all Amtrak services, Long Island Railroad and NJ Transit commuter rail services
New York (Midtown Manhattan/West Side and Port Authority Bus Terminal) 🚌Carey Coach Express »30 min ⌚0600–2400 ⌁1 hr ⌀USD13.
New York (Manhattan hotels) 🚌Gray Line Air Shuttle (800) 451 0455 Q On-demand ⌚0600–2330 ⌁45 min–1 hr ⌀USD16.50.
Queens 🚌Carey Coach Express »30 min ⌚0530–2230 ⌁30 min ⌀USD5.
Queens 🚌TA: Q3 »15 min ⌚0500–0215 ⌀USD1.15. For subway trains F, R
Queens 🚌Green Bus Line: Q10 »15 min ⌚24 hr ⌀USD1.25. For MTA subway trains A, E, J, Z, F and R
Queens 🚕Classic Airport Share Ride Q On-demand ⌀USD23–30.
Queens (subway) 🚇TA: A Train »15 min ⌚24 hr ⌁60–75 min ⌀USD1.50. Take free yellow, white and blue long-stay parking lot bus (15 min frequency) to Howard Beach/JFK Airport Station

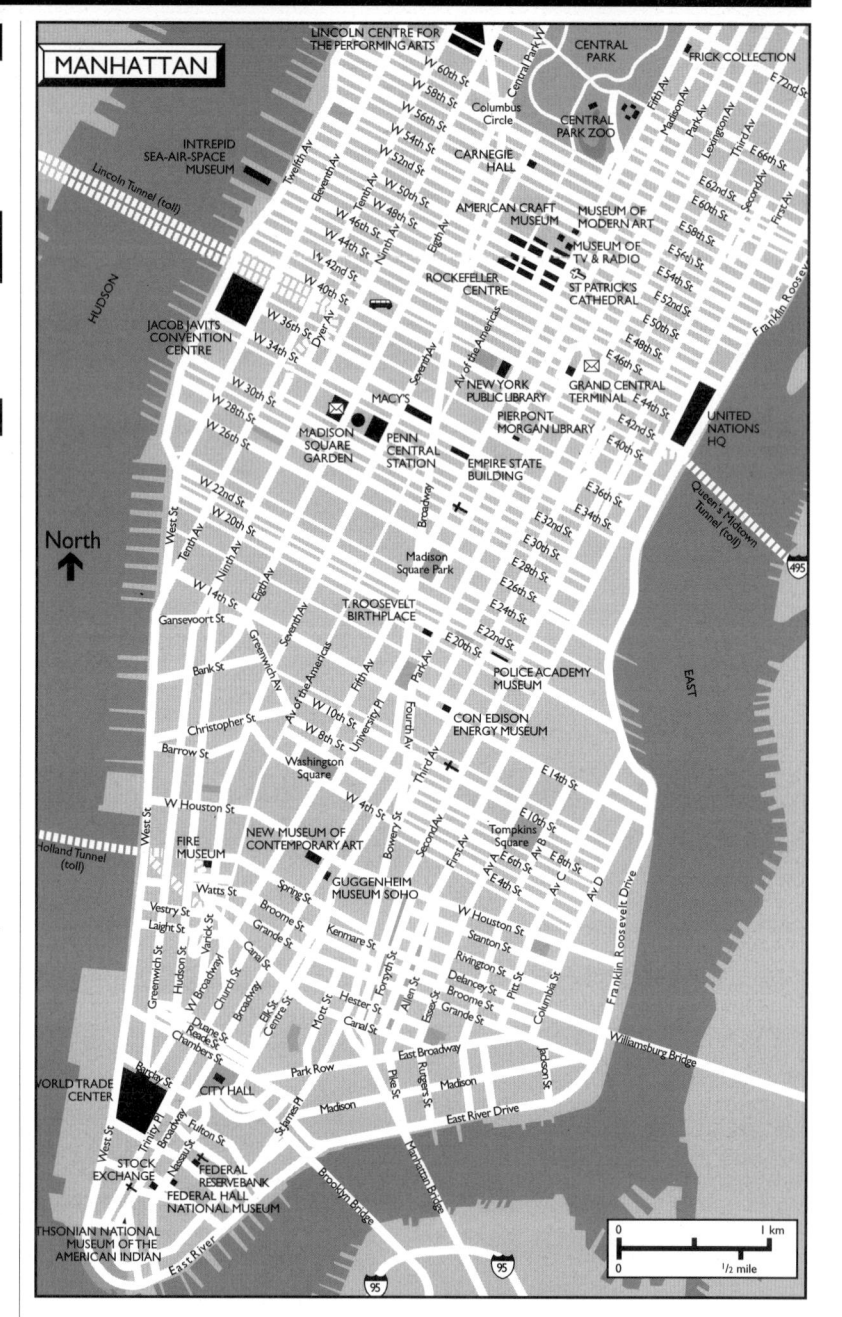

Other towns and cities
Connecticut 🚗Connecticut Limousine »30min–1 hr ⌁1–4 hr ⌚0600–2400 ⌀USD33–40. For Bridgeport/Fairfield, Danbury, Farmington, Greenwich, Hartford, Milford, New Haven, Norwalk, Shelton, Southbury, Stamford, Trumbull and Waterbury CT
Long Island NY (Jamaica Rail stn) 🚌Carey Airport Express »60 min ⌚0530–2230 ⌁1 hr ⌀USD5. For Long Island Railroad
Long Island, NY 🚕Classic Airport Share

ⓟ Phone no. ⓕ Fax no. ⌚ Hours of opening/operation » Frequency of service ⌁ Journey time ⌀ Cost/one-way fare

SECTION TWO • AIRPORT DIRECTORY　　　　　NEW YORK-JFK

Ride » On–demand ⌀USD27–68.
Long Island NY 🚆JFK Flyer »30 min-1 hr ⏱0500-2400 ⌀USD2 For Rockville Center, Valley Stream and Lynbrook
New Jersey 🚆Trans–Bridge Lines »11 day ⏱0730–2015 ⏳1 hr 30 min ⌀USD21 For Clinton, Phillipsburg, Flemington, Frenchtown and Lambertville NJ
New York State (upstate) 🚆Marc 1 » On–demand ⌀USD38–55. Rockland and Putnam counties
Pennsylvania 🚆Trans–Bridge Lines »1–2 hrs ⏱0730–2330 ⏳2 hr 30 min ⌀USD21 For Easton, Bethlehem, Allentown, New Hope and Doylestown PA

Princeton NJ 🚌Princeton Airporter »1–2 hr ⏱0900–2200 ⌀USD29–32. For Princeton, E Brunswick, Jamesburg, Cranbury and Hopewell NJ
Ridgewood NJ 🚌Air Brook Express (201) 670 6697
Westchester NY 🚌Connecticut Limousine »30min–1 hr ⏱0630–2400 ⏳1 hr ⌀USD28. For Rye and White Plains NY
Westchester NY 🚆Westchester Express » On–demand ⌀USD27–47.
Westchester NY 🚆Marc 1 » On–demand ⌀USD20–45.

Regional Air Connections

Albany NY ✈ »Several per day ⏳1 hr
Hartford CT ✈ »Several per day ⏳50 min
Philadelphia PA ✈ »Several per day ⏳50 min
Providence RI ✈ »Several per day ⏳1 hr

TRAVELLER'S NOTES

Terminal 1 is under construction. Porters wear uniforms (and at the other two NY airports) – anyone else offering help with baggage is suspect.

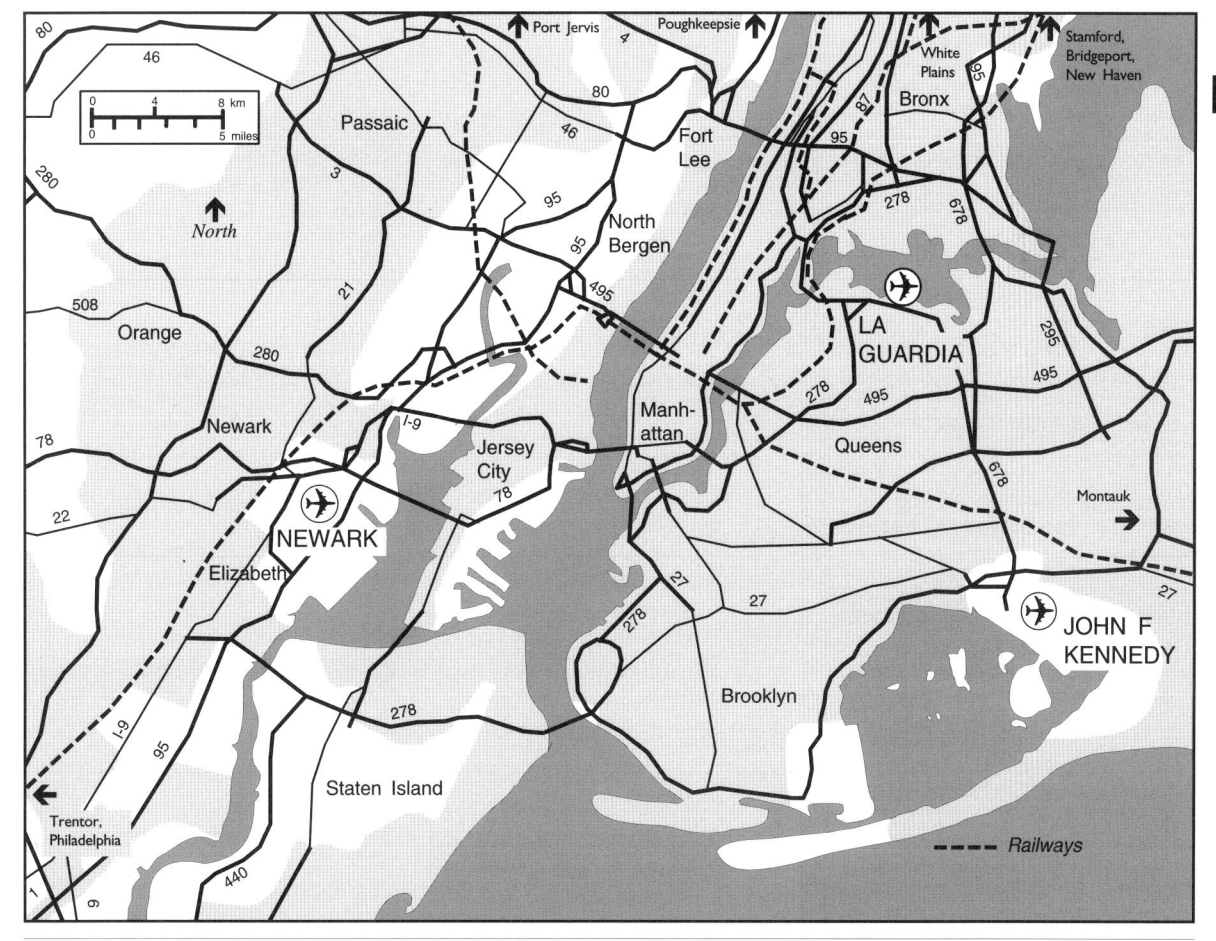

✈ Air 🚆 Rail 🚌 Bus 🚐 Limousine Ⓜ Metro/subway 🚋 Tram 🚁 Helicopter ⛴ Water transport • For map symbols, see p. 9

NEW YORK-LA GUARDIA   SECTION TWO • AIRPORT DIRECTORY ✈✈

NEW YORK-LA GUARDIA — LGA
USA (see page 41)

National ℗ code: 1
Area ℗ code: 718
Local time: Winter GMT-5, Summer GMT-4
New York (La Guardia) Airport, Flushing, NY 11371, USA
℗533 3400
WWW site: http://www.panynj.gov/
Location: 13 km/8 miles NE of New York City

Terminals and Transfers

Terminals
Central Terminal Airlines: All other airlines. Layout: Arrival Level (Baggage Claim, Car Rental, Ground Transportation); Departure Level (Concourse A (Gates A1–A7), B (Gates B1–B8), C (Gates C1–C14), D (Gates D1–D10); Third Floor (Airline Lounges)
US Airways Terminal Airlines: US Airways, US Airways Express, US Airways Shuttle. Layout: Arrival Level (Baggage Claim, Car Rental, Ground Transportation), Departure Level (Gates 1–22)
Delta Terminal Airlines: Business Express, Delta Airlines, Northwest Airlines, NW Airlink. Layout: Arrival Level (Baggage Claim, Car Rental, Ground Transportation), Departure Level (Gates 1–10)
Marine Air Terminal Airlines: Delta Shuttle. Departure Level (Gates 1-6)

Minimum transfer times
International: 1 hr Domestic: 45 min

Transfer between terminals
Bus ≫10–20 min ⊙0500-0200; All terminals ⊘Free

Information

Information and help desks
Information Desk Central Terminal Departure Level ℗476 5000 Airport information, Tourist information

Emergencies
Police All Terminals throughout ℗533 3930
Medical All Terminals throughout ℗476 5575

Lost Property All Terminals throughout ℗533 3935

Airport Facilities

Money
Bank Central Terminal Departure Level
ATM All Terminals throughout
Bureau de change Central Terminal Departure Level Concourse A
Bureau de change Delta Terminal Departure Level
Bureau de change US Airways Terminal Departure Level

Food and drink
Bar All Terminals throughout
Café/light meals All Terminals throughout
Restaurant Central Terminal Departure Level
Restaurant US Airways Terminal Departure Level
Restaurant Delta Terminal Departure Level

Communications
Post box All Terminals throughout
Post office Central Terminal Departures Level ⊙0900–1500 (1600 Wed–Fri)

Shopping
Duty free, departure Central Terminal Departure Level, Concourses A and D
Duty free, departure Delta Terminal Departure Level
Gift Shop All Terminals throughout
News, Stationery & Books All Terminals throughout
Pharmacy Central Terminal Departure Level

Luggage
Left luggage counter Central Terminal Mutual of Omaha, Departure Level between American and United ⊙0630–2030 ⊘USD1.50–5
Left luggage counter US Airways Terminal Mutual of Omaha, Gate 10 ⊙0630–2100 ⊘USD1.50–10
Lockers All Terminals Departure Level ⊙24 hr
Trolleys/carts All Terminals throughout ⊙24 hr ⊘USD1.50

Disabled Travellers

All Terminals Adapted toilets; Lifts

Special car parking; Phones at wheelchair height

Smoking Policy
All Terminals No-smoking throughout

Special Passenger Lounges
American Airlines Admirals Club Central Terminal Departure Level, Concourse D
Continental Airlines Presidents Club Central Terminal Third Floor
Delta Airlines Crown Room Delta Terminal Departure Level
Northwest Airlines World Club Delta Terminal Departure Level
TWA Ambassadors Club Central Terminal Third Floor
United Airlines Red Carpet Club Central Terminal Third Floor
US Airways Club US Airways Terminal Departure Level

Conference and Business Facilities
Conference Room, Central Terminal, Concourse D
Business Centers, Central Terminal ⊙0600–2100 Mon–Fri
Business Centers, US Airways Terminal ⊙0600–2100 Mon–Fri

Airport Hotels
Avis All Terminals Lower Level ℗507 3600
Budget All Terminals Lower Level ℗639 6400
Dollar All Terminals Lower Level ℗779 5600
Hertz All Terminals Lower Level ℗478 5300
National All Terminals Lower Level ℗803 4101

Car Parking
Short-stay Parking Garage and Lots adjacent to terminals ⊘USD4 first 4 hr or part, USD2 per hr thereafter, USD18 per day (max)

℗ Phone no. ℱ Fax no. ⊙ Hours of opening/operation ≫ Frequency of service ⊃ Journey time ⊘ Cost/one-way fare

✈✈ SECTION TWO • AIRPORT DIRECTORY   NEW YORK-LA GUARDIA

Taxis and Chauffeur-driven Cars

Taxis
All terminals New York City (Manhattan) ⊘USD20 plus tolls

Public Transport

Airport to airport
New York-JFK Apt 🚌Carey Coach Express »30 min ⓒ0630–2300 ⊃45 min ⊘USD11.
Newark International Apt 🚌Marc 1 » On-demand ⓒ0700–2300 ⊃1 hr 30 min ⊘USD18.

City & suburbs
Bronx 🚌Marc 1 » On-demand ⊘USD20.
Brooklyn 🚌Carey Coach Express »2 hr ⓒ1045–2045 ⊃30 min ⊘USD7.50.
New York 🚌TA M60 »30 min ⓒ0450-0100 ⊘USD1.50. For 125th St
New York (Grand Central rail stn) 🚌Carey Airport Express »30 min ⓒ0645–2400 ⊃20-30 min ⊘USD10. For Metro–North Railroad
New York (hotels) 🚌Gray Line Air Shuttle » On–demand ⓒ0700–2330 ⊃45 min–1 hr ⊘USD13.50.
New York (Port Authority Bus Terminal) 🚌Carey Coach Express »30 min ⓒ0645–2400 ⊃30-45 min ⊘USD10.
New York Metro/Tri–State Area 🚐Over 80 companies at airport.
New York (Pier 11 Wall Street) 🚢Delta Water Shuttle ⓒMon–Fri ⊃30–45 min ⊘USD15. For East Side (East River at 34th and 62nd St)
Queens 🚌Classic Airport Shuttle » On-demand ⊘USD20–32.
Queens 🚌TA: M60 »30 min ⓒ0450–0100 ⊘USD1.50. For N subway train
Queens 🚌TA: Q48 »15 min ⓒ0530–0030 ⊘USD1.50. For 7 subway train
Queens (Jamaica Station) 🚌Carey Coach Express »1 hr ⓒ0700–2300 ⊃30 min ⊘USD5. For Long Island Railroad trains
Queens 🚌Triboro Coach: Q33, Q47 »10–20 min ⓒ24 hr ⊘US1.25. Connects with E, F, G, R and 7 subway trains

Other towns and cities
Connecticut 🚌Connecticut Limousine »30min–1 hr ⊃1–4 hr ⊘USD33–40. For Bridgeport/Fairfield, Danbury, Farmington, Greenwich, Hartford, Milford, New Haven, Norwalk, Shelton, Southbury, Stamford, Trumbull and Waterbury CT
Long Island, NY 🚌Classic Airport Share Ride » On-demand ⊘USD27–68.
New York (Upstate) 🚌Marc 1 » On-demand ⊘USD30–50. For Rockland and Putnam Counties
Westchester NY 🚐Connecticut Limousine »30 min–1 hr ⓒ0630–2400 ⊃1 hr ⊘USD28. For Rye and White Plains NY
Westchester NY 🚌Marc 1 » On-demand ⊘USD20–40.
Westchester NY 🚌Westchester Express » On-demand ⊘USD22–42.

Regional Air Connections

Albany NY ✈ »Several per day ⊃1 hr
Boston MA ✈ »Several per day ⊃1 hr
Hartford CT ✈ »Several per day ⊃50 min
Manchester NH ✈ »Several per day ⊃1 hr
Philadelphia PA ✈ »Several per day ⊃1 hr
Providence RI ✈ »Several per day ⊃55 min
Syracuse NY ✈ »Several per day ⊃1 hr
Utica NY ✈ »Several per week
Washington DC ✈ »Several per day ⊃1 hr
Worcester MA ✈ »Several per week ⊃1 hr

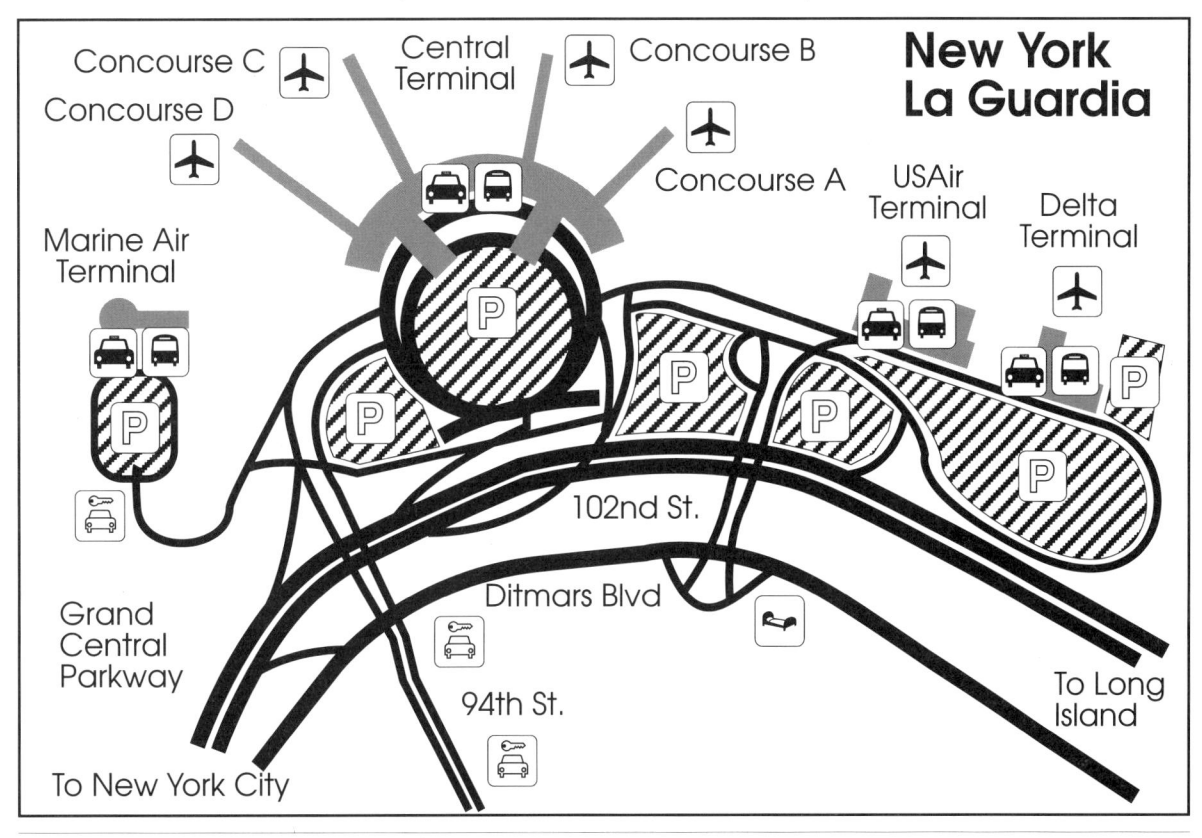

215

New York La Guardia

✈ Air 🚋 Rail 🚌 Bus 🚐 Limousine Ⓜ Metro/subway 🚊 Tram 🚁 Helicopter 🚢 Water transport • For map symbols, see p. 9

NEW YORK-NEWARK — EWR

USA (see page 41)

National ✆ code: 1
Area ✆ code: 201
Local time: Winter GMT-5, Summer GMT-4
Newark International Airport, Tower Rd, Newark, NJ 07114, USA
✆961 6000
🖷961 6259
WWW site: http://www.panynj.gov/
Location: 28 km/16 miles E of New York City

Terminals and Transfers

Terminals
Terminal A Airlines: Aer Lingus (Departures), American Airlines, Chautaugua, Citybird (Departures), Colgan Air, Kiwi, Midway Airlines, Sunjet International, TWA, TW Express, United Airlines (Domestic), United Airlines (International Departures), United Express, US Airways, US Airways Express. Layout: Lower Level (Arrival, Baggage Claim, Car Rental, Ground Transportation), Concourse Level (Gates 10–39), Upper Level (Departure)
Terminal B Airlines: Aer Lingus (Arrivals), Air Alliance (Arrivals), Air Aruba, Air France, Air Jamaica, American Transair, Avianca, British Airways, Carnival Airlines, Citybird (Arrivals), Continental (International Arrivals), Czech Airlines, Delta, Delta Express, El Al Israel, EVA Airways, Korean Air, LOT Polish, Lufthansa, Mexicana, Midwest Express, North American, Northwest, KLM, Philippine Airlines, SAS (Arrivals), Swissair, TAP Air Portugal, United (International Arrivals), Virgin Atlantic, Western Pacific. Layout: Lower Level (Arrival, Baggage Claim, Car Rental, Ground Transportation), Concourse Level (Gates 40–68), Upper Level (Departure)
Terminal C Airlines: Air Alliance (Departures), Air Canada, Air Nova, Alitalia (Departures), America West, Continental Airlines, Continental Express, SAS (Departures). Layout: Lower Level (Arrival, Baggage Claim, Car Rental, Ground Transportation), Concourse Level (Gates 70–134), Upper Level (Departure)

Minimum transfer times
International: 1 hr–2 hr 30 min
Domestic: 1 hr

Transfer between terminals
Monorail ⇒ Frequent; All terminals and long stay parking ⊘Free

Information

Flight enquiries
Aer Lingus ✆(212) 557 1110 Czech Air ✆(212) 765 6022 North American ✆(718) 656 2650 Taesa ✆(718) 656 3018

Information and help desks
Information Desk All Terminals Lower Level ✆961 6000 Airport information, Tourist information

Emergencies

Police All Terminals throughout ✆961 6230
Medical All Terminals throughout ✆961 2525
Lost Property All Terminals Contact airlines ✆961 6230

Airport Facilities

Money
ATM All Terminals throughout
Bank Terminal C Concourse Level, near Gates 70–99 ⓗ0900–1500 Mon–Fri
Bureau de change All Terminals Concourse Level

Food and drink
Bar All Terminals throughout
Café/light meals All Terminals throughout
Restaurant All Terminals Concourse Level

Communications
Fax service All Terminals Concourse Level
Post box All Terminals throughout

Shopping
Duty free, departure All Terminals Concourse Level
Gift Shop All Terminals Concourse Level
News, Stationery & Books All Terminals throughout

Luggage
Left luggage counter Terminal B Mutual of Omaha desk opposite Door 6 ⓗ0700–2000 ⊘USD1.50–10
Lockers All Terminals throughout

Disabled Travellers
All Terminals Lifts Special car parking; Phones adapted for the deaf

Smoking Policy
All Terminals Permitted in bars and bar areas of VIP Lounges and Airline Clubs

Special Passenger Lounges
Lindbergh Lounge Terminal B Concourse Level between Gates 51–57 and 60–68 American Express cardholders
American Airlines Admirals Club Terminal A Concourse Level
Continental Airlines Presidents Club Terminal C Concourse Level
Continental Airlines Presidents Club Terminal B Concourse Level
Delta Airlines Crown Room Terminal B Concourse Level
TWA Ambassadors Club Terminal A Concourse Level
United Airlines Red Carpet Club Terminal A Concourse Level
US Airways Club Terminal A Concourse Level

Conference and Business Facilities
Business Center, All terminals, Concourse Level

Airport Hotels
Mariott Airport ✆623 0006 🖷623 7618 607 rooms Courtesy bus

Car Rental
Alamo All Terminals Monorail Station D2
Avis All Terminals Monorail Station D1 ✆961 4300
Budget All Terminals Monorail Station D2 ✆961 2990

✆ Phone no. 🖷 Fax no. ⓗ Hours of opening/operation ⇒ Frequency of service ⤴ Journey time ⊘ Cost/one-way fare

Dollar All Terminals Monorail Station D2 ✆824 2002
Hertz All Terminals Monorail Station D1 ✆621 2000
National All Terminals Monorail Station D1 ✆622 1270

Car Parking

Long-stay 1 km/½ mile from terminal ⊘USD4 per 4 hr, USD1 per hr thereafter, USD7 per day (max)
Short-stay Adjacent to terminals 3196 spaces ⊘USD4 per 4 hr, USD4 per hr thereafter, USD48 per day (max)

Taxis and Chauffeur-driven Cars

Taxis
All terminals, Lower Level Newark city centre ⊃15 min ⊘USD10
All terminals, Lower Level Manhattan ⊃40 min ⊘USD45 plus tolls

Public Transport

Airport to airport
New York-JFK Apt 🚌Princeton Airporter Van »1–2 hr ⏱0700–2015 ⊃1 hr 15 min ⊘USD19.
New York-La Guardia Apt 🚌Marc 1 »On-demand ⊃1 hr-1hr 30 min ⊘USD18.

City & suburbs
Bronx 🚌Marc 1 » On-demand ⊘USD29.
New York (Grand Central rail stn) 🚆Olympia Trails »20–30 min ⏱0615–2400 ⊃30–60 min ⊘USD7. For Metro–North trains
New York (Midtown Hotels) 🚌Olympia Trails »20–30 min ⏱0615–2400 ⊃30–60 min ⊘USD12.
New York (Pennsylvania rail stn) 🚌Olympia Trails »20–30 min ⏱0615–2400 ⊃30–40 min ⊘USD7. For all Amtrak services, Long Island Railroad and NJ Transit Manhattan services
New York (Port Authority Bus Terminal) 🚌Olympia Trails »10–15 min (30–60 min overnight) ⏱24 hr ⊃30–40 min ⊘USD7.
New York (World Trade Center) 🚌Olympia Trails »20–30 min ⏱0645–0845 ⊃20–40 min ⊘USD7.
New York (Manhattan hotels) 🚌Gray Line Minibus » On-demand ⏱0600–2330 ⊃30 min–1 hr ⊘USD18.50
New York Metro/Tri-State Area lOver 80 companies.

Other towns and cities
Connecticut 🚌Connecticut Limousine »1–2 hr ⏱0815–2315 ⊃1–4 hr ⊘USD36–40. For Bridgeport/Fairfield, Danbury, Farmington, Greenwich, Hartford, Milford, New Haven, Norwalk, Shelton, Southbury, Stamford, Trumbull and Waterbury CT
New Jersey 🚌State Shuttle » On-demand.
New Jersey 🚆Trans–Bridge Lines »3 per day ⏱1015; 1330; 2045. For Hunterdon County (Clinton, Phillipsburg, Flemington, Frenchtown and Lambertville NJ)
New York (Upstate) 🚌Marc 1 » On-demand ⊘USD33–59. For Rockland and Putnam Counties NY
Newark NJ (Penn rail stn) 🚌New Jersey Transit: 302 Airlink »20–30 min ⏱0605–0140 ⊘USD4. For Amtrak, PATH and NJ Transit trains
Northern NJ 🚌Olympic Limousine (800) 822 9797 »45 min–1 hr ⏱0550–0035 ⊘USD15–32. For Ocean and Monmouth Counties NJ
Pennsylvania 🚌Princeton Airporter »Frequent ⏱0900–2100 ⊘USD22. For Yardley and Trevose PA
Pennsylvania 🚆Trans–Bridge Lines »8 per day ⏱0900–2400 ⊃1-2 hr ⊘USD12. For Easton, Bethleham, Allentown, New Hope and Doylestown PA
Princeton NJ 🚆Princeton Airporter »1–2 hr ⏱0715–2215 ⊘USD16–19. For Middlesex and Mercer counties (Princeton, E Brunswick, Jamesburg, Cranbury and Hopewell NJ)
Westchester NY 🚌Marc 1 » On-demand ⊘USD30–48.
Westchester NY 🚌Connecticut Limousine »1-2 hr ⏱0815-2315 ⊃1 hr 30 min ⊘USD32. For Rye and White Plains NY

Regional Air Connections

Albany NY ✈ »Several per day ⊃1 hr
Atlantic City NJ ✈ »Several per day ⊃45 min
Binghamton NY ✈ »Several per day ⊃1 hr
Harrisburg PA ✈ »Several per day ⊃50 min
Hartford CT ✈ »Several per day ⊃1 hr
Ithaca NY ✈ »Several per day ⊃1 hr
New Haven CT ✈ »Several per day ⊃45 min
Philadelphia PA ✈ »Several per day ⊃50 min
Providence RI ✈ »Several per day ⊃1 hr
Wilkes-Barre PA ✈ »Several per day ⊃50 min
Worcester MA ✈ »At least daily ⊃1 hr

NICE — NCE

France (see page 22)

National ✆ code: 33
Area ✆ code: 04
Local time: Winter GMT+1, Summer GMT+2
Aéroport Nice Côte d' Azur, 06056 Nice Cedex, France
✆93 21 30 30
✆93 21 30 29
Location: 6 km/4 miles W of Nice

Terminals and Transfers

Terminals
Terminal 1 Airlines: All international flights. Layout: Ground Level, Arrival; Level 1 Departure; Level 2, offices and facilities; Basement, toilets and Left Luggage
Terminal 2 Airlines: All domestic flights. Layout: Ground Level, Arrival; Level 1 Departure; Basement Level, toilets, left luggage

Minimum transfer times
International: 45 min–1 hr Domestic: 35 min

Transfer between terminals
Bus »8 min peak hours; Terminals 1 and 2 ⊘Free

Information

Flight enquiries
Airport ✆93 21 30 12
Air Afrique ✆93 71 49 71 **Air Algérie** ✆93 83 24 16 **Air France** ✆93 18 89 89

Nice

SECTION TWO • AIRPORT DIRECTORY

Air Inter ℘93 14 84 84 Air Malta ℘92 12 12 27 Air Portugal TAP ℘93 21 34 35 Air UK ℘1 44 56 18 14 Alitalia ℘93 21 46 21 AOM French Airlines ℘92 14 67 77 Austrian Airlines ℘93 18 89 89 British Airways ℘93 21 47 01 British Midland Airways ℘92 14 67 74 Crossair ℘93 21 47 47 Delta Airlines ℘93 21 34 86 Deutsche BA ℘93 21 47 01 Emirates ℘93 21 37 87 Finnair ℘93 21 45 56 Iberia ℘93 83 04 04 KLM ℘1 44 56 18 14 Lot Polish Airlines ℘93 21 46 90 Lufthansa ℘93 83 02 80 Luxair ℘93 18 89 89 Meridiana ℘1 42 61 61 50 Middle East Airlines ℘93 21 42 11 Regional Airlines ℘93 21 34 69 Royal Air Maroc ℘93 83 21 23 Sabena World Airlines ℘93 21 47 60 Saudia ℘93 21 34 90 SAS ℘93 21 34 55 Swissair ℘93 21 47 47 Tunis Air ℘93 21 35 05 Turkish Airlines ℘93 21 44 79

Information and help desks
Information Desk Terminal 1 Central Hall Ground Level ℘93 21 30 12 ⊙0600–last flight *Airport information, Flights Hotel booking, Tourist information*
Information Desk Terminal 1 Arrival Hall ℘93 21 30 12 ⊙0600–last flight *Airport information, Flights Hotel booking, Tourist information*
Information Desk Terminal 2 Luggage claim Area ground Level ℘93 21 30 12 ⊙0600–last flight *Airport information, Flights Hotel booking, Tourist information*

EMERGENCIES
Police Terminal 2 Arrival Hall, Ground Level ℘93 72 71 71
Police Terminal 1 Arrival Hall, Ground Level ℘93 72 71 71
Medical Terminal 1 Information Desks and Vaccination Centre ℘93 21 38 81 ⊙0630–2330
Medical Terminal 2 Information Desk ℘93 21 30 12 ⊙0630–2330
Lost Property Terminal 1 Left Luggage Bureau, Ground Level ℘93 21 31 11
Lost Property Terminal 1 Left Luggage Bureau, Basement ℘93 21 31 11

AIRPORT FACILITIES

Money
ATM Terminal 1 Central Hall, Ground Level ⊙24 hr
Bank Terminal 1 Level 1, opposite Post Office ⊙1000–1600 Mon–Fri
Bureau de change Terminal 1 Central Hall, Ground Level ⊙Jul–Aug 0830–2045; Sep–Jun 0830–1930
Bureau de change Terminal 2 Central Arrival/Departure Halls ⊙0800–2230

Food and drink
Bar Terminal 1 Level 2 ⊙1100–2200
Bar Terminal 1 Ground Level, Central Hall ⊙0630–2200
Bar Terminal 2 Level 1 ⊙0600–2200
Bar Terminal 2 Ground Level, Central Hall ⊙0700–2200
Café/light meals Terminal 1 Level 1, above Central Hall ⊙0700–2200
Café/light meals Terminal 2 Ground Level, Central Hall ⊙0700–2200
Restaurant Terminal 1 Level 2, Le Ciel d'Azur ⊙1100–1500
Restaurant Terminal 1 Level 2, Baie des Anges ⊙1100–2200
Restaurant Terminal 2 Level 1, Le Mercantour ⊙1100–2200

Communications
Post office Terminal 1 Level 1, above Central Hall ⊙0900–1700 Mon-Fri; 0900–1200 Sat
Fax service Terminal 1 Conference & Business centre

Shopping
Duty free, departure Terminal 1 Level 1 Departure Area ⊙All flight times
Shopping mall Terminal 1 Level 1 Departure Area ⊙All flight times
Florist Terminal 2 Level 1 Gallery ⊙0800–2100
Gift Shop Terminal 2 Level 1 Gallery ⊙0800–2100
News, Stationery & Books Terminal 2 Level 1 Gallery ⊙0800–2100

Luggage
Left luggage counter Terminal 1 Basement Level, near toilets
Porters Terminal 1 Ground Level, Arrival/Departure Area ⊙All flight times
Trolleys/carts Terminal 1 Front of Terminal ⊙24 hr ⌀FRF10
Left luggage counter Terminal 2 Level 1, Arrival/Departure Area
Porters Terminal 2 Level 1, Arrival/Departure Area ⊙All flight times
Trolleys/carts Terminal 2 Front of Terminal ⊙24 hr ⌀FRF10

DISABLED TRAVELLERS
Terminal 1 Adapted toilets; Lifts; Special car parking; Phones at wheelchair height; Personal assistance *Doctor via Information Desk 0630–2330*
Terminal 2 Adapted toilets; Lifts; Special car parking; Phones at wheelchair height; Personal assistance *Doctor via Information Desk 0630–2330*

SMOKING POLICY
Terminal 1 No-smoking areas marked throughout
Terminal 2 No-smoking areas marked throughout

SPECIAL PASSENGER LOUNGES
Air France Lounge Terminal 1 Departure Level, after passport control *Club members and First class passengers*
British Airways Executive Club Lounge Terminal 1 Departure Level, after passport control *Club members, First and Business class passengers*

CONFERENCE AND BUSINESS FACILITIES
Business and Conference Centre, Level 1, before Departure Area ℘93 21 30 73 ℻93 21 31 81 *Telephones, Fax service, P*

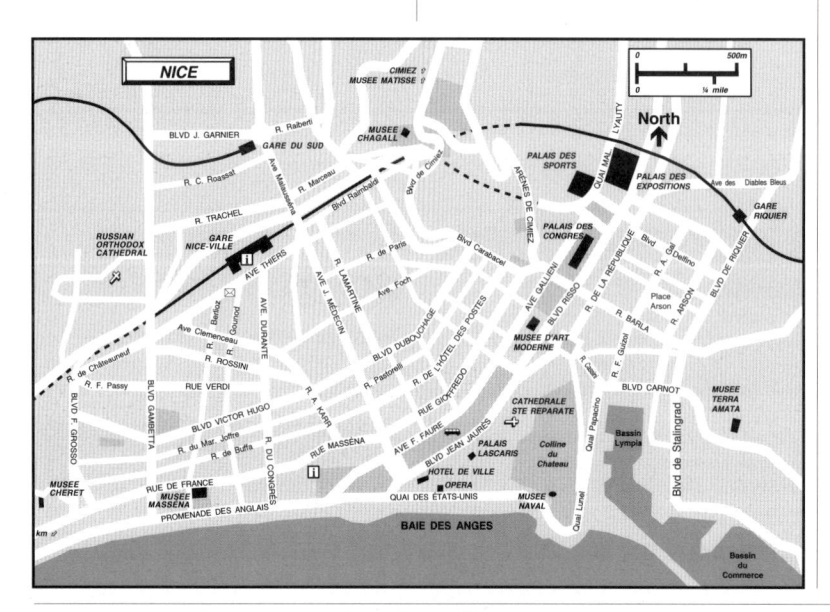

℘ Phone no.   ℻ Fax no.   ⊙ Hours of opening/operation   ≫ Frequency of service   ⊃ Journey time   ⌀ Cost/one-way fare

hotocopier, Secretarial service, Translation/Interpretation service

Airport Hotels

Arenas ℂ93 21 22 50 🅕93 21 63 50 280 rooms *Courtesy bus*
Campanile ℂ93 31 20 20 *Courtesy bus*
Holiday Inn ℂ93 14 80 03 🅕93 07 21 24 *Courtesy bus*
Ibis ℂ93 83 30 30 🅕93 18 14 22 *Courtesy bus*
Novotel ℂ93 31 61 15 🅕93 07 62 25 *Courtesy bus*
Occidental ℂ93 83 91 22 🅕93 21 69 57 *Courtesy bus*

Car Rental

Avis Terminal 1 Ground Level, Arrival Hall ℂ93 21 36 33
Avis Terminal 2 Ground Level, Arrival Hall ℂ93 21 42 80
Budget Terminal 1 Ground Level, Arrival Hall ℂ93 21 36 50
Budget Terminal 2 Ground Level, Arrival Hall ℂ93 21 42 51
EuropCar Terminal 1 Ground Level, Arrival Hall ℂ93 21 36 44
EuropCar Terminal 2 Ground Level, Arrival Hall ℂ93 21 42 53
Hertz Terminal 1 Ground Level, Arrival Hall ℂ93 21 36 72
Hertz Terminal 2 Ground Level, Arrival Hall ℂ93 21 42 72

Car Parking

Long-stay Covered garages in front of Terminal 1; 2400 spaces ⊘FRF80 per day
Short-stay P2 P7 in front of Terminals 1 and 2; 2500 spaces ⊘FRF9 per hr; FRF60 per day

Taxis and Chauffeur-driven Cars

Taxis
Front of terminal, Ground Level ℂ93 80 70 70 City centre ➲10 min ⊘FRF150

Public Transport

City & suburbs
Nice city centre (Gare SNCF rail stn) 🚌Airport Bus »20 min ⏱0605–2325 Mon–Sat ➲20 min ⊘FRF8. *For connections by rail along the Riviera, into Italy, and many other French cities.*
Nice city centre (Gare Routière bus stn) 🚌Auto Nice Transport no 23 »20 min ⏱0605–2325 Mon–Sat ➲20 min ⊘FRF21. *For buses along the Riviera.*

Courtesy/special transport
Nice Gare SNCF rail stn 🚌Airport-Riviera Shuttle ⊘Free.
St Laurent du Var SNCF rail stn 🚌Airport-Riviera Shuttle ⊘Free.

Other towns and cities
Aix-en-Provence 🚌Cars Phocéens »avg 2 hr 30 min ⏱0630–1730 ➲2 hr 45 min ⊘FRF145.
Antibes 🚌Rapides Côte d'Azur »40 min ⏱0750–2115 Mon–Sat ➲1 hr 25 min ⊘FRF42.
Avignon 🚌Cars Phocéens »avg 2 hr 30 min ⏱0630–1730 ➲2 hr 45 min ⊘FRF145.
Cannes 🚁Héli-Inter »avg 20 min ⏱0820–2005 ➲7 min.
Cannes 🚌Airport-Riviera Shuttle »1 hr ⏱0900–2000 ➲1 hr 45 min ⊘FRF70.
Cannes centre 🚌Rapides Côte d'Azur »40 min ⏱0750–2115 Mon–Sat ➲1 hr 25 min ⊘FRF42.
Draguignan 🚌Rapides Varois »1 per day ⏱0912 Mon–Sat ➲1 hr ⊘FRF 72.
Fréjus/St Raphael 🚌Aviabus »avg 2 hr 15 m ⏱0905–1835 Mon–Fri ➲1 hr 15 min ⊘FRF90.
Grasse 🚌SOMA »avg 1 hr 15 min ⏱0900–1945 ➲1 hr ⊘FRF47.
Juan-les-Pins 🚌Rapides Côte d'Azur »40 min ⏱0750–2115 Mon–Sat ➲1 hr 25 min ⊘FRF 42.
Marseille 🚌Cars Phocéens »avg 2 hr 30 min ⏱0630–1730 ➲2 hr 45 min ⊘FRF145.
Menton 🚌Airport-Riviera Shuttle »1 hr 15 min ⏱0910–1930 ➲1 hr 15 min ⊘FRF90.
Monte Carlo 🚁Héli-Inter »avg 20 min ⏱0723–2102 ➲6 min.
Monte Carlo 🚌Airport-Riviera Shuttle »1 hr ⏱0910–1930 ➲45 min ⊘FRF80.
St-Tropez 🚁Héli-Inter »7 per day ⏱0820–2030 ➲28 min.
Toulon 🚌Cars Phocéens ⏱0800–1715 ➲2 hr 30 min ⊘FRF110.

Regional Air Connections
Ajaccio ✈ »Several per day ➲45 min
Bastia ✈ »Several per day ➲45 min
Bologna ✈ »Several per day ➲1 hr 5 min
Calvi ✈ »At least daily ➲40 min
Clermont-Ferrand ✈ »Several per week ➲1 hr 10 min
Figari ✈ »Several per week ➲45 min
Florence ✈ »Several per week ➲1 hr 10 min
Geneva ✈ »Several per day ➲55 min
Lyon ✈ »Several per day ➲50 min
Milan ✈ »Several per week ➲55 min
Rome ✈ »Several per day ➲1 hr
Strasbourg ✈ »Several per week ➲1 hr 10 min
Toulouse ✈ »Several per week ➲1 hr

NORWICH NWI

United Kingdom (see page 41)

National ℂ code: 44
Area ℂ code: 01603
Local time: Winter GMT, Summer GMT+1
Address: Norwich Airport Ltd, Amsterdam Way, Norwich NR6 6JA
ℂ: 411923
🅕: 487523
WWW site: HTTP://WWW vitalo.com/norwichairport

Location: 8 km/5 miles N of Norwich

Terminals and Transfers

Terminals
Main Terminal Airlines: Air UK, Suckling Airways, Peach Air, Air Europa, Eurocypria, Britannia, Spanair, Airtours, Air Malta

Information

Information and help desks ℂ 411923 Flight enqiries, airport information

Airport Facilities

Money
Thomas Cook Bureau de Change ⏱ open during normal operating hours
ATM ⏱ open during normal operating hours

NORWICH • ORLANDO

SECTION TWO • AIRPORT DIRECTORY

Food and drink
Bar ⓞ open during normal operating hours
Café/light meals ⓞ open during normal operating hours

Communications
Post Box

Shopping
Duty free ⓞ open during normal operating hours
News, Stationery & Books ⓞ open during normal operating hours

Luggage
Trolleys/carts

CONFERENCE AND BUSINESS FACILITIES
Stakis Hotel Opposite main terminal
Conference facilities

CAR RENTAL
Avis
Europcar
Hertz

CAR PARKING
Long-stay
Off-airport

TAXIS AND CHAUFFEUR-DRIVEN CARS
Taxis
Available to city centre

PUBLIC TRANSPORT
Other towns and cities
Cambridge 🚂 »Several per day ⊃55 min
Ely 🚂 »1 per hr ⊃1 hr
Great Yarmouth 🚂 »1 per hr ⊃35 min
Ipswich 🚂 »1 per hr ⊃50 min
Peterborough 🚂 »1 per hr ⊃1 hr 35 min
Thetford 🚂 »1 per hr ⊃35 min

REGIONAL AIR CONNECTIONS
Aberdeen ✈ »Several per day ⊃1 hr 50 min
Edinburgh ✈ »Several per day ⊃1 hr 25 min
Manchester ✈ »Several per day ⊃1 hr

220

ORLANDO — MCO
USA (see page 41)

National ⓒ code: 1
Area ⓒ code: 407
Local time: Winter GMT-5, Summer GMT-4
Orlando International Airport, One Airport Blvd, Orlando, FL 32827, USA
ⓟ825 2001
ⓕ825 4079
WWW site:
http://fcn.state.fl.us/goaa
Location: 10 km/6 miles SE of Orlando

TERMINALS AND TRANSFERS
Terminals
Main Terminal Airlines: All airlines.
Layout: Level 1 (Car rental, ground transportation); Level 2 (Arrivals, Baggage Claim), Level 3 (Departures, People Mover shuttles to Gates 1–29, Gates 30–59 and 60–79), Level 4 (Hotel)

Minimum transfer times
International: 1 hr 30 min Domestic: 1 hr
Transfer between terminals
People Mover »Frequent; Main Terminal and Gates
Flight enquiries
Information and help desks
Airport Information Center Main Terminal Level 3, near gates 1–59 and gates 60–99

Emergencies
Police ⓟ825 2075; 825 2076
Lost Property ⓟ825 2111

AIRPORT FACILITIES
Money
ATM Main Terminal throughout
Bank Main Terminal Level 3
Bureau de change Main Terminal Level 2 near baggage claim
Bureau de change Main Terminal Level 3 near gates 1–29 and 60–99

Food and drink
Bar Main Terminal Level 3 throughout
Café/light meals Main Terminal Level 3 throughout
Restaurant Main Terminal Level 3 throughout

Communications
Post box Main Terminal throughout

ⓟ Phone no. ⓕ Fax no. ⓞ Hours of opening/operation » Frequency of service ⊃ Journey time ⓒ Cost/one-way fare

SECTION TWO • AIRPORT DIRECTORY

ORLANDO

Fax service Main Terminal Level 3 in Business Centers

Shopping
Duty free, departure Main Terminal Level 3 and near gates 1–29 and 60–99
Gift Shop Main Terminal Level 3
News, Stationery & Books Main Terminal Level 3
Hairdresser Main Terminal Level 3

Luggage
Left luggage counter Main Terminal Level 3
Lockers Main Terminal Level 3 past security

DISABLED TRAVELLERS

Main Terminal Adapted toilets; Lifts; Special car parking near lifts in parking garages; Phones at wheelchair height; Phones adapted for the deaf ; personal assistance

SMOKING POLICY

Main Terminal Smoking permitted in airport bars and lounges, as well as in bar areas of airline clubs.

SPECIAL PASSENGER LOUNGES

Delta Airlines Crown Room Main Terminal Gates 60–69 Concourse and Gates 70–79 Concourse
US Airways Presidential Suite Main Terminal Gates 50–59 Concourse between gates 50 and 52
United Airlines Red Carpet Club Main Terminal Gates 40–49 Concourse between gates 43 and 45

CONFERENCE AND BUSINESS FACILITIES

Business Centers Main Terminal Level 3 Fax; Photocopy; Conference Rooms

AIRPORT HOTELS

Hyatt Regency Hotel Main Terminal Level 4 near entrance of Gates 60–99 ⓒ825 1234 Ⓕ856 1672 446 rooms, convention space and business facilities

CAR RENTAL

Avis Main Terminal Level 1
Budget Main Terminal Level 1
Dollar Main Terminal Level 1
National Main Terminal Level 1

CAR PARKING

Long-stay Park 'n Ride on airport perimeter ⌀USD4 day
Short-stay Terminal Parking lots and Garages A and B ⌀USD1 per 30 min, USD8 per day (max)

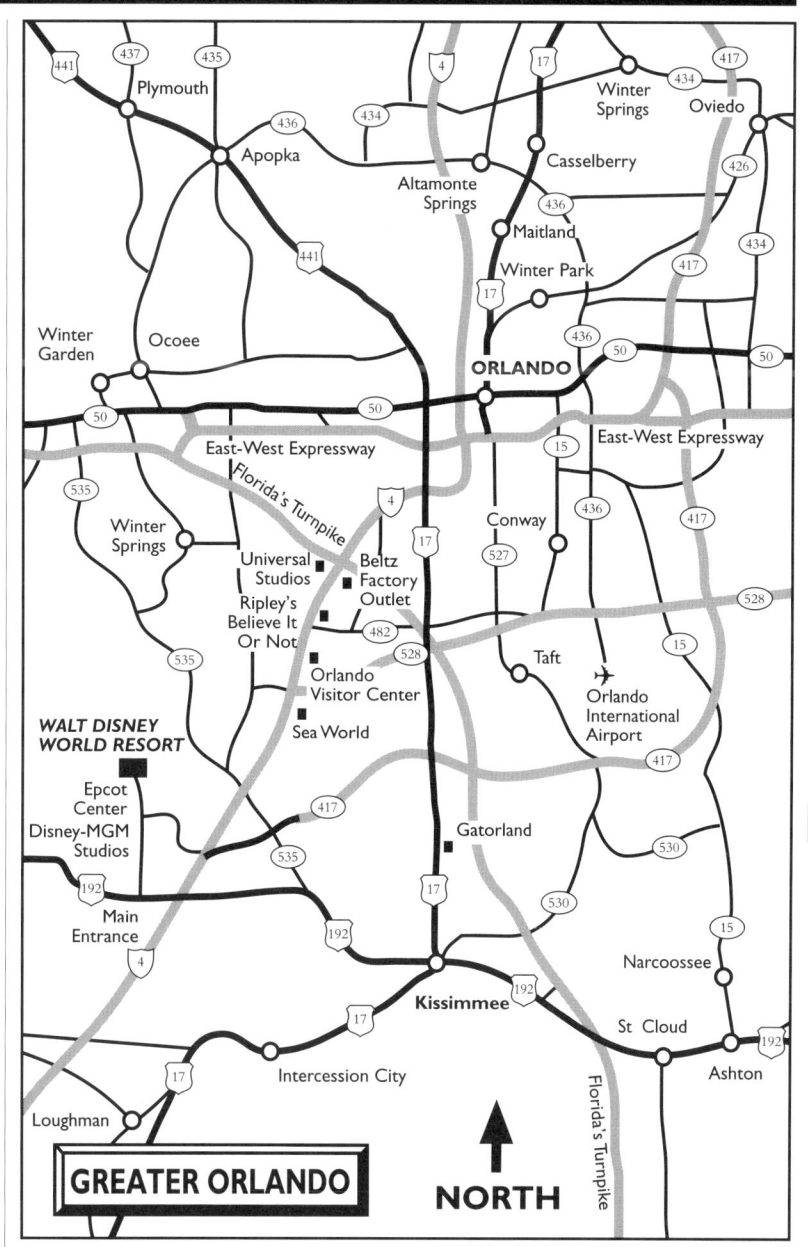

TAXIS AND CHAUFFEUR-DRIVEN CARS

Taxis
Main Terminal Level 2 City centre ➲35 min ⌀USD35

PUBLIC TRANSPORT

City & suburbs
Orlando (city centre) 🚌Lynx: 11 》30 min–1 hr, less Sunday and holidays ⏱0545–2315 ➲45 min ⌀USD0.75 For Amtrak and Pine Street Bus Station (connections to Walt Disney World).
Orlando (city centre) 🚐Mears/Transtar ⌀USD27
Orlando (International Drive) 🚌Lynx: 42 》1 hr ⏱0545–2110 ➲1 hr ⌀USD0.75. For Orlando Convention Center.

GREATER ORLANDO — NORTH

✈ Air 🚆 Rail 🚌 Bus 🚐 Limousine Ⓜ Metro/subway 🚋 Tram 🚁 Helicopter ⛴ Water transport • For map symbols, see p. 9

ORLANDO • OSAKA   SECTION TWO • AIRPORT DIRECTORY

Orlando (International Drive) 🚌Mears/Transtar ⌀USD26
Orlando (Lake Buena Vista) 🚌Mears/Transtar ⌀USD32
Orlando (Walt Disney World) 🚌Mears/Transtar ⌀USD40
Winter Park/Maitland 🚌Mears/Transtar ⌀USD35

Other towns and cities
Melbourne FL 🚌Cocoa Beach Shuttle FL »2 hr ⏱0900–1900 ⤴2 hr 15 min ⌀USD18–25. For Port Canaveral, Coacoa, Merritt Island, Coacoa Beach, Satellite Beach, Indiatlantic, Palm Bay and Titusville FL

REGIONAL AIR CONNECTIONS
Fort Lauderdale FL ✈ »Several per day ⤴50 min
Fort Myers FL ✈ »Several per day ⤴45 min
Gainesville FL ✈ »At least daily ⤴40 min
Jacksonville FL ✈ »Several per day ⤴50 min
Sarasota/Bradenton FL ✈ »Several per day ⤴45 min
Tallahassee FL ✈ »Several per day ⤴1 hr
Tampa/St Petersburg FL ✈ »Several per day ⤴35 min
West Palm Beach FLa »Several per day ⤴50 min

TRAVELLER'S NOTES
Orlando is in the centre of Florida's vacation area and is an alternative to Miami with its well-publicised incidents of car hijacking involving visitors.

OSAKA-KANSAI   KIX
Japan (see page 28)

National ☎ code: 81
Area ☎ code: 06
Local time: Winter GMT+9, Summer GMT+9
Kansai International Airport, Izumisano-shi Osaka 549, Japan
☎724 55 2109
📠724 55 2041
E-mail: kixinfo@ks.kiis.or.jp
WWW site: http://ks.kiis.or.jp/~kixinfo/kix.html
Location: 40 km/25 miles SW of Osaka

TERMINALS AND TRANSFERS

Terminals
Main Terminal Airlines: All airlines. Layout: First (i.e. Ground) Floor International Arrival; Second Floor Domestic Departure and Arrival; Third Floor Shops, restaurants, customs; Fourth Floor International Departure.

Minimum transfer times
International: 1 hr 30 min **Domestic:** 30 min

INFORMATION

Flight enquiries
Airport ☎724 55 2500
Aeroflot ☎271 8471 Air Canada ☎252 4227 (International) ☎0120 89 1890 (Domestic) Air China ☎946 1702 Air France ☎641 1211 Air India ☎264 1781 Air New Zealand ☎0120 300 747 Air Pacific ☎311 2004 Alitalia ☎341 3951 All Nippon Airways ☎534 7733 Ansett Australia ☎346 2556 Asiana Airlines ☎229 3939 Austrian Airlines ☎374 8470 British Airways ☎1020 12 2881 Cathay Pacific Airways ☎245 6731 China Eastern Airlines ☎448 5161 China Southern Airlines ☎448 6655 Continental Micronesia ☎0120 24 2414 Egyptair ☎341 1575 Finnair ☎347 0888 Garuda Indonesian Airlines ☎445 6985 J-Air ☎201 1231 Japan Air System ☎241 5511 Japan Airlines ☎223 2255 (Dom) 223 2345 (Int) Japan Asia Airways ☎0120 747 801 (Dom) ☎223 2258 (Int) Japan Transocean Air ☎201 1231 KLM ☎0120 868 862 Korean Airlines ☎264 3311 Lufthansa ☎341 4966 Malaysian Airlines ☎635 3070 Miat Mongolian Airlines ☎3 3237 1851 Northwest Airlines ☎228 0747 Philippine Airlines ☎444 2541 Qantas Airways ☎0120 207 020 Royal Brunei Airlines ☎343 1567 Royal Nepal Airlines ☎635 3261 SAS ☎0120 67 8101 Singapore Airlines ☎3 3213 3431 South Africa Airways ☎281 2730 Swissair ☎0120 667 788 Thai Airways ☎202 5161 Turkish Airlines ☎441 8690 United Airlines ☎271 5951 VASP Brazilian Airlines ☎444 4441 Vietnam Airlines ☎533 5781

Information and help desks
Information Center Main Terminal Second Floor Airport information ☎724 55 2500 ⏱24 hr
Kansai Tourist Information Center Main Terminal First Floor Tourist information ☎724 56 6025 ⏱0900–2100

EMERGENCIES
Police Main Terminal Second Floor, north of lobby ☎724 56 1234 ⏱24 hr
Medical Main Terminal Second Floor ☎724 56 7185
Lost Property Main Terminal ☎724 55 2500

AIRPORT FACILITIES

Money
Bureau de change Main Terminal First, Second and Fourth Floor
Bank Main Terminal Second Floor
ATM First, Second and Fourth Floor

☎ Phone no. 📠 Fax no. ⏱ Hours of opening/operation » Frequency of service ⤴ Journey time ⌀ Cost/one-way fare

Food and drink
Café/light meals Main Terminal Aeroplaza
Café/light meals Main Terminal Third Floor
Restaurant Main Terminal Second Floor
Restaurant Main Terminal Third Floor
Restaurant Aeroplaza (front of terminal building)

Communications
Post office Main Terminal Second Floor ℗724 55 1980 ⓘ0830–1900

Shopping
Shopping mall Aeroplaza, in front of terminal
Shopping mall Main Terminal Third Floor

Luggage
Trolleys/carts Main Terminal ⌀Free of charge
Left luggage counter Main Terminal First, Second and Fourth floor ⓘ0630–2230

DISABLED TRAVELLERS
Wheelchairs are available free of charge (contact the information counter)

SMOKING POLICY
Restricted

SPECIAL PASSENGER LOUNGES
VIP Room Main Terminal ℗724 55 2328

CONFERENCE AND BUSINESS FACILITIES
Business and Conference Centre Fourth Floor ℗724 56 7151 ℗724 56 7152 ⓘ0800–2000
Business and Conference Centre Nikko Kansai Airport Hotel ℗724 55 1111

AIRPORT HOTELS
Nikko Kansai Airport 576 rooms ℗724 55 1111

CAR RENTAL
Main Terminal First Floor ⓘ0800–2000

CAR PARKING
Short-stay In front of terminal ⌀JPY610 first hr, then JPY 310 per 30 min ('large' cars charged double)

TAXIS AND CHAUFFEUR-DRIVEN CARS
Taxis First Floor

PUBLIC TRANSPORT
Airport to airport
Osaka-Itami Apt 🚌 Limousine Bus ⌚80 min ⌀JPY1700.

City & suburbs
Namba 🚆 Nankai Electric Railway RAPI:T »30 min ⌚29–34 min ⌀JPY1400. Alpha is a non-stop express service, Beta stops between stations. 8-min subway link to Osaka
Namba 🚆 Nankai Electric Railway ⓘ0545–2330 ⌚43 min ⌀890 JPY.
Osaka (rail stn) Airport Limousine »30 min ⌚50 min ⌀JPY1300.
Osaka (rail stn) 🚆 JR Kansai Rapid Service ⌚55–65 min ⌀JPY1160.
Osaka (port – Tempozan) High-speed ferry ⌚30 min ⌀JPY1840.
Shin-Osaka 🚆 Japan Railways (JR) Haruka ⌚45 min ⌀JPY2980. Via Umeda rail stn
Tennoji 🚆 Japan Railways (JR) Haruka ⌚29 min ⌀JPY2270. Via Umeda rail stn

Other towns and cities
Kobe 🚢 Jet Shuttle (K-JET) ⌚27 min ⌀jpy2400.
Kyoto 🚆 Japan Railways (JR) Haruka ⌚75 min ⌀approx JPY3490.

REGIONAL AIR CONNECTIONS
Kochi ✈ »Several per day ⌚40 min
Matsuyama ✈ »Several per day ⌚50 min
Oita ✈ »Several per day ⌚55 min
Takamatsu ✈ »Several per day ⌚45 min
Tokyo ✈ »Several per day ⌚60–70 min

AIRPORT TAX
Passenger Service Facilities Charge Adult (age 12 or older) ⌀JPY2650; Child (age 2 to 11) ⌀JPY1330

TRAVELLER'S NOTES
Built in 1994 on an artificial island, Kansai is one of the busiest airports in Asia, served by a web of excellent high-speed transport services.

OSLO — OSL
Norway (see page 31)

National ℗ code: 47
Area ℗ code: No code required
Local time: Winter GMT+1, Summer GMT+2
Oslo-Fornebu Airport, PO Box 85, Oslo, Norway
℗59 33 40

℗12 41 31
Location: 9 km/5½ miles SW of Oslo

TERMINALS AND TRANSFERS
Terminals
Main Terminal Airlines: All airlines.

Layout: Three passenger Levels, with domestic and international flights from different areas: Domestic Satellite/Piers A and B, International Satellite/Pier C

Minimum transfer times
International: 45 min **Domestic:** 30 min

✈ Air 🚆 Rail 🚌 Bus 🚐 Limousine 🚇 Metro/subway 🚋 Tram 🚁 Helicopter 🚢 Water transport • For map symbols, see p. 9

OSLO

SECTION TWO • AIRPORT DIRECTORY ✈✈

INFORMATION

Flight enquiries
Aeroflot ℂ53 77 17 ℹ12 42 62 Air France ℂ53 83 31 ℹ12 41 11 Alitalia ℂ59 31 71 ℹ12 06 13 Braathens SAFE ℂ53 14 87 British Airways ℂ53 67 08 Delta Airlines ℂ59 70 00 ℹ52 14 87 Finnair ℂ53 97 13 ℂ53 30 11 KLM ℂ53 86 80 ℹ58 38 30 Lufthansa ℂ53 49 94 ℂ53 38 30 Sabena ℂ53 33 00 SAS ℂ59 60 50 ℹ59 69 12

Information and help desks
SAS Information Desk Main Terminal Ground Level Central Hall & Departure Pier C (2 desks) ℂ59 60 50 ⓘ0700–2300 Airport information, Flights, Hotel booking, Tourist information

EMERGENCIES

Police Main Terminal Ground Level outside entrance area ℂ57 69 00 ⓘ24 hr
Medical Main Terminal SAS Desks and Level 1 Domestic Departure Centre ⓘAll flight times
Lost Property Main Terminal SAS Desks and Police Ground Level ℂ59 54 50 ⓘAll flight times

AIRPORT FACILITIES

Money
ATM Main Terminal Arrival Hall after Baggage retrieval ⓘ24 hr
Bank Main Terminal Ground Level Central Area; Level 1 Domestic Area

Food and drink
Bar Main Terminal Levels 1 & 2, and Departure Areas Pier C
Café/light meals Main Terminal Level 1 and Departure Pier Areas B & C
Restaurant Main Terminal Level 2

Communications
Post office Main Terminal Central Hall Level 1
Fax service Main Terminal Service & Communications Centre First Level

Shopping
Duty free, departure Main Terminal

International Pier C Central Area ⓘ0600–2200
Gift Shop Main Terminal International Pier C Central Area ⓘ0600–2200
Hairdresser Main Terminal Ground Level Central Hall
News, Stationery & Books Main Terminal International Pier C Central Area ⓘ0600–2200

Luggage
Left Luggage Counter Main Terminal Ground Level ⌀NOK5–25 per item
Porters Main Terminal Ground Level Central Hall
Trolleys/carts Main Terminal throughout ⓘ24 hr ⌀Free

DISABLED TRAVELLERS

Main Terminal Adapted toilets next to other toilets; Lifts Ground Level Central Area & near passport control; Personal assistance Via airline staff & First Aid Room, all flight times

SMOKING POLICY

Main Terminal Smoking room in Internation Departures/Domestic Second Level

SPECIAL PASSENGER LOUNGES

British Airways Executive Club Lounge Main Terminal Departure Area Club members and Business Class passengers
SAS EuroLounge Main Terminal Departure/Transit Hall of Pier C Royal Viking Club members and Euro Class passengers

CONFERENCE AND BUSINESS FACILITIES

Conference rooms, Level 2 near Caravelle Restaurant ℂ59 61 50 ⓘDuring flight times Telephones

AIRPORT HOTELS

SAS Park Royal Hotel ℂ12 02 20 ℹ12 00 11. 254 rooms

CAR RENTAL

Avis Main Terminal Across access road from terminal ℂ53 05 57
Budget Main Terminal Across access road from terminal ℂ53 79 24
Hertz Main Terminal Across access road from terminal ℂ53 36 47

CAR PARKING

Long-stay Parking Hall 2400 spaces ⌀NOK15 per hr; NOK120 per day
Short-stay Main Terminal area ⌀NOK20 per hr

TAXIS AND CHAUFFEUR-DRIVEN CARS

Taxis
Ground Level outside Main Terminal City centre ➲10 min ⌀NOK100

PUBLIC TRANSPORT

City & suburbs
Oslo city centre 🚌City Transport »30 min ➲20–25 min ⌀NOK 20.
Oslo city centre 🚌SAS Coach »10 min ⓘ0600–2330 ➲15–20 min ⌀NOK35.

REGIONAL AIR CONNECTIONS

Aalesund ✈ »Several per day ➲55 min
Bergen ✈ »Several per day ➲50 min
Copenhagen ✈ »Several per day ➲1 hr 5 min
Fagernes ✈ »Several per week ➲40 min
Gothenburg ✈ »Several per day ➲50 min
Haugesund ✈ »Several per day ➲50 min
Kristiansand ✈ »Several per day ➲45 min
Kristiansund ✈ »Several per week ➲55 min
Sogndal ✈ »Several per day ➲1 hr 5 min
Stavanger ✈ »Several per day ➲50 min
Stockholm ✈ »Several per day ➲55 min
Stord ✈ »Several per day ➲50 min
Trondheim ✈ »Several per day ➲1 hr

TRAVELLER'S NOTES

New airport being constructed at Gardemoen, opening late 1998. All traffic will then transfer from Fornebu to Gardermoen.

ℂ Phone no. ℹ Fax no. ⓘ Hours of opening/operation » Frequency of service ➲ Journey time ⌀ Cost/one-way fare

PALMA DE MALLORCA — PMI

Spain (see page 36)

National ✆ code: 34
Area ✆ code: 71
Local time: Winter GMT+1, Summer GMT+2
✆: 78 90 00
Location: 11km/7mls E of Palma

TERMINALS AND TRANSFERS

Terminals
Main Terminal Airlines: Aero Lloyd, Air Algerie, Air Europa, Air France, Air Nostrum, Aviaco, British Airways, British Midland, Crossair, Condor, Futura, Hapag-Lloyd, Iberia, Lufthansa, LTU, Luxair, Monarch, Sabena, Spanair, Swissair, Transavia Airlines, Portugalia.
Layout: Ground floor: Arrivals; first floor: check-in; second floor: departures

INFORMATION

Flight enquiries
Airport ✆ 789 099
Aero Lloyd ✆ 78 91 57, Air Algerie ✆ 71 72 25, Air Europa ✆ 17 81 00, Air France ✆ 71 35 00, Air Nostrum ✆ 26 00 15, Aviaco ✆ (901) 333 111, British Airways ✆ 26 16 91/78 91 62, British Midland ✆ 26 00 00, Crossair ✆ 26 12 58, Condor ✆ 78 79 99, Futura ✆ 71 79 74, Hapag-Lloyd ✆ 26 49 05, Iberia ✆ 71 01 40, Lufthansa ✆ 78 79 88, LTU ✆ 74 37 22, Luxair ✆ 26 21 93, Monarch ✆ 86 43 62, Sabena 71 35 00, Spanair ✆ 78 94 25, Swissair ✆ (900) 12 12 12, Transavia Airlines ✆ 71 62 71, Portugalia ✆ (902) 100 145

Information and help desks
Ground floor and first floor ✆ 789 520

Emergencies
Police Departures lounge, second floor ✆ 26 46 59
Medical ✆ 789 292

AIRPORT FACILITIES

Money
Bureau de Change Arrivals lounge, ground floor

Food and drink
Bar Departures lounge, second floor ✆ 789 620
Café/light meals Arrivals lounge, ground floor ✆ 789 620
Restaurant Departures lounge, second floor ✆ 789 620

Communications
Post Box

Shopping
Duty free Departures lounge, second floor ✆ 789 280
News, Stationery & Books Departures lounge, second floor ✆ 789 280
Gift Shop Departures lounge, second floor ✆ 789 280

LUGGAGE
Trolleys/carts

DISABLED TRAVELLERS
Lifts

CAR RENTAL
Arrivals lounge, ground floor

CAR PARKING
✆ 789 386

TAXIS AND CHAUFFEUR-DRIVEN CARS
Taxis
City centre ⌀ ESP458

PUBLIC TRANSPORT
City & suburbs
🚌 ⌀ESP285 » avg. 30 min ⏱ 0605–2405

REGIONAL AIR CONNECTIONS
Ibiza ✈ »Several per day ⊃35 min
Menorca ✈ »Several per day ⊃30 min

PARIS-CHARLES DE GAULLE · SECTION TWO • AIRPORT DIRECTORY

PARIS-CHARLES DE GAULLE   CDG

France (see page 22)

National ☎ code: 33
Area ☎ code: 01
Local time: Winter GMT+1, Summer GMT+2
Aéroport Paris Roissy Charles de Gaulle, BP 20101, 95711 Roissy Charles de Gaulle Cedex, Paris, France
☎48 62 12 12
🖶43 35 72 55
Internet e-mail:
http://www.paris.org/accueil/airport
Location: 23 km/16 miles NE of central Paris

TERMINALS AND TRANSFERS

Terminals
Terminal 1 Airlines: All other international flights. Layout: Circular construction, on many Levels, including Arrival, Departure and Transit Levels and the Aerostore shopping Level; 8–9 Departure Piers
Terminal 2 Airlines: Air Canada, Air France, Alitalia, Air Seychelles, Air Inter, Luxair, Lot Polish Airlines, Crossair, Malev Hungarian, Air Madagascar, CSA Czechoslovak, Austrian Airlines, Sabena World Airlines, Swissair, Tyrolean Airways. Layout: Arrivals Level, Departures Level, and shopping and restaurant facilities Level including Boutiquaire shopping area

Minimum transfer times
International: 45 min–1 hr Domestic:45 min–1 hr

Transfer between terminals
Bus ≫8 min; Terminals 1 and 2A/2B/2D ◇Free

INFORMATION

Flight enquiries
Airport ☎48 62 48 80
Aer Lingus ☎47 42 12 50 Aeroflot ☎42 25 43 81 Aerolineas Argentinas ☎42 56 31 16 Air Afrique ☎44 21 32 32 Air Canada ☎43 20 12 00 Air China ☎42 66 16 58 Air France ☎45 35 61 61 Air India ☎42 66 13 72 Air Inter ☎45 46 90 00 Air Lanka ☎42 97 43 42 Air Liberté ☎49 79 09 09 Air Seychelles ☎42 89 85 33 Air UK ☎42 66 57 19 Alitalia ☎40 15 00 21 All Nippon Airways ☎44 31 44 31 Austrian Airlines ☎42 66 34 66 Avianca Colombian Airlines ☎42 60 35 22 British Airways ☎47 78 14 14 British Midland Airways ☎47 42 30 62 Cathay Pacific Airways ☎40 68 98 99 Crossair ☎45 81 11 01 CSA Czechoslovak ☎47 42 18 11 Cyprus Airlines ☎45 01 93 38 Delta Airlines ☎48 62 59 00 Emirates ☎42 94 60 32 Finnair ☎47 42 33 33 Garuda Indonesian Airlines ☎45 62 38 66 Gulf Air ☎47 23 70 70 Japan Airlines ☎44 35 55 00 Jersey European Airlines ☎42 96 02 44 KLM ☎44 56 18 18 Korean Airlines ☎42 61 51 74 Kuwait Airways ☎42 60 30 60 Lot Polish Airlines ☎47 42 05 60 Lufthansa ☎42 65 37 35 Luxair ☎45 35 61 61 Malaysian Airlines ☎47 42 26 00 Malev Hungarian ☎42 61 57 90 Manx Airlines ☎40 74 00 04 Meridiana ☎42 61 61 50 Northwest Airlines ☎42 66 90 00 Philippine Airlines ☎42 96 01 40 Sabena ☎47 42 47 47 Saudia ☎47 23 72 72 Singapore Airlines ☎45 53 90 90 Swissair ☎45 81 11 01 Thai Airways ☎44 20 70 80 Tyrolean Airways ☎45 35 61 61 United Airlines ☎48 97 82 82 Varig Brazilian ☎47 20 03 23

Information and help desks
Information Desk Terminal 2 Ground Level Arrival Area 2A ☎48 62 52 88 ⓗ0700–2300 *Airport information Hotel booking, Tourist information*
Information Desk Terminal 2 Ground Level Arrival Area 2B ☎48 62 40 95 ⓗ0700–2300 *Airport information Hotel booking, Tourist information*
Information Desk Terminal 1 Arrival Area Gate 36 ☎48 62 27 29 ⓗ0700–2300 *Airport information Hotel booking, Tourist information*
Information Desk Terminal 2 Ground Level Arrival Area 2D ☎48 62 12 86 ⓗ0700–2300 *Airport information Hotel booking, Tourist information*

EMERGENCIES

Police Terminal 1 throughout ☎48 62 49 49 ⓗ24 hr
Police Terminal 2 throughout ☎48 63 31 22 ⓗ24 hr
Medical Terminal 1 Aerostore Level and Basement ☎48 62 80 00 ⓗ24 hr
Medical Terminal 2 2A, Basement Level ☎48 62 53 32 ⓗ24 hr
Lost Property Terminal 1 Aerostore Level and Basement ☎48 62 20 85 ⓗ0645–2315
Lost Property Terminal 2 2D, Boutique Area ☎48 62 52 89 ⓗ0645–2315

AIRPORT FACILITIES

Money
ATM Terminal 1 throughout ⓗ24 hr
ATM Terminal 2 ⓗ24 hr
Bank Terminal 1 2D Boutique Area ⓗ0930–1730 Mon–Fri
Bureau de change Terminal 1 Arrival Area, near Gate 34 ⓗ0630–2330
Bureau de change Terminal 2 Levels 2A and 2B ⓗ0630–2330
Bureau de change Terminal 2 Level 2D ⓗ0530–2100

Food and drink
Bar Terminal 1 Departure Lounge Area ⓗAll flight times
Bar Terminal 2 throughout Levels 2A, 2B and 2D and Boutique Area ⓗAll flight times
Café/light meals Terminal 1 Aerostore Level ⓗAll flight times
Café/light meals Terminal 2 throughout ⓗAll flight times
Restaurant Terminal 1 Level 11
Restaurant Terminal 2 throughout Levels 2A, 2B and 2D

Communications
Post office Terminal 1 Aerostore Level ⓗ0900–1900 Mon–Fri ; 0900–1200 Sat
Post box Terminal 1 Transit Level ⓗ0630–2300 Mon–Fri; 0630–1830 Sat
Post office Terminal 2 2D Boutique area ⓗ0630–2300 Mon–Fri; 0630–1830 Sat

Shopping
Duty free, departure Terminal 1 Departure Level ⓗAll flight times
Duty free, arrival Terminal 2 Departure Lounges ⓗAll flight times
Shopping mall Terminal 1 Departure Level ⓗAll flight times
Shopping mall Terminal 2 Departure Level ⓗAll flight times

Luggage
Left luggage counter Terminal 1 Arrival Area ⓗ0645–2115
Left luggage counter Terminal 2 Arrival Area ⓗ0645–2315
Porters Terminal 1 Arrival and Departure

☎ Phone no. 🖶 Fax no. ⓗ Hours of opening/operation ≫ Frequency of service ⊃ Journey time ◇ Cost/one-way fare

Paris Charles De Gaulle

Areas before passport control ⏰All flight times ⊘FRF15 per item
Porters Terminal 2 Arrival and Departure Areas before passport control ⏰All flight times ⊘FRF15 per item
Trolleys/carts Terminal 1 throughout ⏰24 hr ⊘Free
Trolleys/carts Terminal 2 throughout ⏰24 hr ⊘Free

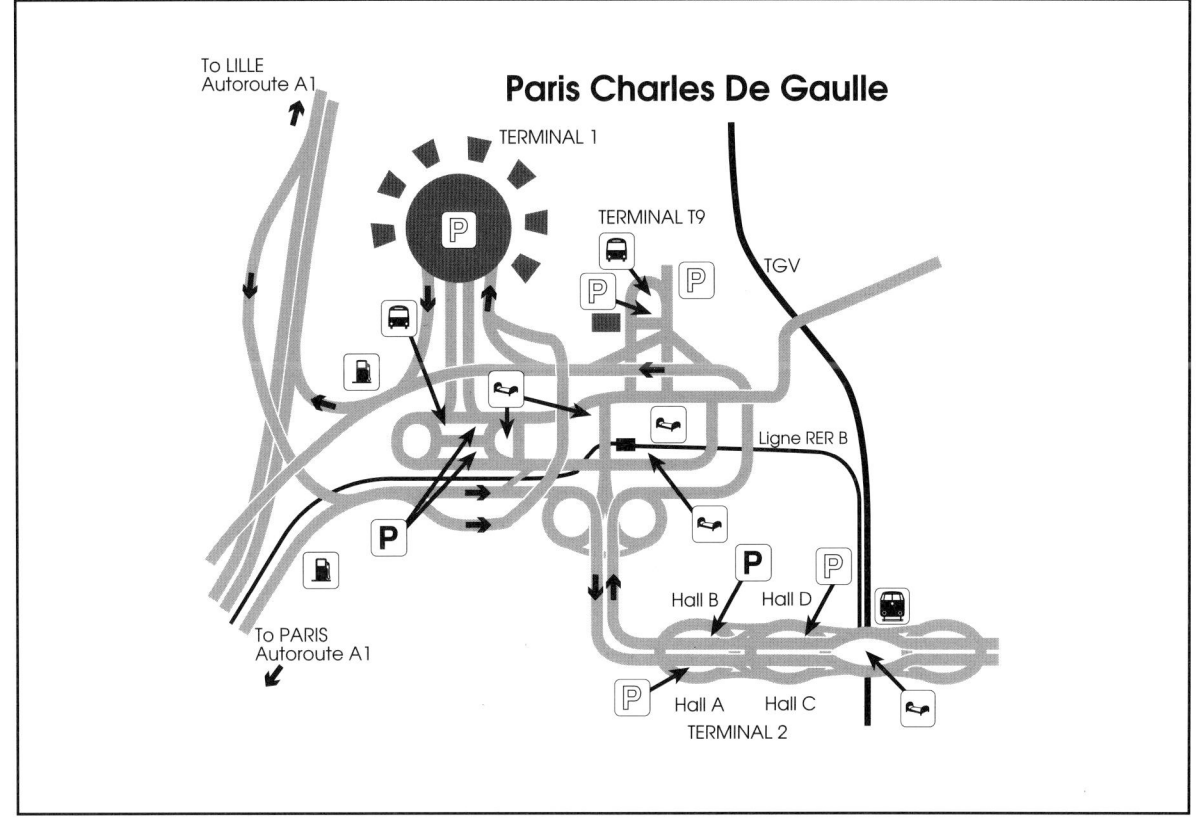

Disabled Travellers

Terminal 1 Adapted toilets; Lifts; Phones at wheelchair height; Personal assistance at Reception Desk; ✆48 62 28 24 0530–2400
Terminal 2 Adapted toilets; Lifts Phones at wheelchair height; Personal assistance at Reception Desk; ✆48 62 59 24 0530–2400

Smoking Policy

Terminal 1 Smoking and no-smoking areas
Terminal 2 Smoking and no-smoking areas

Special Passenger Lounges

GN Lounge Terminal 1 Level 10 *First class passengers*
Aer Lingus First Class Lounge Terminal 1 Level 10 *First class passengers*
Aeroflot First Class Lounge Terminal 1 Level 10 *First class passengers*
Air Canada Lounge Terminal 1 Level 10
Air China Lounge Terminal 1 Level 10 *First class passengers*
Air France VIP Lounge Terminal 2 Levels 2A, 2B and 2D (6 lounges in total) *First and Business class passengers*
Air India Lounge Terminal 1 Level 10 *First and Business class passengers*
Air Lanka Lounge Terminal 1 Level 10 *First and Business class passengers*
Alitalia Lounge Terminal 2 Level 2B *First and Business class passengers*
All Nippon Airways Lounge Terminal 1 Level 10 *First and Business class passengers*
British Airways Executive Club Lounge Terminal 1 Satellite 5 *Club members and First/Business class passengers*
Brymon Airways Lounge Terminal 1 Airside transfer Area
Cathay Pacific Airways Lounge Terminal 1 Level 11
Emirates Lounge Terminal 1 Level 10 *First and Business class passengers*
Finnair Lounge Terminal 1 Level 10 *First and Business class passengers*
Garuda Indonesian Airlines Lounge Terminal 1 Level 10 *First class passengers*
Japan Airlines Lounge Terminal 1 Level 10
KLM Lounge Terminal 1 Level 10 *First and Business class passengers*
Korean Airlines Lounge Terminal 1 Level 10 *First and Business class passengers*
Kuwait Airways Lounge Terminal 1 Level 10 *First and Business class passengers*
Lufthansa Senator Club Lounge Terminal 1 Satellite 6 *Club members and First class passengers*
Malaysian Airlines Lounge Terminal 1 Level 10 *Business class passengers*
Meridiana Lounge Terminal 1 Level 10 *Business class passengers*
Northwest Airlines Lounge Terminal 1 Level 10 *First class passengers*
Saudia Lounge Terminal 1 Level 11
Singapore Airlines Lounge Terminal 1 Level 10 *First class passengers*
Swissair Lounge Terminal 2 Level 2B *First and Business class passengers*
Thai Airways Lounge Terminal 1 Level 10 *First and Business class passengers*
United Airlines Lounge Terminal 1 Level 11
Varig Brazilian Lounge Terminal 1 Level 10 *First class passengers*

Conference and Business Facilities

Business and Conference Centre,

Paris-Charles de Gaulle

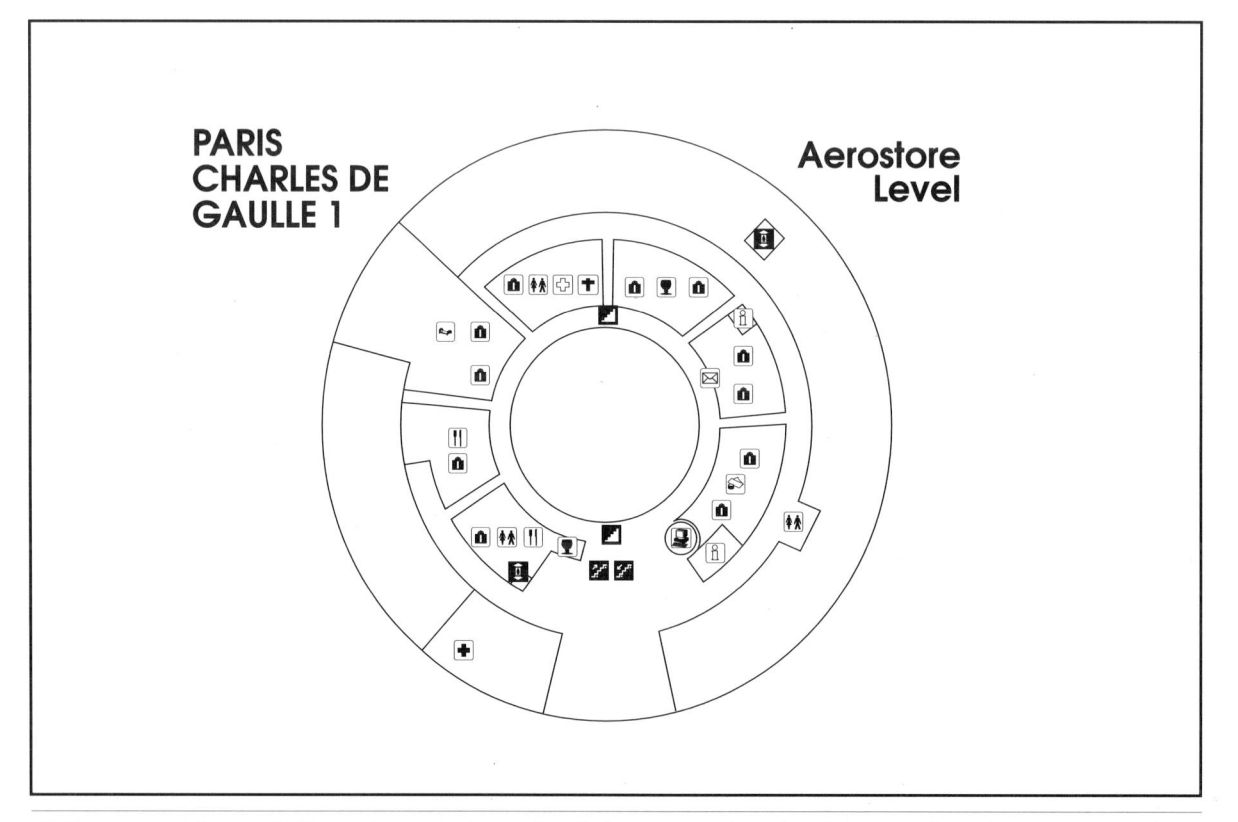

SECTION TWO • AIRPORT DIRECTORY

PARIS CHARLES DE GAULLE 1 — Transfer Level

Satellite 1, Satellite 2, Satellite 3, Satellite 4, Satellite 5, Satellite 6, Satellite 7

PARIS CHARLES DE GAULLE 1 — Aerostore Level

☏ Phone no. ℻ Fax no. ⏱ Hours of opening/operation ≫ Frequency of service ➲ Journey time ◇ Cost/one-way fare

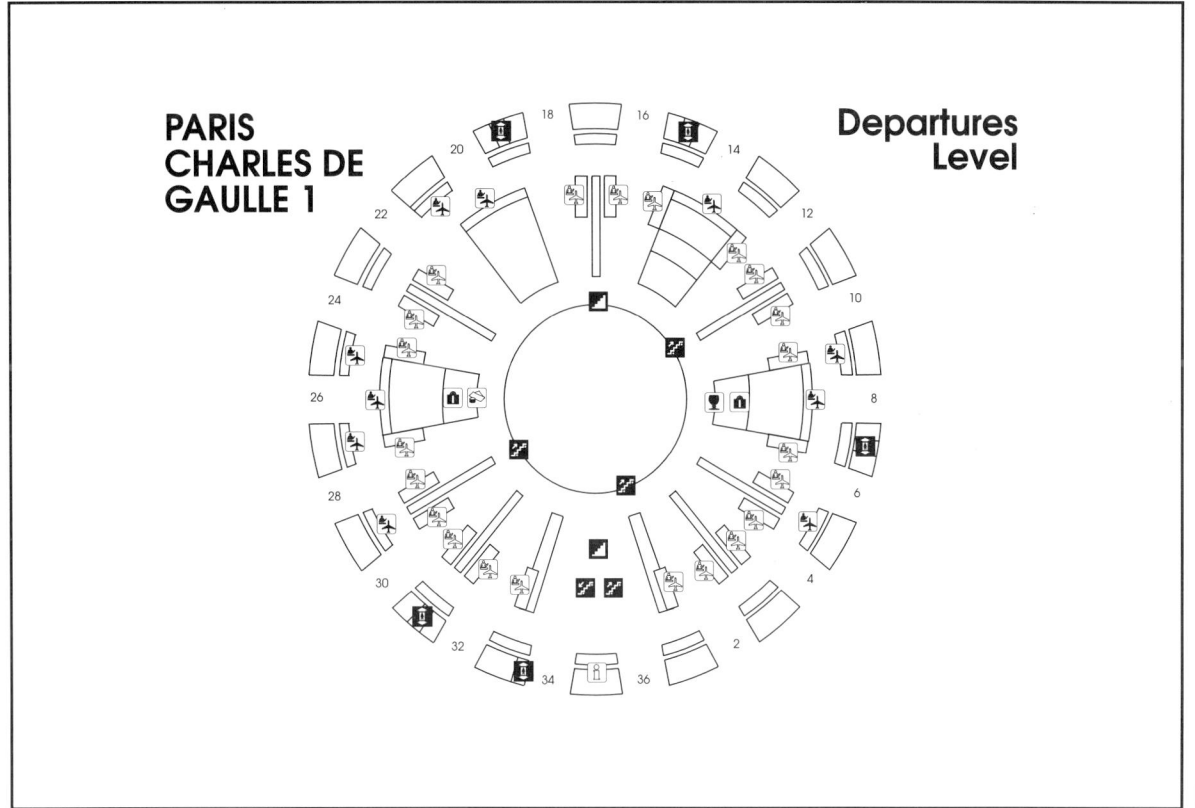

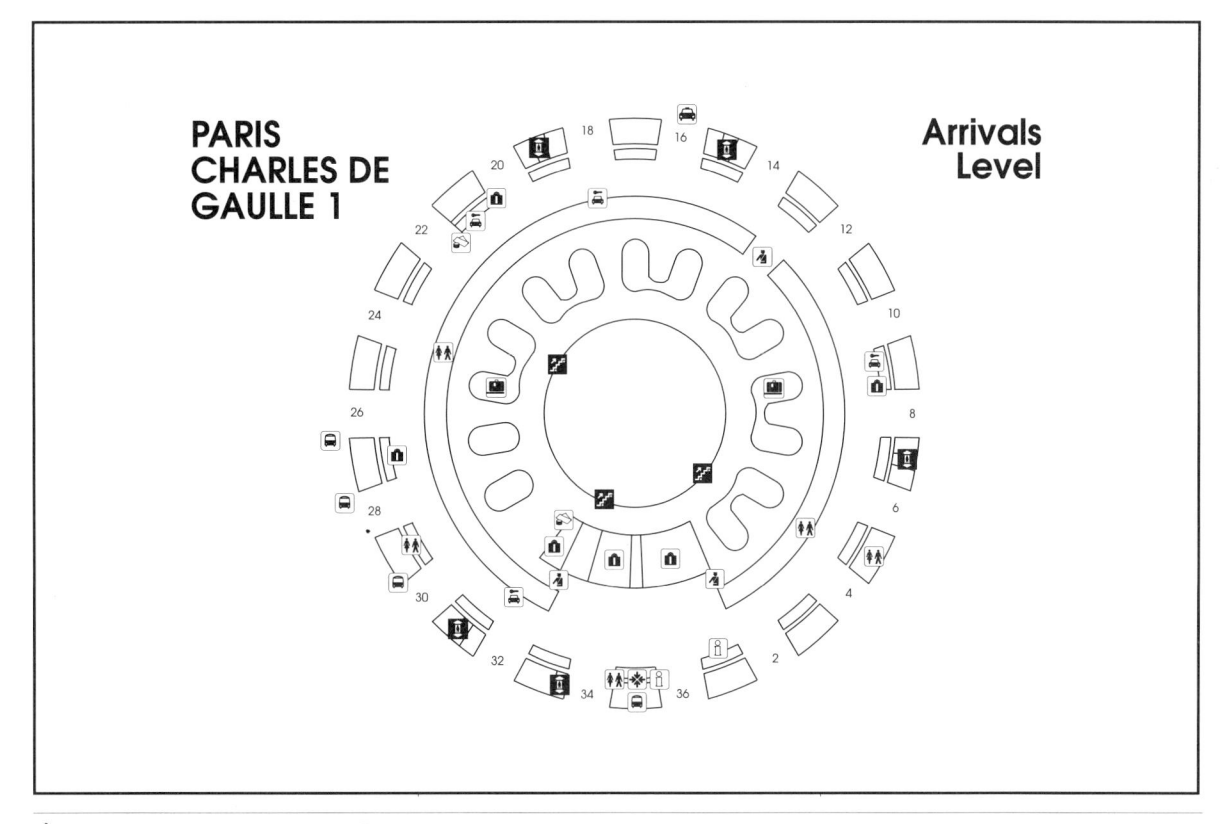

SECTION TWO • AIRPORT DIRECTORY   PARIS-CHARLES DE GAULLE

PARIS CHARLES DE GAULLE 1 — Departures Level

PARIS CHARLES DE GAULLE 1 — Arrivals Level

✈ Air ⛴ Rail 🚌 Bus 🚘 Limousine Ⓜ Metro/subway 🚋 Tram 🚁 Helicopter ⛴ Water transport • For map symbols, see p. 9

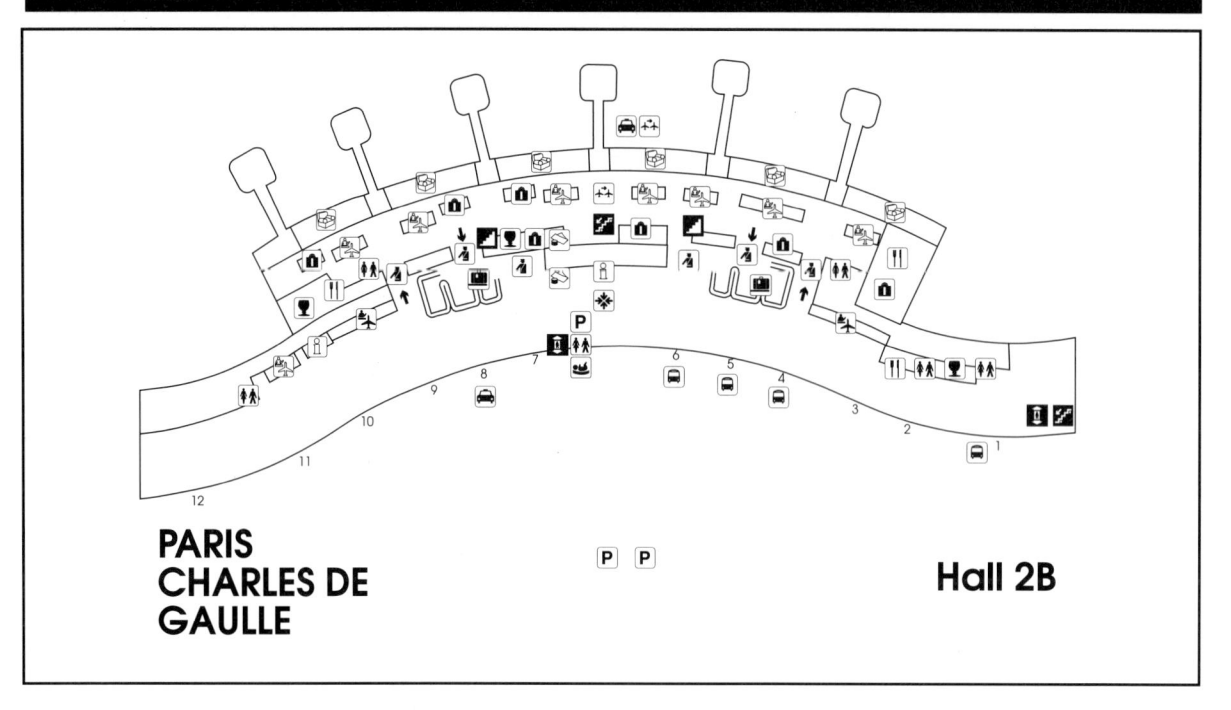

Paris-Charles de Gaulle

SECTION TWO • AIRPORT DIRECTORY

PARIS CHARLES DE GAULLE Hall 2B

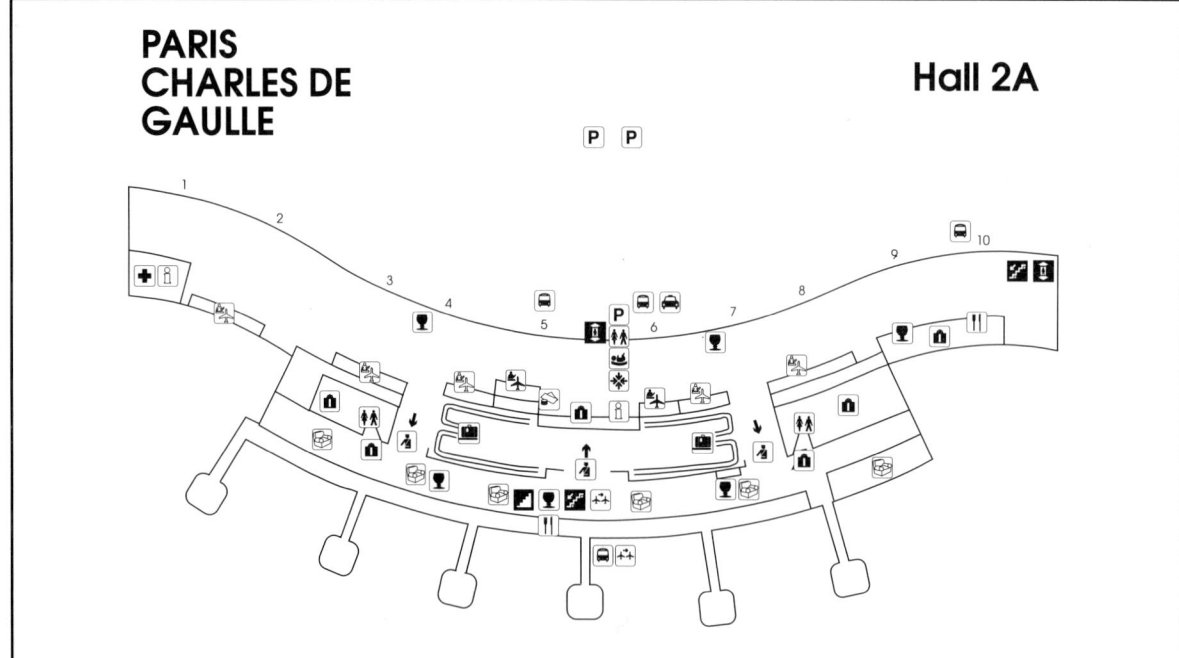

PARIS CHARLES DE GAULLE Hall 2A

Terminal 2D Boutique area ✆48 62 40 95 ⏱0800–1700 Telephones, Fax service, Photocopier, Secretarial service, Translation/Interpretation service
Conference Centre, Terminal 1 ✆48 62 33 06 ⏱0800–1800 Telephones, Fax service, Photocopier, Secretarial service

Airport Hotels

Arcade/Ibis ✆48 62 49 49 *Courtesy bus*
Cocoon ✆48 62 06 16 *Courtesy bus*
Hilton ✆49 19 77 77 *Courtesy bus*
Novotel ✆48 62 00 53 *Courtesy bus*
Sheraton ✆49 19 70 70
Sofitel ✆49 19 29 29 *Courtesy bus*

Car Rental

Avis Terminal 1 Arrival Level ✆48 62 34 34
Avis Terminal 2 Arrival Level ✆48 62 34 34
Budget Terminal 1 Arrival Level ✆48 62 70 21
Budget Terminal 2 Arrival Level ✆48 62 70 21
EuropCar Terminal 1 Arrival Level ✆48

✆ Phone no.   ℱ Fax no.   ⏱ Hours of opening/operation   ≫ Frequency of service   ↪ Journey time   ◇ Cost/one-way fare

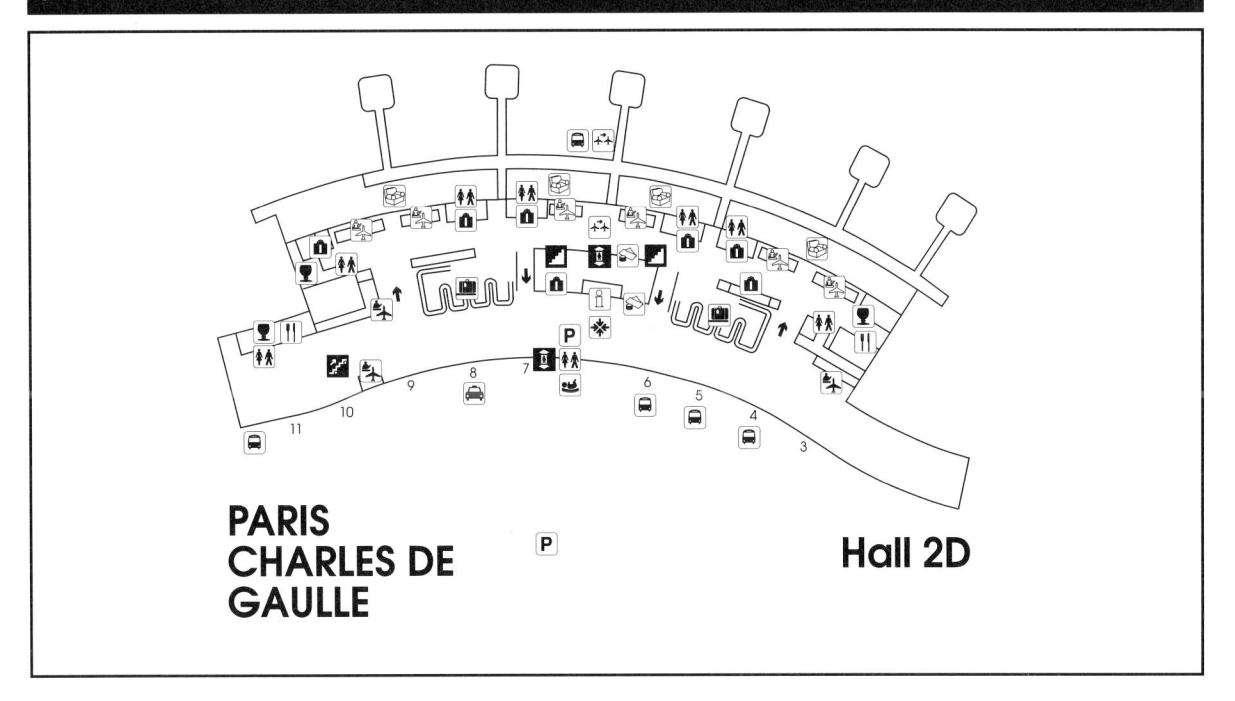

✈✈ SECTION TWO • AIRPORT DIRECTORY   PARIS-CHARLES DE GAULLE

PARIS CHARLES DE GAULLE   **Hall 2D**

PARIS CHARLES DE GAULLE   **Hall 2C**

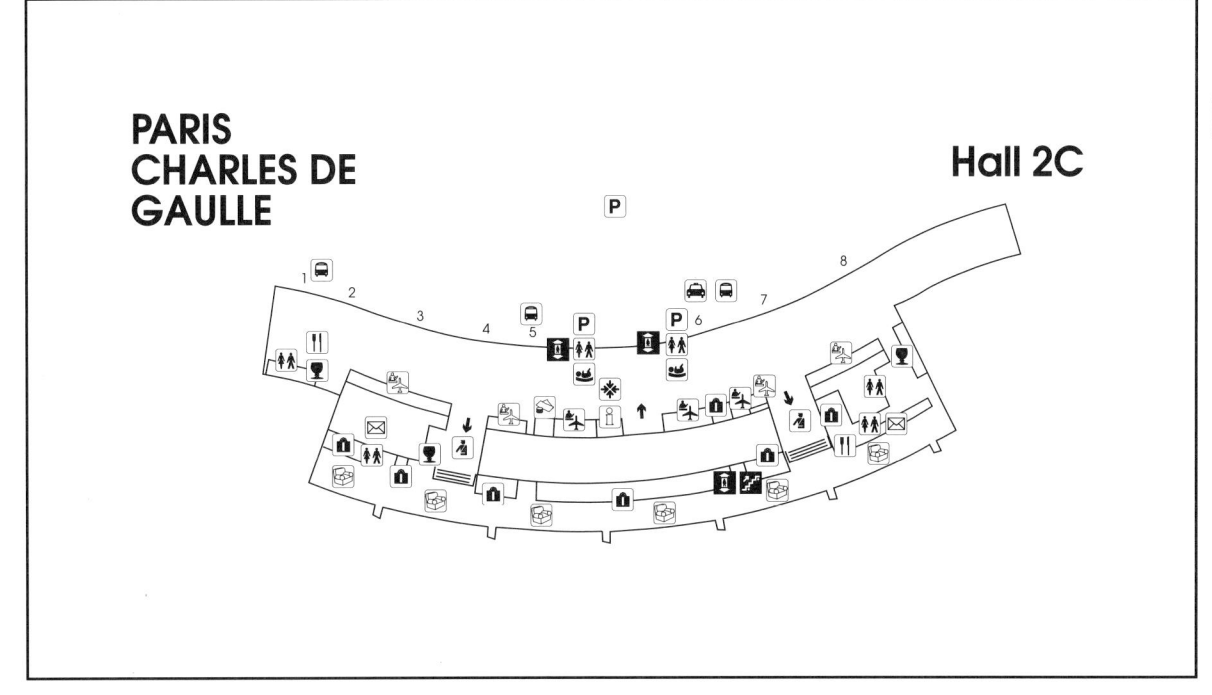

62 33 33
EuropCar Terminal 2 Arrival Level ✆48 62 33 33
Hertz Terminal 1 Arrival Level ✆48 62 29 00
Hertz Terminal 2 Arrival Level ✆48 62 90 00

CAR PARKING

Long-stay Near terminals 1200 spaces
⊘FRF5 per hr; FRF50 per day
Short-stay Near terminals 6090 spaces
⊘FRF10 per hr; FRF100 per day

TAXIS AND CHAUFFEUR-DRIVEN CARS

Taxis
Taxi pick up area outside terminal City centre ➲50 min ⊘FRF200

✈ Air 🚆 Rail 🚌 Bus 🚐 Limousine Ⓜ Metro/subway 🚋 Tram 🚁 Helicopter ⛴ Water transport • For map symbols, see p. 9

Paris–Charles de Gaulle

Taxi pick up area outside terminal Orly Apt ⏲ 1 hr ⬧FRF275

Chauffeur-driven cars
Taxi area outside terminal ℅40 71 84 62

PUBLIC TRANSPORT

Airport to airport
Paris-Orly Airport 🚌 Air France ≫20 min ⏰0600–2300 ⏲50 min ⬧FRF70.
Paris-Orly Airport 🚌 RER B + Orlyval Line B ≫15 min ⏰0545–2350 ⏲1 hr 10 min ⬧FRF97.

City & suburbs
Paris city centre (Gare Montparnasse rail stn) 🚌 Air France ≫15 min ⏰0545–2300 ⏲45 min ⬧FRF65.
Paris city centre (Opéra) 🚌 RATP: Roissybus ≫15 min ⏰0630–2255 ⏲30 min ⬧FRF40.
Paris city centre (Opéra) 🚆 RER Line B ≫15 min ⏰0630–2255 ⏲30 min ⬧FRF40.
Paris city centre (Porte Maillot air terminal) 🚌 Air France ≫15–20 min ⏰0540–2300 ⏲25 min ⬧FRF55.
Paris city centre (Gare du Nord rail stn) 🚆 RER Line B ≫7–15 min ⏰0455–2352 ⏲35 min ⬧FRF45. *For Eurostar.*

Other towns and cities
Angers 🚆 SNCF: TGV ≫4 per day ⏰0856–1825 ⏲1 hr 35 min.
Angoulême 🚆 SNCF: TGV ≫3 per day ⏰0856–1855 ⏲3 hr.
Avignon 🚆 SNCF: TGV ≫7 per day ⏰1005–1846 ⏲3 hr 50 min.
Bordeaux 🚆 SNCF: TGV ≫4 per day ⏰0747–1855 ⏲4 hr.
Le Mans 🚆 SNCF: TGV ≫4 per day ⏰0856–1825 ⏲1 hr 35 min.
Lille 🚆 SNCF: TGV ≫avg 1 hr ⏰0827–2143 ⏲1 hr 22 min. *Connections to Brussels and London via Eurostar.*
Lyon 🚆 SNCF: TGV ≫9 per day ⏰0659–2140 ⏲2 hr.
Marseilles 🚆 SNCF ≫5 per day ⏰1005–1846 ⏲4 hr 47 min.
Montpellier 🚆 SNCF: TGV ≫2 per day ⏰1005; 1705 ⏲4 hr 53 min.
Nantes 🚆 SNCF: TGV ≫4 per day ⏰0837–1825 ⏲2 hr 54 min.
Poitiers 🚆 SNCF: TGV ≫4 per day ⏰0747–1855 ⏲2 hr 14 min.
Tours 🚆 SNCF: TGV ≫4 per day ⏰0747–1855 ⏲1 hr 36 min. *Change at St-Pierre des Corps for Tours.*

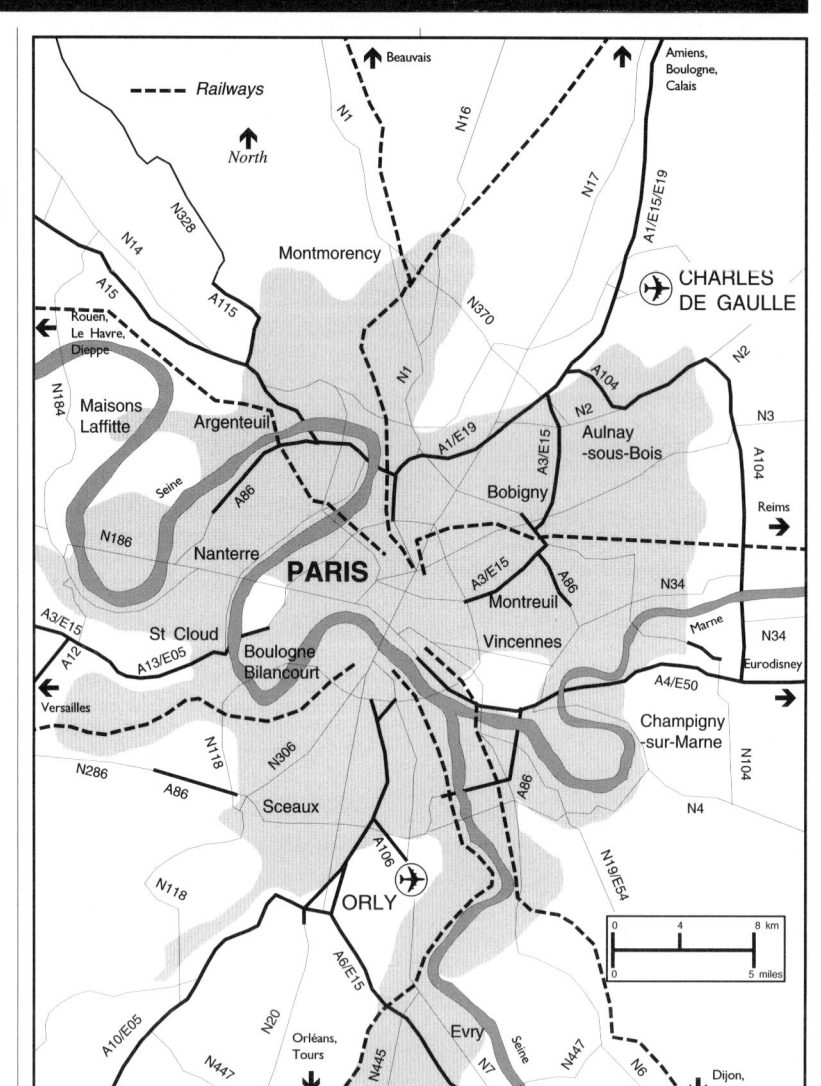

REGIONAL AIR CONNECTIONS

Amsterdam ✈ ≫Several per day ⏲1 hr 5 min
Brussels ✈ ≫Several per day ⏲55 min
Cologne/Bonn ✈ ≫Several per day ⏲1 hr
Düsseldorf ✈ ≫Several per day ⏲1 hr 10 min
Geneva ✈ ≫Several per day ⏲1 hr 05 min
Lille ✈ ≫Several per day ⏲55 min
London ✈ ≫Several per day ⏲1 hr–1 hr 20 min
Lyon ✈ ≫Several per day ⏲1 hr
Marseille ✈ ≫Several per day ⏲1 hr 15 min
Montpellier ✈ ≫Several per day ⏲1 hr 15 min
Rennes ✈ ≫Several per week ⏲1 hr 05 min
Strasbourg ✈ ≫Several per day ⏲1 hr
Toulouse ✈ ≫Several per day ⏲1 hr 15 min

TRAVELLER'S NOTES

The siting of a station at the airport for the ultra-high speed TGV expresses has put most of France within a few hours' reach of Charles de Gaulle. Connections into the city centre are equally good.

℅ Phone no. ℻ Fax no. ⏰ Hours of opening/operation ≫ Frequency of service ⏲ Journey time ⬧ Cost/one-way fare

✈ SECTION TWO • AIRPORT DIRECTORY   PARIS

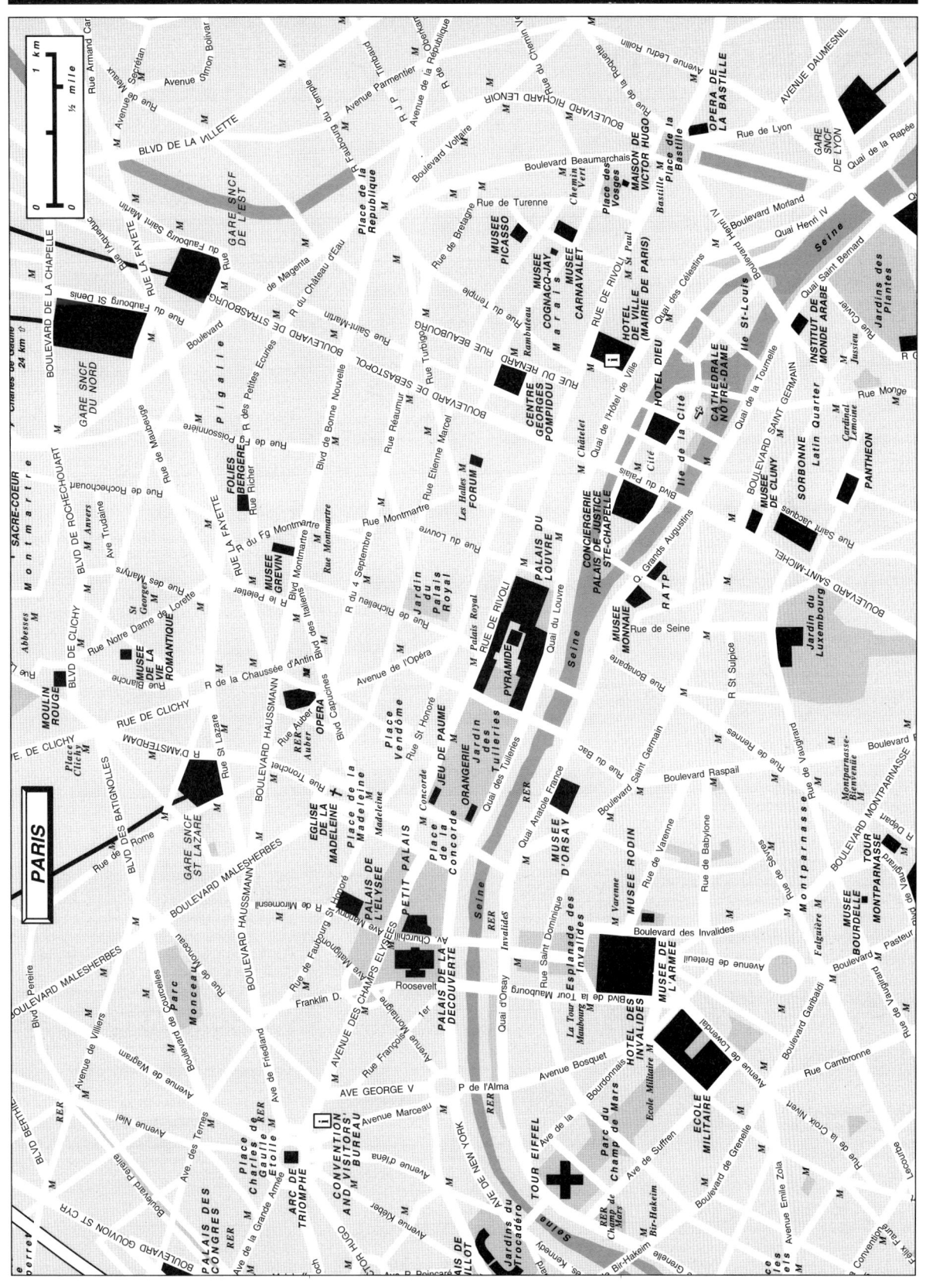

233

✈ Air 🚆 Rail 🚌 Bus 🚐 Limousine Ⓜ Metro/subway 🚋 Tram 🚁 Helicopter ⛴ Water transport • For map symbols, see p. 9

PARIS-ORLY — ORY

France (see page 22)

National ☎ code: 33
Area ☎ code: 01
Local time: Winter GMT+1, Summer GMT+2
Aeroport Paris Orly, 291 Boulevard Raspail, 75675 Paris Cedex 14, France
☎49 75 52 52
http://www.paris.org/accueil/airport
Location: 16 km/10 miles S of central Paris

Terminals and Transfers

Terminals
Orly Sud Airlines: American Airlines, Air France, Air Algérie, Royal Air Maroc, Continental Airlines, Delta Airlines, Icelandair, Iberia, Meridiana, Iran Air, AOM French Airlines, Jat Yugoslav Airlines, Air Malta, Kenya Airways, El Al Israel Airlines, Balkan Bulgarian Airlines, Middle East Airlines, Air Mauritius, Egyptair, Olympic Airways, Pakistan International Airlines, Syrian Arab Airlines, Royal Jordanian Airlines, Tarom Romanian Air, South African Airways, Turkish Airlines, Air Portugal TAP, Tunis Air, USAir, VIASA Venezuelan, . Layout: Ground Level, Baggage Reclaim; Level 1, Arrival; Level 2, Departure, other Levels for Restaurants and other facilities and offices
Orly Ouest Airlines: Air France, British Airways, Air Inter, AOM French Airlines, Air Liberté. Layout: Ground Level, Arrival and Baggage reclaim, Level 1, Departure; Level 2, Restaurants

Minimum transfer times
International: 1 hr Domestic: 50 min

Transfer between terminals
Bus »7 min; Orly Sud and Ouest Terminals ⌀Free
Monorail »Frequent; Orly Sud and Ouest Terminals RER ⌀Free

Information

Flight enquiries
Airport ☎49 75 15 15
Air Algérie ☎42 60 30 62 Air France ☎45 35 61 61 Air Inter ☎45 46 90 00 Air Malta ☎48 74 39 56 Air Portugal TAP ☎44 86 89 89 American Airlines ☎42 98 05 22 AOM French Airlines ☎49 79 12 34 Balkan Bulgarian Airlines ☎47 42 66 66 British Airways ☎98 62 10 22 Continental Airlines ☎42 99 09 09 Delta Airlines ☎47 68 92 92 Egyptair ☎42 66 08 86 El Al Israel Airlines ☎47 42 41 29 Iberia ☎47 23 00 23 Icelandair ☎47 42 52 26 Iran Air ☎42 25 99 06 Jat Yugoslav Airlines ☎42 61 03 44 Kenya Airways ☎47 42 33 11 Meridiana ☎42 61 61 50 Middle East Airlines ☎42 66 93 93 Olympic Airways ☎42 65 92 42 Pakistan International Airlines ☎42 62 92 41 Royal Air Maroc ☎42 66 10 30 Royal Jordanian Airlines ☎42 61 57 45 South African Airways ☎49 27 05 50 Syrian Arab Airlines ☎47 42 11 06 Tarom Romanian Air ☎47 42 25 42 Tunis Air ☎42 66 93 34 Turkish Airlines ☎42 60 28 08 USAir ☎49 10 29 00 VIASA Venezuelan ☎47 42 20 70

Information and help desks
Information Desk Orly Ouest Ground Level ☎49 75 01 39 ⓘ0600–2345 Airport information Hotel booking, Tourist information
Information Desk Orly Sud Ground Level ☎49 75 00 90 ⓘ0600–2345 Airport information Hotel booking, Tourist information

Emergencies
Police Orly Ouest throughout ☎49 75 43 04 ⓘ24 hr
Police Orly Sud throughout ☎49 75 43 04 ⓘ24 hr
Medical Orly Ouest Ground Level, Arrivals Area ☎49 75 43 04 ⓘ24 hr
Medical Orly Sud Level 4, Public Area ☎49 75 45 12 ⓘ24 hr
Lost Property Orly Ouest Ground Level ☎49 75 42 34 ⓘ0830–1705 Sat–Thu; 0830–1530 Fri
Lost Property Orly Sud Ground Level ☎49 75 34 10 ⓘ0830–1705 Sat–Thu; 0830–1530 Fri

Airport Facilities

Money
Bank Orly Sud Ground Level ⓘ0900–1230, 1400–1730 Mon–Fri
Bank Orly Ouest Ground Level ⓘ0900–1730 Mon–Fri
Bureau de change Orly Sud Ground Level ⓘ0630–2330
Bureau de change Orly Ouest Ground Level ⓘ0800–1900 Mon–Fri; 0800–1200 Sat

Food and drink
Bar Orly Sud throughout ⓘ0500–2300
Bar Orly Ouest throughout ⓘ0500–2300
Café/light meals Orly Sud Level 2, Departure Area, and Basement ⓘ1100–2300
Café/light meals Orly Ouest Level 1, Departure Area
Restaurant Orly Sud Level 2, Departure Area ⓘ1130–1500, 1830–2300
Restaurant Orly Ouest Level 2, Departure Area

Communications
Post office Orly Sud Basement Level, landside ⓘ0800–2000 Mon–Fri; 0800–1200 Sat
Post office Orly Ouest Ground Level ⓘ0700–2200 Mon–Fri; 0700–1200 Sat

Shopping
Duty free, departure Orly Sud Level 1 Departure Area ⓘ0645–2230
Duty free, departure Orly Ouest Level 1 Departure Area ⓘ0645–2230
Shopping mall Orly Sud Level 1 Departure Area ⓘ0645–2230
Shopping mall Orly Ouest Level 1 Departure Level ⓘ0645–2230

Luggage
Left luggage counter Orly Sud Ground Level, Baggage Reclaim ⓘ0615–1115
Left luggage counter Orly Ouest Ground Level Baggage Reclaim ⓘ0615–1115
Porters Orly Sud Arrival/Departure Area ⓘAll flight times ⌀FRF20 per item
Porters Orly Ouest Arrival/Departure Area ⓘAll flight times ⌀FRF20 per item
Trolleys/carts Orly Sud throughout ⓘ24 hr
Trolleys/carts Orly Ouest throughout ⓘ24 hr

Disabled Travellers
Orly Sud Adapted toilets; Lifts; Phones at wheelchair height; Personal assistance ☎49 75 30 70, 0530–2300
Orly Ouest Adapted toilets; Lifts; Phones at wheelchair height; Personal assistance ☎46 75 18 18, 0600–2345

☎ Phone no. ℻ Fax no. ⓘ Hours of opening/operation » Frequency of service ⊃ Journey time ⌀ Cost/one-way fare

SECTION TWO • AIRPORT DIRECTORY   PARIS-ORLY

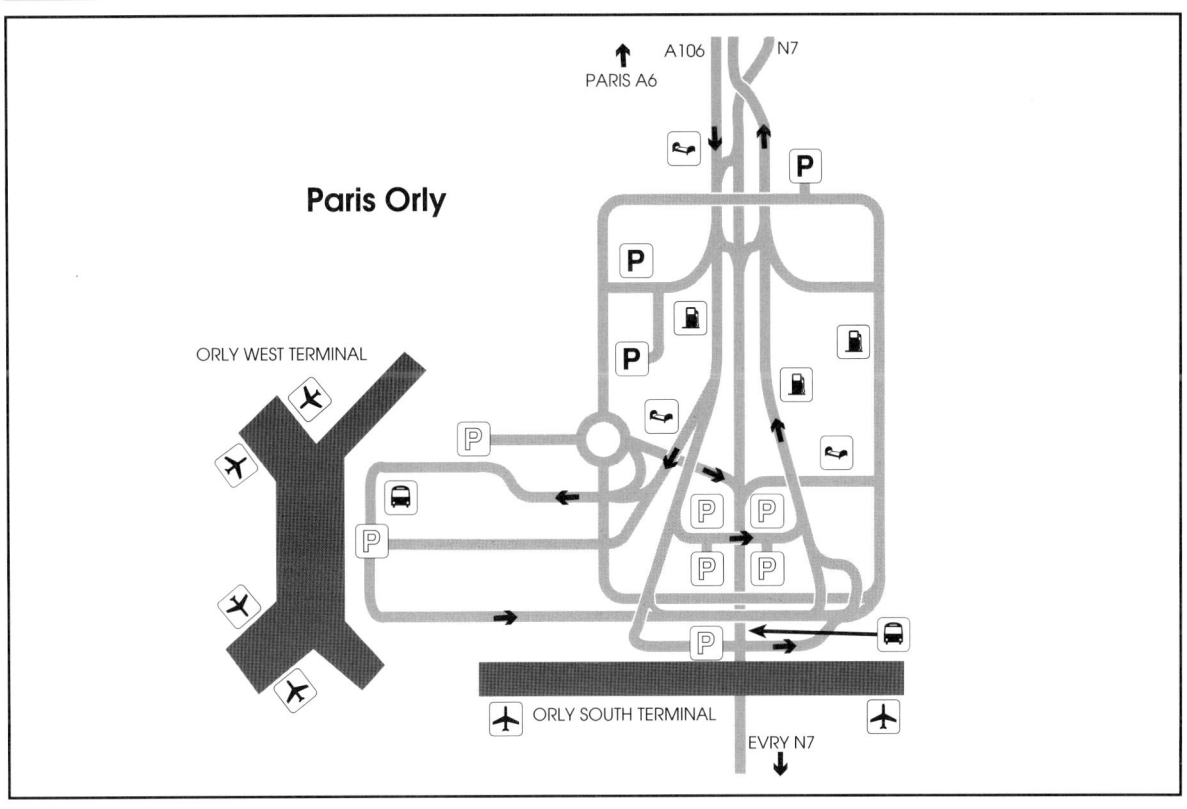

Paris Orly

SMOKING POLICY

Orly Sud No-smoking areas available
Orly Ouest No-smoking areas available

SPECIAL PASSENGER LOUNGES

Air France VIP Lounge Orly Sud Ground Level
All charter flights ICARE VIP Lounge Orly Sud Level 1 airside
American Airlines Salon Espace Orly Sud Level 2 airside
Delta Airlines VIP Lounge Orly Sud Level 1 airside

CONFERENCE AND BUSINESS FACILITIES

Business rooms, Orly Ouest ✆49 75 12 33 ⓞ0800–1900 *Telephones, Fax service, Power points, Photocopier*
Conference rooms, Orly Sud ✆49 75 12 33 ⓞ0800–1700 *Telephones, Fax service*

AIRPORT HOTELS

Hilton Orly ✆45 12 45 12 ⓕ49 78 06 75. 357 rooms *Courtesy bus*
Ibis ✆46 87 35 50. 300 rooms *Courtesy bus*
Mercure ✆46 87 23 37 ⓕ46 87 71 92. 194 rooms *Courtesy bus*
Novotel ✆43 63 85 65 *Courtesy bus*

CAR RENTAL

Avis Orly Sud Ground Level, Baggage Reclaim ✆49 75 44 91
Avis Orly Ouest Ground Level Arrival Area ✆49 75 44 91
Budget Orly Sud Ground Level, Baggage Reclaim ✆49 75 56 00
Budget Orly Ouest Ground Level Arrival Area ✆49 75 56 00
EuropCar Orly Sud Ground Level, Baggage Reclaim ✆49 75 47 47
EuropCar Orly Ouest Ground Level Arrival Area ✆49 75 47 47
Hertz Orly Sud Ground Level, Baggage Reclaim ✆49 75 84 84
Hertz Orly Ouest Ground Level Arrival Area ✆49 75 84 84

CAR PARKING

Long-stay Near Terminals Sud and Ouest 6680 spaces ⊘FRF10 per 50 min; FRF100 per day
Off-airport Free shuttle bus from terminals 2760 spaces ⊘FRF5 per hr; FRF50 per day
Short-stay Near Terminals Sud and Ouest 365 spaces ⊘FRF2 per 6 min; max 2 hr

TAXIS AND CHAUFFEUR-DRIVEN CARS

Taxis
Front of Terminal Charles de Gaulle Apt ⊃ 1 hr ⊘FRF275
Front of terminal City centre ⊃15 min ⊘FRF145

Chauffeur-driven cars
Front of terminal ✆40 71 84 62

PUBLIC TRANSPORT

Airport to airport
Paris-Charles de Gaulle Apt ✈Air France »20 min ⓞ0600–2300 ⊃50 min ⊘FRF70.
Paris-Charles de Gaulle Apt ▬RER B »4–7 min ⓞ0630–2230 ⊃1 hr 5 min ⊘FRF97. *Via Orlyval bus to Antony RER stn*

City & suburbs
Paris city centre (Denfert-Rochereau metro stn) ▄RATP Orlybus »15 min ⊃25 min ⊘FRF30.
Paris city centre (Invalides, Gare Montparnasse rail stn) ▄Air France »15–20 min ⓞ0540–2300 ⊃25 min ⊘FRF40.
Paris city centre ⌁ Hélifrance ⊃15 min

✈ Air ▬ Rail ▄ Bus ⇌ Limousine Ⓜ Metro/subway ⇌ Tram ⌁ Helicopter ⛴ Water transport • For map symbols, see p. 9

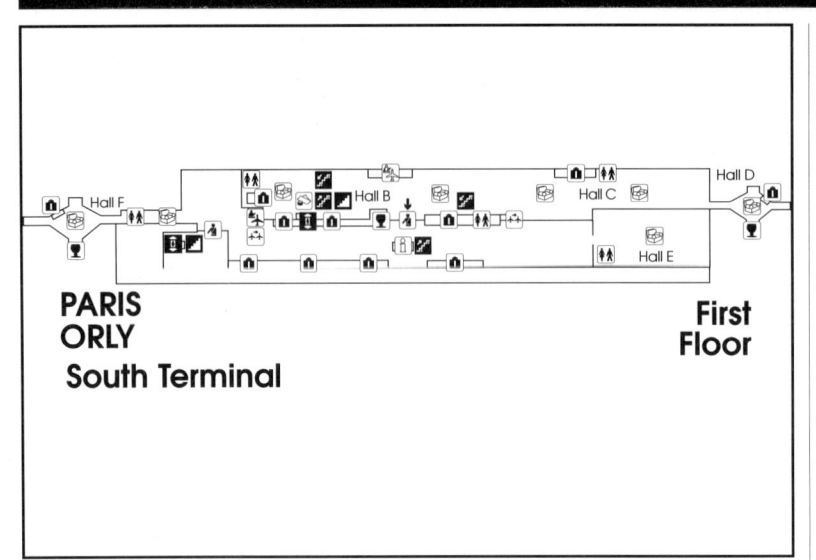

PARIS-ORLY

SECTION TWO • AIRPORT DIRECTORY

PARIS ORLY South Terminal — First Floor

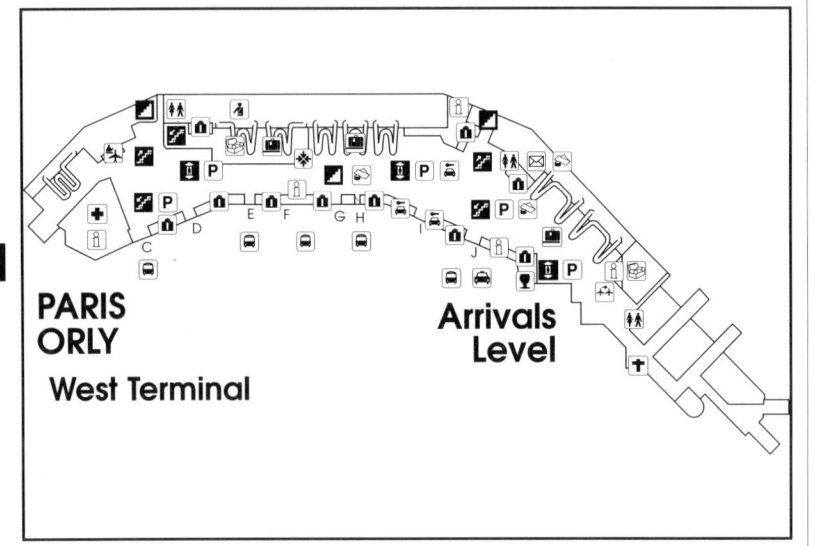

PARIS ORLY West Terminal — Arrivals Level

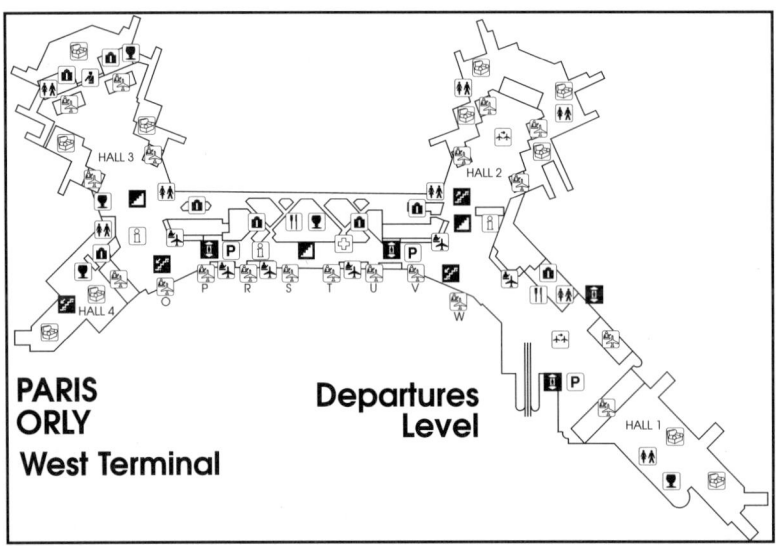

PARIS ORLY West Terminal — Departures Level

◇FRF500.
Paris city centre (St- Michel/Notre Dame)
🚇 RER Line A »avg 15 min
⏰0504–2334 ➲24 min ◇FRF42.50. *Via Orlyval bus to Antony RER stn.*
Paris city centre (St- Michel/Notre Dame)
🚇 RER Line C »15 min ⏰0535–2317
➲35 min ◇FRF52.

REGIONAL AIR CONNECTIONS

Amsterdam ✈ »Severl per day ➲1 hr 10 min
Avignon ✈ »Several per week ➲1 hr 10 min
Basel ✈ »Several per day ➲55 min
Beziers ✈ »Several per week ➲1 hr 10 min
Biarritz ✈ »Several per day ➲1 hr 10 min
Bordeaux ✈ »Several per day ➲55 min
Brest ✈ »Several per day ➲1 hr 05 min
Brussels ✈ »Several per week ➲1 hr
Clermont Ferrand ✈ »Several per day ➲50 min
Grenoble ✈ »Several per day ➲55 min
La Rochelle ✈ »At least daily ➲1 hr 10 min
Lille ✈ »Several per week ➲45 min
Limoges ✈ »Several per week ➲1 hr 05 min
London City Apt ✈ »Several per week ➲1 hr
London Heathrow Apt ✈ »Several per day ➲1 hr 10 min
Lorient ✈ »At least daily ➲1 hr
Lyon Bron Apt ✈ »Several per day ➲55 min
Marseille ✈ »Several per day ➲1 hr 10 min
Montpellier ✈ »Several per day ➲1 hr 10 min
Mulhouse ✈ »Several per day ➲55 min
Nantes ✈ »Several per day ➲55 min
Nimes ✈ »Several per day ➲1 hr 10 min
Quimper ✈ »At least daily ➲1 hr 05 min
Rennes ✈ »At least daily ➲1 hr
St Brieuc ✈ »Several per weekr ➲1 hr 05 min
Strasbourg ✈ »Several per day ➲1 hr
Toulouse Blagnac Apt ✈ »Several per day ➲1 hr 05 min

TRAVELLER'S NOTES

Though lacking the TGV connections of Charles de Gaulle, Orly is very convenient for the centre of Paris and the Métro system (no point in the city centre is more than 500 metres from a Métro station).

✆ Phone no. 🖷 Fax no. ⏰ Hours of opening/operation » Frequency of service ➲ Journey time ◇ Cost/one-way fare

SECTION TWO • AIRPORT DIRECTORY   PERTH

PERTH   PER

Australia (see page 14)

National ✆ code: 61
Area ✆ code: 09
Local time: Winter GMT+8,
Summer GMT+8
Perth International Airport, Perth,
WA, Australia
✆478 8888
🖷277 7537
Location: 12 km/7 miles from Perth

TERMINALS AND TRANSFERS

Terminals
International Terminal Airlines: British Airways, Cathay Pacific Airways, Garuda Indonesian Airlines, Malaysian Airlines, Air New Zealand, Qantas Airways, Singapore Airlines, Thai Airways, Air Zimbabwe. Layout: Upper and Lower Floor
Domestic Terminal Airlines: Ansett Australia. Layout: Upper and Lower Floor

Minimum transfer times
International: 1–2 hr **Domestic:** 30 min–1 hr 30 min

Transfer between terminals
Bus ≫30 min; International and Domestic Terminals

INFORMATION

Information and help desks
Information Desk International Terminal Arrival Lounge.

AIRPORT FACILITIES

Money
Bank International Terminal

Thomas Cook bureau de change International Terminal

Food and drink
Bar International Terminal ⏲24 hr
Bar Domestic Terminal
Café/light meals International Terminal ⏲24 hr
Café/light meals Domestic Terminal
Restaurant International Terminal ⏲24 hr
Restaurant Domestic Terminal

Communications
Post office International Terminal

Shopping
Duty free, departure International Terminal
Duty free, departure Domestic Terminal

DISABLED TRAVELLERS

International Terminal Adapted toilets; Lifts; Phones at wheelchair height
Domestic Terminal Adapted toilets; Lifts; Phones at wheelchair height

SPECIAL PASSENGER LOUNGES

Ansett Australia Lounge Domestic Terminal First and Business Class
Ansett Australia Lounge International Terminal
British Airways Lounge International Terminal
Qantas Airways Lounge International Terminal
Singapore Airlines Lounge International Terminal

AIRPORT HOTELS

Maracoonda Motel ✆277 7777 Courtesy bus

CAR RENTAL

Avis International Terminal
Budget International Terminal
Hertz International Terminal
Thrifty International Terminal

TAXIS AND CHAUFFEUR-DRIVEN CARS

Taxis
City centre ✏AUD15

PUBLIC TRANSPORT

City & suburbs
Perth (city centre) 🚌Perth Airport Bus Services ≫30 min ⏲0600–2230 ➔1 hr 20 min ✏AUD6. From International and Domestic Terminals

REGIONAL AIR CONNECTIONS

Albany WA ✈ ≫Several per day ➔1 hr
Carnarvon WA ✈ ≫At least daily ➔1 hr 10 min
Geraldton WA ✈ ≫Several per day ➔1hr 5 min
Kalgoorlie WA ✈ ≫Several per day ➔1 hr 5 min
Rottnest Island WA ✈ ≫Several per day ➔15 min
Southern Cross WA ✈ ≫Several per week ➔1 hr 5 min

✈ Air 🚆 Rail 🚌 Bus 🚗 Limousine Ⓜ Metro/subway 🚋 Tram 🚁 Helicopter ⛴ Water transport • For map symbols, see p. 9

PHILADELPHIA   SECTION TWO • AIRPORT DIRECTORY

PHILADELPHIA   PHL
USA (see page 41)

National ✆ code: 1
Area ✆ code: 215
Local time: Winter GMT-5,
Summer GMT-4
Philadelphia International Airport,
Philadelphia, PA 19153, USA
✆937 6800
WWW site: http://www.phl.org/
Location: 12 km/7 miles SW of
Philadelphia

TERMINALS AND TRANSFERS

Terminals
Terminal A Airlines: Air Jamaica, Air Mobility Command (International Arrivals), American Airlines, American Eagle, British Airways, Charters, Midway Airlines, Midwest Express, Swissair, US Airways (Transatlantic Arrivals and Departures). Layout: First Floor (Airport Rail Line, Baggage Claim, Car Rental, Ground Transportation); Second Floor (Departure, Gates A1–A11)
Terminal B Airlines: US Airways (Domestic and International Arrivals and Departures). Layout: First Floor (Airport Rail Line, Baggage Claim, Car Rental, Ground Transportation); Second Floor (Departure, Gates B1–B16)
Terminal C Airlines: US Airways. Layout: First Floor (Airport Rail Line, Baggage Claim, Car Rental, Ground Transportation); Second Floor (Departure, Gates C17–C30)
Terminal D Airlines: Air Canada, Air Mobility Command (Departures), America West Airlines, Continental Airlines, United Airlines, United Express. Layout: First Floor (Airport Rail Line, Baggage Claim, Car Rental, Ground Transportation); Second Floor (Departure, Gates D3–D11)
Terminal E Airlines: Delta Airlines, Delta Connection, Delta Express, Northwest Airlines, TWA, TW Express, Valuejet. Layout: First Floor (Airport Rail Line, Baggage Claim, Car Rental, Ground Transportation); Second Floor (Departure, Gates E1–E11)

Minimum transfer times
International: 1 hr 30 min Domestic: 40 min

Transfer between terminals
Bus »10 min; All terminals and parking ⌀Free

INFORMATION

Flight enquiries
Airport ✆937 6937

Information and help desks
Information Desk All Terminals throughout Airport information, Tourist information
Travel Center All Terminals Departure Area

EMERGENCIES
Police All Terminals throughout ✆937 6711
Medical Terminal A Bridge between Terminals A and B ⏱0800–2200 ✆492 2196
Lost Property Terminal C First Floor

AIRPORT FACILITIES

Money
ATM All Terminals throughout
Bureau de change Terminal A Second Floor
Bureau de change Terminal D Second Floor
Thomas Cook bureau de change Terminal A ⏱0600–2100
Thomas Cook bureau de change Terminal C ⏱0900–1700
Thomas Cook bureau de change Terminal D (mobile cart) ⏱0700–1900

Food and drink
Bar All Terminals throughout
Café/light meals All Terminals throughout
Restaurant All Terminals Second Floor

Communications
Post office Terminal A Second Floor
Post office Terminal C Second Floor
Post box All Terminals throughout

Shopping
Duty Free, departure, Terminal A Concourse
Gift Shop All Terminals Second Floor
News, Stationery & Books All Terminals Second Floor

Luggage
Lockers All Terminals Second Floor (by Security) ⌀USD2-4 per day
Trolleys/Carts All Terminals throughout ⌀USD1.50

DISABLED TRAVELLERS
All Terminals Adapted toilets; Lifts Phones at wheelchair height; Phones adapted for the deaf

SMOKING POLICY
All Terminals Permitted in cocktail lounges

SPECIAL PASSENGER LOUNGES
American Airlines Admirals Club Terminal A Second Floor
British Airways Executive/Speedwing Lounge Terminal A Second Floor
Delta Airlines Crown Room Terminal E Second Floor
United Airlines Red Carpet Club Terminal D Second Floor
US Airways Club Terminal B Second Floor
US Airways Club Terminal C Second Floor
US Airways Envoy Lounge Terminal A Second Floor

CONFERENCE AND BUSINESS FACILITIES
Business Center 1, Terminal A (Departures) ✆492 2654 ⏱0600–2100 Telephones, Fax service, Photocopier, Travel advice

AIRPORT HOTELS
Airport Marriott Terminal B via skybridge 419 rooms ✆492 9000

CAR RENTAL
Alamo All Terminals First Floor
Avis All Terminals First Floor
Budget All Terminals First Floor
Dollar All Terminals First Floor
Hertz All Terminals First Floor
National All Terminals First Floor

✆ Phone no. ℱ Fax no. ⏱ Hours of opening/operation » Frequency of service ➲ Journey time ⌀ Cost/one-way fare

SECTION TWO • AIRPORT DIRECTORY

PHILADELPHIA • PRAGUE

CAR PARKING

Long-stay 1 km/½ mile from terminal (take free shuttle bus) ⌀USD6.50 per day (max)
Short-stay Across from terminals ⌀USD2.50 per 30 min, USD30 per day (max)

TAXIS AND CHAUFFEUR-DRIVEN CARS

Taxis
All Terminals First Floor Philadelphia City centre ⌑20 min ⌀USD20

PUBLIC TRANSPORT

City & suburbs
Chester PA ⟶SEPTA: 37 »30–60 min ⓘ0450-0035 ⌀USD1.60.
Elmwood PA ⟶SEPTA: U »35–75 min ⌀USD1.60.
Philadelphia (Metro Area) ⟶Over 30 companies at airport.
Philadelphia (30th Street rail stn) ⟶SEPTA: R1 »30 min ⓘ0600–2400 ⌑20 min ⌀USD5. For all Amtrak and SEPTA Regional Rail services
Philadelphia (Suburban rail stn ⟶SEPTA R1 »30 min ⓘ0600–2400 ⌑20 min ⌀USD6. For all SEPTA Regional Rail services
Philadelphia city centre ⟶SEPTA R1 »30 min ⓘ0600–2400 ⌑20 min ⌀USD5.
Philadelphia PA (69th St. Terminal) ⟶SEPTA 108 »30–60 min ⓘ0605-0025 ⌀USD1.60.

REGIONAL AIR CONNECTIONS

Allentown PA ✈ »Several per day ⌑40 min
Atlantic City NJ ✈ »Several per day ⌑40 min
Baltimore MD ✈ »Several per day ⌑40 min
Harrisburg PA ✈ »Several per day ⌑45 min
Hartford CT ✈ »Several per day ⌑55 min
Lancaster PA ✈ »Several per day ⌑45 min
Newburgh NY ✈ »At least daily ⌑1 hr
New York NY ✈ »Several per day ⌑45 min
Reading PA ✈ »Several per day ⌑35 min
Salisbury MD ✈ »Several per day ⌑50 min
State College PA ✈ »Several per day ⌑1 hr
Washington DC ✈ »Several per day ⌑1 hr
Westchester County NY ✈ »Several per day ⌑1 hr
Wilkes-Barre PA ✈ »Several per day ⌑40 min
Williamsport PA ✈ »Several per day ⌑55 min

TRAVELLER'S NOTES

The public transportation system is reliable and cheap, though better avoided at night. The downtown area is comparatively small and it is not worth hiring a car if you are staying within the city.

Prague (PRAHA)   PRG

Czech Republic (see page 20)

239

National ✆ code: 420
Area ✆ code: 02
Local time: Winter GMT+1, Summer GMT+2
Prague-Ruzyne Airport, 160 08 Praha 6, Czech Republic.
✆2011 1111 (see Traveller's Notes) ℻325169 (Gen. Manager); 360922
Location: 16 km/10 miles W of Prague

TERMINALS AND TRANSFERS

Terminals
Main Terminal Airlines: All airlines. Layout: Public Hall and Transit Hall, each with Ground Floor and First Floor; Arrival Hall, Departure Hall
New Terminal Opened June 1997

Minimum transfer times
International: 55 min **Domestic:** 40 min

Transfer between terminals
Bus »30 min; Main and New Terminals (from mid 1997)

INFORMATION

Flight enquiries
Airport ✆2011 1111
Adria Airways ✆2421 2526; 2421 2762
Aeroflot ✆ext 4318; 2481 2683 Air Algérie ✆ext 3457; 2422 9110; 2421 3554 Air France ✆ext 4321; 2422 7164-6 Air Ostrava ✆3406, 3645; 2403 2734; 2403 2732 Air Ukraine ✆(069) 6627 730 Alitalia ✆ext 3284; 2481 0079 ℻361784 Austrian Airlines ✆ext 4519, 4324; 231 1872; 231 3378 Balkan Bulgarian Airlines ✆ext 4563; 367763 ℻269082 British Airways ✆ext 4421; 232 9080 ℻232 9615 British Midland Airways ✆ext 4495; 2423 9280 Crossair ✆2481 2111; 2481 2678 CSA Czechoslovak ✆ext 3314; 2481 5110 Delta Airlines ✆ext 4267; 269477 ℻267141 El Al Israel Airlines ✆ext 3526, 4526; 2421 7349 Eurowings ✆ext 3400, 3634 Finnair ✆2421 1986 ℻2421 4552 Jat Yugoslav Airlines ✆ext 4467 KLM ✆ext 4322; 2422 8678; 2422 8680 Lot Polish Airlines ✆ext 4535; 231 7524 Lufthansa ✆ext 4570, 4516; 2481 1007; 2481 0994 Malev Hungarian ✆ext 4361; 24812671; 2481 2700 ℻367766 Orbi Georgian Airways ✆2325 742; 2324 642 Sabena World Airlines ✆ext 4323; 4540 Swissair ✆2481 2111; 2481 2678 Syrian Arab Airlines ✆ext 4480; 32 21 53 Tatra Air ✆ext 2224, 3534 Topair ✆316 5554; 316 6737 Tunis Air ✆2422 2673; 2422 6302

Information and help desks
Airport Information Desk Main Terminal Public Hall near exit ✆ext 4433, 4533, 4512 ℻321391 ⓘ24 hr Airport, Flights, Hotel booking, Tourist Information
AVE Main Terminal Public Hall ✆3164266, 3343106 ⓘ0700–2200,
Hotel booking
Cedok Main Terminal Public Hall ✆367802 ℻367803 ⓘ0700–2200 Hotel booking, Tourist Information

EMERGENCIES

Police Main Terminal Airport security, Public Hall Ground Floor ✆3118 558 ⓘ24 hr
Police Main Terminal Police emergency number ✆158 ⓘ24 hr
Medical Main Terminal First aid service number ✆ext 3301, 3302 ⓘ24 hr
Lost Property Main Terminal Arrival Hall, CSA Desk ✆ext 4283, 4285 ⓘ24 hr
Lost Property Main Terminal COAH

✈ Air ⟶ Rail ⟶ Bus ⟶ Limousine ⓂMetro/subway ⟶ Tram ⟶ Helicopter ⟶ Water transport • For map symbols, see p. 9

PRAGUE

SECTION TWO • AIRPORT DIRECTORY

Desk (for AZ, DL LH passengers) ⓒext 4483

AIRPORT FACILITIES

Money
Bank Main Terminal Transit Hall ⓞ24 hr
Bank Main Terminal Arrival Hall ⓞ24 hr
Bureau de change Main Terminal Public Hall ⓞ24 hr
Bureau de change Main Terminal Transit Hall ⓞ24 hr
ATM Main Terminal Public Hall (3) ⓞ24 hr

Food and Drink
Café/light meals Main Terminal Public Hall, First Floor ⓞMay–Oct 0700–2200; Nov–Apr 0800–1800
Restaurant Main Terminal Transit Hall, First Floor ⓞ1000–2000

Communications
Post office Main Terminal Public Hall, Basement ⓞ0800–1800

Shopping
Duty free, arrival Main Terminal Arrival Hall ⓞ0700–2000
Duty free, arrival Main Terminal Transit Hall ⓞ0700–2000
Florist Main Terminal Public Hall, Ground Floor ⓞ0700–2200
News, Stationery & Books Main Terminal Public Hall, Ground Floor ⓞMay–Oct 0600–2200; Nov–Apr 0600–2000
Shopping mall Main Terminal Public Hall, First Floor ⓞMay–Oct 0800–2200; Nov–Apr 0800–1800

Luggage
Left Luggage Counter Main Terminal Public Hall ⓞ24 hr ⌀CZK20 per item per day
Trolleys/carts Main Terminal throughout ⓞ24 hr ⌀Free
Porters Main Terminal throughout ⓞ24 hr ⌀CZK5–10
Trolleys/carts Main Terminal Extra-large porters trolleys, far right of Main Hall ⓞ24 hr

DISABLED TRAVELLERS
Main Terminal Adapted toilets Public Hall, First Floor, and Transit Hall; Special car parking New car park (under construction); Personal assistance CSA Desk, ext 3297; COAH Desk, ext 3315

SMOKING POLICY
Main Terminal No-smoking throughout
New Terminal No-smoking throughout

SPECIAL PASSENGER LOUNGES
All airlines First Class Lounge Main Terminal Operated by CSA/COAH
British Midland Airways Diamond Club Lounge Main Terminal

CONFERENCE AND BUSINESS FACILITIES
Representative Lounge, ⓒext 4490 Telephones, Fax service, Power points

CAR RENTAL
Avis Main Terminal Main Hall ⓒext 4270
Budget Main Terminal Main Hall ⓒext 3253
EuropCar Main Terminal Main Hall ⓒext 3207
Hertz Main Terminal Main Hall ⓒext 4340
Eurodollar Main Terminal Main Hall ⓒext 4554
A Rent Car Main Terminal Main Hall ⓒext 4370
Alamo Main Terminal Main Hall ⓒext 3534

CAR PARKING
Long-stay Behind short-stay car park 1550 spaces ⌀CZK360 first day, CZK120 per extra day
Short-stay Front of terminal 250 spaces ⌀CZK30 per hr

TAXIS AND CHAUFFEUR-DRIVEN CARS

Taxis
Front of Main Terminal Fix-Car (avoid unlicensed taxis) ➲25 min ⌀CZK400

Chauffeur-driven cars
Lincoln Limousine ⓒ401 9063 ⌀CZK900–1500 per hr, 7000–12000 per day

PUBLIC TRANSPORT

City & suburbs
Prague city centre 🚌CSA: Airport Bus » 30 min ⓞ0530–2400 ➲20 min ⌀CZK30.
Prague city centre (Dejvická metro stn) 🚌CEDAZ » 1 hr and acc to demand ⓞ0600–2200 ➲20 min ⌀CZK60. Also operates between scheduled times if sufficient passengers. From metro stn to city centre is 3 stops on Line A.
Prague city centre (Dejvická metro stn) 🚌Municipal bus 119 » 10 min ⓞ0600–2300 ➲30 min ⌀CZK12.
Prague city centre (Hotel Penta) 🚌CSA » ⓞFor CSA flight times ➲30 min ⌀CZK75. CSA flights can be checked in at Hotel Penta.
Prague city centre (Nam. Republicky metro stn) 🚌CEDAZ ⓒ 3344368 » 1 hr and according to demand ⓞ0600–2200 ➲30 min ⌀CZK90.

REGIONAL AIR CONNECTIONS
Berlin ✈ »Several per week ➲55 min
Bratislava ✈ »Several per day ➲55 min
Brno ✈ »At least daily ➲50 min
Budapest ✈ »Several per day ➲1 hr
Munich ✈ »Several per day ➲55 min
Nuremberg ✈ »Several per week ➲1 hr
Ostrava ✈ »Several per day ➲1 hr
Salzburg ✈ »Several per week ➲1 hr
Vienna ✈ »Several per day ➲55 min

TRAVELLER'S NOTES
Tel nos prefixed 'ext' are extensions of the main airport number 2011. Only ext 1111 is direct-dial from outside.

ⓒ Phone no. ⓕ Fax no. ⓞ Hours of opening/operation » Frequency of service ➲ Journey time ⌀ Cost/one-way fare

REYKJAVIK

KEF

Iceland (see page 24)

National ☎ code: 354
Local time: Winter GMT, Summer GMT
Address: Leifur Eiríksson Air Terminal, PO Box 1015, 235 Keflavík Airport, Iceland
☎: 425 0600
℻: 425 0610
Location: 50 km/30 miles SW of Reykjavík

TERMINALS AND TRANSFERS

Terminals
Main Terminal Airlines: Icelandair, Air Atlanta, SAS, Greenlandair, Lufthansa, Canada 3000, Cargolux Layout: Ground floor arrivals and departures lounge. First floor: passenger facilities.

INFORMATION

Flight enquiries
Airport ☎ 425 0200

Information and help desks
Tourist Information Ground floor, arrivals lounge Tourist information, travel information

Emergencies
Police ☎ 425 0655
Lost Property ☎ 425 0226

AIRPORT FACILITIES

Money
Bureau de Change First floor ⓘ 24 hr
Bureau de Change Ground floor ⓘ 24 hr

Food and drink
Bar First floor
Café/light meals Ground floor
Restaurant First floor
Restaurant Ground floor

Communications
Post Office Ground floor ⓘ 0530–2100 Stamps, express mail service, postcards
Post Office First floor ⓘ 0530–2100 Stamps, express mail service, postcards

Shopping
Duty free First floor
Duty free Ground floor
Gift Shop First floor

Luggage
Trolleys/carts

DISABLED TRAVELLERS

Lifts, disabled toilets

SPECIAL PASSENGER LOUNGES

Icelandair Saga Class business lounge first floor

CAR RENTAL

Avis ☎ 425 0760 Ground floor, arrivals lounge
Hertz ☎ 425 0221 Ground floor, arrivals lounge

CAR PARKING

Short-stay Available
Long-stay USD3.80 per day

TAXIS AND CHAUFFEUR-DRIVEN CARS

Taxis
Reykjavík city centre ◇ USD63 ☎ 2 11515 Outside terminal building

PUBLIC TRANSPORT

City & suburbs
Reykjavík city centre 🚌 Flybus ⓘ serves all arrivals and departures ☎ 91 621011 Pick-up outside terminal building

REGIONAL AIR CONNECTIONS

Akureyri ✈ »Several per day ⊃45 min
Isafjordur ✈ »At least daily ⊃40 min
Vestmannaeyja ✈ »Several per day ⊃25 min

RIO DE JANEIRO-INTERNATIONAL GIG

Brazil (see page 17)

National ☎ code: 55
Area ☎ code: 021
Local time: Winter GMT-2, Summer GMT-3
Rio de Janeiro International Airport, Rio de Janeiro 21942-900, Brazil
☎398 4597; 398 4203; 398 4145; 398 4133; 398 4134
📠393 2288
Location: 15 km/9 miles N of Rio de Janeiro

Terminals and Transfers

Terminals
Main Terminal Airlines: All airlines.

Minimum transfer times
International: 1–2 hr Domestic: 1 hr

Information

Flight enquiries
Airport ☎398 4132; 398 4477; 398 4499; 398 4498

Information and help desks
Information Desk Main Terminal ☎398 4132; 398 4133 📠 ⏰0000–2400 Airport information, Flights

Airport Facilities

Money
Bank Main Terminal 3rd floor
ATM Main Terminal

Food and Drink
Café/light meals Main Terminal Third Floor ⏰0600–1200
Restaurant Main Terminal Luxor Hotel ⏰0600–1200
Restaurant Main Terminal Third Floor ⏰0600–1200

Communications
Post office Main Terminal Third Floor ⏰0600–2000

Shopping
Duty free, arrival Main Terminal
Duty free, departure Main Terminal

Luggage
Left Luggage Counter Main Terminal Second Floor, sector green
Lockers Main Terminal Second Floor, all sectors

Disabled Travellers

Main Terminal Adapted toilets; Lifts; Phones at wheelchair height; Personal assistance

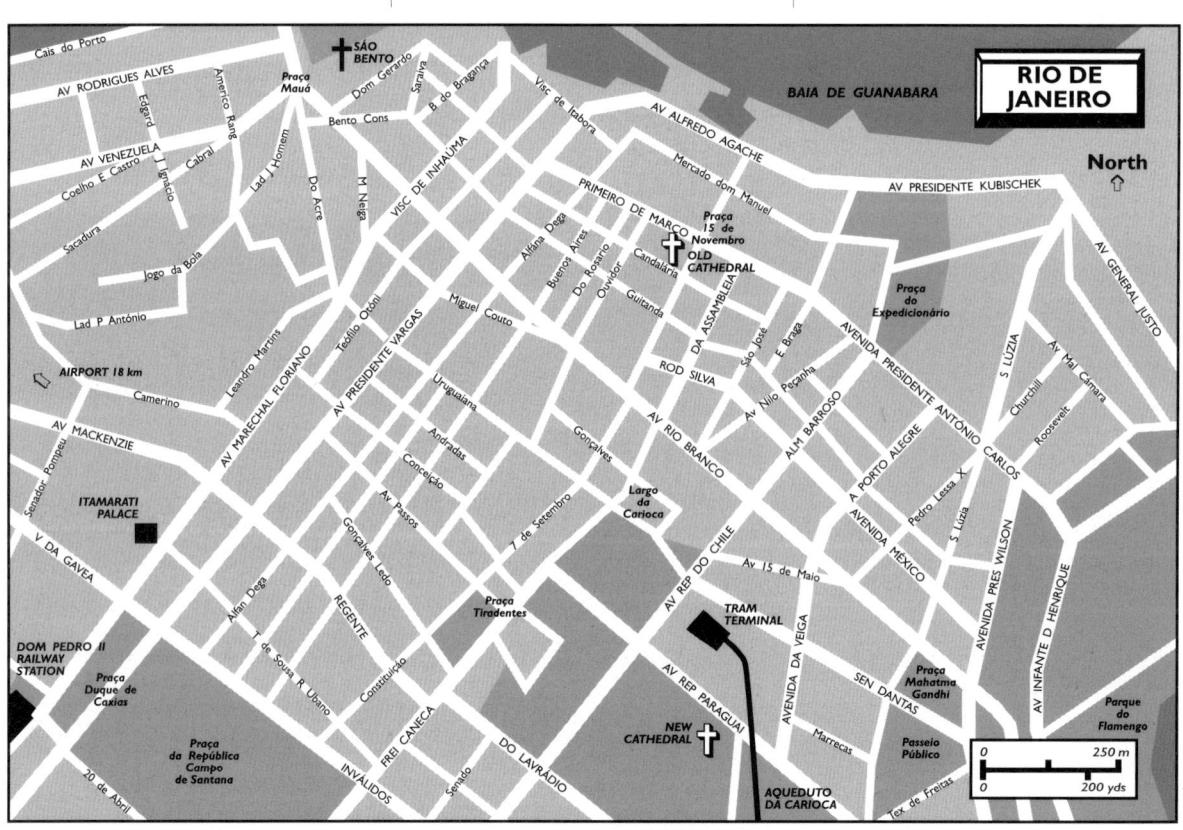

☎ Phone no. 📠 Fax no. ⏰ Hours of opening/operation ≫ Frequency of service ➲ Journey time ◊ Cost/one-way fare

SECTION TWO • AIRPORT DIRECTORY — RIO DE JANEIRO • RIYADH

SPECIAL PASSENGER LOUNGES

Varig Brazilian Business Travel Lounge
Main Terminal *Business class passengers*

CONFERENCE AND BUSINESS FACILITIES

Business facilities, Airport administration

AIRPORT HOTELS

Luxor ✆398 3222; 398 3223
Pousada Galeao ✆398 3852; 398 3853

CAR RENTAL

Hertz Main Terminal
Localiza Main Terminal
Mega Rent Car Main Terminal
SPR Main Terminal
Unidas Rent-a-car Main Terminal

CAR PARKING

Short-stay 1266 spaces ⌀BRC3.30 per 1 hr; BRC30.00 per day

TAXIS AND CHAUFFEUR-DRIVEN CARS

Taxis
City centre ⌀USD20

PUBLIC TRANSPORT

Airport to airport
Rio de Janeiro-Santos Dumont Apt 🚌 30 min ⏱0600–2130 ⟳40 min ⌀USD2.

City & suburbs
Rio de Janeiro city centre (downtown bus depot) 🚌 »30 min ⏱0520–2300 ⟳1 hr ⌀USD2.50.
São Conrado 🚌 »30 min ⏱0530–2050 ⟳40 min ⌀USD2. *Calls at the hotels in the beach area before terminating at São Conrado*

REGIONAL AIR CONNECTIONS

São Paulo ✈ »Several per day ⟳50 min
Victoria (Brazil) ✈ »Several per day ⟳1 hr

TRAVELLER'S NOTES

Duty-free shops are not especially cheap, and you may have to leave bags outside the shopping area – not a safe arrangement. Air-conditioned taxis have fixed rates; buy a ticket at the counter near the arrivals gate before getting into the taxi. Hire charge is per vehicle, so it is worth the possibility of sharing with other passengers.

RIYADH — RUH
Saudi Arabia (see page 35)

National ✆ code: 966
Area ✆ code: 01
Local time: Winter GMT+3, Summer GMT+3
King Khaled International Airport, PO Box 22531, Riyadh, Saudi Arabia
✆221 1000
📠221 1637
Location: 35 km/21½ miles N of Riyadh

TERMINALS AND TRANSFERS

Terminals
Terminal 1 Airlines: All other international flights. Layout: Two Levels. Ground Level, Arrival; Level 1, Departure
Terminal 2 Airlines: Saudia (International flights). Layout: Two Levels. Ground Level, Arrival; Level 1, Departure
Terminal 3 Airlines: All domestic flights, Saudia (Domestic flights). Layout: Two Levels. Ground Level, Arrival; Level 1, Departure

Minimum transfer times
International: 1 hr 30 min–3 hr Domestic: 1 hr

INFORMATION

Flight enquiries
Airport ✆221 3400/4444

EMERGENCIES

Police Terminal 3 throughout Airport ⏱24 hr
Police Terminal 1 throughout Airport ⏱24 hr
Police Terminal 2 throughout Airport ⏱24 hr
Lost Property Terminal 3 Monitored by Airport Police
Lost Property Terminal 1 Monitored by Airport Police
Lost Property Terminal 2 Monitored by Airport Police

AIRPORT FACILITIES

Money
Bank Terminal 1 ⏱24 hr
Bank Terminal 2 ⏱24 hr
Bank Terminal 3 ⏱24 hr

Food and drink
Café/light meals Terminal 1 Departure Area ⏱24 hr
Café/light meals Terminal 2 Departure Area ⏱24 hr
Café/light meals Terminal 3 Departure Areas ⏱24 hr

Communications
Post office Terminal 1 ⏱0700–0200
Post office Terminal 2 ⏱0700–0200
Post office Terminal 3 ⏱0700–0200

Shopping
Gift Shop Terminal 1 Departure Hall ⏱All flight times
Gift Shop Terminal 2 Departure Lounge ⏱All flight times
Gift Shop Terminal 3 Departure Lounge ⏱All flight times

DISABLED TRAVELLERS

Terminal 1 Lifts
Terminal 2 Lifts
Terminal 3 Lifts

SMOKING POLICY

Terminal 1 Smoking permitted throughout
Terminal 2 Smoking permitted throughout
Terminal 3 Smoking permitted throughout

SPECIAL PASSENGER LOUNGES

All international flights VIP Lounge Terminal 1

✈ Air 🚆 Rail 🚌 Bus 🚐 Limousine Ⓜ Metro/subway 🚋 Tram 🚁 Helicopter ⛴ Water transport • For map symbols, see p. 9

RIYADH • ROME

Saudia VIP Lounge Terminal 2
Saudia VIP Lounge Terminal 3

CONFERENCE AND BUSINESS FACILITIES

Conference centre, Airport Sahara Hotel ℂ220 2525

AIRPORT HOTELS

Airport Sahara ℂ220 2525

CAR RENTAL

Avis Terminal 1 Ground Level Arrival
Avis Terminal 2 Ground Level Arrival
Avis Terminal 3 Ground Level Arrival
Budget Terminal 1 Ground Level Arrival
Budget Terminal 2 Ground Level Arrival
Budget Terminal 3 Ground Level Arrival

CAR PARKING

Short-stay 11400 spaces ⌀SAR1 per hr; SAR24 per day

TAXIS AND CHAUFFEUR-DRIVEN CARS

Taxis
City centre ⊃30 min ⌀SAR50

PUBLIC TRANSPORT

City & suburbs
Riyadh city centre 🚌SAPTCO »40 min ⏱0600–0100 ⊃35 min ⌀SAR5.

REGIONAL AIR CONNECTIONS

Amman ✈ »Several per week ⊃1 hr 5 min
Bahrain ✈ »Several per week ⊃1 hr 5 min
Dhahran ✈ »Several per day ⊃1 hr
Gassim ✈ »Several per day ⊃55 min
Jeddah ✈ »Several per day ⊃1 hr 40 min
Qaisumah ✈ »at least daily ⊃55 min

ROME-FIUMICINO (ROMA)   FCO

Italy (see page 27)

National ℂ code: 39
Area ℂ code: 06
Local time: Winter GMT+1, Summer GMT+2
Aeroporto Intercontinentale Leonardo da Vinci, Fiumicino Aeroporto, 00050 Fiumicino, Italy
ℂ6595 1
ℂ6595 3776
Location: 26 km/16 miles SW of Rome

TERMINALS AND TRANSFERS

Terminals
International Terminal Airlines: All international flights except Alitalia. Layout: Three Levels. Level 1, Arrival; Level 2, Departure and Piers; Level 3, restaurants/lounges
Domestic Terminal Airlines: All domestic flights, Alitalia. Layout: Three Levels. Level 1, Arrival; Level 2, Departure and Piers; Level 3, Executive Centre

Minimum transfer times
International: 45 min–2 hr **Domestic:** 45 min

INFORMATION

Flight enquiries
Airport ℂ6595 1 3640
Aer Lingus ℂ6595 1 3162 Aeroflot ℂ6595 1 4345 Aerolineas Argentinas ℂ6595 1 4245 Air Afrique ℂ6595 1 4418 Air Algérie ℂ6595 1 4497 Air France ℂ6595 1 4080 Air India ℂ6595 1 4006 Air Lanka ℂ6595 1 3717 Air Malta ℂ6595 1 3465 Air Mauritius ℂ6595 1 5789 Air Portugal TAP ℂ5695 1 3703 Alitalia ℂ6595 1 6563 Austrian Airlines ℂ6595 1 4083 Balkan Bulgarian Airlines ℂ6595 1 3701 British Airways ℂ6595 1 4190 Canadian Airlines International ℂ6595 1 4117 Cathay Pacific Airways ℂ6595 1 3781 China Airlines ℂ6595 1 3924 Croatia Airlines ℂ6595 1 5854 CSA Czechoslovak ℂ6595 1 4047 Delta Airlines ℂ6595 1 4065 Egyptair ℂ6595 1 4261 El Al Israel Airlines ℂ6595 1 4018 Emirates ℂ6595 1 3196 Ethiopian Airlines ℂ6595 1 4088 Finnair ℂ6595 1 3660 Garuda Indonesian Airlines ℂ6595 1 4042 Ghana Airways ℂ6595 1 3184 Iberia ℂ6595 1 4232 Iran Air ℂ6595 1 4013 Japan Airlines ℂ6595 1 3840 Kenya Airways ℂ6595 1 4200 KLM ℂ6595 1 4046 Korean Airlines ℂ6595 1 3450 Kuwait Airways ℂ5695 1 4569 Lot Polish Airlines ℂ5695 1 4688 Lufthansa ℂ5695 1 4153 Luxair ℂ5695 1 3138 Malev Hungarian ℂ5695 1 3480 Middle East Airlines ℂ5695 1 4236 Nigeria Airways ℂ5695 1 3191 Olympic Airways ℂ5695 1 3481 Pakistan International Airlines

---

ℂ Phone no. ℉ Fax no. ⏱ Hours of opening/operation » Frequency of service ⊃ Journey time ⌀ Cost/one-way fare

✈ SECTION TWO • AIRPORT DIRECTORY ROME

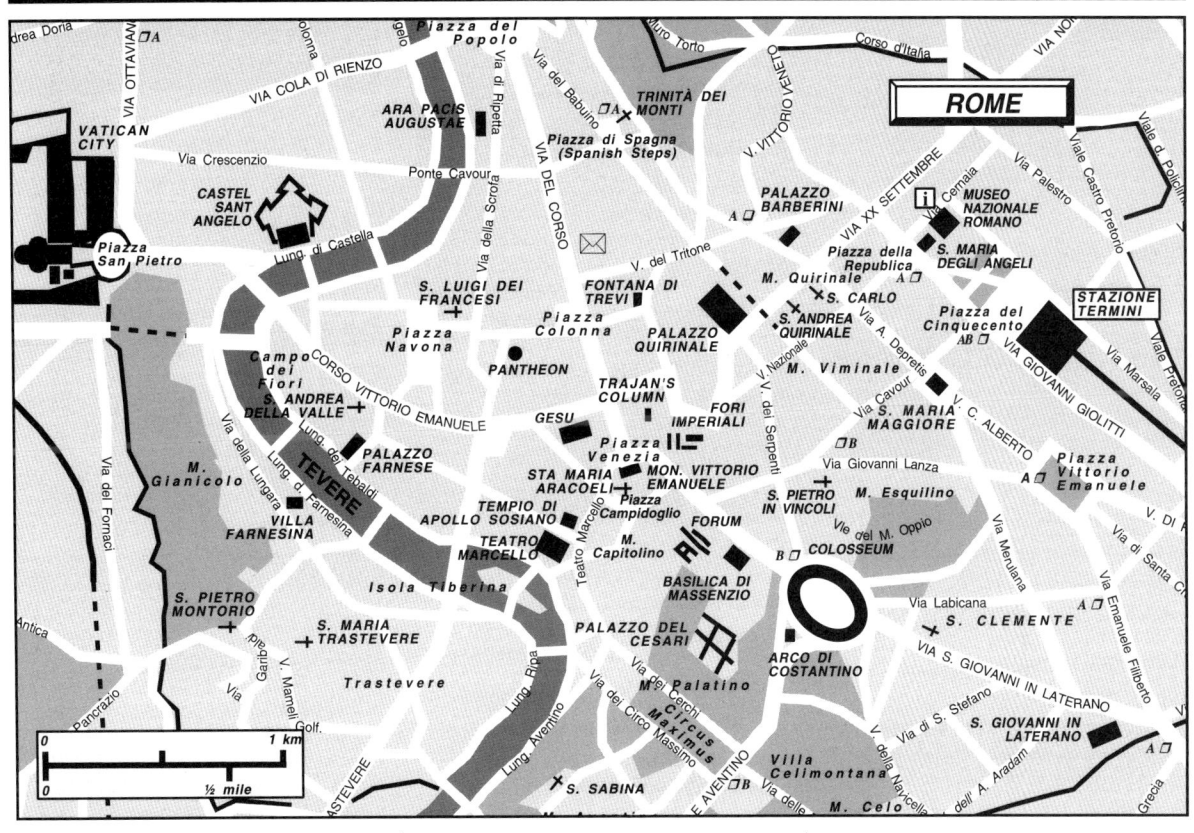

©5695 1 4240 Philippine Airlines ©5695 1 4131 Qantas Airways ©5695 1 3396 Royal Air Maroc ©5695 1 3484 Royal Jordanian Airlines ©5695 1 3071 Sabena World Airlines ©5695 1 4020 Saudia ©5695 1 4527 SAS ©5695 1 4070 Singapore Airlines ©5695 1 3524 Swissair ©5695 1 4087 Syrian Arab Airlines ©5695 1 4315 Tarom Romanian Air ©5695 1 4033 Tunis Air ©5695 1 4128 Turkish Airlines ©5695 1 4375 United Airlines ©5695 1 3063 Varig Brazilian ©5695 1 3323 VIASA Venezuelan ©5695 1 3853 Yemen Airways ©5695 1 3323

Information and help desks
Hotel Courtesy Desk International Terminal Arrival Area ©6595 1 ⓣAll flight times Hotel booking
Tourist Information Desk International Terminal Arrival Area ©6595 3371 ⓣAll flight times Airport information, Flights Hotel booking, Tourist information

EMERGENCIES

Police International Terminal Arrival and Departure Areas ©65011504/511 ⓣ24 hr
Police Domestic Terminal Departure Area ©65010036 ⓣ24 hr
Medical International Terminal First Aid Centre near International Terminal ©6595 3133/3134 ⓣ24 hr
Medical Domestic Terminal First aid Centre near International Terminal ©6595 3133/34 ⓣ24 hr
Lost Property International Terminal Baggage Reclaim Areas ©6595 4252 ⓣ24 hr
Lost Property Domestic Terminal Baggage Reclaim Areas ©6563 4568/9 ⓣ0700–2400

AIRPORT FACILITIES

Money
ATM International Terminal Arrival Hall ⓣ24 hr
ATM Domestic Terminal Arrival/Departure Areas ⓣ24 hr
Bank International Terminal Arrival Hall ⓣ0825–1335, 1510–1600 Mon–Fri
Bank Domestic Terminal Departure Hall ⓣ0825–1335, 1510–1600 Mon–Fri
Bureau de change International Terminal Departure Hall ⓣ0700–2100
Bureau de change International Terminal Arrival Area ⓣ0730–2300
Bureau de change Domestic Terminal Arrival Hall ⓣ0700–2100

Food and drink
Café/light meals International Terminal Departure Gate 33 ⓣ0630–2230
Café/light meals International Terminal Departure Gate 25 ⓣ0730–2230
Café/light meals International Terminal Check-in Hall ⓣ24 hr
Café/light meals International Terminal Arrival Hall ⓣ0730–2230
Café/light meals Domestic Terminal Check in Hall & Departure Pier ⓣ0600–2200/0615–2230
Restaurant (2) International Terminal Main Departure Concourse Third Level ⓣ1130–2230/1130–1500
Restaurant Domestic Terminal Level 3 Departure ⓣ1130–2245

Communications
Post office International Terminal Main Departure Concourse and Arrival Hall ⓣ0800–2100/0800–1850
Fax service International Terminal Executive Centre Level 3 Domestic Terminal ⓣ0800–2100
Post box Domestic Terminal Departure Hall ⓣ0800–1250, 1350–1850
Fax service Domestic Terminal Level 3 Executive Centre ⓣ0800–2100

Shopping
Duty free, departure International Terminal Main Departure Concourse ⓣ0700–2300
Shopping mall International Terminal Main Departure Concourse ⓣ0700–2300

✈ Air ⬚ Rail ⬚ Bus ⬚ Limousine Ⓜ Metro/subway ⬚ Tram ⬚ Helicopter ⬚ Water transport • For map symbols, see p. 9

ROME

Luggage
Left Luggage Counter International Terminal Arrival Area ⓞ24 hr
Left Luggage Counter Domestic Terminal Arrival Area ⓞ0700–2300
Porters International Terminal Departure/Arrival ⓞAll flight times ⌀ITL3500 per item
Trolleys/carts International Terminal throughout ⓞ24 hr ⌀Free
Trolleys/carts Domestic Terminal throughout ⓞ24 hr ⌀Free

Disabled Travellers
International Terminal Adapted toilets; Lifts; Special car parking Level 4 of multi-storey car park; Personal assistance First Aid Centre 24 hr
Domestic Terminal Adapted toilets; Lifts Personal assistance First Aid Centre 24 hr

Smoking Policy
International Terminal No-smoking zones at all Boarding Gates
Domestic Terminal No-smoking zones at all Boarding Gates

Special Passenger Lounges
Alitalia Sala Leonardo da Vinci International Terminal Main Departure Concourse Club members and First class passengers
Alitalia Club Lounge Freccia Alata Domestic Terminal Departure Hall Club members
Alitalia Sala Club Lounge Ulysse Domestic Terminal Departure Hall Club members
All international flights **Easy Roma Lounge** International Terminal Level 1 Departure Transit passengers
All other international flights **Le Navi Lounge** International Terminal Near Gate 34 First class passengers and members of airline clubs
Delta Airlines Delta Lounge International Terminal Departure Hall First class passengers

Conference and Business Facilities
Executive Centre, Level 3 of Domestic Terminal ©6595 2607 ⓞ0800–2100 Telephones, Fax Service, Power Points, Modem Points, Photocopier, Secretarial Service, Translation/Interpretation Service
I Mosaici, Level 4 of International Terminal ©6595 7361/2 ⓞ0615–1915 Telephones, Fax Service, Modem Points, Power Points, Internet Access, Photocopier, Secretarial Service, Reading Room, TV

Car Rental
Avis International Terminal Courtesy phones in Arrival Hall ©65011531
Avis Domestic Terminal Courtesy phones in Arrival Hall ©65011531
Budget International Terminal Courtesy phones in Arrival Hall ©6529133/34
Budget Domestic Terminal Courtesy phones in Arrival Hall ©6529133/34
EuropCar International Terminal Courtesy phones in Arrival Hall ©6595 3560
EuropCar Domestic Terminal Courtesy phones in Arrival Hall ©6595 3560
Hertz International Terminal Courtesy phones in Arrival Hall ©6501448
Hertz Domestic Terminal Courtesy phones in Arrival Hall ©6501448

Car Parking
Long-stay Near motorway 1900 spaces ⌀ITL13000 per day for first 8 days; ITL6500 per day thereafter
Short-stay Between terminals 1600 spaces ⌀ITL3500 first hr; ITL6500 up to 6 hr; ITL26000 per day

Taxis and Chauffeur-driven Cars
Taxis
Outside Arrival Hall both terminals City centre ⌀ITL14000

Chauffeur-driven cars
Arrival Hall both terminals &Intercom service

Public Transport
City & suburbs
Rome, Tiburtina rail stn 🚌Rome city buses ⓞ2330–0600 ⌀ITL7000.
Rome city centre (Termini central rail stn) 🚆»20–30 min ⓞ0738–2208 ↻35 min ⌀ITL13000. Airport stn connected to airport terminals by walkway

Regional Air Connections
Alghero ✈ »Several per day ↻1 hr 5 min
Ancona ✈ »Several per day ↻1 hr 5 min
Bari ✈ »Several per day ↻1 hr
Bologna ✈ »Several per day ↻55 min
Brindisi ✈ »Several per day ↻1 hr 5 min
Cagliari ✈ »Several per day ↻1 hr
Catania ✈ »Several per day ↻1 hr 10 min
Florence ✈ »Several per day ↻1 hr 5 min
Genoa ✈ »Several per day ↻1 hr
Lamezia Terme ✈ »Several per day ↻1 hr 5 min
Milan ✈ »Several per day ↻1 hr 5 min
Naples (Italy) ✈ »Several per day ↻45 min
Nice ✈ »Several per day ↻1 hr 10 min
Olbia ✈ »Several per day ↻45 min
Palermo ✈ »Several per day ↻1 hr
Parma ✈ »Several per week ↻1 hr
Pisa ✈ »Several per day ↻45 min
Reggio Calabria ✈ »Several per day ↻1 hr 5 min
Trieste ✈ »Several per day ↻1 hr 10 min
Turin ✈ »Several per day ↻1 hr 5 min
Venice ✈ »Several per day ↻1 hr 5 min
Verona ✈ »Several per day ↻1 hr

© Phone no. ⓕ Fax no. ⓞ Hours of opening/operation » Frequency of service ↻ Journey time ⌀ Cost/one-way fare

ST LOUIS — STL

USA (see page 41)

National ✆ code: 1
Area ✆ code: 314
Local time: Winter GMT-6, Summer GMT-5
Lambert–St Louis International Airport, St Louis, MO 63145, USA
✆426 8000
WWW site: http://www.st-louis.mo.us/st-louis/airport/
Location: 16 km/10 miles NW of St Louis

Terminals and Transfers

Terminals
Main Terminal Airlines: All other airlines. Layout: Lower Level (Baggage Claim, Car Rental, Ground Transportation, Concourse A (Gates 1–15), B (Gates 16–24), C (Gates 25–59), D (Gates 60–76), Upper Level (Departure)
East Terminal Airlines: American Trans Air, Charter Airlines, Lone Star Airlines, Southwest Airlines. Layout: Lower Level (Baggage Claim, Customs, Ground Transportation, Customs, Gates 77–86), Upper Level (Departure)

Minimum transfer times
International: 1 hr Domestic: 40 min

Information

Flight enquiries
Airport ✆426 8000

Information and help desks
Information Desk Main Terminal Lower Level, entrance to Concourse B ✆426 2955 ⏰1000–2000 Airport information, Tourist information

Emergencies

Police Main Terminal Lower Level ✆426 8100
Medical All Terminals throughout ✆426 8100
Lost Property Main Terminal Lower Level ✆426 8100

Airport Facilities

Money
ATM All Terminals throughout
Bank Main Terminal Lower Level ⏰0730–1730 Mon–Sat; 1300–1700 Sun
Bureau de change Main Terminal Lower Level ⏰1430–1730

Food and drink
Bar Main Terminal Lower Level ⏰24 hr
Café/light meals Main Terminal Lower Level (All Concourses), Upper Level
Restaurant Main Terminal Upper Level ⏰0700–2400

Communications
Fax service Main Terminal throughout
Post office Main Terminal Lower Level ⏰0830–1030 Mon–Fri
Post box All Terminals throughout

Shopping
Gift Shop Main Terminal throughout
News, Stationery & Books All Terminals throughout
Hairdresser Main Terminal Lower Level ⏰0800–2000

Luggage
Left luggage counter Main Terminal Contact airlines
Lockers Main Terminal throughout ⌀USD0.50

Disabled Travellers
All Terminals Adapted toilets; Lifts Special car parking; Phones at wheelchair height; Phones adapted for the deaf

Smoking Policy
All Terminals Permitted only in Smoking lounges

Special Passenger Lounges
American Airlines Admirals Club Main Terminal Lower Level
TWA Ambassadors Club Main Terminal Lower Level, C Concourse

Car Rental
Alamo Main Terminal Lower Level
Avis Main Terminal Lower Level
Budget Main Terminal Lower Level
Dollar Main Terminal Lower Level
Enterprise Main Terminal Lower Level
Hertz Main Terminal Lower Level
National Main Terminal Lower Level
Payless Main Terminal Lower Level
Thrifty Main Terminal Lower Level

Car Parking
Long-stay On airport perimeter (free shuttle bus) ⌀USD2–3 first 6 hr, USD6.50 per day (max)
Short-stay Across from terminals ⌀USD0.75 per 30 min, USD18 per day (max)

Taxis and Chauffeur-driven Cars

Taxis
Main Terminal City centre ➔20–25 min ⌀USD25

Public Transport

City & suburbs
St Louis metro area lOver 10 companies At airport.
St Louis city centre m Bi-State Transit: MetroLink LRT »7–15 min ⏰0500–2400 ➔35 min ⌀USD1. 0530–2330 Sun
St Louis city centre lAirport Express 429 4950 ➔30 min ⌀USD10.
For **downtown** St Louis, Midtown and Clayton areas.

Other towns and cities
Cedar Rapids IA 🚌Burlington Trailways »1 day ⏰0320 ➔11 hr 30 min
For Hanibal MO, Quincy IL, Fort Madison, Burlington, Davenport and Iowa City IA
Joplin MO 🚌Greyhound Lines »2 day ⏰0835; 1815 ➔7 hr.
For Rolla, Fort Leonard Wood and Springfield MO
Kansas City MO 🚌Greyhound Lines »2 day ⏰1410; 1830 ➔4 hr 30 min.
For Columbia MO (University of Missouri)
Clayton MO lAirport Express 429 4950 ⌀USD10.

Regional Air Connections
Bloomington IL »Several per day ➔50 min

St Louis • St Petersburg — Section Two • Airport Directory

Burlington IA ✈ »Several per day ⊃50 min
Cape Girardeau MO ✈ »Several per week ⊃45 min
Cedar Rapids-Iowa City IA ✈ »Several per day ⊃55 min
Champaign IL ✈ »Several per day ⊃50 min
Chicago IL ✈ »Several per day ⊃1 hr
Columbia MO ✈ »Several per day ⊃40 min
Decatur IL ✈ »Several per day ⊃45 min
Fort Leonard Wood MO ✈ »Several per week ⊃45 min
Indianapolis IN ✈ »Several per day ⊃1 hr
Kansas City MO ✈ »Several per day ⊃1 hr
Marion IL ✈ »Several Per day ⊃50 min
Moline IL ✈ »Several per day ⊃1 hr
Paducah KY ✈ »Several per week ⊃50 min
Peoria IL ✈ »Several per day ⊃50 min
Quincy IL ✈ »Several per day ⊃40 min
Springfield IL ✈ »Several per day ⊃35 min
Springfield MO ✈ »Several per day ⊃55 min

Traveller's Notes
The MetroLink light railway connects the airport with downtown St. Louis and visitor attractions.

St Petersburg — LED
Russia (see page 34)

National ✆ code: 7
Area ✆ code: 0812
Local time: Winter GMT+3, Summer GMT+4
St Petersburg-Pulkovo International Airport, Pulkova 2, 196210 St Petersburg, Russia
✆104 33 02
℻104 37 02
Location: 17 km/10½ miles S of St Petersburg

Terminals and Transfers

Terminals
Terminal 1 Airlines: All domestic flights. Layout: Domestic Terminal: 3 Level Building
Terminal 2 Airlines: All international flights. Layout: One Level. Ground Level, check-in and baggage reclaim, Departure/Transit Area

Minimum transfer times
International: 1–3 hr Domestic: 1 hr

Transfer between terminals
Bus Terminals 1 and 2

Information

Flight enquiries
Airport ✆104 34 44

Information and help desks
Information Desk Terminal 1 Arrival Foyer ⓘAll flight times Airport information, Flights Hotel booking, Tourist information
Information Desk Terminal 2 Departure Foyer and Baggage Reclaim Area ⓘAll flight times Airport information, Flights Hotel booking, Tourist information

Emergencies

Police Terminal 1 Ground Level ✆123 87 02 ⓘ24 hr
Police Terminal 2 Administrative Offices Area Ground Level ✆1043482/81&1042732 ⓘ24 hr
Medical Terminal 2 Arrivals area ✆1229734 ⓘ24 hr
Medical Terminal 1 Arrivals area Ground Level ✆104 17 69 ⓘ24 hr
Lost Property Terminal 1 ⓘ24 hr
Lost Property Terminal 2 Near Baggage Reclaim Area ✆123 83 61; 104 34 58 ⓘ24 hr

Airport Facilities

Money
Bank Terminal 1 First Level ⓘ24 hr
Bank Terminal 2 Departure Hall before Customs ⓘ24 hr

Food and drink
Bar Terminal 1 Second Level & ground Level ⓘ1200–2200
Bar Terminal 2 In Departures after Immigration ⓘ24 hr
Bar Terminal 2 Administrative Offices Area ⓘ0100–2000
Restaurant Terminal 1 Second Level ⓘ1000–1900
Restaurant Terminal 2 First Level ⓘ0900–2200

Communications
Post office Terminal 1 First Level ⓘ24 hr

Shopping
Duty free, arrival Terminal 2 Baggage Retrieval Area ⓘAll flight times
Duty free, departure Terminal 2 Departure Area Level 1 after Immigration ⓘAll flight times
Gift Shop Terminal 2 Departure Area near duty free shop ⓘAll flight times

---

✆ Phone no. ℻ Fax no. ⓘ Hours of opening/operation » Frequency of service ⊃ Journey time ⊘ Cost/one-way fare

SECTION TWO • AIRPORT DIRECTORY — ST PETERSBURG

Luggage
Left Luggage Counter Terminal 1 Arrivals Ground Level ⓢ24 hr

Smoking Policy
Terminal 1 Smoking permitted throughout
Terminal 2 Smoking permitted throughout

Special Passenger Lounges
All international flights Business Class Lounge Terminal 2 Arrivals and Departure Areas Level 1 Business and First class passengers

Conference and Business Facilities
Conference rooms, Pulkovskaya Hotel ⓒ264 50 22/51 22

Airport Hotels
Pulkovskaya ⓒ264 50 22/51 22 ⓕ264 63 96

Car Rental
Terminal 1 At Pulkovskaya Hotel ⓒ264 50 22/51 22
Terminal 2 At Pulkovskaya Hotel ⓒ264 50 22/51 22

Car Parking
Long-stay Outside Terminal ⌀RUR 10000–15000 per day
Short-stay Outside Terminal

Taxis and Chauffeur-driven Cars
Taxis
Outside Arrival Area City centre ⤳40 min ⌀USD 30

Public Transport
City & suburbs
St Petersburg city centre (via Metro stn)
🚌 Bus No 39 »25 min ⤳15 min ⌀RUR1000. *From Terminal 1. Advisable to use taxis*
St Petersburg city centre (via Metro stn)
🚌 Bus No 13 »15 min ⌀RUR1000. *From Terminal 2. Advisable to use taxis*

Regional Air Connections
Helsinki ✈ »Several per day ⤳1 hr
Kaliningrad ✈ »Several per week ⤳50 min
Moscow ✈ »Several per day ⤳1 hr 20 min
Tallinn ✈ »Several per week ⤳35 min

Traveller's Notes
Taxis are less expensive than in Moscow. Complete a currency declaration form on arrival, get receipts each time you change money, and fill in a similar form on departure.

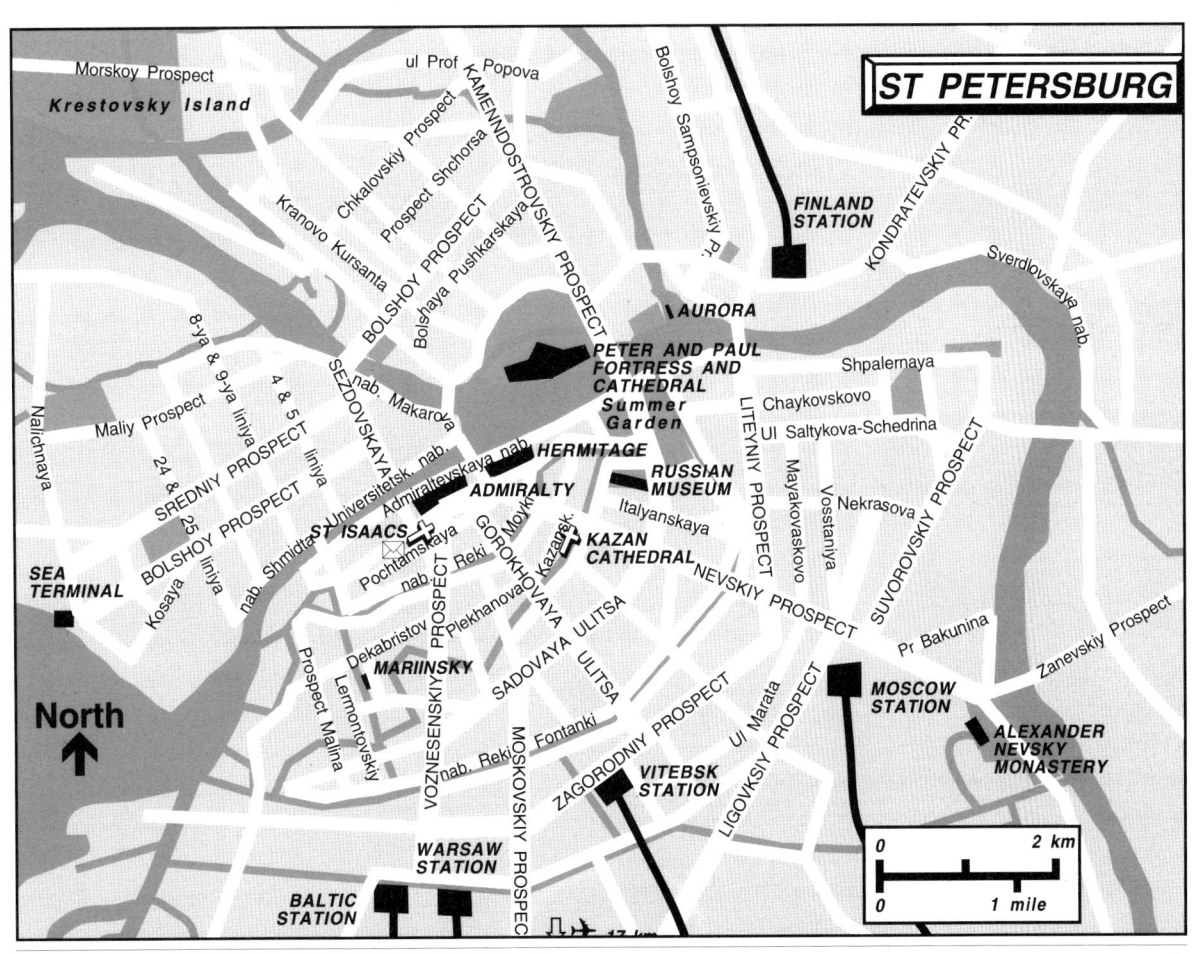

✈ Air 🚆 Rail 🚌 Bus 🚘 Limousine Ⓜ Metro/subway 🚋 Tram 🚁 Helicopter ⛴ Water transport • For map symbols, see p. 9

SAN DIEGO — SAN

USA (see page 41)

National ✆ code: 1
Area ✆ code: 619
Local time: Winter GMT-8, Summer GMT-7
San Diego International Airport, Lindbergh Field, PO Box 488, San Diego, CA 92212, USA
✆291 3100
WWW site: http://www.san.org
Location: 3 km/2 miles NW of San Diego

TERMINALS AND TRANSFERS

Terminals
Terminal 1 Airlines: Aeromexico, Alaska Airlines, America West Airlines, Continental Airlines, Southwest, TWA, United Airlines, US Airways. Layout: All services, Gates 1–19
Terminal 2 Airlines: American Airlines, British Airways, Delta Airlines, Frontier Airlines, Midwest Express, Northwest Airlines, Reno Air, Western Pacific Airlines. Layout: First Floor (Baggage Claim, Car Rental, Ground Transportation), Second Floor (Departures, Gates 20–32)

Minimum transfer times
Commuter Terminal Airlines: Alaska Commuter, American Eagle, Northwest Airlink, Skywest Continental Connection, Skywest Delta Connection, US Airways Express, United Express,.
International: 1 hr Domestic: 30 min–1 hr

Transfer between terminals
Bus Q Frequent; All terminals ⌀Free

INFORMATION

Information and help desks
Traveller's Aid Terminal 1 West Wing
✆231 7361 ⏱0700–2200 Airport information, Tourist information
Traveller's Aid Terminal 2 First Floor
✆231 7361 ⏱0700–2200 Airport information, Tourist information

EMERGENCIES

Police All Terminals throughout ✆231 5260
Medical All Terminals throughout ✆231 5260
Lost Property All Terminals throughout ✆231 5260

AIRPORT FACILITIES

Money
ATM All Terminals throughout
Bank Terminal 1 Main Lobby
⏱0830–1630 Mon–Thu; 0830–1800 Fri

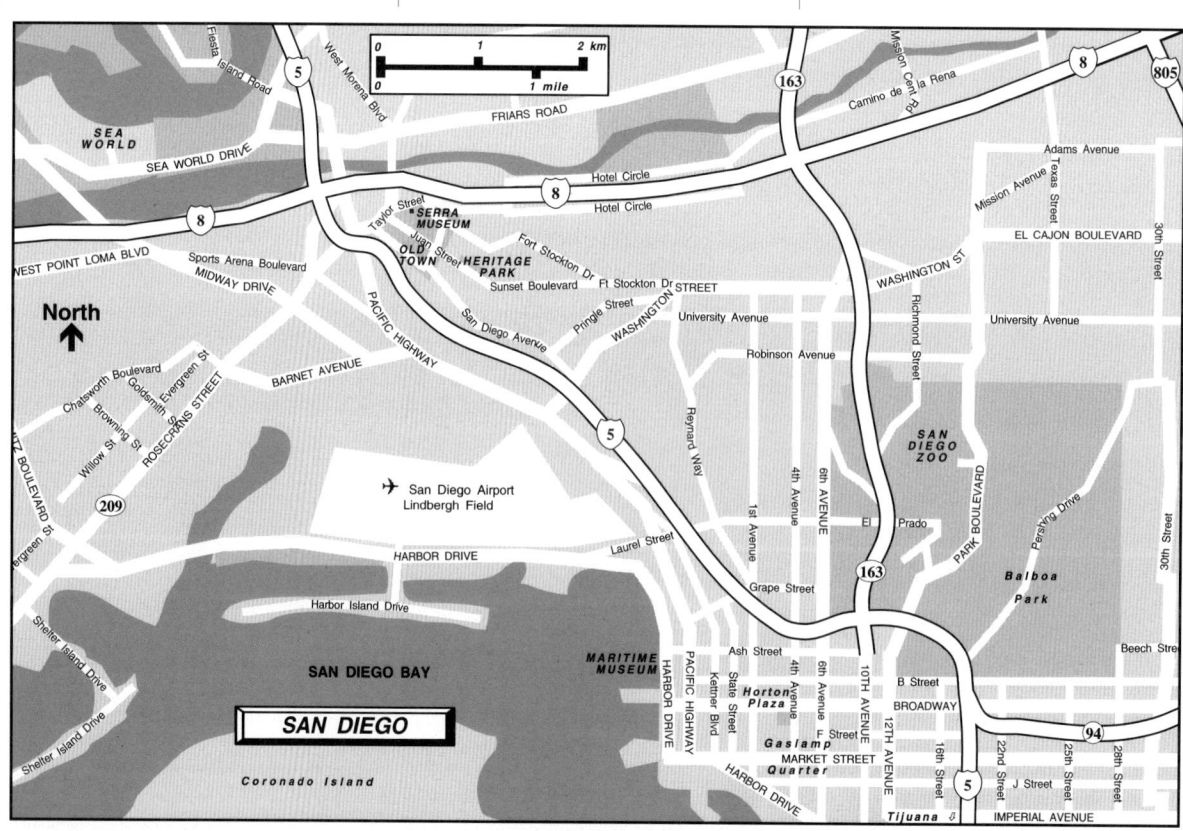

✆ Phone no. ℻ Fax no. ⏱ Hours of opening/operation » Frequency of service ⤴ Journey time ⌀ Cost/one-way fare

SECTION TWO • AIRPORT DIRECTORY — SAN DIEGO

Food and drink
Bar All Terminals throughout
Café/light meals Terminal 1 Main Lobby ⏱0800–2200
Café/light meals Terminal 2 Second Floor ⏱0800–2200

Communications
Post box All Terminals throughout

Shopping
Gift Shop All Terminals throughout
News, Stationery & Books All Terminals throughout

Disabled Travellers
All Terminals Adapted toilets; Lifts

Smoking Policy
All Terminals No-smoking throughout

Special Passenger Lounges
American Airlines Admirals Club Terminal 2 Second Floor
United Airlines Red Carpet Club Terminal 1 West Rotunda

Car Rental
Alamo All Terminals Baggage Claim
Avis All Terminals Baggage Claim
Budget All Terminals Baggage Claim
Dollar All Terminals Baggage Claim
Enterprise All Terminals Baggage Claim
Hertz All Terminals Baggage Claim
National All Terminals Baggage Claim
Sears All Terminals Baggage Claim
Thrifty All Terminals Baggage Claim

Car Parking
Off-airport 2 km/1 mile from terminals (take free shuttles)
Short-stay Adjacent to terminals ⌀USD1 per hr, USD18 per day (max)

Taxis and Chauffeur-driven Cars
Taxis
In front of terminals City centre ➲10 min ⌀USD10

Public Transport
City & suburbs
San Diego (Amtrak/Santa Fe Depot) 🚌San Diego Transit 2 »12–30 min ⏱0530–0100 ➲10 min ⌀USD1.50. For all Amtrak and Coast Express Rail (Coaster) services
San Diego city centre 🚌San Diego Transit 2 »12–30 min ⏱0530–0100 ➲15 min ⌀USD1.50.
San Diego (Metro Area) ➡Over 15 companies at airport.
San Diego (military bases) Peerless 554 1700.

Other towns and cities
Coronado CA ➡Coronado Livery Co 435 6310.

Regional Air Connections
Burbank CA ✈ »Several per day ➲50 min
Las Vegas NV ✈ »Several per day ➲1 hr
Los Angeles CA ✈ »Several per day ➲45 min
Ontario CA ✈ »At least daily ➲40 min
Orange County CA ✈ »Several per week ➲35 min
Palm Springs CA ✈ »Several per week ➲35 min
Phoenix AZ ✈ »Several per day ➲1 hr
Santa Barbara CA ✈ »Several per day ➲1 hr

SAN FRANCISCO   SECTION TWO • AIRPORT DIRECTORY ✈✈

SAN FRANCISCO   SFO
USA (see page 41)

National © code: 1
Area © code: 650
Local time: Winter GMT-8,
Summer GMT-7
San Francisco International Airport,
PO Box 8097, San Francisco, CA
94128, USA
©876 2377

WWW site:
http://www.ci.sf.ca.us/sfo
Location: 19 km/12 miles SE of San Francisco

TERMINALS AND TRANSFERS

Terminals
South Terminal Airlines: Air Canada, Alaska Airlines, America West Airlines, American Trans Air, Continental Airlines, Delta Airlines, Northwest Airlines, Skywest/Delta Connection, Southwest, TWA, US Airways. Layout: Lower Level (Arrival, Baggage Claim, Car Rental, Ground Transportation), Upper Level (Departure, Ground Transportation), Concourse A (Gates 1–15), B (Gates 20–36), C (Gates 40–48)
International Terminal Airlines: Aeroflot, Air China, Air France, Allegro Airlines, Asiana Airlines, British Airways, China Airlines, China Eastern, Eva Air, Japan Airlines, KLM, Korean Airlines, LACSA, Lufthansa, Mexicana, Northwest Airlines (International), Philippine Airlines, Singapore Airlines, TACA International Airlines, United Airlines (International), Virgin Atlantic. Layout: Lower Level (Arrival, Baggage Claim, Customs, Car Rental), Upper Level (Departure, Ground Transportation). Concourse D (Gates 50–59)
North Terminal Airlines: American Airlines, Canadian Airlines International, Frontier Airlines, Reno Air, Shuttle By United, United Airlines (Domestic), United Express, Vanguard Airlines, Western Pacific. Layout: Lower Level (Arrival, Baggage Claim, Car Rental, Ground Transportation), Upper Level (Departure, Ground Transportation), Concourse E (Gates 60–68), Concourse F (Gates 69–90)

Minimum transfer times
International: 1 hr 45 min Domestic: 50 min

INFORMATION

Flight enquiries
Aeroflot ©(415) 434 2300 Air Canada ©876 7461 Air China ©877 0825 Alaska Airlines ©875 8600 Allegro Airlines ©583 8891 American Airlines ©877 6113 American Trans Air ©877 0412 America West ©877 0214 Asiana ©877 3016 Canadian Airlines ©877 5905 Continental Airlines ©876 2612 Delta Airlines &©877 1017 Eva Airways ©876 7422 Frontier Airlines ©876 1765 Hawaiian Airlines ©877 6913 Japan Airlines ©8773260

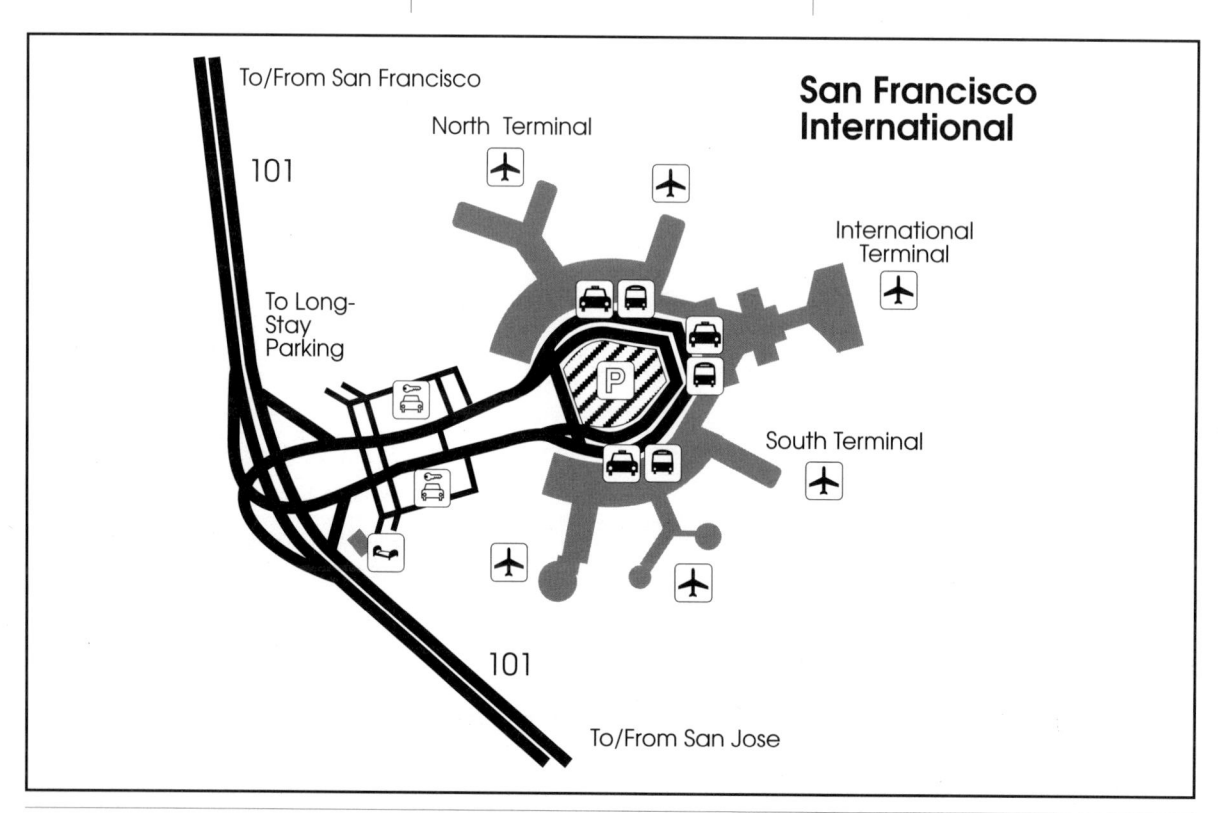

© Phone no. ® Fax no. ⓞ Hours of opening/operation » Frequency of service ➲ Journey time ◇ Cost/one-way fare

SECTION TWO • AIRPORT DIRECTORY

SAN FRANCISCO

Korean Air ✆(415) 956 6373 LACSA ✆877 8412 Lufthansa ✆876 7348 Mexicana ✆877 4905 Midwest Express ✆877 4905 Midwest Express ✆877 0170 Northwest (Domestic) ✆877 5004 Northwest International ✆877 6913 Philippine ✆877 4800 Shuttle By United ✆876 3069 Singapore ✆876 7372 Skywest/Delta Connection ✆877 1017 Southwest Airlines ✆877 0222 TACA ✆877 8412 TWA ✆877 4112 United ✆876 3069 US Airways ✆877 4680 Vanguard Airlines ✆876 2608 Western Pacific Airlines ✆877 3060

Information and help desks

Hotel Information Desk All Terminals Lower Level
Information Desk All Terminals Lower Level ⏱0800–2400 Airport information, Tourist information
Traveller's Aid All Terminals Upper Level ✆877 0444 ⏱0900–2100 (except 0900–1700 South Terminal) Tourist information

EMERGENCIES

Police International Terminal Upper Level ✆876 2424
Medical International Terminal Lower Level ⏱24 hr ✆794 5600
Lost Property International Terminal Upper Level, Police Desk ✆876 2261

AIRPORT FACILITIES

Money
ATM All Terminals throughout
Bank International Terminal Upper Level ⏱0900–1800 Mon–Thur, 0900–1900 Fri
Bank North Terminal Mezzanine ⏱0900–1800 Mon–Thur, 0900–1900 Fri
Bureau de change International Terminal Upper Level ⏱0630–2230
Bureau de change International Terminal Upper Level (Bank of America) ⏱0700–2300
Bureau de change International Terminal (Lower Level) ⏱0800–1900

Food and drink
Bar All Terminals throughout
Café/light meals All Terminals throughout
Restaurant All Terminals throughout

Communications
Fax service All Terminals Upper Level
Post box All Terminals Upper Level

Shopping
Duty free, All Terminals Upper Level
Duty free, departure International Terminal Departure Area
Gift Shop All Terminals throughout
Hairdresser International Terminal

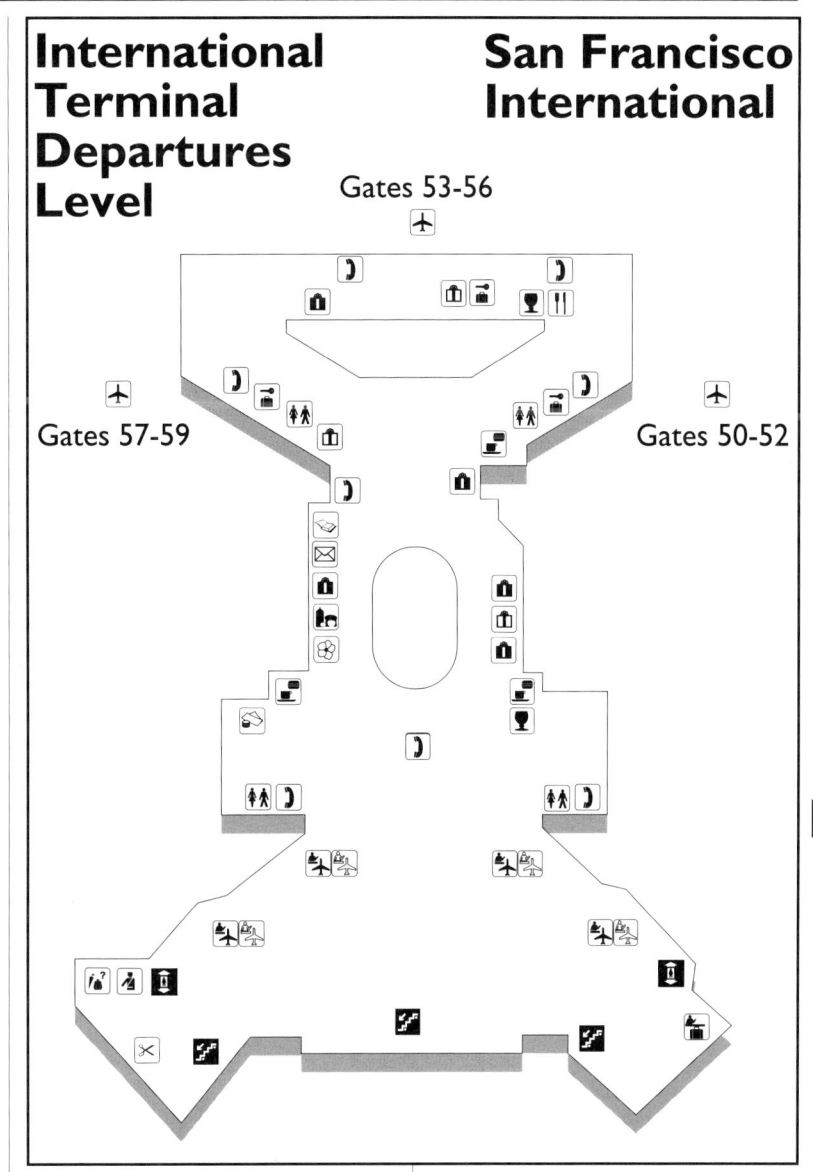

International Terminal Departures Level

San Francisco International

Gates 53-56

Gates 57-59

Gates 50-52

Between North and International Terminals ⏱0800–1800
News, Stationery & Books All Terminals Upper Level

Luggage
Left luggage counter International Terminal between International and South Terminals ⏱0700–2300
Lockers All Terminals Boarding Areas (past Security) ⏱24 hr ◇USD2 per day
Trolleys/carts All Terminals throughout ⏱24 hr ◇USD1.50

DISABLED TRAVELLERS

All Terminals Adapted toilets; Lifts Special car parking Parking Garage, All Levels, near elevators; Phones at wheelchair height; Phones adapted for the deaf; Personal assistance Contact airlines

SMOKING POLICY

Smoking Rooms in all Terminals

SPECIAL PASSENGER LOUNGES

Alaska Airlines Board Room South Terminal Upper Level Concourse B (near Gate 22 and 24)
American Airlines Admirals Club North Terminal Upper Level Concourse E (opposite Gate 62)
British Airways Executive Lounge International Terminal Upper Level 4th

253

✈ Air 🚆 Rail 🚌 Bus 🚐 Limousine 🚇 Metro/subway 🚋 Tram 🚁 Helicopter ⛴ Water transport • For map symbols, see p. 9

SAN FRANCISCO

SECTION TWO • AIRPORT DIRECTORY

Room International Terminal Upper Level Gate 54 (to lower level)
United Airlines Domestic Red Carpet Room North Terminal Mezzanine Level
United Airlines Domestic Red Carpet Room North Terminal Upper Level (near Gate 80)

CONFERENCE AND BUSINESS FACILITIES

VIP Conference Room, North Terminal

CAR RENTAL

Alamo All Terminals Lower Level ℂ347 9911
Avis All Terminals Lower Level ℂ877 3156
Budget All Terminals Lower Level ℂ877 6850
Dollar All Terminals Lower Level ℂ692 1200
Hertz All Terminals Lower Level ℂ877 6681
National All Terminals Lower Level ℂ877 4740

CAR PARKING

Long-stay On airport perimeter (free 24 hr shuttle bus) ⌀USD11 per day
Off-airport At airport Valet Parking ⌀USD32 per day, ⌀USD45 after 24 hrs
Short-stay Parking Garage connected to terminals ⌀USD3 per hr, USD22 per day (max)

TAXIS AND CHAUFFEUR-DRIVEN CARS

Taxis
City centre ⊃30 min ⌀USD29

PUBLIC TRANSPORT

Airport to airport
San Jose International Apt 🚌Santa Cruz Airporter »2 hrs ⏲0800–2200 ⊃1 hr ⌀USD25.
San Jose International Apt 🚌United Airlines South Bay Flyer »1 hr ⏲0650–2150 ⊃1 hr ⌀USD25.
Sonoma County Airport 🚌Sonoma County Airport Express »1 hr ⏲0500–2400 ⊃1 hr 55 min ⌀USD18.

City & suburbs
Colma CA (BART rail stn) 🚌SamTrans: 3X »20–30 min ⏲0600–2350 ⊃15 min ⌀USD1. For all Bay Area Rapid Transit (BART) services.
Concord CA (hotels) 🚌Black Tie Airport Shuttle »1–2 hr ⏲0630–2200 ⊃1 hr 20 min ⌀USD27. For Lafayette and Walnut Creek CA

Floor (USO Elevator)
China Airlines Dynasty Lounge International Terminal Upper Level Concourse D Gate 54 (to lower level)
Continental Airlines Presidents Club South Terminal Upper Level between Continental and Southwest ticket counters
Delta Airlines Crown Room South Terminal Mezzanine Level (take elevator next to Delta counter)
Japan Airlines Sakura Lounge International Terminal Upper Level Concourse D Gate 54 (to lower level)
Lufthansa Lufthansa Lounge International Terminal Upper Level Concourse D Gate 54 (to lower level)

Northwest Airlines Worldclub International Terminal Upper Level (by Connector and Noise Abatement)
Philippine Airlines Mabuhay Lounge International Terminal Upper Level Concourse D (to lower level)
Singapore Airlines Silver Kris Lounge International Terminal Upper Level (near AT & T Communication Center)
TWA Ambassador Club South Terminal Upper Level Concourse B (near Gate 21 and 23)
US Airways Club South Terminal Mezzanine Level Concourse A (above Gate 11)
United Airlines International Red Carpet

ℂ Phone no. ℱ Fax no. ⏲ Hours of opening/operation » Frequency of service ⊃ Journey time ⌀ Cost/one-way fare

254

SECTION TWO • AIRPORT DIRECTORY

SAN FRANCISCO

Dublin/Pleasanton CA 🚌San Ramon Valley Airporter Express »1–2 hrs ⏱0630–2200 ➲1 hr ⌀USD27. For Alamo, Danville and San Ramon CA

Marin County CA 🚌Marin Airporter »30 min ⏱0530–2400 ➲45 min ⌀USD10–14. For Sausalito, Mill Valley, Larkspur, San Rafael, Terra Linda, Ignacio and Novato CA

Millbrae CA (Caltrain rail stn) 🚌Caltrain–SFO Shuttle »10-30 min ⏱0500–2310 ➲15 min ⌀Free. For all Caltrain services (meets all trains to/from San Francisco and San Jose/Gilroy)

Napa CA 🚌Evans Airport Service »1–2 hrs ⏱0630–2245 ➲1 hr 25 min ⌀USD14–15. For Vallejo CA

Palo Alto (Stanford Shopping Ctr.) CA 🚌SamTrans: 7F Expr. »30 min–1 hr ⏱0555–0115 ⌀USD1. For San Mateo, Belmont, San Carlos and Redwood City CA

Redwood City CA 🚌SamTrans: 7B Local »30 min–1 hr ⏱0535–0115 ⌀USD1. For Burlingame, San Mateo, Belmont and San Carlos CA

San Francisco city centre 🚐Over 20 companies.

San Francisco (downtown hotels) 🚌SFO Airporter »30 min ⏱0630–2400 ➲50 min ⌀USD9.

San Francisco (Fisherman's Wharf) 🚌Wharf Airporter »30 min ⏱0710–2310 ➲1 hr ⌀USD10. Also for San Francisco Civic Center area.

San Francisco (Transbay Terminal) 🚌SamTrans: 7F Expr. »30–45 min ⏱0600–2400 ➲30 min ⌀USD2.50. Luggage not permitted. For AC Transit, Golden Gate Transit, San Francisco Municipal Railway (MUNI) and Greyhound bus services.

San Francisco (city centre) 🚌SamTrans: 7B »30 min–1 hr ⏱0540–0115 ➲1 hr ⌀USD1. For South San Francisco and Brisbane CA

San Francisco city centre hotels 🚌Pacific Airporter »30 min ⏱0720–2250 ➲45–55 min ⌀USD10.

San Francisco (Union Square Hotels) 🚌SFO Airporter »30 min ⏱0615–2345 ➲45 min ⌀USD10.

San Jose city centre 🚌United Airlines South Bay Flyer »1 hr ⏱0650–2150 ➲1 hr 15 min ⌀USD15. Also for Santa Clara and San Jose Airport CA

Santa Rosa CA 🚌Santa Rosa Airporter »1 hr ⏱0635–2335 ➲1 hr 25 min ⌀USD18. For San Rafael, Petaluma and Rohnert Park CA

Santa Rosa CA 🚌Sonoma County Airport Express »1 hr ⏱0500–2400 ➲1 hr 45 min ⌀USD18. For Petaluma, Rohnert Park and Sonoma County Airport CA

Sonoma CA 🚌Sonoma Airporter »5 day ⏱0805–2140 ➲1 hr 30 min ⌀USD20–25. For Black Point, Sears Point, Temelec, El Verano, Boyes Hot Springs, Agua Caliente, Glen Ellen, Kenwood and Oakmont CA

Sonoma County CA 🚌Santa Rosa Airporter »4 day ⏱0635;0935;1335;1735 ➲2 hr 40 min ⌀USD35. For Healdsburg, Cloverdale, Hopland and Ukiah CA

Other towns and cities

Modesto CA 🚌Reliable Airport Shuttle »3 day Mon–Fri only ⏱0805; 1405; 2030 ⌀USD29–38. For Livermore, Tracy and Manteca CA

Monterey CA 🚌Monterey/Salinas Airbus »6 day ⏱0930;1230;1530;1800;2030 ➲2–3 hr ⌀USD35. For Salinas and Marina CA

Santa Cruz CA 🚌Santa Cruz Airporter »2 hrs ⏱0800–2200 ➲1–3 hrs ⌀USD25–40. For San Jose, Scotts Valley, Santa Cruz, Soquel/Capitola, Aptos and Watsonville CA

REGIONAL AIR CONNECTIONS

Fresno CA ✈ »Several per day ➲50 min
Merced CA ✈ »Several per week ➲40 min
Modesto CA ✈ »Several per day ➲35 min
Monterey CA ✈ »Several per day ➲35 min
Redding CA ✈ »Several per day ➲1 hr
Reno NV ✈ »Several per day ➲55 min
Sacramento CA ✈ »Several per day ➲40 min
San Luis Obispo CA ✈ »Several per day ➲1 hr
Santa Rosa CA ✈ »Several per day ➲40 min

TRAVELLER'S NOTES

Enclosed passageways allow for convenient transfers between terminals. The city's public transportation system is extensive and is much cheaper than taxis.

✈ Air 🚆 Rail 🚌 Bus 🚐 Limousine 🚇 Metro/subway 🚋 Tram 🚁 Helicopter ⛴ Water transport • For map symbols, see p. 9

SANTIAGO

SCL

Chile (see page 19)

National ☏ code: 56
Area ☏ code: 02
Local time: Winter GMT-3,
Summer GMT-4
Santiago-Comodoro Arturo Merino Benitez International Airport, Santiago, Chile
☏601 9001; 601 9500; 601 9654
🖷601 9416
Location: 14 km/8½ miles NW of Santiago

Terminals and Transfers

Terminals
Main Terminal Airlines: All airlines.

Minimum transfer times
International: 1 hr–1 hr 30 min Domestic: 30 min

Information

Flight enquiries
Airport ☏601 9709

Information and help desks
Information Desk Main Terminal Main Hall ☏601 9709; 601 9320 ⏱0900–2100 *Airport information*

Airport Facilities

Money
Bank Main Terminal ⏱0900–1400 Mon–Fri

Food and Drink
Bar Main Terminal ⏱0700–2400
Restaurant Main Terminal ⏱0700–2400

Communications
Post office Main Terminal Main Hall ⏱0830–1830

Shopping
Gift Shop Main Terminal Departure Lounge

Car Rental

American Main Terminal
Automovilclub Main Terminal
Avis Main Terminal
Budget Main Terminal
Dollar Main Terminal
Galerias Main Terminal
Hertz Main Terminal
Lider Main Terminal
National Main Terminal
Value Main Terminal

Car Parking

Long-stay 500 spaces
Short-stay 600 spaces

Taxis and Chauffeur-driven Cars

Taxis
City centre ⤳20 min ⊘USD20

Public Transport

City & suburbs
Santiago city centre (bus terminal, Moneda St) 🚌Tour Express ⏱0700–2215 ⊘USD1.50.
Santiago city centre (Los Heroes subway station) 🚌Metro Bus »15 min ⏱0630–2300 ⊘USD0.79.

Regional Air Connections

Concepcion (Chile) ✈ »Several per day ⤳1 hr
La Serena ✈ »Several per day ⤳50 min

Airport Tax

Departure tax of USD12.50 on international and domestic flights.

☏ Phone no. 🖷 Fax no. ⏱ Hours of opening/operation » Frequency of service ⤳ Journey time ⊘ Cost/one-way fare

SECTION TWO • AIRPORT DIRECTORY SÃO PAULO

SÃO PAULO-GUARULHOS GRU

Brazil (see page 17)

National ✆ code: 55
Area ✆ code: 011
Local time: Winter GMT-2,
Summer GMT-3
São Paulo Guarulhos International Airport, 07141 Guarulhos, São Paulo, Brazil
✆945 2111
🖷912 3335
Location: 25 km/15½ miles from São Paulo

TERMINALS AND TRANSFERS

Terminals
Terminal 1 Airlines: All other airlines.
Terminal 2 Airlines: Varig Brazilian.

Minimum transfer times
International: 1 he–1 hr 30 min
Domestic: 1 hr

INFORMATION

Flight enquiries
Airport ✆945 2111

Information and help desks
Information Desk Terminal 1 Wings A, B and C, Second Floor (3 desks) ✆945 2945🖷912 3335 ⏲24 hr *Airport information, Flights*
Tourist Information Desk Terminal 1 First Floor ✆945 2380 🖷239 3604 ⏲0800–2200 Mon–Fri; 0900–2100 Sat–Sun, *Tourist Information*

EMERGENCIES

Lost Property Terminal 1 Contact airport police

AIRPORT FACILITIES

Money
Bank Terminal 1 ⏲0800–2200
ATM Terminal 1 ⏲24 hr
ATM Terminal 2 ⏲24 hr

Food and Drink
Bar Terminal 1 Third Floor ⏲0800–2300
Café/light meals Terminal 1 Departure gates ⏲0600–2200
Café/light meals Terminal 1 Second Floor ⏲24 hr
Café/light meals Terminal 2 Departure gates ⏲0600–2200
Café/light meals Terminal 2 Second Floor ⏲0700–2200
Restaurant Terminal 1 Second Floor ⏲1300–1500, 1800–2100
Restaurant Terminal 1 Third Floor ⏲0600–2300

Communications
Post office Terminal 1 Third Floor ⏲0800–2100 Mon–Sat; 0800–1300 Sun

Shopping
Gift Shop Terminal 1 Mezzanine Floor

Luggage
Left Luggage Counter Terminal 1 ⏲24 hr
Lockers Terminal 1 ⏲24 hr

DISABLED TRAVELLERS

Terminal 1 Adapted toilets; Lifts; Phones at wheelchair height; Personal assistance
Terminal 2 Adapted toilets; Lifts; Phones at wheelchair height; Personal assistance

SPECIAL PASSENGER LOUNGES

VIP Domestic Lounge Terminal 2
VIP International Lounge Terminal 1

CONFERENCE AND BUSINESS FACILITIES

Meeting rooms, 3 rooms ✆945 3090
Conference halls, 2 halls ✆945 3090

CAR RENTAL

Avis Terminal 1
Hertz Terminal 1
Interlocadora Terminal 1
Localiza Terminal 1
Locarauto Terminal 1
My Car Terminal 1

Nobre Rent-a-Car Terminal 1
Unidas Rent-a-Car Terminal 1

CAR PARKING

Long-stay 3150 spaces ✐USD1.50 per 4 hr; USD5 per day; USD37 per week

TAXIS AND CHAUFFEUR-DRIVEN CARS

Taxis
✆940 2975 City centre ➲30 min ✐USD24

PUBLIC TRANSPORT

Airport to airport
São Paulo-Congonhas Airport 🚌 EMTU »1 hr ⏲0600–2200.
Congonhas Airport 🚖 Wilson Taxis Aereo ⏲0800–1800 ➲15 min ✐USD120.

City & suburbs
São Paulo (Avenida Paulista Hotel District) 🚌 EMTU »1 hr ⏲0700–2100 ➲50 min ✐USD9. *Calls at each hotel*
São Paulo city centre 🚌 EMTU »30 min ⏲0530–2300 ➲40 min ✐USD7.50.

Other towns and cities
Campinas 🚌 Caprioli Turismo ⏲0900–2230 ➲1 hr 30 min ✐USD10.
Santos 🚌 Translitoral ⏲0630–1100 and 1530- ➲1 hr ✐USD10.

REGIONAL AIR CONNECTIONS

Asuncion ✈ »Several per day ➲1 hr
Belo Horizonte ✈ »Several per day ➲1 hr
Campinas ✈ »Several per day ➲30 min
Rio de Janeiro ✈ »Several per day ➲1 hr
São Jose ✈ »Several per day ➲50 min
Varginha ✈ »At least daily ➲45 min

TRAVELLER'S NOTES

São Paulo is Brazil's most prosperous city, and one of the most active cultural centres of the country. Just one hour away from the city are Brazil's most sophisticated beach resorts.

SEATTLE

SEA

USA (see page 41)

National ✆ code: 1
Area ✆ code: 206
Local time: Winter GMT-8,
Summer GMT-7
Seattle-Tacoma International
Airport, PO Box 68727, Seattle,
WA 98168-0727, USA
✆443 5388
℻439 7725
WWW site: http://www.portseattle.org
Location: 21 km/13 miles S of Seattle

TERMINALS AND TRANSFERS

Terminals
Main Terminal Airlines: AirBC/Air Canada, Alaska Airlines, America West Airlines, American Airlines, Canadian Airlines, Continental Airlines, Delta Airlines, Frontier Airlines, Harbour Airlines, Horizon Air, Reno Air, Southwest Airlines, TWA, US Airways, Western Pacific Airlines. Layout: Transit Level (People Mover), Baggage Level (Baggage Claim, Car Rental, Ground Transportation), Ticketing Level (Departure). Concourse A (Gates A1–A7), B (Gates B1–B15), C (Gates C1–C18), D (Gates D1–D11)
North Satellite Terminal Airlines: Shuttle By United, United Airlines, United Express. Layout: Transit Level (People Mover), Ticketing Level (Gates N1–N16)
South Satellite Terminal Airlines: Aeroflot, American Airlines (International arrivals), Asiana Airlines, British Airways, China Eastern, EVA Air, Hawaiian Airlines, Martinair Holland, Northwest Airlines, Asiana Airlines, SAS Scandinavian Airlines. Layout: Transit Level (People Mover), Ticketing Level (Customs, Gates S1–S15)

Minimum transfer times
International: 1 hr 30 min Domestic: 1 hr 10 min

Transfer between terminals
Bus; Terminals and parking lots ⌀Free
People mover ≫2 min; All terminals ⌀Free

INFORMATION

Flight enquiries
Alaska Airlines ✆433 3100 China Eastern ✆343 5583 Continental Airlines ✆624 1740 EVA Air ✆242 8888 Frontier Airlines ✆431 2025 TWA ✆447 9400

Information and help desks
Ground Transportation Main Terminal Baggage Level ✆431 5906 ⓗ0900–2300
Traveller's Aid Main Terminal Upper Level ✆433 5288 ⓗ0900–2100 Tourist information
Visitor Information Desk Main Terminal Baggage Level (across from Carousel 8) ✆433 5217 ⓗ0930–1930 Tourist information

EMERGENCIES

Police All Terminals throughout ✆433 5400
Lost Property Main Terminal Mezzanine Floor ✆433 5312 ⓗ0700–1730 Mon–Fri, 1000–1730 Sat, 1300–1700 Sun Mon–Sat
Medical ✆433 5327

AIRPORT FACILITIES

Money
ATM Main Terminal throughout
Bank Main Terminal ⓗ0900–2000 Mon–Sat, 1100–1700 Sun
Thomas Cook bureau de change Main Terminal Ticketing Level Concourse B ⓗ0600–2200
Thomas Cook bureau de change Main Terminal Ticketing Level Concourse D ⓗ0600–2000
Thomas Cook bureau de change South Satellite Terminal Transit Level Food and drink

Food and drink
Bar All Terminals throughout
Café/light meals All Terminals throughout
Restaurant Main Terminal Ticketing Level (Centre) ⓗ1030–2100

Communications
Fax service Main Terminal Ticketing Level (Business Center near Gate C-2)
Fax service North Satellite Terminal (across from Gate N-2)
Fax service South Satellite Terminal (across from Gate S-8)
Fax service All Terminals Business Centers
Internet All Terminals Throughout
Post box All Terminals throughout

Shopping
Duty free, departure Main Terminal Ticketing Level Concourse B and C
Duty free, departure North Satellite Terminal Ticketing Level
Duty free, departure South Satellite Terminal Ticketing Level
Gift Shop Main Terminal Ticketing Level, all Concourses
Gift Shop North Satellite Terminal Ticketing Level
Gift Shop South Terminal Ticketing Level (Centre)
Hairdresser Main Terminal Ticketing Level (Centre) ⓗ0800–1900 Mon–Fri; 0900–1600 Sat ✆248 2969
News, Stationery & Books All Terminals Ticketing Level

Luggage
Left luggage counter Main Terminal Baggage Level (between Carousels 9 and 12) ⓗ0530–0030 ✆433 5333
All Terminals Throughout
Porters All Terminals Contact airline
Trolleys/Carts All Terminals Throughout

DISABLED TRAVELLERS

All Terminals Adapted toilets; Lifts; Special car parking Third and Fourth Levels; Phones at wheelchair height; Phones adapted for the deaf; Personal assistance

SMOKING POLICY

All Terminals No-smoking throughout

SPECIAL PASSENGER LOUNGES

Alaska Airlines Board Room Main Terminal Ticketing Level Concourse D
American Airlines Admirals Club Main Terminal Ticketing Level Concourse C
Asiana Airlines Lounge South Satellite Terminal Mezzanine Level
British Airways First Class Lounge South Satellite Terminal Mezzanine Level
Delta Airlines Crown Room Main Terminal Ticketing Level Concourse B
Eva Air Lounge South Satellite Terminal

✆ Phone no. ℻ Fax no. ⓗ Hours of opening/operation ≫ Frequency of service ➔ Journey time ⌀ Cost/one-way fare

SECTION TWO • AIRPORT DIRECTORY — SEATTLE

Mezzanine Level
Hawaiian Airlines Lounge South Satellite Terminal Mezzanine Level
Northwest Airlines Worldclub South Satellite Terminal Ticketing Level
SAS Scanorama Lounge South Satellite Terminal Ticketing Level
United Airlines Red Carpet Club North Satellite Terminal Ticketing Level

CONFERENCE AND BUSINESS FACILITIES

Conference Hall, Main Terminal ℂ433 5605
Business Communications Center, Main Terminal Ticketing Level ℂ433 5605 Telephones, Fax service, Photocopier, Internet
Business Communications Center, Main Terminal Ticketing Level Concourse C ℂ433 5605 Telephones, Fax service, Photocopier, Internet
Conference Room, Main Terminal ℂ433 5605

CAR RENTAL

Advantage Main Terminal Baggage Level ℂ824 0161
Alamo Main Terminal Baggage Level ℂ433 0182
Avis Main Terminal Baggage Level ℂ433 5231
Budget Main Terminal Baggage Level ℂ243 2400
Dollar Main Terminal Baggage Level ℂ433 5825
Hertz Main Terminal Baggage Level ℂ248 1300
National Main Terminal Baggage Level ℂ433 5501
Thrifty Main Terminal Baggage Level ℂ242 7565

CAR PARKING

Long-stay Main Terminal Parking Garage ⌀USD10 per day
Off-airport Free shuttle from Main Terminal
Short-stay Main Terminal Parking Garage (Third Floor) ⌀Free first 30 min, then USD4 per 2 hr

TAXIS AND CHAUFFEUR-DRIVEN CARS

Taxis
Main Terminal, Baggage Level City centre ⊃20 min ⌀USD25

PUBLIC TRANSPORT

Airport to airport
Bellingham Airport ⎯Airporter Shuttle »1–2 hrs ◷0630–2300 (1900 Sat) ⊃2 hr 40 min ⌀USD29.
Vancouver International Airport BC ⎯Quick Shuttle »1–2 hrs ◷0745–1930 ⊃3 hr 25 min ⌀CAD38.

City and suburbs
Seattle (downtown hotels) ⎯Gray Line Downtown Express Bus »30 min ◷0500–2400 ⊃ Baggage Level ⌀USD7.50
Seattle city centre ⎯Metro: 174 (local), 184 (nights), 194 (exp) »30 min ◷0530–0030 (0700 Sun) ⌀USD1.10.
Seattle–Tacoma (metro area) ⎯Over 20 companies At Airport.

Other cities and towns
Bellevue WA ⎯Shuttle Express 622 1424.
Bellevue ⎯Metro: 340 Local »30 min–1 hr 0540–2115 ⊃1 hr ⌀USD1.10. For Burien, Renton, Southcenter, SeaTac Mall and Tukwila WA
Bellingham/Northwest WA ⎯Airporter Shuttle »1–2 hrs ◷0630–2300 (2100Sat) ⊃1–3 hrs ⌀USD15–35. For Anacortes, Anacortes Ferry to San Juan Islands, Oak Harbor, La Connor, Bellingham, Mt. Vernon, Marysville, Stanwood, Alaska Ferry Terminal, Ferndale and Blaine WA
Bremerton WA ⎯Bremerton–Kitsap Airporter »1 hr ◷0540–2325 ⊃1 hr ⌀USD17. For Bremerton, Silverdale, Northwest Tacoma Gig Harbor, Port Orchard, Purdy, Gorst, Poulsbo and Bangor Submarine Base WA
Everett WA ⎯Shuttle Express 622 1424.
Centralia WA ⎯Centralia Sea-Tac Airporter (800) 773 9490. For Chehalis, Olympia, Lacy and Tumwater
Fort Lewis/McChord AFB WA ⎯Fort Lewis/McChord AFBAirporter (800) 562 7948.
Olympia WA ⎯Capital Airporter ℂ(360) 754 7113. For Tacoma, Olympia, Tumwater, Lacey, Evergreen College, Centralia, Chehalis, Fife, Puyallup, Sumner, Shelton and Hoodsport/Union WA
Port Angeles WA ⎯Olympic Van Tours ℂ(360) 452 3858 For Sequim WA
Portland OR ⎯Greyhound Lines »2 day ◷1235; 1710 ⊃4 hrs. For Tacoma, Ft. Lewis, Olympia, Centralia, Kelso, Longview and Vancouver WA
Vancouver BC ⎯Quick Shuttle »1–2 hrs ◷0745–1930 ⊃3 hr 50 min ⌀CAD38. For Everett and Bellingham Airport WA
Vancouver BC ⎯Greyhound Lines »1 day ◷1030 ⊃5 hr. For Everett, Mt. Vernon, Bellingham, Blaine WA and New Westminster BC

REGIONAL AIR CONNECTIONS

Astoria OR ✈ »Several per day ⊃40 min
Bellingham WA ✈ »Several per day ⊃40 min
Eastsound WA ✈ »Several per day ⊃40 min
Friday Harbor WA ✈ »Several per day ⊃50 min
Moses Lake WA ✈ »Several per day ⊃45 min
Oak Harbor WA ✈ »Several per day ⊃25 min
Pasco WA ✈ »Several per day ⊃1 hr
Port Angeles WA ✈ »Several per day ⊃30 min
Portland OR ✈ »Several per day ⊃50 min
Seattle Lake Union WA ✈ »Several per day ⊃30 min
Spokane WA ✈ »Several per day ⊃55 min
Vancouver BC ✈ »Several per day ⊃50 min
Victoria BC ✈ »Several per day ⊃45 min
Wenatchee WA ✈ »Several per day ⊃40min
Yakima WA ✈ »Several per day ⊃40 min

TRAVELLER'S NOTES

In keeping with its "laid–back" image, Seattle may be the only airport in North America with an open–air Massage Bar (located in the Main Terminal Ticketing Level at the entrance to Concourse C) ◷0900–2100.

SEOUL   SEL

South Korea (see page 36)

National ✆ code: 82
Area ✆ code: 02
Local time: Winter GMT+9, Summer GMT+9
Kimpo International Airport, Seoul, South Korea
✆660 2812/2813
☎661 9724/663 8833
Location: 17 km/10 miles W of Seoul

Terminals and Transfers

Terminals
Terminal 1 Airlines: Aeroflot, Air France, All Nippon Airways, British Airways, Cathay Pacific Airways, Delta Airlines, Japan Airlines, Japan Air System, KLM Royal Dutch Airlines, Northwest Airlines, Philippine Airlines, Singapore Airlines, Thai Airways International, United Airlines, VASP Brazilian Airlines, Air Canada. Layout: Three Floors
Terminal 2 Airlines: Korean Air, Asiana Airlines, Lufthansa German Airlines, Continental Micronesia, Garuda Indonesia, Malaysia Airlines, Qantas Airways, Swiss Air Transport, Vietnam Airlines, Air New Zealand, Air China, China Eastern Airlines. Layout: First Floor, Arrival and facilities; Second Floor, Departure, check-in and facilities; Third Floor, Departure, shops and catering; Fourth Floor, Transit Area, catering
Domestic Terminal Airlines: Korean Air, Asiana Airlines.

Minimum transfer times
International: 2 hr Domestic: 1 hr 40 min. Between Domestic Terminals: 1 hr

Transfer between terminals
Airport Shuttle Bus ≫6 min ⏱0630–last flight; International passenger terminals 1 and 2 and the Domestic terminal ⌀Free

Information

Flight enquiries
Airport ✆662 2111 (Internat'l); ✆664 7511 (Domestic)

Information and help desks
Airport Information Counter First Floor of each terminal Arrival ✆665 0088 ⏱daily 30 min prior to first flight and until last flight ✆660 2471 (Terminal 1); 660 2482 (Terminal 2); 660 2475 (Domestic). Airport information.

Emergencies

Lost Property Terminal 1 Second Floor ✆660 2664; Terminal 2 First floor ✆660 2673 ⏱0900–1800

Airport Facilities

Money
Bank Terminal 1 First floor ✆662 1341
Bank Terminal 1 Second floor ✆663 5001
Bank Terminal 2 Third floor ✆662 1341
Bank Terminal 2 First floor ✆663 5000
Bank Domestic Terminal Third floor ✆662 1341
Bureau de Change Terminal 1 Second floor ✆664 2386/8
Bureau de Change Terminal 2 First floor ✆664 0101/4

Food and drink
Restaurant Terminal 1 2, ⏱0630–2200
Café/light meals Terminal 1 First and Second Floors ⏱0630–2200
Restaurant Terminal 2 2, ⏱0630–2200
Café/light meals Terminal 2 First and Second Floors ⏱0630–2200
Café/light meals Domestic Terminal First and Second Floors ⏱0630–2200

Communications
Post office Terminal 1 Second floor ⏱0700–2000 ✆665 1501/3
Post office Terminal 2 Second floor ⏱0700–2000 ✆665 5448

Shopping
Duty free, departure Terminal 1 Third Floor ⏱30 min prior to the first flight until the last
Duty free, departure Terminal 2 Third Floor ⏱30 min prior to the first flight until the last

Luggage
Left luggage counter Terminal 1, Second Floor ⏱0700–30 mins prior to the last flight ⌀KRW1500 per suitcase ✆663 4922
Left luggage counter Terminal 2, Second Floor ⏱0700–30 mins prior to the last flight ⌀KRW1500 per suitcase ✆665 7171/664 3125
Left luggage counter Domestic Terminal, First Floor ⏱0700–30 mins prior to the last flight ⌀KRW1500 per suitcase ✆661 8607

Disabled Travellers

Terminal 1 Adapted toilets; Lifts.
Terminal 2 Adapted toilets; Lifts.
Domestic Terminal Adapted toilets; Lifts.

Special Passenger Lounges

Northwest Airlines World Club, Terminal 1 Third Floor ⏱0700–1 hr prior to last flight departure First class passengers and executive passengers
Cathay Pacific Airlines First Class Lounge, Terminal 1 Third Floor ⏱0810–1740 First class and business class passengers
Japan Airlines Sakura Lounge, Terminal 1 Third Floor ⏱0700–1830 First class passengers
Singapore Airlines Silver Kris Lounge, Terminal 1 Third Floor ⏱All flight times First class and business class passengers
Thai Airways Royal Orchid Lounge, Terminal 1 Third Floor ⏱All flight times First class and business class passengers
Morning Calm Lounge, Terminal 1 Third Floor ⏱All flight times First class and business class passengers travelling with British Airways, Air France, KLM, Royal Dutch Airlines and Philippine Airlines
United Airlines Red Carpet Club, Terminal 1 Third Floor ⏱All flight times First class passengers, Red Carpet Club members and Clipper Club members
Delta Airlines First Class Lounge, Terminal 1 Third Floor ⏱1300–1800 First class and business class passengers, south-east Asia route passengers
All Nippon Airways Lounge, Terminal 1 Third Floor ⏱0900–1700 Club ANA passengers
Japan Air System Rainbow Lounge, Terminal 1 Third Floor ⏱1200–1500 Business class passengers and Rainbow club members
Asiana Airlines Asiana Lounge, Terminal 2 West Side Third Floor and Fourth Floor of the CIQ area ⏱0700–2030 First class and business class passengers
Morning Calm Lounge, Terminal 2

✆ Phone no.   ☎ Fax no.   ⏱ Hours of opening/operation   ≫ Frequency of service   ⊃ Journey time   ⌀ Cost/one-way fare

SEOUL

Fourth Floor of the CIQ area
⏰0700–2030 First class and prestige class passengers travelling with Swiss Air, Lufthansa, Garuda Indonesia, Malaysia Airlines, Vietnam Airlines and Qantas Airways
Korean Airlines Morning Calm Lounge, Terminal 2 West Side Third Floor
⏰0640–2030 First class and prestige class passengers

Airport Hotels

Green World ✆653 1999
Nostalgia ✆691 0071
Regent ✆694 3111

Car Rental

Dae-Han Terminal 1 ✆664 7684
Keum-Ho Terminal 1 ✆665 5711
Sam-Bo Terminal 1 ✆661 0101
Hertz Terminal 1 ✆665 9105
Keum-Ho Terminal 2 ✆665 9106
Avis Terminal 2 ✆666 1121

Cheju Domestic Terminal ✆664 5486
Keum-Ho Domestic Terminal ✆661 5486
Halla Domestic Terminal ✆665 2760

Car Parking

Short-stay 6500 spaces ⌀KRW1000 first 30 min; KRW500 per each 15 min thereafter; KRW40,000 per 24 hr (higher rates for large vehicles) ✆660 2515/6

Taxis and Chauffeur-driven Cars

Taxis
Outside terminals City centre ⤳30 min ⌀KRW1000–3000

Public Transport

City & suburbs
Seoul (city centre and hotels) 🚌 Airport Express bus 600, 601, 602 »7–10 min

⏰0505–the last flight ⤳40 min ⌀KRW800. No additional luggage space
Seoul (city centre and hotels) 🚌 KAL Limousine Bus Lines 1, 2, 3, 4 »5–8 min. ⤳40 min. For information ✆667 0386 9

Regional Air Connections

Chinju ✈ »Several per day ⤳1 hr
Kangnung ✈ »Several per day ⤳50 min
Kunsan ✈ »Several per day ⤳50 min
Kwangju ✈ »Several per day ⤳50 min
Mokpo ✈ »Several per day ⤳55 min
Pohang ✈ »Several per day ⤳55 min
Pusan ✈ »Several per day ⤳1 hr
Sokcho ✈ »Several per day ⤳50 min
Taegu ✈ »Several per day ⤳50 min
Ulsan ✈ »Several per day ⤳55 min
Yechon ✈ »Several per day ⤳45 min

Airport Tax

Departure tax is KRW9000 (International); KRW3000 (Domestic)

SINGAPORE   SIN

Singapore (see page 35)

National ✆ code: 65
Area ✆ code: No code required
Local time: Winter GMT+8, Summer GMT+8
Singapore Changi Airport, PO Box 1, Singapore 918141
✆ Terminal 1: 1800 542 9727;
Terminal 2: 1800 542 9792
✆Terminal 1: 1800 542 6990;
Terminal 2: 1800 545 6223
Internet e-mail: caasinet@pacific.net.sg
WWW site: http://www.changi.airport.com.sg
Location: 23 km/13 miles E of Singapore city centre

Terminals and Transfers

Terminals
Terminal 1 Airlines: Yunnan Airlines, Region Air, Pelangi Air, Air India, Alitalia, British Airways, Biman Bangladesh Airlines, Bouraq Indonesia Airlines, Eva Air, Air China, China Airlines, Cathay Pacific Airways, China Southern Airlines, Emirates, Garuda Indonesian Airlines, Gulf Air, Air Seychelles, Indian Airlines, Japan Airlines, Korean Airlines, KLM, Kuwait Airways, Lufthansa, Middle East Airlines, Air Mauritius, Egyptair, China Eastern Airlines, Merpati Nusantara Airlines, Lauda-Air, All Nippon Airways, Northwest Airlines, Air New Zealand, CSA Czechoslovak, Asiana Airlines, Pakistan International Airlines, Air Niugini, Qantas Airways, Royal Nepal Airlines, Royal Jordanian Airlines, South African Airways, Sempati Air, SAS, Aeroflot, Saudia, China Southwest, Thai Airways, Turkish Airlines, United Airlines, Air Lanka, Royal Air Cambodge, Vietnam Airlines. Layout: Level 1 Arrival, Level 2 Departure, Level 3 Viewing Hall (restaurants and services), Basement Areas 1 (shops and private car pick-up point) and 2 (supermarket, bank and public bus station)
Terminal 2 Airlines: All other airlines. Layout: Level 1 Arrival, Level 2 Departure Hall, Level 3 Viewing Mall (shops, restaurants and services), Basement (shops, supermarket, banks and bus station)

✈ Air 🚆 Rail 🚌 Bus 🚐 Limousine 🚇 Metro/subway 🚋 Tram 🚁 Helicopter ⛴ Water transport • For map symbols, see p. 9

Singapore

SECTION TWO • AIRPORT DIRECTORY

Minimum transfer times
International: 1 hr

Transfer between terminals
Skytrain Terminals 1 and 2 ⊕0600–1300 ◇Free

INFORMATION

Flight enquiries
Airport ℂ1800 542 4422 or 541 8590 (Term 1); 541 8845 (Term 2) Aeroflot ℂ541 89 95 Air China ℂ542 82 92 Air France ℂ542 12 34 Air India ℂ542 84 44 Air Lanka ℂ545 92 42 Air Mauritius ℂ542 12 34 Air New Zealand ℂ535 82 66 Air Niugini ℂ250 48 68 Air Seychelles ℂ255 73 73 Alitalia ℂ543 15 09 All Nippon Airways ℂ543 09 55 Asiana Airlines ℂ545 25 84 Biman Bangladesh Airlines ℂ542 0067 Bouraq Indonesia Airlines ℂ227 56 88 British Airways ℂ542 25 55 Cathay Pacific Airways ℂ542 25 52 China Airlines ℂ542 12 34 China Eastern Airlines ℂ323 26 32 China Southern Airlines ℂ542 03 38 China Southwest ℂ225 21 77 CSA Czechoslovak ℂ737 98 44 Delta Airlines ℂ225 87 00 Egyptair ℂ542 94 96 Emirates ℂ543 00 01 Eva Air ℂ543 01 03 Finnair ℂ545 18 37 Garuda Indonesian Airlines ℂ542 12 34 Gulf Air ℂ543 07 33 Indian Airlines ℂ225 49 49 Japan Airlines ℂ542 59 08 KLM ℂ542 12 34 Korean Airlines ℂ542 06 23 Kuwait Airways ℂ545 72 95 Lauda-Air ℂ542 12 34 Lufthansa ℂ542 12 34 Malaysian Airlines ℂ541 68 15 Merpati Nusantara Airlines ℂ542 12 34 Middle East Airlines ℂ542 63 82 Myanmar Airways International ℂ545 47 33 Northwest Airlines ℂ542 12 34 Pakistan International Airlines ℂ542 59 09 Pelangi Air ℂ336 67 77 Philippine Airlines ℂ542 54 22 Qantas Airways ℂ542 29 05 Royal Air Cambodge ℂ541 68 15 Royal Brunei Airlines ℂ542 42 22 Royal Jordanian Airlines ℂ545 79 73 Royal Nepal Airlines ℂ339 55 35 Saudia ℂ545 20 41 SAS ℂ542 34 33 Sempati Air ℂ542 99 31 Silk Air ℂ540 31 65 Singapore Airlines ℂ542 88 45 South African Airways ℂ227 79 11 Swissair ℂ542 66 22 Thai Airways ℂ542 83 33 Turkish Airlines ℂ542 42 13 United Airlines ℂ542 42 44 Vietnam Airlines ℂ338 81 88 Yunnan Airlines ℂ542 82 92

Information and help desks
CAAS Information Counter Terminal 1 Levels 1 and 2 (2 desks) Airport information, Flights.
CAAS/Passenger Information Counter Terminal 2 Levels 1 and 2 (2 desks) Airport information, Flights.

EMERGENCIES

Medical Terminal 2 Departure Area ℂ543 2223 ⊕0800–2230
Medical Terminal 1 Level 2, Departure Lounge ℂ543 2223 ⊕0800-2400
Medical Terminal 2 Public Area ℂ543 2223 ⊕24 hr
Lost Property (SATS) Terminal 1 ℂ541 8554 ⊕24 hr
Lost Property (SATS) Terminal 2 ℂ541 8875 ⊕24 hr
Lost Property (CIAS) Terminal 1 ℂ541 3132 ⊕24 hr
Lost Property (CIAS) Terminal 2 ℂ541 3152 ⊕24 hr

AIRPORT FACILITIES

Money
Bureau de change Terminal 1 Departure Check-in Hall and Lounge, Arrival Hall ⊕24 hr
Bureau de change Terminal 2 Departure Check-in Hall and Lounge, Arrival Hall, ⊕24 hr

Food and drink
Restaurant Terminal 1 Level 3 (2 locations) ⊕1030–2300 and 1130–2300
Café/light meals Terminal 1 Level 3 (2 locations) ⊕0700–2300 and 24hr
Café/light meals Terminal 1 Level 1 (2 locations) ⊕0800–2300, 0630–2300
Restaurant Terminal 1 Departure Lounge ⊕24 hr
Bar Terminal 1 Departure lounge (various locations)
Café/light meals Terminal 2 Level 3, Public Area (3 locations) ⊕24 hr, 1100–2300, 0700–2330
Restaurant Terminal 2 Departure Lounge

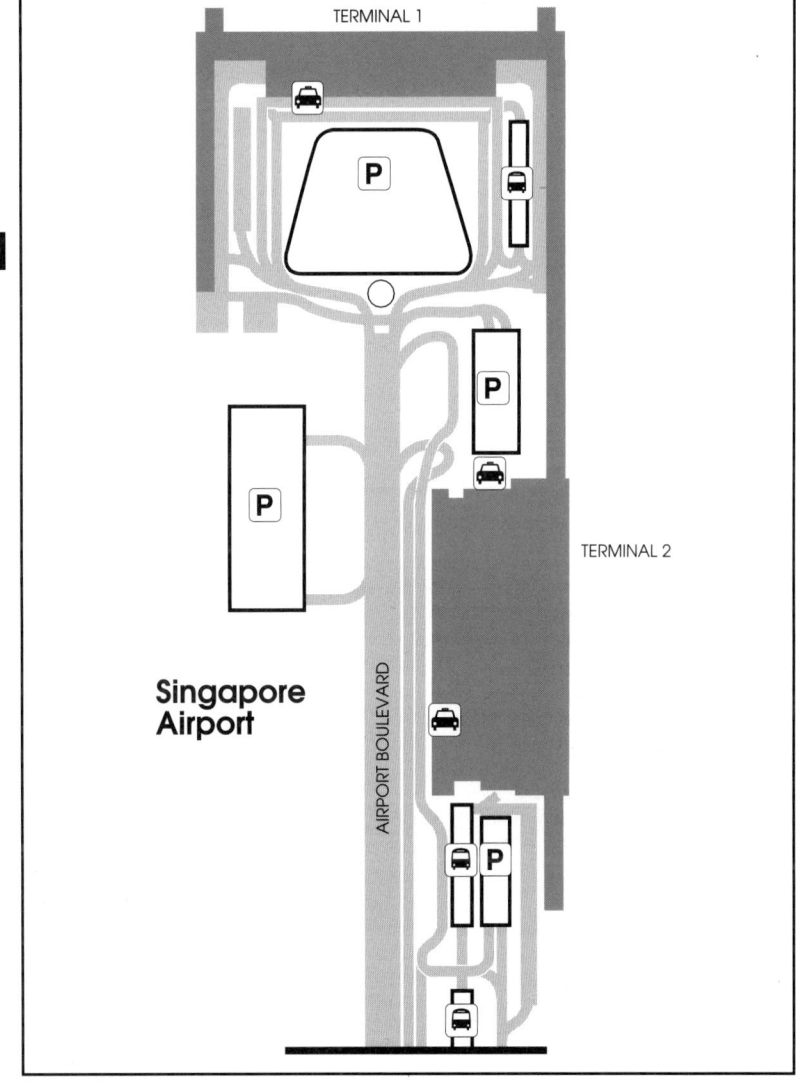

ℂ Phone no. ℱ Fax no. ⊕ Hours of opening/operation » Frequency of service ⊃ Journey time ◇ Cost/one-way fare

SECTION TWO • AIRPORT DIRECTORY

SINGAPORE

SINGAPORE TERMINAL 1 — Arrivals Level

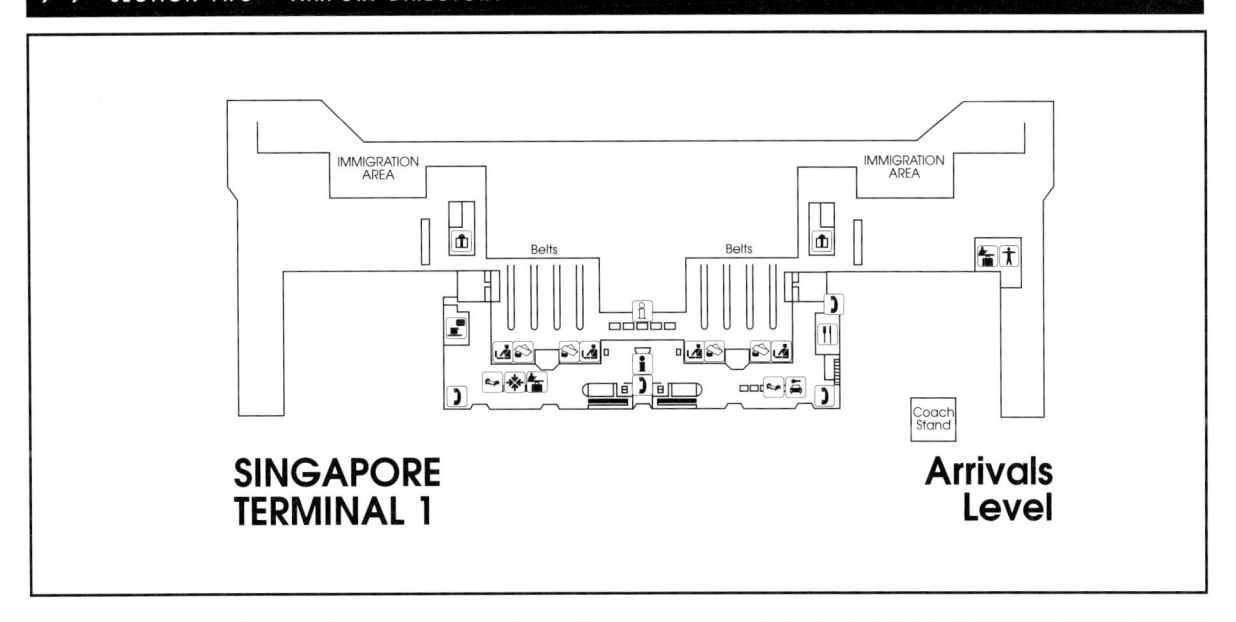

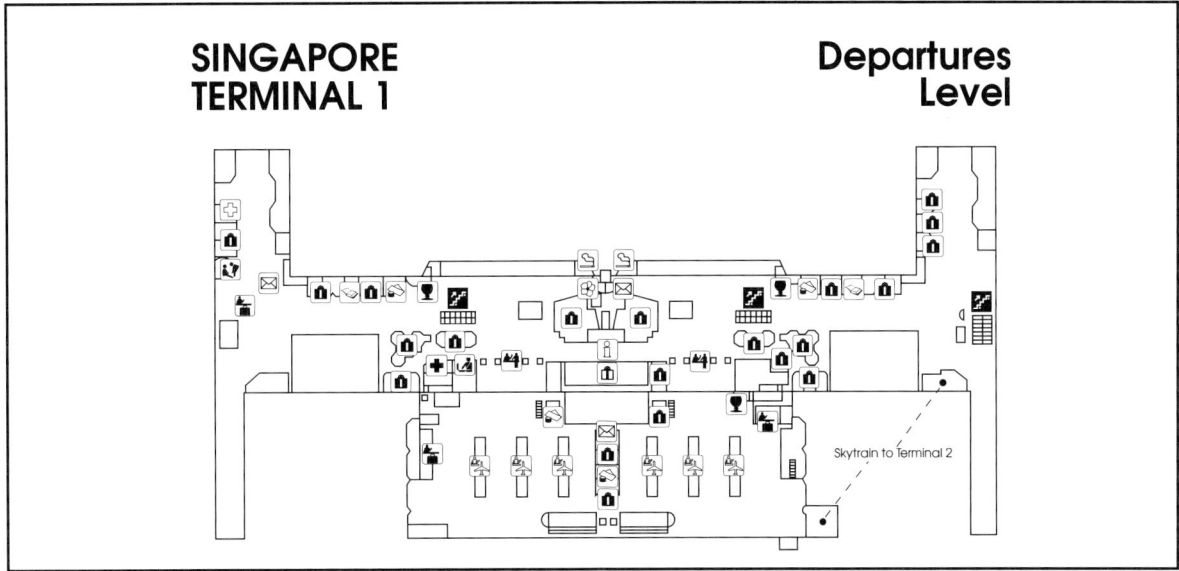

SINGAPORE TERMINAL 1 — Departures Level

⏱24 hr
Bar Terminal 2 Departure Lounge and finger piers
Restaurant Terminal 2 Level 3 (5 locations) ⏱0700–2300 (2); 1030–2400; 1100, 1200–1500, 1800–2200

Communications
Fax service Terminal 1 Departure Hall, Level 2
Post office Terminal 1 Level 2 ⏱24 hrs
Fax service Terminal 2 Departure Hall, Level 2
Post office Terminal 2 Level 2 ⏱24 hr

Shopping
Shopping mall Terminal 1 Level 2
Duty free, arrival Terminal 1 Level 1 ⏱24 hr
Duty free, departure Terminal 1 Level 2 ⏱24 hr
Duty free, arrival Terminal 2 Level 1 Arrival Hall ⏱24 hr
Shopping mall Terminal 2 Level 2 Departure Hall
Duty free, departure Terminal 2 Level 2 ⏱24 hr

Luggage
Left luggage counter Terminal 1 Level 1 and 2 ⏱24 hr ⊘SGD3–5 per day
Porters Terminal 1 Departure Check-in Hall ⏱24 hr ⊘Free
Trolleys/carts Terminal 1 Outside Departure Check-in Hall ⏱24 hr ⊘Free
Left luggage counter Terminal 2 Level 1 Arrival Hall, Level 2 Departure Hall ⏱24 hr ⊘SGD3–5 per day
Porters Terminal 2 Departure Check-in Hall ⏱24 hr ⊘Free
Trolleys/carts Terminal 2 Outside Departure Check-in Hall ⏱24 hr ⊘Free

Disabled Travellers
Terminal 1 Adapted toilets; Lifts; Personal assistance
Terminal 2 Adapted toilets; Lifts; Personal assistance
For wheelchair hire ✆543 1118 ⏱24 hr

✈ Air ⛴ Rail 🚌 Bus 🚗 Limousine Ⓜ Metro/subway 🚋 Tram 🚁 Helicopter ⛵ Water transport • For map symbols, see p. 9

Singapore

SECTION TWO • AIRPORT DIRECTORY

SINGAPORE TERMINAL 2 — Arrivals Level

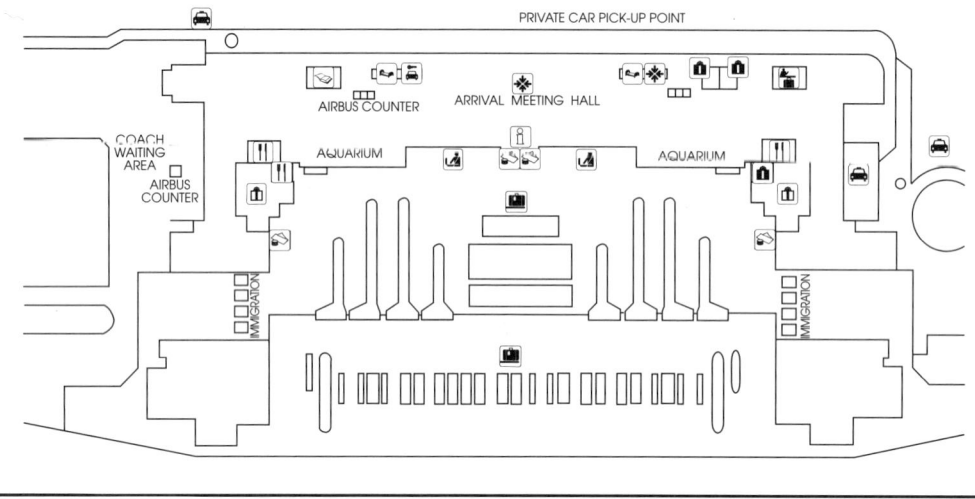

SINGAPORE TERMINAL 2 — Departures Level

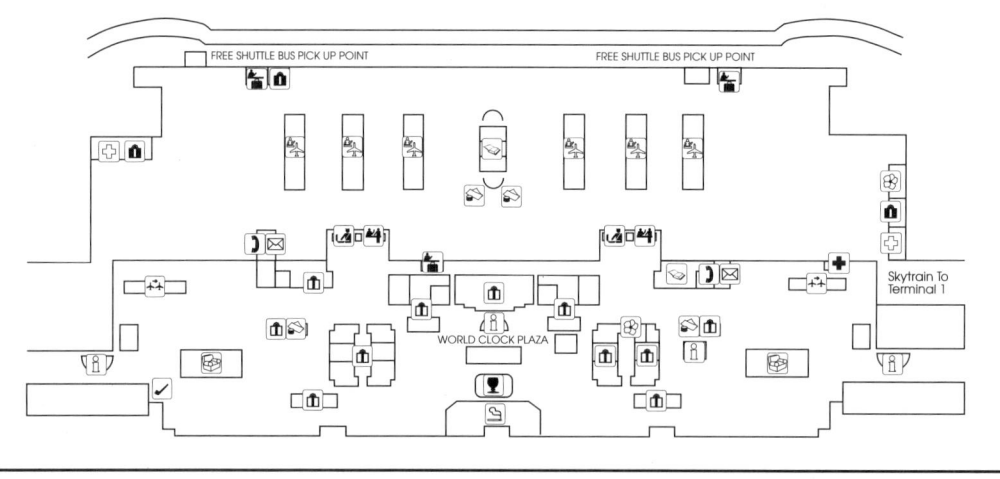

Smoking Policy

Terminal 1 Two smoking rooms in Transit Area
Terminal 2 One smoking room in Transit Area

Special Passenger Lounges

Air France Lounge Terminal 2 Level 3
Air New Zealand Lounge Terminal 1 Level 3
All Nippon Airways Lounge Terminal 1 Level 3
British Airways VIP Lounge Terminal 1 Level 3
Cathay Pacific Airways VIP Lounge Terminal 1 Level 3
China Airlines Lounge Terminal 1 Level 3
Finnair Lounge Terminal 2 Level 3
Japan Airlines Lounge Terminal 1 Level 3
Malaysian Airlines VIP Lounge Terminal 2 Level 3
Northwest Airlines Lounge Terminal 1 Level 3
Philippine Airlines VIP Lounge Terminal 2 Level 3
Qantas Airways VIP Lounge Terminal 1 Level 3
Royal Brunei Airlines Lounge Terminal 2 Level 3
Singapore Airlines VIP Lounge Terminal 2 Level 3
Swissair Lounge Terminal 2 Level 3
Thai Airways VIP Lounge Terminal 1 Level 3
United Airlines Lounge Terminal 1 Level 3

☏ Phone no. ℻ Fax no. ⏱ Hours of opening/operation » Frequency of service ↪ Journey time ◇ Cost/one-way fare

SECTION TWO • AIRPORT DIRECTORY

SINGAPORE

CONFERENCE AND BUSINESS FACILITIES

Business Centre, Transit Hotel, Level 3, Departure Lounge, Terminal 2 ✆543 0911 ⏱0700-2300 Fax service, Photocopier, Secretarial service, Translation/Interpretation service.

AIRPORT HOTELS

Transit Hotel (Terminal 1) ✆543 09 11 ℻545 83 65; 50 rooms
Transit (Terminal 2) ✆542 8122; 56 rooms

CAR RENTAL

Avis Terminal 1 Arrival Hall, Level 1 ✆542 81 69
Avis Terminal 2 Arrival Hall, Level 1 ✆542 81 69
Sintat Terminal 1 Arrival Hall, Level 1 ✆542 3876
Sintat Terminal 2 Arrival Hall, Level 1 ✆542 38 76

CAR PARKING

Short-stay Car parks A, B, C and D spaces ⌀A, B, C: SGD0.90 per 30 min (0700–2400); D: SGD0.45/30 min (0001–0700)
Long-stay ⌀SGD0.15 per 24 hr

TAXIS AND CHAUFFEUR-DRIVEN CARS

Taxis
Outside Arrival Hall, both terminals City centre ⌀Meter + SGD3

PUBLIC TRANSPORT

City ⟲ suburbs
Singapore, Bukit Merah 🚌 Singapore Bus Services ⏱0600–2400 ⌀SGD1.30.
City 🚌 Airbus ⏱0700–2400 ⌀SGD5. Three routes covering all main city hotels Singapore (Raffles City and Orchard Road areas) 🚌Public bus line 16/16E ⌀SGD1.40.

REGIONAL AIR CONNECTIONS

Bandung ✈ ⟫At least daily ⏱55 min
Ho Chi Minh City ✈ ⟫Several per day ⏱50 min
Jakarta ✈ ⟫Several per day ⏱30–40 min
Kuala Lumpur ✈ ⟫Several per day ⏱50–55 min
Kuantan ✈ ⟫Several per week ⏱45 min
Medan ✈ ⟫Several per day ⏱20–30 min
Phnom Penh ✈ ⟫At least daily ⏱55–60 min
Phuket ✈ ⟫Several per day ⏱40–45 min
Tioman ✈ ⟫Several per day ⏱40 min

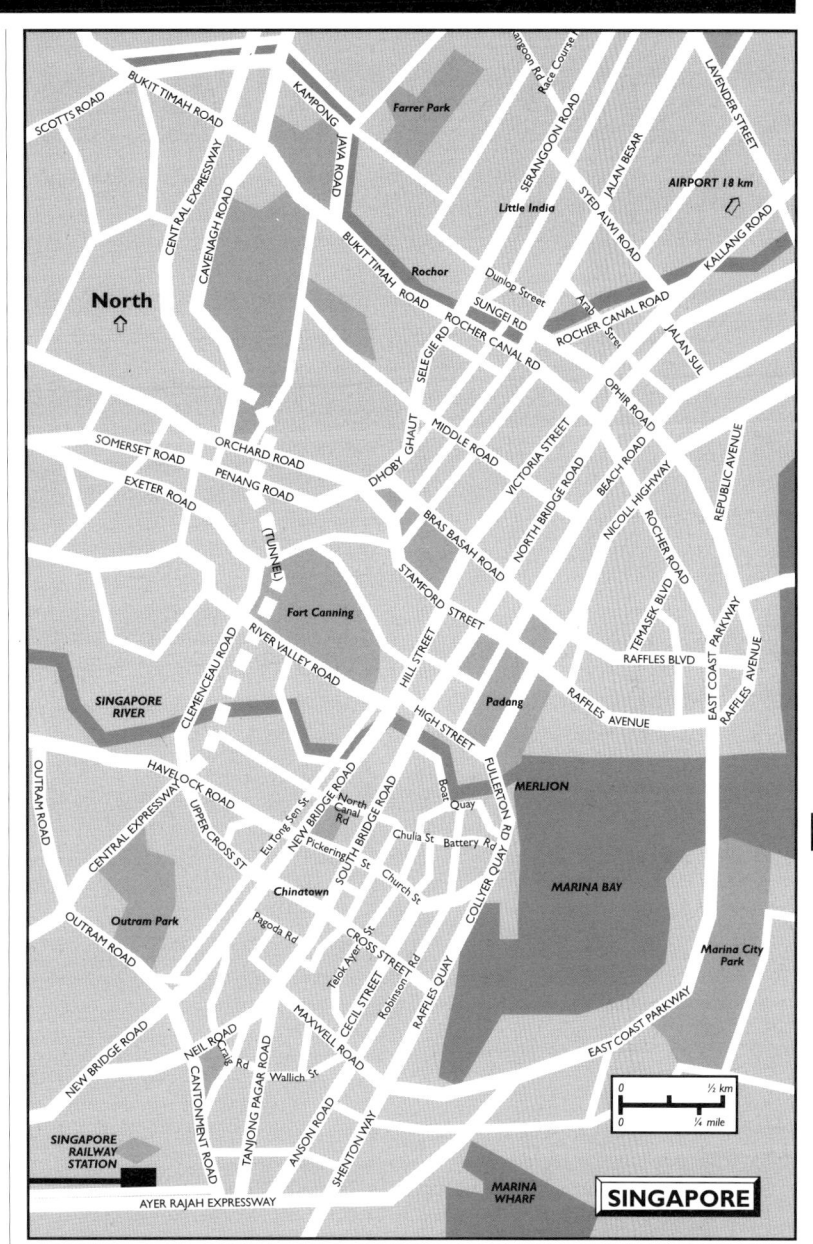

TRAVELLER'S NOTES

For a new food experience, take the lift near McDonald's on the Arrival Level and go to Basement 1 Food Centre: a complete Singapore hawkers' market with Chinese and Malay food. It's essentially the airport staff cafeteria, but the public are quite welcome.

✈ Air 🚆 Rail 🚌 Bus 🚐 Limousine Ⓜ Metro/subway 🚋 Tram 🚁 Helicopter ⛴ Water transport • For map symbols, see p. 9

STOCKHOLM   SECTION TWO • AIRPORT DIRECTORY

STOCKHOLM-ARLANDA ARN

Sweden (see page 37)

National ✆ code: 46
Area ✆ code: 08
Local time: Winter GMT+1, Summer GMT+2
Stockholm-Arlanda Airport, 190 45 Stockholm-Arlanda, Sweden
✆797 6000
🖷593 62096
Internet e-mail: luftfartsverket@arn.lfv.se
WWW site: http//www.lfv.se
Location: 45 km/28 miles N of Stockholm

TERMINALS AND TRANSFERS

Terminals
Terminal 2 Airlines: Alitalia, Austrian Airlines, Braathens SAFE, Finnair, Maersk Air, Nordic European Airlines (domestic/international scheduled flights), Sabena, Swissair, Transwede Airways. Layout: Three Levels.
Terminal 3 Airlines: All other domestic flights. Layout: Satellite of Terminal 2
Terminal 4 Airlines: SAS (domestic flights). Layout: Three Levels with satellite extension and Falcon Aviation
Terminal 5 Airlines: All other international flights. Layout: Three Levels with 2 satellite extensions
Sky City Layout: Facilities and shops.

Minimum transfer times
International: 30 min–1 hr **Domestic:** 15–25 min

Transfer between terminals
Bus ⟫5 min; Terminals 2, 3, 4, 5 and Sky City ⟠Free

INFORMATION

Flight enquiries
Airport ✆797 6100 (all flight enquiries except SAS domestic flights ✆7975050

Information and help desks
CAA Information Desk Terminal 2 Arrival/Departure Hall ✆797 61 00 ⏱24 hr Airport information, Flights Hotel booking, Tourist information
CAA Information Desk Terminal 4 Arrival/Departure Hall ✆797 61 00 ⏱All flight times Airport information, Flights, Hotel booking, Tourist information
CAA Information Desk Terminal 5 Departure Hall ✆797 61 00 ⏱24 hr Airport information, Flights, Hotel booking, Tourist information

EMERGENCIES
Police Terminal 5 Level 4 above Departure Hall ✆797 9000
Medical Sky City, Arlanda Medical Centre Via Information Desk
Lost Property Terminal 5 Arlanda Service Level 1 ✆797 60 80

AIRPORT FACILITIES

Money
ATM Terminal 2 ⏱24 hr
ATM Terminal 4 ⏱24 hr
ATM Terminal 5 ⏱24 hr
ATM Sky City ⏱24 hr
Bank Terminal 5 Arrival Hall ⏱0900–1500 Mon–Fri
Bank Terminal 5 Baggage Claim Area ⏱0730–2230
Bank Terminal 5 Departure Hall ⏱0630–2100
Bank Sky City ⏱0900–1600 Mon–Fri
Bureau de change Terminal 2 Departure Hall ⏱0530–2230
Bureau de change Terminal 5 (5 locations) Departure Hall ⏱0530–2030
Bureau de change Sky City ⏱All flight times

Food and drink
Bar Terminal 2 Transit Area
Bar Terminal 5 Departure/Transit Area
Bar Terminal 4 Sky City Level 1
Café/light meals Terminal 2 Level 1 and Departure Area
Café/light meals Terminal 3
Café/light meals Terminal 4
Café/light meals Terminal 5 Departure/Arrival Hall
Café/light meals Sky City
Restaurant Terminal 2 Departure/Arrival Hall
Restaurant Terminal 2 Transit Hall
Restaurant Terminal 4
Restaurant Terminal 5 Departure Hall
Restaurant Terminal 5 Arrival Hall
Restaurant Terminal 5 Transit Hall Pier A
Restaurant Terminal 5 Transit Hall Pier B
Restaurant Sky City

Communications
Fax service Terminal 2 CAA Information counter ⏱24 hr
Fax service Terminal 4 SAS Service Centre ⏱All flight times
Fax service Terminal 5 Arlanda Service
Fax service Terminal 5 CAA Information desk ⏱24 hr
Fax service Sky City
Post office Sky City ⏱0830–1800 Mon–Fri

Shopping
Duty free, departure Terminal 2 Transit Hall ⏱All flight times
Shopping mall Terminal 2 Transit Area ⏱All flight times
Shopping mall Terminal 4 Sky City ⏱All flight times
Duty free, departure Terminal 5 Transit Hall Piers A and B ⏱All flight times
Shopping mall Terminal 5 Transit Area ⏱All flight times
Shopping mall Sky City ⏱All flight times

Luggage
Left Luggage Counter Terminal 2 Near CAA Information desk
Lockers Terminal 2 ⏱24 hr
Trolleys/carts Terminal 2 ⏱24 hr ⟠SEK1
Left Luggage Counter Terminal 4 CAA Information desk
Lockers Terminal 4 Sky City Level 1 ⏱24 hr
Trolleys/carts Terminal 4 ⏱24 hr ⟠SEK1
Left Luggage Counter Terminal 5 Arlanda Service ⏱0600–2330
Lockers Terminal 5 Level 1 Departure Hall ⏱24 hr
Trolleys/carts Terminal 5 Departure Hall Level 1 ⏱24 hr ⟠SEK1

DISABLED TRAVELLERS
Terminal 2 Adapted toilets; Lifts; Personal assistance Via airline or at check-in
Terminal 4 Adapted toilets; Lifts Phones at wheelchair height; Personal assistance Via airlines or at check-in
Terminal 5 Adapted toilets; Lifts; Personal assistance Via airlines or at check-in

---

✆ Phone no. 🖷 Fax no. ⏱ Hours of opening/operation ⟫ Frequency of service ⟳ Journey time ⟠ Cost/one-way fare

SMOKING POLICY

Terminal 5 Very limited smoking area near Satellite end

SPECIAL PASSENGER LOUNGES

All airlines **Lindbergh Lounge** Terminal 2 Business class passengers
SAS Stockholm Lounge Terminal 4 SK passengers and LHcard holders
All other international flights **Linné Lounge** Terminal 5 Transit Hall Business class passengers and card holders of AF, CA, IB, KL, (Aircardplus), LO, LY, MA, OK, SU, TE, TK, TP, OV
British Airways Executive Club Lounge Terminal 5 Between Transit Halls Club members and AAcard holders
SAS EuroClass Lounge Terminal 5 Departure Area Level 3 Business class passengers of SK and BT, FI, JZ, LH, SK, TG, UA
SAS Royal Viking Club Lounge Terminal 5 Between Transit Halls Club members, LHcard holders and First class passengers of TG

CONFERENCE AND BUSINESS FACILITIES

Arlanda Conference Room, Sky City ℂ797 62 00 ℉593 620 61 ⏰0730–2300 Mon–Fri; 0900–1800 Sat–Sun
Telephones, Fax service, Power points, Modem Points, Photocopier, Secretarial service

AIRPORT HOTELS

Day hotel rooms 3 rooms in Terminal 5 Departures/Arrivals area. Book in person via Information Desks
Good Morning Hotels ℂ655 0100
Nova Park ℂ(018) 349000
Radisson SAS SkyCity ℂ590 77300 ℉595 781 00. 230 rooms
Radisson Arlandia ℂ593 61800

CAR RENTAL

Avis Airport car hire area. Free Phones in terminal for shuttle bus ℂ797 9970
Budget Airport car hire area. Phones in terminal ℂ797 8470
EuropCar/Interrent Airport car hire area. Phones in terminal ℂ593 60940
Hertz Airport car hire area Phones in terminal for shuttle bus ℂ797 99 00

CAR PARKING

Long-stay Beyond Arlandia Hotel (shuttle bus) 5000 spaces ⌀SEK10 per hr; SEK60 per day for the first 3 days then SEK10 per day
Short-stay Multi-storey and open space next to terminals 4000 spaces ⌀SEK10 first hr; SEK25 per hr thereafter; SEK120 per day

TAXIS AND CHAUFFEUR-DRIVEN CARS

Taxis
Taxi stands outside terminals ℂ797 5078
City centre ⌚40 min ⌀Choice of fixed prices and metered

Chauffeur-driven cars
Via SAS Limousines Desks terminals 4 and 5 SAS Limousines ℂ797 3700

PUBLIC TRANSPORT

Airport to airport
Stockholm-Bromma Apt 🚌 SL ≫20 min ⏰0710–2040 ⌚50 min ⌀SEK50.

City & suburbs
Stockholm city centre 🚆 SJ ≫5–10 min ⏰0430–2300 ⌚40 min ⌀SEK50.

Other towns and cities
Enköping 🚆 UL.
Uppsala 🚆 UL ≫15 min ⌀SEK75.
Västerås 🚆 SJ

REGIONAL AIR CONNECTIONS

Borlange ✈ ≫Several per day ⌚35 min
Copenhagen ✈ ≫Several per day ⌚1 hr 10 min
Gothenburg ✈ ≫Several per day ⌚1 hr
Hagfors ✈ ≫Several per week ⌚45 min
Halmstad ✈ ≫Several per day ⌚1 hr
Helsingborg ✈ ≫Several per day ⌚1 hr
Helsinki ✈ ≫Several per day ⌚55 min
Jonköping ✈ ≫At least daily ⌚45 min
Kalmar ✈ ≫Several per day ⌚50 min
Karlstad ✈ ≫Several per day ⌚45 min
Kramfors ✈ ≫Several per day ⌚1 hr
Kristianstad ✈ ≫Several per day ⌚1 hr
Linköping ✈ ≫Several per week ⌚45 min
Malmö ✈ ≫Several per day ⌚1 hr 5 min
Mora ✈ ≫Several per day ⌚1 hr 5 min
Norrköping ✈ ≫Several per week ⌚35 min
Örebro ✈ ≫Several per week ⌚35 min
Örnsköldsvik ✈ ≫Several per day ⌚1 hr 5 min
Oslo ✈ ≫Several per day ⌚55 min
Ostersund ✈ ≫Several per day ⌚1 hr
Ronneby ✈ ≫Several per day ⌚55 min
Sundsvall ✈ ≫Several per day ⌚50 min
Trollhättan ✈ ≫Several per week ⌚55 min
Visby ✈ ≫Several per day ⌚45 min

TRAVELLER'S NOTES

To collect refunds on gifts and souvenirs when leaving Sweden, go to the tax-free collection counter at the airport hall with documents and the items.

Strasbourg — SXB

France (see page 22)

National ℂ code: 33
Local time: Winter GMT+1, Summer GMT+2
Address: Aeroport International Strasbourg-Entzheim, Direction Commerciale, F-67960 Entzheim
ℂ: 88 64 67 67
℻: 88 64 67 64
Location: 16kms/10mls W of Strasbourg

Terminals and Transfers

Terminals
Main Terminal Airlines: Air InterEurope, Air France, Air Liberté, Air Littoral, British Airways, Sabena, TAT. Layout: two floors; arrivals and departures lounge on ground floor.

Information

Flight enquiries
Airport ℂ 88 64 67 67
Air Inter Europe/Air France ℂ 08 02 80 28 02, Air Liberté ℂ 08 03 09 09 09/88 64 69 00, Air Littoral ℂ 88 68 65 30, British Airways ℂ 88 64 69 24, Sabena ℂ 88 64 67 80, TAT ℂ 08 03 80 58 05
Information and help desks Ground floor, arrivals lounge. Photocopying, tourist information, taxi booking service

Emergencies
Police Ground floor, departures lounge
Medical Ground floor, arrivals lounge
Lost Property Ground floor, arrivals lounge

Airport Facilities

Money
Bureau de Change ℂ 88 64 69 80
ATM Ground floor, main transit area
ATM Ground floor, departures lounge by Sabena desk

Food and drink
Bar Ground floor, main transit area ⓞ 0530–2300 ℂ 88 68 80 48
Bar First floor ⓞ 0530–2300 ℂ 88 68 80 48
Bar Ground floor, arrivals lounge c 0530–2300 ℂ 88 68 80 48
Restaurant First floor ⓞ 1130–2200 ℂ 88 68 80 48
Restaurant First floor ⓞ 1130–1500 Sun–Fri ℂ 88 68 80 48

Shopping
Duty free Ground floor, departures lounge ℂ 88 68 90 09
Gift Shop Ground floor, main transit area ⓞ 0530–2300 Mon–Sun ℂ 88 68 60 16
Gift Shop Ground floor, departure lounge ⓞ 0530–2300 Mon–Sun ℂ 88 68 60 16

Luggage
Trolleys/carts Ground floor, departures lounge

Disabled Travellers

Lift, disabled toilets

Conference and Business Facilities

ℂ 88 64 67 67

Car Rental

Avis Ground floor, arrivals lounge ℂ 88 68 82 53
Budget Ground floor, arrivals lounge ℂ 88 64 69 40
Europcar Ground floor, arrivals lounge ℂ 88 68 95 55
Hertz Ground floor, arrivals lounge ℂ 88 64 69 50/88 68 67 67

Car Parking

Short-stay P0 ⊘ free per first 15 min then FRF10 per hr; FRF300 per day. ℂ 88 64 69 49
Long-stay P1/P2 ⊘ FRF10 per hr; FRF20 per 2 hr; FRF30 per 2–4 hr; FRF45 per 4–6 hr; FRF65 per 6–12 hr; FRF100 per first 24 hr. ℂ 88 64 69 49
Underground P3 ⊘ FRF10 per hr; FRF20 per 2 hr; FRF30 per 2–4 hr; FRF50 per 4–6 hr; FRF75 per 6–12 hr; FRF120 per first 24 hr. ℂ 88 64 69 49

Taxis and Chauffeur-driven Cars Taxis

Strasbourg Taxis available to city centre

Public Transport

City & suburbs
Strasbourg (place de la gare) 🚌 Navette Bus ⊘ FRF37 » 30 min Mon–Fri (avg. 1 hr Sat–Sun) ➲ 25 min ⓞ 0530–2330 Mon–Fri; 0600–2300 Sat–Sun

Other cities and towns
Colmar 🚆 »Several per day ➲35 min
Kehl am Läger 🚌 Navette Bus ⊘ FRF42 ➲ 25 min ⓞ 0850–1935 Mon–Fri
Offenbourg Bahnhof 🚌 Navette Bus ⊘ FRF58 ➲ 50 min ⓞ 0850–1935 Mon–Fri
Metz 🚆 »Several per day ➲1 hr 20 min
Nancy 🚆 »Several per day ➲1 hr 15 min

Regional Air Connections

Clermont-Ferrand ✈ »Several per day ➲1 hr 15 min
Lille ✈ »Several per day ➲1 hr 10 min
Lyon ✈ »Several per day ➲55 min
St Etienne ✈ »Several per day ➲1 hr 15 min

ℂ Phone no. ℻ Fax no. ⓞ Hours of opening/operation » Frequency of service ➲ Journey time ⊘ Cost/one-way fare

Stuttgart   STR

Germany (see page 22)

National ✆ code: 49
Area ✆ code: 711
Local time: Winter GMT+1, Summer GMT+2
Address: Flughafen Stuttgart GmbH, Postfach 23 04 61, 70624 Stuttgart
✆: 948 0
🖷: 948 2241
Location: 13 km/21 miles S of Stuttgart

TERMINALS AND TRANSFERS

Terminals
Three Terminals Airlines: Air France, Alitalia, Austrian Airlines, British Airways, Condor, Czech Airlines, Delta Airlines, Deutsche BA, Deutsche Lufthansa, Eurowings, Hapag Lloyd, Iberia, Istanbul Airlines, KLM, LOT, LTU, Malev, Olympic Airways, Onur Air, Regional Airlines, Sabena, SAS, Swissair, Turkish Airlines, Tyrolean Airways

Minimum transfer times
30 min

INFORMATION

Flight enquiries
Airport ✆ 948 3388 ⊙ 0600–2300 Mon–Sun
Air France ✆ 948 4711, Alitalia ✆ 7 90 81 21, Austrian Airlines ✆ 948 4350, British Airways ✆ 948 47 67, Condor ✆ 948 27 59, Czech Airlines ✆ 948 40 20, Delta Airlines ✆ 948 49 69, Deutsche BA ✆ 948 47 67, Deutsche Lufthansa ✆ 948 44 69, Eurowings ✆ 948 49 67, Hapag Lloyd ✆ 948 47 97, Iberia ✆ 948 47 70, Istanbul Airlines ✆ 948 40 12, KLM ✆ 948 27 67, LOT ✆ 948 46 97, LTU ✆ 948 44 24, Malev ✆ 948 22 76, Olympic Airways ✆ 948 49 94, Onur Air ✆ 948 41 11, Regional Airlines ✆ 948 46 92, Sabena ✆ 948 30 00, SAS ✆ 79 90 56 59, Swissair ✆ 948 43 50, Turkish Airlines ✆ 948 47 27, Tyrolean Airways ✆ 948 43 50

Information and help desks
Information Terminal 1, departures ⊙ 0500–2230 ✆ 948 2790 ⊙ 0530–2230
Hotel Reservations Terminal 1, arrivals

Emergencies
Police ✆ 948 2121
Medical ✆ 948 3387
Lost Property ✆ 948 3355

AIRPORT FACILITIES

Money
Bureau de Change Terminal 1, arrivals ⊙ 0730–2100 Mon–Sat; 0830–2100 Sun ✆ 948 44 91
ATM Terminal 1, arrivals

Food and drink
Café/light meals Terminal 1 ⊙ 0430–2000
Café/light meals Terminal 3 ⊙ 0430–2000
Restaurant Terminal 1 ⊙ 0530–2400 ✆ 948 2137
Restaurant Terminal 3 ⊙ 0530–2400 ✆ 948 2720

Communications
Post Office Terminal 1 ⊙ 0700–1840 Mon–Fri; Sat–Sun 0830–1400

Shopping
Duty free Terminal 1 ⊙ 0430–2400
Duty free Terminal 3 ⊙ 0430–2400
News, Stationery & Books Terminal 1
Gift Shop Terminal 1

Luggage
Lockers Terminal 3 ⌀ DEM0.50–DEM1 per item per 24 hr
Trolleys and carts Available

DISABLED TRAVELLERS

Disabled toilets, lifts, telephones, special parking facilities

SPECIAL PASSENGER LOUNGES

Lufthansa Lounge Terminal 1
British Airways Lounge Terminal 1
Swissair Lounge Terminal 1
Diners Club Lounge Terminal 3

CONFERENCE AND BUSINESS FACILITIES

Terminal 1 ⊙ 0700–2200 ✆ 948 4582/2700 Interpreter, typing service, catering

CAR RENTAL

Alamo Terminal 1, arrivals ⊙ 0800–2200 ✆ 948 4422
Avis Terminal 1, arrivals ⊙ 0800–2200 ✆ 948 4451
Hertz Terminal 1, arrivals ⊙ 0800–2200 ✆ 948 4339/4448

CAR PARKING

Short-stay ⌀ DEM2–3 per 30 min; DEM20–35 per day
Long-stay ⌀ DEM1–2 per 30 min; DEM18–25 per day; DEM80–90 per week

TAXIS AND CHAUFFEUR-DRIVEN CARS

Taxis
Stuttgart City centre ⌀ DEM50.

PUBLIC TRANSPORT

City & suburbs
🚆 ⌀ ≫ Stuttgart Hbf ➡ VVS ⟳ 27 min ≫ 10–20 min ✆ 2092 4733

Other towns and cities
Karlsruhe ➡ ≫Several per day ⟳1 hr 20 min

REGIONAL AIR CONNECTIONS

Saarbrucken ✈ ≫1 per day ⟳30 min

SYDNEY   SYD

Australia (see page 14)

National ✆ code: 61
Area ✆ code: 02
Local time: Winter GMT+11, Summer GMT+10
Sydney (Kingsford Smith) International Airport, Airport Central, Level 10, 241 O'Riordan Street, Mascot, NSW 2020, Australia
✆667 9111
fax 667 1592
Location: 9 km/6 miles S of Sydney

Airport Facilities

Money
Thomas Cook bureau de change
International Terminal Landside arrivals
⏱0530–last flight
Thomas Cook bureau de change
International Terminal Landside departures ⏱0530–last flight
Thomas Cook bureau de change
International Terminal Airside arrivals
⏱0530–last flight
Thomas Cook bureau de change
International Terminal Airside departures
⏱0530–last flight

Food and drink
Bar International Terminal Landside departures

Terminals and Transfers

Terminals
International Terminal Airlines: All other airlines, Qantas Airways (Flight numbers QF1 to QF399). Layout: Ground Floor, Arrival; First Floor, Departure
Ansett Terminal Airlines: Ansett Australia, KLM (Flights 4028–4249), Malaysian Airlines (Flights 122–123 and 9019–9128), United Airlines (Except flights 815–863).
Commuter Centre Terminal R Airlines: Ansett Australia (Flights 7150–7225).
Qantas Terminal Airlines: Qantas Airways.

Minimum transfer times
International: 1–2 hr **Domestic:** 30 min–1 hr

Transfer between terminals
Bus ≫15–30 min; Domestic and International Terminals ⌀AUD2.50 (Adult); AUD1.50 (Child)

Information

Information and help desks
Hotel Reservations Desk International Terminal Tourism information centre ✆9667 6051 ⏱0500–2200 Hotel booking.
Travellers Information Service International Terminal Arrival Level 1

Emergencies

Medical International Terminal Departures Level 2 ✆9317 3944 ⏱0800–1700 Mon-Fri; 0800–1400 Sat, Sun

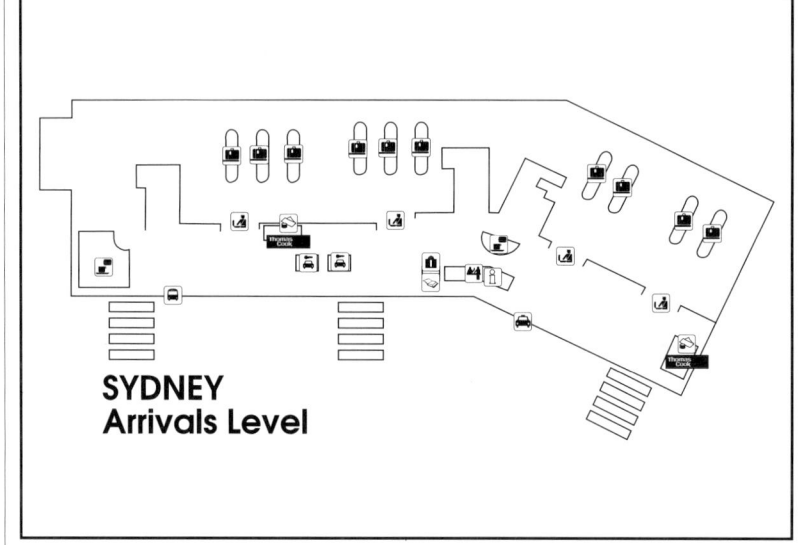

SYDNEY Arrivals Level

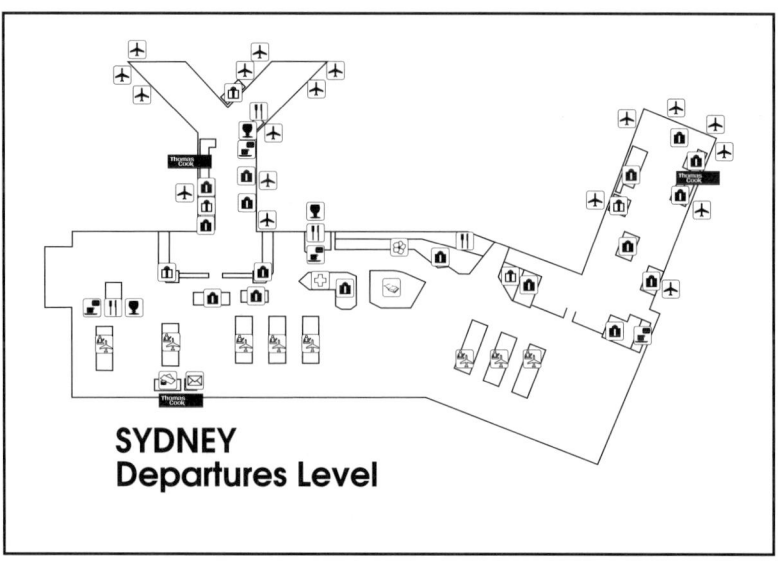

SYDNEY Departures Level

✆ Phone no. fax Fax no. ⏱ Hours of opening/operation ≫ Frequency of service ⤳ Journey time ⌀ Cost/one-way fare

SECTION TWO • AIRPORT DIRECTORY

SYDNEY

Bar International Terminal Landside arrivals
Bar International Terminal Airside departures
Café/light meals International Terminal Departures level ⓒ0600–2230
Restaurant International Terminal Third floor ⓒ1200–1430 and 1730–2000

Communications

Post office International Terminal Departures Level 2 ⓒ0700–1700 daily

Shopping

Duty free, arrival International Terminal Arrival hall ⓒOpen for all flights
Duty free, departure International Terminal Departure hall ⓒOpen for all flights
Pharmacy International Terminal Departure hall ⓒOpen for all flights
Shopping mall International Terminal ⓒOpen for all flights

Luggage

Lockers International Terminal Arrival Level 1 opposite the information counter and Departures Level 2 ⓒ0500–last flight ⬦AUD6–10 per day
Trolleys/Carts Available from trolley bays in car park and on departures concourse ⬦AUD2

DISABLED TRAVELLERS

International Terminal Adapted toilets; Lifts; Special car parking; Phones at wheelchair height
Ansett Terminal Adapted toilets; Lifts; Special car parking; Phones at wheelchair height
Commuter Centre Terminal R Adapted toilets; Lifts; Special car parking; Phones at wheelchair height
Qantas Terminal Adapted toilets; Lifts; Special car parking; Phones at wheelchair height

SMOKING POLICY

International Terminal Smoking restricted throughout terminal
Ansett Terminal Smoking restricted throughout terminal

SPECIAL PASSENGER LOUNGES

Air New Zealand Lounge International Terminal First class passengers
Ansett Australia Lounge International Terminal
British Airways Lounge International Terminal
Cathay Pacific Airways Lounge International Terminal
Japan Airlines Lounge International Terminal
Qantas Airways Captain's Club Lounge International Terminal
Singapore Airlines Lounge International Terminal
Thai Airways Lounge International Terminal
United Airlines Lounge International Terminal

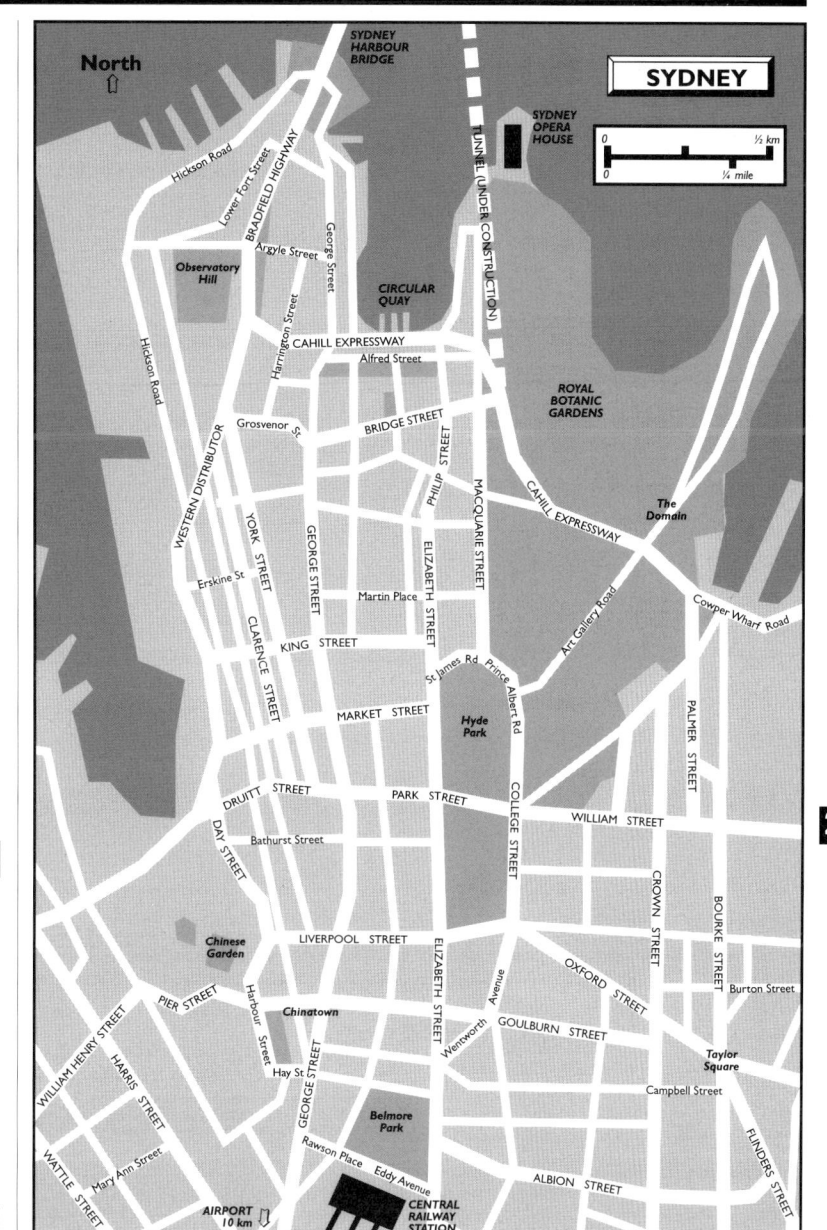

AIRPORT HOTELS

Airport Hilton International ⓒ597 0122
Airport Sydney International Motor Inn ⓒ556 1555
Sheraton Sydney Airport ⓒ317 2200
Sydney Airport Parkroyal ⓒ330 0600
Novotel Brighton Beach ⓒ597 7111

CAR RENTAL

Avis International Terminal ⓒ667 0667
Budget International Terminal ⓒ669 2121
Hertz International Terminal ⓒ669 2444
Thrifty International Terminal ⓒ669 6677

✈ Air 🚆 Rail 🚌 Bus 🚐 Limousine Ⓜ Metro/subway 🚋 Tram 🚁 Helicopter ⛴ Water transport • For map symbols, see p. 9

SYDNEY • TAIPEI   SECTION TWO • AIRPORT DIRECTORY

Car Parking
Long-stay Near the domestic terminals and past the Heliport ⌀AUD10 per day (minimum charge AUD20) ✆669 6163. Free shuttle available to Domestic (»10–15 min) and International (»30 min) Terminals.
Short-stay In front of International Terminal ⌀AUD2.50 per 30 min; AUD20 per 24 hr ✆669 3693

Taxis and Chauffeur-driven Cars
Taxis
Legion Cabs ✆289 9000 City centre ⟿30 min ⌀AUD16–20
ABC Radio Cabs ✆9897 4000 City centre ⟿30 min ⌀AUD16–20

Public Transport
City & suburbs
Sydney (Kings Cross) 🚆 Kingsford Smith Bus Service »10–15 min ⏲0600–last flight ⌀AUD6 ✆667 3221
Sydney city centre 🚆 Airport Express Bus: Service 350/300 »15 min ⏲0555–2300 ⟿40 min ⌀AUD5.50 ✆131 500

Courtesy/special transport
Darling Harbour 🚆 Airporter Bus Service »30 min ⏲0530–2300 ⌀AUD6.

Other towns and cities
Wollongong NSW 🚆 Nowra Coaches »Five times daily ⏲0730–1815 ⟿1 hr 45 min ⌀AUD15.

Regional Air Connections
Canberra ACT ✈ »Several per day ⟿50 min
Coffs Harbour NSW ✈ »Several per day ⟿55 min
Cooma NSW ✈ »Several per day ⟿55 min
Maitland NSW ✈ »Several per day ⟿35 min
Moruya NSW ✈ »Several per day ⟿45 min
Newcastle NSW ✈ »Several per day ⟿30 min
Singleton NSW ✈ »At least daily ⟿50 min
Taree NSW ✈ »At least daily ⟿50 min

Traveller's Notes
Taxis are plentiful and not expensive. Customs and quarantine regulations are strict – be careful to make appropriate declarations on your in-bound flight.

272

Taipei-Chiang Kai Shek   TPE
Taiwan (see page 38)

National ✆ code: 886
Area ✆ code: 02
Local time: Winter GMT+8, Summer GMT+8
Taipei-Chiang Kai Shek International Airport, PO Box 9, Taipei, Taiwan
✆398 2001
📠383 4801
Location: 40 km/25 miles SW of Taipei

Terminals and Transfers
Terminals
Main Terminal Airlines: All international flights.

Minimum transfer times
International: 1 hr

Information
Flight enquiries
Airport ✆398 2050
Cathay Pacific Airways ✆398 2388 **China Airlines** ✆398 2968 **Malaysian Airlines** ✆383 4855 **Northwest Airlines** ✆398 2471 **Philippine Airlines** ✆398 2419 **Singapore Airlines** ✆398 2491 **Thai Airways** ✆398 2404 **United Airlines** ✆398 2781

Information and help desks
Airport Information Desk Main Terminal Departure Lobby ✆398 2143 ⏲0800–2000 *Airport information.*
Tourist Information Desk Main Terminal Arrival Lobby ✆383 4631 ✆383 4250 ⏲0630–0200 *Tourist information*

Emergencies
Lost Property Main Terminal Area B1 from stairs, near UA counter ✆398 2538

Airport Facilities
Money
Bank Main Terminal Various, all floors ⏲0600–2200

Food and drink
Restaurant Main Terminal Third Floor, Departure Hall ⏲0930–2400
Café/light meals Main Terminal Arrival Hall ⏲0600–2200
Café/light meals Main Terminal Departure Concourse; ⏲0600–2130
Café/light meals Main Terminal Basement Level ⏲0730–1930

✆ Phone no.   📠 Fax no.   ⏲ Hours of opening/operation   » Frequency of service   ⟿ Journey time   ⌀ Cost/one-way fare

SECTION TWO • AIRPORT DIRECTORY — TAIPEI

Communications
Post office Main Terminal South end of Departure Lobby (2 others) ⓣ0900–1700 Mon–Fri; 0900–1200 Sat

Shopping
Shopping mall Main Terminal Near Departure Concourse
Duty free, departure Main Terminal Near boading gates no. 6 and no. 17

Luggage
Left luggage counter Main Terminal Departure Hall ⓣ0800–2000

DISABLED TRAVELLERS
Main Terminal Adapted toilets; Lifts; Phones at wheelchair height

SPECIAL PASSENGER LOUNGES
EG Lounge Main Terminal North of Terminal, Second Floor
Cathay Pacific Airways Lounge Main Terminal South of Terminal, Fourth Floor
China Airlines Lounge Main Terminal North of Terminal Fourth Floor
Korean Airlines EVA VIP Lounge Main Terminal South of Terminal, Fourth Floor
Malaysian Airlines Lounge Main Terminal South of Terminal, Second Floor
Northwest Airlines Lounge Main Terminal South of Terminal, Second Floor
Philippine Airlines PR Lounge Main Terminal South of Main Terminal, Second Floor
Singapore Airlines SQ Lounge Main Terminal South of Main Terminal, Second Floor
Thai Airways TG Lounge Main Terminal South of Main Terminal, Second Floor
United Airlines UA Lounge Main Terminal North of Main Terminal, Second Floor

CONFERENCE AND BUSINESS FACILITIES
Conference Room, Airport Hotel, 2 km/1 mile from terminal ⓒ(Hotel) 383 3666 ⓕ(Hotel) 383 3546

AIRPORT HOTELS
Airport Hotel ⓒ383 3666 ⓕ383 3546 *Courtesy bus*

CAR RENTAL
Avis Main Terminal Arrival lobby
Union Main Terminal Arrival lobby

CAR PARKING
Short-stay 2317 spaces ⌀TWD 30 first hr, then TWD 20 per 30 min; TWD 490 per day

TAXIS AND CHAUFFEUR-DRIVEN CARS
Taxis
City centre ⟶Approx 40 min ⌀Approx TWD750–900 (meter+service charge)

PUBLIC TRANSPORT
Airport to airport
Taipei Sung Shan Apt 🚌Taiwan Bus Co »15–20 min ⓘEarly am–late pm ⟶40–50 min ⌀TWD115. *Calls at several hotels, Taipei rail stn, Taipei-Chungluen bus terminal, Sung Shan domestic airport.*

City & suburbs
Taipei (Howard Plaza Hotel) 🚌Gray Line
Taipei city centre 🚌 ⟶Approx 60 min ⌀TWD65.

Other towns and cities
Kaohsiung City 🚌
Hsinchu 🚌
Taichung 🚌
Tainan 🚌

REGIONAL AIR CONNECTIONS
Chiayi ✈ »Several per day ⟶45 min
Hualien ✈ »Several per day ⟶35 min
Kaohsiung ✈ »Several per day ⟶50 min
Kinmen ✈ »Several per day ⟶55 min
Makung ✈ »Several per day ⟶45 min
Pingtung ✈ »Several per day ⟶1 hr
Taichung ✈ »Several per day ⟶35 min
Tainan ✈ »Several per day ⟶45 min
Taitung ✈ »Several per day ⟶50 min

AIRPORT TAX
Airport tax of TWD300 is payable on international departures.

TRAVELLER'S NOTES
The domestic airport is Sung Shan (TSA). Allow 3 hours between arrival and departure if transferring from an international flight to TPE flight and a domestic one from TSA or vice versa.

✈ Air 🚆 Rail 🚌 Bus 🚐 Limousine Ⓜ Metro/subway 🚋 Tram 🚁 Helicopter ⛴ Water transport • For map symbols, see p. 9

TEESSIDE MME

United Kingdom (see page 41)

National ✆ code: 44
Area ✆ code: 01325
Local time: Winter GMT, Summer GMT+1
Address: Teesside International Airport, Darlington, Co. Durham DL2 1LU
✆: 332811
🖷: 332810
Location: 10 km/6 miles E of Darlington

TERMINALS AND TRANSFERS

Terminals
Main Terminal Airlines: Air Kilroe, Air UK, British Midland. Layout: two international and two domestic departure gates. Main terminal on one level only.

INFORMATION

Flight enquiries
Air Kilroe ✆ (0161) 436 2055, Air UK (0345) 666 777, British Midland ✆ (0345) 554 554

Information and help desks
Information desk Outside entrance to terminal building ✆ 332 811 flight information, general enquiries

AIRPORT FACILITIES

Money
Thomas Cook Bureau de Change Main terminal and international arrivals hall ✆ 333809

Food and drink
Bar Passenger terminal main concourse
Café/light meals International departure hall and British Midland departure hall
Restaurant Passenger terminal main concourse

Communications
Post box Main terminal

Shopping
Duty free International departure lounge ✆ 333881
News, Stationery & Books Main concourse
Gift Shop Back of main terminal, next to security area

Luggage
Trolleys/carts

DISABLED TRAVELLERS

Telephones, disabled toilets, wheelchairs

SPECIAL PASSENGER LOUNGE

British Midland Diamond Lounge By gate 4, departure lounge

CONFERENCE AND BUSINESS FACILITIES

Airport information centre facsimile, telephone, telex, postal facilities ✆ 332 811
VIP/CIP Lounge available for business use ✆ 332 811

CAR RENTAL

Avis Main arrivals hall ✆ 332091
Hertz Main arrivals hall ✆ 332600
Europcar Main arrivals hall ✆ 333329

CAR PARKING

Opposite terminal building ⊘ GBP free per first 20 min; GBP1 up to 4 hr; GBP3 per 24hr for first 48 hr; GBP2 per day 3–14 days; GBP16 per 7 days; GBP30 per 14 days or over. Maximum charge GBP30.

TAXIS AND CHAUFFEUR-DRIVEN CARS

Taxis
Arrivals hall, opposite car hire desk ✆ 332177

PUBLIC TRANSPORT

City & suburbs
Darlington city centre 🚌 United Buses ≫ 30 min ✆ 468 771

Other towns and cities
Hartlepool 🚌 ≫1 per hr ↻30 min
Middlesbrough 🚌 ≫1 per hr ↻30 min
York 🚌 ≫1 per hr ↻1 hr

✆ Phone no. 🖷 Fax no. ⏱ Hours of opening/operation ≫ Frequency of service ↻ Journey time ⊘ Cost/one-way fare

TEL AVIV　　　　　　　　　　　TLV

Israel (see page 26)

National ✆ code: 972
Area ✆ code: 03
Local time: Winter GMT+2,
Summer GMT+3
Tel Aviv-Ben Gurion Intenational Airport, PO Box 7 Ben Gurion Airport 70100, Tel Aviv, Israel
✆971 0111
🖷971 0367
Location: 20 km/12 miles SE of Tel Aviv

TERMINALS AND TRANSFERS

Terminals
Terminal 1 Airlines: All international flights.
Terminal 2 Airlines: Some international flights and all domestic flights.

Minimum transfer times
International: 1 hr 30 min **Domestic:** 1 hr 30 min

INFORMATION

Flight enquiries
Airport ✆971 0111

Information and help desks
Information Desk International Terminal ✆971 0111 Airport information.
Tourist Information Desk International Terminal ✆971 1485 Tourist information, hotel reservations ⏰24 hr

EMERGENCIES

Lost Property International Terminal ⏰24 hr

AIRPORT FACILITIES

Money
Bureau de change International Terminal Departure Hall ⏰All flight times
Bureau de change International Terminal Arrival Hall ⏰24 hr

Food and drink
Restaurant International Terminal Departure Lounge ⏰0700–last flight
Restaurant International Terminal East of the terminal ⏰0600–2400
Café/light meals International Terminal Departure Hall ⏰24 hr

Communications
Post office International Terminal ⏰24 hr Sun-Thu; 1400– Fri; 2100– Sat

Shopping
Duty free, departure International Terminal Departure Hall
Shopping mall International Terminal

Luggage
Left luggage counter International Terminal ⏰24 hrs

DISABLED TRAVELLERS

International Terminal Adapted toilets; Lifts; Phones at wheelchair height

SPECIAL PASSENGER LOUNGES

El Al Israel Airlines King David and Jetset Club International Terminal Also open to passengers of other airlines

CAR RENTAL

Avis International Terminal
Budget International Terminal
Hertz International Terminal

CAR PARKING

Long-stay 500 spaces ⌀ILS6 per day

TAXIS AND CHAUFFEUR-DRIVEN CARS

Taxis
City centre ⌀NIS 16

PUBLIC TRANSPORT

City & suburbs
Tel Aviv (central bus station) 🚌Egged, DAN, United Tours 475 »30–60 min ⏰0400–2359 (except Fri mid p.m.–Sat sunset) ➲45 min ⌀NIS 8.80.
Tel Aviv city centre 🚌 United Tours: bus 222 »1 hr ⏰0400–2359 (except Fri mid p.m.–Sat sunset) ➲45 min ⌀NIS10.50 (central station) NIS14 (hotel district – stops at most major hotels)

Other towns and cities
Be'er Sheva 🚌Egged ⏰No service Fri mid p.m.–Sat sunset ⌀NIS27.50.
Haifa 🚌Egged »30 min ⏰0700–2000 (except Fri mid p.m.–Sat sunset) ⌀NIS25
Jerusalem 🚌Egged »15–20 min ⏰0634–2340 (except Fri mid p.m.–Sat sunset) ⌀NIS18.30

REGIONAL AIR CONNECTIONS

Haifa ✈ »Several per week ➲30 min
Jerusalem ✈ »Several per week ➲20–30 min
Kiryat Shmona ✈ »At least daily ➲40 min
Masada ✈ »Several per week ➲1 hr
Rosh Pina ✈ »Several per week ➲35 min

AIRPORT TAX

Airport tax is USD13 and is usually included in the price of the ticket.

TENERIFE

Spain (see page 36)

National ✆ code: 34
Area ✆ code: 22
Local time: Winter GMT, Summer GMT+1
Address: Aeropuerto de Tenerife Sur, 38610 Granadilla-Tenerife
✆: 75 91 60
℻: 75 92 47
Location: 13kms/8mls NW of Santa Cruz

TERMINALS AND TRANSFERS

Terminals
Main Terminal Airlines: Air Europa, Iberia, Spanair

Information
Flight enquiries
Air Europa ✆ 75 90 52 ⏰ 0800–2100, Iberia ✆ 75 92 85 ⏰ 0700–1945 (from 0800 Tues and Thurs), Spanair ✆ 75 91 50 ⏰ 0800–1945
Information and help desks
Information Desk ✆ 75 92 00/75 95 10 ⏰ 24 hr Flight enquiries, airport information, lost property

Emergencies
Police ✆ 75 93 57 ⏰ 24 hr
Medical ✆ 75 93 05 ⏰ 24 hr
Lost Property Contact information desk ✆ 75 92 00/75 95 10

AIRPORT FACILITIES

Money
Bureau de Change ✆ 75 92 64/75 92 93 ⏰ 0800–1400 Mon–Fri

Food and drink
Café/light meals ✆ 75 95 20 ⏰ 24 hr
Café/light meals ✆ 75 95 20 ⏰ 0700–2300

Communications
Post office ✆ 75 90 00 ext. 596 25 ⏰ 0900–1300 Mon–Fri

Shopping
Duty free
News, Stationery & Books ✆ 75 92 79 ⏰ 0700–2200
Gift Shop ✆ 75 90 30 ⏰ 0600–2200

Luggage
Trolleys/carts ✆ 75 92 29 ⏰ 24 hr

DISABLED TRAVELLERS
✆ 75 92 29

CAR RENTAL
Atesa ✆ 75 94 75 ⏰ 0600–2400
Auto Reisen ✆ 75 93 64 ⏰ 0600–2400
Avis ✆ 77 06 56 ⏰ 0600–2400
Cicar ✆ 75 93 29 ⏰ 0600–2400
EuropCar ✆ 75 94 70 ⏰ 0600–2400
Hertz ✆ 75 90 59 ⏰ 0600–2400

TAXIS AND CHAUFFEUR-DRIVEN CARS

Taxis
Las Américas ⬌ ESP2200
Santa Cruz ⬌ ESP7000
Tenerife Sur to Tenerife Norte ⬌ ESP7400
Puerto de la Cruz ⬌ ESP10000
(T) 75 90 09 ⏰ 24 hr

PUBLIC TRANSPORT

Airport to Airport
Tenerife Sur to Tenerife Norte 🚌 340 » 4 per day ⏰ 0945; 1400; 2000; 2300 ⬌ ESP1075
Tenerife Norte to Tenerife Sur 🚌 340 » 4 per day ⏰ 0700; 1200; 1720; 2145 ⬌ ESP1075

City & suburbs
Tenerife Sur to Santa Cruz 🚌 341 » 1 per hr ⏰ 0650–0130 ⬌ ESP690
Tenerife Sur to Puerto de la Cruz 🚌 340 » 4 per day ⏰ 0945; 1400; 2000; 2300 ⬌ ESP1075
Tenefire Sur to Playa de las Américas 🚌 487 » 1 per hr ⏰ 0810–2200 ⬌ ESP250

REGIONAL AIR CONNECTIONS
Fuerteventura ✈ »Several per day ⏱45 min
Lanzarote ✈ »Several per day ⏱50 min
Las Palmas ✈ »Several per day ⏱30 min
Santa Cruz Palmas ✈ »Several per day ⏱30 min
Valverde ✈ »2 per day ⏱40 min

✆ Phone no. ℻ Fax no. ⏰ Hours of opening/operation » Frequency of service ⏱ Journey time ⬌ Cost/one-way fare

SECTION TWO • AIRPORT DIRECTORY   TOKYO-NARITA

TOKYO-NARITA   NRT

Japan (see page 28)

National ✆ code: 81
Area ✆ code: 03
Local time: Winter GMT+9, Summer GMT+9
New Tokyo International Airport (Narita Airport), PO Box 80, Narita-shi Chiba 282, Japan
✆476 34 5037
✆476 30 1571
WWW site: http://www.narita-airport.or.jp/airport/
Location: 65 km/40 miles E of Tokyo

TERMINALS AND TRANSFERS

Terminals

Terminal 1 Airlines: American Airlines, Air France, Finnair, Alitalia, British Airways, Canadian Airlines International, Cathay Pacific Airways, Korean Airlines, KLM, Lufthansa, Northwest Airlines, Varig Brazilian, Singapore Airlines, United Airlines, Virgin Atlantic. Layout: South Wing: Level 1 (1F) Arrival; Level 2 Immigration; Level 3 Departure; Level 4 Departure Lobby. Central Building. Level 0(B1F) JR/Keisei Railways Station; Level 1 Service facilities; Level 2 Food & Service facilities; Level 3 Service facilities; Level 4 Food/Shopping; Level 5 Food/Observation Deck

Terminal 2 Airlines: All other airlines.

Layout: Main building: Level 0 (B1F) JR/Kesei Railways Station; Level 1 Arrival lobby; Level 2 Arrival concourse/Shuttle stop; Level 3 Departure lobby/Departure concourses; Level 4 Restaurants and shopping mall, Observation Decks. Satellite building: Level 2 Arrival concourse; Level 3 Departure concourse/shuttle stop. Also includes Domestic Terminal.

Minimum transfer times
International: 1 hr–2 hr 10 min
Domestic: 30 min

Transfer between terminals
Bus ≫10 min; Terminals 1 and 2 ⊘Free

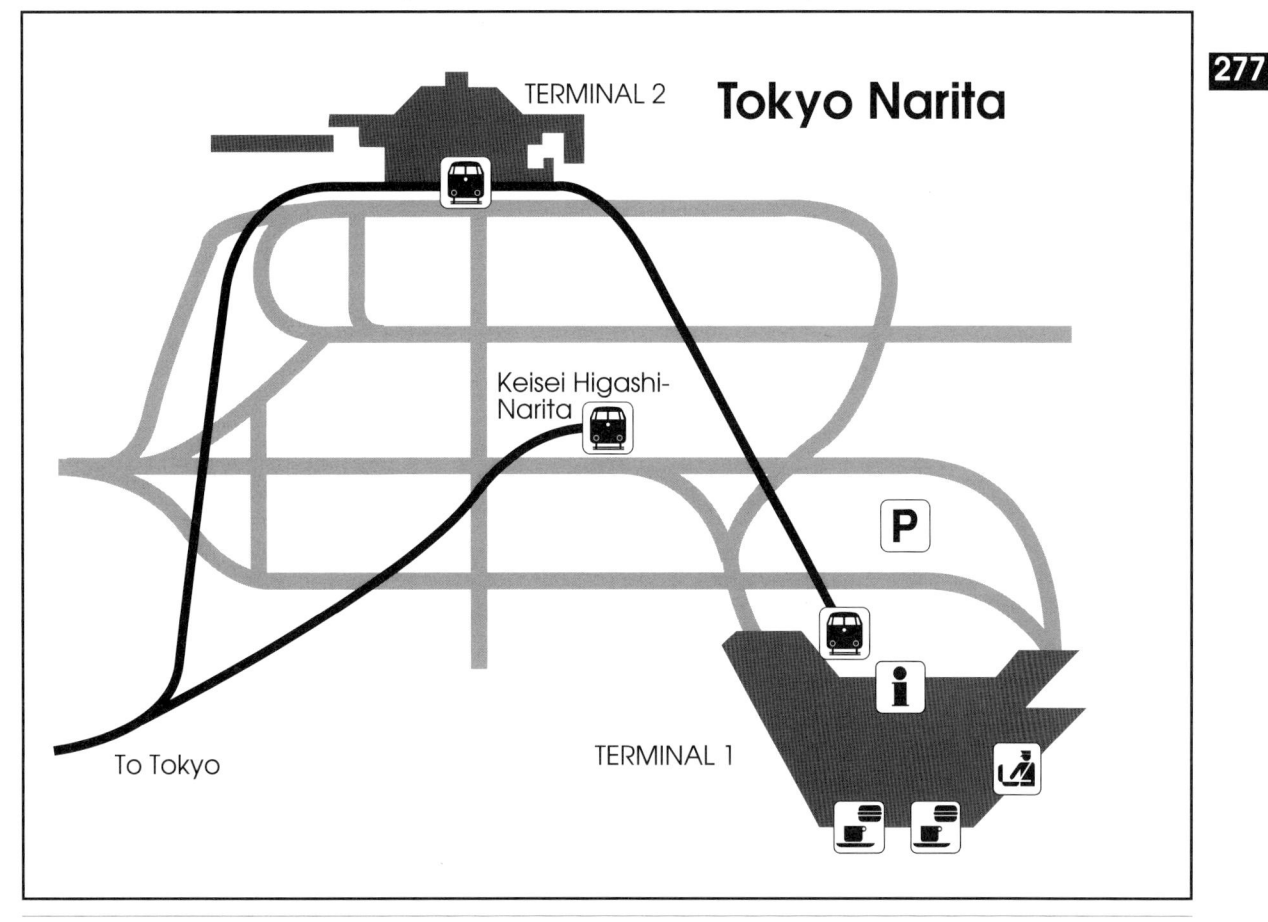

277

✈ Air 🚂 Rail 🚌 Bus 🚐 Limousine 🚇 Metro/subway 🚋 Tram 🚁 Helicopter ⛴ Water transport • For map symbols, see p. 9

TOKYO-NARITA

SECTION TWO • AIRPORT DIRECTORY

Information

Flight enquiries
Airport ✆476 34 5000
Aeroflot ✆0476 343 944 Air China ✆525 107 11 Air France ✆0476 32 7710 Air India ✆0476 348 261 Air Lanka ✆0476 348 350 Air New Zealand ✆0476 348 388 Air Pacific ✆343 513 71 Alitalia ✆0476 32 7811 All Nippon Airways ✆548 912 12 (international) 548 988 00 (domestic) American Airlines ✆321 421 11 Asiana Airlines ✆0476 348 311 Austrian Airlines ✆0476 348 411 Biman Bangladesh Airlines ✆350 279 22 British Airways ✆0476 327 222 Canadian Airlines International ✆0476 327 763 Cathay Pacific Airways ✆0476 327 650 China Eastern Airlines ✆0476 343 945 Continental Micronesia ✆476 348 358 Delta Airlines ✆527 570 00 Egyptair ✆0476 348 391 Finnair ✆0476 327 600 Garuda Indonesian Airlines ✆0476 348 377 Iberia ✆357 835 55 Iran Air ✆0476 348 372 Japan Air System ✆343 811 55 Japan Airlines ✆546 005 11 (international) 546 005 22 (domestic) Japan Asia Airways ✆546 005 33 KLM ✆0476 325 720 Korean Airlines ✆0476 327 561 Lufthansa ✆0476 327 511 Malaysian Airlines ✆0476 348 270 Northwest Airlines ✆0476 327 411 Pakistan International Airlines ✆0476 348 343 Philippine Airlines ✆0476 348 381 Qantas Airways ✆0476 348 285 Sabena World Airlines ✆0476 348 320 SAS ✆0476 348 415 Singapore Airlines ✆0476 327 591 Swissair ✆0476 348 430 Thai Airways ✆0476 348 329 Turkish Airlines ✆0476 348 310 United Airlines ✆381 744 11 Varig Brazilian ✆0476 327 890 Virgin Atlantic ✆0476 324 675

Information and help desks
Information Desk Terminal 1 Arrival Lobby, Level 1
Information Desk Terminal 2 Main building, Level 3 (2 desks)
Information Desk Terminal 2 Arrival Lobby, Level 1 (2 desks)
Information Desk Terminal 1 Level 3, South Wing

Emergencies

Medical Terminal 2 First underground level ✆0476 34 6119 ⊕0900–2200
Medical Terminal 1 First underground level ✆0476 32 88 77 ⊕0900–2200
Lost Property Terminal 2 Main Building Level 3 ✆34 5220
Lost Property Terminal 1 Central Building Level 3 ✆32 2105

Airport Facilities

Money
Bank Terminal 1 first and fourth floor
Bank Terminal 2 first, second and third floor
Bureau de change Terminal 1 First Floor ⊕0630–2300, fourth floor ⊕0700–2200
Bureau de change Terminal 2 First floor ⊕0630–2300, Third Floor ⊕0700–2200

Food and drink
Café/light meals Terminal 1 Central Building, all levels
Café/light meals Terminal 2 Main building, satellites, all levels exc. 0 (B1)
Restaurant Terminal 1 Central Building, levels 1, 2, 4
Restaurant Terminal 2 Main building, level 4

Communications
Post office Terminal 1 fourth floor ⊕0900–2030 ✆476 32 6760
Post office Terminal 1 Level 0 ⊕0900–1700 Mon–Fri; 0900–1230 Sat ✆476 32 6760
Post office Terminal 2 second floor ⊕0900–1700 Mon–Fri; 0900–1230 Sat ✆476 34 2250
Post office Terminal 2 third floor ⊕0900–2030 ✆476 34 2250
Post office Terminal 2 Level 2 ⊕0900–1700 Mon–Fri; 0900–1230 Sat
Fax service Terminal 2 Level 3, Business & Travel Center ⊕0700–2100

Shopping
Duty free, departure Terminal 1 Level 3
Florist Terminal 1 Level 4

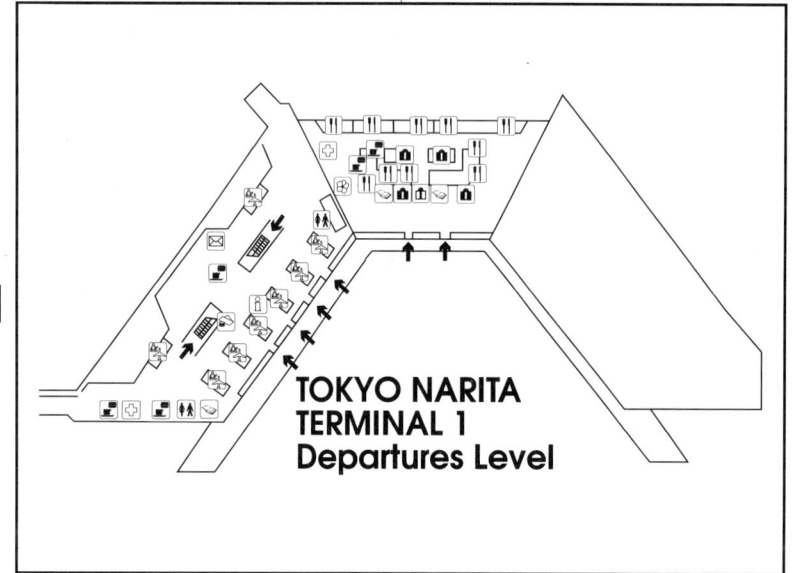

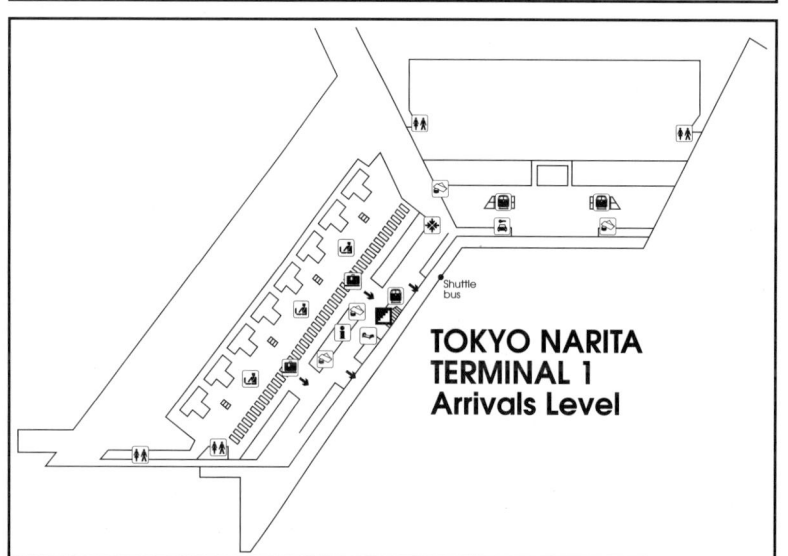

TOKYO NARITA TERMINAL 1 Departures Level

TOKYO NARITA TERMINAL 1 Arrivals Level

✆ Phone no. ℻ Fax no. ⊕ Hours of opening/operation ≫ Frequency of service ⊃ Journey time ◇ Cost/one-way fare

Shopping mall Terminal 1 Level 4
Florist Terminal 2 Level 4
Shopping mall Terminal 2 Level 4
Duty free, departure Terminal 2 Level 3 (main building and satellite)

Luggage

Left luggage counter Terminal 1 South Wing, levels 1 and 4
Trolleys/carts Terminal 1 South Wing, levels 1 and 4
Left luggage counter Terminal 2 Main building, levels 1 and 3
Trolleys/carts Terminal 2 Main Building, levels 1 and 3

Disabled Travellers

Terminal 1 Adapted toilets; Lifts
Terminal 2 Adapted toilets; Lifts

Smoking Policy

Terminal 1 Restricted
Terminal 2 Restricted

Special Passenger Lounges

VIP Lounges Terminal 1 First Floor, Fourth Floor, 5th Floor ⓘ0700–2400 ⓒ476 32 2364 Small lounge JPY7210, large lounge JPY62830
VIP Lounges Terminal 2 First Floor, Second Floor, Fourth Floor ⓘ0700–2400 ⓒ476 32 2364 Small lounge JPY7210, large lounge JPY62830

Conference and Business Facilities

Business & Travel Center, Terminal 2, Level 3 ⓒ476 34 8781 ⓘ0700–2100 Fax service, Photocopier, Secretarial service, Translation/Interpretation service.

Car Rental

Joint reception desk Terminal 2 ⓒ34 8464
Nippon Terminal 1 ⓒ32 8897
Nissan Terminal 1 ⓒ24 1023
Toyota Terminal 1 ⓒ32 8218

Car Parking

Short-stay In front of Terminals 1 and 2 spaces

Taxis and Chauffeur-driven Cars

Taxis
Terminal 1 South Wing, Level 1,
Terminal 2, Level 1 ⓒ32 8282 City centre ⓘ1 hr minimum ⌀JPY22000

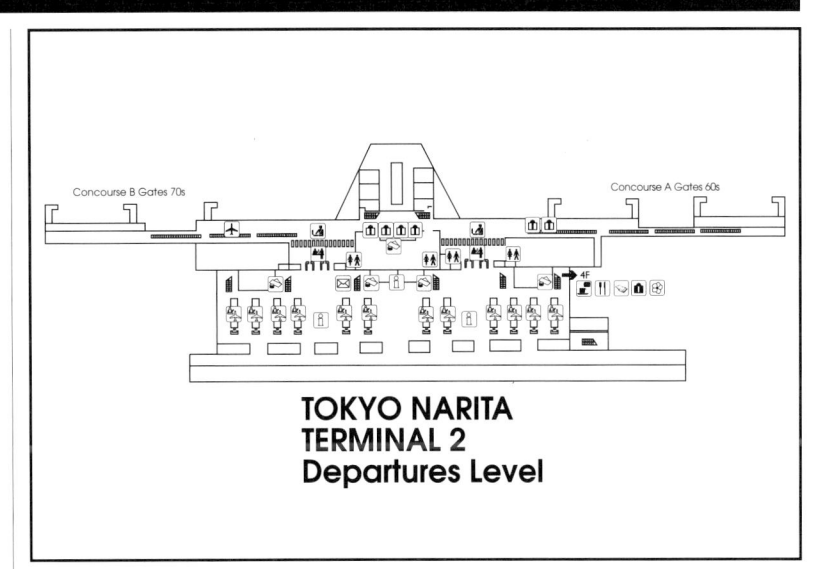

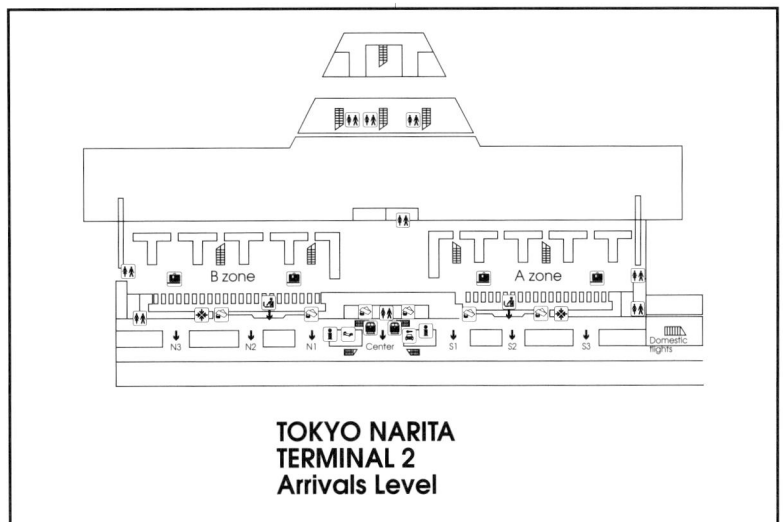

TOKYO NARITA TERMINAL 2 Departures Level

TOKYO NARITA TERMINAL 2 Arrivals Level

Public Transport

Airport to airport
Tokyo-Haneda Apt → Airport Limousine ⓘ75 min ⌀JPY2900. Reservations ⓒ3665 7220

City & suburbs
Tokyo City Air Terminal → Airport Limousine ⓘ10–15 min ⓘ55 min ⌀JPY2700. Reservations ⓒ366 572 20
Tokyo city centre → JR Narita Express ⓘ30 min (1 hr 1013–1413) ⓘ0743–2142 ⓘapprox 1 hr ⌀JPY2890.
Tokyo Ueno → Keisei Electric Railway G Class (Skyliners) ⓘapprox 40 min ⓘ0920–2158 ⓘ60 min ⌀JPY1880.
Tokyo Ueno → Keisei Electric Railway (S Class) ⓘapprox 20 min ⓘ0733–2243 ⓘ1 hr 30 min ⌀JPY980.

Other towns and cities
Yokohama → Airport Limousine ⓘ15–30 min ⓘ2 hr ⌀JPY3300. Reservations ⓒ3665 7220
Yokohama → JR Narita Express ⓘ30 min ⓘapprox 1 hr 40 min ⓘ0743–2143 ⌀JPY4100. Some direct services, but most involve a change of train in Tokyo main rail stn.

Regional Air Connections

Akita ✈ ⓘSeveral per day ⓘ1 hr
Hachijo Jima ✈ ⓘSeveral per day ⓘ45 min
Komatsu ✈ ⓘSeveral per day ⓘ1 hr
Miyake Jima ✈ ⓘSeveral per day ⓘ50 min
Nagoya ✈ ⓘSeveral per day ⓘ60–70 min
Oshima ✈ ⓘSeveral per day ⓘ40 min
Shonai ✈ ⓘSeveral per day ⓘ1 hr

✈ Air Rail Bus Limousine Metro/subway Tram Helicopter Water transport • For map symbols, see p. 9

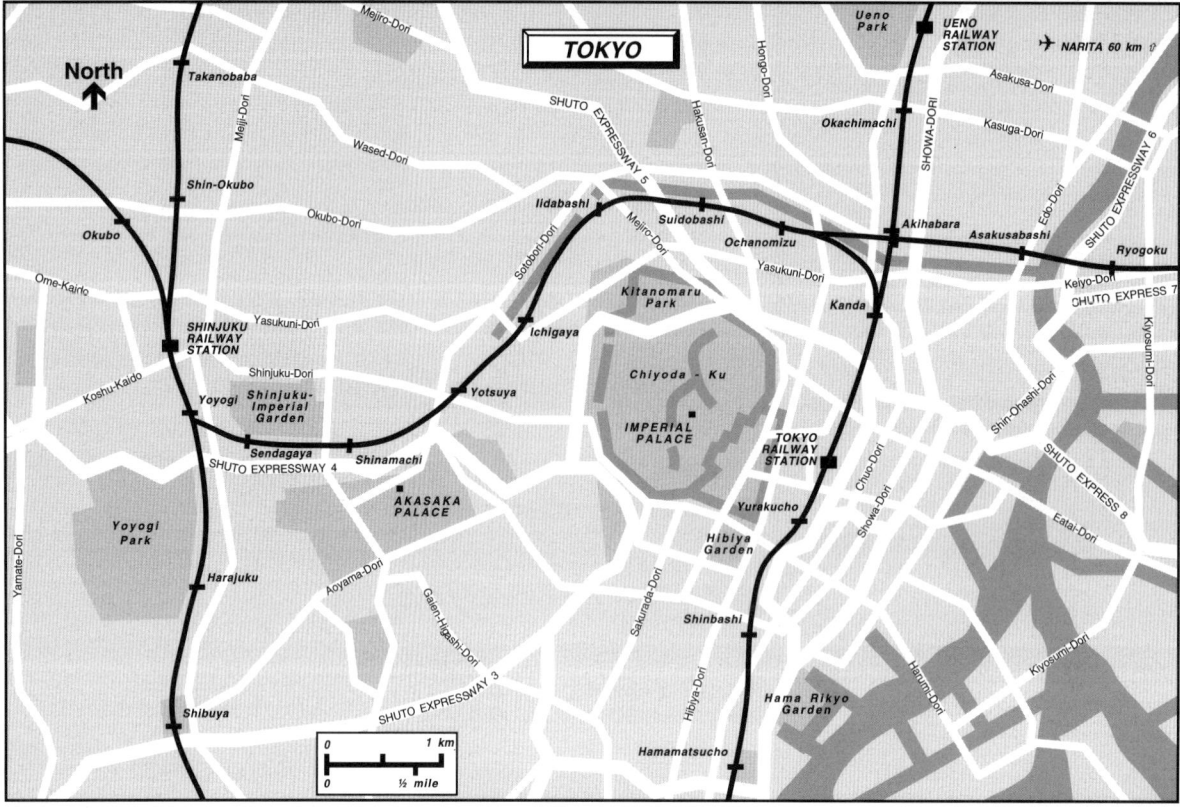

Tokyo-Narita

SECTION TWO • AIRPORT DIRECTORY

Toyama ✈ ≫Several per day ⟃1 hr
Yamagata ✈ ≫Several per day ⟃55 min

TRAVELLER'S NOTES

The airport connects with an extensive rail and metro network covering metropolitan Tokyo, with very fast rail connections to many other cities of Japan.

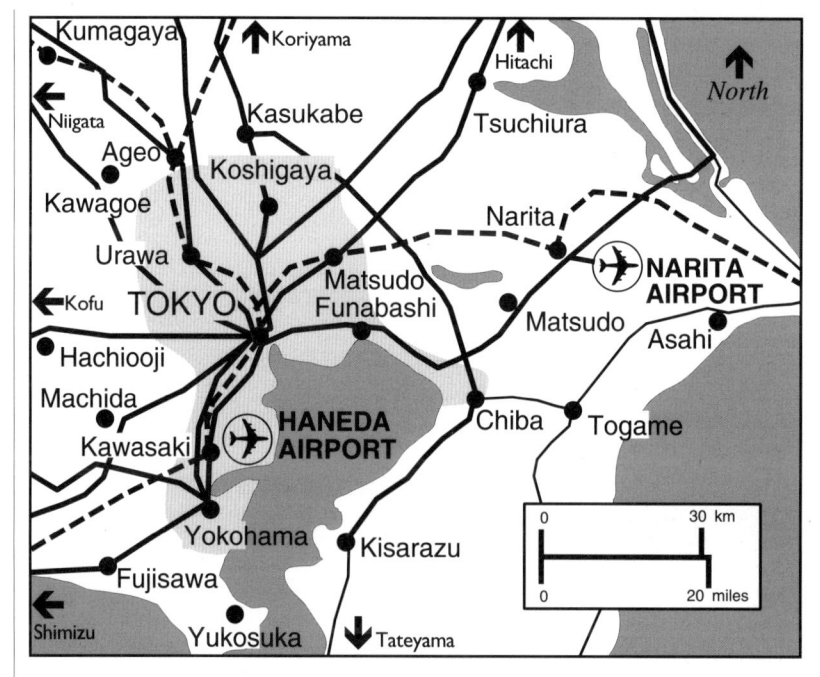

☏ Phone no. ℻ Fax no. ⏱ Hours of opening/operation ≫ Frequency of service ⟃ Journey time ⌀ Cost/one-way fare

SECTION TWO • AIRPORT DIRECTORY

TORONTO — YYZ

Canada (see page 18)

National ✆ code: 1
Area ✆ code: 416
Local time: Winter GMT-5, Summer GMT-4
Lester B. Pearson International Airport, PC 6003, Toronto ON, L5P 1B5, Canada
✆(905) 676 3506
(F)(905) 676 3555
WWW site:
http://www.lbpia.toronto.on.ca
Location: 25 km/15 miles W of Toronto

TERMINALS AND TRANSFERS

Terminals
Terminal 1 Airlines: Aeroflot, Aerolineas Argentinas, Air Club International, Air Transat, Air Ukraine, American Transair, BWIA International, Canada 3000, Canair, Chatauqua Airlines, Comair, Delta Airlines, Henson Piedmont, JARO International, Kelowna Flightcraft, Malev Hungarian, Martinair Holland, Mexicana, Midwest Express Airlines, Northwest Airlines, Olympic, Royal Airlines, Skyservice, Skyway Airlines, TACA International Airlines, TAP Air Portugal, TWA, US Airways, Vistajet. Layout: Lower Level (Arrival, Baggage Claim, Canada Customs, Car Rental, Ground Transportation), Upper Level (Departure, Gates A–L, US Customs/Immigration)
Terminal 2 Airlines: Air Alliance, Air Canada, Air India, Air Jamaica, Air Ontario, Cathay Pacific, Continental Airlines, Cubana, Czech Airlines, EL AL, Finnair, Guyana Airlines, Korean Airlines, LOT Polish Airlines, Lufthansa, Pakistan International, Royal Jordanian, Swissair. Layout: Lower Level (Arrival, Baggage Claim, Car Rental, Canadian Customs/Immigration, Ground Transportation), Upper Level (Departure, Gates 71–115, U.S. Customs/Immigration)
Terminal 3 Airlines: Air France, Air New Zealand, Alitalia, American Airlines, British Airways, Canadian Airlines, Canadian Regional, Corsair, Inter Canadian, KLM, Pemair, Qantas, United Airlines, VASP Brazilian Airlines. Layout: Lower Level (Arrival, Baggage Claim, Car Rental, Ground Transportation), Departure Level (Departure, Gates B7–B22 and C24–C34, US Customs/Immigration)

Minimum transfer times
International: 1 hr 30 min (allow 2 hr+ if changing terminals) Domestic: 45 min (allow 1 hr 30 min if changing terminals)

Transfer between terminals
Bus ≫10 min; All terminals ⌀Free

INFORMATION

Flight enquiries
Airport ✆247 7678 (Term 1 & 2); ✆ (905) 612 5100 (Term 3)
Terminal 1: Air Club International ✆(905) 676 2772; (905) 676 2772 Air Europe Italy ✆(905)612 8330 Air Niagara ✆(905)671 2702 Air Transat ✆(905) 678 1011 Air Ukraine ✆(905) 676 2692 American Transair ✆(905) 676 2772 BWIA International ✆(905) 676 2692 Canada 3000 ✆674 2661 Canair ✆(905) 676 2772 Malev Hungarian ✆944 0093 Martinair Holland ✆365 9833 Olympic ✆(905) 676 4842 Rich International ✆(905) 676 2692 Royal Airlines ✆(905) 677 7289
Terminal 2: Air Canada ✆969 5551 Air India ✆(905) 676 0002; (905) 676 0002; (905) 676 0003 Air Nova ✆925 2311 Air Ontario ✆925 2311 Czech Airlines ✆363 3174 EL AL ✆864 9779 Guyana Airways ✆485 8111 Lufthansa ✆368 4777 Pakistan International ✆(905) 677 9479 Royal Jordanian ✆962 3955
Terminal 3: Alitalia ✆(905) 676 2886 Canadian Airlines ✆798 2280 Canadian Regional ✆798 2280 Inter Canadian ✆798 2211 KLM ✆(905) 612 0556 VASP Brazilian Airlines ✆(905) 612 8989

Information and help desks
Hotel and Travel Reservations Terminal 2 Lower Level ✆(905) 672 6933 Hotel booking
Immigrant Reception and Information Services All Terminals Lower Level Hotel booking, Tourist information
Information Desk Terminal 1 Lower Level ✆(905) 676 3506; 247 7678 ⏲1000–2300 Airport information
Information Desk Terminal 2 Lower Level ✆(905)676 3506; 247 7678 ⏲0800–2300 Airport information
Information Desk Terminal 3 Lower Level ✆(905) 612 5100 ⏲0700–2400 Airport information
Traveller's Aid Terminal 1 Lower Level

Toronto Pearson International

Toronto

SECTION TWO • AIRPORT DIRECTORY

Terminal 1 International
TORONTO PEARSON

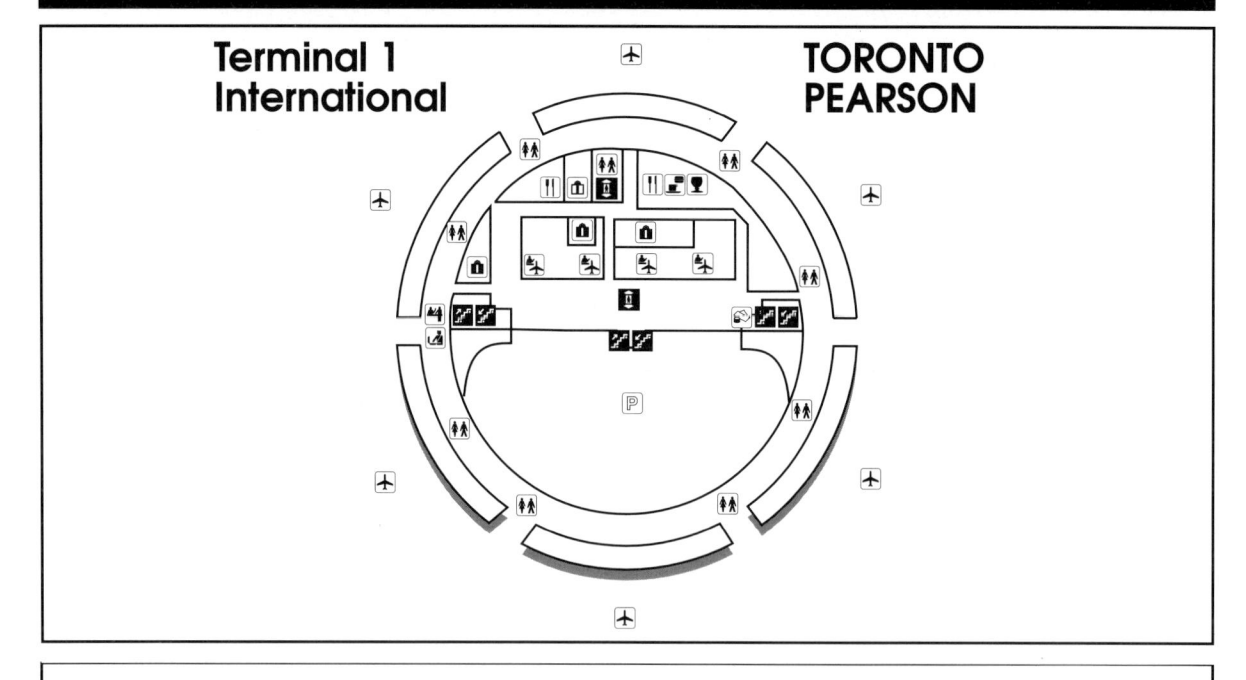

Terminal 2 International
TORONTO PEARSON

International Departures Gates 101–107

U.S. Departures

Canada Departures Gates 70–86

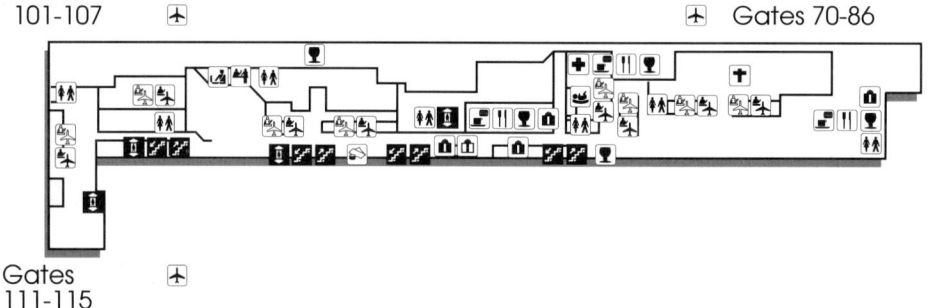

Gates 111–115

©(905) 676 2868 Hotel booking, Tourist information
Traveller's Aid Terminal 2 Lower Level
©(905) 676 2869 Hotel booking, Tourist information
Traveller's Aid Terminal 3 Lower Level
©(905) 612 5890 Hotel booking, Tourist information

Emergencies

Police All Terminals ©(905) 676 3033
Medical Terminal 1 Lower Level
⊙0600–2359
Medical Terminal 2 Upper Level
⊙0600–2359
Medical Terminal 3 Upper Level
⊙0600–2359
Lost Property Terminal 1 Lower Level
©(905) 676 7749
Lost Property Terminal 2 Lower Level
©(905) 676 7749
Lost Property Terminal 3 Lower Level
©(905) 612 0535

Airport Facilities

Money
ATM All Terminals throughout
Bureau de change All Terminals throughout

Food and drink
Bar All Terminals throughout
Café/light meals All Terminals throughout
Restaurant Terminal 1 Upper Level
⊙1200–1900
Restaurant Terminal 2 Upper Level

© Phone no. Ⓕ Fax no. ⊙ Hours of opening/operation ≫ Frequency of service ➲ Journey time ⊘ Cost/one-way fare

✈✈ SECTION TWO • AIRPORT DIRECTORY   TORONTO

Terminal 3 Departures Level — Toronto Pearson

To Gates C24-C34
To Gates B7-B22
Int'l Check-In
Canada Check-In
U.S.A. Check-In

🕐1200–1900
Restaurant Terminal 3 Upper Level
🕐1200–2300

Communications
Fax service Terminal 1 Traveller's Support Services, Lower Level 🕐24 hr
Fax service Terminal 2 International Arrivals 🕐0500–2359
Fax service Terminal 3 International Arrivals 🕐0500–2359

Shopping
Hairdresser Terminal 2 Lower Level
Duty free, departure All Terminals Departure Level 🕐0530–2300
Gift Shop All Terminals throughout
News, Stationery & Books All Terminals throughout

Luggage
Left luggage All Terminals Lower Level
Porters All Terminals throughout

DISABLED TRAVELLERS

All Terminals Adapted toilets; Lifts Special car parking; Phones adapted for the deaf

SMOKING POLICY

All Terminals No-smoking throughout, except in designated bars/restaurants

SPECIAL PASSENGER LOUNGES

Air Canada Maple Leaf Lounge Terminal 2 Upper Level
Air France/KLM Rembrandt Room Terminal 3 Upper Level
American Airlines Admirals Club Terminal 3 Upper Level
British Airways Speedwing Terminal 3 Upper Level
Canadian Airlines International Empress Lounge Terminal 3 Upper Level
Delta Crown Room Terminal 1 Upper Level

CONFERENCE AND BUSINESS FACILITIES

Travellers Support Services, Terminal 1, Lower Level 🕐24 hr Photocopier, Fax service
Travellers Support Services, Terminal 2, Lower Level 🕐0500–2359 Photocopier, Fax service
Travellers Support Services, Terminal 3, Lower Level 🕐0500–2359 Photocopier, Fax service

AIRPORT HOTELS

Sheraton Gateway ℂ(905) 672 7000 ℉(905) 672 7100 474

CAR RENTAL

Avis All Terminals Lower Level Parking Garages ℂ213 8400
Budget All Terminals Lower Level Parking Garages ℂ(905) 676 0311
Hertz All Terminals Lower Level Parking Garages ℂ(905) 676 3241
Thrifty Canada All Terminals Lower Level Parking Garages ℂ(905) 673 8811
National All Terminals Lower Level Parking Garages ℂ(905) 676 2647
Dollar All Terminals Lower Level Parking Garages

CAR PARKING

Long-stay Adjacent to all terminals ⌀CAD16 per day
Off-airport Etobicoke/Mississauga 2 companies
Short-stay Adjacent to all terminals ⌀CAD4 per hr (CAD6 per hr at Terminal 3)

TAXIS AND CHAUFFEUR-DRIVEN CARS

Taxis
City centre ➔30–40 min ⌀CAD40

PUBLIC TRANSPORT

City & suburbs
Brampton ON 🚍GO Transit: 6534 For Bramalea, Malton, Yorkdale and York Mills ON
Mississauga ON 🚍Mississauga Transit: 7 🕐Mon–Fri only ⌀CAD2.
Toronto (Islington Subway Station) 🚍Pacific Western Airport Express ⟫40 min 🕐0625–0045 ➔25 min ⌀CAD6.75.
Toronto (Lawrence West Subway Station) 🚍TTC: 58A ⟫15–30 min Mon–Fri; longer Sat–Sun 🕐0530–0130 ➔45 min–1 hr ⌀CAD4. Transfer to subway at Lawrence West
Toronto city centre 🚍Pacific Western Airport Express ⟫20 min 🕐0625–0045 ➔45 min ⌀CAD12.50.
Toronto metro area 🚖Over 10 companies at Airport.

283

✈ Air 🚆 Rail 🚌 Bus 🚘 Limousine Ⓜ Metro/subway 🚋 Tram 🚁 Helicopter 🚢 Water transport • For map symbols, see p. 9

TORONTO

SECTION TWO • AIRPORT DIRECTORY

York Mills (Subway) ON 🚌 Pacific Western Airport Express »40 min ⓗ 0625–0045 ↪35–40 min ⬦CAD8.30

Yorkdale (Subway) ON 🚌 Pacific Western Airport Express »40 min ⓗ 0625 0045 ↪25 min ⬦CAD7.25

Other towns and cities

Chatham ON 🚌 Robert Q's Airbus »1–4 hr ⓗ 0800–0145 ↪3 hr 30 min ⬦CDN46. For Dutton/Rodney, Ridgetown and Tilbury ON

Guelph ON 🚌 Red Car Airport Service For Elora, Fergus and Rockwood ON

Hamilton ON 🚌 Trentway–Wagar »7 day ⓗ 0800–2359 ↪1 hr 15 min. For Oakville and Burlington ON

Kingston ON 🚌 Trentway–Wagar »3 day ⓗ 1430; 1900; 2130 ↪4 hr. For Bowmanville, Newcastle, Port Hope, Cobourg, Grafton, Colborne, Brighton, Trenton, Belleville, Marysville, Napanee and Odessa ON (Reservations required for some destinations).

London ON 🚌 Robert Q's Airbus »1–2 hr ⓗ 0800–0145 ↪2 hr 15 min ⬦CAD40. For St. Thomas and Woodstock ON

Niagara Falls ON 🚌 Niagara Airbus. For Beamsville, Fonthill, Fort Erie, Grimsby, Niagara-on-the-Lake, Port Colborne, Ridgeway, Stephenville, St Catharines, St Davids, Thorold, Vineland, Virgil and Welland ON

North Bay ON 🚌 Northern Airport Service »2–3 day ⓗ 1400; 1500 (Sat); 1830 ↪4 hr 15 min ⬦CAD55. For Bracebridge, Burks Falls, Callander, Emsdale, Gravenhurst, Huntsville, Powassan, Trout Creek, South River and Sundridge ON

Ontario province 🚌 Classique Airline Service. For Ajax, Beaverton, Blackstock, Bowmanville, Brooklin, Burketon, Caesarea, Claremont, Columbus, Courtice, Enniskillen, Goodwood, Green Bank, Hampton, Kendal, Kirby, Leasdale, Leskard, Maple Beach, Myrtle, Nestleton, Newcastle, Newtonville, Orono, Oshawa, Pickering, Port Bolster, Port Perry, Seagrave, Sunderland, Tyrone, Uxbridge, Victoria Corners and Whitby ON

Ontario province, southwest 🚌 Airways Transit. For Ancaster, Burlington, Cambridge, Hamilton, Kitchener, Oakville, Milton, Stoney Creek and Waterloo ON

Orilla ON 🚌 Simcoe County Airport Service. For Barrie, Coldwater, Midland, Penetanguishene and Orilla ON

Owen Sound ON 🚌 Penetang–Midland Coach Lines. For Alliston, Angus, Barrie, Bolton, CFB Borden, Collingwood, Creemore, Elmvale, Kleinburg, Meaford, Midland, Nobleton, Orilla, Owen Sound, Palgrave, Stayner, Thornbarrie, Tottenham and Wasaga Beach ON

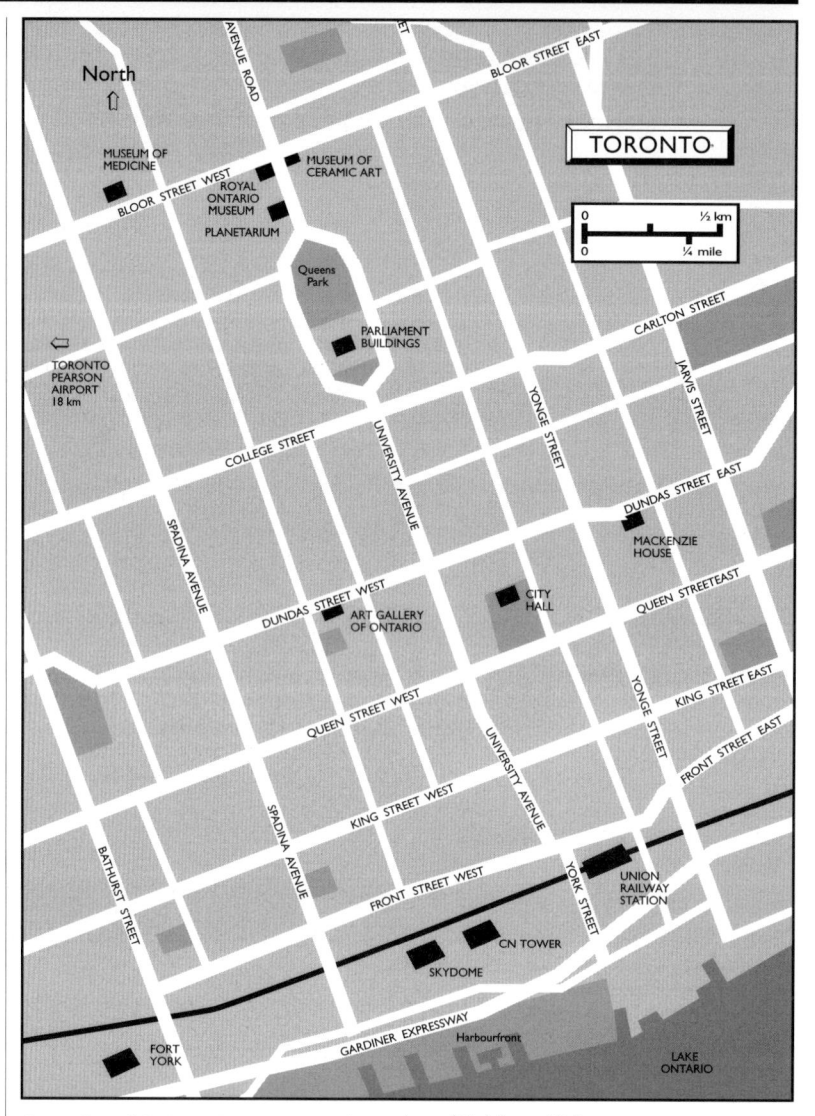

Owen Sound ON 🚌 Grey–Bruce Airbus. For Arthur, Durham, Grand Valley, Hanover, Kincardine, Markdale, Mt Forest, Orangeville, Port Elgin, Shelburne, South Hampton and Walkerton ON

Peterborough ON 🚌 Century Airline Service. For Bewdley, Bridgenorth, Cavan, Douro, Emily, Ennismore, Keene, Lakefield, Lindsay, Millbrook, North and South Monaghan, Omemee, Otonabee, Selwyn and Smith ON

Port Elgin ON 🚌 Canar Coach Service. For Kincardine, Southhampton and Walkerton ON

Sarnia ON 🚌 Robert Q's Airbus »1–3 hr ⓗ 0800–0145 ↪4 hr ⬦CDN46. For Strathroy ON

Simcoe ON 🚌 Airlink Airport Service. For Brantford, Delhi and Paris ON

Stratford ON 🚌 Stratford Airporter. For Clinton, Goderich, Mitchell, Seaforth and St Marys ON

York ON 🚌 Air York Airport Service. For Aurora, Jacksons Point, Keswick, Holland Landing, Markham, Mt Albert, Newmarket, Queensville, Richmond Hill, Sharon, Stouffville, Sutton, Thornhill and Vaughan ON

REGIONAL AIR CONNECTIONS

Kingston ON ✈ »Several per day ↪1 hr
London ON ✈ »Several per day ↪40 min
North Bay ON ✈ »Several per day ↪1 hr
Ottawa ON ✈ »Several per day ↪50 min
Pembroke ON ✈ »Several per week ↪1 hr
Pittsburgh PA ✈ »Several per day ↪1 hr
Sarnia ON ✈ »Several per day ↪50 min
Windsor ON ✈ »Several per day ↪1 hr

ⓟ Phone no. ⓕ Fax no. ⓗ Hours of opening/operation » Frequency of service ↪ Journey time ⬦ Cost/one-way fare

TOULOUSE TLS

France (see page 22)

National ✆ code: 33
Area ✆ code: 05
Local time: Winter GMT+1,
Summer GMT+2
Address: Aéroport International de Toulouse-Blagnac, Chambre de Commerce et d'industrie de Toulouse, BP 103, 31703 Blagnac Cedex, France
✆: 61 42 44 00
ⓕ: WWW site:
http://www.toulouse.cci.fr
Location: 10kms/6mls NW of Toulouse

TERMINALS AND TRANSFERS

Terminals
Main Terminal Air Afrique, Air Algérie, Air France, Air Inter Europe, Air Liberté, Air Littoral, Air Toulouse, Air Transport Pyrénées, Brit Air, British Airways, Crossair, K.L.M., Lufthansa, Proteus Airlines, Royal Air Maroc, T.A.T. European Airlines, Tunisair. Layout: Arrivals Level, ground floor. Departures Level, first floor.

Information Flight enquiries
Airport ✆61 42 44 65/64
Air Afrique ✆61 99 04 07, Air Algérie ✆61 30 05 14, Air France ✆0 802 802 802, Air Inter Europe ✆0 802 802 802, Air Liberté ✆61 15 71 71, Air Littoral ✆0 803 834 834, Air Toulouse ✆61 71 89 90, Air Transport Pyrénées ✆61 71 10 00, Brit Air ✆61 71 27 27, British Airways ✆61 16 37 52, Crossair ✆61 71 10 00, K.L.M. ✆61 71 10 00, Lufthansa ✆61 71 10 00, Proteus Airlines ✆61 71 10 00, Royal Air Maroc ✆61 21 97 52, T.A.T. European Airlines ✆61 71 06 03, Tunisair ✆61 62 99 70

Information and help desks
Arrivals Level, ground floor Flight information, tourist information, hotel reservations, lost property

EMERGENCIES
Police ✆61 71 08 70
Medical Departures and Arrivals Level
Lost Property Information desk, Arrivals Level, ground floor

AIRPORT FACILITIES

Money
Bank Arrivals Level, ground floor
⏰0800–1900 Mon–Fri; 1000–1200 and 1330–1800 Sat–Sun ✆61 30 06 61
Bureau de Change Departures Level, first floor ⏰0600–2130 Mon–Fri, 0630–2130 Sat–Sun
ATM Arrivals Level, ground floor

Food and drink
Bar Departures and Arrivals Level
Restaurant Departures and Arrivals Level ✆61 30 02 75

Communications
Post office Departures Level, first floor
⏰1300–1600 Mon–Fri ✆61 71 52 99

Shopping
Duty free Departures Level, first floor ✆61 30 00 09
News, Stationery & Books Departures Level, first floor ✆61 30 05 50
Gift Shop Departures Level, first floor

DISABLED TRAVELLERS
Contact individual airlines

CONFERENCE AND BUSINESS FACILITIES
✆61 30 42 84

AIRPORT HOTELS
Hotel Ibis ✆61 30 01 00 ⓕ61 30 02 83; 88 rooms

CAR RENTAL
Ada ✆61 30 00 33
Avis ✆61 30 04 94
Budget ✆61 71 85 80
Citer ✆61 30 00 01
Europcar ✆61 30 02 30
Eurorent ✆61 71 20 33
Hertz ✆61 30 00 26

CAR PARKING
Short-stay P1 ⌀First 30 min free;
⌀FRF11 per 1hr; ⌀FRF17 per 2hr;
⌀FRF35 per 12 hr; ⌀FRF44 per 24 hr;
⌀FRF100 per day thereafter
Long-stay P1 and P4 ⌀First 30 min free;
⌀FRF11 per 1hr; ⌀FRF17 per 2hr;
⌀FRF35 per 12 hr; ⌀FRF44 per 24 hr;
⌀FRF28 per day thereafter

TAXIS AND CHAUFFEUR-DRIVEN CARS

Taxis
City centre ⌀FRF100 ✆61 30 02 54

PUBLIC TRANSPORT

City & suburbs
Toulouse (Gare Routière Pierre Sémard) 🚍 »20 min ⏰0520–2100 ➲20 min ⌀FRF25 ✆61 30 04 89

Other towns and cities
Lourdes 🚆 »Several per day ➲2 hr
Tarbes 🚆 »Several per day ➲1 hr 40 mins

VANCOUVER   SECTION TWO • AIRPORT DIRECTORY

Vancouver   YVR
Canada (see page 18)

National ✆ code: 1
Area ✆ code: 604
Local time: Winter GMT-8,
Summer GMT-7
Vancouver International Airport,
PO Box 23750, Richmond, BC,
V7B 1Y7, Canada
✆276 6208
℻276 7755; 270 0610
WWW site: http://www.yvr.ca
Location: 13 km/8 miles SW of
Vancouver

Terminals and Transfers

Terminals
Domestic Terminal Airlines: All other airlines. Layout: Arrivals Level (Baggage Claim, Customs, Car Rental, Ground Transportation); Departure Level (Gates); Level 3 (Airline Lounges)
International Terminal Airlines: All international flights. Layout: Arrivals Level: (Baggage Claim, Car Rental, Customs, Ground Transportation), Departure Level (Gates, US Customs)

Minimum transfer times
International: 1 hr 30 min Domestic: 45 min

Transfer between terminals
Bus ≫10–15 min; Main Terminal (Levels 1 and 3) and parking ⊘Free

Information

Information and help desks
Customer Service Counter International Terminal Departures Level ✆303 4053 ⏱0445–2400 Airport information
Customer Service Counter Domestic Terminal Departures Level ✆276 6117 ⏱0445–2400 Airport information
Tourism InfoCentre International Terminal Departures Level ✆303 3603 ⏱0700–0100 Tourist information
Tourism InfoCentre Domestic Terminal Departures Level ✆303 3602 ⏱0715–2300 Tourist information

Airport Facilities

Money
ATM All Terminals throughout ⏱24 hr

Bank All Terminals throughout ⏱0515–2145
Bureau de change Domestic Terminal Departures Level South ⏱0830–1630
Bureau de change Domestic Terminal Departures Level North ⏱0815–1615
Bureau de change International Terminal Arrivals Level ⏱0745–2345
Bureau de change International Terminal Departures Level (3 locations) ⏱0515–1700
Bureau de change International Terminal Departures holdroom ⏱0915–1715

Food and drink
Bar All Terminals Departure Level
Café/light meals All Terminals throughout
Restaurant All Terminals throughout

Communications
Post box All Terminals throughout

Shopping
Duty free, departure All Terminals throughout
Florist Domestic Terminal Departures Level
Florist International Terminal Arrivals ⏱0900–2200
Gift Shop All Terminals throughout
News, Stationery & Books All Terminals throughout
Hairdresser All Terminals Departures Level (in the link between terminals) ⏱0830–1730
Shopping mall All Terminals Departures Level

Luggage
Trolleys/carts All Terminals throughout ⏱24 hr ⊘Free
Left luggage counter Domestic Terminal Arrivals Level ⏱0500–2300 ⊘CAD1.75–4.75 day
Left luggage counter International Terminal Arrivals Level ⏱0500–00100 ⊘CAD1.75–4.75 day

Disabled Travellers
All Terminals Adapted toilets; Lifts Special car parking; Phones at wheelchair height; Phones adapted for the deaf; Personal assistance; visual paging

Smoking Policy
All Terminals Permitted in smoking rooms only

Special Passenger Lounges
Air Canada Maple Leaf Lounge Domestic Terminal Level 3
Air Canada Maple Leaf Lounge International Terminal Level 3
Air Canada Maple Leaf Lounge International Terminal Transborder Level 3
British Airways Lounge International Terminal Level 4
Canadian Airlines International Empress Club Lounge Domestic Terminal Level 3
Canadian Airlines International Empress Club Lounge International Terminal Level 3
Canadian Airlines International Empress Club Lounge International Terminal Transborder Level 3
Cathay Pacific Lounge International Terminal Level 4
Japan Airlines Executive Lounge International Terminal Level 3
Korean Airlines Morning Calm Lounge International Terminal Level 4

Conference and Business Facilities
International Reception Lobby, International Terminal
Business Centre, International Terminal, Arrival Level ✆303 4511 ⏱0500–0100

Car Rental
Alamo All Terminals Arrivals Level
Avis All Terminals Arrivals Level
Budget All Terminals Arrivals Level
Hertz All Terminals Arrivals Level
Thrifty All Terminals Arrivals Level
Tilden All Terminals Arrivals Level

Car Parking
Long-stay 3 min from terminal (24 hr free shuttle bus) ⊘CAD2 per hr, CAD7 per day (max)
Short-stay Adjacent to terminal ⊘CAD4 per hr; CAD20 per day max

---
✆ Phone no. ℻ Fax no. ⏱ Hours of opening/operation ≫ Frequency of service ➲ Journey time ⊘ Cost/one-way fare

SECTION TWO • AIRPORT DIRECTORY

VANCOUVER

TAXIS AND CHAUFFEUR-DRIVEN CARS

Taxis
City centre ↪45 min ◇CAD19–26

PUBLIC TRANSPORT

Vancouver International Airport BC 🚌Quick Shuttle »1–2 hrs »1–2 hr ⓘ0530–2315 ↪3 hr 25 min ◇CAD38.

City & suburbs
»1–2 hr ⓘ0530–2315
Ladner BC 🚌BC Transit: 404 »30 min–1 hr ⓘ0600–2400 ◇CAD1.50–2.25. For Richmond BC and BC Ferries to Vancouver Island and Gulf Islands (direct service to ferries during summer; at other times transfer to bus 604 at Ladner Exchange)
New Westminster BC (SkyTrain) 🚌BC Transit: 100 »15 min–1 hr ⓘ0600–2400 ↪1 hr ◇CAD1.50–3. Transfer to bus 20 or SkyTrain for city centre
Vancouver BC city centre 🚐Over 10 companies ◇CAD26.
Vancouver BC (city centre hotels) 🚌Airporter »15 min ⓘ0615 0010 ◇CAD9.
Vancouver BC (Pacific Central rail stn) 🚌Airporter »30 min ⓘ0615–0010 ◇CAD9. For Amtrak, Rocky Mountaineer, VIA Rail and all intercity bus lines

Other towns and cities
Seattle WA (centre city) 🚌Quick Coach Lines »1–2 hr ⓘ0530–2315 ↪3 hr 50 min ◇CAD31
Whistler BC (Ski Area) 🚌Perimeter Transportation »2 hr ⓘ0830–1930 Apr–Nov; ⓘ0930–2230 Dec–Apr ◇CAD43. 1100–1830 Apr–Nov; 0930–2230 Dec–Apr

REGIONAL AIR CONNECTIONS

Campbell River Municipal Apt BC ✈ »Several per day ↪40 min
Ganges Harbor BC ✈ »Several per day ↪30 min
Gillies Bay BC ✈ »Several per day ↪1 hr
Kamloops BC ✈ »Several per day ↪50 min
Kelowna BC ✈ »Several per day ↪55 min
Montague BC ✈ »At least daily ↪25 min
Nanaimo BC ✈ »Several per day ↪20–30 min
Penticton BC ✈ »Several per day ↪55 min
Port Alberni BC ✈ »Several per day ↪1 hr
Powell River BC ✈ »Several per day ↪30 min
Qualicum BC ✈ »Several per day ↪30 min
Seattle WA ✈ »Several per day ↪50 min
Victoria BC ✈ »Several per day ↪35 min

AIRPORT TAXES

To finance new facilities at the airport, an Airport Improvement Fee is imposed on departure: CAD5–15

TRAVELLER'S NOTES

A key international gateway between the Asia Pacific region and North America. Volunteers – the Greencoats – are on hand throughout the terminal buildings to assist passengers from 0700–2100 daily. The New International Terminal is the first terminal of its kind built in North America especially for connecting passengers.

✈ Air 🚆 Rail 🚌 Bus 🚐 Limousine Ⓜ Metro/subway 🚋 Tram 🚁 Helicopter ⛴ Water transport • For map symbols, see p. 9

VIENNA (WIEN)
VIE
Austria (see page 15)

National ✆ code: 43
Area ✆ code: 01
Local time: Winter GMT+1, Summer GMT+2
Vienna International Airport, PO Box 1 1-1300 Wien, Austria
✆7007 0
⒡7007 3001
Location: 18 km/11 miles SE of Vienna

TERMINALS AND TRANSFERS

Terminals
Terminal 1 Airlines: All other airlines.
Terminal 2 Airlines: British Airways, KLM, Lufthansa, Lauda-Air.

Minimum transfer times
International: 30 min Domestic: 30 min

INFORMATION

Flight enquiries
Airport ✆7007 2233
Adria Airways ✆7007 5992 ⒡522 37 57
Aeroflot ✆7007–2834 ⒡512–150178 Air China ✆7007 5327 ⒡7007–5328 Air France ✆7007 2065 ⒡7007 6720 Air Malta ✆0663 87 76 88 ⒡407 3254 Air Mauritius ✆713 90 60 ⒡713–9052 Air Portugal TAP ✆513 39 77 ⒡512 25 52 Alitalia ✆7007 2643 ⒡7007 5237 All Nippon Airways ✆7007 3737 ⒡7007 3738 Asiana Airlines ✆7007– 8113 ⒡7007–8115 Austrian Airlines ✆7007 2520 ⒡68 55 05 Balkan Bulgarian Airlines ✆7007 2611 ⒡587 60 48 British Airways ✆7007 2646 ⒡7007 2637 Croatia Airlines ✆7007 5962 ⒡7007 5963 CSA Czechoslovak ✆7007 5913 ⒡7007 5914 Cyprus Airlines ✆713 23 71 ⒡713 06 22 Delta Airlines ✆7007 3459 ⒡7007 3752 Egyptair ✆7007 2063 ⒡58 745 32 20 El Al Israel Airlines ✆7007 2647 ✆7007 5247 Eva Air ✆7007 5581 ⒡7007 5584 Finnair ⒡587 55 48 ⒡587 91 27 Iberia ✆7007 2915 ⒡586 76 30 Iran Air ✆7007 2876 ⒡586 66 99 KLM ✆7007 2978 ✆7007 5569 Lauda-Air ✆7007 3746 ✆7007 3799 Lot Polish Airlines ✆7007 2785 ⒡7007 5354 Malaysian Airlines ✆7007 5152 ⒡7007 5153 Olympic Airways ✆7007 2913 ✆7007 5560 Royal Jordanian Airlines ✆7007 3313 ✆7007 5369 Sabena ✆7007 2817 ⒡7007 2649 SAS ✆7007 2660 ⒡7007 6744 Singapore Airlines ✆7007 3450 ✆7007 3010 Swissair ✆7007 2520 ⒡505 14 34 Tarom Romanian Air ✆7007 2728 ⒡581 88 00 16 Tunis Air ✆7007 5996 ⒡581 42 08 Turkish Airlines ✆7007 2959 ✆7007 2914 Ukraine International Airlines ✆712 96 83 ⒡713 40 36

Information and help desks
Information Desk Terminal 1 Arrival Hall after Baggage retrieval ⓞAll flight times Airport information, Flights
Information Desks in Departure and Transit Halls Terminal 1 Near Central Check-in, East Pier (1 desk), West Pier (1 desk) ✆7007 2233 ⓞ24 hr Airport information, Flights
Tourist Information Desk Terminal 1 Arrival Hall after baggage retrieval ⓞAll flight times Hotel booking, Tourist information

EMERGENCIES
Police ✆7007 133 ⓞ24 hr
Medical Medical Centre near Domestic Departure ✆7007 144 ⓞ24 hr
Lost Property Terminal 1 Information Counter in Arrival Hall ✆7007 2522 ⓞ24 hr

AIRPORT FACILITIES

Money
Bank Arrival Hall ⓞ0800–1230 and 1330–1500 (until 1730 Thurs)
Bank Departure Hall ⓞ0800–1230 and 1330–1500 (until 1730 Thurs)
Bank World Trade Centre (opposite the Arrival Hall) ⓞ0800–1230 and 1330–1500 (until 1730 Thurs)
Bureau de change Throughout departure and arrival hall ⓞ0600–2000

Food and drink
Bar Airside ⓞ0700–2200
Bar Airside ⓞ0600–2030
Café/light meals Airside ⓞ0600–2100
Café/light meals Arrival Area ⓞ0600–2400
Café/light meals Departure Area ⓞ0600–2100
Café/light meals Departure Area ⓞ1030–1830
Restaurant Departure Area ⓞ0630–2100
Restaurant Departure Area ⓞ1100 onwards

Communications
Post office Terminal 1 Departure Hall on boundary of Terminals 1 and 2 ⓞ0730–1900 daily

Shopping
Duty free, departure Transit Area, East Pier, West Pier ⓞAll flight times
Pharmacy Terminal 1 Check-in Area
Shopping mall Terminals 1 and 2 Check-in Area, Transit Area, East Pier, West Pier ⓞAll flight times

Luggage
Left Luggage Counter Terminal 1 Arrival Hall ⓞ24 hr ◇ATS30 per item per day
Porters Terminal 1 Arrival/Departure ⓞAll flight times ◇ATS20 per item
Trolleys/carts Terminal 1 Arrival/Departure Halls ⓞ24 hr ◇Free

DISABLED TRAVELLERS
Terminal 1 Adapted toilets; Central, West Pier, Arrival Lifts Arrival/Departure Levels 1–2 Special car parking; Parking Area 3 Phones at wheelchair height; Personal assistance
Terminal 2 Adapted toilets; Central and East Pier Lifts Arrival/Departure Levels 1–2 Special car parking; Parking Area 3 Phones at wheelchair height

SMOKING POLICY
Terminal 1 Smoking permitted at bars and in lounges
Terminal 2 Smoking permitted at bars and in lounges

SPECIAL PASSENGER LOUNGES
Diners Club Lounge Transit Area Diners Club cardholders and guests
Grand Danube Lounge Transit Area Danube Aviator Club members and passengers of certain airline clubs
All airlines Petite Danube Lounge West Pier Danube Aviator Club members and passengers of certain airlines
Austrian Airlines Travel Club Lounge West Pier Frequent flyers and First class passengers
Austrian Airlines Business Class Lounge

✆ Phone no. ⒡ Fax no. ⓞ Hours of opening/operation ≫ Frequency of service ⊃ Journey time ◇ Cost/one-way fare

SECTION TWO • AIRPORT DIRECTORY

VIENNA

Transit Area
British Airways Lounge East Pier Executive Club members and First and Business class passengers
Lufthansa/Lauda Air Lounge Transit Area First and Business class passengers

CONFERENCE AND BUSINESS FACILITIES

VIP and Business Centre, Transit Area Level 2 ☎7007 3300, 3400 ℻7007 3250 ⏰0700–2230 Telephones, Fax service, Power points, Modem Points, Photocopier, Secretarial service, Translation/ Interpretation service, Travel advice
Concorde Business Club, Concorde Business Park, 5 min from airport ☎0222 706 3231 0 Telephones, Fax service, Power points, Modem Points, Photocopier, Secretarial service, Translation/ Interpretation service
World Trade Centre, 100 m opposite Arrival Hall ☎7007 6000 ℻7007 6027 Telephones, Fax service, Power points, Modem Points, Photocopier, Secretarial service, Translation/Interpretation service

AIRPORT HOTELS

Novotel Airport ☎701 07 0 ℻707 3239. 183 guests
Sofitel Vienna Airport ☎70151 0 ℻7062828. 143 rooms

CAR RENTAL

Avis Arrival Hall ☎7007 2700
Budget Arrival Hall ☎7007 2711/3659
Hertz Arrival Hall ☎7007 2661/5395
EuropCar Arrival Hall ☎7007 3316
Sixt Arrival Hall ☎7007 6517
Airport Jet-Set Service Arrival Hall ☎7007 3140
Mazur Arrival Hall ☎7007 6422

CAR PARKING

Long-stay 5878 spaces ⊘ATS120 per day
Off-airport Three multi-storey buildings 3149 spaces ⊘ATS180 per day
Short-stay 357 spaces ⊘ATS320 per day

TAXIS AND CHAUFFEUR-DRIVEN CARS

Taxis
Arrival Hall, North Stand ☎7007 5910/2717 City centre ⏳20 min ⊘ATS350

Chauffeur-driven cars
Arrival Hall by arrangement ☎7007 3140/6422/5910

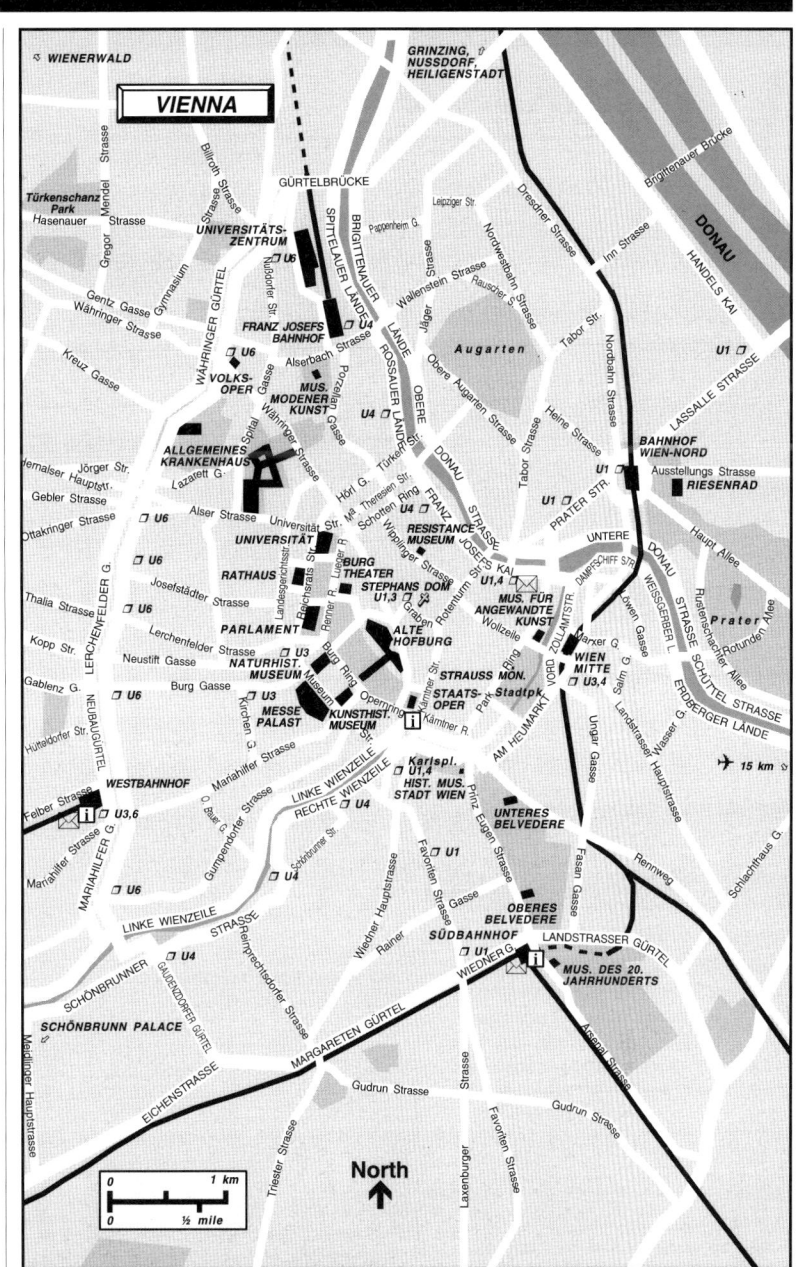

PUBLIC TRANSPORT

City & suburbs
Vienna city centre (City Air Terminal) 🚌Bundesbus ⟫20 min ⏰0430–2400 ⏳20 min ⊘ATS70.
Vienna city centre (main rail stns) 🚆ÖBB ⟫approx 30 min ⏰0503–2223 ⏳30 min ⊘ATS34.

Other towns and cities
Bratislava 🚌Bundesbus ⟫9 daily ⏰0820–2250 ⏳1hr 10 min ⊘ATS 74.
Budapest 🚌Bundesbus ⟫3 daily ⏰0715–1915 ⏳3hr 20 min ⊘ATS 290.

REGIONAL AIR CONNECTIONS

Budapest ✈ ⟫Several per day ⏳55 min
Graz ✈ ⟫Several per day ⏳45 min
Innsbruck ✈ ⟫Several per day ⏳50 min
Klagenfurt ✈ ⟫Several per day ⏳55 min
Linz ✈ ⟫Several per day ⏳40 min
Ljubljana ✈ ⟫Several per week ⏳1 hr
Munich ✈ ⟫Several per day ⏳55 min
Prague ✈ ⟫Several per day ⏳55 min
Salzburg ✈ ⟫Several per day ⏳55 min
Zagreb ✈ ⟫Several per day ⏳1 hr

✈ Air 🚆 Rail 🚌 Bus 🚐 Limousine 🚇 Metro/subway 🚋 Tram 🚁 Helicopter ⛴ Water transport • For map symbols, see p. 9

Warsaw

WAW

Poland (see page 33)

National ✆ code: 48
Area ✆ code: 22
Local time: Winter GMT+1,
Summer GMT+2
Warsaw-Okecie International
Airport, Zwirky i Wigury Str No 1,
00-906 Warsaw, Poland
✆650 30 00
🖷846 68 24
Location: 10 km/6 miles SW of
Warsaw

Terminals and Transfers

Terminals
Main Terminal Airlines: All airlines.
Layout: Three Levels. Ground Level,
Arrivals; Level 2, Departures; Level 3,
offices and administration

Minimum transfer times
International: 40 min Domestic: 35 min

Information

Flight enquiries
Airport ✆952/953
Aeroflot ✆628 25 57 Air Algérie ✆650 25 12/846 70 46 Air Baltic Corporation ✆650 41 21/650 31 21 Air France ✆650 45 08/650 45 09 Air Moldova ✆650 40 25 Air Ukraine ✆650 40 60 Alitalia ✆846 78 46 American Airlines ✆625 04 67 Austrian Airlines ✆650 35 16/650 35 18 Balkan Bulgarian Airlines ✆650 45 13 Belavia – Belarussian Airways ✆650 23 14 British Airways ✆628 94 31/628 39 91 CSA Czechoslovak ✆650 45 14 Delta Airlines ✆650 45 02 El Al Israel Airlines ✆630 66 16/630 66 18/830 09 56 Finnair ✆695 08 11 KLM ✆650 44 44 Lithuanian Airlines ✆650 26 46/650 26 47 Lot Polish Airlines ✆628 75 80 Lufthansa ✆630 25 55 Malev Hungarian ✆635 58 40/635 58 41 Sabena World Airlines ✆627 02 30 SAS ✆826 42 46 Swissair ✆827 50 16 Tarom Romanian Air ✆827 39 65 Tuni Air ✆652 04 92

Information and help desks
Airport Information Desks Departure and Arrival levels ✆650 41 00/650 39 43/846 17 00/846 17 31 ⏱0600–2200 daily

Emergencies

Police ✆650 25 82
Medical Level 3 ⏱24 hr ✆650 19 99 (✆94 from within airport)
Lost Property ✆650 41 22

Airport Facilities

Money
ATM Departure and Arrival Level
Bank Departure Level ⏱0730–1700 Mon–Fri; 0730–2300 Sat
Bureau de change Throughout Departure and Arrival Level

Food and drink
Café/light meals ⏱0600–2200
Restaurant Two restaurants ⏱0830–2000 and 0600–2100
Bar 0600–2200

Communications
Post office Departure Level ⏱0800–2000 Mon–Fri

Shopping
Shopping Mall ⏱0600–2200

Luggage

Left Luggage Counter Arrival Level ⏱24 hr ◇PLZ0.50 per 24 hr plus 1.5% of luggage value

Disabled Travellers

Main Terminal Adapted toilets; Lifts

Smoking Policy

Main Terminal Smoking restricted throughout

Special Passenger Lounges

VIP Lounges Two in Transit area ⏱0600–2200

Conference and Business Facilities

Conference rooms, VIP Areas and Administration Area

Airport Hotels

Falcon Transit Hotel Departure Level ✆650 48 91

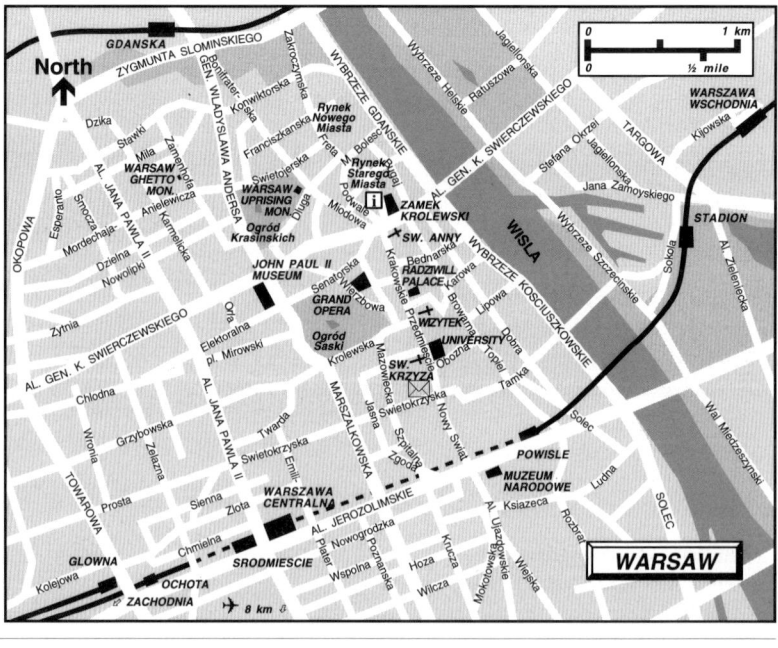

✆ Phone no. 🖷 Fax no. ⏱ Hours of opening/operation ≫ Frequency of service ➲ Journey time ◇ Cost/one-way fare

SECTION TWO • AIRPORT DIRECTORY

WARSAW • WASHINGTON-DULLES

CAR RENTAL
Air Tours Poland ✆650 40 20
Avis Arrival Level ✆650 46 70
Budget Arrival Level ✆46 73 10
Fly & Drive ✆650 23 38/650 23 37
Eurodollar Arrival Level ✆650 47 33/606 92 02
EuropCar Arrival Level ✆650 44 54/50 44 53
Eurotranspol Arrival Level ✆650 48 75
Hertz Arrival Level ✆650 28 96

CAR PARKING
Long-stay ⌀PLZ12 per first day; PLZ10 per day up to seven days; PLZ8 per day after first seven days
Short-stay Multi-storey opposite terminal entrance ⌀PLZ2 per 30 min; PLZ3.5 per hr; PLZ5 per 1.5 hr; PLZ6.5 per 2 hr; PLZ8 per 2.5 hr; PLZ1 per each additional 30 min
Short-stay Ground level car park ⌀PLZ1.5 per 30 min; PLZ3 per 1 hr; PLZ4.5 per 1.5 hr; PLZ6 per 2 hr; PLZ1 per each additional 30 min

TAXIS AND CHAUFFEUR-DRIVEN CARS
Taxis In front of terminals City centre ⏱15 min ⌀PLZ1.2 per 1 km ✆919

Chauffeur-driven cars Front of terminals City centre ⏱15 min

PUBLIC TRANSPORT
City & suburbs
Warsaw city centre 🚌Municipal Bus no 175/188 »10–15 ⏱30–40 min ⏰0450–2310 ⌀PLZ1.4.
Major Hotels 🚌Airport-City Coach »20 min ⏰0600–2300 ⏱15–20 min ⌀PLZ5.70

REGIONAL AIR CONNECTIONS
Berlin ✈ »Several per week ⏱1 hr 20 min
Gdansk ✈ »Several per day ⏱1 hr
Katowice ✈ »Several per week ⏱50 min
Kraków ✈ »Several per day ⏱45 min
Vienna ✈ »Several per day ⏱1 hr 15 min

WASHINGTON-DULLES   IAD
USA (see p. 37)

291

National ✆ code: 1
Area ✆ code: 202
Local time: Winter GMT-5, Summer GMT-4
Washington–Dulles International Airport, PO Box 17045, Washington, DC 20041, USA
✆572 2700
📠572 6817
Internet e-mail: metwashairports.com
WWW site: http://www.met-washairports.com/Dulles
Location: 42 km/26 miles W of Washington

TERMINALS AND TRANSFERS
Terminals
Main Terminal Airlines: All airlines.
Layout: Lower Level (Baggage Claim, Car Rental, Ground Transportation), Upper Level (Departure, A Concourse–C and D Concourses served by Mobile Lounge Shuttle)

Minimum transfer times
International: 1 hr 30 min Domestic: 45 min

Transfer between terminals
Bus » Frequent; Main Terminal and parking lots ⌀Free

INFORMATION
Information and help desks
Information Desk Main Terminal Lower Level ✆(703)572 2700 ⏰0830–1700 Airport information
International Visitor Information Desk Main Terminal Lower Level West End (located within the Greeters Area of the International Arrivals Building) ✆(703) 260 3378 ⏰0700–1900 Airport information, Tourist information
Traveller's Aid Main Terminal Lower Level East End ✆(703)572 8296 ⏰1000–2100 Mon–Fri; 1000–1800 Sat Tourist information

EMERGENCIES
Police Main Terminal throughout ✆(703)572 2950
Medical Main Terminal throughout ✆(703)572 6899; (703) 572 2970
Lost Property Main Terminal Airport Police ✆(703)572 2950

AIRPORT FACILITIES
Money
ATM Main Terminal throughout ⏰24 hr
Bureau de change Main Terminal Upper Level
Bureau de change Main Terminal Upper Level International Arrivals
Thomas Cook bureau de change Main Terminal Midfield C and D Concourses

Food and drink
Bar Main Terminal throughout
Café/light meals Main Terminal throughout ⏰24 hr
Restaurant Main Terminal Upper Level (through Security) ⏰12000–2000

Communications
Post office (self service) Main Terminal Lower Level West End ⏰24 hr
Post box Main Terminal throughout
Fax service Main Terminal Business Centers

Shopping
Duty free, departure Main Terminal Upper Level ⏰0700–2300
Duty free, departure Main Terminal C

✈ Air 🚆 Rail 🚌 Bus 🚘 Limousine 🚇 Metro/subway 🚋 Tram 🚁 Helicopter ⛴ Water transport • For map symbols, see p. 9

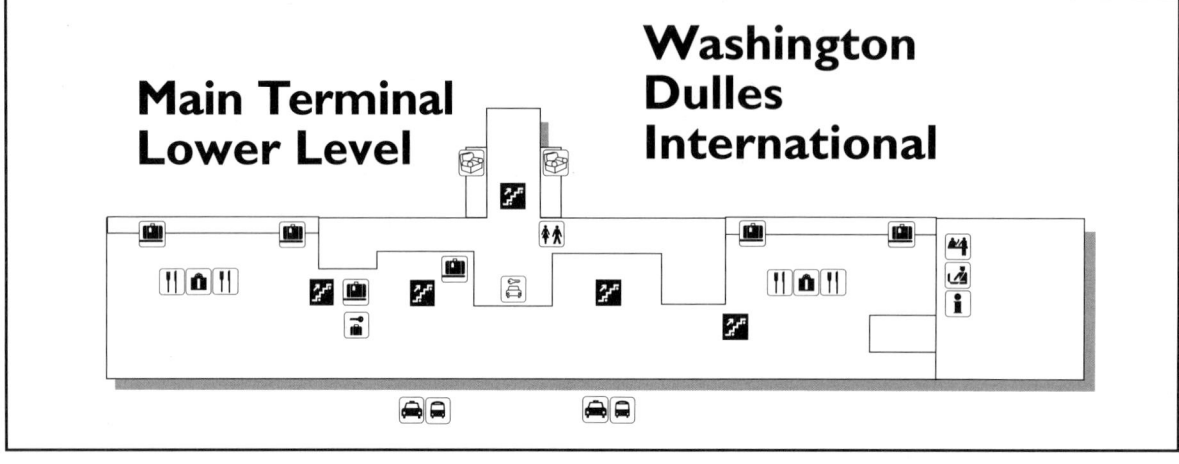

WASHINGTON-DULLES

SECTION TWO • AIRPORT DIRECTORY

Main Terminal Upper Level
Washington Dulles International

C Gates Shuttle D Gates Shuttle

Main Terminal Lower Level
Washington Dulles International

Concourse ⓒ 0700–2300
Gift Shop Main Terminal Main Floor, C Concourse ⓒ 0700–2300
News, Stationery & Books Main Terminal throughout

Luggage
Lockers Main Terminal Upper Level (behind Security) ⓒ 24 hr ⓒ(703) 661 8200
Trolleys/carts Main Terminal throughout ⓒ 24 hr ⓒ USD1.50
Porters Main Terminal throughout

DISABLED TRAVELLERS
Main Terminal Adapted toilets; Lifts East and West end of Main Terminal Phones at wheelchair height; Personal assistance

SMOKING POLICY
Main Terminal No-smoking throughout (Midfield contains 2 smoking rooms)

SPECIAL PASSENGER LOUNGES
Air France Club Lounge Main Terminal

Lower Level A Concourse
American Airlines Admirals Club Main Terminal Midfield D Concourse
ANA Club Main Terminal Lower Level A Concourse
British Airways Club Lounge Main Terminal Midfield D Concourse
Japan Airlines Sakura Lounge Main Terminal Lower Level A Concourse
Lufthansa Club Lounge Main Terminal Lower Level A Concourse
United Airlines Red Carpet Club Main Terminal Midfield C and D Concourses

CONFERENCE AND BUSINESS FACILITIES
Business Center, Main Terminal Upper Level East End ⓒ(703) 661 8864 ⓒ 0600–2100 Fax service, Photocopier, Travel advice

AIRPORT HOTELS
Marriott Washington Dulles Airport ⓒ(703) 471 9500 ⓕ(703) 661 8714 368 rooms Courtesy bus

CAR RENTAL
Alamo Main Terminal Lower Level
Avis Main Terminal Lower Level
Budget Main Terminal Lower Level
Enterprise Main Terminal Lower Level
Hertz Main Terminal Lower Level
National Main Terminal Lower Level

CAR PARKING
Long-stay Airport Perimeter (Free Shuttle to Terminal) ⓒ USD1 per hr; USD5 per day (max)
Short-stay Adjacent to Main Terminal ⓒ USD4 per hr; USD27 per day (max)

TAXIS AND CHAUFFEUR-DRIVEN CARS
Taxis
City centre ⊃30 min ⓒ USD45

PUBLIC TRANSPORT
Airport to airport
Washington-National Airport
🚌 Washington Flyer »1 hr

ⓒ Phone no. ⓕ Fax no. ⓒ Hours of opening/operation » Frequency of service ⊃ Journey time ⓒ Cost/one-way fare

✈︎✈︎ SECTION TWO • AIRPORT DIRECTORY   WASHINGTON

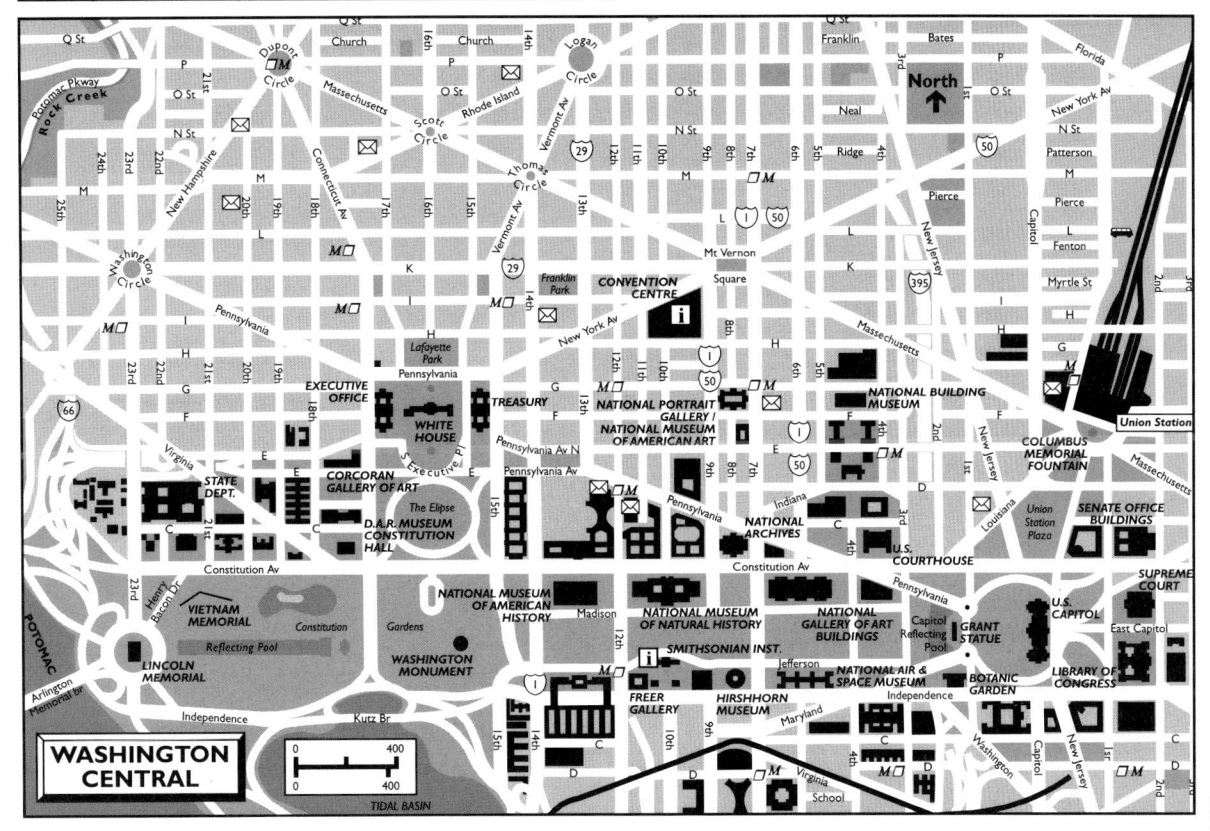

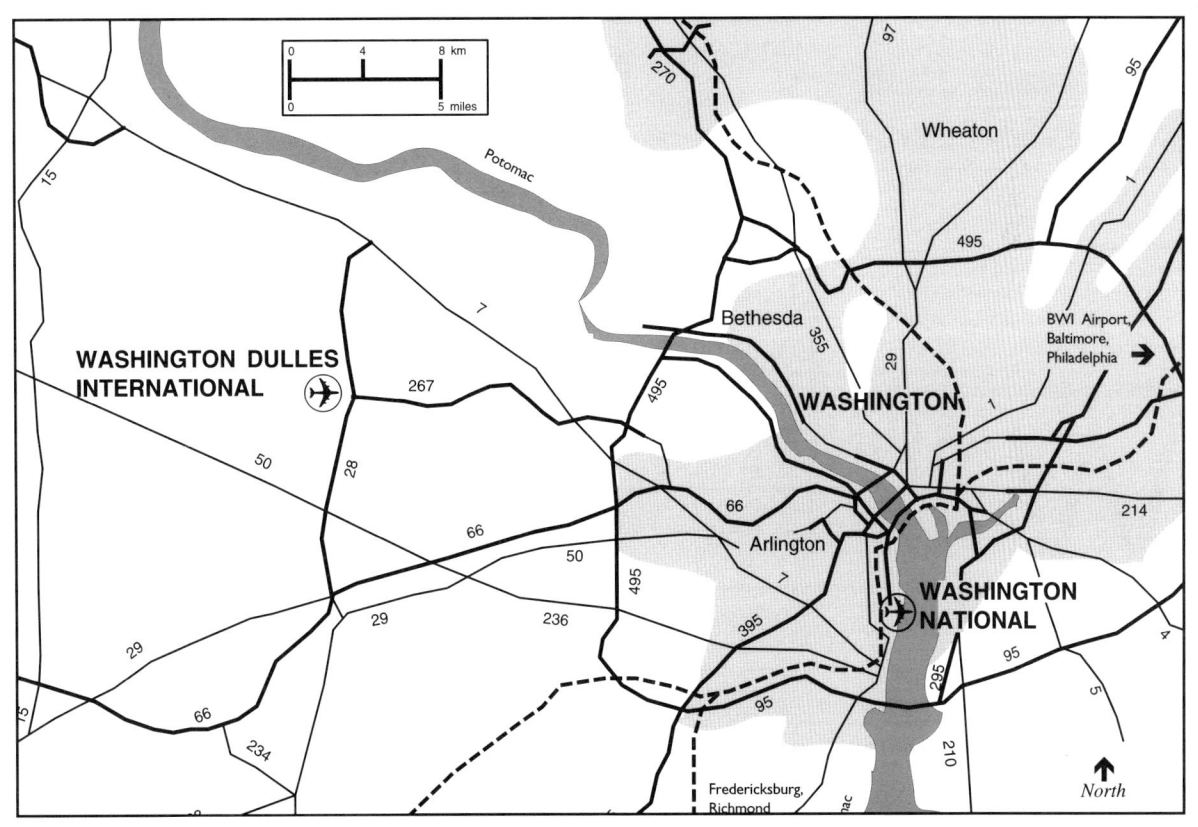

✈︎ Air 🚆 Rail 🚌 Bus 🚘 Limousine Ⓜ Metro/subway 🚋 Tram 🚁 Helicopter ⛴ Water transport • For map symbols, see p. 9

WASHINGTON-DULLES • WASHINGTON-NATIONAL   SECTION TWO • AIRPORT DIRECTORY

Washington Dulles International

16th & K Sts) 🚌Washington Flyer »30 min ⓘ0530–2200 ➲45 min ⊘USD16.
Washington (Union rail stn/Amtrak) ➡Royal Airport Shuttle (800) 653 0888.
Washington metro area ➡Over 40 companies.

Other towns and cities
Quantico VA ➡Dafre Airport Shuttle (703) 680 0987.
For Stafford County VA
Richmond VA ➡Groome Transportation (804) 222 7222.
For Fredericksburg VA

REGIONAL AIR CONNECTIONS

Allentown PA ✈ »Several per day ➲1 hr
Baltimore-Washington International Apt MD ✈ »Several per day ➲30 min
Charlottesville VA ✈ »Several per day ➲35 min
Harrisburg PA ✈ »Several per day ➲40 min
Lynchburg VA ✈ »Several per day ➲50 min
Newport News VA ✈ »Several per day ➲50 min
Norfolk VA ✈ »Several per day ➲55 min
Philadelphia PA ✈ »Several per day ➲50 min
Pittsburgh PA ✈ »Several per day ➲1 hr
Richmond VA ✈ »Several per day ➲40 min
Roanoke VA ✈ »Several per day ➲55 min
State College PA ✈ »Several per day ➲50 min

TRAVELLER'S NOTES

Public transport is ultra-modern, comfortable and, within the city centre, safe.

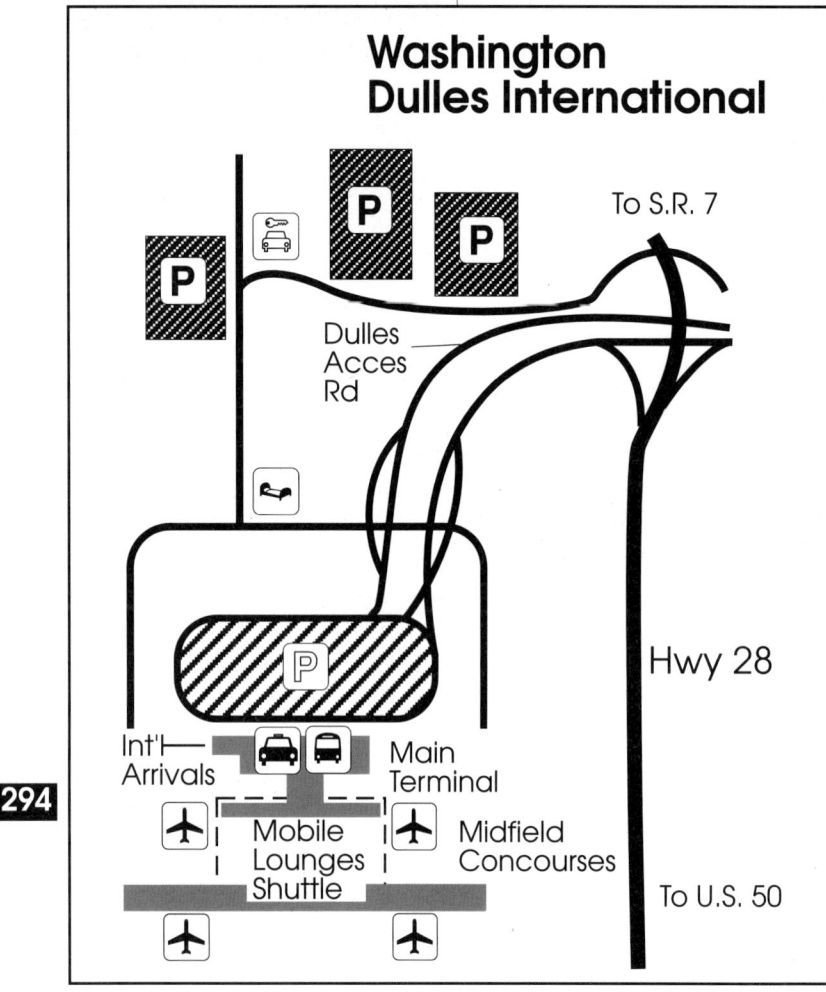

ⓘ0500–2300 ➲45 min ⊘USD16.
Fairfax County VA 🚌Fairfax Connector.
West Falls Church VA (Metro Orange Line) 🚌Washington Flyer 30 min ⓘ0630–2300 ➲20 min ⊘USD8. For Metrorail services
Washington city centre (Airports Terminal

WASHINGTON-NATIONAL
USA (see page 41)

National ☎ code: 1
Area ☎ code: 202
Local time: Winter GMT-5, Summer GMT-4
Washington–National Airport, Washington, DC 20001, USA
☎572 2700

📠572 6817
Internet e-mail: metwashairports.com
WWW site: http://www.metwashairports.com/National
Location: 5 km/3 miles S of Washington

TERMINALS AND TRANSFERS

Terminals
Terminal A Airlines: Continental, Delta Shuttle, Midway, Northwest, TWA, TW Express, US Airways Shuttle Layout: Level 2 (Arrivals, Baggage Claim, Ground Transportation, Departures, Gates 1–6E),

☎ Phone no. 📠 Fax no. ⓘ Hours of opening/operation » Frequency of service ➲ Journey time ⊘ Cost/one-way fare

SECTION TWO • AIRPORT DIRECTORY — WASHINGTON-NATIONAL

Lower Level (Departures, Gates 7C–9). Terminal B Airlines: America West, Delta, **Delta Connection Layout:** Level 1 (Arrivals, Baggage Claim, Ground Transportation), Level 2 (Concourses, Gates 10–15), Level 3 (Departure). Terminal C Airlines: Air Canada, American, American Eagle, Midwest Express, United, US Airways, US Airways Express Layout: Level 1 (Arrivals, Baggage Claim, Ground Transportation), Level 2 (Concourses, Gates 10–15), Level 3 (Departure).

Minimum transfer times
International: 1 hr Domestic: 45 min
Transfer between terminals
Bus »Frequent; Terminals, Metrorail, Rental Cars, parking lots ⊘Free

INFORMATION
Information and help desks
Information Center Terminal B Level 2 Airport, tourist information
Information Center Terminal C Level 2 Airport, tourist information
Traveller's Aid Terminal A Level 2 Tourist information
Traveller's Aid Terminal B Level 1 Tourist information
Police Terminal A Lower Level
Police Terminal B Level 2 ℂ(703) 417 8034
Medical ℂ(703) 417 8200
Lost Property ℂ(703)417 8035

AIRPORT FACILITIES

Money
ATM All Terminals throughout ⓞ24 hr
Bureau de change All Terminals Business Service Centres

Food and drink
Bar All Terminals throughout
Café/light All terminals throughout ⓞ0600–2200
Restaurant All terminals throughout ⓞ0600–2200
Post office Terminal A Level 2 ⓞ0830–1700 Mon–Fri; 0830–1200 Sat
Post box All Terminals throughout
Fax service All Terminals Business Service Centers

Shopping
Duty free, departure, Terminal C, near Air Canada
Gift Shop All Terminals throughout

News, Stationery & Books All terminals throughout

Luggage
Lockers All Terminals Level 2 (behind Security) ⓞ24 hr

DISABLED TRAVELLERS
All Terminals Adapted toilets; Lifts; Phones at wheelchair height; Phones Adapted for the deaf; Special car parking; Personal assistance

SMOKING POLICY
All Terminals No-smoking throughout

SPECIAL PASSENGER LOUNGES
American Airlines Admirals Club
Continental Presidents Club
Delta Crown Room
TWA Ambassadors Club
United Airlines Red Carpet Club
US Airways Club

CONFERENCE AND BUSINESS FACILITIES
Business Service Centers ℂ(703) 419 8383 and (703) 419 8386 ⓞ0600–2100
Currency Exchange, Fax service, Photocopier, Travel advice

CAR RENTAL
Alamo Parking Garage A
Avis Parking Garage A
Budget Parking Garage A
Enterprise Parking Garage A
Hertz Parking Garage A
National Parking Garage A

CAR PARKING
Long-stay Parking Garage A, B and C adjacent to terminals ⊘USD2 per hr; USD12 per day (max)
Long-stay Remote Parking (take shuttle bus) ⊘USD1 per hr; USD8 per day (max)
Short-stay Hourly Lot A and Parking Garage B and C adjacent to terminals ⊘USD4 per hr; USD28 per day (max)

TAXIS AND CHAUFFEUR-DRIVEN CARS

Taxis
City centre ⊃15 min ⊘USD12

PUBLIC TRANSPORT

Airport to airport
Washington-Dulles Airport
🚌Washington Flyer »1 hr ⓞ0500–2300 ⊃45 min ⊘USD16.

City & suburbs
Washington city centre Metrorail: Blue and Yellow lines »5–10 min ⓞ0530–2400 ⊃18 min ⊘USD1
Washington city centre (Airports Terminal 16th & K Sts) 🚌Washington Flyer »30 min ⓞ0530–2200 ⊃45 min ⊘USD16.
Washington metro area 🚗Over 40 companies.

Other towns and cities
Quantico VA 🚗Dafre Airport Shuttle (703) 680 0987.
For Stafford County VA
Richmond VA 🚗Groome Transportation (804) 222 7222.
For Fredericksburg VA

REGIONAL AIR CONNECTIONS
Allentown PA ✈ »Several per day ⊃1 hr
Baltimore-Washington International Apt MD ✈ »Several per day ⊃30 min
New York-La Guardia ✈ »Several per day ⊃1 hr
New York-Newark NJ ✈ »Several per day ⊃1 hr
Norfolk VA ✈ »Several per day ⊃1 hr
Philadelphia PA ✈ »Several per day ⊃1 hr
Pittsburgh PA ✈ »Several per day ⊃1 hr
Raleigh/Durham NC ✈ »Several per day ⊃55 min
Richmond VA ✈ »Several per day ⊃45 min
Salisbury MD ✈ »Several per day ⊃45 min

TRAVELLER'S NOTES
Direct Metrorail service to the city centre is one reason why National Airport is a convenient alternative for domestic flights.

ZURICH   SECTION TWO • AIRPORT DIRECTORY ✈✈

ZÜRICH   ZRH
Switzerland (see page 38)

National ✆ code: 41
Area ✆ code: 01
Local time: Winter GMT+1,
Summer GMT+2
Zürich Flughafen, 8058 Zürich,
Switzerland
✆816 2211
🅕816 5010
Location: 12 km/7½ miles N of
Zürich

TERMINALS AND TRANSFERS

Terminals
Terminal A Airlines: Crossair, Austrian Airlines, Sabena, Delta Airlines, Singapore Airlines. Layout: Basement, car park; Level 1, Arrival; Level 2, Departure
Terminal B Airlines: All other airlines. Layout: Basement, car park and rail station; Level 2, duty free shopping and other services; Level 3, Departure

Minimum transfer times
International: 40 min Domestic: 40 min

INFORMATION

Flight enquiries
Airport ✆812 71 11
Aer Lingus ✆816 2830 **Aeroflot** ✆816 4048 **Aerolineas Argentinas** ✆816 2829 **Air Algérie** ✆816 3548 **Air Canada** ✆816 3038 **Air China** ✆816 3090 **Air France** ✆816 2411 **Air Lanka** ✆816 3556 **Air Madagascar** ✆816 4051 **Air Malta** ✆816 3012 **Air Mauritius** ✆816 3335 **Air Portugal TAP** ✆816 2417 **Alitalia** ✆816 2415 **American Airlines** ✆816 4242 **Austrian Airlines** ✆816 2543 **Balkan Bulgarian Airlines** ✆816 2823 **British Airways** ✆816 2980 **Cathay Pacific Airways** ✆816 4433 **Crossair** ✆816 4170 **CSA Czechoslovak** ✆816 2430 **Cyprus Airlines** ✆816 4414 **Delta Airlines** ✆816 2460 **Egyptair** ✆816 2462 **El Al Israel Airlines** ✆816 4337 **Finnair** ✆816 2815 **Garuda Indonesian Airlines** ✆816 3036 **Iberia** ✆816 3671 **Japan Airlines** ✆816 3566 **Kenya Airways** ✆816 2888 **KLM** ✆816 2408 **Korean Airlines** ✆816 2948 **Lot Polish Airlines** ✆816 2461 **Lufthansa** ✆816 2800 **Malaysian Airlines** ✆816 4060 **Malev Hungarian** ✆816 2476 **Middle East Airlines** ✆816 4324 **Olympic Airways** ✆816 2438 **Sabena** ✆816 2410 **SAS** ✆816 2400 **Singapore Airlines** ✆816 2870 **South African Airways** ✆816 2843 **Tarom Romanian Air** ✆816 2834 **Thai Airways** ✆816 4323 **Tunis Air** ✆816 2824 **Turkish Airlines** ✆816 2825 **TWA** ✆816 4003 **Varig Brazilian** ✆816 2549 **VIASA Venezuelan** ✆816 4210

Information and help desks
Airport Information Desk Terminal A Arrival Hall ✆812 7209 ⏱0600–2200 *Airport information, Hotel booking.*
Airport Information Desk Terminal B Arrival Hall ✆812 7216 ⏱0700–2200 *Airport information, Hotel booking.*
Tourist Information Desk Terminal A Arrival Hall ✆816 35 11 ⏱0900–2000 *Tourist information*

EMERGENCIES

Police Terminal A Building PA ✆816 2421
Lost Property Terminal A Arrival Level 1 ✆157 1015 ⏱0600–2330
Lost Property Terminal B Jet Aviation desk ✆816 4954 ⏱0830–1700
Lost Property Terminal B Swissair desk ✆812 5200 ⏱0600–2300

AIRPORT FACILITIES

Money
Bank Terminal A Departure, Arrival and Transit Levels ⏱0630–2300
Bank Terminal B Departure, Arrival and Transit Levels ⏱0630–2200
Bureau de change Terminal A Departure, Arrival and Transit Levels ⏱0630–2300
Bureau de change Terminal B Departure, Arrival and Transit Levels, rail station, car park ⏱0630–2200

Food and drink
Bar Terminal A throughout ⏱1100–2300
Café/light meals Terminal A throughout ⏱0600–2000
Restaurant Terminal A throughout ⏱0600–2000
Bar Terminal B throughout ⏱1100–2300
Café/light meals Terminal B throughout ⏱0600–2000
Restaurant Terminal B throughout ⏱0600–2000

Communications
Post box Terminal A Departure Hall
Post office Terminal B Plaza shopping area, Second Floor car park B ⏱0700–2000 Mon-Fri; 0700–1200 Sat
Post box Terminal B Departure Hall

Shopping
Duty free, departure Terminal A Transit Area ⏱0600–2330
Duty free, departure Terminal B Transit Area ⏱0600–2330
Pharmacy Terminal B Plaza Shopping Centre, Second Floor, Transit Area and Car Park B ⏱0800–2000
Shopping mall Terminal B Plaza Shopping Centre, Second Floor car park B ⏱0800–2000

Luggage
Porters Terminal A throughout ⌀CHF3 per item
Trolleys/carts Terminal A throughout ⌀Free
Left luggage counter Terminal A ⌀CHF2 per item per day
Porters Terminal B throughout ⌀CHF3 per item
Trolleys/carts Terminal B throughout ⌀Free
Left luggage counter Terminal B ⌀CHF2 per item per day

DISABLED TRAVELLERS

Terminal A Adapted toilets; Lifts; Phones at wheelchair height
Terminal B Adapted toilets; Lifts; Phones at wheelchair height

SPECIAL PASSENGER LOUNGES

British Airways Executive Club Terminal B Transit Area
Lufthansa Lounge Terminal B Transit Area
Singapore Airlines SQ Lounge Terminal B Transit Area
Swissair Lounge Terminal A Transit Area
Swissair Lounge Terminal B Transit Area

CONFERENCE AND BUSINESS FACILITIES

Airport Conference Centre, Terminal B ✆816 3719 🅕816 4716
Airport Forum, Building PA ✆816 3422 🅕816 4455

✆ Phone no. 🅕 Fax no. ⏱ Hours of opening/operation » Frequency of service ⊃ Journey time ⌀ Cost/one-way fare

SECTION TWO • AIRPORT DIRECTORY

ZURICH

AIRPORT HOTELS

Airport ℂ810 4444 ℻810 9708
Hilton ℂ810 3131 ℻810 9366
Novotel ℂ810 3111 ℻810 8185

CAR RENTAL

Avis Terminal A ℂ813 00 84
Budget Terminal A ℂ813 31 31
EuropCar Terminal A ℂ813 20 44
Eurorent Terminal A ℂ816 35 24
Hertz Terminal A ℂ814 05 11

CAR PARKING

Short-stay Below airport 5400 spaces
◇CHF2–4 per hr, CHF26–36 per day, CHF98–132 per week

TAXIS AND CHAUFFEUR-DRIVEN CARS

Taxis
Arrival Terminals A and B ⌁20–30 min
◇CHF40

PUBLIC TRANSPORT

Airport to airport
Geneva Apt ⇌SBB/CFF »60 min
⌚0537–1943 ⌁approx 3 hr 20 min
◇CHF128.

City & suburbs
Zürich city centre ▦ »15 min ⌁20–30 min ◇SFR 5.10.
Zürich (Hbf – central rail stn) ⇌SBB/CFF
»15 min ⌚0537–0021 ⌁10–12 min
◇CHF5.10.

Other towns and cities
Basel ⇌SBB/CFF »30–90 min
⌚0739–2341 ⌁1 hr 12 min–1 hr 25.
Much more frequent service by changing at Zurich Hbf
Chur ⇌SBB »2 hr ⌚0653–1853 ⌁2 hr 46 min

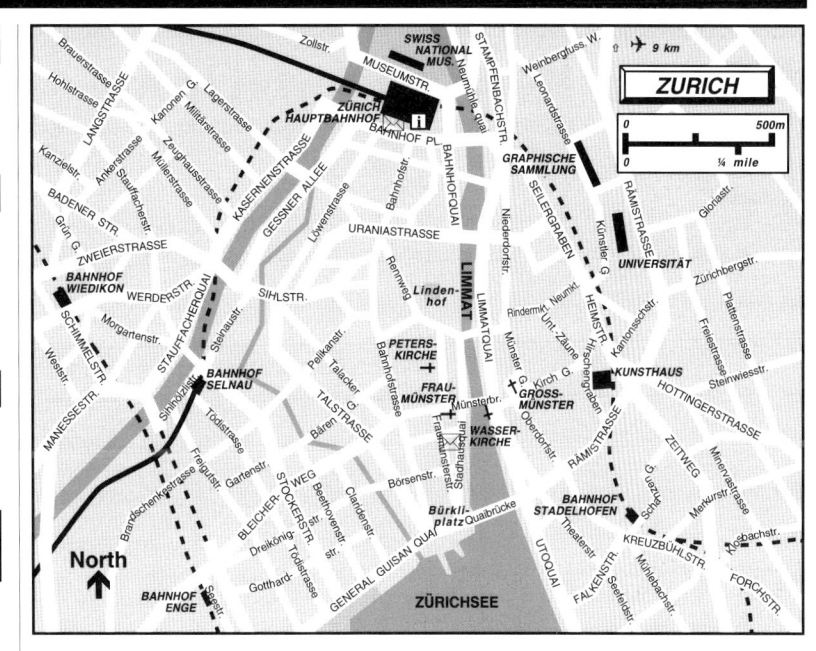

Geneva ⇌SBB/CFF »2 hr ⌚0535–2037
⌁3 hr 30 min
Lausanne ⇌SBB/CFF »2 hr
⌚0637–2037 ⌁3 hr 10 min
Luzern ⇌SBB/CFF »1 hr ⌚0833–2033
(0601–0013 with change at Zürich Hbf)
⌁1 hr 17 min.
St Gallen ⇌SBB/CFF »20–40 min
⌚0614–2327 ⌁60–65 min
Winterthur ⇌SBB/CFF »20–30 min
⌚0614–2327 ⌁15–18 min
Zug ⇌SBB/CFF »1 hr ⌚0833–2033
(0601–0013 with change at Zürich Hbf)
⌁1 hr 28 min.

REGIONAL AIR CONNECTIONS

Basel ✈ »Several per day ⌁25–30 min
Friedrichshafen ✈ »Several per week ⌁30 min
Geneva ✈ »Several per day ⌁45–50 min
Innsbruck ✈ »Several per day ⌁50 min
Linz ✈ »Several per day ⌁1 hr
Lugano ✈ »Several per day ⌁45 min
Luxembourg ✈ »Several per day ⌁1 hr
Lyon ✈ »Several per day ⌁1 hr
Mulhouse ✈ »Several per day ⌁30 min
Munich ✈ »Several per day ⌁55 min
Nuremberg ✈ »At least daily ⌁1 hr
Salzburg ✈ »Several per day ⌁55 min
Strasbourg ✈ »Several per day ⌁40 min
Stuttgart ✈ »Several per day ⌁45 min
Turin ✈ »Several per day ⌁1 hr

TRAVELLER'S NOTES

The rail link with Zürich Hbf puts the airport at the heart of the European rail network, with connections to towns and cities thoroughout the Alps and central Europe.

✈ Air ⇌ Rail ▦ Bus ⇌ Limousine ▦ Metro/subway ⇌ Tram ⌁ Helicopter ⇌ Water transport • For map symbols, see p. 9

DESTINATION INDEX

AALBORG • ANTWERP   SECTION THREE • DESTINATION INDEX

Page references are to the beginning of the airport entry in Section Two, in which more details of the airport and the connection can be found. Places in the USA, Canada and Australia in this index are followed by their respective state or province designation. Other places are designated by their country only if there are two or more places of the same name in the index, e.g. Manchester (UK) is differentiated from Manchester NH.

Aalborg from Copenhagen page 111 ✈ »Several per day ⊃45 min

Aalesund from Oslo page 223 ✈ »Several per day ⊃55 min

Aberdeen from Glasgow page 131 ✈ »Several per day ⊃55 min

Aberdeen from Norwich page 220 ✈ »Several per day ⊃1 hr 50 min

Abilene TX from Dallas/Fort Worth page 113 ✈ »Several per day ⊃1 hr

Abu Dhabi (city centre) from Abu Dhabi page 58 🚌 »30 min ⊃30 min

Abu Dhabi from Dubai page 119 ✈ »Several per week ⊃35 min

Acapulco from Mexico City page 187 ✈ »Several per day ⊃50 min

Accra from Lagos page 153 ✈ »Several per day ⊃50 min

Accra from Lagos page 153 ✈ »Several per day ⊃50 min

Acton MA from Boston page 85 🚌

Adelaide SA from Melbourne page 186 ✈ »Several per day ⊃45 min

Agadir from Casablanca page 86 ✈ »At least daily ⊃1 hr

Aguascalientes from Mexico City page 187 ✈ »Several per day ⊃55–60 min

Aigle from Geneva page 130 🚆 SBB » 1hr ⊃ 1hr 20min

Aix-en-Provence from Nice page 217 🚌 »avg 2 hr 30 min ⊃2 hr 45 min

Aix-les-Bains from Lyon page 178 🚆 »5 per day Mon–Fri, 1 per day Sat, Sun ⊃1 hr 25 min

Ajaccio from Nice page 217 ✈ »Several per day ⊃45 min

Akita from Tokyo-Narita page 277 ✈ »Several per day ⊃1 hr

Akureyri from Reykjavik page 241 ✈ »Several per day ⊃45 min

Alamo CA from San Francisco page 252 🚆 »1–2 hrs ⊃50 min

Albany GA from Atlanta page 67 ✈ »Several per day ⊃55 min

Albany NY from Boston page 85 ✈ »Several per day ⊃45 min

Albany NY from New York-JFK page 209 ✈ »Several per day ⊃1 hr

Albany NY from New York-La Guardia page 214 ✈ »Several per day ⊃55 min

Albany NY from New York-Newark page 216 ✈ »Several per day ⊃1 hr

Albany NY from Philadelphia page 238 ✈ »Several per day ⊃1 hr

Albany WA from Perth page 237 ✈ »Several per day ⊃1 hr

Albany WA from Perth page 237 ✈ »Several per day ⊃1 hr

Albert Lee MN from Minneapolis/St Paul page 161 🚌 »2 per day ⊃2 hr 5 min

Albury NS from Melbourne page 186 ✈ »Several per day ⊃45 min

Alexandria (Egypt) from Cairo page 83 ✈ »Several per day ⊃30–50 min

Alexandria LA from Houston page 142 ✈ »Several per day ⊃1 hr

Alexandria MN from Minneapolis/St Paul page 161

Alghero from Rome-Fiumicino page 244 ✈ »Several per day ⊃1 hr 5 min

Alicante from Barcelona page 75 ✈ »Several per day ⊃55 min

Alicante from Madrid page 180 ✈ »Several per day ⊃55 min

Alice Springs from Adelaide page 59 ✈ »Several per day ⊃60 min

Allentown PA from New York-Newark page 216 🚌 »8 per day ⊃2 hr

Allentown/Bethlehem PA from New York-Newark page 216 ✈ »Several per day ⊃45 min

Allentown PA from Philadelphia page 239 ✈ »Several per day ⊃40 min

Alor Settar from Kuala Lumpur page 151 ✈ »Several per day ⊃50 min

Amersfoort from Amsterdam page 61 🚆 »avg 15 min ⊃39 min

Ames IA from Minneapolis/St Paul page 161 🚌 »2 per day ⊃5 hr

Amherst MA from Boston page 85 🚌

Amman from Jeddah page 146 ✈ »Several per week ⊃1 hr

Amman from Riyadh page 243 ✈ »Several per week ⊃1 hr 5 min

Amsterdam (city centre) from Amsterdam page 61 🚆 »30 min ⊃40 min

Amsterdam (city centre) from Amsterdam page 61 🚌 »avg 15 min by day, 1 hr at night ⊃17 min

Amsterdam from Brussels page 90 ✈ »Several per day ⊃40 min

Amsterdam from Düsseldorf page 122 ✈ »Several per day ⊃50 min

Amsterdam from Hamburg page 135 ✈ »Several per day ⊃60–65 min

Amsterdam from London-City page 157 ✈ »Several per day ⊃50 min

Amsterdam from London-Gatwick page 160 ✈ »Several per day ⊃1 hr 5 min

Amsterdam from London-Heathrow page 164 ✈ »Several per day ⊃1 hr 5 min

Amsterdam from London-Stansted page 173 ✈ »Several per day ⊃1 hr

Amsterdam from Paris-Charles de Gaulle page 226 ✈ »Several per day ⊃1 hr 5 min

Amsterdam from Paris-Orly page 234 ✈ »Several per day ⊃1 hr 10 min

Anacortes WA (San Juan Islands Ferry) from Seattle page 258 🚌 »1–2 hrs ⊃2 hr 40 min

Anacortes WA from Seattle page 258 🚌 »1–2 hrs ⊃2 hr 20 min

Ancona from Rome-Fiumicino page 244 ✈ »Several per day ⊃1 hr 5 min

Andover MA from Boston page 85 🚌

Angers from Paris-Charles de Gaulle page 226 🚆 »4 per day ⏰0856–1825 ⊃1 hr 35 min

Angoulême from Paris-Charles de Gaulle page 226 🚆 »3 per day ⏰0856–1855 ⊃3 hr.

Ankara (city centre) from Ankara page 64 🚌 ⊃30 min

Ankara from Istanbul page 143 ✈ »Several per day ⊃1 hr

Annaba from Lyon page 178 ✈ »Several per week ⊃45 min

Annapolis MD from Baltimore/Washington page 72 🚌 SuperShuttle »2 hr

Annecy from Lyon page 178 🚌 »according to demand

Anniston AL from Atlanta page 67 🚌

Antalya from Ankara page 64 ✈ »At least daily ⊃1 hr 5 min

Antibes from Nice page 217 🚆 »40 min ⊃1 hr 25 min

Antwerp from Amsterdam page 61 ✈ »Several per day ⊃40 min

Antwerp from Amsterdam page 61 🚆 ⊃1 hr 55 min

Antwerp from Brussels page 90 🚆 »1 hr ⊃50 min

298

» Frequency of service ⊃ Journey time   For details of fares, etc, see individual airport entries, Section Two

SECTION THREE • DESTINATION INDEX

ANTWERP • BELFAST

Antwerp from London-City page 157 ✈ »Several per day ◷1 hr

Antwerp from London-Gatwick page 160 ✈ »Several per day ◷1 hr 10 min

Antwerp from London-Heathrow page 164 ✈ »Several per week ◷1 hr 10 min

Antwerpen see **Antwerp**

Anvers see **Antwerp**

Appleton WI from Chicago-O'Hare page 106 ✈ »Several per day ◷45 min

Aptos CA from San Francisco page 252 🚌 »2 hr ◷2 hr 30 min

Arad from Bucuresti page 92 ✈ »2 per day ◷2 hr

Århus from Copenhagen page 111 ✈ »Several per day ◷35 min

Armenia (Colombia) from Bogota page 84 ✈ »Several per week ◷50 min

Arvada CO from Denver page 118 🚌 RTD SkyRide AA »1 hr ◷1 hr 10 min

Aspen CO from Denver page 118 🚌 »1 hr

Aspen CO from Denver page 118 🚌 »30 min .

Aspen CO from Denver page 118 ✈ »Several per day ◷40 min

Astoria OR from Seattle page 259 ✈ »Several per day ◷40 min

Asturias from Madrid page 180 ✈ »Several per day ◷1 hr

Asunción from Buenos Aires page 95 ✈ »Several per day ◷50 min

Asunción from São Paulo-Guarulhos page 257 ✈ »Several per day ◷1 hr

Athens (city centre – Avenue Syngrou) from Athens page 65 🚌 ◷20 min

Athens (city centre – Omonia Square) from Athens page 65 🚌 »20–30 min ◷30 min

Athens (city centre – Syntagma Square) from Athens page 65 🚌 »20–30 min

Athinai see **Athens**

Atlanta GA (city centre) from Atlanta page 67 🚌

Atlanta GA (city centre) from Atlanta page 67 🚆 »4–8 min ◷15 min

Atlanta GA (downtown hotels) from Atlanta page 67 🚌 »20 min ◷15 min

Atlantic City NJ from New York-Newark page 216 ✈ »Several per day ◷45 min

Atlantic City NJ from Philadelphia page 238 ✈ »Several per day ◷40 min

Atlantic City NJ from Philadelphia page 239 ✈ »Several per day ◷40 min

Auburn AL from Atlanta page 67 🚌

Auckland (city centre) from Auckland page 69 🚌 »30 min

Augusta ME from Boston page 85 ✈ »Several per day ◷50 min

Austin TX from Houston page 142 ✈ »Several per day ◷45 min

Austin TX from Dallas/Fort Worth page 113 ✈ »Several per day ◷45 min

Avignon from Lyon page 178 🚆 »1 per day ◷1hr 30 min

Avignon from Nice page 217 🚌 »avg 2 hr 30 min ◷2 hr 45 min

Avignon from Paris-Charles de Gaulle page 226 🚆 »7 per day ◷3 hr 50 min

Avignon from Paris-Orly page 234 ✈ »Several per week ◷1 hr 10 min

Baguio from Manila page 185 ✈ »At least daily ◷40–50 min

Bahrain from Riyadh page 243 ✈ »Several per week ◷1 hr 5 min

Bakersfield CA from Los Angeles page 174 🚌 »8 day ◷2 hr 30 min

Bakersfield CA from Los Angeles page 174 🚌 »3 day ◷2 hr 30 min

Bakersfield CA from Los Angeles page 174 ✈ »Several per day ◷45 min

Bâle, Basle see **Basel**

Baltimore-Washington International Apt MD from Washington-Dulles page 291 🚌

Baltimore-Washington International Apt MD from Washington-Dulles page 291 ✈ »Several per day ◷30 min

Baltimore MD from Philadelphia page 239 ✈ »Several per day ◷40 min

Bandar Lampung from Jakarta page 145 ✈ »Several per day ◷55 min

Bandung from Jakarta page 145 ✈ »Several per day ◷40 min

Bandung from Singapore page 261 ✈ »At least daily ◷55 min

Banff/Lake Louise AB from Calgary page 98 🚌 Brewster Airport Express »2 day ⓘ1230; 1800 ◷ 3hr 45 min

Banff AB from Calgary page 98 🚌 Laidlaw »2 day ⓘ1200; 1500 ◷ 2hr

Bang Pakaew from Bangkok page 72 🚌

Bangkok (city centre) from Bangkok page 72 🚌

Bangkok (Hualampong rail stn) from Bangkok page 72 🚇 »13 per day ◷45 min

Bangkok (rail stn) from Bangkok page 72 ◷1 hr

Bangkok from Kuala Lumpur page 151 ✈ »Several per day ◷1 hr

Bangkok Emerald Buddha Temple (Snam Luang) from Bangkok page 72 🚌

Bangkok, Klong Toey from Bangkok page 72 🚌

Bangor ME from Boston page 85 ✈ »Several per day ◷1 hr

Bangor ME from Boston page 85 🚌 »2 hrs ◷5–6 hrs

Bangrak from Bangkok page 72

Barcelona (city centre – Plaza Cataluña) from Barcelona page 75 🚌 »15 min ◷35 min

Barcelona (city centre – Plaza España) from Barcelona page 75 🚌 »1 hr 20 min ◷40 min

Barcelona (city centre – Sants rail stn) from Barcelona page 75 🚇 »30 min ◷23 min

Barcelona from Madrid page 180 ✈ »Several per day ◷1 hr

Bari from Rome-Fiumicino page 244 ✈ »Several per day ◷1 hr

Barquisimeto from Caracas page 85 ✈ »Several per week ◷40 min

Barra from Glasgow page 131 ✈ »Several per week ◷1hr 05 min

Barrabermeja from Bogota page 84 ✈ »At least daily ◷57 min

Basel see also **Mulhouse/Basel**

Basel from Milan-Malpensa page 194 ✈ »At least daily ◷1 hr

Basel from Geneva page 130 ✈ »5 per day ◷45 min

Basel from Paris-Orly page 234 ✈ »Several per day ◷55 min

Basel from Zürich page 296 ✈ »Several per day ◷25–30 min

Basel from Zürich page 296 🚇 »30–90 min ◷1 hr 12 min–1 hr 25

Bastia from Lyon page 178 ✈ »Several per week ◷60–65 min

Bastia from Nice page 217 ✈ »Several per day ◷45 min

Bathurst Island from Darwin page 115 ✈ »2 per day ◷30 min

Baton Rouge LA from New Orleans page 209 ✈ »At least daily ◷30 min

Be'er Sheva from Tel Aviv page 275

Beaumont TX from Houston page 142 ✈ »Several per day ◷30 min

Beaumont/Port Arthur TX from New Orleans page 209 ✈ »At least daily ◷1 hr

Beaver Creek CO from Denver page 118 🚌 »1 hr

Beaver Creek CO from Denver page 118 🚌 »30 min

Beaver Creek CO from Denver page 118 🚌 »1 hr

Bedford (UK) from London-Gatwick page 160 🚇 »avg 20 min ◷37 min

Bedwell Harbor BC from Vancouver page 286 ✈ »At least daily ◷45 min

Beijing (city centre) from Beijing page 67 🚌 »30 min ◷approx 45 min

Bejaia from Lyon page 178 ✈ »Several per week ◷45 min

Belfast (city centre) from Belfast-International page 78 🚌 »30 min ◷30–40 min

Belfast from Birmingham page 82 ✈ »Several per day ◷55 min

Belfast from Glasgow page 131 ✈ »Several per day ◷45 min

299

Remember . . .
The destinations in this index can be reached directly from the gateway airport. Many more local and long-distance transport connections may be available from the centre of the city. Consult the current edition of the *Thomas Cook European Timetable* (Europe) or *Thomas Cook Overseas Timetable* (rest of the world).

✈ Air 🚆 Rail 🚌 Bus 🚐 Limousine Ⓜ Metro/subway 🚋 Tram 🚁 Helicopter ⛴ Water transport

Belfast from London-Gatwick page 160 ✈ »Several per day ⏱1 hr 20 min

Belfast from London-Heathrow page 164 ✈ »Several per day ⏱1 hr 15 min

Belfast from London-Stansted page 173 ✈ »Several per day ⏱1 hr 15 min

Belfast from Manchester page 183 ✈ »Several per day ⏱55 min

Bellevue WA from Seattle page 258 🚌

Bellingham WA (Alaska Ferry Terminal) from Seattle page 258 🚌 »1–2 hrs ⏱2 hr 25 min

Bellingham WA from Seattle page 258 ✈ »Several per day ⏱40 min

Bellingham WA from Seattle page 258 🚌 »1–2 hrs ⏱2 hr 30 min

Bellingham WA Apt from Seattle page 258 🚌 »1–2 hrs ⏱2 hr 40 min

Bellingham WA from Seattle page 259 ✈ »Several per day ⏱40 min

Belo Horizonte from São Paulo-Guarulhos page 257 ✈ »Several per day ⏱1 hr

Benidorm from Alicante page 60 🚆 Ferrocarrilis de la Generalitat Valenciana »1 hr ⏱1 hr 8 min

Benton Harbor MI from Chicago-O'Hare page 106 🚌United Limo »2 day ⏱4 hr 5 min

Bergen from Oslo page 223 ✈ »Several per day ⏱50 min

Berkshire County MA from Boston page 85 🚌

Berlin (Zoo rail stn) from Berlin page 80 🚌 »approx 10 min ⏱25 min

Berlin from Düsseldorf page 122 ✈ »Several per day ⏱1 hr 5 min

Berlin from Frankfurt page 126 ✈ »Several per day ⏱1 hr 5 min

Berlin from Hamburg page 135 ✈ »Several per day ⏱1 hr

Berlin from Munich page 203 ✈ »Several per day ⏱1 hr 10 min

Berlin from Prague page 239 ✈ »Several per week ⏱55 min

Berlin from Warsaw page 290 ✈ »Several per week ⏱1 hr 20 min

Bern from Geneva page 130 🚌 SBB »1hr ⏱2hr

Bern from Geneva page 130 ✈ »16 per day ⏱2hr

Berne from Munich page 203 ✈ »At least daily ⏱55 min

Bethlehem PA from New York-Newark page 216 🚌 »8 per day ⏱1 hr 30 min

Bethlehem PA see also **Allentown/Bethlehem**

Béziers from Paris-Orly page 234 ✈ »Several per week ⏱1 hr 10 min

Biarritz from Paris-Orly page 234 ✈ »Several per day ⏱1 hr 10 min

Biel from Geneva page 130 🚌 SBB »1hr ⏱1hr 40min

Bielefeld from Düsseldorf page 122 🚌 »avg 20 min ⏱1 hr 55 min

Bilbao from Barcelona page 75 ✈ »Several per day ⏱1 hr

Bilbao from Madrid page 180 ✈ »Several per day ⏱50 min

Billund from Copenhagen page 111 ✈ »Several per day ⏱35 min

Bimini North Spb from Miami page 189 ✈ »Several per day ⏱30 min

Binghamton NY from New York-La Guardia page 214 ✈ »Several per day ⏱1 hr

Binghamton NY from New York-Newark page 216 ✈ »Several per day ⏱1 hr

Binghamton NY from Philadelphia page 238 ✈ »At least daily ⏱55 min

Birmingham (UK) (city centre – St Martin's Circus) from Birmingham page 82 🚌 »20 min ⏱30 min

Birmingham (UK) from Belfast-International page 78 ✈ »Several per day ⏱1hr 05 min

Birmingham (UK) from Dublin page 120 ✈ »Several times daily ⏱55 min

Birmingham (UK) from Glasgow page 131 ✈ »Several per day ⏱1hr

Birmingham (UK) from London-Gatwick page 160 ✈ »Several per week ⏱55 min

Birmingham (UK) Apt from London-Heathrow page 164 🚌 »avg 2 hr ⏱2 hr 45 min

Birmingham AL from Atlanta page 67 ✈ »Several per day ⏱45 min

Birmingham AL from Atlanta page 67 🚌

Birmingham Apt from London-Gatwick page 160 🚌 »avg 3 hr ⏱4 hr 30 min

Birmingham AL from New Orleans page 209 ✈ »Several per day ⏱1 hr

Bisha from Jeddah page 146 ✈ »At least daily ⏱1 hr

Blackpool from Belfast-International page 78 ✈ »Several per day ⏱50 min

Blackpool from Dublin page 120 ✈ »At least daily ⏱50 min

Blaine WA from Seattle page 258 🚌 »1–2 hrs ⏱3 hr 20 min

Bloemfontein from Johannesburg page 147 ✈ »Several per day ⏱55 min

Bloomington IL from Chicago-O'Hare page 106 ✈ »Several per day ⏱50 min

Bloomington IN from Chicago-O'Hare page 106 ✈ »At least daily ⏱30 min

Bloomington-Normal IL from St Louis page 247 ✈ »Several per day ⏱45 min

Boca Raton FL from Miami page 189 🚌

Bogota (city centre) from Bogota page 84 🚌 »15 min ⏱30 min

Bologna from Milan-Linate page 192 ✈ »Several per day ⏱45 min

Bologna from Nice page 217 ✈ »Several per day ⏱1 hr 5 min

Bologna from Rome-Fiumicino page 244 ✈ »Several per day ⏱55 min

Bombay see **Mumbai**

Bonaire from Caracas page 85 ✈ »Several per week ⏱50 min

Bonn see also **Cologne/Bonn**

Bonn from Düsseldorf page 122 🚌 »avg 20 min ⏱1 hr 07 min

Bonn from Frankfurt page 126 🚌 »avg 1 hr (day), 2 hr (night) ⏱1 hr 41 min

Borås city centre from Gothenburg page 133 🚌 »1 hr ⏱35 min

Bordeaux from Lyon page 178 ✈ »Several per day ⏱60 min

Bordeaux from Paris-Charles de Gaulle page 226 🚆 SNCF: TGV »4 per day ⏱4 hr

Bordeaux from Paris-Orly page 234 ✈ »Several per day ⏱55 min

Borlange from Stockholm-Arlanda page 266 ✈ »Several per day ⏱35 min

Bornholm from Copenhagen page 111 ✈ »Several per day ⏱35 min

Boston MA (city centre – Back Bay rail stn) from Boston page 85 🚆 »4–8 min ⏱15 min

Boston MA (city centre – North rail stn) from Boston page 85 🚆 »4–8 min ⏱15 min

Boston MA (city centre – Rowes Wharf) 🚌 »15 min ⏱7 min

Boston MA (city centre – South rail stn) from Boston page 85 🚆 »4–8 min ⏱15 min

Boston MA (city centre) from Boston page 85 🚆 »4–12 min ⏱7 min

Boston MA (city centre) from Boston page 85 🚌

Boston MA (downtown hotels) from Boston page 85 🚌 »30 min

Boston MA from New York-La Guardia page 214 ✈ »Several per day ⏱1 hr

Boulder CO from Denver page 118 🚌 »1 hr ⏱1 hr 30 min

Boulder CO from Denver page 118 🚌 »1 hr

Bourgoin from Lyon page 178 🚌 »4 per day ⏱40 min

Bradenton FL see **Sarasota/Bradenton**

Bradford see also **Leeds/Bradford**

Bradford from Leeds page 155 🚆 » Frequent ⏱ 25 min

Brainerd MN from Minneapolis/St Paul page 161 🚌

Brainerd MN from Minneapolis/St Paul page 161 ✈ »Several per day ⏱50 min

Braintree MA from Boston page 85 🚌 »30 min

Bratislava from Munich page 203 ✈ »At least daily ⏱1 hr

Bratislava from Prague page 239 ✈ »Several per day ⏱55 min

Bratislava from Vienna page 288 🚌 »9 daily ⏱1hr 10 min

Breckenridge CO from Denver page 118 🚌 »1 hr

Bremen from Amsterdam page 61 ✈ »Several per day ⏱1 hr

Bremen from Berlin page 80 ✈ »Several pr day ⏱1 hr

Bremen from Frankfurt page 126 ✈ »Several per day ⏱55 min

Bremen from Frankfurt page 126 🚌 »avg 1 hr ⏱5 hr 11 min

» Frequency of service ⏱ Journey time   For details of fares, etc, see individual airport entries, Section Two

SECTION THREE • DESTINATION INDEX — BREMERTON • CHAMBÉRY

Bremerton WA from Seattle page 258 ⇒ »1 hr ⊃1 hr 10 min

Bremerton WA from Seattle page 259 ⇒ Bremerton–Kitsap Airporter »1 hr ⊃1 hr

Brest from Paris-Orly page 234 ✈ »Several per day ⊃1 hr 05 min

Bridgetown centre from Bridgetown page 88 ⇒ » ⊃45 min

Brighton from London-Gatwick page 160 ⇒ »avg 30 min ⊃45 min

Brighton from London-Gatwick page 160 ⇒ »avg 20 min ⊃37 min

Brighton from London-Heathrow page 164 ⇒ »avg 2 hr ⊃1 hr 55 min

Brighton from London-Stansted page 173 ⇒ »avg 2 hr ⊃3 hr 20 min

Brindisi from Rome-Fiumicino page 244 ✈ »Several per day ⊃1 hr 5 min

Bristol from Dublin page 120 ✈ »Several per day ⊃1 hr

Bristol from London-Gatwick page 160 ⇒ »2 hr ⊃3 hr

Bristol from London-Heathrow page 164 ⇒ »avg 1 hr ⊃2 hr

Brno from Prague page 239 ✈ »At least daily ⊃50 min

Broken Hill from Adelaide page 59 ✈ »3 per day ⊃60 min

Bronx NY from New York-JFK page 209 ⇒ »On–demand

Bronx NY from New York-Newark page 216 ⇒ »On-demand

Bronx NY from New York-La Guardia page 214 ⇒ »On-demand

Brookings SD from Minneapolis/St Paul page 161 ✈ »At least daily ⊃55 min

Brooklyn NY (subway) from New York-JFK page 209 ⇒ »30 min

Brooklyn NY from New York-La Guardia page 214 ⇒ »2 hr ⊃30 min

Brownwood TX from Dallas/Fort Worth page 113 ✈ »At least daily ⊃45 min

Brussels (Centrale/Centraal rail stn) from Brussels page 90 ⇒ »30 min ⊃24 min

Brussels (Nord/Noord rail stn) from Brussels page 90 ⇒ »1 hr ⊃35 min

Brussels from Amsterdam page 61 ✈ »Several per day ⊃50 min

Brussels from Düsseldorf page 122 ✈ »Several per day ⊃50 min

Brussels from Frankfurt page 126 ✈ »Several per day ⊃1 hr

Brussels from London-City page 157 ✈ »Several per day ⊃1 hr

Brussels from London-Gatwick page 160 ✈ »Several per day ⊃1 hr 05min

Brussels from London-Heathrow page 164 ✈ »Several per day ⊃1 hr

Brussels from London-Stansted page 173 ✈ »At least daily ⊃1 hr

Brussels from Paris-Charles de Gaulle page 226 ✈ »Several per day ⊃55 min

Brussels from Paris-Orly page 234 ✈ »Several per week ⊃1 hr

Bruxelles see **Brussels**

Bucaramanga from Bogota page 84 ✈ »At least daily ⊃1 hr

Budapest (city centre) from Budapest page 93 ⇒ »30 min ⊃15 min

Budapest from Istanbul page 143 ✈ »Several per week ⊃1 hr

Budapest from Prague page 239 ✈ »Several per day ⊃1 hr

Budapest from Vienna page 288 ✈ »Several per day ⊃55 min

Budapest from Vienna page 288 ⇒ »3 daily ⊃3hr 20 min

Buenos Aires (city centre – Hotel Gran Colon) from Buenos Aires page 95 ⇒ »15 min (0900–1800); 30 min (1800–2000) ⊃35 min

Bujumbura from Nairobi page 205 ✈ »Several per week ⊃35 min

Bulawayo from Harare page 137 ✈ »Several per day ⊃50 min

Bullhead City AZ from Las Vegas page 154 ⇒ Best way

Burbank CA from Las Vegas page 154 ✈ »Several per day ⊃55 min

Burlington IA from Chicago-O'Hare page 106 ✈ »Several per day ⊃45 min

Burlington IA from St Louis page 247 ✈ »Several per day ⊃50 min

Burlington VT from Boston page 85 ✈ »Several per day ⊃1 hr

Burlington VT from Boston page 85 ⇒ »2 per day ⊃6–9 hrs

Burlington/Mount Vernon WA from Seattle page 258 ⇒ »1–2 hrs ⊃1 hr 50 min

Buxton from Manchester page 183 ⇒ »approx. every 30 min ⊃1 hr 20 min

Cagliari from Rome-Fiumicino page 244 ✈ »Several per day ⊃1 hr

Cairo (city centre – Atabah Sq.) from Cairo page 83 ⇒ »1 hr ⊃1 hr

Cairo (city centre – Tahrir Sq.) from Cairo page 83 ⇒ »1 hr ⊃1 hr

Cairo from Jeddah page 146 ✈ »Several per day ⊃1 hr

Calgary AB from Edmonton page 125 ✈ »Several per day ⊃40 min

Cali from Bogota page 84 ✈ »Several per day ⊃50 min

Calvi from Nice page 217 ✈ »At least daily ⊃40 min

Camarillo CA from Los Angeles page 174 ⇒ »7 per day ⊃1 hr 30 min

Cambridge from London-Gatwick page 160 ⇒ »1 hr ⊃3 hr

Cambridge from London-Heathrow page 164 ⇒ »1 hr ⊃2 hr 10 min

Cambridge from Norwich page 220 ⇒ »Several per day ⊃55 min

Campinas from São Paulo-Guarulhos page 257 ⇒ ⊃1 hr 30 min

Campinas from São Paulo-Guarulhos page 257 ✈ »Several per day ⊃30 min

Canberra ACT from Melbourne page 186 ✈ »Several per day ⊃55 min

Canberra ACT from Sydney page 270 ✈ »Several per day ⊃50 min

Cannes from Nice page 217 ⇒ Heli-Inter »avg 20 min ⊃7 min

Cannes centre from Nice page 217 ⇒ »40 min ⊃1 hr 25 min

Cannon Falls MN from Minneapolis/St Paul page 161 ⇒ »2 per day ⊃45 min

Cap-de-la-Madeleine PQ from Montréal-Mirabel page 199 ⇒ »2 per day

Cape Cod MA (South Shore) from Boston page 85 ⇒

Cape Cod MA from Boston page 85 ⇒

Cape Town (city centre) from Cape Town page 99 ⇒ ⊃1 hr

Caracas (city centre) from Caracas page 85 ⇒ »20 min ⊃30 min

Cardiff from Belfast-International page 78 ✈ »At least daily ⊃1hr 10 min

Cardiff from Dublin page 120 ✈ »At least daily ⊃45 min

Cardiff from Manchester page 183 ✈ »At least daily ⊃45 min

Carlisle from Newcastle page 207 ⇒ »1 hr ⊃1 hr 30 min

Carlsbad CA from Los Angeles page 174 ✈ »Several per day ⊃40 min

Carnarvon WA from Perth page 237 ✈ »At least daily ⊃1 hr 10 min

Cartersville GA from Atlanta page 67 ⇒

Casablanca (city centre) from Casablanca page 104 ⇒ ⊃40 min

Castlegar BC from Calgary page 98 ✈ »Several per day ⊃1 hr

Catania from Rome-Fiumicino page 244 ✈ »Several per day ⊃1 hr 10 min

Cedar Rapids IA from Chicago-O'Hare page 106 ✈ »Several per day ⊃55 min

Centralia WA from Seattle page 258 ⇒

Chambéry from Lyon page 178 ⇒ »5 per day Mon–Fri, 1 per day Sat, Sun ⊃1 hr

Chambéry from Lyon page 178 ⇒ »1 per day exc Sat ⊃1 hr

Chambéry Gare from Geneva page 130 SNCF ⇒ ⓘ 0915, 1315, 1900, 2115 (Sat and Sun 0915 and 1900 only) ⊃ 1hr

---

Remember...
The destinations in this index can be reached directly from the gateway airport. Many more local and long-distance transport connections may be available from the centre of the city. Consult the current edition of the *Thomas Cook European Timetable* (Europe) or *Thomas Cook Overseas Timetable* (rest of the world).

✈ Air ⇐ Rail ⇒ Bus ⇐ Limousine Ⓜ Metro/subway ⇐ Tram ⇐ Helicopter ⇐ Water transport

Champaign IL from Chicago-O'Hare page 106 ✈ »Several per day ↻55 min

Champaign IL from St Louis page 247 ✈ »Several per day ↻50 min

Chania from Athens page 65 ✈ »Several times per day ↻45 min

Charleston SC from Atlanta page 67 ✈ »Several per day ↻1 hr

Charlotte NC from Atlanta page 67 ✈ »Several per day ↻1 hr

Charlottesville VA from Washington-Dulles page 291 ✈ »Several per day ↻35 min

Charlottetown PEI from Halifax page 134 ✈ »Several per day ↻35 min

Chattanooga TN from Atlanta page 67 ✈ »Several per day ↻50 min

Cherry Hill NJ from New York-JFK page 209 🚌

Cherry Hill NJ from New York-Newark page 216 🚌

Chester (UK) from Manchester page 183 🚆 »approx. 2 hr ↻approx. 2 hr

Chester PA from Philadelphia page 238 ✈ »15–60 min

Chester PA from Philadelphia page 239 🚆SEPTA: 37 »30–60 min ⊙0450-0035

Chester from Liverpool page 157 🚌 » 30 min ↻ 40 min

Cheyenne WY from Denver page 118 🚌 »1–2 hr

Cheyenne WY from Denver page 118 ✈ »Several per day ↻40 min

Chiang Mai from Bangkok page 72 🚆 »6 per day ↻12–13 hr

Chiayi from Taipei-Chiang Kai Shek page 272 ✈ »Several per day ↻45 min

Chicago IL (city centre) from Chicago-O'Hare page 106 🚇 CTA: Blue Line »5–15 min ↻35 min

Chicago IL (downtown hotels) from Chicago-O'Hare page 106 🚌 ↻45–60 min

Chicago IL (downtown hotels) from Chicago-O'Hare page 106 ✈ »5–10 min ↻45–60 min

Chicago IL (metro area) from Chicago-O'Hare page 106 🚌

Chicago IL (North Shore suburbs) from Chicago-O'Hare page 106 🚌 »5–10 min ↻45–60 min

Chicago IL from St Louis page 247 ✈ »Several per day ↻1 hr

Chicago-Midway Apt IL from Chicago-O'Hare page 106 🚌 »1 hr ↻35 min

Chico CA from San Francisco page 252 ✈ »Several per day ↻1 hr

Chinju from Seoul page 211 ✈ »Several per day ↻1 hr

Chios from Athens page 65 ✈ »Several times per day ↻50 min

Chur from Zürich page 296 🚆 »2 hr ↻2 hr 46 min

Clayton MO from St Louis page 247 🚌

Clermont-Ferrand from Lyon page 178 ✈ »Several per week ↻30-35 min

Clermont-Ferrand from Nice page 217 ✈ »Several per week ↻1 hr 10 min

Clermont-Ferrand from Paris-Orly page 234 ✈ »Several per day ↻50 min

Clermont-Ferrand from Strasbourg page 268 ✈ »Several per day ↻1 hr 15 min

Cloverdale CA from San Francisco page 252 🚌 »4 day ↻2 hr 10 min

Cluj from Bucuresti page 92 ✈ »4 per day ↻1 hr

Coffs Harbour NSW from Sydney page 270 ✈ »Several per day ↻55 min

College Station TX from Dallas/Fort Worth page 113 ✈ »Several per day ↻1 hr

College Station TX from Houston page 142 ✈ »Several per day ↻35 min

Colma CA from San Francisco page 252 🚌 »20–30 min ↻15 min

Colmar from Strasbourg page 268 🚌 »Several per day ↻35 min

Cologne from Frankfurt page 126 ✈ »avg 1 hr Day/2 hr night ↻2 hr

Cologne/Bonn from Amsterdam page 61 ✈ »Several per day ↻1 hr

Cologne/Bonn from Berlin page 80 ✈ »Several per day ↻1 hr 5 min

Cologne/Bonn from Frankfurt page 126 ✈ »Several per day ↻45 min

Cologne/Bonn from Hamburg page 135 ✈ »Several per day ↻55–75 min

Cologne/Bonn from Munich page 203 ✈ »Several per day ↻1 hr 5 min

Cologne/Bonn from Paris-Charles de Gaulle page 226 ✈ »Several per day ↻1 hr

Colombo (city centre – Fort Station) from Colombo page 110 🚌 »Twice daily ↻1 hr 15 min

Colombo (city centre) from Colombo page 110 🚌 Central Transport Board »avg 30 min ↻45 min

Colonia from Buenos Aires page 95 ✈ »Several per week ↻18 min

Colorado Springs CO from Denver page 118 ✈ »Several per day ↻30 min

Columbia MO from St Louis page 247 🚌 »2 day ↻2 hr 10 min. For University of Missouri

Columbia MO from St Louis page 247 ✈ »Several per day ↻40 min

Columbia SC from Atlanta page 67 ✈ »Several per day ↻55 min

Columbus GA from Atlanta page 67 ✈ »Several per day ↻40 min

Columbus OH from Chicago page 105 ✈ »Several per day ↻1 hr

Comox BC from Vancouver page 286 ✈ »Several per day ↻40 min

Concepción (Chile) from Rio de Janeiro-International page 242 ✈ »Several per day ↻1 hr

Concepcion (Chile) from Santiago page 256 ✈ »Several per day ↻1 hr

Concord MA from Boston page 85 🚌

Concord NH from Boston page 85 🚌 Concord Trailways »1–2 hrs ↻2 hrs 15 min

Concord/Walnut Creek CA (hotels) from San Francisco page 252 🚌 »1–2 hr ↻1 hr

Connecticut from New York-JFK page 209 🚌

Connecticut from New York-La Guardia page 214 🚌 »On–demand

Connecticut from New York-Newark page 216 🚌

Constantine from Lyon page 178 ✈ »Several per day ↻35–40 min

Cooma NSW from Sydney page 270 ✈ »Several per day ↻55 min

Copenhagen (city centre) from Copenhagen page 111 🚆 »10–15 min ↻20–30 min

Copenhagen from Hamburg page 135 ✈ »Several per day ↻55–60 min

Copenhagen from Oslo page 223 ✈ »Several per day ↻1 hr 5 min

Copenhagen from Stockholm-Arlanda page 266 ✈ »Several per day ↻1 hr 10 min

Copper Mountain CO from Denver page 118 🚌 »1 hr

Copper Mountain CO from Denver page 118 🚌 »1 hr

Corfu from Athens page 65 ✈ »Several per day ↻50 min

Corpus Christi TX from Houston page 142 ✈ »Several per day ↻45 min

Coruña, Corunna see **La Coruña**

Coventry from Birmingham page 82 🚌 »20 min ↻30 min

Coventry from Birmingham page 82 🚆 »1 hr ↻15 min

Cracow see **Kraków**

Cranbrook BC from Calgary page 98 ✈ »Several per day ↻40 min

Crestwood/Alsip IL from Chicago-O'Hare page 106 🚌 »1 hr ↻1 hr

Crewe from Manchester page 183 🚆 »approx. 1 per hr ↻25 min

Culiacan from Mexico City page 187 ✈ »Several per day ↻45–50 min

Curacao from Caracas page 85 ✈ »Several per week ↻50 min

Dallas–Fort Worth (metro area) from Dallas/Fort Worth page 113 🚌

Dallas–Fort Worth (metro area) from Dallas/Fort Worth page 113 🚌 Classic Shuttle

Dallas–Fort Worth (metro area) from Dallas/Fort Worth page 113 🚌 »20 min ↻30 min

Dallas–Fort Worth (metro area) from Dallas/Fort Worth page 113 🚌

Dallas (city centre) from Dallas/Fort Worth page 113 🚌 »30 min

SECTION THREE • DESTINATION INDEX — DALLAS • EDMONTON

Dallas/Fort Worth TX from Houston page 142 ✈ »Several per day ⊃55 min

Dalton GA from Atlanta page 67 🚌

Danville CA from San Francisco page 252 🚆 »1–2 hrs ⊃50 min

Danville IL from Chicago-O'Hare page 106 ✈ »At least daily ⊃50 min

Darling Harbour NSW from Sydney page 270 🚢 »30 min

Darlington city centre from Teesside page 274 🚆 United Buses » 30 min © 468 771

Davis CA from San Francisco page 252 🚆 »7 day ⊃2 hr

Dayton OH from Chicago-O'Hare page 106 ✈ »Several per day ⊃1 hr

Decatur IL from Chicago-O'Hare page 106 ✈ »At least daily ⊃50 min

Decatur IL from St Louis page 247 ✈ »Several per day ⊃45 min

Decorah IA from Minneapolis/St Paul page 161 🚆 from Miami page 189 🚌

Delhi (city centre) from Delhi page 116 🚆 ⊃45 min

Den Haag from Amsterdam page 61 🚆 »avg 15 min in day/avg 1 hr at night

Denton TX from Dallas/Fort Worth page 113 🚆

Denver CO (city centre) from Denver page 118 🚌 »1 hr

Denver CO (metro area – hotels) from Denver page 118 🚌 »15 min

Denver CO (metro area) from Denver page 118 🚌 » According to demand

Denver CO (metro area) from Denver page 118 🚌 »30 min–1 hr

Derby from East Midlands page 124 🚆 ⊃30 min

Des Moines IA from Minneapolis/St Paul page 161 🚆 »2 per day ⊃5 hr 30 min

Des Moines IA from Minneapolis/St Paul page 161 ✈ »Several per day ⊃1 hr

Detroit MI from Chicago page 105 ✈ »Several per day ⊃1 hr

Dhahran from Bahrain page 70 ✈ »Several per day ⊃25 min

Dhahran from Riyadh page 243 ✈ »Several per day ⊃1 hr

Dillon CO from Denver page 118 🚌 »1 hr

Disneyland CA from Los Angeles page 174 🚆 »30 min ⊃1 hr 15 min

Doha from Abu Dhabi page 58 ✈ »Several per day ⊃50 min

Doha from Bahrain page 70 ✈ »Several per day ⊃45 min

Doha from Dubai page 119 ✈ »Several per day ⊃1 hr

Dominica Cane Field from Bridgetown page 88 ✈ »Several per week ⊃55 min

Dortmund from Amsterdam page 61 ✈ »Several per day ⊃50 min

Dortmund from Düsseldorf page 122 🚆 »avg 30 min ⊃1 hr 15 min

Dortmund from Frankfurt page 126 🚆 »avg 1 hr ⊃3 hr 15 min

Dortmund from Hamburg page 135 ✈ »Several per week ⊃55 min

Dorval (Gare Dorval) from Montréal page 197 🚆 STCUM: 204 »30 min–1 hr ⊃10 min

Dothan AL from Atlanta page 67 ✈ »Several per day ⊃1 hr

Douglas Lake BC from Vancouver page 286 ✈ »At least daily ⊃55 min

Doylestown PA from New York-Newark page 216 🚆 »3 per day ⊃2 hrs

Draguignan from Nice page 217 🚆 »1 per day ⊃1 hr

Dresden from Düsseldorf page 122 ✈ »Several per day ⊃1 hr 10 min

Dresden from Frankfurt page 126 ✈ »Several per day ⊃1 hr

Dresden from Hamburg page 135 ✈ »Several per day ⊃55–70 min

Dresden from Munich page 203 ✈ »Several per day ⊃1 hr

Dresden from Paris-Charles de Gaulle page 226 ✈ »Several per week ⊃1 hr

Dubai from Abu Dhabi page 58 ✈ »Several per week ⊃35 min

Dublin (Ireland) (city centre – bus stn and Heuston rail stn) from Dublin page 120 🚆 »avg 15 min ⊃25 min

Dublin (Ireland) (city centre) from Dublin page 120 🚆 »avg 15 min ⊃30 min

Dublin (Ireland) from London-Stansted page 173 ✈ »Several per day ⊃1 hr 10 min

Dublin (Ireland) from Manchester page 183 ✈ »Several per day ⊃50 min

Dublin (Ireland) from Glasgow page 131 ✈ »Several per day ⊃45 min

Dublin (Ireland) from London-City page 157 ✈ »Several per day ⊃1 hr 5 min

Dublin from Belfast-International page 78 🚆 »avg 3 hr ⊃3 hr

Dublin from Birmingham page 82 ✈ »Several per day ⊃1 hr

Dublin CA from San Francisco page 252 🚆 »1–2 hrs

Dubuque IA from Chicago-O'Hare page 106 ✈ »Several per day ⊃1 hr

Duluth MN from Minneapolis/St Paul page 161 ✈ »Several per day ⊃50 min

Dundee from Aberdeen page 57 🚆 Scotrail »avg 1 hr ⊃1 hr 15 min

Dundee from Aberdeen page 57 ✈ »daily ⊃30 min

Durban from Johannesburg page 147 ✈ »Several per day ⊃1 hr

Durham NH from Boston page 85 🚆 »1–2 hrs ⊃2 hrs 30 min

Durham from Newcastle page 207 🚆 » 30 min ⊃15 min

Düsseldorf (city centre – Hbf – central rail stn) from Düsseldorf page 122 🚆 DB »20 min ⊃11 min

Düsseldorf (city centre) from Düsseldorf page 122 🚆 »20 min ⊃26 min

Düsseldorf from Amsterdam page 61 ✈ »Several per day ⊃50 min

Düsseldorf from Berlin page 80 ✈ »Several per day ⊃1 hr

Düsseldorf from Brussels page 90 ✈ »Several per day ⊃40 min

Düsseldorf from Frankfurt page 126 ✈ »Several per day ⊃50 min

Düsseldorf from Frankfurt page 126 🚆 »avg 1 hr (day), 2 hr (night) ⊃2 hr 29 min

Düsseldorf from Hamburg page 135 ✈ »Several per day ⊃55 min

Düsseldorf from Munich page 203 ✈ »Several per day ⊃1 hr 10 min

Düsseldorf from Paris-Charles de Gaulle page 226 ✈ »Several per day ⊃1 hr 10 min

East Midlands from Belfast-International page 78 ✈ »Several per day ⊃1hr 05 min

East Midlands from Glasgow page 131 ✈ »At least daily ⊃1hr 05 min

Easton PA from New York-Newark page 216 🚆 »8 per day ⊃1 hr 15 min

Eau Claire WI from Minneapolis/St Paul page 161 🚌

Eau Claire WI from Minneapolis/St Paul page 161 ✈ »Several per day ⊃35 min

Edinburgh from Belfast-International page 78 ✈ »At least daily ⊃50 min

Edinburgh from Birmingham page 82 ✈ »Several per day ⊃1 hr

Edinburgh from East Midlands page 124 ✈ »Several per day ⊃55 min

Edinburgh from Glasgow page 131 🚆 »avg 1 hr ⊃1 hr 45 min

Edinburgh from London-Heathrow page 164 ✈ »Several per day ⊃1 hr 15 min

Edinburgh from London-Stansted page 173 🚆 »1 per day ⊃12 hr

Edinburgh from London-Stansted page 173 ✈ »At least daily ⊃1 hr 20 min

Edinburgh from Norwich page 220 ✈ »Several per day ⊃1 hr 25 min

Edmonton AB from Calgary page 98 🚌 Greyhound »1 day ⓒ1320; 0040 ⊃3 hrs 35 min

Edmonton AB from Calgary page 98 ✈ »Several per day ⊃40 min

Remember . . .
The destinations in this index can be reached directly from the gateway airport. Many more local and long-distance transport connections may be available from the centre of the city. Consult the current edition of the *Thomas Cook European Timetable* (Europe) or *Thomas Cook Overseas Timetable* (rest of the world).

✈ Air 🚆 Rail 🚌 Bus 🚐 Limousine Ⓜ Metro/subway 🚋 Tram 🚁 Helicopter 🚢 Water transport

Eindhoven from Amsterdam page 61 ✈ »Several per day ⏱40 min

Eindhoven from Amsterdam page 61 🚆 »avg 30 min ⏱1 hr 24 min

El Yopal from Bogota page 84 ✈ »Several per week ⏱50 min

Elgin from Aberdeen page 57 🚆 Scotrail »5-8 per day ⏱1 hr 30 min

Elkhart IN from Chicago-O'Hare page 106 🚆 »1–2 hrs ⏱3 hr 25 min

Eller from Düsseldorf page 122 🚆 S-Bahn S7 »avg 20 min ⏱21 min

Elmwood PA from Philadelphia page 238 🚆 »35–75 min

Ely from Norwich page 220 🚆 »1 per hr ⏱1 hr

Enköping from Stockholm-Arlanda page 266 🚆 UL

Enschede from Amsterdam page 61 ✈ »At least daily ⏱30 min

Erfurt from Düsseldorf page 122 ✈ »Several per week ⏱1 hr 10 min

Erfurt from Munich page 203 ✈ »Several per week ⏱55 min

Erzerum from Ankara page 64 ✈ »Several per day ⏱1 hr 10 min

Esbjerg from Copenhagen page 111 ✈ »Several per day ⏱50 min

Essen from Düsseldorf page 122 🚆 »avg 30 min ⏱39 min

Eugene OR from Seattle page 258 ✈ »Several per day ⏱1 hr

Evansville IN from St Louis page 247 ✈ »Several per day ⏱55 min

Everett WA from Seattle page 258 🚆

Fagernes from Oslo page 223 ✈ »Several per week ⏱40 min

Fairfax County VA from Washington-Dulles page 291 🚆 from San Francisco page 252 🚆 »8 day ⏱1 hr 20 min

Faro from Lisbon page 156 ✈ »Several per day ⏱40 min

Fergus Falls MN from Minneapolis/St Paul page 161 ✈ »Several per day ⏱1 hr

Fez from Casablanca page 104 ✈ »Several per week ⏱50 min

Figari from Nice page 217 ✈ »Several per week ⏱45 min

Firenze see **Florence**

Flemington NJ from New York-Newark page 216 🚆 »3 per day

Florence from Milan-Linate page 192 ✈ »At least daily ⏱55 min

Florence from Nice page 217 ✈ »Several per week ⏱1 hr 10 min

Florence from Rome-Fiumicino page 244 ✈ »Several per day ⏱1 hr 5 min

Florida Keys FL from Miami page 189 🚌

Florida Keys FL from Miami page 189 🚌

Fort Collins CO from Denver page 118 🚆 »1–2 hr

Fort Lauderdale FL from Orlando page 222 ✈ »Several per day ⏱50 min

Fort Lauderdale FL from Miami page 189 🚌

Fort Lauderdale FL from Nassau page 206 ✈ »Several per day ⏱55–60 min

Fort Lauderdale/Hollywood FL from Miami page 189 ✈ »Several per day ⏱30 min

Fort Leonard Wood MO from St Louis page 247 🚆 »2 day ⏱3 hr 15 min

Fort Leonard Wood MO from St Louis page 247 ✈ »Several per week ⏱45 min

Fort Lewis/McChord AFB WA from Seattle page 258 🚌

Fort McMurray AB from Edmonton page 125 ✈ »Several per day ⏱1 hr

Fort Myers FL from Miami page 189 ✈ »Several per day ⏱45 min

Fort Myers FL from Miami page 189 🚌

Fort Myers FL from Orlando page 222 ✈ »Several per day ⏱45 min

Fort Wayne IN from Chicago-O'Hare page 106 ✈ »Several per day ⏱1 hr

Fort Worth TX (city)centre from Dallas/Fort Worth page 113 🚆 »30 min

Framingham MA from Boston page 85 🚆 »30 min

Frankfurt from Berlin page 80 ✈ »Several per day ⏱1 hr 5 min

Frankfurt from Brussels page 90 ✈ »Several per day ⏱1 hr

Frankfurt from Düsseldorf page 122 ✈ »Several per day ⏱1 hr

Frankfurt from Düsseldorf page 122 🚆 »4 per day ⏱2hr 30min

Fredericksburg VA from Washington-Dulles page 291 🚌

Fredericton NB from Halifax page 134 ✈ »Several per day ⏱45 min

Freeport from Miami page 189 ✈ »Several per day ⏱45 min

Freeport NY from Nassau page 206 ✈ »Several per day ⏱40 min

Fréjus/St Raphael from Nice page 217 🚆 »avg 2 hr 15 m ⏱1 hr 15 min

Fresno CA from Los Angeles page 174 ✈ »Several per day ⏱1 hr

Fresno CA from San Francisco page 252 ✈ »Several per day ⏱55 min

Fribourg from Geneva page 130 🚆 SBB » 1hr ⏱ 1hr 30min

Friday Harbor WA from Seattle page 258 ✈ »Several per day ⏱1 hr

Friedrichshafen from Frankfurt page 126 ✈ »Several per day ⏱50 min

Friedrichshafen from Zürich page 296 ✈ »Several per week ⏱30 min

Frisco CO from Denver page 118 🚌 »1 hr

Fuerteventura from Tenerife page 276 ✈ »Several per day ⏱45 min

Gainesville FL from Orlando page 222 ✈ »At least daily ⏱40 min

Gaithersburg MD from Washington-Dulles page 291

Galveston TX from Houston page 142 🚆 »1 hr

Galway from Dublin page 120 ✈ »At least daily ⏱1 hr

Ganges Harbor BC from Vancouver page 286 ✈ »Several per day ⏱30 min

Gassim from Riyadh page 243 ✈ »Several per day ⏱55 min

Gaziantep from Ankara page 64 ✈ »At least daily ⏱1 hr 10 min

Gdansk from Warsaw page 290 ✈ »Several per day ⏱1 hr

Geneva from Nice page 217 ✈ »Several per day ⏱55 min

Geneva from Paris-Charles de Gaulle page 226 ✈ »Several per day ⏱1 hr 05 min

Geneva from Zürich page 296 ✈ »Several per day ⏱45–50 min

Geneva from Zürich page 296 🚆 »2 hr ⏱3 hr 30 min

Geneva Apt from Lyon page 178 🚆 »4–5 per day ⏱1hr 40 min

Geneva Apt from Zürich page 296 🚆 »60 min ⏱approx 3 hr 20 min

Genoa (Genova) from Rome-Fiumicino page 244 ✈ »Several per day ⏱1 hr

George from Cape Town page 84 ✈ »At least daily ⏱1 hr

George Town (Cayman Is) from Nassau page 206 ✈ »At least daily ⏱40 min

Geraldton WA from Perth page 237 ✈ »Several per day ⏱1hr 5 min

Gillies Bay BC from Vancouver page 286 ✈ »Several per day ⏱1 hr

Glasgow (city centre) from Glasgow page 131 🚌 »15–20 min ⏱25 min

Glasgow from Belfast-International page 78 ✈ »Several per day ⏱45 min

Glasgow from Dublin page 120 ✈ »Several Daily ⏱1 hr

Glasgow from London-Heathrow page 164 ✈ »Several per day ⏱1 hr 15 min

Glasgow from London-Stansted page 173 ✈ »Several per day ⏱1 hr 15 min

Glasgow Apt from East Midlands page 124 ✈ »At least daily ⏱55 min

Glen Park (Gary) IN from Chicago-O'Hare page 106 🚆 »1 hr ⏱1 hr 55 min

Goodland KS from Denver page 118 ✈ »Several per week ⏱1 hr

Göteborg see **Gothenburg**

Gothenburg from Copenhagen page 111 ✈ »Several per day ⏱55 min

Gothenburg from Oslo page 223 ✈ »Several per day ⏱50 min

Gothenburg from Stockholm-Arlanda page 266 ✈ »Several per day ⏱1 hr

Granbury TX from Dallas/Fort Worth page 113 🚆

Grand Canyon AZ from Las Vegas page 154 ✈ »Several per day ⏱1 hr

Grand Prairie AB from Edmonton page 125 ✈ »Several per day ⏱1 hr

---

» Frequency of service ⏱ Journey time   For details of fares, etc, see individual airport entries, Section Two

SECTION THREE • DESTINATION INDEX — GRAND RAPIDS • HOUSTON

Grand Rapids MI from Chicago-O'Hare page 106 ✈ »Several per day ↻45 min

Grand Rapids, MI from Chicago page 105 ✈ »Several per day ↻55 min

Grasse from Nice page 217 🚌 »avg 1 hr 15 min ↻1 hr

Graz from Munich page 203 ✈ »Several per week ↻1 hr

Graz from Vienna page 288 ✈ »Several per day ↻45 min

Great Yarmouth from Norwich page 220 🚆 »1 per hr ↻35 min

Green Bay WI from Chicago-O'Hare page 106 ✈ »Several per day ↻1 hr

Green Bay WI from Minneapolis/St Paul page 161 ✈ »Several per day ↻1 hr

Greenfield MA from Boston page 85 🚆

Greenville/Spartanburg SC from Atlanta page 67 ✈ »Several per day ↻50 min

Grenada from Bridgetown page 88 ✈ »Several per day ↻50 min

Grenoble from Lyon page 178 🚌 »9–13 per day ↻1 hr 5 min

Grenoble from Lyon page 178 🚆 »2 per day ↻1 hr 7 min

Grenoble from Paris-Orly page 234 ✈ »Several per day ↻55 min

Grenoble from Geneva page 130 Pl. Verdun 🚌 ⊙ 0915, 1315, 1900, 2115 (Sat and Sun 0915 and 1900 only) ↻1hr 45 min

Groningen from Amsterdam page 61 ✈ »At least daily ↻30 min

Guatemala City from Mexico City page 187 ✈ »At least daily ↻45–55 min

Guelph ON from Toronto page 281 🚆 from London-Gatwick page 160 ✈ »Several per day ↻50 min

Guernsey from London-Heathrow page 164 ✈ »Several per day ↻1 hr 5 min

Guernsey from London-Stansted page 173 ✈ »At least daily ↻1 hr 10 min

Gunnison CO from Denver page 118 ✈ »Several per day ↻50 min

Gurnee IL from Chicago-O'Hare page 106 🚌 »90 min ↻35 min

Hachijo Jima from Tokyo-Narita page 277 ✈ »Several per day ↻45 min

Hagerstown MD from Baltimore/Washington page 72 ✈ »Several per day ↻50 min

Hagfors from Stockholm-Arlanda page 266 ✈ »Several per week ↻45 min

Hague ,The see **Den Haag**

Haifa from Tel Aviv page 275 ✈ »Several per week ↻30 min

Haifa from Tel Aviv page 275 🚆 »30 min

Haikou from Hong Kong page 112 ✈ »Several times per week ↻60–70 min

Halmstad from Stockholm-Arlanda page 266 ✈ »Several per day ↻1 hr

Hamburg (city centre) from Hamburg page 135 🚆 »10 min ↻approx 30 min

Hamburg (Hbf–main rail stn) from Hamburg page 135 🚌 »20 min ↻30 min

Hamburg from Berlin page 80 ✈ »Several per day ↻1 hr

Hamburg from Copenhagen page 111 ✈ »Several per day ↻50 min

Hamburg from Düsseldorf page 122 ✈ »Several per day ↻1 hr

Hamburg from Frankfurt page 126 ✈ »Several per day ↻1 hr 5 min

Hamburg from Frankfurt page 126 🚆 »avg 1 hr ↻6 hr

Hamilton (NZ) from Auckland page 69 ✈ »At least daily ↻35 min

Hamilton ON from Toronto page 281 🚆 »7 per day ↻1 hr 15 min

Hammond IN from Chicago-O'Hare page 106 🚌 »1 hr ↻1 hr 35 min

Hannover see **Hanover (Germany)**

Hanover (Germany) from Munich page 203 ✈ »Several per day ↻1 hr 10 min

Hanover (Germany) from Frankfurt page 126 ✈ »Several per day ↻55 min

Hanover NH from Boston page 85 🚌

Harare (city centre) from Harare page 137 🚌 »1 hr ↻15 min

Harlingen TX from Houston page 142 ✈ »Several per day ↻55 min

Harrisburg PA from Philadelphia page 238 ✈ »Several per day ↻45 min

Harrisburg PA from Washington-Dulles page 291 ✈ »Several per day ↻40 min

Harrisburg PA from Baltimore/Washington page 72 ✈ »Several per day ↻35 min

Harrogate from Leeds/Bradford page 155 🚆 » Frequent ↻ 40 min

Hartford CT from Boston page 85 ✈ »Several per day ↻45 min

Hartford CT from Boston page 85 🚌 »3 per day ↻3 hr

Hartford CT from New York-JFK page 209 ✈ »Several per day ↻50 min

Hartford CT from New York-La Guardia page 214 ✈ »Several per day ↻50 min

Hartford CT from New York-Newark page 216 ✈ »Several per day ↻1 hr

Hartford CT from Philadelphia page 238 ✈ »Several per day ↻55 min

Hartlepool from Teesside page 274 🚆 »1 per hr ↻30 min

Harvey IL from Chicago-O'Hare page 106 🚌 »1 hr ↻1 hr 20 min

Haugesund from Oslo page 223 ✈ »Several per day ↻50 min

Hayman Island from Cairns page 96 ✈ »daily ↻1 hr 30 min

Healdsburg CA from San Francisco page 252 🚌 »4 day ↻1 hr 55 min

Helgoland from Hamburg page 135 ✈ »Several per week ↻45–60 min

Helsingborg from Stockholm-Arlanda page 266 ✈ »Several per day ↻1 hr

Helsingborg H/P from Copenhagen page 111 ✈ »Several per day ↻15 min

Helsinki (city centre) from Helsinki page 137 🚆 »15–20 min ↻25–30 min

Helsinki from Moscow-Sheremetyevo page 200 ✈ »Several per day ↻1 hr 50 min

Helsinki from St Petersburg page 248 ✈ »Several per day ↻1 hr

Helsinki from Stockholm-Arlanda page 266 ✈ »Several per day ↻55 min

Hengelo from Amsterdam page 61 🚆 NS »5 per day ↻3 hr

Heraklion from Athens page 65 ✈ »Several times per day ↻45–50 min

Hibbing/Chisholm MN from Minneapolis/St Paul page 161 ✈ »Several per day ↻1 hr

Hillsboro TX from Dallas/Fort Worth page 113 🚌

Hilo HI from Honolulu page 140 ✈ »Several per day ↻50 min

Ho Chi Minh City from Kuala Lumpur page 151 ✈ »At least daily ↻45–55 min

Ho Chi Minh City from Singapore page 261 ✈ »Several per day ↻50 min

Homestead FL from Miami page 189 🚌 »3 per day ↻1 hr 5 min

Hong Kong Central (Macau Ferry) Area from Hong Kong page 112 🚌 »12–15 min

Hong Kong Island, Causeway Bay from Hong Kong page 112

Hong Kong Island, Central/Wan Chai from Hong Kong page 112 🚌

Hong Kong Island, Quarry Bay/North Point from Hong Kong page 112 🚌

Honolulu HI (all downtown hotels) from Honolulu page 140 🚌 »20 min

Honolulu HI (city centre) from Honolulu page 140 🚌 »30 min

Honolulu HI (metro area) from Honolulu page 140 🚌

Hoolehua HI from Honolulu page 140 ✈ »Several per day ↻25 min

Houston Ellington Field TX from Houston page 142 ✈ »Several per day ↻25 min

Houston TX from Dallas/Fort Worth page 113 ✈ »Several per day ↻55 min

---

Remember . . .
The destinations in this index can be reached directly from the gateway airport. Many more local and long-distance transport connections may be available from the centre of the city. Consult the current edition of the *Thomas Cook European Timetable* (Europe) or *Thomas Cook Overseas Timetable* (rest of the world).

✈ Air 🚆 Rail 🚌 Bus 🚘 Limousine Ⓜ Metro/subway 🚋 Tram 🚁 Helicopter ⛴ Water transport

Houston TX from New Orleans page 209 🚌 Greyhound »2 day ⊙0945; 1615 ⊃8 hr 15 min.

Houston TX from New Orleans page 209 ✈ »Several per day ⊃1 hr

Houston-Hobby Apt TX from Houston page 142 🚌 »30 min

Houston-Hobby Apt TX from Houston page 142 ✈ »Several per day ⊃25 min

Hsinchu from Taipei-Chiang Kai Shek page 272 🚌

Hua Hin from Bangkok page 72 ✈ »At least daily ⊃30 min

Hualien from Taipei-Chiang Kai Shek page 272 ✈ »Several per day ⊃35 min

Huddersfield from Leeds/Bradford page 155 🚆 » Frequent ⊃ 25 min

Hudson WI from Minneapolis/St Paul page 161 🚌

Hull from Leeds/Bradford page 155 🚆 » 1 hr ⊃ 1 hr

Huntsville AL from Atlanta page 67 ✈ »Several per day ⊃50 min

Hyannis MA from Boston page 85 ✈ »Several per day ⊃35 min

Hyannis MA from Boston page 85 🚌 »1 hr ⊃3 hr 30 min

Hyderabad from Karachi page 148 ✈ »Several per week ⊃45 min

Ibague from Bogota page 84 ✈ »Several per week ⊃30 min

Ibiza from Barcelona page 75 ✈ »Several per day ⊃40 min

Ibiza from Madrid page 180 ✈ »Several per day ⊃1 hr

Ibiza from Palma page 225 ✈ »Several per day ⊃35 min

Ikaria from Athens page 65 ✈ »Several per week ⊃50 min

Imperial County Apt CA from Los Angeles page 174 ✈ »Several per day ⊃1 hr

Indianapolis IN from Chicago-O'Hare page 106 ✈ »Several per day ⊃50 min

Indianapolis IN from St Louis page 247 ✈ »Several per day ⊃1 hr

Indianapolis, IN from Chicago page 105 ✈ »Several per day ⊃45 min

Inland Empire CA from Los Angeles page 174 🚌

Innsbruck from Vienna page 288 ✈ »Several per day ⊃50 min

Innsbruck from Zürich page 296 ✈ »Several per day ⊃50 min

Inverness from Glasgow page 131 ✈ »Several per week ⊃40 min

Inverness from Aberdeen page 57 🚆 Scotrail »5-8 per day ⊃2 hr 15 min

Inyokern CA from Los Angeles page 174 ✈ »Several per day ⊃50 min

Ipoh from Kuala Lumpur page 151 ✈ »Several per day ⊃35 min

Ipswich from Norwich page 220 🚆 »1 per hr ⊃50 min

Ironwood MN from Minneapolis/St Paul page 161 ✈ »At least daily ⊃55 min

Isafjordur from Reykjavik page 241 ✈ »At least daily ⊃40 min

Islamabad from Karachi page 148 ✈ »Several per week ⊃2 hr

Islamorada FL from Miami page 189 🚌 »3 per day ⊃2 hr 10 min

Islay from Glasgow page 131 ✈ »Several per week ⊃45 min

Isle of Man from Belfast-International page 78 ✈ »Several per day ⊃35 min

Isle of Man from Dublin page 120 ✈ »At least daily ⊃35 min

Isle of Man from Glasgow page 131 ✈ »At least daily ⊃55 min

Isle of Man from London-Heathrow page 164 ✈ »Several per day ⊃1 hr 10 min

Isle of Man from Manchester page 183 ✈ »Several per day ⊃45 min

Istanbul from Ankara page 64 ✈ »Several per day ⊃1 hr 5 min

Istanbul city bus terminal (Sishane) from Istanbul page 143 🚌 »approx. 1 hr ⊃30 min

Ithaca NY from New York-Newark page 216 ✈ »Several per day ⊃1 hr

Iwami from Osaka-Kansai page 222 ✈ »At least daily ⊃1 hr

Ixtapa/Zihuatanejo from Mexico City page 187 ✈ »Several per day ⊃50–55 min

Izmir from Athens page 65 ✈ »Several per week ⊃55 min

Izumo from Osaka-Kansai page 222 ✈ »Several per day ⊃50–65 min

Jackson MS from New Orleans page 209 ✈ »At least daily ⊃50 min

Jacksonville FL from Atlanta page 67 ✈ »Several per day ⊃1 hr

Jacksonville FL from Orlando page 222 ✈ »Several per day ⊃50 min

Jaipur from Delhi page 116 ✈ »Several per week ⊃50 min

Jakarta (city centre) from Jakarta page 145 🚌 »30 min ⊃45–60 min

Jakarta from Kuala Lumpur page 151 ✈ »Several per day ⊃1hr

Jakarta from Singapore page 261 ✈ »Several per day ⊃30–40 min

Jamaica NY from New York-JFK page 209 🚌 »30 min ⊃1 hr

Janesville WI from Chicago-O'Hare page 106 🚌 »90 min – 2 hr ⊃1 hr 30 min

Jerez de la Frontera from Madrid page 180 ✈ »Several per day ⊃55 min

Jersey from Birmingham page 82 ✈ »At least daily ⊃55 min

Jersey from East Midlands page 124 ✈ »At least daily ⊃1 hr

Jersey from London-Gatwick page 160 ✈ »Several per day ⊃1 hr

Jersey from London-Heathrow page 164 ✈ »Several per day ⊃55 min

Jersey from London-Stansted page 173 ✈ »At least daily ⊃1 hr 10 min

Jerusalem from Tel Aviv page 275 ✈ »Several per week ⊃20–30 min

Jerusalem from Tel Aviv page 275 🚌 »15–20 min

Jinan from Beijing page 67 ✈ »Several per day ⊃45–60 min

Joensuu from Helsinki page 137 🚌 »0900 ⊃8 hr

Johannesburg (city centre) from Johannesburg page 147 🚌 »30 min

Johnson County TX from Dallas/Fort Worth page 113 🚌 Zephyr

Johor Bahru from Kuala Lumpur page 151 ✈ »Several per day ⊃45 min

Jonköping from Copenhagen page 111 ✈ »Several per day ⊃55 min

Jonköping from Stockholm-Arlanda page 266 ✈ »At least daily ⊃45 min

Joplin MO from St Louis page 247 🚌 »2 day ⊃7 hr 30 min

Juan-les-Pins from Nice page 217 🚌 »40 min ⊃1 hr 25 min

Kahului HI from Honolulu page 140 ✈ »Several per day ⊃35 min

Kalamata from Athens page 65 ✈ »At least daily ⊃50 min

Kalamazoo MI from Chicago-O'Hare page 106 ✈ »Several per day ⊃45 min

Kalaupapa HI from Honolulu page 140 ✈ »Several per day ⊃50 min

Kalgoorlie WA from Perth page 237 ✈ »Several per day ⊃1 hr 5 min

Kalibo from Manila page 185 ✈ »Several per day ⊃55 min

Kaliningrad from St Petersburg page 248 ✈ »Several per week ⊃50 min

Kalmar from Copenhagen page 111 ✈ »Several per day ⊃50 min

Kalmar from Stockholm-Arlanda page 266 ✈ »Several per day ⊃50 min

Kamloops BC from Vancouver page 286 ✈ »Several per day ⊃50 min

Kangnung from Seoul page 211 ✈ »Several per day ⊃50 min

Kansas City MO from St Louis page 247 🚌 »2 day ⊃4 hr 30 min

Kansas City MO from St Louis page 247 ✈ »Several per day ⊃1 hr

Kaohsiung from Taipei-Chiang Kai Shek page 272 ✈ »Several per day ⊃50 min

Kaohsiung from Taipei-Chiang Kai Shek page 272 🚌

Kapalua HI from Honolulu page 140 ✈ »Several per day ⊃35 min

Karachi (city centre) from Karachi page 148 🚌 »30 min ⊃30 min

Kariba from Harare page 137 ✈ »Several per day ⊃45 min

Karlsruhe from Stuttgart page 269 🚆 »Several per day ⊃1 hr 20 min

Karlstad from Stockholm-Arlanda page 266 ✈ »Several per day ⊃45 min

Karlstad from Gothenburg page 133 🚆 »6 per day ⊃3 hr

» Frequency of service ⊃ Journey time   For details of fares, etc, see individual airport entries, Section Two

Karup from Copenhagen page 111 ✈ »Several per day ⏱45 min

Katherine from Darwin page 115 ✈ »2 per day ⏱50 min

Katowice from Warsaw page 290 ✈ »Several per week ⏱50 min

Kauai Island HI from Honolulu page 140 ✈ »Several per day ⏱35 min

Kavala from Athens page 65 ✈ »At least daily ⏱60–70 min

Keene NH from Boston page 85 🚌 »1 per day ⏱4 hr 30 min

Kefallinia from Athens page 65 ✈ »Several per week ⏱1 hr

Kehl am Läger from Strasbourg page 268 🚌 Navette Bus ⏱25 min

Kelowna BC from Vancouver page 286 ✈ »Several per day ⏱55 min

Kelowna BC from Calgary page 98 ✈ »Several per day ⏱1 hr

Kelowna BC from Calgary page 98 🚌 Greyhound »1 day ⏰1215 ⏱11 hr.

Kenmore WA from Seattle page 258 ✈ »At least daily ⏱1 hr

Kennebunkport ME from Boston page 85 🚐

Kenosha WI from Chicago-O'Hare page 106 🚐 »90 min ⏱1 hr

Kerkyra see **Corfu**

Kerry from Dublin page 120 ✈ »At least daily ⏱50 min

Kerteh from Kuala Lumpur page 151 ✈ »Several per day ⏱55 min

Key Largo FL from Miami page 189 🚌 »3 per day ⏱1 hr 40 min

Key West FL from Miami page 189 ✈ »Several per day ⏱50 min

Key West FL from Miami page 189 🚌 »3 per day ⏱4 hr 45 min

Keystone CO from Denver page 118 🚐 »1 hr

Kharkov from Kiev page 149 ✈ »Several per week ⏱1 hr 15 min

Khon Kaen from Bangkok page 72 ✈ »Several per day ⏱55 min

Kiel from Hamburg page 135 🚌 »2 hr ⏱1 hr

Kiev from Moscow-Sheremetyevo page 200 ✈ »Several per day ⏱1 hr 45 min

Kigali from Nairobi page 205 ✈ »Several per week ⏱30 min

Killeen TX from Dallas/Fort Worth page 113 🚌

Killeen TX from Dallas/Fort Worth page 113 ✈ »Several per day ⏱50 min

Killeen TX from Houston page 142 ✈ »Several per day ⏱50 min

King Island TS from Melbourne page 186 ✈ »At least daily ⏱45 min

Kingston (Jamaica) (city centre) from Kingston page 121 🚌 ⏱30 min

Kingston (Jamaica) from Miami page 189 ✈ »Several per day ⏱45 min

Kingston ON from Toronto page 281 ✈ »Several per day ⏱50 min

Kingston ON from Toronto page 281 🚌 »3 day ⏱4 hr

Kinmen from Taipei-Chiang Kai Shek page 272 ✈ »Several per day ⏱55 min

Kirkwall from Aberdeen page 57 ✈ »3 per day ⏱45 min

Kirkwall from Glasgow page 131 ✈ »Several per week ⏱1hr 10 min

Kiryat Shmona from Tel Aviv page 275 ✈ »At least daily ⏱40 min

Kishinev from Kiev page 149 ✈ »Several per week ⏱1 hr 20 min

Kisumu from Nairobi page 205 ✈ »Several per week ⏱1 hr

Kithira from Athens page 65 ✈ »At least daily ⏱50 min

Klagenfurt from Vienna page 288 ✈ »Several per day ⏱55 min

Knoxville TN from Atlanta page 67 ✈ »Several per day ⏱55 min

København see **Copenhagen**

Kochi from Osaka-Kansai page 222 ✈ »Several per day ⏱40 min

Köln see **Cologne**

Komatsu from Tokyo-Narita page 277 ✈ »Several per day ⏱1 hr

Kona HI from Honolulu page 140 ✈ »Several per day ⏱40 min

Kos from Athens page 65 ✈ »At least daily ⏱50 min

Kota Bharu from Kuala Lumpur page 151 ✈ »Several per day ⏱50 min

Kowloon, Tong MTR stn from Hong Kong page 112 🚇

Kowloon, Tsim Sha Tsui from Hong Kong page 112 🚇

Kraków from Warsaw page 290 ✈ »Several per day ⏱45 min

Kramfors from Stockholm-Arlanda page 266 ✈ »Several per day ⏱1 hr

Krefeld from Düsseldorf page 122 🚄 avg 20 min ⏱51 min

Kristiansand from Oslo page 223 ✈ »Several per day ⏱45 min

Kristianstad from Copenhagen page 111 ✈ »Several per week ⏱35 min

Kristianstad from Stockholm-Arlanda page 266 ✈ »Several per day ⏱1 hr

Kristiansund from Oslo page 223 ✈ »Several per week ⏱55 min

Kuala Lumpur (city centre) from Kuala Lumpur page 151 🚌 »15 min ⏱60 min

Kuala Lumpur from Singapore page 261 ✈ »Several per day ⏱50–55 min

Kuala Terengg from Kuala Lumpur page 151 ✈ »Several per week ⏱45 min

Kuantan from Kuala Lumpur page 151 ✈ »Several per day ⏱40 min

Kuantan from Singapore page 261 ✈ »Several per week ⏱45 min

Kunsan from Seoul page 211 ✈ »Several per day ⏱50 min

Kuwait from Bahrain page 70 ✈ »Several per day ⏱1 hr

Kwangju from Seoul page 211 ✈ »Several per day ⏱50 min

Kyïv see **Kiev**

Kyoto from Osaka-Kansai page 222 🚄 ⏱1 hr 30 min–1 hr 40 min

L'Isle-d'Abeau from Lyon page 178 🚌 »3 per day ⏱33 min

La Coruña from Madrid page 180 ✈ »Several per day ⏱1 hr

La Crosse WI from Minneapolis/St Paul page 161 🚌 »2 per day ⏱3 hr 45 min

La Porte IN from Chicago-O'Hare page 106 🚐 »1–2 hrs ⏱1 hr 40 min

La Rochelle from Paris-Orly page 234 ✈ »At least daily ⏱1 hr 10 min

La Serena from Rio de Janeiro-International page 242 ✈ »Several per day ⏱50 min

Ladner BC from Vancouver page 286 🚌 »30 min–1 hr

Lafayette IN from Chicago-O'Hare page 106 ✈ »At least daily ⏱45 min

Lafayette LA from New Orleans page 209 🚌 Greyhound »4 day ⏰0945; 1300; 1615; 2000 ⏱3 hr.

Lafayette LA from New Orleans page 209 🚌 Greyhound »4 day ⏰0945; 1300; 1615; 2000 ⏱3 hr.

Lagos (city centre) from Lagos page 153 🚌 ⏱40 min

Lahore from Karachi page 148 ✈ »Several per week ⏱1 hr 45 min

Lake Charles LA from Houston page 142 ✈ »Several per day ⏱45 min

Lakewood CO from Denver page 118 🚌 »1 hr ⏱1 hr 15 min

Lakewood WA from Seattle page 258 🚌

Lamar CO from Denver page 118 ✈ »Several per week ⏱45 min

Lamezia Terme from Rome-Fiumicino page 244 ✈ »Several per day ⏱1 hr 5 min

Lampugnano from Milan-Malpensa page 194 🚌 »1 hr ⏱30 min

Lanai City HI from Honolulu page 140 ✈ »Several per day ⏱30 min

Lancaster CA see also **Palmdale/Lancaster CA**

Lancaster PA from Philadelphia page 238 ✈ »Several per day ⏱45 min

Langkawi from Kuala Lumpur page 151 ✈ »Several per day ⏱50–70 min

Lansing MI from Chicago-O'Hare page 106 ✈ »Several per day ⏱55 min

Lanzarote from Tenerife page 276 ✈ »Several per day ⏱50 min

Remember . . .
The destinations in this index can be reached directly from the gateway airport. Many more local and long-distance transport connections may be available from the centre of the city. Consult the current edition of the *Thomas Cook European Timetable* (Europe) or *Thomas Cook Overseas Timetable* (rest of the world).

LAOAG • LONDON — SECTION THREE • DESTINATION INDEX

Laoag from Manila page 185 ✈ »Several per week ⏱50–60 min

Laramie WY from Denver page 118 ✈ »Several per day ⏱40 min

Larkspur CA from San Francisco page 252 🚆 »30 min ⏱50 min

Las Palmas from Tenerife page 276 ✈ »Several per day ⏱30 min

Las Piedras from Caracas page 85 ✈ »Several per day ⏱40 min

Las Vegas NV from San Diego page 250 ✈ »Several per day ⏱1 hr

Las Vegas NV from Los Angeles page 174 ✈ »Several per day ⏱55 min

Laughlin NV from Las Vegas page 154 🚌 Best Way

Launceston TS from Melbourne page 186 ✈ »Several per day ⏱55 min

Lausanne from Geneva page 130 🚆 SBB » 30 min ⏱ 50 min

Lausanne from Zürich page 296 🚆 »2 hr ⏱3 hr 10 min

Laval PQ (Sheraton Centre) from Montréal-Mirabel page 199 🚌 »On-demand

Laval (Sheraton Centre) from Montréal page 197 🚌 Connaisseur » On-demand

Lawrence MA from Boston page 85 🚌

Lawton OK from Dallas/Fort Worth page 113 ✈ »Several per day ⏱55 min

Le Havre from Brussels page 90 ✈ »Several per week ⏱1 hr 5 min

Le Havre from London-Gatwick page 160 ✈ »Several per week ⏱45 min

Le Mans from Paris-Charles de Gaulle page 226 🚆 »4 per day ⏰0856–1825 ⏱1 hr 35 min

La Serena from Santiago page 256 ✈ »Several per day ⏱50 min

Leeds from Manchester page 183 🚆 ⏱2 hr

Leeds/Bradford from Belfast-International page 78 ✈ »Several per day ⏱1hr 05 min

Leeds/Bradford from Dublin page 120 ✈ »Several per day ⏱1 hr

Leeds/Bradford from Glasgow page 131 ✈ »Several per week ⏱1hr

Leeds/Bradford from London-Gatwick page 160 ✈ »Several per week ⏱1 hr 15 min

Leeds/Bradford from London-Heathrow page 164 ✈ »Several per day ⏱55 min

Lefkas see **Preveza/Lefkas**

Leicester from Birmingham page 82 🚆 »2 hr (3 hr Sun) ⏱1 hr 30 min

Leicester from East Midlands page 124 🚆 »1 hr peak times, slower off-peak ⏱1 hr–1 hr 15 min

Leipzig from Düsseldorf page 122 ✈ »Several per week ⏱1 hr 5 min

Leipzig from Frankfurt page 126 ✈ »Several per day ⏱55 min

Leipzig from Hamburg page 135 ✈ »Several per week ⏱55–70 min

Leipzig from Munich page 203 ✈ »Several per day ⏱1 hr

Lemnos from Athens page 65 ✈ »At least daily ⏱1 hr

Leon/Guanajuato from Mexico City page 187 ✈ »Several per day ⏱50 min

Lethbridge AB from Calgary page 98 ✈ »Several per day ⏱40 min

Lille from Lyon page 178 🚆 »1 per day ⏱3 hr 20 min

Lille from Paris-Charles de Gaulle page 226 🚆 »avg 1 hr ⏱1 hr 22 min.

Lille from Paris-Charles de Gaulle page 226 ✈ »Several per day ⏱55 min

Lille from Paris-Orly page 234 ✈ »Several per week ⏱45 min

Lille from Strasbourg page 268 ✈ »Several per day ⏱1 hr 10 min

Lilongwe from Harare page 137 ✈ »Several per day ⏱1 hr 5 min

Limoges from Lyon page 178 ✈ »Several per week ⏱60 min

Limoges from Paris-Orly page 234 ✈ »Several per week ⏱1 hr 05 min

Linkoping from Gothenburg page 133 ✈ »2 per day ⏱40 min

Linköping from Stockholm-Arlanda page 266 ✈ »Several per week ⏱45 min

Linz from Frankfurt page 126 ✈ »Several per day ⏱1 hr 5 min

Linz from Vienna page 288 ✈ »Several per day ⏱40 min

Linz from Zürich page 296 ✈ »Several per day ⏱1 hr

Lisbon (city centre – Cais do Sodre rail stn) from Lisbon page 156 🚌

Lisbon (city centre – Santa Apolonia rail stn) from Lisbon page 156 🚌 »15–20 min ⏱30 min

Lisbon from Barcelona page 75 ✈ »Several per day ⏱50 min

Lisbon from Madrid page 180 ✈ »Several per day ⏱ 1 hr 10 min

Little Rock AR from Dallas/Fort Worth page 113 ✈ »Several per day ⏱1 hr

Littleton CO from Denver page 118 🚆 »1 hr ⏱1 hr 30 min

Littleton MA from Boston page 85 🚌

Livermore CA from San Francisco page 252 🚆 »3 day Mon–Fri only

Liverpool from Belfast-International page 78 ✈ »Several per day ⏱50 min

Liverpool from Dublin page 120 ✈ »Several per day ⏱45 min

Liverpool from Manchester page 183 🚆 »approx. 1 hr (1020–2120) ⏱45 min

Ljubljana from Vienna page 288 ✈ »Several per week ⏱1 hr

Lome from Lagos page 153 ✈ »Several per week ⏱40 min

London (Canary Wharf) from London-City page 157 🚌 »12 min Mon–Fri; 20–30 min Sat, Sun ⏱8 min

London (city centre – Euston and King's Cross rail stns) from London-Heathrow page 164 🚌 »20–30 min ⏱1 hr–1 hr 25 min

London (city centre – Victoria rail stn) from London-Gatwick page 160 🚆 »avg 20 min ⏱35 min

London (city centre – Victoria rail stn) from London-Gatwick page 160 🚌 »15 min (day); 30 min–1 hr (after 2100) ⏱30 min

London (City of London) from London-Gatwick page 160 🚌 »avg 15 min ⏱30–45 min

London (Liverpool St rail stn) from London-City page 157 🚌 »20–30 min ⏱25 min

London from Amsterdam page 61 ✈ »Several per week ⏱50–70 min

London from Birmingham page 82 🚆 »30 min ⏱85 min

London from Brussels page 90 ✈ »Several per week ⏱1 hr–1 hr 10 min

London from Dublin page 120 ✈ »Several per week ⏱1 hr 5 min–1 hr 10 min

London from Glasgow page 131 🚌 »avg 2 hr ⏱7 hr

London from Manchester page 183 ✈ »Several per day ⏱1 hr

London from Manchester page 183 🚆 »4 per day ⏱3 hr 30 min

London from Milan-Linate page 192 ✈ »At least daily ⏱55 min–1 hr

London from Paris-Charles de Gaulle page 226 ✈ »Several per day ⏱1 hr–1 hr 20 min

London-Gatwick Apt from Birmingham page 82 🚌

London-Gatwick Apt from Glasgow page 131 🚌 »1 per day ⏱9 hr 45 min

London-Gatwick Apt from London-Heathrow page 164 🚌 »avg 30 min ⏱1 hr

London-Gatwick Apt from Manchester page 183 🚌 »2 hr (0825–1825) ⏱7 hr

London-Heathrow Apt from Birmingham page 82 🚌

London-Heathrow Apt from Glasgow page 131 🚌 »1 per day ⏱8 hr 30 min

London-Heathrow Apt from London-Gatwick page 160 🚌 »15 min a.m.; 30 min p.m. ⏱1 hr

London-Heathrow Apt from London-Stansted page 173 🚌 »avg 2 hr 30 min ⏱1 hr 20 min

London-Heathrow Apt from Manchester page 183 🚌 »2 hr (0825–1825)

London-Luton Apt from Birmingham page 82 🚌

London-Luton Apt from London-Gatwick page 160 🚌 »avg 1 hr 25 min ⏱3 hr

London-Luton Apt from London-Heathrow page 164 🚌 »avg 2 hr ⏱50 min

London-Stansted Apt from London-Gatwick page 160 🚌 »avg 1 hr 30 min ⏱4 hr 30 min

» Frequency of service ⏱ Journey time   For details of fares, etc, see individual airport entries, Section Two

London-Stansted Apt from London-Heathrow page 164 🚌 »avg 2 hr ⏱1 hr 40 min

Long Island NY from Boston page 85 ✈ »Several per day ⏱55 min

Long Island NY from New York-La Guardia page 214 🚌 »On-demand

Longmont CO from Denver page 118 🚌 »1–2 hr

Longview TX from Dallas/Fort Worth page 113 ✈ »Several per day ⏱50 min

Longview WA from Seattle page 258 🚌 »2 day ⏱3 hr

Lopez Island WA from Seattle page 258 ✈ »Several per day ⏱1 hr

Lorient from Paris-Orly page 234 ✈ »At least daily ⏱1 hr

Los Angeles CA (metro area) from Los Angeles page 174 🚌

Los Angeles CA (Union rail stn) from Los Angeles page 174 🚌 »30–60 min ⏱1 hr

Los Angeles CA from Las Vegas page 154 ✈ »Several per day ⏱1 hr

Louisville, KY from Chicago page 105 ✈ »Several per day ⏱55 min

Lourdes from Toulouse page 285 🚆 »Several per day ⏱2 hr

Loveland CO from Denver page 118 🚌 »1–2 hr

Lubang from Manila page 185 ✈ »Several per week ⏱45 min

Lucerne from Zürich page 296 🚆 »1 hr ⏱1 hr 17 min

Lugano from Zürich page 296 ✈ »Several per day ⏱45 min

Lusaka from Harare page 137 ✈ »Several per week ⏱55 min

Luxembourg from Zürich page 296 ✈ »Several per day ⏱1 hr

Luzern see **Lucerne**

Lvov from Kiev page 149 ✈ »Several per day ⏱1 hr 30 min

Lyon (Perrache rail stn) from Lyon page 178 🚌 »20 min ⏱40 min

Lyon from Paris-Charles de Gaulle page 226 ✈ »Several per day ⏱1 hr

Lyon from Zürich page 296 ✈ »Several per day ⏱1 hr

Lyon-Bron Apt from Paris-Orly page 234 ✈ »Several per day ⏱55 min

Lyon from Strasbourg page 268 ✈ »Several per day ⏱55 min

Maastricht from Amsterdam page 61 ✈ »Several per day ⏱40 min

Maastricht from Amsterdam page 61 🚆 »avg 30 min ⏱2 hr 21 min

Maastricht from London-Stansted page 173 ✈ »Several per day ⏱1 hr

Mackay from Cairns page 96 ✈ »Several per day ⏱2 hr

Macon GA from Atlanta page 67 ✈ »Several per day ⏱35 min

Madinah from Jeddah page 146 ✈ »Several per day ⏱50 min

Madison WI from Chicago-O'Hare page 106 🚌 »90 min–2 hr ⏱3 hr

Madison WI from Chicago-O'Hare page 106 ✈ »Several per day ⏱45 min

Madison WI from Minneapolis/St Paul page 161 ✈ »Several per day ⏱55 min

Madras from Colombo page 110 ✈ »Several per week ⏱20 min

Madrid (city centre – Terminal Colon) from Madrid page 180 🚌 »10 min ⏱30 min

Madrid from Barcelona page 75 ✈ »Several per day ⏱1 hr

Maine state (southern) from Boston page 85 🚌

Mainz from Frankfurt page 126 🚆 »20–30 min ⏱29 min

Maitland NSW from Sydney page 270 ✈ »Several per day ⏱35 min

Makung from Taipei-Chiang Kai Shek page 272 ✈ »Several per day ⏱45 min

Malaga from Madrid page 180 ✈ »Several per day ⏱50 min

Malatya from Ankara page 64 ✈ »At least daily ⏱1 hr 10 min

Malmö 🚌SAS »1 hr ⏱35 min

Malmo from Gothenburg page 133 ✈ »5 per day ⏱35 min

Manchester (UK) (city centre – Piccadilly bus stn) from Manchester page 183 🚌 »30 min ⏱1 hr

Manchester (UK) (city centre – Piccadilly rail stn) from Manchester page 183 🚆 »15 min ⏱15 min

Manchester (UK) from Birmingham page 82 🚌 »approx. every 40 min ⏱approx. 2 hr

Manchester (UK) from Dublin page 120 ✈ »Several per day ⏱1 hr

Manchester (UK) Apt (from London-Gatwick page 160 🚌 »avg 3 hr ⏱8 hr 30 min

Manchester (UK) Apt from Birmingham page 82 🚌

Manchester NH from Boston page 85 ✈ »Several per day ⏱30 min

Manchester NH from Boston page 85 🚌 Concord Trailways »1–2 hrs ⏱1 hr 45 min

Manchester(UK) (city centre – Piccadilly rail stn from Manchester page 183 🚌 GM Buses 747 »1 hr ⏱20 min

Manchester from Norwich page 220 ✈ »Several per day ⏱1 hr

Mangrove Cay from Nassau page 206 ✈ »Several per day ⏱20 min

Manhattan see **New York City NY**

Manila (metro area) from Manila page 185 🚌

Mankato MN from Minneapolis/St Paul page 161 🚌 »4 per day ⏱1 hr 30 min

Mankato MN from Minneapolis/St Paul page 161 ✈ »Several per week ⏱25 min

Mankato MN from Minneapolis/St Paul page 161 🚌 »4 per day ⏱1 hr 30 min

Manteca CA from San Francisco page 252 🚌 »3 day Mon–Fri only

Maple Bay BC from Vancouver page 286 ✈ »At least daily ⏱30 min

Maputo from Johannesburg page 147 ✈ »At least daily ⏱55 min

Mara Lodges from Nairobi page 205 ✈ »Several per week ⏱45 min

Marathon FL from Miami page 189 ✈ »At least daily ⏱40 min

Marathon FL from Miami page 189 🚌 »3 per day ⏱3 hr 10 min

Marco Island FL from Miami page 189 🚌

Marrakech from Casablanca page 104 ✈ »Several per day ⏱40 min

Marseille from Lyon page 178 ✈ »Several per day ⏱50 min

Marseille from Lyon page 178 🚆 SNCF »1 per day ⏱2 hr 35 min

Marseille from Nice page 217 🚌 »avg 2 hr 30 min ⏱2 hr 45 min

Marseille from Paris-Charles de Gaulle page 226 ✈ »Several per day ⏱1 hr 15 min

Marseille from Paris-Charles de Gaulle page 226 🚆 SNCF »5 per day ⏱4 hr 47 min

Marseille from Paris-Orly page 234 ✈ »Several per day ⏱1 hr 10 min

Marsh Harbour from Nassau page 206 ✈ »Several per day ⏱1 hr 5 min

Martha's Vineyard MA from Boston page 85 ✈ »Several per day ⏱35 min

Martigny from Geneva page 130 🚆 SBB »1hr ⏱1 hr 50min

Marysville WA from Seattle page 258 🚌 »1–2 hr ⏱1 hr 10 min

Masada from Tel Aviv page 275 ✈ »Several per week ⏱1 hr

Mason City IA from Minneapolis/St Paul page 161 🚌 »2 per day ⏱3 hr

Massachusetts state (southern) from Boston page 85 🚌

Massachusetts, central and eastern from Boston page 85 🚌

Massachusetts, north central from Boston page 85 🚌

Massachusetts, northwest from Boston page 85 🚌

Matsumoto from Osaka-Kansai page 222 ✈ »Several per day ⏱55 min

Matsuyama from Osaka-Kansai page 222 ✈ »Several per day ⏱50 min

Matteson IL from Chicago-O'Hare page 106 🚌 Tri State Coaches »1 hr ⏱1 hr 30 min

Maturin from Caracas page 85 ✈ »Several per week ⏱50 min

Mazatlan from Mexico City page 187 ✈ »Several per day ⏱25–35 min

---

Remember . . .
The destinations in this index can be reached directly from the gateway airport. Many more local and long-distance transport connections may be available from the centre of the city. Consult the current edition of the *Thomas Cook European Timetable* (Europe) or *Thomas Cook Overseas Timetable* (rest of the world).

✈ Air 🚆 Rail 🚌 Bus Limousine Metro/subway Tram Helicopter Water transport

Mecca from Jeddah page 146 🚌 from Jeddah page 146 🚌 from Minneapolis/St Paul page 161 🚌

Medan from Singapore page 261 ✈ »Several per day ⟳20–30 min

Medicine Hat AB from Calgary page 98 ✈ »Several per day ⟳50 min

Melbourne VIC (city centre – Franklin Street) from Melbourne page 186 🚌 »30 min ⟳45 min

Melbourne FL from Orlando page 222 🚌Cocoa Beach Shuttle FL »2 hr ⟳2 hr 15 min

Menorca from Barcelona page 75 ✈ »Several per day ⟳45 min

Menorca from Palma page 225 ✈ »Several per day ⟳30 min

Menton from Nice page 217 🚌 »1 hr 15 min ⟳1 hr 15 min

Merrilville IN from Chicago-O'Hare page 106 🚌 Tri State Coaches »1 hr ⟳2 hr 15 min

Merrillville IN from Chicago page 105 🚌Tri-State Coach »1 hr ⟳1hr 50 min

Merrimack NH from Boston page 85 🚌 M & L Transportation »30 min ⟳1 hr 30 min

Metz from Strasbourg page 268 🚌 »Several per day ⟳1 hr 20 min

Mexico (city centre) from Mexico City page 187 🚇 ⟲0600–2400 Mon–Fri; 0600–2030 Sat; 0700–2030 Sun, Pub Hol »4–8 min

Miami FL (city centre) from Miami page 189 🚌 »3 day ⟳15 min. For Miami Bayside Bus Station

Miami FL (Tri–Rail stn) from Miami page 189 🚌 »1-2 hr ⟳15–20 min

Miami FL from Nassau page 206 ✈ »Several per day ⟳1 hr 5 min

Miami FL(city centre) from Miami page 189 🚌

Michiana Regional Apt IN from Chicago-O'Hare page 106 🚌 United Limo »1–2 hrs ⟳2 hr 20 min

Michigan City IN from Chicago-O'Hare page 106 🚌 United Limo »1–2 hrs ⟳1 hr 25 min

Middlesbrough from Newcastle page 207 🚌 »1 hr ⟳1 hr 15 min

Middlesbrough from Teesside page 274 🚌 »1 per hr ⟳30 min

Milan (city centre – Piazza S. Babila) from Milan-Linate page 192 🚌 »30 min ⟳25 min

Milan (city centre – Stazione Centrale) from Milan-Linate page 192 🚌 »0600–1900 ⟳20 min

Milan (city centre – Stazione Centrale) from Milan-Malpensa page 194 🚌 »30 min ⟳1 hr

Milan from Lyon page 178 ✈ »Several per week ⟳55–65 min

Milan from Nice page 217 ✈ »Several per week ⟳55 min

Milan from Rome-Fiumicino page 244 ✈ »Several per day ⟳1 hr 5 min

Milan-Linate Apt from Milan-Malpensa page 194 🚌 »4 daily ⟳75 min

Milan-Malpensa Apt from Milan-Linate page 192 🚌 »4 daily ⟳75 min

Milano see **Milan**

Mill Valley CA from San Francisco page 252 🚌 »30 min ⟳45 min

Millbrae CA from San Francisco page 252 🚌 »10-30 min ⟳15 min

Milos from Athens page 65 ✈ »Several per day ⟳45 min

Milwaukee WI from Chicago-O'Hare page 106 🚌 United Limo »90 min ⟳2 hr

Milwaukee WI from Chicago-O'Hare page 106 ✈ »Several per day ⟳35 min

Milwaukee WI from Chicago page 105 ✈ »Several per day ⟳45 min

Minatitlan from Mexico City page 187 ✈ »Several per day ⟳60–65 min

Minneapolis MN (city centre) from Minneapolis/St Paul page 161 🚌 ⟳30 min

Minneapolis MN (city centre) from Minneapolis/St Paul page 161 🚌

Minneapolis/St Paul MN (metro area) from Minneapolis/St Paul page 161 🚌

Miyake Jima from Tokyo-Narita page 277 ✈ »Several per day ⟳50 min

Mobile AL from New Orleans page 209 🚌Greyhound »2 day ⟲1410; 1815 ⟳30 hr 30 min.

Mokpo from Seoul page 211 ✈ »Several per day ⟳55 min

Moline IL from Chicago-O'Hare page 106 ✈ »Several per day ⟳45 min

Moline IL from St Louis page 247 ✈ »Several per day ⟳1 hr

Mönchengladbach from Düsseldorf page 122 🚌 »20 min ⟳45 min

Moncton NB from Halifax page 134 🚌 Acadian Lines »3 day; 0730, 1315, 1625 ⟳3 hr 30 min.

Moncton NB from Halifax page 134 ✈ »Several per day ⟳35 min

Monte Carlo from Nice page 217 🚌 »1 hr ⟳45 min

Monte Carlo from Nice page 217 🚆 »avg 20 min ⟳6 min

Montego Bay from Kingston page 150 ✈ »Several per day ⟳30–40 min

Montego Bay from Miami page 189 ✈ »Several per day ⟳35 min

Monterey CA from San Francisco page 252 🚌 »2 day ⟳3 hr

Monterey CA from San Francisco page 252 ✈ »Several per day ⟳35 min

Monterey/Salinas CA from San Francisco page 252 🚌 »6 day ⟳2–3 hr

Montevideo from Buenos Aires page 95 ✈ »Several per day ⟳45 min

Montgomery AL from Atlanta page 67 ✈ »Several per day ⟳1 hr

Montgomery County MD from Washington-Dulles page 291 🚌

Montpellier from Lyon page 178 ✈ »Several per week ⟳1 hr

Montpellier from Paris-Charles de Gaulle page 226 🚆 SNCF: TGV »2 per day ⟳4 hr 53 min

Montpellier from Paris-Charles de Gaulle page 226 ✈ »Several per day ⟳1 hr 15 min

Montpellier from Paris-Orly page 234 ✈ »Several per day ⟳1 hr 10 min

Montréal PQ (Downtown Terminal) from Montréal-Mirabel page 199 🚌 »30 min–1 hr ⟳1 hr

Montréal PQ (metro area) from Montréal-Mirabel page 199 🚌

Montréal PQ from Boston page 85 ✈ »Several per day ⟳1 hr

Montréal-Dorval Apt PQ from Montréal-Mirabel page 199 🚌 »30 min–1 hr ⟳35 min

Montreux from Geneva page 130 🚆 SBB » 1hr ⟳ 1hr 15min

Montrose CO from Denver page 118 ✈ »Several per day ⟳1 hr

Morelia from Mexico City page 187 ✈ »Several per day ⟳50–55 min

Moruya NSW from Sydney page 270 ✈ »Several per day ⟳45 min

Mulhouse from Zürich page 296 ✈ »Several per day ⟳30 min

Mulhouse/Basel from Lyon page 178 ✈ »Several per week ⟳55 min

Mumbai (city centre – SEEPZ bus terminal) from Mumbai page 202 🚌 »13 min

Mumbai (city centre) from Mumbai page 202 🚌 »30 min

Mumbai Domestic Apts from Mumbai page 202 🚌 »45 min (day); 2 hr (night)

Münchensee Munich

Munich from Milan-Linate page 192 ✈ »At least daily ⟳1 hr

Munich from Prague page 239 ✈ »Several per day ⟳55 min

Munich from Zürich page 296 ✈ »Several per day ⟳55 min

Münster from Frankfurt page 126 ✈ »Several per day ⟳1 hr

Muscat from Abu Dhabi page 58 ✈ »Several per day ⟳55 min

Muscat from Dubai page 119 ✈ »Several per day ⟳50 min

Muscat from Mumbai page 202 ✈ »Several per week ⟳50 min

Mykonos from Athens page 65 ✈ »Several per day ⟳45 min

Mytilene from Athens page 65 ✈ »Several per day ⟳45 min

Nagoya from Tokyo-Narita page 277 ✈ »Several per day ⟳60–70 min

Nairobi (city centre) from Nairobi page 205 🚌 » approx. 30 min ⟳35–40 min

Nakhon Ratchasima from Bangkok page 72 ✈ »At least daily ⏱45 min

Namba from Osaka-Kansai page 222 🚌 »43 min

Namba from Osaka-Kansai page 222 🚌 T »30 min ⏱29–34 min

Nanaimo BC from Vancouver page 286 ✈ »Several per day ⏱20–30 min

Nancy from Strasbourg page 268 🚆 »Several per day ⏱1 hr 15 min

Nantes from Paris-Charles de Gaulle page 226 🚆 SNCF: TGV »4 per day ⏱2 hr 54 min

Nantes from Paris-Orly page 234 ✈ »Several per day ⏱55 min

Nantucket MA from Boston page 85 ✈ »Several per day ⏱45 min

Napa CA from San Francisco page 252 🚌 »1–2 hrs ⏱1 hr 30 min

Naples (Italy) from Rome-Fiumicino page 244 ✈ »Several per day ⏱45 min

Naples FL from Miami page 189 🚌

Naples FL from Miami page 189 ✈ »Several per day ⏱45 min

Nashville TN from Atlanta page 67 ✈ »Several per day ⏱55 min

Nassau (city centre) from Nassau page 206 🚌 »Irregular ⏱30 min

Nawabshah from Karachi page 148 ✈ »Several per week ⏱55 min

Naxos from Athens page 65 ✈ »At least daily ⏱45 min

Nayuki from Nairobi page 205 ✈ »Several per week ⏱45 min

Negril from Kingston page 150 ✈ »At least daily ⏱45 min

Neiva from Bogota page 84 ✈ »Several per week ⏱50 min

Neuchâtel from Geneva page 130 🚆 SBB » 1hr ⏱ 1hr 20min

Neumünster from Hamburg page 135 🚆 »2 hr ⏱1 hr

New Hampshire from Boston page 85 🚌

New Hampshire seacoast from Boston page 85 🚌

New Hampshire state (southern) from Boston page 85 🚌

New Haven CT from New York-Newark page 216 ✈ »Several per day ⏱45 min

New Jersey from New York-JFK page 209 🚌 »11 day ⏱1 hr 30 min

New Jersey state from New York-Newark page 216 🚌 »45 min–1 hr

New Plymouth from Auckland page 69 ✈ »At least daily ⏱50 min

Newport from Cardiff page 103 🚆 » 30 min ⏱ 30 min

New Ulm MN from Minneapolis/St Paul page 161 🚌

New Westminster BC (SkyTrain) from Vancouver page 286 🚌 »15 min–1 hr ⏱1 hr

New York City NY (Columbia University) from New York-La Guardia page 214 🚌 »30 min

New York City NY (E Fourth St and Pier 11 Wall Street) 🚢 Delta Water Shuttle ⏱30–45 min

New York City NY (Grand Central rail stn) from New York-JFK page 209 🚌 »30 min ⏱1 hr

New York City NY (hotels) from New York-Newark page 216 🚌 »On-demand ⏱30 min–1 hr

New York City NY (Manhattan) from New York-JFK page 209 🚇 »15 min ⏱60–75 min

New York City NY (Port Authority Bus Terminal) from New York-La Guardia page 214 🚌 »30 min ⏱40 min

New York City NY (Port Authority Bus Terminal) from New York-Newark page 216 🚌 »10–15 min (30–60 min overnight) ⏱30–40 min

New York City NY (World Trade Center) from New York-Newark page 216 🚌 »20–30 min ⏱20–40 min

New York NY (metro area)/Tri-State Area) from New York-JFK page 209 🚌

New York NY from Philadelphia page 238 ✈ »Several per day ⏱45 min

New York NY metro/Tri-State area from New York-La Guardia page 214 🚌

New York NY metro/Tri-State area from New York-Newark page 216 🚌

New York state (upstate) from New York-JFK page 209 🚌 »On–demand

New York-JFK Apt NY from New York-Newark page 216 🚌 »Frequent ⏱1 hr 30 min

New York-La Guardia Apt NY from New York-JFK page 209 🚌 »30 min ⏱45 min

New York-Newark Apt NJ from New York-JFK page 209 🚌 »Frequent ⏱1 hr 30 min

New York-Newark Apt NJ from New York-La Guardia page 214 🚌 »On-demand ⏱1 hr 30 min

Newark NJ (Penn rail stn) from New York-Newark page 216 🚌 »20–30 min

Newburyport MA from Boston page 85 🚌 »1–2 hrs ⏱1 hr 30 min

Newcastle (UK) from Manchester page 183 ✈ »Several per day ⏱55 min

Newcastle NSW from Sydney page 270 ✈ »Several per day ⏱30 min

Nice (Gare SNCF rail stn) from Nice page 217 🚌 »20 min ⏱20 min

Nice (Gare SNCF rail stn) from Nice page 217 🚆 from Paris-Orly page 234 ✈ »Several per day ⏱1 hr 10 min

Nice from Lyon page 178 ✈ »Several per day ⏱50 min

Nong Khai from Bangkok page 72 🚆 »3 per day ⏱10–11 hrs

Norfolk/Virginia Beach VA from Baltimore/Washington page 72 ✈ »Several per day ⏱1 hr

Norfolk VA from Washington-Dulles page 291 ✈ »Several per day ⏱55 min

Norrköping from Stockholm-Arlanda page 266 ✈ »Several per week ⏱35 min

Norrkoping from Gothenburg page 133 ✈ »2 per day ⏱1 hr

North Bay ON from Toronto page 281 ✈ »Several per day ⏱1 hr

North Bay ON from Toronto page 281 🚌 »2–3 day ⏱4 hr 15 min

North Plymouth MA from Boston page 85 🚌 »1 hr ⏱1 hr 15 min

Northampton MA from Boston page 85 🚌

Norwalk CA from Los Angeles page 174 🚇 Metro Rail: Green Line »7–20 min ⏱25 min

Norwich from London-Heathrow page 164 🚌 »Day avg 2 hr ⏱3 hr 15 min

Norwich from London-Stansted page 173 🚌 »avg 2 hr ⏱2 hr

Norwich from Manchester page 183 ✈ »At least daily ⏱50 min

Notre Dame IN from Chicago-O'Hare page 106 🚌 »1–2 hrs ⏱2 hr 40 min

Nottingham from East Midlands page 124 🚌 »approx. 1 hr ⏱1 hr

Novato CA from San Francisco page 252 🚌 »30 min ⏱1 hr 20 min

Nuremberg from Berlin page 80 ✈ »At least daily ⏱1 hr 10 min

Nuremberg from Düsseldorf page 122 ✈ »Several per week ⏱1 hr

Nuremberg from Frankfurt page 126 ✈ »Several per day ⏱45 min

Nuremberg from Prague page 239 ✈ »Several per week ⏱1 hr

Nuremberg from Zürich page 296 ✈ »At least daily ⏱1 hr

Nürnberg see **Nuremberg**

Nyon from Geneva page 130 🚆 SBB »30min ⏱25min

Oak Harbor WA from Seattle page 258 🚌 »2 hr ⏱3 hr 35 min

Oak Harbor WA from Seattle page 258 ✈ »Several per day ⏱35 min

Oakland International Apt CA from San Francisco page 252 🚌 »1 hr ⏱1 hr

Oakville ON from Toronto page 281 🚌 »7 day ⏱40 min

Oaxaca from Mexico City page 187 ✈ »Several per day ⏱50–55 min

Odense from Copenhagen page 111 ✈ »Several per day ⏱35 min

Remember...
The destinations in this index can be reached directly from the gateway airport. Many more local and long-distance transport connections may be available from the centre of the city. Consult the current edition of the *Thomas Cook European Timetable* (Europe) or *Thomas Cook Overseas Timetable* (rest of the world).

Offenburg • Phnom Penh — Section Three • Destination Index

Offenburg Bahnhof 🚌 Navette Bus ⊘ FRF58 ⟳ 50 min ⌚ 0850–1935 Mon–Fri

Ogunquit ME from Boston page 85 🚌

Oita from Osaka-Kansai page 222 ✈ »Several per day ⟳ 55 min

Oklahoma City OK from Dallas/Fort Worth page 113 ✈ »Several per day ⟳ 1 hr

Olbia from Milan-Linate page 192 ✈ »At least daily ⟳ 1 hr

Olbia from Rome-Fiumicino page 244 ✈ »Several per day ⟳ 45 min

Olympia WA from Seattle page 258 🚆 »2 day ⟳ 1 hr 35 min

Olympia WA from Seattle page 258 🚌

Ontario CA from Los Angeles page 174 ✈ »Several per day ⟳ 35 min

Ontario CA from San Diego page 250 ✈ »At least daily ⟳ 40 min

Ontario province from Toronto page 281 🚆 from Toronto page 281 🚆

Ontario CA from Las Vegas page 154 ✈ »Several per day ⟳ 50 min

Opelika AL from Atlanta page 67 🚌

Oporto see **Porto**

Orange County Apt CA from Los Angeles page 174 🚆 »30 min, 60 min evening ⟳ 1 hr 45 min

Orange County CA from Las Vegas page 154 ✈ »Several per day ⟳ 55 min

Osaka (port) 🚢 ⟳ 30 min

Osaka (rail stn) from Osaka-Kansai page 222 🚌 »30 min ⟳ 65 min

Osaka (rail stn) from Osaka-Kansai page 222 🚆 ⟳ 55–65 min

Osaka-Itami Apt from Osaka-Kansai page 222 🚆 ⟳ 85 min

Oshima from Tokyo-Narita page 277 ✈ »Several per day ⟳ 40 min

Oshkosh WI from Chicago-O'Hare page 106 ✈ »Several per day ⟳ 50 min

Oslo (city centre) from Oslo page 223 🚆 »10 min ⟳ 15–20 min

Ostersund from Stockholm-Arlanda page 266 ✈ »Several per day ⟳ 1 hr

Ostrava from Prague page 239 ✈ »Several per day ⟳ 1 hr

Ottawa ON from Montréal-Mirabel page 199 🚌

Ottawa ON from Montréal-Mirabel page 199 ✈ »Several per day ⟳ 45 min

Ottawa ON from Toronto page 281 ✈ »Several per day ⟳ 50 min

Ottawa ON from Montréal page 197 🚆 Voyageur »5 per day ⌚ 1200, 1400, 1540; 1800; 1940 ⟳ 1 hr 40 min

Owatonna MN from Minneapolis/St Paul page 161 🚆 »2 per day ⟳ 1 hr 30 min

Owen Sound ON from Toronto page 281 🚆

Oxford from London-Heathrow page 164 🚌 »avg 30 min ⟳ 1 hr 25 min

Oxnard CA from Los Angeles page 174 🚆 »7 per day ⟳ 1 hr 45 min

Oxnard/Ventura CA from Los Angeles page 174 🚆 »7 day ⟳ 1 hr 30 min

Oxnard/Ventura CA from Los Angeles page 174 ✈ »Several per day ⟳ 35 min

Padang from Kuala Lumpur page 151 ✈ »Several per day ⟳ 25 min

Paducah KY from St Louis page 247 ✈ »Several per week ⟳ 55 min

Palembang from Jakarta page 145 ✈ »Several per day ⟳ 1 hr

Palermo from Rome-Fiumicino page 244 ✈ »Several per day ⟳ 1 hr

Palm Springs CA from Los Angeles page 174 🚌

Palm Springs CA from Los Angeles page 174 ✈ »Several per day ⟳ 45 min

Palm Springs CA from San Diego page 250 🚌

Palma, Mallorca from Barcelona page 75 ✈ »Several per day ⟳ 40 min

Palmdale CA from Los Angeles page 174 ✈ »Several per day ⟳ 35 min

Palmdale/Lancaster CA from Los Angeles page 174 🚆 »7 per day ⟳ 2 hr

Palm Springs CA from Las Vegas page 154 ✈ »Several per day ⟳ 50 min

Palo Alto CA from San Francisco page 252 🚆 »30 min

Pamplona from Barcelona page 75 ✈ »Several per week ⟳ 55 min

Panama City FL from Atlanta page 67 ✈ »Several per day ⟳ 1 hr

Paris (city centre – Gare du Nord rail stn) from Paris-Charles de Gaulle page 226 🚆 »7–15 min ⟳ 35 min

Paris (city centre – Invalides, Gare Montparnasse rail stn) from Paris-Orly page 234 🚆 »15–20 min ⟳ 25 min

Paris (city centre – Opéra) from Paris-Charles de Gaulle page 226 🚌 »15 min ⟳ 30 min

Paris (city centre – Opéra) from Paris-Charles de Gaulle page 226 🚌 »15 min ⟳ 30 min

Paris (city centre – Porte Maillot air terminal) from Paris-Charles de Gaulle page 226 🚌 »15–20 min ⟳ 25 min

Paris (city centre – St-Michel/Notre Dame) from Paris-Orly page 234 🚆 »avg 15 min ⟳ 24 min

Paris (city centre) from Paris-Orly page 234 🚁 ⟳ 15 min

Paris (Gare de Lyon rail stn) from Lyon page 178 🚆 »3 per day ⟳ 2hr 3 min

Paris from London-City page 157 ✈ »Several per week ⟳ 1 hr

Paris from Lyon page 178 ✈ »Several per day ⟳ 50–60 min

Paris-Charles de Gaulle Apt from Lyon page 178 ✈ »1 per day ⟳ 2 hr 5 min

Paris-Charles de Gaulle Apt from Paris-Orly page 234 🚌 »20 min ⟳ 50 min

Paris-Charles de Gaulle Apt from Paris-Orly page 234 🚌 »4–7 min ⟳ 1 hr 5 min

Paris-Orly Apt from Paris-Charles de Gaulle page 226 🚌 »15 min ⟳ 1 hr 10 min

Parma from Rome-Fiumicino page 244 ✈ »Several per week ⟳ 1 hr

Paros from Athens page 65 ✈ »Several per day ⟳ 45 min

Pasadena CA from Los Angeles page 174 🚆 »60 min ⟳ 1 hr

Pasay City, Makati, Manila from Manila page 185 🚌 ⟳ approx 30 min

Pascagoula MS from New Orleans page 209 🚆 Coastliner/Mississippi Gulf Service »9 day ⌚ 0800–2330

Pasco WA from Seattle page 258 ✈ »Several per day ⟳ 55 min

Peace River AB from Edmonton page 125 ✈ »At Least daily ⟳ 1 hr

Pembroke ON from Toronto page 281 ✈ »Several per week ⟳ 1 hr

Penang from Kuala Lumpur page 151 ✈ »Several per day ⟳ 45 min

Pennsylvania state from New York-JFK page 209 🚆 »1–2 hrs ⟳ 2 hr 30 min

Pensacola FL from Atlanta page 67 ✈ »Several per day ⟳ 1 hr

Peoria IL from Chicago-O'Hare page 106 🚌

Peoria IL from Chicago-O'Hare page 106 ✈ »Several per day ⟳ 55 min

Pereira from Bogota page 84 ✈ »Several per week ⟳ 50 min

Perth WA (city centre) from Perth page 237 🚆 »30 min ⟳ 1 hr 20 min

Petaluma CA from San Francisco page 252 🚆 »1 hr ⟳ 1 hr 15 min

Peterborough from Norwich page 220 🚆 »1 per hr ⟳ 1 hr 35 min

Phoenix AZ from Las Vegas page 154 ✈ »Several per day ⟳ 1 hr

Philadelphia (city centre) from Philadelphia page 238 🚌

Philadelphia (Suburban rail stn) from Philadelphia page 238 🚆 »30 min ⟳ 20 min

Philadelphia PA from New York-JFK page 209 ✈ »Several per day ⟳ 50 min

Philadelphia PA from New York-La Guardia page 214 ✈ »Several per week ⟳ 1 hr

Philadelphia PA from New York-Newark page 216 🚌

Philadelphia from Baltimore/Washington page 72 ✈ »Several per day ⟳ 40 min

Philadelphia PA (30th St Stn) from Baltimore/Washington page 72 🚆 Amtrak »25 day ⌚ 0510–0035 ⟳ 1 hr 20 min

Phitsanulok from Bangkok page 72 🚆 »11 per day ⟳ 4 hr 40 min – 6 hr 50 min

Phnom Penh from Kuala Lumpur page 151 ✈ »At least daily ⟳ 45 min

Phnom Penh from Singapore page 261 ✈ »At least daily ⟳ 55–60 min

---

» Frequency of service ⟳ Journey time   For details of fares, etc, see individual airport entries, Section Two

SECTION THREE • DESTINATION INDEX PHUKET • ROANOKE

Phuket from Kuala Lumpur page 151 ✈ »At least daily ↻15–20 min

Phuket from Singapore page 261 ✈ »Several per day ↻40–45 min

Pingtung from Taipei-Chiang Kai Shek page 272 ✈ »Several per day ↻1 hr

Piraeus from Athens page 65 🚌 »approx 60 min ↻30–40 min

Pisa from Milan-Linate page 192 ✈ »Several per day ↻50 min

Pittsburgh PA from Baltimore/Washington page 72 ✈ »Several per day ↻1 hr

Plymouth from Bristol page 89 ✈ »4 per week ↻35 min

Plymouth from London-Heathrow page 164 ✈ »Several per day ↻1 hr 5 min

Pohang from Seoul page 211 ✈ »Several per day ↻55 min

Poitiers from Paris-Charles de Gaulle page 226 🚆 SNCF: TGV »4 per day ↻2 hr 14 min

Poole from London-Heathrow page 164 🚌 »1 hr 45 min ↻2 hr 10 min

Porlamar from Caracas page 85 ✈ »Several per day ↻40 min

Port Alberni BC from Vancouver page 286 ✈ »Several per day ↻1 hr

Port Angeles WA from Seattle page 258 🚌 from Seattle page 258 ✈ »Several per day ↻30 min

Port Antonio from Kingston page 150 ✈ »At least daily ↻15 min

Port Elgin ON from Toronto page 281 🚌 from Seattle page 258 🚌 »1 hr ↻1 hr

Port Harcourt from Lagos page 153 ✈ »Several per week ↻1 hr

Port of Spain from Bridgetown page 88 ✈ »Several per day ↻55 min

Portage IN from Chicago-O'Hare page 106 🚐 »1–2 hrs ↻1 hr 10 min

Port Augusta from Adelaide page 59 ✈ »3 per day ↻60 min

Portland ME from Boston page 85 ✈ »Several per day ↻40 min

Portland ME from Boston page 85 🚌 »2 hrs ↻2 hrs 30 min

Portland OR from Seattle page 258 ✈ »Several per day ↻50 min

Portland OR from Seattle page 258 🚌 »3 day ↻4 hrs

Portland VIC from Melbourne page 186 ✈ »Several per day ↻50–55 min

Port Lincoln from Adelaide page 59 ✈ »Several per day ↻50 min

Porto from Lisbon page 156 ✈ »Several per day ↻45 min

Porto from Madrid page 180 ✈ »Several per day ↻30 min

Portsmouth NH from Boston page 85 🚌 »1–2 hrs ↻2 hr

Powell River BC from Vancouver page 286 ✈ »Several per day ↻30 min

Poza Rica from Mexico City page 187 ✈ »Several per week ↻50 min

Prague (city centre – Dejvická metro stn) from Prague page 239 🚐CEDAZ » 1 hr and acc to demand ↻20 min

Prague (city centre – Dejvická metro stn) from Prague page 239 🚌 » 10 min ↻30 min

Prague (city centre – Hotel Penta) from Prague page 239 🚌 » ↻30 min

Prague (city centre – Nam. Republicky metro stn) from Prague page 239 🚐CEDAZ tel 3344368 » 1 hr and according to demand ↻30 min

Prague (city centre) from Prague page 239 🚌 » 30 min ↻20 min

Prague from Budapest page 93 ✈ »Several per day ↻1 hr

Prague from Frankfurt page 126 ✈ »Several per day ↻1 hr 5 min

Prague from Munich page 203 ✈ »Several per week ↻1 hr

Prague from Vienna page 288 ✈ »Several per day ↻55 min

Praha see **Prague**

Preston from Liverpool page 157 🚆 » 1 hr ↻1 hr

Preveza/Lefkas from Athens page 65 ✈ »At least daily ↻1 hr

Princeton NJ from New York-JFK page 209 🚐 »Frequent

Pristina from Istanbul page 143 ✈ »Several per week ↻20 min

Providence RI from Boston page 85 ✈ »Several per week ↻30 min

Providence RI from Boston page 85 🚌 »1–2 hrs ↻1 hr 15 min

Provincetown MA from Boston page 85 🚌 »2 per day Mon–Fri ↻4 hr

Puebla from Mexico City page 187 ✈ »Several per week ↻35 min

Pueblo CO from Denver page 118 ✈ »Several per day ↻40 min

Puerto Escondido from Mexico City page 187 ✈ »At least daily ↻55–60 min

Puerto Ordaz from Caracas page 85 ✈ »Several per day ↻1 hr

Punta D'Este from Buenos Aires page 95 ✈ »Several per week ↻50 min

Pusan from Seoul page 211 ✈ »Several per day ↻1 hr

Québec PQ from Montréal-Mirabel page 199 🚌 »2 per day

Québec PQ from Montréal-Mirabel page 199 ✈ »At least daily ↻45 min

Queens NY (Jamaica stn) from New York-La Guardia page 214 🚌 »1 hr ↻30 min

Queens NY from New York-JFK page 209 🚌 »30 min ↻30 min

Queens NY from New York-La Guardia page 214 🚌 »15 min

Queens NY from New York-La Guardia page 214 🚌 »30 min

Queretaro from Mexico City page 187 ✈ »Several per week ↻50 min

Racine WI from Chicago-O'Hare page 106 🚐 »90 min ↻1 hr 15 min

Rajkot from Mumbai page 202 ✈ »Several per week ↻50 min

Ratingen from Düsseldorf page 122 🚌 »avg 20 min ↻35 min

Reading (UK) from London-Heathrow page 164 🚌 »avg 30 min ↻45–70 min.

Reading PA from Philadelphia page 238 ✈ »Several per day ↻35 min

Redding CA from San Francisco page 252 ✈ »Several per day ↻1 hr

Reggio Calabria from Rome-Fiumicino page 244 ✈ »Several per day ↻1 hr 5 min

Rennes from Paris-Charles de Gaulle page 226 ✈ »Several per week ↻1 hr 05 min

Rennes from Paris-Orly page 234 ✈ »At least daily ↻1 hr

Reno NV from San Francisco page 252 ✈ »Several per day ↻50 min

Rhinelander WI from Minneapolis/St Paul page 161 ✈ »Several per day ↻1 hr

Rhode Island state from Boston page 85 🚌

Rhode Island, northern from Boston page 85 🚌

Rhodes from Athens page 65 ✈ »Several times per day ↻55 min

Richmond VA from Washington-Dulles page 291 🚐

Richmond VA from Washington-Dulles page 291 ✈ »Several per day ↻40 min

Richmond VA from Baltimore/Washington page 72 ✈ »Several per day ↻40 min

Ridgedale Center MN from Minneapolis/St Paul page 161 🚐

Riga from Helsinki page 137 ✈ »Several per day ↻55 min

Rio de Janeiro (city centre – downtown bus depot) from Rio de Janeiro-International page 242 🚌 »30 min ↻1 hr

Rio de Janeiro from São Paulo-Guarulhos page 257 ✈ »Several per day ↻1 hr

Rio de Janeiro-Santos Dumont Apt from Rio de Janeiro-International page 242 🚌 30 min ↻40 min

Riyadh (city centre) from Riyadh page 243 🚌 »40 min ↻35 min

Riyadh from Bahrain page 70 ✈ »Several per week ↻1 hr 5 min

Riyadh from Jeddah page 146 ✈ »Several per day ↻1 hr 30 min

Roanoke VA from Washington-Dulles page 291 ✈ »Several per day ↻1 hr

---

Remember . . .
The destinations in this index can be reached directly from the gateway airport. Many more local and long-distance transport connections may be available from the centre of the city. Consult the current edition of the *Thomas Cook European Timetable* (Europe) or *Thomas Cook Overseas Timetable* (rest of the world).

✈ Air   🚆 Rail   🚌 Bus   🚐 Limousine   Ⓜ Metro/subway   🚋 Tram   🚁 Helicopter   ⛴ Water transport

ROCHE HARBOR • SANTA CRUZ — SECTION THREE • DESTINATION INDEX

Roche Harbor WA from Seattle page 258 ✈ »Several per day ⏲1 hr

Rochester MN from Minneapolis/St Paul page 161 🚌

Rochester MN from Minneapolis/St Paul page 161 🚆 »3 per day ⏲1 hr 45 min

Rochester MN from Minneapolis/St Paul page 161 ✈ »Several per day ⏲40 min

Rock Sound from Nassau page 206 ✈ »At least daily ⏲1 hr

Rockford IL from Chicago-O'Hare page 106 🚌 »90 min – 2 hr ⏲1 hr 15 min

Rockland ME from Boston page 85 ✈ »Several per day ⏲55 min

Rodez from Lyon page 178 ✈ »Several per week ⏲50 min

Rodossee Rhodes

Rohnert Park CA from San Francisco page 252 🚆 »1 hr ⏲1 hr 30 min

Rohnert Park CA from San Francisco page 252 🚆 »1 hr ⏲1 hr 15 min

Rolla MO from St Louis page 247 🚆 »2 day ⏲2 hr 35 min

Roma see Rome

Rome (city centre – Termini central rail stn) from Rome-Fiumicino page 244 🚆 »20–30 min ⏲35 min

Rome from Nice page 217 ✈ »Several per day ⏲1 hr

Rosario WA from Seattle page 258 ✈ »Several per day ⏲1 hr

Rosh Pina from Tel Aviv page 275 ✈ »Several per week ⏲35 min

Rotterdam from Amsterdam page 61 🚌 »avg 30 min by day/1 hr at night ⏲47 min

Rotterdam from London-City page 157 ✈ »Several per day ⏲1 hr

Rotterdam from London-Gatwick page 160 ✈ »Several per day ⏲1 hr 10 min

Rotterdam from London-Heathrow page 164 ✈ »Several per day ⏲1 hr 10 min

Rotterdam from London-Stansted page 173 ✈ »Several per week ⏲1 hr

Rottnest Island WA from Perth page 237 ✈ »Several per day ⏲15 min

Rutland VT from Boston page 85 🚆 »2 per day ⏲5–7 hrs

Rye NY from New York-Newark page 216 🚌 »1–2 hr

Saarbrücken from Düsseldorf page 122 ✈ »Several per week ⏲50 min

Saarbrücken from Munich page 203 ✈ »At least daily ⏲1 hr 10 min

Sacramento CA from San Francisco page 252 🚆 »7 day ⏲2 hr 30 min

Sacramento CA from San Francisco page 252 🚌 »Several per day ⏲40 min

Saginaw MI from Chicago-O'Hare page 106 ✈ »Several per day ⏲55 min

St Brieuc from Paris-Orly page 234 ✈ »Several per weekr ⏲1 hr 05 min

St Cloud MN from Minneapolis/St Paul page 161 🚌

St Cloud MN from Minneapolis/St Paul page 161 ✈ »Several per day ⏲45 min

St Etienne from Lyon page 178 🚆 Satobus »5–6 per day ⏲1 hr 10 min–1 hr 25 min

St Etienne from Strasbourg page 268 ✈ »Several per day ⏲1 hr 15 min

St Gallen from Zürich page 296 🚌 »20–40 min ⏲60–65 min

St George UT from Las Vegas page 154 ✈ »Several per day ⏲40 min

St John NB from Halifax page 134 ✈ »Several per day ⏲35 min

St Laurent du Var SNCF rail stn from Nice page 217 🚆 @index:St Louis MO from St Louis page 247 🚆 »7–15 min ⏲35 min

St Louis MO (metro area) from St Louis page 247 🚌

St Lucia Vigie Apt from Bridgetown page 88 ✈ »Several per day ⏲35–45 min

St Paul MN (downtown hotels) from Minneapolis/St Paul page 161 🚌

St Paul MN from Minneapolis/St Paul page 161 🚌 from Minneapolis/St Paul page 161 🚆 »4 per day ⏲1 hr 15 min

St Petersburg (city centre – from Metro stn) from St Petersburg page 248 🚆 »25 min ⏲15 min

St Vincent from Bridgetown page 88 ✈ »Several per day ⏲40 min

Saarbrucken from Stuttgart page 269 ✈ »1 per day ⏲30 min

Salinas CA from San Francisco page 252 🚆 »2 day ⏲3 hr 35 min

Salisbury MD from Philadelphia page 238 ✈ »Several per day ⏲50 min

Salisbury MD from Baltimore/Washington page 72 ✈ »Several per day ⏲35 min

Salzburg from Berlin page 80 ✈ »Several per day ⏲1 hr

Salzburg from Frankfurt page 126 ✈ »Several per day ⏲1 hr

Salzburg from Prague page 239 ✈ »Several per week ⏲1 hr

Salzburg from Vienna page 288 ✈ »Several per day ⏲55 min

Salzburg from Zürich page 296 ✈ »Several per day ⏲55 min

Samos from Athens page 65 »Several times per day ⏲1 hr

Samrong from Bangkok page 72

San Andros from Nassau page 206 ✈ »Several per day ⏲1 hr

San Antonio TX from Dallas/Fort Worth page 113 ✈ »Several per day ⏲1 hr

San Antonio TX from Houston page 142 ✈ »Several per day ⏲50 min

San Diego (city centre) from San Diego page 250 🚆 »12–30 min ⏲15 min

San Diego CA (Amtrak/Santa Fe Depot) from San Diego page 250 🚆 »12–30 min ⏲10 min

San Diego CA (military bases) from San Diego page 250 🚌

San Diego CA from Los Angeles page 174 ✈ »Several per day ⏲45 min

San Diego CA from Las Vegas page 154 ✈ »Several per day ⏲1 hr

San Fernando from Manila page 185 ✈ »At least daily ⏲1 hr

San Francisco CA (city centre) from San Francisco page 252 🚆 »30 min ⏲1 hr

San Francisco CA (City Hall) from San Francisco page 252 🚆 »30 min ⏲30 min

San Francisco CA (downtown hotels) from San Francisco page 252 🚆 »30 min ⏲50 min

San Francisco CA (Financial District) from San Francisco page 252 🚆 »30 min

San Francisco CA (Transbay Terminal) from San Francisco page 252 🚆 »5 day ⏲30 min

San Francisco CA (Transbay Terminal) from San Francisco page 252 🚆 »30 min ⏲30 min

San Francsco CA (Union Square Hotels) from San Francisco page 252 🚆 »30 min ⏲45 min

San Jose (Philippines) from Manila page 185 ✈ »Several per week ⏲45–55 min

San Jose CA (city centre) from San Francisco page 252 🚆 »1 hr ⏲1 hr 15 min

San Jose CA from Los Angeles page 174 ✈ »Several per day ⏲1 hr

San Jose Cabo from Mexico City page 187 ✈ »At least daily ⏲1 hr

San Jose International Apt CA from San Francisco page 252 🚆 »2 hrs ⏲1 hr

San Jose International Apt CA from San Francisco page 252 🚆 »1 hr ⏲1 hr

San Luis Obispo CA from Los Angeles page 174 ✈ »Several per day ⏲1 hr

San Luis Potosi from Mexico City page 187 ✈ »Several times per day ⏲45–75 min

San Pedro Sula from Mexico City page 187 ✈ »Several per week ⏲1 hr

San Rafael CA (Transportation Center) from San Francisco page 252 🚆 »30 min ⏲55 min

San Ramon CA from San Francisco page 252 🚆 »1–2 hrs ⏲50 min

San Salvador (Bahamas) from Nassau page 206 ✈ »Several per week ⏲1 hr

Santa Ana CA from Los Angeles page 174 ✈ »Several per day ⏲30 min

Santa Barbara CA from Los Angeles page 174 🚆 »7 day ⏲2 hr 30 min

Santa Clarita CA from Los Angeles page 174 🚌

Santa Cruz CA from San Francisco page 252 🚆 »2 per day ⏲1 hr 40 min

---

» Frequency of service ⏲ Journey time   For details of fares, etc, see individual airport entries, Section Two

SECTION THREE • DESTINATION INDEX

SANTA CRUZ • STOCKHOLM

Santa Cruz CA from San Francisco page 252 🚌 »2 hrs ⏱2 hr

Santa Cruz Palmas from Tenerife page 276 ✈ »Several per day ⏱30 min

Santa Fe from Buenos Aires page 95 ✈ »Several per week ⏱1 hr

Santa Maria CA from Los Angeles page 174 ✈ »Several per day ⏱50 min

Santa Monica CA from Los Angeles page 174 🚌 »20–60 min ⏱35 min

Santa Rosa CA from San Francisco page 252 🚌 »1 hr ⏱1 hr 45 min

Santa Rosa CA from San Francisco page 252 ✈ »Several per day ⏱40 min

Santiago (city centre – bus terminal, Moneda St) from Santiago page 256

Santiago (city centre – Los Heroes subway stn) from Santiago page 256 🚌 »15 min

Santos from São Paulo-Guarulhos page 257 ⏱1 hr

São São Conrado from Rio de Janeiro-International page 242 🚌 »30 min ⏱40 min

São Jose from São Paulo-Guarulhos page 257 ✈ »Several per day ⏱50 min

São Paulo (Avenida Paulista Hotel District) from São Paulo-Guarulhos page 257 EMTU »1 hr ⏱50 min

São Paulo (city centre) from São Paulo-Guarulhos page 257 EMTU »30 min ⏱40 min

São Paulo from Rio de Janeiro-Intn'l page 208 ✈ »Several per day ⏱50 min

São Paulo-Congonhas Apt from São Paulo-Guarulhos page 257 🚁 Wilson Taxis Aereo ⏱15 min

São Paulo-Congonhas Apt from São Paulo-Guarulhos page 257 🚌 EMTU » 1 hr

Sarasota/Bradenton FL from Miami page 189 ✈ »Several per day ⏱1 hr

Sarasota/Bradenton FL from Orlando page 222 ✈ »Several per day ⏱45 min

Sarnia ON from Toronto page 281 ✈ »Several per day ⏱55 min

Sauk Center MN from Minneapolis/St Paul page 161 🚌

Sausalito CA from San Francisco page 252 🚌 »30 min ⏱35 min

Savannah GA from Atlanta page 67 ✈ »Several per day ⏱1 hr

Scotts Valley CA from San Francisco page 252 🚌 »2 HR ⏱1 hr 45 min

Scottsbluff NE from Denver page 118 ✈ »Several per day ⏱50 min

Seattle–Tacoma WA (metro area) from Seattle page 258 🚌

Seattle–Tacoma WA (metro area) from Seattle page 258 🚌 »On-demand

Seattle Lake WA from Seattle page 258 ✈ »Several per day ⏱20 min

Seattle WA (city centre) from Seattle page 258 🚌 »30 min

Seattle WA (downtown hotels) from Seattle page 258 🚌 »20 min ⏱Lower Level

Seattle WA from Vancouver page 286 ✈ »Several per day ⏱50 min

Semarang from Jakarta page 145 ✈ »Several per day ⏱1 hr

Seoul (city centre) and hotels from Seoul page 211 🚌 »7–10 min ⏱40 min

Seoul (city centre) and hotels from Seoul page 211 🚌 »5–8 min ⏱40 min

Sequim WA from Seattle page 258 🚌 from Belfast-International page 78 ✈ »Several per week ⏱1hr

Seville from Madrid page 180 ✈ »Several per day ⏱55 min

Shannon from Dublin page 120 ✈ »Several per day ⏱45 min

Shantou from Hong Kong page 112 ✈ »Several times per day ⏱50–60 min

Sheffield from Birmingham page 82 🚌 »Twice daily; once only Sun ⏱2 hr

Sheffield from Manchester page 183 🚌 »approx. every 40 min ⏱1 hr 40 min

Sheffield from Leeds/Bradford page 155 🚌 » Frequent ⏱ 1 hr 20 min

Sheppard AFB TX from Dallas/Fort Worth page 113 ✈

Sherbrooke PQ from Montréal page 197 »1 day ⏱2020

Shetland Isles from Aberdeen page 57 ✈ »4 per day ⏱1 hr

Shin-Osaka from Osaka-Kansai page 222 🚌 ⏱45 min

Shonai from Tokyo-Narita page 277 ✈ »Several per day ⏱1 hr

Shreveport LA from Houston page 142 ✈ »Several per day ⏱1 hr

Shreveport LA from New Orleans page 209 🚌 Greyhound »2 day ⏰1300, 2000 ⏱8 hr.

Silverdale WA from Seattle page 258 🚌 »1 hr ⏱1 hr 30 min

Simcoe ON from Toronto page 281 🚌 Serves Brantford

Singapore (city centre) from Singapore page 261 🚌

Singapore (Raffles City and Orchard Road areas) from Singapore page 261 🚌

Singapore from Kuala Lumpur page 151 ✈ »Several per day ⏱55 min

Singapore, Bukit Merah from Singapore page 261 🚌

Singleton NSW from Sydney page 270 ✈ »At least daily ⏱50 min

Sioux Falls SD from Minneapolis/St Paul page 161 ✈ »Several per day ⏱1 hr

Skiathos from Athens page 65 ✈ »Several times per day ⏱40 min

Skiros from Athens page 65 ✈ »At least daily ⏱45 min

Sogndal from Oslo page 223 ✈ »Several per day ⏱1 hr 5 min

Sokcho from Seoul page 211 ✈ »Several per day ⏱50 min

Sonderborg from Copenhagen page 111 ✈ »Several per day ⏱40 min

Sonoma CA from San Francisco page 252 🚌 »5 day ⏱1 hr 30 min

Soquel/Capitola CA from San Francisco page 252 🚌 »2 hr ⏱2 hr 15 min

South Andros from Nassau page 206 ✈ »Several per day ⏱40 min

South Bend IN from Chicago-O'Hare page 106 🚌 »1–2 hr ⏱2 hr 20 min

South Bend IN from Chicago-O'Hare page 106 ✈ »Several per day ⏱40 min

South Philadelphia PA from Philadelphia page 238 🚌 »20–40 min

Southampton from Brussels page 90 ✈ »Several per week ⏱1 hr 5 min

Southern Cross WA from Perth page 237 ✈ »Several per week ⏱1 hr 5 min

Southport from Liverpool page 157 🚌 » Frequent ⏱ 45 min

Spokane WA from Seattle page 258 ✈ »Several per day ⏱50 min

Springfield IL from Chicago-O'Hare page 106 ✈ »Several per day ⏱55 min

Springfield IL from St Louis page 247 ✈ »Several per day ⏱35 min

Springfield MO from St Louis page 247 🚌 »2 day ⏱5 hr

Springfield MO from St Louis page 247 ✈ »Several per day ⏱1 hr

Stapleton Transfer Station CO from Denver page 118 🚌 »30 min–1 hr ⏱40 min

State College PA from Philadelphia page 238 ✈ »Several per day ⏱1 hr

State College PA from Washington-Dulles page 291 ✈ »Several per day ⏱50 min

Stavanger from Oslo page 223 ✈ »Several per day ⏱50 min

Ste-Foy PQ from Montréal-Mirabel page 199 🚌 »2 per day

Steamboat Springs CO from Denver page 118 ✈ »Several per day ⏱50 min

Stella Maris from Nassau page 206 ✈ »Several per week ⏱45 min

Sterling IL from Chicago-O'Hare page 106 ✈ »Several per week ⏱35 min

Stockholm (city centre) from Stockholm-Arlanda page 266 🚌 SJ »5–10 min ⏱40 min

Stockholm from Copenhagen page 111 ✈ »Several per day ⏱1 hr 10 min

Stockholm from Helsinki page 137 ✈ »Several per day ⏱55 min

Remember . . .
The destinations in this index can be reached directly from the gateway airport. Many more local and long-distance transport connections may be available from the centre of the city. Consult the current edition of the *Thomas Cook European Timetable* (Europe) or *Thomas Cook Overseas Timetable* (rest of the world).

✈ Air 🚂 Rail 🚌 Bus 🚐 Limousine Ⓜ Metro/subway 🚊 Tram 🚁 Helicopter ⛴ Water transport

STOCKHOLM • TOULOUSE — SECTION THREE • DESTINATION INDEX

Stockholm from Oslo page 223 ✈ »Several per day ⏱55 min

Stockholm-Bromma Apt from Stockholm-Arlanda page 266 🚌 SL »20 min ⏱50 min

Stockport from Manchester page 183 🚌 »30 min ⏱40 min

Stockton CA from San Francisco page 252 🚌

Stord from Oslo page 223 ✈ »Several per day ⏱50 min

Stornaway from Glasgow page 131 ✈ »Several per week ⏱1hr

Strasbourg from Brussels page 90 ✈ »At least daily ⏱1 hr 5 min

Strasbourg from Lyon page 178 ✈ »Several per week ⏱55 min

Strasbourg from Milan-Linate page 192 ✈ »At least daily ⏱55 min

Strasbourg from Munich page 203 ✈ »Several per week ⏱1 hr 5 min

Strasbourg from Nice page 217 ✈ »Several per week ⏱1 hr 10 min

Strasbourg from Paris-Charles de Gaulle page 226 ✈ »Several per day ⏱1 hr

Strasbourg from Paris-Orly page 234 ✈ »Several per day ⏱1 hr

Strasbourg from Zürich page 296 ✈ »Several per day ⏱40 min

Stratford ON from Toronto page 281 🚌 from Berlin page 80 ✈ »Several per day ⏱1 hr 10 min

Stuttgart from Düsseldorf page 122 ✈ »Several per day ⏱1 hr

Stuttgart from Frankfurt page 126 ✈ »Several per day ⏱45 min

Stuttgart from Munich page 203 ✈ »Several per day ⏱55 min

Stuttgart from Zürich page 296 ✈ »Several per day ⏱45 min

Summit County CO from Denver page 118 🚌 »1 hr

Sunderland from Newcastle page 207 🚌 » Frequent ⏱30 min

Sundsvall from Stockholm-Arlanda page 266 ✈ »Several per day ⏱50 min

Sundsvall from Gothenburg page 133 ✈ »6 per day ⏱1 hr 10 min

Sydney NSW (city centre) from Sydney page 270 🚌 »15 min ⏱20 min

Sydney NSW (Kings Cross) from Sydney page 270 🚌 »20 min ⏱20 min

Sydney NS from Halifax page 134 ✈ »Several per day ⏱1 hr

Sydney NS from Halifax page 134 🚌 Acadian Lines »4 day ⓘ0845; 1315; 1625; 1900 (New Glasgow only) ⏱6 hrs.

Swansea from Cardiff page 103 🚆 » 30 min ⏱ 1 hr

Swansea city centre from Cardiff page 103 🚌 South Wales Transport Flight Path ⓘ Mon–Sun 24 hr ◊ GBP8 single; GBP14 return » 1 hr 30 min.

Syracuse NY from Philadelphia page 238 ✈ »Several per day ⏱55 min

Syracuse NY from Toronto page 281 ✈ »Several per day ⏱55 min

Syros Island from Athens page 65 ✈ »Several times per day ⏱35 min

Tacoma WA (Bus Station) from Seattle page 258 🚌 »2 day ⏱25 min

Tacoma WA from Seattle page 258 🚌 »1 hr ⏱35 min

Tacoma WA from Seattle page 258 🚌

Taegu from Seoul page 211 ✈ »Several per day ⏱50 min

Taichung from Taipei-Chiang Kai Shek page 272 ✈ »Several per day ⏱35 min

Taichung from Taipei-Chiang Kai Shek page 272 🚌

Taif from Jeddah page 146 ✈ from Helsinki page 137 ✈ »Several per day ⏱35 min

Tainan from Taipei-Chiang Kai Shek page 272 ✈ »Several per day ⏱45 min

Tainan from Taipei-Chiang Kai Shek page 272 🚌

Taipei (city centre) from Taipei-Chiang Kai Shek page 272 🚌 ⏱approx 60 min

Taipei (Howard Plaza Hotel) from Taipei-Chiang Kai Shek page 272 🚌

Taipei Sung Shan Apt from Taipei-Chiang Kai Shek page 272 🚌 »15–20 min ⏱40–50 min

Taitung from Taipei-Chiang Kai Shek page 272 ✈ »Several per day ⏱50 min

Takamatsu from Osaka-Kansai page 222 ✈ »Several per day ⏱45 min

Tallahassee FL from Atlanta page 67 ✈ »Several per day ⏱55 min

Tallahassee FL from Orlando page 222 ✈ »Several per day ⏱1 hr

Tallinn from St Petersburg page 248 ✈ »Several per week ⏱35 min

Tampa/St Petersburg FL from Orlando page 222 ✈ »Several per day ⏱35 min

Tampico from Mexico City page 187 ✈ »Several per day ⏱55 min

Tangier from Casablanca page 104 ✈ »At least daily ⏱55 min

Tarbes from Toulouse page 285 🚌 »Several per day ⏱1 hr 40 mins

Taree NSW from Sydney page 270 ✈ »At least daily ⏱50 min

Teesside from London-Heathrow page 164 ✈ »Several per day ⏱1 hr 10 min

Tel Aviv (central bus stn) from Tel Aviv page 275 🚌 »30–60 min ⏱45 min

Tel Aviv (city centre) from Tel Aviv page 275 🚌 »1 hr ⏱45 min

Tel Aviv from Cairo page 83 ✈ »Several per day (not Sat) ⏱1 hr 10 min

Telegraph Harbour BC from Vancouver page 286 ✈ »At least daily ⏱15 min

Temple TX from Dallas/Fort Worth page 113 🚌

Tennoji from Osaka-Kansai page 222 🚆 ⏱29 min

Tepic from Mexico City page 187 ✈ »Several per day ⏱15 min

Terre Haute IN from Chicago-O'Hare page 106 ✈ »At least daily ⏱45 min

Texarkana AR from Dallas/Fort Worth page 113 ✈ »Several per day ⏱1 hr

The Bight from Nassau page 206 ✈ »Several per week ⏱55 min

Thessaloniki from Athens page 65 ✈ »Several times per day ⏱50 min

Thetford from Norwich page 220 🚌 »1 per hr ⏱35 min

Thira from Athens page 65 ✈ »Several times per day ⏱50 min

Thousand Oaks CA from Los Angeles page 174 🚌 »7 per day ⏱1 hr 15 min

Timisoara from Bucuresti page 92 ✈ »4 per day ⏱1 hr

Tioman from Kuala Lumpur page 151 ✈ »Several per day ⏱60 min

Tioman from Singapore page 261 ✈ »Several per day ⏱40 min

Tirana from Istanbul page 143 ✈ »Several per week ⏱45 min

Tokushima from Osaka-Kansai page 222 ✈ »Several per day ⏱30 min

Tokyo (City Air Terminal) from Tokyo-Narita page 277 🚌 »10–15 min ⏱55 min

Tokyo (city centre) from Tokyo-Narita page 277 🚌 »30 min (1 hr 1013–1413) ⏱approx 1 hr

Tokyo from Osaka-Kansai page 222 ✈ »Several per day ⏱60–70 min

Tokyo Ueno from Tokyo-Narita page 277 🚌 »approx 40 min ⏱60 min

Tokyo Ueno from Tokyo-Narita page 277 🚌 »approx 20 min ⏱1 hr 30 min

Tokyo-Haneda Apt from Tokyo-Narita page 277 🚌 ⏱75 min

Tomah WI from Minneapolis/St Paul page 161 🚌 »1 per day ⏱4 hr 25 min

Torino see **Turin**

Toronto ON (Islington Subway Station) from Toronto page 281 🚌 »40 min ⏱25 min

Toronto ON (Lawrence West Subway Station) from Toronto page 281 🚌 »15–30 min Mon–Fri; longer Sat–Sun ⏱45 min–1 hr

Toronto ON (metro area) from Toronto page 281 🚌

Torrance CA from Los Angeles page 174 🚌 »20–60 min ⏱45 min

Toulouse from Lyon page 178 ✈ »Several per day ⏱50–55 min

Toulouse from Nice page 217 ✈ »Several per week ⏱1 hr

Toulouse from Paris-Charles de Gaulle page 226 ✈ »Several per day ⏱1 hr 15 min

Toulouse Blagnac Apt from Paris-Orly page 234 ✈ »Several per day ⏱1 hr 05 min

» Frequency of service ⏱ Journey time   For details of fares, etc, see individual airport entries, Section Two

SECTION THREE • DESTINATION INDEX

TOURS • WASHINGTON

Tours from Paris-Charles de Gaulle page 226 🚆 SNCF: TGV »4 per day ⏱1 hr 36 min.

Townsville from Cairns page 96 ✈ »Several per day ⏱50 min

Toyama from Tokyo-Narita page 277 ✈ »Several per day ⏱1 hr

Toyooka from Osaka-Kansai page 222 ✈ »Several per day ⏱40 min

Tracy CA from San Francisco page 252 🚆 »3 day

Treasure Cay from Nassau page 206 ✈ »Several per day ⏱35 min

Trevose PA from New York-JFK page 209 🚌

Trieste from Rome-Fiumicino page 244 ✈ »Several per day ⏱1 hr 10 min

Trollhättan from Stockholm-Arlanda page 266 ✈ »Several per week ⏱55 min

Trondheim from Oslo page 223 ✈ »Several per day ⏱1 hr

Tuguegarao from Manila page 185 ✈ »Several per week ⏱55 min

Turin from Rome-Fiumicino page 244 ✈ »Several per day ⏱1 hr 5 min

Turin from Zürich page 296 ✈ »Several per day ⏱1 hr

Turku from Helsinki page 137 ✈ »Several per day ⏱35 min

Turku from Helsinki page 137 🚆 »avg 1 hr ⏱2 hr 30 min

Tuskegee AL from Atlanta page 67 🚌

Tyler TX from Dallas/Fort Worth page 113 🚆

Tyler TX from Dallas/Fort Worth page 113 ✈ »Several per day ⏱45 min

Tyler TX from Houston page 142 ✈ »Several per day ⏱50 min

Tysons Corner VA from Washington-Dulles page 291 🚌

Ubon Ratchathani from Bangkok page 72 🚆 »6 per day ⏱9–12 hr

Ukiah CA from San Francisco page 252 🚆 »4 day ⏱2 hr 40 min

Ulsan from Seoul page 211 ✈ »Several per day ⏱55 min

Uppsala from Stockholm-Arlanda page 266 🚆 UL »15 min

Utica NY from New York-La Guardia page 214 ✈ »Several per week

Utrecht from Amsterdam page 61 🚆 »avg 30 min ⏱22 min.

Vacaville CA from San Francisco page 252 🚆 »7 day ⏱1 hr 30 min

Vail CO from Denver page 118 🚌 »30 min

Vail CO from Denver page 118 🚌 »1 hr

Vail CO from Denver page 118 🚌 »1 hr

Valdosta GA from Atlanta page 67 ✈ »Several per day ⏱55 min

Valence from Lyon page 178 🚆 »2 per day ⏱1 hr 20 min

Valence from Lyon page 178 🚌 »1 per day ⏱30 min

Valencia from Barcelona page 75 ✈ »Several per day ⏱1 hr

Valencia from Madrid page 180 ✈ »Several per day ⏱50 min

Vallejo CA from San Francisco page 252 🚆 »8 day ⏱1 hr

Vallejo CA from San Francisco page 252 🚌 »1–2 hrs ⏱1 hr 10 min

Valverde from Tenerife page 276 ✈ »2 per day ⏱40 min

Van Nuys CA from Los Angeles page 174 🚆 »30 min ⏱1 hr

Vancouver BC (city centre) from Vancouver page 286 🚌

Vancouver BC (city centre) hotels) from Vancouver page 286 🚐 »15 min

Vancouver BC (Pacific Central rail stn) from Vancouver page 286 🚐 »30 min

Vancouver BC from Seattle page 258 🚐 »3 day ⏱5 hr

Vancouver WA from Seattle page 258 🚐 »1 day ⏱3 hr 50 min

Vancouver BC from Calgary page 98 🚐Greyhound »1 day ⓒ1700 ⏱15 hr.

Varginha from São Paulo-Guarulhos page 257 ✈ »At least daily ⏱45 min

Västerås from Stockholm-Arlanda page 266 🚐 SJ

Venezia see **Venice**

Venice from Milan-Linate page 192 ✈ »Several per day ⏱55 min

Venice from Milan-Malpensa page 194 ✈ »Several per day ⏱45 min

Venice from Rome-Fiumicino page 244 ✈ »Several per day ⏱1 hr 5 min

Ventura CA see also **Oxnard/Ventura CA**

Ventura CA from Los Angeles page 174 🚐 »7 per day ⏱2 hr

Ventura County CA from Los Angeles page 174 🚐

Veracruz from Mexico City page 187 ✈ »Several per day ⏱50 min

Vermont state (southern) from Boston page 85 🚌

Vermont state from Boston page 85 🚌

Verona from Rome-Fiumicino page 244 ✈ »Several per day ⏱1 hr

Vestmannaeyja from Reykjavik page 241 ✈ »Several per day ⏱25 min

Victoria (Brazil) from Rio de Janeiro-International page 242 ✈ »Several per day ⏱1 hr

Victoria BC from Seattle page 258 ✈ »Several per day ⏱45 min

Victoria BC from Vancouver page 286 ✈ »Several per day ⏱35 min

Victoria Falls from Harare page 137 ✈ »Several per day ⏱1 hr

Vienna (city centre – City Air Terminal) from Vienna page 288 🚐 »20 min ⏱20 min

Vienna (city centre – main rail stns) from Vienna page 288 🚐 »approx 30 min ⏱30 min

Vienna from Budapest page 93 ✈ »Several per day ⏱1 hr

Vienna from Munich page 203 ✈ »Several per day ⏱1 hr

Vienna from Prague page 239 ✈ »Several per day ⏱55 min

Vienna from Warsaw page 290 ✈ »Several per day ⏱1 hr 15 min

Vienne from Lyon page 178 🚆 »2 per day ⏱40 min

Vientiane from Bangkok page 72 ✈ »At least daily ⏱1 hr

Vigo from Madrid page 180 ✈ »Several per day ⏱1 hr

Villefontaine from Lyon page 178 🚆 »3 per day ⏱25 min

Vilnius from Moscow-Sheremetyevo page 200 ✈ »At least daily ⏱1 hr 45 min

Virac from Manila page 185 ✈ »Several per week ⏱55 min

Visby from Stockholm-Arlanda page 266 ✈ »Several per day ⏱45 min

Waco TX from Dallas/Fort Worth page 113 🚐

Waco TX from Dallas/Fort Worth page 113 ✈ »Several per day ⏱45 min

Waco TX from Houston page 142 ✈ »Sveral per day ⏱50 min

Walla Walla WA from Seattle page 258 ✈ »Several per day ⏱1 hr

Walsall from Birmingham page 82 🚆 »30 min Mon–Sat; 1 hr Sun ⏱1 hr 20 min

Walvis Bay from Cape Town page 99 ✈ »Several per week ⏱1 hr

Wanganui from Auckland page 69 ✈ »At least daily ⏱1 hr

Warrington from Liverpool page 157 🚆 » Frequent ⏱ 25 min

Warsaw (city centre) from Warsaw page 290 🚐 »20 min ⏱20–25 min

Warsaw from Budapest page 93 ✈ »Several per day ⏱1 hr 15 min

Warszawa see **Warsaw**

Washington DC (Union Sta) from Baltimore/Washington page 72 🚆Amtrak »25 day ⓒ0510–0035 ⏱25 min

Washington DC (Dulles) from Baltimore/Washington page 72 ✈ »Several per day ⏱30 min

Washington DC (National) from Baltimore/Washington page 72 ✈ »Several per day ⏱30 min

Washington DC (Union Sta) from Baltimore/Washington page 72 🚆MARC »20 day ⓒ0700–2045 Mon–Fri ⏱35 min

Washington DC (Airport Shuttle Terminal) from Baltimore/Washington page 72 🚐SuperShuttle »1 hr ⓒ0500–0030

Washington DC (city centre – Airports Terminal 16th & K Sts) from Washington-Dulles page 291 🚐 »30 min ⏱45 min

---

Remember . . .
The destinations in this index can be reached directly from the gateway airport. Many more local and long-distance transport connections may be available from the centre of the city. Consult the current edition of the *Thomas Cook European Timetable* (Europe) or *Thomas Cook Overseas Timetable* (rest of the world).

✈ Air 🚆 Rail 🚌 Bus 🚐 Limousine Ⓜ Metro/subway 🚋 Tram 🚁 Helicopter ⛴ Water transport

WASHINGTON • ZWOLLE — SECTION THREE • DESTINATION INDEX

Washington DC (metro area) from Washington-Dulles page 291

Washington DC (Union rail stn/Amtrak) from Washington-Dulles page 291

Washington DC from Philadelphia page 238 ✈ »Several per day ⏱1 hr

Washington DC from New York-La Guardia page 214 ✈ »Several per day ⏱1 hr

Washington-National Apt DC from Washington-Dulles page 291 »1–2 hrs ⏱45 min

Washington-National Apt DC from Washington-Dulles page 291

Waterloo IA from Minneapolis/St Paul page 195 ✈ »Several per day ⏱1 hr

Watsonville CA from San Francisco page 252 »2 hr ⏱3 hr

Wausa WI from Minneapolis/St Paul page 195 ✈ »Several per day ⏱1 hr

Weihai from Beijing page 67 ✈ »Several per week ⏱1 hr

Wellington from Auckland page 69 ✈ »Several per day ⏱1 hr

Wells ME from Boston page 85

Wenatchee WA from Seattle page 258 ✈ »Several per day ⏱40min

West Falls Church VA (Metro Orange Line) from Washington-Dulles page 291 »15–30 min

West Palm Beach FL from Miami page 189 ✈ »Several per day ⏱40 min

Westchester County NY from Boston page 85 ✈ »Several per day ⏱1 hr

Westchester County NY from New York-JFK page 209 »30 min–1 hr

Westchester County NY from New York-La Guardia page 214 »On–demand

Westchester County NY from New York-La Guardia page 214 »On–demand

Westchester County NY from Philadelphia page 238 ✈ »Several per day ⏱1 hr

Westchester NY from New York-JFK page 209 »On–demand

Westchester NY from New York-JFK page 209 »On–demand

Westchester NY from New York-La Guardia page 214 »30 min–1 hr

Westchester NY from New York-Newark page 216 »On-demand

Westford MA from Boston page 85

Westlake Village CA from Los Angeles page 174 »7 day ⏱1 hr 10 min

West Palm Beach FL from Orlando page 222 ✈ »Several per day ⏱50 min

Westsound WA from Seattle page 258 ✈ »Several per day ⏱1 hr

Westwood CA (UCLA) from Los Angeles page 174 »12 min, 60 min evenings ⏱50 min

Whakatane from Auckland page 69 ✈ »At least daily ⏱50 min

Whangarei from Auckland page 69 ✈ »Several per day ⏱40 min

White River Junction VT from Boston page 85 »1 per day ⏱4–5 hr

Wichita Falls TX from Dallas/Fort Worth page 113

Wichita Falls TX from Dallas/Fort Worth page 113 ✈ »Several per day ⏱50 min

Wick from Aberdeen page 57 ✈ »2 per day ⏱45 min.

Wigan from Liverpool page 157 » Frequent ⏱45 min

Wien see Vienna

Wilkes-Barre PA from New York-Newark page 216 ✈ »Several per day ⏱50 min

Wilkes-Barre PA from Philadelphia page 238 ✈ »Several per day ⏱40 min

Williamsport PA from Philadelphia page 238 ✈ »Several per day ⏱55 min

Willmar MN from Minneapolis/St Paul page 195

Wilmington DE (Amtrak Stn) from Baltimore/Washington page 72 Amtrak »25 day ⏰0510–0035 ⏱1 hr

Windsor ON from Toronto page 281 Serves London and Sarnia

Winona MN from Minneapolis/St Paul page 195

Winona MN from Minneapolis/St Paul page 195 »2 per day ⏱3 hr 5 min

Winterthur from Zürich page 296 »20–30 min ⏱15–18 min

Woburn MA from Boston page 85 »30 min

Woking from London-Heathrow page 164 »30 min ⏱50 min

Wollongong NSW from Sydney page 270 »Five times daily ⏱1 hr 45 min

Wolverhampton from Birmingham page 82 »1 hr ⏱40 min

Woodland Hills CA from Los Angeles page 174 »7 per day ⏱45 min

Woods Hole MA from Boston page 85 »2 hrs ⏱1 hr 45 min

Woodstock ON from Toronto page 281 »1–2 hr ⏱1 hr 30 min

Worcester MA from Boston page 85 »4 per day

Worcester MA from New York-La Guardia page 214 ✈ »Several per day ⏱1 hr

Worcester MA from New York-Newark page 216 ✈ »At least daily ⏱1 hr

Yakima WA from Seattle page 258 ✈ »Several per day ⏱40 min

Yamagata from Tokyo-Narita page 277 ✈ »Several per day ⏱55 min

Yangon from Bangkok page 72 ✈ »Several per day ⏱45 min

Yangon from Kuala Lumpur page 151 ✈ »Several per week ⏱1 hr

Yantai from Beijing page 67 ✈ »Several per day ⏱60–75 min

Yardley PA from New York-JFK page 209

Yarmouth NS from Halifax page 134 ✈ »At least daily ⏱40 min

Yechon from Seoul page 260 ✈ »Several per day ⏱45 min

Yokohama from Tokyo-Narita page 277 »15–30 min ⏱2 hr

Yokohama from Tokyo-Narita page 277 »30 min ⏱approx 1 hr 40 min

Yonago from Osaka-Kansai page 222 ✈ »Several per day ⏱1 hr

York (UK) from Birmingham page 82 »Twice daily, once only Sun ⏱2 hr 30 min

York from Leeds/Bradford page 155 » Frequent ⏱30 min

York from Teesside page 274 »1 per hr ⏱1 hr

York ME from Boston page 85

York Mills ON (subway) from Toronto page 281 »40 min ⏱35–40 min

Yorkdale ON (subway) from Toronto page 281 »40 min ⏱25 min

Zacatecas from Mexico City page 187 ✈ »Several per day ⏱60–65 min

Zagreb from Vienna page 288 ✈ »Several per day ⏱1 hr

Zakinthos from Athens page 65 ✈ »Several times per day ⏱55 min

Zhengzhou from Beijing page 67 ✈ »At least daily ⏱60–75 min

Zug from Zürich page 296 »1 hr ⏱1 hr 28 min

Zumbrota MN from Minneapolis/St Paul page 195 »2 per day ⏱1 hr 10 min

Zurich from Geneva page 130 ✈ »20 per day ⏱50 min

Zürich (city centre) from Zürich page 296 »15 min ⏱20–30 min

Zürich (Hbf – central rail stn) from Zürich page 296 »15 min ⏱10–12 min

Zürich from Frankfurt page 126 ✈ »Several per day ⏱55 min

Zürich from Lyon page 178 ✈ »Several per day ⏱60–70 min

Zürich from Milan-Linate page 192 ✈ »Several per day ⏱55 min

Zürich from Munich page 203 ✈ »Several per day ⏱1 hr

Zwolle from Amsterdam page 61 »1 hr ⏱1 hr 19 min

» Frequency of service ⏱ Journey time For details of fares, etc, see individual airport entries, Section Two

READER SURVEY

The Thomas Cook International Air Travel Handbook 1998 is the second edition of an annual guide to key airports around the world. We would like your comments and criticisms to help us improve each new edition, so that it best meets the needs of the majority of our readers. You will help us in this by completing and returning a copy of this questionnaire. We will acknowledge every reply, and to show our appreciation we will offer you a £1.00/$2.00 discount off your next purchase from Thomas Cook Publishing's range of travel guidebooks and timetables. We also invite you to use this form to contribute information for future editions; the senders of what are in our opinion the most useful contributions will be credited in the next edition and receive a free copy of that edition upon publication.

Your name: Mr/Mrs/Ms/Other _____
First name or initials _____
Last or family name _____
Address (please include postal or zip code)
_____
_____
_____

Daytime telephone no. _____
Fax number _____

Is your main use of this book as:
❏ A business traveller
❏ A travel trade professional
❏ An air travel industry professional
❏ A travel planner for others
❏ Other (Please specify:_____)

Did you obtain this book
❏ Direct from Thomas Cook Publishing
❏ Through an appointed overseas agent of Thomas Cook Publishing (please specify which: _____)
❏ From a branch of Thomas Cook
❏ From a bookshop or book trade source

Which of the airports have you looked up in this book?
_____
Did you find all the information you were looking for?
❏ Yes ❏ No. If 'No', what was missing:?
_____
_____

We intend to cover more international airports in future editions. Which airports do you think we should add?
_____
_____

Please use this space to contribute any corrections or additions of fact on any airport in this book. In particular, any hints and tips that we can pass on from you to your fellow-travellers, by way of the **Traveller's Notes** *feature, will be appreciated.*
_____
_____
_____
_____
_____

Please rate the categories of information and sections in the book for their usefulness to you. If you indicate 'needs more detail' please specify in the box below. U= Useful; NU =Not useful; MD= Could be useful but needs more detail.

	U	NU	MD
Section One			
Country by country travel facts	❏	❏	❏
A–Z of air travel	❏	❏	❏
Section Two			
Basic airport address, etc.	❏	❏	❏
Terminals and Transfers	❏	❏	❏
Information	❏	❏	❏
Emergencies	❏	❏	❏
Airport Facilities:			
Money	❏	❏	❏
Food and drink	❏	❏	❏
Communications	❏	❏	❏
Shopping	❏	❏	❏
Luggage	❏	❏	❏
Disabled Travellers	❏	❏	❏
Smoking Policy	❏	❏	❏
Special Passenger Lounges	❏	❏	❏
Conference and Business Facilities	❏	❏	❏
Car Rental	❏	❏	❏
Car Parking	❏	❏	❏
Taxis and Chauffeur-driven Cars	❏	❏	❏
Public Transport	❏	❏	❏
Regional Air Connections	❏	❏	❏
Terminal plans	❏	❏	❏
Airport maps	❏	❏	❏
City and regional maps	❏	❏	❏
Section Three:			
Destination index	❏	❏	❏

More detail needed on:
_____
_____

Please use this space for any other criticisms or comments you wish to make:
_____
_____
_____
_____

Please the completed survey form to:
The Project Editor, International Air Travel Handbook, Thomas Cook Publishing, PO Box 227, Thorpe Wood, Peterborough PE3 6PU, United Kingdom.
Fax: 01733 (+44 1733 from overseas) 503596

Or e-mail your comments to: publishing@thomascook.com

ADVERTISEMENT

ESSENTIAL GUIDES FOR THE INTERNATIONAL TRAVELLER FROM THOMAS COOK PUBLISHING

THOMAS COOK EUROPEAN TIMETABLE

First choice amongst rail travellers, and now in its 124th year. Covers 50,000 rail and ferry services across 35 countries and published monthly to ensure constant accuracy. An essential complement to the International Air Travel Handbook.
Published monthly. Price £8.40

THOMAS COOK OVERSEAS TIMETABLE

The widest-ranging guide to rail and bus services in every country outside Europe. Clear and accurate timetables are accompanied by general advice on public transport options. Ideal for advance planning and en route reference.
Published bi-monthly. Price £8.40

THOMAS COOK GUIDE TO EUROPEAN NIGHT TRAINS

Accurate and up-to-date timetables for national and international sleeping car and couchette services throughout the Continent, as well as a guide to travelling by sleeper. Motorail services and booking information have also been included.
Published in May and October. Price £7.95

These publications are available from bookshops and Thomas Cook shops, or direct from Thomas Cook Publishing, (Dept IATH), PO Box 227, Thorpe Wood, Peterborough, PE3 6PU, UK, telephone 01733 (+44 1733) 503571/2 (extra for postage and packing)

Thomas Cook